Mirrors & Windows

Connecting with Literature

"The whole purpose of education
is to turn mirrors into windows."

— Sydney J. Harris

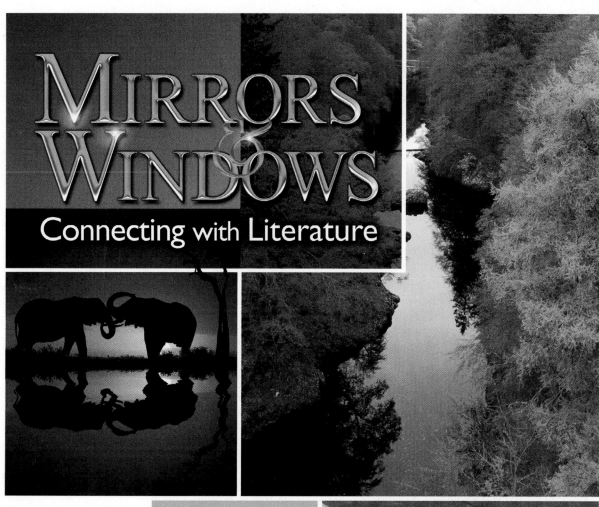

MIRRORS & WINDOWS
Connecting with Literature

Level V

EMC
Publishing

ST. PAUL • LOS ANGELES • INDIANAPOLIS

Staff Credits

Senior Editor: Brenda Owens
Associate Editors: Keri Henkel Stifter, Stephanie Djock
Assistant Editors: Julie Nelson, Brendan Curran
Editorial Assistants: Erin Saladin, Lindsay Ryan
Writer: Stephanie Djock
Marketing Managers: Bruce Ayscue, Laurie Skiba
Permissions Coordinator: Valerie Murphy
Copy Editors: Alison Baker, Nancy Papsin
Proofreaders: Nancy Papsin, Carol Rogers
Indexer: Terry Casey
Photo Researchers: Brendan Curran, Paul Spencer
Production Editor: Deanna Quinn
Cover Designer: Leslie Anderson
Text Design and Page Layout Lead: Matthias Frasch
Page Layout Designers: Matthias Frasch, Jack Ross, Lisa Beller, Jennifer Wreisner
Production Specialist: Petrina Nyhan

Literary Acknowledgments: Literary Acknowledgments appear following the Glossary of Vocabulary Words. We have made every effort to trace the ownership of all copyrighted material and to secure permission from copyright holders. In the event of any question arising as to the use of any material, we will be pleased to make the necessary corrections in future printings. Thanks are due to the authors, publishers, and agents for permission to use the materials indicated.

Art and Photo Credits: Art and Photo Credits appear following the Literary Acknowledgments.

ISBN 978-0-82194-180-5 (Preview Copy)

© 2009 by EMC Publishing, LLC
875 Montreal Way
St. Paul, MN 55102
E-mail: educate@emcp.com
Web site: www.emcp.com

Printed in the United States of America

18 17 16 15 14 13 12 11 10 09 08 07   1 2 3 4 5 6 7 8 9 10

Consultants, Reviewers, and Focus Group Participants

Jean Martorana, Reading
   Specialist/English Teacher
Desert Vista High School
Phoenix, Arizona

Tracy Pulido, Language Arts
   Instructor
West Valley High School
Fairbanks, Arkansas

Cindy Johnston, English Teacher
Argus High School
Ceres, California

Susan Stoehr, Language Arts
   Instructor
Aragon High School
San Mateo, California

John Owens, Reading Specialist
St. Vrain Valley Schools
Longmont, Colorado

Fred Smith, Language Arts
   Instructor
St. Bernard High School
Uncasville, Connecticut

Penny Austin-Richardson,
   English Department Chair
Seaford Senior High School
Seaford, Delaware

Cecilia Lewis, Language Arts
   Instructor
Mariner High School
Cape Coral, Florida

Jane Feber, Teacher
Mandarin Middle School
Jacksonville, Florida

Dorothy Fletcher, Language Arts
   Instructor
Wolfson Senior High School
Jacksonville, Florida

Tamara Doehring, English/
   Reading Teacher
Melbourne High School
Melbourne, Florida

Patti Magee, English Instructor
Timber Creek High School
Orlando, Florida

Margaret J. Graham, Language
   Arts/Reading Teacher
Elizabeth Cobb Middle School
Tallahassee, Florida

Elizabeth Steinman, English
   Instructor
Vero Beach High School
Vero Beach, Florida

Wanda Bagwell, Language Arts
   Department Chair
Commerce High School
Commerce, Georgia

Betty Deriso, Language
   Department Chairperson
Crisp County High School
Cordele, Georgia

Dr. Peggy Leland, English
   Instructor
Chestatee High School
Gainsville, Georgia

Matthew Boedy, Language Arts
   Instructor
Harlem High School
Harlem, Georgia

Patty Bradshaw, English
   Department Chair
Harlem High School
Harlem, Georgia

Dawn Faulkner, English
   Department Chair
Rome High School
Rome, Georgia

Carolyn C. Coleman, AKS
   Continuous Improvement
   Director
Gwinnett County Public Schools
Suwanee, Georgia

Elisabeth Blumer Thompson,
   Language Arts Instructor
Swainsboro High School
Swainsboro, Georgia

Toi Walker, English Instructor
Northeast Tifton County High
   School
Tifton, Georgia

Jeanette Rogers, English
   Instructor
Potlatch Jr.-Sr. High School
Potlach, Idaho

Gail Taylor, Language Arts
   Instructor
Rigby High School
Rigby, Idaho

Carey Robin, Language Arts
   Instructor
St. Francis College Prep
Brookfield, Illinois

Patricia Meyer, English
   Department Chair
Glenbard East High School
Lombard, Illinois

Liz Rebmann, Language Arts
   Instructor
Morton High School
Morton, Illinois

Helen Gallagher, English
   Department Chair
Main East High School
Park Ridge, Illinois

Rosemary Ryan, Dean of Students
Schaumburg High School
Schaumburg, Illinois

Donna Cracraft, English
   Department Co-Chair/IB
   Coordinator
Pike High School
Indianapolis, Indiana

Consultants, Reviewers, and Focus Group Participants (cont.)

K. C. Salter, Language Arts
   Instructor
Knightstown High School
Knightstown, Indiana

Lisa Broxterman, Language Arts
   Instructor
Axtell High School
Axtell, Kansas

Shirley Wells, Language Arts
   Instructor
Derby High School
Derby, Kansas

Karen Ann Stous, Speech &
   Drama Teacher
Holton High School
Holton, Kansas

Martha-Jean Rockey, Language
   Arts Instructor
Troy High School
Troy, Kansas

Shelia Penick, Language Arts
   Instructor
Yates Center High School
Yates Center, Kansas

John Ermilio, English Teacher
St. Johns High School
Shrewsbury, Massachusetts

James York, English Teacher
Waverly High School
Lansing, Michigan

Mary Spychalla, Gifted Education
   Coordinator
Valley Middle School
Apple Valley, Minnesota

Shari K. Carlson, Advanced ILA
   Teacher
Coon Rapids Middle School
Coon Rapids, Minnesota

Rebecca Benz, English Instructor
St. Thomas Academy
Mendota Heights, Minnesota

Michael F. Graves, Professor
   Emeritus
University of Minnesota
330A Peik Hall
Minneapolis, Minnesota

Kathleen Nelson, English
   Instructor
New Ulm High School
New Ulm, Minnesota

Adonna Gaspar, Language Arts
   Teacher
Cooper High School
Robbinsdale, Minnesota

Sara L. Nystuen, English
   Department Chair; AP Instructor
Concordia Academy
Roseville, Minnesota

Tom Backen, English Teacher
Benilde-St. Margaret's School
St. Louis Park, Minnesota

Daniel Sylvester, Jr. High English
   & American Experience Teacher
Benilde-St. Margaret's School
St. Louis Park, Minnesota

Jean Borax, Literacy Coach
Harding High School
St. Paul, Minnesota

Erik Brandt, English Teacher
Harding High School
St. Paul, Minnesota

Kevin Brennan, High School
   English Teacher
Cretin-Derham Hall
St. Paul, Minnesota

Nissa Dalager, Teacher/
   Consultant/Writer
St. Paul, Minnesota

Anna Newcombe, English
   Instructor
Harding High School
St. Paul, Minnesota

Rosemary Ruffenach, Language
   Arts Teacher, Consultant, and
   Writer
St. Paul, Minnesota

Nancy Papsin, English Teacher/
   Educational Consultant
White Bear Lake, Minnesota

Shannon Umfleet,
   Communication Arts Instructor
Northwest High School
Cedar Hill, Missouri

Ken Girard, Language Arts
   Instructor
Bishop LeBlond High School
St. Joseph, Missouri

Jessica Gall, Language Arts
   Instructor
Fremont High School
Fremont, Nebraska

Michael Davis, Language Arts
   Instructor
Millard West High School
Omaha, Nebraska

Lisa Larnerd, English Teacher
Basic High School
Henderson, Nevada

Jo Paulson, Title I Reading
   Teacher
Camino Real Middle School
Las Cruces, New Mexico

Stacy Biss, Language Arts
   Instructor
Hackensack High School
Hackensack, New Jersey

J. M. Winchock, Reading
   Specialist, Adult Literacy
   Instructor
Hillsborough High School
Hillsborough, New Jersey

Consultants, Reviewers, and Focus Group Participants (cont.)

Matthew Cahn, Department of English & Related Arts Supervisor
River Dell High School
Oradell, New Jersey

Jean Mullooly, Language Arts Instructor
Holy Angels High School
Trenton, New Jersey

Fenice Boyd, Assistant Professor, Learning and Instruction
State University of New York at Buffalo
Buffalo, New York

Michael Fedorchuk, Assistant Principal
Auburn High School
Auburn, New York

Robert Balch, English Instructor
Beacon High School
Beacon, New York

Rene A. Roberge, Secondary English/AP English Instructor
Hudson Falls High School
Hudson Falls, New York

Melissa Hedt, Literacy Coach
Asheville Middle School
Asheville, North Carolina

Jane Shoaf, Educational Consultant
Durham, North Carolina

Kimberly Tufts, Department Chair for ELA
Cranberry Middle School
Elk Park, North Carolina

Cheryl Gackle, English Instructor
Kulm High School
Kulm, North Dakota

Barbara Stroh, English Department Chair
Aurora High School
Aurora, Ohio

Mary Jo Bish, Language Arts Instructor
Lake Middle School
Millbury, Ohio

Judy Ellsesser-Painter, Language Arts Instructor
South Webster High School
South Webster, Ohio

Adele Dahlin, English Department Chair
Central Catholic High School
Toledo, Ohio

Joshua Singer, English Instructor
Central Catholic High School
Toledo, Ohio

Debbie Orendorf, Language Arts Instructor
Berlin Brothers Valley High School
Berlin, Pennsylvania

Dona Italiano, English Teacher/ Language Arts Coordinator
Souderton Area High School
Souderton, Pennsylvania

Tina Parlier, Secondary English Instructor
Elizabethton High School
Elizabethton, Tennessee

Wayne Luellen, English Instructor
Houston High School
Germantown, Tennessee

Ed Farrell, Senior Consultant
Emeritus Professor of English Education
University of Texas at Austin
Austin, Texas

Terry Ross, Secondary Language Arts Supervisor
Austin Independent School District
Austin, Texas

Angelia Greiner, English Department Chair
Big Sandy High School
Big Sandy, Texas

Sharon Kremer, Educational Consultant
Denton, Texas

E. J. Brletich, Supervisor of English/Language Arts
Spotsylvania City School
Fredericksburg, Virginia

Jeffrey Golub, Educational Consultant
Bothell, Washington

Clifford Aziz, Language Arts Instructor
Washington High School
Tacoma, Washington

Becky Palmer, Reading Teacher
Madison Middle School
Appleton, Wisconsin

Mary Hoppe, English Teacher
Bonduel High School
Bonduel, Wisconsin

Lou Wappel, English, Humanities & Guidance Instructor
St. Lawrence Seminary High School
Mount Calvary, Wisconsin

Gregory R. Keir, Language Arts Instructor
East Elementary School
New Richmond, Wisconsin

CONTENTS IN BRIEF

Unit 1 Fiction

Unit 2 Nonfiction

Unit 3 Poetry

Unit 4 Drama

DIRECTED READING

Unit 5 Folk Literature

Unit 6 Independent Readings

LANGUAGE ARTS RESOURCES

LANGUAGE ARTS WORKSHOPS

Speaking & Listening

Writing

Test Practice

Reading Skills

Writing Skills

Revising and Editing Skills

INDEPENDENT READING

UNIT 1

Fiction

> "Stories ought to judge and interpret the world."
>
> —Cynthia Ozick

Has anyone ever played a trick on you? Put too much pressure on you? Given you a memorable piece of advice? Think of a time you had to make a difficult decision or a time you worked really hard to accomplish something. As you read the stories in this unit, notice how the challenges and experiences of their characters both mirror your own and portray a greater message about the world around them.

COFER   MAUPASSANT   ATWOOD   POE   TAN   O'BRIEN

1

INTRODUCTION TO FICTION

"The man who opened the door that day is the hero of my life. How do I say this without sounding sappy? Blurt it out—the man saved me."

—Tim O'Brien in "On the Rainy River"

If you're interested in reading a horror story, mystery, romance, or work of science fiction, you'll want to browse the fiction section of a bookstore or library. A person who enjoys chilling tales might pick up a story by Edgar Allan Poe, such as "The Masque of the Red Death" (page 83). Someone who likes reading about intense personal conflict might be in the mood for Tim O'Brien's "On the Rainy River" (page 137). Fiction has something for everyone.

THE GENRE OF FICTION

Genre is a type or category of literary composition, such as fiction, nonfiction, poetry, and drama. The genre known as **fiction** includes any work of **prose** (writing other than poetry and drama) that tells an invented or imaginary story. Fiction is a popular choice for people who read primarily for entertainment. Its two main forms are the short story and the novel. A **short story** is a brief work of fiction. A good short story is crafted carefully to develop a plot, a conflict, characters, a setting, a mood, and a theme, all within a relatively few pages. The majority of the selections in this unit are short stories. The **novel,** a close cousin of the short story, is a long work of fiction. A novel typically features an involved plot, many characters, and numerous settings.

Classic Short Stories

What makes a short story worthy of being considered "a classic"? Why are there certain stories that throughout the decades most people have heard of and many people have read? Take a look at the stories listed below. Have you read any of them? If you have, why do you think they have withstood the test of time?

- "The Lady with the Dog," by Anton Chekhov
- "The Lottery" by Shirley Jackson
- "The Tell-Tale Heart" by Edgar Allan Poe
- "To Build a Fire" by Jack London
- "Why I Live at the P.O." by Eudora Welty

"The whole purpose of education is to turn mirrors into windows."

— Sydney J. Harris

Think about when you were young and about to start school for the first time. When you stood in front of the mirror, your view was focused on your own reflection and limited by your own experience. Then the windows of learning began to open your mind to new ideas and new experiences, broadening both your awareness and your curiosity.

As you discovered reading and the power of words, you learned to connect with what you read and to examine your own ideas and experiences. And the more you read, the more you learned to connect with the ideas and experiences of other people from other times and other places. Great literature provides *mirrors* that help you reflect on your own world and *windows* that lead you into new worlds.

EMC's literature program, *Mirrors and Windows: Connecting with Literature,* provides opportunities for you to explore new worlds full of people, cultures, and perspectives different from your own. This book contains stories, essays, plays, and poems by outstanding authors from around the globe. Reading these selections will expand your appreciation of literature and your world view. Studying them will help you examine universal themes such as honesty, integrity, and justice and common emotions such as fear, pride, and belonging. You may already have thought about some of these ideas and feelings yourself.

As you read the selections in this book, try to see yourself in the characters, stories, and themes. Also try to see yourself as a citizen of the world—a world from which you have much to learn and to which you have much to offer.

ELEMENTS OF FICTION

A good reader is an active participant. As you read, consider each of the elements discussed below.

Plot

The **plot** is the series of events related to a central *conflict,* or struggle. Typically, the plot introduces a conflict, develops it, and eventually resolves it. The plot often contains all or some of the following parts: exposition, rising action, climax, falling action, and resolution. The **exposition,** or introduction, sets the tone or mood, introduces the characters and setting, and provides necessary background information. In the **rising action,** the conflict is developed and intensified. The **climax** is the high point of interest or suspense, and the **falling action** consists of all the events that follow the climax. The **resolution,** or dénouement (dā' nü män´), is the point at which the central conflict is ended, or resolved. (See Understanding Plot, page 12.)

Point of View

Point of view is the vantage point from which the story is told. The one who tells a story is the **narrator.** In **first-person point of view,** the story is told by someone who participates in or witnesses the action; this person uses words such as *I* and *we* in telling the story. In **third-person point of view,** the narrator usually stands outside the action and observes, using words such as *he, she, it,* and *they.* There are two types of third-person point of view: limited point of view and omniscient point of view. In *limited point of view,* the thoughts of only the narrator or a single character are revealed. In *omniscient point of view,* the thoughts of all the characters are revealed. (See Understanding Point of View, page 42.)

Characters

The **characters** are the individuals that take part in the action of a story. The **protagonist** is the main character in a literary work, whereas the **antagonist** is the character or force in conflict with the protagonist. **Characterization** is the act of creating or describing a character. Writers create characters using three major techniques: showing what characters say, do, or think; showing what other characters say or think about them; and describing what physical features, dress, and personality the characters display. (See Understanding Character, page 60.)

Setting

The **setting** of a literary work is the time and place in which it occurs, together with all the details used to create a sense of a particular time and place. Setting helps establish a context and a mood. **Mood,** or atmosphere, is the emotion created in the reader by part or all of a story. (See Understanding Setting, page 80.)

Memorable Literary Settings

The settings some writers of fiction create are so vivid and creative that they become real to readers. From the list below, which of the settings do you recognize? What is it that makes these settings seem so real?

- Middle-earth
- Hogwart's Academy
- Hundred Acre Wood
- Green Gables
- Neverland
- Narnia
- Oz

Theme

The **theme** is the central idea or perception about life that is revealed through a literary work. A *stated theme* is presented directly, whereas an *implied theme* must be inferred. Most works of fiction do not have a stated theme but rather several implied themes. (See Understanding Theme, page 106.)

Author's Style

Style is the manner in which something is said or written. A writer's style is characterized by such elements as word choice (or *diction*), sentence structure and length, and other recurring features that distinguish his or her work from that of another. You can think of literary style as the author's personal signature. Some authors are known for using certain literary devices, such as irony. **Irony** is the difference between appearance and reality—in other words, what seems to be and what really is. The three types of irony are as follows:

- *dramatic irony:* something is known by the writer or audience but unknown to the characters
- *verbal irony:* a character says one thing but means another
- *irony of situation:* an event occurs that is contrary to what is expected by the characters or the audience

FICTION READING MODEL

BEFORE READING DURING READING AFTER READING

BUILD BACKGROUND

- Read the **Build Background** feature to see if there are any hints about what happens in the story. Note also the years the author lived in the **Meet the Author** feature to get an idea about the time period in which the author wrote.

ANALYZE LITERATURE

- The **Analyze Literature** feature will focus on one or more literary techniques or elements that are used in the selection. You will be asked to pay attention to things such as plot, characters, setting, and theme.

SET PURPOSE

- Use the purpose explained in the **Set Purpose** feature or preview the text to create a purpose of your own. What do the art and quotations that accompany the story suggest to you about what it is about?

USE READING SKILLS

- Before reading, apply reading skills, such as analyzing text structure and previewing new vocabulary words. The **Use Reading Skills** feature will give you instructions on how to apply the skills while you read, such as using a graphic organizer.

BEFORE READING **DURING READING** AFTER READING

USE READING STRATEGIES

- **Ask questions** about things that seem unusual or interesting or things you do not understand.
- **Make predictions** about what is going to happen next.
- **Visualize** by forming pictures in your mind to help you see the story's characters or action. Imagine how the characters might say their lines.
- **Make inferences,** or educated guesses, about what is not stated directly. Things may be implied or hinted at, or they may be left out altogether. Sometimes, you must infer what the common understanding of a situation would be in the time period in which it was written.

- **Clarify,** or check that you understand what you read. Go back and reread any confusing or difficult parts before continuing.

ANALYZE LITERATURE

- Pay attention to the **literary elements** that stand out as you read the story. Are the characters engaging and lifelike? Is there a strong central conflict or theme?

MAKE CONNECTIONS

- Notice where there are **connections** between the story and your life or the world beyond the story. What feelings or thoughts do you have while reading the story?

BEFORE READING DURING READING **AFTER READING**

REFER TO TEXT

- **Remember details** like characters' names, location or setting, and important action in the story.
- **Determine the sequence** of events, the order in which things happen in the story.
- Try to **summarize** the story in a sentence or two.

REASON WITH TEXT

- **Interpret** the events of the story to help you clarify meaning.
- **Analyze** the text by breaking down information into smaller pieces and figuring out how those pieces fit into the story as a whole.

- **Evaluate** the text. **Draw conclusions** by bringing together what you have read and using it to make a decision or form an opinion.

ANALYZE LITERATURE

- **Apply** the ideas that you understand about the characters, plot, or theme to see if they help you answer any additional questions. **Review** how the author's use of literary elements increased your understanding or enjoyment of the story.

EXTEND THE TEXT

- **Extend** your reading beyond the story by exploring ideas through writing or doing other creative projects.

The Open Window

BEFORE READING
A Short Story by Saki

BUILD BACKGROUND

Social Context In **"The Open Window,"** Framton Nuttel, a nervous and depressed man who is new in town, pays a formal visit to Mrs. Sappleton. While Framton awaits the arrival of Mrs. Sappleton, her niece, Vera, tries to enliven the conversation by telling Framton a story—with shocking results.

As a newcomer to the community, Framton carries a letter of introduction when he arrives at the Sappleton home. This letter serves as a kind of social résumé and states the newcomer's family connections, qualifications, reputation, and interests. This type of letter was common in nineteenth-century England, the period in which this story is set.

Reader's Context Think about a social situation in which you were expected to behave in a certain way. Did you behave in the manner expected of you? Why or why not?

ANALYZE LITERATURE: Character and Characterization

A **character** is an individual who takes part in the action of a literary work. The main character or *protagonist* is the central figure in a literary work. Authors use techniques of **characterization** to create a character. Such techniques include showing what a character says, does, or thinks; showing what other characters say or think about him or her; and describing the character's physical features, dress, and personality.

SET PURPOSE

Think about the expectations you have about how people will behave when you meet them. We live in a fairly informal society, yet we still expect certain pleasantries and polite acts. Considering that "The Open Window" takes place in a formal society, how do you expect the characters of this story to act? As you read, look for different ways the characters are created and think about whether the characters behave according to your expectations.

MEET THE AUTHOR

Hector Hugh Munro (1870–1916) was born in Scotland. He later took the pseudonym **Saki.** Though he is mostly known for his witty short stories, of which this selection is an example, some of Saki's stories, such as "Sredni Vashtar" and "The Muse on the Hill," are rather somber. Saki's literary career was cut short when, at the age of forty-four, he volunteered for active duty in World War I and was killed in action.

USE READING SKILLS

Draw Conclusions When you **draw conclusions,** you gather pieces of information and then decide what the information means. You can draw conclusions about the characters in a story by using a Conclusions Chart like the one below. In the first column, record important things a character says or does. In the second column, record the conclusion you can draw about the character based on his or her words or actions.

Character's Words or Actions	My Conclusion About the Character

PREVIEW VOCABULARY

Use the context clues in the sentences below to figure out the meanings of the underlined words from the selection.

1. A <u>self-possessed</u> speaker in any situation, she was not upset by the disruptive audience.
2. The foamy waves <u>engulfed</u> the children's sand castle.
3. Nervous and unsure, the boy <u>falteringly</u> took his date's hand.
4. Suffering from paranoia, the patient lived with the <u>delusion</u> that others wished to harm him.
5. The <u>ghastly</u> news photographs of the war shocked and upset viewers.

THE Open WINDOW

A Short Story by **Saki**

It was certainly an unfortunate coincidence that he should have paid his visit on this tragic anniversary.

self • pos • sessed
(self' pə zest´) *adj.*,
confident; composed

du • ly (dü´ lē) *adv.*, as
required; sufficiently

"My aunt will be down presently,[1] Mr. Nuttel," said a very self-possessed young lady of fifteen; "in the meantime you must try and put up with me."

Framton Nuttel endeavored[2] to say the correct something which should duly flatter the niece of the moment without unduly discounting[3] the aunt that was to come. Privately he doubted more than ever whether these formal visits on a succession of total strangers would do much towards helping the nerve cure which he was supposed to be undergoing.

"I know how it will be," his sister had said when he was preparing to migrate to this rural retreat; "you will bury yourself down there and not speak to a living soul, and your nerves will be worse than ever from moping. I shall just give you letters of introduction to all the people I know there. Some of them, as far as I can remember, were quite nice."

5

DURING READING

USE READING STRATEGIES

Make Inferences What can you guess about Framton Nuttel from his doubts about formal visits?

---

1. **presently.** Soon, in a little while
2. **endeavored.** Tried; attempted
3. **unduly discounting.** Improperly disregarding

The Girl by the Window, Harry Morley.

Framton wondered whether Mrs. Sappleton, the lady to whom he   15
was presenting one of the letters of introduction, came into the nice division.

"Do you know many of the people round here?" asked the niece
when she judged that they had had sufficient silent communion.[4]

"Hardly a soul," said Framton. "My sister was staying here, at the   20
rectory,[5] you know, some four years ago, and she gave me letters of
introduction to some of the people here."

He made the last statement in a tone of distinct regret.

"Then you know practically nothing about my aunt?" pursued the
self-possessed young lady.   25

---

4. **communion.** Sharing of thoughts
5. **rectory.** A residence of a parish priest

"Only her name and address," admitted the caller. He was wondering whether Mrs. Sappleton was in the married or widowed state. An undefinable something about the room seemed to suggest masculine habitation.

30 "Her great tragedy happened just three years ago," said the child; "that would be since your sister's time."

"Her tragedy?" asked Framton; somehow in this restful country spot tragedies seemed out of place.

"You may wonder why we keep that window wide open on an October afternoon," said the niece, indicating a large French window that opened on to a lawn.

"It is quite warm for the time of the year," said Framton; "but has that window got anything to do with the tragedy?"

"Out through that window, three years ago to a day, her husband and her two young brothers went off for their day's shooting. They never came back. In crossing the moor to their favorite snipe-shooting[6] ground they were all three engulfed in a treacherous piece of bog.[7] It had been that dreadful wet summer, you know, and places that were safe in other years gave way suddenly without warning.

45 Their bodies were never recovered. That was the dreadful part of it." Here the child's voice lost its self-possessed note and became falteringly human. "Poor aunt always thinks that they will come back some day, they and the little brown spaniel that was lost with them, and walk in at that window just as they used to do. That is why the window is kept

50 open every evening till it is quite dusk. Poor dear aunt, she has often told me how they went out, her husband with his white waterproof coat over his arm, and Ronnie, her youngest brother, singing, 'Bertie, why do you bound?'[8] as he always did to tease her, because she said it got on her nerves. Do you know, sometimes on still, quiet evenings like

55 this, I almost get a creepy feeling that they will all walk in through that window—"

She broke off with a little shudder. It was a relief to Framton when the aunt bustled into the room with a whirl of apologies for being late in making her appearance.

"I hope Vera has been amusing you?" she said. "She has been very interesting," said Framton.

"I hope you don't mind the open window," said Mrs. Sappleton briskly; "my husband and brothers will be home directly from

DURING READING

USE READING STRATEGIES

Ask Questions Is there anything that puzzles you about the information Vera gives Framton? Write a question about it.

en • gulf (in gulf´) v., swallow up

fal • ter • ing • ly (fôl´ tər iŋ lē) adv., uncertainly; unsteadily

DURING READING

USE READING STRATEGIES

Predict What do you think will happen in Framton's meeting with Vera's aunt? How will it go?

---

6. **snipe-shooting.** Bird-hunting
7. **bog.** Wet, spongy ground ~ ▷ moor / marsh
8. '**Bertie…bound?**' Line from a popular song

shooting, and they always come in this way. They've been out for snipe in the marshes today, so they'll make a fine mess over my poor carpets. So like you men-folk, isn't it?"

She rattled on cheerfully about the shooting and the scarcity of birds, and the prospects for duck in the winter. To Framton, it was all purely horrible. He made a desperate but only partially successful effort to turn the talk on to a less <u>ghastly</u> topic; he was conscious that his hostess was giving him only a fragment of her attention, and her eyes were constantly straying past him to the open window and the lawn beyond. It was certainly an unfortunate coincidence that he should have paid his visit on this tragic anniversary.

Hunters and Dogs, Joseph Cusachs y Cusachs.

65

70

75

80

85 **ghast • ly** (gastˊ lē) *adj.,* horrible; frightful

90

"The doctors agree in ordering me complete rest, <u>an absence of mental excitement</u>, and avoidance of anything in the nature of violent physical exercise," announced Framton, who labored under the tolerably widespread <u>delusion</u> that total strangers and chance acquaintances are hungry for the least detail of one's ailments and infirmities,[9] their cause and cure. "On the matter of diet they are not so much in agreement," he continued.

"No?" said Mrs. Sappleton, in a voice which only replaced a yawn at the last moment. Then she suddenly brightened into alert attention—but not to what Framton was saying.

DURING READING

ANALYZE LITERATURE

Characterization What does Framton think is a good topic for conversation? What does this fact suggest about his character?

100 **de • lu • sion** (di lüˊ zhən) *n.,* false belief or opinion

---

9. **infirmities.** Physical weaknesses or defects

"Here they are at last!" she cried. "Just in time for tea, and don't they
105 look as if they were muddy up to the eyes!"

Framton shivered slightly and turned towards the niece with a look
intended to <u>convey</u> sympathetic comprehension. The child was staring
out through the open window with dazed horror in her eyes. In a chill
shock of nameless fear Framton swung around in his seat and looked in
110 the same direction.

In the deepening twilight three figures were walking across the lawn
towards the window; they all carried guns under their arms, and one of
them was additionally burdened with a white coat hung over his shoulders. A tired brown spaniel kept close at their heels. Noiselessly they
115 neared the house, and then a hoarse young voice chanted out of the
dusk: "I said, Bertie, why do you bound?"

Framton grabbed wildly at his stick and hat; the hall-door,
the gravel-drive, and the front gate were dimly noted stages in
his headlong retreat. A cyclist coming along the road had to
run into the hedge to avoid <u>imminent</u> collision.

"Here we are, my dear," said the bearer of the white mackintosh,[10] coming in through the window; "fairly muddy, but
most of it's dry. Who was that who bolted out as we came up?"

"A most extraordinary man, a Mr. Nuttel," said Mrs. Sappleton;
125 "could only talk about his illnesses, and dashed off without a word of
good-bye or apology when you arrived. One would think he had seen a
ghost."

"I expect it was the spaniel," said the niece calmly; "he
told me he had a horror of dogs. He was once hunted into a
cemetery somewhere on the banks of the Ganges by a pack of
pariah dogs,[11] and had to spend the night in a newly dug grave
with the creatures snarling and grinning and foaming just
above him. Enough to make any one lose their nerve."

Romance[12] at short notice was her speciality. ❖

con • vey (kən vā´) v.,
make known

DURING READING

USE READING STRATEGIES

Visualize Picture the scene of the
returning hunters in your mind. How
might that scene seem frightening or
pleasing in different contexts?

im • mi • nent
(im´ ə nənt) adj., coming
soon; threatening

DURING READING

ANALYZE LITERATURE

Characterization
How would you describe the
character of Vera? Why?

---

10. **mackintosh.** Waterproof outer coat
11. **Ganges**…**dogs.** *Ganges*—river in India; *pariah dogs*—stray dogs, outcast and rejected by others
12. **Romance.** A made-up story

Why would someone make up a story to shock another person? Is it wrong to do
so, or is it a harmless joke? Explain your answer.

AFTER READING

REFER TO TEXT PG 7, 8 ▶ ▶ ▶	▶ REASON WITH TEXT	
1a. List questions Vera asks Framton about the "people round here" and about her aunt.	1b. Infer why Vera asks these questions.	**Understand** Find meaning
2a. Identify what Framton knows about the Sappletons before his visit.	2b. Examine Saki's ideas about the social conventions of the time period. What point is he trying to make?	**Apply** Use information
3a. How does Vera direct Framton's attention to the open window? How does Framton respond?	3b. Explain why Vera wants Framton to notice the window. How does Framton's response to Vera's comments about the window allow Vera to create "romance at short notice"?	**Analyze** Take things apart
4a. Record how Framton reacts to the arrival of the hunters and how Mrs. Sappleton reacts to Framton's departure.	4b. Conclude whether Framton would have confronted Vera about her story if he had been a braver sort. Explain your reasoning.	**Evaluate** Make judgments
5a. What does Vera suggest is the reason for Framton's quick departure?	5b. Explain the purpose of Vera's story about Framton Nuttel.	**Create** Bring ideas together

ANALYZE LITERATURE: Character and Characterization

How would you describe the characters of Vera and Framton to a friend who hasn't read "The Open Window"? Give examples from the text that show how Vera and Framton are characterized.

EXTEND THE TEXT

Writing Options

Creative Writing Using what you have learned about Framton and his sister from the story, and filling in the rest with your imagination, write the **letter of introduction** Framton presents to Mrs. Sappleton. Keep in mind that the Nuttels and Sappletons belong to "polite society."

Narrative Writing Reread the story and look for clues that indicate what Framton is thinking and feeling during his visit to the Sappleton home. Then write a three-paragraph **personal essay** from Framton's point of view that describes his experience at the Sappleton home and the effect it had on him and his health, as well as his opinion about the Sappleton family, especially Vera.

Collaborative Learning

Perform a Skit Work with a partner to write a skit, or short play, about two characters in a conventional social situation who find things are not turning out as expected. Examples of conventional social situations include attending a party, having dinner at a restaurant, going on a date, or hanging out at a local club or mall. Once you have written and rehearsed your skit, act it out for your class.

Critical Literacy

Research and Compare Social Conventions
Research the social conventions of another time period in American or world history. Provide as much information as you can to explain the reasons behind the conventions. Then write a report comparing and contrasting these conventions (or rules of etiquette) with modern conventions for similar situations.

 Go to **www.mirrorsandwindows.com** for more.

Understanding Plot

PLOT

A **plot** is a series of related events that drive a story. Have you ever been so wrapped up in a book that you find yourself staying up until the early hours of the morning to finish it or flipping to the end of the book to see how it turns out? Books and stories that are hard to put down usually have an interesting or exciting plot.

ELEMENTS OF PLOT

A car is built around a frame, which gives it shape and stability. In the same way, the plot is the frame that gives a story its structure. In general, the main parts of a plot's framework are as follows:

Exposition: The characters are introduced, the setting is established, and necessary background information is provided.

Rising Action: The main character encounters and tries to solve a problem. This results in a conflict developing and becoming more and more intense.

Climax: At this crucial moment, the main character has to take action or make a decision. Sometimes, fate intervenes and forces the character's hand.

Falling Action: This part of a story explores the events that follow the climax, including the results of the main character's action or decision.

Resolution: This part of a story is sometimes called the dénouement (dā nü mä´). At this point, the conflict is resolved.

A **Plot Diagram** is a useful tool for keeping track of all the parts of a plot. To create a Plot Diagram, draw a pyramid shape and make notes on it about each part of the plot. Below is a Plot Diagram of the story "Cinderella."

Plot Diagram

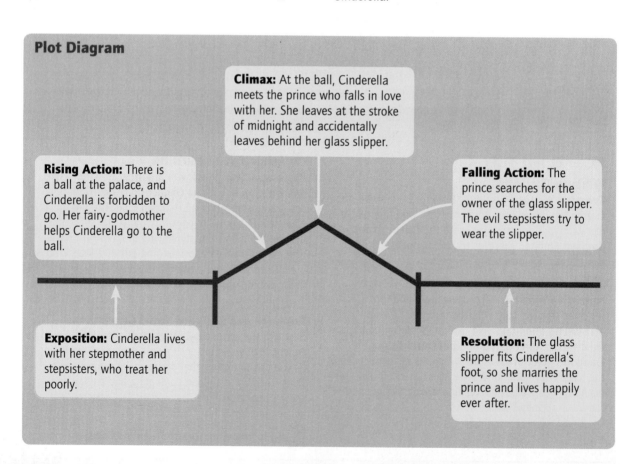

Climax: At the ball, Cinderella meets the prince who falls in love with her. She leaves at the stroke of midnight and accidentally leaves behind her glass slipper.

Rising Action: There is a ball at the palace, and Cinderella is forbidden to go. Her fairy-godmother helps Cinderella go to the ball.

Falling Action: The prince searches for the owner of the glass slipper. The evil stepsisters try to wear the slipper.

Exposition: Cinderella lives with her stepmother and stepsisters, who treat her poorly.

Resolution: The glass slipper fits Cinderella's foot, so she marries the prince and lives happily ever after.

PLOT AND CONFLICT

A plot revolves around some type of **conflict,** or struggle. Usually, throughout the course of a story, a central conflict is introduced, developed, and resolved.

An *internal conflict* is a struggle that takes place within the character. For instance, the barber in "Lather and Nothing Else" (page 45) struggles with his conscience as he decides whether or not to murder his customer.

An *external conflict* is a struggle that takes place between a character and some outside force. One type of external conflict is between a character and nature. This type is demonstrated in "Through the Tunnel" (page 29) as Jerry attempts to swim through the treacherous sea tunnel. Another type of external conflict is between two main characters, such as Jing-mei rebelling against her mother's expectations in "Two Kinds" (page 69). A third type of external conflict is between a character and society. In "On the Rainy River" (page 137), the narrator's desire to ignore the draft is in direct conflict with the expectations of society.

Notable Conflicts

A compelling conflict is central to a memorable plot. Do you recognize any of the protagonist-antagonist pairs below?
- Aslan vs. The White Witch
- Snowball vs. Napoleon
- Hester Prynne vs. Roger Chillingworth
- Jekyll vs. Hyde
- Ebenezer Scrooge vs. greed

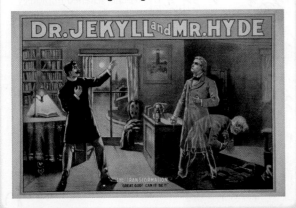

PLOT AND ORGANIZATION

A story has to have a beginning, a middle, and an end. A story's plot, therefore, is often framed by time. Some stories focus on one hour in a person's life; others may span one hundred years. For instance, "The Open Window" (page 6) takes place in an afternoon, whereas "Two Kinds" spans many years.

Most stories are told in **chronological order,** where the writer unfolds events in the order in which they occurred. A **flashback** interrupts the chronological sequence of a literary work and presents an event that occurred earlier. Sometimes, writers play with time sequence and may use flashbacks to reveal what has happened at a prior time. For instance, in "Cranes" (page 132), Sôngsam remembers the time when he and his childhood friend, Tôkchae, capture a crane. This flashback helps explain Sôngsam's later actions concerning his treatment of Tôkchae.

> Once, Sôngsam and Tôkchae were about twelve, they had set a trap here, unbeknown to the adults, and caught a crane, a Tanjông crane. They had tied the crane up, even binding its wings, and paid it daily visits, patting its neck and riding on its back. Then one day they overheard the neighbors whispering: someone had come from Seoul with a permit from the governor-general's office to catch cranes as some kind of specimens. Then and there the two boys had dashed off to the field.
>
> —from "Cranes" by Hwang Sun-wôn

PLOT AND FORESHADOWING

Writers can use **foreshadowing,** or the act of presenting hints to events that will occur later in a story, to build interest and suspense. In "The Monkey's Paw" (page 15), Sergeant-Major Morris's grave tone as he recounts how he came by the paw suggests that the paw does more harm than good.

The Monkey's Paw

BUILD BACKGROUND

Literary Context A horror story, **"The Monkey's Paw"** creates in the reader a sense of dread. British short story writer W. W. Jacobs achieves this suspenseful effect by introducing into the ordinary, everyday life of the White family an odd object—a monkey's paw. This paw was brought home by Sergeant-Major Morris from a tour of duty in India, which, at the time of the story, was controlled by Britain. As the White family soon discovers, the lives of those who fall under the spell of the paw are forever changed.

"The Monkey's Paw" was published in 1902, and its success over the years lies in its classic horror elements: a dark, misty night; a mysterious stranger; the magical powers of an object; the temptation of greed; and the struggle against humankind's ultimate enemy—fate. This story has been adapted for film, television, and stage productions.

Reader's Context If you were granted three wishes, what would they be? Describe what your life would be like if these wishes were granted. What unintended consequences might come of these wishes?

ANALYZE LITERATURE: Plot and Foreshadowing

Plot is a series of events related to a central conflict, or struggle. A typical plot introduces a conflict, develops it, and eventually resolves it. **Foreshadowing,** or the act of presenting materials that hint at events to occur later in the story, can help advance the plot by creating suspense. Several events foreshadow the ending of "The Monkey's Paw."

SET PURPOSE

The idea of three wishes is common in literature, folktales, and oral tradition. This concept is introduced early in "The Monkey's Paw." Using what you know about other stories in which wishes are granted and about "The Monkey's Paw," predict what will happen in the story. As you read the story and learn about wishes that were granted, predict what this information may foreshadow.

MEET THE AUTHOR

William Wymark (W. W.) Jacobs (1863–1943) was born in London, England, and grew up in a house along a Thames River wharf, where his father worked. Although never a seaman himself, he drew on his childhood memories to write comic tales about the misadventures of sailors, though many of these tales were set on land. *Many Cargoes* was Jacobs's first collection of such stories. Jacobs gained enough success as a writer to quit his job in civil service in 1899. Although his work is collected in more than twenty volumes, he is best known for his horror story "The Monkey's Paw."

USE READING SKILLS

Sequence of Events
Sequence refers to the order in which things happen. In short stories, events are not always told to readers in the order in which they occurred; this is why it is important to write down events.

As you read "The Monkey's Paw," use a Time Line like the one below to keep track of the events in the story. As you create your Time Line, circle any events you think might foreshadow something to come.

Sergeant-major visits

PREVIEW VOCABULARY

Use the context clues in the sentences below to figure out the meanings of the underlined words from the selection.

1. Gregor has been <u>maligned</u> because he hangs out with people who get in trouble.
2. The teacher listened <u>dubiously</u> to Antonio's excuse for being late to class.
3. Katarina <u>attributes</u> her success to both talent and hard work.
4. The <u>avaricious</u> man loved his wealth so much that he would not even help his poor mother.
5. Clark's <u>apathy</u> was a sharp contrast to his usual enthusiasm and excitement.

The Monkey's Paw

"Hold it up in your right hand and wish aloud," said the sergeant-major, "but I warn you of the consequences."

A Short Story by **W. W. Jacobs**

Without, the night was cold and wet, but in the small parlor of Laburnum Villa the "blinds were drawn," and the fire burned brightly.

Father and son were at chess, the former, who possessed ideas about the game involving radical changes, putting his king into such sharp and unnecessary perils that it even provoked comment from the white-haired old lady knitting placidly by the fire.

"Hark at the wind," said Mr. White, who, having seen a fatal mistake after it was too late, was <u>amiably</u> desirous of preventing his son from seeing it.

"I'm listening," said the latter, grimly surveying the board as he stretched out his hand. "Check."

"I should hardly think that he'd come tonight," said his father, with his hand poised over the board.

ANALYZE LITERATURE

Foreshadowing What atmosphere does the description of the weather create? What kind of events might the weather foreshadow?

"Mate,"[1] replied the son.

"That's the worst living so far out," bawled Mr. White, with sudden and unlooked-for violence. "Of all the beastly, slushy, out-of-the-way places to live in, this is the worst. Pathway's a bog, and the road's a torrent. I don't know what people are thinking about. I suppose because only two houses in the road are let; they think it doesn't matter."

"Never mind, dear," said his wife soothingly. "Perhaps you'll win the next one."

Mr. White looked up sharply, just in time to intercept a knowing glance between mother and son. The words died away on his lips, and he hid a guilty grin in his thin gray beard.

"There he is," said Herbert White, as the gate banged loudly and heavy footsteps came toward the door.

The old man rose with hospitable haste, and opening the door, was heard condoling with the new arrival. The new arrival also condoled with himself, so that Mrs. White said, "Tut, tut!" and coughed gently as her husband entered the room, followed by a tall, burly man, beady of eye and rubicund of visage.[2]

"Sergeant-Major Morris," he said, introducing him.

The sergeant-major shook hands, and taking the proffered seat by the fire, watched contentedly while his host got out whisky and

tumblers and stood a small copper kettle on the fire.

At the third glass, his eyes got brighter, and he began to talk; the little family circle regarding with eager interest this visitor from distant parts, as he squared his broad shoulders in the chair and spoke of wild scenes and doughty[3] deeds; of wars and plagues and strange peoples.

"Twenty-one years of it," said Mr. White, nodding at his wife and son. "When he went away he was a slip of a youth in the warehouse. Now look at him."

---

1. **Mate.** The winning move in chess, capturing an opponent's king, is announced with "checkmate."
2. **rubicund of visage.** Pink-faced
3. **doughty.** Brave

ami • a • bly (ā´ mē ə blē) *adv.,* pleasantly

"He don't look to have taken much harm," said Mrs. White politely.

"I'd like to go to India myself," said the old man, "just to look round a bit, you know."

"Better where you are," said the sergeant-major, shaking his head. He put down the empty glass, and sighing softly, shook it again.

"I should like to see those old temples and fakirs[4] and jugglers," said the old man. "What was that you started telling me the other day about a monkey's paw or something, Morris?"

"Nothing," said the soldier hastily. "Leastways, nothing worth hearing."

"Monkey's paw?" said Mrs. White curiously.

"Well, it's just a bit of what you might call magic, perhaps," said the sergeant-major offhandedly.

His three listeners leaned forward eagerly. The visitor absentmindedly put his empty glass to his lips and then set it down again. His host filled it for him.

"To look at," said the sergeant-major, fumbling in his pocket, "it's just an ordinary little paw, dried to a mummy."

He took something out of his pocket and proffered it. Mrs. White drew back with a grimace, but her son, taking it, examined it curiously.

"And what is there special about it?" inquired Mr. White as he took it from his son, and having examined it, placed it upon the table.

"It had a spell put on it by an old fakir," said the sergeant-major, "a very holy man. He wanted to show that fate ruled people's lives, and that those who interfered with it did so to their sorrow. He put a spell on it so that three separate men could each have three wishes from it."

His manner was so impressive that his hearers were conscious that their light laughter jarred somewhat.

"Well, why don't you have three, sir?" said Herbert White cleverly.

The soldier regarded him in the way that middle age is wont to regard presumptuous youth. "I have," he said quietly, and his blotchy face whitened.

"And did you really have the three wishes granted?" asked Mrs. White.

"I did," said the sergeant-major, and his glass tapped against his strong teeth.

"And has anybody else wished?" persisted the old lady.

"The first man had his three wishes. Yes," was the reply. "I don't know what the first two were, but the third was for death. That's how I got the paw."

His tones were so grave that a hush fell upon the group.

USE READING STRATEGIES

Predict In this passage, what do you learn about the three wishes made possible by the monkey's paw? Predict what you think will happen in the story.

"If you've had your three wishes, it's no good to you now, then, Morris," said the old man at last. "What do you keep it for?"

The soldier shook his head. "Fancy, I suppose," he said slowly. "I did have some idea of selling it, but I don't think I will. It has caused enough mischief already. Besides, people won't buy. They think it's a fairy tale, some of them, and those who do think anything of it, want to try it first and pay me afterward."

"If you could have another three wishes," said the old man, eyeing him keenly, "would you have them?"

"I don't know," said the other. "I don't know."

He took the paw, and dangling it between his forefinger and thumb, suddenly threw it upon the fire. White, with a slight cry, stooped down and snatched it off.

---

4. **fakirs.** People who, for religious purposes, live a thoughtful life of poverty and self-denial

pre • sump • tu • ous (pri zum[p]′ chə wəs) *adj.*, arrogant; tending to assume

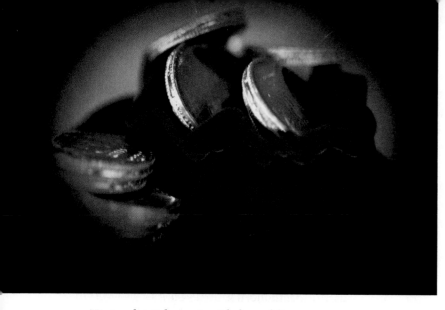

"Better let it burn," said the soldier solemnly.

"If you don't want it, Morris," said the other, "give it to me."

"I won't," said his friend doggedly. "I threw it on the fire. If you keep it, don't blame me for what happens. Pitch it on the fire again like a sensible man."

The other shook his head and examined his new possession closely. "How do you do it?" he inquired.

"Hold it up in your right hand and wish aloud," said the sergeant-major, "but I warn you of the consequences."

"Sounds like the *Arabian Nights*," said Mrs. White, as she rose and began to set the supper. "Don't you think you might wish for four pairs of hands for me?"

Her husband drew the talisman[5] from his pocket, and then all three burst into laughter as the sergeant-major, with a look of alarm on his face, caught him by the arm.

"If you must wish," he said gruffly, "wish for something sensible."

Mr. White dropped it back into his pocket, and placing chairs, motioned his friend to the table. In the business of supper, the talisman was partly forgotten, and afterward the three sat listening in an enthralled fashion to a second installment of the soldier's adventures in India.

"If the tale about the monkey's paw is not more truthful than those he has been telling us," said Herbert, as the door closed behind their guest, just in time for him to catch the last train, "we shan't make much out of it."

"Did you give him anything for it, Father?" inquired Mrs. White, regarding her husband closely.

"A trifle," said he, coloring slightly. "He didn't want it, but I made him take it. And he pressed me again to throw it away."

"Likely," said Herbert, with pretended horror. "Why, we're going to be rich, and famous and happy. Wish to be an emperor, Father, to begin with; then you can't be henpecked."

He darted round the table, pursued by the <u>maligned</u> Mrs. White armed with an antimacassar.[6]

Mr. White took the paw from his pocket and eyed it <u>dubiously</u>. "I don't know what to wish for, and that's a fact," he said slowly. "It seems to me I've got all I want."

"If you only cleared the house, you'd be quite happy, wouldn't you?" said Herbert, with his hand on his shoulder. "Well, wish for two hundred pounds, then; that'll just do it." His father, smiling shamefacedly at his own credulity, held up the talisman, as his son, with a solemn face, somewhat marred by a wink at his

ANALYZE LITERATURE

Foreshadowing How does Herbert's joking about the monkey's paw contrast with the atmosphere established by the sergeant-major? What might Herbert's attitude foreshadow?

---

5. **talisman.** Magic charm
6. **antimacassar.** Cover on a chair or sofa, which prevents soiling

ma • ligned (mə līngd´) *adj.,* slandered
du • bi • ous • ly (dü´ bē əs lē) *adv.,* skeptically; doubtfully

mother, sat down at the piano and struck a few impressive chords.

"I wish for two hundred pounds," said the old man distinctly.

A fine crash from the piano greeted the words, interrupted by a shuddering cry from the old man. His wife and son ran toward him.

"It moved," he cried, with a glance of disgust at the object as it lay on the floor. "As I wished, it twisted in my hand like a snake."

"Well, I don't see the money," said his son as he picked it up and placed it on the table, "and I bet I never shall."

"It must have been your fancy, Father," said his wife, regarding him anxiously.

He shook his head. "Never mind, though; there's no harm done, but it gave me a shock all the same."

They sat down by the fire again while the two men finished their pipes. Outside, the wind was higher than ever, and the old man started nervously at the sound of a door banging upstairs. A silence unusual and depressing settled upon all three, which lasted until the old couple rose to retire for the night.

"I expect you'll find the cash tied up in a big bag in the middle of your bed," said Herbert, as he bade them good night, "and something horrible squatting up on top of the wardrobe watching you as you pocket your ill-gotten gains."

He sat alone in the darkness, gazing at the dying fire, and seeing faces in it. The last face was so horrible and so simian that he gazed at it in amazement. It got so vivid that, with a little uneasy laugh, he felt on the table for a glass containing a little water to throw over it. His hand grasped the monkey's paw, and with a little shiver, he wiped his hand on his coat and went up to bed.

In the brightness of the wintry sun next morning as it streamed over the breakfast table, he laughed at his fears. There was an air of <u>prosaic</u> wholesomeness about the room that it had lacked on the previous night, and the

dirty, shrivelled little paw was pitched on the sideboard with a carelessness which betokened[7] no great belief in its virtues.

"I suppose all old soldiers are the same," said Mrs. White. "The idea of our listening to such nonsense! How could wishes be granted in these days? And if they could, how could two hundred pounds hurt you, Father?"

"Might drop on his head from the sky," said the frivolous Herbert.

"Morris said the things happened so naturally," said his father, "that you might if you so wished <u>attribute</u> it to coincidence."

"Well, don't break into the money before I come back," said Herbert as he rose from the table. "I'm afraid it'll turn you into a mean, <u>avaricious</u> man, and we shall have to disown you."

USE READING STRATEGIES

Ask Questions Write down any questions you have about the events of the story so far. Then continue reading and see if your questions are answered.

His mother laughed, and following him to the door, watched him down the road; and returning to the breakfast table, was very happy at the expense of her husband's credulity. All of which did not prevent her from scurrying to the door at the postman's knock, nor prevent her from referring somewhat shortly to retired sergeant-majors of bibulous[8] habits when she found that the post brought a tailor's bill.

"Herbert will have some more of his funny remarks, I expect, when he comes home," she said, as they sat at dinner.

"I dare say," said Mr. White, pouring himself out some beer. "But for all that, the thing moved in my hand; that I'll swear to."

---

7. **betokened.** Indicated
8. **bibulous.** Tending to drink too much

---

pro • sa • ic (prō zā′ ik) *adj.*, commonplace; dull
at • trib • ute (a tri′ byüt′) *v.*, think of as resulting from
av • a • ri • cious (a′ və ri′ shəs) *adj.*, greedy

"You thought it did," said the old lady soothingly.

"I say it did," replied the other. "There was no thought about it; I had just-What's the matter?"

His wife made no reply. She was watching the mysterious movements of a man outside, who, peering in an undecided fashion at the house, appeared to be trying to make up his mind to enter. In mental connection with the two hundred pounds, she noticed that the stranger was well dressed, and wore a silk hat of glossy newness. Three times he paused at the gate, and then walked on again. The fourth time he stood with his hands upon it, and then with sudden resolution flung it open and walked up the path. Mrs. White at the same moment placed her hands behind her, and hurriedly unfastening the strings of her apron, put that useful article of apparel beneath the cushion of her chair.

She brought the stranger, who seemed ill at ease, into the room. He gazed at her furtively, and listened in a preoccupied fashion as the old lady apologized for the appearance of the room, and

ANALYZE LITERATURE

Foreshadowing What does the description of the visitor suggest about what he might have come to say? How is this an example of foreshadowing?

her husband's coat, a garment that he usually reserved for the garden. She then waited, as patiently as her sex would permit, for him to broach his business; but he was at first strangely silent.

"I—was asked to call," he said at last, and stooped and picked a piece of cotton from his trousers. "I come from Maw and Meggins." The old lady started. "Is anything the matter?" she asked breathlessly. "Has anything happened to Herbert? What is it? What is it?"

Her husband interposed. "There, there, Mother," he said hastily. "Sit down, and don't jump to conclusions. You've not brought bad news, I'm sure, sir," and he eyed the other wistfully.

"I'm sorry—" began the visitor.

"Is he hurt?" demanded the mother wildly.

The visitor bowed in assent. "Badly hurt," he said quietly, "but he is not in any pain."

"Oh, thank God!" said the old woman, clasping her hands. "Thank God for that! Thank—"

She broke off suddenly as the sinister meaning of the assurance dawned upon her, and she saw the awful confirmation of her fears in the other's <u>averted</u> face. She caught her breath, and turning to her slower-witted husband, laid her trembling old hand upon his. There was a long silence.

"He was caught in the machinery," said the visitor at length in a low voice.

"Caught in the machinery," repeated Mr. White, in a dazed fashion, "yes."

He sat staring blankly out at the window, and taking his wife's hand between his own, pressed it as he had been wont to do

Unconscious of his wife's shriek, the old man smiled faintly, put out his hands like a sightless man, and dropped, a senseless heap, to the floor.

a · vert · ed (ə vʉrt´ ed) adj., turned away

USE READING STRATEGIES

Visualize Imagine in your mind Mrs. White's physical reaction to the news of the stranger.

in their old courting days nearly forty years before.

"He was the only one left to us," he said, turning gently to the visitor. "It is hard."

The other coughed, and rising, walked slowly to the window. "The firm wished me to convey their sincere sympathy with you in your great loss," he said, without looking round. "I beg that you will understand I am only their servant and merely obeying orders."

There was no reply. The old woman's face was white, her eyes staring, and her breath <u>inaudible</u>. On the husband's face was a look such as his friend the sergeant-major might have carried into his first action.

"I was to say that Maw and Meggins disclaim all responsibility," continued the other. "They admit no liability at all, but in consideration of your son's services, they wish to present you with a certain sum as compensation."

Mr. White dropped his wife's hand, and rising to his feet, gazed with a look of horror at his visitor. His dry lips shaped the words, "How much?"

"Two hundred pounds," was the answer.

Unconscious of his wife's shriek, the old man smiled faintly, put out his hands like a sightless man, and dropped, a senseless heap, to the floor.

In the huge new cemetery, some two miles distant, the old people buried their dead, and came back to a house steeped in shadow and silence. It was all over so quickly that at first they could hardly realize it, and remained in a state of expectation as though of something else to happen—something else that was to lighten this load, too heavy for old hearts to bear.

But the days passed, and expectation gave place to resignation—the hopeless resignation of the old, sometimes miscalled <u>apathy</u>. Sometimes they hardly exchanged a word, for now they had nothing to talk about, and their days were long to weariness.

It was about a week after, that the old man, waking suddenly in the night, stretched out his hand and found himself alone. The room was in darkness, and the sound of subdued weeping came from the window. He raised himself in bed and listened.

"Come back," he said tenderly. "You will be cold."

"It is colder for my son," said the old woman, and wept afresh.

The sound of her sobs died away on his ears. The bed was warm, and his eyes heavy with sleep. He dozed fitfully, and then slept, until a sudden wild cry from his wife awoke him with a start.

"*The paw!*" she cried wildly. "The monkey's paw!"

He started up in alarm. "Where? Where is it? What's the matter?"

She came stumbling across the room toward him. "I want it," she said quietly. "You've not destroyed it?"

"It's in the parlor, on the bracket," he replied, marvelling. "Why?"

She cried and laughed together, and bending over, kissed his cheek.

"I only just thought of it," she said hysterically. "Why didn't I think of it before? Why didn't *you* think of it?"

---

in • au • di • ble (i[ˈ] nôˈdə bəl) *adj.*, that cannot be heard
ap • a • thy (aˈ pə thē) *n.*, indifference; lack of emotion

"Think of what?" he questioned.

"The other two wishes," she replied rapidly. "We've only had one."

"Was not that enough?" he demanded fiercely.

"No," she cried triumphantly. "We'll have one more. Go down and get it quickly, and wish our boy alive again."

The man sat up in bed and flung the bedclothes from his quaking limbs. "Good God, you are mad!" he cried, aghast.

"Get it," she panted. "Get it quickly, and wish—Oh, my boy, my boy!"

Her husband struck a match and lit the candle. "Get back to bed," he said unsteadily. "You don't know what you are saying."

"We had the first wish granted," said the old woman feverishly. "Why not the second?"

"A coincidence," stammered the old man.

"Go and get it and wish," cried his wife, quivering with excitement.

The old man turned and regarded her, and his voice shook. "He has been dead ten days, and besides he—I would not tell you else, but—I could only recognize him by his clothing. If he was too terrible for you to see then, how now?"

"Bring him back," cried the old woman, and dragged him toward the door. "Do you think I fear the child I have nursed?"

He went down in the darkness, and felt his way to the parlor, and then to the mantelpiece. The talisman was in its place, and a horrible fear that the unspoken wish might bring his mutilated son before him ere he could escape from the room seized upon him, and he caught his breath as he found that he had lost the direction of the door. His brow cold with sweat, he felt his way round the table, and groped along the wall until he found himself in the small passage with the unwholesome thing in his hand.

Even his wife's face seemed changed as he entered the room. It was white and expectant, and to his fears, seemed to have an unnatural look upon it. He was afraid of her.

"*Wish!*" she cried, in a strong voice.

"It is foolish and wicked," he faltered.

"*Wish!*" repeated his wife.

He raised his hand. "I wish my son alive again." The talisman fell to the floor, and he regarded it fearfully. Then he sank trembling into a chair as the old woman, with burning eyes, walked to the window and raised the blind.

He sat until he was chilled with the cold, glancing occasionally at the figure of the old woman peering through the window. The candle-end, which had burned below the rim of the china candlestick, was throwing pulsating shadows on the ceiling and walls, until, with a flicker larger than the rest, it expired. The old man, with an unspeakable sense of relief at the failure of the talisman, crept back to his bed, and a minute or two afterward the old woman came silently and apathetically beside him.

Neither spoke, but lay silently listening to the ticking of the clock. A stair creaked, and a squeaky mouse scurried noisily through the wall. The darkness was oppressive, and after lying for some time screwing up his courage, he took the box of matches, and striking one, went downstairs for a candle.

At the foot of the stairs the match went out, and he paused to strike another; and at the same moment a knock, so quiet and stealthy as to be scarcely audible, sounded on the front door.

The matches fell from his hand and spilled in the passage. He stood motionless, his breath suspended until the knock was repeated. Then he turned and fled swiftly back to his room, and closed the door behind him. A third knock sounded through the house.

"*What's that?*" cried the old woman, starting up.

"A rat," said the old man in shaking tones—"a rat. It passed me on the stairs." His wife sat up in bed listening. A loud knock resounded through the house.

"It's Herbert!" she screamed. "It's Herbert!"

She ran to the door, but her husband was before her, and catching her by the arm, held her tightly.

"What are you going to do?" he whispered hoarsely.

"It's my boy; it's Herbert!" she cried, struggling mechanically. "I forgot it was two miles away. What are you holding me for? Let go. I must open the door."

"For God's sake, don't let it in," cried the old man, trembling.

"You're afraid of your own son," she cried, struggling. "Let me go. I'm coming, Herbert; I'm coming."

There was another knock, and another. The old woman, with a sudden wrench, broke free and ran from the room. Her husband followed to the landing, and called after her appealingly as she hurried downstairs. He heard the chain rattle back and the bottom bolt drawn slowly and stiffly from the socket. Then the old woman's voice, strained and panting.

"The bolt," she cried loudly. "Come down. I can't reach it."

But her husband was on his hands and knees, groping wildly on the floor in search of the paw. If he could only find it before the

The House of Mystery,
1926. Sydney Lee. Harris Museum and Art Gallery, Preston, UK.

thing outside got in. A perfect fusillade[9] of knocks reverberated through the house, and he heard the scraping of a chair as his wife put it down in the passage against the door. He heard the creaking of the bolt as it came slowly back, and at the same moment he found the monkey's paw, and frantically breathed his third and last wish.

The knocking ceased suddenly, although the echoes of it were still in the house. He heard the chair drawn back, and the door opened. A cold wind rushed up the staircase, and a long, loud wail of disappointment and misery from his wife gave him courage to run down to her side, and then to the gate beyond. The street lamp flickering opposite shone on a quiet and deserted road. ❖

9. **fusillade.** Simultaneous discharge of many firearms

> **ANALYZE LITERATURE**
>
> **Plot** What is the climax of the story? How can you tell?

 **MIRRORS & WINDOWS**

"It had a spell put on it by an old fakir.... He wanted to show that fate ruled people's lives, and that those who interfered with it did so to their sorrow." What role does fate play in people's lives? What role do individual choices play? Explain your answer.

AFTER READING

REFER TO TEXT ▸ ▸ ▸ ▸	▸ REASON WITH TEXT	
1a. State the warning that the sergeant-major gives Mr. White.	1b. Infer what might have happened to make the sergeant-major feel this way about the monkey's paw.	**Understand** **Find meaning**
2a. Recall the spell that was put on the monkey's paw by the fakir. Why did the fakir put the spell on the paw?	2b. Apply the fakir's idea to real life. What does the story reveal about the role of fate in human life?	**Apply** **Use information**
3a. Identify a quotation or action taken by the sergeant-major, Mr. White, and Mrs. White that shows each believes in the power of the monkey's paw.	3b. Compare the ideas the sergeant-major, Mr. White and Mrs. White have about the monkey's paw. Identify who believes most strongly in the power of the paw.	**Analyze** **Take things apart**
4a. Name Mr. White's first wish.	4b. Determine what human weakness led to Mr. White's wish. Describe how you would have handled the situation in Mr. White's place.	**Evaluate** **Make judgments**
5a. Identify the limit the fakir put on the monkey's paw.	5b. Do you believe that fate, coincidence, or your own actions determine your future? Explain. What would you do if the monkey's paw still had power and you had a chance to use it?	**Create** **Bring ideas together**

ANALYZE LITERATURE: Plot and Foreshadowing

Look over your Time Line and use the events you listed to create a Plot Diagram like the one on page 12. What examples of foreshadowing did you find as you recorded events? What effect did they have on you as a reader?

Writing Options

Creative Writing Something terrible must have happened to the sergeant-major when he made his wishes, but readers are never told what. Write a **horror story** from the sergeant-major's point of view that tells about the wishes he made and the consequences of those wishes. Before you begin writing your story, brainstorm ideas for the plot using a Plot Diagram like the one on page 12. You might also want to brainstorm ideas for how you want to create the characters and setting.

Expository Writing Imagine "The Monkey's Paw" is going to be included in a suspense anthology. Write a one-page **analytical introduction** to be included in the anthology in which you discuss the use of foreshadowing in the story. Use the notes you took while reading or skim the story to find examples of foreshadowing. Introduce the story, describe examples of foreshadowing, and explain the impact of each example. Summarize how the foreshadowing contributes to suspense.

Media Literacy

Write a Public Service Announcement Imagine that there is an e-mail scam going on. Recipients of the scam e-mails are invited to purchase a monkey's paw for $199.99. The e-mail promises that the monkey's paw has magical powers and will grant the purchaser three wishes. Write a public service announcement warning people about this scam. A public service announcement is a brief, informative article intended to help the community.

Collaborative Learning

Videotape a Performance of the Story In a small group, write a dramatization of one scene in "The Monkey's Paw." Choose a scene that is particularly effective in creating suspense or dread. Choose roles and practice your scene. Then videotape it. Use props, simple costumes, lighting, and music to help create the scene and mood. Share your videotape with the class.

 Go to **www.mirrorsandwindows.com** for more.

READING ASSESSMENT

1. Which quotation best illustrates the sergeant-major's feelings about the monkey's paw?
   A. "Well, it's just a bit of what you might call magic, perhaps."
   B. "To look at...it's just an ordinary little paw, dried to a mummy."
   C. "It had a spell put on it by an old fakir...He wanted to show that fate ruled people's lives, and that those who interfered with it did so to their sorrow."
   D. "I threw it on the fire. If you keep it, don't blame me for what happens. Pitch it on the fire again like a sensible man."
   E. "If you must wish...wish for something sensible."

2. Which event indicates the conclusion of the plot?
   A. The sergeant-major throws the monkey's paw on the fire.
   B. Mr. White wishes for two hundred pounds.
   C. Herbert dies.
   D. Mrs. White begs her husband to wish for Herbert to return to life.
   E. Mr. White makes his third wish, and the knocking stops.

3. Which statement best describes the theme of the story?
   A. The story examines the role of fate in human lives.
   B. The story exposes the credulous nature of humans.
   C. The story shows that humans are inherently curious and greedy.
   D. The story demonstrates the maxim "look before you leap."
   E. The story illustrates that money cannot buy happiness.

4. Which of the following could be considered an antonym of the word *avaricious?*
   A. doubtful
   B. greedy
   C. lovely
   D. generous
   E. kind

5. What was Mr. White's last wish? Explain how you know what he wished for and what you think motivated him to make the wish.

GRAMMAR & STYLE

Subject-Verb Agreement

A noun that describes or stands for one person, place, thing, or idea is **singular.** Examples are *sergeant-major, paw,* and *fire.* A noun that describes or stands for more than one person, place, thing, or idea is **plural.** Examples are *perils, houses,* and *visitors.* In a sentence, a verb must be singular if the noun that serves as its subject is singular. It must be plural if the noun that serves as its subject is plural. This rule for agreement is true regardless of the number of words or phrases that come between the subject and verb.

EXAMPLES

singular agreement: The simian <u>face</u> in the flames <u>grows</u> more vivid.

plural agreement: <u>Wishes</u> related to the monkey's paw <u>come</u> true so naturally.

singular agreement: <u>Herbert</u> <u>tells</u> his father to wish for money.

plural agreement: <u>Three terrible events</u> <u>happen</u> to the White family because of the curse of the monkey's paw.

If the sentence contains a compound subject, the verb must be plural.

EXAMPLES

incorrect: <u>Mr. White and Mrs. White</u> <u>has</u> one son.

correct: <u>Mr. White and Mrs. White</u> <u>have</u> one son.

incorrect: <u>Sergeant-Major Morris and Mr. White</u> <u>uses</u> the monkey's paw to make a wish.

correct: <u>Sergeant-Major Morris and Mr. White</u> <u>use</u> the monkey's paw to make a wish.

Collective nouns, such as *team, family, committee,* or *class,* take a singular verb when the group is acting as a whole, but they take a plural verb if the members are acting as individuals.

EXAMPLES

incorrect: The <u>family</u> <u>welcome</u> the sergeant-major.

correct: The <u>family</u> <u>welcomes</u> the sergeant-major.

incorrect: The <u>family</u> <u>was</u> divided in their response to the monkey's paw.

correct: The <u>family</u> <u>were</u> divided in their response to the monkey's paw.

In the case of a *linking verb,* which connects the subject with a word or words in the predicate that describe the subject, the linking verb agrees with its subject, not with the predicate noun or predicate adjective that follows it.

EXAMPLE

incorrect: The monkey's paw's greatest <u>danger</u> <u>are</u> its wishes.

correct: The monkey's paw's greatest <u>danger</u> <u>is</u> its wishes.

Words of amount or time may be singular or plural. Use a singular verb with words and phrases that refer to single units: fractions, measurements, amounts of money, weights, volumes, or specific intervals of time when the intervals refer to a specific unit.

EXAMPLE

Four <u>hours</u> <u>seems</u> like a lifetime when you are waiting for news. (Four hours is being equated with a lifetime.)

Use a plural verb when the amount or the time is considered to be a number of separate units.

EXAMPLE

The three <u>wishes</u> <u>were</u> used up quickly.

REVIEW TERMS

- **subject:** the doer of the action
- **predicate:** the part of the sentence that contains the verb phrase, including the objects, or recipients, of the action
- **linking verb:** a verb that does not express an action; rather, it connects the subject with a word or words in the predicate that describe or rename the subject

Identify Subjects and Verbs

Copy the following sentences onto your own paper. Underline the subject once and the verb twice.

1. Sergeant-Major Morris tries to get the Whites to take the monkey's paw seriously.
2. Mr. White and his adult son play chess.
3. In the light of the flames writhes the monkey's paw.
4. Is there anything Mrs. White could do to bring her son back?
5. At first, Mrs. White doesn't believe in the powers of the monkey's paw.
6. The sergeant-major shook hands and took the seat by the fire.
7. Herbert was alive, and the monkey's paw was responsible.
8. The matches fell from his hand and spilled in the passage.
9. The man from Herbert's place of employment appears at the door nervously.
10. Mr. White and his wife are aware that their lives will never be the same again.

Correct Subject-Verb Agreement

Rewrite the following sentences to correct errors in subject-verb agreement.

1. Mr. White wish for money.
2. The money come from an unexpected source.
3. The wishes often comes with a price.
4. The warnings of the sergeant-major goes unheeded.
5. Nobody think ahead when offered wishes.
6. Herbert goes to work and never come home again.
7. Mr. and Mrs. White blames the monkey's paw for Herbert's death.
8. Good horror stories has suspense and a compelling plot.
9. "The Monkey's Paw" and other stories focuses on the role of fate in people's lives.
10. A character like the sergeant-major add mystery and intrigue to a story.

Improve a Paragraph

Rewrite the following paragraph so that the verbs agree with the subjects.

"The Monkey's Paw" are a horror story about a cursed monkey paw. Sergeant-Major Morris bring the paw back with him from India and show it to the White family. The Whites is fascinated by the monkey's paw and demands to hear the story. Hesitantly, the sergeant-major tell them the story. At first, the family do not believe him, until the first of three wishes are made. This wish cause the family a lot of pain and sorrow. The monkey's paw is truly cursed.

Use Subject-Verb Agreement

Write a note to a teacher about what a club, team, or other group you are involved with is doing. Use subjects that refer to yourself, other group members, and to the group as a whole. After drafting your note, check for subject-verb agreement by underlining the subject of each sentence once and the verb twice. Make corrections as necessary.

EXTEND THE SKILL

Imagine you are responsible for testing your classmates' knowledge of subject-verb agreement. Write a quiz that can be used to evaluate whether or not a person understands what subject-verb agreement is all about. Write an answer key for the quiz, as well. Then, exchange the quiz you wrote with one your classmate wrote. Take the quiz your classmate wrote and see how well you do. Also evaluate whether the quiz you took is an effective way to check your knowledge or if another means would work better.

Through the Tunnel

BUILD BACKGROUND

Literary Context **"Through the Tunnel"** is the story of a boy named Jerry and his mother on vacation. When the two first arrive at their destination, they spend their time together on "the safe beach," but Jerry's thoughts are on "the wild bay." What Jerry experiences in that bay will help him to leave behind the familiar world of childhood and enter the unfamiliar world of adulthood. As you read, watch for the many layers of meaning in this carefully crafted tale about a literal passage and a rite of passage.

Reader's Context Jerry challenges himself and accomplishes something quite difficult. When have you tested yourself by accomplishing something that at first seemed impossible? How did that experience change you?

ANALYZE LITERATURE: Conflict and Symbol

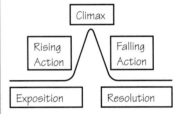

A plot revolves around a central **conflict,** or struggle. There are two types of conflicts: external and internal. In an *external conflict,* the main character struggles against another character, the forces of nature, society or social norms, or fate. In an *internal conflict,* a struggle takes place within a character.

Symbols are things that stand for or represent both themselves and something else. In "Through the Tunnel," Jerry's external struggle with wanting to go through the tunnel is symbolic of his internal struggle.

SET PURPOSE

What ideas come to mind when you think of the word "tunnel"? Based on these ideas and what you've read in the Build Background and Analyze Literature sections, consider how a tunnel could be symbolic. As you read, try to determine why the tunnel is so important to Jerry and what it symbolizes.

MEET THE AUTHOR

Doris Lessing (b. 1919) was born in Kermanshah, Persia (now Baktharan, Iran), and lived for many years in Africa. She set her first novel, *The Grass Is Singing,* in Africa. Lessing's experimental novel *The Golden Notebook* has become a classic of feminist literature. When asked about rites of passage in her own life, Lessing said, "What I'm on the lookout for now is the unexpected, for things that come from outside and that I never thought might happen. Sometimes you have to watch for them so you don't automatically say no to the new, simply because you're in the habit of saying no to everything that comes along. I'm constantly changing my perspective on my own life. I see the past differently, and that's a wonderful thing."

USE READING SKILLS

Text Organization
Understanding the way a story is organized can help you understand the story itself. One way to track the organization of a story is to use a Plot Diagram. Review the elements of plot in the Understanding Plot feature on page 12. Then draw a Plot Diagram like the one below. As you read, record on your Plot Diagram events, dialogue, or details that represent each element of plot.

```
                 Climax

   Rising                  Falling
   Action                  Action

  Exposition              Resolution
```

PREVIEW VOCABULARY

Use the context clues in the sentences below to figure out the meanings of the underlined words from the selection.

1. The boy felt bad about stealing the ball, and his feelings of <u>contrition</u> led him to return it.
2. The knight always behaved with the utmost <u>chivalry</u>, sparing those he beat in duels and aiding damsels in distress.
3. We stood outside in the darkness, our only source of light the <u>luminous</u> full moon.
4. It amazed us that the old rubber raft was still <u>buoyant</u> after all these years.
5. It had been a calm day for sailing, so the sudden <u>surge</u> of water caught us unprepared.

Through the Tunnel

The Rocks at Belle-Ile, the Wild Coast, 1886. Claude Monet. Musée d'Orsay, Paris, France.

A Short Story by **Doris Lessing**

Going to the shore on the first morning of the vacation, the young English boy stopped at a turning of the path and then over the crowded beach he knew so well from other years. His mother walked on in front of him, carrying a bright striped bag in one hand. Her other arm, swinging loose, was very white in the sun. The boy watched that white, naked arm, and turned his eyes, which had a frown behind them, toward the bay and back again to his mother. When she felt he was not with her, she swung around. "Oh, there you are, Jerry!" she said. She looked impatient, then smiled. "Why, darling, would you rather not come with me? Would you rather—" She frowned, <u>conscientiously</u>

con • sci • en • tious • ly (kän[t]′ shē en[t]′ shəs lē) *adv.,* in a manner governed by doing what one knows is right

worrying over what amusements he might secretly be longing for, which she had been too busy or too careless to imagine. He was very familiar with that anxious, apologetic smile. <u>Contrition</u> sent him running after her. And yet, as he ran, he looked back over his shoulder at the wild bay; and all morning, as he played on the safe beach, he was thinking of it.

Next morning, when it was time for the routine of swimming and sunbathing, his mother said, "Are you tired of the usual beach, Jerry? Would you like to go somewhere else?"

"Oh, no!" he said quickly, smiling at her out of that unfailing impulse of contrition—a sort of <u>chivalry</u>. Yet, walking down the path with her, he blurted out, "I'd like to go and have a look at those rocks down there."

She gave the idea her attention. It was a wild looking place, and there was no one there; but she said, "Of course, Jerry. When you've had enough, come to the big beach. Or just go straight back to the villa, if you like." She walked away, that bare arm, now slightly reddened from yesterday's sun, swinging. And he almost ran after her again, feeling it unbearable that she should go by herself, but he did not.

She was thinking, Of course he's old enough to be safe without me. Have I been keeping him too close? He mustn't feel he ought to be with me. I must be careful.

ANALYZE LITERATURE

Conflict What conflict is Jerry's mother facing in this paragraph? Is this an internal or external conflict?

He was an only child, eleven years old. She was a widow. She was determined to be neither possessive nor lacking in devotion. She went worrying off to her beach.

As for Jerry, once he saw that his mother had gained her beach, he began the steep descent to the bay. From where he was, high up among red-brown rocks, it was a scoop of moving bluish green fringed with white. As he went lower, he saw that it spread among small promontories and inlets of rough, sharp rock, and the crisping, lapping surface showed stains of purple and darker blue. Finally, as he ran sliding and scraping down the last few yards, he saw an edge of white surf and the shallow, <u>luminous</u> movement of water over white sand, and, beyond that, a solid, heavy blue.

He ran straight into the water and began swimming. He was a good swimmer. He went out fast over the gleaming sand, over a middle region where rocks lay like discolored monsters under the surface, and then he was in the real sea—a warm sea where irregular cold currents from the deep water shocked his limbs.

When he was so far out that he could look back not only on the little bay but past the promontory that was between it and the big beach, he floated on the <u>buoyant</u> surface and looked for his mother. There she was, a speck of yellow under an umbrella that looked like a slice of orange peel. He swam back to shore, relieved at being sure she was there, but all at once very lonely.

On the edge of a small cape that marked the side of the bay away from the promontory was a loose scatter of rocks. Above them, some boys were stripping off their clothes. They came running, naked, down to the rocks. The English boy swam toward them, but kept his distance at a stone's throw. They were of that coast; all of them were burned smooth dark brown and speaking a language he did not understand. To be with them, of them, was a craving that filled his whole body. He swam a little closer; they turned and watched him with narrowed, alert dark eyes. Then one smiled and waved. It was enough. In a minute, he had swum in and was on the rocks beside them, smiling with a desperate, nervous supplication. They shouted cheerful greetings at him; and then, as he preserved his nervous, uncompre-hending smile, they understood that he was a

con • tri • tion (kən tri´ shən) n., remorse
chiv • al • ry (shi´ vəl rē) n., sense of courage and honor
lu • mi • nous (lü´ mə nəs) adj., shining; bright
buoy • ant (boi´ ənt) adj., having power to keep something afloat

foreigner strayed from his own beach, and they proceeded to forget him. But he was happy. He was with them.

They began diving again and again from a high point into a well of blue sea between rough, pointed rocks. After they had dived and come up, they swam around, hauled themselves up, and waited their turn to dive again. They were big boys—men, to Jerry. He dived, they watched him; and when he swam around to take his place, they made way for him. He felt he was accepted and he dived again, carefully, proud of himself.

Soon the biggest of the boys poised himself, shot down into the water, and did not come up. The others stood about, watching. Jerry, after waiting for the sleek brown head to appear, let out a yell of warning; they looked at him idly and turned their eyes back toward the water. After a long time, the boy came up on the other side of a big dark rock, letting the air out of his lungs in a sputtering gasp and a shout of triumph. Immediately the rest of them dived in. One moment, the morning seemed full of chattering boys; the next, the air and the surface of the water were empty. But through the heavy blue, dark shapes could be seen moving and groping.

Jerry dived, shot past the school of underwater swimmers, saw a black wall of rock looming at him, touched it, and bobbed up at once to the surface, where the wall was a low barrier he could see across. There was no one visible; under him, in the water, the dim shapes of the swimmers had disappeared. Then one, and then another of the boys came up on the far side of the barrier of rock, and he understood that they had swum through some gap or hole in it. He plunged down again. He could see nothing through the stinging salt water but the blank rock. When he came up the boys were all on the diving rock, preparing to attempt the feat again. And now, in a panic of failure, he yelled up, in English, "Look at me! Look!" and he began splashing and kicking in the water like a foolish dog.

They looked down gravely, frowning. He knew the frown. At moments of failure, when he clowned to claim his mother's attention, it was with just this grave, embarrassed inspection that she rewarded him. Through his hot shame, feeling the pleading grin on his face like a scar that he could never remove, he looked up at the group of big brown boys on the rock and shouted, *"Bonjour! Merci! Au revoir! Monsieur, monsieur!"*[1] while he hooked his fingers round his ears and waggled them.

Water surged into his mouth; he choked, sank, came up. The rock, lately weighted with boys, seemed to rear up out of the water as their weight was removed. They were flying down past him, now, into the water; the air was full of falling bodies. Then the rock was empty in the hot sunlight. He counted one, two, three....

At fifty, he was terrified. They must all be drowning beneath him, in the watery caves of the rock! At a hundred, he stared around him at the empty hillside, wondering if he should yell for help. He counted faster, faster, to hurry them up, to bring them to the surface quickly,

ANALYZE LITERATURE

Symbol What does the rock barrier prevent Jerry from doing? What might this barrier symbolize in the story?

---

1. *"Bonjour!...monsieur!"* [French] "Hello! Thank you! Goodbye! Sir, sir!"

surge (sərj) v., to rise and fall

to drown them quickly—anything rather than the terror of counting on and on into the blue emptiness of the morning. And then, at a hundred and sixty, the water beyond the rock was full of boys blowing like brown whales. They swam back to the shore without a look at him.

He climbed back to the diving rock and sat down, feeling the hot roughness of it under his thighs. The boys were gathering up their bits of clothing and running off along the shore to another promontory. They were leaving to get away from him. He cried openly, fists in his eyes. There was no one to see him, and he cried himself out.

It seemed to him that a long time had passed, and he swam out to where he could see his mother. Yes, she was still there, a yellow spot under an orange umbrella. He swam back to the big rock, climbed up, and dived, into the blue pool among the fanged and angry boulders. Down he went, until he touched the wall of rock again. But the salt was so painful in his eyes that he could not see.

He came to the surface, swam to shore and went back to the villa to wait for his mother. Soon she walked slowly up the path, swinging her striped bag, the flushed, naked arm dangling beside her. "I want some swimming goggles," he panted, defiant and <u>beseeching</u>.

She gave him a patient, inquisitive look as she said casually, "Well, of course, darling."

USE READING STRATEGIES

Make Inferences What inferences can you make about Jerry based on the fact that he cries when the boys leave?

But now, now, now! He must have them this minute, and no other time. He nagged and pestered until she went with him to a shop. As soon as she had bought the goggles, he grabbed them from her hand as if she were going to claim them for herself, and was off, running down the steep path to the bay.

Jerry swam out to the big barrier rock, adjusted the goggles, and dived. The impact of the water broke the rubber-enclosed vacuum, and the goggles came loose. He understood that he must swim down to the base of the rock from the surface of the water. He fixed the goggles tight and firm, filled his lungs, and floated, face down, on the water. Now, he could see. It was as if he had eyes of a different kind—fish eyes that showed everything clear and delicate and wavering in the bright water.

Under him, six or seven feet down, was a floor of perfectly clean, shining white sand, rippled firm and hard by the tides. Two grayish shapes steered there, like long, rounded pieces of wood or slate. They were fish. He saw them nose toward each other, poise motionless, make a dart forward, swerve off, and come around again. It was like a water dance. A few inches above them the water sparkled as if sequins were dropping through it. Fish again—<u>myriads</u> of minute fish, the length of his fingernail, were drifting through the water, and in a moment he could feel the innumerable tiny touches of them against his limbs. It was like swimming in flaked silver. The great rock the big boys had swum through rose sheer out of white sand—black, tufted lightly with greenish weed. He could see no gap in it. He swam down to its base.

Again and again he rose, took a big chestful of air, and went down. Again and again he groped over the surface of the rock, feeling it, almost hugging it in the desperate need to find the entrance. And then, once, while he was clinging to the black wall, his knees came up

---

be • seech • ing (bi sēch´iŋ) *adj.,* in an earnest manner
myr • i • ad (mir´ ē əd) *n.,* indefinitely large number

The Act of Breathing Respiration, or the act of breathing, brings oxygen into your lungs. From there, the oxygen is transferred to your bloodstream and distributed to the cells of your body. At the same time, carbon dioxide is released by your cells, transported to your lungs, and expelled when you breathe out. The urge to breathe is triggered by the pressure of carbon dioxide in your blood. Some divers hyperventilate before they dive, to eliminate most of the carbon dioxide in the blood. This can delay the breathing reflex for a minute or more. The official world record for free diving is held by Audrey Mestre, who dove 125 meters (about 410 feet) and was underwater for two minutes and three seconds. Holding your breath for this long is extremely dangerous. Every year, divers black out underwater and die. In fact, Mestre died on a free dive in 2003.

and he shot his feet out forward and they met no obstacle. He had found the hole.

He gained the surface, clambered about the stones that littered the barrier rock until he found a big one, and, with this in his arms, let himself down over the side of the rock. He dropped, with the weight, straight to the sandy floor. Clinging tight to the anchor of stone, he lay on his side and looked in under the dark shelf at the place where his feet had gone. He could see the hole. It was an irregular, dark gap; but he could not see deep into it. He let go of his anchor, clung with his hands to the edge of the hole, and tried to push himself in.

He got his head in, found his shoulders jammed, moved them in sidewise, and was inside as far as his waist. He could see nothing ahead. Something soft and clammy touched his mouth; he saw a dark frond moving against the grayish rock, and panic filled him. He thought of octopuses, of clinging weed. He pushed himself out backward and caught a glimpse, as he retreated, of a harmless tentacle of seaweed drifting in the mouth of the tunnel. But it was enough. He reached the sunlight, swam to shore, and lay on the diving rock. He looked down into the blue well of water. He knew he must find his way through that cave, or hole, or tunnel, and out the other side.

First, he thought, he must learn to control his breathing. He let himself down into the water

with another big stone in his arms, so that he could lie effortlessly on the bottom of the sea. He counted. One, two, three. He counted steadily. He could hear the movement of blood in his chest. Fifty-one, fifty-two….His chest was hurting. He let go of the rock and went up into the air. He saw that the sun was low. He rushed to the villa and found his mother at her supper. She said only "Did you enjoy yourself?" and he said "Yes."

All night the boy dreamed of the water-filled cave in the rock, and as soon as breakfast was over he went to the bay.

That night, his nose bled badly. For hours he had been under water, learning to hold his breath, and now he felt weak and dizzy. His mother said, "I shouldn't overdo things, darling, if I were you."

That day and the next, Jerry exercised his lungs as if everything, the whole of his life, all that he would become, depended upon it. Again his nose bled at night, and his mother insisted on his coming with her the next day. It was a torment to him to waste a day of his careful self-training, but he stayed with her on that other beach, which now seemed a place for small children, a place where his mother might lie safe in the sun. It was not his beach.

ANALYZE LITERATURE

Conflict What conflict has Jerry encountered? Is it an internal conflict or an external conflict? How do you know?

He did not ask for permission, on the following day, to go to his beach. He went, before his mother could consider the complicated rights and wrongs of the matter. A day's rest, he discovered, had improved his count by ten. The big boys had made the passage while he counted a hundred and sixty. He had been counting fast, in his fright. Probably now, if he tried, he could get through the long tunnel, but he was not going to try yet. A curious, most unchildlike <u>persistence</u>, a controlled impatience, made him wait. In the meantime, he lay underwater on the white sand, littered now by stones he had brought down from the upper air, and studied the entrance to the tunnel. He knew every jut and corner of it, as far as it was possible to see. It was as if he already felt its sharpness about his shoulders.

He sat by the clock in the villa, when his mother was not near, and checked his time. He was <u>incredulous</u> and then proud to find he could hold his breath without strain for two minutes. The words "two minutes," authorized by the clock, brought close the adventure that was so necessary to him.

In another four days, his mother said casually one morning, they must go home. On the day before they left, he would do it. He would do it if it killed him, he said defiantly to himself. But two days before they were to leave—a day of triumph when he increased his count by fifteen—his nose bled so badly that he turned dizzy and had to lie limply over the big rock like a bit of seaweed, watching the thick red blood flow on to the rock and trickle slowly down to the sea. He was frightened. Supposing he turned dizzy in the tunnel? Supposing he died there, trapped? Supposing— his head went around, in the hot sun, and he almost gave up. He thought he would return to the house and lie down, and next summer, perhaps, when he had another year's growth in him—*then* he would go through the hole.

But even after he had made the decision, or thought he had, he found himself sitting up on the rock and looking down into the water; and he knew that now, this moment, when his nose had only just stopped bleeding, when his head was still sore and throbbing—this was the moment when he would try. If he did not do it now, he never would. He was trembling with fear that he would not go; and he was trembling with horror at that long, long tunnel under the rock, under the sea. Even in the open sunlight, the barrier rock seemed very wide and very heavy; tons of rock pressed down on where he would go. If he died there, he would lie until one day—perhaps not before next year—those big boys would swim into it and find it blocked.

He put on his goggles, fitted them tight, tested the vacuum. His hands were shaking. Then he chose the biggest stone he could carry and slipped over the edge of the rock until half of him was in the cool, enclosing water and half in the hot sun. He looked up once at the empty sky, filled his lungs once, twice, and then sank fast to the bottom with the stone. He let it go and began to count. He took the edges of the hole in his hands and drew himself into it, wriggling his shoulders in sidewise as he remembered he must, kicking himself along with his feet.

Soon he was clear inside. He was in a

per • sis • tence (pər sis´ tən[t]s) *n.*, stubborn continuance; tenacity
in • cred • u • lous (in[´] kre´ jə ləs) *adj.*, showing disbelief

small rockbound hole filled with yellowish-gray water. The water was pushing him up against the roof. The roof was sharp and pained his back. He pulled himself along with his hands—fast, fast— and used his legs as levers. His head knocked against something; a sharp pain dizzied him. Fifty, fifty-one, fifty-two…. He was without light, and the water seemed to press upon him with the weight of rock. Seventy-one, seventy-two…. There was no strain on his lungs. He felt like an inflated balloon, his lungs were so light and easy, but his head was pulsing.

He was being continually pressed against the sharp roof, which felt slimy as well as sharp. Again he thought of octopuses, and wondered if the tunnel might be filled with weed that could tangle him. He gave himself a panicky, convulsive kick forward, ducked his head, and swam. His feet and hands moved freely, as if in open water. The hole must have widened out. He thought he must be swimming fast, and he was frightened of banging his head if the tunnel narrowed.

> **USE READING STRATEGIES**
>
> **Visualize** Imagine the scene described in this paragraph. If you were to draw Jerry in this scene, what would the expression on his face be?

A hundred, a hundred and one….The water paled. Victory filled him. His lungs were beginning to hurt. A few more strokes and he would be out. He was counting wildly; he said a hundred and fifteen, and then, a long time later, a hundred and fifteen again. The water was a clear jewel-green all around him. Then he saw, above his head, a crack running up through the rock. Sunlight was falling through it, showing the clean, dark rock of the tunnel, a single mussel shell, and darkness ahead.

He was at the end of what he could do. He looked up at the crack as if it were filled with air and not water, as if he could put his mouth to it to draw in air. A hundred and fifteen, he heard himself say inside his head—but he had said that long ago. He must go on into the blackness ahead, or he would drown. His head was swelling, his lungs cracking. A hundred and fifteen, a hundred and fifteen pounded through his head, and he feebly clutched at rocks in the dark, pulling himself forward, leaving the brief space of sunlit water behind. He felt he was dying. He was no longer quite conscious. He struggled on in the darkness between lapses into unconsciousness. An immense, swelling pain filled his head, and then the darkness cracked with an explosion of green light. His hands, groping forward, met nothing; and his feet, kicking back, propelled him out into the open sea.

He drifted to the surface, his face turned up to the air. He was gasping like a fish. He felt he would sink now and drown; he could not swim the few feet back to the rock. Then he was clutching it and pulling himself up on to it. He lay face down, gasping. He could see nothing but a red-veined, clotted dark. His eyes must have burst, he thought; they were full of blood. He tore off his goggles and a gout of blood went into the sea. His nose was bleeding, and the blood had filled the goggles.

He scooped up handfuls of water from the cool, salty sea, to splash on his face, and did not know whether it was blood or salt water he tasted. After a time, his heart quieted, his eyes cleared, and he sat up. He could see the local boys diving and playing half a mile away. He did not want them. He wanted nothing but to get back home and lie down.

In a short while, Jerry swam to shore and climbed slowly up the path to the villa. He flung himself on his bed and slept, waking at the sound of feet on the path outside. His mother was coming back. He rushed to the bathroom, thinking she must not see his face with bloodstains, or tearstains, on it. He came out of the bathroom and met her as she walked into the villa, smiling, her eyes lighting up.

"Have a nice morning?" she asked, laying her hand on his warm brown shoulder.

"Oh, yes, thank you," he said.

"You look a bit pale." And then, sharp and anxious, "How did you bang your head?"

"Oh, just banged it," he told her.

She looked at him closely. He was strained; his eyes were glazed-looking. She was worried.

And then she said to herself, Oh, don't fuss! Nothing can happen. He can swim like a fish.

They sat down to lunch together.

"Mummy," he said, "I can stay under water for two minutes—three minutes, at least." It came bursting out of him.

"Can you, darling?" she said. "Well, I shouldn't overdo it. I don't think you ought to swim any more today."

She was ready for a battle of wills, but he gave in at once. It was no longer of the least importance to go to the bay. ❖

MIRRORS & WINDOWS

Why must we prove things to ourselves? Why take risks when we don't have to? Do greater risks have greater meaning? Explain your answer.

REFER TO TEXT ▶ ▶ ▶ ▶	▶ REASON WITH TEXT	
1a. List things Jerry does to prepare himself for swimming through the tunnel.	1b. In your own words, explain why Jerry doesn't tell his mother what he is attempting to do.	**Understand** Find meaning
2a. Quote Jerry's statement that shows how determined he is to swim through the tunnel.	2b. Why is Jerry so determined? Relate Jerry's experience to a time when you or somebody you know has been very determined.	**Apply** Use information
3a. Record details about the bay.	3b. What dangers does the bay hold? Infer why the bay is attractive to Jerry.	**Analyze** Take things apart
4a. Recall how Jerry's mother reacts when she realizes he is not with her on the way to the beach. How does she react when he wants to go to the bay?	4b. Evaluate whether Jerry's mother has prepared him well for his journey to young adulthood. Use evidence from the text to support your response.	**Evaluate** Make judgments
5a. How does Jerry's journey end? What does the bay mean to him at the end of the story?	5b. Explain Jerry's disinterest in the bay at the end of the story. Is this what you expected of Jerry? Why or why not?	**Create** Bring ideas together

ANALYZE LITERATURE: Conflict and Symbol

What are the main conflicts in "Through the Tunnel"? How are they resolved? Scan the story for references to the bay and the beach. What does each represent to Jerry? How is the symbolic use of these locations related to the plot?

ATWOOD

Literature
CONNECTION

Canadian writer **Margaret Atwood** (b. 1939) published her first poem when she was just nineteen. Since then, she has won many prizes for her writing. **"Death of a Young Son by Drowning"** was written in 1970 and published in *Selected Poems*.

Death of a Young Son by Drowning

A Poem by **Margaret Atwood**

He, who navigated with success
the dangerous river of his own
    birth
once more set forth

5   on a voyage of discovery
into the land I floated on
but could not touch to claim.

His feet slid on the bank,
the currents took him;
he swirled with ice and trees in
    the swollen water

10   and plunged into distant regions,
his head a bathysphere;[1]
through his eyes' thin glass
    bubbles

he looked out, reckless
    adventurer
on a landscape stranger than
    Uranus
15   we have all been to and some
    remember.

---

1. **bathysphere.** Strong steel diving sphere used for deep-sea observation

There was an accident; the air locked,
he was hung in the river like a heart.
They retrieved the swamped body,
cairn[2] of my plans and future charts,
20 with poles and hooks
from among the nudging logs.

It was spring, the sun kept shining,
     the new grass
leapt to solidity;
my hands glistened with details.

25 After the long trip I was tired of
     waves.
My foot hit rock. The dreamed sails
collapsed, ragged.

I planted him in his country like a
     flag. ❖

---

2. **cairn.** Heap of stones piled up as a memorial
or landmark

REFER TO TEXT ▶ ▶ ▶ ▶	▶ REASON WITH TEXT	
1a. According to the title, what happens to the son?	1b. According to lines 7–9 and 16–17, what happens to the son?	**Understand** **Find meaning**
2a. What details are given about the boy in the poem?	2b. What characteristics do the boy in the poem and Jerry in "Through the Tunnel" share?	**Apply** **Use information**
3a. How does this poem relate to the story "Through the Tunnel"?	3b. Which do you prefer, "Through the Tunnel" or "Death of a Young Son by Drowning"? Why?	**Evaluate** **Make judgments**

TEXT ◄—TO—► TEXT CONNECTION

Compare the experience of Jerry's mother in "Through the Tunnel" and the mother of the son in the poem. Contrast Jerry's experience with the experience of the son in the poem. What do you think the speaker of Atwood's poem would tell Jerry in response to his decision to go through the tunnel?

EXTEND THE TEXT

Writing Options

Creative Writing Imagine you plan to make a movie about a journey from childhood to adulthood to a film producer. Brainstorm another actual journey that might show a similar symbolic journey. Create a **storyboard** that shows the key points of your story. You may want to begin by creating a Plot Diagram for your story. In it, highlight the inciting incident, the key points of plot development, and the resolution of the central conflict.

Narrative Writing Write a **narrative paragraph,** or paragraph that tells a story, for classmates about an experience you had that challenged you, taught you a lesson, or gave you an opportunity to prove yourself. In your paragraph, describe the experience and what you learned or gained from it. Consider using an instructive or inspirational tone. Begin by brainstorming a list of possible experiences you could write about. Once you've narrowed your list to one experience, jot down a list of details. Then begin drafting your paragraph.

Collaborative Learning

Conduct an Interview Talk with a family member or friend about an experience that marked his or her transition from childhood to young adulthood. Before you have this conversation, write a series of questions that will help you gather details on the time and place as well as the individual's feelings about himself or herself and others before, during, and after the experience.

Lifelong Learning

Create a Coming-of-Age Presentation Many cultures have formal coming-of-age ceremonies to mark a child's emergence into young adulthood. Use the Internet to search for these kinds of ceremonies, and choose one ceremony that interests you. Research such things as the steps involved in the ceremony and what the ceremony means to the young adult participating in it. Based on your research, create a multimedia presentation about the ceremony. Include pictures and, if possible, sound and video, to really make your presentation come alive.

 Go to **www.mirrorsandwindows.com** for more.

READING ASSESSMENT

1. What conflicting feelings does Jerry's mother have about him?
   A. She worries that he spends too much time alone, but she doesn't like his friends.
   B. She wants him by her, but she doesn't want to smother him.
   C. She hates to see him grow up, but she pushes him to act less childish.
   D. She fears he will leave her, but she wants him to meet new people.
   E. She loves his independent streak, but she wishes he would conform more.

2. Which quotation best explains why Jerry finds the boys appealing?
   A. "They were of that coast; all of them burned smooth dark brown and speaking a language he did not understand."
   B. "They shouted cheerful greetings at him."
   C. "They were big boys—men, to Jerry."
   D. "To be with them, of them, was a craving that filled his whole body."
   E. "Then one smiled and waved. It was enough."

3. Which comparison best describes the experience of both Jerry and the mother in "Death of a Young Son by Drowning"?
   A. Neither completes their journey successfully.
   B. Both have similar purposes for their journey, the move from childhood to adulthood.
   C. Neither cares about the people who might worry about them.
   D. Both wonder about the purpose of their journey.
   E. Both are weary yet satisfied at the end of their journey.

4. Which of the following words is a synonym for the word *Surge?*
   A. plunge
   B. swell
   C. attack
   D. judge
   E. imply

5. Jerry first becomes interested in the tunnel when he sees the other boys swimming through it, and he longs to be with them. Yet when he actually swims through the tunnel, he is alone. What does this suggest about Jerry's motivations and symbolic journey?

GRAMMAR & STYLE

Parallel Structure

A sentence exhibits parallel structure, or **parallelism,** when the same grammatical forms are used to express ideas of equal—or parallel—importance. Parallelism can add emphasis and rhythm to a sentence. Words, phrases, and clauses that have the same form and function in a sentence are called parallel. Notice how Doris Lessing uses parallelism in the sentence below from "Through the Tunnel."

EXAMPLE

> Jerry <u>dived</u>, <u>shot</u> past the school of underwater swimmers, <u>saw</u> a black wall of rock looming at him, <u>touched</u> it, and <u>bobbed</u> up at once to the surface, where the wall was a low barrier he could see across.

In this example, all the verbs are in the past tense. Study the additional examples below for other ways of using parallel structure.

EXAMPLE

> He was <u>trembling with fear</u> that he would not go; and he was <u>trembling with horror</u> at the long, long tunnel under the rock, under the sea.

In this example, the parallel structure of the phrases "trembling with fear" and "trembling with horror" links together both clauses of the sentence and reflects the inner debate waging inside of Jerry's head. On the one hand, Jerry is scared that he will not have the courage to attempt the swim through the tunnel, and, on the other hand, he is scared of having the courage and actually swimming through the tunnel.

EXAMPLES

> **nonparallel:** Jerry's mother thought he might enjoy swimming or to play on the beach.
> **parallel:** Jerry's mother thought he might enjoy swimming or playing on the beach.
>
> **nonparallel:** A day at the beach usually includes warm sun, splashing waves, and gulls swooping.

> **parallel:** A day at the beach usually includes warm sun, splashing waves, and swooping gulls.
> **nonparallel:** Jerry was swimming with grace and he swam with speed as he dove below the deep, dark waves of the blue sea.
> **parallel:** Jerry was swimming with grace and speed as he dove below the deep, dark waves of the blue sea.

Note that in the first example, "swimming" and "playing" are in the same form. In the second example, all the items in the list include an adjective followed by a noun. In the third example, you'll notice that the lack of parallel structure makes the sentence awkward and wordy. In the parallel sentence, the words "grace" and "speed" describe how Jerry was swimming.

Parallelism is commonly used as a **rhetorical device,** or a technique used by a speaker or writer to achieve a particular effect, especially to persuade or influence. The use of parallel structure in this way is most often seen in speeches or essays.

What Great Writers Do

Aside from making sentences grammatically correct, parallel structure can add a type of excitement or urgency to writing. Read the sentence below from "Through the Tunnel" by Doris Lessing. How does she use parallelism? How does it affect the impact of the sentence?

He counted faster, faster, to hurry them up, to bring them to the surface quickly, to drown them quickly— anything rather than the terror of counting on and on into the blue emptiness of the morning.

Identify Parallel Structure

Copy the following sentences onto your own paper and evaluate them. If a sentence demonstrates parallelism, circle the words that create parallelism. If the sentence does not demonstrate parallelism, underline the term or terms you would change to make the sentence parallel.

1. Getting away from his mother and swimming in the bay were the reasons Jerry did not want to go to the safe beach.
2. In order to swim through the tunnel, Jerry needed to train and getting goggles.
3. While Jerry was in the tunnel, he was counting, kicking, and his thoughts were about whether he would make it.
4. Jerry's mother liked sunbathing, walking, and reminded her son "not to overdo it."
5. Jerry wanted to join the older boys and swim through the tunnel.

Correct Parallel Structure

Rewrite the following sentences to correct errors in parallelism.

1. The wild bay represents being grown up to Jerry, whereas the safe beach is standing for childhood.
2. Jerry's feelings are conflicted between longs to go to the bay and contrition for making his mother anxious.
3. The older boys are jumping, diving, swimming underwater, and speak a foreign language.
4. Jerry sitting on the rock and cries like a baby after they leave him.
5. Jerry's mother sits on the safe beach unaware that her son is doggedly trying a dangerous activity and risks his life.

Improve a Paragraph

Copy the following paragraph onto your paper and correct the sentences so that each demonstrates correct parallelism.

Doris Lessing's "Through the Tunnel" recounts the experience of Jerry, a young boy who is determined to prove his manhood. He scoffs at the safe beach where his mother is lying contentedly in the sun and instead is pursuing the allure of the more dangerous neighboring beach. There, sitting aloft on a rock, he watches a group of boys dive beneath the surface of the waves and are holding their breaths for a long time. Eager to prove that he is as good as they are, he breaches the waves, diving down deep to the sandy bottom, and swiftly kicks up to the surface. He cannot hold his breath for very long so he decided to train himself to hold his breath longer. Each day as the crying of the gulls echoes over the beach and the crash of the surf bounces off the rocks, Jerry is practicing holding his breath for longer periods of time. Finally, after days of practice, he decides to test himself and he swam through the tunnel.

Use Parallel Structure in Your Writing

Did Jerry do the right thing in risking his own life to try and conquer the tunnel? Write a letter to Jerry that expresses your opinion about his decision. If you agree that he did the right thing, offer your support. If you think he was foolish, tell him why you think so. Once you have finished a draft, exchange your letter with a classmate and check for correct use of parallelism.

EXTEND THE SKILL

Many speeches, such as Abraham Lincoln's Gettysburg Address, Martin Luther King Jr.'s "I Have a Dream" speech, and John F. Kennedy's Inaugural Address, use parallelism. Use the library or Internet to find a copy of one of these speeches, or a different speech that interests you, and identify examples of parallelism in the speech you choose. How might the use of parallel structure influence the effect of the speech on its listeners?

Understanding Point of View

POINT OF VIEW

The saying, "It all depends on how you look at it," suggests that the meaning or judgment of a matter can vary if you shift your **point of view,** or vantage point or perspective. In literature, it is much the same; so much depends on who is telling the story—whose point of view is interpreting the action.

TYPES OF NARRATION

The **first-person point of view,** or first-person narration, tells a story from the *I* or *we* perspective of someone who participated in or witnessed the action. For example, "Lather and Nothing Else" (page 45) is told from the point of view of the barber, and you see events and other characters through his eyes and through his biases. First-person point of view can make the story seem more emotionally authentic, as in "Lather and Nothing Else." However, it may also make you question the validity of what you are told, as in "Two Kinds" (page 69) when the narrator suggests that her mother's insistence that Jing-mei become a prodigy is only to satisfy her pride.

> But I'm shaking like a regular murderer. From his throat a stream of blood would flow on the sheet, over the chair, down on my hands, onto the floor. I would have to close the door. But the blood would go flowing along the floor, warm, indelible, not to be staunched, until it reached the street like a small scarlet river.
> —from "Lather and Nothing Else" by Hernando Téllez

Second-person point of view uses the word *you* and is relatively rare. It addresses the reader directly, positioning the reader within the story. Although "On the Rainy River" (page 137) is mostly told from the first-person point of view, the narrator slips into second-person narration in order to make you imagine how you would react in a similar situation.

> You're at the bow of a boat on the Rainy River. You're twenty-one years old, you're scared, and there's a hard squeezing pressure in your chest. What would you do? Would you jump? Would you feel pity for yourself?
> —from "On the Rainy River" by Tim O'Brien

He, she, and *it* are the pronouns marking **third-person point of view,** where the narrator stands outside the action and observes. The third-person point of view has two variations: limited point of view and omniscient point of view. *Limited point of view* only gives the reader an insight into the mind of the narrator or of one other character. "Like the Sun" (page 200), for instance, lets us know Sekhar's thoughts but not those of the principal. The *omniscient point of view* reveals the thoughts of all characters, such as in "Through the Tunnel" (page 29) where the mother's worries are revealed as is Jerry's longing to explore the neighboring beach.

> She frowned, conscientiously worrying over what amusements he might secretly be longing for, which she had been too busy or too careless to imagine. He was very familiar with that anxious, apologetic smile. Contrition sent him running after her. And yet, as he ran, he looked back over his shoulder at the wild bay; and all morning, as he played on the safe beach, he was thinking of it.
> —from "Through the Tunnel" by Doris Lessing

TYPES OF NARRATORS

Whether the story is in first- or third-person, the **narrator** is the storyteller. Sometimes, the narrator is a character in the story, as is the case with "Two Kinds" and "Lather and Nothing Else," but other

times the narrator stands apart from the action. Not all narrators are created equal, however. Some narrators, whether in a first-person or third-person story, are reliable; you can trust their account of the events. Some, however, are unreliable narrators. For instance, in "Two Kinds," Jing-mei's conviction that her mother only wants her to succeed so that her mother may boast about it to others taints most of the interactions between mother and daughter told by the character.

The narrator of the third-person story "The Moment Before the Gun Went Off" (page 51) can also be questioned because the events of the story are not merely described; they are also commented upon. The narrator's remarks show a particular personality or opinion that may not strike you as reliable. In other words, you may have your own interpretation of character and events. Notice how the narrator comments on the situation in the example given below.

> There will be an inquiry; there had better be, to stop the assumption of yet another case of brutality against farm workers, although there's nothing in doubt—an accident, and all the facts fully admitted by Van der Vyver.
> —from "The Moment Before the Gun Went Off" by Nadine Gordimer

DETERMINING POINT OF VIEW

To figure out the point of view of a story, ask yourself the following questions. Remember that critical readers will examine whether or not the narrator is reliable before believing everything the narrator says.

- Who is telling the story?
- Is the narrator a character in the story?
- Does the narrator simply present the story or offer commentary on the story?
- What biases, attitudes, or opinions do you think the narrator has? How might these assumptions color his or her view?
- How might the story be different if told from another character's point of view?

Famous Narrators

When a story is told from a first-person point of view, readers hear the narrator's voice in an up-close and personal way. In the following short excerpts, see if you can figure out what distinguishes each narrator's voice.

"I had been to school most all the time and could spell and read and write just a little, and could even say the multiplication table up to six times seven is thirty-five, and I don't reckon I could ever get any further than that if I was to live forever. I don't take no stock in mathematics, anyway."
— Huckleberry Finn, from *The Adventures of Huckleberry Finn*

"In the morning, when I was fighting my way to school against the wind, I couldn't see anything but the road in front of me; but in the late afternoon, when I was coming home, the town looked bleak and desolate to me."
— Jim Burden, from *My Ántonia*

"The snow began to drive thickly. I seized the handle to essay another trial; when a young man without a coat, and shouldering a pitchfork, appeared in the yard behind."
— Mr. Lockwood, from *Wuthering Heights*

Lather and Nothing Else

BUILD BACKGROUND

Historical Context **"Lather and Nothing Else"** is set in Colombia, a country that has been in political turmoil for much of the twentieth and twenty-first centuries. In 1948, disputes between the two major political parties, the Liberals and the Conservatives, worsened when the leader of the Liberal Party, Jorge Eliecer Gaitán, was assassinated in the city of Bogotá. Riots broke out in the city, and fighting soon spread to the countryside. The period was called La Violencia (The Violence) because of the high number of fatalities, about 200,000.

This story explores the dilemma of a barber and secret revolutionary who encounters the leader of the enemy party while at work. With the enemy captured by the barber's chair, the barber's internal conflict rages: Should he kill the man or do his job?

Reader's Context If you worked serving the public and discovered you were serving someone who had harmed people you cared about, how might you behave?

ANALYZE LITERATURE: Point of View and Internal Monologue

Point of view is the perspective from which a story is told. Stories are often written from a *first-person point of view*, in which the narrator uses words such as *I* and *we*. In this selection, the narrator is the town barber, and the story is told from his point of view. This story uses **internal monologue,** or the private thoughts and emotions of the narrator, to allow the reader to get inside the head of the narrator.

SET PURPOSE

Have you ever struggled with a decision? What kinds of thoughts ran through your head? As you read, notice how the narrator reveals his private, internal thoughts as he struggles with his dual roles of good barber and loyal revolutionary. Keep a list of reasons the barber has to support each action he might take.

MEET THE AUTHOR

Hernando Téllez (1908–1966) was born in Bogotá, Colombia. Politician, reporter, and writer, he served in the Colombian Parliament, and he later served as Colombia's ambassador to the United Nations Educational, Scientific, and Cultural Organization (UNESCO) in Paris. Téllez was a journalist as well as a fiction writer. He worked for many of Colombia's newspapers and magazines and published many articles about politics. His short story collection *Ashes for the Wind and Other Stories* includes "Lather and Nothing Else."

USE READING SKILLS

Classify Information
Classifying information is a way of organizing the information you read by putting it into categories. The key to classifying is to choose categories that fit the information. For "Lather and Nothing Else," useful categories of classification could be the positives and negatives the barber presents for killing the captain. Create a graphic organizer like the one below to use as you read. In the "Pro" column, list the positive arguments the barber presents; in the "Con" column, list the negative arguments.

Pro	Con

PREVIEW VOCABULARY

Use the context clues in the sentences below to figure out the meanings of the underlined words from the selection.

1. The astronauts landed near the radio beacon that was <u>emitting</u> a faint signal.
2. In contrast to her brother Allen, who was utterly irresponsible, Ellen was highly <u>conscientious</u>.
3. Dean was frightened of heights, but he <u>ventured</u> up the ladder to rescue his neighbor's kitten.
4. <u>Rejuvenated</u> by the retreat, Salima felt ten years younger.
5. The markers are supposed to be washable, but the ink has been <u>indelible</u> to scrubbing.

Lather and Nothing Else

A Short Story by **Hernando Téllez**

And so, which will it be? Murderer or hero?

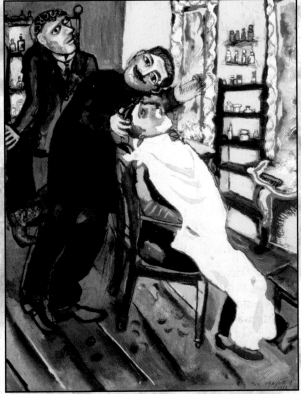

At the Barber's, 1912. Marc Chagall. Musée National d'Art Moderne, Paris, France.

He came in without a word. I was stropping[1] my best razor. And when I recognized him, I started to shake. But he did not notice. To cover my nervousness, I went on honing[2] the razor. I tried the edge with the tip of my thumb and took another look at it against the light.

Meanwhile he was taking off his cartridge-studded[3] belt with the pistol holster suspended from it. He put it on a hook in the wardrobe and hung his cap above it. Then he turned full around toward me and, loosening his tie, remarked, "It's hot as the devil, I want a shave." With that he took his seat.

I estimated he had a four-days' growth of beard, the four days he had been gone on the

---

1. **stropping.** Sharpening by rubbing back and forth on a thick piece of leather, or strop
2. **honing.** Sharpening
3. **cartridge-studded.** Adorned with bullets

last foray after our men. His face looked burnt, tanned by the sun.

I started to lay on the first coat of lather. He kept his eyes closed.

I started to work carefully on the shaving soap. I scraped some slices from the cake, dropped them into the mug, then added a little lukewarm water, and stirred with the brush. The lather soon began to rise.

"The fellows in the troop must have just about as much beard as I." I went on stirring up lather. "But we did very well, you know. We caught the leaders. Some of them we brought back dead; others are still alive. But they'll all be dead soon."

"How many did you take?" I asked.

"Fourteen. We had to go pretty far in to find them. But now they're paying for it. And not one will escape; not a single one."

He leaned back in the chair when he saw the brush in my hand, full of lather. I had not yet put the sheet on him. I was certainly flustered. Taking a sheet from the drawer, I tied it around my customer's neck.

He went on talking. He evidently took it for granted that I was on the side of the existing regime.

"The people must have gotten a scare with what happened the other day," he said.

"Yes," I replied, as I finished tying the knot against his nape, which smelt of sweat.

"Good show, wasn't it?"

"Very good," I answered, turning my attention now to the brush. The man closed his eyes wearily and awaited the cool caress of the lather.

I had never had him so close before. The day he ordered the people to file through the schoolyard to look upon the four rebels hanging there, my path had crossed his briefly. But the sight of those mutilated bodies kept me from paying attention to the face of the man who had been directing it all and whom I now had in my hands.

It was not a disagreeable face, certainly. And the beard, which aged him a bit, was not unbecoming. His name was Torres. Captain Torres.

I started to lay on the first coat of lather. He kept his eyes closed.

"I would love to catch a nap," he said, "but there's a lot to be done this evening."

I lifted the brush and asked, with pretended indifference: "A firing party?"

"Something of the sort," he replied, "but slower."

"All of them?"

"No, just a few."

I went on lathering his face. My hands began to tremble again. The man could not be aware of this, which was lucky for me. But I wished he had not come in. Probably many of our men had seen him enter the shop. And with the enemy in my house I felt a certain responsibility.

I would have to shave his beard just like any other, carefully, neatly, just as though he were a good customer, taking heed that not a single pore should emit a drop of blood. Seeing to it that the blade did not slip in the small whorls.[4] Taking care that the skin was left clean, soft, shining, so that when I passed the back of my hand over it not a single hair should be felt. Yes. I was secretly a revolutionary, but at the same time I was a conscientious barber, proud of the way I did my job. And that four-day beard presented a challenge.

I took up the razor, opened the handle wide, releasing the blade, and started to work, downward from one sideburn. The blade responded to perfection. The hair was tough and hard; not very long, but thick. Little by

---

4. **whorls.** Clusters or curls of hair

for • ay (fôr´ ā) *n.*, raid; attack
re • gime (rā zhēm´ or ri jēm´) *n.*, government; administration in power
e • mit (ē mit´) *v.*, discharge; send out
rev • o • lu • tion • ar • y (re' və lü´ shə ner' ē) *n.*, one who seeks to overthrow a government
con • sci • en • tious (kän[t]´ shē en[t]´ shəs) *adj.*, scrupulous; governed by what one knows is right

little the skin began to show through. The razor gave its usual sound as it gathered up layers of soap mixed with bits of hair. I paused to wipe it clean, and taking up the strop once more went about improving its edge, for I am a painstaking barber.

The man, who had kept his eyes closed, now opened them, put a hand out from under the sheet, felt of the part of his face that was emerging from the lather, and said to me, "Come at six o'clock this evening to the school."

"Will it be like the other day?" I asked, stiff with horror.

"It may be even better," he replied.

"What are you planning to do?"

"I'm not sure yet. But we'll have a good time."

Once more he leaned back and shut his eyes. I came closer, the razor on high.

"Are you going to punish all of them?" I timidly <u>ventured</u>.

"Yes, all of them."

The lather was drying on his face. I must hurry. Through the mirror, I took a look at the street. It appeared about as usual; there was the grocery shop with two or three customers. Then I glanced at the clock, two-thirty.

The razor kept descending. Now from the other sideburn downward. It was a blue beard, a thick one. He should let it grow like some poets, or some priests. It would suit him well. Many people would not recognize him. And that would be a good thing for him, I thought, as I went gently over all the throat line. At this point you really had to handle your blade skillfully, because the hair, while scantier, tended to fall into small whorls. It was a curly beard. The pores might open, <u>minutely</u>, in this area and let out a tiny drop of blood. A good barber like myself stakes his reputation on not permitting that to happen to any of his customers.

And this was indeed a special customer. How many of ours had he sent to their death? How many had he mutilated? It was best not to think about it. Torres did not know I was

Soldiers, 1914–15. Marc Chagall. Coll. M.Z. Gordeyeva, St. Petersburg, Russia.

his enemy. Neither he nor the others knew it. It was a secret shared by very few, just because that made it possible for me to inform the revolutionaries about Torres's activities in the town and what he planned to do every time he went on one of his raids to hunt down rebels. So it was going to be very difficult to explain how it was that I had him in my hands and then let him go in peace, alive, clean-shaven.

His beard had now almost entirely disappeared. He looked younger, several years younger than when he had come in. I suppose that always happens to men who enter and leave barbershops. Under the strokes of my razor Torres was <u>rejuvenated</u>; yes, because I am a good barber, the best in this town, and I say this in all modesty.

---

ven • ture (ven[t]′ shər) *v.,* do at some risk
mi • nute • ly (mī nūt′ lē) *adv.,* to a very small degree
re • ju • ve • nate (ri jü′ və nāt′) *v.,* make to feel young again

A little more lather here under the chin, on the Adam's apple, right near the great vein.[5] How hot it is! Torres must be sweating just as I am. But he is not afraid. He is a <u>tranquil</u> man, who is not even giving thought to what he will do to his prisoners this evening. I, on the other hand, polishing his skin with this razor but avoiding the drawing of blood, careful with every stroke—I cannot keep my thoughts in order.

Confound the hour he entered my shop! I am a revolutionary but not a murderer. And it would be so easy to kill him. He deserves it. Or does he? No! No one deserves the sacrifice others make in becoming assassins. What is to be gained by it? Nothing. Others and still others keep coming, and the first kill the second, and then these kill the next, and so on until everything becomes a sea of blood. I could cut his throat, so, swish, swish! He would not even have time to moan, and with his eyes shut he would not even see the shine of the razor or the gleam in my eye.

But I'm shaking like a regular murderer. From his throat a stream of blood would flow on the sheet, over the chair, down on my hands, onto the floor. I would have to close the door. But the blood would go flowing along the floor, warm, <u>indelible</u>, not to be staunched,[6] until it reached the street like a small scarlet river.

I'm sure that with a good strong blow, a deep cut, he would feel no pain. He would not suffer at all. And what would I do then with the body? Where would I hide it? I would have to flee, leave all this behind, take shelter far away, very far away. But they would follow until they caught up with me. "The murderer of Captain Torres. He slit his throat while he was shaving him. What a cowardly thing to do!"

And others would say, "The avenger of our people. A name to remember"—my name here.

"He was the town barber. No one knew he was fighting for our cause."

And so, which will it be? Murderer or hero? My fate hangs on the edge of this razor blade.

I can turn my wrist slightly, put a bit more pressure on the blade, let it sink in. The skin will yield like silk, like rubber, like the strop. There is nothing more tender than a man's skin, and the blood is always there, ready to burst forth. A razor like this cannot fail. It is the best one I have.

But I don't want to be a murderer. No, sir. You came in to be shaved. And I do my work honorably. I don't want to stain my hands with blood. Just with lather, and nothing else. You are an executioner; I am only a barber. Each one to his job. That's it. Each one to his job.

The chin was now clean, polished, soft. The man got up and looked at himself in the glass. He ran his hand over the skin and felt its freshness, its newness.

"Thanks," he said. He walked to the wardrobe for his belt, his pistol, and his cap. I must have been very pale, and I felt my shirt soaked with sweat. Torres finished adjusting his belt buckle, straightened his gun in its holster, and smoothing his hair mechanically, put on his cap. From his trousers pocket he took some coins to pay for the shave. And he started toward the door. On the threshold he stopped for a moment, and turning toward me, he said, "They told me you would kill me. I came to find out if it was true. But it's not easy to kill. I know what I'm talking about." ❖

---

5. **great vein.** Carotid artery—large blood vessel in the neck
6. **staunched.** Stopped

---

tran • quil (traŋ´ kwəl) *adj.*, calm; serene
in • del • i • ble (in del´ lə bəl) *adj.*, permanent; incapable of being erased or removed

---

MIRRORS & **W**INDOWS

Which is more important: loyalty to one's profession or loyalty to one's beliefs and ideals? How far is it appropriate to go in order to stand up for what you believe in? Explain your answer.

REFER TO TEXT ▷ ▷ ▷ ▷	▷ REASON WITH TEXT	
1a. Describe Torres's entrance into the barbershop and the barber's reaction.	1b. Draw conclusions about what is revealed about each character based on the details in this scene.	**Understand** **Find meaning**
2a. Indicate what the narrator ultimately decides to do to Torres.	2b. Given what you know about Torres, predict how he will treat the barber in the future. Explain your response.	**Apply** **Use information**
3a. Recall when the narrator last crossed paths with Torres. What kept him from looking at Torres's face then?	3b. Contrast the narrator's experience with Torres in the barbershop with the last time they crossed paths.	**Analyze** **Take things apart**
4a. State why Torres came into the barbershop.	4b. Decide how you would have handled the situation if you were the barber. Explain your response.	**Evaluate** **Make judgments**
5a. List some of the acts Torres has led or committed against the revolutionaries.	5b. Develop a statement about the use of violence to bring about political change. Consider these questions: Is political violence ever justified? How can political change be brought about if the party in power will not allow compromise?	**Create** **Bring ideas together**

ANALYZE LITERATURE: Point of View and Internal Monologue

Skim the story to find passages that reveal the narrator's love of his work and those that reveal his dedication to the revolution. How would this story differ if told from the point of view of another customer in the barbershop? from Torres's point of view? What is compelling about the use of internal monologue?

EXTEND THE TEXT

Writing Options

Creative Writing Torres says, "They told me you would kill me. I came to find out if it was true. But it's not easy to kill. I know what I'm talking about." How do you think the barber feels when he hears this? Is he worried that Torres knows who he is? Does he wish he had killed Torres when he had the chance? Does Torres admire the barber or condemn him? Write a **dialogue** between Torres and the barber. Alternately, write a dialogue between the barber and a fellow revolutionary or Torres and one of his colleagues about the meeting in the barbershop.

Applied Writing "Lather and Nothing Else" provides a detailed description of each step the barber takes in shaving Torres's beard. Write **step-by-step instructions** for a task you perform so frequently that you can do it even when you are nervous. Your instructions should be clear enough that someone who has never performed that task will know how to proceed.

Media Literacy

Analyze Point of View in News Reporting Imagine that you are a news reporter preparing a story on political unrest. Research an example of political instability in the world. What are the basic issues of the conflict? What methods are various parties using to support their causes? Prepare two different five-minute television news reports on the conflict. In one, report from the point of view of the ruling party. In the other, report from the point of view of the resistance.

Collaborative Learning

Create a Graphic Novel Sometimes stories take on a whole new meaning if they are told mostly in pictures instead of words. With a group, create a short graphic novel, which is similar to a comic book, of the story "Lather and Nothing Else." If no one in your group enjoys drawing, try creating pictures on the computer.

 Go to **www.mirrorsandwindows.com** for more.

The Moment Before the Gun Went Off

BUILD BACKGROUND

Historical Context In 1948, an all-white South African government ensured white political and economic dominance under law through the system of *apartheid*, a policy of racial segregation and political and economic discrimination. The government forced blacks to live in independent homelands or in separated urban townships. Officials required blacks to carry identification papers and revoked their South African citizenship. During the 1950s, as more and more apartheid laws came into being, resistance grew among black communities. Apartheid in South Africa finally came to an end in 1991. **"The Moment Before the Gun Went Off"** takes place in South Africa as the policy of apartheid was being dismantled. It appeared in the 1991 collection *Jump and Other Stories*.

Reader's Context Write about a time when you became aware of a social situation that was unfair or a stereotype that was inaccurate.

ANALYZE LITERATURE: Point of View and Narrator

Point of view is the vantage point from which a story is told. The person who tells a story is the **narrator.** A narrator may be a participant or witness of the action or he or she may stand outside the action. A narrator may be all knowing or limited in his or her knowledge. He or she may be reliable or unreliable. A Fact and Opinion Chart (see Use Reading Skills at right) will help you decide about the credibility of the narrator in "The Moment Before the Gun Went Off."

SET PURPOSE

Remember that this story takes place as apartheid in South Africa is coming to an end. Consider how people inside and outside of South Africa might have viewed events that had a racial component. As you read, compare your expectations to the narrator's observations.

MEET THE AUTHOR

Nadine Gordimer (b. 1923) was born in a small mining town outside Johannesburg, South Africa, in 1923. She began writing at a young age, publishing her first short story in a South African magazine while still in her teens. In 1949, she published *Face to Face,* her first collection of short stories. An English-speaking Jew living in South Africa during apartheid, Gordimer, who has been called "the conscience of South Africa," has been politically active for most of her life and has written much about race relations in her native land. Gordimer, who has written both fiction and nonfiction, said, "Nothing I say in essays and articles will be as true as my fiction." In 1991, she won the Nobel Prize for literature.

USE READING SKILLS

Distinguish Fact from Opinion One way to discuss fact and opinion as it is related to fiction is to examine how a narrator tells a story. "The Moment Before the Gun Went Off" is a fictional story, but within the story are facts about the shooting along with the narrator's opinions. Looking closely at the facts and opinions the narrator chooses to include can help you decide how the narrator feels about the events and characters of the story. Make a Fact and Opinion Chart like the one below to take notes on the facts and opinions the narrator presents.

Fact	Opinion

PREVIEW VOCABULARY

Use the context clues in the sentences below to figure out the meanings of the underlined words from the selection.

1. Instead of going out on Saturday, Dan spent his time on <u>domestic</u> activities.
2. An example of <u>divestment</u> for social good is the withdrawal of many American companies from South Africa during apartheid.
3. The photographer planned to <u>cull</u> her best shots and send them to the gallery owner.
4. Officials ordered an <u>inquiry</u> into the matter.
5. Anton acted <u>callously</u> when he insulted Lori in front of a group of others.

The Moment Before the Gun Went Off

A Short Story by **Nadine Gordimer**

Marais Van der Vyver shot one of his farm laborers, dead. An accident, there are accidents with guns every day of the week—children playing a fatal game with a father's revolver in the cities where guns are <u>domestic</u> objects, nowadays, hunting mishaps like this one, in the country—but these won't be reported all over the world. Van der Vyver knows his will be. He knows that the story of the Afrikaner[1] farmer—regional leader of the National Party[2] and commandant[3] of the local security commando[4]—shooting a black man who worked for him will fit exactly *their* version of South Africa, it's made for them.

They'll be able to use it in their boycott and <u>divestment</u> campaigns, it'll be another piece of evidence in their truth about the country. The papers at home will quote the story as it has

---

1. **Afrikaner.** A South African of European descent whose native language is Afrikaans
2. **National Party.** Ruling political party in South Africa from 1948–1994 that initiated the policy of apartheid
3. **commandant.** Commanding officer
4. **commando.** An organized force of Boer troops in South Africa. Boers are South Africans of Dutch or Huguenot descent.

---

do • mes • tic (də mes´ tik) *adj.,* relating to the household or family
di • vest • ment (dī ves[t]´ mənt) *n.,* reduction of investments for social or political reasons; selling of assets

---

The moment before the gun went off was a moment of high excitement.

appeared in the overseas press, and in the back and forth he and the black man will become those crudely drawn figures on anti-apartheid banners, units in statistics of white brutality against blacks quoted at the United Nations—he, whom they will gleefully be able to call "a leading member" of the ruling Party.

People in the farming community understand how he must feel. Bad enough to have killed a man, without helping the Party's, the government's, the country's enemies as well. They see the truth of that. They know, reading the Sunday papers, that when Van der Vyver is quoted saying he is "terribly shocked," he will "look after the wife and children," none of those Americans and English, and none of those people at home who want to destroy the white man's power will believe him. And how they will sneer when he even says of the farm boy (according to one paper, if you can trust any of those reporters), "He was my friend, I always took him hunting with me." Those city and overseas people don't know it's true: farmers usually have one particular black boy they like to take along with them in the lands; you could call it a kind of friend, yes, friends are not only your own white people, like yourself, whom you take into your house, pray with in church, and work with on the Party committee. But how can those others know that? They don't want to know it. They think all blacks are like the bigmouth agitators in town. And Van der Vyver's face in the photographs, strangely opened by distress—everyone in the district remembers Marais Van der Vyver as a little boy who would go away and hide himself if he caught him smiling at him, and everyone knows him now as a man who hides any change of expression round his mouth behind a thick, soft mustache, and in his eyes by always looking at some object in hand, a leaf or a crop fingered, pen or stone picked up, while concentrating on what he is saying, or while listening to you. It just goes to show what shock can do; when you look at the newspaper photographs you feel like apologizing, as if you had stared in on some room where you should not be.

There will be an <u>inquiry</u>; there had better be, to stop the assumption of yet another case of brutality against farm workers, although there's nothing in doubt—an accident, and all the facts fully admitted by Van der Vyver.

> **in · qui · ry** (in kwir´ē) *n.*, investigation into a matter of public interest

He made a statement when he arrived at the police station with the dead man in his *bakkie*.[5] Captain Beetge knows him well, of course; he gave him brandy. He was shaking, this big, calm, clever son of Willem Van der Vyver, who inherited the old man's best farm. The black was stone dead, nothing to be done for him. Beetge will not tell anyone that after the brandy Van der Vyver wept. He sobbed, snot running onto his hands, like a dirty kid. The captain was ashamed for him, and walked out to give him a chance to recover himself.

Marais Van der Vyver left his house at three in the afternoon to <u>cull</u> a buck from the family of kudu[6] he protects in the bush areas of his farm. He is interested in wildlife and sees it as the farmers' sacred duty to raise game as well as cattle. As usual, he called at his shed to pick up Lucas, a twenty-year-old farmhand who had shown mechanical aptitude and whom Van der Vyver himself had taught to maintain tractors and other farm machinery. He hooted, and Lucas followed the familiar routine, jumping onto the back of the truck. He liked to travel standing up there, spotting game before his employer did. He would lean forward, bracing against the cab below him.

Van der Vyver had a rifle and .30 caliber ammunition beside him in the cab. The rifle was one of his father's, because his own was at the gunsmith's in town. Since his father died (Beetge's sergeant wrote "passed on") no one had used the rifle, and so when he took it from a cupboard he was sure it was not loaded. His father had never allowed a loaded gun in the house, he himself had been taught since childhood never to ride with a loaded weapon in a vehicle. But this gun was loaded. On a dirt track, Lucas thumped his fist on the cab roof three times to signal: look left. Having seen the white-ripple-marked flank of a kudu, and its fine horns raking through disguising bush, Van der Vyver drove rather fast over a pothole. The jolt fired the rifle. Upright, it was pointing straight through the cab roof at the head of Lucas. The bullet pierced the roof and entered Lucas's brain by way of his throat.

That is the statement of what happened. Although a man of such standing in the

---

5. *bakkie.* Pickup truck
6. **kudu.** African antelope

> **cull** (kəl) *v.*, control the size of a herd by removal; select from a group

district, Van der Vyver had to go through the ritual of swearing that it was the truth. It has gone on record, and will be there in the archive of the local police station as long as Van der Vyver lives, and beyond that, through the lives of his children, Magnus, Helena, and Karel— unless things in the country get worse, the example of black mobs in the town spreads to the rural areas and the place is burned down as many urban police stations have been. Because nothing the government can do will appease the agitators and the whites who encourage them. Nothing satisfies them, in the cities: blacks can sit and drink in white hotels now, the Immorality Act has gone, blacks can sleep with whites… It's not even a crime anymore.

Van der Vyver has a high, barbed security fence round his farmhouse and garden which his wife, Alida, thinks spoils completely the effect of her artificial stream with its tree ferns beneath the jacarandas.[7] There is an aerial soaring like a flagpole in the backyard. All his vehicles, including the truck in which the black man died, have aerials that swing their whips when the driver hits a pothole: they are part of the security system the farmers in the district maintain, each farm in touch with every other by radio, twenty-four hours out of twenty-four. It has already happened that infiltrators from over the border have mined remote farm roads, killing white farmers and their families out on their own property for a Sunday picnic. The pothole could have set off a land mine, and Van der Vyver might have died with his farm boy. When neighbors use the communications system to call up and say they are sorry about "that business" with one of Van der Vyver's boys, there goes unsaid: it could have been worse.

It is obvious from the quality and fittings of the coffin that the farmer has provided money for the funeral. And an elaborate funeral means a great deal to blacks; look how they will deprive themselves of the little they have, in their lifetime, keeping up payments to a burial society so they won't go in boxwood[8]

to an unmarked grave. The young wife is pregnant (of course) and another little one, a boy wearing red shoes several sizes too large, leans under her jutting belly. He is too young to understand what has happened, what he is witnessing that day, but neither whines nor plays about; he is solemn without knowing why. Blacks expose small children to everything, they don't protect them from the sight of fear and pain the way whites do theirs. It is the young wife who rolls her head and cries like a child, sobbing on the breast of this relative and that. All present work for Van der Vyver or are the families of those who work; in the weeding and harvest seasons, the women and children work for him too, carried at sunrise to the fields, wrapped in their blankets, on a truck, singing. The dead man's mother is a woman who can't be more than in her late thirties (they start bearing children at puberty), but she is heavily mature in a black dress, standing between her own parents, who were already working for old Van der Vyver when Marais, like their daughter, was a child. The parents hold her as if she were a prisoner or a crazy woman to be restrained. But she says nothing, does nothing. She does not look up; she does not look at Van der Vyver, whose gun went off in the truck, she stares at the grave. Nothing will make her look up; there need be no fear that she will look up, at him. His wife, Alida, is beside him. To show the proper respect, as for any white funeral, she is wearing the navy blue and cream hat she wears to church this summer. She is always supportive, although he doesn't seem to notice it; this coldness and reserve—his mother says he didn't mix well as a child—she accepts for herself but regrets that it has prevented him from being nominated, as he should be, to stand as the Party's parliamentary candidate for the district. He does not let her clothing, or that of anyone else gathered

---

7. **jacarandas.** A type of creeping, flowering tropical tree
8. **boxwood.** Close-grained, heavy, hard wood

Homage to Chris Hani, 1993. Willie Bester. Private collection.

closely, make contact with him. He, too, stares at the grave. The dead man's mother and he stare at the grave in communication like that between the black man outside and the white man inside the cab the moment before the gun went off.

The moment before the gun went off was a moment of high excitement shared through the roof of the cab, as the bullet was to pass, between the young black man outside and the white farmer inside the vehicle. There were such moments, without explanation, between them, although often around the farm the farmer would pass the young man without returning a greeting, as if he did not recognize him. When the bullet went off what Van der

Critical Viewing

This piece celebrates the life of Chris Hani, a political activist who fought against the South African apartheid and was assassinated in 1993. His death helped stimulate the nation toward taking steps to end apartheid. What strikes you the most about this piece of art? If you were to create a piece of art celebrating Lucas's life, what images would you include?

Vyver saw was the kudu stumble in fright at the report and gallop away. Then he heard the thud behind him, and past the window saw the young man fall out of the vehicle. He was sure he had leapt up and toppled—in fright, like the buck. The farmer was almost laughing with relief, ready to tease, as he opened his door, it did not seem possible that a bullet passing through the roof could have done harm.

The young man did not laugh with him at his own fright. The farmer carried him in his arms, to the truck. He was sure, sure he could not be dead. But the young black man's blood was all over the farmer's clothes, soaking against his flesh as he drove.

How will they ever know, when they file newspaper clippings, evidence, proof, when they look at the photographs and see his face—guilty! guilty! they are right!—how will they know, when the police stations burn with all the evidence of what has happened now, and what the law made a crime in the past? How could they know that *they do not know.* Anything. The young black <u>callously</u> shot through the negligence of the white man was not the farmer's boy; he was his son. ❖

cal • lous • ly (kaˊ ləs lē) *adv.,* insensitively; uncaringly

---

 Given what you know about South Africa at the time the story takes place, how would you have reacted to hearing this story in the news? Are there current news stories that make you wonder about bias or accuracy?

AFTER READING

REFER TO TEXT ▶ ▶ ▶ ▶	▶ REASON WITH TEXT	
1a. Identify assumptions the community makes about Van der Vyver's feelings about the incident.	1b. Explain whether these assumptions are accurate.	**Understand** **Find meaning**
2a. Point out in the text what Van der Vyver assumed about the gun.	2b. Given the setting of the story, what might the loaded gun have symbolized?	**Apply** **Use information**
3a. What did Van der Vyver do in the police station? List signs that show that he contributed to the funeral.	3b. Decide how Van der Vyver felt about Lucas. What leads you to this conclusion?	**Analyze** **Take things apart**
4a. Describe how Lucas died.	4b. Assess whether Van der Vyver should be found guilty of murder. Judge whether he should be convicted in the court of public opinion. Justify your response.	**Evaluate** **Make judgments**
5a. Name stereotypes Lucas and Van der Vyver will come to represent in the press.	5b. How might people revise their perceptions of the story if they knew of the true relationship between Lucas and Van der Vyver?	**Create** **Bring ideas together**

ANALYZE LITERATURE: Point of View and Narrator

 Describe the narrator and his or her point of view. Scan the story for comments the narrator makes that show his or her biases or assumptions. How do you think the narrator feels toward Van der Vyver?

EXTEND THE TEXT

Writing Options

Creative Writing The narrator talks about how the story will play in the overseas press. Write a brief **news story** that reports on this event. In your story, provide some political background about South Africa and some imagined quotations from relevant figures. Remember to use the 5 Ws: *who, what, when, where,* and *why.* If possible, answer the question of *how.* Try to keep your article free of any bias or opinions and instead report the facts objectively. Include a brief, vivid headline for your story.

Narrative Writing To further explore point of view, write a **retelling** of part of the story from the point of view of one of the characters. For example, you could write from the point of view of Van der Vyver, Lucas, or Lucas's mother. Choose a part of the story that allows the character's actions, feelings, and thoughts about other characters to be clearly expressed.

Lifelong Learning

Create a Time Line of Apartheid in South Africa
Use the library and Internet to research the history of apartheid in South Africa. In your own words, define apartheid and the restrictions it imposed on nonwhite members of the South African population. Create a Time Line showing events leading up to apartheid in South Africa, when the policy began, major events that happened under the policy, and how it came to an end. Also include events that have occurred since the end of apartheid. Once your Time Line is in order, find pictures or other visual aids to illustrate the events. Post your Time Line and pictures on a classroom bulletin board.

Critical Literacy

Role-play a Conversation Imagine that Van der Vyver and Lucas's mother have a conversation many years after Lucas's death. They have both aged and changed, and the situation in South Africa has evolved, too. How would such a conversation start? What would they talk about? How do you imagine each feels? With a partner, role-play the conversation between Van der Vyver and Lucas's mother.

 Go to **www.mirrorsandwindows.com** for more.

READING ASSESSMENT

1. Which statement best summarizes the narrator's feelings about whites in South Africa?
   A. They all treat blacks badly.
   B. They are misrepresented in the press and misunderstood by the world.
   C. They have good relationships with the blacks they know.
   D. They are under attack and deserve sympathy in South Africa.
   E. The black agitators make them look bad, though the black country folk understand them.

2. Which description best fits the narrator?
   A. an American reporter stationed in South Africa reporting on a racial issue
   B. a black South African commenting on the death of a friend
   C. a white South African who feels Van der Vyver is a traitor to his race
   D. a white South African who feels white South Africans are misunderstood
   E. a black South African who is close to both blacks and whites in his community

3. Which events show the complicated relationship between Van der Vyver and Lucas?

   A. Van der Vyver sometimes shares excitement with Lucas but other times ignores him.
   B. Van der Vyver spends money on Lucas's funeral but refuses to go to it.
   C. Van der Vyver is saddened by Lucas's death, but more worried about what people will think.
   D. Van der Vyver thinks of Lucas as a friend but fails to acknowledge him as a son.
   E. Van der Vyver admits publicly that Lucas is his son but will not talk to Lucas.

4. Choose the word that best completes the following sentence: Instead of showing sympathy to the grieving family, the _____ landlord evicted them from their home.
   A. domestic
   B. inquiring
   C. callous
   D. ingenuous
   E. ignorant

5. Analyze the character of Van der Vyver. How would you describe him to a friend who has never read the story? Give examples from the story that illustrate key points of his character.

GRAMMAR & STYLE

Pronoun and Antecedent Agreement

A **pronoun** is used in place of a noun. Sometimes, a pronoun refers to a specific person or thing. The most common types of pronouns are listed in the chart below.

Type of Pronoun	Definition	Examples
personal pronoun	used in place of the name of a person or thing	I, me, we, us, he, she, it, him, her, you, they, them
indefinite pronoun	points out a person, place, or thing, but not a specific or definite one	one, someone, anything, other, all, few, nobody
reflexive pronoun	refers back to a noun previously used; adds –self and –selves to other pronoun forms	myself, herself, yourself, themselves, ourselves
intensive pronoun	emphasizes a noun or pronoun	me *myself*, he *himself*, you *yourself*, they *themselves*, we *ourselves*
interrogative pronoun	asks a question	who, whose, whom, what, which
demonstrative pronoun	points out a specific person, place, idea, or thing	this, these, that, those
relative pronoun	introduces an adjective clause	that, which, who, whose, whom
singular pronoun	used in place of the name of one person or thing	I, me, she, her, he, him, it
plural pronoun	used in place of more than one person or thing	we, us, you, they, them
possessive pronoun	shows ownership or possession	mine, yours, his, hers, ours, theirs, its

The word that a pronoun stands for is called its **antecedent.** The antecedent clarifies the meaning of the pronoun. The pronoun may appear in the same sentence as its antecedent or in a following sentence.

EXAMPLES

Marais Van der Vyver shot one of his farm laborers, dead. (*Marais Van der Vyver* is the antecedent of *his*.)

Nadine Gordimer wrote the story "The Moment Before the Gun Went Off." She was born in South Africa. (*Nadine Gordimer* is the antecedent of *she*.)

When you use a pronoun, be sure it refers clearly to its antecedent. A pronoun should agree in both number (singular or plural) and gender (masculine, feminine, or neutral) with its antecedent.

Sometimes, problems in pronoun and antecedent agreement can arise when indefinite pronouns are involved. Most indefinite pronouns are singular, but some are plural, and others can be both singular and plural. Study the list below.

singular: another, anybody, anyone, anything, each, each other, either, everybody, everyone, everything, much, neither, nobody, no one, nothing, one, one another, other, somebody, someone, something

plural: both, few, many, several, others

singular or plural: all, any, more, most, none, some

If the indefinite pronoun is singular, its antecedent should be singular. If the indefinite pronoun is plural, its antecedent should be plural.

If the indefinite pronoun can be singular or plural and you do not know the gender of the antecedent, use both the masculine and feminine pronoun forms, connected by *or*.

EXAMPLE

<u>Everyone</u> grieved the loss in <u>his or her</u> own way.

Identify Pronouns and Antecedents

Copy the following passage from "The Moment Before the Gun Went Off" into your notebook. Then compile a list of all the pronouns in the passage; next to each pronoun, write two things: 1) the type of pronoun it is, and 2) its antecedent.

Marais Van der Vyver left his house at three in the afternoon to cull a buck from the family of kudu he protects in the bush areas of his farm. He is interested in wild-life and sees it as the farmers' sacred duty to raise game as well as cattle. As usual, he called at his shed to pick up Lucas, a twenty-year-old farmhand who had shown mechanical aptitude and whom Van der Vyver himself had taught to maintain tractors and other farm machinery. He hooted, and Lucas followed the familiar routine, jumping onto the back of the truck. He liked to travel standing up there, spotting game before his employer did. He would lean forward, bracing against the cab below him.

Understand Pronoun and Antecedent Agreement

Complete the following sentences by using the correct pronoun in each blank.

1. Nadine Gordimer began writing at an early age, publishing _____ first story in a South African magazine while _____ was still in _____ teens.
2. Black South Africans living during apartheid had to carry _____ identification papers with _____ wherever _____ went. _____ were also denied South African citizenship.
3. "The Moment Before the Gun Went Off" is a story that takes place during apartheid. _____ main character is a white farmer. _____ name is Marais Van der Vyver. _____ shot _____ farmhand, Lucas.

4. Readers will be surprised at the ending of the story; _____ will likely find _____ ironic.
5. Van der Vyver claimed _____ and Lucas were friends, but some people did not believe _____. _____ thought Van der Vyver was just trying to defend _____.
6. When Van der Vyver arrived at the police station, _____ told Captain Beetge what had happened and _____ began to cry. Captain Beetge felt sorry for _____ and left the room so that _____ could collect _____.
7. Lucas's mother stands by _____ grave and remains silent. _____ stares at _____ son's grave, and _____ does not look at anyone. Beside _____, _____ daughter-in-law sobs loudly.
8. The narrator is upset about how other people will view the accident and suggests that _____ will see _____ as just another example of brutality against the farm workers.
9. Van der Vyver could understand the pain of the grieving widow and mother. _____ had just lost a person who was very special to _____.

Use Pronoun and Antecedent Agreement in Your Writing

Think of a famous historical figure whose life you find interesting. Write a profile of the person you choose. Once you have finished a draft of your profile, circle each pronoun and underline its antecedent. Then carefully check to make sure the pronouns and antecedents all agree. If you are unsure, ask a classmate to check your work.

EXTEND THE SKILL

Imagine you are in a book club that is reading "The Moment Before the Gun Went Off." You are responsible for writing the discussion questions to go with the story. Write five questions that would generate discussion about the story; each of the five questions should include at least one pronoun and its antecedent.

Understanding Character

CHARACTER

"He is such a character!" You've probably heard that remark before. Usually, it means that somebody is acting in a certain way that makes him or her identifiable or unique. How people tend to act and think is a reflection of their character, or personality. Similarly, the people you encounter in the pages of a book are characters with distinctive traits.

TYPES OF CHARACTERS

A **character** is an individual that takes part in a literary work. All characters have some role to play in bringing a story to life. The characters around whom a story is centered are the *major characters.* In "Two Kinds" (page 69) for instance, Jing-mei and her mother are major characters. Their conflicted relationship is what creates most of the action in the story. Jing-mei's piano teacher, her aunt, and her cousin are *minor characters.* Minor characters play lesser roles in the story and may give the major characters points of interaction.

Major characters can also be classified as either protagonists or antagonists. The **protagonist** has the central role in a story; the **antagonist** works against the protagonist, and this friction creates conflict.

Have you ever noticed how some characters you remember long after reading and others you quickly forget? The difference could be attributed to whether the character is a *flat character* or a *round character.* Luis in "Catch the Moon" (page 63) is a round character. He shows emotional complexity and development such as exhibiting apathy and disgust over his work at the junkyard at one moment and then pride and purpose in the same work at the end of the story. Many characters that you encounter in fables and fairy tales, however, are flat, exhibiting only a single quality. Some flat characters play into common notions of how certain people think and behave. Such characters are considered stereotypes.

Another way to consider character is by noting static characters and dynamic characters. *Static characters* remain the same throughout the course of the story; the events in the plot do not alter them. *Dynamic characters,* on the other hand, are affected by plot

events and therefore undergo change. Luis in "Catch the Moon" is a dynamic character. Over the course of the story, he learns the value of work and gains a greater respect for his father. His father, Jorge, however, is a static character. His attitude toward work and Luis changes little by the end of the story.

The force that drives a character to think, feel, or behave in a certain way is called **motivation.** Motivation can be relatively simple—the desire to shine in society, for example, or to exact revenge for an insult. It can also be complex, consisting of more than one need.

Memorable Minor Characters

Even though minor characters play lesser roles in fiction than major characters, they are often essential to the development of the story. Look at the list of minor characters below and the stories they are in. How would the stories be different without these characters?

- Bertha Rochester in *Jane Eyre*
- Mr. Peggotty in *David Copperfield*
- The woodsman in "Snow White and the Seven Dwarfs"
- Charlotte Lucas in *Pride and Prejudice*

CHARACTERIZATION

The act of creating or describing a character is called **characterization.** There are three main techniques that an author uses to form a character: showing what characters say, do, or think; showing what other characters say or think about them; and describing the physical features, dress, and personality of the characters. The first two methods are examples of *indirect characterization,* in which the writer shows what a character is like and allows the reader to judge that character.

In the following passage from "On the Rainy River" (page 137), O'Brien describes the man who helps his character, Tim, make his decision whether or not to go to war. Since this description is Tim's impression of Elroy, it is considered an indirect characterization.

Elroy Berdahl: eighty-one years old, skinny and shrunken and mostly bald. He wore a flannel shirt and brown work pants. In one hand, I remember, he carried a green apple, a small paring knife in the other. His eyes had the bluish gray color of a razor blade, the same polished shine, and as he peered up at me I felt a strange sharpness, almost painful, a cutting sensation, as if his gaze were somehow slicing me open.
—from "On the Rainy River"
by Tim O'Brien

The third technique is considered *direct characterization,* in which the writer tells what the character is like. For example, in "Two Friends" (page 95), Maupassant directly describes Monsieur Morissot: "He was a watchmaker by trade and a man who liked to make the most of his leisure."

In the following excerpt from "The Open Window" (page 6), Saki's comment that Framton believed that everyone was interested in hearing the details of his health is a direct characterization that suggests Framton is self-interested.

"The doctors agree in ordering me complete rest, an absence of mental excitement, and avoidance of anything in the nature of violent physical exercise," announced Framton, who labored under the tolerably widespread delusion that total strangers and chance acquaintances are hungry for the least detail of one's ailments and infirmities, their cause and cure.
—from "The Open Window" by Saki

The **dialogue,** or conversations among characters, is also revealing. The content of the dialogue is a form of indirect characterization. A character may speak in a **dialect,** or version of a language spoken by the people of a particular place, time, or social group, which can indicate the character's ethnic or geographical background. For example, when Neffie in "Who Said We All Have to Talk Alike" (page 157) uses the words "worman" and "torelet," she is speaking in dialect, which makes her character more distinctive.

Another example of dialogue revealing character is in "Two Kinds" in the following conversation between Jing-mei and her mother. In this passage, we learn about Jing-mei's frustration with her mother and her mother's expectation of her daughter from what they say and how they say it.

"Why don't you like me the way I am? I'm *not* a genius! I can't play the piano. And even if I could, I wouldn't go on TV if you paid me a million dollars!" I cried.

My mother slapped me. "Who ask you be genius?" she shouted. "Only ask you be your best. For you sake. You think I want you be genius? Hnnh! What for! Who ask you!"
—from "Two Kinds" by Amy Tan

Take a look at the Characterization Chart below. As you read a story, you can fill in a similar graphic organizer to characterize an important figure both directly and indirectly.

Character: Jing-mei	
Characterization Clue	**What It Reveals**
What she says: "Why don't you like me the way I am?"	Jing-mei feels that her mother does not understand her.
What she does: She yells at her mother.	She is very frustrated with her mother.
What others say about her: "If she had as much talent as temper she would be famous now."	Jing-mei has a short temper.

Catch the Moon
A Short Story by Judith Ortiz Cofer

Two Kinds
A Short Story by Amy Tan

BEFORE READING

BUILD BACKGROUND

Literary Context **"Catch the Moon"** was published in *An Island Like You*, Judith Ortiz Cofer's first short story collection. Luis Cintrón, the story's protagonist, has just spent six months in juvenile hall. Upon his release, he returns to work in his father's junkyard and is bitter and angry about his situation. When his father challenges him to search for a specific item in the junkyard, Luis discovers more than what he set out to find.

Amy Tan's **"Two Kinds"** is part of a novel titled *The Joy Luck Club*. The main character Jing-mei, a girl growing up in San Francisco's Chinatown, struggles to define her own future apart from her mother's expectations of her. Fighting her mother as well as cultural attitudes, Jing-mei chooses her own path and, years later, comes to understand her mother's desires and motivations.

As you read these stories, consider the following questions: What kind of relationship between parent and child is described in each story? What different ideas about success do the characters in the stories have? How does each protagonist grow or change throughout his or her story?

Reader's Context Think about a conflict you have experienced with an authority figure. What caused the conflict? How was it resolved?

USE READING SKILLS

Compare and Contrast **Comparing** explores the similarities between things, whereas **contrasting** explores their differences.

As you read "Catch the Moon" and "Two Kinds," take notes on the similarities and differences in the characters. In a Venn Diagram, like the one shown, show similarities inside the space that overlaps, and show differences in the outer spaces.

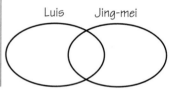

Luis   Jing-mei

COMPARE LITERATURE: Character and Characterization

A **character** is an individual that takes part in the action of a literary work. Authors use techniques of **characterization,** such as direct description, portrayal of behavior, and representation of thoughts and feelings, to create a character. Both Luis in "Catch the Moon" and Jing-mei in "Two Kinds" are *dynamic characters,* or characters who change, as both characters struggle to find their own way. *Static characters* do not change. As you read, take notes about the characters of Luis and Jing-mei. Look for similarities and differences between them.

MEET THE AUTHORS

Judith Ortiz Cofer (b. 1952) said, "...early on I instinctively knew storytelling was a form of empowerment, that the women in my family were passing on power from one generation to another through fables and stories." Like many of the teens in her story, Cofer was born in Puerto Rico and moved with her parents to the United States as a child.

Amy Tan (b. 1952) would have become a doctor and a concert pianist if she had followed her parents' wishes. Instead, she turned to reading as a refuge from family pressure and as an adult began writing fiction. She describes writing her first story about a Chinese-American girl's relationship with her mother as "a magic turning point." The story

helped her understand her own relationship with her mother. "I realized this was the reason for writing fiction. Through...creating something that never happened, I came closer to the truth."

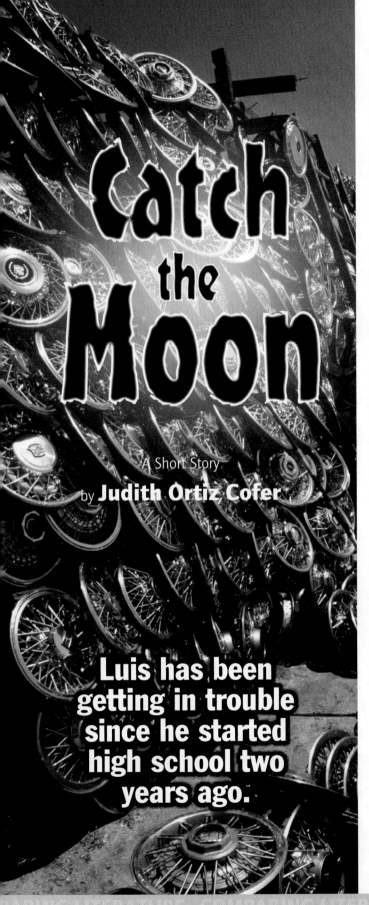

Catch the Moon

A Short Story

by **Judith Ortiz Cofer**

Luis has been getting in trouble since he started high school two years ago.

Luis Cintrón sits on top of a six-foot pile of hubcaps and watches his father walk away into the steel jungle of his car junkyard. Released into his old man's custody after six months in juvenile hall—for breaking and entering—and he didn't even take anything. He did it on a dare. But the old lady with the million cats was a light sleeper, and good with her aluminum cane. He has a scar on his head to prove it.

Now Luis is wondering whether he should have stayed in and done his full time. Jorge Cintrón of Jorge Cintrón & Son, Auto Parts and Salvage, has decided that Luis should wash and polish every hubcap in the yard. The hill he is sitting on is only the latest couple of hundred wheel covers that have come in. Luis grunts and stands up on top of his silver mountain. He yells at no one, "Someday, son, all this will be yours," and sweeps his arms like the Pope blessing a crowd over the piles of car sandwiches and mounds of metal parts that cover this acre of land outside the city. He is the "Son" of Jorge Cintrón & Son, and so far his father has had more than one reason to wish it was plain Jorge Cintrón on the sign.

Luis has been getting in trouble since he started high school two years ago, mainly because of the "social group" he organized—a bunch of guys who were into harassing the local authorities. Their thing was taking something to the limit on a dare or, better still, doing something dangerous, like breaking into a house, not to steal, just to prove that they could do it. That was Luis's specialty, coming up with very complicated plans, like military strategies, and assigning the "jobs" to guys who wanted to join the Tiburones.

Tiburón means "shark," and Luis had gotten the name from watching an old movie about a Puerto Rican gang called the Sharks[1] with his father. Luis thought it was one of the dumbest films he had ever seen. Everybody sang their

---

1. **Sharks.** Fictional Puerto-Rican gang from the movie *West Side Story*

lines, and the guys all pointed their toes and leaped in the air when they were supposed to be slaughtering each other. But he liked their name, the Sharks, so he made it Spanish and had it air-painted on his black T-shirt with a killer shark under it, jaws opened wide and dripping with blood. It didn't take long for the other guys in the barrio[2] to ask about it.

Man, had they had a good time. The girls were interested too. Luis outsmarted everybody by calling his organization a social club and registering it at Central High. That meant they were legal, even let out of last-period class on Fridays for their "club" meetings. It was just this year, after a couple of botched jobs, that the teachers had started getting suspicious. The first one to go wrong was when he sent Kenny Matoa to *borrow* some "souvenirs" out of Anita Robles's locker. He got caught. It seems that Matoa had been reading Anita's diary and didn't hear her coming down the hall. Anita was supposed to be in the gym at that time but had copped out with the usual female excuse of cramps. You could hear her screams all the way to Market Street.

She told the principal all she knew about the Tiburones, and Luis had to talk fast to convince old Mr. Williams that the club did put on cultural activities such as the Save the Animals

talent show. What Mr. Williams didn't know was that the animal that was being "saved" with the ticket sales was Luis's pet boa, which needed quite a few live mice to stay healthy and happy. They kept E.S. (which stood for "Endangered Species") in Luis's room, but she belonged to the club and it was the members' responsibility to raise the money to feed their mascot. So last year they had sponsored their first annual Save the Animals talent show, and it had been a great success. The Tiburones had come dressed as Latino Elvises and did a grand finale to "All Shook Up" that made the audience go wild. Mr. Williams had smiled when Luis talked, maybe remembering how the math teacher, Mrs. Laguna, had dragged him out in the aisle to rock-and-roll with her. Luis had gotten out of that one, but barely.

His father was a problem too. He objected to the T-shirt logo, calling it disgusting and <u>vulgar</u>. Mr. Cintrón prided himself on his own neat, elegant style of dressing after work, and on his manners and large vocabulary, which he picked up by taking correspondence courses in just

2. **barrio** (bä´ rē ō). Spanish-speaking neighborhood in the United States

vul • gar (vul´ gər) *adj.,* lacking in cultivation, perception, or taste

about everything. Luis thought that it was just his way of staying busy since Luis's mother had died, almost three years ago, of cancer. He had never gotten over it.

All this was going through Luis's head as he slid down the hill of hubcaps. The tub full of soapy water, the can of polish, and the bag of rags had been neatly placed in front of a makeshift table made from two car seats and a piece of plywood. Luis heard a car drive up and someone honk their horn. His father emerged from inside a new red Mustang that had been totaled. He usually dismantled every small feature by hand before sending the vehicle into the *cementerio*,[3] as he called the lot. Luis watched as the most beautiful girl he had ever seen climbed out of a vintage[4] white Volkswagen Bug. She stood in the sunlight in her white sundress waiting for his father, while Luis stared. She was like a smooth wood carving. Her skin was mahogany,[5] almost black, and her arms and legs were long and thin, but curved in places so that she did not look bony and hard—more like a ballerina. And her ebony[6] hair was braided close to her head. Luis let his breath out, feeling a little dizzy. He had forgotten to breathe. Both the girl and his father heard him. Mr. Cintrón waved him over.

"Luis, the señorita here has lost a wheel cover. Her car is twenty-five years old, so it will not be an easy match. Come look on this side." Luis tossed a wrench he'd been holding into a toolbox like he was annoyed, just to make a point about slave labor. Then he followed his father, who knelt on the gravel and began to point out every detail of the hubcap. Luis was hardly listening. He watched the girl take a piece of paper from her handbag.

"Señor Cintrón, I have drawn the hubcap for you, since I will have to leave soon. My home address and telephone number are here, and also my parents' office number." She handed the paper to Mr. Cintrón, who nodded.

"Sí, señorita, very good. This will help my son look for it. Perhaps there is one in that stack there." He pointed to the pile of caps that Luis was supposed to wash and polish. "Yes, I'm almost certain that there is a match there. Of course, I do not know if it's near the top or the bottom. You will give us a few days, yes?"

Luis just stared at his father like he was crazy. But he didn't say anything because the girl was smiling at him with a funny expression on her face. Maybe she thought he had X-ray eyes like Superman, or maybe she was mocking him.

"Please call me Naomi, Señor Cintrón. You know my mother. She is the director of the funeral home…." Mr. Cintrón seemed surprised at first; he prided himself on having a great memory. Then his friendly expression changed to one of sadness as he recalled the day of his wife's burial. Naomi did not finish her sentence. She reached over and placed her hand on Mr. Cintrón's arm for a moment. Then she said "Adiós" softly, and got in her shiny white car. She waved to them as she left, and her gold bracelets flashing in the sun nearly blinded Luis.

Mr. Cintrón shook his head. "How about that," he said as if to himself. "They are the Dominican owners of Ramirez Funeral Home." And, with a sigh, "She seems like such a nice young woman. Reminds me of your mother when she was her age."

Hearing the funeral parlor's name, Luis remembered too. The day his mother died, he had been in her room at the hospital while his father had gone for coffee. The alarm had gone off on her monitor and nurses had come running in, pushing him outside. After that, all he recalled was the anger that had made him punch a hole in his bedroom wall. And after-

---

3. *cementerio* (sā mən tā′ rē ō). [Spanish] Cemetery
4. **vintage.** Dating from the past
5. **mahogany** (mə hä′ gə nē). Deep brown color, named after a type of wood
6. **ebony.** Black

---

make • shift (māk′ shift′) *adj.*, crude and temporary substitute
dis • man • tle (dis man′ təl) *v.*, divide into pieces
mock (mäk) *v.*, treat with contempt or ridicule

ward he had refused to talk to anyone at the funeral. Strange, he did see a black girl there who didn't try like the others to talk to him, but actually ignored him as she escorted family members to the viewing room and brought flowers in. Could it be that the skinny girl in a frilly white dress had been Naomi? She didn't act like she had recognized him today, though. Or maybe she thought that he was a jerk.

Luis grabbed the drawing from his father. The old man looked like he wanted to walk down memory lane. But Luis was in no mood to listen to the old stories about his falling in love on a tropical island. The world they'd lived in before he was born wasn't his world. No beaches and palm trees here. Only junk as far as he could see. He climbed back up his hill and studied Naomi's sketch. It had obviously been done very carefully. It was signed "Naomi Ramirez" in the lower right-hand corner. He memorized the telephone number.

Luis washed hubcaps all day until his hands were red and raw, but he did not come across the small silver bowl that would fit the VW. After work he took a few practice Frisbee shots across the yard before showing his father what he had accomplished: rows and rows of shiny rings drying in the sun. His father nodded and showed him the bump on his temple where one of Luis's flying saucers had gotten him.

"Practice makes perfect, you know. Next time you'll probably decapitate[7] me." Luis heard him struggle with the word *decapitate,* which Mr. Cintrón pronounced in syllables. Showing off his big vocabulary again, Luis thought. He looked closely at the bump, though. He felt bad about it.

"They look good, hijo." Mr. Cintrón made a sweeping gesture with his arms over the yard. "You know, all this will have to be classified. My dream is to have all the parts divided by year, make of car, and condition. Maybe now that you are here to help me, this will happen."

"Pop…" Luis put his hand on his father's shoulder. They were the same height and build, about five foot six and muscular. "The judge

said six months of free labor for you, not life, okay?" Mr. Cintrón nodded, looking distracted. It was then that Luis suddenly noticed how gray his hair had turned—it used to be shiny black like his own—and that there were deep lines in his face. His father had turned into an old man and he hadn't even noticed.

"Son, you must follow the judge's instructions. Like she said, next time you get in trouble, she's going to treat you like an adult, and I think you know what that means. Hard time, no breaks."

"Yeah, yeah. That's what I'm doing, right? Working my hands to the bone instead of enjoying my summer. But listen, she didn't put me under house arrest, right? I'm going out tonight."

"Home by ten. She did say something about a curfew, Luis." Mr. Cintrón had stopped smiling and was looking upset. It had always been hard for them to talk more than a minute or two before his father got offended at something Luis said, or at his sarcastic tone. He was always doing something wrong.

Luis threw the rag down on the table and went to sit in his father's ancient Buick, which was in mint[8] condition. They drove home in silence.

After sitting down at the kitchen table with his father to eat a pizza they had picked up on the way home, Luis asked to borrow the car. He didn't get an answer then, just a look that meant "Don't bother me right now." Before bringing up the subject again, Luis put some ice cubes in a Baggie and handed it to Mr. Cintrón, who had made the little bump on his head worse by rubbing it. It had GUILTY written on it, Luis thought.

"Gracias, hijo." His father placed the bag on the bump and made a face as the ice touched his skin.

---

7. **decapitate.** Behead
8. **mint.** As if newly made, as a coin would be if it came straight from the mint (the place where it was made)

They ate in silence for a few minutes more; then Luis decided to ask about the car again.

"I really need some fresh air, Pop. Can I borrow the car for a couple of hours?"

"You don't get enough fresh air at the yard? We're lucky that we don't have to sit in a smelly old factory all day. You know that?"

"Yeah, Pop. We're real lucky." Luis always felt irritated that his father was so grateful to own a junkyard, but he held his anger back and just waited to see if he'd get the keys without having to get in an argument.

"Where are you going?"

"For a ride. Not going anywhere. Just out for a while. Is that okay?"

His father didn't answer, just handed him a set of keys, as shiny as the day they were manufactured. His father polished everything that could be polished: doorknobs, coins, keys, spoons, knives, and forks, like he was King Midas[9] counting his silver and gold. Luis thought his father must be really lonely to polish utensils only he used anymore. They had been picked out by his wife, though, so they were like <u>relics</u>. Nothing she had ever owned could be thrown away. Only now the dishes, forks, and spoons were not used to eat the yellow rice and red beans, the fried chicken, or the mouth-watering sweet plantains[10] that his mother had cooked for them. They were just kept in the cabinets that his father had turned into a museum for her. Mr. Cintrón could cook as well as his wife, but he didn't have the heart to do it anymore. Luis thought that maybe if they ate together once in a while things might get better between them, but he always had something to do around dinnertime and ended up at a hamburger joint. Tonight was the first time in months they had sat down at the table together.

Luis took the keys. "Thanks," he said, walking out to take his shower. His father kept looking at him with those sad, patient eyes. "Okay. I'll be back by ten, and keep the ice on that egg," Luis said without looking back.

He had just meant to ride around his old barrio, see if any of the Tiburones were hanging out at El Building, where most of them lived. It wasn't far from the single-family home his father had bought when the business started paying off: a house that his mother lived in for three months before she took up residence at St. Joseph's Hospital. She never came home again. These days Luis wished he still lived in that tiny apartment where there was always something to do, somebody to talk to.

Instead Luis found himself parked in front of the last place his mother had gone to: Ramirez Funeral Home. In the front yard was a huge oak tree that Luis remembered having climbed during the funeral to get away from

Doing something that had a beginning, middle, and an end did something to your head.

people. The tree looked different now, not like a skeleton, as it had then, but green with leaves. The branches reached to the second floor of the house, where the family lived.

For a while Luis sat in the car allowing the memories to flood back into his brain. He remembered his mother before the illness changed her. She had not been beautiful, as his father told everyone; she had been a sweet lady, not pretty but not ugly. To him, she had been the person who always told him that she was proud of him and loved him. She did that every night when she came to his bedroom door to say good-night. As a joke he would sometimes ask her, "Proud of what? I haven't done anything." And she'd always say, "I'm just

9. **King Midas.** Legendary king who is given the power of turning everything he touches into gold
10. **plantains.** Banana-like fruit

rel • ic (re´ lik) *n.,* memento from a past time

proud that you are my son." She wasn't perfect or anything. She had bad days when nothing he did could make her smile, especially after she got sick. But he never heard her say anything negative about anyone. She always blamed *el destino*, fate, for what went wrong. He missed her. He missed her so much. Suddenly a flood of tears that had been building up for almost three years started pouring from his eyes. Luis sat in his father's car, with his head on the steering wheel, and cried, "Mami,[11] I miss you."

When he finally looked up, he saw that he was being watched. Sitting at a large window with a pad and a pencil on her lap was Naomi. At first Luis felt angry and embarrassed, but she wasn't laughing at him. Then she told him with her dark eyes that it was okay to come closer. He walked to the window, and she held up the sketch pad on which she had drawn him, not crying like a baby, but sitting on top of a mountain of silver disks, holding one up over his head. He had to smile.

The plate-glass window was locked. It had a security bolt on it. An alarm system, he figured, so nobody would steal the princess. He asked her if he could come in. It was soundproof too. He mouthed the words slowly for her to read his lips. She wrote on the pad, "I can't let you in. My mother is not home tonight." So they looked at each other and talked through the window for a little while. Then Luis got an idea. He signed to her that he'd be back, and drove to the junkyard.

Luis climbed up on his mountain of hubcaps. For hours he sorted the wheel covers by make, size, and condition, stopping only to call his father and tell him where he was and what he was doing. The old man did not ask him for explanations, and Luis was grateful for that. By lamppost light, Luis worked and worked, beginning to understand a little why his father kept busy all the time. Doing something that had a beginning, a middle, and an end did something to your head. It was like the satisfaction Luis got out of planning "adventures" for his Tiburones, but there was another element involved here that had nothing to do with showing off for others. This was a treasure hunt. And he knew what he was looking for.

Finally, when it seemed that it was a hopeless search, when it was almost midnight and Luis's hands were cut and bruised from his work, he found it. It was the perfect match for Naomi's drawing, the moon-shaped wheel cover for her car, Cinderella's shoe. Luis jumped off the small mound of disks left under him and shouted, "Yes!" He looked around and saw neat stacks of hubcaps that he would wash the next day. He would build a display wall for his father. People would be able to come into the yard and point to whatever they wanted.

Luis washed the VW hubcap and polished it until he could see himself in it. He used it as a mirror as he washed his face and combed his hair. Then he drove to the Ramirez Funeral Home. It was almost pitch-black, since it was a moonless night. As quietly as possible, Luis put some gravel in his pocket and climbed the oak tree to the second floor. He knew he was in front of Naomi's window—he could see her shadow through the curtains. She was at a table, apparently writing or drawing, maybe waiting for him. Luis hung the silver disk carefully on a branch near the window, then threw the gravel at the glass. Naomi ran to the window and drew the curtains aside while Luis held on to the thick branch and waited to give her the first good thing he had given anyone in a long time. ❖

---

11. **Mami.** [Spanish] Mom

MIRRORS & WINDOWS

What kinds of challenges does a person who wants to make positive changes in his or her life face? In what ways can that person deal with setbacks and obstacles?

REFER TO TEXT ▶ ▶ ▶ ▶	▶ REASON WITH TEXT	
1a. Recall why Luis spends six months in juvenile hall.	1b. What is the underlying reason for Luis's disruptive behavior? Conclude whether he is a typical gang member and explain your response.	**Understand** Find meaning
2a. Repeat what Luis's mother often said to him when she was alive.	2b. Make some generalizations about how people react to the death of a loved one. What kind of reaction do you think Luis's mother would have liked?	**Apply** Use information
3a. Identify things Luis does to show he is a good son.	3b. Infer why Luis wants to create a new relationship with his father.	**Analyze** Take things apart
4a. What does Luis think of his father?	4b. Judge Luis's treatment of his father. Is it justified? Explain.	**Evaluate** Make judgments
5a. Luis's act of giving the hubcap to Naomi represents a turning point in his life. List two things he has done since his mother died that he is probably not proud of.	5b. What do you think about the romantic element in the story as it is related to Luis's turning point? Write a note to the author about her inclusion of this bit of romance.	**Create** Bring ideas together

TWO *Kinds*

In all of my imaginings, I was filled with a sense that I would soon become perfect.

A Short Story by **Amy Tan**

My mother believed you could be anything you wanted to be in America. You could open a restaurant. You could work for the government and get good retirement. You could buy a house with almost no money down. You could become rich. You could become instantly famous.

"Of course you can be prodigy,[1] too," my mother told me when I was nine. "You can be best anything. What does Auntie Lindo know? Her daughter, she is only best tricky."

America was where all my mother's hopes lay. She had come here in 1949 after losing everything in China: her mother and father, her family home, her first husband, and two

---

1. **prodigy.** Person who has extraordinary talent, especially a child

A street in Chinatown in San Francisco, California.

daughters, twin baby girls. But she never looked back with regret. There were so many ways for things to get better.

We didn't immediately pick the right kind of prodigy. At first my mother thought I could be a Chinese Shirley Temple.[2] We'd watch Shirley's old movies on TV as though they were training films. My mother would poke my arm and say, "Ni kan"—You watch. And I would see Shirley tapping her feet, or singing a sailor song, or pursing her lips into a very round O while saying, "Oh my goodness."

"Ni kan," said my mother as Shirley's eyes flooded with tears. "You already know how. Don't need talent for crying!"

Soon after my mother got this idea about Shirley Temple, she took me to a beauty training school in the Mission district and put me in the hands of a student who could barely hold the scissors without shaking. Instead of getting big fat curls, I emerged with an uneven mass of crinkly black fuzz. My mother dragged me off to the bathroom and tried to wet down my hair.

"You look like Negro Chinese," she <u>lamented</u>, as if I had done this on purpose.

The instructor of the beauty training school had to lop off these soggy clumps to make my hair even again. "Peter Pan is very popular these days," the instructor assured my mother. I now had hair the length of a boy's, with straight-across bangs that hung at a slant two inches above my eyebrows. I liked the haircut and it made me actually look forward to my future fame.

In fact, in the beginning, I was just as excited as my mother, maybe even more so. I pictured this prodigy part of me as many different images, trying each one on for size.

2. **Shirley Temple.** Well-known child star of the 1930s

la • ment (lə ment´) v., grieve; express regret

I was a dainty ballerina girl standing by the curtains, waiting to hear the right music that would send me floating on my tiptoes. I was like the Christ child lifted out of the straw manger, crying with holy indignity. I was Cinderella stepping from her pumpkin carriage with sparkly cartoon music filling the air.

In all of my imaginings, I was filled with a sense that I would soon become *perfect*. My mother and father would adore me. I would be beyond reproach. I would never feel the need to sulk for anything.

But sometimes the prodigy in me became impatient. "If you don't hurry up and get me out of here, I'm disappearing for good," it warned. "And then you'll always be nothing."

Every night after dinner, my mother and I would sit at the Formica kitchen table. She would present new tests, taking her examples from stories of amazing children she had read in *Ripley's Believe It or Not*, or *Good Housekeeping, Reader's Digest*, and a dozen other magazines she kept in a pile in our bathroom. My mother got these magazines from people whose houses she cleaned. And since she cleaned many houses each week, we had a great assortment. She would look through them all, searching for stories about remarkable children.

The first night she brought out a story about a three-year-old boy who knew the capitals of all the states and even most of the European countries. A teacher was quoted as saying the little boy could also pronounce the names of the foreign cities correctly.

"What's the capital of Finland?" my mother asked me, looking at the magazine story.

All I knew was the capital of California, because Sacramento was the name of the street we lived on in Chinatown. "Nairobi!" I guessed, saying the most foreign word I could think of. She checked to see if that was possibly one way to pronounce "Helsinki" before showing me the answer.

The tests got harder—multiplying numbers in my head, finding the queen of hearts in a deck of cards, trying to stand on my head without using my hands, predicting the daily temperatures in Los Angeles, New York, and London.

One night I had to look at a page from the Bible for three minutes and then report everything I could remember. "Now Jehosophat[3] had riches and honor in abundance and…that's all I remember, Ma," I said.

And after seeing my mother's disappointed face once again, something inside of me began to die. I hated the tests, the raised hopes and failed expectations. Before going to bed that night, I looked in the mirror above the bathroom sink and when I saw only my face staring back—and that it would always be this ordinary face—I began to cry. Such a sad, ugly girl! I made high-pitched noises like a crazed animal, trying to scratch out the face in the mirror.

And then I saw what seemed to be the prodigy side of me—because I had never seen that face before. I looked at my reflection, blinking so I could see more clearly. The girl staring back at me was angry, powerful. This girl and I were the same. I had new thoughts, willful thoughts, or rather thoughts filled with lots of won'ts. I won't let her change me, I promised myself. I won't be what I'm not.

So now, on nights when my mother presented her tests, I performed listlessly, my head propped on one arm. I pretended to be bored. And I was. I got so bored I started counting the bellows of the foghorns out on the bay while my mother drilled me in other areas. The sound was comforting and reminded me of the cow jumping over the moon. And the next day, I played a game with myself, seeing if

---

3. **Jehosophat** (ji hä′ sə fat′). One of the kings of the country of Judah in the ninth century BCE.

re • proach (ri prōch′) *n.,* blame; disapproval
list • less • ly (list′ ləs lē) *adv.,* without energy or enthusiasm

The actress Shirley Temple.

my mother would give up on me before eight bellows. After a while I usually counted only one, maybe two bellows at most. At last she was beginning to give up hope.

Two or three months had gone by without any mention of my being a prodigy again. And then one day my mother was watching *The Ed Sullivan Show*[4] on TV. The TV was old and the sound kept shorting out. Every time my mother got halfway up from the sofa to adjust the set, the sound would go back on and Ed would be talking. As soon as she sat down, Ed would go silent again. She got up, the TV broke into loud piano music. She sat down. Silence. Up and down, back and forth, quiet and loud. It was like a stiff embraceless dance between her and the TV set. Finally she stood by the set with her hand on the sound dial.

She seemed entranced by the music, a little frenzied piano piece with this mesmerizing quality, sort of quick passages and then teasing,

lilting[5] ones before it returned to the quick, playful parts.

"Ni kan," my mother said, calling me over with hurried hand gestures. "Look here."

I could see why my mother was fascinated by the music. It was being pounded out by a little Chinese girl, about nine years old, with a Peter Pan haircut. The girl had the sauciness of a Shirley Temple. She was proudly modest like a proper Chinese child. And she also did this fancy sweep of a curtsy, so that the fluffy skirt of her white dress cascaded slowly to the floor like the petals of a large carnation.

In spite of these warning signs, I wasn't worried. Our family had no piano and we couldn't afford to buy one, let alone reams of sheet music and piano lessons. So I could be generous in my comments when my mother bad-mouthed the little girl on TV.

"Play note right, but doesn't sound good! No singing sound," complained my mother.

"What are you picking on her for?" I said carelessly. "She's pretty good. Maybe she's not the best, but she's trying hard." I knew almost immediately I would be sorry I said that.

"Just like you," she said. "Not the best. Because you not trying." She gave a little huff as she let go of the sound dial and sat down on the sofa.

The little Chinese girl sat down also to play an encore of "Anitra's Dance" by Grieg. I remember the song, because later on I had to learn how to play it.

Three days after watching *The Ed Sullivan Show*, my mother told me what my schedule would be for piano lessons and piano practice. She had talked to Mr. Chong, who lived on the first floor of our apartment building. Mr. Chong was a retired piano teacher, and my mother had traded house-

---

4. *The Ed Sullivan Show.* Weekly TV variety show popular in the 1950s and 1960s
5. **lilting.** Cheerful and lively

cleaning services for weekly lessons and a piano for me to practice on every day, two hours a day, from four until six.

When my mother told me this, I felt as though I had been sent to hell. I whined and then kicked my foot a little when I couldn't stand it anymore.

"Why don't you like me the way I am? I'm *not* a genius! I can't play the piano. And even if I could, I wouldn't go on TV if you paid me a million dollars!" I cried.

My mother slapped me. "Who ask you be genius?" she shouted. "Only ask you be your best. For you sake. You think I want you be genius? Hnnh! What for! Who ask you!"

"So ungrateful," I heard her mutter in Chinese. "If she had as much talent as she has temper, she would be famous now."

Mr. Chong, whom I secretly nicknamed Old Chong, was very strange, always tapping his fingers to the silent music of an invisible orchestra. He looked ancient in my eyes. He had lost most of the hair on top of his head and he wore thick glasses and had eyes that always looked tired and sleepy. But he must have been younger than I thought, since he lived with his mother and was not yet married.

I met Old Lady Chong once and that was enough. She had this peculiar smell like a baby that had done something in its pants. And her fingers felt like a dead person's, like an old peach I once found in the back of the refrigerator; the skin just slid off the meat when I picked it up.

I soon found out why Old Chong had retired from teaching piano. He was deaf. "Like Beethoven!" he shouted to me. "We're both listening only in our head!" And he would start to conduct his frantic silent sonatas.[6]

Our lessons went like this. He would open the book and point to different things, explaining their purpose: "Key! Treble! Bass!

No sharps or flats! So this is C major! Listen now and play after me!"

And then he would play the C scale a few times, a simple chord, and then, as if inspired by an old, unreachable itch, he gradually added more notes and running trills and a pounding bass until the music was really something quite grand.

I would play after him, the simple scale, the simple chord, and then I just played some nonsense that sounded like a cat running up and down on top of garbage cans. Old Chong smiled and applauded and then said, "Very good! But now you must learn to keep time!"

So that's how I discovered that Old Chong's eyes were too slow to keep up with the wrong notes I was playing. He went through the motions in half-time. To help me keep rhythm, he stood behind me, pushing down on my right shoulder for every beat. He balanced pennies on top of my wrists so I would keep them still as I slowly played scales and arpeggios.[7] He had me curve my hand around an apple and keep that shape when playing chords. He marched stiffly to show me how to make each finger dance up and down, staccato,[8] like an obedient little soldier.

He taught me all these things, and that was how I also learned I could be lazy and get away with mistakes, lots of mistakes. If I hit the wrong notes because I hadn't practiced enough, I never corrected myself. I just kept playing in rhythm. And Old Chong kept conducting his own private reverie.[9]

So maybe I never really gave myself a fair chance. I did pick up the basics pretty quickly,

6. **sonatas** (sə nä´ təs). Instrumental music, usually written for the piano

7. **arpeggios** (är pe´ jē ōs). Chords in which the same notes are played rapidly one after another instead of at the same time

8. **staccato** (stə kä´ tō). With each sound or note played distinctly

9. **reverie.** Daydream

and I might have become a good pianist at that young age. But I was so determined not to try, not to be anybody different, that I learned to play only the most earsplitting preludes, the most <u>discordant</u> hymns.

Over the next year, I practiced like this, dutifully in my own way. And then one day I heard my mother and her friend Lindo Jong both talking in a loud bragging tone of voice so others could hear. It was after church, and I was leaning against the brick wall, wearing a dress with stiff white petticoats. Auntie Lindo's daughter, Waverly, who was about my age, was standing farther down the wall, about five feet away. We had grown up together and shared all the closeness of two sisters squabbling over crayons and dolls. In other words, for the most part, we hated each other. I thought she was snotty. Waverly Jong had gained a certain amount of fame as "Chinatown's Littlest Chinese Chess Champion."

"She bring home too many trophy," lamented Auntie Lindo that Sunday. "All day she play chess. All day I have no time do nothing but dust off her winnings." She threw a scolding look at Waverly, who pretended not to see her.

"You lucky you don't have this problem," said Auntie Lindo with a sigh to my mother.

And my mother squared her shoulders and bragged: "Our problem worser than yours. If we ask Jing-mei wash dish, she hear nothing but music. It's like you can't stop this natural talent."

And right then, I was determined to put a stop to her foolish pride.

A few weeks later, Old Chong and my mother conspired to have me play in a talent show which would be held in the church hall. By then, my parents had saved up enough to buy me a secondhand piano, a black Wurlitzer spinet with a scarred bench. It was the show-piece of our living room.

For the talent show, I was to play a piece called "Pleading Child" from Schumann's[10]

Scenes from Childhood. It was a simple, moody piece that sounded more difficult than it was. I was supposed to memorize the whole thing, playing the repeat parts twice to make the piece sound longer. But I dawdled over it, playing a few bars and then cheating, looking up to see what notes followed. I never really listened to what I was playing. I daydreamed about being somewhere else, about being someone else.

The part I liked to practice best was the fancy curtsy: right foot out, touch the rose on the carpet with a pointed foot, sweep to the side, left leg bends, look up and smile.

My parents invited all the couples from the Joy Luck Club to witness my debut.[11] Auntie Lindo and Uncle Tin were there. Waverly and her two older brothers had also come. The first two rows were filled with children both younger and older than I was. The littlest ones got to go first. They recited simple nursery rhymes, squawked out tunes on miniature violins, twirled Hula-Hoops, pranced in pink ballet tutus, and when they bowed or curtsied, the audience would sigh in unison, "Awww," and then clap enthusiastically.

When my turn came, I was very confident. I remember my childish excitement. It was as if I knew, without a doubt, that the prodigy side of me really did exist. I had no fear what-soever, no nervousness. I remember thinking to myself, This is it! This is it! I looked out over the audience, at my mother's blank face, my father's yawn, Auntie Lindo's stiff-lipped smile, Waverly's sulky expression. I had on a white dress layered with sheets of lace, and a pink bow in my Peter Pan haircut. As I sat down I envisioned people jumping to their feet and Ed Sullivan rushing up to introduce me to everyone on TV.

---

10. **Schumann's.** Refers to a musical composition by Robert Schumann, a German composer from the first half of the nineteenth century

11. **debut.** First public appearance of a performer or show

dis • cord • ant (dis′ kôrd′ n′t) *adj.*, not harmonious

And I started to play. It was so beautiful. I was so caught up in how lovely I looked that at first I didn't worry how I would sound. So it was a surprise to me when I hit the first wrong note and I realized something didn't sound quite right. And then I hit another, and another followed that. A chill started at the top of my head and began to trickle down. Yet I couldn't stop playing, as though my hands were bewitched. I kept thinking my fingers would adjust themselves back, like a train switching to the right track. I played this strange jumble through two repeats, the sour notes staying with me all the way to the end.

When I stood up, I discovered my legs were shaking. Maybe I had just been nervous and the audience, like Old Chong, had seen me go through the right motions and had not heard anything wrong at all. I swept my right foot out, went down on my knee, looked up and smiled. The room was quiet, except for Old Chong, who was beaming and shouting, "Bravo! Bravo! Well done!" But then I saw my mother's face, her stricken[12] face. The audience clapped weakly, and as I walked back to my chair, with my whole face quivering as I tried not to cry, I heard a little boy whisper loudly to his mother, "That was awful," and the mother whispered back, "Well, she certainly tried."

And now I realized how many people were in the audience, the whole world it seemed. I was aware of eyes burning into my back. I felt the shame of my mother and father as they sat stiffly throughout the rest of the show.

We could have escaped during intermission. Pride and some strange sense of honor must have anchored my parents to their chairs. And so we watched it all: the eighteen-year-old boy with a fake mustache who did a magic show and juggled flaming hoops while riding a unicycle. The breasted girl with white makeup who sang an aria[13] from *Madame Butterfly*[14] and got honorable mention. And the eleven-year-old boy who won first prize playing a tricky violin song that sounded like a busy bee.

After the show, the Hsus, the Jongs, and the St. Clairs from the Joy Luck Club came up to my mother and father.

"Lots of talented kids," Auntie Lindo said vaguely, smiling broadly.

"That was somethin' else," said my father, and I wondered if he was referring to me in a humorous way, or whether he even remembered what I had done.

Waverly looked at me and shrugged her shoulders. "You aren't a genius like me," she said matter-of-factly. And if I hadn't felt so bad, I would have pulled her braids and punched her stomach.

But my mother's expression was what devastated me: a quiet, blank look that said she had lost everything. I felt the same way, and it seemed as if everybody were now coming up, like gawkers at the scene of an accident, to see what parts were actually missing. When we got on the bus to go home, my father was humming the busy-bee tune and my mother

---

12. **stricken.** Affected or overcome with illness or misfortune
13. **aria** (är´ ē ə). Elaborate vocal solo in an opera
14. ***Madame Butterfly*.** Opera by the Italian composer Puccini

was silent. I kept thinking she wanted to wait until we got home before shouting at me. But when my father unlocked the door to our apartment, my mother walked in and then went to the back, into the bedroom. No accusations. No blame. And in a way, I felt disappointed. I had been waiting for her to start shouting, so I could shout back and cry and blame her for all my misery.

I assumed my talent-show <u>fiasco</u> meant I never had to play the piano again. But two days later, after school, my mother came out of the kitchen and saw me watching TV.

"Four clock," she reminded me as if it were any other day. I was stunned, as though she were asking me to go through the talent-show torture again. I wedged myself more tightly in front of the TV.

"Turn off TV," she called from the kitchen five minutes later.

I didn't budge. And then I decided. I didn't have to do what my mother said anymore. I wasn't her slave. This wasn't China. I had listened to her before and look what happened. She was the stupid one.

She came out from the kitchen and stood in the arched entryway of the living room. "Four clock," she said once again, louder.

"I'm not going to play anymore," I said nonchalantly. "Why should I? I'm not a genius."

She walked over and stood in front of the TV. I saw her chest was heaving up and down in an angry way.

"No!" I said, and I now felt stronger, as if my true self had finally emerged. So this was what had been inside me all along.

"No! I won't!" I screamed.

She yanked me by the arm, pulled me off the floor, snapped off the TV. She was frighteningly strong, half pulling, half carrying me toward the piano as I kicked the throw rugs under my feet. She lifted me up and onto the hard bench. I was sobbing by now, looking at her bitterly. Her chest was heaving even more and her mouth was open, smiling crazily, as if she were pleased I was crying.

"You want me to be someone that I'm not!" I sobbed. "I'll never be the kind of daughter you want me to be!"

"Only two kinds of daughters," she shouted in Chinese. "Those who are obedient and those who follow their own mind! Only one kind of daughter can live in this house. Obedient daughter!"

"Then I wish I wasn't your daughter. I wish you weren't my mother," I shouted. As I said these things, I got scared. It felt like worms and toads and slimy things crawling out of my chest, but it also felt good, as if this awful side of me had surfaced, at last.

"Too late change this," said my mother shrilly.

fi • as • co (fē as´ kō[´]) *n.*, total failure

And I could sense her anger rising to its breaking point. I wanted to see it spill over. And that's when I remembered the babies she had lost in China, the ones we never talked about. "Then I wish I'd never been born!" I shouted. "I wish I were dead! Like them."

It was as if I had said the magic words. Alakazam!—and her face went blank, her mouth closed, her arms went slack, and she backed out of the room, stunned, as if she were blowing away like a small brown leaf, thin, brittle, lifeless.

It was not the only disappointment my mother felt in me. In the years that followed, I failed her so many times, each time asserting

So she surprised me. A few years ago, she offered to give me the piano, for my thirtieth birthday. I had not played in all those years. I saw the offer as a sign of forgiveness, a tremendous burden removed.

"Are you sure?" I asked shyly. "I mean, won't you and Dad miss it?"

"No, this is your piano," she said firmly. "Always your piano. You only one can play."

"Well, I probably can't play anymore," I said. "It's been years."

"You pick up fast," said my mother, as if she knew this was certain. "You have natural talent. You could been genius if you want to."

"No, I couldn't."

"You just not trying," said my mother.

> It was as if I had said the magic words. Alakazam!—and her face went blank, her mouth closed, her arms went slack, and she backed out of the room, stunned, as if she were blowing away like a small brown leaf, thin, brittle, lifeless.

my own will, my right to fall short of expectations. I didn't get straight A's. I didn't become class president. I didn't get into Stanford. I dropped out of college.

For unlike my mother, I did not believe I could be anything I wanted to be. I could only be me.

And for all those years, we never talked about the disaster at the recital or my terrible accusations afterward at the piano bench. All that remained unchecked, like a betrayal that was now unspeakable. So I never found a way to ask her why she had hoped for something so large that failure was inevitable.

And even worse, I never asked her what frightened me the most: Why had she given up hope?

For after our struggle at the piano, she never mentioned my playing again. The lessons stopped. The lid to the piano was closed, shutting out the dust, my misery, and her dreams.

And she was neither angry nor sad. She said it as if to announce a fact that could never be disproved. "Take it," she said.

But I didn't at first. It was enough that she had offered it to me. And after that, every time I saw it in my parents' living room, standing in front of the bay windows, it made me feel proud, as if it were a shiny trophy I had won back.

Last week I sent a tuner over to my parents' apartment and had the piano reconditioned, for purely sentimental reasons. My mother had died a few months before, and I had been getting things in order for my father, a little bit at a time. I put the jewelry in special silk pouches. The sweaters she had knitted in yellow, pink, bright orange—all the colors I hated—I put those in mothproof boxes. I found some old Chinese silk dresses, the kind with little slits up the sides. I rubbed the old silk against my skin, then wrapped them in tissue and decided to take them home with me.

After I had the piano tuned, I opened the lid and touched the keys. It sounded even richer than I remembered. Really, it was a very good piano. Inside the bench were the same exercise notes with handwritten scales, the same secondhand music books with their covers held together with yellow tape. I opened up the Schumann book to the dark little piece I had played at the recital. It was on the left-hand side of the page, "Pleading Child." It looked more difficult than I remembered. I played a few bars, surprised at how easily the notes came back to me.

And for the first time, or so it seemed, I noticed the piece on the right-hand side. It was called "Perfectly Contented." I tried to play this one as well. It had a lighter melody but the same flowing rhythm and turned out to be quite easy. "Pleading Child" was shorter but slower; "Perfectly Contented" was longer but faster. And after I played them both a few times, I realized they were two halves of the same song. ❖

 **MIRRORS & WINDOWS** Why do some children excel quickly and others struggle? Is it wrong for parents to have expectations for their children? When might the expectations parents have become a negative thing?

REFER TO TEXT ▶ ▶ ▶ ▶	▶ REASON WITH TEXT	
1a. Identify what Jing-mei's mother sees on TV that influences her first effort to make Jing-mei a prodigy. What does she see later that gives her the idea for piano lessons?	1b. Describe how Jing-mei's mother's comparisons of Jing-mei with children on television eventually make Jing-mei feel.	**Understand** **Find meaning**
2a. Quote the "magic words" Jing-mei says to her mother in an argument.	2b. Relate Jing-mei's experience to your own: Explain how you reacted on one occasion when you said something you couldn't take back that hurt somebody.	**Apply** **Use information**
3a. According to Jing-mei's mother, what are the two kinds of Chinese daughters?	3b. Relate the two paired pieces in the piano songbook at the end of the story to Jing-mei's life.	**Analyze** **Take things apart**
4a. Recall how Jing-mei's mother responds when Jing-mei says, "I'm *not* a genius!"	4b. Judge whether Jing-mei or her mother had Jing-mei's best interests in mind.	**Evaluate** **Make judgments**
5a. List ways Jing-mei rebels against her mother.	5b. Summarize when, if ever, is it appropriate to rebel against an authority figure.	**Create** **Bring ideas together**

COMPARE LITERATURE: Character and Characterization
- What traits do the main characters of each story have in common? How are they different?
- Compare the relationships between Luis and his father and Jing-mei and her mother. How do these relationships help characterize Luis and Jing-mei?

EXTEND THE TEXT

Writing Options

Creative Writing Imagine that Luis and Jing-mei meet as adults, and they tell each other their stories. Write a **dialogue** between them in which they discuss what they each learned from their experiences.

Expository Writing In a five-paragraph **compare-and-contrast essay,** compare and contrast the relationship between Luis and Jorge Cintrón, with the relationship between Jing-mei and her mother. What is the source of conflict in each relationship? How is each relationship shaped by grief and loss? What other similarities and differences do you see? Use your response to the second Compare Literature: Character and Characterization prompt on page 78 as a starting point.

Media Literacy

Analyze Ideas of Success Identify the ideas about success expressed directly or indirectly by Mr. Cintrón and by Jing-mei's mother. Then choose four or five television shows, movies, or advertisements that show images of success. Analyze how success is defined in each case. Then consider your own ideas of success. Create a visual presentation in which you compare the different ideas about success and offer your opinions about these ideas.

Collaborative Learning

Debate Ideas About Extracurricular Activities
Some adults push children into activities at a very young age. Others limit activities because of time, cost, or other concerns. Students have varied opinions on involvement, too. Hold a class debate on whether extracurricular activities should be limited. Divide into two groups, one in favor of extracurricular involvement from an early age, and one opposed to it. Work in your groups to prepare your arguments. Each group will have three minutes to present its initial arguments. Then each group will have two minutes to respond to the other group's arguments. Finally, each group will have two minutes for a concluding statement.

 Go to **www.mirrorsandwindows.com** for more.

READING ASSESSMENT

1. Which statement best describes Luis at the beginning of "Catch the Moon"?
   A. surly and troubled
   B. repentant and hopeful of a fresh start
   C. disgusted with himself
   D. hateful and afraid
   E. obedient and eager to please

2. Which pair of words best describes Mr. Cintrón's and Luis's attitudes toward owning a junkyard?
   A. embarrassment and pride
   B. pride and anger
   C. gratitude and shame
   D. relief and annoyance
   E. happiness and sadness

3. What motivates Jing-mei's mother to push Jing-mei to be a prodigy?
   A. fear that her daughter will never make something of herself
   B. love of fame and fortune
   C. certainty in Jing-mei's talent and her own lost dreams
   D. hope for a better life for her daughter
   E. desire for her daughter to succeed and pride

4. Which of the following passages from the selections is an example of irony?
   A. The day his mother died, he had been in her room at the hospital while his father had gone for coffee.
   B. For a while Luis sat in the car allowing the memories to flood back into his brain.
   C. I looked at my reflection, blinking so I could see more clearly. The girl staring back at me was angry, powerful.
   D. "Pleading Child" was shorter but slower; "Perfectly Contented" was longer but faster. And after I played them both a few times, I realized they were two halves of the same song.
   E. Luis has been getting in trouble since he started high school two years ago, mainly because of the "social group" he organized—a bunch of guys who were into harassing the local authorities.

5. Compare and contrast the conflicts faced by Luis in "Catch the Moon" and by Jing-mei in "Two Kinds." Consider the type of conflict and how each is resolved.

Understanding Setting

SETTING

Readers have the opportunity to experience the world through the pages of novels and short stories. The stories in this unit take you from Europe's plague-swept cities in "The Masque of the Red Death" (page 83) to the busy streets of San Francisco's Chinatown in "Two Kinds" (page 69). The details of the settings make these selections colorful and vivid.

The **setting** of a story is the time and place in which it occurs. Setting can include the following: geographical location, time period, socio-economic conditions, and a specific room or building. In the story "Two Friends" (page 95), the geographical setting is Paris, and the time period is the late nineteenth century. These details are very important to the way readers understand "Two Friends." The story would make little sense to readers if they did not know it takes place in the middle of a war. Details, like the names of the nearby villages, help locate the story in a specific place and create a lifelike impression.

Notice how the details in the following excerpt create a backdrop for character and action:

> On the opposite bank they could see the village of Argenteuil, which looked deserted and dead. The hills of Orgemont and Sannois dominated the horizon, and the great plain which stretches as far as Nanterre was empty, completely empty, with nothing to be seen but its leafless cherry trees and gray earth.
>
> —from "Two Friends"
> by Guy de Maupassant

ELEMENTS OF SETTING

Mood

One reason why setting is important is that it provides background for the story. In "Two Friends," readers are told that Paris is under siege and the people are starving. This information is important in under-

standing the motivations of the two main characters that drive them to fish during a battle.

Equally significant is the use of setting in creating a connection between the characters of a story and the context in which they are placed. This connection helps explain why characters speak or act in a certain way. In "The Masque of the Red Death," the readers are told that the Red Death is ravaging the city outside the castle. This helps explain why the prince is determined to keep his guests locked up in the castle.

Setting also helps establish mood. **Mood,** or atmosphere, is the emotion created in the reader by part or all of a story. The mood of a story, for example, might be mysterious, happy, frightening, peaceful, serious, or tense. Details in the setting contribute to mood.

In "The Masque of the Red Death," the description of the setting frequently shifts from the flamboyant reveleries of the guests to the solemn tolling of the clock, which creates a mood of discomfort. If you feel apprehensive about looming death as you read this story, you are responding sensitively to the text.

> …the night is waning away; and there flows a ruddier light through the blood-colored panes; and the blackness of the sable drapery appals; and to him whose foot falls upon the sable carpet, there comes from the near clock of ebony a muffled peal more solemnly emphatic than any which reaches *their* ears who indulge in the more remote gaieties of the other apartments.
>
> —from "The Masque of the Red Death"
> by Edgar Allan Poe

Sensory Details

Authors carefully select and arrange details to achieve a particular effect. The outdoor setting of "Two Friends" has an abundance of details that readers can hear, see, and smell. These are called **sensory details** because they appeal to several or all of the five senses (sight, sound, taste, touch, smell).

But suddenly, the bank beneath them shook with a dull rumble which seemed to come from underground.

The distant cannon were starting to fire again.

Morissot turned his head, and above the bank, over to the left, he saw the great bulk of Mont Valérien. On the mountainside was a white plume of smoke, showing where the gunpowder had just bellowed out.

Almost immediately another jet of smoke spurted from the fort on the summit, and a few seconds later the rumble of another detonation reached their ears.

Other cannon shots followed, and every now and then the mountain spat out its deadly breath, exhaled its clouds of milky vapor, which rose slowly into the calm sky above.

—from "Two Friends"
by Guy de Maupassant

One way to keep track of the details in a story is to use a Sensory Details Chart, like the one created for "Two Friends." If there are no specific details related to one of the senses, you can use other details to ask questions or make inferences about those senses.

Critical Viewing

Setting can play a large part in establishing the mood of the story. Look at the picture below. If this picture were the setting of a story, what kind of mood might the story have? Why do you think so? Write the outline of a story with the place in the picture as the setting.

"Two Friends"

Sound
rumble of cannon fire

Smell
smoky smell of the gunpowder

Sight
white plume of smoke, clouds of milky vapor, great bulk of Mont Valérien

Taste
possibly the taste of acrid smoke drifting off the mountain

Touch
shaking ground from each cannon blast

The Masque of the Red Death

BUILD BACKGROUND

Historical Context Although the Red Death is a fictional disease, the Black Death was a deadly epidemic of bubonic plague that spread over Asia and Europe in the fourteenth century. The name *Black Death* comes from the black sores the plague causes on its victims' skin. In just five years, the bubonic plague wiped out a third of the population of Europe.

Like many of Edgar Allan Poe's short stories, **"The Masque of the Red Death"** is a horror story. To avoid the terrifying, fatal disease spreading across the land, Prince Prospero takes a thousand friends to a remote fortress. Poe uses detailed description to set a vivid scene. As the Red Death causes turmoil outside, the protected crowd celebrates until a mysterious stranger appears at midnight in the midst of a masquerade party.

Reader's Context When have you tried to avoid someone or something? Were you successful, or did you eventually have to face what you were avoiding?

ANALYZE LITERATURE: Setting and Symbol

The **setting** of a literary work is the time and place in which it occurs, together with all the details used to create a sense of that particular time and place. In fiction, the setting is usually revealed through description. In some cases, part of the setting acts as a **symbol,** a thing that stands for or represents both itself and something else. In this story, Poe uses vivid details to create a dramatic and symbolic setting.

SET PURPOSE

Think about what you usually expect from a good horror story. As you read "The Masque of the Red Death," look for elements of a good horror story and find out if Poe's creation meets your expectations of what a horror story should be. Consider especially the setting of the story and how it compares with the settings of other horror stories you've read.

MEET THE AUTHOR

Edgar Allan Poe (1809–1849) wrote, "Those who dream by day are cognizant of many things which escape those who only dream at night." Poe may have dreamed by day to escape his tragic life. After losing both parents before he was three, Poe was raised by John Allan, a Virginia merchant. The two quarreled and, to spite his guardian, Poe had himself expelled from West Point. Allan then cut off his financial support, and Poe spent the rest of his life near poverty. Tragedy struck again when Poe's young wife, Virginia, died early in their marriage. Perhaps as a result of Poe's suffering, his writing often deals with characters wobbling on the edge of insanity.

USE READING SKILLS

Meaning of Words When you come across an unfamiliar word, the text around it may provide clues to its meaning. A common type of context clues is **comparison clues.**

Words and phrases including *such as, like, also, similarly, just as,* and *in the same way* signal comparisons and indicate that the unfamiliar word is like something that might be more familiar to you.

EXAMPLE: "The sagacious advice my grandfather offered me was similar to the wise advice he gave my father at my age."

This selection has many difficult vocabulary words. Look for comparison clues as you read.

PREVIEW VOCABULARY

Use the comparison clues in the sentences below to figure out the meanings of the underlined words from the selection.

1. The nervous speaker's perspiration was as <u>profuse</u> as someone who had just run several miles.
2. The rock climber taking the most dangerous route up the mountain was as <u>dauntless</u> as if he were hiking a small hill.
3. A person who wears only purple and listens to marching band music early in the morning could be described as <u>eccentric</u>; a person who refuses to eat food that is green could be described in the same way.

The Masque of the Red Death

A Short Story by **Edgar Allan Poe**

All these and security were within. Without was the "Red Death."

The "Red Death" had long devastated the country. No pestilence had ever been so fatal, or so hideous. Blood was its Avatar[1] and its seal—the redness and the horror of blood. There were sharp pains, and sudden dizziness, and then <u>profuse</u> bleeding at the pores, with dissolution.[2] The scarlet stains upon the body and especially upon the face of the victim, were the pest ban[3] which shut him out from the aid and from the sympathy of his fellow-men. And the whole seizure, progress, and termination of the disease, were the incidents of half an hour.

But the Prince Prospero was happy and <u>dauntless</u> and <u>sagacious</u>. When his dominions

---

1. **Avatar.** God in human form. In this case, the term refers to the disease in human form.
2. **dissolution.** Death
3. **pest ban.** Official declaration that an individual has the plague

> **pro • fuse** (prə fyüs´) *adj.*, plentiful; available in great amounts
> **daunt • less** (dônt´ ləs) *adj.*, fearless; daring
> **sa • ga • cious** (sə gā´ shəs) *adj.*, wise

were half depopulated, he summoned to his presence a thousand hale and light-hearted friends from among the knights and dames of his court, and with these retired to the deep seclusion of one of his castellated abbeys.[4] This was an extensive and magnificent structure, the creation of the prince's own <u>eccentric</u> yet august taste. A strong and lofty wall girdled it in. This wall had gates of iron. The courtiers, having entered, brought furnaces and massy hammers and welded the bolts. They resolved to leave means neither of ingress nor egress to the sudden impulses of despair or of frenzy from within. The abbey was amply provisioned. With such precautions the courtiers might bid defiance to contagion. The external world could take care of itself. In the meantime it was folly to grieve, or to think. The prince had provided all the appliances of pleasure. There were buffoons,[5] there were improvisatori,[6] there were ballet-dancers, there were musicians, there was Beauty, there was wine. All these and security were within. Without was the "Red Death."

It was toward the close of the fifth or sixth month of his seclusion, and while the pestilence raged most furiously abroad, that the Prince Prospero entertained his thousand friends at a masked ball of the most unusual magnificence.

It was a voluptuous scene, that masquerade. But first let me tell of the rooms in which it was held. There were seven—an imperial suite. In many palaces, however, such suites form a long and straight vista, while the folding doors slide back nearly to the walls on either hand, so that the view of the whole extent is scarcely impeded. Here the case was very different; as might have been expected from the duke's love of the *bizarre*. The apartments were so irregularly disposed[7] that the vision embraced but little more than one at a time. There was a sharp turn at every twenty or thirty yards, and at each turn a novel effect. To the right and left, in the middle of each wall, a tall and narrow Gothic[8] window looked out upon a closed corridor which pursued the windings of the suite. These windows were of stained glass whose color varied in accordance

---

4. **castellated abbeys.** Fortified structures built to use as or resemble monasteries

5. **buffoons.** Clowns

6. **improvisatori.** Poets who make up, or improvise, their poems as they perform

7. **disposed.** Arranged

8. **Gothic.** In the style of architecture prevalent in Western Europe in the twelfth through the sixteenth centuries

ec • cen • tric (ik sen´ trik) *adj.,* odd or unusual in behavior or appearance

with the prevailing hue of the decorations of
the chamber into which it opened. That at the
eastern extremity was hung, for example, in
blue—and vividly blue were its windows. The
second chamber was purple in its ornaments
and tapestries, and here the panes were purple.
The third was green throughout, and so were
the casements.[9] The fourth was furnished and
lighted with orange—the fifth with white—the
sixth with violet. The seventh apartment was
closely shrouded in black velvet tapestries that
hung all over the ceiling and down the walls,
falling in heavy folds upon a carpet of the same
material and hue. But in this chamber only, the
color of the windows failed to correspond with
the decorations. The panes here were scarlet—a
deep blood color. Now in no one of the seven
apartments was there any lamp or candela-
brum, amid the profusion of golden ornaments
that lay scattered to and fro or depended
from the roof. There was no light of any kind
emanating from lamp or candle within the suite
of chambers. But in the corridors that followed
the suite, there stood, opposite to each
window, a heavy tripod, bearing a brazier[10] of
fire, that projected its rays through the tinted
glass and so glaringly illumined the room. And
thus were produced a multitude of gaudy and
fantastic appearances. But in the western or
black chamber the effect of the fire-light that
streamed upon the dark hangings through the
blood-tinted panes was ghastly in the extreme,
and produced so wild a look upon the coun-
tenances of those who entered, that there were
few of the company bold enough to set foot
within its precincts at all.

It was in this apartment, also, that there
stood against the western wall, a gigantic clock
of ebony.[11] Its pendulum swung to and fro
with a dull, heavy, monotonous clang; and
when the minute-hand made the circuit of the
face, and the hour was to be stricken, there
came from the brazen[12] lungs of the clock a
sound which was clear and loud and deep
and exceedingly musical, but of so peculiar

a note and emphasis that, at each lapse of
an hour, the musicians of the orchestra were
constrained[13] to pause, momentarily, in their
performance, to hearken[14] to the sound; and
thus the waltzers perforce ceased their evolutions; and there was a brief disconcert of the
whole gay company; and, while the chimes
of the clock yet rang, it was observed that the
giddiest grew pale, and the more aged and
sedate passed their hands over their brows as if
in confused revery or meditation. But when the
echoes had fully ceased, a light laughter at once
pervaded the assembly; the musicians looked
at each other and smiled as if at their own
nervousness and folly, and made whispering
vows, each to the other, that the next chiming
of the clock should produce in them no similar
emotion; and then, after the lapse of sixty
minutes (which embrace three thousand and
six hundred seconds of the Time that flies),
there came yet another chiming of the clock,
and then were the same disconcert and tremu-
lousness and meditation as before.

But, in spite of these things, it was a gay
and magnificent revel. The tastes of the duke
were peculiar. He had a fine eye for colors and
effects. He disregarded the *decora*[15] of mere
fashion. His plans were bold and fiery, and his
conceptions glowed with barbaric lustre.

There are some who would have thought
him mad. His followers felt that he was not. It
was necessary to hear and see and touch him to
be *sure* that he was not.

He had directed, in great part, the movable
embellishments of the seven chambers, upon

---

9. **casements.** Windows
10. **brazier.** Metal pan designed to hold charcoal or coal used for light and heat
11. **ebony.** Black or dark-colored wood
12. **brazen.** Brass
13. **constrained.** Forced
14. **hearken.** Listen
15. *decora.* What is considered suitable or proper

coun • te • nance (kaun´ t'n ən[t]s or kaůnt´ nən[t]s) *n.*,
face
dis • con • cert (dis' kən sůrt´) *v.*, agitate; fluster

occasion of this great *fête*;[16] and it was his own guiding taste which had given character to the masqueraders. Be sure they were grotesque. There were much glare and glitter and piquancy[17] and phantasm[18]— much of what has been since seen in "Hernani."[19] There were arabesque figures with unsuited limbs and appointments. There were delirious fancies such as the madman fashions. There were much of the beautiful, much of the <u>wanton</u>, much of the *bizarre*, something of the terrible, and not a little of that which might have excited disgust. To and fro in the seven chambers there stalked, in fact, a multitude of dreams. And these—the dreams—writhed in and about, taking hue from the rooms, and causing the wild music of the orchestra to seem as the echo of their steps. And, anon, there strikes the ebony clock which stands in the hall of the velvet. And then, for a moment, all is still, and all is silent save the voice of the clock. The dreams are stiff-frozen as they stand. But the echoes of the chime die away—they have endured but an instant—and a light, half-subdued laughter floats after them as they depart. And now again the music swells, and the dreams live, and writhe to and fro more merrily than ever, taking hue from the many-tinted windows through which stream the rays from the tripods. But to the chamber which lies most westwardly of the seven there are now none of the maskers who venture; for the night is waning away; and there flows a ruddier light through the blood-colored panes; and the blackness of the sable[20] drapery appals; and to him whose foot falls upon the sable carpet, there comes from the near clock of ebony a muffled peal more solemnly emphatic than any which reaches *their* ears who indulge in the more remote gaieties of the other apartments.

But these other apartments were densely crowded, and in them beat feverishly the heart of life. And the revel went whirlingly on, until at length there commenced the sounding of midnight upon the clock. And then the music ceased, as I have told; and the evolutions of the waltzers were quieted; and there was an uneasy cessation of all things as before. But now there were twelve strokes to be sounded by the bell of the clock; and thus it happened, perhaps that more of thought crept, with more of time, into the meditations of the thoughtful among those who revelled. And thus too, it happened, perhaps, that before the last echoes of the last chime had utterly sunk into silence, there were many individuals in the crowd who had found leisure to become aware of the presence of a masked figure which had arrested the attention of no single individual before. And the rumor of this new presence having spread itself whisperingly around, there arose at length from the whole company a buzz, or murmur, expressive of disapprobation[21] and surprise—then, finally, of terror, or horror, and of disgust.

In an assembly of phantasms such as I have painted, it may well be supposed that no ordinary appearance could have excited such sensation. In truth the masquerade license of the night was nearly unlimited; but the figure in

---

16. *fête* (fet). A large, carefully planned party
17. **piquancy.** In this case, state of being charming
18. **phantasm.** In this case, a product of fantasy
19. **"Hernani."** A drama of 1830 on which an opera known for its use of color and imagination was based
20. **sable.** Of the color black
21. **disapprobation.** Disapproval

wan • ton (wôn´ t'n) *adj.,* without appropriate restraint or shame; immoral

question had out-Heroded Herod,[22] and gone beyond the bounds of even the prince's indefinite decorum. There are chords in the hearts of the most reckless which cannot be touched without emotion. Even with the utterly lost, to whom life and death are equally jests, there are matters of which no jest can be made. The whole company, indeed, seemed now deeply to feel that in the costume and bearing of the stranger neither wit nor propriety existed. The figure was tall and gaunt, and shrouded from head to foot in the habiliments[23] of the grave. The mask which concealed the visage was made so nearly to resemble the countenance of a stiffened corpse that the closest scrutiny must have had difficulty in detecting the cheat. And yet all this might have been endured, if not approved, by the mad revellers around. But the mummer had gone so far as to assume the type of the Red Death. His vesture was dabbled in *blood*—and his broad brow, with all the features of the face, was besprinkled with the scarlet horror.

When the eyes of Prince Prospero fell upon this <u>spectral</u> image (which, with a slow and solemn movement, as if more fully to sustain its *rôle*, stalked to and fro among the waltzers) he was seen to be convulsed, in the first moment with a strong shudder either of terror or distaste; but, in the next, his brow reddened with rage.

"Who dares"—he demanded hoarsely of the courtiers who stood near him—"who dares insult us with this <u>blasphemous</u> mockery? Seize him and unmask him—that we may know whom we have to hang, at sunrise, from the battlements!"[24]

It was in the eastern or blue chamber in which stood the Prince Prospero as he uttered these words. They rang throughout the seven rooms loudly and clearly, for the prince was a bold and robust man, and the music had become hushed at the waving of his hand.

It was in the blue room where stood the prince, with a group of pale courtiers by his side. At first, as he spoke, there was a slight rushing movement of this group in the direction of the intruder, who, at the moment was also near at hand, and now, with deliberate and stately step, made closer approach to the speaker. But from a certain nameless awe with which the mad assumptions of the mummer had inspired the whole party, there were found none who put forth hand to seize him; so that, unimpeded, he passed within a yard of the prince's person; and, while the vast assembly, as if with one impulse, shrank from the centres of the rooms to the walls, he made his way uninterruptedly, but with the same solemn and measured step which had distinguished him from the first, through the blue chamber to the purple—through the purple to the green—through the green to the orange—through this again to the white—and even thence to the violet, ere a decided movement had been made to arrest him. It was then, however, that the Prince Prospero, maddening with rage and the shame of his own momentary cowardice, rushed hurriedly through the six chambers, while none followed him on account of a deadly terror that had seized upon all. He bore aloft a drawn dagger, and had approached, in rapid impetuosity, to within three or four feet of the retreating figure, when the latter, having attained the extremity of the velvet apartment,

There are chords in the hearts of the most reckless which cannot be touched without emotion.

---

22. **out-Heroded Herod.** Herod the Great was a ruler who ordered the death of all boys under two years of age in Bethlehem, hoping to kill the baby Jesus. This reference suggests that the stranger has done something even worse.
23. **habiliments.** Clothes
24. **battlements.** Elevated platforms of earth or stone with an open space used to protect soldiers

---

spec • tral (spek´ trəl) *adj.,* ghostlike
blas • phe • mous (blas´ fə məs) *adj.,* insulting or showing disrespect or scorn for God or anything sacred

turned suddenly and confronted his pursuer. There was a sharp cry—and the dagger dropped gleaming upon the sable carpet, upon which, instantly afterward, fell prostrate in death the Prince Prospero. Then, summoning the wild courage of despair, a throng of the revellers at once threw themselves into the black apartment, and, seizing the mummer, whose tall figure stood erect and motionless within the shadow of the ebony clock, gasped in unutterable horror at finding the grave cerements[25] and corpse-like mask, which they handled with so violent a rudeness, untenanted by any tangible form.

And now was acknowledged the presence of the Red Death. He had come like a thief in the night. And one by one dropped the revellers in the blood-bedewed[26] halls of their revel, and died each in the despairing posture of his fall. And the life of the ebony clock went out with that of the last of the gay. And the flames of the tripods expired. And Darkness and Decay and the Red Death held illimitable dominion[27] over all. ❖

25. **cerements.** Strips of cloth used to wrap a dead body and prepare it for burial
26. **blood-bedewed.** *Bedew* means "to moisten as with dew." In this case, the halls are moistened with blood.
27. **dominion.** Control

MIRRORS & WINDOWS

Do people of wealth and privilege have a responsibility to society or a right to do whatever they please regardless of who is affected? Explain your answer.

REFER TO TEXT ▶ ▶ ▶ ▶	▶ REASON WITH TEXT	
1a. List steps the prince's friends take to make themselves safe from the Red Death.	**1b.** Determine why the appearance of a stranger under these circumstances would be so alarming.	**Understand** **Find meaning**
2a. Describe or sketch the seventh room.	**2b.** Consider what aspects of this story would make it a good chioce for filming. Use the text to support your opinions.	**Apply** **Use information**
3a. What do you think life is like inside the fortress?	**3b.** Contrast life inside the fortress with what is going on outside the fortress. How else could the prince have dealt with the problem of the plague?	**Analyze** **Take things apart**
4a. Quote the narrator's comments in the second paragraph of the story about life outside the abbey.	**4b.** Evaluate whether the prince's plan to withdraw from the suffering world was ethical. Explain your answer.	**Evaluate** **Make judgments**
5a. State what happened to the prince and his friends.	**5b.** Write an epilogue, or a conclusion, to the story from the point of view of someone who was invited but chose not to enter the abbey. In the epilogue, explain what happened to this person and why he or she chose not to enter the abbey.	**Create** **Bring ideas together**

ANALYZE LITERATURE: Setting and Symbol *use quotes*

In your own words, describe the setting of this story. In what ways is the setting important to this story? Which elements of the setting of this story are symbols? What do they represent?

what's the theme

Informational Text
CONNECTION

Like the Red Death in Poe's story, the Black Death, or bubonic plague, was a rampant killer. Though many people associate plague with the distant past, it is still a dangerous disease that kills thousands of people every year. Luckily, we now have a solid understanding of how this deadly disease is transmitted and treatments for it. The following Fact Sheet from the Centers for Disease Control and Prevention (CDC) was written to answer common questions about plague.

To read the map on page 90, look for a legend, or key. This part of the map will tell you what the various colors, shadings, styles of lines, and symbols mean. If you are unable to identify the states, refer to another map.

Questions and Answers About Plague

A Fact Sheet and Map by the Centers for Disease Control

Q. How is plague transmitted?

A. By fleas that become infected with bacteria *Yersinia pestis* that cause plague.

Q. How do people get plague?

A. By the bite of fleas infected with the plague bacteria.

Q. What is the basic transmission cycle?

A. Fleas become infected by feeding on rodents, such as chipmunks, prairie dogs, ground squirrels, mice, and other mammals that are infected with the bacteria *Yersinia pestis*. Fleas transmit the plague bacteria to humans and other mammals during the feeding process. The plague bacteria are maintained in the blood systems of rodents.

Q. Could you get plague from another person?

A. Yes, when the other person has plague pneumonia and coughs droplets containing the plague bacteria into air that is breathed by a noninfected person.

Q. What are the signs and symptoms of plague?

A. The typical sign of the most common form of human plague is a swollen and very tender lymph gland, accompanied by pain. The swollen gland is called a "bubo" (hence the term "bubonic plague"). Bubonic plague should be suspected when a person develops a swollen gland, fever, chills, headache, and extreme exhaustion, and has a history of possible exposure to infected rodents, rabbits, or fleas.

Q. What is the incubation period for plague?

A. A person usually becomes ill with bubonic plague 2 to 6 days after being infected. When bubonic plague is left untreated, plague bacteria invade the bloodstream. When plague bacteria multiply in the bloodstream, they spread rapidly throughout the body and cause a severe and often fatal condition. Infection of the lungs with the plague bacterium causes the pneumonic form of plague, a severe respiratory illness. The infected person may experience high fever, chills, cough, and breathing difficulty, and expel bloody sputum. If plague patients are not given specific antibiotic therapy, the disease can progress rapidly to death.

Q. What is the mortality rate of plague?

A. About 14% (1 in 7) of all plague cases in the United States are fatal.

Q. How many cases of plague occur in the U.S.?

A. Human plague in the United States has occurred as mostly scattered cases in rural areas (an average of 10 to 20 persons each year). Globally, the World Health Organization reports 1,000 to 3,000 cases of plague every year.

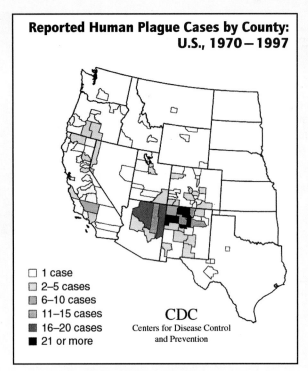

Reported Human Plague Cases by County: U.S., 1970–1997

- ☐ 1 case
- ☐ 2–5 cases
- ☐ 6–10 cases
- ☐ 11–15 cases
- ■ 16–20 cases
- ■ 21 or more

CDC
Centers for Disease Control and Prevention

Q. How is plague treated?

A. According to treatment experts, a patient diagnosed with suspected plague should be hospitalized and medically isolated. Laboratory tests should be done, including blood cultures for plague bacteria and microscopic examination of lymph gland, blood, and sputum samples. Antibiotic treatment should begin as soon as possible after laboratory specimens are taken. Streptomycin is the antibiotic of choice.

Gentamicin is used when streptomycin is not available. Tetracyclines and chloramphenicol are also effective. Persons who have been in close contact with a plague patient, particularly a patient with plague pneumonia, should be identified and evaluated. The U.S. Public Health Service requires that all cases of suspected plague be reported immediately to local and state health departments and that the diagnosis be confirmed by the CDC. As required by the International Health Regulations, the CDC reports all U.S. plague cases to the World Health Organization.

Q. Is the disease seasonal in its occurrence?

A. No, plague can be acquired at any time during the year.

Q. Where is plague most common?

A. Look at the map that shows reported cases of human plague between 1970–1997 by patient's county of residence. Generally, plague is most common in the southwestern states, particularly New Mexico and Arizona.

Q. Who is at risk for getting plague?

A. Outbreaks in people occur in areas where housing and sanitation conditions are poor. These outbreaks can occur in rural communities or in cities. They are usually associated with infected rats and rat fleas that live in the home. ❖

REFER TO TEXT ▶ ▶ ▶ ▶	▶ REASON WITH TEXT	
1a. In what kinds of places in the United States do plague outbreaks occur?	**1b.** Why are outbreaks probably more common in these areas?	**Understand** **Find meaning**
2a. Can you get plague from another person? Why or why not?	**2b.** Would it be reasonable to avoid people you thought might have the plague? Explain.	**Apply** **Use information**
3a. What additional questions do you have about plague?	**3b.** How would you evaluate the information provided about plague by the CDC? Support your answer with evidence from the text.	**Evaluate** **Make judgments**

TEXT ←TO→ TEXT CONNECTION

How might the information in this selection have helped the people in "The Masque of the Red Death"? What does "The Masque of the Red Death" tell us about how people deal with the unknown?

EXTEND THE TEXT

Writing Options

Creative Writing Write the **invitation** Prince Prospero might have used to ask his thousand friends to the fortress. Think about the mood that Prince Prospero wanted to create at his fortress and consider his sense of style. Keep these in mind as you choose your wording. Once you have finished the writing, choose appropriate paper, fonts, and art to complete the invitation.

Descriptive Writing For an audience of interested classmates, write a **descriptive paragraph** about a setting of your choice. Think of a fascinating place that is relatively small—for example, a building, house, park, farm, or museum rather than a country or planet. Try to include significant details that reveal something about the individuals that inhabit the setting. Freewriting about the place or creating a Sensory Details Chart can help you gather ideas. Try to create a specific mood through your description.

Collaborative Learning

Make a Map The detailed description of the fortress on pages 84–85 is quite complex and can be difficult to visualize. With a partner, read the description again and create a map of the fortress. Use an overhead perspective. Once you have established the layout of the rooms, color and furnish them as they are described in the story. When you are finished, compare your map with the maps of other pairs to see if you depicted the fortress in the same way.

Lifelong Learning

Research an Epidemic Use the Internet, books, newspapers, and magazines to research a current epidemic. Find out where the disease is most prevalent, how it spreads, what the symptoms are, and who is most at risk. Using the information you have gathered, create a Frequently Asked Questions (FAQ) document about the disease. Use the CDC's document about plague as a model. Use language that is easy for a general audience to understand, and include maps and other graphics as necessary.

 Go to **www.mirrorsandwindows.com** for more.

READING ASSESSMENT

1. At the beginning of the party, how did the scene inside the abbey contrast with the scene outside the abbey?
   A. Inside was lavish entertainment, while outside death ran rampant.
   B. Inside was beautifully decorated, while outside was filled with simple dwellings.
   C. Inside people worried about the plague, while outside they were beyond concern.
   D. Inside people worked for a cure, while outside people died like flies.
   E. Inside people fearlessly enjoyed each other's company, while outside, people were constantly shunned for fear of plague.

2. How were Prince Prospero and his friends different from other people?
   A. They escaped the Red Death by carefully putting themselves out of its reach.
   B. They were immune to the Red Death.
   C. They survived the Red Death.
   D. They faced the Red Death fearlessly.
   E. None of the above.

3. Which statement most accurately compares severity of plague outbreaks in the contemporary United States to the spread of the Red Death in Poe's story?

   A. The severity of plague outbreaks in the contemporary United States is similar to the severity of the Red Death outbreak.
   B. The severity of plague outbreaks in the contemporary United States far exceeds the severity of the Red Death outbreak.
   C. Plague outbreaks in the contemporary United States are rare and scattered, whereas plague ran rampant in Poe's story.
   D. Plague is fairly common in the contemporary United States, but not nearly as severe as in Poe's story.
   E. In neither case is the disease common.

4. Which of the following words best describes the prince in Poe's story?
   A. sagacious
   B. blasphemous
   C. dauntless
   D. spectral
   E. eccentric

5. Describe the setting of "The Masque of the Red Death." Explain how the setting contributed to the mood of the story.

UNDERSTAND THE CONCEPT

APPLY THE SKILL

Idioms, Metaphors, and Similes

An **idiom** is an expression that can't be understood from the meanings of its separate words but must be learned as a whole. Idioms are often confusing to people who are learning a new language or even to people who stumble across an unfamiliar idiom.

EXAMPLE

Prince Prospero was <u>tickled pink</u> by the idea of a costume party.

The phrase "tickled pink" is an idiom. Nobody actually tickled Prince Prospero, nor did he turn pink. Do you see how idioms can be confusing? What this idiom actually means is Prince Prospero was delighted by the idea of a costume party.

Look at the list of idioms below. How many do you understand?

all thumbs	cost an arm and
asleep at the	a leg
wheel	down the line
back out	fill someone in
bank on some-	from the get-go
thing/someone	heavy-handed
beat someone to	in the red
the punch	jump at the
bee in your bonnet	chance
bend over back-	know the ropes
wards	let sleeping dogs
beside one's self	lie
beyond the pale	like nobody's
bite the bullet	business
bring the house	off the wall
down	on your own
bury the hatchet	pig in a poke
caught dead	

Often, idioms are based on metaphors. A **metaphor** is a figure of speech in which one thing is spoken or written of as if it were another. This figure of speech invites the reader to make a comparison between the two "things" involved. The two things are the writer's actual subject, or the *tenor* of the metaphor, and the thing to which the subject is likened, or the *vehicle* of the metaphor. To interpret a metaphor, identify the tenor and vehicle and determine what the two have in common.

EXAMPLE

Prince Prospero <u>bent over backwards</u> to make sure his guests were comfortable.

In this example, the idiom "bent over backwards" means "was extremely helpful." This idiom is also a metaphor, where a person being helpful is compared to a very flexible person doing a backbend. Review the list of idioms listed in the first column. Which are based on metaphors? What two things are being compared in each?

A **simile** uses *like* or *as* to make a comparison. Like a metaphor, it can be broken into a tenor and vehicle.

EXAMPLE

People were <u>dropping like flies</u>.

The simile above contains the idiom "dropping like flies." The tenor is "people," and the vehicle is "flies." The idiom means that people were dying quickly.

Figurative language, such as idioms, similes, and metaphors, is meant to be understood imaginatively. To understand idioms, similes, or metaphors, you may need to use context clues—or these figures of speech may provide context clues that help you understand other vocabulary words.

REVIEW TERMS

- **idiom:** an expression that can't be understood from the meanings of its separate words but must be learned as a whole
- **metaphor:** a figure of speech in which one thing is spoken or written of as if it were another
- **simile:** a figure of speech that uses *like* or *as* to make a comparison

Exercise A

Copy the following sentences onto your own paper. Underline any idioms, similes, or metaphors. Write I, S, or M to identify each phrase or clause.

1. Profuse as water during the spring thaw, blood poured from the victims.
2. They had no fool for a leader, but rather one sagacious as an owl.
3. The prince had some eccentric, off-the-wall ideas about decorating.
4. Upon seeing the newcomer, the prince's usually ruddy countenance turned to snow.
5. Death is a powerful king whose dominion extends to all who walk the earth.

Exercise B

Since idioms are often confusing for people who are new to the English language to learn, something that might be helpful is an illustration. Using the list of idioms on page 92, choose five and create illustrations for them. The illustrations should get at what the idiom means figuratively instead of literally. Below each illustration, write a brief explanation of the idiom. For example, if you were going to illustrate the idiom "tickled pink," you would draw a picture of someone looking very happy and pleased. Below the picture, you would write, "To be 'tickled pink' is to be happy or pleased."

Exercise C

Choose one of the stories in this unit to either reread or read for the first time. As you read, keep a list of all the similes, metaphors, and idioms that you find. Then, choose any five of the similes, metaphors, or idioms and use them in a poem. The poem can be about any subject matter, but it should create a mood similar to that of "The Masque of the Red Death."

Exercise D

Following are sentences that use vocabulary words and idioms, metaphors, and similes. Choose the letter of the sentence that *most nearly means* the same as the original sentence.

1. Although the idea was quite disconcerting, the prince had to bite the bullet and realize that he could not hide from the Red Death.
    A. Although the idea was quite appealing, the prince had to accept the truth that he could not hide from the Red Death.
    B. Although the idea was quite upsetting to him, the prince had to accept the truth that he could not hide from the Red Death.
    C. Although the idea was quite disturbing to him, the prince ignored the fact that he could not hide from the Red Death.

2. The spectral hand gently brushed his cheek and felt like a cool breeze drifting across his face.
    A. The ghostly hand gently brushed his cheek and felt like a gentle breeze blowing across his face.
    B. The gnarled hand gently brushed his cheek and felt like a gentle breeze blowing across his face.
    C. The soft hand gently brushed his cheek and felt like a gentle breeze blowing across his face.

EXTEND THE SKILL

Choose at least ten vocabulary words from stories in this unit. Using those words as answers, create a crossword puzzle. Here's the tricky part: The clues for the crossword puzzle should be in the form of similes, metaphors, or idioms. The clues can be written as fill-in-the-blank or in other ways.

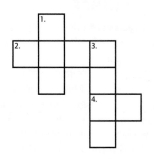

Two Friends

BUILD BACKGROUND

Literary Context **"Two Friends"** is the story of two men trying to lead normal lives in Paris while their country is at war and their city is under siege. The selection is an example of a literary style called *Naturalism,* which was popular in the early twentieth century. Naturalists saw actions and events as resulting inevitably from biological or environmental forces rather than from free will. Closely observed details, a lack of emotion, and accurate historical background are three characteristics that mark the work of Maupassant and other Naturalist writers. Watch for these characteristics as you read.

Reader's Context When have you taken a risk to do something that you truly wanted to do? Was the risk worth it?

ANALYZE LITERATURE: Mood and Irony

Mood, or the emotion created in the reader by part or all of a literary work, is often closely tied to a story's setting. In "Two Friends," details of the setting, such as the time of year, the conditions under which the characters live, and the landscape affect the mood.

Maupassant was known for his use of **irony,** or the difference between appearance and reality. *Dramatic irony* occurs when something is known by the reader or audience but unknown to the characters; *verbal irony* occurs when a character says one thing but means another; and *irony of situation* occurs when an event violates the expectations of the characters, the reader, or the audience.

SET PURPOSE

Read the Build Background section above. As you read "Two Friends," determine why the story is a good example of Naturalism. Consider how Maupassant's use of mood and irony are related to the Naturalist style.

MEET THE AUTHOR

Guy de Maupassant (1850–1893) was born in Normandy, France. After joining the French army and fighting in the Franco-Prussian War, Maupassant moved to Paris, where he met many writers and began to write himself. Maupassant was greatly influenced by Naturalism. Rejecting Romanticism, which valued emotion and the imagination over reason, Naturalist writers sought to portray human beings and the society in which they lived as truthfully as possible. Maupassant wrote six novels and more than three hundred short stories. He is widely considered to be the greatest French writer of short stories.

USE READING SKILLS

Sequence of Events Sequence refers to the order in which things happen. As you read "Two Friends," take notes on the key events in the story. An effective way to organize this information is by creating a Sequence Map. A Sequence Map uses pictures and captions to record key events. Each picture is in a box connected by arrows to show sequence.

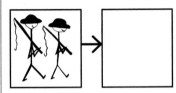

Two friends
go fishing in a
war zone

PREVIEW VOCABULARY

Use the context clues in the sentences below to figure out the meanings of the underlined words from the selection.

1. Carla was <u>fanatical</u> about the roller coaster; she rode it at least twenty times.
2. After he returned from the war, Byron became <u>pensive</u> and lost in thought.
3. Jamal was about to <u>indulge</u> in a pint of ice cream when he remembered that he was trying to lose weight for wrestling.
4. After a five-mile hike in the scorching sun, the hikers found <u>respite</u> in the cool lake.
5. Gina was <u>unperturbed</u> by her friends' teasing; she liked Tony so much that her friends' opinions didn't matter.

Two Friends

A Short Story by
Guy de Maupassant

The Marshes of Arleux, 1871. Jean-Baptiste-Camille Corot.

"It's too bad for you that you've fallen into my hands. But war is war."

Paris was under siege,[1] in the grip of famine, at its last gasp. There were few sparrows on the rooftops now, and even the sewers were losing some of their inhabitants. The fact is that people were eating anything they could get their hands on.

One bright January morning Monsieur Morissot was strolling dejectedly along one of the outer boulevards, with an empty stomach and his hands in the pockets of his old army trousers. He was a watchmaker by trade and a man who liked to make the most of his leisure. Suddenly, he came upon one of his close friends, and he stopped short. It was Monsieur Sauvage, whom he had got to know on fishing expeditions.

Every Sunday before the war it was Morissot's custom to set off at the crack of dawn with his bamboo rod in his hand and a tin box slung over his back. He would catch the Argenteuil train and get off at Colombes, from where he would walk to the island of Marante. The minute he reached this land of his dreams he would start to fish—and he would go on fishing till it got dark.

---

1. **siege.** Cutoff of supplies by an enemy military force

Parisians waiting in line for food during the siege.

And it was here, every Sunday, that he met a tubby, jolly little man by the name of Sauvage. He was a haberdasher[2] from the Rue Notre-Dame-de-Lorette, and as <u>fanatical</u> an angler[3] as Morissot himself. They often spent half the day sitting side by side, rod in hand, with their feet dangling over the water. And they had become firm friends.

There were some days when they hardly spoke to each other. On other occasions they would chat all the time. But they understood

---

2. **haberdasher.** Seller of clothing, usually men's
3. **angler.** Person who fishes

---

fa • nat • ic • al (fə na´ ti kəl) *adj.,* interested to the point of obsession

each other perfectly without needing to exchange any words, because their tastes were so alike and their feelings identical.

On spring mornings at about ten o'clock, when the <u>rejuvenated</u> sun sent floating over the river that light mist which moves along with the current, warming the backs of the two enthusiastic fishermen with the welcome glow of a new season, Morissot would say to his neighbor:

"Ah! It's grand here, isn't it?"

And Monsieur Sauvage would reply:

"There's nothing I like better."

This simple exchange of words was all that was needed for them to understand each other and confirm their mutual appreciation.

In the autumn towards the close of day, when the sky was blood-red and the water reflected strange shapes of scarlet clouds which reddened the whole river, and the glowing sun set the distant horizon ablaze, making the two friends look as though they were on fire, and touching with gold the russet leaves which were already trembling with a wintry shudder, Monsieur Sauvage would turn to Morissot with a smile and say:

"What a marvelous sight!"

And Morissot, equally taken up with the wonder of it all, but not taking his eyes off his float, would answer:

"It's better than walking down the boulevards, eh?"

As soon as the two friends had recognized each other, they shook hands warmly, feeling quite emotional over the fact that they had come across each other in such different circumstances. Monsieur Sauvage gave a sigh and remarked:

"What a lot has happened since we last met!"

Morissot, in mournful tones, lamented:

"And what awful weather we've been having! This is the first fine day of the year."

And, indeed, the sky was a cloudless blue, brilliant with light.

They started to walk on together side by side, <u>pensive</u> and melancholy. Then Morissot said:

"And what about those fishing trips, eh? *There's* something worth remembering!"

"When shall we be able to get back to it?" mused Monsieur Sauvage.

They went into a little café and drank a glass of absinthe.[4] Then they resumed their stroll along the boulevards.

Morissot suddenly stopped and said:

"What about another glass of the green stuff, eh?"

"Just as you wish," consented Monsieur Sauvage, and they went into a second bar.

When they came out they both felt very fuzzy, as people do when they drink alcohol on an empty stomach. The weather was very mild. A gentle breeze caressed their faces.

Monsieur Sauvage, who felt even more fuddled[5] in this warm air, stopped and said:

"What about it, then? Shall we go?"

"Go where?"

"Fishing!"

---

4. **absinthe.** Green, licorice-flavored alcoholic beverage
5. **fuddled.** Confused

> **re • ju • ve • nat • ed** (ri jü´ və nāt´ əd) *adj.,* renewed; made young again
> **pen • sive** (pen[t]´ siv) *adj.,* thoughtful

HISTORY
CONNECTION

The Franco-Prussian War In the mid-1800s, many small countries united into an increasingly large Prussia, which would eventually become Germany. As Prussia grew in power and influence, Napoleon, the emperor of neighboring France, grew nervous. In July 1870, Napoleon declared war on Prussia, and the Franco-Prussian War began. By September, the German troops had captured Napoleon and won several crucial victories. They then surrounded the French capital, Paris, hoping to starve and frighten the citizens into surrender. "Two Friends" is set in the period during which Paris was under siege.

"But where can we go?"

"To our island, of course. The French front-line is near Colombes. I know the colonel in command—fellow called Dumoulin. I'm sure we'd have no trouble in getting through."

Morrisot began to quiver with excitement.

"Right!" he said. "I'm your man!"

And the two friends separated and went off to get their fishing tackle.

An hour later they were striding down the main road together. They reached the villa in which the colonel had set up his headquarters. When he heard their request, he smiled at their eccentric enthusiasm but gave them permission. They set off once again, armed with an official pass.

They soon crossed the frontline, then went through Colombes, which had been evacuated, and now found themselves on the fringe of the area of vineyards which rise in terraces[6] above the Seine. It was about eleven o'clock.

On the opposite bank they could see the village of Argenteuil, which looked deserted

and dead. The hills of Orgemont and Sannois dominated the horizon, and the great plain which stretches as far as Nanterre was empty, completely empty, with nothing to be seen but its leafless cherry trees and gray earth.

Pointing towards the high ground Monsieur Sauvage muttered:

"The Prussians are up there."

And as the two friends gazed at the deserted country-side, they felt almost paralyzed by the sense of uneasiness which was creeping through them.

The Prussians! They had never so much as set eyes on them, but for four months now they had been aware of their presence on the outskirts of Paris, occupying part of France, looting, committing <u>atrocities,</u> reducing people to starvation…the invisible yet all-powerful Prussians. As they thought of them, a kind of supersti-tious dread was added to their natural hatred for this unknown, victorious race.

"What if we should happen to run into some of them?" said Morissot nervously.

Monsieur Sauvage gave the sort of reply which showed that cheerful Parisian banter survived in spite of everything.

"Oh, we'll just offer them some nice fish to fry!"

Even so, they were so worried by the silence of the surrounding countryside that they hesitated about going any further.

---

6. **terraces.** Flat areas formed on a slope and used to grow plants

a • troc • i • ty (ə trä´ sə tē) *n.,* cruel, horrible act

> *And as the two friends gazed at the deserted countryside, they felt almost paralyzed by the sense of uneasiness which was creeping through them.*

It was Monsieur Sauvage who finally made up his mind.

"Come on!" he said. "We'll go on—but we must keep a sharp lookout!"

And they scrambled down the slope of one of the vineyards, bent double, crawling on their hands and knees, taking advantage of the cover afforded by the vines, keeping their eyes wide open and their ears on the alert.

All that now separated them from the river-bank was a strip of open ground. They ran across it, and as soon as they reached the river, they crouched amongst the dry rushes.

Morissot pressed his ear to the ground to see if he could detect the sound of marching feet. He could hear nothing. They were alone, completely alone.

They told each other there was nothing to worry about, and started to fish.

Opposite them the deserted island of Marante concealed them from the other bank. The little building which once housed the restaurant was closed and shuttered, and looked as though it had been abandoned for years.

It was Monsieur Sauvage who caught the first fish—a gudgeon. Morissot caught the second, and then, almost without a pause, they jerked up their rods time after time to find a little silvery creature wriggling away on the hook. This really was a miraculous draft of fishes.

They carefully placed each fish into a fine-meshed net which was suspended in the water at their feet. And as they did so they were overcome by a delightful sense of joy, the kind of joy you only experience when you resume something you really love after being deprived of it for a long time.

A kindly sun was shedding its warmth across their backs. They were so absorbed that they no longer heard, or thought, or paid the least attention to the outside world. What did anything matter now? They were fishing!

But suddenly, the bank beneath them shook with a dull rumble which seemed to come from underground.

The distant cannons were starting to fire again.

Morissot turned his head, and above the bank, over to the left, he saw the great bulk of Mont Valérien. On the mountainside was a white plume of smoke, showing where the gunpowder had just bellowed out.

Almost immediately another jet of smoke spurted from the fort on the summit, and a few seconds later the rumble of another detonation reached their ears.

Other cannon shots followed, and every now and then the mountain spat out its deadly breath, exhaled its clouds of milky vapor, which rose slowly into the calm sky above.

"There they go again!" said Monsieur Sauvage with a shrug of his shoulders.

Morissot, who was anxiously watching the feather on his float as it bobbed up and down, was suddenly filled with the anger of a peace-loving man for these maniacs who <u>indulge</u> in fighting.

"They've got to be really stupid," he growled, "to go on killing each other like that!"

"They're worse than animals," said Monsieur Sauvage.

---

in • dulge (in dulj´) *v.*, take pleasure freely

Morissot, who had just caught another fish, called out:

"And it'll never be any different so long as we have governments!"

"Oh, no," disagreed Monsieur Sauvage. "The Republic[7] would never have declared war…"

"Look!" interrupted Morissot. "Under kings you have war against other countries. Under republican governments you have civil war."

And they began to argue, in a calm and friendly way, sorting out all the world's great political problems with the commonsense approach of mild and reasonable men. On one point they were in absolute agreement: mankind would never be free. And as they talked, Mont Valérien went thundering on without <u>respite</u>, demolishing French homes with its cannonades,[8] pounding lives to dust, crushing human beings to pulp, putting an end to so many dreams, to so many long-awaited joys, so much long-expected happiness, tearing into the hearts of all those wives and daughters and mothers with pain and suffering that would never be eased.

"Such is life," said Monsieur Sauvage.

"Better to call it death," laughed Morissot.

But at that moment they both gave a start, scared by the feeling that somebody had been walking just behind them. They looked round and saw standing above them four men, four tall, bearded men, armed to the teeth, dressed like liveried[9] footmen, with flat military caps on their heads—and rifles which they were pointing straight at the two friends.

The fishing rods dropped from their hands and went floating down the river.

In a matter of seconds they were seized, tied up, hustled along, thrown into a boat and carried across to the island.

Behind the building which they had thought deserted they saw a group of about twenty German soldiers.

A sort of hairy giant who was sitting astride a chair and smoking a large clay pipe asked them in excellent French:

"Well, messieurs, did the fishing go well?"

One of the soldiers placed at the officer's feet the net full of fish which he had been careful to bring along. The Prussian smiled and said:

"Well, well! I can see you didn't do badly at all!… But I have to deal with a very different matter. Now, listen to me carefully, and don't get alarmed… As far as I am concerned you are a couple of spies sent out here to keep an eye on me. I've caught you and I've every right to shoot you. You were obviously pretending to

---

7. **The Republic.** Representative government that ruled France from 1848 to 1852, before Napoleon's rise to power
8. **cannonades.** Constant shooting of cannons
9. **liveried.** In uniform

---

res • pite (res´ pət) *n.,* rest or temporary relief

fish as a cover for your real purposes. It's too bad for you that you've fallen into my hands. But war is war…Now, since you've come out here past your own lines, you're bound to have a password so you can get back. Just give me that password and I'll spare your lives."

The two friends, ghastly pale, stood there side by side with their hands trembling. They said nothing.

"Nobody will ever get to know about it," continued the officer. "You will go back without any trouble, and the secret will go with you…If you refuse to cooperate, you'll die—straight away. So take your choice!"

They stood there motionless, keeping their mouths firmly shut.

The Prussian, who was still quite calm, pointed in the direction of the river and said:

"Just think! In five minutes you'll be at the bottom of that river. In five minutes! You must have families. Think of them!"

The rumbling of the cannon was still coming from Mont Valérien.

The two fishermen simply stood there, refusing to speak. The German now gave some orders in his own language. Then he moved his chair some distance away from the prisoners. Twelve men marched up and formed a line twenty yards from them with their rifles at their sides.

"I'll give you one minute to make up your minds," called the officer. "And not two seconds more."

Then he jumped to his feet, went up to the two Frenchmen, took Morissot by the arm, and led him to one side. Then he said to him in a very low voice:

"Quick! Just let me have that password! Your friend won't know you've told me. I'll make it look as though I've taken pity on you both."

Morissot said nothing.

The Prussian then dragged Monsieur Sauvage to one side and made the same proposition to him.

Monsieur Sauvage said nothing.

So they were pushed together again, side by side.

It was then that Morissot happened to glance down at the net full of gudgeon which was lying in the grass a few yards away.

A ray of sunlight fell on the heap of glittering fish, which were still quivering with life. As he looked at them he felt a momentary weakness. In spite of his efforts to hold them back, tears filled his eyes.

"Farewell, Monsieur Sauvage," he mumbled.

And Monsieur Sauvage replied:

"Farewell, Monsieur Morissot."

They shook hands, trembling uncontrollably from head to foot.

"Fire!" shouted the officer.

Twelve shots rang out simultaneously.

Monsieur Sauvage fell like a log onto his face. Morissot, who was taller, swayed, spun round, then collapsed on top of his friend, with his face staring up at the sky and the blood welling from where his coat had been burst open across his chest.

The German shouted out more orders. His men went off and came back with some lengths of rope and a few heavy stones which they fastened to the feet of the two bodies. Then they carried them to the riverbank.

All the time Mont Valérien continued to rumble, and now it was capped by a great mountain of smoke.

Two soldiers got hold of Morissot by the head and feet. Two others lifted up Monsieur Sauvage in the same way. The two bodies were swung violently backwards and forwards, then thrown with great force. They curved through the air, then plunged upright into the river, with the stones dragging them down, feet first.

The water spurted up, bubbled, swirled round, then grew calm again, with little waves rippling across to break against the bank. There was just a small amount of blood discoloring the surface.

The officer, still quite unperturbed, said, half aloud:

"Well, now it's the fishes' turn."

As he was going back towards the building, he noticed the net full of gudgeon lying in the grass. He picked it up, looked at the fish, then smiled, and called out:

"Wilhelm!"

A soldier came running up. He was wearing a white apron. The Prussian officer threw across to him the catch made by the two executed fishermen, and gave another order:

"Fry me these little creatures—straight away, while they're still alive. They'll be delicious!"

Then he lit his pipe again. ❖

un • per • turbed (un pər tʉrb'd´) *adj.,* not bothered

If you had been living in Paris during the siege, as Morissot and Sauvage were, what would you have done? Why do you think people would be willing to risk their lives for a simple activity, like fishing?

AFTER READING

REFER TO TEXT ▶ ▶ ▶ ▶	▶ REASON WITH TEXT	
1a. Recall what Monsieur Sauvage says he and Morissot will do if they meet some Prussians.	1b. Explain why the officer's last line is ironic.	**Understand** **Find meaning**
2a. Describe how the two men felt once they finally started fishing again.	2b. Generalize about appreciating what you have based on the experience of these two men.	**Apply** **Use information**
3a. Locate three passages in the story that show what kind of friendship Morissot and Sauvage have.	3b. Analyze why these two men were such good friends.	**Analyze** **Take things apart**
4a. State the consequences the officer gives for giving and not giving the password.	4b. Consider what you would have done had you been captured and questioned about the password. Defend your response.	**Evaluate** **Make judgments**
5a. According to the first paragraph, what is Paris like?	5b. How does the friendship of the two men contrast with the setting and action of the story? Explain what point Maupassant might have been trying to make about individual lives versus external forces.	**Create** **Bring ideas together**

ANALYZE LITERATURE: Mood and Irony

The story contains several images of beauty. What mood is created by these images? How does this mood contrast with the one created by the conditions under which the characters live? What is happening on Mont Valérien as the characters seek relief from stress in its shadow? Why is this ironic?

Writing Options

Creative Writing Imagine an additional scene at the end of the story, in which the officer is enjoying his fish dinner with a few of his men. What do they discuss? What is their reaction to what just happened? Write a **screenplay** that continues the story. A screenplay consists of dialogue; for ideas on how to write dialogue, see how Guy de Maupassant does it in the story. A screenplay also contains stage directions, or directions on the actions characters should take (for example, "Officer sits down.") and the way the characters should say their lines. Try to include all these elements in your screenplay.

Persuasive Writing Was it wise for the two friends in the story to go fishing during a war? Should they have just stayed home? Write a five-paragraph **persuasive essay** in which you take a position on whether or not the two friends were foolish to go fishing. In your first paragraph, introduce the title and author of the story and state your position. Use the next three paragraphs to argue three points in support of your position. Use evidence from the story to support your ideas. Also use these paragraphs to refute any arguments someone might take against your position. In the fifth paragraph, restate your position as part of your conclusion.

Lifelong Learning

Present on Naturalism Naturalists believe that events result inevitably from biological or environmental forces rather than from free will. Research Naturalism to learn more about this literary movement. Then analyze "Two Friends" as an example of Naturalism. For example, consider whether Morissot and Sauvage were victims of uncontrollable forces, or whether they exercised bad judgment in crossing the front line. Prepare a brief presentation that explains what Naturalism is and how "Two Friends" fits or does not fit the mold.

Media Literacy

Create a Flier Imagine you are a friend of Morissot or Sauvage. Create a flier to advertise that your friend is missing. Review the story for details about the character and use your imagination to draw the character's face and provide a written description of his physical appearance and habits, the date and time of his disappearance, and information for contacting authorities.

 Go to **www.mirrorsandwindows.com** for more.

READING ASSESSMENT

1. Why is the location of Monsieur Morissot and Monsieur Sauvage's latest meeting ironic?
   - A. They had never run into each other while walking along the boulevard before the war.
   - B. Monsieur Morissot used to say "It's better than walking down the boulevards, eh?" when they were fishing.
   - C. Monsieur Sauvage had been trying to avoid Monsieur Morissot.
   - D. Monsieur Morissot had been looking for Monsieur Sauvage at their usual fishing spot but ran into him on the way home.
   - E. Monsieur Sauvage didn't recognize his friend in the unusual location.

2. How do the characters react when they start fishing?
   - A. They get frustrated that there are as few fish in the river as there are sparrows in Paris.
   - B. They have the same old conversation they always have while fishing.
   - C. They start fighting because one is worried and the other relaxes.
   - D. They continue to worry.
   - E. They stop worrying and start enjoying themselves.

3. Why is the officer's last statement ironic?
   - A. He caught the two friends like they caught the fish.
   - B. The officer doesn't even like fish.
   - C. Monsieur Sauvage had said that if they met any Prussians they'd just offer them some fish to fry.
   - D. The last thing Monsieur Morissot noticed before he died was the net of fish they had caught.
   - E. The two friends had purposefully kept the fish alive in a net.

4. Which of the following is a synonym of the word *unperturbed?*
   - A. pensive
   - B. rejuvenated
   - C. fanatical
   - D. indulgent
   - E. None of the above

5. Describe the setting of the story and explain how it contributes to the mood.

GRAMMAR & STYLE

Sentence Variety

By varying the type of sentence you use in your writing, you can make it more interesting. Combining and expanding sentences can connect related ideas, make sentences longer and smoother, and make a paragraph more interesting to read.

A **simple sentence** consists of one independent clause and no subordinate clauses. A simple sentence is called an independent clause because it has a subject and a predicate. It may have a compound subject, a compound predicate, and any number of phrases.

EXAMPLE

Monsieur Morissot [subject] loves to fish [predicate].

A **compound sentence** consists of two independent clauses joined by a semicolon or by a comma and a coordinating conjunction. The most common coordinating conjunctions are *and, or, nor, for, but, so,* and *yet.* Each part of the compound sentence has its own subject and verb.

EXAMPLE

Monsieur Morissot can't fish during the war [independent clause]; [semicolon] he takes walks instead [independent clause].

A **complex sentence** consists of one independent clause and one or more subordinate clauses. A subordinate clause has a subject and a verb, but it doesn't express a complete thought.

EXAMPLE

While he was walking [subordinate clause], he ran into Monsieur Sauvage [independent clause].

A **compound-complex sentence** has two or more independent clauses and one or more subordinate clauses.

EXAMPLE

While the men were fishing [subordinate clause], the Prussians found them [independent clause], and [coordinating conjunction] they were taken prisoner [independent clause].

Another way to vary your sentences is to vary the way you begin them. For example, instead of starting a sentence with a subject, start with a modifier, a phrase, or a clause.

subject: <u>They</u> fish and talk.

one-word modifier: <u>Frequently</u>, they fish and talk.

prepositional phrase: <u>During the siege</u>, they could not fish and talk often.

participial phrase: <u>Thinking about fishing</u>, they devised a daring plan.

subordinate clause: <u>Since they had come so far</u>, they decided to fish despite their fears.

What Great Writers Do

Notice the sentence variety that Guy de Maupassant uses in this passage from "Two Friends."

An hour later they were striding down the main road together. They reached the villa in which the colonel had set up his headquarters. When he heard their request, he smiled at their eccentric enthusiasm but gave them permission. They set off once again, armed with an official pass.

REVIEW TERMS

- **subject:** the doer of the action
- **predicate:** the part of the sentence that contains the verb phrase, including the objects, or recipients, of the action
- **clause:** a group of words that functions as one part of speech and that contains both a subject and a verb
- **phrase:** a group of words that functions as one part of speech but does not have both a subject and a verb
- **independent clause:** a complete sentence with a subject and a verb
- **subordinate clause:** a clause that contains a subject and a verb but cannot stand alone because it does not express a complete thought

Identify Sentence Structure

For each sentence, identify whether it is simple, compound, complex, or compound-complex. Some of the sentences are from "Two Friends."

1. The men may have been drawn to fish because they enjoyed the activity, but they may also have been motivated by hunger.
2. Knowing the officer in command, Monsieur Sauvage was able to get a pass.
3. Fearful of the Prussians, the men were unable to enjoy themselves at first, but once they got into the water, they were quite happy.
4. The weather was very mild.
5. There were few sparrows on the rooftops now, and even the sewers were losing some of their inhabitants.
6. Almost immediately another jet of smoke spurted from the fort on the summit, and a few seconds later the rumble of another detonation reached their ears.

Improve Sentence Variety

Rewrite the following paragraph using a variety of sentence structures and beginnings. Choose structures and beginnings that will help the paragraph flow more smoothly and clearly for the reader.

> Two friends decide to go fishing. Their names are Monsieur Morissot and Monsieur Sauvage. There is a war going on. Monsieur Morissot asks what they will do if they meet any Prussians. Monsieur Sauvage says, "Oh, we'll just offer them some nice fish to fry!" They do meet some Prussians. A Prussian officer notices their net of fish. He has the two men killed. He asks the cook to fry up the fish for him.

Improve a Paragraph

The following paragraph is full of run-on sentences. Break up the sentences to form simple, compound, complex, and compound-complex sentences so that the paragraph is easier to understand.

> Guy de Maupassant's short story, "Two Friends," follows the ill-conceived fishing trip of Monsieur Morissot and Monsieur Sauvage as they decide to go fishing in the middle of a battle because the men are hungry because there is no food to eat in the city because of the Prussian soldiers who have laid siege to Paris. As the battle rages just out of sight, the men contentedly fish in the river and remember happier times and discuss philosophical questions about life and death and the current situation involving the Prussian siege and talk about days gone by. Unfortunately, they are caught by the Prussians, who are convinced that Monsieur Morissot and Monsieur Sauvage are French spies, and the Prussian captain questions the two men and he decides to execute them right there on the riverbank and then he takes their fish and has his cook fry up the fish for his dinner.

Use Varied Sentence Structures in Your Writing

Write a paragraph about friendship for a teen magazine. After drafting your paragraph, check for variety in your sentence structure. Which type of sentence structure did you use most often? Do you think that type is appropriate for your audience? As you prepare your final draft, alter your sentence structure as needed for variety and appropriateness for your audience.

EXTEND THE SKILL

Choose a paragraph from the story "Two Friends." Rewrite the paragraph using only one type of sentence. Then do the same thing again using another type of sentence. What happens when you do this? Based on this experiment, write a paragraph that explains why sentence variety is necessary to quality writing.

Understanding Theme

THEME

Theme is a central idea in a literary work. You can also think of theme as the author's message. Some literary works have more than one theme, with one theme being more dominant than others. Do not confuse theme with plot. Plot outlines the events of the story; it is the answer to the question, "What happens?" The theme, however, answers the question, "What is the point?"

In traditional literature, such as fables or fairy tales, the theme is the moral of the story. The greedy dog of Aesop's fable snaps at his reflection in a river, and the bone he was enjoying falls from his jaws and is swept away by the current. The theme is obvious: The greedy lose what they have in trying to get more than their fair share. The moral of "Cinderella," featuring literature's most neglected stepdaughter, is also clear: Goodness triumphs over wickedness. In case we miss the point, Cinderella is industrious and beautiful, whereas her stepsisters are lazy and rather funny looking. The reader does not have to dig deep to find the theme.

Modern literature, however, tends to be more sophisticated. That is partly because our worldview has shifted, and partly because the aim of the modern storyteller is somewhat different. There may be a moral in a modern tale, and in some stories, there are certainly clear consequences to human action. But most of today's authors would be embarrassed if a reader could so easily locate meaning that the story is reduced to a one-sentence moral.

ELEMENTS OF THEME

Symbol

Sometimes, the theme can be found in the symbolism of a work of literature. A **symbol** is anything that stands for or represents both itself and something else. This might be a *conventional symbol*, or an object with which many people have associations. For instance, in "The Masque of the Red Death" (page 83), the ornate clock represents time, and the clock's solemn chiming is a reminder that life is limited.

The symbol may also be *personal* or *idiosyncratic*, one that assumes its secondary meaning because of the way the writer uses it. In that case, your job as a reader is to look for all the possible associations that could be attached to the symbolic object. In "A White Heron" (page 185), the heron is a personal symbol; it represents the innocence and freedom of nature being hunted and contained by a materialistic modern society.

Common Symbols

Symbols exist not only in literature but also in folklore, art, music, and other areas of life. Every day, you likely encounter symbols that automatically mean something to you. Some of the most common symbols are listed below.

- dove = peace
- green = envy
- night = darkness; things hidden; evil
- rose = beauty
- shamrock = luck; Ireland
- owl = wisdom

Plot and Characterization

Consider plot and characterization when you are analyzing a work's theme. The writer's attitude toward events and characters can point to a theme, as can a pattern of events. For instance, in "The Leap" (page 119), the narrator's mother is constantly overcoming adversity despite incredible odds. Her attitude to make the best of a situation and not allow tragedy to stop her allows the reader to understand her motivations at the end of the story. What theme might the author be suggesting here? At this point, you'll need to think about the author's attitude toward the events. Does she find them comical, tragic, or ironic? Once you figure out the author's viewpoint, in combination with the patterns in plot and character, you can start to think about theme.

TYPES OF THEME

As you know by now, most works of fiction do not directly state the theme. When the theme is presented directly, it is called a **stated theme.** For example, at the end of "On the Rainy River" (page 137), O'Brien tells his readers why he went to war and what that decision meant about the nature of courage. The story itself is centered on how he reached this decision.

> The day was cloudy. I passed through towns with familiar names, through the pine forests and down to the prairie, and then to Vietnam, where I was a soldier, and then home again. I survived, but it's not a happy ending. I was a coward. I went to the war.
>
> —from "On the Rainy River"
> by Tim O'Brien

Sometimes, a story's character voices a theme, as Neffie does in "Who Said We All Have to Talk Alike?" (page 157) when she comments on her employer's insistence that Neffie speak like her. The events of the story lead Neffie to this comment.

In contrast, Alice Walker presents her story but leaves the reader to draw conclusions about the theme of

"Everyday Use" (page 109). Such an *implied theme* requires the reader to make inferences, or guesses, about the author's message and perception of the events in the story.

DISCOVERING THEMES

To discover the theme or themes in a literary work, you can ask yourself questions about the work and make inferences based on your reading. You may find yourself asking the following questions as you explore the author's intentions in the story:

- What is the message?
- What does the author want me to think about?
- What seems to motivate the characters?
- What causes situations to change or events to happen?

After you find a general theme, consider refining it. For example, truth is a dominant theme in "Like the Sun" (page 200), in which the author examines the effects of complete honesty on people. However, it is not enough to say that "Like the Sun" is a story about truth. You must examine what Narayan is saying *about* truth. Keep in mind that while a theme should have a universal application and should make a complete statement, it should make no mention of specific characters or events from the story.

Popular Themes in Literature

One of the common themes in literature is that of the American dream—the idea that in America anyone can succeed and find greatness. Literary works that contain this theme include the following:

- *The Great Gatsby* by F. Scott Fitzgerald
- *The Joy Luck Club* by Amy Tan
- *Of Mice and Men* by John Steinbeck
- *The Adventures of Huckleberry Finn* by Mark Twain
- *Death of a Salesman* by Arthur Miller

Everyday Use

BUILD BACKGROUND

Social Context **"Everyday Use,"** like many of Alice Walker's writings, explores the idea of African-American heritage. Walker examines the role heritage and culture play in an individual's understanding of his or her life and identity. In a conflict between a sophisticated young woman and her less worldly sister and mother, two different interpretations of heritage are presented. "Everyday Use" is enriched by Walker's use of symbols. In particular, the contested quilts become the central metaphor of the story. "Everyday Use" was published in the collection *In Love and Trouble: Stories of Black Women.*

Reader's Context Do you think family heirlooms are important? Why? If you have a family heirloom you cherish, what makes it important to you? What would you like to pass on to future generations?

ANALYZE LITERATURE: Theme and Metaphor

A **theme** is a central message or perception about life that is conveyed through a literary work. A theme is not the same as a topic, or subject. Rather, it is a broad statement about a topic. African-American heritage is the subject of "Everyday Use," but it is not the theme.

A **metaphor** is a figure of speech in which one thing is spoken or written about as if it were another. In "Everyday Use," Walker uses quilts metaphorically.

SET PURPOSE

As you read, try to determine what the author is saying about heritage. In other words, what is the theme of the story? Also consider how the metaphorical use of quilts helps to advance the theme of the story.

MEET THE AUTHOR

Alice Walker (b. 1944), the daughter of Georgia sharecroppers, gained national recognition with the publication of her novel *The Color Purple,* which earned a Pulitzer Prize and was made into a movie starring Oprah Winfrey. Of particular interest to Walker is her inheritance from the African-American women who came before her. In her book *In Search of Our Mothers' Gardens*, she says, "And so our mothers and grandmothers have, more often than not anonymously, handed on the creative spark, the seed of the flower they themselves never hoped to see." Walker often focuses on African-American women, and a central theme of her writing is that "not enough credit has been given to the black woman who has been oppressed beyond recognition."

USE READING SKILLS

Compare and Contrast When you **compare** one thing to another, you describe the similarities. **Contrasting** describes the differences.

As you read "Everyday Use," take notes on how the narrator, Maggie, and Dee view their heritage. Pay attention, too, to how Dee's ideas have changed.

One way to organize this information is by creating a chart like the one below. As you encounter an object, an activity, or another aspect that shows how the characters react to their heritage, make a note in the chart.

Maggie	Dee	Mother

PREVIEW VOCABULARY

Use the context clues in the sentences below to figure out the meanings of the underlined words from the selection.

1. The <u>homely</u> afghan has a simple pattern.
2. Before throwing the ball, the pitcher sneaked a <u>furtive</u> look at the man on first base.
3. Andrew <u>recomposed</u> himself after the heated tennis match.
4. <u>Rifling</u> through the desk drawer, I found a wedding picture of my parents.
5. After receiving several warnings, the children talking loudly in the movie theater were <u>ushered</u> out.

Everyday USE

A Short Story by **Alice Walker**

for your grandmama

"Maggie can't appreciate these quilts!…She'd probably be backward enough to put them to everyday use."

I will wait for her in the yard that Maggie and I made so clean and wavy yesterday afternoon. A yard like this is more comfortable than most people know. It is not just a yard. It is like an extended living room. When the hard clay is swept clean as a floor and the fine sand around the edges lined with tiny, irregular grooves, anyone can come and sit and look up into the elm tree and wait for the breezes that never come inside the house. Maggie will be nervous until after her sister goes: she will stand hopelessly in corners, <u>homely</u> and ashamed of the burn scars down her arms and legs, eying her sister with a mixture of envy and awe. She thinks her sister has held life always in the palm of one hand, that "no" is a word the world never learned to say to her.

You've no doubt seen those TV shows where the child who has "made it" is confronted, as a surprise, by her own mother and father, tottering in weakly from backstage.[1] (A pleasant surprise, of course: What would they do if parent and child came on the show only to curse out and insult each other?) On TV mother and child embrace and smile into each other's faces.

Sometimes the mother and father weep, the child wraps them in her arms and leans across the table to tell how she would not have made

---

1. **TV shows…backstage.** Refers to *This Is Your Life*, a 1950s television show in which celebrities were surprised by family and friends from their past

home • ly (hōmʹ lē) *adj.*, simple; plain

it without their help. I have seen these programs.

Sometimes I dream a dream in which Dee and I are suddenly brought together on a TV program of this sort. Out of a dark and soft-seated limousine I am <u>ushered</u> into a bright room filled with many people. There I meet a smiling, gray, sporty man like Johnny Carson[2] who shakes my hand and tells me what a fine girl I have. Then we are on the stage and Dee is embracing me with tears in her eyes. She pins on my dress a large orchid, even though she has told me once that she thinks orchids are tacky flowers.

In real life I am a large, big-boned woman with rough, man-working hands. In the winter I wear flannel nightgowns to bed and overalls during the day. I can kill and clean a hog as mercilessly as a man. My fat keeps me hot in zero weather. I can work outside all day, breaking ice to get water for washing; I can eat pork liver cooked over the open fire minutes after it comes steaming from the hog. One winter I knocked a bull calf straight in the brain between the eyes with a sledge hammer and had the meat hung up to chill before nightfall. But of course all this does not show on television. I am the way my daughter would want me to be: a hundred pounds lighter, my skin like an uncooked barley pancake. My hair glistens in the hot bright lights. Johnny Carson has much to do to keep up with my quick and witty tongue.

But that is a mistake. I know even before I wake up. Who ever knew a Johnson with a quick tongue? Who can even imagine me looking a strange white man in the eye? It seems to me I have talked to them always with one foot raised in flight, with my head turned in whichever way is farthest from them. Dee,

though. She would always look anyone in the eye. Hesitation was no part of her nature.

"How do I look, Mama?" Maggie says, showing just enough of her thin body enveloped in pink skirt and red blouse for me to know she's there, almost hidden by the door.

"Come out into the yard," I say.

Have you ever seen a lame animal, perhaps a dog run over by some careless person rich enough to own a car, sidle up to someone who is ignorant enough to be kind to him? That is the way my Maggie walks. She has been like this, chin on chest, eyes on ground, feet in shuffle, ever since the fire that burned the other house to the ground.

Dee is lighter than Maggie, with nicer hair and a fuller figure. She's a woman now, though sometimes I forget. How long ago was it that the other house burned? Ten, twelve years? Sometimes I can still hear the flames and feel Maggie's arms sticking to me, her hair smoking and her dress falling off her in little black papery flakes. Her eyes seemed stretched open, blazed open by the flames reflected in them. And Dee. I see her standing off under the sweet gum tree she used to dig gum out of; a look of concentration on her face as she watched the last dingy gray board of the house fall in toward the red-hot brick chimney. Why don't you do a dance around the ashes? I'd wanted to ask her. She had hated the house that much.

I used to think she hated Maggie, too. But that was before we raised the money, the church and me, to send her to Augusta[3] to school. She used to read to us without pity; forcing words, lies, other folks' habits, whole lives upon us two, sitting trapped and ignorant underneath her voice. She washed us in a river of make-believe, burned us with a lot of knowledge we didn't necessarily need to know.

---

2. **Johnny Carson.** Former host of *The Tonight Show*
3. **Augusta.** City in Georgia where Paine College is located

---

ush • er (u´ shər) *v.,* escort; conduct

side[5] in '49. Cows are soothing and slow and don't bother you, unless you try to milk them the wrong way.

I have deliberately turned my back on the house. It is three rooms, just like the one that burned, except the roof is tin; they don't make shingle roofs any more. There are no real windows, just some holes cut in the sides, like the portholes in a ship, but not round and not square, with rawhide holding the shutters up on the outside. This house is in a pasture, too, like the other one. No doubt when Dee sees it she will want to tear it down. She wrote me once that no matter where we "choose" to live, she will manage to come see us. But she will never bring her friends. Maggie and I thought about this and Maggie asked me, "Mama, when did Dee ever *have* any friends?"

She had a few. <u>Furtive</u> boys in pink shirts hanging about on washday after school. Nervous girls who never laughed. Impressed with her they worshiped the well-turned phrase, the cute shape, the <u>scalding</u> humor that erupted like bubbles in lye.[6] She read to them.

When she was courting Jimmy T she didn't have much time to pay to us, but turned all her faultfinding power on him. He *flew* to marry a cheap city girl from a family of ignorant flashy people. She hardly had time to <u>recompose</u> herself.

Pressed us to her with the serious way she read, to shove us away at just the moment, like dimwits, we seemed about to understand.

Dee wanted nice things. A yellow organdy[4] dress to wear to her graduation from high school; black pumps to match a green suit she'd made from an old suit somebody gave me. She was determined to stare down any disaster in her efforts. Her eyelids would not flicker for minutes at a time. Often I fought off the temptation to shake her. At sixteen she had a style of her own: and knew what style was.

I never had an education myself. After second grade the school was closed down. Don't ask me why: in 1927 colored asked fewer questions than they do now. Sometimes Maggie reads to me. She stumbles along good-naturedly but can't see well. She knows she is not bright. Like good looks and money, quickness passed her by. She will marry John Thomas (who has mossy teeth in an earnest face) and then I'll be free to sit here and I guess just sing church songs to myself. Although I never was a good singer. Never could carry a tune. I was always better at a man's job. I used to love to milk till I was hooked in the

---

4. **organdy.** Sheer cotton fabric
5. **hooked in the side.** Kicked by a cow
6. **lye.** Substance used to make soap

fur • tive (fur′ tiv) *adj.,* sneaky; stealthy
scald • ing (skôl′ diŋ) *adj.,* unpleasantly severe
re • com • pose (rē′ kəm pōz′) *v.,* restore calmness of mind

When she comes I will meet—but there they are!

Maggie attempts to make a dash for the house, in her shuffling way, but I stay her with my hand. "Come back here," I say. And she stops and tries to dig a well in the sand with her toe.

It is hard to see them clearly through the strong sun. But even the first glimpse of leg out of the car tells me it is Dee. Her feet were always neat-looking, as if God himself had shaped them with a certain style. From the other side of the car comes a short, stocky man. Hair is all over his head a foot long and hanging from his chin like a kinky mule tail. I hear Maggie suck in her breath. "Uhnnnh," is what it sounds like. Like when you see the wriggling end of a snake just in front of your foot on the road. "Uhnnnh."

Dee next. A dress down to the ground, in this hot weather. A dress so loud it hurts my eyes. There are yellows and oranges enough to throw back the light of the sun. I feel my whole face warming from the heat waves it throws out. Earrings gold, too, and hanging down to her shoulders. Bracelets dangling and making noises when she moves her arm up to shake the folds of the dress out of her armpits. The dress is loose and flows, and as she walks closer, I like it. I hear Maggie go "Uhnnnh" again. It is her sister's hair. It stands straight up like the wool on a sheep. It is black as night and around the edges are two long pigtails that rope about like small lizards disappearing behind her ears.

"Wa-su-zo-Tean-o!"[7] she says, coming in in that gliding way the dress makes her move. The short stocky fellow with the hair to his navel is all grinning and he follows up with "Asalamalakim,[8] my mother and sister!" He moves to hug Maggie but she falls back, right up against the back of my chair. I feel her trembling there and when I look up I see the perspiration falling off her chin.

"Don't get up," says Dee. Since I am stout it takes something of a push. You can see me trying to move a second or two before I make

it. She turns, showing white heels through her sandals, and goes back to the car. Out she peeks next with a Polaroid. She stoops down quickly and lines up picture after picture of me sitting there in front of the house with Maggie cowering behind me. She never takes a shot without making sure the house is included. When a cow comes nibbling around the edge of the yard she snaps it and me and Maggie *and* the house. Then she puts the Polaroid in the back seat of the car, and comes up and kisses me on the forehead.

Meanwhile Asalamalakim is going through motions with Maggie's hand. Maggie's hand is as limp as a fish, and probably as cold, despite the sweat, and she keeps trying to pull it back. It looks like Asalamalakim wants to shake hands but wants to do it fancy. Or maybe he don't know how people shake hands. Anyhow, he soon gives up on Maggie.

"Well," I say. "Dee."

"No, Mama," she says. "Not 'Dee,' Wangero Leewanika Kemanjo!"

"What happened to 'Dee'?" I wanted to know.

"She's dead," Wangero said. "I couldn't bear it any longer, being named after the people who oppress me."

"You know as well as me you was named after your aunt Dicie," I said. Dicie is my sister. She named Dee. We called her "Big Dee" after Dee was born.

"But who was she named after?" asked Wangero.

"I guess after Grandma Dee," I said.

"And who was *she* named after?" asked Wangero.

"Her mother," I said, and saw Wangero was getting tired. "That's about as far back as I can trace it," I said. Though, in fact, I probably could have carried it back beyond the Civil War through the branches.

---

7. **Wa-su-zo-Tean-o.** Greeting in an African dialect
8. **Asalamalakim.** Muslim greeting

"Well," said Asalamalakim, "there you are."

"Uhnnnh," I heard Maggie say.

"There I was not," I said, "before 'Dicie' cropped up in our family, so why should I try to trace it that far back?"

He just stood there grinning, looking down on me like somebody inspecting a Model A car.[9] Every once in a while he and Wangero sent eye signals over my head.

"How do you pronounce this name?" I asked.

"You don't have to call me by it if you don't want to," said Wangero.

"Why shouldn't I?" I asked. "If that's what you want us to call you, we'll call you."

"I know it might sound awkward at first," said Wangero.

"I'll get used to it," I said. "Ream it out again."

Well, soon we got the name out of the way. Asalamalakim had a name twice as long and three times as hard. After I tripped over it two or three times he told me to just call him Hakim-a-barber. I wanted to ask him was he a barber, but I didn't really think he was so I didn't ask.

"You must belong to those beef-cattle peoples down the road," I said. They said "Asalamalakim" when they met you, too, but they didn't shake hands. Always too busy: feeding the cattle, fixing the fences, putting up salt-lick shelters,[10] throwing down hay. When the white folks poisoned some of the herd the men stayed up all night with rifles in their hands. I walked a mile and a half just to see the sight.

Hakim-a-barber said, "I accept some of their doctrines, but farming and raising cattle is not my style." (They didn't tell me, and I didn't ask, whether Wangero (Dee) had really gone and married him.)

We sat down to eat and right away he said he didn't eat collards[11] and pork was unclean. Wangero, though, went on through the chitlins and corn bread, the greens and everything else. She talked a blue streak over the sweet potatoes. Everything delighted her. Even the fact that we still used the benches her daddy made for the table when we couldn't afford to buy chairs.

"Oh, Mama!" she cried. Then turned to Hakim-a-barber. "I never knew how lovely these benches are. You can feel the rump prints," she said, running her hands underneath her and along the bench. Then she gave a sigh and her hand closed over Grandma Dee's butter dish. "That's it!" she said. "I knew there was something I wanted to ask you if I could

---

9. **Model A car.** One of the first American cars
10. **salt-lick shelters.** Structures that protect cows from the heat of the sun and contain blocks of salt for them to lick
11. **collards.** Leafy green vegetables

doc • trine (däk´ trən) *n.*, teaching; belief

Lone Star Quilt, 1930.
Private collection.

have." She jumped up from the table and went over in the corner where the churn stood, the milk in it clabber[12] by now. She looked at the churn and looked at it.

"This churn top is what I need," she said. "Didn't Uncle Buddy whittle it out of a tree you all used to have?"

"Yes," I said.

"Uh huh," she said happily. "And I want the dasher, too."

"Uncle Buddy whittle that, too?" asked the barber.

Dee (Wangero) looked up at me.

"Aunt Dee's first husband whittled the dash," said Maggie so low you almost couldn't hear her. "His name was Henry, but they called him Stash."

"Maggie's brain is like an elephant's," Wangero said, laughing. "I can use the churn top as a centerpiece for the <u>alcove</u> table," she said, sliding a plate over the churn, "and I'll

think of something artistic to do with the dasher."

When she finished wrapping the dasher the handle stuck out. I took it for a moment in my hands. You didn't even have to look close to see where hands pushing the dasher up and down to make butter had left a kind of sink in the wood. In fact, there were a lot of small sinks; you could see where thumbs and fingers had sunk into the wood. It was beautiful light yellow wood, from a tree that grew in the yard where Big Dee and Stash had lived.

After dinner Dee (Wangero) went to the trunk at the foot of my bed and started <u>rifling</u> through it. Maggie hung back in the kitchen over the dishpan. Out came Wangero with two

---

12. **clabber.** Sour milk

al • cove (al′ kōv′) *n.*, relating to a section or an area of a room that is recessed or set back
ri • fle (rī′ fəl) *v.*, shuffle; move quickly through

quilts. They had been pieced by Grandma Dee and then Big Dee and me had hung them on the quilt frames on the front porch and quilted them. One was in the Lone Star pattern. The other was Walk Around the Mountain. In both of them were scraps of dresses Grandma Dee had worn fifty and more years ago. Bits and pieces of Grandpa Jarrell's Paisley shirts. And one teeny faded blue piece, about the size of a penny matchbox, that was from Great Grandpa Ezra's uniform that he wore in the Civil War.

"Mama," Wangero said sweet as a bird. "Can I have these old quilts?"

I heard something fall in the kitchen, and a minute later the kitchen door slammed.

"Why don't you take one or two of the others?" I asked. "These old things was just done by me and Big Dee from some tops your grandma pieced before she died."

"No," said Wangero. "I don't want those. They are stitched around the borders by machine."

"That'll make them last better," I said.

"That's not the point," said Wangero. "These are all pieces of dresses Grandma used to wear. She did all this stitching by hand. Imagine!" She held the quilts securely in her arms, stroking them.

"Some of the pieces, like those lavender ones, come from old clothes her mother handed down to her," I said, moving up to touch the quilts. Dee (Wangero) moved back just enough so that I couldn't reach the quilts. They already belonged to her.

"Imagine!" she breathed again, clutching them closely to her bosom.

"The truth is," I said, "I promised to give them quilts to Maggie, for when she marries John Thomas."

She gasped like a bee had stung her.

"Maggie can't appreciate these quilts!" she said. "She'd probably be backward enough to put them to everyday use."

"I reckon she would," I said. "God knows I been saving 'em for long enough with nobody using 'em. I hope she will!" I didn't want to bring up how I had offered Dee (Wangero) a quilt when she went away to college. Then she had told me they were old-fashioned, out of style.

"But they're *priceless!*" she was saying now, furiously; for she has a temper. "Maggie would put them on the bed and in five years they'd be in rags. Less than that!"

"She can always make some more," I said. "Maggie knows how to quilt."

Dee (Wangero) looked at me with hatred. "You just will not understand. The point is these quilts, *these* quilts!"

"Well," I said, stumped. "What would *you* do with them?"

"Hang them," she said. As if that was the only thing you *could* do with quilts.

Maggie by now was standing in the door. I could almost hear the sound her feet made as they scraped over each other.

"She can have them, Mama," she said, like somebody used to never winning anything, or having anything reserved for her. "I can 'member Grandma Dee without the quilts."

I looked at her hard. She had filled her bottom lip with checkerberry snuff and it gave her face a kind of dopey, hangdog look. It was Grandma Dee and Big Dee who taught her how to quilt herself. She stood there with her scarred hands hidden in the folds of her skirt. She looked at her sister with something like fear but she wasn't mad at her. This was Maggie's portion. This was the way she knew God to work.

When I looked at her like that something hit me in the top of my head and ran down to the soles of my feet. Just like when I'm in church and the spirit of God touches me and I get happy and shout. I did something I never had done before: hugged Maggie to me, then dragged her on into the room, snatched the quilts out of Miss Wangero's hands and dumped them into Maggie's lap. Maggie just sat there on my bed with her mouth open.

"Take one or two of the others," I said to Dee.

But she turned without a word and went out to Hakim-a-barber.

"You just don't understand," she said, as Maggie and I came out to the car.

"What don't I understand?" I wanted to know.

"Your heritage," she said. And then she turned to Maggie, kissed her, and said, "You ought to try to make something of yourself, too, Maggie. It's really a new day for us. But from the way you and Mama still live you'd never know it."

She put on some sunglasses that hid everything above the tip of her nose and her chin. Maggie smiled; maybe at the sunglasses. But a real smile, not scared. After we watched the car dust settle I asked Maggie to bring me a dip of snuff. And then the two of us sat there just enjoying, until it was time to go in the house and go to bed. ❖

MIRRORS & WINDOWS

What role does your family, culture, and geographical location play in shaping who you are? Why do people sometimes want to change or avoid being influenced by these things?

AFTER READING

REFER TO TEXT ▶ ▶ ▶ ▶	▶ REASON WITH TEXT	
1a. Recall the comparison the narrator makes when Maggie first comes out into the yard.	1b. Contrast Maggie and Dee in personality and appearance.	**Understand** **Find meaning**
2a. Write Dee's new name. Why did she change her name?	2b. List other reasons somebody might have for changing his or her name. Predict how other people would react to a name change like Dee's.	**Apply** **Use information**
3a. List things Wangero appreciates in the house. How had she felt about these things before?	3b. Contrast Wangero's ideas about her heritage to those of Maggie and her mother.	**Analyze** **Take things apart**
4a. Quote what Wangero says Maggie would do with the quilts and what she would do with the quilts.	4b. Assess who values the quilts more, Wangero or Maggie. Explain your response.	**Evaluate** **Make judgments**
5a. What is significant about the pieces of the quilts Wangero wants?	5b. Discuss what pieces of fabric or what scenes and symbols a quilt significant to your life might contain.	**Create** **Bring ideas together**

ANALYZE LITERATURE: Theme and Metaphor

What is the theme of "Everyday Use"? How do the quilts serve as a metaphor that helps illustrate that theme? What other metaphors are present in the story?

EXTEND THE TEXT

Writing Options

Creative Writing Consider the characters of Dee and Maggie. How are they alike? How are they different? How does each of them understand her heritage? Write two separate **journal entries** — one from Dee's point of view and one from Maggie's point of view — giving each character's reaction to the events of the day. In your journal entries, try to accurately represent the personalities and ideas of the characters. Share your journal entries with the class to get an idea of the different ways people understand Dee and Maggie.

Expository Writing Imagine that a magazine that focuses on celebrating heritage is going to republish "Everyday Use." Write a three-paragraph **introduction** that focuses on the theme of the story. In your introduction, examine how Walker develops the theme. Use evidence from the text, including quotations, to support your ideas. You can use your graphic organizer from prereading and your response to the Analyze Literature questions as a starting points.

Lifelong Learning

Create a Museum Exhibit Many people today learn about the past by visiting museums. Choose a time period of American history in which you are interested. Within that time period, choose one specific aspect of life and do research about it. For example, you might choose to research how women were involved in the Civil War or how people in the Midwest survived the Great Depression. As part of your research, see if you can find historical documents such as letters, diaries, or old newspaper articles. A good place to look for these documents is the Library of Congress website. Use your research to create a display of pictures or descriptions of artifacts and other items you would include in a museum exhibit. Create captions for the artifacts describing what they are and their significance to the time period. Share your exhibit with your class.

Media Literacy

Stage a Talk Show The mother in "Everyday Use" dreams about appearing on a television talk show. As a class, stage a talk show in which Dee, Maggie, and the mother discuss the problem of who should get the quilts. Have one student play the host and moderate the discussion, and other students play Dee, Maggie, and the mother. By the end of your show, the position of each family member should be clear, whether or not the problem is actually resolved. Consider allowing the rest of the class, as the audience, to vote on who gets the quilts.

 Go to **www.mirrorsandwindows.com** for more.

READING ASSESSMENT

1. Which is not a way that Dee shows her new sense of heritage?
    - A. in her newfound diet
    - B. by changing her name
    - C. in using new greetings
    - D. in her new appreciation for handcrafted items
    - E. by changing the way she dresses

2. How does the name "Dee" differ for the narrator and for Dee (Wangero)?
    - A. To the narrator, it is just a name; to Wangero, it is a reminder of her past.
    - B. It reminds the narrator of the kind of child Dee was; it reminds Wangero of a life of poverty.
    - C. It makes the narrator think back to the time of slavery, but it makes Wangero think of a new day.
    - D. The narrator thinks of her mother, whereas Wangero thinks it sounds old-fashioned.
    - E. To the narrator, it is a family name, whereas Wangero associates it with oppression.

3. Why does Maggie cherish the quilts?
    - A. She sees them as works of art.
    - B. They have kept her warm.
    - C. They remind her of her grandmother.
    - D. She knows they are part of her heritage.
    - E. She thinks they will be worth a lot of money.

4. Which of the following words means "to escort or conduct"?
    - A. scald
    - B. recompose
    - C. rifle
    - D. usher
    - E. All of the above

5. Wangero says to her mother, "You just don't understand." When her mother asks what she doesn't understand, Wangero says, "Your heritage." Do you think Wangero is correct in her assessment of her mother's understanding? Explain your answer with evidence from the story.

THE LEAP
A Short Story by Louise Erdrich

BEFORE READING

BUILD BACKGROUND

Literary Context Anna Avalon is a former trapeze artist. Her daughter is the narrator of **"The Leap."** The story portrays a complex mother/daughter relationship and how it changes over the years. The story reminds us that love never lessens with age and that memories of events often remain as vivid as the day on which they happened.

"The Leap" has appeared in various publications: first in *Harper's Magazine;* later in a 1994 anthology, *In Praise of Mothers;* and finally, in a significantly altered form, in Louise Erdrich's novel *Tales of Burning Love.*

Reader's Context When has somebody protected you or saved you from getting hurt? If somebody in your family were in danger, what would you do to help the person? What kinds of risks would you take?

ANALYZE LITERATURE: Theme and Anecdote

A **theme** is a central message or perception about life that is conveyed through a literary work. An **anecdote** is a short account of an interesting, amusing, or biographical incident. In "The Leap," Erdrich presents several anecdotes that work together to develop a theme.

SET PURPOSE

Consider the title and the art throughout the story and how a leap might be related to the theme of the story. Predict who makes a leap, why, and what the consequences are. Then, as you read, adjust your prediction as you learn more.

MEET THE AUTHOR

Louise Erdrich (b. 1954) is the mother of six children. Being a mother has deepened her art, she says. "I find myself emotionally engaged in ways I wouldn't have been otherwise. I wouldn't understand certain things that I'm starting to get now."

Erdrich's unique heritage has shaped her writing, too. Like many of the characters in her books, she is of mixed Native American descent: Her mother is French Chippewa (Ojibwa) and her father is German American. While Erdrich was growing up in North Dakota, her parents worked as teachers on a reservation. Today, she is a member of the Turtle Mountain Band of Chippewa. Some of Erdrich's novels include *The Beet Queen, Love Medicine, Tracks, Four Souls,* and *The Painted Drum.*

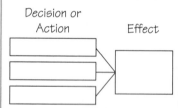

USE READING SKILLS

Cause and Effect When you evaluate cause and effect, you look for a logical relationship between a cause or causes and one or more effects. It's like a train of dominoes: When the first domino falls, it sets in motion all the other dominoes.

In "The Leap," the narrator points out several times how one decision or action leads to another. As you read the story, use a graphic organizer like the one below. Write down different decisions or actions made by the narrator's mother and the effect they have on the narrator and other people.

Decision or
Action   Effect

PREVIEW VOCABULARY

Use the context clues in the sentences below to figure out the meanings of the underlined words from the selection.

1. Many artists make <u>replicas</u> of their works so that more than one copy exists.
2. The opening <u>vignette</u> of the movie was a shot of a couple seated in a park.
3. The marble <u>edifice</u> with the majestic dome is the state capitol building.
4. Mike struggled to <u>extricate</u> himself from the ties of the neighborhood gang.
5. Kim's shoes were a size too small and painfully <u>constricting</u>.

The Acrobat, c. 1900s.
Marc Chagall. Musée d'Art
Moderne de la Ville de Paris,
Paris, France.

THE LEAP

A Short Story by
Louise Erdrich

My mother once said that I'd be amazed at how many things a person can do within the act of falling.

M y mother is the surviving half of a blindfold trapeze act, not a fact I think about much even now that she is sightless, the result of encroaching and stubborn cataracts.[1] She walks slowly through her house here in New Hampshire, lightly touching her way along walls and running her hands over knickknacks, books, the drift of a grown child's belongings and castoffs. She has never upset an object or as much as brushed a magazine onto the floor. She has never lost her balance or bumped into a closet door left carelessly open.

It has occurred to me that the catlike precision of her movements in old age might be the result of her early training, but she shows so little of the drama or flair one might expect from a performer that I tend to forget the Flying Avalons. She has kept no sequined costume, no photographs, no fliers or posters from that part of her youth. I would, in fact, tend to think that all memory of double somersaults and heart-stopping catches had left her arms and legs were it not for the fact that sometimes, as I sit sewing in the room of the rebuilt house in which I slept as a child, I hear the crackle, catch a whiff of smoke from the stove downstairs, and suddenly the room goes dark, the stitches burn beneath my fingers, and I am sewing with a needle of hot silver, a thread of fire.

I owe her my existence three times. The first was when she saved herself. In the town square a <u>replica</u> tent pole, cracked and splintered, now stands cast in concrete. It commemorates the disaster that put our town smack on the front page of the Boston and New York tabloids.[2] It is from those old newspapers, now historical records, that I get my information. Not from my mother, Anna of the Flying Avalons, nor from any of her

---

1. **cataracts.** Clouding of the lenses of the eyes or their membranes that prevents the passage of light
2. **tabloids.** Small newspapers often containing sensationalized material and many photographs

rep • li • ca (re′ pli kə) *n.,* an exact copy

in-laws, nor certainly from the other half of her particular act, Harold Avalon, her first husband. In one news account it says, "The day was mildly overcast, but nothing in the air or temperature gave any hint of the sudden force with which the deadly gale[3] would strike."

I have lived in the West, where you can see the weather coming for miles, and it is true that out here we are at something of a disadvantage. When extremes of temperature collide, a hot and cold front, winds generate instantaneously behind a hill and crash upon you without warning. That, I think, was the likely situation on that day in June. People probably commented on the pleasant air, grateful that no hot sun beat upon the striped tent that stretched over the entire center green. They bought their tickets and surrendered them in anticipation. They sat. They ate carmelized popcorn and roasted peanuts. There was time, before the storm, for three acts. The White Arabians of Ali-Khazar rose on their hind legs and waltzed. The Mysterious Bernie folded himself into a painted cracker tin,[4] and the Lady of the Mists made herself appear and disappear in surprising places. As the clouds gathered outside, unnoticed, the ringmaster cracked his whip, shouted his introduction, and pointed to the ceiling of the tent, where the Flying Avalons were perched.

They loved to drop gracefully from nowhere, like two sparkling birds, and blow kisses as they threw off their plumed helmets and high-collared capes. They laughed and flirted openly as they beat their way up again on the trapeze bars. In the final vignette of their act, they actually would kiss in midair, pausing, almost hovering as they swooped past one another. On the ground, between bows, Harry Avalon would skip quickly to the front rows and point out the smear of my mother's lipstick, just off the edge of his mouth. They made a romantic pair all right, especially in the blindfold sequence.

That afternoon, as the anticipation increased, as Mr. and Mrs. Avalon tied sparkling strips of cloth onto each other's face and as they puckered their lips in mock kisses, lips destined "never again to meet," as one long breathless article put it, the wind rose, miles off, wrapped itself into a cone, and howled. There came a rumble of electrical energy, drowned out by the sudden roll of drums. One detail not mentioned by the press, perhaps unknown—Anna was pregnant at the time, seven months and hardly showing, her stomach muscles were that strong. It seems incredible that she would work high above the ground when any fall could be so dangerous, but the explanation—I know from watching her go blind—is that my mother lives comfortably in extreme elements. She is one with the constant dark now, just as the air was her home, familiar to her, safe, before the storm that afternoon.

From opposite ends of the tent they waved, blind and smiling, to the crowd below. The ringmaster removed his hat and called for silence, so that the two above could concentrate. They rubbed their hands in chalky powder, then Harry launched himself and swung, once, twice, in huge calibrated[5] beats across space. He hung from his knees and on the third swing stretched wide his arms, held his hands out to receive his pregnant wife as she dove from her shining bar.

It was while the two were in midair, their hands about to meet, that lightning struck the main pole and sizzled down the guy wires,[6] filling the air with a blue radiance that Harry Avalon must certainly have seen through the cloth of his blindfold as the tent buckled and

---

3. **gale.** A strong wind that ranges from thirty-two to sixty-three miles per hour
4. **cracker tin.** Cracker box
5. **calibrated.** Precisely adjusted or measured
6. **guy wires.** Wires attached to the tent pole and used as reinforcement or guides for the performers

---

vig • nette (vin yet´) *n.*, a brief scene

the <u>edifice</u> toppled him forward, the swing continuing and not returning in its sweep, and Harry going down, down into the crowd with his last thought, perhaps, just a prickle of surprise at his empty hands.

My mother once said that I'd be amazed at how many things a person can do within the act of falling. Perhaps, at the time, she was teaching me to dive off a board at the town pool, for I associate the idea with midair somersaults. But I also think she meant that even in that awful doomed second one could think, for she certainly did. When her hands did not meet her husband's, my mother tore her blindfold away. As he swept past her on the wrong side, she could have grasped his ankle, the toe-end of his tights, and gone down clutching him. Instead, she changed direction. Her body twisted toward a heavy wire and she managed to hang on to the braided metal, still hot from the lightning strike. Her palms were burned so terribly that once healed they bore no lines, only the blank scar tissue of a quieter future. She was lowered, gently, to the sawdust ring just underneath the dome of the canvas roof, which did not entirely settle but was held up on one end and jabbed through, torn, and still on fire in places from the giant spark, though rain and men's jackets soon put that out.

Three people died, but except for her hands my mother was not seriously harmed until an overeager rescuer broke her arm in <u>extri-cating</u> her and also, in the process, collapsed a portion of the tent bearing a huge buckle that knocked her unconscious. She was taken to the town hospital, and there she must have hemor-rhaged,[7] for they kept her, confined to her bed, a month and a half before her baby was born without life. Harry Avalon had wanted to be buried in the circus cemetery next to the original Avalon, his uncle, so she sent him back with his brothers. The child, however, is buried around the corner, beyond this house and just down the highway. Sometimes I used to walk there just to sit. She was a girl, but I rarely thought of her as a sister or even as a separate person really. I suppose you could call it the <u>egocentrism</u> of a child, of all young children, but I considered her a less finished version of myself.

When the snow falls, throwing shadows among the stones, I can easily pick hers out from the road, for it is bigger than the others and in the shape of a lamb at rest, its legs curled beneath. The carved lamb looms larger as the years pass, though it is probably only my eyes, the vision shifting, as what is close to me

---

7. **hemorrhaged.** Suffered internal bleeding

ed • i • fice (e´ də fəs) *n.*, massive building or structure
ex • tri • cate (ek´ strə kāt') *v.*, free from entanglement or difficulty
e • go • cen • trism (ē' gō sen´ tri' zəm) *n.*, self-centeredness

blurs and distances sharpen. In odd moments, I think it is the edge drawing near, the edge of everything, the unseen horizon we do not really speak of in the eastern woods. And it also seems to me, although this is probably an idle fantasy, that the statue is growing more sharply etched, as if, instead of weathering itself into a <u>porous</u> mass, it is hardening on the hillside with each snowfall, perfecting itself.

It was during her confinement in the hospital that my mother met my father. He was called in to look at the set of her arm, which was complicated. He stayed, sitting at her bedside, for he was something of an armchair traveler and had spent his war quietly, at an air force training grounds, where he became a specialist in arms and legs broken during parachute training exercises. Anna Avalon had been to many of the places he longed to visit— Venice, Rome, Mexico, all through France and Spain. She had no family of her own and was taken in by the Avalons, trained to perform from a very young age. They toured Europe before the war, then based themselves in New York. She was illiterate.

It was in the hospital that she finally learned to read and write, as a way of overcoming the boredom and depression of those weeks, and it was my father who insisted on teaching her. In return for stories of her adventures, he graded her first exercises. He bought her her first book, and over her bold letters, which the pale guides of the penmanship pads could not contain, they fell in love.

I wonder if my father calculated the exchange he offered: one form of flight for another. For after that, and for as long as I can remember, my mother has never been without a book. Until now, that is, and it remains the greatest difficulty of her blindness. Since my father's recent death, there is no one to read to her, which is why I returned, in fact, from my failed life where the land is flat. I came home to read to my mother, to read out loud, to read long into the dark if I must, to read all night.

Once my father and mother married, they moved onto the old farm he had inherited but didn't care much for. Though he'd been thinking of moving to a larger city, he settled down and broadened his practice in this valley. It still seems odd to me, when they could have gone anywhere else, that they chose to stay in the town where the disaster had occurred, and which my father in the first place had found so <u>constricting</u>. It was my mother who insisted upon it, after her child did not survive. And then, too, she loved the sagging farmhouse with its scrap of what was left of a vast acreage of woods and hidden hay fields that stretched to the game park.

I owe my existence, the second time then, to the two of them and the hospital that brought them together. That is the debt we take for granted since none of us asks for life. It is only once we have it that we hang on so dearly.

I was seven the year the house caught fire, probably from standing ash. It can rekindle,[8] and my father, forgetful around the house and perpetually exhausted from night hours on call, often emptied what he thought were ashes from cold stoves into wooden or cardboard containers. The fire could have started from a flaming box, or perhaps a buildup of

---

8. **rekindle.** To catch fire again

> **por • ous** (pôr´ əs) *adj.,* having pores; allowing liquids to absorb or pass through itself
> **con • strict • ing** (kən strict´ iŋ) *adj.,* limiting; compressing

creosote[9] inside the chimney was the <u>culprit</u>. It started right around the stove, and the heart of the house was gutted. The babysitter, fallen asleep in my father's den on the first floor, woke to find the stairway to my upstairs room cut off by flames. She used the phone, then ran outside to stand beneath my window.

When my parents arrived, the two volunteers had drawn water from the fire pond and were spraying the outside of the house, preparing to go inside after me, not knowing at the time that there was only one staircase and that it was lost.

On the other side of the house, the superannuated[10] extension ladder broke in half. Perhaps the clatter of it falling against the walls woke me, for I'd been asleep up to that point.

As soon as I awakened, in the small room that I now use for sewing, I smelled the smoke. I followed things by the letter then, was good at memorizing instructions, and so I did exactly what was taught in the second-grade home fire drill. I got up, I touched the back of my door before opening it. Finding it hot, I left it closed and stuffed my rolled-up rug beneath the crack. I did not hide under my bed or crawl into my closet. I put on my flannel robe, and then I sat down to wait.

Outside, my mother stood below my dark window and saw clearly that there was no rescue. Flames had pierced one side wall, and the glare of the fire lighted the massive limbs and trunk of the vigorous old elm that had probably been planted the year the house was built, a hundred years ago at least. No leaf touched the wall, and just one thin branch scraped the roof. From below, it looked as though even a squirrel would have had trouble jumping from the tree onto the house, for the breadth of that small branch was no bigger than my mother's wrist.

Standing there, beside Father, who was preparing to rush back around to the front of the house, my mother asked him to unzip her dress. When he wouldn't be bothered, she made him understand. He couldn't make his hands work, so she finally tore it off and stood there in her pearls and stockings. She directed one of the men to lean the broken half of the extension ladder up against the trunk of the tree. In surprise, he complied. She ascended. She vanished. Then she could be seen among the leafless branches of late November as she made her way up and, along her stomach, inched the length of a bough that curved above the branch that brushed the roof.

Once there, swaying, she stood and balanced. There were plenty of people in the crowd and many who still remember, or think they do, my mother's leap through the ice-dark air toward that thinnest extension, and how she broke the branch falling so that it cracked in her hands, cracked louder than the flames as she vaulted with it toward the edge of the roof, and how it hurtled down end over end without her, and their eyes went up, again, to see where she had flown.

I didn't see her leap through air, only heard the sudden thump and looked out my window. She was hanging by the backs of her heels from the new gutter we had put in that year, and she was smiling. I was not surprised to see her, she was so matter-of-fact. She tapped on the window. I remember how she did it, too. It was the friendliest tap, a bit <u>tentative</u>, as if she was afraid she had arrived too early at a friend's house. Then she gestured at the latch, and when I opened the window she told me to raise it wide and prop it up with the stick so it wouldn't crush her fingers. She swung down, caught the ledge, and crawled through the opening. Once she was in my room, I realized she had on only underclothing, a bra of the heavy stitched cotton women used to wear and

---

9. **creosote.** Flammable tar deposited from wood smoke on chimney walls

10. **superannuated.** Very old; ready for retirement

---

cul • prit (kul′ prət) *n.,* one guilty of a crime; the cause of a problem

ten • ta • tive (ten′ tə tiv) *adj.,* hesitant; uncertain

step-in, lace-trimmed drawers. I remember feeling light-headed, of course, terribly relieved, and then embarrassed for her to be seen by the crowd undressed.

I was still embarrassed as we flew out the window, toward earth, me in her lap, her toes pointed as we skimmed toward the painted target of the fire fighter's net.

I know that she's right. I knew it even then. As you fall there is time to think. Curled as I was, against her stomach, I was not startled by the cries of the crowd or the <u>looming</u> faces. The wind roared and beat its hot breath at our back, the flames whistled. I slowly wondered what would happen if we missed the circle or bounced out of it. Then I wrapped my hands around my mother's hands. I felt the brush of her lips and heard the beat of her heart in my ears, loud as thunder, long as the roll of drums. ❖

loom • ing (lüm´ iŋ) *adj.*, appearing exaggeratedly large or distorted

---

MIRRORS & WINDOWS
What lessons can daughters learn from their mothers? What causes conflict between mothers and daughters?

REFER TO TEXT ▶ ▶ ▶ ▶	▶ **REASON WITH TEXT**	
1a. The narrator says of her mother, "I owe her my existence three times." List how the mother saved her daughter three times.	**1b.** Compare the first incident and the third incident.	**Understand** **Find meaning**
2a. The narrator says that her mother "lives comfortably in extreme elements." Cite evidence to support this statement.	**2b.** Apply the skill of living comfortably in extreme elements to other situations. In what situations might this skill be useful?	**Apply** **Use information**
3a. Quote what the narrator says she has returned from to help her mother.	**3b.** Compare the narrator to Anna Avalon. How does the narrator think she measures up?	**Analyze** **Take things apart**
4a. Indicate how risky each of the three acts of saving is.	**4b.** Judge whether Anna is courageous. Explain your response.	**Evaluate** **Make judgments**
5a. Read the Literature Connection "Her Flying Trapeze." What words does Nikki Giovanni use to describe the woman on her flying trapeze?	**5b.** Combine what you know about being a trapeze artist from "The Leap" and from "Her Flying Trapeze." What do you imagine it would be like to be a trapeze artist? Is it appealing to you? Why?	**Create** **Bring ideas together**

ANALYZE LITERATURE: Theme and Anecdote

Describe each of the anecdotes that appear in the story. What has Anna done for her daughter? What has the narrator done for her mother? What has each learned from the other? How do these things help you understand the theme of the story?

Literature
CONNECTION

Nikki Giovanni (b. 1943) is the pen name of Yolande Cornelia Giovanni, a poet, publisher, and educator who gained prominence in the 1960s and 1970s for her poetry and essays on racial issues and the African-American experience. Of her life and her writing, she says, "I'm not a leader. I'm not a guru. I'm just a poet looking at the world."

"Her Flying Trapeze" describes a woman who lives life her own way. Consider how this poem relates to the theme of "The Leap."

Her Flying TRAPEZE

A Poem by **Nikki Giovanni**

Some see the world through rose colored glasses
Some can't see the forest for the trees
A stitch in time will always save nine
She rides through the trees with the greatest of ease
5   Alone on her flying trapeze

Some will tell you the glass is half full
Others see it as mostly empty
An ounce of prevention is one pound of cure
She flies through the sky two tattoos on her thigh
10   Alone on her flying trapeze

Some ride the Steinway's 88
Some drive an 18 wheeler
Some feel like fools in their gasoline mules
She glides through the breeze with an absolute ease
15   Alone on her flying trapeze ❖

ALG. BARNES
-SELLS-FLOTO
and JOHN ROBINSON Combined CIRCUSES

JANET MAY
WORLD'S FOREMOST AERIAL GYMNASTE
IN THRILLING ONE-ARM PLANGES

REFER TO TEXT ▶ ▶ ▶ ▶ ▶	REASON WITH TEXT	
1a. Identify the proverbs, clichés, and "conventional wisdom" in this poem.	1b. Does the woman on the trapeze live her life by conventional wisdom? Explain.	**Understand** **Find meaning**
2a. Quote the line that is repeated several times throughout the poem.	2b. Why do you think the poet repeats this line? What ideas is she trying to convey?	**Apply** **Use information**
3a. What are the advantages and disadvantages of living life by "conventional wisdom"?	3b. How does the way you live your life compare with the way the woman in the poem lives hers?	**Create** **Bring ideas together**

TEXT ◀—TO—▶ TEXT CONNECTION

How is Anna Avalon courageous? How is the woman in "Her Flying Trapeze" courageous? Compare the themes of the two selections.

EXTEND THE TEXT

Writing Options

Creative Writing Imagine you are a historian and are interviewing Anna (as an old woman). You plan to write an article about her experiences as part of the town's history. What kinds of questions would be appropriate for this purpose? Write down questions you would ask Anna. Then, using what you know about the character, write responses to your questions. Compile a **transcript,** or written-down version, of the interview.

Expository Writing What is courage? For a magazine for teenagers, write a one-page **essay** about what courage is, based on the lives of Anna Avalon and the woman in Nikki Giovanni's poem "Her Flying Trapeze." Before you begin writing, think about the ways Anna Avalon and the woman in the poem exhibit courage. Consider how they deal with challenging situations and how they define themselves. Include quotes and paraphrases from the two texts as support for your ideas.

Media Literacy

Promote a Circus Imagine you and your group have been asked to promote the circus that is coming to town. First, identify your target audience. Then brainstorm a list of features that might appeal to that audience. Use this information to write a radio script, design flyers and signs, or come up with other ways to promote the event. Present your promotional materials to the class.

Lifelong Learning

Create a Bibliography The topic of mother-daughter relationships is common in literature. Using the Internet, locate ten works that focus on this topic and create a bibliography to serve as a summer reading list for teenagers. Include a variety of genres on your list, such as fiction, poetry, and nonfiction. For each piece of literature you list, include a brief description, or annotation, that tells a little bit of what the work is about and catches readers' interest.

 Go to **www.mirrorsandwindows.com** for more.

READING ASSESSMENT

1. What most likely motivated Anna Avalon to save her daughter from their burning house?
   A. the desire to show her trapeze skills again
   B. her love for her daughter and need to rescue her
   C. fear of heights
   D. the wish to perform for an audience
   E. a sense of destiny since she had saved her daughter twice before

2. What did Anna learn from watching her mother go blind?
   A. that her mother was not as courageous as she thought
   B. that her mother had saved her life and probably would again
   C. that her mother lived comfortably in extreme elements
   D. that her mother was more courageous than she realized
   E. that her mother had been flying in her own way through reading

3. In what way are the woman in "Her Flying Trapeze" and Anna Avalon similar?

   A. Both are always alone: the woman on her trapeze and Anna in her blindness.
   B. Both are unconventional: the woman avoiding the clichés of life and Anna unafraid to save her daughter's life, though she had retired from the circus.
   C. Both demonstrate fearlessness by flying on the trapeze, an act that would terrify many.
   D. Both are misunderstood and use the trapeze as a way to escape from the world.
   E. Both find solace in swinging up high, but both give up the ease of flight to raise their children.

4. Which of the following is a synonym for the word *extricate?*
   A. buy
   B. replicate
   C. find
   D. free
   E. apply

5. How does the narrator feel about her mother? Write a note to the mother from the narrator explaining how she feels about her and why.

GRAMMAR & STYLE

Comma usage

A comma separates words or groups of words within a sentence. Commas tell the reader to pause at certain spots in the sentence. These pauses help keep the reader from running together certain words and phrases when they should be kept apart.

Use a comma to separate items in a series. The items in a series may be words, phrases, or clauses.

EXAMPLES

words in a series: The people at the circus ate caramel corn, peanuts, and cotton candy.
phrases in a series: The narrator's mother saved her by saving herself, by marrying her father, and by rescuing her from a fire.
clauses in a series: No one knew when the storm came, why it was so severe, or what destruction occurred.

Use a comma when you combine sentences using *and, but, or, nor, yet, so,* or *for.* Place the comma before these words. Remember to use a comma only when you are joining complete sentences.

EXAMPLES

incorrect: The glare of the fire, and the heat of the flames frightened her. ("The glare of the fire" is not a complete sentence, so you would not use a comma before the *and.*)
correct: Flames had pierced one side wall, and the glare of the fire lit the massive limbs and trunk of the vigorous old elm.

Use a comma after an introductory word or phrase.

EXAMPLE

Once my father and mother married, they moved onto the old farm he had inherited but didn't care much for.

Use a comma to set off words or phrases that interrupt sentences. Use two commas if the word or phrase occurs in the middle of the sentence. Use one comma if the word or phrase comes at the beginning or at the end of a sentence.

EXAMPLE

From the opposite ends of the tent they waved, blind and smiling, to the crowd below.

Use a comma between two or more adjectives that modify the same noun.

EXAMPLE

The hot, bright, shooting flames consumed the house.

Use a comma to set off names used in direct address.

EXAMPLE

The narrator's mother, Anna Avalon, was a trapeze artist.

Use a comma to separate parts of a date. Do not use a comma between the month and the year.

EXAMPLES

The party was held on August 2, 1902.
In June 1890, she was born.

Use a comma to separate items in addresses. Do not use a comma between the state and the ZIP code.

EXAMPLE

Her favorite place to travel was Venice, Italy.

REVIEW TERMS

- **comma:** a punctuation mark used to separate words or groups of words within a sentence
- **clause:** a group of words that contains a subject and verb and that functions as one part of speech
- **phrase:** a group of words that is used as a single part of speech but that lacks a subject, verb, or both

Identify Commas

Identify the use of each comma in the following passage from "The Leap" as one of the following: combining sentences, interrupter, introductory word or phrase, or direct address.

> My mother once said that I'd be amazed at how many things a person can do within the act of falling. Perhaps, at the time, she was teaching me to dive off a board at the town pool, for I associate the idea with midair somersaults. But I also think she meant that even in that awful doomed second one could think, for she certainly did. When her hands did not meet her husband's, my mother tore her blindfold away. As he swept past her on the wrong side, she could have grasped his ankle, the toe-end of his tights, and gone down clutching him. Instead, she changed direction. He body twisted toward a heavy wire and she managed to hang on to the braided metal, still hot from the lightning strike.

Correct Comma Use

Rewrite the following sentences so that they are correctly punctuated with commas.

1. The author of "The Leap" Louise Erdrich grew up in North Dakota.
2. Today she is a member of the Turtle Mountain Band of Chippewa.
3. In addition to being a writer she is also a mother and she has six children.
4. "The Leap" appeared first in *Harper's Magazine* then in *In Praise of Mothers* and finally in the novel *Tales of Burning Love.*
5. The narrator of "The Leap" and her mother Anna Avalon have a special relationship.
6. After Anna Avalon fell from the trapeze she spent more than a month recovering in the hospital.

7. The narrator's father taught Anna Avalon to read and this is how they fell in love.
8. Anna Avalon's first husband Harold Avalon died in the trapeze accident.
9. Anna Avalon climbed the tree leaped through the air and landed on the windowsill while the fire blazed around her.
10. The crowd silent and awestruck watched as Anna Avalon vaulted through the air toward the flaming house.
11. The narrator reflects on her mother's experiences often using anecdotes to tell the story.
12. Falling through the air the narrator says gives a person time to think.
13. Nikki Giovanni who was born in 1943 wrote "Her Flying Trapeze."
14. Alone the woman on the trapeze flies through the air.
15. The poem and the story have several things in common including performing a trapeze act.

Use Commas in Your Writing

For a teen magazine featuring stories about parent-child relationships, write a personal account about a time you learned something valuable from a parent, guardian, or other adult figure. Also include in your account a description of how that lesson has affected your way of looking at things. Be sure to use commas correctly in your account.

EXTEND THE SKILL

Imagine you have been asked to create a workbook that teaches fifth-grade students how to use commas correctly. Working in a small group, write a lesson on commas for this age level. Also write exercises that reinforce how to use commas but are also fun and interesting for preteens. If possible, try out your workbook on a group of fifth-graders and get their feedback on it.

READING FICTION INDEPENDENTLY
Theme: Choices

"The headmaster looked stunned. His face was beaded with perspiration. Sekhar felt the greatest pity for him. But he felt he could not help it. No judge delivering a sentence felt more pained and helpless."

—from "Like the Sun"
by R. K. Narayan

Every day, you are faced with choices to make. Most of these choices are small, such as what to eat for breakfast or wear to school. Other decisions you make, however, may alter the course of your life. These choices often put to the test who you are as a person and what you stand for. As you read the selections in this section, determine what choices are made and how those choices reveal the characters' true selves.

USING READING SKILLS WITH FICTION

Identify the Main Idea

The **main idea** is a brief statement of what you think the author wants you to know, think, or feel after reading the text. In some cases, the main idea will actually be stated. Usually in fiction, the author will not tell you what the main idea is, and you will have to infer it.

In general, nonfiction texts have main ideas; literary texts, like the fictional stories in this unit, have themes. Sometimes, the term "main idea" is used to refer to the theme of a literary work. Both deal with the central idea in a written work.

Do not confuse the main idea of a story with the plot; the plot signifies the actions or events that happen to the characters of the story. The main idea is the point or purpose of those actions.

Related to the main idea is the author's purpose. The **author's purpose** is the reason the author wrote that story or what he or she hoped to achieve by doing so. Sometimes, there is a message or a point to the message; the author hopes you will think or feel a certain way about a subject after reading it. The purpose of other stories might be simply to entertain, whether to make you laugh or to scare you. If you can determine the author's purpose, you will be better able to critique or analyze the story for how effective the author was in achieving that purpose.

A good way to find the main or overall idea of a whole selection (or part of a selection) is to gather important details into a Main Idea Map like the one below, which is partially completed for "Cranes" by Hwang Sun-wôn (page 132). Use the details to determine the main or overall thought or message. This will help you to draw conclusions about the main idea when you finish reading.

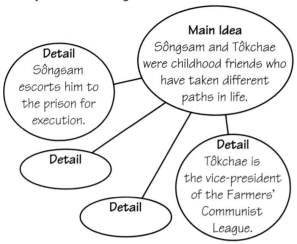

Understand the Author's Approach

The literary elements, the terms and techniques used in literature, make up the author's approach to conveying his or her main idea or theme. Understanding the author's approach in fiction involves recognizing these literary elements:

- **Point of View** This is the vantage point, or perspective, from which a story or narrative is told. (See page 42 for more information on point of view.)
- **Characterization** This is the literary technique writers use to create characters and make them come alive. (See page 60 for more information on characterization.)
- **Mood** This is the atmosphere conveyed by a literary work. Writers create mood by using concrete details to describe the setting, characters, or events. Writers can evoke in the reader an emotional response—such as fear, discomfort, or longing—by working with descriptive language and sensory details. (See page 80 for more information on mood.)

Summarize Basic Events and Ideas

When you **summarize** a story, you recall the main events and points that outline the plot. A **plot** is a series of events related to a **central conflict,** or struggle. A typical plot involves the introduction of a conflict, its development, and its eventual resolution. (See page 12 for more information on plot.) You do not need to restate all minor happenings or details, only the ones that answer the question, "What is this story about?" A basic summary explains who the main characters are, how they relate to one another, what the central conflict is, and what actions the characters take with regards to that conflict.

Framework for Fiction

When reading fiction, you need to be aware of the plot, the characters, and the setting. The following checklist of questions offers a framework for approaching fiction reading.

As you start to read...
☐ From whose perspective is this story told?
☐ Who are the characters? What do I know about them?
☐ Where is the story set?

As you continue reading...
☐ What is the mood of the story?
☐ What do the characters or the setting look like?
☐ What do I predict will happen to the characters at the end?
☐ What is the central conflict?

After you've finished reading...
☐ What happens in the story?
☐ What message or point is the author trying to make?
☐ What am I supposed to understand after reading this?

What Good Readers Do

Use Fix-Up Ideas

If you experience difficulty in comprehending what you're reading, use one of the following Fix-Up Ideas:

☐ Reread
☐ Ask a question
☐ Read in shorter chunks
☐ Read aloud
☐ Retell
☐ Work with a partner
☐ Unlock difficult words
☐ Vary your reading rate
☐ Choose a new reading strategy

CRANES

A Short Story by **Hwang Sun-wôn**

Translated by **Peter H. Lee**

"There's no need to make excuses. You're going to be shot anyway. Why don't you tell the truth here and now?"

Hwang Sun-wôn (1915–2000) faced many difficulties as a Korean writer. From 1910 to 1945, Japan forcibly occupied his country. In an effort to end Korean nationalism during their occupation, the Japanese jailed those who wrote books in Korean. Promising Korean students, such as Hwang, had to go to Japan for college. Despite these obstacles, Hwang wrote extensively, and many consider him the greatest Korean writer of his generation.

"Cranes" is set in a village near the thirty-eighth parallel. Following World War II, Korea was divided at the thirty-eighth parallel. The communist Soviet Union occupied North Korea, and South Korea became a democracy supported by the United Nations. In 1950, North Korea invaded South Korea, beginning the Korean War. Soon other countries became involved. Much of the war was fought around the thirty-eighth parallel. When two childhood friends on opposite sides of the war meet, one of them has a difficult decision to make.

When have you had to make a difficult decision? What was the situation, and how did you decide what to do?

The northern village lay snug beneath the high, bright autumn sky, near the border at the Thirty-eighth Parallel.

White gourds lay one against the other on the dirt floor of an empty farmhouse. Any village elders who passed by extinguished their bamboo pipes first, and the children, too, turned back some distance off. Their faces were marked with fear.

As a whole, the village showed little damage from the war, but it still did not seem like the same village Sôngsam had known as a boy.

At the foot of a chestnut grove on the hill behind the village he stopped and climbed a chestnut tree. Somewhere far back in his mind he heard the old man with a wen[1] shout, "You bad boy, climbing up my chestnut tree again!"

The old man must have passed away, for he was not among the few village elders Sŏngsam had met. Holding on to the trunk of the tree, Sŏngsam gazed up at the blue sky for a time. Some chestnuts fell to the ground as the dry clusters opened of their own accord.

A young man stood, his hands bound, before a farmhouse that had been converted into a Public Peace Police office. He seemed to be a stranger, so Sŏngsam went up for a closer look. He was stunned: this young man was none other than his boyhood playmate, Tŏkchae.

Sŏngsam asked the police officer who had come with him from Ch'ŏnt'ae for an explanation. The prisoner was the vice-chairman of the Farmers' Communist League and had just been flushed[2] out of hiding in his own house, Sŏngsam learned.

Sŏngsam sat down on the dirt floor and lit a cigarette.

Tŏkchae was to be escorted to Ch'ŏngdan by one of the peace police. After a time, Sŏngsam lit a new cigarette from the first and stood up.

"I'll take him with me."

Tŏkchae averted his face and refused to look at Sŏngsam. The two left the village.

Sŏngsam went on smoking, but the tobacco had no flavor. He just kept drawing the smoke in and blowing it out. Then suddenly he thought that Tŏkchae, too, must want a puff. He thought of the days when they had shared dried gourd leaves behind sheltering walls, hidden from the adults' view. But today, how could he offer a cigarette to a fellow like this?

Once, when they were small, he went with Tŏkchae to steal some chestnuts from the old man with the wen. It was Sŏngsam's turn to climb the tree. Suddenly the old man began shouting. Sŏngsam slipped and fell to the ground. He got chestnut burrs all over his bottom, but he kept on running. Only when the

two had reached a safe place where the old man could not overtake them did Sŏngsam turn his bottom to Tŏkchae. The burrs hurt so much as they were plucked out that Sŏngsam could not keep tears from welling up in his eyes. Tŏkchae produced a fistful of chestnuts from his pocket and thrust them into Sŏngsam's...Sŏngsam threw away the cigarette he had just lit, and then made up his mind not to light another while he was escorting Tŏkchae.

They reached the pass at the hill where he and Tŏkchae had cut fodder for the cows until Sŏngsam had to move to a spot near Ch'ŏnt'ae, south of the Thirty-eighth Parallel, two years before the liberation.

Sŏngsam felt a sudden surge of anger in spite of himself and shouted, "So how many have you killed?"

---

1. **wen.** Harmless growth on the skin
2. **flushed.** Exposed or chased from a hiding place

For the first time, Tôkchae cast a quick glance at him and then looked away.

"You! How many have you killed?" he asked again.

Tôkchae looked at him again and glared. The glare grew intense, and his mouth twitched.

"So you managed to kill quite a few, eh?" Sôngsam felt his mind becoming clear of itself, as if some obstruction had been removed. "If you were vice-chairman of the Communist League, why didn't you run? You must have been lying low with a secret mission."

Tôkchae did not reply.

"Speak up. What was your mission?"

Tôkchae kept walking. Tôkchae was hiding something, Sôngsam thought. He wanted to take a good look at him, but Tôkchae kept his face averted.

Fingering the revolver at his side, Sôngsam went on: "There's no need to make excuses. You're going to be shot anyway. Why don't you tell the truth here and now?"

"I'm not going to make any excuses. They made me vice-chairman of the League because I was a hardworking farmer and one of the poorest. If that's a capital offense,[3] so be it. I'm still what I used to be—the only thing I'm good at is tilling the soil." After a short pause, he added, "My old man is bedridden at home. He's been ill almost half a year." Tôkchae's father was a widower, a poor, hardworking farmer who lived only for his son. Seven years before his back had given out, and he had contracted a skin disease.

"Are you married?"

"Yes," Tôkchae replied after a time.

"To whom?"

"Shorty."

"To Shorty?" How interesting! A woman so small and plump that she knew the earth's vastness, but not the sky's height. Such a cold fish! He and Tôkchae had teased her and made her cry. And Tôkchae had married her!

"How many kids?"

"The first is arriving this fall, she says."

Sôngsam had difficulty swallowing a laugh that he was about to let burst forth in spite of himself. Although he had asked how many children Tôkchae had, he could not help wanting to break out laughing at the thought of the wife sitting there with her huge stomach, one span around. But he realized that this was no time for joking.

"Anyway, it's strange you didn't run away."

"I tried to escape. They said that once the South invaded, not a man would be spared. So all of us between seventeen and forty were taken to the North. I thought of evacuating, even if I had to carry my father on my back. But Father said no. How could we farmers leave the land behind when the crops were ready for harvesting? He grew old on that farm depending on me as the prop and the mainstay of the family. I wanted to be with him in his last moments so I could close his eyes with my own hand. Besides, where can farmers like us go, when all we know how to do is live on the land?"

Sôngsam had had to flee the previous June. At night he had broken the news privately to his father. But his father had said the same thing: Where could a farmer go, leaving all the chores behind? So Sôngsam had left alone. Roaming about the strange streets and villages in the South, Sôngsam had been haunted by thoughts of his old parents and the young children, who had been left with all the chores. Fortunately, his family had been safe then, as it was now.

They had crossed over a hill. This time Sôngsam walked with his face averted. The autumn sun was hot on his forehead. This was an ideal day for the harvest, he thought.

When they reached the foot of the hill, Sôngsam gradually came to a halt. In the middle of a field he espied a group of cranes that resembled men in white, all bent over. This had been

---

3. **capital offense.** Crime for which punishment is death

the demilitarized zone[4] along the Thirty-eighth Parallel. The cranes were still living here, as before, though the people were all gone.

Once, Sôngsam and Tôkchae were about twelve, they had set a trap here, unbeknown to the adults, and caught a crane, a Tanjông crane. They had tied the crane up, even binding its wings, and paid it daily visits, patting its neck and riding on its back. Then one day they overheard the neighbors whispering: someone had come from Seoul with a permit from the governor-general's office to catch cranes as some kind of specimens. Then and there the two boys had dashed off to the field. That they would be found out and punished had no longer mattered; all they cared about was the fate of their crane. Without a moment's delay, still out of breath from running, they untied the crane's feet and wings, but the bird could hardly walk. It must have been weak from having been bound.

The two held the crane up. Then, suddenly, they heard a gunshot. The crane flut-

tered its wings once or twice and then sank back to the ground.

The boys thought their crane had been shot. But the next moment, as another crane from a nearby bush fluttered its wings, the boys' crane stretched its long neck, gave out a whoop, and disappeared into the sky. For a long while the two boys could not tear their eyes away from the blue sky up into which their crane had soared.

"Hey, why don't we stop here for a crane hunt?" Sôngsam said suddenly.

Tôkchae was dumbfounded.

"I'll make a trap with this rope; you flush a crane over here."

Sôngsam had untied Tôkchae's hands and was already crawling through the weeds.

Tôkchae's face whitened. "You're sure to be shot anyway"—these words flashed through his

---

4. **demilitarized zone.** Area that is not allowed to be used for military purposes. In this case, that area runs along the border separating North and South Korea.

mind. Any instant a bullet would come flying from Sôngsam's direction, Tôkchae thought.

Some paces away, Sôngsam quickly turned toward him.

"Hey, how come you're standing there like a dummy? Go flush a crane!"

Only then did Tôkchae understand. He began crawling through the weeds.

A pair of Tanjông cranes soared high into the clear blue autumn sky, flapping their huge wings. ❖

Is it wrong to break the rules in order to help a friend? What might the results be, both good and bad, of doing so?

Refer and Reason

1. Recall how Sôngsam and Tôkchae know each other. Compare and contrast the paths the two friends have taken in their lives since they were boys.
2. List mentions of cranes in the story. Interpret what the cranes symbolize or represent in each case.
3. Sôngsam and Tôkchae find themselves on opposite sides in the war. Generate a list of the kinds of disagreements that could create this same kind of tension between two American friends today.

Writing Options

1. Consider the friendship between Sôngsam and Tôkchae and friendships you have experienced.

Write an ode to friendship. In your poem, you may choose to identify the important elements of friendship, explain how friendship affects lives, or praise a particular friend. Use examples from your own experience or from the story to illustrate your ideas in your ode.

2. Suppose your older sister is struggling to understand the symbolism in "Cranes." Write a literary analysis for her, in which you explain the symbolism of cranes in the story. Use your response to the Refer and Reason question 2 to gather ideas for your analysis.

 Go to **www.mirrorsandwindows.com** for more.

On the Rainy River

A Short Story by **Tim O'Brien**

I REMEMBER OPENING UP THE LETTER, SCANNING THE FIRST FEW LINES, FEELING THE BLOOD GO THICK BEHIND MY EYES. I REMEMBER A SOUND IN MY HEAD. IT WASN'T THINKING, IT WAS JUST A SILENT HOWL.

Tim O'Brien (b. 1946) grew up in a small town in Minnesota. In 1968, he was drafted for the Vietnam War. He served in Vietnam and earned a Purple Heart. Much of his writing draws upon his experience in Vietnam. He won the National Book Award for fiction in 1979 for his novel *Going After Cacciato*, which tells the story of a soldier going AWOL and walking to Paris.

O'Brien struggled with the idea of going to war. He explores the role shame and embarrassment played in his decision in the short story **"On the Rainy River."** The story is one of many found in O'Brien's 1990 collection entitled *The Things They Carried*. A review of the book says he moved "beyond the horror of the fighting to examine with sensitivity and insight the nature of courage and fear."

How would you define "courage"? Have you met any courageous people? What made them so?

This is one story I've never told before. Not to anyone. Not to my parents, not to my brother or sister, not even to my wife. To go into it, I've always thought, would only cause embarrassment for all of us, a sudden need to be elsewhere, which is the natural response to a confession. Even now, I'll admit, the story makes me squirm. For more than twenty years I've had to live with it, feeling the shame, trying to push it away, and so by this act of remembrance, by putting the facts down on paper, I'm hoping to relieve at least some of the pressure on my dreams.

Still, it's a hard story to tell. All of us, I suppose, like to believe that in a moral emergency we will behave like the heroes of our youth, bravely and forthrightly, without thought of personal loss or discredit. Certainly that was my conviction back in the summer of 1968. Tim O'Brien: a secret hero. The Lone Ranger. If the stakes ever became high enough—if the evil were evil enough, if the good were good enough—I would simply tap a secret reservoir of courage that had been accumulating inside me over the years. Courage, I seemed to think, comes to us in finite quantities, like an inheritance, and by being frugal and stashing it away, and letting it earn interest, we steadily increase our moral capital in preparation for that day when the account must be drawn down. It was a comforting theory. It dispensed with all those bothersome little acts of daily courage; it offered hope and grace to the repetitive coward; it justified the past while amortizing the future.

In June of 1968, a month after graduating from Macalester College, I was drafted to fight a war I hated. I was twenty-one years old. Young, yes, and politically naive, but even so the American war in Vietnam seemed to me wrong. Certain blood was being shed for uncertain reasons. I saw no unity of purpose, no consensus on matters of philosophy or history or law. The very facts were shrouded in uncertainty: Was it a civil war? A war of national liberation or simple aggression? Who started it, and when, and why? What really happened to the U.S.S. *Maddox* on that dark night in the Gulf of Tonkin? Was Ho Chi Minh a Communist stooge, or a nationalist savior, or both, or neither? What about the Geneva Accords? What about SEATO and the Cold War? What about dominoes?[1] America was divided on these and a thousand other issues, and the debate had spilled out across the floor of the United States Senate and into the streets, and smart men in pinstripes could not agree on even the most fundamental matters of public policy. The only certainty that summer was moral confusion. It was my view then, and still is, that you don't make war without knowing why. Knowledge, of course, is always imperfect, but it seemed to me that when a nation goes to war it must have reasonable confidence in the justice and imperative of its cause. You can't fix your mistakes. Once people are dead, you can't make them undead.

In any case those were my convictions, and back in college I had taken a modest stand against the war. Nothing radical, no hothead stuff, just ringing a few doorbells for Gene McCarthy,[2] composing a few tedious, uninspired editorials for the campus newspaper. Oddly, though, it was almost entirely an intellectual activity. I brought some energy to it, of course, but it was the energy that accompanies almost any abstract endeavor; I felt no personal danger; I felt no sense of an impending crisis in my life. Stupidly, with a kind of smug removal that I can't begin to fathom, I assumed that the problems of killing and dying did not fall within my special province.

The draft notice arrived on June 17, 1968. It was a humid afternoon, I remember, cloudy and very quiet, and I'd just come in from a round of golf. My mother and father were having lunch out in the kitchen. I remember opening up the letter, scanning the first few

---

1. **Gulf of Tonkin…dominoes.** The narrator refers to many events or issues related to the Vietnam War. Claims that American ships had been attacked in the Gulf of Tonkin led to increased U.S. involvement in the war. Ho Chi Minh was a Vietnamese nationalist and Communist leader. SEATO, or the Southeast Asia Treaty Organization, was formed to help protect Southeast Asia from communist expansion. "Dominoes" refers to the domino theory, or the idea that if one country fell to communism, other neighboring countries would also fall.

2. **Gene McCarthy.** Senator Eugene McCarthy was an antiwar candidate who hoped to receive the Democratic nomination to run for president.

A Vietnam War protestor burns a draft card at the 1968 Democratic Party Convention in Chicago, Illinois.

lines, feeling the blood go thick behind my eyes. I remember a sound in my head. It wasn't thinking, it was just a silent howl. A million things all at once—I was too *good* for this war. Too smart, too compassionate, too everything. It couldn't happen. I was above it. I had the world—Phi Beta Kappa and summa cum laude and president of the student body and a full-ride scholarship for grad studies at Harvard. A mistake, maybe—a foul-up in the paperwork. I was no soldier. I hated Boy Scouts. I hated camping out. I hated dirt and tents and mosquitoes. The sight of blood made me queasy, and I couldn't tolerate authority, and I didn't know a rifle from a slingshot. I was a *liberal:* If they needed fresh bodies, why not draft some back-to-the-stone-age hawk? Or some dumb jingo in his hardhat and Bomb Hanoi button? Or one of LBJ's pretty daughters? Or Westmoreland's whole family— nephews and nieces and baby grandson? There

should be a law, I thought. If you support a war, if you think it's worth the price, that's fine, but you have to put your own life on the line. You have to head for the front and hook up with an infantry unit and help spill the blood. And you have to bring along your wife, or your kids, or your lover. A *law,* I thought.

I remember the rage in my stomach. Later it burned down to a smoldering self-pity, then to numbness. At dinner that night my father asked what my plans were.

"Nothing," I said. "Wait."

I spent the summer of 1968 working in an Armour meat-packing plant in my hometown of Worthington, Minnesota. The plant specialized in pork products, and for eight hours a day I stood on a quarter-mile assembly line—more properly, a disassembly line— removing blood clots from the necks of dead pigs. My job title, I believe, was Declotter.

After slaughter, the hogs were decapitated, split down the length of the belly, pried open, eviscerated, and strung up by the hind hocks on a high conveyer belt. Then gravity took over. By the time a carcass reached my spot on the line, the fluids had mostly drained out, everything except for thick clots of blood in the neck and upper chest cavity. To remove the stuff, I used a kind of water gun. The machine was heavy, maybe eighty pounds, and was suspended from the ceiling by a heavy rubber cord. There was some bounce to it, an elastic up-and-down give, and the trick was to maneuver the gun with your whole body, not lifting with the arms, just letting the rubber cord do the work for you. At one end was a trigger; at the muzzle end was a small nozzle and a steel roller brush. As a carcass passed by, you'd lean forward and

> IT WAS A KIND OF SCHIZOPHRENIA. A MORAL SPLIT. I COULDN'T MAKE UP MY MIND. I FEARED THE WAR, YES, BUT I ALSO FEARED EXILE.

swing the gun up against the clots and squeeze the trigger, all in one motion, and the brush would whirl and water would come shooting out and you'd hear a quick splattering sound as the clots dissolved into a fine red mist. It was not pleasant work. Goggles were a necessity, and a rubber apron, but even so it was like standing for eight hours a day under a lukewarm blood-shower. At night I'd go home smelling of pig. I couldn't wash it out. Even after a hot bath, scrubbing hard, the stink was always there—like old bacon, or sausage, a dense greasy pig-stink that soaked deep

into my skin and hair. Among other things, I remember, it was tough getting dates that summer. I felt isolated; I spent a lot of time alone. And there was also that draft notice tucked away in my wallet.

In the evenings I'd sometimes borrow my father's car and drive aimlessly around town, feeling sorry for myself, thinking about the war and the pig factory and how my life seemed to be collapsing toward slaughter. I felt paralyzed. All around me the options seemed to be narrowing, as if I were hurtling down a huge black funnel, the whole world squeezing in tight. There was no happy way out. The government had ended most graduate school deferments; the waiting lists for the National Guard and Reserves were impossibly long; my health was solid; I didn't qualify for CO status—no religious grounds, no history as a pacifist. Moreover, I could not claim to be opposed to war as a matter of general principle. There were occasions, I believed, when a nation was justified in using military force to achieve its ends, to stop a Hitler or some comparable evil, and I told myself that in such circumstances I would've willingly marched off to the battle. The problem, though, was that a draft board did not let you choose your war.

Beyond all this, or at the very center, was the raw fact of terror. I did not want to die. Not ever. But certainly not then, not there, not in a wrong war. Driving up Main Street, past the courthouse and the Ben Franklin store, I sometimes felt the fear spreading inside me like weeds. I imagined myself dead. I imagined myself doing things I could not do—charging an enemy position, taking aim at another human being.

At some point in mid-July I began thinking seriously about Canada. The border lay a few hundred miles north, an eight-hour drive. Both my conscience and my instincts were telling me to make a break for it, just take off and run like hell and never stop. In the beginning the idea seemed purely abstract, the word Canada printing itself out in my head; but after a time I could see particular shapes and images, the sorry details of my own future—a hotel room in Winnipeg, a battered old suitcase, my father's eyes as I tried to explain myself over the telephone. I could almost hear his voice, and my mother's. Run, I'd think. Then I'd think, Impossible. Then a second later I'd think, *Run*.

It was a kind of schizophrenia. A moral split. I couldn't make up my mind. I feared the war, yes, but I also feared exile. I was afraid of walking away from my own life, my friends and my family, my whole history, everything that mattered to me. I feared losing the respect of my parents. I feared the law. I feared ridicule and censure. My hometown was a conservative little spot on the prairie, a place where tradition counted, and it was easy to imagine people sitting around a table at the old Gobbler Café on Main Street, coffee cups poised, the conversation slowly zeroing in on the young O'Brien kid, how the damned sissy had taken off for Canada. At night, when I couldn't sleep, I'd sometimes carry on fierce arguments with those people. I'd be screaming at them, telling them how much I detested their blind, thoughtless, automatic acquiescence to it all, their simple-minded patriotism, their prideful ignorance, their love-it-or-leave-it platitudes, how they were sending me off to fight a war they didn't understand and didn't want to understand. I held them responsible. By God, yes I *did*. All of them—I held them personally and individually responsible—the polyestered Kiwanis boys, the merchants and farmers, the pious churchgoers, the chatty housewives, the PTA and the Lions club and the Veterans of Foreign Wars and the fine upstanding gentry out at the country club. They didn't know Bao Dai from the man in the moon. They didn't know history. They didn't know the first thing about Diem's tyranny, or the nature of Vietnamese nationalism, or the

long colonialism of the French[3]—this was all too damned complicated, it required some reading—but no matter, it was a war to stop the Communists, plain and simple, which was how they liked things, and you were treasonous if you had second thoughts about killing or dying for plain and simple reasons.

I was bitter, sure. But it was so much more than that. The emotions went from outrage to terror to bewilderment to guilt to sorrow and then back again to outrage. I felt a sickness inside me. Real disease.

Most of this I've told before, or at least hinted at, but what I have never told is the full truth. How I cracked. How at work one morning, standing on the pig line, I felt something break open in my chest. I don't know what it was. I'll never know. But it was real. I know that much, it was a physical rupture—a cracking-leaking-popping feeling. I remember

---

3. **Bao Dai...French.** The narrator refers to several people and incidents from Vietnam's history.

dropping my water gun. Quickly, almost without thought, I took off my apron and walked out of the plant and drove home. It was midmorning, I remember, and the house was empty. Down in my chest there was still that leaking sensation, something very warm and precious spilling out, and I was covered with blood and hog-stink, and for a long while I just concentrated on holding myself together. I remember taking a hot shower. I remember packing a suitcase and carrying it out to the kitchen, standing very still for a few minutes, looking carefully at the familiar objects all around me. The old chrome toaster, the telephone, the pink and white Formica on the kitchen counters. The room was full of bright sunshine. Everything sparkled. My house, I thought. My life. I'm not sure how long I stood there, but later I scribbled out a short note to my parents.

What it said exactly, I don't recall now. Something vague. Taking off, will call, love Tim.

I drove north.

It's a blur now, as it was then, and all I remember is a sense of high velocity and the feel of the steering wheel in my hands. I was riding on adrenaline. A giddy feeling, in a way, except there was the dreamy edge of impossibility to it—like running a dead-end maze—no way out—it couldn't come to a happy conclusion and yet I was doing it anyway because it was all I could think to do. It was pure flight, fast and mindless. I had no plan. Just hit the border at high speed and crash through and keep on running. Near dusk I passed through Bemidji, then turned northeast toward International Falls. I spent the night in the car behind a closed-down gas station a half mile from the border. In the morning, after gassing up, I headed straight west along the Rainy River, which separates Minnesota from Canada, and which for me separated one life from another. The land was mostly wilderness. Here and there I passed a motel or bait shop, but otherwise the country unfolded in great sweeps of pine and birch and sumac. Though it was still August, the air already had the smell of October, football season, piles of yellow-red leaves, everything crisp and clean. I remember a huge blue sky. Off to my right was the Rainy River, wide as a lake in places, and beyond the Rainy River was Canada.

For a while I just drove, not aiming at anything, then in the late morning I began looking for a place to lie low for a day or two. I was exhausted, and scared sick, and around noon I pulled into an old fishing resort called the Tip Top Lodge. Actually, it was not a lodge at all, just eight or nine tiny yellow cabins clustered on a peninsula that jutted northward into the Rainy River. The place was in sorry shape. There was a dangerous wooden dock, an old minnow tank, a flimsy tar paper boathouse along the shore. The main building, which stood in a cluster of pines on high ground, seemed to lean heavily to one side, like a cripple, the roof sagging toward Canada. Briefly, I thought about turning around, just giving up, but then I got out of the car and walked up to the front porch.

The man who opened the door that day is the hero of my life. How do I say this without sounding sappy? Blurt it out—the man saved me. He offered exactly what I needed, without questions, without any words at all. He took me in. He was there at the critical time—a silent, watchful presence. Six days later, when it ended, I was unable to find a proper way to thank him, and I never have, and so, if nothing else, this story represents a small gesture of gratitude twenty years overdue.

Even after two decades I can close my eyes and return to that porch at the Tip Top Lodge. I can see the old guy staring at me. Elroy Berdahl: eighty-one years old, skinny and shrunken and mostly bald. He wore a flannel shirt and brown work pants. In one hand, I remember, he carried a green apple, a small paring knife in the other. His eyes had the bluish gray color of a razor blade, the same polished shine, and as he peered up at me I felt a strange sharpness, almost painful, a cutting sensation, as if his gaze were somehow slicing me open. In part, no doubt, it was my own sense of guilt, but even so I'm absolutely certain that the old man took one look and went right to the heart of things—a kid in trouble. When I asked for a room, Elroy made a little clicking sound with his tongue. He nodded, led me out to one of the cabins, and dropped a key in my hand. I remember smiling at him. I also remember wishing I hadn't. The old man shook his head as if to tell me it wasn't worth the bother.

"Dinner at five-thirty," he said. "You eat fish?"

"Anything," I said.

Elroy grunted and said, "I'll bet."

We spent six days together at the Tip Top Lodge. Just the two of us. Tourist season was over, and there were no boats on the river, and the wilderness seemed to withdraw into a great permanent stillness. Over those six days Elroy Berdahl and I took most of our meals together. In the mornings we sometimes went out on long hikes into the woods, and at night we played Scrabble or listened to records or sat reading in front of his big stone fireplace. At times I felt the awkwardness of an intruder, but Elroy accepted me into his quiet routine without fuss or ceremony. He took my presence for granted, the same way he might've sheltered a stray cat—no wasted sighs or pity—and there was never any talk about it. Just the opposite. What I remember more than anything is the man's willful, almost ferocious silence. In all that time together, all those

hours, he never asked the obvious questions: Why was I there? Why alone? Why so preoccupied? If Elroy was curious about any of this, he was careful never to put it into words.

My hunch, though, is that he already knew. At least the basics. After all, it was 1968, and guys were burning draft cards, and Canada was just a boat ride away. Elroy Berdahl was no hick. His bedroom, I remember, was cluttered with books and newspapers. He killed me at the Scrabble board, barely concentrating, and on those occasions when speech was necessary, he had a way of compressing large thoughts into small, cryptic packets of language. One evening, just at sunset, he pointed up at an owl circling over the violet-lighted forest to the west.

"Hey, O'Brien," he said. "There's Jesus."

The man was sharp—he didn't miss much. Those razor eyes. Now and then he'd catch me staring out at the river, at the far shore, and I could almost hear the tumblers clicking in his head. Maybe I'm wrong, but I doubt it.

One thing for certain, he knew I was in desperate trouble. And he knew I couldn't talk about it. The wrong word—or even the right word—and I would've disappeared. I was wired and jittery. My skin felt too tight. After

Cokes—and now I was off on the margins of exile, leaving my country forever, and it seemed so impossible and terrible and sad.

I'm not sure how I made it through those six days. Most of it I can't remember. On two or three afternoons, to pass some time, I helped Elroy get the place ready for winter, sweeping down the cabins and hauling in the boats, little chores that kept my body moving. The days were cool and bright. The nights were very dark. One morning the old man showed me how to split and stack firewood, and for several hours we just worked in silence out behind his house. At one point, I remember, Elroy put down his maul and looked at me for a long time, his lips drawn as if framing a difficult question, but then he shook his head and went back to work. The man's self-control was amazing. He never pried. He never put me in a position that required lies or denials. To an extent, I supposed, his reticence was typical of that part of Minnesota, where privacy still held value, and even if I'd been walking around with some horrible deformity—four arms and three heads—I'm sure the old man would've talked about everything except those extra arms and heads. Simple politeness was part of it. But even more than that, I think, the man understood that words were insufficient. The problem had gone beyond discussion. During that long summer I'd been over and over the various arguments, all the pros and cons, and it was no longer a question that could be decided by an act of pure reason. Intellect had come up against emotion. My conscience told me to run, but some irrational and powerful force

supper one evening I vomited and went back to my cabin and lay down for a few moments and then vomited again; another time, in the middle of the afternoon, I began sweating and couldn't shut it off. I went through whole days feeling dizzy with sorrow. I couldn't sleep; I couldn't lie still. At night I'd toss around in bed, half awake, half dreaming, imagining how I'd sneak down to the beach and quietly push one of the old man's boats out into the river and start paddling my way toward Canada. There were times when I thought I'd gone off the psychic edge. I couldn't tell up from down, I was just falling, and late in the night I'd lie there watching weird pictures spin through my head. Getting chased by the Border Patrol—helicopters and searchlights and barking dogs—I'd be crashing through the woods, I'd be down on my hands and knees—people shouting out my name—the law closing in on all sides—my hometown draft board and the FBI and the Royal Canadian Mounted Police. It all seemed crazy and impossible. Twenty-one years old, an ordinary kid with all the ordinary dreams and ambitions, and all I wanted was to live the life I was born to—a mainstream life—I loved baseball and hamburgers and cherry was resisting, like a weight pushing me toward the war. What it came down to, stupidly, was a sense of shame. Hot, stupid shame. I did not want people to think badly of me. Not my parents, not my brother and sister, not even the folks down at the Gobbler Café. I was ashamed to be there at the Tip Top Lodge. I was ashamed of my conscience, ashamed to be doing the right thing.

Some of this Elroy must've understood. Not the details, of course, but the plain fact of crisis.

Although the old man never confronted me about it, there was one occasion when he came close to forcing the whole thing out into the open. It was early evening, and we'd just finished supper, and over coffee and dessert I asked him about my bill, how much I owed so far. For a long while the old man squinted down at the tablecloth.

"Well, the basic rate," he said, "is fifty bucks a night. Not counting meals. This makes four nights, right?"

I nodded. I had three hundred and twelve dollars in my wallet.

Elroy kept his eyes on the tablecloth. "Now that's an on-season price. To be fair, I suppose we should knock it down a peg or two." He leaned back in his chair. "What's a reasonable number, you figure?"

"I don't know," I said. "Forty?"

"Forty's good. Forty a night. Then we tack on food—say another hundred? Two hundred sixty total?"

"I guess."

He raised his eyebrows. "Too much?"

"No, that's fair. It's fine. Tomorrow, though…I think I'd better take off tomorrow."

Elroy shrugged and began clearing the table. For a time he fussed with the dishes, whistling to himself as if the subject had been settled. After a second he slapped his hands together.

"You know what we forgot?" he said. "We forgot wages. Those odd jobs you done. What we have to do, we have to figure out what your time's worth. Your last job—how much did you pull in an hour?"

"Not enough," I said.

"A bad one?"

"Yes. Pretty bad."

Slowly then, without intending any long sermon, I told him about my days at the pig plant. It began as a straight recitation of the facts, but before I could stop myself I was talking about the blood clots and the water gun and how the smell had soaked into my skin and how I couldn't wash it away. I went on for a long time. I told him about wild hogs squealing in my dreams, the sounds of butchery, slaughterhouse sounds, and how I'd sometimes wake up with that greasy pig-stink in my throat.

When I was finished, Elroy nodded at me.

"Well, to be honest," he said, "when you first showed up here, I wondered about that. The aroma, I mean. Smelled like you was awful damned fond of pork chops." The old man almost smiled. He made a snuffling sound, then sat down with a pencil and a piece of paper. "So what'd this crud job pay? Ten bucks an hour? Fifteen?"

"Less."

Elroy shook his head. "Let's make it fifteen. You put in twenty-five hours here, easy. That's three hundred seventy-five bucks total wages. We subtract the two hundred sixty for food and lodging. I still owe you a hundred and fifteen."

He took four fifties out of his shirt pocket and laid them on the table.

"Call it even," he said.

"No."

"Pick it up. Get yourself a haircut."

The money lay on the table for the rest of the evening. It was still there when I went back to my cabin. In the morning though, I found an envelope tacked to my door. Inside were the four fifties and a two-word note that said EMER-GENCY FUND.

The man knew.

Looking back after twenty years, I sometimes wonder if the events of that summer didn't happen in some other dimension, a place where your life exists before you've lived it, and where it goes afterward. None of it ever seemed real. During my time at the Tip Top Lodge I had the feeling that I'd slipped out of my own skin, hovering a few feet away while some poor yo-yo with my name and face tried to make his way toward a future he didn't understand and didn't want. Even now I can see myself as I was then. It's like watching an old home movie: I'm young and tan and fit. I've got hair—lots of it. I don't smoke or drink. I'm wearing faded blue jeans and a white polo shirt. I can see myself sitting on Elroy Berdahl's dock near dusk one evening, the sky a bright shimmering pink, and I'm finishing up

a letter to my parents that tells what I'm about to do and why I'm doing it and how sorry I am that I've never found the courage to talk to them about it. I ask them not to be angry. I try to explain some of my feelings, but there aren't enough words, and so I just say that it's a thing that has to be done. At the end of the letter I talk about the vacations we used to take up in this north country, at a place called Whitefish Lake, and how the scenery here reminds me of those good times. I tell them I'm fine. I tell them I'll write again from Winnipeg or Montreal or wherever I end up.

On my last full day, the sixth day, the old man took me out fishing on the Rainy River. The afternoon was sunny and cold.

A stiff breeze came in from the north, and I remember how the little fourteen-foot boat made sharp rocking motions as we pushed off from the dock. The current was fast. All around us, I remember, there was a vastness to the world, an unpeopled rawness, just the trees and the sky and the water reaching out toward nowhere. The air had the brittle scent of October.

For ten or fifteen minutes Elroy held a course upstream, the river choppy and silver-gray, then he turned straight north and put the engine on full throttle. I felt the bow lift beneath me. I remember the wind in my ears, the sound of the old outboard Evinrude. For a time I didn't pay attention to anything, just feeling the cold spray against my face, but then it occurred to me that at some point we must've passed into Canadian waters, across that dotted line between two different worlds, and I remember a sudden tightness in my chest as I looked up and watched the far shore come at me. This wasn't a daydream. It was tangible and real. As we came in toward land, Elroy cut the engine, letting the boat fishtail lightly about twenty yards off shore. The old man didn't look at me or speak. Bending down, he opened up his tackle box and busied himself with a bobber and a piece of wire leader, humming to himself, his eyes down.

It struck me then that he must've planned it. I'll never be certain, of course, but I think he meant to bring me up against the realities, to guide me across the river and to take me to the edge and to stand a kind of vigil as I chose a life for myself.

I remember staring at the old man, then at my hands, then at Canada. The shoreline was dense with brush and timber. I could see tiny red berries on the bushes. I could see a squirrel up in one of the birch trees, a big crow looking at me from a boulder along the river. That close—twenty yards—and I could see the delicate latticework of the leaves, the texture of the soil, the browned needles beneath the pines, the configurations of geology and human history. Twenty yards. I could've done it. I could've jumped and started swimming for my life. Inside me, in my chest, I felt a terrible squeezing pressure. Even now, as I write this, I can still feel that tightness. And I want you to feel it—the wind coming off the river, the waves, the silence, the wooded frontier. You're at the bow of a boat on the Rainy River. You're twenty-one years old, you're scared, and there's a hard squeezing pressure in your chest.

What would you do?

Would you jump? Would you feel pity for yourself? Would you think about the family and your childhood and your dreams and all you're leaving behind? Would it hurt? Would it feel like dying? Would you cry, as I did?

I tried to swallow it back. I tried to smile, except I was crying.

Now, perhaps, you can understand why I've never told this story before. It's not just the embarrassment of tears. That's part of it, no doubt, but what embarrasses me much more, and always will, is the paralysis that took my heart. A moral freeze: I couldn't decide, I couldn't act, I couldn't comport myself with even a pretense of modest human dignity.

All I could do was cry. Quietly, not bawling, just the chest-chokes.

At the rear of the boat Elroy Berdahl pretended not to notice. He held a fishing rod in his hands, his head bowed to hide his eyes. He kept humming a soft, monotonous little tune. Everywhere, it seemed, in the trees

and water and sky, a great worldwide sadness came pressing down on me, a crushing sorrow, sorrow like I had never known before. And what was so sad, I realized, was that Canada had become a pitiful fantasy. Silly and hopeless. It was no longer a possibility. Right then, with the shore so close, I understood that I would not do what I should do. I would not swim away from my hometown and my country and my life. I would not be brave. That old image of myself as a hero, as a man

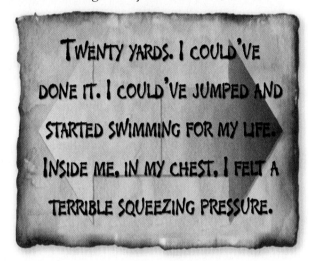

TWENTY YARDS. I COULD'VE DONE IT. I COULD'VE JUMPED AND STARTED SWIMMING FOR MY LIFE. INSIDE ME, IN MY CHEST, I FELT A TERRIBLE SQUEEZING PRESSURE.

of conscience and courage, all that was just a threadbare pipe dream. Bobbing there on the Rainy River, looking back at the Minnesota shore, I felt a sudden swell of helplessness come over me, a drowning sensation, as if I had toppled overboard and was being swept away by the silver waves. Chunks of my own history flashed by. I saw a seven-year-old boy in a white cowboy hat and a Lone Ranger mask and a pair of holstered six-shooters; I saw a twelve-year-old Little League shortstop pivoting to turn a double play; I saw a sixteen-year-old kid decked out for his first prom, looking spiffy in a white tux and a black bow tie, his hair cut short and flat, his shoes freshly polished. My whole life seemed to spill out into the river, swirling away from me, everything I had ever been or ever wanted to be. I couldn't get my breath; I couldn't stay afloat; I couldn't tell which way to swim. A hallucination, I suppose,

and Jane Fonda dressed up as Barbarella, and an old man sprawled beside a pigpen, and my grandfather, and Gary Cooper, and a kind-faced woman carrying an umbrella and a copy of Plato's *Republic,* and a million ferocious citizens waving flags of all shapes and colors—people in hardhats, people in headbands—they were all whooping and chanting and urging me toward one shore or the other. I saw faces from my distant past and distant future. My wife was there. My unborn daughter waved at me, and my two sons hopped up and down, and a drill sergeant named Blyton sneered and shot up a finger and shook his head. There was a choir in bright purple robes. There was a cabbie from the Bronx. There was a slim young man I would one day kill with a hand grenade along a red clay trail outside the village of My Khe.

The little aluminum boat rocked softly beneath me. There was the wind and the sky.

I tried to will myself overboard.

I gripped the edge of the boat and leaned forward and thought, *Now.*

I did try. It just wasn't possible.

All those eyes on me—the town, the whole universe—and I couldn't risk the embarrassment. It was as if there were an audience to my life, that swirl of faces along the river, and in my head I could hear people screaming at me. Traitor! they yelled. Turncoat! I felt myself blush. I couldn't tolerate it. I couldn't endure the mockery, or the disgrace, or the patriotic ridicule. Even in my imagination, the shore just twenty yards away, I couldn't make myself be brave. It had nothing to do with morality. Embarrassment, that's all it was.

And right then I submitted.

but it was as real as anything I would ever feel. I saw my parents calling to me from the far shoreline. I saw my brother and sister, all the townsfolk, the mayor and the entire Chamber of Commerce and all my old teachers and girlfriends and high school buddies. Like some weird sporting event: everybody screaming from the sidelines, rooting me on—a loud stadium roar. Hotdogs and popcorn—stadium smells, stadium heat. A squad of cheerleaders did cartwheels along the banks of the Rainy River; they had megaphones and pompoms and smooth brown thighs. The crowd swayed left and right. A marching band played fight songs. All my aunts and uncles were there, and Abraham Lincoln and Saint George, and a nine-year-old girl named Linda who had died of a brain tumor back in fifth grade, and several members of the United States Senate, and a blind poet scribbling notes, and LBJ, and Huck Finn, and Abbie Hoffman, and all the dead soldiers back from the grave, and the many thousands who were later to die— villagers with terrible burns, little kids without arms or legs—yes, and the Joint Chiefs of Staff were there, and a couple of popes, and a first lieutenant named Jimmy Cross, and the last surviving veteran of the American Civil War,

I would go to the war—I would kill and maybe die—because I was embarrassed not to.

That was the sad thing. And so I sat in the bow of the boat and cried. It was loud now. Loud, hard crying.

Elroy Berdahl remained quiet. He kept fishing. He worked his line with the tips of his fingers, patiently, squinting out at his red and white bobber on the Rainy River. His eyes were flat and impassive. He didn't speak. He was simply there, like the river and the late-summer sun. And yet by his presence, his mute watchfulness, he made it real. He was the true audience. He was a witness, like God, or like the gods, who look on in absolute silence as we live our lives, as we make our choices or fail to make them.

"Ain't biting," he said.

Then after a time the old man pulled in his line and turned the boat back toward Minnesota.

I don't remember saying goodbye. That last night we had dinner together, and I went to bed early, and in the morning Elroy fixed breakfast for me. When I told him I'd be leaving, the old man nodded as if he already knew. He looked down at the table and smiled.

At some point later in the morning it's possible that we shook hands—I just don't remember—but I do know that by the time I'd finished packing the old man had disappeared. Around noon, when I took my suitcase out to the car, I noticed that his old black pickup truck was no longer parked in front of the house. I went inside and waited for a while, but I felt a bone certainty that he wouldn't be back. In a way, I thought, it was appropriate. I washed up the breakfast dishes, left his two hundred dollars on the kitchen counter, got into the car, and drove south toward home.

The day was cloudy. I passed through towns with familiar names, through the pine forests and down to the prairie, and then to Vietnam, where I was a soldier, and then home again. I survived, but it's not a happy ending. I was a coward. I went to the war. ❖

 Is it acceptable to break the law if the law contradicts one's personal beliefs? What options might a person have who does not want to break the law and yet wants to show that he or she disagrees with the law?

Refer and Reason

1. The narrator says, "I was a coward. I went to war." Quote other statements about courage and cowardice in the story. Analyze the narrator's view of courage. If he were to write a dictionary definition of the word *courage*, what would it say?

2. What decision did the narrator make about the Vietnam War? Evaluate his decision. On what was it based? Do you think it was a good decision? Why?

3. Identify the main internal conflicts in this story. Explain how the narrator deals with these conflicts. How does the narrator's way of dealing with conflicts compare with the way you deal with your own internal conflicts?

Writing Options

1. Write a very brief story or anecdote about a difficult decision you have had to make. In your story, describe how you decided what to do and how you felt about your decision afterward.

2. Write a brief analysis of "On the Rainy River" to be used by social studies teachers to determine if the story would be good reading for their class on the United States and the Vietnam War. Make and support a suggestion for or against including the story in the class syllabus.

 Go to **www.mirrorsandwindows.com** for more.

from

The Kite Runner

A Novel Excerpt by

Khaled Hosseini

Khaled Hosseini was born in Kabul, Afghanistan, in 1965 and spent his early life there. When Hosseini was eleven years old, his family moved to Paris, where his father was assigned to a diplomatic post with the Afghan Embassy. In 1980, after the Soviet invasion of Afghanistan, his family immigrated to the United States for political protection and settled in California. *The Kite Runner* is Hosseini's first novel.

The novel describes the experiences of Amir, a young Afghan boy, as his country undergoes dramatic changes. This excerpt is set in winter, when Kabul hosted a kite-fighting tournament in which boys try to cut down their opponents' kites while protecting their own. Kite runners would run to collect the fallen kites. As you read, notice how the kite-fighting tournament provides a chance for the narrator to develop and analyze his relationships with his father and his best friend and servant, Hassan.

What connotations, or emotional associations, does the word *kite* have for you? What images come to your mind when you think of kites? What time of year do you picture? How do these images make you feel?

W inter.

Here is what I do on the first day of snowfall every year: I step out of the house early in the morning, still in my pajamas, hugging my arms against the chill. I find the driveway, my father's car, the walls, the trees, the rooftops, and the hills buried under a foot of snow. I smile. The sky is seamless and blue, the snow so white my eyes burn. I shovel a handful of the fresh snow into my mouth, listen to the muffled stillness broken only by the cawing of crows. I walk down the front steps, barefoot, and call for Hassan[1] to come out and see.

Winter was every kid's favorite season in Kabul, at least those whose fathers could afford to buy a good iron stove. The reason was simple: They shut down school for the icy season. Winter to me was the end of long division and naming the capital of Bulgaria, and the start of three months of playing cards by the stove with Hassan, free Russian movies on Tuesday mornings at Cinema Park, sweet turnip *qurma* over rice for lunch after a morning of building snowmen.

And kites, of course. Flying kites. And running them.

For a few unfortunate kids, winter did not spell the end of the school year. There were the so-called voluntary winter courses. No kid I knew ever volunteered to go to these classes; parents, of course, did the volunteering for them. Fortunately for me, Baba[2] was not one of them. I remember one kid, Ahmad, who lived across the street from us. His father was some kind of doctor, I think. Ahmad had epilepsy and always wore a wool vest and thick black-rimmed glasses—he was one of Assef's regular victims. Every morning, I watched from my bedroom window as their Hazara[3] servant shoveled snow from the driveway, cleared the way for the black Opel. I made a point of watching Ahmad and his father get into the car, Ahmad in his wool vest and winter coat,

his schoolbag filled with books and pencils. I waited until they pulled away, turned the corner, then I slipped back into bed in my flannel pajamas. I pulled the blanket to my chin and watched the snowcapped hills in the north through the window. Watched them until I drifted back to sleep.

I loved wintertime in Kabul. I loved it for the soft pattering of snow against my window at night, for the way fresh snow crunched under my black rubber boots, for the warmth of the cast-iron stove as the wind screeched through the yards, the streets. But mostly because, as the trees froze and ice sheathed the roads, the chill between Baba and me thawed a little. And the reason for that was the kites. Baba and I lived in the same house, but in different spheres of existence. Kites were the one paper-thin slice of intersection between those spheres.

E very winter, districts in Kabul held a kite-fighting tournament. And if you were a boy living in Kabul, the day of the tournament was undeniably the highlight of the cold season. I never slept the night before the tournament. I'd roll from side to side, make shadow animals on the wall, even sit on the balcony in the dark, a blanket wrapped around me. I felt like a soldier trying to sleep in the trenches the night before a major battle. And that wasn't so far off. In Kabul, fighting kites *was* a little like going to war.

As with any war, you had to ready yourself for battle. For a while, Hassan and I used to build our own kites. We saved our weekly allowances in the fall, dropped the money in a little porcelain horse Baba had brought one time from Herat. When the winds of winter began to blow and snow fell in chunks, we

---

1. **Hassan.** Amir's servant. Earlier in the novel, readers learn that Hassan is a member of an ethnic minority group and that he and Amir have an uneasy friendship because of the ethnic difference.
2. **Baba.** Father (Arabic)
3. **Hazara.** Member of a minority ethnic group in Afghanistan

undid the snap under the horse's belly. We went to the bazaar[4] and bought bamboo, glue, string, and paper. We spent hours every day shaving bamboo for the center and cross spars, cutting the thin tissue paper which made for easy dipping and recovery. And then, of course, we had to make our own string, or *tar*. If the kite was the gun, then *tar*, the glass-coated cutting line, was the bullet in the chamber. We'd go out in the yard and feed up to five hundred feet of string through a mixture of ground glass and glue. We'd then hang the line between the trees, leave it to dry. The next day, we'd wind the battle-ready line around a wooden spool. By the time the snow melted and the rains of spring swept in, every boy in Kabul bore telltale horizontal gashes on his fingers from a whole winter of fighting kites. I remember how my classmates and I used to huddle, compare our battle scars on the first day of school. The cuts stung and didn't heal for a couple of weeks, but I didn't mind. They were reminders of a beloved season that had once again passed too quickly. Then the class captain would blow his whistle and we'd march in a single file to our class-rooms, longing for winter already, greeted instead by the specter of yet another long school year.

But it quickly became apparent that Hassan and I were better kite fighters than kite makers. Some flaw or other in our design always spelled its doom. So Baba started taking us to Saifo's to buy our kites. Saifo was a nearly blind old man who was a *moochi* by profession—a shoe repairman. But he was also the city's most famous kite maker, working out of a tiny hovel on Jadeh Maywand, the crowded street south of the muddy banks of the Kabul River. I remember you had to crouch to enter the prison cell-sized store, and then had to lift a trapdoor to creep down a set of wooden steps to the dank basement where Saifo stored his coveted kites. Baba would buy us each three identical kites and spools of glass string. If I changed my mind and asked for a bigger and fancier kite, Baba would buy it for me—but then he'd buy it for Hassan too. Sometimes I wished he wouldn't do that. Wished he'd let me be the favorite.

The kite-fighting tournament was an old winter tradition in Afghanistan. It started early in the morning on the day of the contest and didn't end until only the winning kite flew in the sky—I remember one year the tournament outlasted daylight. People gathered on sidewalks and roofs to cheer for their kids. The streets filled with kite fighters, jerking and tugging on their lines, squinting up to the sky, trying to gain position to cut the opponent's line. Every kite fighter had an assistant—in my case, Hassan—who held the spool and fed the line.

One time, a bratty Hindi kid whose family had recently moved into the neighborhood told us that in his hometown, kite fighting had strict rules and regulations. "You have to play in a boxed area and you have to stand at a right angle to the wind," he said proudly. "And you can't use aluminum to make your glass string."

Hassan and I looked at each other. Cracked up. The Hindi kid would soon learn what the British learned earlier in the century, and what the Russians would eventually learn by the late 1980s: that Afghans are an independent people. Afghans cherish custom but abhor rules. And so it was with kite fighting. The

---

4. **bazaar.** Rows of stalls or shops selling a variety of goods

rules were simple: No rules. Fly your kite. Cut the opponents. Good luck.

Except that wasn't all. The real fun began when a kite was cut. That was where the kite runners came in, those kids who chased the windblown kite drifting through the neighborhoods until it came spiraling down in a field, dropping in someone's yard, on a tree, or a rooftop. The chase got pretty fierce; hordes of kite runners swarmed the streets, shoved past each other like those people from Spain I'd read about once, the ones who ran from the bulls. One year a neighborhood kid climbed a pine tree for a kite. A branch snapped under his weight and he fell thirty feet. Broke his back and never walked again. But he fell with the kite still in his hands. And when a kite runner had his hands on a kite, no one could take it from him. That wasn't a rule. That was custom.

For kite runners, the most coveted prize was the last fallen kite of a winter tournament. It was a trophy of honor, something to be displayed on a mantle for guests to admire. When the sky cleared of kites and only the final two remained, every kite runner readied himself for the chance to land this prize. He positioned himself at a spot that he thought would give him a head start. Tense muscles readied themselves to uncoil. Necks craned. Eyes crinkled. Fights broke out. And when the last kite was cut, all hell broke loose.

Over the years, I had seen a lot of guys run kites. But Hassan was by far the greatest kite runner I'd ever seen. It was downright eerie the way he always got to the spot the kite would land *before* the kite did, as if he had some sort of inner compass.

I remember one overcast winter day, Hassan and I were running a kite. I was chasing him through neighborhoods, hopping gutters, weaving through narrow streets. I was a year older than him, but Hassan ran faster than I did, and I was falling behind.

"Hassan! Wait!" I yelled, my breathing hot and ragged.

He whirled around, motioned with his hand. "This way!" he called before dashing around another corner. I looked up, saw that the direction we were running was opposite to the one the kite was drifting.

"We're losing it! We're going the wrong way!" I cried out.

"Trust me!" I heard him call up ahead. I reached the corner and saw Hassan bolting along, his head down, not even looking at the sky, sweat soaking through the back of his

No rules. Fly your kite. Cut the opponents. Good luck.

shirt. I tripped over a rock and fell—I wasn't just slower than Hassan but clumsier too; I'd always envied his natural athleticism. When I staggered to my feet, I caught a glimpse of Hassan disappearing around another street corner. I hobbled after him, spikes of pain battering my scraped knees.

I saw we had ended up on a rutted dirt road near Isteqlal Middle School. There was a field on one side where lettuce grew in the summer, and a row of sour cherry trees on the other. I found Hassan sitting cross-legged at the foot of one of the trees, eating from a fistful of dried mulberries.

"What are we doing here?" I panted, my stomach roiling with nausea.

He smiled. "Sit with me, Amir agha."

I dropped next to him, lay on a thin patch of snow, wheezing. "You're wasting our time. It was going the other way, didn't you see?"

Hassan popped a mulberry in his mouth. "It's coming," he said. I could hardly breathe and he didn't even sound tired.

"How do you know?" I said.

"I know."

"How can you *know*?"

He turned to me. A few sweat beads rolled from his bald scalp. "Would I ever lie to you, Amir agha?"

fraction of a moment, long enough to leave me with the unsettling feeling that maybe I'd seen it someplace before. Then Hassan blinked and it was just him again. Just Hassan.

"If you asked, I would," he finally said, looking right at me. I dropped my eyes. To this day, I find it hard to gaze directly at people like Hassan, people who mean every word they say.

Suddenly I decided to toy with him a little. "I don't know. Would you?"

"I'd sooner eat dirt," he said with a look of indignation.

"Really? You'd do that?"

He threw me a puzzled look. "Do what?"

"Eat dirt if I told you to," I said. I knew I was being cruel, like when I'd taunt him if he didn't know some big word. But there was something fascinating—albeit in a sick way—about teasing Hassan. Kind of like when we used to play insect torture. Except now, he was the ant and I was holding the magnifying glass.

His eyes searched my face for a long time. We sat there, two boys under a sour cherry tree, suddenly looking, *really* looking, at each other. That's when it happened again: Hassan's face changed. Maybe not *changed*, not really, but suddenly I had the feeling I was looking at two faces, the one I knew, the one that was my first memory, and another, a second face, this one lurking just beneath the surface. I'd seen it happen before—it always shook me up a little. It just appeared, this other face, for a

"But I wonder," he added. "Would you ever ask me to do such a thing, Amir agha?" And, just like that, he had thrown at me his own little test. If I was going to toy with him and challenge his loyalty, then he'd toy with me, test my integrity.

I wished I hadn't started this conversation. I forced a smile. "Don't be stupid, Hassan. You know I wouldn't."

Hassan returned the smile. Except his didn't look forced. "I know," he said. And that's the thing about people who mean everything they say. They think everyone else does too.

"Here it comes," Hassan said, pointing to the sky. He rose to his feet and walked a few paces to his left. I looked up, saw the kite plummeting toward us. I heard footfalls, shouts, an approaching melee of kite runners. But they were wasting their time. Because Hassan stood with his arms wide open, smiling, waiting for the kite. And may God—if He exists, that is—strike me blind if the kite didn't just drop into his outstretched arms. ❖

MIRRORS & WINDOWS

What's the difference between teasing in a friendly way and teasing in a cruel way? Why do friends sometimes taunt and tease each other? How can doing so harm a friendship?

Informational Text
CONNECTION

The Kite Runner was reviewed in many newspapers and magazines shortly after its release in spring 2003. Americans were newly interested in Afghanistan, where the novel is set, because of U.S. military involvement in the country following the terrorist attacks of September 11, 2001. During this military campaign, the United States drove out the fundamentalist Islamic government called the Taliban, which novelist **Edward Hower** mentions in his New York Times book review, **"The Kite Runner: A Servant's Son."**

The Kite Runner:
A Servant's Son

The New York Times

A Review by Edward Hower

This powerful first novel, by an Afghan physician now living in California, tells a story of fierce cruelty and fierce yet redeeming love. Both transform the life of Amir, Khaled Hosseini's privileged young narrator, who comes of age during the last peaceful days of the monarchy, just before his country's revolution and its invasion by Russian forces.

But political events, even as dramatic as the ones that are presented in *The Kite Runner,* are only a part of this story. A more personal plot, arising from Amir's close friendship with Hassan, the son of his father's servant, turns out to be the thread that ties the book together. The fragility of this relationship, symbolized by the kites the boys fly together, is tested as they watch their old way of life disappear.

Amir is served breakfast every morning by Hassan; then he is driven to school in the gleaming family Mustang while his friend stays home to clean the house. Yet Hassan bears Amir no resentment and is, in fact, a loyal companion to the lonely boy, whose mother is dead and whose father, a rich businessman, is often preoccupied. Hassan protects the sensitive Amir from sadistic neighborhood bullies; in turn, Amir fascinates Hassan by reading him heroic Afghan folk tales. Then, during a kite-flying tournament that should be the triumph of Amir's young life, Hassan is brutalized by some upper-class teenagers. Amir's failure to defend his friend will haunt him for the rest of his life.

Hosseini's depiction of pre-revolutionary Afghanistan is rich in warmth and humor but also tense with the friction between the nation's different ethnic groups. Amir's father, or Baba, personifies all that is reckless, courageous and arrogant in his dominant Pashtun tribe. He loves nothing better than watching the Afghan national pastime, buzkashi, in which galloping horsemen bloody one another as they compete to spear the carcass of a goat. Yet he is generous and tolerant enough to respect his son's artistic yearnings and to treat the lowly Hassan with great kindness, even arranging for an operation to mend the child's harelip.

As civil war begins to ravage the country, the teenage Amir and his father must flee for their lives. In California, Baba works at a gas station to put his son through school; on weekends he sells secondhand goods at swap meets. Here too Hosseini provides lively descriptions, showing former professors and doctors socializing as they haggle with their customers over black velvet portraits of Elvis.

Despite their poverty, these exiled Afghans manage to keep alive their ancient standards of honor and pride. And even as Amir grows to manhood, settling comfortably into America and a happy marriage, his past shame continues to haunt him. He worries about Hassan and wonders what has happened to him back in Afghanistan.

The novel's canvas turns dark when Hosseini describes the suffering of his country under the tyranny of the Taliban, whom Amir encounters when he finally returns home, hoping to help Hassan and his family. The final third of the book is full of haunting images: a man, desperate to feed his children, trying to sell his artificial leg in the market; an adulterous couple stoned to death in a stadium during the halftime of a football match; a rouged young boy forced into prostitution, dancing the sort of steps once performed by an organ grinder's monkey.

When Amir meets his old nemesis, now a powerful Taliban official, the book descends into some plot twists better suited to a folk tale than a modern novel. But in the end we're won over by Amir's compassion and his determination to atone for his youthful cowardice.

In *The Kite Runner,* Khaled Hosseini gives us a vivid and engaging story that reminds us how long his people have been struggling to triumph over the forces of violence—forces that continue to threaten them even today. ❖

Refer and Reason

1. List some of Hassan's characteristics and abilities. Make inferences about the narrator and his feelings toward Hassan based on his description of Hassan.
2. Identify examples of honesty and dishonesty in the story. Determine who is more honest, Amir or Hassan. How do you know?
3. Quote what the narrator says at the end of the selection about people who say what they mean. Write a continuation of the story that shows how this assumption might be a problem for Hassan in the future.

Writing Options

1. Write a retelling of the incident described by Amir from Hassan's point of view. Keep in mind what you know about Hassan and his relationship with Amir.
2. For a magazine feature on customs and traditions, write a narrative paragraph describing your participation in a tradition or custom shared by your family, culture, or religion. In your narrative, talk about how the tradition is practiced and what your feeling is toward sharing in the tradition.

 Go to **www.mirrorsandwindows.com** for more.

TEXT ◄—TO—► TEXT CONNECTION

- According to Hower, what is *The Kite Runner* really about? How does the excerpt from *The Kite Runner* you've just read reflect this idea?
- Does the review make you want to read more of the novel? Why?

Who Said We All Have to Talk Alike

In fact, Neffie never really knew that she talked different from most other people.

A Short Story by
Wilma Elizabeth McDaniel

Wilma Elizabeth McDaniel (b. 1918) was born in Oklahoma. Like many people from Oklahoma, Texas, Arkansas, and other Great Plains states, McDaniel moved to California to escape the Dust Bowl in 1936. McDaniel writes poetry, fiction, and drama. McDaniel said of her experience during the Dust Bowl, "You had to have magic and art to survive those Dust Bowl days. We need our art to get through the toughest times."

McDaniel draws upon her life in Oklahoma and her knowledge of not quite fitting in to a new place in **"Who Said We All Have to Talk Alike."** In the story, the Okie accent of Neffie, the protagonist, causes problems for her when she moves to California for a job. As you read, notice how Neffie speaks in *dialect*, or a version of a language spoken by the people of a particular time, place, or social group. Also notice how McDaniel re-spells words to show nonstandard pronunciations. If you have trouble figuring out the meaning of a word that is re-spelled, try saying it aloud.

Describe a situation when you felt out of place. What did you do to deal with the situation?

Who knows how Neffie Pike's speech pattern was formed? Her Ozark[1] family had talked the same way for generations. They added an "r" to many words that did not contain that letter. In spite of this, or because of it, their speech was clear and colorful and to the point. Most people understood what they were talking about, exactly.

Neffie was her parent's daughter. She called a

---

1. **Ozark.** Mountainous area between the Arkansas and Missouri Rivers that lies in Missouri, Arkansas, Oklahoma, and Kansas

> ## 'A widder worman is a free worman, especially if she don't have no children. She ought to be free to come and go like she pleases.'

toilet, "torelet," and a woman, "worman," very comfortably. The teacher at the country school never attempted to change Neffie's manner of speaking. She said that Neffie had a fine imagination and should never allow anyone to squelch it. In fact, Neffie never really knew that she talked different from most other people.

People in the tiny community of Snowball really loved Neffie. She was a good neighbor, unfailingly cheerful and helpful. The appearance of her tall and bony figure at the door of a sickroom or a bereaved family meant comfort and succor. A great woman, everyone in Snowball agreed.

She would have probably lived her life out in the same lumber house if her husband had not died. In the months that followed his death she developed a restless feeling. Home chores, church and charity work did not seem to be enough to occupy her mind. She started to read big town newspapers at the library in nearby Marshall, something new for her. She became especially interested in the out of state employment want ads. She mentioned to neighbors, "They are a lot of good jobs out there in the world."

One day she came home from Marshall and stopped at old Grandma Meade's house. She sat down in a canebottom chair and announced, "I have got me a job in California. I am selling my house and lot to a couple of retired people from Little Rock. They will be moving in the first of June."

Grandma Meade sat in shocked silence for several seconds, then said, "Honey, I do not believe it. I mean that I never in the world imagined that you would consider leaving Snowball. You and Lollis was so happy together here." Her voice trailed off, "Of course

nobody could foretell the Lord would call him so young."

Neffie looked stonily at her and said with her usual clarity, "A widder worman is a free worman, especially if she don't have no children. She ought to be free to come and go like she pleases. After all, I am only fifty-one years old. I can do as much work as I ever did. This job is taking care of two little girls while their mother works at some high paying job. She has already sent me a bus ticket. I would be a fool not to go. Everyone has been to California except me. I always hankered to see the state for myself. Now is my chance to see some of the rest of the world. It may sound foolish, but it will sort of be like having a dorter of my own and grandchildren. I aim to write you a long letter when I get settled down out there."

Neffie left for California on schedule. After two weeks Grandma Meade began to worry a bit. She said, "I thought that Neffie surely would have dropped us a line by now. The last thing she told me was that she would write me a long letter. Well, maybe she hasn't got settled down yet."

A month passed without any word from Neffie.

Bug Harrison was at Grandma Meade's house when Neffie returned the day after Snowball's big Fourth of July celebration.

Neffie put her suitcases down and began at the beginning. "Grandma, you was so right about so many things. I knowed I was in trouble hock-deep, only one minute after I stepped off that bus in California. A purty young worman come forward to meet me and said she was Beryl. I busted out and told her, 'My, you are a purty worman, even purtier than your pitcher.' She kinda shrunk back and looked at me like I had used a cussword. She

stood there holding her little girls' hands and asked me, where on earth did you hear a word like worman, was it a female worm of some kind? She said, 'Worman is woe-man,' like you say woh to a horse.

"Her remark nearly knocked me off my feet. I felt like a fool, and I didn't even know why. My stomach started churning. I durst not say anything to defend myself, because I hadn't done anything wrong.

"We started walking to Beryl's station wagon in the parking lot. I told her that I never was blessed with a dorter or son, either. That set her off again. She said that her children were at a very impressionable age, that I would have to watch my speech and learn the correct pronunciation of words. She did not want them picking up incorrect speech patterns and something she called coll-oke-ism,[2] something I had, and didn't even realize. I decided to shut up and get in the car. The worman had already paid for my fare. I felt that I had to at least give

her a few months' service, if I could stand the punishment at all.

"On our way to Beryl's house, she stopped at a drive-in restaurant and ordered cheeseburgers and milkshakes for all of us. I decided to just eat and listen.

"It was sure a pleasurable drive on to Beryl's home. We followed the same county highway for the entire seven miles. The road was lined on both sides with pams, tall with them fronds waving in the breeze. It reminded me of pitchers I have seen of The Holy Land, really touched my heart. I forgot myself again and said that I never had seen pams before except in pitchers. Quick as a flash Beryl told me, 'They are pall-ms, not pams. There is an l in the word.' After that, I sure buttoned up my mouth. I just said yes or no to anything she asked me.

"Her house turned out to be a real nice place, bright and modern with every type of

---

2. **coll-oke-ism.** Colloquialism, or informal speech

popovers, french toast, corn dodgers, fried mush. You name it, worman, I cooked it for those dolls. It wouldn't be no big deal for the kids here in Snowball, they was raised to eat like that, but it was hog heaven to Pat and Penny."

Grandma Meade had been listening intently, her eyes pinned on Neffie's face. Now she asked, "How did Beryl like your cooking?"

Neffie laughed heartily. She said, "To put it plain, she LOVED it. I can say that she never found any flaw in my cooking, only made one complaint connected with it. I boirled her a fine big cabbage and hamhock dinner and made cornbread for our supper one evening. When we started to sit down at the table, I said that is was a nice change to have a boirled dinner now and then. That set her off like a firecracker. She said, 'That is boil-ed, not boirled.' I decided to let that snide remark pass. I saw she started dishing up the food — she lit in on it like a starving hounddog. That showed what she thought of my cooking, didn't it? My cooking sure helped me get through them weeks as good as I did."

Bug Harrison broke in, "What were your duties during the day?"

Neffie said, "I was hired to take care of the two little girls. That is what I done. I cooked because people have to eat. I always have, always will. That didn't put no extra strain on me. The girls and I played the most of the day. They would sit on each arm of my chair and listen to me tell them about my life back in Arkansas. I didn't hold back nothing. I told them about haunted houses, ghosts, robbers, bank holdups, tornadoes, snakes, tarantulas, times when the river flooded and we had to float on a rooftop to save our lives. Lordy, worman, they just ate it up. They would listen to me with their eyes as big as saucers. I don't quite know why I done it, but I asked the girls not to tell their mother about my stories. They

electrical gadget you could think of. There were four bedrooms, each with a bath. I was so tired and upset over Beryl's attitude that I begged off sitting up to visit with her and the little girls. I ran me a full tub of warm water and took me a long soaking bath. I fell into bed and went sound asleep. Worman, I plumb died away, slept all night without waking up. To show you how hard I slept, there was a fairly severe earthquake in the central part of California where Beryl lived. It even shook a few things off a living room shelf. I tell you, I wouldn't have heard Gabriel blow his horn that night.

"I woke up feeling relieved that it was Monday. Beryl left for work promptly at seven-thirty. That meant the girls and I had the house to ourselves. Worman, I am a telling you, they was two living dolls, Pat and Penny. I made them bran muffins for breakfast and scrambled some eggs. They ate until they nearly foun-dered. It seemed like they had never seen a bran muffin before, asked me if I would cook them the same thing each day.

"I told them I knew how to cook other good old homely dishes, too. Every day, I tried something new on them, biscuits and sausage and milk gravy, buttermilk pancakes, waffles,

I figured I was in bad trouble, but I kept on dropping the noodles into the broth. I was a hundred percent right about the trouble.

were as secretive as little private detectives until a week ago. They got so excited over one of my stories that they forgot theirselves. I was busy in the kitchen putting some homemade noodles into a pot of chicken broth. I heard Pat tell her mother, 'Mom, back in Arkansas where Neffie used to live, they are wormans that can tell fortunes for people. They can look right through your face and tell if you are telling the truth or a lie. They can rub your warts with skunk oirl and say some words and all the warts will fall off, never ever come back.' I figured I was in bad trouble, but I kept on dropping the noodles into the broth. I was a hundred percent right about the trouble.

"Beryl blowed her stack. She marched right back to the kitchen with the girls at her heels. She stood in the door . and said, 'I have been afraid of this very thing. Neffie, I just can't keep you on any longer.'

"At that point Pat and Penny throwed themselves down on the floor and started bawling like two young calves. Pat sobbed out real angry-like, 'Yes, you CAN keep Neffie! She is the best storyteller in the whole world and the best cooker. If she goes home to Arkansas, we won't never have no more biscuits and sausage and gravy.' The tears began to run down her little face.

"Beryl stood there with her face like a flintrock. It looked like she wanted to be nice to me, but that her duty come first with her.

She drawed in her breath and said, 'Neffie, you are as good and kind and honest as you can be, exceptional, but your speech is totally unacceptable. My children are at a very impressionable age. I have tried to overlook it, but they are definitely being influenced in the wrong direction. They say dorter and orter with regularity. The pattern must be eradicated immediately. I shall be happy to pay your traveling expenses home. You can look on this trip out West as my vacation gift to you.' I could see that her mind was made up and she wasn't going to change it.

"I did think to ask her if she had some other baby-sitter in mind. I didn't want to run out and leave her in a bind without one. She said there was a young girl from the college who wanted day work, so she could attend night classes. She thought that would work out great. I got her point. The college girl would be different from me, more to suit Beryl.

"Well, to shorten my story, she bought me a big box of real expensive chocolates and put

chocolate and think over my experience with Beryl. Things kind of cleared up in my mind, like having blinders taken off of my eyes. I saw I had really been ignorant of some things that other folks knowed. I didn't talk right to suit some of them, but that wasn't my fault. *I didn't know we was all supposed to talk the same way.* I thought people hadn't all talked the same since before God tore down their tower at Babel and confused all their tongues.[3] Folks all over the world have talked different ever since then. I guess some of them like Beryl want to go back to pre-Babel days. Anyway, it was sure an eye-opener to me, hurt me, too. Beryl just plain separated herself from

me on the bus with my paid ticket, just like she had promised. She and the girls stood there beside the bus waiting for it to pull out. Penny looked up at me and blew me a kiss. I heard her say as plain as plain could be, 'Neffie, you are a sweet worman.' Then I saw Beryl put her hand over Penny's mouth. Right then, the bus pulled out of the depot and I lost sight of them.

"Worman, I done a lot of thinking as that bus rolled along the highway. I would eat a

me. It was like she took a sharp knife and cut a melon in half, and throwed away the half that was me. You know what you do with a piece of melon you don't want. You throw it with the rinds into the garbage can. Worman, who said that we all have to talk alike? Can anyone tell me that?" ❖

---

3. **tower at Babel…tongues.** Reference to a biblical story in which God makes people speak in different languages to cause confusion

How divisive do you think things like speech patterns really are? What other differences can be divisive? Have you ever judged somebody or been judged yourself because of a trait like a speech pattern? How did you react?

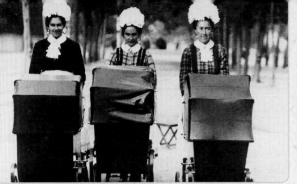

Informational Text
CONNECTION

Contracts are legal documents that describe an agreement between two parties. Both parties sign the contract and agree to abide by its rules. An employment contract outlines the terms of employment, the salary, time off, rules of termination, and the process for grievances. Think about what benefits a contract might have for both an employer and an employee. As you read the contract, consider how a similar contract would have affected Neffie in "Who Said We All Have to Talk Alike."

EMPLOYMENT CONTRACT FOR A NANNY

BETWEEN

1. Ronald and Philipa MacKubin **("the Employer")**
2. Sophie Arnout **("the Nanny")**

It is agreed that the Employer will employ the Nanny on the following terms and conditions:

1. Terms of Employment

1.a. The Nanny is employed to work at the Employer's home at 1265 Fern Glen Drive, Abbisdale, PA, or any other locations that the Employer may require within reason.

1.b. The Nanny will start employment on June 15, 2008, and finish employment at a future time to be determined by both parties.

1.c. The Nanny's duties shall be:
  A. Caring for these children:
   Name: Hugh MacKubin Age: 7
   Name: Linda MacKubin Age: 4
   Name: Jackson MacKubin Age: 2
  B. Babysitting at times agreed in advance
  C. Other duties as specified here: Preparing breakfast and lunch for the children, bathing the children, tidying the children's rooms.

1.d. The Nanny shall normally work the following: Monday–Saturday.

1.e. The Employer and the Nanny shall agree in advance upon the hours to be worked, but the usual hours shall fall between 8:00 am and 6:00 pm. The Nanny is entitled to a break of one half-hour to be taken at an appropriate time when the safety and security of the children is guaranteed.

1.f. The Nanny is entitled to a rest period of no less than 12 hours between the end of working hours on one day and the start of working hours on the next.

1.g. The Nanny shall not engage in any work from a third party, whether paid or unpaid, during the working hours set by the Employer. The Nanny's full attention shall be devoted to the care and attendance of the children in the Nanny's charge.

2. Salary

2.a. The Nanny's salary shall be $800 per week. The salary shall be reviewed once a year after three months of employment. A raise in salary is at the discretion of the Employer.

2.b. The Nanny shall be paid bi-weekly either by check or direct deposit. The Employer shall give the Nanny a pay stub with each payment that details gross pay, deductions, and net pay.

2.c. The Nanny shall receive the following benefits:

A. Accommodation: The Employer shall provide a private room with a single bed and private bath.
B. Meals: The Employer shall provide appropriate ingredients for the Nanny's breakfasts and lunches, though the Nanny is responsible for preparing those meals for herself. The Employer will also provide dinner.
C. Transportation: The Employer shall provide the use of a car during the hours of employment if given two days' advance notice.
D. Pension: The Employer does not provide a pension or other retirement benefits.
E. Health Insurance: The Employer does not provide private health insurance.

2.d. The Nanny shall be reimbursed by the Employer for all reasonable expenses incurred for the purpose of performing her duties. These expenses should be cleared with the Employer in advance when possible. All requests for reimbursements should be accompanied by a receipt or other form of documentation of the expenditure.

2.e. The Employer shall be responsible for reporting to the Internal Revenue Service for income tax and Social Security taxes.

3. Time Off

3.a. In each year, the Nanny is entitled to 10 vacation days with pay. Vacation days must be cleared with the Employer at least two weeks in advance of the first proposed day of vacation. If the proposed time off is not convenient to the Employer, an alternative time must be decided upon.

3.b. The Nanny is entitled to time off with pay for these holidays: Memorial Day, Independence Day, Labor Day, Thanksgiving and the following day, Christmas Eve, Christmas Day, and New Year's Day.

3.c. At the termination of her employment, the Nanny will be paid any vacation days accrued but not taken.

3.d. If the Nanny is unable to work due to sickness or injury, she shall promptly notify the Employer before the start of her working hours. For any absences due to illness or injury lasting more than three days, the Nanny is required to provide the Employer with evidence of her sickness, such as a note of explanation from a doctor.

3.e. The Nanny is entitled to receive full pay for up to five days of sick leave.

4. Termination

4.a. If either party wishes to terminate this contract within the first month of employment, one week's notice must be given. Thereafter, three weeks' notice shall be required.

4.b. The Nanny's employment may be terminated by the Employer at any time for the following:
   A. serious misconduct that either violates this contract or in any way threatens the safety or well-being of the children or property of the Employer, including drunkenness and drug-taking
   B. criminal offenses involving stealing, fraud, violence, or abuse

5. Grievances

5.a. The Employer shall issue a warning to the Nanny about the following:
   A. job incompetence
   B. inappropriate dress or appearance
   C. unreliability in attendance and punctuality
   D. failure to follow instructions given by the Employer

5.b. If a second warning is required, the Nanny is considered "on probation" until it is proven that the unsatisfactory behavior has been corrected. A third incidence of the same behavior may lead to a deduction in pay or termination of employment as the Employer deems appropriate. The Employer shall keep written record of all warnings issued.

5.c. If the Nanny has any reasonable grievances relating to her employment, the matter can be raised with the Employer in a casual manner, if the Nanny deems it appropriate. For more serious grievances, the Nanny should provide a written statement to the Employer. At that point, the Employer will call a meeting with the Nanny to discuss the grievance and rectify the situation to the satisfaction of both parties.

SIGNED by the Employer
DATED

SIGNED by the Nanny
DATED

Refer and Reason

1. Recall why Neffie traveled to California. Analyze her reasons for leaving Snowball. How do you think she felt about leaving?
2. List some of Neffie's characteristics. Assess which of Neffie's characteristics was most important to Beryl. Why do you think this mattered to her so much? What does her decision to fire Neffie tell you about Beryl's character?
3. Identify some of the differences between life in Snowball and life at Beryl's. If Beryl went to live with Neffie for a month, what challenges would she face?

Writing Options

1. Write a postcard from Neffie to Pat and Penny telling them about her life now that she is back in Snowball. Make sure the message on the postcard reflects Neffie's character and speech.
2. Write a contract that Beryl could have her next nanny sign. Use the employment contract you just read as a guide. Add or adjust clauses to reflect some of Beryl's concerns.

TEXT ←TO→ TEXT CONNECTION

Review the Termination section of the contract. If this contract were in place, would Beryl have had just cause to fire Neffie? Explain.

CHEE'S DAUGHTER

CHEE SAT UPRIGHT, A TERRIBLE FEAR
POSSESSING HIM. FOR A MOMENT
HIS MOUTH COULD MAKE NO
SOUND. THEN: "THE LITTLE ONE!
MOTHER, WHERE IS SHE?"

A Short Story by
Juanita Platero and Siyowin Miller

Dine Country, 1996. Nelson Tsosie. Nelson Tsosie Collection, Santa Fe, New Mexico.

"Chee's Daughter" is the story of a traditional Navajo farmer, Chee, whose ways come into conflict with modern society and materialistic values. After Chee's wife dies, his daughter is taken by his in-laws to live with them, according to a Navajo custom that maintains that a girl child belongs with her mother's relatives. Chee struggles to maintain his belief in the promise of the land as he fights to get his daughter back.

Juanita Platero, a Navajo writer, lived at one time on a reservation in New Mexico, the setting for "Chee's Daughter." She began working in collaboration with **Siyowin Miller** in 1929. Most of the stories the two wrote together share the theme of the conflict in values between the old Navajo ways and the new ways of industrial society. As you read, consider why the setting is important to the story.

Have you ever lost something you valued? What were you willing to do to get it back?

The hat told the story, the big, black, drooping Stetson. It was not at the proper angle, the proper rakish angle for so young a Navajo. There was no song, and that was not in keeping either. There should have been at least a humming, a faint, all-to-himself "he he he heya," for it was a good horse he was riding, a slender-legged, high-stepping buckskin that would race the wind with light knee-urging. This was a day for singing, a warm winter day, when the touch of the sun upon the back belied the snow high on distant mountains.

Wind warmed by the sun touched his high-boned cheeks like flicker[1] feathers, and still he rode on silently, deeper into Little Canyon, until the red rock walls rose straight upward from the stream bed and only a narrow piece of blue sky hung above. Abruptly the sky widened where the canyon walls were pushed back to make a wide place, as though in ancient times an angry stream had tried to go all ways at once.

This was home—this wide place in the canyon—levels of jagged rock and levels of rich red earth. This was home to Chee, the rider of the buckskin, as it had been to many generations before him.

He stopped his horse at the stream and sat looking across the narrow ribbon of water to the bare-branched peach trees. He was seeing them each springtime with their age-gnarled limbs transfigured beneath veils of blossom pink; he was seeing them in autumn laden with their yellow fruit, small and sweet. Then his eyes searched out the indistinct furrows of the fields beside the stream, where each year the corn and beans and squash drank thirstily of the overflow from summer rains. Chee was trying to outweigh today's bitter betrayal of hope by gathering to himself these reminders of the integrity of the land. Land did not cheat! His mind lingered deliberately on all the days spent here in the sun caring for the young plants, his songs to the earth and to the life springing from it— "…In the middle of the wide field…Yellow Corn Boy…He has started both ways…" then the harvest and repayment in full measure. Here was the old feeling of wholeness and of oneness with the sun and earth and growing things.

Chee urged the buckskin toward the family compound where, secure in a recess of over-hanging rock, was his mother's dome-shaped hogan,[2] red rock and red adobe like the ground on which it nestled. Not far from the hogan was the half-circle of brush like a dark shadow against the canyon wall-corral for sheep and goats. Farther from the hogan, in full circle, stood the horse corral made of heavy cedar branches sternly interlocked. Chee's long thin lips curved into a smile as he passed his daughter's tiny hogan squatted like a round Pueblo oven beside the corral. He remembered the summer day when together they sat back on their heels and plastered wet adobe all about the circling wall of rock and the woven dome of piñon[3] twigs. How his family laughed when the Little One herded the bewildered chickens into her tiny hogan as the first snow fell.

Then the smile faded from Chee's lips and his eyes darkened as he tied his horse to a corral post and turned to the strangely empty compound. "Someone has told them," he thought, "and they are inside weeping." He passed his mother's deserted loom on the south side of the hogan and pulled the rude wooden door toward him, bowing his head, hunching his shoulders to get inside.

His mother sat sideways by the center fire, her feet drawn up under her full skirts. Her hands were busy kneading dough in the chipped white basin. With her head down, her voice was muffled when she said, "The meal will soon be ready, Son."

Chee passed his father sitting against the wall, hat over his eyes as though asleep. He

---

1. **flicker.** Woodpecker
2. **hogan.** Traditional cone-shaped Navajo house made of logs or strips of wood and covered with mud
3. **piñon.** Small pine tree native to the Southwest

passed his older sister, who sat turning mutton ribs on a crude wire grill over the coals, noticed tears dropping on her hands. "She cared more for my wife than I realized," he thought.

Then because something must be said sometime, he tossed the black Stetson upon a bulging sack of wool and said, "You have heard, then." He could not shut from his mind how confidently he had set the handsome new hat on his head that very morning, slanting the wide brim over one eye: he was going to see his wife, and today he would ask the doctors about bringing her home; last week she had looked so much better.

His sister nodded but did not speak. His mother sniffled and passed her velveteen sleeve beneath her nose. Chee sat down, leaning against the wall. "I suppose I was a fool for hoping all the time. I should have expected this. Few of our people get well from the coughing sickness.[4] But she seemed to be getting better."

His mother was crying aloud now and blowing her nose noisily on her skirt. His father sat up, speaking gently to her.

Chee shifted his position and started a cigarette. His mind turned back to the Little One. At least she was too small to understand what had happened, the Little One who had been born three years before in the sanitarium[5] where his wife was being treated for the coughing sickness, the Little One he had brought home to his mother's hogan to be nursed by his sister, whose baby was a few months older. As she grew fat-cheeked and sturdy-legged, she followed him about like a shadow; somehow her baby mind had grasped that of all those at the hogan who cared for her and played with her, he—Chee—belonged most to her. She sat cross-legged at his elbow when he worked silver at the forge; she rode before him in the saddle when he drove the horses to water; often she lay wakeful on her sheep pelts until he stretched out for the night in the darkened hogan and she could snuggle warm against him.

Chee blew smoke slowly, and some of the sadness left his dark eyes as he said, "It is not as bad as it might be. It is not as though we are left with nothing."

Chee's sister arose, sobs catching in her throat, and rushed past him out the doorway. Chee sat upright, a terrible fear possessing him. For a moment his mouth could make no sound. Then: "The Little One! Mother, where is she?"

His mother turned her stricken face to him. "Your wife's people came after her this morning. They heard yesterday of their daughter's death through the trader at Red Sands."

Chee started to protest, but his mother shook her head slowly. "I didn't expect they would want the Little One either. But there

---

4. **coughing sickness.** Tuberculosis, a disease that affects the lungs
5. **sanitarium.** Institution where tuberculosis patients go to recover their health

BUT CHEE HAD ASKED INSTEAD FOR A PIECE OF LAND FOR A CORNFIELD AND HELP IN BUILDING A HOGAN FAR BACK FROM THE HIGHWAY AND A CORRAL FOR THE SHEEP HE HAD BROUGHT TO THIS MARRIAGE.

is nothing you can do. She is a girl child and belongs to her mother's people; it is custom."

Frowning, Chee got to his feet, grinding his cigarette into the dirt floor. "Custom! When did my wife's parents begin thinking about custom? Why, the hogan where they live doesn't even face the east!"[6] He started toward the door. "Perhaps I can overtake them. Perhaps they don't realize how much we want her here with us. I'll ask them to give my daughter back to me. Surely, they won't refuse."

His mother stopped him gently with her outstretched hand. "You couldn't overtake them now. They were in the trader's car. Eat and rest, and think more about this."

"Have you forgotten how things have always been between you and your wife's people?" his father said.

That night, Chee's thoughts were troubled—half-forgotten incidents became disturbingly vivid—but early the next morning he saddled the buckskin and set out for the settlement of Red Sands. Even though his father-in-law, Old Man Fat, might laugh, Chee knew that he must talk to him. There were some things to which Old Man Fat might listen.

Chee rode the first part of the fifteen miles to Red Sands expectantly. The sight of sandstone buttes near Cottonwood Spring reddening in the morning sun brought a song almost to his lips. He twirled his reins in salute to the small boy herding sheep toward many-colored Butterfly Mountain, watched with pleasure the feathers of smoke rising against treedarkened western mesas from the hogans sheltered there. But as he approached the familiar settlement sprawled in mushroom growth along the highway, he began to feel as though a scene from a bad dream was becoming real.

Several cars were parked around the trading store, which was built like two log hogans side by side, with red gas pumps in front and a sign across the tar-paper roofs: Red Sands Trading Post—Groceries Gasoline Cold Drinks Sandwiches Indian Curios. Back of the trading post an unpainted frame house and outbuildings squatted on the drab, treeless land. Chee and the Little One's mother had lived there when they stayed with his wife's people. That was according to custom—living with one's wife's people—but Chee had never been convinced that it was custom alone which prompted Old Man Fat and his wife to insist that their daughter bring her husband to live at the trading post.

Beside the post was a large hogan of logs, with brightly painted pseudo-Navajo designs on the roof—a hogan with smoke-smudged windows and a garish blue door which faced north to the highway. Old Man Fat had offered Chee a hogan like this one. The trader would build it if he and his wife would live there and Chee would work at his forge, making silver jewelry where tourists could watch him. But Chee had asked instead for a piece of land for a cornfield and help in building a hogan far back from the highway and a corral for the sheep he had brought to this marriage.

A cold wind blowing down from the mountains began to whistle about Chee's ears. It flapped the gaudy Navajo rugs which were hung in one long bright line to attract tourists. It swayed the sign *Navajo Weaver at Work* beside the loom where Old Man Fat's wife sat hunched in her striped blanket, patting the colored thread of a design into place with a

---

6. **"Why, the hogan...face the east."** According to Navajo custom, the door of the hogan faces east.

wooden comb. Tourists stood watching the weaver. More tourists stood in a knot before the hogan where the sign said: *See Inside a Real Navajo Home 25¢*.

Then the knot seemed to unravel as a few people returned to their cars; some had cameras; and there against the blue door Chee saw the Little One standing uncertainly. The wind was plucking at her new purple blouse and wide green skirt; it freed truant strands of soft dark hair from the meager queue[7] into which it had been tied with white yarn.

"Isn't she cunning!" one of the women tourists was saying as she turned away.

Chee's lips tightened as he began to look around for Old Man Fat. Finally he saw him passing among the tourists collecting coins.

Then the Little One saw Chee. The uncertainty left her face, and she darted through the crowd as her father swung down from his horse. Chee lifted her in his arms, hugging her tight. While he listened to her breathless chatter, he watched Old Man Fat bearing down on them, scowling.

As his father-in-law walked heavily across the graveled lot, Chee was reminded of a statement his mother sometimes made: "When you see a fat Navajo, you see one who hasn't worked for what he has."

Old Man Fat was fattest in the middle. There was indolence in his walk even though he seemed to hurry, indolence in his cheeks so plump they made his eyes squint, eyes now smoldering with anger.

Some of the tourists were getting into their cars and driving away. The old man said belligerently to Chee, "Why do you come here? To spoil our business? To drive people away?"

"I came to talk with you," Chee answered, trying to keep his voice steady as he faced the old man.

---

7. **queue.** Braid

"We have nothing to talk about," Old Man Fat blustered and did not offer to touch Chee's extended hand.

"It's about the Little One." Chee settled his daughter more comfortably against his hip as he weighed carefully all the words he had planned to say. "We are going to miss her very much. It wouldn't be so bad if we knew that *part* of each year she could be with us. That might help you too. You and your wife are no longer young people and you have no young ones here to depend upon." Chee chose his next words remembering the thriftlessness of his wife's parents, and their greed. "Perhaps we could share the care of this little one. Things are good with us. So much snow this year will make lots of grass for the sheep. We have good land for corn and melons."

Chee's words did not have the expected effect. Old Man Fat was enraged. "Farmers, all of you! Long-haired farmers! Do you think everyone must bend his back over the shorthandled hoe in order to have food to eat?" His tone changed as he began to brag a little. "We not only have all the things from cans at the trader's, but when the Pueblos come past here on their way to town, we buy their salty jerked[8] mutton, young corn for roasting, dried sweet peaches."

Chee's dark eyes surveyed the land along the highway as the old man continued to brag about being "progressive." *He* no longer was tied to the land. He and his wife made money easily and could *buy* all the things they wanted. Chee realized too late that he had stumbled into the old argument between himself and his wife's parents. They had never understood his feeling about the land—that a man took care of his land and it in turn took care of him. Old Man Fat and his wife scoffed at him, called him

a Pueblo farmer, all during that summer when he planted and weeded and harvested. Yet they ate the green corn in their mutton stews, and the chili paste from the fresh ripe chilis, and the tortillas from the cornmeal his wife ground. None of this working and sweating in the sun for Old Man Fat, who talked proudly of his easy way of living—collecting money from the trader who rented this strip of land beside the highway, collecting money from the tourists.

Yet Chee had once won that argument. His wife had shared his belief in the integrity of the earth, that jobs and people might fail one, but the earth never would. After that first year she had turned from her own people and gone with Chee to Little Canyon.

Old Man Fat was reaching for the Little One. "Don't be coming here with plans for my daughter's daughter," he warned. "If you try to make trouble, I'll take the case to the government man in town."

The impulse was strong in Chee to turn and ride off while he still had the Little One in his arms. But he knew his time of victory would be short. His own family would uphold the old custom of children, especially girl children, belonging to the mother's people. He would have to give his daughter up if the case were brought before the headman of Little Canyon, and certainly he would have no better chance before a strange white man in town.

He handed the bewildered Little One to her grandfather who stood watching every movement suspiciously. Chee asked, "If I brought you a few things for the Little One, would that be making trouble? Some velvet for a blouse,

---

8. **jerked.** Preserved by being cut into strips and dried

or some of the jerky she likes so well…this summer's melon?"

Old Man Fat backed away from him. "Well," he hesitated, as some of the anger disappeared from his face and beads of greed shone in his eyes. "Well," he repeated. Then as the Little One began to squirm in his arms and cry, he said, "No! No! Stay away from here, you and all your family."

The sense of his failure deepened as Chee rode back to Little Canyon. But it was not until he sat with his family that evening in the hogan, while the familiar bustle of meal preparing went on about him, that he began to doubt the wisdom of the things he'd always believed. He smelled the coffee boiling and the oily fragrance of chili powder dusted into the bubbling pot of stew; he watched his mother turning round crusty fried bread in the small black skillet. All around him was plenty— a half of mutton hanging near the door, bright strings of chili drying, corn hanging by the braided husks, cloth bags of dried peaches. Yet in his heart was nothing.

He heard the familiar sounds of the sheep outside the hogan, the splash of water as his father filled the long drinking trough from the water barrel. When his father came in, Chee could not bring himself to tell a second time of the day's happenings. He watched his wiry, soft-spoken father while his mother told the story, saw his father's queue of graying hair quiver as he nodded his head with sympathetic exclamations.

Chee's doubting, acrid thoughts kept forming: Was it wisdom his father had passed on to him, or was his inheritance only the stubbornness of a long-haired Navajo resisting change? Take care of the land and it will take care of you. True, the land had always given him food, but now food was not enough. Perhaps if he had gone to school, he would have learned a different kind of wisdom, something to help him now. A schoolboy might even be able to speak convincingly to this government man whom Old Man Fat threatened to call, instead of sitting here like a clod of earth itself—Pueblo farmer indeed. What had the land to give that would restore his daughter?

In the days that followed, Chee herded sheep. He got up in the half-light, drank the hot coffee his mother had ready, then started the flock moving. It was necessary to drive the sheep a long way from the hogan to find good winter forage. Sometimes Chee met friends or relatives who were on their way to town or to the road camp where they hoped to get work; then there was friendly banter and an exchange of news. But most of the days seemed endless; he could not walk far enough or fast enough from his memories of the Little One or from his bitter thoughts. Sometimes it seemed his daughter trudged beside him, so real he could almost hear her footsteps—the muffled pad-pad of little feet in deerhide. In the glare of a snowbank he would see her vivid face, brown eyes sparkling. Mingling with the tinkle of sheep bells he heard her laughter.

When, weary of following the small sharp hoof marks that crossed and recrossed in the snow, he sat down in the shelter of a rock, it was only to be reminded that in his thoughts he had forsaken his brotherhood with the earth and sun and growing things. If he remembered times when he had flung himself against the earth to rest, to lie there in the sun until he could no longer feel where he left off and the earth began, it was to remember also that now he sat like an alien against the same earth; the belonging together was gone. The earth was one thing and he was another.

It was during the days when he herded sheep that Chee decided he must leave Little Canyon. Perhaps he would take a job silver-smithing for one of the traders in town. Perhaps, even though he spoke little English, he could get a job at the road camp with his cousins; he would ask them about it.

Springtime transformed the mesas. The peach trees in the canyon were shedding fragrance and pink blossoms on the gentled wind. The sheep no longer foraged for the yellow seeds of chamiso[9] but ranged near the hogan with the long-legged new lambs, eating tender young grass.

Chee was near the hogan on the day his cousins rode up with the message for which he waited. He had been watching with mixed emotions while his father and his sister's husband cleared the fields beside the stream.

"The boss at the camp says he needs an extra hand, but he wants to know if you'll be willing to go with the camp when they move it to the other side of the town?" The tall cousin shifted his weight in the saddle.

The other cousin took up the explanation. "The work near here will last only until the new cutoff beyond Red Sands is finished. After that, the work will be too far away for you to get back here often."

That was what Chee had wanted—to get away from Little Canyon—yet he found himself not so interested in the job beyond town as in this new cutoff which was almost finished. He pulled a blade of grass, split it thoughtfully down the center, as he asked questions of his cousins. Finally he said: "I need to think more about this. If I decide on this job, I'll ride over."

Before his cousins were out of sight down the canyon, Chee was walking toward the fields, a bold plan shaping in his mind. As the plan began to flourish, wild and hardy as young tumbleweed, Chee added his own voice softly to the song his father was singing: "...In the middle of the wide field...Yellow Corn Boy...I wish to put in."

Chee walked slowly around the field, the rich red earth yielding to his footsteps. His plan depended upon this land and upon the things he remembered most about his wife's people.

Through planting time Chee worked zeal-ously and tirelessly. He spoke little of the large new field he was planting, because he felt so strongly that just now this was some-thing between himself and the land. The first days he was ever stooping, piercing the ground with the pointed stick, placing the corn kernels there, walking around the field and through it, singing, "...His track leads into the ground...Yellow Corn Boy...his track leads into the ground." After that, each day Chee walked through his field watching for the tips of green to break through; first a few spikes in the center and then more and more, until the corn in all parts of the field was above ground. Surely, Chee thought, if he sang the proper songs, if he cared for this land faithfully, it would not forsake him now, even though through the lonely days of winter he had betrayed the good-ness of the earth in his thoughts.

Through the summer Chee worked long days, the sun hot upon his back, pulling weeds from around young corn plants; he planted squash and pumpkin; he terraced a small piece of land near his mother's hogan and planted carrots and onions and the moisture-loving chili. He was increasingly restless. Finally he told his family what he hoped the harvest from this land would bring him. Then the whole family waited with him, watching the corn: the slender graceful plants that waved

---

9. **chamiso.** Shrubs that form dense thickets

green arms and bent to embrace each other as young winds wandered through the field, the maturing plants flaunting their pollen-laden tassels in the sun, the tall and sturdy parent corn with new-formed ears and a froth of purple, red, and yellow corn beards against the dusty emerald of broad leaves.

Summer was almost over when Chee slung the bulging packs across two pack ponies. His mother helped him tie the heavy rolled pack behind the saddle of the buckskin. Chee knotted the new yellow kerchief about his neck a little tighter, gave the broad black hat brim an extra tug, but these were only gestures of assurance and he knew it. The land had not failed him. That part was done. But this he was riding into? Who could tell?

When Chee arrived at Red Sands, it was as he had expected to find it—no cars on the highway. His cousins had told him that even the Pueblo farmers were using the new cutoff to town. The barren gravel around the Red Sands Trading Post was deserted. A sign banged against the dismantled gas pumps: *Closed until further notice.*

Old Man Fat came from the crude summer shelter built beside the log hogan from a few branches of scrub cedar and the sides of wooden crates. He seemed almost friendly when he saw Chee.

"Get down, my son," he said, eyeing the bulging packs. There was no bluster in his voice today, and his face sagged, looking somewhat saddened, perhaps because his cheeks were no longer quite full enough to push his eyes upward at the corners. "You are going on a journey?"

Chee shook his head. "Our fields gave us so much this year, I thought to sell or trade this to the trader. I didn't know he was no longer here."

Old Man Fat sighed, his voice dropping to an injured tone. "He says he and his wife are going to rest this winter; then after that he'll build a place up on the new highway."

when her husband asked with noticeable deference if she would give him money to buy supplies. Chee surmised that the only income here was from his mother-in-law's weaving.

She peered around the corner of the shelter at the laden ponies, and then she looked at Chee. "What do you have there, my son?" Chee smiled to himself as he turned to pull the pack from one of the ponies, dragged it to the shelter where he untied the ropes. Pumpkins and hard-shelled squash tumbled out, and the ears of corn—pale yellow husks fitting firmly over plump ripe kernels, blue corn, red corn, yellow corn, many-colored corn, ears and ears of it—tumbled into every corner of the shelter.

"Yooooh," Old Man Fat's wife exclaimed as she took some of the ears in her hands. Then she glanced up at her son-in-law. "But we have no money for all this. We have sold almost everything we own—even the brass bed that stood in the hogan."

Old Man Fat's brass bed. Chee concealed his amusement as he started back for another pack. That must have been a hard parting. Then he stopped, for, coming from the cool darkness of the hogan was the Little One, rubbing her eyes as though she had been asleep. She stood for a moment in the doorway, and Chee saw that she was dirty, barefoot, her hair uncombed, her little blouse shorn of all its silver buttons. Then she ran toward Chee, her arms outstretched. Heedless of Old Man Fat and his wife, her father caught her in his arms, her hair falling in a dark cloud across his face, the sweetness of her laughter warm against his shoulder.

It was the haste within him to get this slow waiting game played through to the finish that made Chee speak unwisely. It was the desire

Chee moved as though to be traveling on, then jerked his head toward the pack ponies. "Anything you need?"

"I'll ask my wife," Old Man Fat said as he led the way to the shelter. "Maybe she has a little money. Things have not been too good with us since the trader closed. Only a few tourists come this way." He shrugged his shoulders. "And with the trader gone—no credit."

Chee was not deceived by his father-in-law's unexpected confidences. He recognized them as a hopeful bid for sympathy and, if possible, something for nothing. Chee made no answer. He was thinking that so far he had been right about his wife's parents: their thriftlessness had left them with no resources to last until Old Man Fat found another easy way of making a living.

Old Man Fat's wife was in the shelter working at her loom. She turned rather wearily to swing her before him in the saddle and ride fast to Little Canyon that prompted his words. "The money doesn't matter. You still have something…"

Chee knew immediately that he had over-spoken. The old woman looked from him to the corn spread before her. Unfriendliness began to harden in his father-in-law's face. All the old arguments between himself and his wife's people came pushing and crowding in between them now.

Old Man Fat began kicking the ears of corn back onto the canvas as he eyed Chee angrily. "And you rode all the way over here thinking that for a little food we would give up our daughter's daughter?"

Chee did not wait for the old man to reach for the Little One. He walked dazedly to the shelter, rubbing his cheek against her soft dark hair, and put her gently into her grandmother's lap. Then he turned back to the horses. He had failed. By his own haste he had failed. He swung into the saddle, his hand touching the roll behind it. Should he ride on into town?

Then he dismounted, scarcely glancing at Old Man Fat, who stood uncertainly at the corner of the shelter, listening to his wife. "Give me a hand with this other pack of corn, Grandfather," Chee said, carefully keeping the small bit of hope from his voice.

Puzzled, but willing, Old Man Fat helped carry the other pack to the shelter, opening it to find more corn as well as carrots and round, pale yellow onions. Chee went back for the roll behind the buckskin's saddle and carried it to the entrance of the shelter, where he cut the ropes and gave the canvas a nudge with his toe. Tins of coffee rolled out, small plump cloth bags; jerked meat from several butcherings spilled from a flour sack; and bright red chilis splashed like flames against the dust.

"I will leave all this anyhow," Chee told them. "I would not want my daughter nor even you old people to go hungry."

Old Man Fat picked up a shiny tin of coffee, then put it down. With trembling hands he began to untie one of the cloth bags—dried sweet peaches.

The Little One had wriggled from her grandmother's lap, unheeded, and was on her knees, digging her hands into the jerked meat.

"There is almost enough food here to last all winter." Old Man Fat's wife sought the eyes of her husband.

Chee said, "I meant it to be enough. But that was when I thought you might send the Little One back with me." He looked down at his daughter noisily sucking jerky. Her mouth, both fists, were full of it. "I am sorry that you feel you cannot bear to part with her."

Old Man Fat's wife brushed a straggly wisp of gray hair from her forehead as she turned to look at the Little One. Old Man Fat was looking too. And it was not a thing to see. For in that moment the Little One ceased to be their daughter's daughter and became just another mouth to feed.

"And why not?" the old woman asked wearily.

Chee was settled in the saddle, the bare-footed Little One before him. He urged the buckskin faster, and his daughter clutched his shirtfront. The purpling mesas flung back the echo: "…My corn embrace each other. In the middle of the wide field…Yellow Corn Boy embrace each other." ❖

Do actions always speak louder than words? When you feel an injustice has been done to you, what is the benefit to remaining silent and working out a plan? Why is this difficult?

Literature
CONNECTION

The speaker of **"Freeway 280"** is caught between two cultures, that of Mexican Americans and that of white Americans. In her quest for self-identity, the speaker visits her old neighborhood and is overwhelmed by nostalgia for how things used to be. Before you read, predict how the speaker's emotional experiences will compare to Chee's in "Chee's Daughter."

Lorna Dee Cervantes is a Mexican-American poet who published her first collection of poems, *Emplumada,* in 1981. Cervantes has a keen awareness of the struggles faced by women, especially Hispanic women, in contemporary American society.

Freeway 280

A Poem by **Lorna Dee Cervantes**

Las casitas[1] near the gray cannery,
nestled amid wild abrazos[2] of climbing roses
and man-high red geraniums
are gone now. The freeway conceals it
all beneath a raised scar.

But under the fake windsounds of the open lanes,
in the abandoned lots below, new grasses sprout,
wild mustard remembers, old gardens
come back stronger than they were,
trees have been left standing in their yards.
Albaricoqueros, cerezos, nogales…[3]
Viejitas[4] come here with paper bags to gather greens.

---

1. **Las casitas** (läs kä sē´ täs). [Spanish] Little houses
2. **abrazos** (ä brä´ zōs). [Spanish] Embraces
3. **Albaricoqueros, cerezos, nogales** (äl bä rē kō kä´ rōs, se re´ zōs, nō gä´ les). [Spanish] Apricot, cherry, and walnut trees
4. **Viejitas** (vē yä hē´ täs). [Spanish] Old women

Espinaca, verdolagas, yerbabuena…[5]
I scramble over the wire fence
that would have kept me out.
Once, I wanted out, wanted the rigid lanes
to take me to a place without sun,
without the smell of tomatoes burning
on swing shift[6] in the greasy summer air.

Maybe it's here
en los campos extraños de esta ciudad[7]
where I'll find it, that part of me
mown under
like a corpse
or a loose seed. ❖

---

5. **Espinaca, verdolagas, yerbabuena** (es pē nä´ kä, ver dô lä´ gäs,
yer bä bü ä´ nä). [Spanish] Spinach, purslane (an edible weed), and mint
6. **swing shift.** Work shift between the day and night shifts, for example
4 PM to midnight
7. **en los campos extraños de esta ciudad** (en lōs cäm´ pōs eks trä´
nyōs dä lä cē yü däd). [Spanish] In the strange fields of this city

Refer and Reason

1. List examples of specific words used in the description of the two settings—Chee's home and Old Man Fat's home. Analyze what tone is set by the descriptions. Relate the description of setting to the theme of the story.
2. Describe what happens when Chee brings food to Old Man Fat and his wife. Judge whether Chee is being generous or manipulative when he gives the food to Old Man Fat and his wife.
3. Quote Old Man Fat's wife's comment after Chee says he meant for there to be enough food. Create a new ending for the story that explains what might have happened to Old Man Fat, his wife, and Chee's daughter if they had not accepted Chee's offer.

Writing Options

1. Imagine that you are Chee in winter when he loses faith in the land. Describe a daydream in which your life is the way you want it to be. What are you doing? Who is present? What happens?
2. In this story, we are given descriptions of two contrasting settings: the trading post and Chee's home in Little Canyon. Write two descriptive paragraphs contrasting settings that create different emotions in you. Use specific details to help readers visualize the two settings and understand your feelings about the two places.

 Go to **www.mirrorsandwindows.com** for more.

TEXT ←TO→ TEXT CONNECTION

What has the speaker of "Freeway 280" lost? How does her loss compare with Chee's? How does it compare with Old Man Fat's loss?

Civil Peace

"Nothing puzzles God," he said in wonder.

A Short Story by
Chinua Achebe

Victory, 1947. Jacob Lawrence. Private collection.

Chinua Achebe was born in 1930 in Nigeria. At the time, Nigeria was a British colony. Achebe's first, and perhaps best-known, novel, *Things Fall Apart,* addresses the effects of colonialism and Western influences on the traditional Ibo way of life. The Ibo are one of Nigeria's largest ethnic groups.

"Civil Peace," published in 1971, was probably set in 1970 shortly after the Nigerian civil war ended. The war began in 1967, when the Ibo people tried to secede and form an independent nation, the Republic of Biafra. Achebe has said, "Any good story, any good novel, should have a message, should have a purpose." As you read "Civil Peace," try to determine the message or purpose Achebe intended it to have.

Think about a person you know or have heard about who has survived something—an illness, a natural disaster, a war. What qualities does this person have? What did he or she have to do to survive?

Jonathan Iwegbu counted himself extraordinarily lucky. "Happy survival!" meant so much more to him than just a current fashion of greeting old friends in the first hazy days of peace. It went deep to his heart. He had come out of the war with five inestimable blessings—his head, his wife Maria's head and the heads of three out of their four children. As a bonus he also had his old bicycle—a miracle too but naturally not to be compared to the safety of five human heads.

The bicycle had a little history of its own. One day at the height of the war it was commandeered "for urgent military action." Hard as its loss would have been to him he would still have let it go without a thought had he not had some doubts about the genuineness of the officer. It wasn't his disreputable rags, nor the toes peeping out of one blue and one brown canvas shoes, nor yet the two stars of his rank done obviously in a hurry in biro,[1] that troubled Jonathan; many good and heroic soldiers looked the same or worse. It was rather a certain lack of grip and firmness in his manner. So Jonathan, suspecting he might be amenable to influence, rummaged in his raffia bag and produced the two pounds with which he had been going to buy firewood which his wife, Maria, retailed to camp officials for extra stock-fish and corn meal, and got his bicycle back. That night he buried it in the little clearing in the bush where the dead of the camp, including his own youngest son, were buried. When he dug it up again a year later after the surrender all it needed was a little palm-oil greasing. "Nothing puzzles God," he said in wonder.

He put it to immediate use as a taxi and accumulated a small pile of Biafran money ferrying camp officials and their families across the four-mile stretch to the nearest tarred road. His standard charge per trip was six pounds and those who had the money were only glad to be rid of some of it in this way. At the end of a fortnight he had made a small fortune of one hundred and fifteen pounds.

Then he made the journey to Enugu[2] and found another miracle waiting for him. It was unbelievable. He rubbed his eyes and looked

> **Then he made the journey to Enugu and found another miracle waiting for him.**

again and it was still standing there before him. But, needless to say, even that monumental blessing must be accounted also totally inferior to the five heads in the family. This newest miracle was his little house in Ogui Overside. Indeed nothing puzzles God! Only two houses away a huge concrete edifice some wealthy contractor had put up just before the war was a mountain of rubble. And here was Jonathan's little zinc house[3] of no regrets built with mud blocks quite intact! Of course the doors and windows were missing and five sheets off the roof. But what was that? And anyhow he had returned to Enugu early enough to pick up bits of old zinc and wood and soggy sheets of cardboard lying around the neighborhood before thousands more came out of their forest holes looking for the same things. He got a destitute carpenter with one old hammer, a blunt plane and a few bent and rusty nails in his tool bag to turn this assortment of wood, paper and metal into door and window shutters for five Nigerian shillings or fifty Biafran pounds. He paid the pounds, and moved in with his overjoyed family carrying five heads on their shoulders.

His children picked mangoes near the military cemetery and sold them to soldiers' wives for a few pennies—real pennies this time—and his wife started making breakfast akara balls[4] for neighbors in a hurry to start life again. With his family earnings he took his bicycle to the villages around and bought fresh palm wine which he mixed generously in his rooms with the water which had recently

---

1. **biro.** Ballpoint pen, here used to draw the stars that marked the officer's rank
2. **Enugu.** City in southeast Nigeria
3. **zinc house.** House with a zinc-coated roof
4. **akara balls.** Round bean cakes

started running again in the public tap down the road, and opened up a bar for soldiers and other lucky people with good money.

At first he went daily, then every other day and finally once a week, to the offices of the Coal Corporation where he used to be a miner, to find out what was what. The only thing he did find out in the end was that that little house of his was even a greater blessing than he had thought. Some of his fellow ex-miners who had nowhere to return at the end of the day's waiting just slept outside the

doors of the offices and cooked what meal they could scrounge together in Bournvita tins. As the weeks lengthened and still nobody could say what was what Jonathan discontinued his weekly visits altogether and faced his palm wine bar.

But nothing puzzles God. Came the day of the windfall when after five days of endless scuffles in queues and counter queues in the sun outside the Treasury he had twenty pounds counted into his palms as ex gratia[5] award for the rebel money he had turned in. It was like Christmas for him and for many others like him when the payments began. They called it (since few could manage its proper official name) *egg rasher*.

As soon as the pound notes were placed in his palm Jonathan simply closed it tight over them and buried fist and money inside his trouser pocket. He had to be extra careful because he had seen a man a couple of days earlier collapse into near madness in an instant before that oceanic crowd because no sooner had he got his twenty pounds than some heartless ruffian picked it off him. Though it was not right that a man in such an extremity of agony should be blamed yet many in the queues that day were able to remark quietly on the victim's carelessness, especially after he pulled out the innards of his pocket and revealed a hole in it big enough to pass a thief's head. But of course he had insisted that the money had been in the other pocket, pulling it out too to show its comparative wholeness. So one had to be careful.

Jonathan soon transferred the money to his left hand and pocket so as to leave his right free for shaking hands should the need arise, though by fixing his gaze at such an elevation as to miss all approaching human faces he made sure that the need did not arise, until he got home.

He was normally a heavy sleeper but that night he heard all the neighborhood noises die down one after another. Even the night watchman who knocked the hour on some metal somewhere in the distance had fallen silent after knocking one o'clock. That must have been the last thought in Jonathan's mind before he was finally carried away himself. He couldn't have been gone for long, though, when he was violently awakened again.

"Who is knocking?" whispered his wife lying beside him on the floor.

---

5. **ex gratia.** In kindness, something given as a favor

"I don't know," he whispered back breathlessly.

The second time the knocking came it was so loud and imperious that the rickety old door could have fallen down.

"Who is knocking?" he asked then, his voice parched and trembling.

"Na tief-man and him people," came the cool reply. "Make you hopen de door." This was followed by the heaviest knocking of all.

Maria was the first to raise the alarm, then he followed and all their children.

"Police-o! Thieves-o! Neighbors-o! Police-o! We are lost! We are dead! Neighbors, are you asleep? Wake up! Police-o!"

This went on for a long time and then stopped suddenly. Perhaps they had scared the thief away. There was total silence. But only for a short while.

"You done finish?" asked the voice outside. "Make we help you small. Oya, everybody!"

"Police-o! Tief-man-o! Neighbors-o! we done loss-o! Police-o!..."

There were at least five other voices besides the leader's.

Jonathan and his family were now completely paralyzed by terror. Maria and the children sobbed inaudibly like lost souls. Jonathan groaned continuously.

The silence that followed the thieves' alarm vibrated horribly. Jonathan all but begged their leader to speak again and be done with it.

"My frien," said he at long last, "we don try our best for call dem but I tink say dem all done sleep-o...So wetin we go do now? Sometaim you wan call soja? Or you wan make we call dem for you? Soja better pass police. No be so?"

"Na so!" replied his men. Jonathan thought he heard even more voices now than before and groaned heavily. His legs were sagging under him and his throat felt like sandpaper.

"My frien, why you no de talk again. I de ask you say you wan make we call soja?"

"No."

"Awrighto. Now make we talk business. We no be had tief. We no like for make trouble. Trouble done finish. War done finish and all the katakata wey de for inside.[6] No Civil War again. This time na Civil Peace. No be so?"

"Na so!" answered the horrible chorus.

"What do you want from me? I am a poor man. Everything I had went with this war. Why do you come to me? You know people who have money. We..."

"Awright! We know say you no get plenty money. But we sef no get even anini.[7] So derefore make you open dis window and give one hundred pound and we go commot. Oderwise we de come for inside now to show you guitar-boy like dis..."

---

6. **War done finish and all the katakata...inside.** Nigerian dialect meaning roughly "The war is finished and all that went with it." The word *katakata* may be an onomatopoeic word to represent gunfire.

7. **anini.** Nigerian coin of little value

A volley of automatic fire rang through sky. Maria and the children began to weep aloud again.

"Ah, missisi de cry again. No need for dat. We done talk say we na good tief. We just take our small money and go nwayorly. No molest. Abi we de molest?"

"At all!" sang the chorus.

"My friends," began Jonathan hoarsely. "I hear what you say and I thank you. If I had one hundred pounds…"

"Lookia my frien, no be play we come play for your house. If we make mistake and step for inside you no go like am-o. So derefore…"

"To God who made me; if you come inside and find one hundred pounds, take it and shoot me and shoot my wife and children. I swear to God. The only money I have in this life is this twenty-pounds *egg rasher* they gave me today…"

"OK. Time de go. Make you open dis window and bring the twenty pound. We go manage am like dat."

There were now loud murmurs of dissent among the chorus: "Na lie de man de lie; e get plenty money…Make we go inside and search properly well…Wetin be twenty pound?…"

"Shurrup!" rang the leader's voice like a lone shot in the sky and silenced the murmuring at once. "Are you dere? Bring the money quick!"

"I am coming," said Jonathan fumbling in the darkness with the key of the small wooden box he kept by his side on the mat.

At the first sign of light as neighbors and others assembled to commiserate with him he was already strapping his five-gallon demijohn to his bicycle carrier and his wife, sweating in the open fire, was turning over akara balls in a wide clay bowl of boiling oil. In the corner his eldest son was rinsing out dregs of yesterday's palm wine from old beer bottles.

"I count it as nothing," he told his sympathizers, his eyes on the rope he was tying. "What is *egg rasher*? Did I depend on it last week? Or is it greater than other things that went with the war? I say, let *egg rasher* perish in the flames! Let it go where everything else has gone. Nothing puzzles God." ❖

 **MIRRORS & WINDOWS** Is luck or fate responsible when good things happen? When bad things happen? Can a person be proactive in determining his or her future? Explain your answers.

Refer and Reason

1. List the blessings Jonathan has after the war. Compare and contrast his life before the war to his life after the war.
2. Quote what the thief says when Jonathan asks who is knocking. Evaluate the use of dialect during the robbery scene. How does the use of dialect affect your reading? What effect does the use of dialect have on this scene?
3. Recall what happened to a man who received his *egg rasher* a few days before Jonathan. The narrator says, "Though it was not right that a man in such an extremity of agony should be blamed yet many in the queues that day were able to remark quietly on the victim's carelessness…." What does this statement suggest about the people in the postwar society? Explain why people are often eager to blame victims.

Writing Options

1. Imagine a newsmagazine is writing a feature on Jonathan Iwegbu. Write a personality profile of Jonathan. Consider the kind of person he seems to be based on what he says and does in the story.
2. Consider Achebe's quotation, "Any good story, any good novel, should have a message, should have a purpose." Write a brief essay in which you explain the message or purpose of "Civil Peace."

Go to **www.mirrorsandwindows.com** for more.

A White Heron

A Short Story by
Sarah Orne Jewett

Suddenly this little woods-girl is horror-stricken to hear a clear whistle not very far away.

Louisiana Heron. Rodney Busch. Private collection.

Sarah Orne Jewett (1849–1909) grew up in a small town in rural Maine. Jewett published her first short story as a teenager. In her writing, she celebrated rural Maine and its people.

"A White Heron," one of her short stories published in a collection of the same name, is an example of regional literature. The nineteenth-century regionalists wrote at a time when the United States was being rapidly industrialized. People had to work in factories, and many people moved from the country to the city looking for work. Old-growth forests were being cut down to plant farms to feed city dwellers, and the wild animals that lived in these places were losing their natural habitats. Like much regional literature, "A White Heron" can be seen as a protest against these events.

Which do you prefer, the country or the city? Why?

I

The woods were already filled with shadows one June evening, just before eight o'clock, though a bright sunset still glimmered faintly among the trunks of the trees. A little girl was driving home her cow, a plodding, dilatory, provoking creature in her behavior, but a valued companion for all that. They were going away from whatever light there was, and striking deep into the woods, but their feet were familiar with the path, and it was no matter whether their eyes could see it or not.

There was hardly a night the summer through when the old cow could be found waiting at the pasture bars; on the contrary, it was her greatest pleasure to hide herself away among the high huckleberry bushes, and though she wore a loud bell she had made the discovery that if one stood perfectly still it would not ring. So Sylvia had to hunt for her until she found her,

She waded on through the brook as the cow moved away, and listened to the thrushes with a heart that beat fast with pleasure.

and call Co'! Co'! with never an answering Moo, until her childish patience was quite spent. If the creature had not given good milk and plenty of it, the case would have seemed very different to her owners. Besides, Sylvia had all the time there was, and very little use to make of it. Sometimes in pleasant weather it was a consolation to look upon the cow's pranks as an intelligent attempt to play hide and seek, and as the child had no playmates she lent herself to this amusement with a good deal of zest. Though this chase had been so long that the wary animal herself had given an unusual signal of her whereabouts, Sylvia had only laughed when she came upon Mistress Moolly at the swamp-side, and urged her affectionately homeward with a twig of birch leaves. The old cow was not inclined to wander farther, she even turned in the right direction for once as they left the pasture, and stepped along the road at a good pace. She was quite ready to be milked now, and seldom stopped to browse. Sylvia wondered what her grandmother would say because they were so late. It was a great while since she had left home at half past five o'clock, but everybody knew the difficulty of making this errand a short one. Mrs. Tilley had chased the

hornéd torment[1] too many summer evenings herself to blame anyone else for lingering, and was only thankful as she waited that she had Sylvia, nowadays, to give such valuable assistance. The good woman suspected that Sylvia loitered occasionally on her own account; there never was such a child for straying about out-of-doors since the world was made! Everybody said that it was a good change for a little maid who had tried to grow for eight years in a crowded manufacturing town, but, as for Sylvia herself, it seemed as if she never had been alive at all before she came to live at the farm. She thought often with wistful compassion of a wretched geranium that belonged to a town neighbor.

" 'Afraid of folks,' " old Mrs. Tilley said to herself, with a smile, after she had made the unlikely choice of Sylvia from her daughter's houseful of children, and was returning to the farm. " 'Afraid of folks,' they said! I guess she won't be troubled no great with 'em up to the old place!" When they reached the door of the lonely house and stopped to unlock it, and the cat came to purr loudly, and rub against them, a deserted pussy, indeed, but fat with young robins, Sylvia whispered that this was a beautiful place to live in, and she never should wish to go home.

The companions followed the shady wood-road, the cow taking slow steps, and the child very fast ones. The cow stopped long at the brook to drink, as if the pasture were not half a swamp, and Sylvia stood still and waited, letting her bare feet cool themselves in the shoal water, while the great twilight moths struck softly against her. She waded on through the brook as the cow moved away, and listened to the thrushes with a heart that beat fast with pleasure. There was a stirring in the great boughs overhead. They were full of little birds and beasts that seemed to be wide awake, and going about their world, or else saying goodnight to each other in sleepy twitters. Sylvia herself felt sleepy as she walked along. However, it was not much farther

---

1. **hornéd torment.** Troublesome cow

to the house, and the air was soft and sweet. She was not often in the woods so late as this, and it made her feel as if she were a part of the gray shadows and the moving leaves. She was just thinking how long it seemed since she first came to the farm a year ago, and wondering if everything went on in the noisy town just the same as when she was there; the thought of the great red-faced boy who used to chase and frighten her made her hurry along the path to escape from the shadow of the trees.

Suddenly this little woods-girl is horror-stricken to hear a clear whistle not very far away. Not a bird's whistle, which would have a sort of friendliness, but a boy's whistle, determined, and somewhat aggressive. Sylvia left the cow to whatever sad fate might await her, and stepped discreetly aside into the bushes, but she was just too late. The enemy had discovered her, and called out in a very cheerful and persuasive tone, "Halloa, little girl, how far is it to the road?" and trembling Sylvia answered almost inaudibly, "A good ways."

She did not dare to look boldly at the tall young man, who carried a gun over his shoulder, but she came out of her bush and again followed the cow, while he walked alongside. "I have been hunting for some birds," the stranger said kindly, "and I have lost my way, and need a friend very much. Don't be afraid," he added gallantly. "Speak up and tell me what your name is, and whether you think I can spend the night at your house, and go out gunning early in the morning."

Sylvia was more alarmed than before. Would not her grandmother consider her much to blame? But who could have foreseen such an accident as this? It did not seem to be her fault, and she hung her head as if the stem of it were broken, but managed to answer "Sylvy," with much effort when her companion again asked her name.

Mrs. Tilley was standing in the doorway when the trio came into view. The cow gave a loud moo by way of explanation.

"Yes, you'd better speak up for yourself,

Cows in the Meadow, c.1980. Robert McIntosh.

you old trial! Where'd she tucked herself away this time, Sylvy?" But Sylvia kept an awed silence; she knew by instinct that her grandmother did not comprehend the gravity of the situation. She must be mistaking the stranger for one of the farmer-lads of the region.

The young man stood his gun beside the door, and dropped a lumpy game bag beside it; then he bade Mrs. Tilley good evening, and repeated his wayfarer's story, and asked if he could have a night's lodging

"Put me anywhere you like," he said. "I must be off early in the morning, before day; but I am very hungry, indeed. You can give me some milk at any rate, that's plain."

"Dear sakes, yes," responded the hostess, whose long slumbering hospitality seemed to

be easily awakened. "You might fare better if you went out to the main road a mile or so, but you're welcome to what we've got. I'll milk right off, and you make yourself at home. You can sleep on husks or feathers," she proffered graciously. "I raised them all myself. There's good pasturing for geese just below here towards the ma'sh. Now step round and set a plate for the gentleman, Sylvy!" And Sylvia promptly stepped. She was glad to have something to do, and she was hungry herself.

It was a surprise to find so clean and comfortable a little dwelling in this New England wilderness. The young man had known the horrors of its most primitive housekeeping, and the dreary squalor of that level of society which does not rebel at the companionship of hens. This was the best thrift of an old-fashioned farmstead, though on such a small scale that it seemed like a hermitage. He listened eagerly to the old woman's quaint talk, he watched Sylvia's pale face and shining gray eyes with ever growing enthusiasm, and insisted that this was the best supper he had eaten for a month, and afterward the new-made friends sat down in the doorway together while the moon came up.

Soon it would be berry-time, and Sylvia was a great help at picking. The cow was a good milker, though a plaguy thing to keep track of, the hostess gossiped frankly, adding presently that she had buried four children, so Sylvia's mother, and a son (who might be dead) in California were all the children she had left. "Dan, my boy, was a great hand to go gunning," she explained sadly. "I never wanted for pa'tridges or gray squer'ls while he was to home. He's been a great wand'rer, I expect, and he's no hand to write letters. There, I don't blame him, I'd ha' seen the world myself if it had been so I could.

"Sylvia takes after him," the grandmother continued affectionately, after a minute's pause. "There ain't a foot o' ground she don't know her way over, and the wild creatures counts her one o' themselves. Squer'ls she'll tame to come an' feed right out o' her hands, and all sorts o'birds. Last winter she got the jay-birds to bangeing[2] here, and I believe she'd 'a' scanted herself[3] of her own meals to have plenty to throw out amongst 'em, if I hadn't kep' watch. Anything but crows, I tell her, I'm willin' to help support—though Dan he had a tamed one o' them that did seem to have reason same as folks. It was round here a good spell after he went away. Dan an' his father they didn't hitch,—but he never held up his head ag'in after Dan had dared him an' gone off."

The guest did not notice this hint of family sorrows in his eager interest in something else.

"So Sylvy knows all about birds, does she?" he exclaimed, as he looked round at the little girl who sat, very demure but increasingly sleepy, in the moonlight. "I am making a collection of birds myself. I have been at it ever since I was a boy." (Mrs. Tilley smiled.) "There are two or three very rare ones I have been hunting for these five years. I mean to get them on my own ground if they can be found."

"Do you cage 'em up?" asked Mrs. Tilley doubtfully, in response to this enthusiastic announcement.

"Oh, no, they're stuffed and preserved, dozens and dozens of them," said the ornithologist, "and I have shot or snared every one myself. I caught a glimpse of a white heron three miles from here on Saturday, and I have followed it in this direction. They have never been found in this district at all. The little white heron, it is," and he turned again to look at Sylvia with the hope of discovering that the rare bird was one of her acquaintances.

But Sylvia was watching a hop-toad in the narrow footpath.

"You would know the heron if you saw it," the stranger continued eagerly. "A queer tall white bird with soft feathers and long thin legs. And it would have a nest perhaps in the top of a high tree, made of sticks, something like a hawk's nest."

Sylvia's heart gave a wild beat; she knew that strange white bird, and had once stolen softly near where it stood in some bright green swamp grass, away over at the other side of the woods. There was an open place where the sunshine always seemed strangely yellow and hot, where tall, nodding rushes grew, and her grandmother had warned her that she might sink in the soft black mud underneath and never be heard of more. Not far beyond were the salt marshes just this side the sea itself, which Sylvia wondered and dreamed about, but never had seen, whose great voice could sometimes be heard above the noise of the woods on stormy nights.

"I can't think of anything I should like so much as to find that heron's nest," the handsome stranger was saying. "I would give ten dollars to anybody who could show it to me," he added desperately, "and I mean to spend my whole vacation hunting for it if need be. Perhaps it was only migrating, or had been chased out of its own region by some bird of prey."

Mrs. Tilley gave amazed attention to all this, but Sylvia still watched the toad, not divining, as she might have done at some calmer time, that the creature wished to get to its hole under the doorstep, and was much hindered by the unusual spectators at that hour of the evening. No amount of thought, that night, could decide how many wished-for treasures the ten dollars, so lightly spoken of, would buy.

The next day the young sportsman hovered about the woods, and Sylvia kept him company, having lost her first fear of the friendly lad, who proved to be most kind and sympathetic. He told her many things about the birds and what they knew and where they lived and what they did with themselves. And he gave her a jackknife, which she

---

2. **bangeing.** Hanging around
3. **'a' scanted herself.** Would have deprived herself

thought as great a treasure as if she were a desert-islander. All day long he did not once make her troubled or afraid except when he brought down some unsuspecting singing creature from its bough. Sylvia would have liked him vastly better without his gun; she could not understand why he killed the very birds he seemed to like so much. But as the day waned, Sylvia still watched the young man with loving admiration. She had never seen anybody so charming and delightful; the woman's heart, asleep in the child, was vaguely thrilled by a dream of love. Some premonition of that great power stirred and swayed these young creatures who traversed the solemn woodlands with soft-footed silent

What a spirit of adventure, what wild ambition! What fancied triumph and delight and glory for the later morning when she could make known the secret!

care. They stopped to listen to a bird's song; they pressed forward again eagerly, parting the branches,—speaking to each other rarely and in whispers; the young man going first and Sylvia following, fascinated, a few steps behind, with her gray eyes dark with excitement.

She grieved because the longed-for white heron was elusive, but she did not lead the guest, she only followed, and there was no such thing as speaking first. The sound of her own unquestioned voice would have terrified her,—it was hard enough to answer yes or no when there was need of that. At last evening began to fall, and they drove the cow home together, and Sylvia smiled with pleasure when they came to the place where she heard the whistle and was afraid only the night before.

II

Half a mile from home, at the farther edge of the woods, where the land was highest, a great pine tree stood, the last of its generation. Whether it was left for a boundary mark, or for what reason, no one could say; the woodchoppers who had felled its mates were dead and gone long ago, and a whole forest of sturdy trees, pines and oaks and maples, had grown again. But the stately head of this old pine towered above them all and made a landmark for sea and shore miles and miles away. Sylvia knew it well. She had always believed that whoever climbed to the top of it could see the ocean; and the little girl had often laid her hand on the great rough trunk and looked up wistfully at those dark boughs that the wind always stirred, no matter how hot and still the air might be below. Now she thought of the tree with a new excitement, for why, if one climbed it at break of day, could not one see all the world, and easily discover from whence the white heron flew, and mark the place, and find the hidden nest?

What a spirit of adventure, what wild ambition! What fancied triumph and delight and glory for the later morning when she could make known the secret! It was almost too real and too great for the childish heart to bear.

All night the door of the little house stood open and the whippoorwills came and sang upon the very step. The young sportsman and his old hostess were sound asleep, but Sylvia's great design kept her broad awake and watching. She forgot to think of sleep. The short summer night seemed as long as the winter darkness, and at last when the whippoorwills ceased, and she was afraid the morning would after all come too soon, she stole out of the house and followed the pasture path through the woods, hastening toward the open ground beyond, listening with a sense of comfort and companionship to the drowsy twitter of a half-awakened bird, whose perch she had jarred in passing. Alas, if the great wave of human interest which flooded for the first time this dull little life should sweep away the satisfactions of an existence heart to heart with nature and the dumb life of the forest!

There was the huge tree asleep yet in the paling moonlight, and small and silly Sylvia began with utmost bravery to mount to the top of it, with tingling, eager blood coursing the channels of her whole frame, with her bare feet and fingers, that pinched and held like bird's claws to the monstrous ladder reaching up, up, almost to the sky itself. First she must mount the white oak tree that grew alongside, where she was almost lost among the dark branches and the green leaves heavy and wet with dew; a bird fluttered off its nest, and a red squirrel ran to and fro and scolded pettishly at the harmless housebreaker. Sylvia felt her way easily. She had often

climbed there, and knew that higher still one of the oak's upper branches chafed against the pine trunk, just where its lower boughs were set close together. There, when she made the dangerous pass from one tree to the other, the great enterprise would really begin.

She crept out along the swaying oak limb at last, and took the daring step across into the old pine tree. The way was harder than she thought; she must reach far and hold fast, the sharp dry twigs caught and held her and scratched her like angry talons, the pitch made her thin little fingers clumsy and stiff as she went round and round the tree's great stem, higher and higher upward. The sparrows and robins in the woods below were beginning to wake and twitter to the dawn, yet it seemed much lighter there aloft in the pine tree, and the child knew that she must hurry if her project were to be of any use.

The tree seemed to lengthen itself out as she went up, and to reach farther and farther upward. It was like a great main-mast to the voyaging earth; it must truly have been amazed that morning through all its ponderous frame as it felt this determined spark of human spirit winding its way from higher branch to branch. Who knows how steadily the least twigs held themselves to advantage this light, weak creature on her way! The old pine must have loved

Salt Marsh at Southport, Connecticut, c.1875—81. Martin Johnson Heade. North Carolina Museum of Art.

his new dependent. More than all the hawks, and bats, and moths, and even the sweet voiced thrushes, was the brave, beating heart of the solitary gray-eyed child. And the tree stood still and frowned away the winds that June morning while the dawn grew bright in the east.

Sylvia's face was like a pale star, if one had seen it from the ground, when the last thorny bough was past, and she stood trembling and tired but wholly triumphant, high in the treetop. Yes, there was the sea with the dawning sun making a golden dazzle over it, and toward that glorious east flew two hawks with slow-moving pinions. How low they looked in the air from that height when one had only seen them before far up, and dark against the blue sky. Their gray feathers were as soft as moths; they seemed only a little way from the tree, and Sylvia felt as if she too could go flying away among the clouds. Westward, the woodlands and farms reached miles and miles into the distance; here and there were church steeples, and white villages; truly it was a vast and awesome world!

The birds sang louder and louder. At last the sun came up bewilderingly bright. Sylvia could see the white sails of ships out at sea, and the clouds that were purple and rose-colored and yellow at first began to fade away.

of light and consciousness from your two eager eyes, for the heron has perched on a pine bough not far beyond yours, and cries back to

Where was the white heron's nest in the sea of green branches, and was this wonderful sight and pageant of the world the only reward for having climbed to such a giddy height?

his mate on the nest, and plumes his feathers for the new day!

The child gives a long sigh a minute later when a company of shouting catbirds comes also to the tree, and vexed by their fluttering and lawlessness the solemn heron goes away. She knows his secret now, the wild, light, slender bird that floats and wavers, and goes back like an arrow presently to his home in the green world beneath. Then Sylvia, well satisfied, makes her perilous way down again, not daring to look far below the branch she stands on, ready to cry sometimes because her fingers ache and her lamed feet slip. Wondering over and over again what the stranger would say to her, and what he would think when she told him how to find his way straight to the heron's nest.

"Sylvy, Sylvy!" called the busy old grandmother again and again, but nobody answered, and the small husk bed was empty and Sylvia had disappeared.

The guest waked from a dream, and remembering his day's pleasure hurried to dress himself that might it sooner begin. He was sure from the way the shy little girl looked once or twice yesterday that she had at least seen the white heron, and now she must really

Where was the white heron's nest in the sea of green branches, and was this wonderful sight and pageant of the world the only reward for having climbed to such a giddy height? Now look down again, Sylvia, where the green marsh is set among the shining birches and dark hemlocks; there where you saw the white heron once you will see him again; look, look! a white spot of him like a single floating feather comes up from the dead hemlock and grows larger, and rises, and comes close at last, and goes by the landmark pine with steady sweep of wing and outstretched slender neck and crested head. And wait! wait! do not move a foot or a finger, little girl, do not send an arrow

be made to tell. Here she comes now, paler than ever, and her worn old frock is torn and tattered, and smeared with pine pitch. The grandmother and the sportsman stand in

Whatever treasures were lost to her, woodlands and summertime, remember! Bring your gifts and graces and tell your secrets to this lonely country child!

the door together and question her, and the splendid moment has come to speak of the dead hemlock tree by the green marsh.

But Sylvia does not speak after all, though the old grandmother fretfully rebukes her, and the young man's kind, appealing eyes are looking straight in her own. He can make them rich with money; he has promised it, and they are poor now. He is so well worth making happy, and he waits to hear the story she can tell.

No, she must keep silence! What is it that suddenly forbids her and makes her dumb?

Has she been nine years growing and now, when the great world for the first time puts out a hand to her, must she thrust it aside for a bird's sake? The murmur of the pine's green branches is in her ears, she remembers how the white heron came flying through the golden air and how they watched the sea and the morning together, and Sylvia cannot speak; she cannot tell the heron's secret and give its life away.

Dear loyalty, that suffered a sharp pang as the guest went away disappointed later in the day, that could have served and followed him and loved him as a dog loves! Many a night Sylvia heard the echo of his whistle haunting the pasture path as she came home with the loitering cow. She forgot even her sorrow at the sharp report of his gun and the sight of thrushes and sparrows dropping silent to the ground, their songs hushed and their pretty feathers stained and wet with blood. Were the birds better friends than their hunter might have been,—who can tell? Whatever treasures were lost to her, woodlands and summertime, remember! Bring your gifts and graces and tell your secrets to this lonely country child! ❖

MIRRORS & WINDOWS

Have you ever done something you didn't believe in because you needed the money? What sacrifices do people often make for money? Why does money have so much power over people?

Refer and Reason

1. Identify examples of a bird *motif*, or recurring element, in "A White Heron." Analyze how the motif sheds light on the relationship Sylvia and the young man have with nature.
2. Recall what the young man offers Sylvia if she helps him find the white heron. Evaluate Sylvia's decision to not tell the young man where the white heron nests.
3. At the end of the story, the narrator says, "Whatever treasures were lost to her, woodlands and summertime, remember! Bring your gifts and graces and tell your secrets to this lonely country child!" Compose a list of secrets Sylvia might learn from nature. Explain why she is worthy of such secrets.

Writing Options

1. Write a dialogue between Sylvia and the young man in which she tells him why she won't tell the white heron's secret.
2. Write a note to a friend who has also read this story. In your note, compare the conflict Sylvia faced with an internal conflict you have overcome.

 Go to **www.mirrorsandwindows.com** for more.

The Enchanted Garden

The pale boy was wandering about his shady room furtively, touching with his white fingers the edges of the cases studded with butterflies; then he stopped to listen.

A Short Story by
Italo Calvino

Artist's Garden at Vétheuil, 1880. Claude Monet. National Gallery of Art, Washington, DC.

Born in Santiago de las Vegas, Cuba, **Italo Calvino** (1923–1985) left Cuba for Italy in his youth. There, he joined the Italian Resistance during World War II. After the war, he wrote his first novel, *The Path to the Nest of Spiders,* when he was only twenty-four years old. In the 1950s, Calvino turned his attention to writing fantasy and allegory.

"The Enchanted Garden" is a realistic short story with elements of fantasy. Taken from Calvino's collection *Difficult Loves,* the selection is written in lyrical and sharply realistic prose, particularly the descriptive passages of the garden grounds that Giovannino and Serenella find by chance. Chance is an invisible character in the story, governing among other things the children's discovery of the garden.

If you could design your own paradise, what would it look like?

Giovannino and Serenella were strolling along the railroad tracks. Below was a scaly sea of somber, clear blue; above, a sky lightly streaked with white clouds. The railroad tracks were shimmering and burning hot. It was fun going along the tracks, there were so many games to play—he balancing on one rail and holding her hand while she walked along on the other, or else both jumping from one sleeper[1] to the next without ever letting their feet touch the stones in between. Giovannino and Serenella had been out looking for crabs, and now they had decided to explore the railroad tracks as far as the tunnel. He liked playing with Serenella, for

And it was all quite deserted. The two children crept forward, treading carefully over the gravel...

she did not behave as all the other little girls did, forever getting frightened or bursting into tears at every joke. Whenever Giovannino said, "Let's go there," or "Let's do this," Serenella followed without a word.

Ping! They both gave a start and looked up. A telephone wire had snapped off the top of the pole. It sounded like an iron stork shutting its beak in a hurry. They stood with their noses in the air and watched. What a pity not to have seen it! Now it would never happen again.

"There's a train coming," said Giovannino.

Serenella did not move from the rail. "Where from?" she asked.

Giovannino looked around in a knowledgeable way. He pointed at the black hole of the tunnel, which showed clear one moment, then misty the next, through the invisible heat haze rising from the stony track.

"From there," he said. It was as though they already heard a snort from the darkness of the tunnel, and saw the train suddenly appear, belching out fire and smoke, the wheels mercilessly eating up the rails as it hurtled toward them.

"Where shall we go, Giovannino?"

There were big gray aloes down by the sea, surrounded by dense, impenetrable nettles,

while up the hillside ran a rambling hedge with thick leaves but no flowers. There was still no sign of the train; perhaps it was coasting, with the engine cut off, and would jump out at them all of a sudden. But Giovannino had now found an opening in the hedge. "This way," he called.

The fence under the rambling hedge was an old bent rail. At one point it twisted about on the ground like the corner of a sheet of paper. Giovannino had slipped into the hole and already half vanished.

"Give me a hand, Giovannino."

They found themselves in the corner of a garden, on all fours in a flower bed, with their hair full of dry leaves and moss. Everything was quiet; not a leaf was stirring.

"Come on," said Giovannino, and Serenella nodded in reply.

There were big old flesh-colored eucalyptus trees and winding gravel paths. Giovannino and Serenella tiptoed along the paths, taking care not to crunch the gravel. Suppose the owners appeared now?

Everything was so beautiful: sharp bends in the path and high, curling eucalyptus leaves and patches of sky. But there was always the worrying thought that it was not their garden, and that they might be chased away any moment. Yet not a sound could be heard. A flight of chattering sparrows rose from a clump of arbutus at a turn in the path. Then all was silent again. Perhaps it was an abandoned garden?

But the shade of the big trees came to an end, and they found themselves under the open sky facing flower beds filled with neat rows of petunias and convolvulus, and paths and balustrades[2] and rows of box trees. And up at the end of the garden was a large villa with flashing window panes and yellow-and-orange curtains.

And it was all quite deserted. The two children crept forward, treading carefully

---

1. **sleeper.** British term for a tie supporting a railroad track
2. **balustrades.** Staircase railings held up by posts

over the gravel: perhaps the windows would suddenly be flung open, and angry ladies and gentlemen appear on the terraces to unleash great dogs down the paths. Now they found a wheelbarrow standing near a ditch. Giovannino picked it up by the handles and began pushing it along: it creaked like a whistle at every turn. Serenella seated herself in it and they moved slowly forward, Giovannino pushing the barrow with her on top, along the flower beds and fountains.

Every now and then Serenella would point to a flower and say in a low voice, "That one," and Giovannino would put the barrow down, pluck it, and give it to her. Soon she had a lovely bouquet.

Eventually the gravel ended and they reached an open space paved in bricks and mortar. In the middle of this space was a big empty rectangle: a swimming pool. They crept up to the edge; it was lined with blue tiles and filled to the brim with clear water. How lovely it would be to swim in!

"Shall we go for a dip?" Giovannino asked Serenella. The idea must have been quite dangerous if he asked her instead of just saying, "In we go!" But the water was so clear and blue, and Serenella was never afraid. She jumped off the barrow and put her bunch of flowers in it. They were already in bathing suits, since they'd been out for crabs before. Giovannino plunged in—not from the diving board, because the splash would have made too much noise, but from the edge of the pool. Down and down he went with his eyes wide open, seeing only the blue from the tiles and his pink hands like goldfish; it was not the same as under the sea, full of shapeless green-

black shadows. A pink form appeared above him: Serenella! He took her hand and they swam up to the surface, a bit anxiously. No, there was no one watching them at all. But it was not so nice as they'd thought it would be; they always had that uncomfortable feeling that they had no right to any of this, and might be chased out at any moment.

They scrambled out of the water, and there beside the swimming pool they found a Ping-Pong table. Instantly Giovannino picked up the paddle and hit the ball, and Serenella, on the other side, was quick to return his shot. And so they went on playing, though giving only light taps at the ball, in case someone in the villa heard them. Then Giovannino, in trying to parry a shot that had bounced high, sent the ball sailing away through the air and smack against a gong hanging in a pergola.³ There was a long, somber boom. The two children crouched down behind a clump of ranunculus. At once two menservants in white coats appeared, carrying big trays; when they had put the trays down

on a round table under an orange-and-yellow-striped umbrella, off they went.

Giovannino and Serenella crept up to the table. There was tea, milk, and sponge cake. They had only to sit down and help themselves. They poured out two cups of tea and cut two slices of cake. But somehow they did not feel at all at ease, and sat perched on the edge of their chairs, their knees shaking. And they could not really enjoy the tea and cake, for nothing seemed to have any taste. Everything in the garden was like that: lovely but impossible to enjoy properly, with that worrying feeling inside that they were only there through an odd stroke of luck, and the fear that they'd soon have to give an account of themselves.

Very quietly they tiptoed up to the villa. Between the slits of a Venetian blind they saw a beautiful shady room, with collections of butterflies hanging on the walls. And in the room was a pale little boy. Lucky boy, he

---

3. **pergola.** An arbor

must be the owner of this villa and garden. He was stretched out on a chaise lounge, turning the pages of a large book filled with figures. He had big white hands and wore pajamas buttoned up to the neck, though it was summer.

As the two children went on peeping through the slits, the pounding of their hearts gradually subsided. Why, the little rich boy seemed to be sitting there and turning the pages and glancing around with more anxiety and worry than their own. Then he got up and tiptoed around, as if he were afraid that at any moment someone would come and turn him out, as if he felt that that book, that chaise lounge, and those butterflies framed on the wall, the garden and games and tea trays, the swimming pool and paths, were only granted to him by some enormous mistake, as if he were incapable of enjoying them and felt the bitterness of the mistake as his own fault.

The pale boy was wandering about his shady room furtively, touching with his white fingers the edges of the cases studded with butterflies; then he stopped to listen. The pounding of Giovannino and Serenella's hearts, which had died down, now got harder than

ever. Perhaps it was the fear of a spell that hung over this villa and garden and over all these lovely, comfortable things, the residue of some injustice committed long ago.

Clouds darkened the sun. Very quietly Giovannino and Serenella crept away. They went back along the same paths they had come, stepping fast but never at a run. And

The pounding of Giovannino and Serenella's hearts, which had died down, now got harder than ever.

they went through the hedge again on all fours. Between the aloes they found a path leading down to the small, stony beach, with banks of seaweed along the shore. Then they invented a wonderful new game: a seaweed fight. They threw great handfuls of it in each other's faces till late in the afternoon. And Serenella never once cried.

MIRRORS & WINDOWS

What joy can be found in the simple things in life? Why do people who have a lot of wealth and possessions sometimes miss out on the most simple pleasures?

Refer and Reason
1. List some details about the enchanted garden. Analyze the mood created by the setting's details.
2. Describe the little boy Giovannino and Serenella see. Compare and contrast him with Giovannino and Serenella. What do you think would happen if they met?
3. Identify elements in the garden that emphasize the feeling of otherworldliness. Explain what the phrase "the residue of some injustice committed long ago" might refer to.

Writing Options
1. In a paragraph or two, write a brief story about what the pale little boy did after Giovannino and Serenella left.
2. Write a summary of the theme of the story and give three examples that illustrate this theme.

Go to **www.mirrorsandwindows.com** for more.

Like the Sun

All the time the headmaster was singing, Sekhar went on commenting within himself. He croaks like a dozen frogs. He is bellowing like a buffalo. Now he sounds like loose window shutters in a storm.

A Short Story by **R. K. Narayan**

R. K. Narayan (1906–2001) was born in Madras, India. The author of more than thirty books, Narayan didn't always find writing easy. He once said, "Writing in the beginning is like going uphill. Absolutely terrible. It was all frustration and struggle for more than fifteen years." Narayan persevered, however, and published many short stories, essays, travel pieces, and translations.

Like many of his stories, **"Like the Sun"** is set in the imaginary town of Malgudi in southern India. Through the ordinary experiences of the characters in this town, Narayan portrays the quirkiness of human relationships and the ironies of daily life.

Think of a time you struggled with telling the truth at the risk of hurting someone's feelings or causing someone to be angry with you. What did you decide to do? What was the outcome of your decision?

Truth, Sekhar reflected, is like the sun. I suppose no human being can ever look it straight in the face without blinking or being dazed. He realized that, morning till night, the essence of human relationships consisted in tempering truth so that it might not shock. This day he set apart as a unique day—at least one day in the year we must give and take absolute Truth whatever may happen. Otherwise life is not worth living. The day ahead seemed to him full of possibilities. He told no one of his experiment. It was a quiet resolve, a secret pact between him and eternity.

The very first test came while his wife served him his morning meal. He showed hesitation over a tidbit, which she had thought was her culinary masterpiece. She asked, "Why, isn't it good?" At other times he would have said, considering her feelings in the matter, "I feel full up; that's all."

But today he said, "It isn't good. I'm unable to swallow it." He saw her wince and said to himself, Can't be helped. Truth is like the sun.

His next trial was in the common room when one of his colleagues came up and said, "Did you hear of the death of so and so? Don't you think it a pity?" "No," Sekhar answered. "He was such a fine man—" the other began. But Sekhar cut him short with: "Far from it. He always struck me as a mean and selfish brute."

During the last period, when he was teaching geography for Third Form A, Sekhar received a note from the headmaster: "Please see me before you go home." Sekhar said to himself: It must be about these horrible test papers. A hundred papers in the boys' scrawls; he had shirked this work for weeks, feeling all the time as if a sword were hanging over his head.

The bell rang and the boys burst out of the class.

Sekhar paused for a moment outside the headmaster's room to button up his coat; that was another subject the headmaster always sermonized[1] about.

He stepped in with a very polite "Good evening, sir."

The headmaster looked up at him in a very friendly manner and asked, "Are you free this evening?"

Sekhar replied, "Just some outing which I have promised the children at home—"

"Well, you can take them out another day. Come home with me now."

"Oh…yes, sir, certainly… " And then he added timidly, "Anything special, sir?"

"Yes," replied the headmaster, smiling to himself…"You didn't know my weakness for music?"

"Oh, yes, sir…"

"I've been learning and practicing secretly, and now I want you to hear me this evening. I've engaged a drummer and a violinist to accompany me—this is the first time I'm doing it full dress[2] and I want your opinion. I know it will be valuable."

Sekhar's taste in music was well known. He was one of the most dreaded music critics in the town. But he never anticipated his musical inclinations would lead him to this trial…. "Rather a surprise for you, isn't it?" asked the headmaster. "I've spent a fortune on it behind closed doors…." They started for the headmaster's house. "God hasn't given me a child, but at least let him not deny me the consolation of music," the headmaster said, pathetically, as they walked. He incessantly chattered about music: how he began one day out of sheer boredom; how his teacher at first laughed at him and then gave him hope; how his ambition in life was to forget himself in music.

At home the headmaster proved very ingratiating. He sat Sekhar on a red silk carpet, set before him several dishes of delicacies, and fussed over him as if he were a son-in-law of the house. He even said, "Well, you must listen with a free mind. Don't worry about these test papers." He added half humorously, "I will give you a week's time."

"Make it ten days, sir," Sekhar pleaded.

"All right, granted," the headmaster said generously. Sekhar felt really relieved now—he would attack them at the rate of ten a day and get rid of the nuisance.

The headmaster lighted incense sticks. "Just to create the right atmosphere," he

A hundred papers in the boys' scrawls; he had shirked this work for weeks, feeling all the time as if a sword were hanging over his head.

---

1. **sermonized.** Gave lectures
2. **full dress.** As a dress rehearsal, or final practice before a performance

like loose window shutters in a storm.

The incense sticks burnt low. Sekhar's head throbbed with the medley of sounds that had assailed his eardrums for a couple of hours now. He felt half stupefied. The headmaster had gone nearly hoarse, when he paused to ask, "Shall I go on?" Sekhar replied, "Please don't, sir, I think this will do...." The headmaster looked stunned. His face was beaded with perspiration. Sekhar felt the greatest pity for him. But he felt he could not help it. No judge delivering a sentence felt more pained and help-less. Sekhar noticed that the headmaster's wife peeped in from the kitchen, with eager curiosity. The drummer and the violinist put away their burdens with an air of relief. The headmaster removed his spectacles, mopped his brow, and asked, "Now, come out with your opinion."

"Can't I give it tomorrow, sir?" Sekhar asked tentatively.

"No. I want it immedi-ately—your frank opinion. Was it good?"

"No, sir...," Sekhar replied.

"Oh!...Is there any use continuing my lessons?"

"Absolutely none, sir...," Sekhar said with his voice trembling. He felt very unhappy that he could not speak more soothingly. Truth, he reflected, required as much strength to give as to receive.

explained. A drummer and a violinist, already seated on a Rangoon mat,[3] were waiting for him. The headmaster sat down between them like a professional at a concert, cleared his throat, and began an alapana,[4] and paused to ask, "Isn't it good Kalyani?"[5] Sekhar pretended not to have heard the question. The headmaster went on to sing a full song composed by Thyagaraja[6] and followed it with two more. All the time the headmaster was singing, Sekhar went on commenting within himself. He croaks like a dozen frogs. He is bellowing like a buffalo. Now he sounds

---

3. **Rangoon mat.** Woven mat from the seaport capital of Burma
4. **alapana.** Classical Indian music that is improvised
5. **Kalyani.** Folk song from Mysore, a state in what is now India
6. **Thyagaraja.** Indian composer (1756–1847)

All the way home he felt worried. He felt that his official life was not going to be smooth sailing hereafter. There were questions of increment and confirmation[7] and so on, all depending upon the headmaster's goodwill. All kinds of worries seemed to be in store for him.... Did not Harischandra[8] lose his throne, wife, child, because he would speak nothing less than the absolute Truth, whatever happened?

At home his wife served him with a sullen face. He knew she was still angry with him for his remark of the morning. Two casualties for today, Sekhar said to himself. If I practice it for a week, I don't think I shall have a single friend left.

He received a call from the headmaster in his classroom next day. He went up apprehensively.

"Your suggestion was useful. I have paid off the music master. No one would tell me the truth about my music all these days. Why such antics at my age! Thank you. By the way, what about those test papers?"

"You gave me ten days, sir, for correcting them."

"Oh, I've reconsidered it. I must positively have them here tomorrow...."

A hundred papers in a day! That meant all night's sitting up! "Give me a couple of days, sir...."

"No. I must have them tomorrow morning. And remember, every paper must be scrutinized."

"Yes, sir," Sekhar said, feeling that sitting up all night with a hundred test papers was a small price to pay for the luxury of practicing Truth. ❖

Sekhar felt the greatest pity for him. But he felt he could not help it. No judge delivering a sentence felt more pained and helpless.

---

7. **increment and confirmation.** Raise and recognition for an employee
8. **Harischandra.** Ancient ruler of the Mysore

MIRRORS & WINDOWS

What's the difference between a small lie and a big lie? Is it ever right to tell a lie? What are the consequences of always telling the truth?

Refer and Reason

1. Recall what motivates Sekhar to undertake his "truth" experiment. What can you infer about his character from this motivation?
2. List examples of Sekhar telling the truth. Assess whether it is better to tell the truth or to temper the truth. Distinguish how tempering the truth differs from lying.
3. At the end of the story, Sekhar refers to the "luxury of practicing Truth." Do you think telling the truth is a luxury? When might you relish the chance to tell the truth instead of tempering it to avoid shocking people?

Writing Options

1. A younger friend is learning about truth and lying. Write a fable about telling the truth. Consider Sekhar's conclusions about the truth and your own feelings. Choose an appropriate moral for the fable.
2. You and your best friend discuss whether it is ever ethical to lie. As a way of continuing your conversation, write a reflective essay for your friend on the topic of truth and lying. In your essay, refer to ideas from the story as well as your own experiences.

 Go to **www.mirrorsandwindows.com** for more.

BEE SEASON
by Myla Goldberg

Eliza Naumann, despite the brilliance of the rest of her family members, has never been good at school—until she surprises everyone by winning the fourth-grade spelling bee. Although it begins with a simple spelling bee, this bittersweet coming-of-age novel is ultimately about the joys and sorrows of love.

A TALE OF TWO CITIES
by Charles Dickens

"It was the best of times, it was the worst of times." So begins Charles Dickens's riveting tale of ill-fated love and heroic sacrifice set against the backdrop of the French Revolution. In one of his most popular and powerful novels, Dickens paints an unforgettable portrait of London and Paris at the height of the Reign of Terror.

ACROSS THE GRAIN
by Jean Ferris

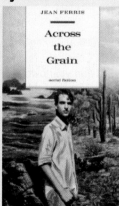

After the death of his mother, seventeen-year-old Will is left under the guardianship of his irresponsible sister, Paige. Readers can sympathize with Will's feelings of loneliness, self-pity, and anger as he struggles to figure out who he is and how best to deal with his situation.

NECTAR IN A SIEVE
by Kamala Markandaya

Rukmani had never met Nathan when they married, but soon their mudwalled home is filled with love. Although barely surviving, they continue to hope that someday they can return to their farm. Set in 1940s India during the last years of English rule, this is a story of love, poverty, industrialization, and determined survival.

DRACULA
by Bram Stoker

In 1887, Irishman Bram Stoker published the best-known of the vampire novels, combining popular folklore with the historical figure Prince Vlad Dracul. In it, English lawyer, Jonathan Harker, visits Castle Dracula in Transylvania on business, only to be imprisoned by his host. Little does he know the danger that will follow.

THINGS FALL APART
by Chinua Achebe

Okonkwo holds a prominent place in his Ibo village in 1890s Nigeria. When Christian missionaries appear, everything begins to fall apart for Okonkwo and his village. In this simple masterpiece, Okonkwo's ruin comes to stand for that of the entire culture as it collides with modern life.

Present a Horror Story

Picture yourself sitting around a campfire in the woods. You and your friends decide to tell spooky stories to pass the time. Good storytellers are able to make stories come alive for their audiences by using not only words but also facial expressions, gestures, and different tones of voice. In this lesson, you will present a horror story to your classmates.

1. Select a story
Using your textbook, the library, or the Internet, find a spooky story or urban legend that interests you. Two horror stories you'll find in Unit 1 are "The Masque of the Red Death" and "The Monkey's Paw."

2. Read the story
Read the story to yourself several times until you are familiar with the order of events and the details that are important to readers' understanding of the story.

3. Map out the story line
Determine the beginning, middle, and end of the story. Decide on good first and last lines for the story, and commit these lines to memory. Don't try to memorize the whole story word for word. Instead, become familiar enough with the main plot elements that you can tell the story in your own words.

4. Visualize the story
What is the setting of the story? What sights, sounds, smells, tastes, and textures attract you as you read? Figure out how to add these to your story using descriptive words and imagery.

5. Create mood and tone
Do you want your audience to laugh nervously or be frightened? Should you use a quiet voice or a forceful voice, or both? Think about how your facial expressions and posture help create tone and mood.

6. Practice
Tell the story often—by yourself in front of a mirror, or to a friend. As you practice, also keep in mind the following elements of verbal communication:
- Watch your **volume.** For a horror story, your volume should vary depending on the action in the story.
- Be sure to **enunciate,** or pronounce your words clearly.
- Pay attention to your **pace.** Do not speak too slowly or too quickly.
- Vary your **pitch,** or **intonation** (the highness or lowness of your voice), to give expression to your narrative.
- Use **stress** to emphasize important ideas.
- Vary your **tone** (the emotional quality of your voice) throughout the narrative.

Speaking Tip
Use simple vocabulary and sentence structure. Your audience will not have time to go back and "reread" what you said. They have to understand it the first time.

Also keep in mind the following nonverbal types of expression:
- eye contact
- facial expressions
- gestures
- body language

Speaking & Listening Rubric

Your presentation will be evaluated on these elements:

Content
- ☑ Clear chronology—beginning, middle, and end
- ☑ Strong opening and closing sentences
- ☑ Simple vocabulary and sentence structure
- ☑ Vivid description

Delivery/Presentation
- ☑ Appropriate volume, enunciation, and pace
- ☑ Effective intonation, stress, and tone to create mood
- ☑ Effective eye contact, facial expressions, gestures, and body language

Plot Analysis

What makes a short story meaningful and satisfying to read? In "The Open Window" by Saki, a young storyteller plays with Mr. Nuttel's mind. A dangerous wish leads to loss in "The Monkey's Paw" by W. W. Jacobs. In "Through the Tunnel" by Doris Lessing, a young boy's risk almost takes his life. In each gripping story, a strong **plot**—the series of events related to a central conflict—creates an electrifying, emotional, or thoughtful experience for the reader.

A **plot analysis** takes a story apart and examines it piece by piece in order to discover what makes it work. An analysis considers how plot elements work together—such as exposition, inciting incident, rising action, climax, falling action, resolution, and dénouement. A plot analysis is a way to interpret the story to gain a deeper understanding of both content and form.

❶ PREWRITE

Select Your Topic
Choose a story from this unit to analyze, perhaps one that was most compelling for you to read, one that interests you most.

Gather Information
Reread the story you have chosen to analyze. Identify what happens in each stage—note that plot elements will vary in order and importance depending on the story. This is how you take the story apart. Copy quotations you may want to refer to in your essay. Write your notes in a Plot Element Chart like the one on page 207.

Once you isolate and examine the plot elements, you can look at the story analytically to see how it works and to gain insight into the plot. When you form a focused observation, write it as your thesis statement.

Organize Your Ideas
To focus your ideas, review your Plot Element Chart and ask yourself these questions: What is the author's most impressive accomplishment in the story? What plot feature offers surprise, shock, or emotional depth? What plot device creates the turning point in the story?

Create an organizational plan for your essay using your Plot Element Chart. Number or list the plot elements in the order they logically appear—the same order they appeared in the story. Highlight information that is important and relevant to your analysis. Cross out irrelevant, unnecessary information.

Write Your Thesis Statement
Examine your notes and write a statement capturing the main point of your plot analysis. This is your **thesis statement.** One student, Lucy Ann Morris, wrote this

Assignment
Choose a story from this unit and write a plot analysis, using the three-part process – prewriting, drafting, and revising.

Purpose
To provide insight into how and why the elements of plot work in a specific story

Audience
Your teacher and classmates; people who have read the story and may or may not have analyzed the plot

Writing Rubric

A successful plot analysis:

☑ states the title, author, and brief summary of the story in the **introduction**

☑ presents a clear **thesis statement** expressing the main idea of the analysis

☑ develops **body paragraphs** that support the thesis, identify what happens in each element of the plot, and cite details and brief quotations from the story

☑ **concludes** by summarizing the analysis and restating the thesis

☑ is written in complete sentences

Plot Element Chart

"The Masque of the Red Death" by Edgar Allan Poe			
	Story Details	Significance / Ideas	Quotations
Exposition	The "Red Death" sweeps the country	The story is horrible and sad from the start	"the horror of blood"
Inciting Incident	Prince Prospero wants to hide from death and have a long party with friends	Who wouldn't try to hide? Still, it's irresponsible for a leader to ignore plague	The prince is "happy and dauntless," in "defiance to contagion"
Rising Action	Prospero hosts a masked ball; clock chimes eerily	The party's grotesque; the clock makes it so no one can really forget the sadness of plague	party "glowed with barbaric lustre"; clock causes "confused revery"
Climax, or Crisis	Man dressed as Red Death appears; when Prospero tries to unmask him, he dies	Prospero is so proud he thought he was protected from his fate	Red Death dressed as "a stiffened corpse"; Prospero shouts, "Who Dares?"
Falling Action	Guests attack Red Death; no one is inside the costume	Red Death comes to the partiers in costume, like they are	Red Death is not human "untenanted by any tangible form"
Resolution	Guests die	This part happens so quickly	"one by one dropped the revellers in the blood-bedewed halls"
Dénouement	Clock stops; flames go out; Red Death wins	Time and life have stopped for these people	"Red Death held illimitable dominion over all"
Thesis Idea: Prince Prospero made the Red Death even more horrible by trying so hard to defy it.			

thesis statement about the plot of Edgar Allan Poe's "The Masque of the Red Death":

> The sad story turns to horror because of Prospero's vain belief that he can escape the fate of the Red Death.

❷ DRAFT

Write your essay by following the three-part framework described on page 208: introduction, body, and conclusion.

Draft Your Introduction

In a plot analysis, the **introduction** identifies the author and title of the story and briefly summarizes its plot or theme. The introduction also states the thesis, establishing the main idea of the analysis. Finally, a good introduction creates interest, drawing readers into the rest of the essay.

The introduction that Lucy wrote during the Draft stage is shown in the first column of the chart on page 209. Her first

What Great Writers Do

Edgar Allan Poe used long and short sentences in "The Masque of the Red Death." Notice the example below:

But the Prince Prospero was happy and dauntless and sagacious. When his dominions were half depopulated, he summoned to his presence a thousand hale and light-hearted friends from among the knights and dames of his court, and with these retired to the deep seclusion of one of his castellated abbeys.

- **Introduction**
  Provide the title, author, and a summary of the story. Include the thesis statement of your analysis.
- **Body**
  Write an in-depth analysis by expanding on the thesis. Include details and quotations from the story to illustrate your points about the plot elements.
- **Conclusion**
  Rephrase the thesis statement, summarize the analysis, and give the essay a sense of closure.

sentence states the title of the story and author and briefly tells what the story is about. Then she provides a general statement about the plot elements. Lastly, she writes the main point of her analysis, her thesis statement. Her sentences, however, are choppy. They do not work well together. How could Lucy improve the flow of her sentences?

Draft Your Body

In the **body,** write about plot elements in the order they occur in the story, starting with exposition and ending with dénouement. State each point you want to make, and support it with evidence—details, ideas, and brief quotations from the text.

Look at the draft of Lucy's first of her four body paragraphs in the left-hand column of the chart on page 209. She begins to prove her thesis by offering specific details from the story, including several quotations.

Referring to your Plot Element Chart, develop your observations about the plot you are analyzing into logical paragraphs. Add supporting details and quotations from the story. Every detail should relate to the main point you make about the plot, as stated in your thesis.

Draft Your Conclusion

Finally, write a good **conclusion** that restates the thesis, summarizes the analysis, and provides closure to the essay. Give your readers, who have read the story, insight. You might describe your response to the plot and whether it worked for you, or connect the plot to a modern-day story, or link the plot structure with one character's development.

How successfully does Lucy conclude the draft of her essay? Read the draft of her conclusion in the chart on page 209.

What Great Writers Do

Edgar Allan Poe (1809–1849) paid as much attention to grammar as to plot. He says:

"The writer who neglects punctuation, or mispunctuates, is liable to be misunderstood. ... For the want of merely a comma, it often occurs that an axiom appears a paradox, or that a sarcasm is converted into a sermonoid."

❸ REVISE

Evaluate Your Draft

The final step is to evaluate your writing. Read your own essay or exchange papers with a classmate to evaluate each other's work. Comment on what has been done well and what can be improved.

Focus on content and organization. The introduction, body, and conclusion should work together to prove the thesis. All paragraphs should relate to the main idea. Use the Revision Checklist on page 210 to guide your evaluation. Write notes on the essay about what changes could be made.

Next, check for language errors. Correctly apply the guidelines in the Grammar & Style Workshops in this unit. Again, use the Revision Checklist to evaluate the writing. Think about how to write more clearly. Challenge any phrases that sound awkward when you say them out loud. Rewrite them until the words sound natural.

DRAFT STAGE		REVISE STAGE	
Introduction "The Masque of the Red Death" by Edgar Allan Poe is a chilling story. The story is about the attempts of Prince Prospero and his friends to escape the Red Death. The Red Death is a plague. Poe combines all the elements of plot to build a horror story full of horror from beginning to end. It's horror because of Prospero's vain belief that he can escape the fate of the Red Death.	*Identifies title and author; briefly summarizes story* *Identifies aspect to be analyzed* *States thesis*	"The Masque of the Red Death" by Edgar Allan Poe is a chilling story. ~~The story is~~ about the attempts of Prince Prospero and his friends to escape the Red Death, ~~The Red Death is~~ a "fatal" and "hideous" plague that is sweeping the land. Poe combines all the elements of plot to build a ~~horror~~ story full of horror from beginning to end. In fact, the sad story turns to horror because of Prospero's vain belief that he can escape the fate of the Red Death.	*Combines sentences* *Adds defining details* *Avoids unnecessary repetition of words; develops thesis*
Body Paragraph Readers learn that the Red Death leaves victims dizzy and bleeding. With red stains all over the face and body. Then we meet the main character, Prince Prospero. The inciting incident introduces the central conflict. Prince Prospero attempts to escape the Red Death. To do so, he takes one thousand friends. They go into a sealed abbey. They hide away, in "defiance to contagion."	*Starts analysis with the beginning of story* *Refers to plot elements* *Uses quotations from the text*	The exposition sets a frightening mood. Readers learn that the Red Death leaves victims dizzy and bleeding, with red stains all over the face and body. Then we meet the main character, Prince Prospero. He is "happy and dauntless," in contrast to the plague. The inciting incident introduces the central conflict, Prince Prospero's desperate attempts to escape the Red Death. To do so, he takes one thousand friends ~~They go~~ into a sealed abbey. They hide away, in "defiance to contagion."	*Includes all plot elements* *Fixes sentence fragment* *Adds details and quotations* *Effectively combines sentences to improve quality of writing*
Conclusion The Prince and his guests, after trying so hard to escape death, are overcome by it right there in there hiding place. The party chamber Prince Prospero meant to keep them all safe became a tomb. Edgar Allan Poe combines all of the plot elements to make this horror story work.	*Brings discussion to end of story* *Summarizes analysis*	It's ironic that the Prince and his guests, after trying so hard to escape death, are overcome by it right there in their hiding place. The party chamber Prince Prospero meant to keep them all safe became a tomb. Edgar Allan Poe combines all of the plot elements to make this horror story work.	*Uses analytical language; corrects word usage; combines sentences to strengthen the connection*

REVISION CHECKLIST

Content and Organization

☐ Are the story's title, author, and brief summary stated in the **introduction?**

☐ Does the **thesis statement** make an important analytical point about the plot?

☐ In the **body,** are the elements of plot arranged in a logical order?

☐ What additional evidence is used to support each plot element?

☐ Does the **conclusion** summarize the analysis, restate the thesis, and provide closure?

☐ Are all sentences effective?

Grammar and Style

☐ Do all subjects and verbs agree? (page 26)

☐ Does the writer use parallel structure? (page 40)

☐ Do all pronouns agree with their antecedents? (page 58)

☐ Are sentences varied in length and structure to add interest? (page 104)

☐ Does the writer use commas correctly? (page 128)

Revise for Content, Organization, and Style

Lucy evaluated her draft and found things to improve. Look at the chart on page 209 (this time, the right-hand column) to see how she revised the three paragraphs we looked at earlier:

• **Introduction:** Lucy combined sentences to reduce wordiness and create a seamless flow in her writing. She defined "Red Death" for readers, using quotations from the story. To avoid overusing the word "horror," she searched for other ways to say it.

• **Body:** Lucy added story details and quotations to prove her points. She made sure to refer to all plot elements. She corrected a sentence fragment and combined sentences to make them less choppy.

• **Conclusion:** By using analytical language, Lucy made a more compelling final point. Combining sentences strengthened the relationship between them. In reworking her last line, she retained her draft idea but created a more resonant closure.

Review the notes you or your partner made regarding your draft. Respond to each comment and effectively revise your essay.

Proofread for Errors

Proofread to check for remaining errors. While you may have corrected errors as you evaluate your essay, you can focus on this purpose during proofreading. Use proofreader's symbols to mark any errors you find. (See Language Arts Handbook 4.1 for a list of proofreader's symbols.) To complete the assignment, print out a final draft and read the entire thing once more before turning it in.

Take a look at Lucy's final draft on the next page. Review how she worked through the three stages of the writing process: Prewrite, Draft, and Revise.

WRITING FOLLOW-UP

Publish and Present

• In small groups, share your plot analyses. Pay attention to what you learn from other students' plot analyses as well as to how they respond to yours.

• Submit your essay to a school or community literary magazine, newsletter, journal, or newspaper.

Reflect

• What did you discover by reading the short story you analyzed a second and third time? What did you miss during the first reading? What is the value of rereading?

• What did you learn from your classmates' reactions to the same story? What is the value of discussing literature? How does insightful conversation help you become a better writer?

STUDENT MODEL

Plotting Horror in Poe's "The Masque of the Red Death"
by Lucy Ann Morris

"The Masque of the Red Death," by Edgar Allan Poe, is a chilling story about the attempts of Prince Prospero and his friends to hide from the Red Death, a "fatal" and "hideous" plague that sweeps the land. Poe combines all the elements of plot to build a story full of horror from beginning to end. In fact, the sad story turns to horror because of Prospero's vain belief that he can escape the fate of the Red Death.

The exposition sets a frightening mood. Readers learn that the Red Death leaves victims dizzy and bleeding, with red stains all over the face and body. Then we meet the main character, Prince Prospero. He is "happy and dauntless," in contrast to the plague. The inciting incident introduces the central conflict, Prince Prospero's desperate attempt to escape the Red Death. To do so, he takes one thousand friends into a sealed abbey. They hide away, in "defiance to contagion."

The action rises when Prince Prospero hosts a masked ball in seven rooms of his fortress. The guests cannot forget about the plague, however, and neither can readers. One room scares the guests because a red light shines through the window. A huge and eerie clock chimes each hour. Both remind the guests of death. The rising action peaks when a stranger appears, dressed as "a stiffened corpse," and "shrouded from head to foot in the habiliments of the grave."

The corpselike figure frightens everyone. Prince Prospero shouts, "Who dares?" and demands that his guests capture and unmask this person. When his guests understandably shrink from the terrifying figure, the Prince grabs his dagger and chases him. The corpse turns and confronts the Prince, bringing the plot to its climax. The Prince screams, drops his dagger, and dies.

The falling action occurs when the guests attack the figure. They discover nothing under his wrappings. He is not a person but is "untenanted by any tangible form." The guests are staring at the Red Death. The central conflict resolves as "one by one dropped the revellers in the blood-bedewed halls." Soon they are all dead. The dénouement ties up loose ends. As the story closes, Poe writes that when the guests lie dead on the floor, the clock stops chiming and the lights go out. The Red Death has won. It holds "illimitable dominion over all."

Edgar Allan Poe combines all of the plot elements to make this horror story work. Though the reader may expect the ending, the dénouement is horrifying because of how hard the partiers try to ignore the plague. In spite of hiding, the guests cannot escape death.

What is the writer's thesis statement?

How does the writer organize her essay?

What language of analysis does the writer use?

How does the writer incorporate references to plot elements?

How does the writer integrate details and quotations from the story into her sentences?

Where does the writer restate her thesis?

Reading Skills

MAKE INFERENCES

People make inferences all the time. You walk into the gym and see several volley-balls on the floor and a volleyball net set up in the center of the room; you infer that your gym class will play volleyball this period. You see your friend frantically studying his notes for biology class and infer that he has a test that day. **Making inferences** means combining clues with your prior knowledge to make an educated guess about what is happening or is about to happen.

As you read, you gather clues from the text and use your prior knowledge to fill in the gaps. For example, read the following passage from "The Monkey's Paw" by W. W. Jacobs, which comes just after the sergeant-major has revealed that the monkey's paw can grant its owner three wishes:

> "Well, why don't you have three, sir?" said Herbert White cleverly. The soldier regarded him in the way that middle age is wont to regard presumptuous youth. "I have," he said quietly, and his blotchy face whitened.

From the way the sergeant-major lowers his voice and turns pale, you might infer that something horrible happened when he made his wishes. You can test this inference by reading on and gathering more clues.

One way to make inferences while you read is to use an Inference Chart like the one below. In the first column, write part of a text or details about a character, event, or setting in a text. In the second column, write the conclusion you've drawn about the meaning of the text or details.

Text or Details	My Conclusion
The sergeant-major lowers his voice and his face goes white.	Something terrible happened when the sergeant-major used the paw.

Answering Multiple-Choice Questions

When you are taking a test that only gives you a certain amount of time to answer a number of questions, here are a few tips to keep in mind:

1. Answer the easy questions first. If you get stumped by a question, skip to the next question and come back to the difficult one.
2. Rule out answers you know are incorrect. When you have eliminated several answers, it's easier to make an educated guess about the remaining choices.
3. Keep track of time. If you are short on time, focus on the questions you can answer quickly.
4. Skip questions you are unable to answer. It's better to spend your time on questions you can answer than to spend a lot of time trying to figure out a very difficult question.

Test-Taking Tips
- Read the passage carefully.
- Read and consider all of the answer choices before you choose the one that best responds to the question.
- Refer to the passage when answering the questions.

PRACTICE

Directions: Read the following story. The questions that come after it will ask you to make inferences using the clues in the passage.

Prose Fiction: This passage is Lon Otto's short story "Love Poems."

He has written her a St. Valentine's Day love poem. It is very beautiful; it expresses, embodies a passionate, genuine emotion, emotion of a sort he hardly realized himself capable of, tenderness that
5 is like the tenderness of a better man. At the same time, the imagery is hard, diamond clear, the form intricate yet unobtrusive. He says the poem out loud to himself over and over. He cannot believe it, it is so good. It is the best poem he has ever
10 written.

He will mail it to her tonight. She will open it as soon as it arrives, cleverly timed, on St. Valentine's Day. She will be floored, she will be blown away by its beauty and passion. She will put it away
15 with his other letters, loving him for it, as she loves him for his other letters. She will not show it to anyone, for she is a private person, which is one of the qualities he loves in her.

After he has mailed the poem to her, written out
20 in his interesting hand, he types up a copy for his own files. He decides to send a copy to one of the more prestigious literary magazines, one into which he has not yet been admitted. He hesitates about the dedication, which could lead to embar-
25 rassment, among other things, with his wife. In the end he omits the dedication. In the end he decides to give a copy also to his wife. In the end he sends a copy also to a woman he knows in England, a poet who really understands his work.
30 He writes out a copy for her, dedicated to her initials. It will reach her a few days late, she will think of him thinking of her a few days before St. Valentine's Day.

Multiple Choice

1. Which of the following statements is most likely true of the man in the story?
   A. He is one of the most important poets of his time.
   B. He has beautiful handwriting.
   C. He is a loyal husband.
   D. He takes himself very seriously.

2. Which of the following adjectives *best* describes the man?
   F. loving
   G. self-absorbed
   H. talented
   J. humble

3. Which of the following is an antonym for the word *prestigious* (line 22)?
   A. obscure
   B. famous
   C. important
   D. ridiculous

4. Based on the passage, what can we infer about the lady to whom the man sends poems and letters?
   F. She and the man correspond often.
   G. She doesn't like poems and letters.
   H. She lives in England.
   J. She reads a lot of poetry.

Constructed Response

5. Why, do you think, does the man love the woman's quality of being a private person? Use information from the passage to explain your answer.

Writing Skills

REFLECTIVE ESSAY

When you write a reflective essay, you look back on, or *reflect* on, your past experiences, thoughts, and feelings and examine the ways they've shaped who you are today. A good example of a reflective essay is "How Reading Changed My Life" by Anna Quindlen, an excerpt of which can be found in Unit 2.

> Yet there was always in me, even when I was very small, the sense that I ought to be somewhere else. And wander I did, although, in my everyday life, I had nowhere to go and no imaginable reason on earth why I should want to leave. The buses took to the interstate without me; the trains sped by. So I wandered the world through books.
>
> —from "How Reading Changed My Life" by Anna Quindlen

Many standardized tests include sections that ask you to demonstrate your writing ability by composing an essay in response to a prompt, or topic. Some writing prompts ask you to express your thoughts and feelings about something that has happened to you. When you respond to an expressive or a reflective prompt, keep the following tips in mind:

- Narrow the topic to one specific aspect, experience, or event about which you have something to say.
- Don't just tell what happened, but explain how it affected you, what you learned, or how it changed your thinking.
- Include an introduction in which you identify your narrowed topic, a body in which you explain the topic and your insights about it, and a conclusion in which you sum up your reflections on the topic.

Because you will be evaluated in part on your ability to use standard English, you should also pay attention to grammar, usage, capitalization, spelling, and punctuation.

Writing Tips

- Practice writing in different formats and in real situations.
- Share your writing with others and get feedback.
- Strive for your writing to be well-developed and well-organized.
- Use precise, clear, and concise language.

PRACTICE

Timed Writing: 30 minutes

Assignment: Write a reflective essay for an interested reader about a book, movie, or play that has had a significant impact on you. Explain why it has been important.

As you write, make sure that you accomplish these tasks:

- Write about a specific book, movie, or play and explain the impact it has had on you, always keeping your audience and purpose in mind.

- Include sufficient detail so that the reader gets a sense of the content of the book, movie, or play and understands why it has been important to you.
- Organize the information in your essay so that the reader can follow it.
- Choose precise, descriptive words that show your insight into the subject and audience.
- Use a variety of sentence structures to make the writing interesting.
- Proofread your writing for errors in grammar, usage, spelling, punctuation, and capitalization.

Revising and Editing Skills

Some standardized tests ask you to read a draft of an essay and answer questions about how to improve it. As you read the draft, watch for errors like these:

- incorrect spellings
- disagreement between subject and verb; inconsistent verb tense; incorrect forms for irregular verbs; sentence fragments and run-ons; double negatives; and incorrect use of frequently confused words, such as *affect* and *effect*
- missing end marks, incorrect comma use, and lowercased proper nouns and proper adjectives
- unclear purpose, unclear main ideas, and lack of supporting details
- confusing order of ideas and missing transitions
- language that is inappropriate to the audience and purpose, and mood that is inappropriate for the purpose

PRACTICE

Directions: For each underlined section in the passage that follows, choose the revision that most improves the writing. If you think the original version is best, choose "MAKE NO CHANGE."

(1) Earlier this year I had to do a book report, and my teacher suggested I write about a book called "Of Mice and Men" by John Steinbeck. (2) Although I was relieved to see it was a short book. By the time I finished this book I was so glad my teacher suggested I should read it. (3) I really likes the two main characters, Lenny and George. (4) They took care of each other; even though sometimes it was difficult. (5) This reminded me of the relationship between me and my brother.

1. A. MAKE NO CHANGE.
   B. Of Mice and Men
   C. Of Mice And Men
   D. *Of Mice and Men*

2. F. MAKE NO CHANGE.
   G. Although I was relieved to see it was a short book; by the time I finished reading it I was glad my teacher suggested I should read it.

H. Although I was relieved to see it was a short book, by the time I finished reading it I was glad my teacher suggested it.
J. Although, I was relieved to see it was a short book by the time I finished this book I was glad my teacher suggested for me to read it.

3. A. MAKE NO CHANGE.
   B. liked
   C. have liked
   D. will like

4. F. MAKE NO CHANGE.
   G. each other, but even though
   H. each other, even though
   J. each other even though

5. A. MAKE NO CHANGE.
   B. My brother and I
   C. My brother and me
   D. I and my brother

UNIT 2

Nonfiction

QUINDLEN

HUGHES

SEATTLE

"'Tis strange but true; for truth is always strange; Stranger than fiction."
— Lord George Gordon Byron

A natural disaster takes the lives of tens of thousands of people. One couple's stand against racism changes a nation. Two families in different parts of the world suffer through the same war. These are just some of the real people and events you will discover in this unit. As you read, you will look at the world through someone else's eyes—eyes not too different from your own.

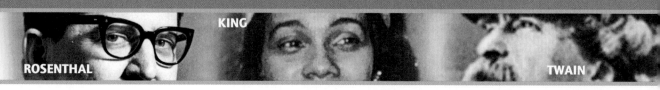

ROSENTHAL   KING   TWAIN

INTRODUCTION TO NONFICTION

"Writing can be a pretty desperate endeavor, because it is about some of our deepest needs: our need to be visible, to be heard, our need to make sense of our lives, to wake up and grow and belong."

—Anne Lamott in "Short Assignments"

"Truth is stranger than fiction" is an old saying that suggests real life is as interesting as literature. Whether or not you agree with this bit of folk wisdom, it is certain that well-crafted nonfiction can be just as gripping as a novel or short story. If you have ever delved into the biography of a remarkable person, like the one Langston Hughes wrote about Harriet Tubman (page 261), or if you've read an essay like "The Trouble with Television" (page 279) that really made you stop and think, you're already familiar with nonfiction.

THE GENRE OF NONFICTION

Nonfiction writing deals with real, not imagined, people, places, things, and events. It also explores thoughts and ideas. Popular types of nonfiction, like biographies, autobiographies, and memoirs, feature well-rounded characters, colorful settings, significant themes, and many other elements you will recognize from reading fiction. Other types of nonfiction, like essays and speeches, generally focus on developing or proving a central idea. Nonfiction that is intended mainly to share information falls into the category of informational texts.

Young Adult Nonfiction

Many schools and libraries create recommended reading lists to encourage teenagers to read. The following nonfiction works appear on several of these lists. Do any of the titles sound interesting to you?

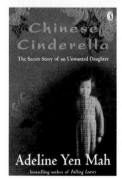

Drive: The Story of My Life by Larry Bird

A Girl from Yamhill by Beverly Cleary

The Road from Coorain by Jill K. Conway

Chinese Cinderella by Adeline Yen Mah

My Life in Dog Years by Gary Paulsen

FORMS OF NONFICTION

Biography, Autobiography, and Memoir

A **biography** is the story of a person's life told by someone other than that person. An **autobiography** is the story of a person's life, written by that person. Like other types of personal narratives, the autobiography expresses the first-person point of view and uses the pronoun "I." A **memoir** is a type of autobiography that focuses on one incident or period in a person's life. Memoirs are often based on an individual's memories of, and reactions to, historical events. (See Understanding Biography, Autobiography, and Memoir, page 232.)

Essay

Another form of nonfiction, the **essay,** is a short work that presents a single main idea, or *thesis,* about a particular topic. Different types of essays include *narrative, expository* or *informative, descriptive,* and *persuasive.* (See Understanding the Essay, page 276.)

Speech

A **speech** is a public address that was originally delivered orally. Many historically significant speeches were recorded in writing and are widely read today. (See Understanding Speeches, page 296.)

Lines from Historically Significant Speeches

"I say to the House as I said to ministers who have joined this government, I have nothing to offer but blood, toil, tears, and sweat."
—Winston Churchill,
Blood, Toil, Tears, and Sweat Speech, 1940

"And so let us always meet each other with a smile, for the smile is the beginning of love, and once we begin to love each other naturally we want to do something."
—Mother Teresa,
Nobel Lecture Speech, 1979

"Yet I do not come here to lament. For I find in Berlin a message of hope, even in the shadow of this wall, a message of triumph."
—Ronald Reagan,
Tear Down This Wall Speech, 1987

Informational Text

A form of nonfiction writing with which you are probably quite familiar is the informational text. An **informational text** aims to convey or explain information. Because of the Internet and easy access to most publications, people today have more information available at their fingertips than ever before. Included as informational texts are articles, how-to writing, web pages, visual media such as photographs and charts, and advertisements. (See Understanding Informational Text, page 316.)

AUTHOR'S PURPOSE IN NONFICTION

A writer's **purpose** is his or her aim, or goal. All writers of nonfiction have some sort of purpose in mind when they are writing. The following chart lists some of the *modes,* or forms, and purposes of writing. Remember that a piece of writing can have more than one purpose. For example, a nonfiction work may open with a brief story, or narrative, to introduce the topic or to make a point. It may then incorporate description, factual information, and a persuasive appeal to convince the reader to adopt a particular point of view.

Mode of Writing	Purpose	Examples
expository	to inform	news article, research report
narrative	to express thoughts or ideas, or to tell a story	personal account, memoir
descriptive	to portray a person, place, object, or event	travel brochure, personal profile
persuasive	to convince people to accept a position and respond in some way	editorial, petition

NONFICTION READING MODEL

BUILD BACKGROUND

- Make predictions about what the author will have to say by reading the title and the **Build Background** feature, and by looking over the vocabulary words.
- Read the **Meet the Author** feature to see if the information about the author gives you an idea about his or her area of interest or expertise.

ANALYZE LITERATURE

- The **Analyze Literature** feature will focus on one or more literary techniques or elements. What elements does the author use to achieve an effect?

SET PURPOSE

- Use the purpose explained in the **Set Purpose** feature or preview the text to create a purpose of your own. You may want to set the purpose of discovering the author's aim, or reason for writing.

USE READING SKILLS

- The **Use Reading Skills** feature will give you instructions on how to apply certain skills while you read, such as using a graphic organizer.

USE READING STRATEGIES

- **Ask questions** about things that seem unusual or interesting or things you don't understand. For instance, you might ask why the author chose to present information in a certain way.
- **Make predictions** about what's going to happen next. As you read, gather more clues that will either confirm or change your predictions.
- **Visualize** by forming pictures in your mind to help you see what is described in the selection.
- **Make inferences,** or educated guesses, about what is not stated directly. Connect what you read to your prior knowledge.

- **Clarify,** or check that you understand, what you read. Go back and reread any confusing or difficult parts before continuing.

ANALYZE LITERATURE

- Determine which **literary elements** stand out as you read. What point of view is used? How does the author use the literary elements to make his or her point?

MAKE CONNECTIONS

- Notice where there are **connections** between the selection and your life or the world beyond the story. In what ways does the topic affect you?

REFER TO TEXT

- **Remember details,** such as events and people. It may help to take notes to remember important facts.
- **Determine the sequence of events,** or the order in which things happen.
- Try to **summarize** the selection in a sentence or two.

REASON WITH TEXT

- **Interpret** the events or information in the selection to help clarify meaning.
- **Analyze** the text by breaking down information into smaller pieces and figuring out how those pieces fit into the story as a whole.

- **Evaluate** the text. **Draw conclusions** by bringing together what you have read and using it to make a decision or form an opinion.

ANALYZE LITERATURE

- **Apply** what you understand about the narrator, theme, and type of writing to see if they help you answer any additional questions. Review how the author uses literary elements.

EXTEND THE TEXT

- **Extend** your reading beyond the selection by exploring ideas through writing or doing other creative projects.

Montgomery Boycott

BEFORE READING

A Memoir by Coretta Scott King

BUILD BACKGROUND

Historical Context "Montgomery Boycott" is an excerpt from Coretta Scott King's memoir *My Life with Martin Luther King, Jr.* In the 1950s, a series of nonviolent protests began, with the goal of ending segregation (forced separation of African Americans and Caucasians) in public facilities, such as lunch counters, bathrooms, and buses. One method of nonviolent protest is a *boycott*, or a planned refusal to buy, sell, or use something in order to punish, persuade, or make a statement. In 1955, civil rights activists organized a successful boycott of the city buses of Montgomery, Alabama. The boycott began after Rosa Parks was arrested for not giving up to a white passenger her seat on a bus.

Reader's Context What injustices do you feel are worth protesting? Why are protests important? How would life in the United States be different if no one ever protested?

ANALYZE LITERATURE: Point of View

Point of view is the vantage point, or perspective, from which a story is told—in other words, who is telling the story. This narrative was written in *first-person* point of view. We know this because Coretta Scott King, the narrator, uses words such as *I* and *we*. She is a participant in or witness of the action.

SET PURPOSE

Based on what you know about boycotts from the Build Background section above, read to find out about the impact of the Montgomery bus boycott. Also consider how Mrs. King's point of view affects the trustworthiness of the account and how the narrative would be different if it were told from someone else's point of view.

MEET THE AUTHOR

Coretta Scott King (1927–2006) grew up in Alabama, where she watched buses transporting white children pass by as she walked five miles to school. Early experiences such as this made King determined to be treated as an equal. She continued her education at Antioch College in Ohio, and then moved to Boston to study music. There she met Martin Luther King Jr., whom she married in 1953. The couple moved to Montgomery, Alabama, where they fought for civil rights.

King said of the Montgomery bus boycott, "I came to the realization that we had been thrust into the forefront of a movement to liberate oppressed people, not only in Montgomery but also throughout our country, and this movement had worldwide implications."

USE READING SKILLS

Importance of Details
Coretta Scott King includes in her memoir many references to different dates, people, and places. Some of these details are *major,* or very important to your understanding of the memoir. Details that are not as important are *minor.* Use a Details Chart like the one below to write down major details. Next to each detail record why it is important to the memoir.

Detail	Importance to memoir

PREVIEW VOCABULARY

Use the context clues in the sentences below to figure out the meanings of the underlined words from the selection.

1. She was <u>aptly</u> described in the yearbook as charming, popular, and smart—words that fit her perfectly.
2. Nature preserves are often <u>serene</u> places, allowing for quiet reflection.
3. You need to express yourself more <u>coherently</u>; your essay is confusing and disorganized.
4. Her blind date was <u>devoid</u> of charm or wit, and his lack of appeal made her wish the evening would end.
5. The sports reporter's <u>exaltation</u> of the running back made the boy one of the town's most celebrated heroes.

Montgomery

Rosa Parks was not in a revolutionary state of mind. She had not planned to do what she did.

Martin Luther King Jr. and Coretta Scott King.

Boycott

A Memoir by **Coretta Scott King**

DURING READING

USE READING STRATEGIES

Clarify How do the details in this paragraph support King's claim that the Montgomery City Bus Lines treated the black customers "like cattle"?

Of all the facets of segregation in Montgomery,[1] the most degrading were the rules of the Montgomery City Bus Lines. This Northern-owned corporation outdid the South itself. Although seventy percent of its passengers were black, it treated them like cattle—worse than that, for nobody insults a cow. The first seats on all buses were reserved for whites. Even if they were unoccupied and the rear seats crowded, Negroes would have to stand at the back in case some whites might get aboard; and if the front seats happened to be occupied and

10   more white people boarded the bus, black people seated in the rear were

---

1. **Montgomery.** Capital of the state of Alabama

forced to get up and give them their seats. Furthermore—and I don't think Northerners ever realized this—Negroes had to pay their fares at the front of the bus, get off, and walk to the rear door to board again. Sometimes the bus would drive off without them after they had paid their fare. This would happen to elderly people or pregnant women, in bad weather or good, and was considered a great joke by the drivers. Frequently the white bus drivers abused their passengers, called them niggers, black cows, or black apes. Imagine what it was like, for example, for a black man to get on a bus with his son and be subjected to such treatment.

There had been one incident in March 1955 when fifteen-year-old Claudette Colvin refused to give up her seat to a white passenger. The high school girl was handcuffed and carted off to the police station. At that time Martin[2] served on a committee to protest to the city and bus-company officials. The committee was received politely—and nothing was done.

The fuel that finally made that slow-burning fire blaze up was an almost routine incident. On December 1, 1955, Mrs. Rosa Parks, a forty-two-year-old seamstress whom my husband <u>aptly</u> described as "a charming person with a radiant personality," boarded a bus to go home after a long day working and shopping. The bus was crowded, and Mrs. Parks found a seat at the beginning of the Negro section. At the next stop more whites got on. The driver ordered Mrs. Parks to give her seat to a white man who boarded; this meant that she would have to stand all the way home. Rosa Parks was not in a revolutionary frame of mind. She had not planned to do what she did. Her cup had run over. As she said later, "I was just plain tired, and my feet hurt." So she sat there, refusing to get up. The driver called a policeman, who arrested her and took her to the courthouse. From there Mrs. Parks called E. D. Nixon, who came down and signed a bail bond[3] for her.

Mr. Nixon was a fiery Alabamian. He was a Pullman porter[4] who had been active in A. Philip Randolph's Brotherhood of Sleeping Car Porters and in civil-rights activities. Suddenly he also had had enough; suddenly, it seemed, almost every Negro in Montgomery had had enough. It was spontaneous combustion. Phones began ringing all over the Negro section of the city. The Women's Political Council suggested

15

20

25

40

45

apt • ly (apt´ lē) *adv.,* fittingly; appropriately

DURING READING

USE READING STRATEGIES

Make Inferences What can you infer about the mood of Rosa Parks's confrontation and arrest by the information given in this paragraph? Do you think it was a dramatic scene? Why or why not?

---

2. **Martin.** Dr. Martin Luther King Jr. (1929–1968), leader of the American Civil Rights movement who was assassinated in 1968

3. **bail bond.** Formal pledge to pay the full amount of bail assigned by the court if the prisoner being released does not appear in court as scheduled

4. **Pullman porter.** Attendant in a railroad car that has seats that can be converted to berths for sleeping

a one day boycott of the buses as a protest. E. D. Nixon courageously agreed to organize it.

The first we knew about it was when Mr. Nixon called my husband early in the morning of Friday, December 2. He had already talked to Ralph Abernathy.[5] After describing the incident, Mr. Nixon said, "We have taken this type of thing too long. I feel the time has come to boycott the buses. It's the only way to make the white folks see that we will not take this sort of thing any longer."

Martin agreed with him and offered the Dexter Avenue Church as a meeting place. After much telephoning, a meeting of black ministers and civic leaders was arranged for that evening. Martin said later that as he approached his church Friday evening, he was nervously wondering how many leaders would really turn up. To his delight, Martin found over

A segregated bus in Texas, 1956.

forty people, representing every segment of Negro life, crowded into the large meeting room at Dexter. There were doctors, lawyers, businessmen, federal-government employees, union leaders, and a great many ministers. The latter were particularly welcome, not only because of their influence, but because it meant that they were beginning to accept Martin's view that "Religion deals with both heaven and earth…. Any religion that professes to be concerned with the souls of men and is not concerned with the slums that doom them, the economic conditions that strangle them, and the social conditions that cripple them, is a dry-as-dust religion." From that very first step, the Christian ministry provided the leadership of our struggle, as Christian ideals were its source.

DURING READING

USE READING STRATEGIES

Predict Make a prediction about what you think will happen at the meeting.

---

5. **Ralph Abernathy.** A leader of the Civil Rights movement

The meeting opened with brief devotions.[6] Then, because E. D. Nixon was away at work, the Reverend L. Roy Bennett, president of the Interdenominational[7] Ministerial Alliance, was made chairman. After describing what had happened to Mrs. Parks, Reverend Bennett said, "Now is the time to move. This is no time to talk; it is time to act."

90

Martin told me after he got home that the meeting was almost wrecked because questions or suggestions from the floor were cut off. However, after a stormy session, one thing was clear: however much they differed on details, everyone was unanimously for a boycott. It was set for Monday, December 5. Committees were organized; all the ministers present promised to urge their congregations to take part. Several thousand leaflets were printed on the church mimeograph machine[8] describing the reasons for the boycott and urging all Negroes not to ride buses "to work, to town, to school, or anyplace on Monday, December 5." Everyone was asked to come to a mass meeting at the Holt Street Baptist Church on Monday evening for further instructions. The Reverend A. W. Wilson had offered his church because it was larger than Dexter and more convenient, being in the center of the Negro district.

100

105

Saturday was a busy day for Martin and the other members of the committee. They hustled around town talking with other leaders, arranging with the Negro-owned taxi companies for special bulk fares and with the owners of private automobiles to get the people to and from work. I could do little to help because Yoki was only two weeks old, and my physician, Dr. W. D. Pettus, who was very careful, advised me to stay in for a month. However, I was kept busy answering the telephone, which rang continuously, and coordinating from that central point the many messages and arrangements.

110

115

Our greatest concern was how we were going to reach the fifty thousand black people of Montgomery, no matter how hard we worked. The white press, in an outraged exposé, spread the word for us in a way that would have been impossible with only our resources.

As it happened, a white woman found one of our leaflets, which her Negro maid had left in the kitchen. The <u>irate</u> woman immediately telephoned the newspapers to let the white community know what the blacks were up to. We laughed a lot about this, and Martin later said that we owed them a great debt.

120

i • rate (ī rāt´) *adj.,* angry

On Sunday morning, from their pulpits, almost every Negro minister in town urged people to honor the boycott.

125

---

6. **devotions.** Prayers
7. **Interdenominational.** Cooperative effort among leaders of different religious groups
8. **mimeograph machine.** Early form of copy machine that used a roller with ink on it

DURING READING

ANALYZE LITERATURE

Point of View What insights into Martin Luther King Jr. and the boycott are readers offered by receiving this information from the point of view of Coretta Scott King?

com • ply (kəm plī´) v., act in accordance with a rule or request

se • rene (sə rēn´) adj., calm; peaceful

Martin came home late Sunday night and began to read the morning paper. The long articles about the proposed boycott accused the NAACP[9] of planting Mrs. Parks on the bus—she had been a volunteer secretary for the Montgomery chapter—and likened the boycott to the tactics of the White Citizens' Councils.[10] This upset Martin. That awesome conscience of his began to gnaw at him, and he wondered if he were doing the right thing. Alone in his study, he struggled with the ques-

135 tion of whether the boycott method was basically unchristian. Certainly it could be used for unethical ends. But, as he said, "We are using it to give birth to freedom…and to urge men to comply with the law of the land. Our concern was not to put the bus company out of business, but to put justice in business." He recalled Thoreau's words, "We can no

140 longer lend our cooperation to an evil system," and he thought, "He who accepts evil without protesting against it is really cooperating with it." Later Martin wrote, "From this moment on I conceived of our movement as an act of massive noncooperation. From then on I rarely used the word *boycott.*"

145 Serene after his inner struggle, Martin joined me in our sitting room. We wanted to get to bed early, but Yoki began crying and the telephone kept ringing. Between interruptions we sat together talking about the prospects for the success of the protest. We were both filled with doubt. Attempted boycotts had failed in Montgomery and other cities. Because

150 of changing times and tempers, this one seemed to have a better chance, but it was still a slender hope. We finally decided that if the boycott was 60 percent effective we would be doing all right, and we would be satisfied to have made a good start.

A little after midnight we finally went to bed, but at five-thirty the

155 next morning we were up and dressed again. The first bus was due at 6 o'clock at the bus stop just outside our house. We had coffee and toast in the kitchen; then I went into the living room to watch. Right on time, the bus came, headlights blazing through the December darkness, all lit up inside. I shouted, "Martin! Martin, come quickly!" He ran in and stood

160 beside me, his face lit with excitement. There was not one person on that usually crowded bus!

We stood together waiting for the next bus. It was empty too, and this was the most heavily traveled line in the whole city. Bus after empty bus paused at the stop and moved on. We were so excited we could

---

9. **NAACP.** National Association for the Advancement of Colored People
10. **White Citizens' Councils.** Groups started in Mississippi in 1954 that had the goal of defeating desegregation in the South

hardly speak <u>coherently</u>. Finally Martin said, "I'm going to take the car and see what's happening in other places in the city."

He picked up Ralph Abernathy, and they cruised together around the city. Martin told me about it when he got home. Everywhere it was the same. A few white people and maybe one or two blacks in otherwise

co • her• ent • ly
(kō hār´ ənt lē) *adv.*, in a way capable of being understood

Rosa Parks at her trial on March 19, 1956.

empty buses. Martin and Ralph saw extraordinary sights—the sidewalks crowded with men and women trudging to work; the students of Alabama State College walking or thumbing rides; taxi cabs with people clustered in them. Some of our people rode mules; others went in horse-drawn buggies. But most of them were walking, some making a round trip of as much as twelve miles. Martin later wrote, "As I watched them I knew that there is nothing more majestic than the determined courage of individuals willing to suffer and sacrifice for their freedom and dignity."

Martin rushed off again at nine o'clock that morning to attend the trial of Mrs. Parks. She was convicted of disobeying the city's segregation ordinance and fined ten dollars and costs. Her young attorney, Fred D. Gray, filed an appeal. It was one of the first clearcut cases of a Negro

DURING READING

USE READING STRATEGIES

Visualize Picture in your mind the scene described in this paragraph.

180

APPLY THE MODEL

DURING READING

USE READING SKILLS

Importance of Details What is significant about Rosa Parks's trial?

being convicted of disobeying the segregation laws—usually the charge was disorderly conduct or some such thing.

The leaders of the movement called a meeting for three o'clock in the afternoon to organize the mass meeting to be held that night. Martin was a bit late, and as he entered the hall, people said to him, "Martin, we have elected you to be our president. Will you accept?"

190   It seemed that Rufus A. Lewis, a Montgomery businessman, had proposed Martin, and he had been unanimously elected. The people knew, and Martin knew, that the post was dangerous, for it meant being singled out to become the target of the white people's anger and vengeance. Martin said, "I don't mind. Somebody has to do it, and if you

195 think I can, I will serve."

Then other officers were elected. Rev. L. Roy Bennett became vice-president; Rev. E. N. French, corresponding secretary; Mrs. Erna A. Dungee, financial secretary; and E. D. Nixon, treasurer. After that they discussed what to call the organization. Someone suggested the Negro

200 Citizens' Committee. Martin did not approve, because that sounded like an organization of the same spirit as the White Citizens' Council. Finally, Ralph Abernathy proposed calling the organization the Montgomery Improvement Association, the MIA, and this name was unanimously approved.

205   Fear was an invisible presence at the meeting, along with courage and hope. Proposals were voiced to make the MIA a sort of secret society, because if no names were mentioned it would be safer for the leaders. E. D. Nixon opposed that idea. "We're acting like little boys," he said. "Somebody's name will be known, and if we're afraid, we might just

210 as well fold up right now. The white folks are eventually going to find out anyway. We'd better decide now if we are going to be fearless men or scared little boys."

That settled that question. It was also decided that the protest would continue until certain demands were met. Ralph Abernathy was made

215 chairman of the committee to draw up the demands.

Martin came home at six o'clock. He said later that he was nervous about telling me he had accepted the presidency of the protest movement, but he need not have worried, because I sincerely meant what I said when I told him that night, "You know that whatever you do, you

220 have my backing."

Reassured, Martin went to his study. He was to make the main speech at the mass meeting that night. It was now six-thirty, and—this was the way it was usually to be—he had only twenty minutes to prepare what he thought might be the most decisive speech of his life. He said

afterward that thinking about the responsibility and the reporters and television cameras, he almost panicked. Five minutes wasted and only fifteen minutes left. At that moment he turned to prayer. He asked God "to restore my balance and be with me in a time when I need Your guidance more than ever."

How could he make his speech both militant enough to rouse people to action and yet <u>devoid</u> of hate and resentment? He was determined to do both.

Martin and Ralph went together to the meeting. When they got within four blocks of the Holt Street Baptist Church, there was an enormous traffic jam. Five thousand people stood outside the church 235 listening to loudspeakers and singing hymns. Inside it was so crowded, Martin told me, the people had to lift Ralph and him above the crowd and pass them from hand to hand over their heads to the platform. The crowd and the singing inspired Martin, and God 240 answered his prayer. Later Martin said, "That night I understood what the older preachers meant when they said, 'Open your 245 mouth and God will speak for you.'"

First the people sang "Onward, Christian Soldiers" in a tremendous 250 wave of five thousand voices. This was followed by a prayer and a reading of the Scriptures. Martin was introduced. People 255 applauded; television lights beat upon him. Without any notes at all he began to speak. Once again he told the story of Mrs. 260 Parks, and rehearsed some of the wrongs black people were suffering. Then he said, "But there comes a time when people get tired. We are here this evening to say to those who have mistreated us so long that we are tired, tired of being segregated and humiliated, tired of 265 being kicked about by the brutal feet of oppression."

DURING READING

ANALYZE LITERATURE

Point of View Does this perspective on Martin Luther King Jr. differ from what is commonly known about him? Why or why not?

de • void (də void´)
adj., completely without

Martin Luther King Jr.

The audience cheered wildly, and Martin said, "We have no alternative but to protest. We have been amazingly patient…but we come here tonight to be saved from the patience that makes us patient with anything less than freedom and justice."

270 Taking up the challenging newspaper comparison with the White Citizens' Council and the Klan,[11] Martin said, "They are protesting for the perpetuation of injustice in the community; we're protesting for the birth of justice…their methods lead to violence and lawlessness. But in our

275 protest there will be no cross burnings; no white person will be taken from his home by a hooded Negro mob and brutally murdered…we will be guided by the highest principles of law and order."

Having roused the audience for militant action, Martin now set limits upon it. His study of nonviolence and his love of Christ informed his words. He said, "No one must be intimidated to keep them from riding the buses. Our method must be persuasion, not coercion. We will only say to the people, 'Let your conscience be your guide.'…Our actions must be guided by the deepest principles of the Christian faith…. Once again we must hear the words of Jesus, 'Love your enemies. Bless them that curse you. Pray for them that despitefully use you.' If we fail to do this, our protest will end up as a meaningless drama on the stage of history, and its memory will be shrouded in the ugly garments of shame…. We must not become bitter and end up by hating our white brothers. As Booker

290 T. Washington[12] said, 'Let no man pull you so low as to make you hate him.'" Finally, Martin said, "If you will protest courageously, and yet with dignity and Christian love, future historians will say, 'There lived a great people—a black people—who injected new meaning and dignity into the veins of civilization.' This is our challenge and our overwhelming

295 responsibility."

As Martin finished speaking, the audience rose cheering in exaltation. And in that speech my husband set the keynote and the tempo of the movement he was to lead from Montgomery onward. ❖

DURING READING

USE READING STRATEGIES

Make Inferences Why, do you think, was the policy of nonviolence important to this stage of the Civil Rights movement?

co • er • cion
(kō ur´ zhən) n., act of force through threats or violence

ex • al • ta • tion
(ek' sôl´ tā´ shən) n., feeling of great joy and pride

---

11. **the Klan.** Group begun as the Ku Klux Klan in Tennessee in 1866 for the purpose of militantly defeating any efforts of nonwhites to attain equal rights with white Americans
12. **Booker T. Washington.** (1856–1915) Founder of the teachers' college for African Americans that later became Tuskegee Institute

MIRRORS & WINDOWS

"Fear was an invisible presence at the meeting, along with courage and hope." When have you been both fearful and courageous at the same time? What does it mean to you that tremendous leaders like Martin Luther King Jr. also experienced fear?

AFTER READING

REFER TO TEXT ▶ ▶ ▶ ▶	▶ REASON WITH TEXT	
1a. Recall which aspect of segregation Coretta Scott King found most degrading. How were African-American passengers treated on buses? What cruel joke did the bus drivers play?	1b. Describe the laws that allowed the mistreatment of African-American bus passengers. How did people react to such laws?	**Understand** **Find meaning**
2a. Identify Dr. King's concerns about the boycott. What term does he use instead of *boycott?*	2b. Examine how Dr. King reconciled the idea of a boycott with his own beliefs.	**Apply** **Use information**
3a. List the rules or limits Dr. King placed on protests.	3b. Analyze why Dr. King was insistent that the protests be nonviolent.	**Analyze** **Take things apart**
4a. State what Dr. King finds majestic. What sight prompts him to say he finds it so?	4b. Judge whether or not the decision to boycott Montgomery buses was a good one for the organizers of the Civil Rights movement. Explain your answer.	**Evaluate** **Make judgments**
5a. Name the alternative forms of transportation used by the people who were boycotting the buses.	5b. Have you ever done something that caused you hardship, in order to support a cause you believed in? If not, would you? Explain.	**Create** **Bring ideas together**

ANALYZE LITERATURE: Point of View

What private, internal thoughts of Dr. King's do we read in the selection that we might not have learned had another more distant biographer compiled this information? Why is it important to consider the point of view in which a piece is written?

EXTEND THE TEXT

Writing Options

Creative Writing Write a **leaflet** to promote the Montgomery Bus Boycott. Your purpose is to get the proper information to people and to convince them to join in the boycott. The leaflet should be persuasive, as well as informative.

Expository Writing Pretend you are a reporter for the *Montgomery Herald* on December 5, 1955. Write a one-page **news report** of the first day of the bus boycott. Use the selection for factual information, and use your imagination to fill in the gaps. You may wish to include comments from individuals involved on both sides. For example, you might quote a bus company executive and a person supporting the boycott.

Lifelong Learning

Conduct a Survey Conduct a survey in your school about racial issues. First, with a group, brainstorm a list of the data you would like to gather with your survey. Write questions based on the information you want to gather. Represent the results in charts and graphs, and display them in your school.

Media Literacy

Analyze Civil Rights Coverage Research coverage of the Civil Rights movement in newspapers and magazines and on the radio, television, and the Internet. How objective is each report? Whom does each report quote, and how long is each quotation? Does each story appear at or near the beginning, middle, or end of the medium? Can you tell what the reporter thinks of the movement? Write a report on your overall impression of the stories you investigated.

 Go to **www.mirrorsandwindows.com** for more.

Understanding Biography, Autobiography, and Memoir

BIOGRAPHY, AUTOBIOGRAPHY, AND MEMOIR

A man types his life story with one toe. A courageous and determined woman leads slaves to freedom. A family is forced to leave home and live in a horse stall because of their ethnicity. Reading about other people's lives can be a fascinating experience. Perhaps this is why biography, autobiography, and memoir are such popular forms of writing.

Biography

A **biography** is the story of a person's life, told by someone other than that person.

Writers of biographies often rely on such primary sources as letters, diaries, journals, and interviews, which are also forms of nonfiction. A **source** is evidence of an event, idea, or a development. A **primary source** is direct evidence, or proof that comes straight from those involved. The use of sources helps biographers and other writers find the most accurate and trustworthy information.

Most biographers write about people who are well-known, such as athletes, performers, writers, or political figures, but this isn't always the case. Langston Hughes's "Harriet Tubman: The Moses of Her People" (page 261) is about Harriet Tubman, an escaped slave who leads other slaves to freedom. Notice how Hughes selects only the most telling of Tubman's experiences to convey what is remarkable about this woman.

> During the first years of her own freedom, Harriet spent most of her time showing others how to follow in her footsteps. Her fame as a fearless leader of "freedom bands" spread rapidly. Shortly large rewards were offered by the slaveholders for her capture. But she was never captured, and she never lost any of her followers to the slave catchers.
>
> —from "Harriet Tubman: The Moses of Her People" by Langston Hughes

Autobiography and Memoir

An **autobiography** is the story of a person's life, written by that person. Sometimes confused with autobiography is **memoir.** Though the two terms are often used interchangeably, the main difference between an autobiography and a memoir is that, generally, an autobiography includes all or most of the significant experiences of the subject's life, whereas a memoir typically focuses on one or more particular incidents or people who have been important to the memoirist. For example, the autobiography *My Left Foot* (page 235) revolves around Brown's struggle to communicate with others and live with cerebral palsy.

The memoir *The Diving Bell and the Butterfly* (page 241) is about specific events in Jean-Dominique Bauby's life following his stroke. Unlike Brown's more comprehensive story, Bauby's experiences are limited to a specific time, and the author reflects on why the particular instance is important to him. For instance, in the chapter "Paris," notice how Bauby recalls his two trips to the hospital following his stroke and tells the reader the significance of the difference between the two trips.

> Yet since taking up residence in my diving bell, I have made two brief trips to the world of Paris medicine to hear the verdict pronounced on me from the diagnostic heights. On the first occasion, my emotions got the better of me when my ambulance happened to pass the ultra modern high-rise where I once followed the reprehensible calling of editor in chief of a famous women's magazine.
>
> …The second time I went to Paris, four months later, I was unmoved by it. The streets were decked out in summer finery, but for me it was still winter, and what I saw through the ambulance windows was just a movie background.
>
> —from *The Diving Bell and the Butterfly* by Jean-Dominique Bauby

Another difference between the two forms is the order in which events unfold. Autobiographies are often written in chronological order, with details arranged in the order in which they occurred. Memoirs are usually less structured.

While autobiography and memoir clearly fall into the category of nonfiction, it is up to their authors to choose which details to include and which to leave out, as well as where to begin and end the retelling of events. This filtering of information allows writers to shape their stories to be understood by readers in a certain way.

Notable Autobiographies

- *The Confessions of St. Augustine* by St. Augustine of Hippo
- *Black Elk Speaks* by Black Elk and John J. Neihardt
- *The Autobiography of Benjamin Franklin* by Benjamin Franklin
- *The Story of My Life* by Helen Keller
- *Walden* by Henry David Thoreau
- *Black Boy* by Richard Wright
- *The Autobiography of Mark Twain* by Mark Twain

With a New Foreword by EDWARD P. JONES

60TH ANNIVERSARY EDITION

BLACK BOY

RICHARD WRIGHT

The Restored Text Established by The Library of America

HOW TO READ BIOGRAPHY, AUTOBIOGRAPHY, AND MEMOIR

When you are getting ready to read a biography, autobiography, or memoir, there are several approaches you can take. The approach you use, however, will depend on your purpose for reading. Below are two common purposes for reading biography, autobiography, and memoir and the approach you might take reading with each purpose. Keep in mind that these two purposes will often overlap.

- **Read to find out about a person's life.** Christy Brown learned to write using his feet instead of his hands. This is a remarkable feat. The pages of biographies, autobiographies, and memoirs are

filled with the interesting, moving, heroic, or heart-warming events of people's lives. Therefore, it is logical to approach biographies, autobiographies, and memoirs as a means of learning more about the lives of others. If you read with this purpose, you can use a graphic organizer like a Time Line (see below) to keep track of important events. As you read, look for details about time and place and fill them in on your Time Line. As an example, part of the Time Line below is filled in for "Harriet Tubman: The Moses of Her People."

Harriet Tubman is born in Maryland

Harriet is hit on the head with an iron weight; this results in epilepsy

Harriet is made a field slave

- **Read to learn more about someone's character.** Imagine the biography of a public figure you've always admired has recently been published. You read it because you want to know what this person is really like in his or her everyday life. To read with this purpose, a Cluster Chart like the one below can be useful. This Cluster Chart is partially filled out to record information about the character of Christy Brown.

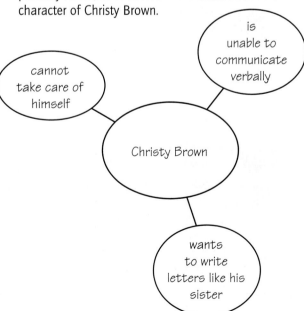

cannot take care of himself

is unable to communicate verbally

Christy Brown

wants to write letters like his sister

from My Left Foot
An Autobiography by Christy Brown

from The Diving Bell and the Butterfly
A Memoir by Jean-Dominique Bauby

BUILD BACKGROUND

Literary Context *My Left Foot* is the autobiography of Christy Brown. This remarkable man was unable to control the movements of his body because of cerebral palsy, yet he learned to write and type with his left foot. This excerpt describes Brown's birth and early childhood, including the event that proved his mother's conviction that it was "his body that [was] shattered, not his mind."

The Diving Bell and the Butterfly is the memoir of Jean-Dominique Bauby. In 1995, Bauby suffered a massive stroke that left him completely paralyzed with the exception of his left eyelid. This excerpt includes two chapters from the memoir. In "The Alphabet," Bauby describes the system that enables him to communicate. In "Paris," he describes two very different visits to the city where he once lived and worked.

Christy Brown and Jean-Dominique Bauby both overcame physical challenges to communicate. As you read, consider the following questions:
- What unique ways of communicating do Brown and Bauby discuss in these selections?
- What feelings or attitudes do Brown and Bauby express toward their physical challenges?

Reader's Context Describe a time when someone had confidence in your abilities.

USE READING SKILLS

Cause and Effect When you evaluate cause and effect, you look for the relationship between a cause or causes and one or more effects. As you read these two selections, use a Cause-Effect Organizer like the one below. Note the events (causes) and results of the events (effects) in your chart.

Causes		Effects
	→	

COMPARE LITERATURE: Metaphor and Theme

A **metaphor** is a comparison in which one thing is spoken or written about as if it were another. For example, "The basketball was a comet arching down the court." As you read the two selections, look for metaphors the writers use. Also think about how the title *The Diving Bell and the Butterfly* can work as a metaphor for the lives of both Bauby and Brown.

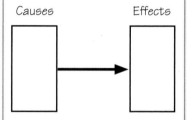

The **theme** of a literary work is the author's central message or insight into human nature or behavior. As you read these selections, note the metaphors the authors use, and consider how these metaphors may be related to the theme each writer conveys.

MEET THE AUTHORS

Christy Brown (1932–1981) was born in Dublin, Ireland, one of thirteen surviving children. Although it took him fifteen years, using one toe to type, to complete his first novel, he published seven books during his lifetime. Brown said, "I have made myself articulate and understood to people in many parts of the world, and this is something we all wish to do whether we are crippled or not."

BROWN

Jean-Dominique Bauby (1952–1997) was editor-in-chief of *Elle*, a highly respected French fashion magazine, until a stroke in 1995 left him paralyzed and unable to communicate except by blinking one eye. By blinking as a special alphabet was read aloud to him, Bauby composed *The Diving Bell and the Butterfly*. He died two days after the book was published in France, where it topped the best seller list.

BAUBY

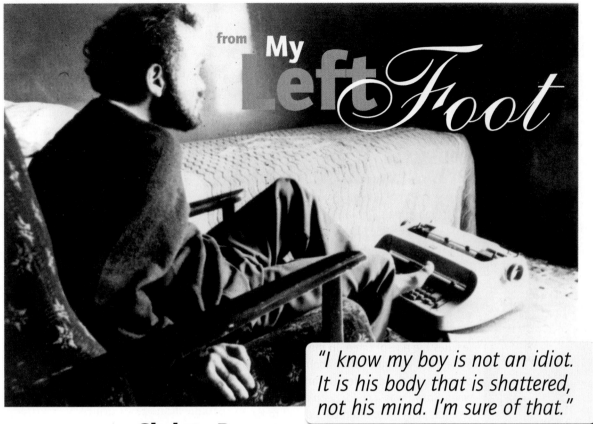

from My Left Foot

> "I know my boy is not an idiot. It is his body that is shattered, not his mind. I'm sure of that."

An Autobiography by **Christy Brown**

I was born in the Rotunda Hospital on June 5th, 1932. There were nine children before me and twelve after me, so I myself belong to the middle group. Out of this total of twenty-two, seventeen lived, but four died in infancy, leaving thirteen still to hold the family fort.

Mine was a difficult birth, I am told. Both mother and son almost died. A whole army of relations queued up[1] outside the hospital until the small hours of the morning, waiting for news and praying furiously that it would be good.

After my birth, Mother was sent to recuperate for some weeks, and I was kept in the hospital while she was away. I remained there for some time, without name, for I wasn't baptized until my mother was well enough to bring me to church.

It was Mother who first saw that there was something wrong with me. I was about four months old at the time. She noticed that my head had a habit of falling backward whenever she tried to feed me. She attempted to correct this by placing her hand on the back of my neck to keep it steady. But when she took it away, back it would drop again. That was the first warning sign. Then she became aware of other defects as I got older. She saw that my hands were clenched nearly all of the time and were inclined to twine behind my back, my mouth couldn't grasp the teat of the bottle because even at that early age my jaws would either lock together tightly, so that it was impossible for her to open them, or they would suddenly become limp and fall loose, dragging my whole mouth to one side.[2] At six months I could not sit up without having a mountain

---

1. **queued up.** Joined a line of people
2. **my jaws...whole mouth to one side.** These behaviors are typical of someone with severe cerebral palsy, a condition which is caused by lack of oxygen to the brain and which often occurs in a difficult childbirth.

SCIENCE CONNECTION

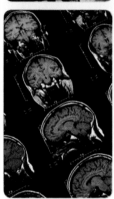

Cerebral Palsy Christy Brown was born with cerebral palsy, paralysis caused by a brain disorder. He displayed the common symptoms of this disorder, including the inability to sit or hold his head up unsupported, clenched hands, uncontrollable bouts of clenched or slack jaw, and convulsive motion. The early signs of cerebral palsy are usually detected before a child reaches the age of three. In the United States, it is estimated that about 500,000 people have the disorder. Unfortunately, when Brown was a child, people with cerebral palsy were often considered to be mentally deficient because of difficulties expressing themselves.

of pillows around me. At twelve months it was the same.

Very worried by this, Mother told my father her fears, and they decided to seek medical advice without any further delay. I was a little over a year old when they began to take me to hospitals and clinics, convinced that there was something definitely wrong with me, something which they could not understand or name, but which was very real and disturbing.

Almost every doctor who saw and examined me labeled me a very interesting but also a hopeless case. Many told Mother very gently that I was mentally defective and would remain so. That was a hard blow to a young

USE READING STRATEGIES

Ask Questions If Christy Brown were in your classroom right now, what would you want to ask him about his childhood?

mother who had already reared five healthy children. The doctors were so very sure of themselves that Mother's faith in me seemed almost an <u>impertinence</u>. They assured her that nothing could be done for me. She refused to accept this truth, the inevitable truth—as it then seemed—that I was beyond cure, beyond saving, even beyond hope. She could not and would not believe that I was an imbecile, as the doctors told her. She had nothing in the world to go by, not a scrap of evidence to support her <u>conviction</u> that, though my body was crippled, my mind was not. In spite of all the doctors and specialists told her, she would not agree. I don't believe she knew why—she just knew, without feeling the smallest shade of doubt.

Finding that the doctors could not help in any way beyond telling her not to place her trust in me, or, in other words, to forget I was a human creature, rather to regard me as just something to be fed and washed and then put away again, Mother decided there and then to take matters into her own hands. I was *her* child, and therefore part of the family. No matter how dull and incapable I might grow up to be, she was determined to treat me on the same plane as the others, and not as the "queer one" in the back room who was never spoken of when there were visitors present.

That was a <u>momentous</u> decision as far as my future life was concerned. It meant that I would always have my mother on my side to help me fight all the battles that were to come, and to inspire me with new strength

im • per • ti • nence (im' pʉr´ tə nən[t]s) *n.,* inappropriate, insolent action
con • vic • tion (kən vik´ shən) *n.,* strong belief
mo • men • tous (mō men´ təs) *adj.,* very important

when I was almost beaten. But it wasn't easy for her because now the relatives and friends had decided otherwise. They contended that I should be taken kindly, sympathetically, but not seriously. That would be a mistake. "For your own sake," they told her, "don't look to this boy as you would to the others; it would only break your heart in the end." Luckily for me, Mother and Father held out against the lot of them. But Mother wasn't content just to say that I was not an idiot: she set out to prove it, not because of any rigid sense of duty, but out of love. That is why she was so successful.

At this time she had the five other children to look after besides the "difficult one," though as yet it was not by any means a full house. They were my brothers, Jim, Tony, and Paddy, and my two sisters, Lily and Mona, all of them very young, just a year or so between each of them, so that they were almost exactly like steps of stairs.

Four years rolled by, and I was now five, and still as helpless as a newly born baby. While my father was out at bricklaying,[3] earning our bread and butter for us, Mother was slowly, patiently pulling down the wall, brick by brick, that seemed to thrust itself between me and the other children, slowly, patiently penetrating beyond the thick curtain that hung over my mind, separating it from theirs. It was hard, heart-breaking work, for often all she got from me in return was a vague smile and perhaps a faint gurgle. I could not speak or even mumble, nor could I sit up without support on my own, let alone take steps. But I wasn't inert or motionless. I seemed, indeed, to be convulsed with movement, wild, stiff, snakelike movement that never left me, except in sleep. My fingers twisted and twitched continually, my arms twined backwards and would often shoot out suddenly this way and that, and my head lolled and sagged sideways. I was a queer, crooked little fellow.

Mother tells me how one day she had been sitting with me for hours in an upstairs room, showing me pictures out of a great big storybook that I had got from Santa Claus last Christmas and telling me the names of different animals and flowers that were in them, trying without success to get me to repeat them. This had gone on for hours while she talked and laughed with me. Then at the end of it she leaned over me and said gently into my ear:

"Did you like it, Chris? Did you like the bears and the monkeys and all the lovely flowers? Nod your head for yes, like a good boy."

But I could make no sign that I had understood her. Her face was bent over mine hopefully. Suddenly, involuntarily, my queer hand reached up and grasped one of the dark curls that fell in a thick cluster about her neck. Gently she loosened the clenched fingers, though some dark strands were still clutched between them.

Then she turned away from my curious stare and left the room, crying. The door closed behind her. It all seemed hopeless. It looked as though there was some justification for my relatives' <u>contention</u> that I was an idiot and beyond help.

They now spoke of an institution.

"Never!" said my mother almost fiercely, when this was suggested to her. "I know my boy is not an idiot. It is his body that is shattered, not his mind. I'm sure of that."

Sure? Yet inwardly, she prayed God would give her some proof of her faith. She knew it was one thing to believe but quite another thing to prove.

I was now five, and still I showed no real sign of intelligence. I showed no apparent

---

3. **bricklaying.** Building with layers of bricks and mortar

con • ten • tion (kən ten[t]´ shən) *n.*, argument

Critical Viewing

Cite specific details of this painting that contribute to its overall mood. How does the painting's mood reflect Brown's feelings during his childhood?

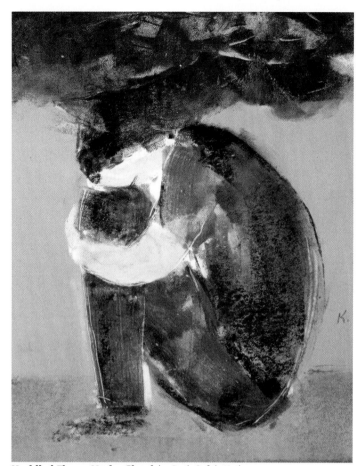

Huddled Figure Under Cloud, by Ruth Sofair Ketler.

interest in things except with my toes—more especially those of my left foot. Although my natural habits were clean, I could not aid myself, but in this respect my father took care of me. I used to lie on my back all the time in the kitchen or, on bright warm days, out in the garden, a little bundle of crooked muscles and twisted nerves, surrounded by a family that loved me and hoped for me and that made me part of their own warmth and humanity. I was lonely, imprisoned in a world of my own, unable to communicate with others, cut off, separated from them as though a glass wall stood between my existence and theirs, thrusting me beyond the sphere of their lives and activities. I longed to run about and play with the rest, but I was unable to break loose from my bondage.

Then, suddenly, it happened! In a moment everything was changed, my future life molded into a definite shape, my mother's faith in me rewarded and her secret fear changed into open triumph.

It happened so quickly, so simply after all the years of waiting and uncertainty, that I can see and feel the whole scene as if it had happened last week. It was the afternoon of a cold, gray December day. The streets outside glistened with snow, the white sparkling flakes stuck and melted on the windowpanes and hung on the boughs of the trees like molten silver. The wind howled dismally, whipping up little whirling columns of snow that rose and fell at every fresh gust. And over all, the dull, murky sky stretched like a dark canopy, a vast infinity of grayness.

Inside, all the family were gathered round the big kitchen fire that lit up the little room with a warm glow and made giant shadows dance on the walls and ceiling.

In a corner Mona and Paddy were sitting, huddled together, a few torn school primers[4] before them. They were writing down little sums onto an old chipped slate, using a bright piece of yellow chalk. I was close to them, propped up by a few pillows against the wall, watching.

---

4. **primers.** First books used to teach young children

It was the chalk that attracted me so much. It was a long, slender stick of vivid yellow. I had never seen anything like it before, and it showed up so well against the black surface of the slate that I was fascinated by it as much as if it had been a stick of gold.

Suddenly, I wanted desperately to do what my sister was doing. Then—without thinking or knowing exactly what I was doing, I reached out and took the stick of chalk out of my sister's hand—with my left foot.

I do not know why I used my left foot to do this. It is a puzzle to many people as well as to myself, for, although I had displayed a curious interest in my toes at an early age, I had never attempted before this to use either of my feet in any way. They could have been as useless to me as were my hands. That day, however, my left foot, apparently by its own volition, reached out and very impolitely took the chalk out of my sister's hand.

I held it tightly between my toes, and, acting on an impulse, made a wild sort of scribble with it on the slate. Next moment I stopped, a bit dazed, surprised, looking down at the stick of yellow chalk stuck between my toes, not knowing what to do with it next, hardly knowing how it got there. Then I looked up and became aware that everyone had stopped talking and was staring at me silently. Nobody stirred. Mona, her black curls framing her chubby little face, stared at me with great big eyes and open mouth. Across the open hearth,[5] his face lit by flames, sat my father, leaning forward, hands outspread on his knees, his shoulders tense. I felt the sweat break out on my forehead.

My mother came in from the pantry with a steaming pot in her hand. She stopped midway between the table and the fire, feeling the tension flowing through the room. She followed their stare and saw me in the corner. Her eyes looked from my face down to my foot, with the chalk gripped between my toes. She put down the pot.

Then she crossed over to me and knelt down beside me, as she had done so many times before.

"I'll show you what to do with it, Chris," she said, very slowly and in a queer, choked way, her face flushed as if with some inner excitement.

Taking another piece of chalk from Mona, she hesitated, then very deliberately drew, on the floor in front of me, *the single letter "A."*

"Copy that," she said, looking steadily at me. "Copy it, Christy."

I couldn't.

I looked about me, looked around at the faces that were turned toward me, tense, excited faces that were at that moment frozen, immobile, eager, waiting for a miracle in their midst.

The stillness was profound. The room was full of flame and shadow that danced before my eyes and lulled my taut nerves into a sort of waking sleep. I could hear the sound of the water tap dripping in the pantry, the loud ticking of the clock on the mantelshelf, and the soft hiss and crackle of the logs on the open hearth.

I tried again. I put out my foot and made a wild jerking stab with the chalk which produced a very crooked line and nothing more. Mother held the slate steady for me.

"Try again, Chris," she whispered in my ear. "Again."

---

5. **hearth.** Fireplace

vo • li • tion (vō li′ shən) *n.*, free will
taut (tôt) *adj.*, tense

USE READING STRATEGIES

Make Inferences Why is Brown's mother crying?

I did. I stiffened my body and put my left foot out again, for the third time. I drew one side of the letter. I drew half the other side. Then the stick of chalk broke and I was left with a stump. I wanted to fling it away and give up. Then I felt my mother's hand on my shoulder. I tried once more. Out went my foot. I shook, I sweated and strained every muscle. My hands were so tightly clenched that my fingernails bit into the flesh. I set my teeth so hard that I nearly pierced my lower lip. Everything in the room swam till the faces around me were mere patches of white. But—I drew it—*the letter "A."* There it was on the floor before me. Shaky, with awkward, wobbly sides and a very uneven center line. But it *was* the letter "A." I looked up. I saw my mother's face for a moment, tears on her cheeks. Then my father stooped and hoisted me on to his shoulder.

I had done it! It had started—the thing that was to give my mind its chance of expressing itself. True, I couldn't speak with my lips. But now I would speak through something more lasting than spoken words—written words.

That one letter, scrawled on the floor with a broken bit of yellow chalk gripped between my toes, was my road to a new world, my key to mental freedom. It was to provide a source of relaxation to the tense, taut thing that was I, which panted for expression behind a twisted mouth. ❖

Describe a time when you were determined to accomplish something. How did your determination impact the people around you?

REFER TO TEXT ▶ ▶ ▶ ▶	▶ REASON WITH TEXT	
1a. List the details Christy Brown shares about his birth. What did his mother notice when he was about four months old, and what did doctors tell her?	**1b.** Explain why the doctors may have suggested this solution.	**Understand** **Find meaning**
2a. Recall the decision Brown's mother made about where he would grow up.	**2b.** Examine the reasons why the decision made by Brown's mother was so crucial to his future.	**Apply** **Use information**
3a. Identify the incidents Christy shares about his mother's efforts to make him respond to her.	**3b.** Infer how Christy felt about the incident that occurred when his mother was trying to get him to respond to the picture book. Use evidence from the text to support your answer.	**Analyze** **Take things apart**
4a. Name the character traits of Brown's mother.	**4b.** Describe how Christy feels about his mother. Use evidence from the text to support your answer.	**Evaluate** **Make judgments**
5a. Of what importance is the title of Christy Brown's autobiography?	**5b.** Who are some people you admire because of what they had to overcome in order to succeed? What are some of their achievements?	**Create** **Bring ideas together**

from
The Diving Bell
and the Butterfly

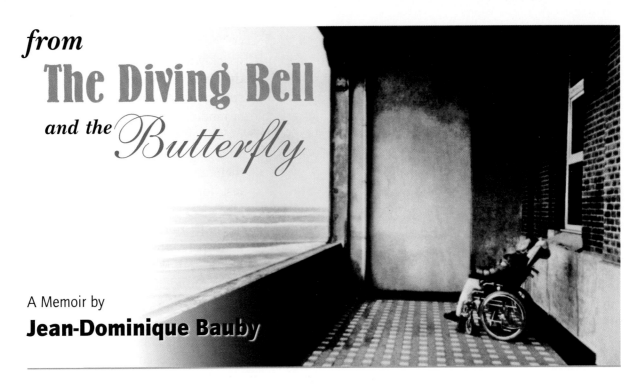

A Memoir by
Jean-Dominique Bauby

*My old life still burns within me,
but more and more of it is reduced to the ashes of memory.*

———— The Alphabet ————

I am fond of my alphabet letters. At night, when it is a little too dark and the only sign of life is the small red spot in the center of the television screen, vowels and consonants dance for me to a Charles Trenet[1] tune: "Dear Venice, sweet Venice, I'll always remember you…" Hand in hand, the letters cross the room, whirl around the bed, sweep past the window, wriggle across the wall, swoop to the door, and return to begin again.

E S A R I N T U L O M D P C F B V H G J Q Z Y X K W

The jumbled appearance of my chorus line stems not from chance but from cunning calculation. More than an alphabet, it is a hit parade in which each letter is placed according to the frequency of its use in the French language. That is why E dances proudly out in front, while W labors to hold on to last place. B resents being pushed back next to V, and haughty J—which begins so many sentences in French—is amazed to find itself so near the rear of the pack. Rolypoly G is annoyed to have to trade places with H, while T and U, the tender components of *tu*,[2] rejoice that they have not been separated. All this reshuffling has a purpose: to make it easier for those who wish to communicate with me.

It is a simple enough system. You read off the alphabet (ESA version, not ABC) until, with a blink of my eye, I stop you at the letter to be noted. The maneuver is repeated for the letters that follow, so that fairly soon you have

USE READING STRATEGIES

Clarify What determines the order of Bauby's alphabet? Why would an English speaker probably have a different alphabet?

---

1. **Charles Trenet.** Popular French singer
2. ***tu.*** French pronoun meaning *you*, used when addressing friends and family members

Inside a Diving Bell A diving bell is an early type of diving equipment consisting of a container open only at the bottom and supplied with compressed air by a hose. How might it feel to be inside a diving bell? In his book *The Diving Bell and the Butterfly*, Bauby uses a diving bell to represent his paralysis and a butterfly to represent his imagination.

a whole word, and then fragments of more or less intelligible sentences. That, at least, is the theory. In reality, all does not go well for some visitors. Because of nervousness, impatience, or <u>obtuseness</u>, performances vary in the handling of the code (which is what we call this method of transcribing my thoughts). Crossword fans and Scrabble players have a head start. Girls manage better than boys. By dint of practice, some of them know the code by heart and no longer even turn to our special notebook—the one containing the order of the letters and in which all my words are set down like the Delphic oracle's.

Indeed, I wonder what conclusions anthropologists of the year 3000 will reach if they ever chance to leaf through these notebooks, where <u>haphazardly</u> scribbled remarks like "The physical therapist is pregnant," "Mainly on the legs," "Arthur Rimbaud,"[3] and "The French team played like pigs" are interspersed with unintelligible gibberish, misspelled words, lost letters, omitted syllables.

USE READING SKILLS

Cause and Effect The narrator has invented a system of communication. What are the effects when nervous visitors try to use the system?

Nervous visitors come most quickly to grief. They reel off the alphabet tonelessly, at top speed, jotting down letters almost at random; and then, seeing the meaningless result, exclaim, "I'm an idiot!" But in the final analysis, their anxiety gives me a chance to rest, for they take charge of the whole conversation, providing both questions and answers, and I am spared the task of holding up my end. <u>Reticent</u> people are much more difficult. If I ask them, "How are you?" they answer, "Fine," immediately putting the ball back in my court. With some, the alphabet becomes an artillery barrage, and I need to have two or three questions ready in advance in order not to be swamped. <u>Meticulous</u> people never go wrong: they scrupulously note down each letter and never seek to unravel the mystery of a sentence before it is complete. Nor would they dream of completing a single word for you. Unwilling to chance the smallest error, they will never take it upon themselves to provide the "room" that follows "mush," the "ic" that follows "atom," or the "nable" without which neither "intermi" nor "abomi" can exist. Such scrupulousness makes for laborious progress, but at least you avoid the misunderstandings in which impulsive visitors bog down when they neglect to verify their intuitions. Yet I understood the poetry of such mind games one day when, attempting to ask for my glasses (*lunettes*), I was asked what I wanted to do with the moon (*lune*).

---

3. **Arthur Rimbaud.** French Symbolist poet (1854–1891)

ob • tuse • ness (äb tüs´ nes) *n.,* state of demonstrating slow intellect; dullness
hap • haz • ard • ly (hap' ha´ zərd lē) *adv.,* done in a manner marked by lack of plan, order, or direction
ret • i • cent (re´ tə sənt) *adj.,* inclined to be silent or uncommunicative in speech
me • tic • u • lous (mə ti´ kyə ləs) *adj.,* marked by extreme or excessive care in the treatment of details

The Eiffel Tower, 1935. Raoul Dufy. Private collection.

Critical Viewing

Bauby says that what he saw on his second trip to Paris was "straight out of a Dufy canvas." Look at the art on this page. How does this painting help you to understand his metaphor?

Paris

I am fading away. Slowly but surely. Like the sailor who watches the home shore gradually disappear, I watch my past recede. My old life still burns within me, but more and more of it is reduced to the ashes of memory.

Yet since taking up residence in my diving bell,[4] I have made two brief trips to the world of Paris medicine to hear the verdict pronounced on me from the diagnostic heights. On the first occasion, my emotions got the better of me when my ambulance happened to pass the ultra modern high-rise where I once followed the <u>reprehensible</u> calling of editor in chief of a famous women's magazine. First I recognized the building next door—a sixties antiquity, now scheduled to be demolished, according to the billboard out front. Then I saw our own glass facade, airily reflecting clouds and airplanes. On the sidewalk were a few of those familiar-looking faces that one passes every day for ten years without ever being able to put a name to them. When I thought I glimpsed someone I actually knew, walking behind a woman with her hair in a bun and a burly man in work clothes, I nearly unscrewed my head to see. Perhaps someone had caught sight of my ambulance from our sixth floor offices. I shed a few tears as we passed the corner café where I used to drop in for a bite. I can weep quite discreetly. People think my eye is watering.

The second time I went to Paris, four months later, I was unmoved by it. The streets were decked out in summer finery,

ANALYZE LITERATURE

Metaphor Why might Bauby use a diving bell as a metaphor for his paralysis? Can you think of other metaphors that would apply?

4. **diving bell.** Diving apparatus consisting of a container open only at the bottom and supplied with compressed air by a hose

rep • re • hen • si • ble (re′ pri hen[t]′ sə bəl) *adj.,* worthy of or deserving disapproval or censure

but for me it was still winter, and what I saw through the ambulance windows was just a movie background. Filmmakers call the process a "rear screen projection," with the hero's car speeding along a road that unrolls behind him on a studio wall. Hitchcock films owe much of their poetry to the use of this process in its early,

unperfected stages. My own crossing of Paris left me indifferent. Yet nothing was missing—housewives in flowered dresses and youths on roller skates, revving buses, messengers cursing on their scooters. The Place de l'Opéra, straight out of a Dufy[5] canvas. The treetops foaming like surf against glass building fronts, wisps of cloud in the sky. Nothing was missing, except me. I was elsewhere. ❖

---

5. **Dufy.** Raoul Dufy, French painter (1877–1953), whose cityscapes are characterized by bright colors

MIRRORS & WINDOWS

Have you ever spent time with someone who is unable to communicate in a conventional way? Describe your experience. Of the types of visitors Bauby describes in "The Alphabet," which would describe you if you were to visit him?

REFER TO TEXT ▶ ▶ ▶ ▶	▶ REASON WITH TEXT	
1a. In "The Alphabet," recall what Bauby's lifeline is to the outside world.	1b. Summarize how the alphabet facilitates communication between Bauby and his visitors.	**Understand** **Find meaning**
2a. List the ways Bauby categorizes his visitors in terms of how they communicate with him.	2b. Which visitors does Bauby prefer? How do you know this?	**Apply** **Use information**
3a. In "Paris," what cinematic technique does Bauby describe?	3b. Infer why Bauby compares his second trip to Paris to a "rear screen projection."	**Analyze** **Take things apart**
4a. Quote a line from Bauby's memoir that reflects his attitude about life.	4b. Evaluate Bauby's attitude toward life. Has he given up? What does he have left to live for besides his visitors? Use the text to support your answer.	**Evaluate** **Make judgments**
5a. Explain why Bauby cries during his first trip to Paris. What does this reveal about him?	5b. Propose why Bauby might have written a memoir about his experiences.	**Create** **Bring ideas together**

COMPARE LITERATURE: Metaphor and Theme

What two metaphors does Brown use in the last paragraph of the excerpt from *My Left Foot* to describe what the letter *A* that he draws means to him? What does Bauby mean when he says that "the alphabet becomes an artillery barrage"? What other metaphors can you find in the selections? What is the main theme of each excerpt? How do the metaphors help advance the themes?

EXTEND THE TEXT

Writing Options

Creative Writing Imagine that Brown and Bauby are touring high schools together, talking about living with disabilities. Write a **dialogue** in which the two discuss their attitudes toward their physical challenges. Consider these questions: How does Brown feel about the challenges he faced? How does Bauby feel? Does being born with a disability, as Brown was, and becoming paralyzed later in life, as Bauby was, affect their feelings in different ways? Explain.

Expository Writing For a high school literary magazine, write a two- or three-paragraph **critical essay** in which you identify and evaluate each writer's theme. How are the themes similar and how are they different? Use evidence from the selections to support your ideas.

Media Literacy

Write a News Story Imagine that you are a medical reporter doing research for a newspaper feature story. Your assignment is to provide a guide to five or six websites on cerebral palsy or another disability. Create a graphic organizer to track and organize information as you analyze the websites. Your chart should help you evaluate the trustworthiness of each site as a source of information. Consider the following questions: Who created the site? How recently has it been updated? Does the information seem reliable? Is it presented in a way that is easy to navigate? In your newspaper feature, give each site a rating and explain its strengths and weaknesses.

Collaborative Learning

Communicate in a New Way Write down something you would like to communicate to a partner. Then figure out a way to communicate without talking or writing as you usually do. Make your own communication board or alphabet, or draw or write with the hand you don't usually use, your mouth, or your foot. With your partner, take turns using the new method of communication to deliver the message you wrote down earlier, and see if each partner can understand the message.

 Go to **www.mirrorsandwindows.com** for more.

READING ASSESSMENT

1. In the excerpt from *My Left Foot*, when Christy Brown was a very young child he was diagnosed with which of the following disorders?
   A. cystic fibrosis
   B. cerebral palsy
   C. meningitis
   D. leukemia
   E. muscular dystrophy

2. In the excerpt from *My Left Foot*, the word *momentous* on page 236 most nearly means
   A. temporary.
   B. immediate.
   C. ominous.
   D. very important.
   E. sad.

3. Which of the following best describes Christy's mother in the excerpt from *My Left Foot*?
   A. humorous
   B. downcast
   C. determined
   D. whimsical
   E. None of the above

4. The author of *The Diving Bell and the Butterfly*, Jean-Dominique Bauby, was the victim of which of the following?
   A. an auto accident
   B. a heart attack
   C. a fall
   D. a stroke
   E. an infection

5. The word *obtuseness* on page 242 of "The Alphabet" most nearly means
   A. dullness.
   B. suspicion.
   C. insight.
   D. guilt.
   E. gentleness.

6. In the excerpt from *The Diving Bell and the Butterfly*, which of the following best describes the author's tone at the end of the section entitled "Paris"?
   A. hilarious
   B. ironic
   C. sad
   D. enthusiastic
   E. All of the above

7. Which of these two narratives did you find more inspiring, and why? In one or two paragraphs, explain your choice.

from **Desert Exile** The Uprooting of a Japanese-American Family

BUILD BACKGROUND

Historical Context In this excerpt from her autobiography **Desert Exile: The Uprooting of a Japanese-American Family,** Yoshiko Uchida tells about her experience as one of more than 120,000 Americans of Japanese ancestry who were relocated to internment camps during World War II. The United States government made the decision to relocate people based on suspicions that Japanese Americans might help Japan, which was allied with Germany and Italy in the war. *Desert Exile* is a story of survival, pride, ingenuity, and the power of community during difficult times.

Reader's Context When, if ever, have you lived communally with people outside of your immediate family? Have you been to camp, a retreat, or a group overnight? What are the positive and negative aspects of communal living?

ANALYZE LITERATURE: Description and Euphemism

Description is a type of writing that portrays a character, an object, or a scene. Descriptions make use of *sensory details*—words that describe how things look, sound, smell, taste, or feel.

A **euphemism** is an indirect word or phrase used in place of a direct statement that might be considered overly harsh or offensive. For example, a euphemism for *garbage dump* is *landfill.*

SET PURPOSE

As you read this selection, imagine that you have been asked to create a museum exhibit about the Japanese internment camps. Read this account with the purpose of learning what the camps were like from one young woman's perspective. Consider the types of details Uchida uses to describe the camp.

MEET THE AUTHOR

Yoshiko Uchida (1921–1992) was born in California, the child of parents who had immigrated from Japan before her birth. On December 7, 1941, she was studying for final exams at the University of California at Berkeley when news of the Japanese attack on Pearl Harbor came over the radio. In May of 1942, she and her family were relocated to Tanforan racetrack, a makeshift camp in California. Five months later, they were sent to Topaz, an internment camp in Utah. Uchida was released in 1943 to accept a graduate fellowship at Smith College. Her books *Journey to Topaz: A Story of the Japanese-American Evacuation* and *Desert Exile: The Uprooting of a Japanese-American Family* focus on internment experiences.

USE READING SKILLS

Sequence of Events
Sequence refers to the order in which things happen. When you read certain types of writing, such as an autobiography, a novel, a short story, a biography, or a history book, it is often useful to keep track of the sequence of events. Make a Time Line by drawing a line and dividing it into equal parts like the one shown below. As you read the selection, add key events and the places at which they occur.

Arrival at
Tanforan

PREVIEW VOCABULARY

Use the context clues in the sentences below to figure out the meanings of the underlined words from the selection.

1. Hurrying to finish the book, Maria took only a <u>cursory</u> glance at the last few chapters.
2. The air in the windowless attic was hot and stale because there was little <u>ventilation</u>.
3. All the campers are in the <u>communal</u> mess hall, where they are having lunch together.
4. Humanity's <u>baser</u> instincts include greed, vengefulness, and a territorial tendency.
5. We tried to pacify Ron with apologies and gifts, but nothing seemed to <u>assuage</u> his anger.

from Desert EXILE

SHIVERING IN THE COLD, WE PRESSED CLOSE TOGETHER TRYING TO SHIELD MAMA FROM THE WIND.

An Autobiography by

Yoshiko Uchida

The Uprooting of a Japanese-American Family

Critical Viewing

Examine the title of the painting and brainstorm a list of your reactions to the title. Does the title suggest that the image is an everyday occurrence? How does it affect your response to the images in the painting?

American Diary: October 16, 1942, 1997. Roger Shimomura. Private collection.

As the bus pulled up to the grandstand, I could see hundreds of Japanese Americans jammed along the fence that lined the track. These people had arrived a few days earlier and were now watching for the arrival of friends or had come to while away the empty hours that had suddenly been thrust upon them.

As soon as we got off the bus, we were directed to an area beneath the grandstand where we registered and filled out a series of forms. Our baggage was inspected for contra- band,[1] a <u>cursory</u> medical check made, and our living quarters assigned. We were to be housed in Barrack 16, Apartment 40. Fortunately, some friends who had arrived earlier found us and offered to help us locate our quarters.

It had rained the day before, and the hundreds of people who had trampled on the track had turned it into a miserable mass of

---

1. **contraband.** Smuggled goods

cur • so • ry (kurs´ rē *or* kurs´ ə rē) *adj.,* hasty; rapidly performed

SOCIAL STUDIES
CONNECTION

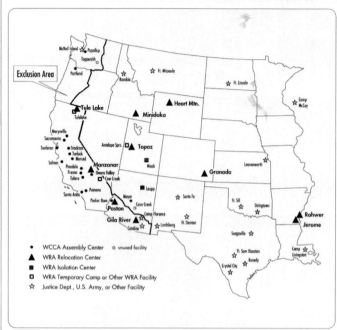

Exclusion Area

- • WCCA Assembly Center
- ▲ WRA Relocation Center
- ■ WRA Isolation Center
- □ WRA Temporary Camp or Other WRA Facility
- ☆ Justice Dept., U.S. Army, or Other Facility
- ○ unused facility

Executive Order 9066 Less than three months after the Japanese attack on Pearl Harbor on December 7, 1941, President Franklin D. Roosevelt issued Executive Order 9066, which required people of Japanese descent living mainly in areas along the West Coast of the United States to move into special camps because they were thought to be a threat to the security of the United States. This type of forced confinement is called *internment*. Internees included the Issei, Japanese immigrants; Nisei, American-born children of Japanese immigrants; Kibei, American-born Japanese who were educated mostly in Japan; and Sansei, children of Nisei. After the war ended, internees were allowed to return to their homes, but Executive Order 9066 was not officially terminated until 1976. Since then, the United States has offered reparations, or sums of money to make up for lost opportunities, to families who were dislocated.

slippery mud. We made our way on it carefully, helping my mother, who was dressed just as she would have been to go to church. She wore a hat, gloves, her good coat, and her Sunday shoes, because she would not have thought of venturing outside our house dressed in any other way.

Everywhere there were black tar-papered barracks[2] that had been hastily erected to house the eight thousand Japanese Americans of the area who had been uprooted from their homes. Barrack 16, however, was not among them, and we couldn't find it until we had traveled half the length of the track and gone beyond it to the northern rim of the racetrack compound.

Finally one of our friends called out, "There it is, beyond that row of eucalyptus trees." Barrack 16 was not a barrack at all, but a long stable raised a few feet off the ground with a broad ramp the horses had used to reach their stalls. Each stall was now numbered, and ours was number 40. That the stalls should have

been called "apartments" was a euphemism so <u>ludicrous</u> it was comical.

When we reached stall number 40, we pushed open the narrow door and looked uneasily into the vacant darkness. The stall was about ten by twenty feet and empty except for three folded army cots lying on the floor. Dust, dirt, and wood shavings covered the linoleum that had been laid over manure-covered boards, the smell of horses hung in the air, and the whitened corpses of many insects still clung to the hastily whitewashed walls.

High on either side of the entrance were two small windows, which were our only source of daylight. The stall was divided into two sections by Dutch doors[3] worn down by teeth marks, and each stall in the stable was separated from the adjoining one only by

---

2. **barracks.** Large, plain, often temporary housing
3. **Dutch doors.** Doors split horizontally so that the top and bottom halves can be opened separately

---

lu • di • crous (lü´ də krəs) *adj.,* laughably absurd or foolish

A line forms outside the Tanforan Assembly Center, 1942. San Bruno, CA.

hall,[4] which was located beneath the grandstand.

The sun was going down as we started along the muddy track, and a cold, piercing wind swept in from the bay. When we arrived, there were six long, weaving lines of people waiting to get into the mess hall. We took our place at the end of one of them, each of us clutching a plate and silverware borrowed

rough partitions that stopped a foot short of the sloping roof. The space, while perhaps a good source of <u>ventilation</u> for the horses, deprived us of all but visual privacy, and we couldn't even be sure of that because of the crevices and knotholes in the dividing walls.

Because our friends had already spent a day as residents of Tanforan, they had become adept at scrounging for necessities. One found a broom and swept the floor for us. Two of the boys went to the barracks where mattresses were being issued, stuffed the ticking with straw themselves, and came back with three for our cots.

Nothing in the camp was ready. Everything was only half-finished. I wondered how much the nation's security would have been threatened had the army permitted us to remain in our homes a few more days until the camps were adequately prepared for occupancy by families.

By the time we had cleaned out the stall and set up the cots, it was time for supper. Somehow, in all the confusion, we had not had lunch, so I was eager to get to the main mess

from friends who had already received their baggage.

Shivering in the cold, we pressed close together trying to shield Mama from the wind. As we stood in what seemed a bread line for the <u>destitute</u>, I felt degraded, humiliated, and overwhelmed with a longing for home. And I saw the unutterable sadness on my mother's face.

This was only the first of many lines we were to endure, and we soon discovered that waiting in line was as inevitable a part of Tanforan as the north wind that swept in from the bay, stirring up all the dust and litter of the camp.

Once we got inside the gloomy, cavernous mess hall, I saw hundreds of people eating at wooden picnic tables, while those who had already eaten were shuffling aimlessly over the wet cement floor. When I reached the serving table and held out my plate, a cook reached

---

4. **mess hall.** Room or building where a group of people eat

ven • ti • la • tion (ven' tə lā´ shən) *n.,* movement of air in a room
des • ti • tute (des´ tə tüt') *n.,* those living in poverty

into a dishpan full of canned sausages and dropped two onto my plate with his fingers. Another man gave me a boiled potato and a piece of butterless bread.

With five thousand people to be fed, there were few unoccupied tables, so we separated from our friends and shared a table with an elderly man and a young family with two crying babies. No one at the table spoke to us, and even Mama could seem to find no friendly word to offer as she normally would have done. We tried to eat, but the food wouldn't go down.

"Let's get out of here," my sister suggested.

We decided it would be better to go back to our barrack than to linger in the depressing confusion of the mess hall. It had grown dark by now, and since Tanforan had no lights for nighttime occupancy, we had to pick our way carefully down the slippery track.

Once back in our stall, we found it no less depressing, for there was only a single electric light bulb dangling from the ceiling, and a one-inch crevice at the top of the north wall admitted a steady draft of the cold night air. We sat huddled on our cots, bundled in our coats, too cold and miserable even to talk. My sister and I worried about Mama, for she wasn't strong and had recently been troubled with neuralgia,[5] which could easily be aggravated by the cold. She in turn was worrying about us, and of course we all worried and wondered about Papa.

Suddenly we heard the sound of a truck stopping outside.

"Hey, Uchida! Apartment 40!" a boy shouted.

I rushed to the door and found the baggage boys trying to heave our enormous "camp bundle" over the railing that fronted our stall.

"What ya got in here anyway?" they shouted good-naturedly as they struggled with the <u>unwieldy</u> bundle. "It's the biggest thing we got on our truck!"

I grinned, embarrassed, but I could hardly wait to get out our belongings. My sister and I fumbled to undo all the knots we had tied into the rope around our bundle that morning and eagerly pulled out the familiar objects from home.

We unpacked our blankets, pillows, sheets, tea kettle, and, most welcome of all, our electric hot plate. I ran to the nearest washroom to fill the kettle with water, while Mama and Kay made up the army cots with our bedding. Once we hooked up the hot plate and put the kettle on to boil, we felt better. We sat close to its warmth, holding our hands toward it as though it were our fireplace at home.

Before long some friends came by to see us, bringing with them the only gift they had—a box of dried prunes. Even the day before, we wouldn't have given the prunes a second glance, but now they were as welcome as the boxes of Maskey's chocolates my father used to bring home from San Francisco.

Mama managed to make some tea for our friends, and we sat around our steaming kettle, munching gratefully on our prunes. We spent most of the evening talking about food and the lack of it, a concern that grew obsessive over the next few weeks, when we were constantly hungry.

Our stable consisted of twenty-five stalls facing north, which were back to back with an equal number facing south, so we were surrounded on three sides. Living in our stable were an assortment of people—mostly small family units—that included an artist, my father's barber and his wife, a dentist and his wife, an elderly retired couple, a group of Kibei bachelors (Japanese born in the United States but educated in Japan), an insurance salesman and his wife, and a widow with two daugh-

---

5. **neuralgia** (nŭ ral´ jə). Pain along the path of a nerve

un • wiel • dy (un´ wēl´ dē) *adj.,* hard to manage because of weight or shape

ters. To say that we all became intimately acquainted would be an understatement. It was, in fact, <u>communal</u> living, with semiprivate cubicles provided only for sleeping.

Our neighbors on one side spent much of their time playing cards, and at all hours of the day we could hear the sound of cards being shuffled and money changing hands. Our other neighbors had a teenage son who spent most of the day with his friends, coming home to his

Children playing Monopoly at an internment camp.

stall at night only after his parents were asleep. Family life began to show signs of strain almost immediately, not only in the next stall but throughout the entire camp.

One Sunday our neighbor's son fell asleep in the rear of his stall with the door bolted from inside. When his parents came home from church, no amount of shouting or banging on the door could awaken the boy.

"Our stupid son has locked us out," they explained, coming to us for help.

I climbed up on my cot and considered pouring water on him over the partition, for I knew he slept just on the other side of it. Instead I dangled a broom over the partition and poked and prodded with it, shouting, "Wake up! Wake up!" until the boy finally bestirred himself and let his parents in. We became good friends with our neighbors after that.

About one hundred feet from our stable were two latrines and two washrooms for our section of camp, one each for men and women. The latrines were crude wooden structures

containing eight toilets, separated by partitions but having no doors. The washrooms were divided into two sections. In the front section was a long tin trough spaced with spigots of hot and cold water, where we washed our faces and brushed our teeth. To the rear were eight showers, also separated by partitions but lacking doors or curtains. The showers were difficult to adjust, and we either got scalded by torrents of hot water or shocked by an icy blast of cold. Most of the Issei[6] were unaccustomed to showers, having known the luxury of soaking in deep, pine-scented tubs during their years in Japan, and found the showers virtually impossible to use.

Our card-playing neighbor scoured the camp for a container that might serve as a tub and eventually found a large wooden barrel. She rolled it to the showers, filled it with warm water, and then climbed in for a pleasant and

6. **Issei (ē[´] sā´).** The first generation of Japanese immigrants to the United States

com • mu • nal (kə myü´ n'l) *adj.,* of or relating to a community

The Manzanar Relocation Center in Southern California during World War II.

leisurely soak. The greatest compliment she could offer anyone was the use of her private tub.

The lack of privacy in the latrines and showers was an embarrassing hardship especially for the older women, and many would take newspapers to hold over their faces or squares of cloth to tack up for their own private curtain. The army, obviously ill-equipped to build living quarters for women and children, had made no attempt to introduce even the most common of life's civilities into these camps for us.

During the first few weeks of camp life, everything was <u>erratic</u> and in short supply. Hot water appeared only sporadically, and the minute it was available, everyone ran for the showers or the laundry. We had to be clever and quick just to keep clean, and my sister and I often walked a mile to the other end of the camp, where hot water was in better supply, in order to boost our morale with a hot shower.

Even toilet paper was at a premium, for new rolls would disappear as soon as they were placed in the latrines. The shock of the evacuation compounded by the short supply of every necessity brought out the <u>baser</u> instincts of the internees, and there was little <u>inclination</u> for anyone to feel responsible for anyone else. In the early days, at least, it was everyone for himself or herself.

One morning I saw some women emptying bed pans into the troughs where we washed our faces. The sight was enough to turn my stomach, and my mother quickly made several large signs in Japanese cautioning people

er • rat • ic (i ra′ tik) *adj.,* having no fixed purpose
ba • ser (bā′ sər) *adj.,* less decent
in • cli • na • tion (in′ klə nā′ shən) *n.,* tendency to do something

against such unsanitary practices. We posted them in conspicuous spots in the washroom and hoped for the best.

Across from the latrines was a double barrack, one containing laundry tubs and the other equipped with clotheslines and ironing boards. Because there were so many families with young children, the laundry tubs were in constant use. The hot water was often gone by 9:00 A.M. and many women got up at 3:00 and 4:00 in the morning to do their wash, all of which, including sheets, had to be done entirely by hand.

We found it difficult to get to the laundry before 9:00 A.M. and by then every tub was taken and there were long lines of people with bags of dirty laundry waiting behind each one. When we finally got to a tub, there was no more hot water. Then we would leave my mother to hold the tub while my sister and I rushed to the washroom, where there was a better supply, and carried back bucketfuls of hot water, as everyone else learned to do. By the time we had finally hung our laundry on lines outside our stall, we were too exhausted to do much else for the rest of the day.

For four days after our arrival, we continued to go to the main mess hall for all our meals. My sister and I usually missed breakfast because we were assigned to the early shift, and we simply couldn't get there by 7:00 A.M. Dinner was at 4:45 P.M. which was a terrible hour, but not a major problem, as we were always hungry. Meals were uniformly bad and skimpy, with an abundance of starches such as beans and bread. I wrote to my non-Japanese friends in Berkeley shamelessly asking them to send us food, and they obliged with large cartons of cookies, nuts, dried fruit, and jams.

We looked forward with much anticipation to the opening of a half dozen smaller mess halls located throughout the camp. But when ours finally opened, we discovered that the preparation of smaller quantities had absolutely no effect on the quality of the food. We went eagerly to our new mess hall only to be confronted at our first meal with chili con carne, corn, and butterless bread. To assuage our disappointment, a friend and I went to the main mess hall, which was still in operation, to see if it had anything better. Much to our amazement and delight, we found small lettuce salads, the first fresh vegetables we had seen in many days. We ate ravenously and exercised enormous self-control not to go back for second and third helpings.

The food improved gradually, and by the time we left Tanforan five months later, we had fried chicken and ice cream for Sunday dinner. By July tubs of soapy water were installed at the mess hall exits so we could wash our plates and utensils on the way out. Being slow eaters, however, we usually found the dishwater tepid and dirty by the time we reached the tubs, and we often rewashed our dishes in the washroom.

Most internees got into the habit of rushing for everything. They ran to the mess halls to be first in line; they dashed inside for the best tables and then rushed through their meals to get to the washtubs before the suds ran out. The three of us, however, seemed to be at the end of every line that formed and somehow never managed to be first for anything.

One of the first things we all did at Tanforan was to make our living quarters as comfortable as possible. A pile of scrap lumber in one corner of camp melted away like snow on a hot day as residents salvaged whatever they could to make shelves and crude pieces of furniture to supplement the army cots. They also made ingenious containers for carrying their dishes to the mess halls, with handles and lids that grew more and more elaborate in a sort of unspoken competition.

Because of my father's absence, our friends helped us in camp, just as they had in Berkeley, and we relied on them to put

as • suage (ə swāj´) v., to calm; relieve

up shelves and build a crude table and two benches for us. We put our new camp furniture in the front half of our stall, which was our "living room," and put our three cots in the dark, windowless rear section, which we promptly dubbed "the dungeon." We ordered some print fabric by mail and sewed curtains by hand to hang at our windows and to cover our shelves. Each new addition to our stall made it seem a little more like home.

One afternoon about a week after we had arrived at Tanforan, a messenger from the administration building appeared with a telegram for us. It was from my father, telling us he had been released on parole from Montana and would be able to join us soon in camp. Papa was coming home. The wonderful news had come like an unexpected gift, but even as we hugged each other in joy, we didn't quite dare believe it until we actually saw him. ❖

MIRRORS & WINDOWS

Do you think what happened to the Uchida family could happen again in the United States? Could it happen in other parts of the world? Explain your answer.

REFER TO TEXT ▶ ▶ ▶ ▶	▶ REASON WITH TEXT	
1a. Name the place where the narrator and her family were sent. Where did they finally find their housing?	1b. Explain what made the family's new situation bearable.	**Understand** **Find meaning**
2a. Quote the sentence that shows how the narrator felt when she first went to the mess hall. What lifted the spirits of her and her family?	2b. Apply what you know about the mess hall and the Uchidas to explain why the situation at the mess hall was so troubling to the Uchidas.	**Apply** **Use information**
3a. List some of the problems of communal living.	3b. Identify ways people dealt with the problems of communal living. How were relationships among people affected by the lifestyle in the camp?	**Analyze** **Take things apart**
4a. Recall the improvements made in the internees' living conditions.	4b. Summarize the character traits of the Uchida family and the other Japanese-American families who tried to create a better environment in which to live.	**Evaluate** **Make judgments**
5a. Infer Uchida's attitude toward relocation.	5b. Compare and contrast the forcing of Japanese Americans into internment centers with the forcing of Jews into concentration camps. Explain the similarities and differences.	**Create** **Bring ideas together**

ANALYZE LITERATURE: Description and Euphemism

Reread the selection, and then single out a paragraph or two of description that you think is especially effective. What sensory details does Uchida use to make the description clear and vivid? What euphemisms did you find in the selection? How does Uchida use them to create tone, or attitude?

Informational Text
CONNECTION

On February 19, 1976, **President Gerald R. Ford** signed **Proclamation 4417** to terminate Executive Order 9066, the document responsible for the internment during World War II of more than 120,000 people of Japanese descent. In 1981, the Commission on Wartime Relocation and Internment of Civilians (CWRIC) held several public hearings at which Japanese Americans who had been confined during World War II testified about their experiences. In 1988, President Ronald Reagan signed the Civil Liberties Act, which provided each surviving internee with $20,000 in reparations. As part of this act, the Civil Liberties Education Fund was created to help teach people about the internment.

PROCLAMATION 4417:
Termination of Executive Order 9066

A Government Document by
President Gerald R. Ford

In this Bicentennial Year,[1] we are <u>commemorating</u> the anniversary dates of many of the great events in American history. An honest reckoning,[2] however, must include a recognition of our national mistakes as well as our national achievements. Learning from our mistakes is not pleasant, but as a great philosopher once <u>admonished</u>, we must do so if we want to avoid repeating them.

February 19th is the anniversary of a sad day in American history. It was on that date in 1942, in the midst of the response to the hostilities that began on December 7, 1941, that Executive Order No. 9066 was issued, subsequently enforced by the criminal penalties of a <u>statute</u> enacted March 21, 1942, resulting in the uprooting of loyal Americans. Over one hundred thousand persons of Japanese ancestry were removed from their homes, detained in special camps, and eventually relocated.

The tremendous effort by the War Relocation Authority[3] and concerned Americans for the welfare of these Japanese Americans may add perspective to that story, but it does not erase the setback to fundamental American principles. Fortunately, the Japanese-American community in Hawaii was spared the <u>indignities</u> suffered by those on our mainland.

We now know what we should have known then—not only was that evacuation

---

1. **Bicentennial Year.** The year 1976 marked the two-hundredth anniversary (bicentennial) of the 1776 declaration of an independent United States.
2. **reckoning.** Settling of accounts
3. **War Relocation Authority.** This group was established by President Franklin D. Roosevelt in 1942 to supervise the removal and relocation of internees and to provide for their needs.

---

com • mem • o • rate (kə me´ mə rāt') *v.*, remember by having a ceremony or celebration
ad • mon • ish (ad' mä´ nish) *v.*, express disapproval
stat • ute (sta´ chüt') *n.*, law
in • dig • ni • ty (in dig´ nə tē) *n.*, humiliating treatment

wrong, but Japanese Americans were and are loyal Americans. On the battlefield and at home, Japanese Americans—names like Hamada, Mitsumori, Marimoto, Noguchi, Yamasaki, Kido, Munemori and Miyamura—have been and continue to be written in our history for the sacrifices and the contributions they have made to the well-being and security of this, our common Nation.

The Executive Order that was issued on February 19, 1942, was for the sole purpose of <u>prosecuting</u> the war with the Axis Powers,[4] and ceased to be effective with the end of those hostilities. Because there was no formal statement of its termination, however, there is concern among many Japanese Americans that there may yet be some life in that <u>obsolete</u> document. I think it appropriate, in this our Bicentennial Year, to remove all doubt on that matter, and to make clear our commitment in the future.

Now, therefore, I, Gerald R. Ford, President of the United States of America, do hereby proclaim that all the authority <u>conferred</u> by

Executive Order No. 9066 terminated upon the issuance of Proclamation No. 2714, which formally proclaimed <u>cessation</u> of the hostilities of World War II on December 31, 1946.

I call upon the American people to affirm with me this American Promise—that we have learned from the tragedy of that long-ago experience forever to treasure liberty and justice for each individual American, and resolve that this kind of action shall never again be repeated.

Gerald R. Ford
The White House, 1976 ❖

---

4. **Axis Powers.** The Axis powers—Germany, Italy, and Japan—were the forces that opposed the United States and its allies in World War II.

---

pros • e • cute (prä′ si kyüt′) v., engage in
ob • so • lete (äb′ sə lēt) adj., outdated; of no further use
con • fer (kən fur′) v., give to something or someone, as from a position of authority
ces • sa • tion (se sā′ shən) n., stopping of an action

REFER TO TEXT ▷ ▷ ▷ ▷	▷ REASON WITH TEXT	
1a. Recall what reference to history President Ford makes at the beginning of the proclamation.	1b. Explain why you think Ford makes this reference.	**Understand** **Find meaning**
2a. How does Ford describe the decision taken in 1942 to relocate Japanese Americans in internment camps?	2b. Identify the audience Ford had in mind for this proclamation.	**Analyze** **Take things apart**
3a. According to Ford, what lesson can be learned from "the tragedy of that long-ago experience"?	3b. Judge whether you think issuing this proclamation was a valuable act. Explain your answer.	**Evaluate** **Make judgments**

TEXT ◄—ᵀᴼ—► TEXT CONNECTION

- What do you think was Ford's purpose in delivering Proclamation 4417? What was Uchida's purpose in writing *Desert Exile*? Which text do you think is more effective in achieving its purpose? Why?
- How do you think Uchida reacted to Proclamation 4417? Explain your answer.

EXTEND THE TEXT

Writing Options

Creative Writing   Imagine that you are the narrator of *Desert Exile* and that, while interned at Tanforan, you write a letter to President Roosevelt describing conditions there and conveying your opinions about the internment of Japanese Americans. Write a **letter** of two or three paragraphs, making sure you express yourself with a firm but respectful tone.

Persuasive Writing   On February 29, 1872, Senator Carl Schurz made the following statement at a Senate session: "My country, right or wrong; if right, to be kept right; and if wrong, to be set right." For the Op-Ed page of a newspaper, write a **persuasive article** arguing that the quotation is or is not important today. Include a thesis statement in your introduction, and then use reasons with examples and evidence to support your main idea.

Collaborative Learning

Analyze the Effect of Time and Place   Together with a small group, use the Internet to research World War II propaganda posters from the United States, Germany, and Japan. Print out examples of posters from each country, and make a list of the key messages advertised by each. Then discuss the following questions: How are these messages similar? How are they different? What conditions in each country and in the world at large contributed to the need for each poster? What kinds of propaganda posters might be well received in the United States today?

Speaking and Listening

Tell a Japanese Folk Tale   Yoshiko Uchida wrote a number of stories for children based on Japanese folk tales. Read one of her stories, or a Japanese folk tale by another author, several times until you are very familiar with its main ideas. You do not need to memorize the folk tale word for word. Volunteer to tell your story to a small group of children at your local library, elementary school, or community center. Use eye contact, vocal inflection, pitch, and gestures to make the story interesting and vivid.

 Go to **www.mirrorsandwindows.com** for more.

READING ASSESSMENT

1. Which of the following is the historical background for this selection?
   A.   the Spanish-American War
   B.   World War I
   C.   World War II
   D.   the Vietnam War
   E.   None of the above

2. The word *cursory* on page 247 most nearly means
   A.   predatory.
   B.   preliminary.
   C.   hasty.
   D.   somber.
   E.   expected.

3. Which of the following *best* describes Uchida's purpose for writing *Desert Exile*?
   A.   to persuade readers to feel sympathy
   B.   to inform readers about life in the internment camps
   C.   to entertain readers with an interesting story
   D.   to inspire readers to write their own autobiographies
   E.   All of the above

4. At the end of the selection, what does the narrator reveal about Papa?
   A.   He is being sent to a camp in Montana.
   B.   He will soon be joining the family at Tanforan.
   C.   He has written a book about his experiences as an internee.
   D.   He has been drafted into the army.
   E.   He has died.

5. In Proclamation 4417, why does Ford refer to an "American Promise"?
   A.   to inspire Americans to protect the liberty of all citizens
   B.   to persuade Americans to accept the internment as part of the past
   C.   to entertain the audience with interesting language
   D.   to inform Americans about their potential
   E.   None of the above

6. Based on this account, what sort of a person do you think the narrator is? Write a character sketch of the narrator, supporting your main ideas with specific details drawn from the autobiography.

GRAMMAR & STYLE

Colons and Semicolons

A **colon** is a punctuation mark used to mean "note what follows." A colon can be used in these ways:

• to introduce a list of items

EXAMPLE

The Uchidas' friends sent them the following things: cookies, nuts, dried fruit, and jams.

• to introduce a long or formal statement or a quotation (In this case, the first word of the statement or quotation should be capitalized.)

EXAMPLE

This line from Uchida's autobiography describes the family's living quarters: "Dust, dirt, and wood shavings covered the linoleum that had been laid over manure-covered boards..."

• to separate two independent clauses when the second clause explains or summarizes the first clause

EXAMPLE

People in the camp learned to rush everywhere: There were so many people that everyone ran to be first in line.

• to separate the hour from the minutes when stating a time, to follow the greeting in a business letter, and to separate the chapter and verse numbers of religious works

EXAMPLE

In the camp, breakfast was served at 7:00 a.m.

Do not use a colon in the following situations: after a verb, between a preposition and its object(s), or after *because* or *as*.

EXAMPLES

After a Verb
incorrect: Two of Uchida's writing strengths are: her use of detail and her tone.
correct: Two of Uchida's writing strengths are her use of detail and her tone.

Between a Preposition and its Object
incorrect: People in the camps suffered from: cold, hunger, and shock.

correct: People in the camps suffered from cold, hunger, and shock.

After *because* or *as*
incorrect: Showering in the camps was difficult for older people because: there was little hot water.
correct: Showering in the camps was difficult for older people because there was little hot water.

A **semicolon** joins two closely related independent clauses. Using a semicolon in place of a comma and a coordinating conjunction such as *and, but, so, or, nor, for,* or *yet* adds emphasis to the second clause. The semicolon signals a pause longer than that of a comma but shorter than that of a period.

EXAMPLE

Her family made the most of their situation; they tried to make their living quarters as homelike as possible.

Use a semicolon between items in a series if the items contain commas.

EXAMPLE

The Uchidas were hungry because meal times were inconvenient; the mess hall was crowded, uncomfortable, and ill-equipped; and there was never enough food served.

Use a semicolon between independent clauses joined by a conjunctive adverb (*however, therefore, furthermore,* etc.) or a transitional phrase (for example, *as a result, in other words,* etc.).

EXAMPLE

Mr. Uchida was released on parole; therefore, he would soon join his family.

REVIEW TERMS
• **colon:** a punctuation mark used to mean "note what follows"
• **semicolon:** a punctuation mark that joins two closely related sentences
• **independent clause:** a group of words that contains a subject and a verb and expresses a complete thought

Use Colons and Semicolons

Review each item below. If any colons or semicolons are missing, rewrite the sentences adding colons or semicolons where they are needed. If the sentence is correct, write "Correct."

1. Some works by Yoshiko Uchida are *Journey to Topaz: A Story of the Japanese-American Evacuation, The Invisible Thread: An Autobiography,* and *The Terrible Leak.*
2. Uchida taught in an elementary school until she was released from the camp Topaz she then earned a master's degree in education.
3. The relocation of Japanese Americans to internment camps began in the 1940s the order repealing this action, however, was not issued until 1976.
4. That many women in the camps got up at 400 in the morning to do laundry shows just how desperate people were to have hot water.
5. What is made clear by Uchida is this: The government did not adequately prepare the camps for women and children.
6. The Uchidas tried to make their living quarters comfortable; and their neighbors helped them.
7. In 1976, President Ford terminated Executive Order 9066; in 1988, internees were given reparations.
8. The Civil Liberties Education Fund was created to teach people about the internment education is one of the best ways to avoid the same thing happening again.
9. Uchida points out some positive aspects of the internment; a sense of unity, family togetherness, and pride in survival.
10. Proclamation 4417 was delivered to: remind people of the internment, admit fault, and resolve not to repeat the mistake.

Improve a Paragraph

Rewrite the following paragraph, correcting errors in the use of colons and semicolons.

Traditionally, elders in Japanese society are given much respect by the younger generations however, the Issei, who were immigrants to the United States, were not given positions of authority in the camps. Instead, the government assigned such positions to the Nisei. The Nisei were: born in the United States, had American citizenship, and seemed less of a threat to national security than the generation before them. This violation of tradition created cultural conflict in the camps Uchida describes these types of conflicts in her autobiography.

Use Colons and Semicolons in Your Writing

Using semicolons is a way to add variety to writing. Two short sentences can be joined with a semicolon to make one longer sentence. Or, a semicolon joining two independent clauses can add emphasis to the second clause; this is the case in the example below, from *Desert Exile*:

They ran to the mess halls to be first in line; they dashed inside for the best tables and then rushed through their meals to get to the washtubs before the suds ran out.

Write five factual statements about Yoshiko Uchida. In each statement, add variety to your writing by using either a colon or a semicolon.

EXTEND THE SKILL

Choose an essay or a news article on a topic that interests you. Read the text carefully, and then write a brief summary of it, using your own words. Use at least one colon and one semicolon in your writing.

Harriet Tubman: The Moses of Her People

BUILD BACKGROUND

Historical Context During the mid-1800s, the Underground Railroad helped slaves escape into northern states and Canada. The Underground Railroad was not actually a railroad, as Langston Hughes explains in **"Harriet Tubman: The Moses of Her People."** It was so named because it helped slaves move quickly and easily toward their destination of freedom. Safe places where escaped slaves could hide were called "stations," and people who helped slaves move to freedom were called "conductors." Harriet Tubman, an escaped slave herself, was one of the most famous conductors on the Underground Railroad. She returned from safety to the South nineteen times and helped hundreds of slaves to escape. Langston Hughes featured Tubman in his book *Famous American Negroes.*

Reader's Context To what lengths have you gone or would you go for what you believe is right?

ANALYZE LITERATURE: Style and Allusion

Style is the manner in which something is said or written. As you read, think about how you would describe both the diction, or word choice, and the grammatical structure of "Harriet Tubman: The Moses of Her People."

An **allusion** is a reference to a well-known person, event, object, or work from history or literature. There is an allusion to Moses, a character from the Bible, in the title of this selection. Moses led the Israelites out of slavery in Egypt into the Promised Land.

SET PURPOSE

A good biographer selects details and events that paint a vivid picture of the biography's subject for the reader. As you read, think about why Langston Hughes might have selected specific incidents, allusions, and anecdotes. Then consider how these details contribute to the overall portrait of Harriet Tubman.

MEET THE AUTHOR

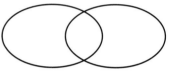

Langston Hughes (1902–1967) came from a family of abolitionists, or people who fought in the 1800s for the end of slavery in the United States. Hughes started writing at an early age and published poetry and fiction in his high school's magazine. After attending Columbia University for one year, he worked at a series of odd jobs while developing his skills as a writer. He then attended Lincoln University in Pennsylvania and graduated in 1929. By that time, he had published two books of poetry and had become known as a versatile and gifted poet. For twenty years, Hughes worked as a columnist for an African-American weekly publication, the *Chicago Defender.*

USE READING SKILLS

Compare and Contrast When you compare and contrast, you note and explore the similarities and differences between two or more things. In his biographical sketch of Harriet Tubman, Langston Hughes uses a number of allusions to people from history. Use a Venn Diagram like the one below to compare and contrast the characteristics and accomplishments of two of these people and think about why Hughes alludes to them in his biography.

Person 1   Person 2

PREVIEW VOCABULARY

A **synonym** is a word that has the same or nearly the same meaning as another word. Read each item below. Then choose the synonym for the vocabulary word.

1. bondage
   - A. disadvantage
   - B. slavery
   - C. poverty
2. faltering
   - A. wavering
   - B. criticizing
   - C. praising
3. capacity
   - A. fault
   - B. ability
   - C. powerlessness
4. compensation
   - A. contract
   - B. payment
   - C. analysis

"I never run my train off the track, and I never lost a passenger."

Harriet Tubman, c. 1945. William H. Johnson. National Museum of American Art, Washington, DC.

HARRIET TUBMAN
THE MOSES OF HER PEOPLE

A Biography by **Langston Hughes**

"Then we saw the lightning, and that was the guns; and then we heard the thunder, and that was the big guns; and then we heard the rain falling and that was the drops of blood falling; and when we came to get in the crops, it was dead men that we reaped." So the escaped slave, Harriet Tubman, described one of the battles of the War between the North and South in which she took part, for she was in the thick of the fighting. Before the War, like Frederick Douglass,[1] Harriet

Tubman devoted her life to the cause of freedom, and after the War to the advancement of her people.

Like Douglass she was born in Maryland a slave, one of eleven sons and daughters. No one kept a record of her birth, so the exact year is not known. But she lived so long and so much was written about her that most of the

---

1. **Frederick Douglass** (c.1818–1895). African-American leader, writer, and diplomat

The Story of Moses In the Bible, Moses is the leader who gained freedom for his people, the Hebrews, who were enslaved in Egypt in the 1400s BCE. According to the Bible, Moses, like Harriet Tubman, was born a slave, but he did not live a slave's life; instead, he was adopted by the daughter of the Pharaoh of Egypt and brought up as a royal prince. After he discovered his true identity, he dedicated himself to delivering his people from slavery. The Egyptians were cursed with a number of plagues, and the Pharaoh reluctantly agreed to free the Hebrews.

other facts of her life are accurately recorded. She was a homely child, morose, wilful, wild, and constantly in rebellion against slavery. Unlike Phillis Wheatley[2] or Douglass, Harriet had no teaching of any sort, except the whip. As a little girl, on the very first day that she was sent to work in the Big House,[3] her mistress whipped her four times. Once she ran away and hid in a pig sty for five days, eating the scraps thrown to the pigs. "There were good masters and mistresses, so I've heard tell," she once said, "but I didn't happen to come across any of them."

Harriet never liked to work as a servant in the house, so perhaps because of her rebellious nature, she was soon ordered to the fields. One day when she was in her early teens something happened that affected her whole life. It was evening and a young slave had, without permission, gone to a country store. The overseer[4] followed him to whip him. He ordered Harriet to help tie him up. As Harriet refused, the slave ran. The overseer picked up a heavy iron weight from the scales and threw it. But

he did not hit the fellow. He struck Harriet's head, almost crushing her skull, and leaving a deep scar forever. Unconscious, the girl lingered between life and death for days. When at last she was able to work again, Harriet still suffered fits of unconsciousness. These lasted all her life. They would come upon her at any time, any place, and it would seem as if she had suddenly fallen asleep. Sometimes in the fields, sometimes leaning against a fence, sometimes in church, she would "go to sleep"[5] and no one could wake her until the seizure had passed. When she was awake, this did not affect her thinking. But her master thought the blow had made her half-witted. Harriet continued to let him believe this. Meanwhile, she prayed God to deliver her from bondage.

When she was about twenty-four years old, she married a jolly, carefree fellow named Tubman, who did not share her concern for leaving the slave country. A few years later, when her old master died, Harriet heard that she and two of her brothers were to be sold, so they decided to run away, together. It was dangerous to tell anyone. Harriet had no chance to let even her mother know directly. But on the evening that she was leaving, she went about the fields and the slaves quarters singing:

"When that old chariot comes
I'm gwine to leave you.
I'm bound for the Promised Land…"

---

2. **Phillis Wheatley** (c.1753–1784). African-born American poet, who was brought to this country as a slave

3. **Big House.** Owner's house on a plantation

4. **overseer.** One who controlled and directed the slaves on a plantation

5. **"go to sleep."** Tubman was an epileptic; epilepsy, a disorder of the nervous system characterized by periods of unconsciousness, convulsions, or seizures, is caused by brain damage resulting from a head injury.

bond • age (bän´ dij) *n.,* slavery

And the way she sang that song let her friends and kinfolks[6] know that to Harriet the Promised Land right then meant the North, not heaven. That night she left the Brodas Plantation on the Big Buckwater River never to return. Before dawn her brothers became frightened and went back to the slave huts before their absence was discovered. But Harriet went on alone through the woods by night, hiding by day, having no map, unable to read or write, but trusting God, instinct, and the North star to guide her. By some miracle she eventually got to Philadelphia, found work there, and was never again a slave.

But Harriet could not be happy while all her family were slaves. She kept thinking about them. So, some months later, she went back to Maryland, hoping to persuade her husband to come North with her. He said he did not wish to go. She led others Northward, however, and, within two years of her own escape, she had secretly returned to the South three times to rescue two brothers, a sister and her children, and a dozen more slaves. The Fugitive Slave Law of 1850[7] now made it dangerous for runaways to stop anywhere in the United States, so Harriet led her followers to Canada where she spent a winter begging, cooking, and praying for them. Then she returned to Maryland to rescue nine more Negroes.

During the first years of her own freedom, Harriet spent most of her time showing others how to follow in her footsteps. Her fame as a fearless leader of "freedom bands" spread rapidly. Shortly large rewards were offered by the slaveholders for her capture. But she was never captured, and she never lost any of her followers to the slave catchers. One reason for this was that once a slave made up his mind to go with her and started out, Harriet did not permit any turning back. Perhaps her experience with her two brothers when she first ran

Harriet Tubman escape, disguised as a man, c. 1934 or 1935. Bernarda Bryson Shahn.

away accounted for this insistence. Her method of preventing frightened or weak travelers on the freedom road from returning to slavery, and perhaps being whipped into betraying the others, was simple. Harriet Tubman carried a pistol. When anyone said he could not, or would not go on, Harriet pulled her gun from the folds of her dress and said, "You *will* go on—or you'll die." The strength or the courage to continue was always forthcoming when her <u>faltering</u> companions looked into the muzzle of Harriet's gun. Through swamp and thicket, rain and cold, they went on toward the North. Thus everyone who started out with Harriet Tubman lived to thank her for freedom.

Long before the War between the States came, so many slaves were escaping, and so many white people in the North were helping them, that the routes to freedom became known as the "Underground Railroad." Secret

---

6. **kinfolks.** Family
7. **Fugitive Slave Law of 1850.** Law that made it illegal to offer protection to escaping slaves

fal • ter • ing (fôl′ t[ə] riŋ) *adj.,* hesitant; uncertain; wavering

"stations" where escaping slaves might be hidden, warmed, and fed were established in homes, barns, and sometimes even churches along the way. The Quakers[8] were especially helpful and active in this regard. And a strong Anti-Slavery Society supported such activities. Slave owners were losing thousands of dollars worth of slaves by escape every year. Harriet Tubman became known as a "conductor" on the Underground Railroad. She was not the only "conductor" but she was the most famous, and one of the most daring. Once she brought as many as twenty-five slaves in a single band to freedom.

Another time she had in her party of runaways a big strong slave worth $1500. His name was Josiah Bailey and the Maryland countryside was plastered with posters offering a reward for his capture. There were ads in the papers for his return. On the way through New York City a friend of freedom recognized Bailey from the description in the papers and said, "I'm glad to meet a man whose head is worth fifteen hundred dollars!" Josiah was so shocked at being recognized and so afraid that he would be captured that a mood of deep despair descended upon him and he would not speak the rest of the trip. When the train was carrying the runaways across the bridge at Buffalo into Canada, Bailey would not even look at the wonder of Niagara Falls.[9] But when they got on free soil and he was finally safe, he burst into song, and nobody could stop him from singing. He cried that at last, thanks to God, he was in Heaven! Harriet Tubman said, "Well, you old fool, you! You might at least have looked at Niagara Falls on the way to Heaven."

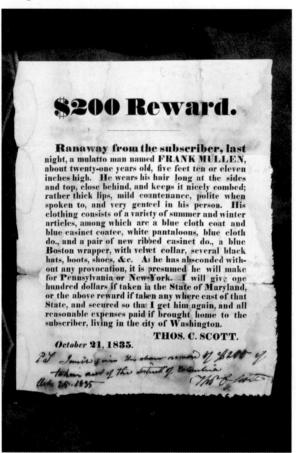

$200 Reward.

Ranaway from the subscriber, last night, a mulatto man named FRANK MULLEN, about twenty-one years old, five feet ten or eleven inches high. He wears his hair long at the sides and top, close behind, and keeps it nicely combed; rather thick lips, mild countenance, polite when spoken to, and very genteel in his person. His clothing consists of a variety of summer and winter articles, among which are a blue cloth coat and blue casinet coatee, white pantaloons, blue cloth do., and a pair of new ribbed casinet do., a blue Boston wrapper, with velvet collar, several black hats, boots, shoes, &c. As he has absconded without any provocation, it is presumed he will make for Pennsylvania or New-York. I will give one hundred dollars if taken in the State of Maryland, or the above reward if taken any where east of that State, and secured so that I get him again, and all reasonable expenses paid if brought home to the subscriber, living in the city of Washington.

THOS. C. SCOTT.

October 21, 1835.

Poster announcing a runaway slave.

Harriet had a great sense of humor. She enjoyed telling the story on herself of how, not being able to read, she once sat down and went to sleep on a park bench right under a sign offering a big reward for her capture. When she began to make speeches to raise money for the cause of freedom, she often told jokes, sang, and sometimes even danced. She might have been a great actress, people said, because without makeup she could hollow out her cheeks and wrinkle her brow to seem like a very old woman. She would make her body shrink and cause her legs to totter when she chose to so disguise herself. Once, making a trip to Maryland to rescue some relatives, she had to pass through a village where she was known. She bought two hens, tied them by their feet and hung them heads down around her neck, then went tottering along. Sure enough, a slave catcher came up the street who might, she thought, recognize her, tottering or not. So she

---

8. **Quakers.** Members of a Protestant sect who practice simplicity in their religious services and hold world peace as a primary goal

9. **Niagara Falls.** Giant waterfall divided by an island; one side is in Niagara, New York, in the United States; the other side is in Niagara, Ontario, in Canada.

unloosed the squalling chickens in the middle of the street and dived after them, purposely not catching them so she could run down the road in pursuit and out of the slave catcher's sight, while all the passersby laughed.

Sometimes, knowing that her band of fugitives was pursued by angry masters, she would get on a train headed South—because nobody would suspect that runaway slaves would be going South. Sometimes she would disguise the women in her party and herself as men. Babies would be given a sleeping medicine to keep them quiet and then wrapped up like bundles. Sometimes she would wade for hours up a stream to throw the hounds off scent. In the dark of night when there was no North star, she would feel the trunks of trees for the moss that grows on the northern side, and that would serve as a guide toward freedom. Often when all seemed hopeless—although she never told her followers she had such feelings— Harriet would pray. One of her favorite prayers was, "Lord, you've been with me through six troubles. Be with me in the seventh." Some people thought that Harriet Tubman led a charmed life because, within twelve years, she made nineteen dangerous trips into the South rescuing slaves. She herself said, "I never run my train off the track, and I never lost a passenger."

Her father and mother were both over seventy years of age when she rescued them and brought her parents North to a home she had begun to buy in Auburn, New York. At first they stayed in St. Catharines, Canada, where escaped slaves were safe, since, in 1833, Queen Victoria[10] had declared all slavery illegal. But it was too cold for the old folks there. And Harriet's work was not on foreign soil. She herself seemed to have no fear of being captured. She came and went about the United States as she chose. And became so famous that, although she never sought the spotlight, it was hard for her not to be recognized wherever she was. Once at a great woman's suffrage

Photograph of Harriet Tubman, c. 1880.

meeting where her old head wound had caused her to go sound asleep in the audience, she was recognized, and awoke to find herself on the platform. Her speech for women's rights was roundly applauded. In those days neither Negroes nor women could vote. Harriet believed both should, so, like Frederick Douglass, she followed the woman's suffrage movement closely.

In appearance "a more ordinary specimen of humanity could hardly be found," but there was no one with a greater <u>capacity</u> for leadership than she had. Among the slaves,

---

10. **Queen Victoria** (1819–1901). Queen of Great Britain and Ireland from 1837 to 1901

ca • pac • i • ty (kə pa´ sə tē) *n.,* ability; qualification

Harriet Tubman with slaves she helped escape.

where she walked in secret, Harriet began to be known as Moses. And at the great public meetings of the North, as the Negro historian William Wells Brown wrote in 1854, "all who frequented anti-slavery conventions, lectures, picnics, and fairs, could not fail to have seen a black woman of medium size, upper front teeth gone, smiling <u>countenance</u>, attired in coarse but neat apparel, with an old-fashioned reticule or bag suspended by her side, who, on taking her seat, would at once drop off into a sound sleep…. No fugitive was ever captured who had Moses for a leader." She was very independent. Between rescue trips or speeches, she would work as a cook or a scrubwoman. She might borrow, but she never begged money for herself. All contributions went toward the cause of freedom in one way or another, as did most of what she earned.

But when the War between the States began and she became a nurse for the Union Armies, and then a military scout and an invaluable intelligence agent behind the Rebel lines, she was promised some <u>compensation</u>. Technically she was not a registered nurse,[11] and being a woman, she could not be a soldier. Yet she carried a Union pass, traveled on government transports, did dangerous missions in Confederate territory, and gave advice to chiefs of staffs. But she never got paid for this, although she had been promised $1800 for certain assignments. To Harriet this made no difference until, after the War, she badly

---

11. **registered nurse.** Nurse who has completed training and passed a state examination

coun • te • nance (kaủn´ t'n ən[t]s) *n.,* look on a person's face; face
com • pen • sa • tion (käm pən sā´ shən) *n.,* payment for service

needed money to care for her aged parents. <u>Petitions</u> were sent to the War Department and to Congress to try to get the $1800 due her. But it was never granted.

Harriet Tubman's war activities were amazing. She served under General Stevens at Beaufort, South Carolina. She was sent to Florida to nurse those ill of dysentery, smallpox, and yellow fever.[12] She was with Colonel Robert Gould Shaw at Fort Wagner. She organized a group of nine Negro scouts and river pilots and, with Colonel Montgomery, led a Union raiding <u>contingent</u> of three gunboats and about 150 Negro troops up the Combahee River. As reported by the Boston *Commonwealth*,[13] for July 10, 1863, they "under the guidance of a black woman, dashed into the enemy's country, struck a bold and effective blow, destroying millions of dollars worth of commissary stores, cotton and lordly dwellings, and striking terror into the heart of rebeldom, brought off near 800 slaves and thousands of dollars worth of property." Concerning Harriet Tubman, it continued, "Many and many times she has penetrated the enemy's lines and discovered their situation and condition, and escaped without injury, but not without extreme hazard."

One of the songs Harriet sang during the War was:

> "Of all the whole creation in the East or in the West,
> The glorious Yankee nation is the greatest and the best.
> Come along! Come along! Don't be alarmed,
> Uncle Sam is rich enough to give you all a farm."

But Harriet Tubman never had a farm of her own. Her generous nature caused her to give away almost all the money she ever got her hands on. There were always fugitives, or relatives, or causes, or friends in need. She was over forty years old when Abraham Lincoln signed the Emancipation Proclamation, making legal for all the freedom she had struggled to secure. She lived for almost fifty years after the War was over. Some people thought she was a hundred years old when she died in 1913. Certainly she was over ninety.

A number of books have been written about her. The first one, *Scenes in the Life of Harriet Tubman*, by Sarah H. Bradford, appeared in 1869, and the proceeds from its sale helped Harriet pay for her cottage. She wrote her friend, Frederick Douglass, who had hidden her and her runaway slaves more than once in his home in Rochester, for a letter about her book. In his reply he compared their two careers:

"The difference between us is very marked. Most that I have done and suffered in the service of our cause has been in public, and I have received much encouragement at every step of the way. You, on the other hand, have labored in a private way. I have wrought in the day—you in the night. I have had the applause of the crowd and the satisfaction that comes of being approved by the <u>multitude</u>, while the most that you have done has been witnessed by a few trembling, scared and footsore bondsmen[14] and women, whom you have led out of the house of bondage, and whose heartfelt, *God bless you*, has been your only reward. The midnight sky and the silent stars have been the witnesses of your devotion to freedom and of your heroism."

When years later, in her old age, a reporter for *The New York Herald Tribune*[15] came to interview her one afternoon at her home in

---

12. **dysentery, smallpox, and yellow fever.** *Dysentery*—intestinal inflammation that can be caused by unsanitary conditions; *smallpox*—viral disease causing fever and skin eruptions; *yellow fever*—viral disease (carried by a mosquito) that causes high fever
13. **Commonwealth.** Daily newspaper in Boston
14. **bondsmen.** Slaves
15. **The New York Herald Tribune.** Daily newspaper in New York City

---

pe • ti • tion (pə ti´ shən) *n.,* formal document containing an earnest request
con • tin • gent (kən tin´ jənt) *n.,* group forming part of a larger group, such as troops
mul • ti • tude (məl´ tə tüd´) *n.,* masses; large number of people considered as a unit

Auburn, he wrote that, as he was leaving, Harriet looked toward an orchard nearby and said, "Do you like apples?"

On being assured that the young man liked them, she asked, "Did you ever plant any apples?"

The writer confessed that he had not.

"No," said the old woman, "but somebody else planted them. I liked apples when I was young. And I said, 'Some day I'll plant apples myself for other young folks to eat.' And I guess I did."

Her apples were the apples of freedom. Harriet Tubman lived to see the harvest. Her home in Auburn, New York, is preserved as a memorial to her planting. ❖

Must personal sacrifice always be required of a good leader? Using examples of political, business, or social leaders who are well known in recent history, explain your answer.

REFER TO TEXT ▶ ▶ ▶ ▶	▶ **REASON WITH TEXT**	
1a. Identify the event that affected Harriet Tubman's entire life following its occurrence.	1b. Describe how Tubman used this event to her advantage. What doors did this event open for her?	**Understand** Find meaning
2a. Quote from the biography what Tubman did to prevent weak or frightened travelers from turning back.	2b. Examine what this action by Tubman says about her personality. What was she trying to accomplish by responding to travelers in this way?	**Apply** Use information
3a. Name the ways Tubman contributed to the war effort.	3b. What is surprising about Tubman's role in the war? What social conventions did she defy?	**Analyze** Take things apart
4a. List the methods Tubman used to avoid being captured.	4b. Evaluate Tubman's effectiveness as a "conductor" on the Underground Railroad. What character traits did she possess that set her apart as a leader?	**Evaluate** Make judgments
5a. What motivated Tubman to take the risks that she took? How was she rewarded for her work?	5b. Explain why Tubman might have followed the women's suffrage movement. What do the two movements—freedom for the slaves and suffrage for women—have in common?	**Create** Bring ideas together

ANALYZE LITERATURE: Style and Allusion

How does Hughes's style and use of allusions show the heroic nature of Harriet Tubman's character? Give some examples from the text.

Verse

When Is-rael was in E-gypt's land, Let my peo-ple go! Oppressed so hard they could not stand, Let my peo-ple go!

Literature CONNECTION

As a form of religious folk song, spirituals (originally called "jubilees") developed in the eighteenth century and focused on the daily lives and concerns of slaves. Spirituals such as **"Go Down, Moses"** were intended to be sung chorally, or in a call-and-response pattern between an individual singer and a chorus. "Go Down, Moses" presents an *allegory*, or work in which characters, events, or settings represent something else — the enslaved Israelites in the Old Testament represent the African-American slaves.

GO DOWN, MOSES

A Traditional Spiritual

1

When Israel was in Egypt's land,
Let my people go!
Oppressed so hard they could not stand,
Let my people go!

Chorus
"Go down, Moses,
'Way down in Egypt's land,
Tell old Pharaoh
    To let my people go!"

2

"Thus spoke the Lord," bold Moses said,
"Let my people go!
If not, I'll smite[1] your firstborn dead,
Let my people go!"

(Repeat Chorus)

3

"No more shall they in bondage toil,[2]
Let my people go!
Let them come out with Egypt's spoil,[3]
Let my people go!"

(Repeat Chorus) ❖

---

1. **smite.** Kill
2. **...in bondage toil.** The word *bondage* means "slavery," and the word *toil* means "to work hard."
3. **spoil.** Riches

REFER TO TEXT	REASON WITH TEXT	
1a. According to the song, who is "in Egypt's land"?	1b. Summarize what life was like for these people in Egypt.	**Understand** **Find meaning**
2a. State the message Moses repeatedly gives Pharaoh.	2b. How is Moses portrayed in the song? What kind of character traits does he possess? Identify lines from the song to support your answer.	**Apply** **Use information**
3a. Recall with what Moses threatens Pharaoh. By whose authority does he make this threat?	3b. Explain why someone living in slavery might have found the story of the delivery of the Israelites from slavery so appealing. Why might Moses have been a hero to a slave?	**Create** **Bring ideas together**

TEXT ←TO→ TEXT CONNECTION

- Compare and contrast the Biblical figure of Moses with Harriet Tubman, the conductor on the Underground Railroad. How are they similar? How are they different?
- Compare Harriet Tubman's song on page 262 with "Go Down, Moses." In what ways are they alike and different? Consider their themes and word choices.

EXTEND THE TEXT

Writing Options

Creative Writing Imagine that you are a former slave who has traveled north to freedom with Harriet Tubman. In the years since then, you have been fortunate enough to get an education and obtain a university degree. You recently read about Harriet Tubman in the newspapers, and you have decided to request a meeting with her to thank her personally for the sacrifices she made. Create a **dialogue** that you might have with Tubman at the meeting.

Expository Writing The people you come in contact with on a regular basis usually play some role in shaping who you are. Choose a person who has in some way influenced your life, and write a one-page **biographical sketch** of that person. A biographical sketch is a brief account of a person's life and accomplishments. In your biographical sketch, try to use an allusion to another person to highlight the character of the person you are writing about, much like Hughes does in his biography of Harriet Tubman.

Collaborative Learning

Create an Illustrated Children's Book Together with a small group, use Internet or library resources to carry out more research on the life of Harriet Tubman. Then create an illustrated children's book that tells the story of Tubman's life. The audience for your book will be eight- to ten-year-olds. When you have finished your work, present your book to a class of third- or fourth-grade students, and invite them to offer you feedback.

Media Literacy

Create a Website Spirituals like "Go Down, Moses" (page 269) are religious and emotional songs often based on biblical stories of deliverance. Find other spirituals common during the 1800s, and design a website that explains the meanings the songs may have had for those who sang them. Try to find recordings of these spirituals to hear how they sound, and use links on your website to inform viewers where they may go on the Internet to hear the recordings.

 Go to **www.mirrorsandwindows.com** for more.

READING ASSESSMENT

1. Which of the following is *not* true of Harriet Tubman?
   A. She risked her personal safety to help others.
   B. She was born free.
   C. She became a nurse for the Union armies.
   D. She carried a pistol.
   E. None of the above

2. On page 263, the word *faltering* most nearly means
   A. criticizing.
   B. lingering.
   C. wavering.
   D. advancing.
   E. angering.

3. In this selection, the author's tone could best be described as
   A. skeptical.
   B. philosophical.
   C. ironic.
   D. admiring.
   E. introspective.

4. During the Civil War, Harriet Tubman worked in each of the following jobs *except*
   A. nurse.
   B. scout.
   C. shopkeeper.
   D. intelligence collector.
   E. None of the above

5. Hughes uses the allusion between Moses and Tubman to show that Tubman
   A. wanted to visit Egypt.
   B. led her people to freedom.
   C. used threats to make the slave owners listen to her cause.
   D. was an eloquent speaker.
   E. None of the above

6. Harriet Tubman exhibited extraordinary courage and perseverance. Think of another person who has these qualities—either someone you know personally or someone you've heard or read about—and write a description of his or her personality and accomplishments.

GRAMMAR & STYLE

Consistent Use of Verb Tenses

Verbs have different forms, called **tenses,** which are used to tell the time in which an action takes place. In your writing and speaking, you most commonly use the simple tenses, which are **present, past,** and **future.**

The **present tense** tells that an action happens now—in present time.

EXAMPLE

She <u>helps</u> slaves get to freedom.

The **past tense** tells that an action happened in the past—prior to the present time.

EXAMPLE

She <u>helped</u> slaves get to freedom.

The **future tense** tells that an action will happen in the future.

EXAMPLE

She <u>will help</u> slaves get to freedom.

The **perfect tenses** of verbs also express present, past, and future time, but they show that the action continued and was completed over a period of time or that the action will be completed in the present or future. The perfect tense is formed by using *has, have,* or *had* with the past participle.

The **present perfect tense** tells that an action continued and was completed over a period of time.

EXAMPLE

She <u>has helped</u> slaves get to freedom.

The **past perfect tense** tells that an action was completed before another action took place in the past.

EXAMPLE

She <u>had helped</u> slaves get to freedom.

The **future perfect tense** tells than an action will be completed before another action will take place in the future.

EXAMPLE

She <u>will have helped</u> slaves get to freedom.

The **progressive** form of a verb is used to express continuing action or state of being. The progressive form is made of the appropriate tense of the verb *be* and the present participle of the verb.

EXAMPLES

present progressive: She <u>is helping</u> slaves get to freedom.
past progressive: She <u>was helping</u> slaves get to freedom.
future progressive: She <u>will be helping</u> slaves get to freedom.

Good writers use verb tenses consistently in their writing. This means they do not switch from present to past, or vice versa, without justification.

EXAMPLE

inconsistent: Harriet Tubman <u>put</u> her life in danger to help others. She <u>is</u> always there to help anyone in need. [The verb *put* is in the past tense; the verb *is* is in the present tense.]
consistent: Harriet Tubman <u>put</u> her life in danger to help others. She <u>was</u> always there to help anyone in need. [The verbs *put* and *was* are both in the past tense.]

One instance where it is acceptable to switch tenses is when you are writing about literature, as in the example below. You'll notice that even though Langston Hughes is no longer alive, the present tense is still used to describe his work. However, Harriet Tubman is described in the past tense.

EXAMPLE

Langston Hughes writes about what Harriet Tubman was like as a person. He highlights not only her actions but also her courageous and selfless character.

REVIEW TERMS

- **present participle:** verb form that is an action adjective; it ends in *–ing.*
- **past participle:** verb form that is an action adjective; it ends in *–ed.*

Identify Verb Tenses

Copy the following passages from "Harriet Tubman: The Moses of Her People" onto your own paper. Then, underline the verbs and identify their tenses.

1. Long before the War between the States came, so many slaves were escaping, and so many white people in the North were helping them, that the routes to freedom became known as the "Underground Railroad." Secret "stations" where escaping slaves might be hidden, warmed, and fed were established in homes, barns, and sometimes even churches along the way.

2. But Harriet Tubman never had a farm of her own. Her generous nature caused her to give away almost all the money she ever got her hands on.

3. A number of books have been written about her. The first one, *Scenes in the Life of Harriet Tubman,* by Sarah H. Bradford, appeared in 1869, and the proceeds from its sale helped Harriet pay for her cottage.

4. During the first years of her own freedom, Harriet spent most of her time showing others how to follow in her footsteps. Her fame as a fearless leader of "freedom bands" spread rapidly.

5. Harriet had a great sense of humor. She enjoyed telling the story on herself of how, not being able to read, she once sat down and went to sleep on a park bench right under a sign offering a big reward for her capture.

6. Once, making a trip to Maryland to rescue some relatives, she had to pass through a village where she was known. She bought two hens, tied them by their feet and hung them heads down around her neck, then went tottering along.

7. Harriet never liked to work as a servant in the house, so perhaps because of her rebellious nature, she was soon ordered to the fields. One day when she was in her early teens something happened that affected her whole life.

Correct Errors in Verb Tense

Rewrite the paragraph shown, correcting any inconsistencies in the use of verb tenses.

Langston Hughes compared Harriet Tubman to Moses. Both of these well-known historical figures are responsible for leading their people out of slavery. Moses leads the Hebrews from their captivity by the Egyptians, and Harriet Tubman provided a means for slaves to flee from the South to the North by using the Underground Railroad. Both of these leaders will have to risk their own lives to help others. This perhaps wasn't always easy to do. It takes a lot of courage and perseverance.

Use Verb Tenses Consistently in Your Writing

Choose one of your favorite authors and write a two-paragraph biographical sketch of him or her. Pay close attention to the verb tenses you choose to use, and try to use them consistently throughout the two paragraphs. When you have finished your draft, exchange it with a partner. Your partner should check carefully for consistent use of verb tenses. Rewrite any sentences that contain errors.

EXTEND THE SKILL

Write a series of directions to describe the steps in a process, such as preparing a meal or playing a certain video game. Be sure that you use verb tenses consistently in your directions.

VOCABULARY & SPELLING

Word Meanings in Synonyms, Antonyms, Homophones, and Homographs

A **synonym** is a word that has the same, or nearly the same, meaning as another word. An **antonym** has the opposite, or nearly the opposite, meaning as another word. Using the word *harsh* as an example, a synonym of *harsh* would be *cruel*. An antonym would be *kind*.

When you are learning new words, expanding your reach to take in other words that have similar or opposite meanings is an effective way to build your overall vocabulary. Because you are creating associations—connections and contexts between words—you are more likely to remember the meanings of the words.

One way of using synonyms and antonyms to make many connections to new words is to create a Concept Map. In a Concept Map, you list synonyms, antonyms, examples, non-examples, and contextual sentences for the word you are studying. Look at the Concept Map below for the word *curious*.

A **homophone** is a word that has the same pronunciation as another word but a different meaning and/or spelling. For example, the words *sight, site,* and *cite* are homophones. A **homograph** is a word that has the same spelling as another word but has a different meaning and sometimes, a different pronunciation. For example, the word *produce* can be a verb meaning "to make" or a noun meaning "products grown on a farm."

Spelling Tip

Be aware that homophones and homographs are words that are easily confused and will often be missed by computer software that checks for spelling. Use homophones and homographs to build your vocabulary by creating connections to words you already know.

Contextual sentences

The **curious** child had almost touched the hot burner on the stove before his mother stopped him.

Since she had always been interested in birds, we found her indifference to tanagers **curious.**

Synonyms

inquisitive, inquiring, odd, rare, recondite

Antonyms

incurious, indifferent, trite, superficial

CURIOUS

Examples

child, cat, antique vase, message, news report

Non-examples

telephone, cliché

Exercise A

Circle the letter of the correct answer choice.

1. Which of the following is a synonym for *petition?*
   A. request
   B. answer
   C. letter

2. Which of the following is a synonym for *multitude?*
   A. multiple
   B. large number
   C. small number

3. Which of the following is an antonym for *bondage?*
   A. slavery
   B. idea
   C. freedom

4. Which of the following is *not* a synonym of *capacity?*
   A. ability
   B. knowledge
   C. amount

5. A homophone for the word *pear* means which of the following?
   A. cut
   B. squeeze
   C. intersect

6. A homograph for the word *bow* means which of the following?
   A. front of a ship
   B. cast of a play
   C. baby cradle

Exercise B

One of the qualities of Harriet Tubman that is highlighted by Langston Hughes in his biography is her courage. With a partner, write down eight synonyms of the word *courage*. Use a thesaurus if necessary.

Then use at least five of these words in a descriptive paragraph about a person you know who has shown courage.

Exercise C

Create a Concept Map for two of the following vocabulary words from "Harriet Tubman: The Moses of Her People."

bondage

faltering

capacity

countenance

compensation

petition

contingent

multitude

Exercise D

Homophones can be confusing for people who are just learning English. One thing that can help is a visual dictionary, or a dictionary with pictures next to the words. With a partner, brainstorm a list of five words that have homophones. Then for each word and its homophone(s), create an illustration for a picture dictionary.

EXTEND THE SKILL

Create a list of ten vocabulary words from the selections in this unit. Use these words to create a crossword puzzle. As your clues for the crossword puzzle, ask people to identify synonyms, antonyms, homophones, and homographs. Try to think of clever ways to phrase the clues so the answers aren't necessarily obvious.

Understanding the Essay

THE ESSAY

You've heard it before—your teacher tells you to write an essay on a particular topic. Essays, however, are not only homework assignments. Many of the nonfiction works you encounter are versions of the essay form. An **essay** is a short nonfiction work that presents a single main idea, or thesis, about a particular topic.

TYPES OF ESSAYS

The three most common types of essays are expository, persuasive, and personal. Some essays are a combination of these types.

- An **expository essay** explores a topic with the goal of informing or enlightening readers. In his essay "The Trouble with Television" (page 279), Robert MacNeil writes about the influence of television on the lives of Americans.
- A **persuasive essay** aims to convince the reader to accept a certain point of view. "The Trouble with Television" is also an example of a persuasive essay, in which Robert MacNeil tries to convince readers that passive and uncritical viewing of television is harmful to viewers.
- A **personal essay** explores a topic related to the life or interests of the writer. Personal essays are characterized by an intimate and informal style or tone. The excerpt from *How Reading Changed My Life* (page 287) by Anna Quindlen is a personal essay.

THESIS STATEMENT AND SUPPORTING DETAILS

Perhaps the most important part of an essay is its thesis. The **thesis** is the essay's main idea—essentially, the nucleus around which the rest of the essay is built. If you're able to identify an essay's thesis, you will be able to better determine the writer's purpose and locate points in the essay that support the thesis. In most essays, the thesis is somewhere near the end of the introduction. An exception is the personal essay, where the thesis might be positioned near the end of the essay by way of pointing out a moral or offering a reflection on what has come before.

To support the thesis statement, an essay must have **supporting details** such as facts, examples, statistics, or quotations, or the writer's personal experiences. To locate the supporting details in an essay, try creating an outline. An example of a partial outline for "The Trouble with Television" is provided below.

I. Main idea: People watch a lot of television.

    A. Supporting detail: By the age of 20, a person will have watched 20,000 hours of television.

    B. Supporting detail: The only thing people do more than watch television is eat and sleep.

II. Main idea: Television discourages concentration.

    A. Supporting detail: It requires no effort to watch television; instead, viewers "surrender" attention.

    B. Supporting detail: Television holds viewers' attention through constant stimulation, making everything else seem boring.

Writers of persuasive essays use methods of presenting details called deductive and inductive reasoning. **Deductive reasoning** involves starting with a general idea and, using examples and facts, moving toward a precise conclusion. Think about an upside-down triangle, wide on top and narrowing to a point. That's the way deductive reasoning works.

Inductive reasoning is the opposite—a right-side-up triangle. The writer starts with specific details and builds upon them to reach a general, broader conclusion.

ESSAY ORGANIZATION

There are several different ways to organize an essay. The most common methods of organization are listed in the chart to the right.

METHOD	CHARACTERISTICS	EXAMPLE
Chronological Order	• Events are given in the order in which they occurred. • Events are connected by transition words such as *when, next, then, finally*, and *at last.* • Personal essays, because they tell a story, are often written in chronological order.	The day we arrived, a hot, humid afternoon had splintered into thunderstorms as the last rays of the sun dipped into the rest of the United States...Two days later, I leaned against the wall of our apartment building on McKibbin Street wondering where New York ended and the rest of the world began. —from "Something Could Happen to You" (page 362) by Esmeralda Santiago
Order of Importance	• Details are presented in order of importance or familiarity. • Details are connected by transition words such as *more important, less important, most important*, and *least important.*	People a hundred years from now should be able to grasp the enormity of this attack by visiting this sacred ground...Recalling these attacks and their aftermath will remind people today that we need to be unyielding in completing the war on terror. —from "Getting It Right at Ground Zero" (page 347) by Rudolph Giuliani
Comparison and Contrast Order	• When comparing two things (or ideas), like apples and oranges, there are two methods of organization: 1) List all the characteristics of apples, usually in one paragraph, followed by all the characteristics of oranges; or 2) list one characteristic of apples and compare it with one characteristic of oranges. Follow this with another characteristic applied to both apples and oranges. • The things being compared are connected by transition words such as *likewise, similarly, in contrast, a different kind*, and *another difference.*	I have clear memories of that sort of life, of lifting the rocks in the creek that trickled through Naylor's Run to search for crayfish...But at base it was never any good. The best part of me was always at home, within some book that had been laid flat on the table to mark my place, its imaginary people waiting for me to return and bring them to life. —from *How Reading Changed My Life* (page 287) by Anna Quindlen
Cause and Effect Order	• One or more causes are presented followed by one or more effects, or one or more effects are presented followed by one or more causes. • Transition words that indicate cause and effect include *one cause, another effect, as a result, consequently*, and *therefore.*	The trouble with television is that it discourages concentration...In the case of news, this practice, in my view, results in inefficient communication. I question how much of television's nightly news effort is really absorbable and understandable. —from "The Trouble with Television" (page 279), by Robert MacNeil

THE TROUBLE WITH TELEVISION

BUILD BACKGROUND

Cultural Context **"The Trouble with Television"** was first printed in *Reader's Digest* magazine. In this persuasive essay, Robert MacNeil—himself a prominent television journalist—presents his ideas about the often negative ways that he thinks television viewing affects Americans. Television news, for example, has frequently been criticized for its superficiality, since only two or three minutes can be allocated for any particular story on national news programs. Entertainment on television has also been criticized for its inclusion of violent scenes and sexual content. On the other hand, television has been praised for its immediacy and prompt response to breaking news, and such programs as travel and science documentaries have played an important role in conveying information and educating viewers.

Reader's Context How much television do you watch every week? In your opinion, what are some of the advantages of television? What are some of the drawbacks?

ANALYZE LITERATURE: Thesis and Argument

A **thesis** is a main idea that is supported in a work of nonfiction. An **argument** is a form of persuasion that makes a case to the audience for accepting or rejecting a course of action. As you read, use clues from the text to state Robert MacNeil's thesis in your own words. Then track MacNeil's arguments to see how well he supports his case.

SET PURPOSE

Based on the title of this essay, what do you think is the trouble with television? Make a prediction about what arguments the essay will make against television viewing. Read to find out if your prediction is correct.

MEET THE AUTHOR

Robert MacNeil (b. 1931) was born in Montreal, Canada. He worked in radio in both New York City and in Ottawa, Canada, before being hired by NBC as a correspondent. After spending many years traveling the globe as a journalist, MacNeil returned to the United States and, in 1975, began editing and hosting a public television news program called *The Robert MacNeil Report.* During the next two decades, he also wrote and hosted many documentaries and published several successful books. Upon MacNeil's retirement in 1995, Jim Lehrer, who co-hosted the TV news program after its first few months, said of MacNeil, "He's the man of television who realized that television was more than an electric box that made sounds and transmitted moving pictures, that it was also an instrument for transmitting the words and ideas of serious people."

USE READING SKILLS

Author's Viewpoint In persuasive writing, the **author's viewpoint** is an assertion, or statement of belief, he or she makes. An assertion is supported with details. As you read the essay, figure out MacNeil's main viewpoint and use a graphic organizer like the one below to keep track of the supporting details of that viewpoint. Then decide whether or not the support for MacNeil's viewpoint is convincing to you as a reader.

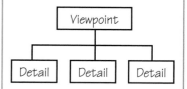

PREVIEW VOCABULARY

Use the context clues in the sentences below to figure out the meanings of the underlined words from the selection.

1. The children were surprised to find <u>gratification</u> in completing the chores they had dreaded.
2. The rights to life, liberty, and the pursuit of happiness are not always <u>inherent</u>—sometimes, people must struggle for them.
3. The traveler knew that arriving at the airport on time was an <u>imperative</u>, so she left the hotel early.
4. My grandfather wants to <u>bequeath</u> me his gold pocket watch.
5. Philip was a stubborn child who believed that getting his way was his <u>inalienable</u> right.

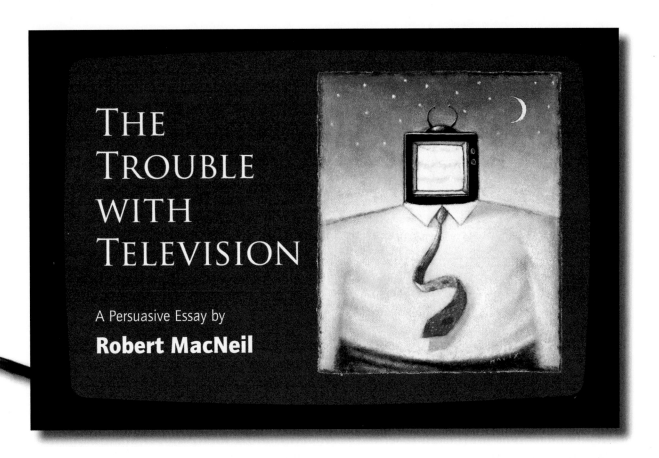

THE TROUBLE WITH TELEVISION

A Persuasive Essay by
Robert MacNeil

The only things Americans do more than watch television are work and sleep.

It is difficult to escape the influence of television. If you fit the statistical averages, by the age of 20 you will have been exposed to at least 20,000 hours of television. You can add 10,000 hours for each decade you have lived after the age of 20. The only things Americans do more than watch television are work and sleep.

Calculate for a moment what could be done with even a part of those hours. Five thousand hours, I am told, are what a typical college undergraduate spends working on a bachelor's degree. In 10,000 hours you could have learned enough to become an astronomer or engineer. You could have learned several languages <u>fluently</u>. If it appealed to you, you could be reading Homer[1] in the original

Greek or Dostoevski[2] in Russian. If it didn't, you could have walked around the world and written a book about it.

The trouble with television is that it discourages concentration. Almost anything interesting and rewarding in life requires some constructive, consistently applied effort. The dullest, the least gifted of us can achieve things that seem miraculous to those who never concentrate on anything. But television encourages us to apply no effort. It sells us instant

---

1. **Homer.** Greek epic poet of the eighth century BCE
2. **Dostoevski.** Fyodor Dostoevski (usually spelled Dostoyevski), Russian novelist (1821–1881)

flu • ent • ly (flü´ ənt lē) *adv.*, smoothly; easily

The History of Television Television originated in the late 1800s with experiments in transmitting images electronically. At the 1900 World's Fair in Paris, the International Congress of Electricity first began using the word *television*. In the 1920s, Charles Jenkins and John Baird transmitted the first moving silhouette images over wire circuits. After the first televised presidential speech was shown at the 1939 World's Fair, the American public began to get excited about this new technology. By 1960, 85 percent of American households owned a television set, and more than 500 commercial stations were in operation. Today, there are more than 1,500 television stations in the United States, and more than 98 percent of American households own at least one television.

gratification. It diverts us only to divert, to make the time pass without pain.

Television's variety becomes a narcotic,[3] not a stimulus. Its serial,[4] kaleidoscopic exposures force us to follow its lead. The viewer is on a perpetual guided tour: thirty minutes at the museum, thirty at the cathedral, then back on the bus to the next attraction—except on television, typically, the spans allotted are on the order of minutes or seconds, and the chosen delights are more often car crashes and people killing one another. In short, a lot of television usurps one of the most precious of all human gifts, the ability to focus your attention yourself, rather than just passively surrender it.

Capturing your attention—and holding it—is the prime motive of most television programming and enhances its role as a profitable advertising vehicle. Programmers live in constant fear of losing anyone's attention—anyone's. The surest way to avoid doing so is to keep everything brief, not to strain the attention of anyone but instead to provide constant stimulation through variety, novelty, action and movement. Quite simply, television operates on the appeal to the short attention span.

It is simply the easiest way out. But it has come to be regarded as a given, as inherent in the medium itself: as an imperative, as though General Sarnoff,[5] or one of the other august[6] pioneers of video, had bequeathed to us tablets of stone commanding that nothing in television shall ever require more than a few moments' concentration.

In its place that is fine. Who can quarrel with a medium that so brilliantly packages

---

3. **narcotic.** Something that dulls the senses
4. **serial.** Appearing in a series of parts that follow an order
5. **General Sarnoff.** David Sarnoff (1891–1971), pioneer in radio and television broadcasting
6. **august.** Worthy of respect

grat • i • fi • ca • tion (gra' tə fə kā' shən) *n.*, satisfaction
stim • u • lus (stim' yə ləs) *n.*, something that causes action
per • pet • u • al (pər pe' chə wəl) *adj.*, continuing forever
u • surp (yu̇ sʉrp') *v.*, take away without the right to do so
in • her • ent (in hir' ənt) *adj.*, natural
im • per • a • tive (im per' ə tiv) *n.*, requirement
be • queath (bi kwēth') *v.*, hand down; pass on

escapist[7] entertainment as a mass-marketing tool? But I see its values now pervading[8] this nation and its life. It has become fashionable to think that, like fast food, fast ideas are the way to get to a fast-moving, impatient public.

In the case of news, this practice, in my view, results in inefficient communication. I question how much of television's nightly news effort is really absorbable and understandable. Much of it is what has been aptly described as "machine gunning with scraps." I

think its technique fights coherence. I think it tends to make things ultimately boring and dismissible (unless they are accompanied by horrifying pictures) because almost anything is boring and dismissible if you know almost nothing about it.

I believe that TV's appeal to the short attention span is not only inefficient communication but decivilizing as well. Consider the casual assumptions that television tends to cultivate: that complexity must be avoided, that visual stimulation is a substitute for thought, that verbal precision is an anachronism.[9] It may be old-fashioned, but I was taught that thought is words, arranged in grammatically precise ways.

There is a crisis of literacy in this country. One study estimates that some 30 million adult Americans are "functionally illiterate" and cannot read or write well enough to answer a want ad or understand the instructions on a medicine bottle.

Literacy may not be an <u>inalienable</u> human right, but it is one that the highly literate Founding Fathers might not have found unreasonable or even unattainable. We are not only not attaining it as a nation, statistically

speaking, but we are falling further and further short of attaining it. And, while I would not be so simplistic as to suggest that television is the cause, I believe it contributes and is an influence.

Everything about this nation—the structure of the society, its forms of family organization, its economy, its place in the world—has become more complex, not less. Yet its dominating communications instrument, its principal form of national linkage, is one that sells neat resolutions to human problems that usually have no neat resolutions. It is all symbolized in my mind by the hugely successful art form that television has made central to the culture, the thirty-second commercial: the tiny drama of the earnest housewife who finds happiness choosing the right toothpaste.

---

7. **escapist.** Designed purposely for escaping from reality or routine
8. **pervading.** Becoming spread throughout every part of
9. **anachronism.** Thing that seems to be out of its proper place in history

> in • alien • able (in āl′ yə nə bəl) *adj.,* not able to be taken away; incapable of being surrendered or transferred

When before in human history has so much humanity collectively surrendered so much of its leisure to one toy, one mass diversion? When before has virtually an entire nation surrendered itself wholesale to a medium for selling?

Some years ago Yale University law professor Charles L. Black, Jr. wrote: "...forced feeding on trivial fare is not itself a trivial matter." I think this society is being force fed with trivial fare, and I fear that the effects on our habits of mind, our language, our tolerance for effort, and our appetite for complexity are only dimly perceived. If I am wrong, we will have done no harm to look at the issue <u>skeptically</u> and critically, to consider how we should be resisting it. I hope you will join with me in doing so. ❖

skep • ti • cal • ly (skep´ ti k[ə] lē) *adv.,* critically; with doubt

---

"The only things Americans do more than watch television are work and sleep." Is this statement surprising? Is it alarming? Is watching television any more harmful than playing video games? Explain your answers. What kind of influence has watching television had on you and on people you know?

AFTER READING

REFER TO TEXT ▶ ▶ ▶ ▶	▶ REASON WITH TEXT	
1a. List two things that a television viewer could do with those hours spent watching television.	1b. Discuss why you think MacNeil includes specific examples of what a person could have achieved in the hours spent watching television.	**Understand** **Find meaning**
2a. Quote what MacNeil says about the effect television has on the people who watch it.	2b. Examine why television has this effect. Who or what is responsible for the effect?	**Apply** **Use information**
3a. State MacNeil's opinion of television's nightly news shows.	3b. Analyze the validity of MacNeil's support for his opinion about the nightly news on television.	**Analyze** **Take things apart**
4a. Name the problems MacNeil sees in the way television appeals to a short attention span.	4b. Conclude what MacNeil means by the statement, "Television's variety becomes a narcotic, not a stimulus."	**Evaluate** **Make judgments**
5a. MacNeil gives many examples of the trouble he sees with television. Do you agree with MacNeil's opinion? Do you think there is a problem with television? Give evidence to support your viewpoint.	5b. Specify why you watch television. Do you usually have a purpose for watching when you turn on the television? Explain.	**Create** **Bring ideas together**

ANALYZE LITERATURE: Thesis and Argument

What is the thesis of MacNeil's essay? What arguments does MacNeil use to advance his thesis? What evidence is given to support the arguments?

Writing Options

Creative Writing Suppose that you want to encourage students at your school to limit the time they spend watching television. Create a **public awareness poster** that focuses on either the negative effects of watching too much television or the positive effects of *not* watching too much television. Be sure to include specific examples on your public awareness poster.

Applied Writing Heated debate continues in the United States on the subject of violence on television. Write a **business letter** to the programming executives of one or more television networks in which you discuss whether or not violence on television is harmful to society. In your letter, make recommendations to the executives as to how the network or station's programs could be more entertaining, helpful, or beneficial.

Collaborative Learning

Participate in a Panel Discussion Consider MacNeil's assertion that television is "decivilizing" the nation. Hold a panel discussion in which some students from your class support this idea and others argue that television benefits the nation. One student should act as the moderator. A representative for each position should give an opening statement about the issue. Then the moderator or members of the audience can ask questions and give each presenter a chance to reply.

Media Literacy

Analyze Television Commercials Select three very different television programs that air at different times, such as a morning news program, an afternoon soap opera, and an evening sitcom. Answer these questions about each commercial aired during the programs: What is the commercial selling? What techniques are used to sell the product? How often is this specific product advertised thoughout the show? Do you see any similarities in the products advertised? To whom would this commercial be most appealing? Write a brief report comparing and contrasting the types of commercials. You might publish the results in your school or local paper.

 Go to **www.mirrorsandwindows.com** for more.

READING ASSESSMENT

1. Which of the following is <u>not</u> a type of nonfiction?
   A. autobiography
   B. essay
   C. novel
   D. letter
   E. personal narrative

2. On page 279, the word *fluently* most nearly means
   A. abundantly.
   B. sparsely.
   C. smoothly.
   D. relentlessly.
   E. eagerly.

3. The author's attitude toward television might best be described as
   A. enthusiastic.
   B. hostile.
   C. admiring.
   D. skeptical.
   E. All of the above

4. Which of the following is the thesis of MacNeil's essay?
   A. Everything about this nation—the structure of the society, its forms of family organization, its economy, its place in the world—has become more complex, not less.
   B. The trouble with television is that it discourages concentration.
   C. Capturing your attention—and holding it—is the prime motive of most television programming and enhances its role as a profitable advertising vehicle.
   D. There is a crisis of literacy in this country.
   E. It has become fashionable to think that, like fast food, fast ideas are the way to get to a fast-moving, impatient public.

5. Reread the selection. Then, in a paragraph or two, explain why you either agree or disagree with MacNeil on the subject of television. Give reasons for your opinion.

Irregular Verbs

Verb forms change to show when an action happened. The many forms of the verb are based on its three principal parts: the present, the past, and the past participle. A past participle is a verb form indicating a past or completed action, as in "By the time she arrived, I <u>had opened</u> the door." For all regular verbs, –d or –ed are added to form the past and the past participle.

EXAMPLE

present	discover
past	discovered
past participle	(has, have) discovered

Some regular verbs change their spelling when –d or –ed is added.

EXAMPLE

present	hurry
past	hurried
past participle	(has, have) hurried

Verbs that do not follow the regular pattern of adding –d or –ed are called **irregular verbs.** Some of these irregular verbs have the same spelling for their past and past participle forms. Some have the same spelling in all three principal parts. Other irregular verbs have three different forms. When you are not sure whether a verb is regular or irregular, look up the verb in a dictionary. Many of the common irregular verbs are shown in the chart on the right.

REVIEW TERMS

- **irregular verb:** a verb that does not follow the regular pattern of adding –d or –ed to form the past and the past participle
- **past participle:** a verb form indicating a past or completed action

Present	Past	Past Participle (following *has* or *have*)
begin	began	begun
bring	brought	brought
buy	bought	bought
catch	caught	caught
creep	crept	crept
drink	drank	drunk
feel	felt	felt
get	got	got/gotten
grow	grew	grown
keep	kept	kept
know	knew	known
lay	laid	laid
lead	led	led
leave	left	left
lend	lent	lent
lose	lost	lost
make	made	made
pay	paid	paid
ring	rang	rung
say	said	said
seek	sought	sought
sell	sold	sold
sit	sat	sat
sleep	slept	slept
spring	sprang or sprung	sprung
swim	swam	swum
swing	swung	swung
teach	taught	taught
think	thought	thought
throw	threw	thrown
win	won	won
write	wrote	written

Identify Regular or Irregular Verbs

In the following passage from "The Trouble with Television," identify each of the underlined verbs as either regular or irregular.

Literacy <u>may not be</u> an inalienable human right, but it <u>is</u> one that the highly literate Founding Fathers might not <u>have found</u> unreasonable or even unattainable. We <u>are</u> not only not attaining it as a nation, statistically speaking, but we are falling further and further short of attaining it. And, while I <u>would not be</u> so simplistic as to suggest that television is the cause, I <u>believe</u> it contributes and is an influence.

Everything about this nation—the structure of the society, its forms of family organization, its economy, its place in the world—<u>has become</u> more complex, not less. Yet its dominating communications instrument, its principal form of national linkage, is one that sells neat resolutions to human problems that usually have no neat resolutions. It is all symbolized in my mind by the hugely successful art form that television <u>has made</u> central to the culture, the thirty-second commercial: the tiny drama of the earnest housewife who <u>finds</u> happiness choosing the right toothpaste.

Use Irregular Verbs Correctly

Write the correct past form of the verb given in parentheses.

1. When people first (buy) televisions, they (have) few options of what to watch.

2. Robert MacNeil (write) "The Trouble with Television" for *Reader's Digest* magazine.

3. Consumers (catch) on to the concept of television early and (get) excited about it.

4. MacNeil (host) a news program on public television and (publish) several books.

5. As Americans (grow) accustomed to watching television, it (affect) their attention spans more and more.

Form Irregular Verbs

Write the correct form indicated for each verb.
1. begin (past participle)
2. say (past)
3. win (past participle)
4. make (past)
5. get (past participle)
6. throw (past)
7. feel (past participle)
8. leave (past)
9. pay (past participle)
10. sell (past)

Use Irregular Verbs in Your Writing

What was the last television program you watched that you really enjoyed? What made you decide to watch it? Was it recommended by friends? Was it advertised? Write a summary of the television program and explain in a paragraph what prompted you to watch it. Use a variety of irregular verbs in your writing, and underline each past and past participle form.

EXTEND THE SKILL

Make up your own quiz to test your classmates' knowledge of correct irregular verb forms. Use a variety of question types, including multiple choice, true and false, fill-in-the-blank, and short answer. Also draw up an answer key. Then call on volunteers to take the test. You might designate a suitable prize for the competitor with the highest score.

from *How Reading Changed My Life*

BUILD BACKGROUND

Literary Context This selection is taken from ***How Reading Changed My Life*** (1998), a book-length essay in which Anna Quindlen describes her passion for books. "Reading has always been my home, my sustenance, my great invincible companion," says Quindlen. "Yet of all the many things in which we recognize some universal comfort...reading seems to be the one in which the comfort is most undersung, at least publicly.... I did not read from a sense of superiority, or advancement, or even learning. I read because I loved it more than any other activity on earth."

Reader's Context What book or story has been particularly memorable for you? What about it makes it memorable?

ANALYZE LITERATURE: Purpose and Style

A writer's **purpose** is his or her aim, or goal. This purpose might be to inform, to describe, to persuade, to entertain, to enlighten, or to tell a story, or some combination of these goals. **Style** is the manner in which something is said or written. A writer's style depends on diction, or word choice, and grammatical structures.

SET PURPOSE

Preview the essay by reading the quotations and looking at the artwork. How can reading change a person's life? Why do you think Quindlen would write about such a thing? As you read, try to determine Quindlen's purpose and evaluate how her writing style advances her purpose.

MEET THE AUTHOR

Anna Quindlen (b. 1953) was born in Philadelphia, Pennsylvania. After

graduating from Barnard College in 1974, she became a reporter for the *New York Post*. Later, she joined the *New York Times*, where she worked until 1995, writing popular columns such as "About New York" and "Life in the 30s." In 1992, Quindlen won a Pulitzer Prize for her nationally syndicated column, "Public and Private." She has also written four novels, numerous nonfiction books, and two children's books. Her novel *One True Thing* was adapted for the screen in 1998. Currently, Quindlen writes a regular column for *Newsweek*.

USE READING SKILLS

Summarize The ability to summarize a piece of writing, or recap its main ideas or events in your own words, is important to a successful reading experience. As you read the excerpt from *How Reading Changed My Life*, use a graphic organizer like the one below to summarize each part of the essay.

Topic:
Introduction:
Body:
Conclusion:

PREVIEW VOCABULARY

Use the context clues in the sentences below to figure out the meanings of the underlined words from the selection.

1. The <u>raucous</u> pep rally shook the rafters of the gym and energized the players for the game.
2. The investigative report detailed the <u>covert</u> operations of the government's intelligence division.
3. The <u>eloquent</u> orator impressed the audience with her powerful, moving words.
4. Mrs. Carmichael scoffed at the <u>exclusivity</u> of the club, which would not admit a candidate for membership without intensive screening.
5. When the prices were <u>plummeting</u> after the holidays, Latif bought a new stereo.

from
How Reading Changed My Life

A Personal Essay by **Anna Quindlen**

> And then there were books, a kind of parallel universe in which anything might happen and frequently did, a universe in which I might be a newcomer but was never really a stranger.

Woman Reading, 1922. Marc Chagall.
Private collection.

The stories about my childhood, the ones that stuck, that got told and retold at dinner tables, to dates as I sat by red-faced, to my own children by my father later on, are stories of running away. Some are stories of events I can't remember, that I see and feel only in the retelling: the toddler who wandered down the street while her mother was occupied with yet another baby and was driven home by the police; the little girl who was seen by a neighbor ambling down the alley a block north of her family's home; the child who appeared on her grandparents' doorstep and wasn't quite sure whether anyone knew she'd come so far on her own.

Other times I remember myself. I remember taking the elevated train to downtown Philadelphia because, like Everest, it was there, a spired urban Oz so other from the quiet flat streets of the suburbs where we lived. I remember riding my bicycle for miles to the neighborhood where my aunt and uncle lived, a narrow avenue of brick row houses with long boxcar backyards. I remember going to the

Literacy in America In its 1991 National Literacy Act, Congress defined *literacy* as "an individual's ability to read, write, and speak in English, and compute and solve problems at levels of proficiency necessary to function on the job and in society, to achieve one's goals, and develop one's knowledge and potential." Soon after this definition was released, the 1992 National Adult Literacy Survey showed that 21–23 percent of American adults, or roughly 40 million people, function at the lowest possible literacy level. Numerous studies have linked illiteracy to poverty, unemployment, and crime.

airport with my parents when I was thirteen and reading the destinations board, seeing all the places I could go: San Juan, Cincinnati, Los Angeles, London. I remember loving motels; the cheap heavy silverware on airplanes; the smell of plastic, disinfectant, and mildew on the old Greyhound buses. I remember watching trains click by, a blur of grey and the diamond glitter of sunshine on glass, and wishing I was aboard.

The odd thing about all this is that I had a lovely childhood in a lovely place. This is the way I remember it; this is the way it was. The neighborhood where I grew up was the sort of place in which people dream of raising children—pretty, privileged but not rich, a small but satisfying spread of center-hall colonials, old roses, rhododendrons, and quiet roads. We walked to school, wandered wild in the

summer, knew everyone and all their brothers and sisters, too. Some of the people I went to school with, who I sat next to in sixth and seventh grade, still live there, one or two in the houses that their parents once owned.

Not long ago, when I was in town on business, I determined to test my memories against the reality and drove to my old block, my old school, the homes of my closest friends, sure that I had inflated it all in my mind. But the houses were no smaller, the flowers no less bright. It was as fine as I had remembered— maybe more so, now when so much of the rest of the world has come to seem dingy and diminished.

Yet there was always in me, even when I was very small, the sense that I ought to be somewhere else. And wander I did, although, in my everyday life, I had nowhere to go and no imaginable reason on earth why I should want to leave. The buses took to the interstate without me; the trains sped by. So I wandered the world through books. I went to Victorian England in the pages of *Middlemarch* and *A Little Princess,* and to Saint Petersburg before the fall of the tsar with *Anna Karenina.* I went to Tara, and Manderley, and Thornfield Hall, all those great houses, with their high ceilings and high drama, as I read *Gone with the Wind, Rebecca,* and *Jane Eyre.*

When I was in eighth grade I took a scholarship test for a convent school, and the essay question began with a quotation: "It is a far, far better thing that I do, than I have ever done; it is a far, far better rest that I go to, than I have ever known." Later, over a stiff and awkward lunch of tuna-fish salad, some of the other girls at my table were perplexed by the source of the quotation and what it meant, and I was certain, at that moment, weeks before my parents got the letter from the nuns, that the scholarship was mine. How many times had I gone up the steps to the guillotine with Sydney Carton as he went to that far, far better rest at the end of *A Tale of Two Cities?*

Like so many of the other books I read, it never seemed to me like a book, but like a place I had lived in, had visited and would visit again, just as all the people in them, every blessed one—Anne of Green Gables, Heidi, Jay Gatsby, Elizabeth Bennet, Scarlett O'Hara, Dill and Scout, Miss Marple, and Hercule Poirot—were more real than the real people I knew. My home was in that pleasant place outside Philadelphia, but I really lived somewhere else. I lived within the covers of books and those books were more real to me than any other thing in my life. One poem committed to memory in grade school survives in my mind. It is by Emily Dickinson: "There is no Frigate like a Book / To take us Lands away / Nor any coursers like a Page / Of prancing Poetry."

Perhaps only a truly discontented child can become as seduced by books as I was. Perhaps restlessness is a necessary <u>corollary</u> of devoted literacy. There was a club chair in our house, a big one, with curled arms and a square ottoman;[1] it sat in one corner of the living room, catty-corner to the fireplace, with a barrel table next to it. In my mind I am always sprawled in it, reading with my skinny, scabby legs slung over one of its arms. "It's a beautiful day," my mother is saying; she said that always, often, autumn, spring, even when there was a fresh snowfall. "All your friends are outside." It was true; they always were. Sometimes I went out with them, coaxed into the street, out into the fields, down by the creek, by the lure of

what I knew intuitively was normal childhood, by the promise of being what I knew instinctively was a normal child, one who lived, <u>raucous</u>, in the world.

I have clear memories of that sort of life, of lifting the rocks in the creek that trickled through Naylor's Run to search for crayfish, of laying pennies on the tracks of the trolley and running to fetch them, flattened, when the trolley had passed. But at base it was never any good. The best part of me was always at home, within some book that had been laid flat on the table to mark my place, its imaginary people waiting for me to return and bring them to life. That was where the real people were, the trees that moved in the wind, the still, dark waters.

---

1. **ottoman.** Cushioned footstool

cor • ol • lar • y (kôr´ ə ler' ē) *n.,* something that naturally follows; result
rau • cous (rô´ kəs) *adj.,* boisterous

I won a bookmark in a spelling bee during that time with these words of Montaigne upon it in gold: "When I am reading a book, whether wise or silly, it seems to me to be alive and talking to me." I found that bookmark not long ago, at the bottom of a box, when my father was moving.

In the years since those days in that club chair I have learned that I was not alone in this, although at the time I surely was, the only child I knew, or my parents knew, or my friends knew, who preferred reading to playing kick-the-can or ice-skating or just sitting on the curb breaking sticks and scuffing up dirt with a sneaker in summer. In books I have traveled, not only to other worlds, but into my own. I learned who I was and who I wanted to be, what I might aspire to, and what I might dare to dream about my world and myself. More powerfully and persuasively than from the "shalt nots" of the Ten Commandments, I learned the difference between good and evil, right and wrong. One of my favorite childhood books, *A Wrinkle in Time,* described that evil, that wrong, existing in a different dimension from our own. But I felt that I, too, existed much of the time in a different dimension from everyone else I knew. There was waking, and there was sleeping. And then there were books, a kind of parallel universe in which anything might happen and frequently did, a universe in which I might be a newcomer but was never really a stranger. My real, true world. My perfect island.

Years later I would come to discover, as Robinson Crusoe did when he found Man Friday, that I was not alone in that world or on that island. I would discover (through reading, naturally) that while I was sprawled, legs akimbo,[2] in that chair with a book, Jamaica Kincaid was sitting in the glare of the Caribbean sun in Antigua reading in that same way that I did, as though she was starving and the book was bread. When she was grown-up, writing books herself, winning awards for her work, she talked in one of her memoirs of ignoring her little brother when she was supposed to be looking after him: "I liked reading a book much more than I liked looking after him (and even now I like reading a book more than I like looking after my own children…)."

While I was in that club chair with a book, Hazel Rochman and her husband were in South Africa, burying an old tin trunk heavy with hardcovers in the backyard, because the police might raid their house and search it for banned books. Rochman, who left Johannesburg for Chicago and became an editor for the American Library Association's *Booklist,* summed up the lessons learned from that night, about the power of reading, in a way I would have recognized even as a girl. "Reading makes immigrants of us all," she wrote years later. "It takes us away from home, but, most important, it finds homes for us everywhere."

While I was in that club chair with a book, Oprah Winfrey was dividing her childhood between her mother in Milwaukee and her father in Nashville, but finding her most consistent home between the covers of her books. Even decades later, when she had

Yet there was always in me, even when I was very small, the sense that I ought to be somewhere else.

---

2. **akimbo.** Set in a bent position

become the host of her eponymous[3] talk show, one of the world's highest-paid entertainers, and the founder of an on-air book club that resulted in the sale of millions of copies of serious literary novels, Winfrey still felt the sting as she talked to a reporter from *Life* magazine: "I remember being in the back hallway when I was about nine—I'm going to try to say this without crying—and my mother threw the door open and grabbed a book out of my hand and said, 'You're nothing but a something-something bookworm. Get your butt outside! You think you're better than the other kids.' I was treated as though something was wrong with me because I wanted to read all the time!"

Reading has always been my home, my <u>sustenance</u>, my great <u>invincible</u> companion. "Book love," Trollope called it. "It will make your hours pleasant to you as long as you live." Yet of all the many things in which we recognize some universal comfort—God, sex, food, family, friends—reading seems to be the one in which the comfort is most undersung, at least publicly, although it was really all I thought of, or felt, when I was eating up book after book, running away from home while sitting in that chair, traveling around the world and yet never leaving the room. I did not read from a sense of superiority, or advancement, or even learning. I read because I loved it more than any other activity on earth.

Develop the Power
that is within you

**Get ahead. Books are free
at your Public Library**

By the time I became an adult, I realized that while my satisfaction in the sheer act of reading had not <u>abated</u> in the least, the world was often as hostile, or at least as blind, to that joy as had been my girlfriends banging on our screen door, begging me to put down the book— "that stupid book," they usually called it, no matter what book it happened to be. While we pay lip service to the virtues of reading, the truth is that there is still in our culture something that suspects those who read too much, whatever reading too much means, of being lazy, aimless dreamers, people who need to grow up and come outside to where real life is, who think themselves superior in their separateness.

There is something in the American character that is even secretly hostile to the act of aimless reading, a certain hale[4] and heartiness that is suspicious of reading as anything more than a tool for advancement. This is a country that likes confidence but despises hubris,[5] that associates the "nose in the book" with the same sense of <u>covert</u> superiority that Ms. Winfrey's

---

3. **eponymous** (i pä´ nə məs). One for which something is named after
4. **hale.** Retaining exceptional health and vigor
5. **hubris.** Exaggerated pride or self-confidence

---

sus • te • nance (sus´ tə nən[t]s) *n.,* nourishment
in • vin • ci • ble (in[´] vin[t] zə bəl) *adj.,* incapable of being conquered, overcome, or subdued
a • bate (ə bāt´) *v.,* decrease in force or intensity
co • vert (kō´ vərt[´]) *adj.,* not openly shown, engaged in, or avowed

sanctioned[7] reading only if there was some point to it. Students at the nation's best liberal arts colleges who majored in philosophy or English were constantly asked what they were "going to do with it," as though intellectual pursuits for their own sake had had their day, and lost it in the press of business. Reading for pleasure was replaced by reading for purpose, and a kind of dogged self-improvement: whereas an executive might learn far more from *Moby Dick* or *The Man in the Grey Flannel Suit,* the book he was expected to have read might be *The Seven Habits of Highly Successful People.* Reading for pleasure, spurred on by some interior compulsion, became as suspect as getting on the subway to ride aimlessly from place to place, or driving from nowhere to nowhere in a car. I like to do both those things, too, but not half so much as reading.

For many years I worked in the newspaper business, where every day the production of the product stands as a flimsy but <u>eloquent</u> testimony to the thirst for words, information, experience. But, for working journalists, reading in the latter half of the twentieth century was most often couched as a series of problems to be addressed in print: were children in public schools reading poorly? Were all Americans reading less? Was the printed word giving way to the spoken one? Had television and the movies supplanted[8] books? The journalistic answer, most often, was yes, yes, yes, yes,

mother did. America is also a nation that prizes sociability and community, that accepts a kind of psychological domino effect: alone leads to loner, loner to loser. Any sort of turning away from human contact is suspect, especially one that interferes with the go-out-and-get-going <u>ethos</u> that seems to be at the heart of our national character. The image of American presidents that stick are those that portray them as men of action: Theodore Roosevelt on safari, John Kennedy throwing a football around with his brothers. There is only Lincoln as solace to the inveterate[6] reader, a solitary figure sitting by the fire, saying, "My best friend is a person who will give me a book I have not read."

There also arose, as I was growing up, a kind of careerism in the United States that

---

6. **inveterate.** Firmly established by long persistence; habitual
7. **sanctioned.** Given approval or consent
8. **supplanted.** To take the place of

---

e • thos (ē´ thäs´) *n.,* distinguishing character, sentiment, moral nature, or guiding beliefs of a person, group, or institution
el • o • quent (e´ lə kwənt) *adj.,* marked by forceful and fluent expression

buttressed[9] by a variety of statistics that, as so often happens, were massaged to prove the point: reading had fallen upon hard times. And in circles devoted to literary criticism, among the professors of literature, the editors and authors of fiction, there was sometimes a kind of horrible <u>exclusivity</u> surrounding discussions of reading. There was good reading, and there was bad reading. There was the worthy and the trivial. This was always couched[10] in terms of taste, but it tasted, smelled, and felt unmistakably like snobbery.

None of this was new, except, in its discovering, to me. Reading has always been used as a way to divide a country and a culture into the literati[11] and everyone else, the intellectually worthy and the hoi polloi.[12] But in the fifteenth century Gutenberg invented the printing press, and so began the process of turning the book from a work of art for the few into a source of information for the many. After that, it became more difficult for one small group of people to lay an exclusive claim to books, to seize and hold reading as their own. But it was not impossible, and it continued to be done by critics and scholars. When I began to read their work, in college, I was disheartened to discover that many of them felt that the quality of poetry and prose, novels and history and biography, was <u>plummeting</u> into some intellectual bargain basement. But reading saved me from despair, as it always had, for the more I read the more I realized it had always been thus, and that apparently an essential part of studying literature, whether in 1840, 1930, or 1975, was to conclude that there had once been a golden age, and it was gone. "The movies consume so large a part of the leisure of the country that little time is left for other things," the trade magazine of the industry, *Publishers Weekly,* lamented in 1923. "The novel can't compete with cars, the movies, television, and liquor," the French writer Louis-Ferdinand Céline said in 1960.

There was certainly no talk of comfort and joy, of the lively subculture of those of us who forever fell asleep with a book open on our bedside tables, whether bought or borrowed. Of those of us who comprise the real clan of the book, who read not to judge the reading of others but to take the measure of ourselves. Of those of us who read because we love it more than anything, who feel about bookstores the way some people feel about jewelers. The silence about this was odd, both because there are so many of us and because we are what the world of books is really about. We are the people who once waited for the newest installment of Dickens's latest novel and who kept battered copies of *Catcher in the Rye* in our back pockets and our backpacks. We are the ones who saw to it that *Pride and Prejudice* never went out of print.

But there was little public talk of us, except in memoirs like Ms. Kincaid's. Nothing had changed since I was a solitary child being given

Reading for pleasure, spurred on by some interior compulsion, became as suspect as getting on the subway to ride aimlessly from place to place, or driving from nowhere to nowhere in a car.

---

9. **buttressed.** Supported or strengthened
10. **couched.** To phrase in a specified manner
11. **literati** (lĭ' tə rä' tē). Persons interested in literature or the arts
12. **hoi polloi** (hôi' pə lôi'). General population; masses

---

ex • clu • siv • i • ty (eks' klü' si' və tē) *n.,* quality or state of being limiting or restrictive
plum • met • ing (plu' mət iŋ) *adj.,* dropping sharply and abruptly

embossed[13] leather bookmarks by relatives for Christmas. It was still in the equivalent of the club chairs that we found one another: at the counters in bookstores with our arms full, at the front desks in libraries, at school, where teachers introduced us to one another—and, of course, in books, where book-lovers make up a lively subculture of characters. "Until I feared I would lose it, I never loved to read. One does not love breathing," says Scout in *To Kill a Mockingbird*.

Reading is like so much else in our culture, in all cultures: the truth of it is found in its people and not in its pundits[14] and its professionals. If I believed what I read about reading I would despair. But instead there are letters from readers to attend to, like the one from a girl who had been given one of my books by her mother and began her letter, "I guess I am what some people would call a bookworm."

"So am I," I wrote back. ❖

---

13. **embossed.** Ornamented with raised work, such as gold lettering
14. **pundits.** People who give opinions in an authoritative manner

 **MIRRORS & WINDOWS**

Must reading for pleasure be something every educated, well-rounded person does? How does reading compare with other forms of entertainment? Why might someone think reading is a better way to spend one's time?

AFTER READING

REFER TO TEXT ▶ ▶ ▶ ▶	▶ REASON WITH TEXT	
1a. Summarize the stories Quindlen's family members like to recount about her early childhood.	1b. Explain what these stories reveal about Quindlen's personality. How does Quindlen tie running away to reading?	**Understand** **Find meaning**
2a. List the things Quindlen has learned about herself from reading.	2b. Examine the reasons why Quindlen continues to read, even now that she is an adult and has fulfilled many of her aspirations.	**Apply** **Use information**
3a. Recall what Quindlen says she has in common with Jamaica Kincaid and Oprah Winfrey.	3b. Infer why Quindlen writes about the reading experiences of well-known people like Kincaid, Winfrey, and others in her essay.	**Analyze** **Take things apart**
4a. Quote what Quindlen says was the common perception of what constitutes good reading and bad reading.	4b. Evaluate the judgments Quindlen makes about different types of literature. Do you agree or disagree with her? Why?	**Evaluate** **Make judgments**
5a. What does Quindlen read by scholars and critics of literature that she finds disheartening?	5b. Do you think advancements in technology and new forms of entertainment have changed the role of reading for pleasure? Why or why not?	**Create** **Bring ideas together**

ANALYZE LITERATURE: Purpose and Style

What do you think is Quindlen's principal purpose in writing *How Reading Changed My Life*? How does Quindlen accomplish this aim? What are some things you noticed about Quindlen's style of writing? How does her style contribute to accomplishing her purpose?

Writing Options

Creative Writing For an essay contest meant to promote literacy, write a five-paragraph **reflective essay** about your own reading experiences. Like Quindlen, use a lot of sensory details and descriptive phrases to help the reader relive your experience. Include quotations about reading from others in your essay as Quindlen does.

Expository Writing Develop a **summer reading list** of ten books you recommend for students your age. Write a brief description of each book to make it sound interesting to your peers. Include a quotation from the book to act as a "hook" to further intrigue your peers. Post your list on the classroom bulletin board.

Collaborative Learning

Design a Book Jacket Working with a small group, read the rest of *How Reading Changed My Life.* (You can assign different segments of the book to each group member.) Then, working together, design an appropriate book jacket. On the front cover, draw an illustration that reflects the spirit of the book. On the inside flap of the cover, summarize the book's content, using quotations from the book where appropriate. On the back cover, write a biographical paragraph about Anna Quindlen.

Media Literacy

Create a Calendar Search the Internet for quotations about reading. You will find many quotations by famous authors and poets, but also try to include quotations by people like athletes, musicians, and actors. Choose your twelve favorite quotations. Then find an image, either a photograph or a fine art print, to illustrate or enhance each quotation. Use the quotations and images to create a calendar for avid readers. When you are finished, give this calendar to someone who will appreciate it.

 Go to **www.mirrorsandwindows.com** for more.

READING ASSESSMENT

1. At the beginning of the selection, which of the following does the author say was the distinguishing characteristic of the stories about her childhood?
   A. eating ice cream
   B. learning to ride a bicycle
   C. flying a plane
   D. running away
   E. playing with her sibling

2. On page 289, the word *raucous* most nearly means
   A. boisterous.
   B. spectacular.
   C. exaggerated.
   D. blatant.
   E. interesting.

3. On page 292, the word *eloquent* most nearly means
   A. funny.
   B. abrupt.
   C. expressive.
   D. somber.
   E. None of the above

4. Which of the following lines from the essay best represents one of Quindlen's key points?
   A. "The odd thing about all this is that I had a lovely childhood in a lovely place."
   B. "Perhaps only a truly discontented child can become as seduced by books as I was."
   C. "In books I have traveled, not only to other worlds, but into my own."
   D. "There is something in the American character that is even secretly hostile to the act of aimless reading..."
   E. None of the above

5. What are your three favorite books? In a paragraph or two, identify and explain your choices.

Understanding Speeches

SPEECHES

When you think about giving a speech, you might envision yourself standing in front of a group of people, trembling and sweating, your eyes darting back and forth, your hands nervously clenching your note cards. Speaking in front of a crowd is not always easy. Many people throughout history, however, have been in the same situation, and their speeches were so significant that they were reprinted to be read over and over again. You will read two such famous speeches in this unit.

A **speech** is a public address that was originally delivered orally. The nature of a speech, whether formal or informal, is usually determined by the situation or context in which it is presented. Formal speeches generally call for a greater degree of preparation. A *formal speech* situation might exist when presenting an assigned speech to classmates, or giving a presentation to a community group or ceremony. The more formal a speech is the more preparation it requires. *Informal speech* situations are more casual and might include telling a story among friends, giving a pep talk to your team at halftime, or presenting a toast at a dinner table. The three main types of speeches are impromptu, memorized, and extemporaneous speeches.

TYPES OF SPEECHES

Impromptu Speech
A speech that requires no advance preparation is called an **impromptu speech.** If you were to give this type of speech, you would simply get up and talk. For example, if you were surprised by a gift or

an award, you might be called upon to give a brief speech that was not written or rehearsed. The famous line spoken by Neil Armstrong from the surface of the moon, "That's one small step for man, one giant leap for mankind," could be considered an impromptu speech.

Memorized Speech
A **memorized speech** requires more preparation in that the speaker writes and memorizes the speech word for word. This is difficult to do, and memorized speeches sometimes seem stiff and devoid of expression.

Extemporaneous Speech
Most speeches that have become famous are **extemporaneous speeches,** or speeches that are prepared and rehearsed ahead of time. If you were to give this type of speech, you would prepare and refer to notes or outlines, and you would rehearse until you felt comfortable giving the speech. The speech delivered by John F. Kennedy from which came the line, "Ask not what your country can do for you—ask what you can do for your country," is an example of an extemporaneous speech.

ELEMENTS OF SPEECHES

Most of the time, speeches are delivered orally to a public audience. When you are able to read a copy of a speech, however, you have more of a chance to absorb and reflect on its message. To understand and analyze a speech you are reading, it helps to consider the elements that make up a speech.

Purpose
When a person writes a piece for publication, he or she has a **purpose,** or goal. The same is true when a person gives a speech. The most common purposes for giving a speech are to either explain something or to convince people to accept a position and respond in some way. Historical speeches are also often connected to an occasion of some sort. Elie Wiesel delivered his speech "Keep Memory Alive" (page 299) when he accepted the Nobel Peace Prize in 1986. The purpose of his speech was to urge listeners to act and not to remain silent when they know that others are suffering.

Main Idea
The main idea, or central message, of a speech is stated directly, usually in the introduction. More often than not, however, the main idea is implied, or not directly declared. For instance, in "Yonder Sky That Has Wept Tears of Compassion" (page 309), Chief Seattle's main idea, which is that his people must learn to live with the white man in order to not be forgotten, is implied.

Good speakers understand the need to support their main ideas. Common types of support include facts and statistics, firsthand experiences or examples, opinions of experts, logical reasoning, comparisons and contrasts, research results, and appeals to emotion. Chief Seattle uses a variety of support. He points to the high cost of life to his people by fighting with the white settlers, draws on his own experiences, and appeals to the honor of the president of the United States to treat his people with dignity and respect.

Rhetorical Devices

Rhetorical devices are techniques used by speakers to achieve a particular effect, especially to persuade or influence. Three common types of rhetorical devices are listed below:

- **Parallelism** Using this rhetorical device, a writer emphasizes the equal value or weight of two or more ideas by expressing them in the same grammatical form.
- **Repetition** This is the intentional reuse of a sound, word, phrase, or sentence.

Writers often use repetition to emphasize ideas. Notice how in his "Keep Memory Alive" speech, Elie Wiesel uses both parallelism and repetition:

> I remember: it happened yesterday or eternities ago. A young Jewish boy discovered the kingdom of night. I remember his bewilderment. I remember his anguish. It all happened so fast. The ghetto. The deportation. The sealed cattle car. The fiery altar upon which the history of our people and the future of mankind were meant to be sacrificed. I remember: he asked his father: 'Can this be true?'
> — from "Keep Memory Alive"
> by Elie Wiesel

- **Rhetorical Question** This kind of question is asked for effect but is not meant to be answered. A rhetorical question will draw attention to the purpose of the speech. In "Yonder Sky That Has Wept Tears of Compassion," Chief Seattle asks rhetorical questions.

> How then can we be brothers? How can your God become our God and renew our prosperity and awaken in us dreams of returning greatness?
> — from "Yonder Sky That Has Wept Tears of Compassion" by Chief Seattle

Ethos, Pathos, and Logos

There are many speakers who will try to persuade others to take their point of view, such as a lawyer giving opening and closing arguments to a jury or a politician soliciting votes. Persuasive speakers form arguments by using something called ethos, pathos, and logos.

Ethos refers to the character of the person giving the argument. There are several techniques speakers use to establish ethos in a persuasive argument.

1. They align themselves with others who are known for their expertise or goodness. By quoting from people the audience is likely to know and respect, they show that they know what they are talking about and win the audience's respect, as well.
2. They show that they share the values held by their audiences. For example, if someone is talking to a group of animal rights activists, he or she can establish ethos by showing a concern for animals, even if he or she will later go on to disagree with certain specific animal rights positions.
3. They acknowledge other viewpoints. This shows that they know and understand the positions of those who disagree with them. As a result, they come across as fair-minded.

Pathos is persuasion based on arousing emotions, including passion, love, hate, joy, fear, guilt, patriotism, sympathy, pity, sorrow, envy, and anger. Pathos provides a personal appeal that has the power to move listeners, change attitudes, and produce actions.

Having established credibility, or ethos, and having used pathos to heighten the emotions of the audience, speakers also consider logos. **Logos** is based on logic, or reason. A person who uses logos strives to convince the audience through a clear, logical argument that his or her position is the correct one.

Keep Memory Alive

BUILD BACKGROUND

Cultural Context Elie Wiesel, a Holocaust survivor, has fought against violence and oppression of people around the globe. **"Keep Memory Alive"** is part of the speech he gave when accepting the Nobel Peace Prize in 1986. In accepting the award, Wiesel explains why he has vowed never again to be silent when human beings are suffering. Wiesel is internationally known for his writings about the Holocaust. One of the most famous of these books is the memoir entitled *Night* (1960), a vivid account of his life as a teenager in a Nazi concentration camp.

Reader's Context Have you ever witnessed something you believed was wrong? What did you do about it?

ANALYZE LITERATURE: Parallelism and Tone

Parallelism is a rhetorical device in which a writer emphasizes the equal value or weight of two or more ideas by expressing them in the same grammatical form. An example is "To speak is to risk everything," in which "to speak" and "to risk" are parallel elements.

Tone is the emotional attitude toward the reader or toward the subject implied by a literary work.

SET PURPOSE

As you read the speech, look for examples of parallelism, and think of adjectives you might use to describe Wiesel's tone. Also respond to the text by remaining aware of your own feelings, ideas, and judgments about the truth or the effectiveness of the writing.

MEET THE AUTHOR

Elie Wiesel (b. 1928) was born in the close-knit Jewish community of Sighet, Transylvania, now a part of Romania. When he was fifteen years old, he and his family were deported to the Nazi death camp of Auschwitz in Poland. His mother and younger sister died there. Wiesel and his father were later transferred to Buchenwald, another concentration camp, where his father died. Years later, in France, Wiesel was reunited with his two older sisters. In 1955, ten years after the end of World War II, Wiesel was encouraged to "bear witness" to the atrocities of the Holocaust he had seen and experienced. He has done so through writing, speaking, and teaching. For young people, Wiesel offers this advice: "Always favor the person who is tolerant enough to understand that there are no absolute answers, but there are absolute questions."

USE READING SKILLS

Main Idea The **main idea** of a piece of writing is the central point that the author develops with supporting details. In some cases, the main idea is actually stated. If it isn't stated, you will have to infer it. A good way of finding the main idea of a selection is to gather important details into a Main Idea Map like the one below. As you read "Keep Memory Alive," add details to your own map. When you finish reading, use the details to determine the main idea and draw conclusions about it.

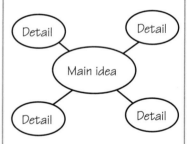

PREVIEW VOCABULARY

Use the context clues in the sentences below to figure out the meanings of the underlined words from the selection.
1. For an experience that <u>transcends</u> the ordinary, try our super-deluxe spa relaxation package.
2. I couldn't believe Luisa was so <u>presumptuous</u> as to ask such a personal question.

Keep Memory Alive

A Speech by **Elie Wiesel**

It all happened so fast. The ghetto. The deportation. The sealed cattle car.

It is with a profound sense of humility that I accept the honor you have chosen to bestow upon me. I know: your choice <u>transcends</u> me. This both frightens and pleases me.

It frightens me because I wonder: do I have the right to represent the multitudes who have perished? Do I have the right to accept this great honor on their behalf? I do not. That would be <u>presumptuous</u>. No one may speak for the dead, no one may interpret their mutilated dreams and visions.

It pleases me because I may say that this honor belongs to all the survivors and their children, and through us, to the Jewish people with whose destiny I have always identified.

I remember: it happened yesterday or eternities ago. A young Jewish boy[1] discovered the kingdom of night. I remember his bewilderment. I remember his anguish. It all happened so fast. The ghetto. The deportation. The sealed cattle car. The fiery altar upon which the history of our people and the future of mankind were meant to be sacrificed.[2]

I remember: he asked his father: "Can this be true? This is the 20th century, not the Middle Ages. Who would allow such crimes to be committed? How could the world remain silent?"

And now the boy is turning to me: "Tell me," he asks. "What have you done with my future? What have you done with your life?"

And I tell him that I have tried. That I have tried to keep memory alive, that I have tried to fight those who would forget. Because if we forget, we are guilty, we are accomplices.

And then I explained to him how naive we were, that the world did know and remain silent. And that is why I swore never to be silent whenever and wherever human beings endure suffering and humiliation. We must always take sides. Neutrality helps the oppressor, never the victim. Silence encourages the tormentor, never the tormented. ❖

---

1. **A young Jewish boy.** Wiesel refers to himself as a boy.
2. **The ghetto…sacrificed.** Wiesel refers to what the Jews suffered—first being forced into ghettos, then being deported, and finally being killed in sealed cattle cars or being sent to gas chambers at concentration camps.

---

tran • scend (tran[t] send´) *v.,* rise above or go beyond the limits of
pre • sump • tu • ous (pri zum[p]´ chə wəs) *adj.,* going too far; overstepping bounds

The Holocaust Between 1933 and 1945, approximately six million Jews and members of other minorities in European countries were persecuted and systematically killed by the Nazis, followers of Adolf Hitler, who believed in the superiority of the Aryan race. This dark period is known as the Holocaust. By 1939, Jews in Germany had been stripped of their rights and forced into small, segregated parts of cities, called ghettos. The Nazis planned to wipe out the entire Jewish population. Finding other methods of execution insufficient, the Nazis forced millions of Jews into concentration camps in Eastern Europe. Once there, many were immediately killed in gas chambers, and others were forced to labor as slaves until they died. The photo to the left is one of the gas chambers. Survivors like Elie Wiesel remind us of the importance of fighting intolerance and prejudice.

MIRRORS & WINDOWS To what degree can one individual speaking out against oppression make a difference? Give examples from history and from your own experiences to support your opinion.

REFER TO TEXT ▶ ▶ ▶ ▶	▶ REASON WITH TEXT	
1a. Recall how Wiesel feels about accepting the award.	1b. Summarize what Wiesel means in his opening statement about his reactions to the award.	**Understand** **Find meaning**
2a. Quote the question the boy asks of his father. Quote the questions he asks of the adult Wiesel.	2b. Examine how the answers to those questions have affected Wiesel and the way he lives.	**Apply** **Use information**
3a. Recite the two-word phrase Wiesel repeats four times near the end of the speech.	3b. Analyze how this repeated phrase ties in with the theme, or central message, of the speech as a whole.	**Analyze** **Take things apart**
4a. Quote the answers the adult Wiesel gives to the questions posed by Wiesel as a young boy.	4b. Wiesel uses the device of a dialogue between himself as a boy and himself as an adult. Judge the effectiveness of this device.	**Evaluate** **Make judgments**
5a. State what Wiesel says neutrality does. State what he says silence does.	5b. Explain why you think people often remain silent or are reluctant to become involved when they witness oppression or suffering.	**Create** **Bring ideas together**

ANALYZE LITERATURE: Parallelism and Tone

What example of parallelism can you find in the last paragraph of the selection? How does this use of parallelism emphasize Wiesel's closing point? What words would you use to describe Wiesel's tone? How do parallelism and tone contribute to the effectiveness of the speech?

Informational Text
CONNECTION

"No News from Auschwitz" was published in *The New York Times* in 1958. Assigned to cover news in Poland during that year, **A. M. Rosenthal** (1922–2006) visited Auschwitz, a concentration camp that had, in part, been turned into a museum. Auschwitz had been liberated in 1944, but little news about it had appeared in American newspapers. Rosenthal's article stands as a sober reminder to readers not to forget the horror of the Holocaust. Rosenthal later became managing editor of *The New York Times.*

ROSENTHAL

The New York Times   April 14, 1958

No News from Auschwitz

A News Article by A. M. Rosenthal

Brzezinka, Poland[1]—The most terrible thing of all, somehow, was that at Brzezinka the sun was bright and warm, the rows of graceful poplars were lovely to look upon, and on the grass near the gates children played.

It all seemed frighteningly wrong, as in a nightmare, that at Brzezinka the sun should ever shine or that there should be light and greenness and the sound of young laughter. It would be fitting if at Brzezinka the sun never shone and the grass withered, because this is a place of unutterable terror.

And yet every day, from all over the world, people come to Brzezinka, quite possibly the most <u>grisly</u> tourist center on earth. They come for a variety of reasons—to see if it could really have been true, to remind themselves not to forget, to pay <u>homage</u> to the dead by the simple act of looking upon their place of suffering.

Brzezinka is a couple of miles from the better-known southern Polish town of Oświęcim.[2] Oświęcim has about 12,000 inhabitants, is situated about 171 miles from Warsaw, and lies in a damp, marshy area at the eastern end of the pass called the Morsavian Gate. Brzezinka and Oświęcim together formed part of that minutely organized factory of torture and death that the Nazis called Konzentrationslager Auschwitz.

By now, fourteen years after the last batch of prisoners was herded naked into the gas chambers by dogs and guards, the story of Auschwitz has been told a great many times. Some of the inmates have written of those memories of which sane men cannot conceive. Rudolf Franz Ferdinand Hoess, the superintendent of the camp, before he was executed wrote his detailed memoirs of mass exterminations and the experiments on living bodies. Four million people died here, the Poles say.

And so there is no news to report about Auschwitz. There is merely the <u>compulsion</u> to write something about it, a compulsion that grows out of a restless feeling that to have visited Auschwitz and then turned away without having said or written anything would somehow be a most <u>grievous</u> act of discourtesy to those who died here.

Brzezinka and Oświęcim are very quiet places now; the screams can no longer be heard. The tourist walks silently, quickly at first to get it over with and then, as his mind peoples the barracks

---

1. **Brzezinka** (b' zhə zēn´ kä), **Poland.** Site of Birkenau, a concentration camp close to Auschwitz
2. **Oświęcim** (ôsh' fyen´ chēm). Polish name for Auschwitz

gris • ly (griz´ lē) *adj.,* horrifying
hom • age (ä´ mij) *n.,* display of respect or honor
com • pul • sion (kəm pul´ shən) *n.,* overwhelming desire or urge
griev • ous (grē´ vəs) *adj.,* serious or grave

and the chambers and the dungeons and flogging posts, he walks draggingly. The guide does not say much either, because there is nothing much for him to say after he has pointed.

For every visitor there is one particular bit of horror that he knows he will never forget. For some it is seeing the rebuilt gas chamber at Oświęcim and being told that this is the "small one."

For others it is the fact that at Brzezinka, in the ruins of the gas chambers and the crematoria[3] the Germans blew up when they retreated, there are daisies growing.

There are visitors who gaze blankly at the gas chambers and the furnaces because their minds simply cannot <u>encompass</u> them, but stand shivering before the great mounds of human hair behind the plate-glass window or the piles of babies' shoes or the brick cells where men sentenced to death by suffocation were walled up.

One visitor opened his mouth in a silent scream simply at the sight of boxes—great stretches of three-tiered wooden boxes in the women's barracks. They were about six feet wide, about three feet high, and into them from five to ten prisoners were shoved for the night. The guide walks quickly through the barracks. Nothing more to see here.

A brick building where sterilization experiments were carried out on women prisoners. The guide tries the door—it's locked. The visitor is grateful that he does not have to go in, and then flushes with shame.

A long corridor where rows of faces stare from the walls. Thousands of pictures, the photographs of prisoners. They are all dead now, the men and women who stood before the cameras, and they all knew they were to die.

They all stare blank-faced, but one picture, in the middle of a row, seizes the eye and wretches the mind. A girl, twenty-two years old, plumply pretty, blond. She is smiling gently, as at a sweet, treasured thought. What was the thought that passed through her young mind and is now her memorial on the wall of the dead at Auschwitz?

Into the suffocation dungeons the visitor is taken for a moment and feels himself strangling. Another visitor goes in, stumbles out, and crosses herself. There is no place to pray in Auschwitz.

The visitors look pleadingly at each other and say to the guide, "Enough."

There is nothing new to report about Auschwitz. It was a sunny day and the trees were green and at the gates the children played. ❖

---

3. **crematoria** (krē' mə tōr´ ē ə). Crematoriums, or places where the bodies of the dead are burned

en • com • pass (in kum´ pəs) v., enclose or include

REFER TO TEXT ▷ ▷ ▷ ▶	▶ REASON WITH TEXT	
1a. Identify the sharp contrast Rosenthal establishes in the first two paragraphs of the article.	1b. Describe the effect Rosenthal creates through this sharp contrast.	**Understand** **Find meaning**
2a. State why there is "no news to report" about Auschwitz.	2b. Analyze why Rosenthal has a "compulsion" to write about Auschwitz.	**Analyze** **Take things apart**
3a. List the two reasons people come to Brzezinka from all over the world.	3b. Judge whether you feel it would be valuable for you to visit Brzezinka.	**Evaluate** **Make judgments**

TEXT ←TO→ TEXT CONNECTION

How would A. M. Rosenthal evaluate Elie Wiesel's speech, "Keep Memory Alive"? How would Wiesel evaluate Rosenthal's article, "No News from Auschwitz"?

EXTEND THE TEXT

Writing Options

Creative Writing Imagine that you are being honored for achievement in a particular field that appeals to you: sports, performing arts, journalism, teaching, or social work. Write a **speech** you might give on the occasion of accepting this award. In your speech, offer the audience some insights about why the field you have chosen is important and beneficial to society as a whole.

Persuasive Writing Speak out against oppression. Write an **editorial** for the school newspaper about an issue of injustice that bothers you. In your editorial, state your opinions clearly; provide facts, examples, and experts to support your opinions; and try to persuade readers to take action to end this injustice.

Collaborative Learning

Analyze Speeches Use the Internet to find a complete version of Elie Wiesel's Nobel Prize acceptance speech. Then work with two or three classmates to find another speech by Wiesel, or another acceptance speech for the Nobel Prize. With your group, analyze the speeches. Identify the main message of each speech, the purpose of each speech, and any rhetorical devices, such as parallelism, that the speaker uses. Also compare the speeches. Read aloud passages that illustrate your main points.

Lifelong Learning

Present Holocaust Research Choose a subject related to the Holocaust to research. The U.S. Holocaust Memorial Museum in Washington, DC, offers a good overview that might help you narrow your topic. Once you have selected a topic, use the Internet, library, and other sources to learn more about it. Prepare an oral presentation with visual aids on your subject. Try to anticipate questions other students may ask, and prepare answers for those questions.

 Go to **www.mirrorsandwindows.com** for more.

READING ASSESSMENT

1. This selection is excerpted from a speech that Wiesel delivered when he received which of the following?
   A. the Medal of Freedom
   B. the Pulitzer Prize
   C. the Nobel Prize
   D. an Academy Award
   E. the Edgar Award

2. On page 299, the word *presumptuous* most nearly means
   A. resonant.
   B. ingratiating.
   C. disagreeable.
   D. going too far.
   E. None of the above

3. Which passage best describes the main idea of Wiesel's speech?
   A. "It is with a profound sense of humility that I accept the honor you have chosen to bestow upon me."
   B. "We must always take sides. Neutrality helps the oppressor, never the victim. Silence encourages the tormentor, never the tormented."
   C. "A young Jewish boy discovered the kingdom of night."

   D. "And then I explained to him how naive we were, that the world did know and remain silent."
   E. "No one may speak for the dead, no one may interpret their mutilated dreams and visions."

4. Elie Wiesel's primary focus in this selection is on which of the following?
   A. retribution
   B. analysis
   C. remembrance
   D. choice
   E. All of the above

5. In Rosenthal's news article, what does he find "frighteningly wrong" about his visit to Auschwitz?
   A. that there could be beauty and laughter at a place with such a terrible history
   B. that no one at Auschwitz acknowledges the Holocaust took place
   C. that the tours do not provide enough historical information
   D. that after fourteen years, there is nothing left to see at Auschwitz
   E. None of the above

6. In a brief essay, identify and discuss two or three examples of parallelism in the speech. How does parallelism contribute to the forceful effect of the speech as a whole?

GRAMMAR & STYLE

UNDERSTAND THE CONCEPT   APPLY THE SKILL

Capitalization

While the concept of capitalization may seem simple—capitalize proper nouns and adjectives—knowing what and when to capitalize can sometimes be confusing. Listed below are important capitalization rules.

Capitalize the **pronoun "I."**

EXAMPLE

I read Wiesel's speech and was moved by it.

The **first word of a sentence** should be capitalized.

EXAMPLE

The first day of the week is Sunday.

Proper nouns are capitalized. A proper noun names a specific person, place, or thing. The following types of proper nouns should be capitalized.
- names of people: Elie Wiesel
- months, days, and holidays: June, Monday, Christmas Day
- names of religions, languages, races, and nationalities: German, Jewish, Polish, Hispanic, African American
- names of clubs, organizations, businesses, and institutions: Volunteers of America, Smithsonian Institution
- names of awards, prizes, and medals: Nobel Prize, Guggenheim Fellowship

A **proper adjective** is either an adjective formed from a proper noun or a proper noun used as an adjective. Either way, proper adjectives are capitalized.

EXAMPLES

Swiss cheese
Spanish class
Bunsen burner

Geographical names of specific places are capitalized, including terms such as *lake, mountain, river,* or *valley,* if they are used as part of a name. Do not capitalize general names for places.

EXAMPLES

capitalized:	Rhine River
	Auschwitz
not capitalized:	the river
	the concentration camp

Geographical directions are capitalized if they are part of a specific name of a commonly recognized region. Do not capitalize such words as *east(ern), west(ern), north(ern),* and *south(ern)* if they are used only to indicate direction.

EXAMPLES

capitalized:	Near East
	Pacific Northwest
	South Africa
not capitalized:	south of the Rhine River
	north side of the road
	western countries

Historical events are capitalized, as are **special events** and **recognized periods of time.**

EXAMPLES

World War II
Industrial Revolution
the Holocaust

The first and last words and all major words in between are capitalized in the **titles of artworks and literary works,** including short stories, songs, and poems. Articles and prepositions are not capitalized unless they follow colons in titles.

EXAMPLES

Night
"Keep Memory Alive"

REVIEW TERMS
- **proper noun:** noun that names a specific person, place, or thing
- **proper adjective:** adjective formed from a proper noun or a proper noun that is used as an adjective

Identify Capitalized Words

For each capitalized word in the following passage, identify the capitalization rule.

> Between 1933 and 1945, approximately six million Jews and members of other minorities in European countries were persecuted and systematically killed by the Nazis, followers of Adolf Hitler, who believed in the superiority of the Aryan race. This dark period is known as the Holocaust. By 1939, Jews in Germany had been stripped of their rights and forced into small, segregated parts of cities, called ghettos. The Nazis planned to wipe out the entire Jewish population. Finding other methods of execution insufficient, the Nazis forced millions of Jews into concentration camps in Eastern Europe. Once there, many were immediately killed in gas chambers, and others were forced to labor as slaves until they died. Survivors like Elie Wiesel remind us of the importance of fighting intolerance and prejudice.

Correct Errors in Capitalization

Rewrite the following sentences, correcting any errors in capitalization.

1. On September 1, 1939, adolf hitler and the nazis invaded poland; as a result, Britain and france declared war on germany, and World war II began.

2. The jewish people in many european Countries were forced by the nazis into concentration camps.

3. The largest of the concentration camps was auschwitz; rosenthal visited this camp and wrote a newspaper article about it.

4. Elie wiesel was awarded the nobel prize in 1986.

5. The Japanese attack on pearl harbor in December of 1941 brought the united states into the War.

6. The concentration camp auschwitz is located in eastern europe.

7. Elie Wiesel wrote a Memoir entitled *night;* it was made a book club selection by oprah winfrey.

8. the united states holocaust memorial museum is in washington, DC.

9. This Museum is dedicated to remember the Holocaust.

10. The museum is open sunday through saturday.

11. Many movies have been made about the Holocaust, including *schindler's list.*

12. The young diarist anne frank wrote about her family's experiences during the Holocaust in her journal.

13. Survivors of the Holocaust are often asked to tell their stories; i find the stories very moving.

Use Capitalization in Your Writing

Think of a historical site of interest you've visited or would like to visit. After doing some research on the site, write a tourist brochure about it. In your brochure, include all the information people who would want to visit the site would need, including its hours of operation and directions to get there. Pay close attention to capitalization as you write. If you are uncertain as to whether a word should be capitalized, look it up in a dictionary or on the Internet.

EXTEND THE SKILL

Find a magazine article on a topic that interests you. Choose two paragraphs. In those two paragraphs, mark every capitalized word, and see if you can explain why each word is capitalized.

VOCABULARY & SPELLING

Word Origins

The English language expands constantly and gathers new words from different sources. Understanding the source of a word can help you unlock its meaning.

One source of new words is the names of people and places associated with the things being named. Words named for people and places are called **eponyms.**

EXAMPLE

The word *braille* is named for Louis Braille, a French teacher of the visually impaired who was blind himself and who developed a written language for the blind.

Another source for new words is **acronyms.** Acronyms are words formed from the first letter or letters of the major parts of terms.

EXAMPLE

The word *scuba* is an acronym for "self-contained underwater breathing apparatus."

The English language contains many words taken from other languages. These are known as **borrowed words.**

A number of words borrowed from Spanish are actually Native American in origin. When Spanish explorers arrived in the Americas, they found plants and animals for which they didn't have words. They turned to the native peoples for the names of these things. Later, English speakers borrowed these same words from Spanish.

EXAMPLES

chile, chocolate, cocoa, tomato (Nahuatl)
condor, llama, puma (Quechua)
guava, papaya (Arawak)
iguana (Arawak and Carib)
manatee, potato (Taino)

In 1066, England was conquered by the Normans, a people from northern France. As a result, the English language was greatly influenced by Norman French. So many French words entered the English language that today it is impossible to write a paragraph in English without using many words of French origin.

EXAMPLES

banquet
en masse
faux pas
gourmet
government
harmony
loyalty

More than seven million Germans immigrated to America from the seventeenth to the twentieth centuries. These immigrants brought with them their language, and gradually, German words made their way into English.

EXAMPLES

fest
hamster
kindergarten
nickel
waltz
wander

In addition to words borrowed from European languages, English also encompasses words brought by immigrants from Japan, China, and other Asian countries.

EXAMPLES

bonsai, tsunami, origami (Japanese)
gung ho, kung fu, wok (Chinese)

Etymology is the study of the origins of words. In a good dictionary, you will find the origin of each word. For example, the word *holocaust* is listed as coming from Latin, French, and Greek words all having to with fire or burning.

REVIEW TERMS

- **eponym:** word named for a person or a place
- **acronym:** word formed from the first letter or letters of the major parts of terms
- **borrowed word:** word borrowed from another language

Exercise A

Match each word in Column A with its language of origin in Column B by writing the correct letter in the blank. Use a dictionary if necessary.

Column A	Column B
_____1. kumquat	A. French
_____2. tattoo	B. Malay
_____3. amok	C. Spanish
_____4. mariachi	D. Chinese
_____5. roulette	E. Tahitian

Exercise B

Research the origins of the following eponyms. Write a sentence explaining how they came to be words in the English language.

1. forsythia
2. ferris wheel
3. diesel engine
4. graham cracker
5. shrapnel
6. silhouette
7. Bunsen burner
8. boycott
9. Caesar salad
10. sandwich
11. chauvinistic
12. decibel

Exercise C

Research the origins of the following acronyms. Write out what each letter of the acronym means.

1. HMO
2. UNESCO
3. ETA
4. CNN
5. NASA
6. HTTP
7. NCAA
8. DNA
9. BBC
10. FBI
11. DVD
12. ATM

Exercise D

Research the etymology of the following borrowed words to the best of your ability. Write a short description of where each of the words came from.

1. à la carte
2. déjà vu
3. macabre
4. embargo
5. pronto
6. renegade
7. karaoke
8. rickshaw
9. barbecue
10. quartz
11. jungle
12. toboggan

EXTEND THE SKILL

Visit an ethnic restaurant in your area, or locate a menu from one by doing an Internet search. Collect a list of ethnic foods served at that restaurant. If there are no descriptions of the foods on the menu, ask one of the servers what they are, or research them on the Internet. Then use that list to plan a menu for a dinner party with an ethnic theme. Include a beverage, appetizer, entrée, side dish, and dessert.

Yonder Sky That Has Wept Tears of Compassion

A Speech by Chief Seattle

BEFORE READING

BUILD BACKGROUND

Historical Context Soon after the Washington Territory was organized in 1853, Governor Isaac Stevens visited to inform Chief Seattle about a proposed treaty that would relocate Seattle's people to reservations. In his speech **"Yonder Sky That Has Wept Tears of Compassion,"** delivered in 1854, Seattle responds to this news. Seattle's frequent use of natural imagery underscores the connection between his people and the land, even as he agrees to consider the conditions of the treaty. Seattle's speech first appeared in print in 1887, when it was translated by Dr. Henry A. Smith. However, there is some doubt about whether Smith's translation accurately captures the chief's actual words.

Reader's Context Imagine that you are told you have to move to another state. How would you react?

ANALYZE LITERATURE: Mood and Imagery

Mood, or atmosphere, is the emotion created in the reader by all or part of a literary work. **Imagery** is language that creates word pictures or *images*. A writer can create mood by working carefully with imagery. Both mood and imagery involve the use of *sensory details,* or words that appeal to the five senses.

SET PURPOSE

Chief Seattle delivered this speech at a time when change for Native Americans was becoming inevitable. As you read, think about the kind of mood Seattle creates with his speech and how the imagery he uses contributes to the mood. What does the mood and imagery reflect in regard to Seattle's feelings about the whites and about his own people?

MEET THE AUTHOR

Chief Seattle (c.1786–1866) was born in what is today part of the state of Washington. His father was a member of the Suquamish tribe, and his mother was of the Duwamish. The Native Americans in Washington Territory did not have hereditary chiefs. Instead, they awarded the title "chief" to those who, like Seattle, were skilled warriors, speakers, and leaders. As a man, he became known for his diplomacy and ability to negotiate agreements with white officials. In 1850, the town of Seattle was named after him. After his people were removed to reservations, he continued to comply with the U.S. government, even though he was frustrated by the declining health and increasing poverty of his people.

USE READING SKILLS

Classify Information To **classify** information is to put items that share one or more characteristics into categories, or groups. As you read Chief Seattle's speech, use a graphic organizer like the one below to write down examples of specific images that reference nature. Classify the images into the categories of earth, water, or sky.

Image	Category
Today is fair. Tomorrow it may be overcast with clouds.	Sky

PREVIEW VOCABULARY

An **antonym** is a word that has a meaning opposite from that of another word. For each vocabulary word below, choose the correct antonym.

1. reproach
   A. criticism
   B. praise
   C. explanation
2. impulsive
   A. passionate
   B. taciturn
   C. prudent
3. receding
   A. conflicting
   B. disobeying
   C. advancing
4. sequestered
   A. conspicuous
   B. proportional
   C. sensitive
5. stolidly
   A. massively
   B. emotionally
   C. apologetically

YONDER SKY THAT HAS WEPT TEARS OF COMPASSION

A Speech by

Chief Seattle

Scorched Earth, **Clear-cut Logging on Native Sovereign Land, Shaman Coming to Fix,** 1991. Lawrence Paul Yuxweluptun, National Gallery of Canada, Ottawa.

To us the ashes of our ancestors are sacred and their resting place is hallowed ground.

Yonder sky that has wept tears of compassion upon my people for centuries untold, and which to us appears changeless and eternal, may change. Today is fair. Tomorrow it may be overcast with clouds. My words are like the stars that never change. Whatever Seattle says the great chief at Washington[1] can rely upon with as much certainty as he can upon the return of the sun or the seasons. The white chief says that big chief at Washington sends us greetings of friendship and goodwill. This is kind of him for we know he has little need of our friendship in return. His people are many. They are like the grass that covers vast prairies. My people are few. They resemble the scattering trees of a storm-swept plain. The great—and I presume—good white chief sends us word that he wishes to buy our lands but is willing to allow us enough to live comfortably. This indeed appears just, even generous, for the red man no longer has rights that he need respect, and the

offer may be wise also, as we are no longer in need of an extensive country.

There was a time when our people covered the land as the waves of a wind-ruffled sea cover its shell-paved floor, but that time long since passed away with the greatness of tribes that are now but a mournful memory. I will not dwell on, nor mourn over, our untimely decay, nor <u>reproach</u> my paleface brothers with hastening it as we too may have been somewhat to blame.

Youth is <u>impulsive</u>. When our young men grow angry at some real or imaginary wrong, and <u>disfigure</u> their faces with black paint, it

---

1. **great chief at Washington.** President of the United States. Franklin Pierce was president at the time of Seattle's speech.

> **re • proach** (ri prōch´) *v.,* accuse; blame
> **im • pul • sive** (im pul´ siv) *adj.,* likely to act without a lot of planning or thought
> **dis • fig • ure** (dis fi´ gyər) *v.,* disguise

Native Americans in Puget Sound Long before Washington became a state in 1889, the people of the Suquamish Nation and the Duwamish lived in the Puget Sound area, which today includes the city of Seattle. The Point Elliott Treaty of 1855 made Puget Sound a part of the United States and relocated the Suquamish to the Port Madison Indian Reservation. The Duwamish were expected to live with other tribes on their reservations.

denotes that their hearts are black, and that they are often cruel and relentless, and our old men and old women are unable to restrain them. Thus it has ever been. Thus it was when the white man first began to push our forefathers westward. But let us hope that the hostilities between us may never return. We would have everything to lose and nothing to gain. Revenge by young men is considered gain, even at the cost of their own lives, but old men who stay at home in times of war, and mothers who have sons to lose, know better.

Our good father at Washington—for I presume he is now our father as well as yours, since King George[2] has moved his boundaries further north—our great and good father, I say, sends us word that if we do as he desires he will protect us. His brave warriors will be to us a bristling[3] wall of strength, and his wonderful ships of war will fill our harbors so that our ancient enemies far to the northward—the Hydas and Tsimpsians—will cease to frighten our women, children, and old men. Then in reality will he be our father and we his children. But can that ever be? Your God is not our God!

Your God loves your people and hates mine. He folds his strong protecting arms lovingly about the pale face and leads him by the hand as a father leads his infant son—but He has forsaken His red children—if they really are His. Our God, the Great Spirit, seems also to have forsaken us. Your God makes your people wax strong every day. Soon they will fill all the land. Our people are ebbing away like a rapidly <u>receding</u> tide that will never return. The white man's God cannot love our people or He would protect them. They seem to be orphans who can look nowhere for help. How then can we be brothers? How can your God become our God and renew our prosperity and awaken in us dreams of returning greatness? If we have a common heavenly father He must be partial—for He came to His paleface children. We never saw Him. He gave you laws but had no word for his red children whose teeming multitudes once filled this vast continent as stars fill the firmament.[4] No; we are two distinct races with separate origins and separate destinies. There is little in common between us.

To us the ashes of our ancestors are sacred and their resting place is hallowed ground.[5] You wander far from the graves of your ancestors and seemingly without regret. Your religion was written upon tables of stone by the iron finger of your God[6] so that you could not

---

2. **King George.** George III was king of England at the time the United States declared its independence in 1776. Native Americans may have assumed that King George was still ruling England when Seattle gave this speech in 1854.
3. **bristling.** Standing rigid and firm
4. **firmament.** Sky seen as an arch
5. **hallowed ground.** Sacred ground
6. **written...iron finger of your God.** Seattle is referring to the stone tablets containing the Ten Commandments.

re • ced • ing (ri sēd´ iŋ) *adj.,* gradually moving away

forget. The Red Man could never comprehend nor remember it. Our religion is the traditions of our ancestors—the dreams of our old men, given them in the solemn hours of night by the Great Spirit; and the visions of our sachems,[7] and is written in the hearts of our people.

Your dead cease to love you and the land of their nativity[8] as soon as they pass the portals of[9] the tomb and wander way beyond the stars. They are soon forgotten and never return. Our dead never forget the beautiful world that gave them being. They still love its <u>verdant</u> valleys, its murmuring rivers, its magnificent mountains, <u>sequestered</u> vales and verdant-lined lakes and bays, and ever yearn in tender, fond affection over the lonely hearted living, and often return from the Happy Hunting Ground[10] to visit, guide, console and comfort them.

Day and night cannot dwell together. The red man has ever fled the approach of the white man, as the morning mist flees before the morning sun.

However, your proposition seems fair and I think that my people will accept it and will retire to the reservation you offer them. Then we will dwell in peace, for the words of the great white chief seem to be the words of nature speaking to my people out of dense darkness.

It matters little where we pass the <u>remnant</u> of our days. They will not be many. The Indians' night promises to be dark. Not a single star of hope hovers above his horizon. Sad-voiced winds moan in the distance. Grim fate seems to be on the red man's trail, and wherever he goes he will hear the approaching footsteps of his fell destroyer and prepare <u>stolidly</u> to meet his doom, as does the wounded doe that hears the approaching footsteps of the hunter.

A few more moons. A few more winters—and not one of the descendants of the mighty hosts that once moved over this broad land or lived in happy homes, protected by the Great Spirit, will remain to mourn over the graves of a people—once more powerful and hopeful than yours. But why should I mourn at the untimely fate of my people? Tribe follows tribe, and nation follows nation, like the waves of the sea. It is the order of nature, and regret is useless. Your time of decay may be distant, but it will surely come, for even the white man whose God walked and talked with him as friend with friend, cannot be <u>exempt</u> from the common destiny. We may be brothers after all. We will see.

We will ponder your proposition and when we decide we will let you know. But should we accept it, I here and now make this condition that we will not be denied the privilege without <u>molestation</u> of visiting at any time the tombs of our ancestors, friends, and children. Every part of this soil is sacred in the estimation of my people. Every hillside, every valley, every plain and grove, has been hallowed by some sad or happy event in days long vanished. Even the rocks, which seem to be dumb and dead as they swelter in the sun along the silent shore, thrill with memories of stirring

---

7. **sachems.** Holy men
8. **nativity.** Birth
9. **portals of.** Opening to
10. **Happy Hunting Ground.** Heaven; place of afterlife

ver • dant (vʉr´ d'nt) *adj.,* green with vegetation
se • ques • tered (si kwes´ tərd) *adj.,* secluded
rem • nant (rem´ nənt) *n.,* small remaining part
stol • id • ly (stä´ ləd lē) *adv.,* with little emotion
ex • empt (ig zem[p]t´) *adj.,* excused; released
mo • les • ta • tion (mō' les' tā´ shən) *n.,* the annoyance of or disturbance of with hostile intent

events connected with the lives of my people, and the very dust upon which you now stand responds more lovingly to their footsteps than to yours, because it is rich with the blood of our ancestors and our bare feet are conscious of the sympathetic touch. Our departed braves, fond mothers, glad, happy-hearted maidens, and even our little children who lived here and rejoiced here for a brief season, will love these somber solitudes and at eventide[11] they greet shadowy returning spirits. And when the last red man shall have perished, and the memory of my tribe shall have become a myth among the white men, these shores will swarm with the invisible dead of my tribe, and when your children's children think themselves alone in the field, the store, the shop, upon the highway, or in the silence of the pathless woods, they will not be alone. In all the earth there is no place dedicated to solitude. At night when the streets of your cities and villages are silent and you think them deserted, they will throng with the returning hosts that once filled them and still love this beautiful land. The white man will never be alone.

Let him be just and deal kindly with my people, for the dead are not powerless. Dead, did I say? There is no death, only a change of worlds. ❖

---

11. **eventide.** Evening

When have you been in a situation where you've wanted to take revenge? How did you decide what to do? What are the benefits and drawbacks of seeking revenge? What difference can the choice to take revenge or not to take revenge make?

AFTER READING

REFER TO TEXT	REASON WITH TEXT	
1a. List the comparisons Chief Seattle makes in the first paragraph.	1b. Explain why he makes these comparisons.	**Understand** **Find meaning**
2a. State what the white chief wants. What happens to Seattle's people as a result?	2b. Examine the way Seattle feels about what the white chief wants and the way he feels about the downfall of his people.	**Apply** **Use information**
3a. Recall the description Chief Seattle gives of the relationship his people have with the land.	3b. Compare and contrast the white people's relationship with the natural world to that of the Native Americans.	**Analyze** **Take things apart**
4a. Quote the warning Seattle gives the white people.	4b. Evaluate Seattle as a leader. In your opinion, should he have agreed to the demands of the whites or refused to agree?	**Evaluate** **Make judgments**
5a. From the perspective of Chief Seattle, compare his people's religion with the religion of the white people.	5b. Summarize what Seattle thinks about the possibility of his people and white people uniting under the same God.	**Create** **Bring ideas together**

ANALYZE LITERATURE: Mood and Imagery

Make a list of images from the speech that contribute to its mood or moods. Then classify the words according to the moods they help establish. What mood or moods are reflected most strongly? Explain.

EXTEND THE TEXT

Writing Options

Creative Writing Imagine that you are Governor Stevens, the person responsible for informing Chief Seattle about the treaty that would relocate Seattle's people. After you have heard Seattle's speech, write a **letter** to President Franklin Pierce in which you summarize Seattle's main points. Also include in your letter your own impressions of the speech and how the meeting with Seattle went.

Descriptive Writing Think of a place that is important to you. Close your eyes and picture the place in your mind: What does it look like? What sounds and smells stand out? What feeling do you get when you're there? Write two **descriptive paragraphs** for a friend who has never been to that place. In your paragraphs, use imagery and sensory details to establish mood and to make the place come alive.

Collaborative Learning

Research the Authenticity of a Speech People have questioned how much of Chief Seattle's speech was actually said by the tribal leader and how much of it was embellished by Dr. Henry A. Smith, a translator who reportedly wrote down the speech thirty years after hearing it. Several versions of the speech are now in print. Together with a partner or small group, use the Internet to research one of those versions and the arguments for and against its authenticity. Then present your findings to the rest of the class in the form of an informative speech.

Media Literacy

Write a Movie Review Watch a film that portrays interactions between white people and Native Americans. Some possibilities are *The Last of the Mohicans, Little Big Man,* and *I Will Fight No More Forever.* Write a review of the movie for people who want to learn more about Native American culture and history. Would you recommend the movie for this purpose? To what degree does the movie contribute to understanding Native American culture? On what stereotypes, if any, does the movie rely?

 Go to **www.mirrorsandwindows.com** for more.

READING ASSESSMENT

1. Which of the following literary elements is used frequently in Seattle's speech?
   A. rhyme
   B. personification
   C. protagonist
   D. plot
   E. foreshadowing

2. On page 309, the word *reproach* most nearly means
   A. answer.
   B. blame.
   C. praise.
   D. request.
   E. discipline.

3. In the speech, Chief Seattle places great emphasis on which of the following?
   A. the generosity of white people
   B. the tombs of the ancestors
   C. Native American traditions of warfare
   D. future prosperity
   E. the hostile actions of white people

4. On page 311 the word *stolidly* most nearly means
   A. exuberantly.
   B. emotionlessly.
   C. cheerfully.
   D. quickly.
   E. angrily.

5. Chief Seattle requests that if his people decide to accept the offer proposal, his people must be allowed to
   A. not pay taxes to the U.S. government.
   B. collect payment for each acre of land they yield.
   C. visit the tombs of their ancestors without hassle from the U.S. government.
   D. choose the location of the reservation.
   E. None of the above

6. Imagine that you are a member of the Suquamish nation and that you were an eyewitness to the delivery of this speech. In a paragraph or two, speculate on your reactions to the words of Chief Seattle.

Prefixes, Roots, and Suffixes

A **morpheme** is a chunk of a word that has meaning. All words are made up of one or more morphemes. The four main types of morphemes are prefixes, suffixes, word roots, and base words. A **prefix** is a letter or group of letters added to the beginning of a word to change its meaning. A **suffix** is a letter or group of letters added to the end of a word to change its meaning. **Word roots** and **base words** are word parts that form the core of a word. Word roots cannot stand alone as words; base words can stand on their own.

Breaking a word into its parts can help you figure out what the word means. For example, suppose you did not know the meaning of the word *prediction*. You could break it down into three meaningful parts: prediction = *pre–* + *dict* + *–ion*

> *pre–* = a prefix meaning "before"
> *dict* = a word root meaning "say" or "tell"
> *–ion* = a suffix meaning "act of," "state of," or "result of"

Together, the parts create a word that means "the act of telling about something before it happens."

Below are charts of some common prefixes, suffixes, and word roots. Use these charts and a dictionary to complete the exercises.

Common Prefixes

Prefix	Meaning
anti– / ant–	against, opposite
de–	opposite, remove, reduce
dis–	not, opposite of
hyper–	too much, above, extreme
il–, im–, in–, ir–	not
inter–	among, between
per–	through, throughout
post–	after, later
re–	again, back
super–	above, over, exceeding
trans–	across, beyond

Common Suffixes

Noun Suffix	Meaning
–ion / –tion	action or process
–ism	act, state, or system of belief
–ment	action or process
–ness	state of

Adjective Suffix	Meaning
–able / –ible	capable of
–ive	performs or tends toward
–less	without

Verb Suffix	Meaning
–ate	make or cause to be
–ify / –fy	make or cause to be
–ize	bring about, cause to be

Common Word Roots

Word Root	Meaning
aqua	water
aud	hear
bene	good
bibl	book
chron	time
cred	believe, trust
derm	skin
dyn	force, power
fer	carry
flect / flex	bend
gress	go
hydro / hydra	water
ject	throw
locut / loqu	speak
mal	bad
morph	form
ped	foot, child
psych	mind, soul
scrib / script	write

therm	heat
tract	draw
vid / vis	see

Exercise A

For each item below, write the relevant prefix, suffix, or word root, and then identify its meaning. Some items may involve more than one word part. Use a dictionary if necessary.

1. pedagogy
2. extract
3. elation
4. disengage
5. miscalculate
6. chronometer
7. eloquence
8. psychopath
9. beatify
10. tractable
11. rustic
12. irreparable

Exercise B

List four words that contain each of the following roots. Give a brief definition of each word, showing how it is related to the meaning of the root.

1. *ject,* Latin root meaning "to throw"
2. *duc* or *duct,* Latin root meaning "to lead"
3. *port,* Latin root meaning "to carry"
4. *lect,* Greek root meaning "speak, choose"
5. *path,* Greek root meaning "feel, suffer, disease"
6. *scrib,* Latin root meaning "to write"
7. *dyn,* Greek root meaning "force, power"
8. *mal,* Latin root meaning "bad"
9. *cred,* Latin root meaning "to believe or trust"
10. *tract,* Latin root meaning "to draw"
11. *fer,* Latin root meaning "to carry"
12. *morph,* Greek root meaning "form"

Exercise C

Create a verb by combining each of the following words with a suffix. Then use the word in a sentence. Remember, you may have to alter the spelling of the word when you add a suffix.

1. glory
2. standard
3. motive
4. haste
5. familiar
6. reside
7. free
8. commence
9. lovely
10. dye
11. health
12. colloquial

EXTEND THE SKILL

Greek and Latin word roots can be found in many given names. For example, the name *Theodore* means "gift from God." It comes from the Greek roots *theo,* meaning "God," and *doro,* meaning "gift." Using Internet or library resources, research the following names to uncover their Greek or Latin roots.

- Barbara
- Dominic
- Laura
- Lucas
- Melanie
- Timothy
- Valerie
- Victor

Spelling Tip

Some suffixes are spelled differently depending on the word to which they are attached. One suffix, which means "to go" or "to yield," can be spelled as *–cede, –sede,* or *–ceed.* A good thing to remember with this specific suffix is that the only word in the English language that ends in *–sede* is *supersede.* Only the following three words end in *–ceed: exceed, proceed,* and *succeed.* Every other word that ends with the "seed" sound is spelled *–cede.*

Understanding Informational Text

INFORMATIONAL TEXT

If you wanted to find out who won last night's football game, when your favorite band is coming to town, or how to bake a cake, where would you look? Whether you use the Internet, a newspaper, or a cookbook to find out what you need to know, you are using an **informational text,** a form of nonfiction that aims to convey or explain information.

TYPES OF INFORMATIONAL TEXTS

Articles

An **article** is an informational piece of writing about a particular topic, issue, event, or series of events. Articles usually appear in newspapers, popular magazines, or professional journals, or on websites. An *editorial* is a magazine or newspaper article that gives the opinions of the editors or publishers. A *review* is an article that is a critical evaluation of a work, such as a book, play, movie, or musical performance or recording.

How-to-Writing

How-to-writing does exactly that—tells you, in detail, how to do something. Some how-to documents use numbered lists to give instructions; others explain procedures with diagrams or in paragraph form. "How to Write a Short Story" (page 333) uses numbered steps followed by explanations.

Websites

A website is an electronic source of information that is available through the Internet. Anybody can create a website, and the information found there is very rarely monitored or censored. Websites that are created by credible organizations or experts usually contain trustworthy information that could serve as a valuable research source. However, many websites also contain misinformation. Make sure to evaluate the credibility of what you find by checking it against authorized sources.

Graphic Aids

Charts, graphs, maps, diagrams, spreadsheets, drawings, and illustrations are visual materials that present information in understandable ways. When you work with a graphic, look for elements such as its title, labels, column or row headings, a key or legend, a scale or unit of measurement, and its source.

READING CRITICALLY

Just because an article is printed in a reputable newspaper or magazine doesn't mean all the information is reliable or presented objectively. When you read an article critically, you first look for the facts and then look beyond the facts at what the writer is trying to say. Ask yourself these questions:

- What is the writer's main idea? Is it clear?
- What evidence does the writer give to support his or her main idea? For example, does the article contain facts and statistics, quotations from experts, or statements from eyewitnesses?
- Does the evidence come from reliable sources?
- How much evidence is presented? Is it convincing?
- Is there another side of the story? What is a possible opposing viewpoint?

Distinguish Fact from Opinion

A **fact** is a statement that can be proven by direct observation or supported by reliable resources. Every statement of fact is either true or false. An **opinion,** on the other hand, expresses an attitude or a desire, not a fact about the world. You can agree or disagree with an opinion, but not prove it to be true or false.

Opinions can take different forms: *value statements, policy statements,* or *predictions.* Value statements use judgment words, such as *good, bad, nice, cheap, ugly,* and *hopeless.* Policy statements express rules or ideas about how things should be. Words such as *should, should not, must,* or *must not* are often used. Predictions make statements about the future and are signaled by words such as *may, might,* and *could.* Because the future is largely unknowable, predictions are considered opinions.

Both facts and opinions require analysis on the part of the active reader. When evaluating a fact, ask yourself whether it can be proven through observation or by checking a reliable, unbiased source. An opinion can also be evaluated by checking the facts that support it.

Recognize Bias

Something to look out for while you read critically is a writer's bias. **Bias** is a personal judgment about something, or a mental leaning in one direction or the other. You may think bias is a negative thing, but everyone has it in some form.

Look for What's Missing

You should also direct a critical eye to the facts that a writer may have left out. Look for quotations from experts that seem to be out of context or seem inconsistent with other statements the experts have made.

When an informational text is making an argument for or against something, make sure all three parts of the argument exist. The three parts of a good argument are 1) the author's assertion, or statement of belief; 2) facts, figures, statistics, and examples to support the argument; and 3) the opposing viewpoint of the argument, also known as the counterargument. If any of these three parts are missing, you can be fairly certain the argument is flawed.

Be Aware of Propaganda

The intentional use of false arguments to persuade others is called **propaganda.** Propaganda most often appears in nonfiction. There are many types of faulty arguments of which a discerning reader should be aware. They are listed in the chart below.

TYPE OF ARGUMENT	DEFINITION	EXAMPLE	ANALYSIS
Glittering Generality	statement given to make something sound more appealing than it actually is	This video game system is the best one ever made!	Nothing in this statement tells why the video game system is the best.
Spin	a technique of creating manipulative and misleading statements in order to slant public perception of the news	The accident was a minor incident because only twenty-five people were injured.	Someone is interpreting the accident as minor so the public will see it as such.
Stereotype	an overgeneralization about a group of people that is always based on a lack of knowledge or experience	All teenagers want to do is find ways to get into trouble.	There is no proof for this statement, as some teenagers do get into trouble, but others do not.
Circular Reasoning	the error of trying to support an opinion by restating it in different words	That adventure film was exciting because it was full of action.	The "reason" given for the film being exciting is really just another way of saying it was exciting.
Loaded Words	words that stir up strong feelings, either positive or negative	The new coach is incredibly kind and a lot of fun.	This statement is not a reasonable evaluation of the coach's skills or abilities.
Bandwagon Appeal	statement that plays to a person's desire to be part of the crowd — to be like everyone else and do what everyone else is doing	Those who want to be cool wear Star jeans.	This statement doesn't prove, or even say, anything about the quality of the clothing.

We Heard It Before We Saw Anything

BUILD BACKGROUND

Historical Context The tsunami of December 2004 has been called one of the most devastating natural disasters in recorded history. The giant waves, triggered by a severe, undersea earthquake, killed approximately 200,000 people and made millions homeless. A large geographical area in Southeast Asia was affected. Following the disaster, international relief efforts were mounted on an unprecedented scale. In his article **"We Heard It Before We Saw Anything,"** reporter **Julian West** gives an account of the tsunami from the point of view of the people who witnessed it. This article appeared in the *National Post*, a Canadian newspaper, on December 27, 2004.

Reader's Context Have you, or has someone you know, been an eyewitness to a natural disaster? How would you put the power of natural forces, such as wind, fire, or water, into words?

ANALYZE LITERATURE: News Article and Bias

A **news article** reports facts and gives background information about an event that has occurred recently. Journalists who write news articles often structure the text to answer "the five W's," or the questions *Who? What? When? Where?* and *Why?* Another question a news article commonly answers is *How?*

An unreasonable prejudice or mind-set on one side of an issue or another is called **bias.** When journalists report the news, they should do so in an unbiased fashion, or objectively, so that readers can use the facts to form their own conclusions. Read this article critically, looking for bias both in what is written and in what is not stated.

SET PURPOSE

Think about what you know about tsunamis. Then write down a question about something you would like to know about tsunamis. Read the article with the purpose of finding the answer to your question. Start by looking for answers to the questions *Who? What? When? Where? Why?* and *How?* If the article does not answer your question, try to find the answer in another source.

USE READING SKILLS

Fact and Opinion A **fact** is a statement that can be proven by direct observation or a reliable reference guide. Every statement of fact is either true or false. An **opinion** is a statement that expresses an attitude or a desire, not a fact about the world. An opinion can be supported with facts. As you read the news article, distinguish fact from opinion by creating a Fact and Opinion Chart like the one shown below.

Fact: Proof:
Opinion: Support:

PREVIEW VOCABULARY

Use the context clues in the sentences below to figure out the meanings of the underlined words from the selection.

1. Mia <u>unleashed</u> a flood of tears when she heard that her pet hedgehog had died.
2. Jordan <u>appealed</u> to his mother not to enforce the punishment for breaking curfew and to let him go out with his friends.
3. The small tidepool was <u>engulfed</u> with water each time a wave came ashore.
4. Ricardo <u>nestled</u> under heavy blankets in order to keep warm during the camping trip.
5. "Fay, by standing in the doorway, you are <u>hampering</u> my ability to leave the room," said Aidan crossly.

We Heard It Before We Saw Anything

National Post   December 27, 2004

One million people affected by disaster, government says

A News Article by **Julian West**

COLOMBO—The three little girls collecting mussels on the beach in Tangalle, in southeastern Sri Lanka, never had a chance. The wall of water—10 metres high according to some accounts— must have swept over them even before they had time to be frightened.

"We saw them floating in the bay," said Channa Perera, who works for a local real estate agent and had been on higher ground when the tidal wave struck. "There were a lot of other bodies too— mostly fishermen who had been out at sea."

All along Sri Lanka's coast there were reports of devastation as the tsunami struck. Children, fishermen, tourists, hotels, homes and cars were swept away by walls of water as high as a house <u>unleashed</u> by the earthquake.

Government officials said more than one million people, or about 5% of the Indian Ocean island's population, had been affected by the disaster— which came just two weeks after severe monsoon flooding damaged crops and homes.

"It is a huge tragedy and it is unfolding all the time," said Lalith Weerathunga, secretary to the Prime Minister. "The death toll is going up all the time."

More than 4,000 people were reported dead as of last night. About 170 children at an orphanage and a Catholic priest were feared

un • leash (un' lēsh′) v., to free from; to let loose

SCIENCE CONNECTION

Tsunami of 2004 A tsunami is a huge ocean wave or series of waves, usually the result of an earthquake. The Indian Ocean tsunami that occurred on December 26, 2004, was one of the deadliest in recorded history. It was triggered by an earthquake of magnitude 9.0, which is estimated by the U.S. Geologic Survey to have unleashed a force with the energy of more than 20,000 Hiroshima-type atomic bombs. The epicenter of this earthquake was in the ocean west of the Indonesian island of Sumatra. The tsunami was responsible for more than 200,000 deaths in Indonesia, Thailand, Sri Lanka, Malaysia, India, and islands in the Indian Ocean, with millions more injured or homeless.

Indian Ocean Area

the international community for help.

The first many coastal residents knew of the tidal wave that would <u>engulf</u> the island's entire southern and eastern seaboard was when the area was shaken by a massive tremor at about 8 a.m. yesterday.

"We heard it before we saw anything. Everything in the room was shaking," said Piero Crida, an artist who has lived in Talpe, a small beach resort near Galle, for several years. Mr. Crida added: "It's total devastation here. The cafes, the hotels, the small beach shacks have all been destroyed."

Sri Lanka's southern coast is heavily built up with small towns and tourist resorts <u>nestled</u> along the length of the winding beach road from Colombo southward. This is the height of the tourist season and beach resorts along the southern and eastern coasts were jammed with people on holiday.

Although exact casualty figures from each district were not known yesterday—telephones throughout the island were down— as many as 1,000 people were believed to have died in the town of Galle alone.

On the East Coast, which bore the brunt of the tidal wave, rescue efforts will be <u>hampered</u> by bad roads and an infrastructure devastated by 20 years of civil war. Local media reported that plastic landmines, sown during the war, had been uprooted by the floods.

dead after tidal waves pounded it in the town of Mullaithivu, reports said. In the seaside town of Kalutara, holidaymakers staying at a luxury hotel on the seafront described a three-metre wall of water crashing on to the coast.

"We were sitting by the water when people started shouting a wave was coming in," said visiting British car salesman Richard Freeman. "We left everything behind and ran inside."

So great was the force of the water that it not only swept away cafes and guesthouses, but changed the entire geography of the beach. "The sand is now about 15 feet deeper than it was," Mr. Perera said.

President Chandrika Bandaranaike Kumaratunga, who is on holiday in England, has declared a national emergency and <u>appealed</u> to

---

ap • peal (ə pēl´) v., to make an earnest request
en • gulf (in gulf´) v., to flow over and enclose
nes • tle (ne´ səl) v., to settle snugly or comfortably
ham • per (ham´ pər) v., to interfere with the operation of

Devastation after the tsunami.

Although there is a substantial naval presence in the port of Trincomalee, in the east, and the navy is nominally in charge of manning services throughout the eastern coast, Sri Lanka as a whole has no disaster management. Government officials were appealing to

NOTABLE TSUNAMIS

Tsunamis have been reported since ancient times. The first recorded occurred off Syria in 2000 BCE. The most devastating have generated waves up to 35 metres high. Among the most notable:

JULY 17, 1998	An offshore quake triggers a wave that strikes the north coast of Papua-New Guinea killing 2,000 people.
AUGUST 16, 1976	A tsunami kills more than 5,000 people in the Moro Gulf region of the Philippines.
MARCH 28, 1964	Good Friday earthquake in Alaska sends out a wave killing 107 people in the state, four in Oregon and 11 in California.
MAY 22, 1960	A wave up to 35 feet high kills 1,000 in Chile and causes damage in Hawaii, where 61 die, and in the Philippines, Okinawa and Japan.
APRIL 1, 1946	Alaskan quake generates tsunami that destroys North Cape Lighthouse, killing five. Hours later the wave hits Hilo, Hawaii, killing 159.
JAN. 31, 1906	A devastating offshore quake submerges part of Tumaco, Colombia, and washes away every house on the coast between Rioverde, Ecuador, and Micay, Colombia. Death toll estimated at 500 to 1,500.
DEC. 17, 1896	A tsunami washes away part of the main boulevard of Santa Barbara, Calif.
JUNE 15, 1896	The Sanriku tsunami strikes Japan without warning. A wave estimated at more than 70 feet high hits a crowd gathered for a religious festival, killing more than 26,000.
AUG. 27, 1883	The volcano Krakatau generates a wave that sweeps over the shores of nearby Java and Sumatra, killing 36,000.

The Daily Telegraph

people not to crowd the beaches— many locals had headed for the coast to sight-see—and urged them to go to hospitals to help identify the dead.

"I think this is the worst-ever natural disaster in Sri Lanka," said N. D. Hettiarachchi, an official coordinating the government's response. ❖

How is seeing something in person different from seeing something on television or reading about it? What impact did this article have on you?

REFER TO TEXT ▶ ▶ ▶ ▶	▶ REASON WITH TEXT	
1a. Recall the natural disaster that is the main focus for this article.	1b. Discuss why you think the writer begins the article with a description of three little girls collecting mussels on the beach.	**Understand** **Find meaning**
2a. Quote how Lalith Weerathunga, the Prime Minister's secretary, describes the tragedy.	2b. What mood or atmosphere does Lalith Weerathunga's comment help to create?	**Apply** **Use information**
3a. Identify three other direct quotations that Julian West uses in this newspaper article.	3b. Analyze how the direct quotations contribute to the tone and overall effect of the article.	**Analyze** **Take things apart**
4a. List the factual details West reports about the southern and eastern coasts of Sri Lanka.	4b. Describe the effect you think West is trying to create by including these details.	**Evaluate** **Make judgments**
5a. According to the final paragraphs of the article, what appeal is being made by government officials to the people?	5b. Do you think the government appeal is realistic? Do people have a natural impulse to view disasters firsthand, in your opinion? Explain your answer.	**Create** **Bring ideas together**

ANALYZE LITERATURE: News Article and Bias

What are the answers to the "five W's" of this article? Does the author of this newspaper article show any signs of bias? Explain your answer.

INFORMATIONAL TEXT CONNECTION

The author of a news article has a number of choices to make. For example, he or she can tell a story using an objective, third-person point of view. Or a story can be narrated primarily in the first person, through the perspective of eyewitnesses who tell the tale in their own words. In **"Like Being Spun in a Giant Washer,"** author **David Williams** has chosen the second method, as he uses quoted statements from several eyewitnesses to the tsunami.

Daily Mail, London   Dec. 27, 2004

Like Being Spun in a Giant Washer

British girl tells how she dived into path of the tsunami

A News Article by David Williams

THAILAND—Becky Ralph gave a final check to her oxygen tank then rolled backwards into the warm Andaman Sea with five other divers.

Moments later the 25-year-old British art student was hit by the first in a series of huge waves.

"There seemed to be a shudder and then a giant whoosh," said Becky, an experienced diver from Chichester, West Sussex. "I was shot out of the water, back in again and then began to spin. It was like being in a washing machine.

I just went round and round in fast spin, gulping water and fighting to stay alive. I was totally helpless and thought I would drown." Becky, who is on a round-the-world tour with her Australian boyfriend, was visiting the Thai island of Ko Phi Phi, where the Leonardo DiCaprio film *The Beach* was filmed.

It was hit by a 16 ft. wall of water, sweeping 200 holiday bungalows into the water together with holidaymakers, many of whom had been sitting on their terraces enjoying a late breakfast.

"After a few seconds I stopped spinning and began to try to swim but it was impossible," Becky added. "I was just dragged along. The debris of what I think were two boats washed over me.

"Two people, a man and a woman, swept past, one was bleeding from his head and his

eyes were closed. I tried to reach him but he disappeared.

"Everything was moving so fast but I remember a pair of sunglasses with a pink band which someone must have been wearing go past; it was surreal.

"There was a man, a fisherman I think, clinging to an upturned boat and he kept shouting.

"My air tanks were off and I struggled to reach the surface and to control my breathing. I remember my heart thumping, thumping against my suit.

"Suddenly, it all seemed to slow down and I was able to swim to the shore. There was blood coming from one of my ears.

"I think my diving training and luck were all that saved me. As I went to shore, there were two people on what was the remains of the beach and they were being given the kiss of life. A woman was pleading with one of the men not to leave her." Becky's boyfriend, who did not go diving, escaped unhurt.

Elsewhere along the beach, she said, dazed holidaymakers were calling the names of their loved ones. A boy was being cut free from a fishing net. She said she had no idea what had happened to her fellow divers, one of whom was British.

"I should be dead. I am so lucky. I am in shock and about an hour after leaving the water began to shake. I'll look on life very, very differently after this." Another British girl, 24-year-old Amy Harding, works as a diving instructor on Ko Phi Phi.

She was giving a lesson when her group was swept ashore and landed on a hotel roof. She told her brother Mike, in Neston, Cheshire, that she was unhurt but her Israeli boyfriend was missing.

In nearby Phuket, where 48 Britons were injured, company director Christos Angelides had just taken his seat at the breakfast table in the Pounds 300-a-night Sheraton Grande Laguna Hotel. His wife Suzanne began screaming at him to run.

"I looked out of the window and saw a huge tidal wave about 100 metres away and moving towards the beach fast," said father-of-two Mr. Angelides, a director with the clothing and interiors company Next, from Solihull, West Midlands.

"It was the most terrifying moment of my life. We grabbed the children and rushed to the highest part of the hotel, which is the reception area."

The whole dining room cleared within seconds.

"The wave went straight over the beach area and just cleaned everything out. There were lots of shops and restaurants there.

"It hit four rooms at the front of our hotel. They were smashed to pieces.

"The wave was mesmerising. I just stared at it. It's not like a wave you would see someone surfing.

"There was no foam and it wasn't that high. It's just as if a huge body of water is being pushed along at great speed. It swamped everything.

"We felt a slight tremor about two hours before the wave hit, which must have been the initial earthquake." Tim Acton, 25, from Harwich, Essex, was in Khao Lak, 40 miles south of Phuket. He said: "There was just a huge wall of water that came straight up the beach.

"People tried desperately to escape but it was moving too fast. People were caught up in it and just flung around. There was devastation everywhere.

"Buildings have been destroyed, cars overturned and total chaos." Along the miles of devastated Asian coastline, other Britons were telling their stories of survival. ❖

REFER TO TEXT ▶ ▶ ▶ ▶	▶ REASON WITH TEXT	
1a. Where was Becky Ralph when the tsunami hit?	1b. Summarize Becky Ralph's story. What impact do you think the tsunami had on her? Explain.	**Understand** **Find meaning**
2a. List the eyewitnesses who give an account of the tsunami.	2b. Compare and contrast the accounts. Which do you find most compelling? Which leave you with additional questions? Explain your answers.	**Analyze** **Take things apart**
3a. Identify three facts and three opinions in the article.	3b. Evaluate how effective you find the method of narrative reporting, or telling a news story from the point of view of witnesses. What are the advantages of this method? What is lost?	**Evaluate** **Make judgments**

TEXT ←TO→ TEXT CONNECTION

Compare and contrast the method each writer uses to report on the tsunami. Which account do you find more vivid? Which is more meaningful to you? Use support from the articles to explain your answers.

EXTEND THE TEXT

Writing Options

Creative Writing Imagine that you are the president of Sri Lanka. Write a **press release** in which you declare a national state of emergency for your country in the aftermath of the tsunami. A press release is an announcement delivered to the press by a government agency or other organization. Be sure to use the facts gathered from both news articles to help support the need for a declaration of a national state of emergency.

Expository Writing What questions about the tsunami does "We Heard It Before We Saw Anything" leave unanswered? Imagine that you have a chance to interview Julian West, the author of the selection. Write some **interview notes** to use as a reference guide during your conversation with him. In your notes, identify the questions you would like to ask, and discuss reasons for the importance of these questions.

Collaborative Learning

Create Public Awareness What can be done to prepare people who may lie in the path of a tsunami? Together with a small group, use Internet and library resources to research the ideas and opinions of experts. Then, think about how you would get this information to the people who need it, as many of the people affected by the 2004 tsunami live in developing countries. Create a public awareness campaign that outlines what information you would get to people and how you would relate the information to them.

Lifelong Learning

Profile Sri Lanka Using an atlas, an almanac, an encyclopedia, and other reference works, develop a country profile of Sri Lanka. Include material about some or all of the following topics: geographical location, population statistics, recent historical events, religion, the economy, and culture. You may also include maps and photographs. When you have finished your research, post your profile on the class bulletin board.

 Go to **www.mirrorsandwindows.com** for more.

READING ASSESSMENT

1. The greatest impact of the tsunami occurred in which part of Sri Lanka?
   A. the southern coast
   B. the northwestern coast
   C. the northern coast
   D. the western coast
   E. the eastern coast

2. Which of the following statements is *not* supported by information in the selection?
   A. Sri Lanka as a whole has no disaster management.
   B. Rescue efforts would be hampered by bad roads.
   C. The tsunami caused a large buildup of sand on some beaches.
   D. The tsunami affected only about 1 percent of Sri Lanka's population.
   E. None of the above

3. On page 320, the word *hamper* most nearly means
   A. hasten.
   B. enlarge.
   C. anger.
   D. impede.
   E. None of the above`

4. Which of the following statements from "We Heard It Before We Saw Anything" contains an opinion?
   A. More than 4,000 people were reported dead as of last night.
   B. "The sand is now about 15 feet deeper than it was," Mr. Perera said.
   C. "I think this is the worst-ever natural disaster in Sri Lanka," said N. D. Hettiarachchi, an official coordinating the government's response.
   D. Tsunamis have been reported since ancient times.
   E. President Chandrika Bandaranaike Kumaratunga, who is on holiday in England, has declared a national emergency and appealed to the international community for help.

6. Evaluate Julian West's article. What additional information, if any, would you like to see included? Which details, if any, should be excluded? Is the tone objective? If you were a news reporter writing a story about a tragic event, like the 2004 tsunami, how would you approach the situation?

GRAMMAR & STYLE

Sentence Fragments and Run-Ons

A sentence contains a subject and a verb and should express a complete thought. A **sentence fragment** is a phrase or clause that does not express a complete thought but has been punctuated as though it did.

EXAMPLES

complete sentence: A tsunami is a huge ocean wave or series of waves that is usually the result of an earthquake.

sentence fragment: Is usually the result of an earthquake. (The subject is missing.)

sentence fragment: A tsunami. (The verb is missing.)

sentence fragment: A huge ocean wave. (The subject and verb are missing.)

In a **sentence run-on,** two or more sentences have been run together as if they were one complete sentence. There are two types of sentence run-ons: a fused sentence and a comma splice. In a *fused sentence,* no punctuation mark is used between the sentences. In a *comma splice,* a comma has been placed between the two joined sentences and thus used incorrectly.

EXAMPLES

fused sentence: The temperature was below zero on Sunday morning we went skiing anyway.

comma splice: The temperature was below zero on Sunday morning, we went skiing anyway.

You can correct a sentence run-on by dividing it into two separate sentences. You can also correct a run-on by using a semicolon or by joining the sentences with a comma and a coordinating conjunction.

EXAMPLES

The temperature was below zero on Sunday morning. We went skiing anyway.

The temperature was below zero on Sunday morning; we went skiing anyway.

The temperature was below zero on Sunday morning, but we went skiing anyway.

Good writers generally avoid using sentence fragments and run-ons. However, writers sometimes use fragments to create a certain effect. Notice in the following example how the sentence fragment "A very long day" creates a feeling of weariness and adds emphasis to the fact that people had a difficult task to do.

EXAMPLE

It was a long day. A very long day. Everyone was exhausted from trying to clean up after the earthquake.

What Great Writers Do

In the following passage, notice how newspaper writer Julian West avoids using sentence fragments and run-ons by using two separate sentences.

All along Sri Lanka's coast there were reports of devastation as the tsunami struck. Children, fishermen, tourists, hotels, homes and cars were swept away by walls of water as high as a house unleashed by the earthquake.

REVIEW TERMS

- **sentence fragment:** a phrase or clause that does not express a complete thought but has been presented as though it did
- **sentence run-on:** two or more sentences that have been run together as if they were one complete thought
- **fused sentence:** type of run-on in which no punctuation mark is used between two sentences
- **comma splice:** type of run-on in which a comma is placed between two joined sentences

Identify Sentence Fragments and Run-Ons

Identify each of the following as a sentence fragment, a sentence run-on, or a correct sentence.

1. The tsunami of 2004 affected more than one million people the water swept away people's homes and means of making a living.
2. The first tsunami recorded occurred in 2000 BCE off the coast of Syria.
3. Seems very terrible for everyone.
4. A tsunami is triggered by an offshore earthquake.
5. Men, women, and children all died in the tsunami, they never saw it coming.
6. One of the most powerful earthquakes recorded took place in Chile in 1960. Registered 9.5 on the Richter scale.
7. Sri Lanka's southern coast is an area many tourists visit; the tsunami struck at the height of the tourist season.
8. The force of the tsunami was so great it destroyed buildings instantly people did not have any time to react.
9. In 1896, a tsunami hit Santa Barbara, California. Tragic thing.
10. After the tsunami, many countries around the world sent people and resources to help the survivors.

Correct Sentence Fragments and Sentence Run-Ons

Rewrite each item below to correct errors.

1. Seems very unpleasant to me.
2. Sitting in the middle of the backyard, with ears swiveling at the slightest sound.
3. Each time the unemployment rate rose, the stock market fell investors became very nervous.
4. The end of each chapter a fascinating, ironic reversal.
5. The mailbox looked inviting after so many weeks away it was overflowing with magazines.

Improve a Paragraph

Rewrite the paragraph shown below, correcting any sentence fragments or run-ons that you find.

A wide variety of natural disasters plague the populations of the world, they are so dangerous because they often happen unexpectedly. Tornados, floods, earthquakes, mudslides, tsunamis, and so on. What is the best way to prepare for a natural disaster? Early warning systems exist not all parts of the world have access to them, though. Even with early warning systems. Not all the consequences of natural disasters can be avoided. Property is still lost. These systems can save lives, though, people know to seek shelter.

Avoid Sentence Fragments and Run-Ons in Your Writing

Think about a time you've witnessed firsthand or know someone who has witnessed a natural disaster. What was the experience like? Write a paragraph describing how you found out about the natural disaster, what you did to protect yourself from it, and what the results of the natural disaster were. When you have finished a draft, exchange your writing with a classmate and have him or her check it for sentence fragments and run-ons. Correct any errors.

EXTEND THE SKILL

Imagine you are teaching an English Language Learner about writing in complete sentences. How would you explain fragments and run-ons to him or her? Prepare a lesson on sentence fragments and run-ons for a class of English Language Learners. Make sure the lesson is interesting and complete.

Short Assignments

BUILD BACKGROUND

Literary Context Anne Lamott's essay **"Short Assignments"** is from her popular book *Bird by Bird: Some Instructions on Writing and Life.* In *Bird by Bird,* Lamott wants to share "everything that has helped me along the way and what [writing] is like for me on a daily basis." In doing so, she also gives readers "the excuse to do things, go places and explore." "Short Assignments" focuses on one of the most common obstacles to writing.

Reader's Context What problems have you encountered when you have been given a writing assignment?

ANALYZE LITERATURE: Coherence and Colloquialism

Coherence is the logical arrangement and progression of ideas in a piece of writing. Writers achieve coherence by presenting their ideas in a logical sequence and by using transitions to show how their ideas are connected to one another.

A **colloquialism** is an informal use of language, such as "hey" for "hello." The use of colloquialisms helps to establish the tone, or emotional attitude.

SET PURPOSE

When you think of how-to writing, what do you expect to read? Lengthy instructions? A recipe? A diagram with brief explanations? Read "Short Assignments" with the purpose of seeing how it compares with your ideas of what how-to writing should be. Consider especially the way Lamott's writing is organized and her use of colloquialisms. How does the language, tone, and organization of the piece compare with other types of how-to writing?

MEET THE AUTHOR

Anne Lamott (b. 1954) was raised in northern California. She credits her father, also a writer, for teaching her to "be bold and original and to let [herself] make mistakes." Her father's example and her own love of reading helped her realize early the sense of power and connection that good books can elicit. "I came to know," she writes in *Bird by Bird,* "what it was like to have someone speak for me, to close a book with a sense of both triumph and relief, one lonely isolated social animal finally making contact." Lamott's first novel, about her father's death, was published when she was twenty-six. In addition to *Bird by Bird* (1994), Lamott has written five novels, as well as a memoir and several collections of essays.

USE READING SKILLS

Draw Conclusions When you draw conclusions, you gather pieces of information and decide what that information means for you. In this selection, one writer shares her writing process and gives advice on how to conquer obstacles to writing. As you read, record notes on Lamott's advice in the first column of an Application Chart like the one below. In the second column, draw conclusions about what the advice means for you as a writer.

Writing Advice from Anne Lamott	How I Can Apply This Advice
Focus on one small thing at a time.	Start by writing one paragraph.

PREVIEW VOCABULARY

A **synonym** is a word that has the same or nearly the same meaning as another word. For the vocabulary words below, choose the letter that identifies the correct synonym. Use a dictionary to check word meanings if necessary.

1. leer
   A. ogle
   B. replenish
   C. invigorate
2. arresting
   A. halting
   B. striking
   C. gazing

> *"Bird by bird, buddy. Just take it bird by bird."*

Short Assignments

How-to Writing by
Anne Lamott

The first useful concept is the idea of short assignments.

Often when you sit down to write, what you have in mind is an autobiographical novel about your childhood, or a play about the immigrant experience, or a history of—oh, say—say women. But this is like trying to scale a glacier. It's hard to get your footing, and your fingertips get all red and frozen and torn up. Then your mental illnesses arrive at the desk like your sickest, most secretive relatives. And they pull up chairs in a semicircle around the computer, and they try to be quiet but you

know they are there with their weird coppery breath, <u>leering</u> at you behind your back.

What I do at this point, as the panic mounts and the jungle drums begin beating and I realize that the well has run dry and that my future is behind me and I'm going to have to get a job only I'm completely unemployable, is to stop. First I try to breathe, because I'm either sitting there panting like a lapdog or I'm unintentionally making slow

---

leer (lir) *v.*, cast a sidelong glance that is lustful, knowing, or mischievous

NATIONAL BESTSELLER

Anne Lamott
Author of Operating Instructions

b i r d
b y
b i r d

Some Instructions on Writing and Life

***Bird by Bird with Annie* Documentary** Lamott is the subject of the documentary *Bird by Bird with Annie*. Director Freida Lee Mock wanted to make a film about Lamott after hearing her speak at a writer's conference. Mock says, "I was struck by her raucous humor, which was not ego-driven, and by her story of survival."

The film covers a year in Lamott's life. Lamott talks about her childhood: being shy, feeling different, and being teased and rejected. She also talks about being an alcoholic, a mother, a writer, and a born-again Christian. Mock's goal for the film was for viewers to enjoy it and "gain some insight into themselves about humor, life, writing, creativity, artistry, spirituality, acceptance, diversity, lifestyles and surviving."

Lamott's advice to writers is to take it "bird by bird"; Mock's advice to aspiring filmmakers is "seize the moment and just do it."

asthmatic death rattles. So I just sit there for a minute, breathing slowly, quietly. I let my mind wander. After a moment I may notice that I'm trying to decide whether or not I am too old for orthodontia[1] and whether right now would be a good time to make a few calls, and then I start to think about learning to use makeup and how maybe I could find some boyfriend who is not a total and complete fixer-upper and then my life would be totally great and I'd be happy all the time, and then I think about all the people I should have called back before I sat down to work, and how I should probably at least check in with my agent and tell him this great idea I have and see if *he* thinks it's a good idea, and see if *he* thinks I need orthodontia—if that is what he is actually thinking whenever we have lunch together. Then I think about someone I'm really annoyed with, or some financial problem that is driving me crazy, and decide that I must resolve this before I get down to today's work. So I become a dog with a chew toy, worrying it for a while, wrestling it to the ground, flinging it over my shoulder, chasing it, licking it, chewing it, flinging it back over my shoulder. I stop just short of actually barking. But all of this only takes somewhere between one and two minutes, so I haven't actually wasted that much time. Still, it leaves me winded. I go back to trying to breathe, slowly and calmly, and I finally notice the one-inch picture frame that I put on my desk to remind me of short assignments.

It reminds me that all I have to do is to write down as much as I can see through a one-inch picture frame. This is all I have to bite off for the time being. All I am going to do right now, for example, is write that one paragraph that sets the story in my hometown, in the late fifties, when the trains were still running. I am going to paint a picture of it, in words, on my word processor. Or all I am going to do is to describe the main character the very first time we meet her, when she first walks out the front door and onto the porch. I am not even going to describe the expression on her face when she first notices the blind dog sitting behind the wheel of her car—just what I can see through the one-inch picture frame, just one paragraph describing this woman, in the town where I grew up, the first time we encounter her.

---

1. **orthodontia.** Branch of dentistry dealing with irregularities of the teeth and their correction (as by means of braces)

E. L. Doctorow[2] once said that "writing a novel is like driving a car at night. You can see only as far as your headlights, but you can make the whole trip that way." You don't have to see where you're going, you don't have to see your destination or everything you will pass along the way. You just have to see two or three feet ahead of you. This is right up there with the best advice about writing, or life, I have ever heard.

So after I've completely exhausted myself thinking about the people I most resent in the world, and my more <u>arresting</u> financial problems, and, of course, the orthodontia, I remember to pick up the one-inch picture frame and to figure out a one-inch piece of my story to tell, one small scene, one memory, one exchange. I also remember a story that I know I've told elsewhere but that over and over helps me to get a grip: thirty years ago my older brother, who was ten years old at the time, was trying to get a report on birds written that he'd had three months to write, which was due the next day. We were out at our family cabin in Bolinas, and he was at the kitchen table close to tears, surrounded by binder paper and pencils and unopened books on birds, immobilized by the hugeness of the task ahead. Then my father sat down beside him, put his arm around my brother's

It reminds me that all I have to do is to write down as much as I can see through a one-inch picture frame.

shoulder, and said, "Bird by bird, buddy. Just take it bird by bird."

I tell this story again because it usually makes a dent in the tremendous sense of being overwhelmed that my students experience. Sometimes it actually gives them hope, and hope, as Chesterton[3] said, is the power of being cheerful in circumstances that we know to be desperate. Writing can be a pretty desperate endeavor, because it is about some of our deepest needs: our need to be visible, to be heard, our need to make sense of our lives, to wake up and grow and belong. It is no wonder if we sometimes tend to take ourselves perhaps a bit too seriously. So here is another story I tell often.

In the Bill Murray[4] movie *Stripes,* in which he joins the army, there is a scene that takes place the first night of boot camp, where Murray's platoon is assembled in the barracks. They are supposed to be getting to know their sergeant, played by Warren Oates, and one another. So each man takes a few moments to say a few things

---

2. **E. L. Doctorow.** American novelist (b. 1931)
3. **Chesterton.** G. K. Chesterton (1874–1936), a British writer and critic
4. **Bill Murray.** American film and television comedian

ar • rest • ing (ə res´ tiŋ) *adj.,* catching the attention; striking; impressive

about who he is and where he is from. Finally it is the turn of this incredibly intense, angry guy named Francis. "My name is Francis," he says. "No one calls me Francis—anyone here calls me Francis and I'll kill them. And another thing. I don't like to be touched. Anyone here ever tries to touch me, I'll kill them," at which point Warren Oates jumps in and says, "Hey—lighten up, Francis."

This is not a bad line to have taped to the wall of your office.

Say to yourself in the kindest possible way, Look, honey, all we're going to do for now is to write a description of the river at sunrise, or the young child swimming in the pool at the club, or the first time the man sees the woman he will marry. That is all we are going to do for now. We are just going to take this bird by bird. But we are going to finish this *one* short assignment. ❖

 **MIRRORS & WINDOWS** What is your attitude toward receiving unsolicited advice when you are in a frustrating situation? What compels people to want to give advice? When can unsolicited advice be beneficial? When can it be annoying?

REFER TO TEXT ▷ ▷ ▷ ▷ ▶	REASON WITH TEXT	
1a. Quote the sentence in which Lamott explains what writers often have in mind when they first sit down to write.	1b. Summarize what Lamott means when she compares one's first attempts at writing to trying to scale a glacier.	**Understand** Find meaning
2a. Identify the potential obstacles writers face when starting a new writing project.	2b. What is the ultimate goal of Lamott's advice about short assignments? What does she want writers to be able to do?	**Apply** Use information
3a. List the problems or challenges that Lamott discusses in the second paragraph of the essay.	3b. Analyze how the second paragraph creates a humorous tone as Lamott leads up to the mention of the one-inch picture frame.	**Analyze** Take things apart
4a. State the quotation Lamott uses from the novelist E. L. Doctorow. What anecdote does she tell about her older brother when he was ten years old?	4b. Compare the quotation from Doctorow and the anecdote about Lamott's brother. Which one of these passages makes the author's point more effectively, in your opinion?	**Evaluate** Make judgments
5a. Do you think Lamott's advice for writing is helpful? Why or why not?	5b. Propose how Lamott's advice might apply to other aspects of your life. In what other circumstances might the "bird by bird" approach help you to reach your goals?	**Create** Bring ideas together

ANALYZE LITERATURE: Coherence and Colloquialism

How does Lamott organize her essay? How would you evaluate its coherence? The use of colloquialisms helps to establish the tone of Lamott's writing. Identify three examples of colloquialism in this selection. How does the use of colloquialisms affect the tone of the essay?

Informational Text
CONNECTION

You probably read at least one "how-to" article every week. Some common examples of this type of nonfiction writing include owner's manuals, recipes, instructions for pet care, directions for reaching a destination on foot or by road, and directions for assembling a bicycle, toy, or appliance. Informational "how-to" articles on thousands of topics are now available on the Internet. For many young writers, the project of writing a short story may seem impossible. When the task is broken into a series of small steps, however, it may seem a lot easier. As you read **"How to Write a Short Story,"** think about the approach you might take to each step.

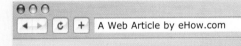

A Web Article by eHow.com

How to Write a Short Story

The model described here is the pyramid plot: The upward slope establishes setting and characters and builds tension; the tip is the climax; and the downward slope is the resolution.

Steps:

1. Choose a narrative point of view. You can write your story as if you were one of the characters (first person), as a detached narrator who presents just one character's thoughts and observations (third-person limited), or as a detached narrator who presents the thoughts and observations of several characters (third-person omniscient). A first-person point of view will refer to the central character as "I" instead of "he" or "she."

2. Create a protagonist, or main character. This should be the most developed and usually the most sympathetic character in your story.

3. Create a problem, or conflict, for your protagonist. The conflict of your story should take one of five basic forms: person vs. person, person vs. himself or herself, person vs. nature, person vs. society, or person vs. God or fate. If you choose a person vs. person conflict, create an antagonist to serve as the person your protagonist must contend with.

4. Establish believable characters and settings, with vivid descriptions and dialogue, to create a story that your readers will care about.

5. Build the story's tension by having the protagonist make several failed attempts to solve or overcome the problem. (You may want to skip this step for shorter stories.)

6. Create a crisis that serves as the last chance for the protagonist to solve his or her problem.

7. Resolve the tension by having the protagonist succeed through his or her own intelligence, creativity, courage or other positive attributes. This is usually referred to as the story's climax.

8. Extend this resolution phase, if you like, by reflecting on the action of the story and its significance to the characters or society.

Tips:

There are many possible variations of this model, all of which allow for perfectly good short stories.

Keep your diction concise, specific and active. For example, say "Steve ate the apple" instead of "The fruit was eaten by someone."

REFER TO TEXT ▶ ▶ ▶ ▶	▶ REASON WITH TEXT	
1a. List the five types of conflicts mentioned in step 3.	1b. From stories you've read or written, give an example of each type of conflict.	**Understand** **Find meaning**
2a. According to this article, what is the first step in writing a short story?	2b. Explain why it is necessary to follow the steps in the order in which in they are given.	**Analyze** **Take things apart**
3a. What can you do to create believable characters and settings?	3b. On a scale of one to ten, with ten being the highest, rank how useful you find this advice to be. Use the text to show which aspects of the advice are useful and which aspects could use improvement.	**Evaluate** **Make judgments**

TEXT ◀──ᵀᴼ──▶ TEXT CONNECTION

- Compare and contrast the two forms of how-to writing you've just read. Which do you find more appealing? Which do you find more useful? Why?
- Based on the advice she gives in "Short Assignments," how do you think Anne Lamott would respond to this "how-to" list of steps? Explain your answer.

EXTEND THE TEXT

Writing Options

Creative Writing Write a **descriptive paragraph** about a friend for someone who has never met this person. Describe what you saw in that friend at the very first moment you met him or her. Include only the details you might see inside Lamott's "one-inch picture frame."

Applied Writing Write **instructions** for something you know how to do well, such as cooking your favorite dish or playing a certain card game. Make sure you provide enough details and explanation for beginners. You may choose to organize your instructions by giving steps, or you may want to include more narration, like Lamott does.

Collaborative Learning

Create Visual Instructions Together with two or three classmates, decide on a common process for which you will provide visual instructions: for example, wrapping a gift, potting a plant, frying an egg, or some other simple activity. As a group, plan a series of photographs that will capture how to perform the activity. Start with a series of sketches that will illustrate what

the photographs should show. Then take the pictures. In your series, use at least three different angles or distances from your subject. Mount the photos on poster board and give each a brief caption explaining the step. Exchange projects with another group and imagine yourselves following the other group's instructions. Give the other group feedback on the success of its project.

Media Literacy

Follow Instructions Use the Internet to find writing contests or publication opportunities. Examine the instructions or guidelines for submitting a piece of writing. Note information such as the deadline, how the manuscript should be formatted, how long the manuscript should be, and what application forms should be used. Make a checklist for yourself. Then prepare a piece of writing for submission by following your list, checking items off when you have completed them.

 Go to **www.mirrorsandwindows.com** for more.

READING ASSESSMENT

1. The object on her desk that reminds the author of "short assignments" is which of the following?
   A. a miniature china dog
   B. a one-inch picture frame
   C. a telephone
   D. a paperweight
   E. a bird

2. On page 331, the word *arresting* most nearly means
   A. enforcing.
   B. striking.
   C. peering.
   D. anticipating.
   E. frightening.

3. Which of these adjectives best describes the author's tone in this selection?
   A. lofty
   B. satirical
   C. colloquial
   D. objective
   E. formal

4. The author's use of the phrase "bird by bird" most nearly means which of the following?
   A. If you begin with one good idea, more ideas will flock to it.
   B. One idea written down is better than two ideas in your head.
   C. Once you begin writing, your ideas will take on a life of their own and fly away.
   D. The best way to tackle a big project is to take it one step at a time.
   E. None of the above

5. On page 329, the word *leer* most nearly means
   A. glance.
   B. strike.
   C. ogle.
   D. pacify.
   E. leave.

6. How does Lamott's advice on how to write compare with the way you write? How can you apply Lamott's advice to your own methods of writing?

GRAMMAR & STYLE

Paragraph Form

A **paragraph** is a carefully organized group of related sentences that focus on or develop a single **main idea.** As the sentences within a paragraph are connected—like links in a chain—so are a series of paragraphs connected to create a longer piece of writing, like an essay, a short story, or a research paper.

Most effective paragraphs have a main idea or point that is developed with **supporting details**—such as examples, sensory details, facts, anecdotes, and quotations. Paragraphs can serve different purposes: to narrate, to describe, to persuade, or to inform. All effective paragraphs, however, share two key elements: unity and a logical method of organization.

Coherence is the logical arrangement and progression of ideas in a piece of writing. When ideas, sentences, and details fit together clearly, the writing is coherent, and readers are able to follow and stay focused. You can achieve coherence by presenting your ideas in the appropriate sequence. To review different ways of organizing your writing, see Understanding the Essay on page 276. Using **transitions,** or words that connect ideas and show the relationship between them, also contributes to a paragraph's coherence.

Read the following paragraph from "Short Assignments." This paragraph is unified and coherent because every sentence flows in logical order and contributes to the main idea—that what Lamott is going to do is look through a one-inch picture frame and write what she sees.

> It reminds me that all I have to do is to write down as much as I can see through a one-inch picture frame. This is all I have to bite off for the time being. All I am going to do right now, for example, is write that one paragraph that sets the story in my hometown, in the late fifties, when the trains were still running. I am going to paint a picture of it, in words,

> on my word processor. Or all I am going to do is to describe the main character the very first time we meet her, when she first walks out the front door and onto the porch. I am not even going to describe the expression on her face when she first notices the blind dog sitting behind the wheel of her car—just what I can see through the one-inch picture frame, just one paragraph describing this woman, in the town where I grew up, the first time we encounter her.

The main idea of a paragraph is often stated directly in a **topic sentence.** The topic sentence can be placed at the beginning, middle, or end of a paragraph. Usually, the topic sentence appears at the beginning of a paragraph and is followed by one or more supporting sentences. In many paragraphs, however, the main idea is implied rather than stated in a topic sentence. This means that the sentences in the paragraph work together to suggest—rather than directly state—the main idea.

REVIEW TERMS

- **paragraph:** a carefully organized group of related sentences that focus on or develop a single main idea
- **main idea:** main point of a paragraph
- **supporting details:** details that support a paragraph's main idea
- **topic sentence:** sentence in a paragraph that states the main idea
- **coherence:** the logical arrangement and progression of ideas in a piece of writing
- **transition:** word that connects ideas and shows the relationship between them

Identify Main Ideas

Read each of the following paragraphs from selections in this unit. Then identify the main idea of each.

1. There was a time when our people covered the land as the waves of a wind-ruffled sea cover its shell-paved floor, but that time long since passed away with the greatness of tribes that are now but a mournful memory. I will not dwell on, nor mourn over, our untimely decay, nor reproach my paleface brothers with hastening it as we too may have been somewhat to blame.

   — from "Yonder Sky That Has Wept Tears of Compassion" by Chief Seattle

2. Capturing your attention — and holding it — is the prime motive of most television programming and enhances its role as a profitable advertising vehicle. Programmers live in constant fear of losing anyone's attention — anyone's. The surest way to avoid doing so is to keep everything brief, not to strain the attention of anyone but instead to provide constant stimulation through variety, novelty, action and movement. Quite simply, television operates on the appeal to the short attention span.

   — from "The Trouble with Television" by Robert MacNeil

Understand Main Ideas and Supporting Details in a Paragraph

Write two supporting sentences for each of the following main ideas. Make sure that each supporting sentence develops the main idea and that all the sentences are related.

1. The weekday hours a high school student can work at a part-time job should (or should not) be limited.
2. Weather extremes have become the norm.
3. Owning a pet is a substantial responsibility.
4. *Bird by Bird* is a book every high school student should read.
5. Canceling recycling programs is not the way to save money in our community.

6. All high schools should require students to wear uniforms.
7. The driving age should be raised from sixteen years old to eighteen years old.
8. Participating in extracurricular activities is beneficial for high school students.
9. Everyone in the United States should learn to speak a second language.
10. The people in the United States need to exercise more and make better food choices.

Write a Paragraph

Organize the sentences below into a single, unified paragraph in which you use a logical method of organization and transitions. Feel free to make changes in the order and wording of the sentences, or even to omit a sentence entirely, so that your paragraph is unified and coherent.

1. Among disputes swirling around school corridors, the issue of cell phones has recently received considerable attention.
2. Critics of the new policies, who include many parents and students, claim that cell phones are a vital aid to safety and security.
3. Other gadgets routinely carried by students these days are high-tech calculators and personal sound systems such as iPods.
4. Several school districts in large cities have either placed severe restrictions on cell phone usage or banned cell phones entirely.
5. Many school administrators argue that cell phones serve as a distraction, are used to arrange after-school fights, and aid students in cheating on tests.

EXTEND THE SKILL

Write down at least five ideas about an activity, a sport, or a hobby in which you participate. Review your list and write five effective topic sentences — one for each of five different paragraphs you might develop about the activity, sport, or hobby.

READING NONFICTION INDEPENDENTLY

Theme: Things That Divide and Things That Unite

"I went home that evening and wrote. I wrote of just about every injustice that I had ever experienced. Kansas, Minnesota, Chicago, New York and Washington were all forged together in the heat of the blast."

—Gordon Parks, from *A Choice of Weapons*

The issue of unity is ever-present on a national level; even the motto of the United States promotes the idea: *E pluribus unum* ("out of many, one"). However, there are several forces that threaten the unity of a country or community, such as racism, poverty, and war. The selections in this section present people who confront division and contemplate the road to unity. As you read, determine what the divisive issue is, as well as what unity means to the authors and how they plan to achieve it.

USING READING SKILLS WITH NONFICTION

Identify Supporting Details

Supporting details are the facts and information that provide the evidence and structure that make up nonfiction writing. To identify supporting details, you need to do the following:

- Locate **basic facts,** such as names, dates, and events.
- **Determine the importance** of those facts to your understanding of the piece. Some facts or details will be more important than others. The main ideas are what the selection is about; the minor ideas and details provide support for the main ones.
- Determine the **mode of writing** the author is using. The possible modes and types of writing that employ those modes are listed on page 219.
- Interpret **subtly stated details.** These details can help clarify the author's stance or purpose, or they may give fuller meaning to the basic facts.
- Understand the **function** of a part of a passage. Is the author providing information, supporting a previously made point, presenting a conflicting argument, building suspense? Pay attention to how your understanding of a topic or your feelings toward it change as you read.
- **Draw conclusions** about how the author uses the supporting details to achieve the desired result. Put together clues from the text with your prior knowledge to make inferences. An Inference Chart like the one following for the excerpt from *A Choice of Weapons* can help you keep track of your ideas.

Inference Chart

Text	What I Infer
"Don't you know colored people can't eat in here?" […] I retreated, too stunned to answer him as I walked out the door.	Parks was not expecting to be treated like that in Washington, DC.
"I purposely sent you out this morning so that you can see just what you're up against."	Stryker is preparing Parks for how to be an effective photographer of social problems in Washington, DC.

Distinguish Fact from Opinion

A **fact** is a statement that can be proven by direct observation. Every statement of fact is either true or false. An **opinion** is a statement that expresses an attitude or a desire, not a fact about the world.

One common type of opinion statement is a *value statement.* A value statement expresses an attitude toward something.

EXAMPLE

> Ancient Greece produced some beautiful and inspiring myths. (The adjectives used to describe myths express an attitude or opinion toward something that cannot be proven.)

A *policy statement* is an opinion that tells not what is but what someone believes should be.

EXAMPLES

> The president should be reelected.
> You must not play your radio during study hall.

A *prediction* makes a statement about the future. Because the future is unpredictable, most predictions can be considered opinions.

EXAMPLES

> People will live longer in the future.
> Tomorrow will be partly cloudy.

When evaluating a fact, ask yourself whether it can be proven through direct observation or by checking a reliable source such as a reference book or an unbiased expert. An opinion is only as good as the facts that support it. When reading, be critical about the statements that you encounter.

Framework for Nonfiction

When reading nonfiction, you need to be aware of what type of writing it is, how it uses supporting details, and what the author's intent is. The following checklist of questions offers a framework for approaching nonfiction reading.

As you start to read...
- ❑ What are the basic facts, such as names, dates, locations, and events?
- ❑ What mode of writing is this: narrative, expository, persuasive, or descriptive?

As you continue reading...
- ❑ What seem to be the most important ideas in this selection?
- ❑ Are there more facts or more opinions?
- ❑ How are the opinions supported?

After you've finished reading...
- ❑ How does the author use supporting details to convey his or her message?
- ❑ What can you infer by the author's choice of words and details about how the author regards the subject or wants the reader to regard the subject?

What Good Readers Do

Monitor Your Reading Progress

All readers encounter difficulty when they read, especially if the reading material is not self-selected. When you have to read something, note problems you are having make a plan to fix them. Here are some common reading obstacles you may need to address:

- ❑ Because I do not understand this part, I will...
- ❑ Because I am having trouble staying interested in the selection, I will...
- ❑ Because the words are too hard, I will...
- ❑ Because the selection is very long, I will...
- ❑ Because I cannot remember what I have just read, I will...

from A Choice of Weapons

A Memoir by **Gordon Parks**

Everyone in the place was staring at me now. I retreated, too stunned to answer him as I walked out the door.

Gordon Parks (1912–2006) was born in Fort Scott, Kansas, the youngest of fifteen children. At the age of twenty-five, he began to pursue photography seriously. Several years later, he moved to Washington, DC. After a stint as a fashion photographer for *Vogue* magazine, Parks worked for twenty years for *Life* and became one of that magazine's premier photographers.

The excerpt from Parks's memoir ***A Choice of Weapons*** was written in the 1960s and records the author's early career as a news photographer encountering the Jim Crow culture of Washington, DC, in the period after the Great Depression.

Have you ever been caught by surprise at the way people around you behave? Describe your experience.

A tall blond girl who said her name was Charlotte came forward and greeted me. "Mr. Stryker will be with you in a minute," she said. She had just gotten the words out when he bounced out and extended his hand. "Welcome to Washington. I'm Roy," were his first words. "Come into the office and let's get acquainted." I will like this man, I thought.

He motioned me to a chair opposite his desk, but before he could say anything his telephone rang. "It's Arthur Rothstein phoning from Montana," Charlotte called from the outer office. The name flashed my thoughts back to the night on the dining car when I first saw it beneath the picture of the farmer and his two sons running toward their shack through the dust storm.

"Arthur? This is Roy."

I'm here I thought; at last I'm here.

As he talked, I observed the chubby face topped with a mane of white hair, the blinking piercingly curious eyes, enlarged under thick bifocal lenses. There was something boyish, something fatherly, something tyrannical, something kind and good about him. He did not seem like anyone I had ever known before.

They talked for about ten minutes. "That was Rothstein," Stryker said, hanging up. "He had bad luck with one of his cameras." The way he said this pulled me in as if I were already accepted, as if I had been there for years. The indoctrination had begun. "Now tell me about yourself and your plans," he said with a trace of playfulness in his voice. I spent a lot of time telling him perhaps more than he bargained for. After I had finished, he asked me bluntly, "What do you know about Washington?"

"Nothing much," I admitted.

"Did you bring your cameras with you?"

"Yes, they're right here in this bag." I took out my battered Speed Graphic and a Roleiflex and proudly placed them on his desk.

He looked at them approvingly and then asked me for the bag I had taken them from. He then took all my equipment and locked it in a closet behind him. "You won't be needing those for a few days," he said flatly. He lit a cigarette and leaned back in his chair and continued, "I have some very specific things I would like you to do this week. And I would like you to follow my instructions faithfully. Walk around the city. Get to know it. Buy yourself a few things—you have money, I suppose."

"Yes, sir."

"Go to a picture show, the department stores, eat in the restaurants and drugstores. Get to know this place." I thought his orders were a bit trivial, but they were easy enough to follow. "Let me know how you've made out in a couple of days," he said after he had walked me to the door.

"I will," I promised casually. And he smiled oddly as I left.

I walked toward the business section and stopped at a drugstore for breakfast. When I sat down at the counter, the white waiter looked at me as though I were crazy. "Get off of that stool," he said angrily. "Don't you know colored people can't eat in here? Go round to the back door if you want something." Everyone in the place was staring at me now. I retreated, too stunned to answer him as I walked out the door.

I found an open hot dog stand. Maybe this place would serve me. I approached the counter warily. "Two hot dogs, please."

"To take out?" the boy in the white uniform snapped.

"Yes, to take out," I snapped back. And I walked down the street, gulping down the sandwiches.

I went to a theater.

"What do you want?"

"A ticket."

"Colored people can't go in here. You should know that."

I remained silent, observing the ticket seller with more surprise than anything else. She looked at me as though I were insane. What is this, I wondered. Was Stryker playing some sort of joke on me? Was this all planned to exasperate me? Such discrimination here in Washington, D.C., the nation's capital? It was hard to believe.

Strangely, I hadn't lost my temper. The experience was turning into a weird game, and I would play it out—follow Roy's instructions to the hilt. I would try a department store now; and I chose the most imposing one in sight, Julius Garfinckel. Its name had confronted me many times in full-page advertisements in fashion magazines. Its owners must have been filled with national pride—their ads were always identified with some sacred Washington monument. Julius Garfinckel. Julius Rosenwald. I lumped them with the names of Harvey Goldstein and Peter Pollack—Jews who had helped shift the course of my life. I pulled myself together and entered the big store, with nothing particular in mind. The men's hats were on my right, so I arbitrarily chose that department. The salesman appeared a little on edge, but he sold me a hat. Then leaving I saw an advertisement for camel's-hair coats on an upper floor. I had wanted one since the early days at the Minnesota Club. It was possible now. The elevator operator's face brought back memories of the doorman at the Park Central Hotel on that first desperate morning in New York.

"Can I help you?" His question was shadowed with arrogance.

"Yes. Men's coats, please." He hesitated for a moment, then closed the door, and we went up.

The game had temporarily ended on the first floor as far as I was concerned. The purchase of the hat had relieved my doubts about discrimination here; the coat was the goal now. The floor was bare of customers. Only four salesmen stood eying me as I stepped from the elevator. None of them offered assistance, so I looked at them and asked to be shown a camel's-hair coat.

No one moved. "They're to your left," someone volunteered.

I walked to my left. There were the coats I wanted, several racks of them. But no one attempted to show them to me.

"Could I get some help here?" I asked.

One man sauntered over. "What can I do for you?"

"I asked you for a camel's-hair coat."

"Those aren't your size."

"Then where are my size?"

"Probably around to my right?" The game was on again. "Then show them to me."

"That's not my department."

"Then whose department is it?"

"Come to think of it, I'm sure we don't have your size in stock."

"But you don't even know my size."

"I'm sorry. We just don't have your size."

"Well, I'll just wait here until you get one my size." Anger was at last beginning to take over. There was a white couch in the middle of the floor. I walked over and sprawled out leisurely on it, took a newspaper from my pocket and pretended to read. My blackness stretched across the white couch commanded attention. The manager arrived, posthaste, a generous smile upon his face. My ruse had succeeded, I thought.

"I'm the manager of this department. What can I do for you?"

"Oh, am I to have the honor of being waited on by the manager? How nice," I said, smiling with equal graciousness.

"Well, you see, there's a war on. And we're very short of help. General Marshall[1] was in here yesterday and *he* had to wait for a salesman. Now please understand that—"

"But I'm not General Marshall, and there's no one here but four salesmen, you and me. But I'll wait right here until they're not so busy. I'll wait right here." He sat down in a chair beside me and we talked for a half hour—about weather, war, food, Washington, and even camel's-hair coats. But I was never shown one. Finally, after he ran out of conversation, he left. I continued to sit there under the gaze of the four puzzled

---

1. **General Marshall.** George C. Marshall (1880–1959), American military leader and statesman

salesmen and the few customers who came to the floor. At last the comfort of the couch made me sleepy; and by now the whole thing had become ridiculous. I wouldn't have accepted a coat if they had given me the entire rack. Suddenly I thought of my camera, of Stryker. I got up and hurried out of the store and to his office. He was out to lunch when I got back. But I waited outside his door until he returned.

"I didn't expect you back so soon," he said. "I thought you'd be out seeing the town for a couple of days."

"I've seen enough of it in one morning," I replied sullenly. "I want my cameras."

"What do you intend to do with them?"

"I want to show the rest of the world what your great city of Washington, D.C., is really like, I want—"

"Okay. Okay." The hint of that smile was on his face again. And now I was beginning to understand it. "Come into my office and tell me all about it," he said. He listened patiently. He was sympathetic; but he didn't return my equipment.

"Young man," he finally began, "you're going to have to face some very hard facts down here. Whatever else it may be, this is a Southern city.[2] Whether you ignore it or tolerate it is up to you. I purposely sent you out this morning so that you can see just what you're up against." He paused for a minute to let this sink in. Then he continued. "You're going to find all kinds of people in Washington, and a good cross-section of the types are right here in this building. You'll have to prove yourself to them, especially the lab people. They are damned good technicians—but they are all Southerners. I can't predict what their attitudes will be toward you, and I warn you I'm not going to try to influence them one way or the other. It's completely up to you. I do think they will respect good craftsmanship. Once you get over that hurdle, I honestly believe you will be accepted as another photographer—not just as a Negro

photographer. There is a certain amount of resentment against even the white photographers until they prove themselves. Remember, these people slave in hot darkrooms while they think about the photographers enjoying all the glamor and getting all the glory. Most of them would like to be on the other end."

We were walking about the building now, and as he introduced me to different people, his words took on meaning. Some smiled and extended their hands in welcome. Others, especially those in the laboratory, kept working and

2. **a Southern city.** A reference to the Jim Crow laws, or official segregation statutes in the South, by which black people were denied many of their basic civil rights

acknowledged me with cold nods, making their disdain obvious. Any triumph over them would have to be well earned, I told myself. Stryker closed the door when we were back in his office. "Go home," he advised, "and put it on paper."

"Put what on paper?" I asked puzzled.

"Your plan for fighting these things you say you just went through. Think it out constructively. It won't be easy. You can't take a picture of a white salesman, waiter or ticket seller and just say they are prejudiced. That isn't enough. You've got to verbalize the experience first, then find logical ways to express it in pictures. The right words too are important; they should underscore your photographs. Think in terms of images and words. They can be mighty powerful when they are fitted together properly."

I went home that evening and wrote. I wrote of just about every injustice that I had ever experienced. Kansas, Minnesota, Chicago, New York and Washington were all forged together in the heat of the blast.

Images and words images and words images and words—I fell asleep trying to arrange an acceptable marriage of them.

Stryker read what I had written with a troubled face. I watched his eyes move over the lines, his brows furrow from time to time. When he had finished, we both sat quietly for a few minutes. "You've had quite a time," he finally said, "but you have to simplify all this material. It would take many years and all the photographers on the staff to fulfill what you have put down here. Come outside; I want to show you something." He took me over to the file and opened a drawer marked "Dorothea Lange."[3] "Spend the rest of the day going through this set of pictures. Each day take on another drawer. And go back and write more specifically about your visual approach to things."

For several weeks I went through hundreds of photographs by Lange, Russell Lee, Jack Delano, Carl Mydans, John Vachon, Arthur Rothstein, Ben Shahn, Walker Evans, John Collier and others. The disaster of the thirties was at my fingertips: the gutted cotton fields, the eroded farmland, the crumbling South, the unending lines of dispossessed migrants, the pitiful shacks, the shameful city ghettos, the breadlines and bonus marchers,[4] the gaunt faces of men, women and children caught up in the tragedy; the horrifying spectacles of sky blackened with locusts, and swirling dust, and towns flooded with muddy rivers. There were some, no doubt, who laid these tragedies to God. But research accompanying these stark photographs accused man himself—especially the lords of the land. In their greed and passion for wealth, they had gutted the earth for cotton; overworked the farms; exploited the tenant farmers and sharecroppers[5] who, broken, took to the highways with their families in search of work. They owned the ghettos as well as the impoverished souls who inhabited them. No, the indictment was against man, not God; the proof was there in those ordinary steel files. It was a raw slice of contemporary America— clear, hideous and beautifully detailed in images and words. I began to get the point....

Using my camera effectively against intolerance was not so easy as I had assumed it would be. One evening, when Stryker and I were in the office alone, I confessed this to him. "Then at least you have learned the most important lesson," he said. He thought for a moment, got up and looked down the corridor, then called me to his side. There was a Negro charwoman mopping the floor. "Go have a talk with her before you go home this evening. See what she has to say about life and things. You might find her interesting."

This was a strange suggestion, but after he had gone I went through the empty building

---

3. **Dorothea Lange** (1895–1965). An American photographer, known especially for her photographs of the Depression
4. **bonus marchers.** In 1932, thousands of needy World War I veterans protested in Washington, DC, demanding payment of the bonus the government had promised them for their war service.
5. **sharecroppers.** People who farm land owned by others in return for a percentage of the crop

Parks describes this photograph as "unsubtle." What message do you think it conveys? What specific images help convey this message?

Charwoman with Mop and Broom by American Flag, 1942. Gordon Parks.

searching for her. I found her in a notary public's office and introduced myself. She was a tall, spindly woman with sharp features. Her hair was swept back from graying temples; a sharp intelligence shone in the eyes behind the steel-rimmed glasses. We started off awkwardly, neither of us knowing my reason for starting the conversation. At first it was a meaningless exchange of words. Then, as if a dam had broken within her, she began to spill out her life story. It was a pitiful one. She had struggled alone after her mother had died and her father had been killed by a lynch mob. She had gone through high school, married and become pregnant. Her husband was accidentally shot to death two days before the daughter was born. By the time the daughter was eighteen, she had given birth to two illegitimate children, dying two weeks after the second child's birth. What's more, the first child had been stricken with paralysis a year before its mother died. Now this woman was bringing up these grandchildren on a salary hardly suitable for one person.

"Who takes care of them while you are at work?" I asked after a long silence.

"Different neighbors," she said, her heavily veined hands tightening about the mop handle.

"Can I photograph you?" The question had come out of an elaboration of thoughts. I was escaping the humiliation of not being able to help.

"I don't mind," she said.

My first photograph of her was unsubtle. I overdid it and posed her, Grant Wood[6] style, before the American flag, a broom in one hand, a mop in the other, staring straight into the camera. Stryker took one look at it the next day and fell speechless.

"Well, how do you like it?" I asked eagerly.

He just smiled and shook his head. "Well?" I insisted.

"Keep working with her. Let's see what happens," he finally replied. I followed her for nearly a month—into her home, her church and wherever she went. "You're learning," Stryker admitted when I laid the photographs out before him late one evening. "You're showing you can involve yourself in other people. This woman has done you a great service. I hope you understand this." I did understand. ❖

---

6. **Grant Wood.** American artist famous for his paintings of the Midwest; his best known work is *American Gothic*

 **MIRRORS & WINDOWS**

What are some things that need to change in today's society? How can you go about changing these things? What are some of the challenges and rewards of attempting to make a positive difference in society?

Refer and Reason

1. Why does Roy Stryker tell the narrator to walk around Washington, DC, without his cameras for a few days? To his surprise, what does the narrator discover on his walks?
2. How is a camera Parks's "choice of weapon"? In what other situations might a camera make a good weapon?
3. What do you think is the significance of Parks's photograph entitled *Charwoman with Mop and Broom by American Flag*?

Writing Options

1. Imagine you are Roy Stryker. Write a journal entry recording your impressions of your first few meetings with Gordon Parks.
2. Research the career of photographer Dorothea Lange, Walker Evans, or another famous American photographer. Then write a brief biographical sketch of the person you have chosen, chronicling that person's major themes and artistic achievements.

 Go to **www.mirrorsandwindows.com** for more.

Getting It Right at Ground Zero

This was mass murder perpetrated by madmen bent on destroying not only American lives but also American values.

An Essay by **Rudolph Giuliani**

Rudolph Giuliani (b. 1944) grew up in a working-class family in Brooklyn, New York, the grandson of Italian immigrants. His government service in New York and Washington, DC, included posts as Associate Attorney General and U.S. Attorney for the Southern District of New York. From 1993 until 2001, Giuliani served two terms as mayor of New York.

The essay **"Getting It Right at Ground Zero"** was published in *Time* magazine in September of 2002 to mark the first-year anniversary of the September 11, 2001, attacks on the World Trade Center. After the collapse of the World Trade Center, the site of the Twin Towers where so many had died became known as "Ground Zero."

What do you think should be done to memorialize the people who died in the September 11th attacks?

Twelve months have passed. The debris is gone. The thousands who worked tirelessly to rescue and recover those who died no longer dig through the night. The twisted remains of New York's two biggest buildings no longer stand as reminders of the worst attack in American history.

But I haven't changed. When I go to ground zero now, I feel as shocked,

New York firefighters carry a body away from the ruins of the World Trade Center.

angry and resolute as I did a year ago. On Sept. 14, 2001, I flew over the site in a helicopter with President George W. Bush and Governor George Pataki. I had been there many times during the three days after the attack, but that was the first time I had seen the smoking ruins from above. It was indescribably awful. A year has done nothing to erase these images from my mind.

What happened at the World Trade Center and the Pentagon and outside Shanksville, Pa., was not a natural disaster or some colossal accident. This was mass murder perpetrated by madmen bent on destroying not only American lives but also American values. These attacks were not just on the people who were killed and injured but also on the very things that define us as a society: religious freedom, equality, economic opportunity and political choice. I learned as a prosecutor that intent matters. When a loved one dies in an accident, of course it's painful. But knowing that your husband or

wife or mother or son is gone because of an intentional act cuts much more deeply.

One way of dealing with this lasting pain is to talk about it. I frequently discuss Sept. 11, often with those who have been most affected by the attacks. I try to confront what was done to us and the importance of being resolute. I've also attended many memorials and funerals, which reinforced a lesson my father taught me long ago about being there for people when they need you most. It's a two-way street. People absorb strength from you, and you get it back from them.

Back at ground zero—16 barren acres, including the footprints of the towers—the debate continues about how best to commemorate the loss. There are many competing pressures and different viewpoints. I am convinced that ground zero must first and foremost be a memorial. All other decisions should flow from that goal. If anything else is added to the site, it should complement and not over-shadow the memorial. People a hundred years from now should be able to grasp the enormity of this attack by visiting this sacred ground. Ground zero is a cemetery. It is the last resting place for loved ones whose bodies were not recovered and whose remains are still within that hallowed ground. We must respect the role these events play in our history.

It is the place where the President came and told the exhausted rescue workers, "I can hear you. The rest of the world hears you, and the people who knocked these buildings down will hear all of us soon." President Bush has been determined to keep his commitment to elimi-nate global terrorism. An appropriately large and enduring tribute at the site will remind future generations of that commitment. Recalling these attacks and their aftermath will remind people today that we need to be unyielding in completing the war on terror. And it will remind people tomorrow that we must never let something like this happen again.

If it were up to me, I'd devote the entire 16 acres to the memorial. A soaring structure should dominate the site, taking its place along New York City's wonderful skyline. It should be visible for miles to demonstrate the spirit of those who gave their lives to defend freedom. There should be a museum and a library. Those who visit should be able to relive the experience in a way that does justice to the enormity of the events. The memorial should echo the goals of the city's Museum of Jewish Heritage, which sits a stone's throw away. The purpose of that

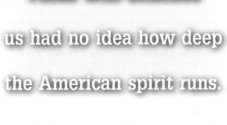

Those who attacked us had no idea how deep the American spirit runs.

museum is to demonstrate the horror of the Holocaust as well as celebrate the survival and strength of the Jewish people. Done correctly, the memorial at ground zero will commemorate the horror and the heroism of Sept. 11.

If we don't do this correctly—if we let some minor memorial be dwarfed by office space—people a hundred years from now will say this generation did not understand the significance of that world-altering day.

Sept. 11 must not lose its resonance as time dulls the sharp edges of our collective memory. Ground zero is the site of the worst attack in the history of this country. I pray it will be the worst attack in the history of this country a hundred years from now. Done correctly, a memorial will inspire people. It should not symbolize the loss of our world before Sept. 11 or of an America that no longer exists. It should symbolize our survival and our triumph.

I'm an optimist. Our way is the way of the future. Nation after nation sees that and embraces democracy. It is not a perfectly smooth road. But it's undeniably the way the world is headed. And that's a good thing.

Because—and I don't mean this belliger-ently—we're right and they're wrong. Those who attacked us had no idea how deep the American spirit runs. I think our grief, rage and resolve have surprised even us. One year later, that might be the most resonant lesson of all. America's resilience—the depth of this nation's character—should never be underestimated. ❖

What is the difference between remembering and memorializing? What purposes should a memorial serve? In what ways can the act of creating a memorial be positive? What are some negative effects of creating a memorial?

KAPLANSKY

Literature CONNECTION

Folksinger and songwriter **Lucy Kaplansky** (b. 1960) grew up in Chicago but moved to New York City at the age of eighteen to pursue a career in music. Today, she still lives and works in New York and co-writes many of her songs with her husband, filmmaker and songwriter Richard Litvin.

The song **"Land of the Living"** was recorded on Kaplansky's 2004 album called *The Red Thread*. The title of the album refers to a Chinese proverb about an invisible, unbreakable red thread that connects people to those who are and will be important to them. How does music help people deal with difficult situations?

Land of the Living

A Song by **Lucy Kaplansky**
and **Richard Litvin**

Late afternoon back in New York town
Waking up as the wheels touch down
Pick up my guitar and walk away
Wish I was going home to stay

Line of taxis, I wait my turn
Tar and asphalt, exhaust and fumes
Beside the road on a patch of ground
Taxi drivers are kneeling down

Beneath the concrete sky I watch them pray
While the people of the world hurry on their way
I think they're praying for us all today
And the stories that fell from the sky that day

Chorus:
This is the land of the living
This is the land that's mine
She still watches over Manhattan
She's still holding onto that torch for life

Back home fire's still burning, I can see it in
    the air
Pictures of faces posted everywhere
They say "hazel eyes, chestnut hair
Mother of two missing down there"

I pass the firemen on duty tonight
Carpets of flowers in candlelight
And thank you in a child's scrawl
Taped to the Third Street firehouse wall

There's shadows of the lost on the faces I see
Brothers and strangers on this island of grief
There's death in the air but there's life on this street
There's life on this street

Chorus:
This is the land of the living
This is the land that's mine
She still watches over Manhattan
She's still holding onto that torch for life

Then I got in a taxi, said "Hudson Street please"
He started the meter and he looked at me
I glanced at his name on the back of his seat
And I looked out the window at the ghost filled
    streets

I noticed cuts on his hand and his face
And I said "You're bleeding, are you okay?"
He said "I'm not so good, got beat up today
And I'm not one of them no matter what they say

I'm just worried about my family
My wife's in the house and she's scared to leave"
And I didn't know what to say
I didn't know what to say
But I said a prayer for him anyway

Chorus:
This is the land of the living
This is the land that's mine
She still watches over Manhattan
She's still holding onto that torch for life ❖

TEXT ←TO→ TEXT CONNECTION

- How does the purpose of Kaplansky's song compare with the purpose of Giuliani's essay? How do the images in the song and essay contribute to their purposes? Which text, the song or the essay, do you find more compelling?
- What do the "brothers and strangers" in "Land of the Living" have in common with the people in Garrison Keillor's reflection, "On This Day in 2001" (page 352)?

Literature CONNECTION

Garrison Keillor (b. 1942) hosts National Public Radio's programs *A Prairie Home Companion* and *The Writer's Almanac.* The latter is a brief daily program in which Keillor reads a poem or other literary work and mentions literary events related to the date in history. On September 11, 2003, Keillor shared these words about the experiences of several people who survived the September 11, 2001, attacks on the World Trade Center in New York City. What do you remember about September 11, 2001?

On This Day in 2001

A Reflection by **Garrison Keillor**

On this day in 2001, it was a clear, crisp, sunny morning in New York City. Students were in their second week of school. People were getting to work in cars, buses, and trains. Alessandra Fremura had planned on leaving for work at 8:00, but her babysitter was 20 minutes late. Virginia DiChiara couldn't get her golden retrievers to come in from the backyard, so she decided to have another cup of coffee. Kenneth Merlo was supposed to go the office, but he decided to spend the morning helping a friend hook up her computer instead of going to his office. Michael Lomonaco stopped in the lobby of the World Trade Center to order some reading glasses from the one-hour eyeglass store. Michael Jacobs was running late when he reached the Trade Center lobby. He rushed to make the elevator, but the doors slid shut in his face. A musician named Michelle Wiley was at home in her apartment. She sat down at her piano in her nightgown and shower shoes, and stared out her window at the Twin Towers before beginning to play.

Refer and Reason

1. List specific images Rudolph Giuliani uses in his essay. How do the images Giuliani uses contribute to the mood?
2. Identify references to the dead and missing in Lucy Kaplansky's song. Why do you think Kaplansky called the song "Land of the Living" when she is talking about an event that killed so many?
3. Why do you think Keillor included in this reflection such everyday details as having a cup of coffee or helping a friend hook up a computer?

Writing Options

1. Imagine that you are a feature writer for a newspaper. Write one of the "stories that fell from the sky that day." In other words, write a brief story about the life of one of the victims of the attacks.
2. In many countries of the world, including the United States, memorials play an important role in national life. Research a particular memorial. Organize your findings into an informational brochure for people who might be interested in the memorial's history and significance.

Go to **www.mirrorsandwindows.com** for more.

from When Heaven and Earth Changed Places

A Memoir by Le Ly Hayslip

Le Ly Hayslip (b. 1949) was born the youngest of six children in a traditional farming village in Vietnam. She was twelve years old when Americans landed in her village, beginning the nightmare of the Vietnam War for her. She survived terrible abuse, imprisonment, and torture. Her father was not as fortunate. After separation from his family, cruel treatment by soldiers on both sides of the war, and distress over the loss of his village, he died by his own hand. In 1970, Hayslip married an American serviceman and moved to the United States. She now lives in Los Angeles, where she has started a relief and world peace organization called the East Meets West Foundation.

When Heaven and Earth Changed Places is an autobiographical account of Hayslip's experiences during the Vietnam War. This excerpt examines her relationship with her father, as well as the difficulty of surviving the ravages of war.

What kinds of things do most parents want for their children?

My father drew me out to arm's length and looked me squarely in the eye. "Now, Bay Ly, do you understand what your job is?"

After my brother Bon went North, I began to pay more attention to my father.

He was built solidly—big-boned—for a Vietnamese man, which meant he probably had well-fed, noble ancestors. People said he had the body of a natural-born warrior. He was a year younger and an inch shorter than my mother, but just as good-looking. His face was round, like a Khmer or Thai,[1] and his complexion was brown as soy from working all his life in the sun. He was

---

1. **Khmer or Thai.** *Khmer*—native of Cambodia; *Thai*—native of Thailand

very easygoing about everything and seldom in a hurry. Seldom, too, did he say no to a request—from his children or his neighbors. Although

Where my mother would instruct me on cooking and cleaning and tell stories about brides, my father showed me the mystery of hammers and explained the customs of our people.

he took everything in stride, he was a hard and diligent worker. Even on holidays, he was always mending things or tending to our house and animals. He would not wait to be asked for help if he saw someone in trouble. Similarly, he always said what he thought, although he knew, like most honest men, when to keep silent. Because of his honesty, his empathy, and his openness to people, he understood life deeply. Perhaps that is why he was so easygoing. Only a half-trained mechanic thinks everything needs fixing.

He loved to smoke cigars and grew a little tobacco in our yard. My mother always wanted him to sell it, but there was hardly ever enough to take to market. I think for her it was the principle of the thing: smoking cigars was like burning money. Naturally, she had a song for such gentle vices—her own habit of chewing betel nuts[2] included:

> *Get rid of your tobacco,*
> *And you will get a water buffalo.*
> *Give away your betel,*
> *And you will get more paddy land.*

Despite her own good advice, she never abstained from chewing betel, nor my father from smoking cigars. They were rare luxuries that life and the war allowed them.

My father also liked rice wine, which we made, and enjoyed an occasional beer, which he purchased when there was nothing else we needed. After he'd had a few sips, he would tell jokes and happy stories and the village kids would flock around. Because I was his youngest daughter, I was entitled to listen from his knee—the place of honor….

Once, when I was the only child at home, my mother went to Da Nang[3] to visit Uncle Nhu, and my father had to take care of me. I woke up from my nap in the empty house and cried for my mother. My father came in from the yard and reassured me, but I was still cranky and continued crying. Finally, he gave me a rice cookie to shut me up. Needless to say, this was a tactic my mother never used.

The next afternoon I woke up, and although I was not feeling cranky, I thought a rice cookie might be nice. I cried a fake cry, and my father came running in.

"What's this?" he asked, making a worried face. "Little Bay Ly[4] doesn't want a cookie?"

I was confused again.

"Look under your pillow," he said with a smile.

I twisted around and saw that, while I was sleeping, he had placed a rice cookie under my pillow. We both laughed, and he picked me up like a sack of rice and carried me outside while I gobbled the cookie.

In the yard, he plunked me down under a tree and told me some stories. After that, he got some scraps of wood and showed me how to make things: a doorstop for my mother and a toy duck for me. This was unheard of—a father doing these things with a child that was not a son! Where my mother would instruct me on cooking and cleaning and tell stories about brides, my father showed me the mystery of hammers and explained the customs of our people.

His knowledge of the Vietnamese went back to the Chinese Wars in ancient times.

---

2. **betel nuts.** Red palm seeds, the fruit of the betel palm; commonly chewed in Southeast Asia
3. **Da Nang.** Seaport in central Vietnam
4. **Little Bay Ly.** Narrator's childhood nickname

I learned how one of my distant ancestors, a woman named Phung Thi Chinh, led Vietnamese fighters against the Han. In one battle, even though she was pregnant and surrounded by Chinese, she delivered the baby, tied it to her back, and cut her way to safety wielding a sword in each hand. I was amazed at this warrior's bravery and impressed that I was her descendant. Even more, I was amazed and impressed by my father's pride in her accomplishments (she was, after all, a humble female) and his belief that I was worthy of her example. *"Con phai theo got chan co ta"* ("follow in her footsteps"), he said. Only later would I learn what he truly meant.

Never again did I cry after my nap. Phung Thi women were too strong for that. Besides, I was my father's daughter, and we had many things to do together.

On the eve of my mother's return, my father cooked a feast of roast duck. When we sat down to eat it, I felt guilty and my feelings showed on my face. He asked why I acted so sad.

"You've killed one of mother's ducks," I said. "One of the fat kind she sells at the market. She says the money buys gold, which she saves for her daughters' weddings. Without gold for a dowry[5]—*con o gia*—I will be an old maid!"

My father looked suitably concerned, then brightened and said, "Well, Bay Ly, if you can't get married, you will just have to live at home forever with me!"

I clapped my hands at the happy prospect.

My father cut into the rich, juicy bird and said, "Even so, we won't tell your mother about the duck, okay?"

I giggled and swore myself to secrecy.

The next day, I took some water out to him in the fields. My mother was due home any time, and I used every opportunity to step

---

5. **dowry.** Property transferred from a woman's family to her husband upon their marriage

He said, "Bay Ly, you see all this here? This is the Vietnam we have been talking about. You understand that a country is more than a lot of dirt, rivers, and forests, don't you?"

I said, "Yes, I understand." After all, we had learned in school that one's country is as sacred as a father's grave.

"Good. You know, some of these lands are battlefields where your brothers and cousins are fighting. They may never come back. Even your sisters have all left home in search of a better life. You are the only one left in my house. If the enemy comes back, you must be both a daughter and a son. I told you how the Chinese used to rule our land. People in this village had to risk their lives diving in the ocean just to find pearls for the Chinese emperor's gown. They had to risk tigers and snakes in the jungle just to find herbs for his table. Their payment for this hardship was a bowl of rice and another day of life. That is why Le Loi, Gia Long, the Trung Sisters, and Phung Thi Chinh fought so hard to expel the Chinese. When the French came,

outside and watch for her. My father stopped working, drank gratefully, then took my hand and led me to the top of a nearby hill. It had a good view of the village and the land beyond it, almost to the ocean. I thought he was going to show me my mother coming back, but he had something else in mind.

it was the same old story. Your mother and I were taken to Da Nang to build a runway for their airplanes. We labored from sunup to sundown and well after dark. If we stopped to rest or have a smoke, a Moroccan would come up and whip our behinds. Our reward was a bowl of rice and another day of life. Freedom is never a gift, Bay Ly. It must be won and won again. Do you understand?"

I said that I did.

"Good." He moved his finger from the patchwork of brown dikes, silver water, and rippling stalks to our house at the edge of the village. "This land here belongs to me. Do you know how I got it?"

I thought a moment, trying to remember my mother's stories, then said honestly, "I can't remember."

He squeezed me lovingly. "I got it from your mother."

"What? That can't be true!" I said. Everyone in the family knew my mother was poor and my father's family was wealthy. Her parents were dead, and she had to work like a slave for her mother-in-law to prove herself worthy. Such women don't have land to give away!

"It's true." My father's smile widened. "When I was a young man, my parents needed someone to look after their lands. They had to be very careful about whom they chose as wives for their three sons. In the village, your mother had a reputation as the hardest worker of all. She raised herself and her brothers without parents. At the same time, I noticed a beautiful woman working in the fields. When my mother said she was going to talk to the matchmaker about this hard-working village girl she'd heard about, my heart sank. I was too attracted to this mysterious tall woman I had seen in the rice paddies. You can imagine my surprise when I found out the girl my mother heard about and the woman I admired were the same.

"Well, we were married and my mother tested your mother severely. She not only had to cook and clean and know everything about children, but she had to be able to manage several farms and know when and how to take the extra produce to the market. Of course,

> I suddenly missed my mother very much and looked down the road to the south, hoping to see her.

she was testing her other daughters-in-law as well. When my parents died, they divided their several farms among their sons, but you know what? They gave your mother and me the biggest share because they knew we would take care of it best. That's why I say the land came from her, because it did."

I suddenly missed my mother very much and looked down the road to the south, hoping to see her. My father noticed my sad expression.

"Hey." He poked me in the ribs. "Are you getting hungry for lunch?"

"No. I want to learn how to take care of the farm. What happens if the soldiers come back? What did you and Mother do when the soldiers came?"

My father squatted on the dusty hilltop and wiped the sweat from his forehead. "The first thing I did was to tell myself that it was my duty to survive—to take care of my family and my farm. That is a tricky job in wartime. It's as hard as being a soldier. The Moroccans were very savage. One day the rumor passed that they were coming to destroy the village. You may remember the night I sent you and your brothers and sisters away with your mother to Da Nang."

"You didn't go with us!" My voice still held the horror of the night I thought I had lost my father.

"Right! I stayed near the village—right on this hill—to keep an eye on the enemy and on our house. If they really wanted to destroy

> "The real problem was to keep things safe and avoid being captured. Their patrols were everywhere."

the village, I would save some of our things so that we could start over. Sure enough, that was their plan.

"The real problem was to keep things safe and avoid being captured. Their patrols were everywhere. Sometimes I went so deep in the forest that I worried about getting lost, but all I had to do was follow the smoke from the burning huts and I could find my way back.

"Once, I was trapped between two patrols that had camped on both sides of a river. I had to wait in the water for two days before one of them moved on. When I got out, my skin was shriveled like an old melon's. I was so cold I could hardly move. From the waist down, my body was black with leeches. But it was worth all the pain. When your mother came back, we still had some furniture and tools to cultivate the earth. Many people lost everything. Yes, we were very lucky."

My father put his arms around me. "My brother Huong—your uncle Huong—had three sons and four daughters. Of his four daughters, only one is still alive. Of his three sons, two

went north to Hanoi and one went south to Saigon. Huong's house is very empty. My other brother, your uncle Luc, had only two sons. One went north to Hanoi, the other was killed in the fields. His daughter is deaf and dumb. No wonder he has taken to drink, eh? Who does he have to sing in his house and tend his shrine[6] when he is gone? My sister Lien had three daughters and four sons. Three of the four sons went to Hanoi and the fourth went to Saigon to find his fortune. The girls all tend their in-laws and mourn slain husbands. Who will care for Lien when she is too feeble to care for herself? Finally, my baby sister Nhien lost her husband to French bombers. Of her two sons, one went to Hanoi and the other joined the Republic, then defected, then was murdered in his house. Nobody knows which side killed him. It doesn't really matter."

My father drew me out to arm's length and looked me squarely in the eye. "Now, Bay Ly, do you understand what your job is?"

I squared my shoulders and put on a soldier's face. "My job is to avenge my family. To protect my family by killing the enemy. I must become a woman warrior like Phung Thi Chinh!"

My father laughed and pulled me close. "No, little peach blossom. Your job is to stay alive—to keep an eye on things and keep the village safe. To find a husband and have babies and tell the story of what you've seen to your children and anyone else who'll listen. Most of all, it is to live in peace and tend the shrine of our ancestors. Do these things well, Bay Ly, and you will be worth more than any soldier who ever took up a sword." ❖

---

6. **shrine.** Altar; place of worship

MIRRORS & WINDOWS

How has the author lived up to her father's advice? What kinds of advice have people you admire given you? How did you apply the advice to your life?

Literature CONNECTION

Nguyen Thi Vinh (b. 1924) was born in the Red River Delta region of northern Vietnam. She is best known for her short stories, but she is also an accomplished poet. Following the Vietnam War, she left her native land to live with relatives in Norway.

The Vietnam War served as the historical context for **"Thoughts of Hanoi,"** which originally appeared in *The Poetry of Nguyen Thi Vinh* (1973). In 1954, the French occupation of Vietnam ended, and Vietnam was temporarily divided into a Communist North and a non-Communist South. When the Northern-backed Vietcong overthrew the government of South Vietnam, civil war erupted. Hanoi, the capital of North Vietnam, was nearly destroyed by bombs.

Thoughts of Hanoi

A Poem by
Nguyen Thi Vinh

The night is deep and chill
as in early autumn. Pitchblack,
it thickens after each lightning flash.
I dream of Hanoi:
5   Co-ngu Road
ten years of separation
the way back sliced by a frontier of hatred.
I want to bury the past
to burn the future
10   still I yearn
still I fear
those endless nights
waiting for dawn.

Brother,
15 how is Hang Dao now?
How is Ngoc Son temple?
Do the trains still run
each day from Hanoi
to the neighboring towns?
20 To Bac-ninh, Cam-giang, Yen-bai,
the small villages, islands
of brown thatch in a lush green sea?

The girls
    bright eyes
25   ruddy cheeks
    four-piece dresses
        raven-bill scarves
    sowing harvesting
        spinning weaving
30   all year round,
the boys
    ploughing
        transplanting
    in the fields
35   in their shops
    running across
        the meadow at evening
    to fly kites
        and sing alternating songs.

40 Stainless blue sky,
    jubilant voices of children
stumbling through the alphabet,
    village graybeards strolling to the temple.
grandmothers basking in twilight sun,
45   chewing betel leaves
while the children run—

Brother,
how is all that now?
Or is it obsolete?
50 Are you like me,
reliving the past,

imagining the future?
Do you count me as a friend
or am I the enemy in your eyes?
55 Brother, I am afraid
that one day I'll be with the March-North Army
meeting you on your way to the South.
I might be the one to shoot you then
or you me
60 but please
not with hatred.

For don't you remember how it was,
you and I in school together,
plotting our lives together?
65 Those roots go deep!

Brother, we are men,
conscious of more
than material needs.
How can this happen to us
70 my friend
my foe?

Refer and Reason

1. What does the speaker of the poem want to do with the past? with the future? Why might the speaker want to do these things?
2. In the memoir, compare and contrast what Bay Ly believes to be her job with what her father desires for her. What is the major difference between these two job descriptions?
3. Evaluate whether the narrator's father is a good father. If not, why not? If so, why do you think so? Use evidence from the text to support your answer.

Writing Options

1. It is obvious from the selection that Le Ly Hayslip's father had a great influence on her. Choose an older relative or a friend whom you admire and who has influenced your values and choices in life. In a biographical sketch, use Hayslip's narrative as a model for your own anecdotes that illustrate the influence of this person.
2. Bay Ly's mother wrote a song about why she should stop chewing betel nuts and why her husband should stop smoking tobacco. Write song lyrics that explain why you or someone you know should stop a particular habit.

Go to **www.mirrorsandwindows.com** for more.

TEXT ←TO→ TEXT CONNECTION

Compare the tone of the narrator of the excerpt from *When Heaven and Earth Changed Places* with that of the speaker of "Thoughts of Hanoi." What emotions does the tone of each selection evoke in you? Which selection did you find more compelling? How did each selection contribute to your understanding of the Vietnam War?

SOMETHING COULD HAPPEN TO YOU

Portrait of a Girl, 1900s. Jesús Guerrero Galván. Private collection.

NEW YORK WAS DARKER THAN I EXPECTED, AND, IN SPITE OF THE CLEANSING RAIN, DIRTIER.

An Autobiography by

Esmeralda Santiago

Esmeralda Santiago (b. 1948) spent her early childhood in Macun, Puerto Rico. At the age of thirteen, she moved with her family to New York City, where she struggled with the culture as well as with the English language. Santiago explores issues of identity in *When I Was Puerto Rican* (1993) and *Almost a Woman* (1998).

"Something Could Happen to You" is a warning that young Esmeralda frequently heard from her mother when they moved to Brooklyn, New York, from Puerto Rico. In this selection from her memoir *Almost a Woman*, Santiago describes her initial reactions to her new city, neighborhood, extended family, and school.

Have you ever visited or moved to a new place? How did it feel to be a newcomer in a strange place?

We came to Brooklyn in search of medical care for my youngest brother, Raymond, whose toes were nearly severed by a bicycle chain when he was four. In Puerto Rico, doctors wanted to amputate the often red and swollen foot, because it wouldn't heal. In New York, Mami hoped doctors could save it.

The day we arrived, a hot, humid afternoon had splintered into thunderstorms as the last rays of the sun dipped into the rest of the United States. I was thirteen and superstitious enough to believe thunder and lightning held significance beyond the meteorological. I stored the sights and sounds of that dreary night into memory as if their meaning would someday be revealed in a flash of insight to forever transform my life. When the insight came, nothing changed, for it wasn't the weather in Brooklyn that was important, but the fact that I was there to notice it.

One hand tightly grasped by Mami, the other by six-year-old Edna, we squeezed and pushed our way through the crowd of travellers. Five-year-old Raymond clung to Mami's other hand, his unbalanced gait drawing sympathetic smiles from people who moved aside to let us walk ahead of them.

At the end of the tunnel waited Tata, Mami's mother, in black lace and high heels, a pronged rhinestone pin on her left shoulder. When she hugged me, the pin pricked my cheek, pierced subtle flower-shaped indentations that I rubbed rhythmically as our taxi hurtled through drenched streets banked by high, angular buildings.

New York was darker than I expected, and, in spite of the cleansing rain, dirtier. Used to the sensual curves of rural Puerto Rico, my eyes had to adjust to the regular, aggressive two-dimensionality of Brooklyn. Raindrops pounded the hard streets, captured the dim silver glow of street lamps, bounced against sidewalks in glistening sparks, then disappeared, like tiny ephemeral jewels, into the darkness. Mami and Tata teased that I was disillusioned because the streets were not paved with gold. But I had no such vision of New York. I was disappointed by the darkness, and fixed my hopes on the promise of light deep within the sparkling raindrops.

Two days later, I leaned against the wall of our apartment building on McKibbin Street wondering where New York ended and the rest of the world began. It was hard to tell. There was no horizon in Brooklyn. Everywhere I looked my eyes met a vertical maze of gray and brown straight-edged buildings with sharp corners and deep shadows. Every few blocks there was a cement playground surrounded by chain link fence. And in between, weedy lots mounded with garbage and rusting cars.

A girl came out of the building next door, a jump rope in her hand. She appraised me shyly; I pretended to ignore her. She stepped on the rope, stretched the ends overhead as if to measure their length, then began to skip, slowly, grunting each time she came down on the sidewalk. Swish splat grunt swish, she turned her back to me, swish splat grunt swish, she faced me again and smiled. I smiled back and she hopped over.

"¿Tú eres hispana?" she asked, as she whirled the rope in lazy arcs.

"No, I'm Puerto Rican."

"Same thing. Puerto Rican, Hispanic. That's what we are here." She skipped a tight circle, stopped abruptly and shoved the rope in my direction. "Want a turn?"

"Sure." I hopped on one leg, then the other. "So, if you're Puerto Rican, they call you Hispanic?"

"Yeah. Anybody who speaks Spanish."

I jumped a circle, like she had done, but faster. "You mean, if you speak Spanish, you're Hispanic?"

"Well, yeah. No, I mean your parents have to be Puerto Rican or Cuban or something."

I whirled the rope to the right, then the left, like a boxer. "Okay, your parents are Cuban, let's say, and you're born here, but you don't speak Spanish. Are you Hispanic?"

She bit her lower lip. "I guess so," she finally said. "It has to do with being from a Spanish country. I mean, you or your parents, like, even if you don't speak Spanish, you're Hispanic, you know?" She looked at me uncertainly. I nodded and returned her rope.

> I WAS DISAPPOINTED BY THE DARKNESS, AND FIXED MY HOPES ON THE PROMISE OF LIGHT DEEP WITHIN THE SPARKLING RAINDROPS.

But I didn't know. I'd always been Puerto Rican, and it hadn't occurred to me that in Brooklyn I'd be someone else.

Later, I asked. "Are we Hispanics, Mami?"

"Yes, because we speak Spanish."

"But a girl said you don't have to speak the language to be Hispanic."

She scrunched her eyes. "What girl? Where did you meet a girl?"

"Outside. She lives in the next building."

"Who said you could go out to the sidewalk? This isn't Puerto Rico. *Algo te puede suceder.*"

"Something could happen to you" was a variety of dangers outside the locked doors of our apartment. I could be mugged. I could be dragged into any of the dark, abandoned buildings on the way to or from school, and be raped and murdered. I could be accosted by gang members into whose turf I strayed. I could be seduced by men who preyed on unchaperoned girls too willing to talk to strangers. I listened to Mami's lecture with downcast eyes and the necessary, respectful expression of humility. But inside, I quaked. Two days in New York, and I'd already become someone else. It wasn't hard to imagine that greater dangers lay ahead.

Our apartment on McKibbin Street was more substantial than any of our houses in Puerto Rico. Its marble staircase, plaster walls, and tiled floors were bound to the earth, unlike the wood and zinc rooms on stilts where I'd grown up. Chubby angels with bare buttocks danced around plaster wreaths on the ceiling. There was a bathtub in the kitchen with hot and cold running water, and a toilet inside a closet with a sink and a medicine chest.

An alley between our bedroom window and the wall of the next building was so narrow that I stretched over to touch the bricks and left my mark on the greasy soot that covered them. Above, a sliver of sky forced vague yellow light into the ground below, filled with empty detergent boxes, tattered clothes, unpaired shoes, bottles, broken glass.

Mami had to go look for work, so Edna, Raymond, and I went downstairs to stay with Tata in her apartment. When we knocked on her door, she was just waking up. I sat at the small table near the cooking counter to read the newspapers that Don Julio, Tata's boyfriend, brought the night before. Edna and Raymond stood in the middle of the room and stared at the small television on a low table. Tata switched it on, fiddled with the knobs and the antenna until the horizontal lines disappeared and black and white cartoon characters chased each other across a flat landscape. The kids sank to the floor cross-legged, their eyes on the screen. Against the wall, under the window, Tata's brother, Tío Chico, slept with his back to us. Every so often, a snore woke him, but he chewed his drool, mumbled, slept again.

While Tata went to wash up in the hall bathroom, I tuned in to the television. A dot bounced over the words of a song being performed by a train dancing along tracks, with dogs, cats, cows, and horses dangling from its windows and caboose. I was hypnotized by the dot skipping over words that looked nothing like they sounded. "Shilbee cominrun demuntin wenshecoms, toot-toot" sang the locomotive, and the ball dipped and rose over "She'll be coming 'round the mountain when she comes," with no toots. The animals, dressed in cowboy hats, overalls, and bandannas, waved pick axes and shovels in the air. The toot-toot was replaced by a bow-wow or a miaow-ow, or a moo-moo. It was joyous

> *"SOMETHING COULD HAPPEN TO YOU" WAS A VARIETY OF DANGERS OUTSIDE THE LOCKED DOORS OF OUR APARTMENT.*

and silly, and made Edna and Raymond laugh. But it was hard for me to enjoy it as I focused on the words whizzing by, on the dot jumping rhythmically from one syllable to the next, with barely enough time to connect the letters to the sounds, with the added distraction of an occasional neigh, bark, or the kids' giggles.

When Tata returned from the bathroom, she made coffee on the two-burner hot plate. Fragrant steam soon filled the small room, and, as she strained the grounds through a well-worn flannel filter, Tío Chico rose as if the aroma were an alarm louder and more insistent than the singing animals on the television screen, the clanking of pots against the hot plate and counter, the screech of the chair legs as I positioned myself so that I could watch both Tata and the cartoons.

"Well, look who we have here," Tío Chico said as he stretched until his long, bony fingers scraped the ceiling. He wore the same clothes as the day before, a faded pair of dark pants and a short-sleeve undershirt, both wrinkled and giving off a pungent sweaty smell. He stepped over Edna and Raymond, who barely moved to let him through. In two long-legged strides, he slipped out to the bathroom. As he shut the door, the walls closed in, as if his lanky body added dimension to the cramped room.

Tata hummed the cartoon music. Her big hands reached for a pan, poured milk, stirred briskly as it heated and frothed. I was mesmerized by her grace, by how she held her head, by the disheveled ash-color curls that framed her high cheekbones. She looked up with mischievous caramel eyes, and grinned without breaking her rhythm.

Tío Chico returned showered and shaved, wearing a clean shirt and pants as wrinkled as the ones he'd taken off. He dropped the dirty clothes in a corner near Tata's bed and made

up his cot. Tata handed me a cup of sweetened *café con leche*, and, with a head gesture, indicated I should vacate the chair for Tío Chico.

"No, no, that's okay," he said, "I'll sit here."

He perched on the edge of the cot, elbows on knees, his fingers wrapped around the mug Tata gave him. Steam rose from inside his hands in a transparent spiral. Tata served Edna and Raymond, then sat with her coffee in one hand and a cigarette in the other talking softly with Tío Chico, who also lit up. I brought my face to the steaming coffee, to avoid the mentholated smoke that curled from their corner of the room to ours, settling like a soft, gray blanket that melted into our clothes and hair.

I couldn't speak English, so the school counselor put me in a class for students who'd scored low on intelligence tests, who had behavior problems, who were marking time until their sixteenth birthday when they could drop out. The teacher, a pretty black woman only a few years older than her students, pointed to a seat in the middle of the room. I didn't dare look anyone in the eyes. Grunts and mutters followed me, and, while I had no idea what they meant, they didn't sound friendly.

The desk surface was elaborately carved. There were many names, some followed by an apostrophe and a year. Several carefully rendered obscenities meant nothing to me, but I appreciated the workmanship of the shadowed letters, the fastidious edges around the *f* and *k*. I guessed a girl had written the cursive message whose *i*s were dotted with hearts and daisies. Below it, several lines of timid, chicken-scratch writing alternated with an aggressive line of block letters.

I pressed my hands together under the desk to subdue their shaking, studied the straight lines and ragged curves chiseled into the desktop by those who sat there before me. Eyes on the marred surface, I focused on the teacher's voice, on the unfamiliar waves of sound that crested over my head. I wanted to float up and out of that classroom, away from the hostile air that filled every corner of it, every crevice. But the more I tried to disappear, the more present I felt, until, exhausted, I gave in, floated with the words, certain that if I didn't, I would drown in them.

On gym days, girls had to wear grass-green, cotton, short-sleeve, bloomer-leg, one-piece outfits that buttoned down the front to an elastic waistband covered with a sash too short to tie into anything but a bulky knot. Grass green didn't look good on anyone, least of all adolescent girls whose faces broke out in red pimples. The gym suit had elastic around the bottom to keep our panties from showing when we fell or sat. On those of us with skinny legs, the elastic wasn't snug enough, so the bloomers hung limply to our knees, where they flapped when we ran.

The uniform, being one piece, made it impossible to go to the bathroom in the three minutes between classes. Instead of wearing it all day, we could bring it to school and change before gym, but no one did, since boys periodically raided the locker room to see our underwear. Proper hygiene during "the curse" was impossible, as we needed at least three hands, so most girls brought notes from their mothers. The problem was that if you didn't wear the uniform on gym days, everyone knew you were menstruating.

One girl bought two gym suits, chopped off the bottom of one, seamed around the

> *BUT THE MORE I TRIED TO DISAPPEAR, THE MORE PRESENT I FELT, UNTIL, EXHAUSTED, I GAVE IN, FLOATED WITH THE WORDS, CERTAIN THAT IF I DIDN'T, I WOULD DROWN IN THEM.*

selvage, and wore the top part under her blouse so that no one could tell if she had her period or not. I asked Mami to do that for me, but she said we didn't have money to waste on such foolishness.

Friday mornings we had Assembly. The first thing we did was to press our right hands to our breasts and sing "The Star Spangled Banner." We were encouraged to sing as loud as we could, and within a couple of weeks, I learned the entire song by heart.

Ojo sé. Can. Juice. ¿Y?
Bye de don surly lie.
Whassoprowow we hell
Add debt why lie lass gleam in.
Whosebrods tripe sand bye ¿Stars?
True de perro los ¡Ay!
Order am parts we wash,
Wha soga lang tree streem in.

I had no idea what the song said or meant, and no one bothered to teach me. It was one of the things I was supposed to know, and, like the daily recitation of "The Pledge of Allegiance," it had to be done with enthusiasm, or teachers gave out demerits.[1] The pledge was printed in ornate letters on a poster under the flag in every classroom. "The Star Spangled Banner," however, remained a mystery for years, its nonsense words the only song I could sing in English from beginning to end. ❖

---

1. **demerits.** Marks entailing loss of privilege

MIRRORS & WINDOWS

Suppose someone tells you that all parents should be as protective as Santiago's mother was and that teenagers don't need to be exposed to the "real world" yet. How would you respond? Why do you think Santiago's mother was so protective? What kinds of things might parents want to protect their teenagers from today?

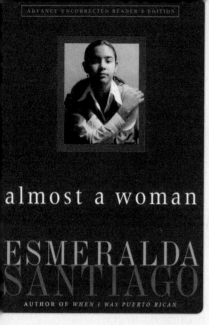

almost a woman

ESMERALDA SANTIAGO

AUTHOR OF *WHEN I WAS PUERTO RICAN*

Literature CONNECTION

"On Loan to the Lonely" is a review of Esmeralda Santiago's *Almost a Woman,* the memoir from which "Something Could Happen to You" has been excerpted. The review appeared in the *St. Paul Pioneer Press* on October 4, 1998. As you read, notice what **Barbara Gutierrez** finds important about the book.

St. Paul Pioneer Press   October 4, 1998

On Loan to the Lonely

Esmeralda Santiago remembers what life was like for a Puerto Rican girl trying to survive in a borrowed country.

A Book Review by **Barbara Gutierrez**

I still remember the initial shock of sitting in my fifth-grade class in New York City and realizing that I could not understand a word the teacher was saying.

I was a newly arrived Cuban refugee,[1] and learning English became a monumental and painful task. Esmeralda Santiago brings back those initial moments of life in the United States in her new memoir, *Almost a Woman.*

A sequel to Santiago's well-received *When I Was Puerto Rican,* the book details the story of a teenager's arrival in Brooklyn from her hometown of Macun and her slow and often painful assimilation[2] into U.S. society. This is a universal tale familiar to thousands of immigrants[3] to this country, but it is made special by Santiago's simplicity and honesty in the telling.

"Negi," as her family affectionately calls the young Santiago, is the oldest of eight children

who arrive with their mother to seek medical care for one of the youngest. Negi leaves behind a father whom she loves but who is separated from her mother and has become emotionally distant from his daughter, as well. She also cherishes her warm memories of island life.

For Negi, 13 at the time, life in this borrowed homeland is full of incongruities[4] and challenges.

Two days after her arrival, a young neighbor asks her if she is Hispanic.

"No, I am Puerto Rican," Negi retorts.

---

1. **refugee.** Person who is granted residence in a country because he or she is in danger in his or her native country
2. **assimilation** (ə si' mə lā´ shən). Process of being absorbed into the culture of the majority population
3. **immigrants.** People who come to a country in order to live there
4. **incongruities** (in' kən grü´ ə tēs). Inconsistencies

"Same thing. Puerto Rican. Hispanic. That's what we are here."

"Two days in New York, and I'd already become someone else. It wasn't hard to imagine that greater dangers lay ahead," Santiago writes.

Life becomes a constant balancing act as Negi tries to embrace an independent life-style without giving up the protective values of her upbringing. Each time she pushes the issue—wanting to date without a chaperone, for instance—her mother warns her: "Algo te puede suceder" or "Something could happen to you."

When her mother loses her factory job, and the only financial sustenance for the family, Negi accompanies her to the local welfare office to act as a translator. The scene is heart-wrenching as the daughter musters the little English she knows to help her family get assistance while retaining integrity and self-respect.

This encounter is a self-defining moment for Negi, who vows to learn enough English to never get "caught between languages."

Headstrong and intelligent, Negi manages not only to learn English but also to excel in school, and she gains acceptance to the prestigious High School of Performing Arts (eventually, she graduates from Harvard).

By far the most interesting part of the work is watching Negi develop her own moral compass in the face of her "mami," a single mother who bore several children out of wedlock but wanted her daughters to fare better and to leave the house in "a white gown en route to a cathedral."

Negi manages to fulfill most of the obligations imposed on her, acting as a role model for her many siblings, working full time and studying part time at a community college and still making the trip home to sleep safely under her mother's roof.

Santiago writes in a straightforward, honest tone without much flourish. Yet her language conveys intimate details of her emotional maturing that allows us to feel privy to a private woman. ❖

Refer and Reason

1. Find a quotation from "Something Could Happen to You" that summarizes the narrator's mother's attitude about her new home. Why might she feel this way?
2. Describe what the narrator of "Something Could Happen to You" learns about being Hispanic. How does she feel about being Hispanic? What are her greatest obstacles as a recent immigrant?
3. Interpret why Gutierrez begins her review "On Loan to the Lonely" by recounting a personal experience. What does Gutierrez have in common with Santiago?

Writing Options

1. Imagine that you are Mami, young Esmeralda's mother. In a series of journal entries, record your impressions of American life soon after your arrival in Brooklyn. Also jot down your thoughts about how Esmeralda seems to be adjusting to life in her new neighborhood.
2. Esmeralda Santiago has said about *Almost a Woman*, "When I began writing this book, I had no idea it would result in a dialogue about cultural identity." For a conference on cultural identity, write a critical essay in which you examine the ideas Santiago expresses about the topic and then compare them to your own.

Go to **www.mirrorsandwindows.com** for more.

TEXT ← TO → TEXT CONNECTION

Considering your own reactions to "Something Could Happen to You," do you think Barbara Gutierrez has evaluated Esmeralda Santiago's book fairly in the review? Why or why not?

An Encounter with an Interviewer

But, good heavens! If you were at his funeral, he must have been dead; and if he was dead, how could he care whether you made a noise or not?

A Humorous Sketch by **Mark Twain**

Mark Twain was the pen name, or pseudonym, chosen by Samuel Langhorne Clemens (1835–1910), who was born in Florida, Missouri, and became one of America's best-loved writers. In the 1890s, Twain suffered a series of financial disasters and had to deal with the death of his wife and two daughters, and the vitality and sly humor of his early work gave way to a dark pessimism.

In 1894, Twain was bankrupt. To pay off his debts, he made a worldwide lecture tour. While lecturing, he was interviewed by many journalists. The experience gave him plenty of material to write his satire **"An Encounter with an Interviewer."**

Have you ever wanted to make fun of a foolish custom or idea? How could you use humor to expose its foolishness?

The nervous dapper, "peart"[1] young man took the chair I offered him, and said he was connected with the "Daily Thunderstorm" and added,—

"Hoping it's no harm, I've come to interview you."

"Come to what?"

"*Interview* you."

"Ah! I see. Yes—yes. Um! Yes—yes. I see."

I was not feeling bright that morning. Indeed, my powers seemed a bit under a cloud. However, I went to the bookcase, and when I had been looking six or seven minutes, I found I was obliged to refer to the young man. I said,—"How do you spell it?"

"Spell what?"

"Interview."

"Oh my goodness! what do you want to spell it for?"

"I don't want to spell it; I want to see what it means."

---

1. **peart.** Lively; chipper

Mark Twain, 1885. Joseph Ferdinand Keppler. Library of Congress.

A portrait of Aaron Burr.

"Well, this is astonishing, I must say. I can tell you what it means, if you—if you—"

"Oh, all right! That will answer, and much obliged to you, too."

"In, *in*, ter, *ter*, *inter*—"

"Then you spell it with an *I*?"

"Why, certainly!"

"Oh, that is what took me so long."

"Why, my *dear* sir, what did *you* propose to spell it with?"

"Well, I—I—hardly know. I had the Unabridged[2] and I was ciphering around the back end, hoping I might tree her among the pictures. But it's a very old edition."

"Why, my friend, they wouldn't have a *picture* of it in even the latest e— My dear sir, I beg your pardon, I mean no harm in the world, but you do not look as—as—intelligent as I had expected you would."

"Oh, don't mention it! It has often been said, and by people who would not flatter and who could have no inducement to flatter, that I am quite remarkable in that way. Yes—yes; they always speak of it with rapture."

"I can easily imagine it. But about this interview. You know it is the custom, now, to interview any man who has become notorious."

"Indeed, I had not heard of it before. It must be very interesting. What do you do it with?"

"Ah, well—well—well— this is disheartening. It *ought* to be done with a club in some cases; but customarily it consists in the interviewer asking questions and the interviewed answering them. It is all the rage[3] now. Will you let me ask you certain questions calculated to bring out the salient points of your public and private history?"

"Oh, with pleasure,—with pleasure. I have a very bad memory, but I hope you will not mind that. That is to say, it is an irregular memory,—singularly irregular. Sometimes it goes in a gallop, and then again it will be as much as a fortnight[4] passing a given point. This is a great grief to me."

---

2. **Unabridged.** Dictionary that has not been condensed
3. **all the rage.** Craze; fad
4. **fortnight.** Two weeks

"Oh, it is no matter, so you will try to do the best you can."

"I will. I will put my whole mind on it."

"Thanks. Are you ready to begin?"

"Ready."

Q. How old are you?

A. Nineteen, in June.

Q. Indeed! I would have taken you to be thirty-five or -six. Where were you born?

A. In Missouri.

Q. When did you begin to write?

A. In 1836.

Q. Why, how could that be, if you are only nineteen now?

A. I don't know. It does seem curious, somehow.

Q. It does, indeed. Whom do you consider the most remarkable man you ever met?

A. Aaron Burr.[5]

Q. But you never could have met Aaron Burr, if you are only nineteen years—

A. Now, if you know more about me than I do, what do you ask me for?

Q. Well, it was only a suggestion— nothing more. How did you happen to meet Burr?

A. Well, I happened to be at his funeral one day, and he asked me to make less noise and—

Q. But, good heavens! If you were at his funeral, he must have been dead; and if he was dead, how could he care whether you made a noise or not?

A. I don't know. He was always a particular kind of man that way.

Q. Still, I don't understand it at all! You say he spoke to you, and that he was dead.

A. I didn't say he was dead.

Q. But, wasn't he dead?

A. Well, some said he was, some said he wasn't.

Q. What did you think?

A. Oh, it was none of my business! It wasn't any of my funeral.

Q. Did you—However, we can never get this matter straight. Let me ask about something else. What was the date of your birth?

A. Monday, October 31st, 1693.

Q. What! Impossible! That would make you a hundred and eighty years old. How do you account for that?

A. I don't account for it at all.

Q. But you said at first you were only nineteen, and now you make yourself out to be one hundred and eighty. It is an awful discrepancy.

A. Why, have you noticed that? (Shaking hands.) Many a time it has seemed to me like a discrepancy, but somehow I couldn't make up my mind. How quick you notice a thing!

Q. Thank you for the compliment, as far as it goes.[6] Had you, or have you, any brothers or sisters?

A. Eh! I—I—I think so—yes—but I don't remember.

Q. Well, this is the most extraordinary statement I ever heard!

A. Why, what makes you think that?

Q. How could I think otherwise? Why, look here! Who is this a picture of on the wall? Isn't that a brother of yours?

A. Oh! yes, yes, yes! Now you remind me of it, that *was* a brother of mine. That's William—*Bill* we called him. Poor old Bill!

Q. Why? Is he dead, then?

A. Ah! well, I suppose so. We never could tell. There was a great mystery about it.

Q. That is sad, very sad. He disappeared, then?

A. Well, yes, in a sort of general way. We buried him.

Q. *Buried* him. *Buried* him, without knowing whether he was dead or not?

A. Oh, no! Not that. He was dead enough.

Q. Well, I confess that I can't understand this. If you buried him, and you knew he was dead—

A. No! no! We only thought he was.

Q. Oh, I see! He came to life again?

A. I bet he didn't.

---

5. **Aaron Burr** (1756–1836). Vice President of the United States from 1801 to 1805

6. **as far as it goes.** Limited though it is

The Power of the Press. This cartoon by Thomas Nast depicts a journalist crushing men with a printing press.

Q. Well, I never heard anything like this. *Somebody* was dead. *Somebody* was buried. Now, where was the mystery?

A. Ah! that's just it! That's it exactly . You see, we were twins,—defunct[7] and I,—we got mixed in the bath-tub when we were only two weeks old, and one of us was drowned. But we didn't know which. Some think it was Bill. Some think it was me.

Q. Well, that *is* remarkable. What do *you* think?

A. Goodness knows! I would give whole worlds to know. This solemn, this awful mystery has cast a gloom over my whole life. But I will tell you a secret now, which I never have revealed to any creature before. One of us had a peculiar mark—a large mole on the back of his left hand; that was *me. That child was the one that was drowned!*

Q. Very well, then, I don't see that there is any mystery about it, after all.

A. You don't? Well, I do. Anyway, I don't see how they could ever have been such a blun-dering lot as to go and bury the wrong child. But, 'sh—don't mention it where the family can hear of it. Heaven knows they have heart-breaking troubles enough without adding this.

Q. Well, I believe I have got material enough for the present, and I am very much obliged to you for the pains you have taken. But I was a good deal interested in that account of Aaron Burr's funeral. Would you mind telling me what particular circumstance it was that made you think Burr was such a remarkable man?

A. Oh! it was a mere trifle! Not one man in fifty would have noticed it at all. When the sermon was over, and the procession all ready to start for the cemetery, and the body all arranged nice in the hearse, he said he wanted to take a last look at the scenery, and so he *got up and rode with the driver—*

Then the young man reverently withdrew. He was very pleasant company, and I was sorry to see him go. ❖

---

7. **defunct.** No longer living; dead

Evaluate the decision of "playing dumb" in order to prove a point to someone. What can be achieved by doing so? What are the drawbacks? What are alternative ways of getting someone to understand your point of view?

Refer and Reason

1. What word does the narrator attempt to look up in the dictionary? Describe the response on the part of the interviewer that reveals his gullibility.
2. Analyze the information the narrator gave to the interviewer. Is it possible the interviewer has "got material enough"? Why or why not? What is the narrator trying to do to the interviewer? Is he successful?
3. Judge whether the narrator's attitude toward the interviewer is understandable. If you were the interviewer, would you have tolerated the narrator's behavior? Explain your answer.

Writing Options

1. Imagine that you are the interviewer. Write a character sketch of Mark Twain, as he appears from your perspective. Share your sketch orally with a small group of classmates, and invite their feedback.
2. Mark Twain was a celebrity when he made his worldwide lecture tour to pay off his debts. Read several magazines to see how they cover celebrities. Then write a celebrity profile of Mark Twain, adopting the style of the magazine you consider most appealing. You will need to read more about Mark Twain in order to write an interesting and accurate article. Use Internet resources, or consult standard reference volumes such as *The Oxford Companion to American Literature*.

 Go to **www.mirrorsandwindows.com** for more.

WARRIORS DON'T CRY: A Searing Memoir of the Battle to Integrate Little Rock's Central High
by Melba Patillo Beals

Fifteen-year-old Melba Patillo became one of the "Little Rock Nine" in 1957, integrating the all-white Central High School. Based on Melba's diaries, this straightforward chronicle allows us a glimpse of what it must have been like to be a teenage warrior, who often wanted to be "just a girl."

NIGHT
by Elie Wiesel

When fifteen-year-old Elie and his family are marched onto a train bound for Auschwitz, he finds out for himself what human beings can do to each other. In this harrowing personal account of his time in a concentration camp, Elie Wiesel conveys a powerful message about how we relate to each other.

DOWN AND OUT IN PARIS AND LONDON
by George Orwell

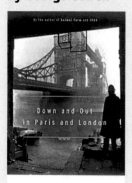

To see what life is really like for people with no money or home, George Orwell takes up life as a street person in 1930s Paris and London. This honest and sometimes humorous account of life in the slums and alleys offers a look at a side of life many people avoid thinking about.

A BRIEF HISTORY OF TIME
by Stephen Hawking

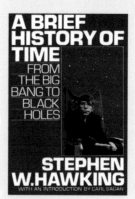

Stephen Hawking, who is confined to a wheelchair as a result of Lou Gehrig's disease, has been called the most brilliant physicist since Einstein. His purpose in this book is to inform his readers, in a clear, accessible way, about the progress being made in understanding the laws that govern the universe.

SILENT DANCING: A Partial Remembrance of a Puerto Rican Childhood
by Judith Ortiz Cofer

In this collection of essays, poems, and stories, Judith Ortiz Cofer shuttles back and forth between her childhood on the island of Puerto Rico and her adolescence in New Jersey, exploring the loneliness of being an immigrant and the difficulty of establishing roots in a military family.

PHINEAS GAGE: A Gruesome but True Story About Brain Science
by John Fleischman

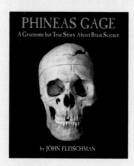

When Phineas Gage ended up with an iron rod in his head due to an accident in 1848, no one believed he would survive. But he did, and his recovery changed the way the medical community understood the human brain. This account describes Gage's harrowing ordeal.

Listen Actively and Take Notes

Have you ever sat in class without really hearing what the teacher said? Sometimes, it's easy to let your mind wander, but when you are in school, it's important to be an active listener and note taker.

Being an active listener is more than just hearing what a speaker says; it's consciously focusing your attention on the speaker with the purpose of gaining information. Review the following tips for being an active listener. Are there ways you can improve your own methods of listening?

Active Listening Strategies

- Focus your total attention on the speaker.
- Avoid distractions by sitting near the front of the classroom.
- Listen with all your senses, imagining what the speaker describes as if you were experiencing it firsthand.
- Set a purpose for listening so that you know what to focus on.
- Listen with an open mind, even if you disagree with the speaker. (See Listening Tip.)
- Adapt to your listening the reading strategies that work best for you. For example, connect the speaker's ideas to what you know, or visualize what the speaker is describing.

Note-Taking Strategies

- Prepare to take notes by bringing a notebook and a pen or pencil.
- Write down the main points.
- Listen for cues that indicate main points. Cues include transitions, repetition, changes in voice, and numbered lists.
- Avoid getting lost in minor details and examples by focusing on how each relates to the main point.
- After the speaker has finished, review your notes, and ask questions to fill in any missing information or clear up points of confusion.

Practice

Imagine that you are listening to Anne Lamott give a lecture on how to improve your writing. Listen as your teacher reads "Short Assignments" aloud or plays an audio recording of it. You'll find that Lamott uses many details and examples to enhance her main ideas, but what you are most concerned with is learning as much as you can from her about how to write. Take notes on the ideas that seem most important. Then discuss the following questions with your class.

1. What purpose did you set for listening?
2. How did you stay focused as you listened?
3. What did you write down as you listened? Did you use any kind of code as you made notes?
4. What questions would you like to ask Lamott about this excerpt if she were speaking to your class?
5. Which of Lamott's ideas or examples is most meaningful to you?

Listening Tip

If you get distracted because you disagree with something a speaker says, make a note of your disagreement so that you can come back to it later. Then refocus on what the speaker is saying. Learn as much as you can about the speaker's views so that you can disagree most effectively during the discussion period.

Note-Taking Tip

Develop a code for making notes. Here are some marks you could use:

? Ask a question about this later.
! I disagree!
★ This is important.

Develop a set of symbols that is meaningful to you, and practice using them. Eventually, you will use the symbols automatically.

Personal Narrative

Assignment
Write a personal narrative about a true story from your life.

Purpose
To understand your story and to share it with readers

Audience
Your teacher and classmates; family and friends; people who do or do not know you

Personal stories have always been an important way for humans to communicate with each other. Telling them helps us to understand what we've been through. Listening to them shows us experiences we might never know on our own. To write *My Left Foot*, Christy Brown had to overcome the very physical challenges he meant to describe. The act of reading so influenced Anna Quindlen's life that she wrote an entire book about it. There is universal truth in a specific and unique personal story. Everyone has a story worth telling.

A **personal narrative** tells a true story from the author's own life, often an important and relevant story. Written in first person, a focused narrative shares the author's thinking, interests, or life events. The narrative reflects on the significance of the topic, and what the author learned or how an experience shaped his or her life.

❶ PREWRITE

Select Your Topic
Talk to parents, siblings, and other relatives. Look through photo albums and scrapbooks, and make a list of memories. Settle on a topic — an event, possession, characteristic, or idea — of personal importance.

Writing Rubric

A well-written personal narrative:

☑ focuses on a single specific incident or experience, stated in the **introduction;** provides enough background for context

☑ states a purpose for exploring the incident in the **thesis statement**

☑ narrates the story in the **body;** includes only relevant details; and uses description, action, and dialogue

☑ **concludes** by ending the narration, reflecting on the topic's significance, and providing satisfying closure for the reader

---

Gather Information
After you've chosen your topic, begin to narrow it down and develop it. Freewrite everything you remember or know about your topic. Use a Details Chart like the one on page 379 to help you stay focused and to generate details to include in your narrative.

Consider why the topic is important to you. The more you work with your topic, the more you may remember. Continue to fill in details. As you begin to understand the story's significance, record these thoughts in the last column of the chart.

Organize Your Ideas
Most personal narratives use **chronological order,** telling about events in the order in which they occurred. Sometimes, however, a writer chooses to start the story at a particularly exciting moment or interesting bit of dialogue and then fills in the earlier events later in the narrative.

As you look at the notes in your chart, decide where you would like to start your narrative. Consider how best to organize the details of your topic.

Write Your Thesis Statement
Write one sentence that zeroes in on the focus of your essay. This is your **thesis statement,** your purpose for writing the narrative. After generating information in his chart, one student, Joshua Tanner, wrote a thesis statement about a significant fishing trip with his father and brother.

Thesis: One morning when I was nine, however, a steelhead managed to change our brotherly relationship forever.

Details Chart

Focus: First Fish				
Beginning	Middle	Sensory Details	End, or Results	Significance
I had never been steelhead fishing before.	John was being his typical teacher self.	The lures were orange, and the fish was rainbow and silver.	We got the fish in and it was a big deal because it was my first.	I want to focus on the importance of my father and brother's fishing relationship.
I was only nine but had been trout fishing.	I got my line tangled, a bird's nest, and Dad asked John to take it and fix it.	The fish crashed, exploded from the water, pulling on the line.	My brother could have given me a hard time but he didn't.	The fish—what are the chances? I was inexperienced. I got lucky?
I had a typical relationship with my dad and older brother.	The fish hit a moment later. This all happened in a matter of minutes.	It was really cold out. I remember being tired. My arms ached.	My dad was proud and happy for me. So was my brother, which surprised me.	My brother should have got the fish. I stole my first steelhead with inexperience.
We fish a lot together. Fishing is a big part of our lives.	It took forever, but we got the fish in.	There was shouting but I didn't understand any of it.	I got my picture in the local hunting and news weekly.	Dad and John are proud. It's been better between us ever since.

❷ DRAFT

Write your essay by following a three-part framework: **introduction, body,** and **conclusion.**

Draft Your Introduction

In a personal narrative, you describe yourself to readers as well as tell a story from your life. Begin your essay in a way that **introduces** the topic and grabs the reader's interest. The introduction sets the tone for the rest of the essay, so your language should be warm and personable, yet clear and informative.

Joshua's essay begins with a brief introduction of his family fishing trips, as shown in the first column of his Details Chart. He layers in a description of his relationship with his brother. He ends with his thesis statement, alerting readers to a specific incident that will change the way the brothers relate. Consider whether your narrative would benefit from an introduction like Joshua's, or whether you prefer beginning with some aspect of the story itself.

What Great Writers Do

Adding descriptive details helps readers visual your subject.

When Anna Quindlen in *How Reading Changed My Life* says, "I remember riding my bicycle for miles to the neighborhood where my aunt and uncle lived," she provides a visual picture for the reader by adding, "a narrow avenue of brick row houses with long boxcar backyards."

- **Introduction**
  Introduce your topic and begin the narrative. Set up the situation and introduce the other people involved. Include your thesis statement.
- **Body**
  Using vivid sensory details, describe what happened. Develop characters and conflicts.
- **Conclusion**
  Narrate the end of the story. Include any conflict resolutions. Mention insights gained. Give your essay closure.

Draft Your Body

In the body, draft the full story. Use details from your Details Chart, and include other details that arise in your memory as well. Try to fully re-experience the event. Rather than simply stating what happened, use dialogue and sensory details to let your reader visualize and experience the action.

Joshua began the body of his essay with the cold, dark start of the day the event happened. Read the draft of his first body paragraph in the left-hand column on page 381. Joshua continued to support his thesis statement by writing dialogue and including action from his story.

Review the paragraph order you decided on. Develop the story into a logical, smooth-flowing narrative. All story elements should refer back to your main purpose for writing it, as stated in your thesis.

Draft Your Conclusion

Lastly, write the **conclusion** of your personal narrative. A good conclusion brings the story to a close in a satisfying way, and at the same time reflects on the story's larger significance. Consider how to add insights you gained. Perhaps you can discuss what you learned, what you know now that you didn't know then, or how things have changed.

Does Joshua conclude his narrative successfully? Look at the draft of his conclusion on page 381.

❸ REVISE

Evaluate Your Draft

You can evaluate your own writing or exchange papers with a classmate and evaluate each other's work. Carefully consider what's done well and what can be improved.

What Great Writers Do

At the end of her personal narrative, *How Reading Changed My Life,* Anna Quindlen asserts the insight of her opinion with a tone of confidence: "Reading is like so much else in our culture, in all cultures: the truth of it is found in its people and not in its pundits and its professionals."

As you read for content and organization, make sure the three parts of the essay — the introduction, body, and conclusion — work together and focus on the thesis. Use the Revision Checklist on page 382 to make this evaluation. Make notes directly on the essay about what changes need to be made.

As you check the language for errors, make sure you have correctly applied the guidelines in the Grammar & Style workshops in this unit. Again, use the Revision Checklist to evaluate the writing. Think, too, about how to make your story vivid. One way to achieve this is to replace any statements telling what happened with description that shows instead of tells.

Revise for Content, Organization, and Style

Joshua evaluated his draft and found a number of things to improve. Look at the right-hand column on page 381 to see how he revised the three paragraphs you looked at earlier.

DRAFT STAGE		REVISE STAGE	

Introduction

My father, John, and I go fishing a lot. The three of us spend hours together in a small rowboat. John is three years older. He is often critical of me. He gets frustrated by my incompetence. He is a born fisherman in a way I am not. One morning when I was nine a steelhead changed our brotherly relationship forever.

Provides story context with background information

States thesis about the specific incident

My father has been taking my older brother John and I ~~go~~ fishing ~~a lot~~ since we could walk. The three of us spend hours together in a small rowboat. John, ~~is~~ three years older, ~~He~~ is often critical of me and ~~He gets~~ frustrated by my incompetence. He is a born fisherman in a way I am not. One morning when I was nine, however, a steelhead changed our brotherly relationship forever.

Creates a more interesting first line

Combines sentences to reduce choppiness and vary length

Uses a good sentence-level transition

Body Paragraph

For my fanatic father and brother, the "morning" of that steelhead trip started at night. Fishing poles got handed out. My father pulled steadily on the oars. Me shivering in the bottom of the boat, watching the dark shoreline and the stars above. At the time, I had little interest in fishing. That day, my brother turns into a steelhead expert with an attitude.

Begins the narrative

Gives reader a visual sense of the event

Describes conflict and keeps readers' interest

For my fanatic father and brother, the "morning" of that steelhead trip started at night. John handed out fishing poles ~~get handed out~~. My father pulled steadily on the oars. ~~Me~~ I shivere~~d~~ing in the bottom of the boat, watching the dark shoreline and the stars above. At the time, I had little interest in fishing. That day, my brother turn~~s~~ed into a steelhead expert with an attitude.

Makes passive sentence active

Fixes verb tense to write parallel sentences; corrects grammatical error: verb tense agreement

Conclusion

There's a newspaper photo of me holding the steelhead. John has his arm slung around my shoulder and a proud smile on his face. We had hamburgers and milkshakes right after that. My hands still smelled like fish. I couldn't shake the feeling that I had stolen a victory rightfully meant for him but John never said a word because on the day John let me have his fish, I finally became a member of "the club."

Finishes telling the story; allows reader to see how his brother changed

Briefly describes the aftermath

~~There's a~~ In the newspaper photo of me holding the steelhead, John has his arm slung around my shoulder and a proud smile on his face. ~~We had hamburgers and milkshakes right after that. My hands still smelled like fish.~~ At first, I couldn't shake the feeling that I had stolen a victory rightfully meant for him. ~~but~~ John never said a word. ~~because~~ On the day he let me have his steelhead, I finally became a member of "the club."

Combines sentences

Deletes details irrelevant to the conclusion

Adds sentence-level transition

Separates sentences for good emphasis

REVISION CHECKLIST

Content and Organization

❑ How is the topic **introduced?** Does the thesis establish the focus of this essay?

❑ Does the **body** develop the narrative using a clear and logical organization?

❑ Is all information relevant and important? Does each detail serve a purpose?

❑ Does the **conclusion** reflect on the topic's significance and provide a satisfying closure for the reader?

❑ Is the language vivid and precise?

Grammar and Style

❑ Does the writer use colons and semi-colons correctly? (page 258)

❑ Are verb tenses consistent? (page 272)

❑ Does the writer use irregular verbs correctly? (page 284)

❑ Are words capitalized correctly? (page 304)

❑ Does the writer avoid sentence fragments and run-ons? (page 326)

❑ Do all paragraphs include a topic sentence and supporting details? (page 336)

- **Introduction:** Joshua improved his introduction by developing his first line. He combined three choppy sentences into one to create smoother, more varied writing. By adding a sentence-level transition, he strengthened the relationship of his thesis to the previous sentences.
- **Body:** Joshua made sure all verbs were consistently in past tense. He changed a passive sentence to active. This also created a nice parallel construction.
- **Conclusion:** Joshua combined two closely related sentences. He deleted details that were unnecessary for his conclusion. Joshua broke a long sentence, one with too much going on in it, into three sentences, giving emphasis to each line.

Review the notes you or your partner made as you evaluated your draft. Then respond to each comment and effectively revise your narrative.

Proofread for Errors

Proofreading checks for remaining errors. While you can make corrections during the evaluation phase, you should focus on it during proofreading. Use proofreader's symbols to mark any errors you find. (See Language Arts Handbook 4.1 for a list of proofreader's symbols.) To complete the assignment, print out a final draft and read the entire essay once more before turning it in.

Take a look at Joshua's final draft on the next page. Review how he worked through the three stages of the writing process: Prewrite, Draft, and Revise.

WRITING FOLLOW-UP

Publish and Present

- Compile a class anthology of personal narratives. Place it in the classroom or your school library so students can access it.
- Print out and give a copy of your essay to all the people who appear in your narrative.

Reflect

- How did writing a personal narrative sharpen or even change your memory of the event? What did you learn about the power and limitations of memory?
- What are other ways to preserve experiences? Why is it important to reflect on personal experiences?

STUDENT MODEL

A First Fish
by Joshua Tanner

My father has been taking my older brother John and I fishing since we could walk. The three of us spend hours together in a small rowboat. John, three years older, is often critical of me and frustrated by my incompetence. He is a born fisherman in a way I am not. One morning when I was nine, however, a steelhead changed our brotherly relationship forever.

For my fanatic father and brother, the "morning" of that steelhead trip started at night. John handed out fishing poles. My father pulled steadily on the oars. I shivered in the bottom of the boat, watching the dark shoreline and the stars above. At the time, I had little interest in fishing. That day, my brother turned into a steelhead expert with an attitude.

"They hit hard, like this," he said and punched me in the shoulder. "You gotta put in a lot of fishing time to hook a steelhead."

"Just hand me the bait," I said.

"There is no bait, stupid," John scoffed.

"Knock it off," my father said. "Josh, check your reel. What d'ya got going there?"

I looked down. I had accidentally released the spool on my reel and tangled the fishing line into a "bird's nest."

"Josh, take your brother's pole," Dad ordered. "John, fix that."

Without a word, John traded poles and set to work untangling my mess. I didn't have a moment to be embarrassed. John's fishing pole, in my hands, suddenly bent double. A steelhead shot out of the water thirty yards downstream. My instincts made me stand, jab the pole into my gut, and reel like crazy.

"That's right, Josh," John shouted. "Hold steady." The fish fought and thrashed. A few times it got so close we saw its black back and dangling pink lure. Then it launched across the river and almost pulled me with it. We saw it explode from the water, trying to throw the hook.

It felt like hours before the fish tired out. It took, in reality, about twenty minutes. Dad and John helped me reel it in. Only when Dad docked the boat did I notice John had managed to untangle my bird's nest.

In the newspaper photo of me holding the steelhead, John has his arm slung around my shoulder and a proud smile on his face. At first, I felt like I had stolen a victory rightfully meant for him. John never said a word. On the day he let me have his steelhead, I finally became a member of "the club."

What will this story be about?
What is the focus, or thesis statement, of this narrative?

How and when does the writer begin telling the story?

What descriptive details help the reader envision the story?

Where does the writer use vivid, precise language?

How does action move the story along?

In what ways does the writer reflect on the incident in the conclusion?

Reading Skills

IDENTIFY THE MAIN IDEA AND SUPPORTING DETAILS

The **main idea** is a brief statement of what you think the author wants you to know, think, or feel after reading the text. In some cases, the main idea will actually be stated. Check the first and last paragraphs for a sentence that sums up the entire passage. Usually, the author will not tell you what the main idea is, and you will have to infer it. To make an inference, you will need to combine all the details from the text with your prior knowledge and draw a conclusion as to the meaning of the passage.

To infer the main idea, ask yourself these questions:
- Who or what is this passage about?
- What does the author want me to know, think, feel, or do about this "who" or "what"?
- If I had to tell someone in one sentence what this passage is about, what would I say?

A good way of inferring the main idea is to gather important details from the selection into a Main Idea Map like the one shown here for the excerpt from *Desert Exile* (page 247). Use the details you have listed to infer the main idea of the selection. (Remember, all the significant details in the selection should relate to the main idea.)

Main Idea Map

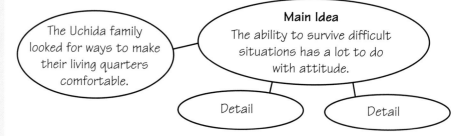

The Uchida family looked for ways to make their living quarters comfortable.

Main Idea
The ability to survive difficult situations has a lot to do with attitude.

Detail

Detail

Test-Taking Tips
- Read the passage carefully.
- Read and consider all of the answer choices before you choose the one that best responds to the question.
- Refer to the passage when answering the questions.

PRACTICE

Directions: Read the following article. The questions that come after it will ask you to identify the main idea and supporting details.

Nonfiction: This excerpt is from "The Roots of Genius? The Odd History of a Famous Old Brain" by Steven Levy.

Albert Einstein's death, in 1955, hasn't stopped his brain from leading a lively existence. Its visit to McMaster University in Ontario, Canada, has led to an article in the June 19 *Lancet* (a British medical journal) affirming that maybe, just maybe, the secrets of relativity were due in part to unusual development of a lobe known for mathematical thought. And then again, maybe not. 5

It was just one more chapter in the twisted history of a brain that was born in 1879, hatched the secret of relativity in 1905 and was liberated from its body by a Princeton pathologist 50 years later. No further news came until the summer of 1978, 10

when I came into the picture; my editor at a
regional magazine asked me to find it. I deduced
that it was still in the hands of the pathologist, Dr.
Thomas Harvey. I tracked him to Wichita, Kans.,
where, after much cajoling, he sighed deeply and
pulled from a cardboard box two glass jars with
the sectioned pieces of Einstein's brain. Eureka!
Harvey told me that so far in his ongoing study
he'd found no variations from the norm.

My article encouraged Berkeley neuroanato-
mist Marian Diamond to get some samples from
Harvey; she counted 73 percent more glial cells
than the norm. (Glial cells help keep the network
of neurons humming.) In 1996, another study
indicated that the Nobel winner's cortex was
"more densely populated with neurons." But there
was no indication that the density led to E=mc².

The McMaster researchers, led by Sandra F.
Witelson, began their work when Dr. Harvey sent
them some samples in 1996, as well as photos
of the brain before sectioning. Unlike brains
in a control group of 35, Einstein's had a short
sylvian fissure (a groove on the side), and a brain
part known as the operculum was undeveloped.
This may have allowed Einstein's parietal lobes,
believed to affect math, music and visual images,
to grow 15 percent wider than average. "The
thing that's compelling," says Witelson, "is that
the differences occur in the region that supports
psychological functions of which Einstein was a
master." The *Lancet* findings may well be a valuable jumping-off point for further research. But
will taking the measure of parietal lobes really
tell us why Einstein stands atop the scientific
pantheon? His genius was unique, a control group
of one. That's why his brain fascinates us, and has
been the subject of "potboilers, poems, screen-
plays and paranoid cloning plots." And that's why,
when I beheld Albert's brain matter bobbing in
the formaldehyde like soggy tofu chunks, my own
mind spun with amazement and wonder. When
it comes to appreciating the most famous brain of
our century, it ain't the meat—it's the emotion.

Multiple Choice

1. Which of the following statements *best* expresses
   the main idea of the article?
   A. Einstein's brain has traveled to many universi-
      ties and is the subject of several studies.
   B. According to Thomas Harvey, Einstein's brain
      is completely normal.
   C. Einstein's genius might be attributable to an
      excess of glial cells or a groove on the side of
      his brain.
   D. Though Einstein's brain shows certain abnor-
      malities, it is far from clear whether his genius
      was the result of biology.

2. Which detail below supports the idea that the
   differences in Einstein's brain occur in regions
   where Einstein was most successful?
   F. Einstein had more glial cells, which keep
      neurons fueled.
   G. Einstein had more neurons than average.
   H. Einstein had a groove on the side of his brain.
   J. Einstein's parietal lobe was 15 percent wider
      than average.

3. In line 18, the word *cajoling* means
   A. coaxing.
   B. nagging.
   C. questioning.
   D. laughing.

4. Which of the following details is *not* included in
   this article?
   F. New discoveries were made about Einstein's
      brain up until 1978.
   G. Glial cells help keep the network of neurons
      in the brain working.
   H. The finding of the *Lancet* provided a start for
      further research.
   J. Einstein died in 1955.

Constructed Response

5. What does Steven Levy, the author, seem to
   believe about Einstein's genius? How can you tell?
   Use information from the passage to support your
   answer.

Writing Skills

PERSUASIVE ESSAY

Many high-stakes tests, including a college entrance exam, ask that you write an essay on a prescribed issue. Prompts on such tests generally introduce the issue and offer two different perspectives or positions on the topic. You are then asked to choose a position and write a persuasive essay supporting this position, using reasons and examples. The essay must be completed within a specified period of time, often 30 minutes.

Scorers will take into account the limited amount of time you had for writing your essay. They will evaluate your ability to do the following:
- take a position on the issue in the prompt
- focus on the topic throughout the essay
- support your ideas logically and thoroughly
- organize your ideas in a logical way
- use language clearly and effectively according to the conventions of standard written English

As with any writing assignment, make sure to apply the basic steps of the writing process: prewrite, draft, and revise. Organize your essay into the three-part framework of introduction, body, and conclusion.

- **Introduction** Identify your topic and include a thesis that states your opinion about it.
- **Body** Provide at least three logical reasons to support your opinion, and to inform and persuade your readers.
- **Conclusion** Rephrase your thesis and give your essay closure.

Writing Tips

Plan your essay by doing the following:
- choosing a position
- listing at least three reasons that support that position
- offering support and examples for each reason
- identifying any counterarguments and responses

PRACTICE

Timed Writing: 30 minutes

Think carefully about the issue presented in the following paragraph and the assignment below. Allow 30 minutes to write your response to the prompt.

Some legislators would like to require all students in public schools to recite the Pledge of Allegiance every day. They believe this measure would improve citizenship and inspire patriotism in students. Opponents of this idea argue that it would take valuable time away from learning and would make the pledge meaningless through repetition. Do you think students should be required to recite the Pledge of Allegiance every day?

Assignment: Write an essay in which you take a position on this issue. You may argue in favor of one of the two points of view given, or you may write about a third perspective on the issue. Support your position with specific reasons and examples.

Revising and Editing Skills

Some standardized tests ask you to read a draft of an essay and answer questions about how to improve it. As you read the draft, watch for errors like these:

- incorrect spellings
- disagreement between subject and verb; inconsistent verb tense; incorrect forms for irregular verbs; sentence fragments and run-ons; double negatives; and incorrect use of frequently confused words, such as *affect* and *effect*
- missing end marks, incorrect comma use, and lowercased proper nouns and proper adjectives
- unclear purpose, unclear main ideas, and lack of supporting details
- confusing order of ideas and missing transitions
- language that is inappropriate to the audience and purpose, and mood that is inappropriate for the purpose

After checking for errors, read each test question and decide which answer is best.

PRACTICE

Directions: In the passage that follows the sentences are numbered. Read each question, and consider each answer to determine which one is best. If you think the original version is best, choose "MAKE NO CHANGE."

(1) The airport is quite far from our house, so in order to get <u>their</u> on time, we left at six in the morning. (2) <u>My uncle's car he drove us to the airport was crammed with suitcases, coats, and carry-on bags, not to mention me, my mother, and my father.</u> (3) My uncle dropped us off at the airport and <u>drives</u> away, leaving us to catch our plane. (4) <u>My parents and me were</u> excited to fly to Germany to visit my grandmother.

1. A. MAKE NO CHANGE.
   B. they're
   C. there
   D. there's

2. F. MAKE NO CHANGE.
   G. My uncle's car—he drove us to the airport—was crammed with suitcases, coats, and carry-on bags, not to mention me, my mother, and my father.
   H. My uncles car he drove us to the airport was crammed with suitcases, coats, and carry-on bags, not to mention me, my mother, and my father.
   J. My uncle's car he drove us to the airport in was crammed with suitcases, coats, and carry-on bags, not to mention me, my mother, and my father.

3. A. MAKE NO CHANGE.
   B. was driving
   C. had been driving
   D. drove

4. F. MAKE NO CHANGE.
   G. Me and my parents were
   H. My parents and I were
   J. My parents and me was

UNIT 3
Poetry

BACA

NYE

SANDBURG

"A poem should not mean
But be." —Archibald MacLeish

Have you ever loved someone so much it hurt? Have you ever known anyone who failed to live up to his or her potential? Have you ever wanted to shout for joy? The poems in this unit show that poetry is so much more than fancy words on a page; rather, it's about the joys, challenges, and experiences that come with being alive.

LEE

KINCAID

MISTRAL

INTRODUCTION TO POETRY

Remember the plants, trees, animal life
 who all have their
tribes, their families, their histories,
 too. Talk to them,
listen to them. They are alive poems.

—from "Remember" by Joy Harjo

What is poetry? It's a love poem tucked in your locker. It's a tribute to a hero or loved one who has died. It's a means of protesting injustice, expressing anger, or shouting with joy. It's a humorous or dramatic way to tell a story. It's a variety of shapes and forms and uses of language. In this unit, you will find that the answer to "What is poetry?" varies from person to person but that all poetry springs from the experience of being human.

THE GENRE OF POETRY

The word "poem" comes from the Greek *poíma,* which means "work," and is derived from *poieín,* "to make." Finding a good definition for poetry is difficult, however, because poems can take so many forms.

Poetry uses imaginative and musical language to communicate experiences, thoughts, or emotions. Of all the literary forms, it packs the most meaning into the fewest words. Because poetry is often arranged in lines and stanzas as opposed to sentences and paragraphs, it has more freedom than prose in its ordering of words and use of punctuation.

There are many different types of poetry. One thing that all poems have in common, however, is precision of language; each word of a poem is carefully chosen to convey a tone, viewpoint, and perception of an object or an experience.

Why Read Poetry?

"We don't read and write poetry because it's cute. We read and write poetry because we are members of the human race. And the human race is filled with passion. And medicine, law, business, engineering, these are noble pursuits and necessary to sustain life. But poetry, beauty, romance, love, these are what we stay alive for."

—Robin Williams, as Mr. Keating in the film
Dead Poets Society

ELEMENTS OF POETRY

A single poem may contain numerous recognizable elements. As you read the poems in this unit, consider the ways they make use of the elements described below.

Speaker and Tone

An essential part of any poem is its speaker. The **speaker** of a poem is the character who speaks in, or narrates, the poem—the voice assumed by the writer. Since the speaker is the voice of the poem, the voice sets the tone. **Tone** is the emotional attitude toward the reader or toward the subject implied by a poem. Examples of different tones include familiar, ironic, playful, sarcastic, serious, and sincere. (See Understanding Speaker and Tone, page 398.)

Setting and Context

The **setting** of a literary work is the time and place in which it occurs, together with all the details used to create a sense of a particular time and place. In poetry, **context** refers to the conditions in which the poem occurs. Context is closely related to setting but focuses more on the environment of the time and place. Two common types of context include historical and cultural. (See Understanding Setting and Context, page 410.)

Structure and Form

Poetry is divided into lines and stanzas as opposed to sentences and paragraphs. A stanza may have any number of lines. The types of stanzas are sometimes referred to by the number of lines in each. For example, a two-line stanza is known as a *couplet.*

There are many different forms of poetry. Some forms, such as sonnets and haiku, follow fixed patterns. Other forms, like free verse, do not follow any pattern at all. (See Understanding Structure and Form, page 418.)

Figurative Language

Figurative language is writing or speech that is meant to be understood imaginatively instead of literally. Figurative language may be used in all types of writing but is especially common in poetry.

- A **metaphor** is a comparison in which one thing is written about as if it were another.
- A **simile** is a comparison that uses *like* or *as.* In "Poetry," for example (page 447), Nikki Giovanni uses many similes: "poetry is motion graceful / as a fawn / gentle as a teardrop / strong like the eye."
- **Personification** is a figure of speech in which an animal, a thing, a force of nature, or an idea is described as if it were human or is given human qualities. (See Understanding Figurative Language, page 444.)

Sight and Sound

There are several elements of poetry that enhance its musical and visual qualities. **Rhythm** is the pattern of beats, or stresses, in a line of poetry. Rhythm can be regular or irregular. A regular rhythmic pattern is called a **meter.** Typically, stressed syllables are marked with a ⌣ and unstressed syllables with a ╱. **Rhyme** is the repetition of sounds in words, as in *day* and *away.*

Imagery is descriptive language that creates a vivid picture in the mind of the reader and appeals to the senses—primarily sight but also sound, touch, taste, and smell. For example, in "Making a Fist" (page 401), Naomi Shihab Nye uses the image of "a melon split wide inside my skin" to describe how her stomach feels as she suffers from motion sickness. (See Understanding Sight and Sound, page 452.)

Poets Throughout History

Do you recognize any of these poets? Several of them are featured in this unit. What do you think it is that makes the works of well-loved poets like these stand the test of time?

William Shakespeare (c. 1564–1616)
Emily Dickinson (1830–1886)
Robert Frost (1874–1963)
Langston Hughes (1902–1967)
Pablo Neruda (1904–1973)
Sylvia Plath (1932–1963)
Lucille Clifton (b. 1936)

POETRY READING MODEL

BEFORE READING   DURING READING   AFTER READING

BUILD BACKGROUND

- **Make predictions** about what the poem will be about by reading the title and the **Build Background** feature, and looking over any footnotes.
- Read the **Meet the Author** feature to see if the information about the author gives you any insights into his or her writing.

ANALYZE LITERATURE

- The **Analyze Literature** feature will focus on literary techniques or elements that are used in the selection. In poetry, the author may use language or structure in a way that supports the meaning of the poem.

SET PURPOSE

- **Preview** the text to set a purpose for reading. A purpose for reading poetry might be to see how the poet creates moods, messages, or images in the reader's mind.

USE READING SKILLS

- Before reading, apply reading skills, such as analyzing text structure and previewing new vocabulary words. The **Use Reading Skills** feature will give you instructions on how to apply the skills while you read, such as using a graphic organizer.

BEFORE READING   **DURING READING**   AFTER READING

USE READING STRATEGIES

- **Ask questions** about things that seem unusual or interesting or things you don't understand. For instance, you might ask why the author chose certain images to express his or her ideas.
- **Make predictions** about what's going to be revealed next in the poem.
- **Visualize** by forming pictures in your mind to help you see any scenes or people described in the poem. Poetry often makes use of strong images.
- **Make inferences,** or educated guesses, about what is not stated directly. Things may be implied or hinted at, or they may be left out altogether.

- **Clarify,** or check that you understand, what you read. Go back and reread any confusing or difficult parts before continuing.

ANALYZE LITERATURE

- Determine which **literary elements** stand out as you read the poem. What point of view does the speaker of the poem have? Which metaphors and similes contribute to the meaning of the poem?

MAKE CONNECTIONS

- Notice where there are **connections** between the selection and your life or the world beyond the poem. In what ways does the topic of the poem apply to you or to people you know?

BEFORE READING   DURING READING   **AFTER READING**

REFER TO TEXT

- **Remember details,** such as the key images.
- Try to **summarize** the selection in a sentence or two. Ask yourself, what is this poem about?

REASON WITH TEXT

- **Interpret** the ideas and images in the poem to help you clarify meaning.
- **Analyze** the text by breaking down information into smaller pieces and figuring out how those pieces fit into the poem as a whole.
- **Evaluate** the text. **Draw conclusions** by bringing

together what you have read and using it to make a decision about what the speaker of the poem is trying to get across.

ANALYZE LITERATURE

- Review how the author's use of **literary elements** increased your understanding or enjoyment of the poem.

EXTEND THE TEXT

- **Extend** your reading beyond the selection by exploring ideas through writing or doing other creative projects.

I Am Offering This Poem

BEFORE READING
A Lyric Poem by Jimmy Santiago Baca

BUILD BACKGROUND

Literary Context "I Am Offering This Poem" was the first love poem written by Jimmy Santiago Baca in the most unlikely place—a maximum-security prison. Baca, who had been homeless for much of his teens, was sent to prison for five years when he was twenty-one and there decided to learn how to read and write. Learning language led him to reading poetry, in particular, Pablo Neruda and Federico García Lorca. Encouraged by another inmate, he sent his poems to poet Denise Levertov at the journal *Mother Jones* for publication. In 1979, Baca's first collection of poetry was published, entitled *Immigrants in Our Own Land.*

Reader's Context What are the basic necessities of life? What do you need for a happy life?

ANALYZE LITERATURE: Image and Imagery

An **image** is a picture formed in the mind of a reader. The vivid language that creates this picture is called **imagery.** Imagery appeals to the senses of sight, sound, touch, taste, and smell.

SET PURPOSE

Why might someone offer a poem to another person? Consider the speaker's reason for offering this poem. To whom do you think the speaker is writing? Why? Throughout the poem, Baca uses a series of images to describe what the poem means. Note how this use of imagery supports the speaker's purpose in offering the poem.

MEET THE AUTHOR

Jimmy Santiago Baca (b. 1952) was born in Santa Fe, New Mexico, of Mexican-Apache heritage. Abandoned by his parents at the age of two, he lived with his grandmother for a while before being placed in an orphanage, from which he ran away at age thirteen. It looked as though Baca's rough childhood would lead him to a life of crime when he was arrested at twenty-one and sentenced to five years in prison. However, while in prison, he learned to read and write, which changed the course of his life. The same year that Baca was released from prison, he published his first collection of poems and earned his GED. Baca says of his call to poetry, "I think language gives us courage. Poetry gives us courage and faith to live with open wounds."

USE READING SKILLS

Text Organization Paying attention to text organization can help you read a poem in small and manageable sections. This poem is divided into *stanzas,* which are the breaks between lines of poetry. The stanzas in "I Am Offering This Poem" vary in number of lines, but each is followed by the phrase "I love you" separated from the stanza. As you read, summarize the main message of each stanza. You may want to use a graphic organizer like the one below to help you as you read. Then discuss with a partner why "I love you" is set apart and repeated.

Stanza	Images	Summary
1		
2		
3		
4		

Chalet in the Snow. Gabrielle Munter. Bridgeman Art Library.

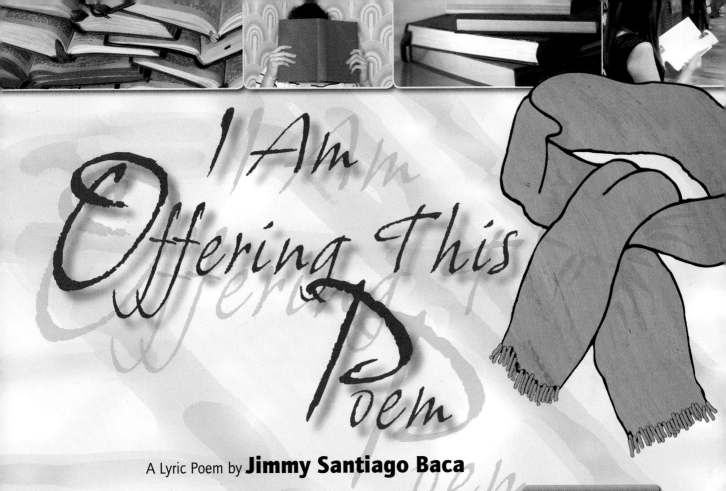

I Am Offering This Poem

A Lyric Poem by **Jimmy Santiago Baca**

DURING READING

USE READING STRATEGIES

Visualize Picture each image in your mind as you read. What feelings do the images create inside you?

I am offering this poem to you,
since I have nothing else to give.
Keep it like a warm coat
when winter comes to cover you,
5   or like a pair of thick socks
the cold cannot bite through,

      I love you,

I have nothing else to give you,
so it is a pot full of yellow corn
10   to warm your belly in winter,
it is a scarf for your head, to wear
over your hair, to tie up around your face,

      I love you,

DURING READING

USE READING STRATEGIES

Make Inferences Why is the metaphorical cabin or hogan "tucked away" in the trees?

Keep it, treasure this as you would
15   if you were lost, needing direction,
in the wilderness life becomes when mature;
and in the corner of your drawer,
tucked away like a cabin or hogan[1]
in dense trees, come knocking,
20   and I will answer, give you directions,
and let you warm yourself by this fire,
rest by this fire, and make you feel safe,

               I love you,

It's all I have to give,
25   and all anyone needs to live,
and to go on living inside,
when the world outside
no longer cares if you live or die;
remember,

30   I love you. ❖

DURING READING

ANALYZE LITERATURE

Image and Imagery What emotions do the images evoke in you? Which images do you find the most powerful?

---

1. **hogan.** A traditional Navajo dwelling made of logs and covered with earth

Why is writing poetry often considered a romantic gesture? What kind of power does poetry have? What messages, both positive and negative, can the act of giving a poem as a gift convey?

AFTER READING

REFER TO TEXT ▶ ▶ ▶ ▶	▶ REASON WITH TEXT	
1a. List the objects to which the poem is likened.	1b. Conclude which emotions or items that can't be held or touched the poem represents.	**Understand** **Find meaning**
2a. Identify a quotation from the poem that explains when life becomes a wilderness.	2b. Apply what you know about Baca's background to speculate on what inspired him to write this poem.	**Apply** **Use information**
3a. Recall what the speaker will do if the recipient of the poem "come[s] knocking."	3b. Infer what feelings and ideas the speaker wants the recipient of the poem to have.	**Analyze** **Take things apart**
4a. How should the recipient keep the poem?	4b. Judge whether or not love is "all anyone needs to live." Explain your answer.	**Evaluate** **Make judgments**
5a. Summarize the last stanza of the poem.	5b. Propose whether or not you think the speaker has actually experienced the difficult times mentioned in the poem. Use evidence from the poem to support your answer.	**Create** **Bring ideas together**

ANALYZE LITERATURE: Image and Imagery

Reread the poem and make a list of the images. To which sense or senses does each image appeal? Describe what the poem would be like if it did not use imagery. How does the use of imagery impact your understanding of the poem?

EXTEND THE TEXT

Writing Options

Creative Writing Greeting cards allow people to express their sentiments in an artistic way. Create a **line of greeting cards** for special occasions that include verses from songs or poems. You may write your own verses or use ones from other sources. The cards can be made by hand or done on a computer. Include art or photos with your cards and display them in your classroom.

Narrative Writing The speaker of this poem gives the gift of poetry to show his love. Imagine you've been asked to write for the holiday edition of a magazine a short **reflective paragraph** about a time someone gave you a meaningful gift. Include in your paragraph a description of how you reacted to the gift and how it affected you.

Lifelong Learning

Research Literacy Programs Jimmy Santiago Baca's life changed when he learned to read, thanks in part to a "Good Samaritan" program where a kind stranger sent him a grammar book. With a partner, do Internet research to find statistics about rates of illiteracy in your state. Find out what literacy programs are available in your community. Then, create a public awareness poster promoting the importance of literacy and drawing attention to one or more of the literacy programs in your community.

Collaborative Learning

Create an Anthology "I Am Offering This Poem" is a poem expressing love. Many poems focus on the topic of love. Using a variety of poetry collections, create an anthology of poems about different types of love, such as romantic love, love among family members, and so on. For each poem you include, write a brief introduction about the author and the poem. Collect all your poems and introductions together in a binder to share with your class.

 Go to **www.mirrorsandwindows.com** for more.

Understanding Speaker and Tone

SPEAKER AND TONE

Poetry has survived the centuries because of its ability to convey emotions and images. One of the reasons so many poems are cherished is that they speak to the reader's heart, mind, or imagination. Yet, who really is speaking? Is it the author? a created character in the poem? The **speaker** of a poem is the character who speaks in, or narrates, the poem—the voice assumed by the writer. The speaker and the writer of the poem are not necessarily the same person.

Since the speaker is the voice of the poem, the voice sets the tone. **Tone** is the emotional attitude toward the reader or toward the subject implied by a poem. Examples of different tones include familiar, ironic, playful, sarcastic, serious, and sincere. Closely related to tone is **mood,** or the emotion created in the reader by the poem.

ELEMENTS OF SPEAKER AND TONE

Voice

Voice is the way a writer uses language to reflect his or her unique personality and attitude toward a topic, form, and audience. The speaker in Joy Harjo's poem, "Remember" (page 407) conveys a sense of earnestness in which she hopes that people will not forget that they are connected to the world around them. The constant repetition of the use of the word "remember" helps express this sense of urgency in the speaker's voice and contributes to the serious tone of the poem.

> Remember you are all people and all people are you.
> Remember you are this universe and this universe is you.
> Remember all is in motion, is growing, is you.
> Remember language comes from this.
> Remember the dance language is, that life is.
> Remember.
> —from "Remember" by Joy Harjo

The voice in "I Am Offering This Poem" is humble as the speaker asks that his love and his poem be accepted and that the reader find comfort in both.

> It's all I have to give,
> and all anyone needs to live,
> and to go on living inside,
> when the world outside
> no longer cares if you live or die;
> remember,
>   I love you.
> —from "I Am Offering This Poem" by
>   Jimmy Santiago Baca

Irony

One aspect of voice to consider is irony. **Irony** is the difference between appearance and reality. Different types of irony include the following:
- *dramatic irony:* something is known by the reader or audience by unknown to the characters
- *verbal irony:* a character says one thing but means another
- *irony of situation:* an event occurs that violates the expectations of the characters, the reader, or the audience

Verbal irony operates when a speaker says one thing but means something quite different. Irony can be subtle, suggesting that the speaker has in mind several different shades of meaning. An ironic statement may also be rather crude and obvious, as in the case of sarcasm. As you read, be aware of this gap between what is said and what is intended.

In "Holidays" (page 437), for example, the speaker uses irony of situation. The poem begins with the speaker reflecting on how she is spending her vacation sitting on the porch looking at the mountains. At the end of the poem, the speaker says, "Perhaps, I will take a nice long nap. Perhaps, while taking my nap, I will have a dream, a dream in which I am not sitting on the porch facing the mountains." That the poem is about the speaker's vacation while the speaker appears not to really want to be on vacation is ironic.

Diction

Diction, when applied to writing, refers to the author's or poet's choice of words and how those word choices express ideas or emotions. As you know, poets choose words very carefully, and every word is important. As you read, consider specific word choices and think about why a poet chooses certain words instead of others.

ASSESSING TONE

Discovering the tone of a poem is more than knowing what the poem is about or what it is trying to accomplish. For example, in "I Am Offering This Poem" and "Remember," we know both speakers offer the reader advice on how to persevere through life's difficult times. In "I Am Offering This Poem," the speaker tells the reader to seek comfort and guidance in the speaker's love and poem. In "Remember," the speaker asks the reader to remember that all people are part of a larger world. Figuring out tone, however, involves going beyond knowing what the poem is about and paying close attention to the words the poem uses. Below are some methods of discovering tone.

Read Aloud To figure out the tone of a poem, first try reading it aloud. Sometimes, hearing the words will help reveal how the speaker feels about the subject.

Notice Words That Stand Out Pay attention to the words in a poem that seem to follow a certain pattern or evoke similar emotions. In "I Am Offering This Poem," the words *warm, treasure, tucked away, rest, safe*, and *love* all express a sense of comfort and security.

Another thing to think about is the connotations of words. The **denotation** of a word is its dictionary definition. The **connotation** of a word is the set of ideas or emotional associations it suggests, in addition to its actual meaning. For example, the connotation of the word *warm* suggests comfort and security, whereas the connotation of the word *stuffy* suggests a feeling of being closed in and uncomfortable.

Consider the Speaker It may also help to consider the speaker as a character instead of as a neutral observer. What bias might the speaker show? What attitude do you think the speaker or poet expresses? What is the speaker not saying that might be important?

Compare and Contrast Comparing poems with similar themes or subjects can help you to analyze the tone of each poem. "Poetry" (page 447) and "Introduction to Poetry" (page 449) both deal with writing poetry. "Shall I compare thee to a summer's day?" (page 421) and "I know I am but summer to your heart" (page 422) are about love. "Dream Variations" (page 456) and "miss rosie" (page 473) celebrate African-American pride. The speaker's voice and perspective are different in each poem, so, naturally, each will have its own particular tone. Consider these adjectives as a starting point for how to describe tone:

hopeful	scared	terrified
sad	thrilled	agitated
wistful	regretful	calm
mournful	impassioned	reluctant
determined	boastful	
celebratory	worried	
joyful	annoyed	
bitter	rebellious	
frustrated	ambivalent	
amused	furious	

Making a Fist

A Lyric Poem by Naomi Shihab Nye

BUILD BACKGROUND

Literary Context In the lyric poem **"Making a Fist,"** the speaker shares a vivid childhood memory about being afraid while on a family road trip. The lessons learned from this experience have remained with the speaker in her adult life. The poem is also a quiet commentary on the things children worry about—worries that often seem exaggerated or amusing from an adult perspective. For example, were you ever afraid of dragonflies sewing your mouth shut? of seeds growing into plants in your stomach? of gum collecting in your digestive system?

Reader's Context As a child, were you ever anxious or frightened when you were sick? Who or what gave you comfort and reassurance? What did you learn from the experience?

ANALYZE LITERATURE: Speaker and Tone

The **speaker** is the character who speaks in, or narrates, a poem. The speaker and the writer of a poem are not necessarily the same person. **Tone** is the emotional attitude toward the reader or toward the subject that is implied in a literary work. Examples of the different tones a work may have include familiar, ironic, angry, playful, serious, or sincere.

SET PURPOSE

Before you read, think about the poem's title. When or why might you make a fist? What situations come to mind? Read to find out what the title means. As you read, visualize the speaker as a child and consider how this image of "making a fist" contributes to the overall tone of the poem.

MEET THE AUTHOR

Naomi Shihab Nye (b. 1952) was born in St. Louis, Missouri, and raised there by her German-American mother and her Palestinian father. She wrote her first poems around the age of six, just after learning to write. She has published numerous books of poetry as well as children's books. Her subjects over the years have included marriage, motherhood, her Palestinian heritage, and travel. Nye has said, "Anyone who feels poetry is an alien or ominous force should consider the style in which human beings think.... We think in poetry. But some people pretend poetry is far away." When asked what advice she would give to young writers, Nye replied, "Read, Read, and then Read some more."

USE READING SKILLS

Main Idea The **main idea** of a piece of writing is a brief statement of what you think the author wants you to know, think, or feel after reading the text. In some cases, the main idea is actually stated. If it isn't stated, you will have to infer it. As you read the poem, find the main idea by gathering important details into a Main Idea Map like the one below. When you finish reading, use the details to determine the main idea and draw conclusions about it.

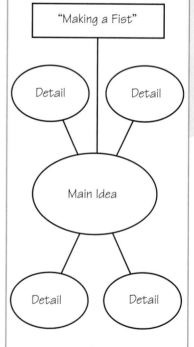

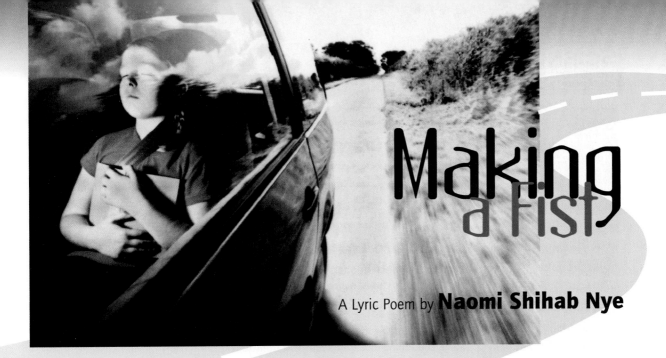

Making a Fist

A Lyric Poem by **Naomi Shihab Nye**

USE READING STRATEGIES

Visualize Describe in words or sketch the images that form in your mind as you read.

For the first time, on the road north of Tampico,[1]
I felt the life sliding out of me,
a drum in the desert, harder and harder to hear.
I was seven, I lay in the car
5   watching palm trees swirl a sickening pattern past the glass.
My stomach was a melon split wide inside my skin.

"How do you know if you are going to die?"
I begged my mother.
We had been traveling for days.
10   With strange confidence she answered,
"When you can no longer make a fist."

Years later I smile to think of that journey,
the borders we must cross separately,
stamped with our unanswerable woes.
15   I who did not die, who am still living,
still lying in the backseat behind all my questions,
clenching and opening one small hand. ❖

ANALYZE LITERATURE

Speaker Think of three or four adjectives to describe the poem's speaker.

---

1. **Tampico** (tam pē´ kō'). Port city on Mexico's east coast

MIRRORS & WINDOWS

What kind of impact can a parent's words have on his or her child? Should a parent always answer a child's questions truthfully? Why or why not?

Motion Sickness Motion sickness is a feeling of nausea, clamminess, and dizziness caused by mixed signals received when a person is in motion. Usually, the feeling occurs when the fluid in the inner ear, called endolymph, tells your brain that you are in motion, but your other senses do not reinforce that message. Car sickness, a form of motion sickness, is often caused by lying down, reading, or doing something else that keeps you from seeing the scenery moving past the car. Seasickness and, more recently, space sickness are other forms of motion sickness. The best cure for motion sickness is to look out a window at scenery in the distance. Getting fresh air and drinking ginger tea can also help.

AFTER READING

REFER TO TEXT ▶ ▶ ▶ ▶	▶ REASON WITH TEXT	
1a. Recall where the speaker and her mother are at the beginning of the poem. How old is the speaker?	1b. Explain why the speaker might remember the trip so vividly.	**Understand** **Find meaning**
2a. Quote the question the speaker asks and her mother's answer.	2b. Examine why the speaker asks this question.	**Apply** **Use information**
3a. State what the speaker says about the "borders" in lines 13–14.	3b. Identify what the "borders" symbolize. What main idea or larger meaning does the speaker find in this childhood memory?	**Analyze** **Take things apart**
4a. Evaluate whether the mother's answer to the speaker's question is a good one. Explain your answer.	4b. How would you respond to a child if he or she asked you the same question as the speaker asked?	**Evaluate** **Make judgments**
5a. Summarize how the speaker sees herself, now that she is an adult.	5b. Compile a list of some of the childhood lessons that remain with people throughout their lives. Do memories of childhood play a positive role in adulthood, in your opinion? Explain.	**Create** **Bring ideas together**

ANALYZE LITERATURE: Speaker and Tone

Reread the poem, and then explain how the speaker's tone changes from the first to the third stanza. What details help to create this change in tone?

Writing Options

Creative Writing Which memories from your childhood remain etched in your mind? Write a one-page **memoir** that shares one of your childhood memories. In your memoir, use vivid details to make the memory really come alive for your readers and relate why the memory is so important that it has remained with you all these years.

Expository Writing Think about the main idea in "Making a Fist" and what you did and did not like about the poem. Write a one-page **persuasive essay** in which you advise a friend who is editing a poetry anthology whether or not to include "Making a Fist" in the collection. Briefly summarize what the poem describes. Then explain your reasons for recommending or not recommending the selection. Finally, summarize your thoughts in a conclusion.

Collaborative Learning

Create a Website The speaker in the poem asks her mother a difficult question. Young children often ask their parents complex questions, and parents don't always know how to answer. Working in a small group, compile a list of ten challenging questions children might ask their parents. An example of a challenging question might be "Why is the sky blue?" Then, if the questions can be answered factually, do research to find the answers. If there are not factual answers to the questions, think of the best and most truthful way to answer the questions. Finally, create the text for a website meant to help parents answer the difficult questions their children ask.

Critical Literacy

Develop Interview Questions Locate one or two of Naomi Shihab Nye's collections of poetry: for example, *Different Ways to Pray* (1980), *Yellow Glove* (1986), or *The Flag of Childhood: Poems from the Middle East* (2002). Read other poems by this author, and think about the common elements among their subjects and themes. Then prepare a list of interview questions for Nye, asking her to comment on ways in which her poetry reflects her life experiences and her most important values. Share your questions with a small group of classmates.

 Go to **www.mirrorsandwindows.com** for more.

READING ASSESSMENT

1. In "Making a Fist," which of the following childhood memories does the speaker recall?
   A. a time when her mother was sick
   B. a time when she did poorly on a test at school
   C. a time when she was sick on a family trip
   D. the first time she rode a bicycle
   E. a time when she got the flu at school

2. In line 10, the word *confidence* most nearly means
   A. trickery.
   B. firm belief.
   C. secrecy.
   D. pride.
   E. happiness.

3. Which of the following best describes the speaker's tone at the end of the poem?
   A. anguished
   B. indifferent
   C. humorous
   D. determined
   E. miserable

4. Which of the following best describes one of the main ideas of the poem?
   A. Getting carsick is not fun.
   B. Life is uncertain, but one must still press on.
   C. Being able to make a fist indicates being alive.
   D. Moms are good at giving advice.
   E. Long car trips are difficult for young children.

5. Which of the following is an example of a metaphor?
   A. "I felt the life sliding out of me."
   B. "I lay in the car / watching palm trees swirl a sickening pattern past the glass."
   C. "My stomach was a melon split wide inside my skin."
   D. "With strange confidence she answered, / 'When you can no longer make a fist.'"
   E. None of the above

6. Reread the final stanza of the poem. Then, in a paragraph explain how you know that the speaker, as an adult, still struggles with her own vulnerability and lack of confidence.

GRAMMAR & STYLE

Phrases

A **phrase** is a group of words used as a single part of speech. A phrase lacks a subject, a verb, or both. Therefore, it cannot be a sentence. There are several different types of phrases, including prepositional, participial, gerund, and infinitive. They are listed in the chart below.

Type of Phrase	Prepositional	Participial	Gerund	Infinitive
What it is	preposition + object + modifiers	participle + objects or modifiers	gerund + modifiers or complements	infinitive + modifiers or complements
What it does	shows the relationship between the object and another word in the sentence using words such as *above, after, against, among, around, at, behind, beside, between, down, for, from, in, like, off, on, through, to, toward, until, upon,* and *with*	describes a noun or pronoun in the sentence	acts as a subject, predicate nominative, direct object, indirect object, or object of a preposition in a sentence	acts as a subject, object, or modifier
How it functions	adjective or adverb	adjective	noun	noun, adjective, or adverb
Example	The girl sat *behind her mother in the car.*	*Riding in the car,* the girl clenched her hand into a fist.	*Walking briskly for half an hour* is a good way to get over car sickness.	The girl hoped *to feel better after she got out of the car.*

REVIEW TERMS

- **preposition:** word or group of words that combines with a noun or pronoun to form a phrase that usually acts as an adverb, an adjective, or a noun, such as "in the house"
- **direct object:** the receiver of an action
- **indirect object:** the receiver of an action when the direct object is received by someone or something, as in "The boy gave the bat to his mom." (*Bat* is the direct object; *mom* is the indirect object.)
- **modifier:** word that adds meaning to a noun, adjective, verb, or adverb
- **participial:** verb form that sometimes can be used like an adjective, such as the words *leaning* and *tumbled* in the sentence "The leaning wall had tumbled."
- **gerund:** noun formed from a verb by the addition of *–ing*
- **complement:** word or group of words added to a sentence to make the sentence complete
- **predicate nominative:** word or group of words that follows a linking verb and identifies the subject
- **object of a preposition:** the noun or pronoun that follows a preposition
- **infinitive:** verb form preceded by the word *to,* as in "to run"

Identify Phrases

Identify each of the underlined phrases in these sentences as prepositional, participial, gerund, or infinitive.

1. Lying in the backseat of the car, the child felt ill.
2. Traveling for days had exhausted her.
3. Her stomach felt like a watermelon split open.
4. She wanted to ask her mother a question.
5. Her mother answered the question with strange confidence.
6. Making a fist gave the child hope.
7. Years later, now an adult, she smiled at that question recalled from the past.
8. She remembered the car trip from her childhood.
9. She was seven years old when she realized her mortality.
10. Her family was on a road trip through the desert.
11. Asking complicated questions is something many children do.
12. Having similar experiences as the poem's speaker is a way children learn.
13. A parent has to be creative to answer a child's questions about life.
14. The poem's speaker came to an understanding at that time in her life.
15. She will never forget her introduction to the adult world.

Understand Phrases

Write a sentence for each of the following phrases.

1. riding in the car
2. to be home soon
3. sleeping peacefully
4. in a strange way
5. from everyday life
6. dropped on the floor
7. to win the game
8. after lunch
9. eating noisily
10. like a flower
11. at 10:00 a.m.
12. to write a poem
13. made a loaf of bread
14. acting strangely
15. thought about summer vacation

Improve a Paragraph

Rewrite the paragraph shown below, adding prepositional, participial, gerund, and infinitive phrases as needed to make the writing more detailed and interesting.

Naomi Shihab Nye often celebrates ordinary people and objects. She creates poetry from everyday scenes. Often, she explores the similarities and differences between cultures. For example, her first novel for young adults, entitled *Habibi*, tells the story of an Arab-American boy who lives in Jerusalem during the 1970s. Nye's poems are also known to reflect her Arab-American heritage. Her literature serves to encourage and bring peace.

Use Phrases in Your Writing

Use library or Internet resources to research the biography of Naomi Shihab Nye. Then write a short biographical sketch of the poet to share with your classmates. In your sketch, use at least one of each of the four different types of phrases: prepositional, participial, gerund, and infinitive.

EXTEND THE SKILL

Pick a sentence at random from each of three or four works that you have read recently or are currently reading, whether it is a textbook, a novel, a magazine, or a how-to appliance manual. Note how many phrases are used in the sentences, and what type of phrase each one is. You might also want to look at sentences in a children's book and compare the phrases with those in a work written for adults.

Remember

BUILD BACKGROUND

Cultural Context Joy Harjo's ancestry includes Native Americans of the Cherokee nation. Once the most dominant people of the southeastern United States, the Cherokees lost half their number in the mid-1700s to a smallpox epidemic. In the 1830s, after gold was discovered on their land, they were forcibly evicted and ordered to settle 1,000 miles to the west, in what is now Oklahoma. The suffering and loss during this journey, known as the "Trail of Tears," are still remembered as one of the most tragic episodes in Native American history. In **"Remember,"** the speaker urges readers to remember their origins and their connections with each other and with the natural world.

Reader's Context What do you think about the human ability to remember the past? Are memories always positive and helpful? When might memories be negative, imprisoning us or holding us back?

ANALYZE LITERATURE: Voice and Theme

Voice is the way a writer uses language to reflect his or her unique personality and attitude toward the topic, form, and audience. A writer expresses voice through tone, word choice, and sentence structure. A **theme** is a central idea in a literary work.

SET PURPOSE

"Remember" comes from Harjo's *How We Became Human.* As you read, watch for hints that suggest the author's attitude on what it means to be truly human. Make a list of the things that Harjo asks the reader to remember. Consider what these things suggest about the personality of the speaker and how each of these things contributes to the overall theme of the poem.

MEET THE AUTHOR

Born in Tulsa, Oklahoma, **Joy Harjo** (b. 1951) is of mixed Muscogee/Creek, Cherokee, French, and Irish heritage. The author of many poetry collections, Harjo is also a songwriter, a musician, and a screenwriter. Harjo's poetry collection entitled *In Mad Love and War* (1990) won several distinguished poetry awards, including the Delmore Schwartz Memorial Prize. Commenting on her poetry, she has said that it relates to "sacred space — I call it a place of grace, or the place in which we're most human.... It's that place in which we understand there is no separation between worlds."

USE READING SKILLS

Draw Conclusions When you **draw conclusions** from a literary work, you gather pieces of information and then decide what that information means. You use evidence from the work, as well as your own prior experience and reasoning ability, to develop a reasonable generalization. As you read the poem, use a graphic organizer like the one shown below. On the left-hand side of the diagram, write details, or evidence from the poem. On the right-hand side, note how these details relate to your own experience or reasoning. Then write a conclusion at the bottom of the diagram.

Evidence in the Text

Experience/ Reasoning

Conclusion

Sunrise at Montserrat, 1935. Andre Masson. Bridgeman Art Library.

Remember

A Lyric Poem by **Joy Harjo**

Remember the sky you were born under,
know each of the star's stories.
Remember the moon, know who she is.
Remember the sun's birth at dawn, that is the
5   strongest point of time. Remember sundown
and the giving away to night.
Remember your birth, how your mother struggled
to give you form and breath. You are evidence of
her life, and her mother's, and hers.
10 Remember your father. He is your life, also.
Remember the earth whose skin you are:
red earth, black earth, yellow earth, white earth
brown earth, we are earth.
Remember the plants, trees, animal life who all have their
15 tribes, their families, their histories, too. Talk to them,
listen to them. They are alive poems.
Remember the wind. Remember her voice. She knows the
origin of this universe.
Remember you are all people and all people
20 are you.
Remember you are this universe and this
universe is you.
Remember all is in motion, is growing, is you.
Remember language comes from this.
25 Remember the dance language is, that life is.
Remember. ❖

Critical Viewing

Review Harjo's poem, then critique *Sunrise at Montserrat.* State what images you see in the painting and cite line numbers that correspond with these images in the text. Do you think *Sunrise at Montserrat* supports the message in Harjo's poem? Why or why not?

USE READING SKILLS

Draw Conclusions
What have you been told about your birth? Why do you think Harjo encourages readers to remember their births?

ANALYZE LITERATURE

Voice What can you tell about Harjo's attitude toward the past based on her repetition of the word *remember?*

MIRRORS & WINDOWS

What are the positive and negative effects of remembering the past? Is it possible to place too much importance on the past? What is the difference between remembering the past and dwelling on the past?

CULTURE
CONNECTION

Creation Stories Across the cultures of the world, creation stories exist to explain the origins of the earth and its life. Although creation stories vary among the Native American tribes of North America, common to all stories is the belief that animals, plants, people, and places are interconnected. In the stories, often animals and people work together to solve problems. Another common element in creation stories is the existence of a supreme being.

AFTER READING

REFER TO TEXT ▶ ▶ ▶ ▶	▶ REASON WITH TEXT	
1a. List the items the speaker asks you to remember in lines 1–6.	**1b.** Explain why such memories might be important.	**Understand** **Find meaning**
2a. Identify the kind of memories on which the speaker focuses in lines 7–10.	**2b.** Show how the awareness of one's family roots might help a person in life.	**Apply** **Use information**
3a. Indicate how, according to line 11, human beings are connected to the earth.	**3b.** Analyze why you think the speaker says "we are earth" (line 13). In what sense do you think that plants, trees, and animals can be "alive poems" (line 16)?	**Analyze** **Take things apart**
4a. State the word that is repeated frequently in the poem.	**4b.** Judge what kind of effect the repetition of this word might have on the poem when it is read aloud. How does the repetition relate to the theme, or central idea, of the poem?	**Evaluate** **Make judgments**
5a. Quote the lines from the end of the poem in which the speaker describes both language and life.	**5b.** If you were writing a poem on the subject of memory, propose which elements or details in "Remember" you might include. What different elements might you add?	**Create** **Bring ideas together**

ANALYZE LITERATURE: Voice and Theme

Reread the poem. Then, in two or three sentences, describe your impression of the poet's voice, or unique personality and attitude. Consider how the poet chooses to speak directly to the reader. How does this choice affect the theme of the poem?

EXTEND THE TEXT

Writing Options

Creative Writing In "Remember," Joy Harjo urges readers to remember their roots. In two or three paragraphs, write a brief **family history** that describes your ethnic and cultural heritage. Make other members of your family the audience for your writing, and share your history at a family gathering.

Applied Writing Imagine the city you live in is considering building a history center to teach visitors about the city's past. Write a **business letter** to the mayor of your city in which you express approval of the plan for a history center and point out the importance of remembering the past. Incorporate into your letter some of the ideas Joy Harjo expresses in her poem about what makes the past significant.

Collaborative Learning

Plan an Oral Interpretation Work in a small group to discuss the most effective methods and formats for an oral interpretation of "Remember." Hold a panel discussion in which you consider the advantages and disadvantages of an individual presentation or a choral reading. How might sound effects or music add to the presentation? Appoint a recorder who will write up the panel's results and share them with the class as a whole.

Media Literacy

Research Native American Myths
When Joy Harjo says that plants, trees, and natural life are "alive poems," she alludes to the fact that Native American myths includes stories about animals and the natural world. Using Internet or library resources, research Native American myths about one of the following animal characters: Coyote, Raven, or Lynx. Share the results of your research with the class in an oral report. At the end of your report, allow time for feedback and questions from your classmates.

 Go to **www.mirrorsandwindows.com** for more.

READING ASSESSMENT

1. In "Remember," the speaker uses the word *remember* as which of the following?
   A. a theme
   B. a stanza
   C. a refrain
   D. a rhyme
   E. an image

2. In line 18, the word *origin* most nearly means
   A. beginning.
   B. cause.
   C. dimension.
   D. effect.
   E. occurrence.

3. Which of the following best states the speaker's theme in the poem?
   A. The world is continually growing and developing.
   B. To understand the universe in all its complexity is impossible.
   C. Human beings should remain aware that we are all interconnected with one another and with nature.
   D. Those who cannot remember the past are condemned to repeat it.
   E. None of the above

4. Which of the following phrases contains an example of personification?
   A. "Remember the sky you were born under…"
   B. "Remember language comes from this."
   C. "Remember your father. He is your life, also."
   D. "Remember the wind. Remember her voice."
   E. "Remember you are all people…"

5. According to the speaker, what are "alive poems"?
   A. stars, moon, and sun
   B. plants, trees, and animals
   C. mother, grandmother, and father
   D. sky, wind, and earth
   E. None of the above

6. Reread the poem, sounding out the words or voicing them silently. Then, in a paragraph or two, explain how "Remember" has some of the qualities of a song or chant.

Understanding Setting and Context

SETTING

In the world of real estate, a common joke is that there are three important issues to consider when assessing a property: location, location, location. In some cases, the geographical, cultural, and chronological (time) location of a poem's subject or composition is of great importance. Understanding time and place in poetry can help you to construct a larger meaning from the words on the page.

The **setting** of a literary work is the time and place in which it occurs, together with all the details used to create a sense of a particular time and place. Poets often create setting by using **sensory details,** or words and phrases that describe how things look, sound, smell, taste, or feel.

Closely tied to setting is **mood,** or the emotion created in the reader by a poem. The language the poet uses to create setting can lead to an emotional response—such as fear, discomfort, longing, or anticipation—in the reader.

Li-Young Lee's poem "Eating Alone" (page 413) is set during the winter, and the oppressive, barren bleakness of the season reflects the loneliness of the poem's speaker. The winter setting of the poem directly reflects the speaker's mood and emphasizes the parallels between the barrenness of the winter season and the barrenness of the speaker's life without his father. Likewise, the reference to the fading color of the autumn leaves and the brief appearance, and quick disappearance, of the cardinal, suggests that all color and happiness in the speaker's life is overpowered by the oppressive bleakness of winter and the speaker's sorrow.

> The garden is bare now. The ground is cold,
> brown and old. What is left of the day flames
> in the maples at the corner of my
> eye. I turn, a cardinal vanishes.
> By the cellar door, I wash the onions,
> Then drink from the icy metal spigot.
> —from "Eating Alone" by Li-Young Lee

The poem "Those Winter Sundays" by Robert Hayden (page 478) is also set during winter. Hayden refers to the "blueblack cold," which emphasizes the sacrifice the speaker's father makes by waking up early, chopping wood, and building a fire to warm his family. Despite the frigid cold, the speaker's father still ventures outside in order to find wood to warm his family. If the poem was set in the summertime, the father's actions would not be as heroic, for he would not be battling the icy, "blueblack" cold.

> Sundays too my father got up early
> and put his clothes on in the blueblack cold,
> then with cracked hands that ached
> from labor in the weekday weather made
> banked fires blaze. No one ever thanked him.
> —from "Those Winter Sundays"
> by Robert Hayden

Winter Scene. John Henry Twachtman.

CONTEXT

In literature, **context** refers to the conditions in which the poem occurs. Context is closely related to setting but focuses more on the environment of the time and place. Two common types of context include historical and cultural.

Interpreting a poem within its *historical context* requires that you have some knowledge of the time period in which it was written or of the events it describes. For example, if a poem is set during the Civil War, you would be better able to interpret the poem if you knew something about the conditions or environment created by the Civil War.

Poems about History

Significant historical events are often commemorated by poems. Some of these poems are listed below. While it is possible for you to understand and appreciate these poems without any knowledge of the historical events they are commemorating, considering the historical context of the poems can greatly enhance your reading experience.

- "Paul Revere's Ride" by Henry Wadsworth Longfellow

- "O Captain! My Captain!" by Walt Whitman

- "In Flanders Field" by John McCrae

- "Ballad of Birmingham" by Dudley Randall

Cultural context is less dependent on a time period than on the culture of the poet, speaker, or subject of the poem. For instance, "The Floral Apron" (page 414) draws on the speaker's culture and the responsibility of elders to pass on their culture and knowledge to the younger generation, as well as the responsibility of the younger generation to learn from its elders. Through demonstrating how to prepare squid, the woman wearing the floral apron passes on her knowledge to the next generation. Understanding the importance in Chinese culture of passing knowledge from generation to generation can contribute to the way you read and understand "The Floral Apron."

Then, she, an elder of the tribe,
without formal headdress, without elegance,
deigned to teach the younger
about the Asian plight.

And although we have traveled far
we would never forget that primal lesson—
on patience, courage, forbearance,
on how to love squid despite squid,
how to honor the village, the tribe,
that floral apron.

> —from "The Floral Apron"
> by Marilyn Chin

Although "The Floral Apron" is about the writer's culture, a poem can also take on a universal or general significance. Joy Harjo's "Remember" (page 407), for example, may be grounded in the poet's belief that people are intimately connected to the world around them, which is a belief shared by many other Native Americans. However, the poem's message and imagery can be understood and enjoyed without the knowledge that Harjo is of Native American descent.

READING STRATEGIES WITH SETTING AND CONTEXT

Use these strategies to help you determine the setting and the historical or cultural context of a poem:
- **Visualize** Consider whether the poem is set in a particular place or at a particular time. Try to picture the images presented in the poem.
- **Use Background Information** Sometimes, reading the comments about a historical era or about the author's life can provide information that further explains the work.
- **Clarify** After reading the poem, read it again while writing down words and references that are unknown or confusing to you. Look up these words in a dictionary or try to find a translation if they are not in a language you know.
- **Ask Questions** What do you need to know about the setting or context to help you understand the poem? Form questions to help you research the subject. Use the library or Internet to find out more.

Eating Alone
A Lyric Poem by Li-Young Lee

The Floral Apron
A Lyric Poem by Marilyn Chin

BEFORE READING

BUILD BACKGROUND

Cultural Context Preparing and sharing food have always been among the ties that bind families and friends together. Historically, before kitchens and dining rooms existed, the hearth or fireside, where food was cooked, was the gathering place of families and clans. It was here that traditions were passed on and life lessons were learned by generation after generation.

In **"Eating Alone,"** the speaker reflects on his loneliness, now that his father is no longer there to sustain and guide him. This poem comes from **Li-Young Lee's** collection *Rose,* published in 1986.

In **"The Floral Apron,"** the speaker comes to recognize ways that preparing a meal can tap into a deep vein of loyalty to an entire culture. "The Floral Apron" is published in **Marilyn Chin's** collection entitled *The Phoenix Gone, the Terrace Empty* (1994).

These poems have several similarities, but they also reveal important differences. As you read, compare and contrast the role preparing food and eating plays in each poem and how food and eating relate to the culture and memories of each speaker.

Reader's Context What kinds of sights, smells, sounds, tastes, and textures do you associate with the kitchen in your home? What feelings or emotions does the kitchen prompt in you?

USE READING SKILLS

**Meaning of Words
Restatement clues** are types of context clues in which ideas are restated, or explained in a different way. In the sentences below, look for restatement clues to help find the meanings of the vocabulary words from the selections.

1. The chicken was <u>braised</u>, or browned by simmering, and served with broccoli.
2. Sometimes, it is difficult to <u>absolve</u>, or forgive, someone who has really hurt your feelings.
3. My father always showed a great deal of <u>forbearance</u>, that is, patience, when my brothers and sisters and I fought.

COMPARE LITERATURE: Setting and Mood

The **setting** of a literary work is the time and place in which it occurs. Setting is often closely linked with **mood,** or the emotion created in the reader by part or all of the work. As you read these poems, pay careful attention to details that suggest the setting of each work. Then consider how the setting relates to the mood of each poem.

MEET THE AUTHORS

Li-Young Lee (b. 1957) was born in Jakarta, Indonesia, the son of Chinese parents. When he was seven, his family immigrated to the United States and settled near Pittsburgh, Pennsylvania. Some common subjects that appear in Lee's poems are the relationship between child and parent and episodes from his childhood. Lee is noted for his use of language to create an atmosphere of silence in many of his poems. Lee has published several award-winning collections of poetry and currently lives in Chicago, Illinois.

LEE

The family of **Marilyn Chin** (b. 1955) brought her to the United States from Hong Kong soon after she was born. Chin believes in the power of poetry to bring about change and states, "What we write can change the world. That may sound a little idealistic but I feel it's very important that poetry make something happen." Chin has taught at a number of universities in the United States and around the world. Her poetry collections include *Dwarf Bamboo* (1987) and *Rhapsody in Plain Yellow* (2002).

CHIN

EATING
ALONE

A Lyric Poem by **Li-Young Lee**

Many Dinners: In Photo Sepia. Gerrit Greve.

I've pulled the last of the year's young onions.
The garden is bare now. The ground is cold,
brown and old. What is left of the day flames
in the maples at the corner of my
5   eye. I turn, a cardinal vanishes.
By the cellar door, I wash the onions,
then drink from the icy metal spigot.[1]

Once, years back, I walked beside my father
among the windfall pears. I can't recall
10   our words. We may have strolled in silence. But
I still see him bend that way—left hand braced
on knee, creaky—to lift and hold to my
eye a rotten pear. In it, a hornet
spun crazily, glazed in slow, glistening juice.

15   It was my father I saw this morning
waving to me from the trees. I almost
called to him, until I came close enough
to see the shovel, leaning where I had
left it, in the flickering, deep green shade.

20   White rice steaming, almost done. Sweet green peas
fried in onions. Shrimp <u>braised</u> in sesame
oil and garlic. And my own loneliness.
What more could I, a young man, want. ❖

---

1. **spigot.** Faucet

braised (brāzd) *adj.,* browned by simmering

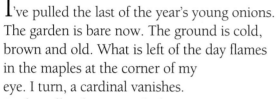

What is the difference between being alone and being lonely? Why is loneliness often such a difficult emotion to deal with?

THE floral apron

A Lyric Poem by
Marilyn Chin

The woman wore a floral apron around her neck,
that woman from my mother's village
with a sharp <u>cleaver</u> in her hand.
She said, "What shall we cook tonight?
5 Perhaps these six tiny squids
lined up so perfectly on the block?"

She wiped her hand on her apron,
pierced the blade into the first.
There was no resistance,
10 no blood, only cartilage
soft as a child's nose. A last
iota of ink[1] made us wince.

Suddenly, the aroma of ginger and scallion[2]
        fogged our senses,
15 and we <u>absolved</u> her for that moment's barbarism.
Then, she, an elder of the tribe,
without formal headdress, without elegance,
<u>deigned</u> to teach the younger
about the Asian <u>plight</u>.

20 And although we have traveled far
we would never forget that <u>primal</u> lesson—
on patience, courage, <u>forbearance</u>,
on how to love squid despite squid,
how to honor the village, the tribe,
25 that floral apron. ❖

---

1. **iota of ink.** Very small quantity of squid's ink
2. **scallion.** Young green onion

cleav • er (klē´ vər) *n.,* heavy cutting tool with a broad blade
ab • solve (eb zälv´) *v.,* forgive
deign (dān) *v.,* condescend; consent to act below one's normal level of dignity
plight (plīt) *n.,* awkward or wretched situation
pri • mal (prī´ məl) *adj.,* fundamental; primitive
for • bear • ance (fôr bar´ ən[t]s) *n.,* patience

MIRRORS & WINDOWS   What lessons should all children be taught? What happens if no one teaches children these lessons?

REFER TO TEXT ▶ ▶ ▶ ▶	▶ REASON WITH TEXT	
1a. Quote the lines from "The Floral Apron" in which the woman describes the squid.	1b. What can you imply about the woman's personality from her description of the squid?	**Understand** **Find meaning**
2a. In "Eating Alone," describe the image that the poet uses in lines 12–14.	2b. Infer what larger ideas about life and death this image suggests.	**Apply** **Use information**
3a. List the sensory details in lines 13–14 of "The Floral Apron." To which sense do these details appeal?	3b. Illustrate how these lines mark an important turning point in the poem as a whole.	**Analyze** **Take things apart**
4a. State the "primal lesson" the speaker of "The Floral Apron" has learned, according to lines 21–24.	4b. Judge whether the lesson learned by the speaker is important. Explain your answer.	**Evaluate** **Make judgments**
5a. What ironic contrast does the speaker in "Eating Alone" establish in the poem's final stanza?	5b. Imagine that you are a close friend of the speaker. Create a letter to him in which you try to comfort him in his loneliness.	**Create** **Bring ideas together**

COMPARE LITERATURE: Setting and Mood

In these two poems, what similarities in setting can you identify? What are some of the differences? In "Eating Alone," how would you describe the mood of the whole poem? In "The Floral Apron," at what point is there a shift in mood? How does the shift contribute to the meaning of the poem?

EXTEND THE TEXT

Writing Options
Creative Writing Imagine that the speakers in "Eating Alone" and "The Floral Apron" meet at a dinner party and begin to discuss their childhood experiences with each other. Write a **dialogue** for these characters in which they exchange memories and comment on the significance that these recollections have for them. Try to make your dialogue consistent with the personalities and character traits of the speakers, as these are revealed in each poem.

Expository Writing Research the background and family histories of Li-Young Lee and Marilyn Chin more fully, using library and Internet resources. Then write a four-paragraph **analysis** in which you discuss the importance of historical context for these two poems. Your audience for this analysis will be younger students who need more detailed background in order to appreciate the poems. In your first paragraph, provide a brief introduction to modern Chinese history. In two body paragraphs, sketch the significance of this history for the families of Lee and Chin. Then summarize your main ideas in a concluding paragraph.

Collaborative Learning
Research the Chinese New Year Few holidays are as rich in traditional and cultural symbolism as the Chinese New Year. Together with a small group, research the foods, songs, costumes, gifts, cultural beliefs, decorations, and parades of the Chinese New Year celebration. Then develop a multimedia presentation to share the results of your research with the class as a whole.

Lifelong Learning
Interview an Older Person Select a grandparent, an older relative, or another older person whom you would like to interview. The goal of your interview will be to acquire more information about that person's life in the past, as well as about his or her attitudes toward cultural heritage. Prepare a list of interview questions for the interviewee, and conduct the interview. When you are finished, write up your notes in the form of a letter that you might send to the interviewee as a token of thanks and appreciation.

Go to **www.mirrorsandwindows.com** for more.

GRAMMAR & STYLE

Sensory Details

To make descriptive writing really come alive, writers use **sensory details,** or images that appeal to one or more of the five senses: sight, hearing, taste, smell, and touch.

Take a look at the first stanza of "Eating Alone" (page 413) as it is printed below. Notice how the detail of the cold ground appeals to the sense of touch. Readers can imagine how it feels to touch cold ground. The image of the "flames in the maples" creates the image of the brilliant red and orange of the late-autumn leaves. This image appeals to the sense of sight.

A single detail can appeal to more than one of the senses. Drinking from an "icy metal spigot" is an example. The reader can feel the icy-cold of the metal spigot and taste the cold, crisp water coming from it.

> I've pulled the last of the year's young
>   onions.
> The garden is bare now. The ground is
>   cold,
> brown and old. What is left of the day
>   flames
> in the maples at the corner of my
> eye. I turn, a cardinal vanishes.
> By the cellar door, I wash the onions,
> then drink from the icy metal spigot.
>   —from "Eating Alone" by Li-Young Lee

REVIEW TERMS
- **image:** picture created by words
- **descriptive writing:** writing used to portray a character, an object, or a scene

What Great Writers Do

LEE

Both Li-Young Lee and Marilyn Chin wrote poems about food. Notice in the following examples how readers can almost smell and taste the food because of the vivid images these poets create with words.

> White rice steaming, almost done. Sweet
>   green peas
> fried in onions. Shrimp braised in sesame
> oil and garlic. And my own loneliness.
> What more could I, a young man, want.
>   —from "Eating Alone" by Li-Young Lee
>
> Suddenly, the aroma of ginger and scallion
>   fogged our senses,
> and we absolved her for that moment's
>   barbarism.
>   —from "The Floral Apron"
>   by Marilyn Chin

CHIN

Instead of simply stating that the young man or the woman in the floral apron "cooked dinner," the poets provide details to help flesh out the image. Lines such as "the aroma of ginger and scallion / fogged our senses" from "The Floral Apron" (page 414), as well as the intimate details from Lee's poem of the steaming white rice, green peas fried with onions, and braised shrimp in sesame oil and garlic, help the reader create his or her own mental picture.

By describing specifically what food is being cooked and how it is being prepared, the poets allow the readers to imagine the savory smells that are wafting through the air and the sound of the hiss and the crackle of the oil as it hits the pan. These details and images make the poems come alive for the reader by providing specific images, sounds, tastes, and smells for the reader to experience.

Identify Sensory Details

For each item below, write a word or phrase that provides the required sensory detail. The sense to which the detail appeals is shown in parentheses.

1. Lines 8–14 of "Eating Alone" (taste)
2. Lines 15–19 of "Eating Alone" (sight)
3. Lines 20–24 of "Eating Alone" (sight and hearing)
4. Lines 20–24 of "Eating Alone" (sight and taste)
5. Lines 1–6 of "The Floral Apron" (sight)
6. Lines 7–12 of "The Floral Apron" (touch)
7. Lines 13–14 of "The Floral Apron" (smell and sight)
8. Line 16 of "The Floral Apron" (sight)

Improve a Paragraph

Rewrite the paragraph shown below, adding sensory details to make it more vivid and appealing.

Woodrow stared at the photograph of the grandparents he had never known. They were probably in their eighties when the picture was taken, he thought. There they sat, side by side on a porch swing. His grandfather wore overalls, a plaid shirt buttoned at the neck, and a narrow-brimmed hat. Grandma Miller wore a checked calico dress and was bare-headed. She had glasses perched on her nose. Both Grandpa and Grandma had an easy, slight smile, and their hands lay comfortably in their laps, as if posing for the photographer on that swing was a welcome task, releasing them for the moment, at least, from more painful chores.

Use Sensory Details in Your Writing

Write a paragraph in which you describe an ideal vacation spot. Use at least five sensory details in your writing, appealing to each one of the five senses: sight, hearing, taste, smell, and touch. You may want to use a Sensory Details Chart like the one below to brainstorm or keep track of details.

Sight	Sound	Smell	Taste	Touch

Visualize Images

Get together with a partner and together choose one of your favorite poems. Then have your partner read the poem aloud while you listen. Close your eyes and visualize the images in the poem. Then read the poem aloud to your partner while he or she visualizes. Talk about how the sensory details in the poem contribute to its tone, mood, and theme. Finally, you and your partner should both sketch the images in the poem that most appeal to your individual senses. Compare your sketches with those of your partner and see which of the images you visualized in the same way.

EXTEND THE SKILL

Review "Eating Alone" and "The Floral Apron." Choose one poem and make a list of the sensory images that you find in the poem. Examine old nature magazines to find visual representations of those images. Try to include images that convey the same mood as the poem. Cut out these images and make a collage of the clippings. Present your collage to the class.

Understanding Structure and Form

STRUCTURES OF POETRY

Stories and essays are divided into paragraphs. Poems, on the other hand, are often divided into **stanzas,** or groups of lines. The type of stanza is determined by the number of lines. Two lines are a *couplet,* three a *tercet* or *triplet,* four a *quatrain,* five a *quintet* or *quintain,* six a *sestet,* seven a *septet,* and eight an *octave.* It is sometimes possible to determine the type of poem by the stanza type, if the poem is not in free verse. The following stanza from "Dream Variations" (page 456) is an example of an octave. The lines below from Shakespeare's sonnet (page 421) are an example of a couplet.

> To fling my arms wide
> In the face of the sun,
> Dance! Whirl! Whirl!
> Till the quick day is done.
> Rest at pale evening…
> A tall, slim tree...
> Night coming tenderly
>   Black like me.
>   —from "Dream Variations"
>   by Langston Hughes

> So long as men can breathe or eyes can see,
> So long lives this, and this gives life to thee.
>   —from "Shall I compare thee to a
>   summer's day?" by William Shakespeare

The briefest of formal structures presented in this unit is the tanka. A **tanka** is a traditional Japanese poem consisting of five lines, with five syllables in the first and third lines and seven syllables in the other lines, for a total syllable count of thirty-one. Tanka use only a few words to express a complex idea. The tanka by Tsukamoto Kunio (page 467) uses the image of a golden leaf to describe a human soul. The poems by Miyazawa Kenji (page 467) and Okamoto Kanoko (page 467) are also examples of tanka.

Poems that consist of four-line, rhyming stanzas (usually *abcb*) that tell a story are called **ballads.**

Ballads are quite popular in folk literature and are very often sung.

A **sonnet** is a fourteen-line poem, usually written in iambic pentameter (five sets of an unstressed-stressed syllable pattern per line). There are two main types of sonnets: *Shakespearean* (or *Elizabethan*) and *Petrarchan* (or *Italian*). The Shakespearean sonnet is divided into three quatrains and a rhyming couplet. "Shall I compare thee to a summer's day?" by William Shakespeare and "I know I am but summer to your heart" by Edna St. Vincent Millay (page 422) are examples of Shakespearean sonnets. The rhyme scheme is usually *abab cdcd efef gg*. The Petrarchan sonnet is divided into an octave and a sestet with a rhyme scheme of *abbaabba cdecde* (or *cdedce* or *cdcdcd*). To learn more about rhyme scheme and meter, see Understanding Sight and Sound on page 452.

FORMS OF POETRY

The form of a poem must suit its content. If a poet wants to tell a story, for instance, the chosen form would probably be a **narrative poem.** "Ex-Basketball Player" by John Updike (page 431) is an example of a narrative poem.

> Once Flick played for the high-school
>   team, the Wizards.
> He was good: in fact, the best. In '46
> He bucketed three hundred ninety points,
> A county record still. The ball loved Flick.
> I saw him rack up thirty-eight or forty
> In one home game. His hands were like
>   wild birds.
>   —from "Ex-Basketball Player"
>   by John Updike

A special type of narrative poem is the **dramatic poem,** which relies on elements of drama, such as monologue or dialogue, to tell the story. (See the Introduction to Drama on pages 503 and 504 for more about monologue and dialogue.)

A **lyric poem** expresses the emotions of a speaker and tends to be musical in style. "Dream Variations" and "I Am Offering This Poem" (page 395) are lyric poems. A common type of lyric poetry is called **free verse.** As you can tell by its name, free verse is poetry that is free from regular rhyme, meter, or stanza division.

Blank verse is unrhymed poetry written in iambic pentameter. Shakespeare used blank verse in his plays. Both sonnets and the lines from Shakespeare's plays are written in iambic pentameter, but only sonnets follow a set rhyme scheme; blank verse does not.

A **prose poem** is a passage of prose that makes such extensive use of poetic language that the line between prose and poetry is blurred. Jamaica Kincaid's piece "Holidays" (page 437) is an example of a prose poem.

> I sit on the porch facing the mountains. I sit on a wicker couch looking out the window at a field of day lilies. I walk into a room where someone—an artist, maybe— has stored some empty canvases. I drink a glass of water. I put the empty glass, from which I have just drunk the water, on a table.
>
> —from "Holidays" by
> Jamaica Kincaid

Two other forms are based on the purpose of the poem. An **ode** is a poem intended to honor or praise someone or something. An **elegy** can usually be recognized by its formal tone that laments the death of someone.

RECOGNIZING STRUCTURE AND FORM

You can determine the structure and form of a poem (if it is not free verse) by looking for these elements:

- Text organization: Is the poem divided into stanzas? How many lines are in the poem or in each stanza?
- Rhyme scheme: Does the poem rhyme? Is there a pattern of a recurring rhyme?

- Content: Is the poem telling a story, expressing an emotion, or presenting an image?
- Style: Is the poem more musical or narrative in style? What tone does it take?

Odes and Elegies

Many classic poems were written as odes and elegies, along with some more recent poems. Do you recognize any of the titles below?

- "Ode to a Nightingale" by John Keats
- "Ode to My Socks" by Pablo Neruda
- "On a Favourite Cat, Drowned in a Tub of Gold Fishes" by Thomas Gray
- "Good Night, Willie Lee, I'll See You in the Morning" by Alice Walker

"Shall I compare thee to a summer's day?"

A Sonnet by William Shakespeare

"I know I am but summer to your heart"
A Sonnet by Edna St. Vincent Millay

BEFORE READING

BUILD BACKGROUND

Literary Context While William Shakespeare is best known for his plays, he was also the most important lyric poet of his time. In Shakespeare's day, the sonnet was the leading form of lyric poetry. A **sonnet** is a fourteen-line poem, usually written in iambic pentameter, that follows one of a number of different rhyme schemes. Shakespeare and his contemporaries produced sonnet sequences, or groups of poems dedicated to the writer's beloved, who could be either a fictional or a real person. Shakespeare so mastered the form that his version, with a distinctive structure and rhyme scheme, is known as the "Shakespearean sonnet."

Edna St. Vincent Millay wrote more than three hundred years after Shakespeare. Though she had several sonnet structures from which to choose, she wrote **"I know I am but summer to your heart"** in the Shakespearean tradition. In fact, her sonnet appears almost to be in dialogue with Shakespeare's **"Shall I compare thee to a summer's day?"** "I know I am but summer to your heart" is included in the book *Collected Poems of Edna St. Vincent Millay* (1981).

Reader's Context Think about someone you love. What would you say in a love poem to him or her? What comparisons might come to mind for the emotions you feel for your loved one?

USE READING SKILLS

Compare and Contrast
Both Shakespeare and Millay write about love, and yet their attitudes toward love are completely different. As you read, explore the similarities and differences in the messages and tones of the two poems. Then use your observations, along with support from the poems, to sum up the main idea of each poem. Use a Venn Diagram like the one below to keep track of your comparisons.

Shakespeare   Millay

COMPARE LITERATURE: Iambic Pentameter and Meter

Iambic pentameter is a type of **meter,** or rhythmic pattern, commonly used in sonnets. Each line consists of five *iambs*, or rhythmic units made up of a weakly stressed syllable followed by a strong one, as in the word *forget*. For example, "Shall I compare thee to a summer's day?" is a line written in iambic pentameter.

⌣ / ⌣ / ⌣ / ⌣ / ⌣ /
Shall I / compare / thee to / a sum / mer's day?

The stress marks indicate strong and weak syllables. As you read each sonnet, listen for the rhythm. Think about how the rhythm of a poem affects the way it is read and understood.

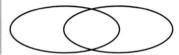

MEET THE AUTHORS

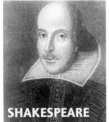

SHAKESPEARE

William Shakespeare (c. 1564–1616) was born in Stratford-upon-Avon, England. Relatively little is known about Shakespeare's life. We know that he worked as an actor, a playwright, and a theater manager in London. Even in his own time, Shakespeare was confident that his writing would bestow immortality on him and his subjects.

Edna St. Vincent Millay (1892–1950) was an American poet and playwright best known for her lyric verse. Millay, who was called "Vincent" by her close friends, was encouraged by her mother to be independent. Millay's unconventional lifestyle and vivid imagery made her a literary celebrity during her lifetime. Like Shakespeare centuries before her, Millay hoped she would live on in her work.

MILLAY

"Shall I compare thee to a summer's day?"

(Sonnet 18)

A Sonnet by
William Shakespeare

The Sonnet. William Mulready.
The Victoria and Albert Museum,
London, England.

Shall I compare thee to a summer's day?
Thou art more lovely and more <u>temperate</u>:
Rough winds do shake the darling buds of May,
And summer's lease hath all too short a date;
5   Sometime too hot the eye of heaven shines,
And often is his gold complexion dimmed;
And every fair from fair sometime declines,
By chance or nature's changing course untrimmed.[1]
But thy eternal summer shall not fade,
10 Nor lose possession of that fair thou ow'st,[2]
Nor shall death brag thou wander'st in his shade,
When in eternal lines to time thou grow'st:
So long as men can breathe or eyes can see,
So long lives this, and this gives life to thee. ❖

---

1. **untrimmed.** Stripped of beauty
2. **ow'st.** Own

tem • per • ate (tem´ pə rət) *adj.*, moderate

MIRRORS & WINDOWS

How do you respond to the speaker's assertion that the "eternal summer" of his beloved will never fade? Is he being realistic, or is this claim merely wish fulfillment? Why do you think so?

Critical Viewing

Compare Homer's *Daydreaming* to Mulready's *The Sonnet* (page 421). Write a short paragraph that describes the mood, or atmosphere, of each painting. Examine the details in the painting such as facial expressions, use of light and darkness, perspective, and setting and show how these details contribute to the overall mood.

Daydreaming, 1880.
Winslow Homer.

"I know I am but *summer* to your heart"

A Sonnet by

Edna St. Vincent Millay

I know I am but summer to your heart,
And not the full four seasons of the year;
And you must welcome from another part
Such noble moods as are not mine, my dear.
5   No gracious weight of golden fruits to sell
Have I, nor any wise and wintry thing;
And I have loved you all too long and well
To carry still the high sweet breast of Spring.
Wherefore I say: O love, as summer goes,
10   I must be gone, <u>steal</u> forth with silent drums,
That you may <u>hail</u> anew the bird and rose
When I come back to you, as summer comes.
Else will you seek, at some not distant time,
Even your summer in another clime.[1] ❖

---

1. **clime.** Climate or season

steal (stēl) *v.,* move silently or cautiously
hail (hāl) *v.,* greet joyfully

 **MIRRORS & WINDOWS** What is the difference between love and infatuation? How might ideas about love change throughout the course of a couple's relationship? Are these changes positive or negative? Why?

CULTURE
CONNECTION

KEATS

WORDSWORTH

HEANEY

The Sonnet From its origin in Italy during the thirteenth century, the sonnet has made its mark throughout Europe and the Americas. In sixteenth-century England, writing sonnets was quite fashionable, and poets and courtiers alike chose love, beauty, and art as their themes. Romantic poets in the eighteenth and nineteenth centuries, such as William Wordsworth and John Keats, added mythology and nature to the list of sonnet subjects and breathed new life into the form. In the twentieth century, German poet Rainer Maria Rilke, Chilean poet Pablo Neruda, American poet Edna St. Vincent Millay, and Irish poet Seamus Heaney continued to use the sonnet to explore a variety of subjects, from human relationships to political statements.

REFER TO TEXT ▶ ▶ ▶ ▶	▶ REASON WITH TEXT	
1a. In Millay's sonnet, identify the comparison the speaker makes in line 1.	1b. Explain what the word *but* in line 1 suggests about the relationship of the speaker and her beloved.	**Understand** **Find meaning**
2a. In Millay's sonnet, list the statements in lines 5–8 that illustrate the comparison the speaker makes in line 1.	2b. Examine what the statements in lines 5–8 suggest about the couple's relationship.	**Apply** **Use information**
3a. In Shakespeare's sonnet, identify the word in line 9 that introduces an important shift in the speaker's focus.	3b. Contrast the poem's last six lines with lines 1–8. How does the speaker's focus shift?	**Analyze** **Take things apart**
4a. In Shakespeare's sonnet, recall what death will not be allowed to do, according to line 11.	4b. Summarize what the speaker is saying about the person he addresses in this sonnet. Judge whether the speaker's prediction about his beloved is true. Explain your answer.	**Evaluate** **Make judgments**
5a. In your own words, state the point that the speaker of each sonnet makes in the sonnet's concluding couplet. Use details from the text to support your answer.	5b. Write a letter from the speaker of each sonnet to the beloved that conveys the same ideas as the sonnet but in modern language.	**Create** **Bring ideas together**

COMPARE LITERATURE: Iambic Pentameter and Meter

How does the use of iambic pentameter in the sonnets contribute to the way they are read aloud? Try changing the meter of some of the lines. What effect do these changes have on the overall impressions created by the sonnets?

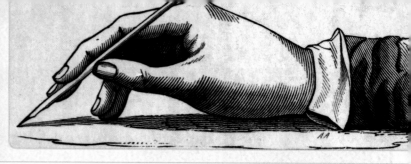

Informational Text
CONNECTION

The sonnet has been a remarkably durable literary form. From the sixteenth century to the mid-twentieth century, numerous major poets in the English language have written sonnets. After 1950, however, many poets began to favor other stanza forms for love poetry or write in free verse. It is surprising, therefore, that at a high school in Portland, Maine, a sonnet-writing contest drew more than sixty entries. In her article **"Well-Versed Approach Merits Poetry Prize,"** newspaper reporter **Joanne Lannin** reports on the first Henry Wadsworth Longfellow poetry-writing contest and profiles the top three writers and their poems.

Portland Press Herald

February 20, 2001

WELL-VERSED APPROACH MERITS POETRY PRIZE

Entries by Portland High School juniors were chosen the three best in a new sonnet-writing contest

A News Article by **Joanne Lannin**

Hayley Shriner, Emily Hricko and Ralph Lerman, all juniors at Portland High School, were never big fans of sonnets.

Like many of their classmates, they found the 14-line poetry structure and the <u>prescribed</u> meter to be <u>archaic</u> and rigid.

Romantic, flowerly verse, like Shakespeare's "Shall I compare thee to a summer's day?" just didn't speak to them.

Despite their <u>misgivings</u>, they each entered a sonnet-writing contest last month.

And, to their delight, they won. Their entries were chosen the three best of the 61 sonnets entered in the first Henry Wadsworth Longfellow poetry-writing contest. They will receive cash prizes and read their sonnets Saturday Feb. 24 at the Longfellow birthday celebration at the Center for Maine History, 489 Congress St. in Portland.

pre • scribed (pri skrībd´) *adj.*, ordered; specific
ar • cha • ic (är kā´ ik) *adj.*, out of date
mis • giv • ing (mis giˊ viŋ) *n.*, doubt

American poet Henry Wadsworth Longfellow (1807–1882) is perhaps best known for his long narrative poems. However, he also wrote a number of sonnets, one of which is included below. Notice how Longfellow's sonnet follows the Petrarchan form.

The Broken Oar

Once upon Iceland's solitary strand
A poet wandered with his book and pen,
Seeking some final word, some sweet Amen,
Wherewith to close the volume in his hand.
The billows rolled and plunged upon the sand,
The circling sea-gulls swept beyond his ken,
And from the parting cloud-rack now and then
Flashed the red sunset over sea and land.
Then by the billows at his feet was tossed
A broken oar; and carved thereon he read,
"Oft was I weary, when I toiled at thee";
And like a man, who findeth what was lost,
He wrote the words, then lifted up his head,
And flung his useless pen into the sea.

Herb Coursen, a poet and former teacher of poetry at Bowdoin College, judged the sonnet-writing contest. Coursen said that 12 to 15 of the entries from PHS could have been prize winners. He chose the three he did because each of them explored an idea with feeling and depth and sustained the energy for the full 14 lines.

"That's hard to do," he said. "You can sense a kind of life within the poems. You can hear the quest going on."

Back in Shakespeare's day—and even in Longfellow's— most poems were written to a certain length and had a rhyme scheme. While free verse has become the standard for most modern poetry, the sonnet's <u>proponents</u> believe its structured rhyme schemes and sing-song rhythm (iambic pentameter) still have a role to play; they have tried to teach today's students that sonnets aren't always about hearts and flowers.

"The sonnet's form imposes discipline and control," said Coursen, who has written 26 books of poetry and eight novels. "As Robert Frost said, 'I'd as soon write poetry without rhyme as play tennis with the net down.' A lot of what passes for poetry today is just lashing a tennis ball out in an open field."

The sonnet-writing contest was the idea of Nancy Merrow, who presides over the Fine Arts Boosters at Portland High School and who wrote the $2,000 Maine Humanities Council and Maine Arts Commission grant that funded the sonnet-writing project.

Merrow is impressed by the fact that Maine has produced so many good sonnet writers, including Longfellow, Edna St. Vincent Millay and Edwin Arlington Robinson. She thought that celebrating them around the time of Longfellow's birthday would make for an interesting cultural event in the life of the school.

"Something in the Maine lifestyle provides a breeding ground for sonnet writing," she wrote in the introduction to the resource guide. "Our environment gets mirrored in our creative choices."

With Coursen's help, Merrow produced a resource guide for teachers and students to

---

pro • po • nent (prə pō´ nənt) n., supporter

use in preparing for the contest. The booklet contains sonnets by Longfellow, St. Vincent Millay, Robinson, Coursen and another current Maine poet, Tom Carper. Coursen, Carper and another Maine poet, Bill Watterson, held workshops in January for students to help them understand the sonnet.

"They were surprised to hear that you could write a sonnet about football and fighter pilots," said Coursen, who read them his poem about a fighter pilot's death.

The student sonnet writers who will read from their work say they surprised themselves with the results of their efforts.

"I thought it would be hard to write with a format," Hricko said, "but in the end it comes out better."

Hricko won the third-place prize of $25. Her poem uses the atmosphere surrounding a snowstorm to mirror her feelings of confusion and sadness that give way to renewed hope.

Shriner's offbeat, first-place poem explores the sound of the word "Utah" and the feelings the word <u>evokes</u>.

"It required a lot of focus," she said. "It has helped me work on theme and structure in all my poetry."

Ralph Lerman wrote his second-place poem about his favorite painting, *Jardin a Giverny* by Claude Monet, and the feelings conjured up by the contradictions of light and space.

"I never knew I had it in me to write good poetry. I was pleasantly surprised," Lerman said.

The reaction to the sonnet-writing contest has been so positive that Merrow plans to take the contest statewide next year.

"I know that not many poets are writing sonnets," Merrow said. "But poetry is sort of like fashion. Sonnets could come back." ❖

---

e • voke (i vōk´) *v.*, draw forth

REFER TO TEXT ▶ ▶ ▶ ▶	▶ REASON WITH TEXT	
1a. Recall how Nancy Merrow, who founded the poetry-writing contest, connect sonnets with Maine.	1b. Paraphrase information from the article that supports Merrow's opinion about sonnets and Maine.	**Understand** **Find meaning**
2a. Quote what reference the poet Herb Coursen says about Robert Frost.	2b. Apply Robert Frost's attitude toward writing poetry without rhyme to sonnet writing.	**Apply** **Use information**
3a. Name what Merrow compares poetry to at the end of the newspaper article.	3b. Create your own comparison for poetry in the form of a metaphor or a simile.	**Create** **Bring ideas together**

TEXT ←TO→ TEXT CONNECTION

- Describe ways sonnets like "Shall I compare thee to a summer's day?" and "I know I am but summer to your heart" might not "speak to" high school students. Then describe ways these two sonnets do "speak to" high school students. Why do you think sonnets are sometimes viewed as being lofty and dull? Use lines from both poems to support your answers.

- What makes writing a poem in a prescribed form, like a sonnet, challenging? What makes it easier than writing in free verse? Why do you think sonnets like those by Shakespeare and Millay have survived through the years?

EXTEND THE TEXT

Writing Options

Creative Writing For an audience of younger students, write a one- or two-paragraph **character sketch** of each of the speakers in these sonnets. In your sketches, use clues and hints from the following aspects of the sonnets to flesh out each speaker's personality: word choice, figurative language, comparisons, predictions, and tone.

Applied Writing Suppose one of your friends is having a hard time understanding the two sonnets you've just read. Write a line-by-line **paraphrase** of each sonnet. Remember, a paraphrase is a restatement of someone else's words in your own words. When you are finished, compare your paraphrases with those of your classmates. Which ideas from the poem did you paraphrase in a similar way? Which parts of your paraphrases are different?

Collaborative Learning

Illustrate a Sonnet Joining with a small group of two or three classmates, create an illustration for one of the sonnets you have just read. First, read both sonnets aloud. Then choose the one that is most visu-ally appealing to the group. Discuss what you visualize when you read the sonnet, and then work together to create the illustration. For example, you might sketch the "darling buds of May" in Shakespeare's sonnet, or you might depict the "golden fruits" from Millay's poem. When all the groups have finished, hang the pictures around the room and invite viewers to guess which sonnet goes with each picture.

Critical Literacy

Create a Lecture Imagine that either Shakespeare or Millay will give a lecture on the meaning of love. Judging only from what you have read in the sonnet by the author of your choice, compose an outline of the lecture. In preparing the outline, ask yourself these questions: According to the sonnet, what is the attitude toward love? Does the author believe that love should be based on physical attraction or on emotion? Would the author recommend falling in love? Be prepared to cite evidence from the sonnet to support the ideas you express in your outline.

 Go to **www.mirrorsandwindows.com** for more.

READING ASSESSMENT

1. Which of the following lines from the poems is an example of personification?
   A. "Thou art more lovely and more temperate"
   B. "Nor shall death brag thou wander'st in his shade"
   C. "And I have loved you all too long and well"
   D. "I must be gone, steal forth with silent drums"
   E. None of the above

2. In "Shall I compare thee to a summer's day?" the speaker answers the opening question by saying that
   A. his beloved reminds him more of spring than of summer.
   B. his beloved is more lovely and more moderate than the weather in summer.
   C. his beloved will inevitably lose her beauty as she ages.
   D. summer weather is usually predictable.
   E. he doesn't like summer weather.

3. A line written in iambic pentameter has which of the following?
   A. five feet with a syllable stressed weakly followed by a strong one

   B. five feet with a syllable stressed strongly followed by a weak one
   C. six feet with a syllable stressed weakly followed by a strong one
   D. four feet with a syllable stressed strongly followed by a weak one
   E. six feet with a syllable stressed weakly followed by a strong one

4. In Millay's sonnet, which of the following *best* describes the speaker's tone?
   A. flowery
   B. irritable
   C. dry
   D. indifferent
   E. sarcastic

5. Although both poets write about love, each speaker displays a unique attitude, or tone, toward his or her subject. For each sonnet, write a paragraph analyzing the speaker's tone. Use specific lines from each poem to support your ideas.

Literal and Figurative Meanings of Words

Literal language is language that means exactly what it says. **Figurative language** is writing or speech meant to be understood imaginatively instead of literally. Many writers, especially poets, use figurative language to create vivid, memorable images and to help readers see and understand things in new ways. Think about the difference in meaning in the following two examples:

EXAMPLES

literal meaning: Sally burned her hand on the hot oven rack.

figurative meaning: Sally's face burned with embarrassment at the humiliating comment.

In the first sentence, the verb *burned* conveys its literal meaning "to injure or damage by exposure to fire or heat." In the second sentence, the verb *burned* is used figuratively to illustrate the emotional impact of a memory or an event.

The most common figures of speech are simile, metaphor, personification, and hyperbole. They are described in the chart below.

Sometimes, a figure of speech is implied, rather than directly stated. For example, examine the concluding couplet of Shakespeare's sonnet:

> So long as men can breathe, or eyes can see,
> So long lives this, and this gives life to thee.

The word *this* almost certainly refers to the sonnet itself. In the final line, Shakespeare implies a comparison between his own poem and a creative force that is strong enough to keep his beloved alive forever.

Sometimes, similes are overused and become clichés, such as "He is as quiet as a mouse," "She was as happy as a clam," or "It was as cold as ice." Avoid using clichés in your writing. Instead, use original similes.

Figure of Speech	Definition	Example
simile	comparison using *like* or *as*	"When I come back to you, as summer comes"
metaphor	comparison in which one thing is spoken of or written about as if it were another	"And summer's lease hath all too short a date"
personification	figure of speech in which an idea, an animal, or a thing is described as if it were a person	"Sometime too hot the eye of heaven shines, / And often is his gold complexion dimmed"
hyperbole	deliberate exaggeration made for effect	"So long as men can breathe or eyes can see, / So long lives this, and this gives life to thee"

REVIEW TERMS

- **literal language:** language that means exactly what it says
- **figurative language:** writing or speech meant to be understood imaginatively instead of literally
- **simile:** comparison using *like* or *as*
- **metaphor:** comparison in which one thing is spoken of or written about as if it were another
- **personification:** figure of speech in which an idea, an animal, or a thing is described as if it were a person
- **hyperbole:** deliberate exaggeration made for effect

Exercise A

For each quotation from the sonnets below, identify it as a simile, metaphor, personification, or hyperbole.

1. "Sometime too hot the eye of heaven shines"
2. "Nor shall death brag thou wander'st in his shade"
3. "But thy eternal summer shall not fade"
4. "I know I am but summer to your heart"
5. "No gracious weight of golden fruits to sell / Have I, nor any wise and wintry thing"
6. "Else will you seek... / Even your summer in another clime"

Exercise B

With a partner, brainstorm a simile, metaphor, personification, and hyperbole for each word listed below. Then use the items you brainstormed for one of the words to write a sonnet about that word.

1. love
2. poverty
3. anger
4. jealousy
5. worry
6. happiness
7. death
8. birth
9. youth
10. family

Exercise C

Rewrite the paragraph shown below, adding figurative language to make it more vivid and appealing. Try to use at least one simile, one metaphor, and one personification.

> After graduating from Vassar College, Edna St. Vincent Millay settled in the Greenwich Village neighborhood of New York City. Her first poetry collection appeared in 1917. Her second volume of poems, *A Few Figs from Thistles* (1920), celebrated the carefree joys of Bohemian life and love. Millay's moral stance was considered daring for her day. Even her

> critics, however, could not deny the spontaneity that she brought to traditional forms such as the sonnet.

Exercise D

Write a paragraph in which you describe a special person in your life, such as a family member, classmate, friend, or adult mentor. Use at least four figures of speech in your writing: one simile, one metaphor, one personification, and one hyperbole.

EXTEND THE SKILL

Choose one of your favorite poems and reread it carefully. Then create a Figurative Language Chart like the one below that lists the figures of speech you can identify in the poem. Of course, not all poems have figurative language. If your favorite poem does not, try changing it by adding figurative language. How does your addition change the poem? Do you like it better with or without figurative language? Why?

Figurative Language Chart

Example of Figurative Language	What Is Compared?	What You Envision
"The black canopy of nighttime sky was painted with dazzling jewels."	The night sky is described as a black canopy or painting. The stars are described as dazzling jewels.	A dark, cloudless night sky filled with bright, twinkling stars

Ex-Basketball Player

BUILD BACKGROUND

Literary Context In **"Ex-Basketball Player,"** John Updike uses unique expressions and vivid imagery to sketch a small-town scene that will be familiar to most readers: trolley tracks, a high school gymnasium, an Esso gas station, and a luncheonette where people hang out and play pinball in their leisure time. The centerpiece of this portrait is Flick Webb, whose glory days are long gone and whose present existence offers an ironic contrast to a time when he could use his talents to the fullest. Although many people believe that taking part in sports can prepare youngsters well for adulthood, Updike's poem seems to suggest a different attitude: We must be careful not to waste our potential in life.

Reader's Context Many people who excel at sports have a brief career, since athletic excellence usually requires youthful energy and vigor. Discuss what outstanding athletes might do after their sports careers are over.

ANALYZE LITERATURE: Narrative Poem and Narrator

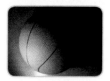

A **narrative poem** is a verse that tells a story. As in works of fiction, the writer of a narrative poem makes choices about different alternatives for storytelling. A **narrator** is a character or speaker who tells a story. The author's choice of narrator is important because it determines how much and what kind of information readers will be given about events and characters.

SET PURPOSE

As you read, consider the narrator's attitude toward Flick. Look for ways the information the narrator discloses reflects how he feels about Flick.

MEET THE AUTHOR

John Updike (b. 1932) was born in Reading, Pennsylvania, and grew up in the nearby town of Shillington. After graduating from Harvard, he worked for several years as a staff writer for the *New Yorker*. Updike's first novel, *The Poorhouse Fair*, was published in 1959. The following year, the novelist achieved international fame with *Rabbit, Run,* a sensitive, realistic portrayal of the manners and morals of middle-class suburban life in the United States. A prolific novelist and story writer (he has published more than sixty books), Updike has achieved renown as one of America's foremost men of letters, and his essays, poems, and reviews are widely admired.

USE READING SKILLS

Importance of Details In "Ex-Basketball Player," the narrator provides a variety of details about Flick Webb. Some of the details are *major,* or important to the way you understand the poem. Other details are *minor,* or not very significant. The details the narrator chooses to include reflect what the narrator thinks about Flick and what he wants readers to believe about Webb.

As you read the poem, use a Details Chart like the one below. For each stanza, record major and minor details. Then summarize the main idea of each stanza based on the details that are given.

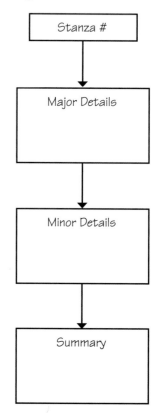

Stanza #

↓

Major Details

↓

Minor Details

↓

Summary

Ex-Basketball Player

A Narrative Poem by **John Updike**

Pearl Avenue runs past the high-school lot,
Bends with the trolley tracks, and stops, cut off
Before it has a chance to go two blocks,
At Colonel McComsky Plaza. Berth's Garage
5   Is on the corner facing west, and there,
Most days, you'll find Flick Webb, who helps Berth out.

Flick stands tall among the idiot pumps—
Five on a side, the old bubble-head style,[1]
Their rubber elbows hanging loose and low.
10 One's nostrils are two S's, and his eyes
An E and O. And one is squat, without
A head at all—more of a football type.

Once Flick played for the high-school team, the Wizards.
He was good: in fact, the best. In '46
15 He bucketed three hundred ninety points,
A county record still. The ball loved Flick.
I saw him rack up thirty-eight or forty
In one home game. His hands were like wild birds.

He never learned a trade, he just sells gas,
20 Checks oil, and changes flats. Once in a while,
As a gag, he dribbles an inner tube,
But most of us remember anyway.
His hands are fine and nervous on the lug wrench.
It makes no difference to the lug wrench, though.

25 Off work, he hangs around Mae's Luncheonette.
Grease-gray and kind of coiled, he plays pinball,
Smokes those thin cigars, nurses lemon phosphates.[2]
Flick seldom says a word to Mae, just nods
Beyond her face toward bright applauding tiers
30 Of Necco Wafers, Nibs, and Juju Beads.[3] ❖

1. **bubble-head style.** Refers to
pumps at early gas stations that were
sometimes topped with glass globes
2. **lemon phosphates.** Soft drinks
made of soda water and syrup
3. **Necco Wafers, Nibs, and Juju
Beads.** Types of candy

MIRRORS & WINDOWS Why are sports stars often held in such high regard by society? Is the idolization of sports stars always a good thing? What are the negative effects of doing so?

REFER TO TEXT ▶ ▶ ▶ ▶	▶ REASON WITH TEXT	
1a. List the details given in the first stanza.	1b. Interpret the purpose of the narrator in including these details in the poem.	**Understand** **Find meaning**
2a. Recall what the narrator describes in lines 7–12.	2b. Show how the description in lines 7–12 is humorous.	**Apply** **Use information**
3a. Quote the line in the poem that puts the narrator into the story.	3b. Infer what the narrator finds most impressive about Flick. Why do you think the narrator finds this impressive?	**Analyze** **Take things apart**
4a. State how the narrator describes Flick's hands in lines 23–24.	4b. From the details in these lines, judge whether Flick is well suited to his job. Why or why not?	**Evaluate** **Make judgments**
5a. Identify three vivid details in the description of Flick at Mae's Luncheonette in the final stanza.	5b. Explain what the inclusion of these details tells you about the narrator's feelings about Flick.	**Create** **Bring ideas together**

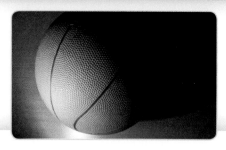

ANALYZE LITERATURE: Narrative Poem and Narrator

What specific features make this poem a narrative poem? How would you judge the narrator's reliability in telling the story about Flick? What information does the narrator leave out? Is the narrator being fair in his portrayal of Flick?

EXTEND THE TEXT

Writing Options

Creative Writing Think about how you might tell the narrative of Flick Webb in a different form, such as a short story or a play. Then, write a scene of **dialogue** focusing on Flick: for example, a conversation between Flick and Berth at the gas station, or an exchange between Flick and another pinball player at Mae's Luncheonette. Make sure the tone and flavor of your dialogue are consistent with the portrayal of Flick in Updike's poem.

Narrative Writing Imagine you are Flick Webb. You have reached old age and have decided to record the story of your life. Write a section of Flick's **memoir,** focusing either on his childhood, his basketball career, or his life after basketball. You'll have to use your imagination, based on what you know about Flick from the poem, to fill in the details of the rest of his life.

Lifelong Learning

Create a Career Portfolio Have you thought much about what profession you'd like to pursue after high school? Choose a career in which you are currently inter-

ested and research it. Then put together a list of things that would be useful to include in a portfolio in order to get a job in your chosen area. For example, if you want to be a teacher, your portfolio might feature things like a college transcript, a list of teaching credentials, and memberships in organizations dedicated to the field of education.

Critical Literacy

Prepare for a Debate "High school sports offer young people valuable preparation for the game of life." Do you agree or disagree? Choose a position, and then write a series of talking points that you might use to support your opinion in a debate on the issue. Your points might include examples, statistics, reasons, or case histories; you might also want to anticipate opposing arguments and prepare to counter them. When you have finished, share your talking points with a classmate who has adopted the opposing side of the issue.

 Go to **www.mirrorsandwindows.com** for more.

Marching Through a Novel

A Lyric Poem by **John Updike**

The Widows of Belguim, c. 1915. Louis Raemaekers.

Each morning my characters
    greet me with misty faces
willing, though chilled, to muster
    for another day's progress
5 through the dazzling quicksand,
    the marsh of blank paper.
With instant obedience
    they change clothes and mannerisms,
drop a speech impediment,
10   develop a motive backwards
to suit the deed that's done.
    They extend skeletal arms
for the handcuffs of contrivance,
    slog through docilely
15 maneuvers of coincidence,
    look toward me hopefully,
their general and quartermaster,
    for a clearer face, a bigger heart.
I do what I can for them,
20   but it is not enough.
Forward is my order,
    though their bandages unravel
and some have no backbones
    and some turn traitor
25 like heads with two faces
    and some fall forgotten
in the trenchwork of loose threads,
    poor puffs of cartoon flak.
Forward. Believe me, I love them
30   though I march them to finish
      them off. ❖

UNDERSTAND THE CONCEPT

Denotation and Connotation

The **denotation** of a word is its dictionary definition. A word's **connotation** is the emotional association the word has in addition to its literal meaning.

Several types of connotation can influence the way you think about a word:

- **positive (favorable) connotation:** words that provoke a positive emotional response

- **negative (unfavorable) connotation:** words that provoke a negative emotional response

- **neutral connotation:** words that cause no emotional reaction

For example, the words *odor* and *fragrance* both have to do with smell, but *odor* has a negative connotation similar to *stinky*, whereas *fragrance* has a positive connotation that suggests smelling good. The best way of learning the connotation of a word is to pay attention to the context in which the word appears.

Different people may have different connotations for words. For example, the word *sunshine* has a positive connotation for many people. They may hear it and think warm and relaxing thoughts. However, if your skin is sensitive to the sun, the word *sunshine* may have a negative connotation for you.

Connotations often express degree. For example, notice the slight differences in meaning among the following words:

- **anger:** intense feeling of displeasure
- **rage:** anger leading to loss of self-control
- **wrath:** desire for revenge
- **fury:** destructive anger

APPLY THE SKILL

Considering connotation is an important step in reading poetry. Poems usually have fewer words than stories or nonfiction pieces, and each word in a poem is carefully chosen. Think about, for example, the character Flick in John Updike's poem "Ex-Basketball Player." Though Flick is a name in the poem, it is also a dictionary word. Look at the dictionary definition below for the word *flick*.

> **flick** (flik) **1.** *n.*, a light sharp jerky movement **2.** *v.*, to strike lightly with a quick sharp motion (flick a bug off your shoulder)

Now that you know the denotation of the word *flick*, think about its connotation. You can use a Response Chart like the one below to keep track of how you think individual words in a poem contribute to the meaning of the poem.

Word	My Thoughts
flick	The connotation of the word *flick* is mostly negative. When I flick a bug off my shoulder, it's usually because I don't want the bug on my shoulder. Maybe Updike chose to name the main character in his poem Flick because Flick, like a bug flicked off someone's shoulder, doesn't really fit in anymore now that he is no longer a basketball star.

REVIEW TERMS

- **denotation:** the dictionary definition of a word
- **connotation:** the emotional association of a word in addition to its literal meaning

Exercise A

Use your prior knowledge, and a dictionary if needed, to identify the denotation of each of the following words or phrases from "Ex-Basketball Player." Then tell whether the word or phrase has a positive, negative, or neutral connotation. Work with a partner to write a sentence that uses the word or phrase correctly. Make sure the sentence is appropriate for the connotation of the word or phrase.

1. idiot (line 7)
2. old (line 8)
3. squat (line 11)
4. best (line 14)
5. rack (line 17)
6. fine (line 23)
7. nervous (line 23)
8. hangs around (line 25)
9. seldom (line 28)
10. bright (line 29)

Exercise B

Rewrite the paragraph shown below, changing key words and phrases to create a description with negative connotations, rather than positive ones.

Flick walked into the classroom late, two minutes after the bell rang. He smiled at Ms. Jefferson, our history teacher, and murmured an apology. Then he took his seat, resting his textbook on the desk. He sat attentively in his desk, drinking in every word Ms. Jefferson said. When called upon five minutes later to identify the causes of the Civil War, he didn't miss a trick. Responding as deftly as he dribbled the basketball on the court, he was able to show that he was solidly prepared for today's oral quiz.

Exercise C

Working with a partner, brainstorm a list of words that have similar meaning, but different connotations. You may use a dictionary or thesaurus to help you. Then sort the words into a chart like the one below, showing which have negative connotations, which have positive connotations, and which have neutral connotations.

Negative	Neutral	Positive
rowdy	loud	boisterous
pushy	firm	assertive
gaudy	bright	colorful
stench	smell	fragrance

EXTEND THE SKILL

Read the following verse below from "Ex-Basketball Player." Then rewrite it, substituting synonyms with different connotations for some of the key words. Read your revised verse out loud to a partner, and discuss how the changes you made affect the mood, tone, and meaning of the verse.

He never learned a trade, he just sells gas,
Checks oil, and changes flats. Once in a
  while,
As a gag, he dribbles an inner tube,
But most of us remember anyway.
His hands are fine and nervous on the lug
  wrench.
It makes no difference to the lug wrench,
  though.

from HOLIDAYS

| BEFORE READING | A Prose Poem by Jamaica Kincaid |

BUILD BACKGROUND

Literary Context In **"Holidays,"** the narrator relates her thoughts and sensations as she confronts a series of choices about what to do and where to go during her vacation. Kincaid's speaker uses a stream-of-consciousness technique, or writing that attempts to show the moment-by-moment flow of feelings, thoughts, and impressions within the mind of a character. In fully developed stream-of-consciousness writing, sentence breaks and punctuation are often abandoned, in order to suggest an unfettered flow of images, ideas, and sensations.

Reader's Context Do you enjoy being by yourself? How do you feel about solitude? Is being alone from time to time a relaxing and enjoyable experience? Why or why not?

ANALYZE LITERATURE: Prose Poem and Style

 A **prose poem** is a work, usually brief and written in prose, that makes such extensive use of poetic language that the line between prose and poetry becomes blurred. **Style** is the manner in which something is said or written. In "Holidays," Kincaid writes in a *stream-of-consciousness* style in which there is a continuous flow of thoughts through the mind of the narrator.

SET PURPOSE

Notice how the narrator's mind travels from subject to subject, image to image, without any apparent logical connection. Is this a realistic portrayal of how people's minds work? Examine the subjects and images the narrator's mind travels to.

MEET THE AUTHOR

 Born on the Caribbean island of Antigua, **Jamaica Kincaid** (b. 1949) is the pseudonym adopted by Elaine Potter Richardson. After completing her secondary education, she traveled to New York, where she worked as a governess and studied photography. Her first published writing was a series of articles for *Ingenue* magazine. As a freelance writer, she went on to publish articles and short stories in the *New Yorker, Rolling Stone, Ms.,* and the *Paris Review.* Her collection *At the Bottom of the River* (1983), from which "Holidays" is excerpted, won the Morton Dauwen Award from the American Academy and Institute of Arts and Letters. Other works of Kincaid include *Annie John, Lucy,* and *Autobiography of My Mother.*

USE READING SKILLS

Summarize A **summary** is a brief statement in your own words of the main ideas, details, and events of a work. Summarizing a poem can help you remember its main points. The key to summarizing well is being able to pick out what is important. As you read the excerpt from "Holidays," think about what you would tell a friend about the poem—look for ideas and details that are important to the meaning of the poem. Use a graphic organizer like the one below to organize your thoughts.

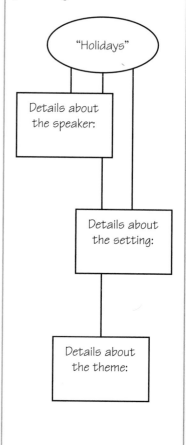

"Holidays"

Details about the speaker:

Details about the setting:

Details about the theme:

from
H O L I D A Y S

A Prose Poem by **Jamaica Kincaid**

I sit on the porch facing the mountains. I sit on a wicker couch looking out the window at a field of day lilies. I walk into a room where someone—an artist, maybe—has stored some empty canvases. I drink a glass of water. I put the empty glass, from which I have just drunk the water, on a table. I notice two flies, one sitting on top of the other, flying around the room. I scratch my scalp, I scratch my thighs. I lift my arms up and stretch them above my head. I sigh. I spin on my heels once. I walk around the dining-room table three times. I see a book lying on the dining-room table and I pick it up. The book is called *An Illustrated Encyclopedia of Butterflies and Moths.* I leaf through the book, looking only at the pictures, which are bright and beautiful. From my looking through the book, the word "thorax"[1] sticks in my mind. "Thorax," I say, "thorax, thorax," I don't know how many times. I bend over and touch my toes. I stay in that position until I count to one hundred. As I count, I pretend to be counting off balls on a ball frame. As I count the balls, I pretend that they are the colors red, green, blue, and yellow. I walk over to the fireplace. Standing in front of the fireplace, I try to write my name in the dead ashes with my big toe. I cannot write my name in the dead ashes with my big toe. My big toe, now dirty, I try to clean by rubbing it vigorously on a clean royal-blue rug. The royal-blue rug now has a dark spot, and my big toe has a strong burning sensation. Oh, sensation. I am filled with sensation. I feel—oh, how I feel. I feel, I feel, I feel. I have no words right now for how I feel. I take a walk down the road in my bare feet. I feel the stones on the road, hard and sharp against my soft, almost pink soles. Also, I feel the hot sun beating down on my bare neck. It is midday. Did I say that? Must I say that? Oh, me, oh my. The road on which I walk barefoot leads to the store— the village store. Should I go to the village store or should I not go to the village store? I can if I want. If I go to the village store, I can buy a peach. The peach will be warm from sitting in a box in the sun. The peach will not taste sweet and the peach will not taste sour. I will know that I am eating a peach only by looking at it. I will not go to the store. I will sit on the porch facing the mountains.

I sit on the porch facing the mountains. The porch is airy and spacious. I am the only person sitting on the porch. I look at myself. I can see myself. That is, I can see my chest, my abdomen, my legs, and my arms. I cannot see my hair, my ears, my face, or my collarbone. I can feel them, though. My nose is moist with sweat. Locking my fingers, I put my hands on my head. I see a bee, a large bumblebee, flying around aimlessly. I remove my hands from resting on my head, because my arms are tired. But also I have just

---

1. **thorax.** The part of the body from the neck to the abdomen

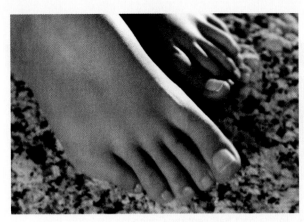

remembered a superstition: if you sit with your hands on your head, you will kill your mother. I have many superstitions. I believe all of them. Should I read a book? Should I make myself something to drink? But what? And hot or cold? Should I write a letter? I should write a letter. I will write a letter. "Dear So-and-So, I am…and then I got the brilliant idea…I was very amusing…I had enough, I said…I saw what I came to see, I thought …I am laughing all the way to the poorhouse. I grinned…I just don't know anymore. I remain, etc." I like my letter. Perhaps I shall keep my letter to myself. I fold up the letter I have just written and put it between the pages of the book I am trying to read. The book is lying in my lap. I look around me, trying to find something on which to focus my eyes. I see ten ants. I count them as they wrestle with a speck of food. I am not fascinated by that. I see my toes moving up and down as if they were tapping out a beat. Why are my toes tapping? I am fascinated by that. A song is going through my mind. It goes, "There was a man from British Guiana, Who used to play a piana. His foot slipped, His trousers ripped…" I see, I see. Yes. Now. Suddenly I am tired. I am yawning. Perhaps I will take a nap. Perhaps I will take a long nap. Perhaps I will take a nice long nap. Perhaps, while taking my nap, I will have a dream, a dream in which I am not sitting on the porch facing the mountains. ❖

"Oh, sensation. I am filled with sensation. I feel—oh, how I feel. I feel, I feel, I feel. I have no words right now for how I feel." When have you experienced the same thing as the speaker? How did you deal with the situation of not knowing how to express yourself?

LITERATURE
CONNECTION

Caribbean Literature In the past half century, Caribbean literature has emerged with great distinction on the world stage. Besides Jamaica Kincaid, leading authors from the West Indies include two writers who have won the Nobel Prize for Literature: V. S. Naipaul (b. 1932) from Trinidad and Derek Walcott (b. 1930) from St. Lucia. Naipaul's early works are set in the Caribbean and focus on the ironic comedy of everyday life as well as on the search for cultural and personal identity. Caribbean imagery, history, and speech patterns play major roles in the works of poet and playwright Derek Walcott.

AFTER READING

REFER TO TEXT	REASON WITH TEXT	
1a. Identify where the speaker is at the beginning and at the end of the poem.	1b. Infer why the speaker is at this particular place. Is this where she typically lives? How can you tell?	**Understand** **Find meaning**
2a. Recall the decision the speaker has to make as she walks down the road. List the other decisions she has to make.	2b. Examine whether these decisions are difficult or important. In what way is the speaker's description of the peach she could buy similar to her own feelings?	**Apply** **Use information**
3a. Quote the part of the poem that indicates what the speaker tries to do with the ashes from the fireplace and what happens as a result.	3b. Analyze the connection between the ash incident and the activity that follows. What feelings does the ash incident invoke? Why?	**Analyze** **Take things apart**
4a. List adjectives that appropriately describe the speaker in this selection.	4b. Evaluate the speaker's attitude about where she is and what she is doing.	**Evaluate** **Make judgments**
5a. What does the speaker decide to do at the end of the poem?	5b. If you were the speaker, how would you feel about going home after this kind of holiday? Explain your answer using evidence from the poem.	**Create** **Bring ideas together**

ANALYZE LITERATURE: Prose Poem and Style

Make a list of the elements of poetry and of prose that you find in the speaker's mental wanderings. How do these elements contribute to the structure of a prose poem? How does the writer's style affect your reading of the poem? What are the challenges of reading stream-of-consciousness writing?

Writing Options

Creative Writing Imagine that you are the speaker in the prose poem. Complete the **letter** that you are considering writing in the second paragraph. Choose an appropriate addressee for the letter, and then use details in the prose poem as a springboard for your writing.

Expository Writing Kincaid uses a stream-of-consciousness technique in "Holidays." See the Build Background section to review what this technique involves. Then write a one-paragraph **analysis** discussing whether or not you enjoy reading this kind of writing. Include in your analysis your reasons for liking or disliking this writing technique and the ways you think it either contributes to or detracts from Kincaid's work.

Collaborative Learning

Plan a Dream Vacation Working with a small group, plan a weeklong trip to a location chosen by your group members. First, find out how much the airfare costs by locating an airline online. Then, locate an Internet site on your destination by entering a key word, such as "Hawaii." Identify a suitable hotel and then write out an itinerary, listing where you will go and what you will do each day.

Lifelong Learning

Learn About Antigua Use an almanac, an atlas, an encyclopedia, or other suitable reference works to gather information on Jamaica Kincaid's native island of Antigua. Look for basic facts, such as land area, population, topography, literacy rate, and life expectancy

for males and females. Also research the island's history as a British colony, independence, the present form of government, and important aspects of the economy. When you have gathered enough information, create a children's book about the island.

 Go to **www.mirrorsandwindows.com** for more.

READING ASSESSMENT

1. Which of the following is an important technique used by Jamaica Kincaid in "Holidays"?
   A. flashback
   B. foreshadowing
   C. repetition
   D. alliteration
   E. personification

2. In paragraph 2, the word *spacious* most nearly means
   A. empty.
   B. large.
   C. enormous.
   D. optimistic.
   E. breezy.

3. Which of the following *best* describes the speaker's most difficult problem while she is on vacation?
   A. There is too much sun.
   B. She doesn't have any money.
   C. She doesn't have time to take a nap.
   D. She wants to go home.
   E. She is restless.

4. At the end of the prose poem, the speaker implies that she is which of the following?

   A. ambitious
   B. frightened
   C. bored
   D. amused
   E. None of the above

5. How does the setting of the poem contribute to its overall mood?
   A. The island setting gives the poem a romantic and adventurous mood.
   B. The speaker dislikes the view of the mountains, and her thoughts contribute to a foreboding mood.
   C. The speaker is annoyed by all of the distractions around her, contributing to a frustrated mood.
   D. The speaker is on vacation and is able to let her mind wander, which contributes to a restless mood.
   E. None of the above

6. Reread the selection. Then, in a paragraph or two, identify the images and details that give the writing a "poetic" quality.

GRAMMAR & STYLE

UNDERSTAND THE CONCEPT | APPLY THE SKILL

Possessives

Nouns that show ownership or possession of things or qualities are called **possessive nouns.** A possessive noun names who or what has something. Possessive nouns can be singular or plural. Study the following rules for making nouns possessive.

- To form the possessive of a singular noun, add an apostrophe and an *–s* to the end of the word. If a singular noun ends in *–s,* you will still add an apostrophe and an *–s.*

EXAMPLES

a comet's orbit   the countess's jewels
a child's toys   the Jones's house

- If a plural noun does not end in *–s,* add an apostrophe and an *–s* to the end of the word to form the possessive. If a plural noun ends with an *–s,* add only an apostrophe.

EXAMPLES

geese's livers
employees' vacation time
two weeks' vacation

- Use an apostrophe and an *–s* to show joint or separate ownership. If two nouns are used to show joint ownership, form only the last noun in the possessive. If two or more nouns are used to show separate ownership, form each noun in the possessive.

EXAMPLES

Mark and Delia's presentation (The presentation belongs to both Mark and Delia collectively.)
Gloria's and Bonnie's red hair (Both Gloria and Bonnie have their own red hair.)

- Use an apostrophe and an *–s* to form the possessive of only the last word in a compound noun.

EXAMPLES

the Secretary General's speech
her brother-in-law's car

- Add an apostrophe and an *–s* to form the possessive of an indefinite pronoun.

EXAMPLES

no one's enemy
everyone's friend
one another's essays

- Some proper names, particularly from ancient times, have an irregular possessive form. Even though the names are singular and end in *–s,* you add only an apostrophe.

EXAMPLES

Hercules' labors
Moses' laws
Sophocles' plays

When a pronoun is in the possessive case, different rules apply than with regular nouns. The chart below contains a list of singular and plural possessive pronouns.

Singular		Plural	
First person	my, mine	**First person**	our, ours
Second person	your, yours	**Second person**	your, yours
Third person	his, her, hers, its	**Third person**	their, theirs

You do not use apostrophes or add an *–s* to possessive pronouns.

EXAMPLES

my dog   her pencil
its foot   their car

REVIEW TERMS

- **possessive case:** form of noun or pronoun that shows ownership
- **compound noun:** noun made up of two or more words
- **indefinite pronoun:** a pronoun that points out a person, place, or thing but not a particular or definite one

Use Possessives Correctly

Use an apostrophe and an —s to form the possessive forms of each of the following words.

1. house
2. antonym
3. parent
4. deer
5. woman
6. business
7. boundary
8. mother-in-law
9. ox
10. playwright
11. goose
12. family

Correct a Sentence

Add an apostrophe and an —s where needed to make the singular and plural possessive forms of words in the following sentences.

1. The speaker vacation takes place in Antigua.
2. The West Indies two Nobel Prize winners are Derek Walcott and V. S. Naipaul.
3. Everyone vacation last summer was wonderful.
4. The memo from the office told her that she had to return to work in three weeks time.
5. "If you sit with your hands on your head, you will kill your mother" is one of the speaker superstitions.
6. In his works, Walcott makes use of the Caribbean imagery and history. He also incorporates the Caribbean people speech pattern into his works.
7. Walcott and Naipaul prize is the Nobel Prize of Literature.
8. Gwen and her sister nose looked very red after spending all day at the beach.
9. Nobel Prize winner V. S. Naipaul early works are set in the Caribbean.
10. The students summer vacation was a blast. They went hiking all over the Caribbean islands.

Improve a Paragraph

Rewrite the paragraph shown below, fixing the possessive forms as needed.

Many people around the world like to go on vacations or holidays. One persons idea of an ideal vacations fun might be to sit on the beach and read. Another person might enjoy the adventure of experiencing a foreign countrys sights and smells. Since traveling can be expensive, families limited budgets might prompt them to go sightseeing around their own communities. Visiting a museums special exhibit or taking a walk through a local park on one of it's trails can be interesting and enjoyable. Big cities are attractive vacation spots for some, whereas others preference might be for the countryside and it's charm. Perhaps the key to a successful vacation is simply doing what one likes.

Use Possessives in Your Writing

Write an opinion column for your school newspaper about whether or not students should have jobs during their summer vacations. As you express your thoughts and feelings on the subject, pay attention to the way you use possessive nouns and pronouns.

EXTEND THE SKILL

Make up your own quiz to test your classmates' knowledge of correct possessive forms. Also draw up an answer key. Then call on volunteers to take the test. You might designate a suitable prize for the competitor with the highest score.

Understanding Figurative Language

TYPES OF FIGURATIVE LANGUAGE

Have you ever read a poem that you simply didn't comprehend? Though the text may be written in your native language, the poet may be using poetic, or figurative, language to describe an image, a scene, or a feeling. By learning to identify these poetic devices, you will be better able to read and understand the language of poetry.

Simile and Metaphor

One of the most frequently used techniques in poetry is to make a comparison between two dissimilar objects, such as between a poem and a tree. How the comparison is made determines whether the writer is using a simile or a metaphor. **Similes** make the comparison by using the word *like* or *as*. In the example below from "Jazz Fantasia" (page 463), a moan is compared to an autumn wind.

> Moan like an autumn wind high in the
>   lonesome treetops
>   —from "Jazz Fantasia" by Carl Sandburg

Metaphors, on the other hand, make a comparison without using *like* or *as,* thus making the stated comparison seem stronger. In a metaphor, the two objects being compared are called the *tenor* and the *vehicle.* The tenor is the actual object being discussed, and the vehicle is the object used to describe it. In the example below from "Poetry" (page 447), the metaphor "a poem is pure energy" compares a poem to pure energy by saying the poem *is* pure energy and then showing how this statement is true.

> a poem is pure energy
> horizontally contained
> between the mind
> of the poet and the ear of the reader
>   —from "Poetry" by Nikki Giovanni

Analogy

Similarly, an **analogy** is a comparison of two things that are alike in some ways by otherwise quite different. Similes are *expressed analogies;* metaphors are *implied analogies.* In Shakespeare's "Shall I compare thee to a summer's day?" (page 421), the speaker makes an analogy between his lover's beauty and personality and the season of summer.

> Shall I compare thee to a summer's day?
> Thou art more lovely and more temperate:
> Rough winds do shake the darling buds
>   of May,
> And summer's lease hath all too short
>   a date
>   —from "Shall I compare thee to a
>   summer's day?" by William Shakespeare

Personification

Another type of figurative language is personification. **Personification** is a figure of speech in which an animal, a thing, an idea, or a force of nature is given human characteristics. "Poetry" by Nikki Giovanni personifies a poem:

> it never says "love me" for poets are
> beyond love
> it never says "accept me" for poems seek not
> acceptance but controversy
> it only says "i am"…
> if it does not sing discard the ear
> for poetry is song
>   —from "Poetry" by Nikki Giovanni

Poems cannot literally speak or sing, for they are abstract and intangible ideas. However, by giving poetry these human qualities, Giovanni allows her readers to better understand the motivations of poetry by allowing them to identify with the poem. Her readers certainly know what it means to speak

and to sing, and what it feels like to ask for love or to provoke an argument. Thus, the use of personification here allows the reader to clearly understand the emotional overtones of Giovanni's view of the purpose and nature of poetry; contrast this figurative language with the uninspired paraphrase, "The purpose of a poem is to spark controversy and to sound beautiful."

Symbolism

Symbolism is another type of literary device that falls into the category of figurative language. A **symbol** is anything that stands for or represents both itself and something else. For example, in the tanka by Okamoto Kanoko (page 467), the speaker uses the symbol of a flower to represent life.

> if I were to stand
> with roots in the ground
> like a flower
> would my life bloom out
> in the color I was born with?
> —Tanka by Okamoto Kanoko

Flowers are often used in literature to symbolize life, health, or beauty, such as the "darling buds of May" in Shakespeare's "Shall I compare thee to a summer's day?" or when someone is compared to a "faded rose" to suggest that he or she was once beautiful but now is no longer so.

When every element of a poem or story, including characters, events, or settings, symbolizes something else, the work is then considered an **allegory.**

Hyperbole

Hyperbole is a type of figurative language in which overstatement, or exaggeration, is used for dramatic effect. The sayings "a flood of tears" or "muscles of steel" are hyperboles.

READING STRATEGIES AND SKILLS WITH FIGURATIVE LANGUAGE

Sometimes, figurative language is hard to understand. If you find you are struggling to understand a poem because of its language, try the following reading strategies and skills:

- **Visualize** Try to picture similes and metaphors in your mind. For example, consider the line "Moan like an autumn wind high in the lonesome tree-tops" from Carl Sandburg's "Jazz Fantasia." Imagine in your mind how the wind sounds as it's blowing through the trees. If you enjoy drawing, create illustrations for the poems you read.

- **Paraphrase** Restate in your own words, or paraphrase, each line or stanza of poetry you struggle to understand. Consider what symbols might represent or ways the tenor and vehicle of a metaphor are related.

- **Connect** For each use of figurative language you encounter in a poem, think about how its main concept relates to a familiar aspect in your life. For example, when reading the line "a poem is pure energy" from Nikki Giovanni's poem, ask yourself what "pure energy" means to you. Is it a young child who never slows down? Is it a scientific concept? Connect what you read to what you understand.

- **Ask Questions** If you are having a hard time understanding a poem, write down specific questions about things that puzzle you. If you want to know why a poet chose to write something a certain way, try looking at other poems by that poet to see if there are any patterns, or read some biographical information on the poet to find clues about his or her writing.

Poetry
A Lyric Poem by Nikki Giovanni

Introduction to Poetry
A Lyric Poem by Billy Collins

COMPARING LITERATURE

BEFORE READING

BUILD BACKGROUND

Literary Context Poetry has been defined in many different ways. The English Romantic poet William Wordsworth (1770–1850) said that poetry was "the spontaneous overflow of powerful feelings." Wordsworth's friend Samuel Taylor Coleridge (1772–1834) put it more directly, saying poetry was "the best words in the best order." **"Poetry"** and **"Introduction to Poetry"** also seek to define what poetry is and what it means to readers.

For the speaker in "Poetry," making verse is a consuming passion, causing poets to "[forget] our lovers or children." The poem "Introduction to Poetry" is about teaching poetry to students, and Billy Collins singles out the dimensions of excitement and discovery in poetry. This poem first appeared in Collins's collection entitled *The Apple that Astonished Paris* (1996). In an interview about "Introduction to Poetry," Collins said, "Often people, when they're confronted with a poem, it's like someone who keeps saying 'what is the meaning of this? What is the meaning of this?' And that dulls us to the other pleasures poetry offers."

Reader's Context What elements of a poem appeal to you most: the sound devices, the images, or the speaker's ideas and feelings?

USE READING SKILLS

Paraphrase Using your own words to describe something you've read is called **paraphrasing.** You can paraphrase a poem by asking "What is it about?" or "What does it mean?" As you read the selections, use a Paraphrase Chart like the one below to paraphrase lines or stanzas.

Line / Stanza
My Paraphrase
My Thoughts

COMPARE LITERATURE: Personification and Paradox

Personification is a figure of speech in which an idea, an animal, or a thing is described as if it were a person. A **paradox** is a seemingly contradictory statement, idea, or event that may actually be true. As you read, notice the way Collins and Giovanni personify poetry and call attention to poetry's often paradoxical qualities.

MEET THE AUTHORS

GIOVANNI

Born in Knoxville, Tennessee, **Nikki Giovanni** (b. 1943) graduated from Fisk University, where she was active in the Civil Rights movement and began to write poetry. Many of her poems have been inspired by African-American family culture, as well as by religious faith, blues music and rhythm, and women's issues. Giovanni has published numerous poetry collections, and she has also authored children's books and essays.

Billy Collins (b. 1941) grew up in New York City. Over the past thirty years, he has authored half a dozen collections of poetry; the most recent is entitled *The Trouble with Poetry* (2005). Collins teaches at Lehman College of the City University of New York. From 2001 to 2003, he served as Poet Laureate of the United States. He describes poetry as "the only surviving history we have of human emotion."

COLLINS

POETRY

A Lyric Poem by **Nikki Giovanni**

Velocita Astratta-Auto in Corsa, 1913. Giacomo Balla.

poetry is motion graceful
as a fawn
gentle as a teardrop
strong like the eye
5   finding peace in a crowded room

we poets tend to think
our words are golden
though emotion speaks too
loudly to be defined
10   by silence

sometimes after midnight or just before
    the dawn
we sit typewriter in hand
pulling loneliness around us
15   forgetting our lovers or children
who are sleeping
ignoring the weary <u>wariness</u>
of our own logic
to compose a poem
20   no one understands it
it never says "love me" for poets are
beyond love
it never says "accept me" for poems seek not
acceptance but controversy
25   it only says "i am" and therefore
i <u>concede</u> that you are too

a poem is pure energy
horizontally contained
between the mind
30   of the poet and the ear of the reader
if it does not sing <u>discard</u> the ear
for poetry is song
if it does not delight discard
the heart for poetry is joy
35   if it does not inform then close
off the brain for it is dead
if it cannot heed the insistent message
that life is precious

which is all we poets
40   wrapped in our loneliness
 are trying to say ❖

war • i • ness (war´ ē nəs) *n.,* caution
con • cede (kən sēd´) *v.,* admit
dis • card (dis kärd´) *v.,* throw away

MIRRORS & WINDOWS   Does poetry serve a purpose in the "real" world? What are the benefits of being able to read and understand poetry?

HUMANITIES
CONNECTION

RAY CHARLES

Blues and Gospel Influences Poetry has often been described as "verbal music." In fact, many poets have been inspired by music or have composed their works with a musical setting in mind. Nikki Giovanni, for example, has been strongly influenced by blues and gospel music. **Blues,** which is usually classified as a type of jazz music, developed in the early twentieth century and combined African harmonies, rhythms, and melodic elements with plainspoken, earthy lyrics and a melancholy, sometimes cynical, mood. Early blues pioneers included W. C. Handy, Ma Rainey, Bessie Smith, and Blind Lemon Jefferson. **Gospel music,** which first developed in southern Protestant churches, is typically intense and joyful. Rooted in African-American work songs, gospel often exhibits a call-and-response structure, in which preacher and congregation answer each other. Outstanding artists associated with gospel music have included Mahalia Jackson, Aretha Franklin, and Ray Charles.

REFER TO TEXT ▶ ▶ ▶ ▶	▶ REASON WITH TEXT	
1a. List the adjectives the speaker uses to describe poetry in lines 1–5.	1b. Describe the emotions these adjectives create in you.	**Understand** **Find meaning**
2a. Identify the characteristics of the poet the speaker presents.	2b. Applying what you know about the speaker's perception of poets, explain the emotional and intellectual qualities this description suggests a poet needs.	**Apply** **Use information**
3a. Quote the surprising statements the speaker makes about poetry in lines 21–24.	3b. Analyze the apparent contradictions in these lines about "love" and "acceptance." Are they really contradictions? What is the speaker trying to say?	**Analyze** **Take things apart**
4a. State four things that poetry *must* do, according to lines 31–38.	4b. Evaluate the speaker's opinions about poetry in these lines. Do you agree or disagree? Support your answer.	**Evaluate** **Make judgments**
5a. How does line 40 echo line 14? To what aspect of a poet's life do these lines call attention?	5b. If you were to choose a single, over-riding element or quality of what poetry is, what would it be, and why?	**Create** **Bring ideas together**

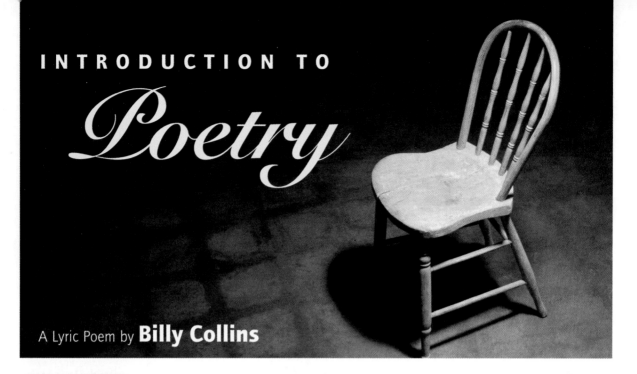

INTRODUCTION TO
Poetry

A Lyric Poem by **Billy Collins**

I ask them to take a poem
and hold it up to the light
like a color slide

or press an ear against its hive.

5   I say drop a mouse into a poem
and watch him <u>probe</u> his way out,

or walk inside the poem's room
and feel the walls for a light switch.

I want them to water-ski
10 across the surface of a poem
waving at the author's name on the shore.

But all they want to do
is tie the poem to a chair with a rope
and torture a confession out of it.

15 They begin beating it with a hose
to find out what it really means. ❖

probe (prōb) *v.*, explore; search

What is the most effective way to read a poem? Does trying to analyze and find special meaning in a poem ruin it or enhance it? Explain your answer.

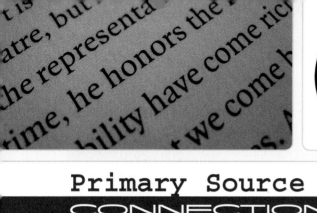

PBS

COLLINS

Primary Source
CONNECTION

Elizabeth Farnsworth of PBS's *Online NewsHour* interviewed former Poet Laureate Billy Collins in December of 2001. In the excerpt from the interview included below, Collins talks about his poem "Introduction to Poetry" and the challenges of writing and reading poetry.

ELIZABETH FARNSWORTH TALKS TO BILLY COLLINS

An Interview by Elizabeth Farnsworth

ELIZABETH FARNSWORTH: I want to talk about this issue of accessibility. I notice that the word "accessible" is used a lot in reviews and discussions of your poetry meaning, I guess, easy to understand. It is a word you like? Do you try to be accessible?

BILLY COLLINS: Well, I've gotten tired of it actually. It's a little overused, not just in application to my work, but a lot of other poets I think. I think accessible just means that the reader can walk into the poem without difficulty. The poem is not, as someone put it, deflective of entry. But the real question is what happens to the reader once he or she gets inside the poem? That's the real question for me, is getting the reader into the poem and then taking the reader somewhere because I think of poetry as a kind of form of travel writing.

ELIZABETH FARNSWORTH: You have a poem that's kind of about this. Read it. We'll keep on with this discussion.

BILLY COLLINS: Well, the poem is called "Introduction to Poetry." It's about the teaching of poetry to students. [Collins reads poem.]

ELIZABETH FARNSWORTH: (Laughs) There's a lot here. Part of it is just you're asking people to approach this with a lighter heart than they sometimes think they should, right?

BILLY COLLINS: I think so. Often people, when they're confronted with a poem, it's like someone who keeps saying "what is the meaning of this? What is the meaning of this?" And that dulls us to the other pleasures poetry offers.

ELIZABETH FARNSWORTH: Is it... Would you say it's something of a cause with you or has been to avoid pomposity? To... It's subtle what you're doing. It isn't that it's easy. It looks very hard to me, but it is... You use the word "hospitable." You're very hospitable to your reader.

BILLY COLLINS: Well, I think I'm making up for previous sins, because when I was in graduate school, I was taught that difficulty was part of the value of poetry, and I committed the sin of difficulty over and over again in my earlier writing. It took quite a while for me just to try to speak more clearly. I'm very aware of the presence of a reader, and that probably is a reaction against a lot of poems that I do read which seem oblivious to my presence as a reader. ❖

REFER TO TEXT ▶ ▶ ▶ ▶	▶ REASON WITH TEXT	
1a. List the things the speaker asks "them" to do to a poem.	1b. Explain what the speaker hopes to accomplish by asking "them" to do this.	**Understand** **Find meaning**
2a. Identify the image in line 4.	2b. What does the image suggest about the nature of poetry?	**Apply** **Use information**
3a. Describe the images that the speaker uses in lines 6–11.	3b. Infer the qualities of poetry suggested by these images.	**Analyze** **Take things apart**
4a. What personification appears in lines 12–14?	4b. Determine how the speaker's tone changes in these lines. Evaluate whether the change in tone is justified or not. Explain your answer.	**Evaluate** **Make judgments**
5a. Paraphrase the last two lines of the poem.	5b. Summarize what the speaker is saying in the last two lines of the poem about how students often approach poetry.	**Create** **Bring ideas together**

COMPARE LITERATURE: Personification and Paradox

In what ways do Giovanni and Collins use personification? How does the use of personification affect the way you feel about and understand the poems? What qualities of poetry could be called paradoxical? What does the fact that paradoxes exist in these poems about poetry say about the nature of poetry?

EXTEND THE TEXT

Writing Options

Creative Writing What is poetry? There are many different ways for people to express what poetry means to them, even without using poetry. Think about what poetry means to you. Then create a **blog entry** that expresses your ideas. Or, create a blog entry that expresses the ideas in either "Poetry" or "Introduction to Poetry."

Persuasive Writing What is the purpose of poetry? Should poetry be taught in high school? If not, why? If so, which poems should be taught? Write a one-page **editorial** for your school newspaper that examines these questions thoughtfully and comes up with some sort of conclusion. Since the purpose of an editorial is usually to persuade others to agree with your opinions, structure your editorial like a persuasive essay: Take a position on the issues addressed, and give logical and supported arguments for believing what you do.

Collaborative Learning

Research a Poet Laureate The United States Poet Laureate program began in 1986, with the first appointment going to Robert Penn Warren. Subsequent laureates, who are appointed by the Librarian of Congress, have included Richard Wilbur, Rita Dove, Robert Pinsky, Louise Glück, and Donald Hall. Using Internet and library resources, research one of the laureates. Then prepare a résumé for that person, listing his or her career achievements.

Critical Literacy

Create a Dialogue Imagine that Nikki Giovanni and Billy Collins are making a joint appearance at a panel discussion about poetry. Write a dialogue between the poets that explores their attitudes about being a poet and writing poems. In your dialogue, you may include points of both agreement and disagreement. When you have finished, join with a partner to role-play your dialogue for an audience of classmates. Then invite feedback from your audience.

 Go to **www.mirrorsandwindows.com** for more.

Understanding Sight and Sound

TECHNIQUES OF SIGHT

The pictures that form in your mind as you read a poem or other work are called **images.** The language that creates those pictures is called **imagery.** Imagery uses **sensory details,** or details that appeal to the five senses, and concrete objects to represent a scene, an emotion, or an experience.

Poets use imagery to connect with readers. A poem that contains well-chosen and carefully-described images is more appealing than a poem that is abstract. In "Introduction to Poetry" (page 449), Billy Collins uses the images of a mouse exploring a maze, a person fumbling for a light in a dark room, and a person waterskiing over the surface of a poem to describe how he wishes his students would approach poetry. Readers can make meaning out of these images by connecting them to what they know about mice and waterskiing.

> I say drop a mouse into a poem
> and watch him probe his way out…
>
> I want them to water-ski
> across the surface of a poem
> waving at the author's name on the shore.
> —from "Introduction to Poetry" by
> Billy Collins

Imagery can also paint a scene so vividly that readers will understand and empathize with what the speaker is feeling, as in the example below from "I Am Offering This Poem" (page 395).

> I am offering this poem to you,
> since I have nothing else to give.
> Keep it like a warm coat
> when winter comes to cover you,
> or like a pair of thick socks
> the cold cannot bite through
> —from "I Am Offering This Poem" by
> Jimmy Santiago Baca

TECHNIQUES OF SOUND

Poets use a variety of techniques to appeal to the sense of hearing. These techniques are listed below.

Rhyme

The first sound device you associate with poetry is very likely to be **rhyme.** The most common type of rhyme is the repetition of sounds at the ends of words that fall at the ends of lines, such as "He gives his harness bells a shake / To ask if there is some mistake," from "Stopping by Woods on a Snowy Evening" (page 477). This type of rhyme is called *end rhyme.* If the rhyming words appear within the lines instead of at the ends, the pattern is called *internal rhyme.* If the rhyme is not exact, meaning that the sounds are somewhat similar but do not quite rhyme, it is considered a *slant rhyme.*

A pattern of end rhymes is called **rhyme scheme.** A rhyme scheme is designated by assigning a different letter of the alphabet to each rhyme. The rhyme scheme of the example below is *aaba.*

> Whose woods these are I think I <u>know</u>.   *a*
> His house is in the village <u>though</u>;   *a*
> He will not see me stopping <u>here</u>   *b*
> To watch his woods fill up with <u>snow</u>.   *a*
> —from "Stopping by Woods on a Snowy
> Evening" by Robert Frost

Assonance, Consonance, and Alliteration

The sounds of letters in other parts of words can also be used for effect. **Assonance** is the repetition of vowel sounds. In "Jazz Fantasia" (page 463), for instance, the speaker states "batter on your banjoes." The short /a/ sound in "batter" and "banjoes" creates a harsh twang, which mimics the distinctive sound of a banjo.

Consonance, on the other hand, is a similarity in consonant sounds in words that otherwise do not rhyme. For example, in "Eight Puppies" (page 480), the words "whimper and whine" share the /wh/ sound, and in

"Simple Song" (page 475), the words "sealed in skin" share the /s/ sound. When you notice that a sound is repeated at the beginning of several words, you have found an example of **alliteration.** The example below from "Jazz Fantasia" contains alliteration.

> ...a <u>r</u>ed moon <u>r</u>ides
> on the <u>h</u>umps of the low river <u>h</u>ills
> —from "Jazz Fantasia" by Carl Sandburg

Onomatopoeia

Onomatopoeia is the use of words or phrases that sound like the things to which they refer. For example, in "Jazz Fantasia," in addition to the words "husha hushahushoo" and "hoo-hoo-hoo," which directly imitate the sounds being made, the words "bang" and "cry" are also examples of onomatopoeia. Both words sound abrupt and harsh, and not only describe a particular sound, but imitate the sound that is being made.

Repetition

The use of **repetition** can add emphasis to an idea. By repeating the word "remember" throughout her poem "Remember" (page 407), Joy Harjo emphasizes that it is vitally important to remember the interconnectedness of all living things. Repetition of entire lines or stanzas also emphasizes ideas, as in Lucille Clifton's "miss rosie" (page 473), where the concluding line "I stand up" is repeated twice.

Rhythm and Meter

By paying attention to the syllables and stresses in words and lines of poetry, poets can create **rhythm** within a verse. The rhythm of a poem is determined by the **meter,** which is a regular rhythmic pattern in poetry. This pattern is determined by the number of beats, or stresses, in each line. Stressed and unstressed syllables are divided into rhythmical units called *feet*. Feet commonly used in poetry are listed in the following chart.

Foot	Description	Example
iamb (iambic)	unstressed syllable followed by a stressed syllable	‿ / insist
trochee (trochaic)	stressed syllable followed by an unstressed syllable	/ ‿ freedom
anapest (anapestic)	two unstressed syllables followed by one stressed syllable	‿ ‿ / unimpressed
dactyl (dactylic)	one stressed syllable followed by two unstressed syllables	/ ‿ ‿ feverish
spondee (spondaic)	two stressed syllables	/ / baseball

The number of feet in a line makes up the meter. Terms used to describe different types of meter include the following:

- *monometer* for a one-foot line
- *dimeter* for a two-foot line
- *trimeter* for a three-foot line
- *tetrameter* for a four-foot line
- *pentameter* for a five-foot line
- *hexameter,* or *Alexandrine,* for a six-foot line
- *heptameter* for a seven-foot line
- *octameter* for an eight-foot line

A complete description of the meter of a line includes both the term for the type of foot used most often in the line and the term for the number of feet in the line. Therefore, a line of poetry with five iambs would be called "iambic pentameter." The most common meters are *iambic tetrameter* and *iambic pentameter*. An example of iambic pentameter is the sonnet "I know I am but summer to your heart" by Edna St. Vincent Millay (page 422).

The Bean Eaters
A Lyric Poem by Gwendolyn Brooks

Dream Variations
A Lyric Poem by Langston Hughes

BEFORE READING

BUILD BACKGROUND

Literary Context In **"The Bean Eaters,"** Gwendolyn Brooks presents a different view of pride. The poem centers on the lives of two people, an "old yellow pair," as the speaker describes them. According to Brooks, this poem was inspired by a painting by Vincent Van Gogh entitled *The Potato Eaters.* Both the poem and the painting provide a glimpse into the everyday lives of poor people who must struggle to get by.

"Dream Variations" deals with a common theme in Langston Hughes's writing—African-American pride. Like much of Hughes's poetry, this poem also reflects the spontaneity and lyricism found in the Harlem jazz music of the poet's time. Hughes was a leading figure in the Harlem Renaissance, a period in which art, literature, and music by African-American artists flourished in Harlem, an area of New York City.

Reader's Context When do you feel a sense of celebration in life? What objects do you have around you in your room? What do they say about who you are?

USE READING SKILLS

Main Idea The **main idea** is a brief statement of what the author wants you to know, think, or feel after reading a text. Use a Main Idea Map like the one below to record details. This will help you to draw conclusions about the main idea.

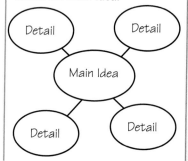

COMPARE LITERATURE: Rhyme and Theme

Rhyme is the repetition of sounds in two or more words or lines of verse. There are several different types of rhyme; see Understanding Sight and Sound (page 452) for a description of these types. A **theme** is a central message or perception about life that is revealed through a literary work. As you read these two poems, compare and contrast the way each one uses rhyme, and consider the themes they share.

MEET THE AUTHORS

BROOKS

Gwendolyn Brooks (1917–2000) was born in Topeka, Kansas, and raised primarily in Chicago, Illinois. In 1950, Brooks became the first African-American writer to win the Pulitzer Prize, which was awarded for her second book of poems, *Annie Allen.* Brooks once remarked, "Even if I had never been published, I knew that I would go on writing, enjoying it and experiencing the challenge."

Langston Hughes (1902–1967) was born in Joplin, Missouri, and grew up in various cities throughout the Midwest. Much of his work concerns the lives of African Americans, particularly those who dwell in cities. Of his identity as an African-American writer, Hughes said, "No great poet has ever been afraid of being himself."

HUGHES

The Potato Eaters, 1885. Vincent Van Gogh. Van Gogh Museum, Amsterdam, the Netherlands.

Critical Viewing

Review Brooks's poem and examine Van Gogh's *The Potato Eaters*. Identify which elements Brooks responds to in this painting. Does viewing this painting contribute to your understanding of the poem? Why or why not?

THE BEAN EATERS

A Lyric Poem by **Gwendolyn Brooks**

They eat beans mostly, this old yellow pair.
Dinner is a casual affair.
Plain chipware[1] on a plain and creaking wood,
Tin flatware.[2]

5 Two who are Mostly Good.
Two who have lived their day,
But keep on putting on their clothes
And putting things away.

And remembering...
10 Remembering, with twinklings and twinges, [3]
As they lean over the beans in their rented back room
    that is full of beads and receipts[4] and dolls and cloths,
    tobacco crumbs, vases and fringes. ❖

---

1. **chipware.** China dishes that have been chipped
2. **flatware.** Forks, knives, and spoons
3. **twinges.** Small stabs of pain
4. **receipts.** Formal written notices acknowledging payment for goods or services

MIRRORS & WINDOWS

Do you know people or have you heard of people who resemble the "old yellow pair"? What is your impression of their lifestyle? How would they describe their philosophy of life?

On the Seekonk, 1892. Edward Mitchell Bannister. National Museum of American Art, Washington, DC.

Dream Variations

A Lyric Poem by **Langston Hughes**

To fling my arms wide
In some place of the sun,
To whirl and to dance
Till the white day is done.
5   Then rest at cool evening
Beneath a tall tree
While night comes on gently,
      Dark like me—
That is my dream!

10   To fling my arms wide
In the face of the sun,
Dance! Whirl! Whirl!
Till the quick day is done.
Rest at pale evening…
15   A tall, slim tree…
Night coming tenderly
      Black like me. ❖

MIRRORS & WINDOWS

What makes you, like the speaker in Hughes's poem, really want to dance and whirl? How do you express those feelings?

HUMANITIES CONNECTION

The Harlem Renaissance The Harlem Renaissance of the 1920s and 1930s was a flowering of African-American art, music, and literature centered in the Harlem neighborhood of New York City. The period is often said to have been sparked by an influential anthology edited by the editor and philosopher Alain Locke, entitled *The New Negro: An Interpretation.* Illustrations for *The New Negro* were created by Aaron Douglas, who went on to become one of the period's most distinguished artists. The above painting, entitled *Aspects of Negro Life: From Slavery through Reconstruction,* is an example of Douglas's work.

AFTER READING

REFER TO TEXT	REASON WITH TEXT	
1a. Quote the lines from "Dream Variations" that suggest the speaker may feel uncomfortable or out of place.	1b. Summarize the speaker's idea of a perfect life.	**Understand** **Find meaning**
2a. List the details in "The Bean Eaters" referring to the physical surroundings and to the activities of the couple.	2b. Infer what these details tell you about the life of "this old yellow pair."	**Apply** **Use information**
3a. Identify at least three examples of repetition or near-repetition in "Dream Variations."	3b. Analyze the use of repetition in the poem and its title.	**Analyze** **Take things apart**
4a. List the words in "Dream Variations" that express the idea of celebration.	4b. Evaluate how realistic it is to search for the kind of life the speaker describes.	**Evaluate** **Make judgments**
5a. Quote lines from each poem that express a form of pride.	5b. Compare and contrast your ideas of what pride means with those of the speaker of "Dream Variations" and the old couple in "The Bean Eaters."	**Create** **Bring ideas together**

COMPARE LITERATURE: Rhyme and Theme

What type or types of rhyme does Brooks use in "The Bean Eaters"? Does her use of rhyme follow a consistent pattern throughout the poem? What rhyme exists in "Dream Variations"? What common theme or themes do both poems share? How does the use of rhyme contribute to the theme of "Dream Variations"?

EXTEND THE TEXT

Writing Options

Creative Writing A tribute is a brief speech that expresses gratitude, respect, honor, or praise. Choose either the speaker in "Dream Variations" or the elderly couple described in "The Bean Eaters," and write a **tribute** that conveys your appreciation for their lives. When you have finished, post your tribute on the classroom bulletin board.

Narrative Writing What does pride mean to you? When have you been most proud of yourself or your friends or family? What were the circumstances or conditions that caused you to realize this pride? For a teen magazine, write a one-page **personal narrative** in which you tell about a time when you felt a great deal of pride in yourself or someone you know. Remember that a personal narrative is a story about an event or experience that is important to you.

Media Literacy

Create a Bibliography Imagine that you work for a publishing house and have been asked to create a list of all the books published by Gwendolyn Brooks or Langston Hughes. Together with a small group, use library or Internet resources to compile a complete bibliography for either of these writers. If you use the Internet, you might begin by typing "Academy of American Poets" into a search engine. Remember to include all the necessary information for each title in your bibliography. (See the Language Arts Handbook, 5.6 Documenting Sources, for the format to use.)

Collaborative Learning

Perform in a Poetry Slam A poetry slam is a competition of the spoken word—part poetry reading and part sports event. Rather than merely reading their poems, poets *perform* them with vocal expression and gestures (although most slams rule out props). At most poetry slams, judges are selected randomly from the audience, and each judge gives each performer a score between 0.0 and 10.0. The audience is encouraged to cheer or boo the judges' scores. Organize a poetry slam in your class. Recruit contestants to write their own poems or to choose poems that others have written.

 Go to **www.mirrorsandwindows.com** for more.

READING ASSESSMENT

1. From details in "The Bean Eaters," you can reasonably infer that the old couple is which of the following?
   A. educated
   B. wealthy
   C. poor
   D. ill
   E. adventurous

2. What do the couple in "The Bean Eaters" do as they eat their dinner?
   A. watch TV
   B. argue
   C. remember
   D. read to each other
   E. discuss the day's events

3. In "Dream Variations," which of the following does the speaker want to do during the day?
   A. attend a performance of a play
   B. write a poem
   C. enjoy life to the fullest
   D. travel to see a relative
   E. take a nap

4. Each stanza of "Dream Variations" includes which of the following?
   A. slant rhyme
   B. a contrast between day and night
   C. a concluding couplet
   D. the word *dream*
   E. None of the above

5. Which of the following contains an example of end rhyme?
   A. "To fling my arms wide / In some place of the sun"
   B. "They eat beans mostly, this old yellow pair. / Dinner is a casual affair."
   C. "Two who are Mostly Good. / Two who have lived their day"
   D. "To whirl and to dance / Till the white day is done."
   E. None of the above

6. Choose either the speaker in "Dream Variations" or the old couple in "The Bean Eaters." Write a note explaining your philosophy of life to the addressee(s), and offer encouragement.

We Real cool

A Lyric Poem by
Gwendolyn Brooks

THE POOL PLAYERS.
SEVEN AT THE GOLDEN SHOVEL.

We real cool. We
Left school. We

Lurk late. We
Strike straight. We

5 Sing sin. We
Thin gin. We

Jazz June. We
Die soon. ❖

Teacher

A Lyric Poem by
Langston Hughes

Ideals are like the stars,
    Always above our reach.
Humbly I tried to learn,
    More humbly did I teach.

5 On all honest virtues
    I sought to keep firm hold.
I wanted to be a good man
    Though I pinched my soul.

But now I lie beneath cool loam
10   Forgetting every dream;
And in this narrow bed of earth
    No lights gleam.

In this narrow bed of earth
    Star-dust never scatters,
15 And I tremble lest the darkness teach
    Me that nothing matters. ❖

GRAMMAR & STYLE

Use Precise Language and Avoid Clichés

Poets have the difficult task of using a limited number of words to express an idea. Because of this, successful poets choose their words very carefully and make every word count by using precise and lively language. Imagine if the first line of "Dream Variations" (page 456) read "To open my arms" instead of "To fling my arms wide." "To open my arms" conjures up a pretty dull image in the reader's mind. "To fling my arms wide," however, creates the image of a person throwing his arms open as wide as he can with energy and excitement. Do you see the difference between the impact of the two lines?

The eighteenth-century British writer Jonathan Swift, who wrote both verse and prose, once defined style as "proper words in proper places." When you write, use words that tell your reader exactly what you mean. Precise and lively language makes your writing more interesting to your reader.

EXAMPLES
dull: The people made noise.
precise: The mob roared its approval.

dull: Remembering, with happiness about good times and sadness about painful times.
precise: Remembering, with twinklings and twinges... (from "The Bean Eaters")

dull: Rest as it gets later into the evening.
precise: Rest at pale evening... (from "Dream Variations")

One thing that precise language is not is wordy. **Wordy** sentences contain more words than necessary to get meaning across. Take a look at the example below.

EXAMPLE
wordy: I most definitely did appreciate your frank and brutal opinion about my abysmal lack of ability to write poetry after I wrote several poems for you to read.
precise: Thank you for your honest opinion about my lack of poetic skill.

As you strive to make your writing precise and interesting, try not to use clichés. A **cliché** is an overused or unoriginal expression: for example, "happy as a clam" or "as cold as ice." Good writers avoid clichés and use more original and colorful ways to express ideas.

EXAMPLES
dull: I found the lecture boring.
cliché: The lecture bored me to tears.
precise: The lecture was so boring I had to pry my eyelids open and pinch myself to stay awake.

dull: He was really poor.
cliché: He was as poor as a mouse.
precise: He was destitute.

What Great Writers Do

Poets, more so than writers of fiction or other genres, have to make the most of every word they choose. Poets do not have the liberty of rambling  on and wasting words; rather, they are experts at using precise language. In the following stanza from "The Bean Eaters," notice how Gwendolyn Brooks creates a complete image using very few well-chosen words.

> They eat beans mostly, this old yellow
>   pair.
> Dinner is a casual affair.
> Plain chipware on a plain and creaking
>   wood,
> Tin flatware.
>
> —from "The Bean Eaters" by
> Gwendolyn Brooks

Fix Wordy Sentences and Clichés

The following sentences are wordy and contain clichés. Read each one and identify the cliché. Then rewrite the sentence so it uses precise and vivid language.

1. It was really incredibly difficult for her to get out of bed that Monday morning because the weather was really cold and in her bed she felt snug as a bug in a rug.
2. It isn't very easy to be happy and cheerful on the outside when you're really feeling totally down in the dumps on the inside.
3. The really bright and shiny necklace attracted the girl's attention like a bee to honey even though it was only costume jewelry and not valuable at all.
4. Sometimes, getting students to read poetry is like pulling teeth because poetry for some reason has a reputation for being hard to understand.
5. Since Sam had studied grammar for many years and really enjoyed putting his ideas into words, when his teacher asked him to write an article for the school newspaper he thought the assignment was a piece of cake.

Use Precise Language

Describe each of the following scenarios in a sentence that uses vivid language to create a precise image.

1. a young boy staring at a bonfire
2. a heavy snowstorm on a city street
3. an angry person leaving a room
4. a snake moving across the ground
5. an audience at a rock concert
6. a river flooding over its banks
7. a baby sleeping
8. a flock of geese flying in the sky
9. a family eating dinner together
10. a cat chasing a ball of yarn

Improve a Paragraph

Rewrite the paragraph shown below, making the language more precise.

> Dora suddenly realized it was nearly 9:00 AM. She had eaten her breakfast slowly, reading through the newspaper. She would have to hurry to make her 10:30 train. She packed her suitcase and checked to see that all the house windows were closed and locked. Then she went out the door and down the stairs. Outside, the weather was fair. Dora reached the bus stop and, to her satisfaction, a bus arrived within two or three minutes.

Use Precise Language in Your Writing

Write a paragraph in which you describe an appliance in your kitchen or in an appliance store. Make your language as precise as you can so that a person reading your description can create a visual picture.

EXTEND THE SKILL

Use library or Internet resources to investigate the origins of the following clichés. Then, for each cliché, invent a fresh way of saying the same thing.

1. bite the dust
2. on cloud nine
3. crying over spilled milk
4. head over heels
5. when push comes to shove
6. busy as a bee
7. angry as a hornet
8. loud enough to wake the dead

JAZZ FANTASIA

BEFORE READING   **A Lyric Poem by Carl Sandburg**

BUILD BACKGROUND

Cultural Context In the poem **"Jazz Fantasia,"** the speaker addresses an audience of jazz musicians, urging them to improvise with energy and gusto. The jazz group plays on typical instruments for this type of music: banjoes, saxophones, drums, trombones, and horns (trumpets). The poet conjures up a variety of images to suggest the moods created by the music, ranging from noisy, aggressive fights to the moaning autumn wind. Written in 1919, soon after the birth of jazz, Sandburg's poem alternates between rowdy celebration and hushed murmurs—ingeniously evoking the wide emotional range of jazz itself.

Reader's Context What kind of music do you like to listen to? How does listening to your favorite music bring vivid, concrete images to mind? How does listening affect your mood?

ANALYZE LITERATURE: Alliteration and Onomatopoeia

Alliteration is the repetition of initial consonant sounds. **Onomatopoeia** is a sound device in which the sound of a word or phrase suggests the thing to which it refers. As you read, look for ways alliteration and onomatopoeia affect the meaning and impact of the poem.

SET PURPOSE

Sandburg intended the verbal sounds of "Jazz Fantasia" to suggest the sound of the musicians themselves. As you read, sound out the lines of the poems, experimenting with tone, pitch, pace, and volume. Look for specific examples of alliteration and onomatopoeia that help the poem sound like a jazz band.

MEET THE AUTHOR

Carl Sandburg (1878–1967) was born in Galesburg, Illinois. At age thirteen, he left school to work at odd jobs. Later on, he worked his way through

college and then held various posts as a news correspondent, advertising writer, and editorial writer. His poems reveal the strong influence of Walt Whitman, though Sandburg managed to develop a highly individual style. Sandburg's verse typically celebrates the American landscape, both rural and urban, and pays tribute to the energy and resourcefulness of ordinary people. In addition to his poetry, he published collections of American folklore. He received two Pulitzer Prizes: one for his *Complete Poems*, and one for his monumental biography of Abraham Lincoln.

USE READING SKILLS

Author's Approach When you are reading poetry, you can sometimes infer the author's approach, or perspective, about a certain topic from a poem he or she has written. Remember, when you infer something, you make an educated guess based on details in the text. As you read "Jazz Fantasia," make three inferences about Carl Sandburg's attitude toward jazz music. Consider the language Sandburg uses, especially the connotations of words, along with the overall feeling you get from the poem.

You may find it useful to use an Inference Chart like the one below. In the first box, write down an inference about the author's viewpoint. In the second box, write down specific lines from the poem that support your inference.

Inference 1	Support from Poem
Inference 2	Support from Poem
Inference 3	Support from Poem

JAZZ FANTASIA

A Lyric Poem by **Carl Sandburg**

Drum on your drums, batter on your banjoes,
sob on the long cool winding saxophones.
Go to it, O jazzmen.

Sling your knuckles on the bottoms of the happy
5 tin pans, let your trombones ooze, and go husha-
husha-hush with the slippery sand-paper.

Moan like an autumn wind high in the lonesome treetops,
moan soft like you wanted somebody terrible, cry like a
racing car slipping away from a motorcycle cop, bang-bang!
10 you jazzmen, bang altogether drums, traps, banjoes, horns,
tin cans—make two people fight on the top of a stairway
and scratch each other's eyes in a clinch[1] tumbling down
the stairs.

Can the rough stuff…now a Mississippi steamboat pushes
15 up the night river with a hoo-hoo-hoo-oo…and the green
lanterns calling to the high soft stars…a red moon rides
on the humps of the low river hills…go to it, O jazzmen. ❖

---

1. **clinch.** Embrace

MIRRORS & WINDOWS

Do you agree or disagree with this statement: Music is only for entertainment; it doesn't mean anything else. Explain your answer.

CULTURE CONNECTION

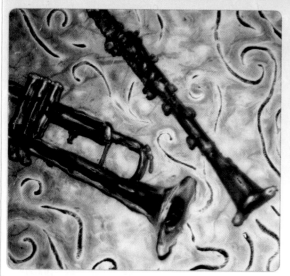

The History of Jazz The history of jazz as a musical style is closely bound to the city of New Orleans, and it is thus not surprising that Sandburg mentions a "Mississippi steamboat" in "Jazz Fantasia." A variety of influences shaped early jazz: African-American work songs, spirituals, the blues, ragtime, military music, and the French heritage of New Orleans. Early pioneers of the form included Buddy Bolden and Jelly Roll Morton. Around the time of World War I, musicians like King Oliver and Louis Armstrong sought work in Chicago, thus popularizing jazz with a larger audience. Nationally famous jazz bands were swift to develop: Among their leaders were Count Basie, Duke Ellington, and Benny Goodman. Distinctive harmonies, syncopated rhythms, and an improvisational style were all hallmarks of jazz. The style defined an era when American novelist F. Scott Fitzgerald referred to the 1920s as "the Jazz Age."

AFTER READING

REFER TO TEXT ▶ ▶ ▶ ▶	▶ REASON WITH TEXT	
1a. Name those to whom this poem is addressed.	1b. Infer what this direct address suggests about the speaker's attitude toward jazz music.	**Understand** **Find meaning**
2a. Quote lines that contain an example of alliteration and an example of onomatopoeia.	2b. Apply what you know about these two sound devices to determine why Sandburg may have used them in the lines you quoted. What effect do these sound devices achieve?	**Apply** **Use information**
3a. List the actions the speaker urges the jazzmen to perform in the second stanza.	3b. Analyze how these actions suggest the broad range of emotional moods that jazz music can convey.	**Analyze** **Take things apart**
4a. Identify two examples of slang or informal speech in the poem.	4b. Judge whether the poet's use of slang is effective. How does it contribute to the mood or overall atmosphere of the poem?	**Evaluate** **Make judgments**
5a. Describe the vivid images in the last four lines of the poem.	5b. Why might a jazz or music fan like (or dislike) this poem? Explain your answer.	**Create** **Bring ideas together**

ANALYZE LITERATURE: Alliteration and Onomatopoeia

Reread the poem. Then, in two or three sentences, explain how "Jazz Fantasia" resembles, but yet is different from, a piece of music. Be sure to include in your explanation how alliteration and onomatopoeia affect the musical quality of the poem.

Writing Options

Creative Writing The speaker in Sandburg's poem addresses a group of musicians, but it is clear that the poet wants to involve you, the reader, in his enthusiastic appreciation of jazz. Imagine that you read this poem soon after it was first published. Write a **literary review** of the poem for your local newspaper in which you share your reactions to "Jazz Fantasia." Be sure to support your opinions with reasons and examples from the text.

Expository Writing The style of "Jazz Fantasia" is probably quite different from other poems you've read. Imagine you want to explain to a friend what this poem is about and how it is unique. Write a three-paragraph **critical analysis** that examines the poem's images, rhythms, and sound devices and how these things contribute to what the poem means to you. Use specific lines from the poem to support your ideas. If there are parts of the poem that don't make sense to you or that you don't care for, include these types of things in your analysis as well.

Collaborative Learning

Develop a Children's Book Work in a small group to develop a short children's book on the history of jazz. In your book, provide simple definitions and descriptions of concepts such as *improvisation, blues,* and *syncopated rhythm.* Also focus on some of the great figures in the development of this musical style, such as Louis Armstrong and Duke Ellington. Add appropriate illustrations to your work: for example, pictures of distinctive jazz instruments. Then share your work with a class of fifth- or sixth-graders.

Lifelong Learning

Prepare an Oral Interpretation Rehearse an oral interpretation of "Jazz Fantasia." Reread the poem carefully, marking it up the way you would develop a script for a performance. Decide where tone, volume, pitch, and pace need variation, and identify words or phrases to which you will give special emphasis. As you are preparing, consider your audience. Ask yourself which aspects of the poem provide the most appeal for the audience, and think about how you can really play up the most appealing aspects. Then present your oral interpretation to a live audience and invite feedback from your listeners.

 Go to **www.mirrorsandwindows.com** for more.

READING ASSESSMENT

1. In "Jazz Fantasia," the speaker addresses a group of
   A. critics.
   B. concertgoers.
   C. musicians.
   D. scholars.
   E. students.

2. In line 1, the word *batter* most nearly means
   A. caress.
   B. strum.
   C. pound.
   D. tune.
   E. None of the above

3. Which of the following best identifies the speaker's attitude toward jazz in the poem?
   A. skeptical
   B. hostile
   C. resigned
   D. appreciative
   E. disapproving

4. Which of the following literary devices does Sandburg use?
   A. sensory details
   B. simile
   C. onomatopoeia
   D. personification
   E. All of the above

5. Which of the following phrases contains an example of alliteration?
   A. "Sling your knuckles on the bottoms of the happy / tin pans"
   B. "a red moon rides / on the humps of the low river hills"
   C. "cry like a / racing car slipping away from a motorcycle cop"
   D. "Can the rough stuff"
   E. All of the above

6. Does music have any power? How do you think Carl Sandburg would respond to this question? Answer the question from Sandburg's point of view using "Jazz Fantasia" as support for your answer.

three tanka

Tanka by Okamoto Kanoko, Miyazawa Kenji, and Tsukamoto Kunio

BEFORE READING

BUILD BACKGROUND

Cultural Context Many readers are familiar with haiku, which are traditional three-line poems that developed in Japanese literature. Like the haiku, the **tanka** is rooted in Japanese tradition. It consists of five lines, with five syllables in the first and third lines and seven syllables in the other lines, for a total syllable count of thirty-one. A tanka uses imagery to evoke emotions, but it is often more philosophical than a haiku. As a verse form, tanka date back to the seventh century and were closely woven into the fabric of court life. Keep in mind that the following tanka are English translations of the Japanese originals and may not reflect the correct number of syllables. Although the original Japanese poems contain the correct syllable count, this may have been lost in translation.

Reader's Context Look around you. What is the most vivid image your brain records? How would you express this image in a concise phrase or sentence?

ANALYZE LITERATURE: Sensory Details and Imagery

Words and phrases that appeal to the five senses (primarily sight but also sound, touch, taste, and smell) are called **sensory details.** An image is a picture in words. Writers often use sensory details to create images. The images in a literary work are referred to, collectively, as the work's **imagery.** As you read these poems, note the images they create in your mind.

SET PURPOSE

While reading each tanka, look for ways to visualize the images in the poems. Identify the specific sensory details that help to create the images. For each tanka, create a sketch of the image and then compare your sketch with those made by your classmates. Did you respond to the same sensory details as your classmates? Why or why not?

USE READING SKILLS

Compare and Contrast When you **compare** one thing to another, you describe similarities between two things; when you **contrast** two things, you describe their differences. As you read the three tanka, look for similarities and differences among them. What can you tell about each poet from his or her poem? To which poem do you most easily relate? Why?

What I Learn about the Poet	
Tanka 1	
Tanka 2	
Tanka 3	

My Reactions to the Tanka	
Tanka 1	
Tanka 2	
Tanka 3	

MEET THE AUTHORS

As an unconventional woman living in a conventional society, **Okamoto Kanoko** (1889–1939) struggled with depression and sought comfort in various forms of religion. She wrote multitudes of tanka in her lifetime and had several books published. Okamoto Kanoko is also highly respected today for her fiction.

Miyazawa Kenji (1896–1933) is known for his creative writing. His life passions were service to poor people, agriculture, and Buddhism.

Tsukamoto Kunio (b. 1922) has published more than one hundred books, including compilations of his own poetry and collections of the verse of other writers.

three tanka

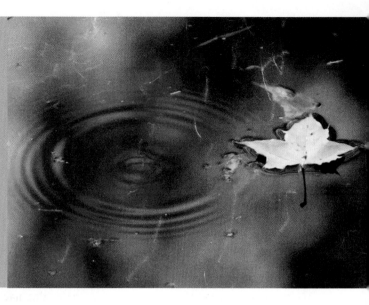

Tanka by **Okamoto Kanoko, Miyazawa Kenji, and Tsukamoto Kunio**

if I were to stand
with roots in the ground
like a flower
would my life bloom out
in the color I was born with? ❖
         —by Okamoto Kanoko

at dawn
on a mountain pass
in the drifting fog
almost imperceptible[1]
the smell of green tomatoes ❖
         —by Miyazawa Kenji

Standing still
in the twilight of a cold
spring evening
I wonder if a soul does not
resemble a leaf of gold ❖
         —by Tsukamoto Kunio

---

1. **imperceptible.** Unable to be seen

MIRRORS & WINDOWS

Suppose a friend asks what the purpose is for writing such a short, seemingly simple poem like a tanka. How would you answer? What could the benefits of tanka be to the average reader?

Kanesaka of Tanba, 1853. Ando Hiroshige II.

Describe what you see in this painting. Identify any similarities you see between the painting and the tanka. What artistic elements do they share? Do they share a similar mood? If so, what artistic details help create this mood? What can you infer about Japanese artistic philosophy based on your experience with this painting and the tanka?

REFER TO TEXT ▶ ▶ ▶ ▶	▶ REASON WITH TEXT	
1a. Recall to what the speaker in Okamoto Kanoko's poem compares himself or herself. According to the speaker in Tsukamoto Kunio's poem, what might the human soul resemble?	1b. Explain why the poets make these two comparisons. What ideas are they trying to convey?	**Understand** Find meaning
2a. Identify the senses to which the images in each of these poems appeal.	2b. What effect do these sensory details have on the reader of tanka?	**Apply** Use information
3a. What is the setting of each of the three tanka?	3b. What kind of mood does the setting of each poem create? What kind of feeling do you get from the mood?	**Analyze** Take things apart
4a. State the theme, if one exists, of each tanka.	4b. Evaluate whether tanka is a form in which it is possible to develop a theme. If not, what might be a purpose for writing tanka?	**Evaluate** Make judgments
5a. Discuss what the speakers of these poems might be like.	5b. Imagine that you are the speaker of one of these poems. What is your life like? What kind of person are you?	**Create** Bring ideas together

ANALYZE LITERATURE: Sensory Details and Imagery

One prominent characteristic of tanka is the way they use sensory details and imagery to stimulate the reader. As you read each poem, think about what you see, hear, feel, smell, or taste. Summarize each image in one sentence.

EXTEND THE TEXT

Writing Options

Creative Writing Write a **tanka** of your own. First, select a topic or theme. Then choose one or two sensory images that appeal vividly to sight, sound, taste, smell, or touch. Finally, pay attention to the syllable requirements for each line as you write your poem. When you have finished your work, share your tanka with a small group.

Expository Writing How does the tanka compare with the other types of poetry? Choose another poem from this unit. In a two-page **compare-and-contrast essay,** discuss the similarities and differences between the poem you chose and the tanka. In your comparison, consider the following elements of poetry: speaker, imagery, rhythm, and theme. Also consider your reactions to the different types of poetry. Which do you enjoy more? Which did you find more compelling? Be sure to cite specific examples from the texts to support your ideas.

Lifelong Learning

Research the History of Haiku Although tanka enjoy classic status in Japan, in the Western world haiku have always been better known. Imagine that you work for a television network that focuses on history and culture. You are going to write the voice-over for a special on the history of haiku. Using library or Internet resources, research the early history of this type of poem. Explore the origins of the poetic form, including its early writers. Learn about Japanese history and culture during the time in which haiku emerged. You might also investigate how haiku have changed over time. Using the information you have collected, write the voice-over for the television program.

Media Literacy

Create an Art Exhibit Much Japanese poetry is closely related to the visual arts. Working with a small group, find and print out or photocopy one piece of art to match each tanka you just read. Choose art that reflects the themes and moods of the poetry. Finally, create an art exhibit that displays the poems and the artworks side by side.

 Go to **www.mirrorsandwindows.com** for more.

READING POETRY INDEPENDENTLY
Theme: Realizations

*"What did I know, what did I know
of love's austere and lonely offices?"*

——from "Those Winter Sundays"
by Robert Hayden

As people get older and have more experiences in life, they often come to realize things they hadn't known before. Children might not understand the sacrifices their parents made until after they grow up and, possibly, become parents themselves, as is true with the speaker in Robert Hayden's poem "Those Winter Sundays" (page 478). In each of the poems you will read in this section, the speaker comes to some sort of realization about himself or herself or about life in general. Look for those realizations as you read.

USING READING SKILLS WITH POETRY

Understand Denotation and Connotation

A word's **denotation** is its dictionary definition. A word's **connotations** are all the positive or negative associations it has in addition to its literal meaning. For example, the words *dirty* and *soiled* both denote "unclean." However, the word *dirty* has negative connotations. For example, it is associated with low morals (as in "a dirty business deal") and unpleasant tasks (as in "a dirty job"). *Soiled,* on the other hand, is rather neutral—neither positive or negative.

Different people have different connotations for words. For example, the word *ocean* has a positive connotation for many people. They may hear it and think peaceful thoughts. However, if you are afraid of water due to a near-drowning incident when you were a child, the word *ocean* may have a negative association for you.

In poetry, the word choices the poets make are intentional to conjure certain images or feelings. Be aware of the connotations of words as you read. One way to do that is to substitute a word that means (denotes) the same thing and see if the feeling of the line holds true. Using a graphic organizer like the one below may help. Decide whether a word is negative, neutral, or positive and put it in the correct column. Then write in other words with the same denotation but different connotations. An example has been done for you.

Connotation Chart

Negative	Neutral	Positive
weird	unusual	unique
freakish	different	remarkable
bizarre	uncommon	extraordinary
abnormal	rare	unequaled
strange	surreal	phenomenal

Use Context Clues

Using **context clues** to find the meaning of an unfamiliar word involves taking a closer look at the context, or the surrounding text, for clues that can help you guess the meaning of the word. There are five main types of context clues:

- **Restatement clues:** This type is found when an author restates an idea, or explains it in a different way. *Apposition* is a direct type of restatement that renames something. Some of the signals for restatement are *that is, in other words,* and *or.*
- **Cause-and-effect clues:** This type requires the reader to make an assumption based on cause and effect. Some words that signal cause and effect are *if...then, when...then, thus, therefore, because,* and *so.*
- **Examples:** Sometimes, a writer will give you examples to help clarify the meaning of a difficult word. These examples may be introduced by expressions like *including, such as, especially,* and *particularly.*
- **Comparison clues:** Words and phrases including *such as, like, also, similarly, just as,* and *in the same way* signal comparisons and indicate that the unfamiliar word is like something that might be more familiar to you.
- **Contrast clues:** Words and phrases such as *however, but, not, except, although,* and *on the other hand* signal that something contrasts, or differs in meaning, from something else.

Determine the Appropriate Meaning for the Context

In poetry, *context* refers to the conditions in which the poem occurs. In a certain context, a word might mean one thing, but in another, it might change. This is especially true in poetry as poets may use figurative language and rely on connotation to carry the meanings of the words, and thus the poem. One way to keep track of the meanings of words is to sort key words and images by general category, such as natural versus man-made objects or words of sight, smell, sound, taste, or touch; or by specific categories, such as bird-related words and images or words that allude to imprisonment.

Framework for Poetry

When reading a poem, you need to be aware of its form, imagery, rhythm, and sound devices. The following checklist of questions offers a framework for approaching poetry.

As you start to read...

❑ In what form is the poem?

❑ What images stand out?

❑ Which words are unfamiliar to me or are used in an unfamiliar way?

As you continue reading...

❑ What is the mood that the images create in the poem?

❑ What sound devices has the poet used?

❑ What is the meter of the poem?

After you've finished reading...

❑ How will reading this poem aloud bring more poetic elements to light?

❑ What is the message or theme of the poem?

❑ Of what does this poem remind me?

What Good Readers Do

Difficult words in a poem can get in the way of your ability to understand the meaning of a poem. Use footnotes, consult a dictionary, or ask someone about words you do not understand. When you come across a word you do not know, say to yourself

Tackle Difficult Vocabulary

❑ The context tells me that this word means...

❑ A dictionary definition provided in the poem shows that the word means...

❑ My work with the word before class helps me know that the word means...

❑ A classmate said that the word means...

❑ I can skip knowing the exact meaning of this word because...

Lucille Clifton (b. 1936) was born in DePew, New York. Educated at Howard University and Fredonia State Teachers College, Clifton has taught poetry at many universities. Expressing pride in her African-American heritage and identity, Clifton has said, "I am a Black woman poet, and I sound like one."

The poem **"miss rosie"** appeared in Lucille Clifton's first poetry collection, *Good Times*, published in 1969. A recurring theme in the collection—human resilience and survival in the face of life's hardships—can be seen in the poem. Clifton uses figurative language, including similes and metaphors, to create a strong, clear picture of the woman who was once known as "Georgia Rose."

When have you had to adjust or recover from a difficult change in your life?

miss rosie

A Lyric Poem by **Lucille Clifton**

when i watch you
wrapped up like garbage
sitting, surrounded by the smell
of too old potato peels
5   or
when i watch you
in your old man's shoes
with the little toe cut out
sitting, waiting for your mind
10   like next week's grocery
i say
when i watch you
you wet brown bag of a woman
who used to be the best looking gal in georgia
15   used to be called the Georgia Rose
i stand up
through your destruction
i stand up ❖

What things have you seen people "stand up for"? Was it worth it for them to do so? Why or why not?

Refer and Reason

1. What details reinforce the portrait of Miss Rosie?
2. What does Miss Rosie's former nickname suggest about her appearance when she was young? How does she live her life now?
3. Why might Miss Rosie have such an effect on the speaker? If you were the speaker, what two things could you do for Miss Rosie?

Writing Options

1. Imagine you are Miss Rosie. Write a journal entry contrasting your present life with your past life, when you were known as "the Georgia Rose."
2. Suppose that you are teaching a Web-based class on creative writing for young adults. You want to show students how figurative language — similes, metaphors, personification, and other figures of speech — can create powerful images. Write three paragraphs of text for a website using "miss rosie" as an example. You may also include examples from other poems if you like.

 Go to **www.mirrorsandwindows.com** for more.

Elderly Lady who lives on Lamont Street, 1942. Gordon Parks. Library of Congress.

Novelist and poet **Marge Piercy** (b. 1936) was born in Detroit, Michigan, during the Great Depression and grew up listening to the stories of her mother and grandmother.

"Simple Song" explores how similarities and differences affect individuals and their relationships.

Do you prefer spending time with people who are similar to you or different from you? Why?

Simple Song

A Lyric Poem by
Marge Piercy

When we are going toward someone we say
You are just like me
your thoughts are my brothers
word matches word
5   how easy to be together.

When we are leaving someone we say:
how strange you are
we cannot communicate
we can never agree
10   how hard, hard and weary to be together.

We are not different nor alike
But each strange in his leather body
sealed in skin and reaching out clumsy hands
and loving is an act
15   that cannot outlive
the open hand
the open eye
the door in the chest standing open.

MIRRORS & WINDOWS

Do you have any friends with whom it is "easy to be together"? What makes them so easy to be with? Do you have any friends who are very different from you? How do you get along with them? What advice about friendships might the speaker of "Simple Song" give you?

Refer and Reason

1. What phases of a relationship are represented in stanzas 1 and 2? How does stanza 3 serve as a response to stanzas 1 and 2?
2. What does it mean to have an "open hand" and an "open eye"? What does the speaker mean by "the door in the chest standing open"?
3. Based on lines 14–18, what might you conclude about the speaker's experience with love?

Writing Options

1. Write a statement of belief about one of the following: friendship, diversity, or interpersonal communication.
2. Theme in a literary work is the writer's central message or insight into human nature or behavior. Write a brief literary analysis in which you identify and discuss Marge Piercy's theme in "Simple Song."

MW Go to **www.mirrorsandwindows.com** for more.

Stopping by Woods on a Snowy Evening

A Lyric Poem by
Robert Frost

Robert Frost (1874–1963) is most often associated with New England, though he was born in San Francisco. He started writing poetry in high school and published his first poem in the New York newspaper *The Independent* in 1894. Of the plain speech and common objects that make up much of his poetry, Frost says, "We write of things we see and we write in accents we hear."

"Stopping by Woods on a Snowy Evening" was written in 1922 and published in 1923. It was one of Frost's favorite poems.

Describe a time when you were captivated by a beautiful scene. Were you able to stop and enjoy it? What appealed to you about the scene?

Whose woods these are I think I know.
His house is in the village, though;
He will not see me stopping here
To watch his woods fill up with snow.

5   My little horse must think it queer - weird
To stop without a farmhouse near
Between the woods and frozen lake
The darkest evening of the year.

He gives his harness bells a shake
10 To ask if there is some mistake.
The only other sound's the sweep
Of easy wind and downy flake.

The woods are lovely, dark, and deep,
But I have promises to keep,
15 And miles to go before I sleep.
And miles to go before I sleep. ❖

 **IRRORS WINDOWS**
What are some things that prevent you from enjoying time in nature? Do you think the idea that people have to be busy all the time is limited to the United States, or is it evident in other parts of the world as well? Why? Explain your answers.

Refer and Reason

1. In some analyses of this poem, it is believed that the speaker is talking about death. Find elements of the poem that would support this interpretation.
2. How well does Frost create a specific mood in this poem? How would you describe the mood?
3. Why might the speaker want to stay? What pulls him to go? Explain what you think the promises are and how the speaker weighs his choices.

Writing Options

1. Write a descriptive advertisement for a vacation spot in a cold climate. Use words that appeal to the senses in order to lure tourists to the area.
2. Write a one-paragraph analysis of how Frost uses meter and rhyme scheme to add to the mood of the poem. (See Understanding Sight and Sound, page 452, for an explanation of meter and rhyme scheme.)

 Go to **www.mirrorsandwindows.com** for more.

THOSE WINTER Sundays

A Lyric Poem by **Robert Hayden**

Sundays too my father got up early
and put his clothes on in the blueblack cold,
then with cracked hands that ached
from labor in the weekday weather made
5   banked fires blaze. No one ever thanked him.

I'd wake and hear the cold splintering, breaking.
When the rooms were warm, he'd call,
and slowly I would rise and dress,
fearing the chronic angers of that house,

10   Speaking indifferently to him,
who had driven out the cold
and polished my good shoes as well.
What did I know, what did I know
of love's austere and lonely offices? ❖

Robert Hayden (1913–1980) grew up in a poor neighborhood of Detroit, Michigan. Building on his personal experiences and on the heritage of African Americans, Hayden wrote poetry that spoke for different groups of people throughout history. Although he wanted to help represent African-American culture in literature, he did not wish to be considered an important writer only because he was African American. "There is no such thing as black literature," Hayden said. "There's good literature and bad. And that's all."

"Those Winter Sundays" was published in Hayden's poetry collection *The Ballad of Remembrance* in 1962. It recalls a single, recurring event from the speaker's childhood and draws from it a moving generalization about the nature of love. The poem is remarkable for its simplicity, beauty, and precision of language.

What things does a parent or guardian do for you that you rarely stop to appreciate?

Early Morning, 1964. Romare Bearden. New Britain Museum of American Art. © Copyright Romare Bearden Foundation. Licensed by VAGA, New York.

 **MIRRORS & WINDOWS**

Why are the things parents do for their children on a daily basis often taken for granted? How might television, including news programs, sitcoms, and dramas, influence the way children view their parents?

Refer and Reason

1. What did the speaker's father want to spare the child?
2. Identify how the speaker's attitude toward his father has changed since the speaker was a child.
3. Explain what the speaker means by "love's austere and lonely offices." Do you agree that the father exhibited love toward his son?

Writing Options

1. Assume that you are the speaker in this poem, that you are now an adult, and that your father is still alive. Write a thank-you letter to your father to let him know how much you appreciate his sacrifices for you when you were a child.
2. Working with a small group, focus for one week on the ways fathers are represented or mentioned on television, in newspapers and magazines, on billboards, and on the radio. Then create a handbook for new fathers. Offer your audience some practical tips as they venture into fatherhood.

 Go to **www.mirrorsandwindows.com** for more.

Eight Puppies

A Lyric Poem by
Gabriela Mistral

Translated by **Doris Dana**

Between the thirteenth and the fifteenth day
the puppies opened their eyes.
Suddenly they saw the world,
anxious with terror and joy.
5 They saw the belly of their mother,
saw the door of their house,
saw a deluge of light,
saw flowering azaleas.

They saw more, they saw all,
10 the red, the black, the ash.
Scrambling up, pawing and clawing
more lively than squirrels,
they saw the eyes of their mother,
heard my rasping cry and my laugh.

15 And I wished I were born with them.
Could it not be so another time?
To leap from a clump of banana plants
one morning of wonders—
a dog, a coyote, a deer;
20 to gaze with wide pupils,
to run, to stop, to run, to fall,
to whimper and whine and jump with joy,
riddled with sun and with barking,
a hallowed child of God, his secret, divine servant. ❖

Gabriela Mistral (1889–1957) was born in Vicuña, Chile, as Lucila Godoy y Alcayaga. Mistral began to write poems while she served as a village schoolteacher. In 1945, Gabriela Mistral became the first Latin American to win the Nobel Prize in Literature.

The poem **"Eight Puppies"** has a single speaker but exhibits two points of view. In lines 1–14, the action is viewed primarily from the perspective of the newborn puppies. In the last stanza (lines 15–24), the point of view shifts to the speaker herself—the human observer who is overcome with admiration and empathy for the wonder of creation that the newborn puppies exemplify.

When you hear the word "puppies," what images come to mind? What feelings does the word invoke?

Ocho Perritos

Los perrillos abrieron sus ojos
del treceavo al quinceavo día.
De golpe vieron el mundo,
con ansia, susto y alegría.
5   Vieron el vientre de la madre,
la puerta suya que es la mía,
el diluvio de la luz,
las azaleas floridas.

Vieron más: se vieron todos,
10 el rojo, el negro, el ceniza,
gateando y aupándose,
más vivos que las ardillas;
vieron los ojos de la madre
y mi grito rasgado, y mi risa.

15 Y yo querría nacer con ellos.
¿Por qué otra vez no sería?
Saltar de unos bananales
una mañana de maravilla,
en can, en coyota, en venada;
20 mirar con grandes pupilas,
correr, parar, correr, tumbarme
y gemir y saltar de alegria,
acribillada de sol y ladridos
hija de Dios, sierva oscura y divina. ❖

MIRRORS & WINDOWS

What experiences have you had with babies—either animal babies or human babies or both? Is it possible to ever regain things like a spirit of playfulness and innocence, or are such things limited to the young? Explain your answers.

Refer and Reason

1. In lines 3–8, what are the physical and emotional results for the puppies when they open their eyes?
2. In lines 13–14, why do you think the speaker places the phrases "their mother" and "my rasping cry and my laugh" so close together?
3. How does the focus of the poem suddenly expand in the poem's final line? In your own words, how would you paraphrase the speaker's thoughts in this line?

Writing Options

1. Mistral's poem is full of vivid sensory images. In a brief critical essay, analyze her use of images appealing to one or more of the five senses in the poem. How does this imagery contribute to the theme, or central message, of the poem as a whole?
2. Use the poem as a springboard for writing a children's tale about a puppy's adventures. In your tale, use the puppy's first-person point of view, and be sure to make the setting, images, and tone consistent with Mistral's portrayal of infancy in "Eight Puppies."

 Go to **www.mirrorsandwindows.com** for more.

Pat Mora (b. 1942) was born in El Paso, Texas, and studied at Texas Western College and the University of Texas at El Paso. She has remarked that part of her reason for writing is that "Hispanic perspectives need to be part of our literary heritage."

Immigration has been a prominent part of the American story for hundreds of years. For much of that time, immigrants have faced the challenge of assimilation, or incorporation into the mainstream of American culture. In **"Immigrants"** and **"Family Ties,"** Pat Mora movingly explores the eagerness, as well as the anxieties, that this challenge sparks for the first few generations in an immigrant family.

Do you have a relative, friend, or neighbor who is either an immigrant or from a family that has recently immigrated to the United States? Describe the experience.

IMMIGRANTS

A Lyric Poem by **Pat Mora**

wrap their babies in the American flag,
feed them mashed hot dogs and apple pie,
name them Bill and Daisy,
buy them blonde dolls that blink blue
5 eyes or a football and tiny cleats
before the baby can even walk,
speak to them in thick English,
       hallo, babee, hallo,
whisper in Spanish or Polish
10 when the babies sleep, whisper
in a dark parent bed, that dark
parent fear, "Will they like
our boy, our girl, our fine american
boy, our fine american girl?" ❖

What do you think it means to be a "fine american boy" or "fine american girl"? What qualities should a "fine american" have? How might recent immigrants to the United States have a different idea of what a "fine american" is than someone who has lived in the United States all of his or her life?

FAMILY TIES

A Lyric Poem by **Pat Mora**

Though I shop for designer jeans,
uniforms make me smile.
Chalk-white uniforms in store windows remind
me of my grandmother who refused to learn English,
5   who laughed with the women from the canneries
when they all filled her small home with the smell of fish,
filled her hands with crumpled dollars in exchange
for the white garments piled in pale pink
boxes throughout the house.

10   My grandmother preferred to shop in the grocery stores,
preferred buying garlic, onion, chile, beans,
to buying me gifts of frilly blouses and barrettes,
hers a life of cooking, cleaning, selling.
But when I shyly showed my *abuelita*
15   my good report card or recited the Pledge of Allegiance,
my grandmother would smile and hand me a uniform,
never the right size, but a gift
I would add to the white stack
at the bottom of my closet. ❖

Refer and Reason

1. What details of "Immigrants" suggest the topic of assimilation into mainstream society?
2. Of what do uniforms remind the speaker of "Family Ties"? Infer why the speaker's grandmother refuses to learn English.
3. Do you think that immigrants should do their best to fit into mainstream culture, or should they preserve at least some aspects of their distinctive native cultures and traditions? Support your answers.

Writing Options

1. Tone is the attitude that a writer takes toward the subject, the characters, or the audience. Write a paragraph in which you identify and comment on the tone in Mora's poems.
2. Imagine you work for an organization that prepares new immigrants for life in the United States. Prepare a brochure that includes key "survival" information for people who have just recently arrived.

Go to **www.mirrorsandwindows.com** for more.

Informational Text
CONNECTION

IMMIGRATION STATISTICS

Map and table compiled from information from the United States Citizenship and Immigration Services and the Department of Homeland Security Office of Immigration Statistics

Every year, thousands of people immigrate to the United States from around the world, and millions of immigrants who have been in the United States for many years become permanent residents. An *immigrant* is someone who leaves his or her native country to settle in another country. A *permanent resident* is an immigrant who has nearly all of the same rights as a citizen.

Immigrants by Intended State of Residence, 2003

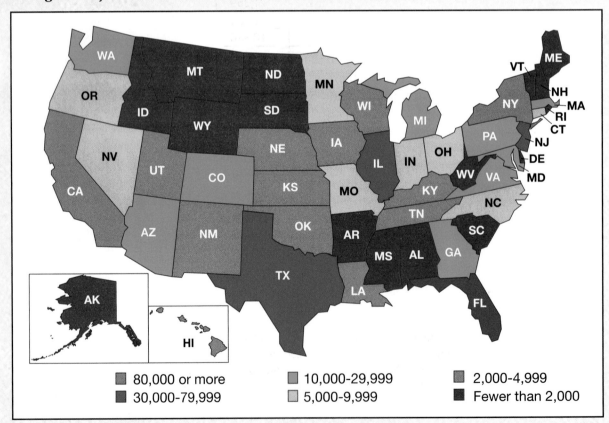

Legend:
- 80,000 or more
- 30,000-79,999
- 10,000-29,999
- 5,000-9,999
- 2,000-4,999
- Fewer than 2,000

Permanent Residents by Region and Country of Birth

Region/Country of Birth	2006 Number	2006 Percent	2005 Number	2005 Percent	2004 Number	2004 Percent
Total	1,266,264	100.0	1,122,373	100.0	957,883	100.0
Region						
Africa	117,430	9.3	85,102	7.6	66,422	6.9
Asia	422,333	33.4	400,135	35.7	334,540	34.9
Europe	164,285	13.0	176,569	15.7	133,181	13.9
North America	414,096	32.7	345,575	30.8	342,468	35.8
Caribbean	146,771	11.6	108,598	9.7	89,144	9.3
Central America	75,030	5.9	53,470	4.8	62,287	6.5
Other North America	192,295	15.2	183,507	16.4	191,037	19.9
Oceania	7,385	0.6	6,546	0.6	5,985	0.6
South America	138,001	10.9	103,143	9.2	72,060	7.5
Unknown	2,734	0.2	5,303	0.5	3,227	0.3
Country of Birth						
Mexico	173,753	13.7	161,445	14.4	175,411	18.3
China, People's Republic	87,345	6.9	69,967	6.2	55,494	5.8
Philippines	74,607	5.9	60,748	5.4	57,846	6.0
India	61,369	4.8	84,681	7.5	70,151	7.3
Cuba	45,614	3.6	36,261	3.2	20,488	2.1
Colombia	43,151	3.4	25,571	2.3	18,846	2.0
Dominican Republic	38,069	3.0	27,504	2.5	30,506	3.2
El Salvador	31,783	2.5	21,359	1.9	29,807	3.1
Vietnam	30,695	2.4	32,784	2.9	31,524	3.3
Jamaica	24,976	2.0	18,346	1.6	14,430	1.5
Korea	24,386	1.9	26,562	2.4	19,766	2.1
Guatemala	24,146	1.9	16,825	1.5	18,920	2.0
Haiti	22,228	1.8	14,529	1.3	14,191	1.5
Peru	21,718	1.7	15,676	1.4	11,794	1.2
Canada	18,207	1.4	21,878	2.0	15,569	1.6
Brazil	17,910	1.4	16,664	1.5	10,556	1.1
Ecuador	17,490	1.4	11,608	1.0	8,626	0.9
Pakistan	17,418	1.4	14,926	1.3	12,086	1.3
United Kingdom	17,207	1.4	19,800	1.8	14,915	1.6
Ukraine	17,142	1.4	22,761	2.0	14,156	1.5
All other countries	457,050	36.1	402,478	35.9	312,801	32.7

TEXT ←TO→ TEXT CONNECTION

- Why do you think so many immigrants reside in California and New York? Infer from the poem "Immigrants" why people immigrate to the United States.
- What are some of the challenges new immigrants to the United States might face? Explain how the two poems by Pat Mora illustrate these challenges.

Melancholia: On the Beach, 1896. Edvard Munch. The Cleveland Art Museum.

THE WAKING

A Villanelle by **Theodore Roethke**

I wake to sleep, and take my waking slow.
I feel my fate in what I cannot fear.
I learn by going where I have to go.

Poet **Theodore Roethke** (1908–1963) was born in Saginaw, Michigan. By helping in his family's greenhouses as a boy, Roethke developed the reverence for nature that is present in much of his poetry.

"The Waking" comments on the speaker's processes of learning as he or she goes through life. The poem, which was published in 1953, is in a complex verse form called a villanelle. In this form, borrowed from French literature, certain lines are repeated at intervals in a 19-line poem, and the poet may use only two rhymes.

When do you feel most awake or alive?

We think by feeling. What is there to know?
5   I hear my being dance from ear to ear.
I wake to sleep, and take my waking slow.

Of those so close beside me, which are you?
God bless the Ground! I shall walk softly there,
And learn by going where I have to go.

10   Light takes the Tree; but who can tell us how?
The lowly worm climbs up a winding stair;
I wake to sleep, and take my waking slow.

Great Nature has another thing to do
To you and me; so take the lively air,
15   And, lovely, learn by going where to go.

This shaking keeps me steady. I should know.
What falls away is always. And is near.
I wake to sleep, and take my waking slow.
I learn by going where I have to go. ❖

"I learn by going where I have to go." What have you learned about yourself and the world around you from the places you've been? What are some things you would still like to know?

Refer and Reason

1. Most people wake and sleep every day. What "once in a lifetime" pair of opposites are hinted at by the ideas of waking and sleeping? What is the "thing" that Great Nature has in store?
2. What might it mean to "think by feeling"? How might this be related to the speaker's learning where he has to go?
3. Imagine that you are the speaker. How would you explain your philosophy of life?

Writing Options

1. Imagine that Theodore Roethke is your English teacher. Write a descriptive paragraph about an experience that made you feel intensely awake. In other words, tell about a time when you experienced life to the fullest.
2. Working with a small group, write and illustrate a public service pamphlet to be distributed to high school students. In the pamphlet, explain the benefits of getting enough sleep. You can use humor or real-life examples to make students want to read your pamphlet.

 Go to **www.mirrorsandwindows.com** for more.

HEART TO HEART: New Poems Inspired by Twentieth-Century American Art
edited by Jan Greenberg

In this collection of poetic responses to famous pieces of twentieth-century American art, readers are invited to choose a work of art and write a response. Including the artwork and biographical information on both the visual artists and poets, the collection is a delightful marriage of art forms.

THE POETRY OF ROBERT FROST
by Robert Frost
edited by Edward Connery Lathem

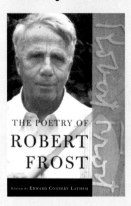

Robert Frost is one of the most well-known poets of all time, and many of his most famous poems are gathered in this collection. In this book, readers will find a broad assortment of Frost's poems, along with essays, interviews, and other writings.

WHAT HAVE YOU LOST?
edited by Naomi Shihab Nye

In this collection for young adults, poets explore the feeling and meaning of loss in words. In her introduction to the book, Nye describes the sources of the poems: "Envelopes from strangers. People I had met only once, who sent me sheaves of poems. Old friends sending messages for the first time in years."

LETTERS TO A YOUNG POET
by Rainer Maria Rilke
translated by Stephen Mitchell

This book is a collection of letters between a young aspiring poet and Rainer Maria Rilke, a famous writer. In his letters, Rilke gives advice on everything from the practical realities of being a poet to the cultivation of solitude and quiet observation.

I SHALL NOT BE MOVED
by Maya Angelou

In funny, honest, and eloquent poems, Maya Angelou's fifth volume of verse speaks about the richness and pain of being African American and struggling to be free. Included is "Our Grandmothers," honoring the history and strength of black women with the repeated refrain, "I shall not be moved."

HOW TO HAIKU: A WRITER'S GUIDE TO HAIKU AND RELATED FORMS
by Bruce Ross

In this book, Bruce Ross walks the reader through the basics of writing haiku, from using patterns and present tense to capturing nature and personal insight. Examples are used to further introduce readers to other forms of haiku that experiment with humor, narratives, and emotional expressions.

Present an Oral Response to Literature

When you present an oral response to literature, you simply state aloud your reactions to something you have read. You present informal oral responses every time your teacher asks you to share your ideas about something you have read. In this workshop, you will present a formal two-minute oral response to poetry.

1. Select a poem

Choose a poem that you feel strongly about. The more interested you are in the poem, the more interesting your presentation will be. Unless the poem you have chosen is in the textbook, make copies of it for the class.

2. Study the poem

Read the poem several times, jotting notes about what stands out for you and what you like or dislike about the poem. Use the information in the Introduction to Poetry, page 390, to help you analyze your poem. You might also review the terms in the Analyze Literature boxes for the selections in this unit.

3. Organize your ideas

Consider the information you have gathered. What is the most important thing you want your audience to know about the poem, or about your opinion of it, when you have completed your presentation? The answer to this question is the main idea of your oral response. Write down this idea, and then list the details that explain or support your main idea, as shown in the following chart. You may use this chart as a guide during your presentation.

Main Idea
Detail or quotation 1
Detail or quotation 2
Detail or quotation 3

4. Practice

Using your chart, practice your response out loud, possibly in front of a mirror. This process will help you access more quickly the words you want to use when you are in front of the audience. It will also help you gauge whether your presentation is too short or too long. Think about what you, as an audience member, find boring or interesting in public speakers, and let those thoughts help you plan a successful presentation.

5. Deliver the response

When it is your turn to speak, pass out your photocopies. Then take your chart with you to the front of the room, take a deep breath, and share your response to the poem you have chosen. Let your enthusiasm for the poem show, and don't worry too much about how you are doing. The point of this exercise is to share ideas.

Organization Tip

Reveal your main idea early in the presentation, and use the rest of your time to support it.

Rehearsal Tip

As you practice, pay attention to and adjust these elements:

- vocal qualities like volume, enunciation, pace, pitch, and stress
- nonverbals like gestures and facial expressions

Speaking & Listening Rubric

Your presentation will be evaluated on these elements:

Content

- ☑ clarity of main idea or ideas
- ☑ use of details to support main idea or ideas
- ☑ organization of ideas
- ☑ overall quality of analysis

Delivery and Presentation

- ☑ appropriate volume, enunciation, and pace
- ☑ appropriate intonation, stress, and tone
- ☑ effective use of gestures and eye contact

Lyric Poem

Lyric poetry works a little like music, combining sound and rhythm. The difference is that a poem makes its melody with words, while expressing the emotions of a speaker. Carl Sandburg makes the music parallel clear in his poem "Jazz Fantasia (page 463)." Jimmy Santiago Baca's poem punctuates "I Am Offering This Poem" (page 395) with a refrain of "I love you." In "Eating Alone" (page 413), Li-Young Lee combines food, seasonal changes, and a memory of his father; what he does not say is as important as what he does.

Since a lyric poem packs a lot of meaning into very few words, its language must be concise. At the same time, the language is imaginative, moving the reader through precise imagery and musical sound. A good poem expresses timeless, universal emotions—love, rage, passion, grief—in startling new ways.

❶ PREWRITE

Select Your Topic
Brainstorm a list of topic ideas, ranging from memories, concerns, possessions, or personal or current events. Choose a topic from your list, one you feel passionately about, to explore in your poem.

Writing Rubric

A good lyric poem

☑ begins by orienting the reader to the main theme

☑ contains, in the body, images that work together to express ideas and emotions about a single central theme

☑ uses precise, vivid language to create effective similes, metaphors, personification, and poetic imagery

☑ closes the poem in a meaningful, insightful, satisfying way

☑ avoids wordiness

Gather Information/Discovery
Creative expression requires being open-minded and risking putting language together in a way that may sound illogical. Discover what you feel is important about your subject. What do you know about your topic? How does it make you feel? What are its sources of passion, joy, or sadness? Let your mind and heart explore your topic in a free way.

To generate ideas, and find your voice, create a Cluster Chart like the one on page 491. Start with a statement like "I have…" or "I want…" or "I am…" at the center of your paper. See what words emerge. Describe the images that come to your mind and freewrite about your ideas.

Organize Your Ideas
Experiment and play with rhyme and meter. Listen to music or take a walk to find a good rhythm. Read poetry that inspires you. To structure the poem, create line breaks at natural places. Cross out words and lines that don't seem to work. Insert new words and lines that enliven your ideas.

Review your Cluster Chart. Make use of whatever surprised or delighted you during your brainstorming. Try combining categories in a new way. Remember to write about your topic in terms of images. In this way, by playing with words, your lines will become poetry.

Cluster Chart

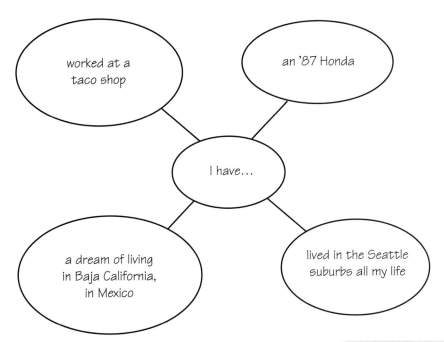

- worked at a taco shop
- an '87 Honda
- I have...
- a dream of living in Baja California, in Mexico
- lived in the Seattle suburbs all my life

Write Your Opening

Now you have a good idea of what you want to express in your poem. Write the first line, or the **opening** of your poem. Based on the ideas in his Cluster Chart, one student, Kevin Rhodes, wrote this opening for a poem about his car:

> My '87 Honda rests on the street,
> collecting sap from the oak

❷ DRAFT

Write your poem by following this three-part framework: **opening, body,** and **conclusion.**

Draft Your Opening Stanza

A poem's **opening** often orients the reader to the subject, provides context, and attracts the reader, compelling him or her to read more. But remember, it's all about language. The beginning of a poem doesn't have to correlate with a logical chronology like stories and essays often do.

The first lines Kevin wrote during the Draft stage are shown in the first column of the chart on page 495. His opening stanza describes three cars, and three different owners. You can see that he tries to use consonance and assonance, letting the sounds of the words create a poetic rhythm. But how could he infuse this first stanza with more imagery?

What Great Writers Do

Don't be afraid of the blank page. Writing poetry is like taking a journey into the unknown. The poet Derek Walcott (b. 1930) said,

"If you know what you are going to write when you're writing a poem, it's going to be average."

- **Opening**
  Identify the topic your poem addresses. Establish a voice.

- **Body**
  Develop the idea of your topic in as many stanzas as needed. Use precise imagery and figurative language to communicate ideas.

- **Conclusion**
  Close the poem with a resounding image or an insightful phrase that conveys a significant experience and leaves readers thinking.

Draft Your Body Stanzas

A poem combines meaning with sound, content with form. In the **body,** as you say what you mean about your topic, experiment with rhyme and meter. Craft vowel and consonant sounds. Replace a predictable word with a synonym that creates alliteration, assonance, or consonance.

Kevin worked the body of his draft by specifically describing his car. Read the draft of his second stanza in the left-hand column of the chart on page 493. Kevin allowed imagery to stand for meaning so his readers could interpret his love for a car in a state of disrepair.

Review your Cluster Chart. Have you made good use of your images? Experiment by adding, deleting, or moving lines. Listen to the rhythm of the lines and to how the words sound together. Effective poems depend on precise word choices, conveying ideas in the fewest possible words. Use only the words necessary to make your meaning clear to your reader.

Draft Your Concluding Stanza

Finally, finish your poem. Just as a song ends musically, a poem's **conclusion** resonates. A good ending makes an impact, both with rhythm and content. It gives the reader a profound experience or a new way to think about the ideas in the poem.

Does Kevin accomplish these things in the conclusion of his poem? Look at the draft of his conclusion in the chart on page 493.

❸ REVISE

What Great Writers Do

In the following lines from her poem "Making a Fist" (page 401), Naomi Shihab Nye doesn't simply say, "I felt sick." Her figurative language and imagery allow for a richer interpretation of the experience.

"palm trees swirl a sickening pattern past the glass"

"My stomach was a melon split wide inside my skin"

"the borders we must cross separately"

What do her lines mean? How would you interpret them? What do her images stand for?

Evaluate Your Draft

As you evaluate your poem or exchange poems with a classmate and evaluate each other's work, think carefully about what's done well and what can be improved.

Read the poem aloud so you can hear the rhythm created by the stressed syllables. If some sentences sound overcomplicated, or too much like prose, edit and simplify them. Make sure the three parts of the poem—the opening, body, and conclusion—work well together. The lines and images should come together for a single expression. Use the Revision Checklist on page 494 to make this evaluation.

Review the poem with word choice in mind, paring down the language when necessary. Apply the guidelines in the Grammar & Style workshops in this unit. Think of ways to make the writing precise and fresh. One way to achieve this is to replace vague words with specific choices—for example, *Honda* rather than *car.*

DRAFT STAGE		REVISE STAGE	
Introduction My car, an old '87 Honda, rests on the street, just sitting there on "the best block in town," although discreet, while my dad's Explorer only gets a boring commute to work. Mom's Acura drives to the store, questing food, while the clerk smiles and secretly smirks.	Identifies the subject; establishes a first-person narrator; uses description; plays with consonance and assonance	My ~~car, an old~~ '87 Honda rests on the street, ~~just sitting there~~ collecting sap from the oak on "the best block in town," although discreet, while my dad's Explorer ~~only gets~~ ~~a boring~~ dreams to explore more than the commute to work. Mom's Acura ~~drives~~ finds the store, questing ~~food~~ the accurate spice, while the clerk smiles and secretly smirks.	Eliminates wordi- ness; adds a vivid image Uses a play on words; replaces vague language with specific words

Body
The car has 200K miles on
it and more to go
The entire car is rust
brown—except for the rear
fender, see the speedometer
broke while I drove slow
past the high school where I
play basketball
I was just bringing it home
tenderly
Fourteen months, two
weeks, and three days ago.
Chip on the windshield
    where a rock hit it,
Seats of vinyl, such fine
    quality so
in winter they're cold
    (heater is lacked).
	Develops theme
	
	Uses imagery to
	convey meaning
	and gentle humor
	
	Uses interesting
	line breaks
		~~The car has~~ 200K miles ~~on it~~ and
		more to go
		~~The entire car is~~ Rust brown—
		except for the rear fender, see
		the speedometer broke while I
		drove slow ~~past the high school~~
		~~where I play basketball~~
		I was just bringing it home
		tenderly
		Fourteen months, two weeks,
		and three days ago.
		Chip on the windshield where a
		rock ~~hit it~~ attacked,
		Seats of vinyl, such fine quality
		so in winter they're cold (heater is
		    lacked).
			Deletes
			wordiness for
			conciseness
			
			Deletes unneces-
			sary information
			
			Uses a word to
			add rhyme and
			consonance

Conclusion The transmission grinds, the main seal leaks, the starter whines, but it gets me to school. It gets me to work, it gets me to my friend's place, where we chill, and talk about the future.	Creates a strong rhythm with lines Stays focused on the topic, yet creates a shift for a good ending	The transmission grinds, the main seal leaks a pool, the starter whines, but it gets me to school. It gets me to ~~work~~ Joe's Tacos (my career), it gets me to my friend's place, where we chill, just dreaming of the day it will get us out of here.	Creates rhyme; uses specific words that also convey a tone of ironic humor Creates a much richer closing line

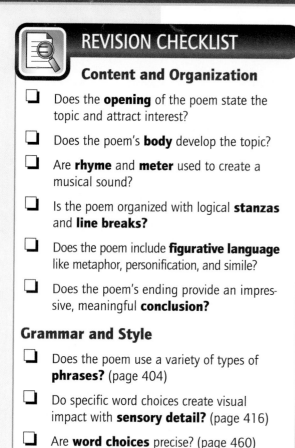

REVISION CHECKLIST

Content and Organization

❏ Does the **opening** of the poem state the topic and attract interest?

❏ Does the poem's **body** develop the topic?

❏ Are **rhyme** and **meter** used to create a musical sound?

❏ Is the poem organized with logical **stanzas** and **line breaks?**

❏ Does the poem include **figurative language** like metaphor, personification, and simile?

❏ Does the poem's ending provide an impressive, meaningful **conclusion?**

Grammar and Style

❏ Does the poem use a variety of types of **phrases?** (page 404)

❏ Do specific word choices create visual impact with **sensory detail?** (page 416)

❏ Are **word choices** precise? (page 460)

Revise for Content, Organization, and Style

Upon evaluation, Kevin found ways to improve the draft of his poem. Look at the chart on page 493 (this time, the right-hand column) to see how he revised the three stanzas we looked at earlier:

- **Opening:** Kevin pared down language by deleting all unnecessary words. He experimented with line breaks and word choice. He added specific visual imagery.
- **Body:** Kevin continued to craft the language of his poem. He replaced vague, predictable words with specific, vivid imagery and rhyming words. He deleted a phrase he didn't think worked for the poem.
- **Conclusion:** In his closing stanza, Kevin establishes an assertive, driving rhythm. He develops his gentle humor and irony. His revised last line adds the surprising idea that the speaker wants his life to change. He brings his poem to a close and gives the reader something to think about and possibly relate to.

Review the notes you or your partner made as you evaluated your draft. Respond to each comment as you revise your poem.

Proofread for Errors

Finally, proofread to check for remaining errors. You may have corrected errors as you evaluated your poem; now you should focus only on proofreading. Use proofreader's symbols to mark any errors you find. (See Language Arts Handbook 4.1 for a list of proofreader's symbols.) To complete the assignment, print out a final draft and read it through once more before turning it in.

Take a look at the final version of Kevin's poem on the next page. Review how he worked through the three stages of the writing process: Prewrite, Draft, and Revise.

WRITING FOLLOW-UP

Publish and Present

- Research literary magazines on the Internet. Choose one and submit your poem for publication.
- Plan and organize an "open mike" poetry reading. Create a sign-up list. Advertise the event. Allow each poet to read up to three original poems.

Reflect

- How is writing poetry different from writing prose? What thinking, planning, and writing skills do you need to write poetry?
- How did writing a poem help you appreciate reading poetry? How might you discover new poets you would enjoy reading?

STUDENT MODEL

My Ride, by Kevin Rhodes

My '87 Honda rests on the street,
collecting sap from the oak
on "the best block in town," although
    discreet,
while my dad's Explorer dreams to explore
more than the commute to work.
Mom's Acura voyages to the store,
questing the accurate spice, while the clerk
smiles and secretly smirks.

200K miles and more to go
Rust brown—except for the rear fender, see
the speedometer broke while I drove slow
I was just bringing it home tenderly
Fourteen months, two weeks, and three days ago.
Chip on the windshield where a rock attacked,
Seats of vinyl, such fine quality so
in winter they're cold (heater is lacked).
The dash is split, but this causes no
    troubles—
I keep a five-dollar bill in the crack.
Fill the gas tank, and the car's value
    doubles.

It is my ride—lady-killer it's not,
but I earned it, I can say with pride,
from the very sweat of my brow's knot
as it dripped into hard-shelled tacos, fried.

The transmission grinds,
the main seal leaks a pool,
the starter whines,
but it gets me to school.
It gets me to Joe's Tacos (my career),
it gets me to my friend's place,
where we chill, just dreaming of the day
it will get us out of here.

What is the writer's topic?

How does he feel about this
topic, and how can you tell?
Name three images that help
to convey this feeling.

Which words in this poem
seem the most precise or vivid
to you?

What types of figurative
language does the writer use
in the poem? Point out examples in each stanza.

Where do you think the writer
says the most with the fewest
words?

Reading Skills

DRAW CONCLUSIONS

You draw conclusions every day, so it makes sense that drawing conclusions is an essential part of reading. When you draw conclusions, you gather pieces of information and then decide what that information means. You look for a key idea and supporting points; from these, you can infer a conclusion.

Test-Taking Tip
When answering multiple-choice questions that ask you to draw conclusions, eliminate any answer choices that contradict information in the text.

Think of drawing conclusions like a mathematical equation: information + information + information = my conclusion. For example, in the poem "The Bean Eaters," page (455), several pieces of information—in this case, details from the poem—indicate that the couple in the poem is poor. Read the stanzas below.

> They eat beans mostly, this old yellow pair.
> Dinner is a casual affair.
> Plain chipware on a plain and creaking wood,
> Tin flatware.
> …Remembering, with twinklings and twinges,
> As they lean over the beans in their rented back room
> that is full of beads and receipts and dolls and cloths,
> tobacco crumbs, vases and fringes.

To keep track of pieces of information that support your conclusion, try using a graphic organizer like the one below.

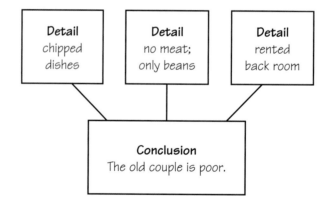

Detail chipped dishes

Detail no meat; only beans

Detail rented back room

Conclusion The old couple is poor.

PRACTICE

Directions: Read the following story. The questions after the story will ask you to draw conclusions based on key ideas and supporting points from this passage.

Prose Fiction: This passage is H. E. Francis's story "Sitting."

In the morning the man and woman were sitting on his front steps. They sat all day. They would not move.

With metronomic regularity, he peered at them through the pane in the front door.

5

They did not leave at dark. He wondered when they ate or slept or did their duties.

At dawn they were still sitting there. They sat through sun and rain.

10 At first only the immediate neighbors called: Who are they? What are they doing there?

He did not know.

Then neighbors from farther down the street called. People who passed and saw the couple called.

15 He never heard the man and woman talk.

When he started getting calls from all over the city, from strangers and city fathers, professionals and clerks, garbage and utilities men, and the postman, who had to walk around them to deliver
20 the letters, he had to do something.

He asked them to leave.

They said nothing. They sat. They stared, indifferent.

He said he would call the police.

The police gave them a talking to, explained the
25 limits of their rights, and took them away in a police car.

In the morning they were back.

The next time the police said they would put them in jail if the jail were not so full, though they
30 would have to find a place for them somewhere, if he insisted.

That is your problem, he said.

No, it is really yours, the police told him, but they removed the pair.

35 When he looked out the next morning, the man and woman were sitting on the steps.

They sat there every day for years.

Winters he expected them to die from the cold.

But he died.

40 He had no relatives, so the house went to the city.

The man and woman went on sitting there.

When the city threatened to remove the man and woman, neighbors and citizens brought a suit against the city: after sitting so long, the man and woman deserved the house.   45

The petitioners won. The man and woman took over the house.

In the morning strange men and women were sitting on front steps all over the city.

Multiple Choice

1. Which of the following conclusions is supported by the passage?
   A. The man and woman on the steps were not real.
   B. The neighbors and postal carrier disliked the man and woman on the steps.
   C. The man who owned the house was insane.
   D. The man and woman wanted the owner's house.

2. Why were there strange men and women sitting on steps around the city on the day after the man and woman took over the house?
   F. They thought it might be fun.
   G. They wanted to make a political statement.
   H. They wanted to take over the houses.
   J. They had nothing better to do.

3. In line 4, the word *metronomic* means
   A. mechanical.
   B. musical.
   C. chaotic.
   D. None of the above

4. Based on the conclusion to the story, which of the following character traits can you infer about the man and woman sitting?
   F. They were friendly.
   G. They were determined.
   H. They were humble.
   J. They were angry.

Constructed Response

5. Is this a realistic story, or not? Cite specific information from the text that supports your answer.

Writing Skills

REFLECTIVE ESSAY

Test-Taking Tip
Use words that are concise, clear, and appropriate. The purpose of your essay is not to impress readers with large vocabulary words but rather to use words that effectively express your ideas.

Many standardized tests include sections that ask you to demonstrate your writing ability by composing an essay in response to a *prompt*. Some prompts ask you to express your thoughts about a particular topic, often something that has happened to you.

You are asked to reflect on an issue, not give a straight report of the facts. Feel free to use "I," and give examples that are meaningful to you from your personal life or experiences. Come up with as many examples as you can and take the time to really explain your examples to fully develop your point of view. An essay with one or two thoughtful, well-developed reasons or examples is more likely to get a high score than an essay with several short, simplistic examples.

Make sure to support your ideas appropriately, and show that you can use language well, but remember: The reflective essay is an opportunity for you to say what you think about an important issue that's relevant to your life.

The position you choose to take will not affect your score. What will be assessed is how well you support that position. Scorers will evaluate your ability to

- develop a point of view and support it with reasons, examples, and other evidence
- organize ideas logically and progress from one idea to another smoothly
- employ varied, precise, and appropriate vocabulary
- use a variety of sentence structures
- avoid errors in grammar, usage, and mechanics

PRACTICE

Timed Writing: 30 minutes
Read the quotation by Helen Keller. Then consider the assignment that follows.

> "Character cannot be developed in ease and quiet. Only through experience of trial and suffering can the soul be strengthened, ambition inspired, and success achieved."

Assignment: Do you agree that character is best developed by going through difficult times? Write a reflective essay in which you support your position by discussing one or more examples from your personal experience, your observations, your reading, or your knowledge of popular culture, the arts, science and technology, or current events.

Revising and Editing Skills

Some standardized tests ask you to read a passage and answer multiple-choice questions about how to improve it. As you read the passage, keep the following tips in mind:

- Pay attention to the writing style used in each passage.
- Consider the elements of writing, such as tone or emphasis, that are included in each underlined part of the passage.
- Be aware of questions with no underlined portions: You may be asked questions about a section of the passage or about the passage as a whole.
- Examine each answer choice and determine how it differs from the others.
- Read and consider all of the answer choices and eliminate the answers that you know are incorrect.
- Determine the answer that best responds to the question.
- Reread the sentence using your selected answer to make sure it is correct.

PRACTICE

Directions: For each underlined section in the passage that follows, choose the revision that most improves the writing. If you think the original version is best, choose "MAKE NO CHANGE."

(1) <u>I always used to think I hated cauliflower.</u> But now I love it. Here's how my opinion changed.

I had many reasons for hating cauliflower. (2) <u>Everybody I knew hated it. The exception to this was my mom.</u> (3) My mom may be smart about most things, but she was <u>out-numbered</u> about this. So I thought that all these other people must be right.

(4) <u>Another reason I had for hating this vegetable was it's appearance.</u> It looks bad, disgusting, just plain yucky. (5) <u>Like pieces of brain in pictures I've seen.</u> (6) I didn't like the idea of eating <u>that.</u>

1. A. MAKE NO CHANGE.
   B. I all ways used to think I hated cauliflower.
   C. I always use to think I hated cauliflower.
   D. I always used to think, I hated cauliflower.

2. F. MAKE NO CHANGE.
   G. Everybody I knew hated it, the exception to this was my mom.

H. Everybody I knew, except my mom, hated it.
J. Excepting for my mom, everybody I knew hated it.

3. A. MAKE NO CHANGE.
   B. out numbered
   C. outnumbered
   D. outnummbered

4. F. MAKE NO CHANGE.
   G. Another reason I had for hating this vegetable, was it's appearance.
   H. Another reason I have for hating this vegetable was it's appearance.
   J. Another reason I have for hating this vegetable is its appearance.

5. A. MAKE NO CHANGE.
   B. It looks like pieces of brain in pictures I've seen.
   C. Like pieces of brain, which I've seen pictures of.
   D. Like pieces of brain, that I've seen in pictures.

6. F. MAKE NO CHANGE.
   G. this vegetable.
   H. cauliflower.
   J. pieces of brain.

UNIT 4

Drama

SHAKESPEARE

GLASPELL

CHEKOV

"Drama is life with the dull bits cut out."

—Alfred Hitchcock

Have you ever seen in someone an unquenchable desire for fame or greatness? Think about a story on the news that made you ask, "What was that person thinking?" Most of the plays you will read in this unit were written long before you were born, but you'll find as you read them that even though times have changed, the desires and behavior of human beings have not.

MACHIAVELLI

KAUFMAN

CAVAFY

501

INTRODUCTION TO DRAMA

ANTIGONE. *Creon, what more do you want than my death?*
CREON. *Nothing.*
That gives me everything.
ANTIGONE. *Then I beg you: kill me.*
—from *Antigone* by Sophocles

Have you ever heard someone referred to as a "drama queen"? Most likely, that person was acting in an exaggerated manner, as if in a play. Although the concept of the "drama queen" is relatively new, drama itself has been around since long before the beginning of recorded history. In this unit, you'll discover drama's ancient roots in the Greek play *Antigone* by Sophocles. You'll also see how drama can be humorous or ironic, as in Anton Chekhov's "A Marriage Proposal."

THE GENRE OF DRAMA

A **drama** is a story told through characters played by actors. This makes a drama, or play, different from other types of literature. Drama is meant to be spoken, acted out, and given movement. When you read the script of a play, try to visualize the actions as they might unfold on a stage or movie screen. Use the playwright's stage directions and notes to help you imagine a live production of the play.

Famous Characters from Plays

Romeo, from *The Tragedy of Romeo and Juliet*
Eliza Doolittle, from *Pygmalion*
Willy Loman, from *Death of a Salesman*
Peter Pan, from *Peter Pan*
Blanche DuBois, from *A Streetcar Named Desire*

Julie Andrews stars as Eliza Doolittle in the 1956 Broadway production of *My Fair Lady*, adapted from *Pygmalion*.

TYPES OF DRAMA

Most dramas can be classified as either comedy or tragedy:

- A **comedy,** in its original sense, was a play with a happy ending. Today, the term is widely used to refer to any humorous work, especially one prepared for the stage or the screen.
- A **tragedy** was originally a drama that told the story of the fall of a person of high status. In more recent times, the word *tragedy* has been used both to describe a play about the downfall of a sympathetic character, or protagonist, and a story with an unhappy ending.

ELEMENTS OF DRAMA

Like the author of a work of fiction, the playwright must combine a number of elements to successfully craft a drama. Those elements compose the script, or written form of the play.

Structure

In creating a drama, the playwright organizes a story into acts and scenes:

- An **act** is a major division of a play. Most plays written in Shakespeare's time, including *The Tragedy of Julius Caesar,* have five acts. Today, one-act and three-act plays are common. "Trifles" and "A Marriage Proposal" are examples of one-act plays.
- Acts are often divided into **scenes,** which are shorter sections that usually mark changes of time and place.

Characters

You get to know a dramatic character largely through his or her actions and speech. As you read, look for clues to a character's motivations and emotional state. Consider how one character plays off of another. The characters in drama, as in prose fiction, can be classified as protagonists or antagonists, flat or round, and major or minor. See Understanding Character in Unit 1 for more information on these types of characters.

In drama, particularly classic drama, there are certain types of characters that are quite common. These character types were fairly standard in Ancient Greek dramas and in Shakespearean drama and may sometimes appear in modern plays.

In tragedies, such as *The Tragedy of Julius Caesar,* the main character (or characters, in this case) is frequently a **tragic hero.** Tragic heroes have a **tragic flaw,** or a weakness of personality, that causes them to make unfortunate choices. They are thus doomed to a tragic end. Early on in *The Tragedy of Julius Caesar,* it is possible to see one of Caesar's tragic flaws: his thirst for power.

A **foil** is a character who contrasts with a central character in order to highlight each other's strengths and, more commonly, weaknesses. In *The Tragedy of Julius Caesar,* Cassius acts as a foil to Brutus. By comparing Cassius's motives in killing Caesar with those of Brutus, we see that Brutus truly believed he was acting on behalf of Rome and not for personal gain.

To offset the heaviness of tragedy, playwrights will often incorporate a more humorous character for comic relief.

Dialogue

One of the elements that makes a drama memorable is the dialogue, meaning, in general, the words spoken by the actors. Unlike a written story, where all the necessary descriptions and thoughts are there for you to read, drama relies primarily on the speech of the characters to tell the story. Badly written dialogue can make a movie or play seem silly or forced; good dialogue will impress the audience with its eloquence or emotional power.

In most cases, the word *dialogue* refers to what the actors (or characters) say aloud to one another. Sometimes, however, characters speak to themselves or to the audience directly. The following are the main types of dialogue in a play, all of which are found in *The Tragedy of Julius Caesar:*

- A **dialogue** is a conversation between two or more characters. The example below is from Act I, Scene iii, in which Casca and Cassius meet to discuss what to do about Caesar:

> CASSIUS. Who's there?
> CASCA.   A Roman.
> CASSIUS.   Casca, by your voice.
> CASCA. Your ear is good. Cassius, what night is this!
> CASSIUS. A very pleasing night to honest men.
> CASCA. Who ever knew the heavens menace so?

- A **monologue** is a long speech made by one character. The following example is from Act III, Scene ii, when Antony addresses the Roman public over the dead body of Julius Caesar:

> **ANTONY.** Friends, Romans, countrymen,
>   lend me your ears!
> I come to bury Caesar, not to praise him.
> The evil that men do lives after them,
> The good is oft interred with their bones;
> So let it be with Caesar. The noble Brutus
> Hath told you Caesar was ambitious;
> If it were so, it was a grievous fault,
> And grievously hath Caesar answer'd it.
> Here, under leave of Brutus and the rest
> (For Brutus is an honorable man,
> So are they all, all honorable men),
> Come I to speak in Caesar's funeral.

- A **soliloquy** is a monologue given by a character alone on stage. In Act III, Scene i, Antony, alone on the stage with the body of Caesar, speaks of his grief and anger:

> **ANTONY.** O, pardon me, thou bleeding
>   piece of earth,
> That I am meek and gentle with these
>   butchers!
> Thou art the ruins of the noblest man
> That ever lived in the tide of times.
> Woe to the hand that shed this costly blood!
> Over thy wounds now do I prophesy
> (Which like dumb mouths do ope their
>   ruby lips
> To beg the voice and utterance of my
>   tongue)
> A curse shall light upon the limbs of men;
> Domestic fury and fierce civil strife
> Shall cumber all the parts of Italy;...
> That this foul deed shall smell above the
>   earth
> With carrion men, groaning for burial.

- An **aside** is a statement intended to be heard by the audience but not by certain other characters on the stage. In Act II, Scene ii, Trebonius, a conspirator, comments on the irony of Caesar's invitation to him:

> **CAESAR.** Remember that you call on me
>   today;
> Be near me, that I may remember you.
> **TREBONIUS.** Caesar, I will; [*Aside.*] and so
>   near will I be,
> That your best friends shall wish I had
>   been further.

Theme

Theme is a central idea in a literary work. Some works may have more than one theme, some themes being more dominant than others. Do not confuse theme with plot. Plot indicates the story; it is the answer to the question, "What happens?" The theme, on the other hand, is the answer to "What is the point?"

When many people think of *The Tragedy of Julius Caesar,* one of the first things that comes to mind is power and ambition. However, saying that "power and ambition" is a theme that runs through the play is not enough. What does the play tell us *about* the nature of power and ambition? What does the play show us about the *effect* of power and ambition on people?

Another important theme addressed in the play is that of loyalty and betrayal. The internal and external conflicts faced by the characters Brutus, Cassius, and

Mark Anthony offer the reader a chance to examine this theme. For instance, these characters struggle with several questions: Is it more important to be loyal to my friends or to be loyal to my country? Is it right to betray my friend if I feel my country will benefit? Is duty to my country a higher priority than personal gain? How important is Rome to me? Am I motivated to act as I do because I think it is in my best interest or in the best interest of Rome? Think about how each of these men responds to these questions and what ultimately happens to him in the play.

In addition to examining the dialogue to discover the characters' motivations and the outcomes of their actions, it is also important to look for motifs. A **motif** is a recurring element in one or more works of literature or art. Often, a motif can be a clue to identifying an important theme in the piece. For instance, throughout *The Tragedy of Julius Caesar,* omens and prophecies play an important role and suggest that fate and destiny are a part of Caesar's story. As you read, decide for yourself how important a role fate plays in determining events.

In dramas, the theme can only be conveyed through the dialogue. Therefore, pay attention to any recurring concepts that the characters discuss. The theme may not be all that obvious, however. You may find that asking yourself these questions, in addition to "What's the point?" could help you discover the theme:
- What is the message?
- What does the playwright want me to think about?
- What seems to motivate the characters?
- What causes situations to change or events to happen?

Stage Directions

Stage directions are the notes provided by the playwright to describe how the play should be presented or performed. They are usually printed in italics and may be enclosed in brackets or parentheses. Stage directions may describe these aspects of the drama:
- the setting, or when and where a scene takes place, as well as any related background information
- the action, or how the actors should move and behave, including when they should enter and exit the stage and how they should employ facial expressions, gestures, and tones of voice
- the special effects, such as the lighting, music, sound effects, costumes, properties (called *props*), and set design

In stage directions, the parts of the stage are often described using the terms *up, down, right, left,* and *center,* which designate stage areas from the point of view of the actors. (See the Parts of the Stage diagram below.)

Parts of the Stage

Up Right	Up Center	Up Left
Right Center	Center	Left Center
Down Right	Down Center	Down Left

READING DRAMA

The structure of a drama is different than that of a short story, essay, or poem. Therefore, to read a drama successfully, you'll need to try a variety of strategies and skills, such as the ones listed below.

- **Read Aloud** As dramas are meant to be performed, you may find that reading aloud can help you better understand their content and language. If you are reading Shakespeare aloud, you may more readily notice the rhyme schemes that appear not only in monologues but also in the dialogues between certain characters. For each play you read from this unit, try reading parts of it aloud with a partner.
- **Paraphrase** When you come across lines that are difficult to understand, try paraphrasing them, or restating them in your own words. To organize your paraphrases, draw a line down the center of a piece of paper. On one side of the paper, write the text as it appears in the play. On the other side, write your paraphrase.
- **Make Inferences** Because information in dramas is only revealed through dialogue and stage directions, you will constantly have to make inferences, or educated guesses, about what the playwright is revealing about characters and themes.

DRAMA READING MODEL

BEFORE READING DURING READING AFTER READING

BUILD BACKGROUND

- **Make predictions** about what the play will be about by reading the title and the **Build Background** feature.
- Read the **Meet the Author** feature to see if the information about the playwright gives you an idea about his or her usual style of writing.

ANALYZE LITERATURE

- The **Analyze Literature** feature will focus on one or more literary techniques or elements that are used in the selection. Dramas include many of the same literary elements as other genres, including characters, dialogue, setting, plot, and theme.

SET PURPOSE

- Use the purpose explained in the **Set Purpose** feature or preview the text to create a purpose of your own.

USE READING SKILLS

- Before reading, apply reading skills, such as analyzing text structure and previewing new vocabulary words. The **Use Reading Skills** feature will give you instructions on how to apply the skills while you read.

BEFORE READING **DURING READING** AFTER READING

USE READING STRATEGIES

- **Ask questions** about things that seem unusual or interesting or things you don't understand.
- **Make predictions** about what's going to happen next in the play. As you read, gather more clues that will either confirm or change your prediction.
- **Visualize** by forming pictures in your mind to help you see the set, actions, and characters described in the play.
- **Make inferences,** or educated guesses, about what is not stated directly. Connect what you read to your prior knowledge of the subject in order to make informed guesses.

- **Clarify,** or check that you understand, what you read. Go back and reread any confusing or difficult parts before continuing.

ANALYZE LITERATURE

- Look for **literary elements** that stand out as you read. Consider how literary elements are used in drama as opposed to fiction or poetry.

MAKE CONNECTIONS

- Notice where there are **connections** between the drama and your life or the world beyond the story.

BEFORE READING DURING READING **AFTER READING**

REFER TO TEXT

- **Remember details,** such as actions and characters' names. Also remember any information about sets, costumes, or tone given in the stage directions.
- Try to **summarize** the play in a paragraph.
- **Determine the sequence** of events, the order in which things happen in the play.

REASON WITH TEXT

- **Interpret** the events in the selection to help you clarify meaning. Why do characters act the way they do?
- **Analyze** the text by breaking down information into smaller pieces and figuring out how those pieces fit into the story as a whole.

- **Evaluate** the text. **Draw conclusions** by bringing together what you have read and using it to make a decision or form an opinion.

ANALYZE LITERATURE

- **Apply** what you understand about the characters, plot, or theme to help you understand parts of the play that are not clear. Review how the author's use of literary elements increased your understanding or enjoyment of the selection.

EXTEND THE TEXT

- **Extend** your reading beyond the selection by exploring ideas through writing or doing other creative projects.

A Marriage Proposal

A One-Act Play by Anton Chekhov

Translated by Theodore Hoffman

BEFORE READING

BUILD BACKGROUND

Social Context "A Marriage Proposal" was written in 1888 or 1889, early in Anton Chekhov's literary career. It is known as a *farce*, or a play about ridiculous situations intended to be humorous. In "A Marriage Proposal," the humor revolves around Ivan Lomov's intended marriage proposal to his neighbor's daughter. The play takes place in the Russian countryside at a time when many wealthy landowners hoped to increase their holdings through marriages that made sense economically. However, as you will see in the play, marriages intended only for economic success did not always result in perfect bliss.

Reader's Context Describe a time when your plans to do something did not turn out as you had expected.

ANALYZE LITERATURE: Dialogue and Stage Directions

In a play, **dialogue** refers to what the characters say aloud to one another. Sometimes, characters also speak to themselves or the audience. When a character makes a statement not intended to be heard by the other characters, it is called an *aside*. An aside is indicated in stage directions.

Stage directions are the notes included in a play, in addition to the dialogue, for the purpose of describing how something should be performed on stage. They indicate setting, lighting, music, sound effects, entrances and exits, properties, and the movement of characters. They are usually printed in italics and enclosed in brackets or parentheses.

SET PURPOSE

This play is supposed to be humorous. Consider how the humor is developed and what form it takes. Pay particular attention to the dialogue and stage directions and determine how they help contribute to the development of the play's humor.

MEET THE AUTHOR

Russian storyteller and dramatist **Anton Chekhov** (1860–1904) is famous for writing both tragedy and comedy. A fan of vaudeville and farces, Chekhov began writing short stories while he was in medical school. After graduating, he started writing one-act plays, like "A Marriage Proposal," that contain a comic look at life in Russia at the time. However, most of Chekhov's success and fame springs from his full-length tragic plays such as *Uncle Vanya*, *The Three Sisters*, and *The Cherry Orchard*.

USE READING SKILLS

Importance of Details In "A Marriage Proposal," Chekhov uses dialogue and stage directions to provide a variety of details about the setting and actions of the characters. Some of the details are *major*, or important to the way you understand the play. Other details are *minor*, or not very significant.

As you read the play, use a Details Chart like the one below to record the major and minor details included in the stage directions. Then summarize the main idea you think the playwright is trying to get across, based on the details that are given.

Major Details	Minor Details	Summary

PREVIEW VOCABULARY

Use the context clues in the sentences below to figure out the meanings of the underlined words from the selection.

1. Because he was so <u>affable,</u> Ben had many friends who enjoyed spending time with him.
2. It was difficult for the <u>hypochondriac</u> to hold a job, as he called in sick to work more often than was acceptable.
3. The teacher would not tolerate any <u>impudence</u> from her students.
4. The banker was charged with <u>embezzlement</u> and sentenced to serve time in jail.

A Marriage Proposal

A One-Act Play by **Anton Chekhov**

Translated by **Theodore Hoffman**

The Smoker. Paul Cezanne. Pushking Museum of Fine Art, Moscow, Russia.

Critical Viewing

Examine the body language of the man in this painting. What can you infer about his state of mind based on his body language and other details in the painting? Write a brief paragraph about his personality, citing specific details to support your description. Would you want this man to ask for your daughter's hand in marriage? Why or why not?

pomp • ous (päm´ pəs)
adj., self-important
af • fa • ble (a´ fə bəl)
adj., being pleasant and at ease in talking with others
hy • po • chon • dri • ac (hī' pə kän´ drē ak') *n.,* person who suffers from *hypochondria,* or depression stemming from imagined illness

Characters

STEPAN STEPANOVITCH CHUBUKOV (ste pän´ ste pä´ nô vich chü bü´ kôf), a landowner, elderly, <u>pompous</u> but <u>affable</u>.

IVAN VASSILEVITCH LOMOV (i vän´ vä sil´ ē yich lô´ môv), healthy, but a <u>hypochondriac</u>; nervous, suspicious. Also a landowner.

NATALIA STEPANOVNA (nä täl´ yə ste pä nôv´ və), Chubukov's daughter; twenty-five but still unmarried.

Chubukov's mansion—the living room

LOMOV *enters, formally dressed in evening jacket, white gloves, top hat. He is nervous from the start.*

CHUBUKOV. [*Rising.*] Well, look who's here! Ivan Vassilevitch! [*Shakes his hand warmly.*] What a surprise, old man! How are you?

LOMOV. Oh, not too bad. And you?

CHUBUKOV. Oh, we manage, we manage. Do sit down, please. You know, you've been neglecting your neighbors, my dear fellow. It's been ages. Say, why the formal dress? Tails, gloves, and so forth. Where's the funeral, my boy? Where are you headed?

LOMOV. Oh, nowhere. I mean, here; just to see you, my dear Stepan Stepanovitch.

10 **CHUBUKOV.** Then why the full dress, old boy? It's not New Year's, and so forth.

LOMOV. Well, you see, it's like this. I have come here, my dear Stepan Stepanovitch, to bother you with a request. More than once, or twice, or more than that, it has been my privilege to apply to you for assistance in

15 things, and you've always, well, responded. I mean, well, you have. Yes. Excuse me, I'm getting all mixed up. May I have a glass of water, my dear Stepan Stepanovitch? [*Drinks.*]

CHUBUKOV. [*Aside.*] Wants to borrow some money. Not a chance! [*Aloud.*] What can I do for you my dear friend?

20 **LOMOV.** Well, you see, my dear Stepanitch…Excuse me, I mean Stepan my Dearovitch…No, I mean, I get all confused, as you can see. To make a long story short, you're the only one who can help me. Of course, I don't deserve it, and there's no reason why I should expect you to, and all

25 that.

CHUBUKOV. Stop beating around the bush! Out with it!

LOMOV. In just a minute. I mean, now, right now. The truth is, I have come to ask the hand…I mean, your daughter, Natalia Stepanovna, I, I want to marry her!

30 **CHUBUKOV.** [*Overjoyed.*] Great heavens! Ivan Vassilevitch! Say it again!

LOMOV. I have come humbly to ask for the hand…

DURING READING

USE READING SKILLS

Importance of Details Describe the relationship between Lomov and Chubukov. Which details contribute to your understanding of this relationship?

CHUBUKOV. [*Interrupting.*] You're a prince! I'm overwhelmed, delighted, and so forth. Yes, indeed, and all that! [*Hugs and kisses* LOMOV.] This is just what I've been hoping for. It's my fondest dream come true. [*Sheds a tear.*] And,
35 you know, I've always looked upon you, my boy, as if you were my own son. May God grant to both of you His Mercy and His Love, and so forth. Oh, I have been wishing for this…But why am I being so idiotic? It's just that I'm off my rocker with joy, my boy! Completely off my rocker! Oh, with all my soul I'm…I'll go get Natalia, and so forth.

40 LOMOV. [*Deeply moved.*] Dear Stepan Stepanovitch, do you think she'll agree?

CHUBUKOV. Why, of course, old friend. Great heavens! As if she wouldn't! Why she's crazy for you! Good God! Like a love-sick cat, and so forth. Be right back. [*Leaves.*]

45 LOMOV. It's cold. I'm gooseflesh all over, as if I had to take a test. But the main thing is, to make up my mind, and keep it that way. I mean, if I take time out to think, or if I hesitate, or talk about it, or have ideals, or wait for real love, well, I'll just never get married! Brrrr, it's cold! Natalia Stepanovna is an excellent housekeeper. She's not too bad looking. She's
50 had a good education. What more could I ask? Nothing. I'm so nervous, my ears are buzzing. [*Drinks.*] Besides, I've just got to get married. I'm thirty-five already. It's sort of a critical age. I've got to settle down and lead a regular life. I mean, I'm always getting palpitations, and I'm nervous, and I get upset so easy. Look, my lips are quivering, and my eyebrow's twitching. The worst thing is the night. Sleeping. I get into bed, doze off, and, suddenly, something inside me jumps. First my head snaps, and then my shoulder blade, and I roll out of bed like a lunatic and try to walk it off. Then I try to go back to sleep, but, as soon as I do, something jumps again! Twenty times a night, sometimes…

[NATALIA STEPANOVNA *enters.*]

NATALIA. Oh, it's only you. All Papa said was: "Go inside, there's a merchant come to collect his goods." How do you do, Ivan Vassilevitch?

LOMOV. How do you do, dear Natalia Stepanovna?

65 NATALIA. Excuse my apron, and not being dressed. We're shelling peas. You haven't been around lately. Oh, do sit down. [*They do.*] Would you like some lunch?

LOMOV. No thanks, I had some.

pal • pi • ta • tion
(paľ pə tā´ shən) *n.,*
throbbing or rapid beating
of the heart

DURING READING

ANALYZE LITERATURE

Dialogue What do you learn about Lomov's character from Lomov's spoken thoughts in lines 45–60?

Natalia. Well, then smoke if you want. [*He doesn't.*] The weather's nice
70 today…but yesterday, it was so wet the workmen couldn't get a thing done.
Have you got much hay in? I felt so greedy I had a whole field done, but
now I'm not sure I was right. With the rain it could rot, couldn't it? I should
have waited. But why are you so dressed up? Is there a dance or something?
Of course, I must say you look splendid, but… Well, tell me, why are you
75 so dressed up?

Lomov. [*Excited.*] Well, you see, my dear Natalia Stepanovna, the truth is,
I made up my mind to ask you to…well, to, listen to me. Of course, it'll
probably surprise you and even maybe make you angry, but… [*Aside.*] It's
so cold in here!

80 **Natalia.** Why, what do you mean? [*A pause.*] Well?

Lomov. I'll try to get it over with. 1 mean, you know, my dear Natalia
Stepanovna that I've known, since childhood, even, known, and had the
privilege of knowing, your family. My late aunt, and her husband, who, as
you know, left me my estate, they always had the greatest respect for your
85 father, and your late mother. The Lomovs and the Chubukovs have always
been very friendly, you might even say affectionate. And, of course, you
know, our land borders on each other's. My Oxen Meadows touch your
birch grove…

Natalia. I hate to interrupt you, my dear Ivan Vassilevitch,
90 but you said: "my Oxen Meadows." Do you really think
they're yours?

Lomov. Why of course they're mine.

Natalia. What do you mean? The Oxen Meadows are ours, not yours!

Lomov. Oh, no, my dear Natalia Stepanovna, they're mine.

95 **Natalia.** Well, this is the first I've heard about it! Where did you get that
idea?

Lomov. Where? Why, I mean the Oxen Meadows that are wedged between
your birches and the marsh.

Natalia. Yes, of course, they're ours.

100 **Lomov.** Oh, no, you're wrong, my dear Natalia Stepanovna, they're mine.

Natalia. Now, come, Ivan Vassilevitch! How long have they been yours?

Lomov. How long! Why, as long as I can remember!

Natalia. Well, really, you can't expect me to believe that!

> **DURING READING**
>
> **ANALYZE LITERATURE**
>
> **Dialogue** What is your opinion of
> Natalia, based on her conversation
> with Lomov to this point?

Lomov. But, you can see for yourself in the deed, my dear
105 Natalia Stepanovna. Of course, there was once a dispute about them, but everyone knows they're mine now. There's nothing to argue about. There was a time when my aunt's grandmother let your father's grandfather's peasants use the land, but they were supposed to bake bricks for her in return.
110 Naturally, after a few years they began to act as if they owned it, but the real truth is…

Natalia. That has nothing to do with the case! Both my grandfather and my great-grandfather said that their land went as far as the marsh, which means that the Meadows are
115 ours! There's nothing whatever to argue about. It's foolish.

Lomov. But I can show you the deed, Natalia Stepanovna.

Natalia. You're just making fun of me… Great Heavens! Here we have the land for hundreds of years, and suddenly you try to tell us it isn't ours. What's wrong with you, Ivan
120 Vassilevitch? Those meadows aren't even fifteen acres, and they're not worth three hundred rubles,[1] but I just can't stand unfairness! I just can't stand unfairness!

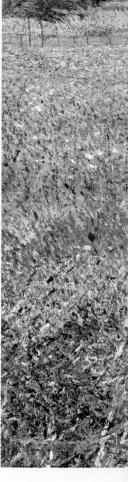

Lomov. But, you must listen to me. Your father's grandfather's peasants, as I've already tried to tell you, they were supposed to bake bricks for my aunt's grandmother. And my aunt's grandmother, why, she wanted to be nice to them…

Natalia. It's just nonsense, this whole business about aunts and grandfathers and grandmothers. The Meadows are ours! That's all there is to it!

130 **Lomov.** They're mine!

Natalia. Ours! You can go on talking for two days and you can put on fifteen evening coats and twenty pairs of gloves, but I tell you they're ours, ours, ours!

Lomov. Natalia Stepanovna, I don't want the Meadows! I'm just acting on
135 principle. If you want, I'll give them to you.

Natalia. I'll give them to *you!* Because they're ours! And that's all there is to it! And if I may say so, your behavior, my dear Ivan Vassilevitch, is very strange. Until now, we've always considered you a good neighbor, even a friend. After all, last year we lent you our threshing machine,[2] even though it meant putting

---

1. **rubles.** Russian currency
2. **threshing machine.** Machine used to separate grain from its stalks and husks

Roman Countryside. Umberto Boccioni. Oil on canvas. Museo Civico di Belle Arti, Lugano, Switzerland.

140 off our own threshing until November. And here you are treating us like a
pack of gypsies. Giving me my own land, indeed! Really! Why that's not being
a good neighbor. It's sheer <u>impudence</u>, that's what it is…

LOMOV. Oh, so you think I'm just a landgrabber? My dear lady, I've never
grabbed anybody's land in my whole life, and no one's going to accuse
145 me of doing it now! [*Quickly walks over to the pitcher and drinks some more
water.*] The Oxen Meadows are mine!

NATALIA. That's a lie. They're ours!

LOMOV. Mine!

NATALIA. A lie! I'll prove it. I'll send my mowers out there today!

150 **LOMOV.** What?

im • pu • dence
(im´ pyə dən[t]s) *n.,*
quality or state of being
impudent, or showing a
lack of respect or regard
for others

NATALIA. My mowers will mow it today!

LOMOV. I'll kick them out!

NATALIA. You just dare!

DURING READING

USE READING SKILLS

Importance of Details List details given about Lomov that are significant to your understanding of his character.

LOMOV. [*Clutching his heart.*] The Oxen Meadows are mine! Do you understand? Mine!

NATALIA. Please don't shout! You can shout all you want in your own house, but here I must ask you to control yourself.

LOMOV. If my heart wasn't palpitating the way it is, if my insides weren't jumping like mad, I wouldn't talk to you so calmly. [*Yelling.*] The
160 Oxen Meadows are mine!

NATALIA. Ours!

LOMOV. Mine!

NATALIA. Ours!

LOMOV. Mine!

165 [*Enter* CHUBUKOV.]

CHUBUKOV. What's going on? Why all the shouting?

NATALIA. Papa, will you please inform this gentleman who owns the Oxen Meadows, he or we?

CHUBUKOV. [*To* LOMOV.] Why, they're ours, old fellow.

170 **LOMOV.** But how can they be yours, my dear Stepan Stepanovitch? Be fair. Perhaps my aunt's grandmother did let your grandfather's peasants work the land, and maybe they did get so used to it that they acted as if it was their own, but…

CHUBUKOV. Oh, no, no…my dear boy. You forget something. The reason
175 the peasants didn't pay your aunt's grandmother, and so forth, was that the land was <u>disputed</u>, even then. Since then it's been settled. Why, everyone knows it's ours.

dis • put • ed
(di spyüt´ əd) *adj.,*
subject to disagreement
or debate

LOMOV. I can prove it's mine.

CHUBUKOV. You can't prove a thing, old boy.

180 **LOMOV.** Yes, I can!

CHUBUKOV. My dear lad, why yell like that? Yelling doesn't prove a thing. Look, I'm not after anything of yours, just as I don't intend to give up

anything of mine. Why should I? Besides, if you're going to keep arguing about it, I'd just as soon give the land to the peasants, so there!

185 **Lomov.** There nothing! Where do you get the right to give away someone else's property?

Chubukov. I certainly ought to know if I have the right or not. And you had better realize it, because, my dear young man, I am not used to being spoken to in that tone of voice, and so forth. Besides which, my dear young
190 man, I am twice as old as you are, and I ask you to speak to me without getting yourself into such a tizzy, and so forth!

Lomov. Do you think I'm a fool? First you call my property yours, and then you expect me to keep calm and polite! Good neighbors don't act like that, my dear Stepan
195 Stepanovitch. You're no neighbor, you're a landgrabber!

DURING READING

USE READING STRATEGIES

Predict Predict who you think will win the argument. Why?

Chubukov. What was that? What did you say?

Natalia. Papa, send the mowers out to the meadows at once!

Chubukov. What did you say, sir?

Natalia. The Oxen Meadows are ours, and we'll never give them up, never,
200 never, never, never!

Lomov. We'll see about that. I'll go to court. I'll show you!

Chubukov. Go to court? Well, go to court, and so forth! I know you, just waiting for a chance to go to court, and so forth. You pettifogging[3] cheater, you! All of your family is like that. The whole bunch of them!

205 **Lomov.** You leave my family out of this! The Lomovs have always been honorable, upstanding people, and not a one of them was ever tried for <u>embezzlement</u>, like your grandfather was.

em • bez • zle • ment
(im be´ zəl mənt) *n.*, stealing money or property entrusted to one's care

Chubukov. The Lomovs are a pack of lunatics, the whole bunch of them!

Natalia. The whole bunch!

210 **Chubukov.** Your grandfather was a drunkard, and what about your other aunt, the one who ran away with the architect? And so forth.

Natalia. And so forth!

Lomov. Your mother limped! [*Clutches at his heart.*] Oh, I've got a stitch in my side…My head's whirling…Help! Water!

---

3. **pettifogging.** Derived from *pettifogger,* or a reference to a lawyer who is dishonest or disreputable

Interior with a Woman in Yellow in Front of a Window. Edouard Vuillard. Private collection. Bridgeman Art Library.

ma • li • cious
(mə li´ shəs) *adj.*, desiring to cause pain, injury, or distress to another; being mean and spiteful

Chubukov. Your father was a gambler.

Natalia. And your aunt was queen of the scandalmongers![4]

Lomov. My left foot's paralyzed. You're a plotter…Oh, my heart. It's an open secret that in the last elections you brib…I'm seeing stars! Where's my hat?

Natalia. It's a low-mean, spiteful…

Chubukov. And you're a two-faced, <u>malicious</u> schemer!

Lomov. Here's my hat…Oh, my heart…Where's the door? How do I get out of here?…Oh, I think I'm going to die…My foot's numb. [*Goes.*]

Chubukov. [*Following him.*] And don't you ever set foot in my house again!

Natalia. Go to court, indeed! We'll see about that!

235 [Lomov *staggers out.*]

Chubukov. The devil with him! [*Gets a drink, walks back and forth excited.*]

Natalia. What a rascal! How can you trust your neighbors after an incident like that?

Chubukov. The villain! The scarecrow!

240 **Natalia.** He's a monster! First he tries to steal our land, and then he has the nerve to yell at you.

Chubukov. Yes, and that turnip, that stupid rooster, has the gall[5] to make a proposal. Some proposal!

Natalia. What proposal?

245 **Chubukov.** Why, he came to propose to you.

Natalia. To propose? To me? Why didn't you tell me before?

---

4. **scandalmongers.** People who circulate gossip meant to hurt or defame other people's characters
5. **gall.** Boldness coupled with arrogance

CHUBUKOV. So he gets all dressed up in his formal clothes. That stuffed sausage, that dried up cabbage!

NATALIA. To propose to me? Ohhhh! [*Falls into a chair and*
250 *starts wailing.*] Bring him back! Back! Go get him! Bring him back! Ohhhh!

DURING READING

ANALYZE LITERATURE

Stage Directions What do the stage directions tell you about Natalia's personality and behavior?

CHUBUKOV. Bring who back?

NATALIA. Hurry up, hurry up! I'm sick. Get him! [*Complete hysterics.*]

CHUBUKOV. What for? [*To her.*] What's the matter with you? [*Clutches his*
255 *head.*] Oh, what a fool I am! I'll shoot myself! I'll hang myself! I ruined her chances!

NATALIA. I'm dying. Get him!

CHUBUKOV. All right, all right, right away! Only don't yell!

[*He runs out.*]

260 **NATALIA.** What are they doing to me? Get him! Bring him back! Bring him back!

[*A pause.* CHUBUKOV *runs in.*]

CHUBUKOV. He's coming, and so forth, the snake. Oof! You talk to him. I'm not in the mood.

265 **NATALIA.** [*Wailing.*] Bring him back! Bring him back!

CHUBUKOV. [*Yelling.*] I told you, he's coming! What agony to be the father of a grown-up daughter. I'll cut my throat some day, I swear I will. [*To her.*] We cursed him, we insulted him, abused him, kicked him out, and now… because you, you…

270 **NATALIA.** Me? It was all your fault!

CHUBUKOV. My fault? What do you mean my fau…? [LOMOV *appears in the doorway.*] Talk to him yourself! [*Goes out.* LOMOV *enters, exhausted.*]

LOMOV. What palpitations! My heart! And my foot's absolutely asleep. Something keeps giving me a stitch in the side…

275 **NATALIA.** You must forgive us, Ivan Vassilevitch. We all got too excited. I remember now. The Oxen Meadows are yours.

LOMOV. My heart's beating something awful. My Meadows. My eyebrows, they're both twitching!

NATALIA. Yes, the Meadows are all yours, yes, yours. Do sit down. [*They sit.*] We were wrong, of course.

DURING READING

USE READING STRATEGIES

Make Inferences Infer why Natalia suddenly changes the way she treats Lomov.

LOMOV. I argued on principle. My land isn't worth so much to me, but the principle…

NATALIA. Oh, yes, of course, the principle, that's what counts. But let's change the subject.

285 **LOMOV.** Besides, I have evidence. You see, my aunt's grandmother let your father's grandfather's peasants use the land…

NATALIA. Yes, yes, yes, but forget all that. [*Aside.*] I wish I knew how to get him going. [*Aloud.*] Are you going to start hunting soon?

LOMOV. After the harvest I'll try for grouse. But oh, my dear Natalia
290 Stepanovna, have you heard about the bad luck I've had? You know my dog, Guess? He's gone lame.

NATALIA. What a pity. Why?

LOMOV. I don't know. He must have twisted his leg, or got in a fight, or something. [*Sighs.*] My best dog, to say nothing of the cost. I paid Mironov
295 125 rubles for him.

DURING READING

USE READING SKILLS

Importance of Details Do you think the details about the dogs are major or minor? Why?

NATALIA. That was too high, Ivan Vassilevitch.

LOMOV. I think it was quite cheap. He's a first class dog.

NATALIA. Why Papa only paid 85 rubles for Squeezer, and he's much better than Guess.

300 **LOMOV.** Squeezer better than Guess! What an idea! [*Laughs.*] Squeezer better than Guess!

NATALIA. Of course he's better. He may still be too young but on points and pedigree,[6] he's a better dog even than any Volchanetsky owns.

LOMOV. Excuse me, Natalia Stepanovna, but you're forgetting he's overshot,[7]
305 and overshot dogs are bad hunters.

NATALIA. Oh, so he's overshot, is he? Well, this is the first time I've heard about it.

LOMOV. Believe me, his lower jaw is shorter than his upper.

NATALIA. You've measured them?

---

6. **pedigree.** Recorded purity of a breed
7. **overshot.** Having the upper jaw extending beyond the lower jaw. An overshot dog is not considered to be good for breeding and may have problems chewing.

310 **LOMOV.** Yes. He's all right for pointing, but if you want him to retrieve…

NATALIA. In the first place, our Squeezer is a thoroughbred, the son
315 of Harness and Chisel, while your mutt doesn't even have a pedigree. He's as old and worn out as a peddler's horse.

LOMOV. He may be old, but I
320 wouldn't take five Squeezers for him. How can you argue? Guess is a dog, Squeezer's a laugh. Anyone you can name has a dog like Squeezer hanging around
325 somewhere. They're under every bush. If he only cost twenty-five rubles you got cheated.

Duck Rising. Eugene Petit.

NATALIA. The devil is in you today, Ivan Vassilevitch! You want to contradict everything. First you pretend the
330 Oxen Meadows are yours, and now you say Guess is better than Squeezer. People should say what they really mean, and you know Squeezer is a hundred times better than Guess. Why say he isn't?

LOMOV. So, you think I'm a fool or a blind man, Natalia Stepanovna! Once and for all, Squeezer is overshot!

335 **NATALIA.** He is not!

LOMOV. He is so!

NATALIA. He is not!

LOMOV. Why shout, my dear lady?

NATALIA. Why talk such nonsense? It's terrible. Your Guess is old enough to
340 be buried, and you compare him with Squeezer!

LOMOV. I'm sorry, I can't go on. My heart…it's palpitating!

NATALIA. I've always noticed that the hunters who argue most don't know a thing.

LOMOV. Please! Be quiet a moment. My heart's falling apart… [*Shouts.*] Shut
345 up!

DURING READING

USE READING STRATEGIES

Clarify Why are the three characters arguing? Is the argument really about the dogs, or is there something else going on?

NATALIA. I'm not going to shut up until you admit that Squeezer's a hundred times better than Guess.

LOMOV. A hundred times worse! His head…My eyes…shoulder…

NATALIA. Guess is half-dead already!

350 **LOMOV.** [*Weeping.*] Shut up! My heart's exploding!

NATALIA. I won't shut up!

[CHUBUKOV *comes in.*]

CHUBUKOV. What's the trouble now?

NATALIA. Papa, will you please tell us which is the better dog, his Guess or
355 our Squeezer?

LOMOV. Stepan Stepanovitch, I implore you to tell me just one thing: Is your Squeezer overshot or not? Yes or no?

CHUBUKOV. Well what if he is? He's still the best dog in the neighborhood, and so forth.

DURING READING

USE READING STRATEGIES

Ask Questions Write down any questions you have about what the characters are doing and why.

LOMOV. Oh, but isn't my dog, Guess, better? Really?

CHUBUKOV. Don't get yourself so fraught up, old man. Of course, your dog has his good points—thoroughbred, firm on his feet, well sprung ribs, and so forth. But, my dear fellow, you've got to admit he has two defects; he's old and he's short in the muzzle.

365 **LOMOV.** Short in the muzzle? Oh, my heart! Let's look at the facts! On the Marunsinsky hunt my dog ran neck and neck with the Count's, while Squeezer was a mile behind them…

CHUBUKOV. That's because the Count's groom hit him with a whip.

LOMOV. And he was right, too! We were fox hunting; what was your dog
370 chasing sheep for?

CHUBUKOV. That's a lie! Look, I'm going to lose my temper…[*Controlling himself.*] my dear friend, so let's stop arguing, for that reason alone. You're only arguing because we're all jealous of somebody else's dog. Who can help it? As soon as you realize some dog is better than yours, in this case
375 our dog, you start in with this and that, and the next thing you know— pure jealousy! I remember the whole business.

LOMOV. I remember too!

CHUBUKOV. [*Mimicking.*] "I remember too!" What do you remember?

Lomov. My heart…my foot's asleep…I can't…

380 **Natalia.** [*Mimicking.*] "My heart…my foot's asleep." What kind of a hunter are you? You should be hunting cockroaches in the kitchen, not foxes. "My heart!"

Chubukov. Yes, what kind of a hunter are you anyway? You should be sitting at home with your palpitations, not tracking down animals. You

385 don't hunt anyhow. You just go out to argue with people and interfere with their dogs, and so forth. For God's sake, let's change the subject before I lose my temper. Anyway, you're just not a hunter.

Lomov. But you, you're a hunter? Ha! You only go hunting to get in good with the count, and to plot, and intrigue, and scheme…Oh, my heart!

390 You're a schemer, that's what!

Chubukov. What's that? Me a schemer? [*Shouting.*] Shut up!

Lomov. A schemer!

Chubukov. You infant! You puppy!

Lomov. You old rat!

395 **Chubukov.** You shut up, or I'll shoot you down like a partridge! You idiot!

Lomov. Everyone knows that—oh, my heart—that your wife used to beat you…Oh, my feet…my head…I'm seeing stars…I'm going to faint! [*He drops into an armchair.*] Quick, a doctor! [*Faints.*]

Chubukov. [*Going on, oblivious.*] Baby! Weakling! Idiot! I'm getting sick.

400 [*Drinks water.*] Me! I'm sick!

Natalia. What kind of a hunter are you? You can't even sit on a horse! [*To her father.*] Papa, what's the matter with him? Look, papa! [*Screaming.*] Ivan Vassilevitch! He's dead.

Chubukov. I'm choking, I can't breathe…Give me air.

405 **Natalia.** He's dead! [*Pulling* Lomov's *sleeve.*] Ivan Vassilevitch! Ivan Vassilevitch! What have you done to me? He's dead! [*She falls into an armchair. Screaming hysterically.*] A doctor! A doctor! A doctor!

Chubukov. Ohhhh…What's the matter? What happened?

410 **Natalia.** [*Wailing.*] He's dead! He's dead!

Chubukov. Who's dead? [*Looks at* Lomov.] My God, he is! Quick! Water! A doctor! [*Puts glass to* Lomov's *lips.*] Here, drink this! Can't drink it—he must

DURING READING

ANALYZE LITERATURE

Dialogue What information does the dialogue between Natalia and her father when they think Lomov is dead give you about their characters?

415 be dead, and so forth…Oh what a miserable life! Why don't I shoot myself! I should have cut my throat long ago! What am I waiting for? Give me a knife! Give me a pistol! [LOMOV *stirs.*] Look, he's coming to. Here, drink some water. That's it.

LOMOV. I'm seeing stars…misty…Where am I?

CHUBUKOV. Just you hurry up and get married, and then the devil with you! She accepts. [*Puts* LOMOV's *hand in* NATALIA's.] She accepts and so forth! I
420 give you my blessing, and so forth! Only leave me in peace!

LOMOV. [*Getting up.*] Huh? What? Who?

CHUBUKOV. She accepts! Well? Kiss her!

NATALIA. He's alive! Yes, yes, I accept.

CHUBUKOV. Kiss each other!

425 **LOMOV.** Huh? Kiss? Kiss who? [*They kiss.*] That's nice. I mean, excuse me, what happened? Oh, now I get it…my heart…those stars…I'm very happy, Natalia Stepanovna. [*Kisses her hand.*] My foot's asleep.

NATALIA. I…I'm happy too.

CHUBUKOV. What a load off my shoulders! Whew!

430 **NATALIA.** Well, now maybe you'll admit that Squeezer is better than Guess?

LOMOV. Worse!

NATALIA. Better!

CHUBUKOV. What a way to enter matrimonial bliss! Let's have some champagne!

LOMOV. He's worse!

NATALIA. Better! Better, better, better, better!

CHUBUKOV. [*Trying to shout her down.*] Champagne! Bring some champagne! Champagne! Champagne!

CURTAIN ❖

DURING READING

USE READING STRATEGIES

Make Inferences Why does Chubukov seem to be so pushy about getting Natalia and Lomov engaged at the end of the play?

MIRRORS & WINDOWS

What do you think makes for a good marriage? How has the thinking about what makes a good marriage changed over time? Will Lomov and Natalia have a good marriage? Explain your answer.

AFTER READING

REFER TO TEXT ▶ ▶ ▶ ▶	▶ REASON WITH TEXT	
1a. Recall what Lomov is planning to do when he visits Chubukov's house.	1b. Conclude whether Lomov's plans will change, given what happens during his visit and the way the play ends.	**Understand** **Find meaning**
2a. List the opposing viewpoints of the two arguments.	2b. Apply what you know about the way people behave in this play to explain why they are arguing.	**Apply** **Use information**
3a. How does the first argument end?	3b. What does Natalia's behavior during the arguments tell you about her character?	**Analyze** **Take things apart**
4a. Identify ways Chekhov uses humor in this play.	4b. How does Chekhov's use of humor contribute to the message of the play?	**Evaluate** **Make judgments**
5a. Summarize the conclusion of the play. Do you think Natalia and Lomov are headed into "matrimonial bliss"?	5b. Write a brief epilogue, or conclusion, to the play that describes Natalia and Lomov's lives after ten years of marriage.	**Create** **Bring ideas together**

ANALYZE LITERATURE: Dialogue and Stage Directions

Review the stage directions throughout the play and indicate which ones seem the most important for the performance of the play. How do the stage directions, together with the dialogue, enhance your perceptions of the characters?

EXTEND THE TEXT

Writing Options

Creative Writing For an online dating service, write a one-paragraph **profile** of Lomov written from Lomov's point of view. In the profile, Lomov should express how he views himself as a potential husband and list the qualities he is looking for in a wife.

Expository Writing For a drama anthology, write a two-paragraph **critical introduction** to this play that focuses on the playwright's statement about society. Consider the following questions: If the play were to have deeper significance than just a comedy, what might Chekhov be trying to say about the way people behave toward each other? What message might a modern audience take away from a performance of this play?

Media Literacy

Create a Television Commercial Go online to find information about different methods of conflict resolution. Then, create the script for a television commercial about solving problems peacefully. In addition to dialogue, include in your script a description of the background music and setting. Finally, either act out your script for your class, or, if you have the equipment, record your commercial.

Lifelong Learning

Research a Russian Writer Fyodor Dostoevsky, Ivan Turgenev, and Leo Tolstoy were all, like Chekhov, nineteenth-century Russian writers. Research one of these authors and read a short story by him. As you read the story, note characteristics of the writer's style, themes, and characters. In an informative speech, present your findings to the class.

 Go to **www.mirrorsandwindows.com** for more.

Understanding Shakespeare

SHAKESPEARE AND HIS WORKS

William Shakespeare (1564–1616) is widely

considered the greatest dramatist the world has known. Today, nearly four hundred years after his death, his plays are still performed for audiences all over the world. As fellow poet Ben Jonson famously put it, Shakespeare's art is "not of an age, but for all time."

[handwritten: he only wrote sonnets & plays]

Little is known about Shakespeare's early life. His mother, Mary Arden Shakespeare, was from a well-to-do, well-connected family. His father, John Shakespeare, was a prosperous glove maker and local politician. William's exact birth date is unknown, but he was baptized in his hometown of Stratford-upon-Avon on April 26, 1564, and tradition has assigned him a birth date of April 23, which was also the date of his death fifty-two years later.

[handwritten: all his plays only had five acts]

Shakespeare attended the Stratford grammar school, where he probably studied classical literature in Latin and Greek, as was typical for students of that era. He did not go on to a university. At the age of eighteen, he married Anne Hathaway, eight years his senior. The couple's first child, a daughter whom they named Susanna, was born shortly thereafter. In 1585, the couple had twins, Hamnet and Judith. There is no record of what Shakespeare did in the years directly after the twins were born. He may have worked for a while as a schoolteacher, as there are many references to teaching in his plays. However, it is clear that by 1592, he had moved to London, leaving his family behind while he pursued a life in the theater. Shakespeare continued to provide for his family and to expand his holdings in Stratford while living in London.

[handwritten: did most of his writing in 1580]

Once in London, Shakespeare soon made himself known as a successful actor and playwright. His history plays *Henry the Sixth,* Parts 1, 2, and 3, and *The Tragedy of Richard the Third* established him as a significant force in London theater. In 1593, all London theaters were forced to close because of an outbreak of the plague. During their shutdown, Shakespeare turned to narrative poetry, producing *Venus and Adonis* and *The Rape of Lucrece,* both dedicated to a wealthy patron, the Earl of Southampton.

When the theaters reopened the following year, Shakespeare became a partner in a theater company known as the Lord Chamberlain's Men. The group soon became the most popular acting troupe in London and performed regularly at the court of Queen Elizabeth I. In 1599, the troupe was wealthy enough to build its own theater, which was called the Globe. When Queen Elizabeth died in 1603, Shakespeare's company found a new patron in her successor, King James I, and the name of the company was changed to the King's Men.

Although Shakespeare continued to act in the troupe, writing the material soon became his primary vocation. In the span of twenty years, he penned at least thirty-seven plays, including comedies such as *All's Well That Ends Well, The Merchant of Venice, A Midsummer Night's Dream, The Taming of the Shrew,* and *Twelfth Night, or What You Will;* tragedies such as *Hamlet, Julius Caesar, King Lear, Macbeth, Othello, and Romeo and Juliet;* romances such as *The Tempest* and *The Winter's Tale;* and histories such as *The Life of Henry the Fifth.*

[handwritten: everyone went to his plays]

Shakespeare's birthplace.

[handwritten: groundlings- ppl who stood on the ground; didn't get seats]

The last play Shakespeare wrote on his own was *The Famous History of the Life of King Henry the Eighth,* which was performed in London in 1613. Later that year, he collaborated with John Fletcher on the romance *The Two Noble Kinsmen.* At that time, Shakespeare was probably living again in Stratford, in a large house called New Place that he had bought in 1597. When he died at age fifty-two, survived by his wife and his two daughters, Shakespeare was a wealthy man. He was buried in Holy Trinity Church in Stratford-upon-Avon. Carved in stone above his grave are the following lines, believed to have been written by Shakespeare himself:

> Good frend for Jesus sake forbeare,
>
> To digg the dust enclosed heare:
>
> Blest be ye man yt spares thes stones,
>
> And curst be he yt moves my bones.

RENAISSANCE DRAMA

The Renaissance in England

The word *renaissance* means "rebirth." Historians use the name **Renaissance** to refer to the period between the fifteenth and early seventeenth centuries, when Europe was influenced by a rebirth of interest in Greek and Latin learning and experienced a flowering of literature and the arts.

In England, the Renaissance did not truly begin until 1558, when Queen Elizabeth I ascended to the throne. Elizabeth was a great patron of the arts, and during her reign, from 1558 to 1603—a period known as the **Elizabethan Age**—English literature reached what many people consider its zenith. Shakespeare wrote and produced his plays at the height of the Elizabethan period and throughout much of the **Jacobean period,** from 1603 to 1625, when James I ruled England.

Shakespeare's writing is a good example of the spirit of the Renaissance: His plays often focus on memorable and complex characters from the noble class; his plots often derive from classical sources; and his themes often involve challenges to authority. Since Shakespeare probably studied Greek and Latin in school, he may have read many of the classical works of Rome in their original Latin. He was inspired by classical works and by the history of Rome to write *The Tragedy of Julius Caesar.*

Queen Elizabeth I.

Types of Renaissance Drama

The two most common types of drama during the English Renaissance (sixteenth and seventeenth centuries) were comedies and tragedies. The key difference between the two is that comedies have happy endings and tragedies have unhappy ones. (It is sometimes said that comedies end with wedding bells and tragedies with funeral bells.)

A **comedy** is typically lighthearted, though it may touch on serious themes. Action in a comedy usually progresses from initial order, to humorous misunderstanding or confusion, and back to order again. Stock elements of comedy include mistaken identities, puns and wordplay, and coarse or exaggerated characters. Shakespeare's comedies frequently end with one or more marriages.

A **tragedy** tells the story of the downfall of a person of high status. Often, it celebrates the courage and dignity of its hero in the face of inevitable doom. The hero is typically neither completely good nor completely evil but lives and acts between these extremes. The hero's fall may be brought about by some flaw in his or her character, known as a **tragic flaw.** In Macbeth, that flaw is ambition; in Hamlet, indecisiveness. As you read *The Tragedy of Julius Caesar,* decide who the tragic hero is, and what tragic flaw, if any, the hero possesses.

Other kinds of plays produced during the English Renaissance included histories (plays about events from the past) and romances (plays that contain

highly fantastic elements, such as fairies and magic spells). Also popular were short plays called interludes, as well as elaborate entertainments, called masques, that feature acting, music, and dance. *The Tragedy of Julius Caesar,* while typically classified as a tragedy, can also be considered a history, as it is based on real events from Roman history.

Organization of Renaissance Drama

Shakespeare's plays, like those of other playwrights in his time, are divided into five acts, with various scenes marked by the entrance and exit of characters. The following Plot Diagram and explanation outline the way the action of a Renaissance drama typically unfolds.

Plot Diagram

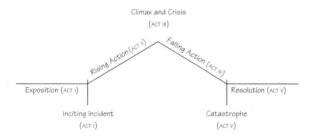

Act I: Exposition and Inciting Incident

The setting and main characters are presented. The *inciting incident* (the event that sets in motion the play's central conflict, or struggle) is introduced.

Act II: Rising Action or Complication

The central conflict is developed further, and suspense builds.

Act III: Climax and Crisis

The suspense peaks in the climax, and something decisive happens to determine the future course of events. The decisive event is called the *crisis;* sometimes, it is the same event as the climax, but not always.

Act IV: Falling Action

The consequences of the crisis lead the action to its inevitable conclusion.

Act V: Catastrophe and Resolution

A final event resolves, or ends, the central conflict. In a tragedy, this event is called the *catastrophe* because it marks the fall of the central character.

The Renaissance Playhouse

The Globe Theater. Illustration by Carol O'Malia.

The Globe Theater, in which *The Tragedy of Julius Caesar* was first performed, is described in one of Shakespeare's plays as a "wooden O." The theater was nearly circular. It had eight sides and was open in the middle. The stage jutted into the center of this open area. Poorer theatergoers called groundlings, who paid a penny apiece for admission, stood around three sides of the stage. Wealthier playgoers could pay an additional penny or two to sit in one of the three galleries set in the walls of the theater.

The stage itself was partially covered with a canopy supported by two pillars. Trapdoors in the stage floor made it possible for actors to appear or disappear. Backstage center was an area known as the tiring house, in which actors could change costumes. This area could be opened for interior scenes. A second-story playing area above the tiring house could be used to represent a hilltop, a castle turret, or a balcony. A third level above the balcony provided a space for musicians and sound effects technicians.

The theater in Shakespeare's day used little in the way of scenery, and few props. The audience had to imagine the setting according to characters' descriptions of it. In a modern performance of a historical play like *The Tragedy of Julius Caesar,* the actors would most likely be dressed in period costumes such as togas. However, in a seventeenth-century performance, the actors wore standard contemporary

Elizabethan dress. (This may explain why in Act I, there is a reference to Caesar wearing a doublet, or elaborate Renaissance vest.) As you read *The Tragedy of Julius Caesar*, you may notice other elements of the play that are historically out of place; these elements are called *anachronisms*. For example, clocks are said to be striking even though clocks that would strike did not exist in Roman times.

Another unrealistic element of plays at the original Globe was that the actors were all men or boys. In Shakespeare's time, it was considered improper for women to act in plays.

Today, the Globe has been reconstructed, and tourists can see Shakespearean plays there as either groundlings or wealthier patrons, depending on the ticket price they are willing to pay.

The Renaissance Audience

Audiences at the Globe and similar theaters included people from all stations of society: laboring people from the lower classes, middle-class merchants, members of Parliament, and lords and ladies. Pickpockets mingled among the noisy, raucous groundlings crowding around the stage. Noblemen and noblewomen sat on cushioned seats in the first-tier balcony. The fanfare of trumpets that signaled the beginning of a play was heard by some twenty-five hundred spectators, a cross-section of the Elizabethan population. As noted in the preface to the First Folio, Shakespeare's plays were written for everyone, from "the most able, to him that can but spell." That may explain why they have such a universal appeal even today.

READING SHAKESPEARE

Shakespeare's Language

Shakespeare used one of the largest vocabularies ever employed by an author. In fact, according to the *Oxford English Dictionary*, Shakespeare actually introduced an estimated three thousand new words into the English language, many of which are in common use today, including *bedazzle, silliness, critical, obscene, hurry,* and *lonely*. Numerous well-known phrases come from his plays, such as "wear my heart upon my sleeve" *(Othello),* "at one fell swoop"

The Globe Theater, 2004.

(Macbeth), "fair play" *(The Tempest),* and "the world is my oyster" *(The Merry Wives of Windsor).*

Shakespeare wrote his plays about four hundred years ago. Since that time, the English language has changed considerably, so you will find that reading Shakespeare presents some special challenges. The meanings and spellings of some of the words he used have changed over the years, and some of the words in his writings are no longer used at all. As you read, refer to the footnotes for definitions of those archaic words. Here are some examples:

- alarum (a trumpet call to battle)
- fleering (mocking)
- hie thee (hurry up)
- howted (hooted; howled)
- Soft! (Wait; Hold on!)
- want (lack)
- wherefore (why)

You will also find that Shakespeare used many contractions that you would not use today, such as *i'* for *in, 'tis* for *it is,* and *veil'd* for *veiled.*

Another thing you'll notice about Shakespeare's writing is that some of his sentences are inverted or arranged in odd patterns, as in the line "But what trade art thou?" Today we might say "What is your trade, or profession?" When you encounter sentence patterns that seem unusual, try rearranging the words.

The footnotes will help you as you read, but try not to get bogged down by them. Remember that a play is a dramatic action and should move quickly. First, try reading through each scene without looking at the footnotes, so that you can get a general sense of what is happening. Then reread each scene, referring to the footnotes to get the details.

If you are having trouble understanding a scene, you might try paraphrasing the lines, translating them into more modern language, as shown below:

Original

    CASSIUS. Brutus, I do observe you now of late;
    I have not from your eyes that gentleness
    And show of love as I was wont to have.

Paraphrase

    CASSIUS. Brutus, I have noticed lately that
    you are not as kind and loving toward me
    as you used to be.

Referencing Lines in Shakespeare

When scholars refer to specific lines within a Shakespeare play, they follow a specific format. Specific lines are formatted in the following way: Act number. Scene number. Line numbers. For example, Caesar's line "Et tu, Brute?" would be cited as III.i.77. You would look in Act III, Scene i, line 77 to find this quotation.

Shakespeare's Poetic Technique

Shakespeare wrote his plays in *blank verse,* or unrhymed iambic pentameter. Each line of iambic pentameter consists of five *iambs,* or rhythmic units, each made up of a weakly stressed syllable followed by a strongly stressed syllable, as in the word *forget.* A simpler way of describing this type of verse is to say that it contains ten syllables in each line, and

every other syllable is stressed. The following are some typical lines:

> The fault, dear Brutus, is not in our stars,
>
> But in our selves, that we are under lings.

To maintain this pattern, the lines are sometimes split between two or more characters. This accounts for the unusual line numbering and formatting in Shakespeare's plays. In the following example, the words spoken by the Soothsayer and Caesar are counted as one line:

    SOOTHSAYER. Beware the ides of March.

    CAESAR.   What
    man is that?

If you scan the dialogue in *The Tragedy of Julius Caesar,* you will find that most of it is written in blank verse, with some variations in stress and syllable count. Shakespeare and other playwrights of his time favored the use of blank verse in drama because they believed that it captured the natural rhythms of English speech, yet still had a noble, heroic quality that would not be present in ordinary prose. You will notice that when Shakespeare does use prose, it is because the characters are speaking informally or are from the lower class. Brutus uses prose in his funeral oration to show humility, and Antony follows with a more formal speech in blank verse.

Persuasive Methods: Ethos, Pathos, and Logos

Thousands of years ago, an ancient Greek philosopher named Aristotle believed that persuasion relied on three complementary concepts that he called *ethos, pathos,* and *logos.* These concepts are still considered crucial to persuasive argument today. In *The Tragedy*

of *Julius Caesar,* Brutus and Antony appeal to all three concepts as they attempt to persuade the Romans of their contrasting views on Caesar's assassination.

- *Ethos* refers to the character of the speaker. Brutus appeals to ethos when he requests, "Believe me for mine honor...."
- *Pathos* is persuasion based on arousing emotions, including passion, love, hate, joy, fear, guilt, patriotism, sympathy, pity, sorrow, envy, and anger. Pathos provides a personal appeal that has the power to move listeners, change attitudes, and produce actions.
- *Logos* is based on logic, or reason. Brutus appeals to logos in Act III, Scene ii, lines 18–19, when he explains that Caesar was killed in order to protect the freedom of the people of Rome. Antony appeals to logos when he relates that he gave Caesar the opportunity three times to be king, but that Caesar refused each time.

VIEWING AND PERFORMING THE PLAY

Shakespeare never meant for his plays to be read in a book; he intended for them to be performed! All drama comes alive when it is presented by actors and is best experienced as a performance. If possible, listen to an audio version of the play or, better yet, view a production of the play on film or on a stage.

You can make the play come to life in the classroom by reading or performing it with other students. Here are some tips to keep in mind as you read aloud or act out the play:

- Although the play is in verse, read naturally, as though you are speaking to a friend. Don't worry about placing stress on every other syllable.
- Pause or stop only when you see a punctuation mark—not at the end of each line.
- Before acting out your lines, go over them with a classmate to be sure you understand what they mean. Once you understand your lines, then you can work on giving your performance the right expression and tone.

Martin Benrath (as Caesar) and Rosel Zech (as Calphurnia) perform in a production of *The Tragedy of Julius Caesar* at the Edinburgh International Arts Festival, 1993.

The Tragedy of Julius Caesar

A Play by William Shakespeare

BUILD BACKGROUND

Historical Context *The Tragedy of Julius Caesar* is based on real events

that occurred in ancient Rome around the years 45 BCE to 42 BCE, as told by the Greek Plutarch. In about 509 BCE, a republic was established in Rome, ruled by elected leaders. Two consuls and a powerful senate made up of noblemen led the government, and tribunes represented the common people. Over the next four hundred years, the Roman Republic grew to become a great power.

In 59 BCE, Julius Caesar was elected consul, a post he shared with Pompey and Crassus. His popularity grew, and the senate feared that this great leader would declare himself king and overthrow the Republic. In 49 BCE, they voted to remove Caesar from power. Caesar responded by initiating a four-year civil war. He returned to Rome triumphant and assumed the title of dictator in 45 BCE. Later that year, he left for Farther Spain to put down a revolt led by Pompey's sons. Soon afterward, he was declared dictator for life. In 44 BCE, a group of conspirators plotted to assassinate him. The play begins with Caesar's return to Rome after his campaign in Spain.

Reader's Context How would you react if a popular military leader declared himself or herself dictator for life of the United States?

ANALYZE LITERATURE: Plot, Conflict, and Inciting Incident

A **plot** is a series of events related to a **central conflict,** or primary struggle. The event that introduces the central conflict is called the **inciting incident.**

SET PURPOSE

Some critics have suggested that *The Tragedy of Julius Caesar* ought to be called *Brutus* because Brutus is really the play's main character. As you read Act I, consider what sort of person Brutus is. Pay attention to his actions, his words, and what other characters say about him. Consider what role Brutus plays in the escalation of the central conflict. What is his role in the inciting incident? How do his actions contribute to the overall tension in the play?

USE READING SKILLS

Paraphrase As you read the play, use the footnotes and vocabulary words to **paraphrase** passages, or translate them into your own words. A Paraphrasing Chart like the one below might help you. Copy important passages into the left column. In the right column, paraphrase them in your own words. An example is given.

Original Passage	Paraphrased Version
What, know you not, / Being mechanical, you ought not walk / Upon a laboring day without the sign / Of your profession? (Flavius, I. i. 2)	Don't you know that since you're a workman, you shouldn't be out walking on a workday without your tools and uniform?

PREVIEW VOCABULARY

Use the context clues in the sentences below to figure out the meanings of the underlined words from Act I.

1. The coach <u>culled</u> the best players; he picked them out from the B squad and moved them up to varsity.
2. We behaved in a <u>servile</u> manner toward the tyrant, obeying her every command.
3. The reporters <u>fawned</u> over the movie star, flattering her shamelessly.
4. The <u>surly</u> cabdriver scowled at the small tip.
5. The words of the wise man proved <u>portentous</u>: Everything happened just as he had foreseen.

Statue of Julius Caesar. National Museum, Naples, Italy.

The Tragedy of Julius Caesar

A Play by **William Shakespeare**

CHARACTERS IN THE PLAY

JULIUS CAESAR

OCTAVIUS CAESAR

MARK ANTONY   *triumvirs[1] after the death of Julius Caesar*

M. AEMILIUS LEPIDUS

CICERO

PUBLIUS   *senators*

POPILIUS LENA

MARCUS BRUTUS

CASSIUS

CASCA

TREBONIUS

CAIUS LIGARIUS   *conspirators against Julius Caesar*

DECIUS BRUTUS

METELLUS CIMBER

CINNA

FLAVIUS *AND* MURELLUS, *tribunes[2]*

ARTEMIDORUS OF CNIDOS, *a teacher of rhetoric[3]*

SOOTHSAYER[4]

CINNA, *a poet*
     Another POET

LUCILIUS

TITINIUS

MESSALA   *friends to Brutus and Cassius*

YOUNG CATO

VOLUMNIUS

FLAVIUS

VARRUS

CLITUS

CLAUDIO

STRATO   *servants to Brutus*

LUCIUS

DARDANIUS

PINDARUS, *servant to Cassius*

CALPHURNIA, *wife to Caesar*

PORTIA, *wife to Brutus*

SENATORS, PLEBEIANS,[5] GUARDS, ATTENDANTS, *etc.*

Time: *Around 44 BCE*
Place: *Rome; near Sardis; near Philippi*

CHARACTERS IN THE PLAY

1. **triumvirs.** In ancient Rome, three administrators who shared power equally among themselves
2. **tribunes.** In ancient Rome, administrators elected to protect the rights of the plebeians, or common people
3. **rhetoric.** Art of public speaking and persuasion
4. **SOOTHSAYER.** Fortune-teller; literally, a truth teller
5. **PLEBEIANS.** Common people of Rome, as opposed to nobles, or patricians

ACT I

SCENE I: A STREET IN ROME

Enter FLAVIUS, MURELLUS, *and certain* COMMONERS *over the stage.*

FLAVIUS.　Hence! home, you idle creatures, get you home!
Is this a holiday? What, know you not,
Being mechanical,[1] you ought not walk
Upon a laboring day without the sign
5　Of your profession?[2] Speak, what trade art thou?

CARPENTER.　Why, sir, a carpenter.

MURELLUS.　Where is thy leather apron and thy rule?
What dost thou with thy best apparel on?
You, sir, what trade are you?

10　**COBBLER.**　Truly, sir, in respect of a fine workman,[3] I am but, as you
would say, a cobbler.[4]

MURELLUS.　But what trade art thou? Answer me directly.[5]

COBBLER.　A trade, sir, that I hope I may use with a safe conscience,
which is indeed, sir, a mender of bad soles.[6]
15　**FLAVIUS.**　What trade, thou knave? thou naughty knave, what trade?

COBBLER.　Nay, I beseech you, sir, be not out with me; yet if you be
out,[7] sir, I can mend you.

MURELLUS.　What mean'st thou by that? Mend me, thou saucy[8]
fellow?

COBBLER.　Why, sir, cobble you.

20　**FLAVIUS.**　Thou art a cobbler, art thou?

COBBLER.　Truly, sir, all that I live by is with the awl:[9] I meddle
with no tradesman's matters, nor women's matters; but withal I
am indeed, sir, a surgeon to old shoes; when they are in great

danger, I recover[10] them. As proper men as ever trod upon
25　neat's-leather[11] have gone upon my handiwork.

FLAVIUS.　But wherefore art not in thy shop today?
Why dost thou lead these men about the streets?

COBBLER.　Truly, sir, to wear out their shoes, to get myself into more
work. But indeed, sir, we make holiday to see Caesar, and
30　to rejoice in his triumph.[12]

ACT I, SCENE I

1. **Being mechanical.**
Being workmen

2. **sign / Of your
profession.** Tools and uniforms

3. **in respect...workman.**
Compared with a master
craftsman

4. **a cobbler.** Pun: *cobbler*
meant both "a shoemaker"
and "a clumsy worker"

5. **directly.** Plainly, without
puns or double-talk

6. **soles.** Pun on the word
souls

7. **if you be out.** Punning
phrase meaning both "if your
shoes are worn out" and "if
you are put out, or angry"

8. **saucy.** Rude or
impertinent

9. **awl.** Cobbler's tool, used
to make holes in leather. The
Cobbler puns on the words
all, *awl*, and *withal* (meaning
"nevertheless").

10. **recover.** Pun meaning
both "to make better" and "to
resole"

11. **neat's-leather.** Calfskin
used to make fine shoes

12. **triumph.** Victory

MURELLUS.   Wherefore rejoice? What conquest brings he home?
What tributaries follow him to Rome,
To grace in captive bonds his chariot-wheels?[13]
You blocks, you stones, you worse than senseless things!
35 O you hard hearts, you cruel men of Rome,
Knew you not Pompey?[14] Many a time and oft
Have you climb'd up to walls and battlements,
To tow'rs and windows, yea, to chimney-tops,
Your infants in your arms, and there have sat
40 The livelong day, with patient expectation,
To see great Pompey pass the streets of Rome;
And when you saw his chariot but appear,
Have you not made an universal shout,
That Tiber trembled underneath her banks
45 To hear the replication of your sounds
Made in her concave shores?[15]
And do you now put on your best attire?
And do you now <u>cull</u> out a holiday?
And do you now strew flowers in his way,
50 That comes in triumph over Pompey's blood?[16]
Be gone!
Run to your houses, fall upon your knees,
Pray to the gods to intermit the plague
That needs must light on this ingratitude.[17]

55 FLAVIUS.   Go, go, good countrymen, and for this fault
Assemble all the poor men of your sort;
Draw them to Tiber banks, and weep your tears
Into the channel, till the lowest stream
Do kiss the most exalted shores of all.

Exeunt[18] *all the* COMMONERS.

60 See whe'er their basest metal be not mov'd;[19]
They vanish tongue-tied in their guiltiness.
Go you down that way towards the Capitol,[20]
This way will I. Disrobe the images,
If you do find them deck'd with ceremonies.[21]

65 MURELLUS.   May we do so?
You know it is the feast of Lupercal.[22]

FLAVIUS.   It is no matter, let no images
Be hung with Caesar's trophies.[23] I'll about,
And drive away the vulgar[24] from the streets;
70 So do you too, where you perceive them thick.
These growing feathers pluck'd from Caesar's wing
Will make him fly an ordinary pitch,[25]

13. **What tributaries...chariot-wheels?** What captured enemies has he brought to Rome, chained to his chariot wheels?

14. **Pompey** (päm´ pē). Roman general and statesman, former triumvir who ruled with Caesar and Crassus, defeated by Caesar in the Roman Civil War and murdered in Egypt

15. **Tiber...shores?** The Tiber River, which runs through Rome, trembled to hear the echo (replication) of the people's shouts in its curved (concave) shores.

cull (kul) *v.,* pick; select

16. **Pompey's blood.** Caesar has just returned from defeating the sons of Pompey in the province of Farther Spain.

17. **Pray...ingratitude.** Murellus warns that the disrespect shown for Pompey may anger the gods and cause them to start a plague in the city.

18. **Exeunt.** They exit (Latin). Exit by two or more people

19. **See...mov'd.** Notice that these base, or lowly, people have been moved by what I said.

20. **Capitol.** Temple of Jupiter on the Capitoline Hill in Rome

21. **Disrobe...ceremonies.** If you find that the statues of Caesar have ceremonies, or ornaments, on them, take them off. (Murellus is worried that Caesar's supporters may have placed kingly garments or crowns on statues of Caesar.)

22. **the feast of Lupercal.** Fertility festival held on February 15

23. **Caesar's trophies.** Decorations honoring Caesar

24. **vulgar.** Common people

25. **pitch.** Height

Who else would soar above the view of men,
And keep us all in <u>servile</u> fearfulness.

Exeunt.

Forget not in your speed, Antonio, / To touch Calphurnia. Caesar, Mark Antony, and Calphurnia, played by Louis Calhern, Marlon Brando, and Greer Garson in the 1953 film *Julius Caesar*.

SCENE II: A PUBLIC PLACE IN ROME, LATER THAT SAME DAY

Enter CAESAR, ANTONY *for the course,*[1] CALPHURNIA, PORTIA, DECIUS, CICERO, BRUTUS, CASSIUS, CASCA, CITIZENS, *and a* SOOTHSAYER; *after them* MURELLUS *and* FLAVIUS.

CAESAR.   Calphurnia!

CASCA.   Peace ho, Caesar speaks.

CAESAR.   Calphurnia!

CALPHURNIA.   Here, my lord.

CAESAR.   Stand you directly in Antonio's[2] way
When he doth run his course. Antonio!

5   ANTONY.   Caesar, my lord?

CAESAR.   Forget not in your speed, Antonio,
To touch Calphurnia; for our elders say,
The barren, touched in this holy chase,
Shake off their sterile curse.[3]

ACT I, SCENE II
1. *for the course.* Antony is ready to run in a ceremonial race held as part of the Lupercal celebration.

2. **Antonio's.** Mark Antony's

3. **The barren...curse.** Caesar's wife, Calphurnia, had not given birth to any children, so Caesar was without an heir. It was believed that a barren woman could become fertile if touched by a runner in the Lupercal race.

ANTONY.   I shall remember:
10   When Caesar says, "Do this," it is perform'd.

CAESAR.   Set on, and leave no ceremony out.

Flourish.[4]

SOOTHSAYER.   Caesar!

CAESAR.   Ha? who calls?

CASCA.   Bid every noise be still; peace yet again!
15   **CAESAR.**   Who is it in the press[5] that calls on me?
    I hear a tongue shriller than all the music
    Cry "Caesar!" Speak, Caesar is turn'd to hear.

✗ **SOOTHSAYER.**   Beware the ides of March.[6]

CAESAR.   What man is that?

BRUTUS.   A soothsayer bids you beware the ides of March.

20   **CAESAR.**   Set him before me, let me see his face.

CASSIUS.   Fellow, come from the <u>throng</u>, look upon Caesar.

CAESAR.   What say'st thou to me now? Speak once again.

SOOTHSAYER.   Beware the ides of March.

CAESAR.   He is a dreamer, let us leave him. Pass.

                Sennet.[7] *Exeunt. Manent*[8] BRUTUS *and* CASSIUS.

25   **CASSIUS.**   Will you go see the order of the course?[9]

BRUTUS.   Not I.

CASSIUS.   I pray you do.

BRUTUS.   I am not gamesome;[10] I do lack some part
    Of that quick spirit that is in Antony.
30   Let me not hinder, Cassius, your desires;
    I'll leave you.

CASSIUS.   Brutus, I do observe you now of late;
    I have not from your eyes that gentleness
    And show of love as I was wont to[11] have.
35   You bear too stubborn and too strange a hand
    Over your friend that loves you.

BRUTUS.   Cassius,
    Be not deceiv'd. If I have veil'd my look,
    I turn the trouble of my countenance
    Merely upon myself.[12] Vexed I am

---

4. **Flourish.** Sounding of trumpets

5. **press.** Press of bodies; crowd

6. **the ides of March.** March 15

throng (thrôn) *n.,* crowd; gang; group

7. **Sennet.** Sounding of trumpets to mark, ceremoniously, an entrance or an exit
8. **Manent.** They remain (Latin).
9. **Will you go see the order of the course?** Will you watch the race?
10. **gamesome.** In the mood for games; merry

11. **was wont to.** Used to

12. **If I...myself.** If I seem distant, my troubled face (countenance) is due to personal matters.

40 Of late with passions of some difference,[13]
    Conceptions only proper to myself,
    Which give some soil, perhaps, to my behaviors;[14]
    But let not therefore my good friends be griev'd
    (Among which number, Cassius, be you one),
45 Nor construe any further my neglect,[15]
    Than that poor Brutus, with himself at war,
    Forgets the shows of love to other men.

CASSIUS. Then, Brutus, I have much mistook your passion,
    By means whereof this breast of mine hath buried
50 Thoughts of great value, worthy cogitations.[16]
    Tell me, good Brutus, can you see your face?

BRUTUS. No, Cassius; for the eye sees not itself
    But by reflection, by some other things.

CASSIUS. 'Tis just,[17]
55 And it is very much lamented, Brutus,
    That you have no such mirrors as will turn
    Your hidden worthiness into your eye,
    That you might see your shadow.[18] I have heard
    Where many of the best respect in Rome
60 (Except immortal[19] Caesar), speaking of Brutus
    And groaning underneath this age's yoke,[20]
    Have wish'd that noble Brutus had his eyes.

BRUTUS. Into what dangers would you lead me, Cassius,
    That you would have me seek into myself
65 For that which is not in me?

CASSIUS. Therefore,[21] good Brutus, be prepar'd to hear;
    And since you know you cannot see yourself
    So well as by reflection, I, your glass,
    Will modestly discover to yourself
70 That of yourself which you yet know not of.
    And be not jealous on me,[22] gentle Brutus:
    Were I a common laughter, or did use
    To stale with ordinary oaths my love
    To every new protester;[23] if you know
75 That I do <u>fawn</u> on men and hug them hard,
    And after scandal[24] them; or if you know
    That I profess myself in banqueting
    To all the rout,[25] then hold me dangerous.

Flourish and shout.

BRUTUS. What means this shouting? I do fear the people
    Choose Caesar for their king.

---

13. **Vexed...passions of some difference.** I have been troubled by conflicting feelings.

14. **Conceptions...behaviors.** Thoughts of my own, which are perhaps soiling, or staining, my behavior

15. **But let not...neglect.** I hope my good friends (including you, Cassius) are not upset and do not interpret (construe) my neglect as meaning anything more.

16. **By means...cogitations.** For that reason, I kept my thoughts (cogitations) to myself.

17. **'Tis just.** That is so.

18. **it is...shadow.** It is too bad you have no mirror to reflect (turn) your inner qualities, so that you could see your worthiness in your reflection (shadow).

19. **immortal.** Cassius may be using this word as a contemptuous exaggeration.

20. **yoke.** Anything that harnesses or reduces to servitude, like the wooden yokes used around the necks of cattle. "[T]his age's yoke" refers to Caesar's rule.

21. **Therefore.** In answer to that

22. **jealous on me.** Suspicious of me

23. **Were I...protester.** If I were someone whom everyone laughed at, or if I were the kind of person to declare my love and loyalty to every new friend

fawn (fôn) *v.,* flatter; show excessive friendliness

24. **scandal.** Slander

25. **profess...rout.** Declare my friendship by holding banquets for the rabble

80 **CASSIUS.**   Aye, do you fear it?
Then must I think you would not have it so.

BRUTUS.   I would not, Cassius, yet I love him well.
But wherefore do you hold me here so long?
What is it that you would <u>impart</u> to me?
85 If it be aught toward the general good,
Set honor in one eye and death i' th' other,
And I will look on both indifferently;[26]
For let the gods so speed me[27] as I love
✗ The name of honor more than I fear death.

90 **CASSIUS.**   I know that virtue to be in you, Brutus,
As well as I do know your outward favor.[28]
Well, honor is the subject of my story:
I cannot tell what you and other men
Think of this life; but, for my single self,
95 ✗ I had as lief not be as live to be
In awe of such a thing as I myself.[29]
I was born free as Caesar, so were you;
We both have fed as well, and we can both
<u>Endure</u> the winter's cold as well as he;
100 For once, upon a raw and gusty day,
The troubled Tiber chafing with[30] her shores,
Caesar said to me, "Dar'st thou, Cassius, now
Leap in with me into this angry flood,
And swim to yonder point?" Upon the word,
105 Accoutred as I was,[31] I plunged in,
And bade him follow; so indeed he did.
The torrent roar'd, and we did buffet[32] it
With lusty sinews,[33] throwing it aside
And stemming it with hearts of controversy;[34]
110 But ere we could arrive the point propos'd,
Caesar cried, "Help me, Cassius, or I sink!"
I, as Aeneas, our great ancestor,
Did from the flames of Troy upon his shoulder
The old Anchises bear, so from the waves of Tiber
115 Did I the tired Caesar.[35] And this man
Is now become a god, and Cassius is
A wretched creature, and must bend his body[36]
If Caesar carelessly but nod on him.
He had a fever when he was in Spain,
120 And when the fit was on him, I did mark
How he did shake—'tis true, this god did shake;
His coward lips did from their color fly,[37]
And that same eye whose bend[38] doth awe the world

---

im • part (im pärt´) *v.*, get
across; give

26. **If it be…indifferently.**
If what you have in mind concerns the good of Rome (the general good), then I do not care if it brings me honor or if it brings me death; I will do what needs to be done.
27. **For let…speed me.** Let the gods bring me good fortune (an oath similar to "By God").
28. **outward favor.**
Appearance
29. **I had…myself.** I would rather not live at all than live in awe of a man who is no better than I am.

en • dure (in dùr´) *v.*, live
through

30. **chafing with.** Raging against

31. **Accoutred as I was.**
Dressed as I was (in battle gear)
32. **buffet** (buf´ it). Strike out or attack
33. **lusty sinews**
(sin´ yüz). Strong muscles
34. **stemming…controversy.** Moving through the water in aggressive competition

35. **I, as Aeneas…Caesar.**
Cassius compares himself to the legendary hero Aeneas (i nē´ əs), who carried his old father, Anchises, out of the burning city of Troy and went on to found Rome.
36. **bend his body.** Bow

37. **His coward lips…fly.**
His lips turned pale.
38. **bend.** Glance

Cassius and Brutus (played by John Gielgud and James Mason) in the 1953 film *Julius Caesar*.

Did lose its luster;[39] I did hear him groan;
125 Aye, and that tongue of his that bade the Romans
Mark him, and write his speeches in their books,
Alas, it cried, "Give me some drink, Titinius,"
As a sick girl. Ye gods, it doth amaze me
A man of such a feeble temper[40] should
130 So get the start of[41] the majestic world
And bear the palm[42] alone.

Shout. Flourish.

BRUTUS. Another general shout!
I do believe that these applauses are
For some new honors that are heap'd on Caesar.

135 **CASSIUS.** Why, man, he doth bestride the narrow world
Like a Colossus,[43] and we petty men
Walk under his huge legs, and peep about
To find ourselves dishonorable graves.
Men at some time are masters of their fates;
140 The fault, dear Brutus, is not in our stars,[44]
But in ourselves, that we are underlings.
Brutus and Caesar: what should be in that "Caesar"?
Why should that name be sounded more than yours?
Write them together, yours is as fair a name;

39. **Did lose its luster.** Lost its gleam

40. **feeble temper.** Weak or sickly constitution
41. **get the start of.** Get ahead of; outdistance
42. **bear the palm.** Carry the prize of victory

43. **Colossus.** Gigantic statue such as the Colossus of Rhodes, said to be so large that ships sailed under its legs

44. **stars.** Reference to the belief that human destiny is governed by the stars

145	Sound them, it doth become[45] the mouth as well;
	Weigh them, it is as heavy; conjure[46] with 'em,
	"Brutus" will start a spirit[47] as soon as "Caesar."
	Now in the names of all the gods at once,
	Upon what meat doth this our Caesar feed
150	That he is grown so great? Age, thou art sham'd!
	Rome, thou hast lost the breed of noble bloods!
	When went there by an age since the great flood
	But it was fam'd with more than with one man?[48]
	When could they say, till now, that talk'd of Rome,
155	That her wide walks encompass'd but one man?
	Now is it Rome indeed and room enough,
	When there is in it but one only man.[49]
	O! you and I have heard our fathers say
	There was a Brutus[50] once that would have brook'd
160	Th' eternal devil to keep his state in Rome
	As easily as a king.[51]

BRUTUS.　That you do love me, I am nothing jealous;[52]
What you would work me to, I have some aim.[53]
How I have thought of this, and of these times,

165　I shall recount hereafter. For this present,
I would not (so with love I might <u>entreat</u> you)
Be any further mov'd.[54] What you have said
I will consider; what you have to say
I will with patience hear, and find a time

170　Both meet[55] to hear and answer such high things.
Till then, my noble friend, chew upon this:
Brutus had rather be a villager
Than to repute himself a son of Rome
Under these hard conditions as this time

175　Is like to lay upon us.

CASSIUS.　I am glad that my weak words
Have struck but thus much show of fire from Brutus.

Enter CAESAR and his TRAIN.[56]

BRUTUS.　The games are done, and Caesar is returning.

CASSIUS.　As they pass by, pluck Casca by the sleeve,
180　And he will (after his sour fashion) tell you
What hath proceeded worthy note today.

BRUTUS.　I will do so. But look you, Cassius,
The angry spot doth glow on Caesar's brow,
And all the rest look like a chidden train:[57]
185　Calphurnia's cheek is pale, and Cicero

---

45. **become.** Suit
46. **conjure.** Do magic; call up spirits
47. **start a spirit.** Call up a ghost; inspire people
48. **But it was...man?** Cassius is saying that every age has had more than one famous person. The "flood" refers to a flood in Greek mythology that drowned everyone but two people who were saved by Zeus because of their virtue.
49. **Now is it Rome...man.** Cassius puns on the words *Rome* and *roam*, emphasizing that in Rome, there is room enough for only one great man, Caesar.
50. **Brutus.** Lucius Junius Brutus, who led the defeat of the Etruscan kings in ancient Rome and then helped to establish the republic
51. **that would have brook'd...king.** Who would rather have had the devil live in Rome than tolerate a king of Rome

en • treat (in trēt´) *v.,* to implore; strongly urge

52. **am nothing jealous.** Do not doubt
53. **aim.** Understanding
54. **For...mov'd.** For right now, I ask you as a friend, please do not urge me any more.
55. **meet.** Appropriate

56. **TRAIN.** Companions; attendants

57. **chidden train.** Group of servants who have been scolded

Looks with such ferret[58] and such fiery eyes
As we have seen him in the Capitol,
Being cross'd in conference[59] by some senators.

CASSIUS.   Casca will tell us what the matter is.

190 CAESAR.   Antonio!

ANTONY.   Caesar?

CAESAR.   Let me have men about me that are fat,
Sleek-headed men and such as sleep a-nights.
Yond Cassius has a lean and hungry look,
195 He thinks too much; such men are dangerous.

don't pay attention

ANTONY.   Fear him not, Caesar, he's not dangerous,
He is a noble Roman, and well given.[60]

CAESAR.   Would he were fatter! but I fear him not.
Yet if my name[61] were liable to fear,
200 I do not know the man I should avoid
So soon as that spare[62] Cassius. He reads much,
He is a great observer, and he looks
Quite through the deeds of men.[63] He loves no plays,
As thou dost, Antony; he hears no music;
205 Seldom he smiles, and smiles in such a sort
As if he mock'd himself, and scorn'd his spirit
That could be mov'd to smile at anything.
Such men as he be never at heart's ease
Whiles they behold a greater than themselves,
210 And therefore are they very dangerous.
I rather tell thee what is to be fear'd
Than what I fear; for always I am Caesar.
Come on my right hand, for this ear is deaf,
And tell me truly what thou think'st of him.

Sennet. Exeunt CAESAR *and his* TRAIN. CASCA *stays.*

215 CASCA.   You pull'd me by the cloak, would you speak with me?

BRUTUS.   Aye, Casca, tell us what hath chanc'd today
That Caesar looks so sad.[64]

CASCA.   Why, you were with him, were you not?

BRUTUS.   I should not then ask Casca what had chanc'd.

220 CASCA.   Why, there was a crown offer'd him; and being offer'd him,
he put it by[65] with the back of his hand thus, and then the people fell
a-shouting.

BRUTUS.   What was the second noise for?

58. **ferret.** Red like the eyes of a ferret, a weasel-like animal

59. **cross'd in conference.** Engaged in debate

60. **well given.** Favorable; sympathetic (toward Caesar)

61. **my name.** A person with my fame and power

62. **spare.** Lean or thin

63. **looks / Quite through... men.** Sees the motivations behind men's actions

64. **sad.** Serious; troubled

65. **put it by.** Pushed it aside

The Rise and Fall of a Leader Gaius Julius Caesar was a Roman general and politician who lived from about 100 BCE to 44 BCE. One of the ablest leaders the world has known, Caesar greatly expanded the Roman Republic. After defeating the king of Pontus, a territory in Asia Minor, he famously declared, "Veni, vidi, vici" (I came, I saw, I conquered). Besides being a powerful military leader, Caesar was a good politician. His reforms improved the lives of the common people, or *plebeians*, who loved him for championing their causes. Some saw Caesar as an ambitious and shrewd self-promoter who hoped to end democracy and become a dictator, and some saw him as a hero, but either way, he was a legend. After his death in 44 BCE, Caesar's name became forever synonymous with power and leadership. The Russian word *czar*, the German *Kaiser*, and the Arabic *qaysar*, all meaning "king" or "ruler," are variations on his name.

    CASCA.   Why, for that too.

225 **CASSIUS.**   They shouted thrice;[66] what was the last cry for?

    CASCA.   Why, for that too.

    BRUTUS.   Was the crown offer'd him thrice?

    CASCA.   Aye, marry,[67] was't,[68] and he put it by thrice, every time gentler than other; and at every putting-by mine honest
230 neighbors shouted.

    CASSIUS.   Who offer'd him the crown?

    CASCA.   Why, Antony.

    BRUTUS.   Tell us the manner of it, gentle Casca.

    CASCA.   I can as well be hang'd as tell the manner of it: it was
235 mere foolery, I did not mark it. I saw Mark Antony offer him a crown—yet 'twas not a crown neither, 'twas one of these coronets[69]—and as I told you, he put it by once; but for all that, to my thinking, he would fain[70] have had it. Then he offer'd it to him again; then he put it by again; but, to my thinking, he

66. **thrice.** Three times

67. **marry.** Oath meaning "truly" or "indeed"
68. **was't.** It was

69. **coronets.** Little crowns
70. **fain.** Willingly; gladly

240 was very loath[71] to lay his fingers off it. And then he offered it
the third time; he put it the third time by; and still[72] as he
refus'd it, the rabblement howted, and clapp'd their chopp'd
hands,[73] and threw up their sweaty nightcaps, and utter'd such
a deal of stinking breath because Caesar refus'd the crown, that
245 it had, almost, chok'd Caesar, for he swounded,[74] and fell down
at it; and for mine own part, I durst[75] not laugh, for fear
of opening my lips and receiving the bad air.[76]

CASSIUS. But soft[77] I pray you; what, did Caesar swound?

CASCA. He fell down in the market-place, and foam'd at
250 mouth, and was speechless.

BRUTUS. 'Tis very like, he hath the falling sickness.[78]

CASSIUS. No, Caesar hath it not; but you, and I,
And honest Casca, we have the falling sickness.[79]

CASCA. I know not what you mean by that, but I am sure
255 Caesar fell down. If the tag-rag people did not clap him and hiss
him, according as he pleas'd and displeas'd them, as they use to do
the players in the theater,[80] I am no true man.

BRUTUS. What said he when he came unto himself?

CASCA. Marry, before he fell down, when he perceiv'd the
260 common herd was glad he refus'd the crown, he pluck'd me ope
his doublet,[81] and offered them his throat to cut. And I had
been a man of any occupation, if I would not have taken him at
a word, I would I might go to hell among the rogues.[82] And so
he fell. When he came to himself again, he said, if he had done
265 or said anything amiss, he desir'd their worships to think it was
his infirmity.[83] Three or four wenches, where I stood, cried,
"Alas, good soul!" and forgave him with all their hearts. But
there's no heed to be taken of them; if Caesar had stabb'd their
mothers, they would have done no less.

270 BRUTUS. And after that, he came thus sad away?

CASCA. Aye.

CASSIUS. Did Cicero say anything?

CASCA. Aye, he spoke Greek.

CASSIUS. To what effect?

275 CASCA. Nay, and I tell you that, I'll ne'er look you i' th' face
again. But those that understood him smil'd at one another,
and shook their heads; but, for mine own part, it was Greek to
me.[84] I could tell you more news too. Murellus and Flavius, for

71. **loath.** Unwilling
72. **still.** Each time
73. **the rabblement… hands.** The crowd hooted and clapped their chapped hands.
74. **swounded.** Swooned; fainted
75. **durst.** Dared
76. **receiving the bad air.** Breathing or smelling the bad odor
77. **soft.** Pause; hold on

78. **falling sickness.** Epilepsy

79. **No…sickness.** Cassius is implying that while Caesar's power increases, the power of others, such as Brutus, Casca, and Cassius himself, declines.

80. **If the tag-rag…theater.** Casca is implying that a noble Roman, unlike Caesar, should be above the approval or disapproval of commoners.

81. **pluck'd me ope his doublet.** Opened his jacket
82. **And…rogues.** If I had been a member of the working class (or, a man of action), I would have taken him literally (cut his throat) and gone to hell with the other scoundrels.
83. **infirmity.** Illness (in Caesar's case, epilepsy)

84. **it was Greek to me.** It made no sense to me.

280 pulling scarfs off Caesar's images, are put to silence.[85] Fare you well. There was more foolery yet, if I could remember it.

CASSIUS. Will you sup with me tonight, Casca?

CASCA. No, I am promis'd forth.[86]

CASSIUS. Will you dine with me tomorrow?

285 **CASCA.** Aye, if I be alive, and your mind hold, and your dinner worth the eating.

CASSIUS. Good, I will expect you.

CASCA. Do so. Farewell both.

Exit CASCA.

BRUTUS. What a blunt fellow is this grown to be!
He was quick mettle[87] when he went to school.

290 **CASSIUS.** So is he now in execution
Of any bold or noble enterprise,
However he puts on this tardy form.[88]
This rudeness is a sauce to his good wit,
Which gives men stomach to digest his words
295 With better appetite.[89]

BRUTUS. And so it is. For this time I will leave you;
Tomorrow, if you please to speak with me,
I will come home to you; or, if you will,
Come home to me, and I will wait for you.

300 **CASSIUS.** I will do so; till then, think of the world.[90]

Exit BRUTUS.

Well, Brutus, thou art noble; yet I see
Thy honorable mettle may be wrought
From that it is dispos'd;[91] therefore it is meet[92]
That noble minds keep ever with their likes;
305 For who so firm that cannot be seduc'd?
Caesar doth bear me hard,[93] but he loves Brutus.
If I were Brutus now and he were Cassius,
He should not humor me.[94] I will this night,
In several hands,[95] in at his windows throw,
310 As if they came from several citizens,
Writings, all tending to the great opinion
That Rome holds of his name; wherein obscurely
Caesar's ambition shall be glanced at.[96]
And after this let Caesar seat him sure,[97]
315 For we will shake him, or worse days endure.

Exit.

---

85. **put to silence.** Deprived of their political posts or executed

86. **I am promis'd forth.** I have a previous engagement.

87. **quick mettle.** Lively spirit
88. **So is he...tardy form.** Casca can still be intelligent in carrying out an important project, even though he puts on a show of being slow and sluggish (tardy).

89. **This rudeness...appetite.** As a sauce makes a meal easier to digest, so does Casca's bluntness make it easier for people to accept the intelligence, or wit, of his words.

90. **think of the world.** Think about the state of the world.

91. **Thy...dispos'd.** Your honorable character can be manipulated (wrought) into something less than honorable.
92. **meet.** Fit; appropriate
93. **bear me hard.** Dislike me
94. **If I...humor me.** If I were in Brutus's place, I would never allow anyone to persuade me to go against Caesar.
95. **In several hands.** In different handwritings
96. **Writings...glanced at.** Letters that speak of how highly regarded Brutus is in Rome and subtly criticize Caesar's ambition
97. **seat him sure.** Make himself secure

Scene III: A Street in Rome, One Month Later

Thunder and lightning. Enter from opposite sides Casca *with his sword drawn and* Cicero.

Cicero. Good even,[1] Casca; brought you Caesar home?
Why are you breathless, and why stare you so?

Casca. Are not you mov'd, when all the sway of earth[2]
Shakes like a thing unfirm? O Cicero,
5   I have seen tempests[3] when the scolding winds
Have riv'd[4] the knotty oaks, and I have seen
Th' ambitious ocean swell, and rage, and foam,
To be exalted with[5] the threat'ning clouds;
But never till tonight, never till now,
10 Did I go through a tempest dropping fire.
Either there is a civil strife in heaven,
Or else the world, too saucy with the gods,
Incenses them to send destruction.[6]

Cicero. Why, saw you anything more wonderful?

15 **Casca.** A common slave—you know him well by sight—
Held up his left hand which did flame and burn
Like twenty torches join'd; and yet his hand,
Not sensible of fire, remain'd unscorch'd.
Besides—I ha' not since put up my sword—
20 Against[7] the Capitol I met a lion,
Who glaz'd[8] upon me, and went <u>surly</u> by,
Without annoying me. And there were drawn
Upon a heap a hundred ghastly women,[9]
Transformed with their fear, who swore they saw
25 Men, all in fire, walk up and down the streets.
And yesterday the bird of night[10] did sit
Even at noon-day upon the market-place,
Howting[11] and shrieking. When these prodigies
Do so conjointly meet, let not men say,
30 "These are their reasons, they are natural";
For I believe they are <u>portentous</u> things
Unto the climate that they point upon.[12]

Cicero. Indeed, it is a strange-disposed[13] time;
But men may construe things after their fashion
35 Clean from the purpose of the things themselves.[14]
Comes Caesar to the Capitol tomorrow?

Act I, Scene III
1. **even.** Evening

2. **all the sway of earth.**
Whole pattern or rule of
things
3. **tempests.** Storms
4. **riv'd.** Split open

5. **exalted with.** Raised up
to

6. **Either…destruction.**
Either there is civil war in
heaven or else the gods are
trying to destroy the world
because they are angry
(incensed) by people's disrespectful (saucy) ways.

7. **Against.** Near
8. **glaz'd.** Gazed or glared

sur • ly (sʉr´ lē) *adj.,* bad-
tempered; hostile

9. **drawn / Upon a heap…
ghastly women.** A hundred
women, white like ghosts,
were gathered in a huddle.
10. **bird of night.** Owl
11. **Howting.** Hooting

por • ten • tous (pôr
ten´ təs) *adj.,* predictive;
foreboding; ominous

12. **When these…upon.**
When these exceptional things
(prodigies) happen all at once
(conjointly)…they are ominous signs of things to come
in the climate, or region, in
which they occur.
13. **strange-disposed.**
Unusual; abnormal
14. **men may…themselves.**
Men are capable of misunderstanding the actual meanings
of things.

CASCA. He doth; for he did bid Antonio
Send word to you he would be there tomorrow.

CICERO. Good night then, Casca; this disturbed sky
Is not to walk in.[15]

40 **CASCA.** Farewell, Cicero.

Exit CICERO.

Enter CASSIUS.

CASSIUS. Who's there?

CASCA. A Roman.

CASSIUS. Casca, by your voice.

CASCA. Your ear is good. Cassius, what night is this!

CASSIUS. A very pleasing night to honest men.

CASCA. Who ever knew the heavens menace so?

45 **CASSIUS.** Those that have known the earth so full of faults.
For my part, I have walk'd about the streets,
Submitting me unto the perilous night;
And thus unbraced,[16] Casca, as you see,
Have bar'd my bosom to the thunder-stone;[17]
50 And when the cross[18] blue lightning seem'd to open
The breast of heaven, I did present myself
Even in the aim and very flash of it.

CASCA. But wherefore[19] did you so much tempt the heavens?
It is the part[20] of men to fear and tremble
55 When the most mighty gods by tokens send
Such dreadful heralds to astonish us.

CASSIUS. You are dull, Casca; and those sparks of life
That should be in a Roman you do want,[21]
Or else you use not. You look pale, and gaze,
60 And put on fear, and cast yourself in wonder,
To see the strange impatience of the heavens;
But if you would consider the true cause
Why all these fires, why all these gliding ghosts,
Why birds and beasts from quality and kind,[22]
65 Why old men, fools, and children calculate,[23]
Why all these things change from their ordinance,[24]
Their natures, and preformed faculties,[25]
To monstrous quality—why, you shall find
That heaven hath infus'd them with these spirits,

15. **not to walk in.** Not safe to walk under

16. **unbraced.** With jacket open
17. **thunder-stone.** Lightning; thunderbolt
18. **cross.** Jagged or zig-zagged

19. **wherefore.** Why
20. **part.** Role

21. **want.** Lack

22. **from quality and kind.** Not displaying their normal characteristics and natures
23. **calculate.** Prophesy
24. **ordinance.** Usual ways of being
25. **preformed faculties.** Innate or inborn qualities

Elizabethan Superstition The people who lived in Shakespeare's day are called Elizabethans, after their great monarch Queen Elizabeth I. The Elizabethans were extremely superstitious. They believed in astrology, magic, witchcraft, good and bad omens, ghosts, fortune-telling, and alchemy. Animals were often considered omens. For instance, owls and ravens were both associated with death. Belief in the supernatural was common, and Queen Elizabeth's successor, James I, wrote a popular work on witchcraft, the *Daemonologie,* in 1599. Do you share any of the beliefs of the Elizabethans? How did Shakespeare's descriptions of the abnormal events of the times affect you? How do you think these descriptions might have affected an Elizabethan audience?

70 To make them instruments of fear and warning
    Unto some monstrous state.[26]
    Now could I, Casca, name to thee a man
    Most like this dreadful night,
    That thunders, lightens, opens graves, and roars
75 As doth the lion in the Capitol—
    A man no mightier than thyself, or me,
    In personal action, yet prodigious[27] grown,
    And fearful, as these strange eruptions are.

    CASCA.   'Tis Caesar that you mean; is it not, Cassius?

80 CASSIUS.   Let it be who it is; for Romans now
    Have thews[28] and limbs like to their ancestors;
    But woe the while,[29] our fathers' minds are dead,
    And we are govern'd with our mothers' spirits;
    Our yoke and sufferance[30] show us womanish.

85 CASCA.   Indeed, they say, the senators tomorrow
    Mean to establish Caesar as a king;

26. **heaven...state.** The gods have filled them with supernatural powers in order to warn the Romans of a terrible, or unnatural, state of affairs or government.

27. **prodigious.** Ominous and enormous

28. **thews.** Sinews or muscles
29. **woe the while.** Pity the times

30. **yoke and sufferance.** Servitude and the acceptance of it

And he shall wear his crown by sea and land,
In every place, save here in Italy.

    CASSIUS.   I know where I will wear this dagger then;
90   Cassius from bondage will deliver Cassius.[31]
    Therein, ye gods, you make the weak most strong;
    Therein, ye gods, you tyrants do defeat;
    Nor stony tower, nor walls of beaten brass,
    Nor airless dungeon, nor strong links of iron,
95   Can be retentive to the strength of spirit;[32]
    But life, being weary of these worldly bars,
    Never lacks power to dismiss itself.
    If I know this, know all the world besides,
    That part of tyranny that I do bear
    I can shake off at pleasure.

Thunder still.

100   **CASCA.**   So can I;
    So every bondman[33] in his own hand bears
    The power to cancel his captivity.

    CASSIUS.   And why should Caesar be a tyrant then?
    Poor man, I know he would not be a wolf
105   But that he sees the Romans are but sheep;
    He were no lion, were not Romans hinds.[34]
    Those that with haste will make a mighty fire
    Begin it with weak straws. What trash is Rome?
    What rubbish and what offal?[35] when it serves
110   For the base matter to illuminate
    So vile a thing as Caesar! But, O grief,
    Where hast thou led me? I, perhaps, speak this
    Before a willing bondman; then I know
    My answer must be made. But I am arm'd,
115   And dangers are to me indifferent.[36]

    CASCA.   You speak to Casca, and to such a man
    That is no fleering tell-tale.[37] Hold, my hand.
    Be factious for redress of all these griefs,[38]
    And I will set this foot of mine as far
    As who goes farthest.

120   **CASSIUS.**   There's a bargain made.
    Now know you, Casca, I have mov'd already
    Some certain of the noblest-minded Romans
    To undergo with me an enterprise
    Of honorable-dangerous consequence;

31. **will deliver Cassius.** That is, by killing himself

32. **Nor stony...spirit.** This idea was later expressed by poet Richard Lovelace: "Stone walls do not a prison make / Nor iron bars a cage," because the spirit cannot be imprisoned or contained.

33. **bondman.** Serf or slave

34. **hinds.** Deer

35. **offal** (ô´ fəl). Trash

36. **I, perhaps...indifferent.** Perhaps you (Casca) are a willing slave of Caesar, in which case you will want to fight me. But I am armed and unafraid of danger.
37. **fleering tell-tale.** Sneering tattletale
38. **Be...griefs.** Form a faction, or political group, to right these wrongs.

125 And I do know, by this they stay[39] for me
In Pompey's Porch;[40] for now, this fearful night,
There is no stir or walking in the streets;
And the complexion of the element
In favor's like[41] the work we have in hand,
130 Most bloody, fiery, and most terrible.

Enter CINNA.

CASCA.   Stand close[42] a while, for here comes one in haste.

CASSIUS.   'Tis Cinna, I do know him by his gait,
He is a friend. Cinna, where haste you so?

CINNA.   To find out you. Who's that? Metellus Cimber?

135 CASSIUS.   No, it is Casca, one incorporate
To our attempts.[43] Am I not stay'd for, Cinna?[44]

CINNA.   I am glad on't.[45] What a fearful night is this!
There's two or three of us have seen strange sights.

CASSIUS.   Am I not stay'd for? Tell me.

CINNA.   Yes, you are.
140 O Cassius, if you could
But win the noble Brutus to our party—

CASSIUS.   Be you content. Good Cinna, take this paper,
And look you lay it in the praetor's[46] chair,
Where Brutus may but find it; and throw this
145 In at his window; set this up with wax
Upon old Brutus'[47] statue. All this done,
Repair[48] to Pompey's Porch, where you shall find us.
Is[49] Decius Brutus and Trebonius there?

CINNA.   All but Metellus Cimber, and he's gone
150 To seek you at your house. Well, I will hie,[50]
And so bestow these papers as you bade me.

CASSIUS.   That done, repair to Pompey's theater.

                                              Exit CINNA.

Come, Casca, you and I will yet, ere day,
See Brutus at his house. Three parts of him
155 Is[51] ours already, and the man entire
Upon the next encounter yields him ours.

---

39. **by this they stay.**. this time, they are waiting me.
40. **Pompey's Porch.** Covered walk, or portico, in front of Pompey's theater
41. **complexion...like.** The sky looks like

42. **close.** Hidden

43. **incorporate / To our attempts.** United in our cause
44. **Am I not stay'd for...?** Are they waiting for me?
45. **on't.** Of it

46. **praetor's** (prē´ terz). Brutus is praetor, or chief magistrate, of Rome.
47. **old Brutus.** Lucius Junius Brutus, founder of the republic and symbol of republican ideals
48. **Repair.** Go
49. **Is.** Are

50. **hie.** Make haste

51. **Is.** Are

CASCA.   O, he sits high in all the people's hearts;
And that which would appear offense in us,
His countenance, like richest alchymy,
160   Will change to virtue and to worthiness.⁵²

CASSIUS.   Him and his worth, and our great need of him,
You have right well conceited.⁵³ Let us go,
For it is after midnight, and ere day
We will awake him and be sure of him.

Exeunt.

52. **that which...worthiness.** Because of this popularity, having Brutus on our side will magically change whatever offensive things we do into something virtuous and worthy in the eyes of the people (just as in the ancient pseudoscience of alchemy, people attempted to change base metals into gold).
53. **conceited.** Described in an elaborate metaphor, or conceit

MIRRORS & WINDOWS

"Yond Cassius has a lean and hungry look, / He thinks too much; such men are dangerous." What immediate response does this statement trigger in you? What do you think Caesar means? When might someone say something like this today?

REFER TO TEXT ▶▶▶▶	▶ REASON WITH TEXT	
1a. Recall the strange events that are reported in Scene iii.	1b. Conclude what you think these occurrences suggest will happen next in Rome.	**Understand** **Find meaning**
2a. List the traits Caesar objects to in Cassius.	2b. Examine why Caesar objects to these traits. What about them seems dangerous to him?	**Apply** **Use information**
3a. Name the work of art to which Cassius compares Caesar.	3b. Identify the arguments Cassius uses to persuade Brutus to join the conspiracy against Caesar.	**Analyze** **Take things apart**
4a. Describe what Caesar does when Antony offers him a crown to wear at the festival. How do the people react when they see this?	4b. Assess Caesar's actions, his words, and the comments the other characters make about him. What is you opinion of Caesar? Do you think the Roman people have reason to fear him? Why or why not?	**Evaluate** **Make judgments**
5a. Explain what the senators plan to do tomorrow. What will Cassius do if that happens?	5b. In your opinion, should one be suspicious of those who are in power? Why or why not? In a democracy, what might occur if a politician became too powerful or too popular?	**Create** **Bring ideas together**

ANALYZE LITERATURE: Plot, Conflict, and Inciting Incident

Why does Cassius speak with Brutus in Scene ii? What struggle within Brutus is introduced in lines 79–89 of that scene? Create a Plot Diagram like the one in Unit 1, Understanding Plot. Use your answers to the preceding questions to note on the diagram the inciting incident and the central conflict, which are both part of the rising action. As you read on, you will add to this Plot Diagram.

Informational Text
CONNECTION

This website presents a guide to the PBS series "In Search of Shakespeare," led by Michael Wood. Though William Shakespeare is, perhaps, the most famous English writer of all time, information about his life is sketchy. That is, while certain facts are well-known (about his parents and his children, for example), there are gaps in the information that have led to numerous speculations on who he really was as a man. Working with the Royal Shakespeare Company (RSC), the documentary crew traveled around England to explore the influences on this influential writer.

As you read a website, pay attention to the purpose of the site and its sources of information. Evaluate whether the sources of information are trustworthy. Look for things like headings, subheadings, and sidebars to help you navigate and find information. Instead of reading every word, skim to find the information you are seeking.

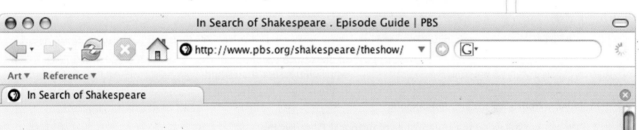

In Search of Shakespeare . Episode Guide | PBS

http://www.pbs.org/shakespeare/theshow/

Art ▾   Reference ▾

In Search of Shakespeare

In Search of Shakespeare
Episode Guide
Introduction

"In Search of Shakespeare" is a four-part series exploring the life of the world's greatest and most famous writer. Surprisingly, it is the first time that a full-scale life of William Shakespeare has been attempted on TV. Presenter-led, mixing travel, adventure, interviews and specially shot documentary and live action sequences with the RSC on the road, this is an innovative TV history series from the award-winning team which made "In the Footsteps of Alexander the Great" and "Conquistadors."

The film set the life of the poet in the turbulent times in which he lived. In Episode One, we are introduced to the dark side of Queen Elizabeth's police state—in a time of surveillance, militarism and foreign wars. Shakespeare

More

Episode 1: A Time of Revolution

Episode 2: The Lost Years

Episode 3: The Duty of Poets

Episode 4: For All Time

http://www.pbs.org/shakespeare/theshow/ ▼

lived through the Spanish Armada, the Gunpowder Plot,[1] the colonization of the New World and the beginnings of British power in America. But most important, he also saw at first hand England's Cultural Revolution; an enforced split with the old medieval English spirit world which was to lead the English people into a brave new Protestant future. A split that Michael Wood argues defined Shakespeare's life.

The series takes the form of a detective story, a documentary search, and a journey.

Royal Shakespeare Company performance of *Macbeth* in London, 2005.

"We set out to film England as if we were working in a foreign country," says producer Rebecca Dobbs: "Journeying to forgotten corners of the landscape, interviewing real life witnesses — for example royal robe makers and heralds, the last surviving master glover, living descendants of Shakespeare's patrons who still treasure stories and documents from his time...What we have done in other shows in Peru or India, we have set out to do in England.

"We are not following the current style of historical TV shows that use re-enactments and tableaux.[2] There is no one dressed up as Will Shakespeare — or Queen Elizabeth! Instead we asked the Royal Shakespeare Company to give us a group of Britain's best young actors and actresses, go on the road and play in the places where his company played.

The Shakespeare Team are led by the director Greg Doran — who has just won this year's Olivier Award for Achievement in the Theatre. Shot documentary style, on and off stage, the successors of Shakespeare's company give us a magical glimpse into how it was done: playing scenes from all Shakespeare's great shows in Tudor Guildhalls, Royal Palaces like Hampton Court, and even in broad daylight, in a surviving intact inn yard in Gloucester, to see what it was like to play in the conditions they did."

But the core of the series is a biography. The story of one Elizabethan, his life, family and friendships, his triumphs and disasters, his loves and his losses.

The four shows follow Shakespeare's life from cradle to grave in a way never hitherto thought possible. In them we see how his life and work were shaped

---

1. **Gunpowder Plot.** In 1605, a group of conspirators tried, unsuccessfully, to blow up the Houses of Parliament in order to kill King James I and members of Parliament and install a new Catholic monarch.

2. **tableaux.** A scene presented by people in costume

by his times; how he created some of the greatest literature in the world, and why we still love him: For in these films we see how Shakespeare in his life and

Hampton Court in London.

work sums up English (and British) history—and the English character too—more than any other person. Decent, humane, open minded, tolerant, witty, bawdy, sexy, diffident, guarded, skeptical, wary of any political system, identifying himself with the "Other"—in his great portrayals of black people, women, the poor, Jews,—and even evil

people—Shakespeare is an artist born out of turbulent times. But also, as his old friend Ben Jonson[3] said: "He was not of an age, but for all time."

3. **Ben Jonson.** (1572–1637) English Renaissance dramatist

REFER TO TEXT ▶ ▶ ▶ ▶	▶ REASON WITH TEXT	
1a. Identify the categories into which the episodes are divided. Summarize what the first episode is about.	1b. Explain why the information presented in the first episode would be important to understanding Shakespeare's life.	**Understand** **Find meaning**
2a. Recall Ben Johnson's opinion of Shakespeare. How is this connected to the title of the fourth episode?	2b. Based on the information provided, infer what information you think the fourth episode will cover.	**Analyze** **Take things apart**
3a. Cite specific examples of how this documentary approaches Shakespeare's life differently than other television shows.	3b. Evaluate how effective you think this approach will be. What benefits and disadvantages do you see about this approach?	**Evaluate** **Make judgments**

TEXT ←TO→ TEXT CONNECTION

Just as Shakespeare used historical writings and speculation to create scenes in the lives of Julius Caesar, Brutus, and Antony, so do modern researchers draw upon their imaginations, as well as historical documents, to present the life of William Shakespeare.

- How do you think Shakespeare would have felt about his life being analyzed in this fashion by the documentary team working with the Royal Shakespeare Company?
- In what cases is it acceptable to use imagination and speculation when discussing history and when is it not appropriate? Explain.

GRAMMAR & STYLE

Active and Passive Voice

Did you know that verbs have voices? The voice of an action verb tells whether the subject of the sentence performs or receives the action. When the subject performs the action of the verb, the verb is in the **active voice.** When the subject receives the action of the verb, the verb is in the **passive voice.** A sentence written in passive voice uses some form of *be* as a helping verb, followed by a past participle. Remember, the forms of *be* are *is, are, was, were, be, am, been,* and *being.*

EXAMPLES

passive: Huge cypress trees were uprooted by the hurricane.
active: The hurricane uprooted the huge cypress trees.

passive: The dentist was bitten by a child patient.
active: The child patient bit the dentist.

passive: The necklace was stolen by the thief.
active: The thief stole the necklace.

A common characteristic of poor writing is the overuse of the passive voice. In general, the active voice makes writing more natural and interesting. Use active verbs to avoid wordiness and awkwardness.

EXAMPLES

passive: An excellent conversation was held by the class. (Notice how this sentence is awkward and does not imitate natural speech.)
active: The class held an excellent conversation.

passive: The award of valor was presented to the firefighter by the fire chief. (Notice how this sentence is not concise and rambles a bit.)
active: The fire chief presented the firefighter with the award of valor.

The active voice is used more frequently than the passive voice because active verbs express ideas more directly. However, there are some situations where it is better to use passive voice:

- when the doer of the action is unknown or unimportant

EXAMPLE

The cathedral was built in 1632. (No one knows who built the cathedral.)

- when you want to emphasize the more important part of the sentence

EXAMPLE

The barn had been struck by lightning. (The barn is more important to the discussion than the lightning.)

- when you are trying to hide responsibility

EXAMPLE

Mistakes were made. (By not naming the agent, responsibility for the mistakes is hidden.)

REVIEW TERMS

- **active voice:** the subject of the sentence performs the action
- **passive voice:** the subject of the sentence receives the action
- **helping verb:** verb that helps the main verb tell about an action
- **past participle:** the form of the verb used in perfect tenses, such as *has gone* (present perfect; *gone,* not *went*), *had seen* (past perfect; *seen,* not *saw*)

Identify Active/Passive Voice

Identify the verbs in the following sentences from and about *The Tragedy of Julius Caesar,* Act I, as either active or passive. (Some spellings have been changed from the original.) Note that in some sentences, only one part may be in passive voice.

1. "When Caesar says, 'Do this,' it is performed."
2. "If I have veiled my look, I turn the trouble of my countenance merely upon myself."
3. "Let not therefore my good friends be grieved."
4. "Then, Brutus, I have much mistaken your passion."
5. Many citizens have wished that Brutus would be the leader of Rome.
6. Cassius complains to Brutus that Caesar is unworthy and weak.
7. "I do believe that these applauses are for some new honors that are heaped on Caesar."
8. Caesar is disturbed by the look of Cassius; he would rather be surrounded by men who don't think as much.
9. "Was the crown offered to him thrice?"
10. "If Caesars had stabbed their mothers, they would have done no less."

Fix Sentence Voice

In this paragraph about *The Tragedy of Julius Caesar,* correct the passive sentences that should be active, and vice versa. Share your rewritten paragraph with a classmate and be prepared to explain why you changed the sentences you did.

In Act I of *The Tragedy of Julius Caesar,* Caesar has returned to Rome from Spain. The senators fear that the people will make him a king. Caesar's growing popularity worries Brutus. Brutus is told by Cassius that Caesar is only a great leader because Romans are so weak. A story about how Caesar nearly drowned and was saved by Cassius is told. A plan is developed to take down Caesar as the night is filled with strange omens. On the ides of March, Caesar is killed by the conspirators. A warning was given to Caesar by his wife, but Caesar did not listen. A speech was given at Caesar's funeral by Mark Antony. He tries to convince the people that Caesar was a good and noble man.

Use Appropriate Voice in Your Writing

A frequent theme in literature is the conflict between the individual and society. From a work of literature you have recently read, select a character who struggles against society. In a brief essay, identify the character and the conflict, and explain why and how his or her struggle is important. Use at least three passive verbs and three active verbs in your essay.

EXTEND THE SKILL

Find a television news channel that broadcasts speeches by politicians or sessions of Congress. Record a few minutes of a speech and write out a transcript of it. Find where the passive voice is used. Select a few examples and write a brief report on how and why the passive voice is used in those instances.

VOCABULARY & SPELLING

UNDERSTAND THE CONCEPT **APPLY THE SKILL**

Using a Dictionary and a Thesaurus

Many times, you will be able to figure out the meaning of an unknown word just by looking at the context in which you found it. Sometimes, though, the context holds no clues or you might need a more precise definition than the context gives you. In those cases, you may need to use reference materials, such as a dictionary or a thesaurus, in order to get an exact meaning.

A dictionary contains a wealth of information about words. In addition to the definition of a word, you can find its part of speech, pronunciation, and etymology. The *etymology* of a word traces its origins back to Old English or another language.

Look at the following dictionary entries for the word *keen*. Parts of the entry are labeled.

A *thesaurus*, a reference book that contains lists of synonyms and antonyms, is a useful companion to the dictionary. The thesaurus is especially helpful when you can't think of the exact word to convey your meaning, or when you want to enliven your writing by using a variety of words.

To use a thesaurus, simply look up a word and find a list of other words that have approximately the same meaning. For example, suppose you had written the following sentence about poet e. e. cummings:

> Modern poet e. e. cummings was famous for his strange use of punctuation.

You decide that *strange* is not exactly the right word. Looking it up in a thesaurus, you find many synonyms, including *odd, unusual, extraordinary, uncommon, eccentric, unconventional,* and *bizarre.* You might revise your sentence to read: Modern poet e. e. cummings was famous for his unconventional use of punctuation.

4 3 5 2 6 7 8

¹**keen** (kēn′) *adj.* [ME *kene* brave, sharp, fr. OE *cēne* brave; akin to OHG *kuoni* brave] (13c) **1** : having a sharp edge or point ⟨a *keen* sword⟩ **2** : having a sharp or piercing effect a *keen* insult **3 a** : having or showing a sharp mind **b** : being particularly perceptive or sensitive ⟨a *keen* eye; a *keen* sense of smell⟩ **4** : showing great enthusiasm ⟨she is very *keen* on horses⟩. *syn* see *sharp, eager.*
— **keen • ly** *adv.* — **keen • ness** (kēn′ nəs) *n.*
²**keen** (kēn′) *n.* [Ir *caoinim,* or "lament"] **1** : a wailing cry of mourning
—*v.* **2** : to make wailing cries of mourning for the dead

1. **Main entry.** A word may have one or more main entries. Here, *keen* meaning "sharp" is listed as a separate entry from *keen* meaning "wail or cry." The main entry shows how a word is spelled and how it may be divided into syllables.
2. **Pronunciation.** The pronunciation is shown by the use of phonetic symbols. See your dictionary for a pronunciation key.
3. **Part-of-speech label.** The part-of-speech label indicates whether a word may be used as a noun (*n.*), verb (*v.*), adjective (*adj.*), or another part of speech.

4. **Etymology.** The etymology gives the origins and history of the word, telling how and approximately when the word came into English. Many terms are abbreviated. Here, ME=Middle English, OE=Old English, OHG=Old High German, and Ir=Irish.
5. **Definitions.** Each definition of a word is numbered (e.g., **1, 2, 3**). Some definitions are broken down into two or more sub-definitions (e.g., **a, b, c**).
6. **Example phrase.** Example phrases are sometimes given to show how the word may be used.
7. **Synonyms.** Synonyms, words with similar meanings, and antonyms, words with opposite meanings, may be given. Some dictionaries may also explain the different shades of meaning carried by each synonym.
8. **Other forms.** Related forms of the word may be given at the end of the entry.

Exercise A

Use a dictionary to find the etymology (the origins) of each of the following words from *The Tragedy of Julius Caesar* and the poem "The Ides of March (page 600)." Also note the pronunciation and the various meanings of each word, if there is more than one.

1. puissant
2. grandiose
3. chastisement
4. corporal
5. entourage
6. infirmity
7. grievous
8. surly
9. fawn
10. visage

Exercise B

The dictionary also provides information about how a word is generally used. A usage label may tell you, for example, that a word is *slang* (informal language only), used only in a certain *dialect* (such as British English), *archaic* (no longer in common usage), or *obsolete* (no longer used at all). With a partner, try to find a word or definition of a word (the meaning may have changed over time) that is labeled archaic or obsolete from the vocabulary words and footnoted words in *The Tragedy of Julius Caesar.* What other words could be used in place of the archaic or obsolete ones?

Exercise C

Using a thesaurus, rewrite the sentences below to replace the overused word *great* with a more interesting or appropriate word or words.

1. The plebeians had a <u>great</u> time at the Lupercalia festival.
2. Returning from Spain, Caesar and his armies had to travel <u>great</u> distances.
3. Julius Caesar was a <u>great</u> Roman ruler.
4. The conspirators' plan was going <u>great</u> until Antony gave his speech.
5. Brutus was awake all night worrying about the <u>great</u> decision he would have to make.

6. It is <u>great</u> to be able to read Shakespeare in high school.
7. Shakespeare was a <u>great</u> playwright; some people believe he was the greatest of all time.
8. Sometimes, it takes a <u>great</u> deal of effort to understand Shakespeare's language.
9. Several <u>great</u> productions of *The Tragedy of Julius Caesar* are available on film.
10. It is perhaps difficult to find a modern playwright who is as <u>great</u> as Shakespeare.

Exercise D

For each of the following vocabulary words from *The Tragedy of Julius Caesar,* use a thesaurus to find its synonyms and at least one antonym.

1. commend
2. surly
3. servile
4. grievous
5. endure
6. cull
7. puissant
8. piteous
9. gracious
10. ambitious

EXTEND THE SKILL

Take one of the speeches from *The Tragedy of Julius Caesar,* such as Brutus's or Antony's speech after the death of Caesar, and rewrite it in modern language using a thesaurus. Without changing the overall meaning, consider choosing related words that convey a different sense. For example, you could use slang instead of formal language in Antony's speech, changing "I come to bury Caesar, not to praise him," to "I come to plant Caesar, not to give him props." Then read your new speech to a partner.

View of Rome [Detail], c.1700s. Antonio Canaletto (Giovanni Antonio Canale).

Act II

Scene 1: Brutus's Garden in Rome, the Ides of March

Enter Brutus *in his orchard.*[1]

Brutus.　What, Lucius, ho!
I cannot by the progress of the stars
Give guess how near to day. Lucius, I say!
I would it were my fault to sleep so soundly.
5　When, Lucius, when? Awake, I say! What, Lucius!

Enter Lucius.

Lucius.　Call'd you, my lord?

Act II, Scene 1
1. ***orchard.*** Garden

Brutus. Get me a taper[2] in my study, Lucius.
When it is lighted, come and call me here.

Lucius. I will, my lord.

Exit Lucius.

10 **Brutus.** It must be by his death; and for my part,
I know no personal cause to spurn[3] at him,
But for the general.[4] He would be crown'd:
How that might change his nature, there's the question.
It is the bright day that brings forth the adder,[5]
15 And that craves[6] wary walking. Crown him that,
And then I grant we put a sting in him
That at his will he may do danger with.[7]
Th' abuse of greatness is when it disjoins
Remorse from power;[8] and to speak truth of Caesar,
20 I have not known when his affections sway'd[9]
More than his reason. But 'tis a common proof[10]
That lowliness[11] is young ambition's ladder,
Whereto the climber-upward turns his face;
But when he once attains the upmost round,[12]
25 He then unto the ladder turns his back,
Looks in the clouds, scorning the base degrees
By which he did ascend. So Caesar may;
Then lest he may, prevent.[13] And since the quarrel
Will bear no color for the thing he is,
30 Fashion it thus: that what he is, augmented,
Would run to these and these extremities;[14]
And therefore think him as a serpent's egg,
Which, hatch'd, would as his kind grow mischievous,
And kill him in the shell.

Enter Lucius.

35 **Lucius.** The taper burneth in your closet,[15] sir.
Searching the window for a flint,[16] I found
This paper, thus seal'd up, and I am sure
It did not lie there when I went to bed.

Gives him the letter.

Brutus. Get you to bed again, it is not day.
40 Is not tomorrow, boy, the ides of March?

Lucius. I know not, sir.

Brutus. Look in the calendar, and bring me word.

Lucius. I will, sir.

Exit Lucius.

---

2. **taper.** Candle

3. **spurn.** Goad or kick
4. **the general.** The general welfare or common good
5. **adder.** Type of poisonous snake
6. **craves.** Requires or demands
7. **we put…with.** Brutus is making the point that power corrupts.
8. **disjoins / Remorse from power.** Makes the powerful no longer merciful
9. **affections sway'd.** Feelings moved him
10. **'tis a common proof.** It is commonly proved or shown
11. **lowliness.** Pretended humility
12. **round.** Rung

13. **prevent.** The word is said by Brutus as a command or exhortation to himself.
14. **since…extremities.** Since our case against Caesar cannot be justified (will bear no color) by Caesar's present behavior, we must state our argument this way: If Caesar's power grows (is augmented), it will reach terrible extremes.

15. **closet.** Room
16. **flint.** Piece of stone that creates a spark with which to light the candle

BRUTUS.   The exhalations[17] whizzing in the air
45   Give so much light that I may read by them.

Opens the letter and reads.

"Brutus, thou sleep'st; awake, and see thyself!
Shall Rome, etc. Speak, strike, redress!"[18]
"Brutus, thou sleep'st, awake!"
Such instigations[19] have been often dropp'd
50   Where I have took[20] them up.
"Shall Rome, etc." Thus must I piece it out:[21]
Shall Rome stand under one man's awe? What, Rome?
My ancestors did from the streets of Rome
The Tarquin[22] drive when he was call'd a king.
55   "Speak, strike, redress!" Am I entreated
To speak and strike? O Rome, I make thee promise,
If the redress will follow, thou receivest
Thy full petition[23] at the hand of Brutus!

Enter LUCIUS.

LUCIUS.   Sir, March is wasted fifteen days.

Knock within.

60   **BRUTUS.**   'Tis good. Go to the gate. Somebody knocks.

Exit LUCIUS.

Since Cassius first did whet[24] me against Caesar,
I have not slept.
Between the acting of a dreadful thing
And the first motion, all the interim is
65   Like a phantasma[25] or a hideous dream.
The genius and the mortal instruments[26]
Are then in council; and the state of a man,
Like to a little kingdom, suffers then
The nature of an insurrection.[27]

Enter LUCIUS.

70   **LUCIUS.**   Sir, 'tis your brother[28] Cassius at the door,
Who doth desire to see you.

BRUTUS.   Is he alone?

LUCIUS.   No, sir, there are more with him.

BRUTUS.   Do you know them?

LUCIUS.   No, sir, their hats are pluck'd about[29] their ears
And half their faces buried in their cloaks,

---

17. **exhalations.** Meteors (omens of important events)

18. **redress.** Right a wrong

19. **instigations.** Letters urging action
20. **took.** Taken
21. **piece it out.** Guess the rest of the sentence

22. **Tarquin.** Last king of Rome

23. **Thy full petition.** All that you ask for

24. **whet.** Sharpen; incite

in • ter • im (in´ tə rəm) *n.,* in-between time

25. **phantasma.** Fantastic imagining
26. **genius and the mortal instruments.** Mental and physical powers
27. **The nature of an insurrection.** A kind of rebellion

28. **brother.** Brother-in-law. Brutus's sister Junia is married to Cassius.

29. **pluck'd about.** Drawn down to

"O Conspiracy..." The conspirators visit Brutus's house.

75   That by no means I may discover them
    By any mark of favor.[30]

    BRUTUS.   Let 'em enter.

                                 Exit LUCIUS.

    They are the faction. O Conspiracy,
    Sham'st thou to show thy dang'rous brow by night,
    When evils are most free? O then, by day

80   Where wilt thou find a cavern dark enough
    To mask thy monstrous <u>visage</u>? Seek none, Conspiracy!
    Hide it in smiles and affability,
    For if thou path, thy native semblance on,
    Not Erebus itself were dim enough

85   To hide thee from prevention.[31]

    Enter the conspirators, CASSIUS, CASCA, DECIUS, CINNA, METELLUS, *and*
    TREBONIUS.

    CASSIUS.   I think we are too bold upon[32] your rest.
    Good morrow, Brutus, do we trouble you?

    BRUTUS.   I have been up this hour, awake all night.
    Know I these men that come along with you?

90   **CASSIUS.**   Yes, every man of them; and no man here
    But honors you, and every one doth wish
    You had but that opinion of yourself

30. **by no means...favor.** I am unable to recognize (discover) them by any familiar characteristic.

vis • age (vi´ zij) *n.,* face; appearance

31. **if thou...prevention.** If you walk about (path) showing your true natures (native semblance), not even the darkest place in hell can hide you. (In Greek and Roman mythology, Erebus was a dark place in the underworld.)
32. **too bold upon.** Intruding upon

Which every noble Roman bears of you.
This is Trebonius.

BRUTUS.   He is welcome hither.[33]

CASSIUS.   This, Decius Brutus.

95   **BRUTUS.**   He is welcome too.

CASSIUS.   This, Casca; this, Cinna; and this, Metellus Cimber.

BRUTUS.   They are all welcome.
What watchful cares[34] do <u>interpose</u> themselves
Betwixt[35] your eyes and night?

100   **CASSIUS.**   Shall I entreat a word?

They whisper.

DECIUS.   Here lies the east; doth not the day break here?

CASCA.   No.

CINNA.   O, pardon, sir, it doth; and yon gray lines
That fret[36] the clouds are messengers of day.

105   **CASCA.**   You shall confess that you are both deceiv'd.
Here, as I point my sword, the sun arises,
Which is a great way growing on the south,
Weighing the youthful season of the year.[37]
Some two months hence, up higher toward the north
110   He first presents his fire, and the high east[38]
Stands, as the Capitol, directly here.

BRUTUS.   Give me your hands all over,[39] one by one.

CASSIUS.   And let us swear our resolution.

BRUTUS.   No, not an oath! If not the face of men,
115   The sufferance of our souls, the time's abuse—
If these be motives weak, break off betimes,[40]
And every man hence to his idle bed;
So let highsighted[41] tyranny range on,
Till each man drop by lottery.[42] But if these
120   (As I am sure they do) bear fire enough
To kindle cowards, and to steel with valor
The melting spirits of women, then, countrymen,
What need we any spur but our own cause
To prick us to redress? what other bond
125   Than secret Romans, that have spoke the word
And will not palter?[43] and what other oath
Than honesty to honesty engag'd

33. **hither.** Here

34. **watchful cares.** Worries that keep a person awake at night

in • ter • pose
(ĭn' tər pōz') *v.*, to place or come between

35. **Betwixt.** Between

36. **fret.** Form a pattern upon

37. **You shall…year.** Casca insists that the sun rises farther to the south because it is still early in the year.
38. **high east.** Due east

39. **all over.** All turned over; palms down, one on top of the other

40. **If not…betimes.** If the sadness on people's faces, our suffering souls, and the abuses, or misdeeds, of our day are not enough to make us keep our promise, then let's break it at once (betimes).
41. **highsighted.** Arrogant
42. **by lottery.** By chance

43. **palter.** Speak in double-talk

That this shall be, or we will fall for it?
Swear priests and cowards, and men cautelous,[44]

130 Old feeble carrions,[45] and such suffering souls
That welcome wrongs; unto bad causes swear
Such creatures as men doubt; but do not stain
The even virtue of our enterprise,
Nor th' insuppressive mettle[46] of our spirits,

135 To think that or our cause or our performance[47]
Did need an oath; when every drop of blood
That every Roman bears, and nobly bears,
Is guilty of a several bastardy,[48]
If he do break the smallest particle

140 Of any promise that hath pass'd from him.

CASSIUS.   But what of Cicero? Shall we sound him?
I think he will stand very strong with us.

CASCA. Let us not leave him out.

CINNA.   No, by no means.

METELLUS.   O, let us have him, for his silver hairs

145 Will purchase us a good opinion,
And buy men's voices to <u>commend</u> our deeds.
It shall be said his judgment rul'd our hands;
Our youths and wildness shall no whit appear,
But all be buried in his gravity.[49]

150 BRUTUS.   O, name him not; let us not break with[50] him,
For he will never follow anything
That other men begin.

CASSIUS.   Then leave him out.

CASCA.   Indeed he is not fit.

DECIUS.   Shall no man else be touch'd but only Caesar?

155 CASSIUS.   Decius, well urg'd. I think it is not meet,[51]
Mark Antony, so well belov'd of Caesar,
Should outlive Caesar. We shall find of him
A shrewd contriver; and you know, his means,
If he improve them, may well stretch so far

160 As to annoy[52] us all; which to prevent,
Let Antony and Caesar fall together.

BRUTUS.   Our course will seem too bloody, Caius Cassius
To cut the head off and then hack the limbs[53]—
Like wrath in death and envy afterwards;[54]

165 For Antony is but a limb of Caesar.

44. **cautelous.** Full of deception

45. **carrions.** Literally, pieces of dead flesh; figuratively, people who are almost dead

46. **insuppressive mettle.** Unyielding nature

47. **or our cause...performance.** Either our cause or our performance

48. **Is guilty...bastardy.** Shows that we are not truly Romans

com • mend (kə mend´) v., to praise

49. **gravity.** Seriousness

50. **break with.** Share the secret with

51. **meet.** Okay; acceptable

52. **annoy.** Hurt

53. **cut the head...the limbs.** Kill Caesar and then also kill his supporters

54. **Like wrath...afterwards.** Brutus is saying that killing Caesar should not be made to seem like a matter of anger or malice.

SOCIAL STUDIES
CONNECTION

The "Limb of Caesar" In line 165 and following, Brutus metaphorically describes Antony as a limb of Caesar. This comparison is a reference to the Elizabethan conception of the king's two bodies. According to Elizabethan notions of kingship, a king had two bodies: a physical and mortal body, and a political and immortal body. Shakespeare is describing Caesar as a typical Elizabethan monarch would be described — as possessing a physical body that will die when the conspirators "cut the head off," as well as possessing the authority of kingship, or a "kingly" body, that will continue to exist even after physical death. Antony, here, is described as the limb of kingship, indicating that he will take on Caesar's political power once Caesar's physical body is destroyed. While this concept had not yet evolved in Caesar's time, it would have had contemporary significance to Shakespeare's audience.

Let's be sacrificers, but not butchers, Caius.
We all stand up against the spirit of Caesar,
And in the spirit of men there is no blood;
O that we then could come by[55] Caesar's spirit,

170 And not dismember Caesar! But, alas,
Caesar must bleed for it! And, gentle friends,
Let's kill him boldly, but not wrathfully;
Let's carve him as a dish fit for the gods,
Not hew him as a carcass[56] fit for hounds;

175 And let our hearts, as subtle masters do,
Stir up their servants to an act of rage,
And after seem to chide 'em.[57] This shall make
Our purpose necessary, and not envious;
Which so appearing to the common eyes,

180 We shall be called purgers,[58] not murderers.
And for Mark Antony, think not of him;
For he can do no more than Caesar's arm
When Caesar's head is off.

CASSIUS.   Yet I fear him,
For in the ingrafted[59] love he bears to Caesar—

185 BRUTUS.   Alas, good Cassius, do not think of him.

55. **come by.** Possess

56. **carcass.** Body of a dead animal
57. **let our hearts...chide 'em.** Let our hearts treat our hands (servants) the way tricky masters do—allow them to do our dirty work, and then scold (chide) them afterward by expressing our regret.
58. **purgers.** Ones who get rid of, or cleanse, something

59. **ingrafted.** Joined together, as the limb of one tree might be joined to the trunk of another

564   UNIT 4 DRAMA

If he love Caesar, all that he can do
Is to himself—take thought[60] and die for Caesar;
And that were much he should, for he is given
To sports, to wildness, and much company.

190 **TREBONIUS.**   There is no fear in him; let him not die,
For he will live, and laugh at this hereafter.

Clock strikes.

BRUTUS.   Peace, count the clock.

CASSIUS.   The clock hath stricken three.

TREBONIUS.   'Tis time to part.

CASSIUS.   But it is doubtful yet
Whether Caesar will come forth today or no;
195 For he is superstitious grown of late,
Quite from the main opinion[61] he held once
Of fantasy, of dreams, and ceremonies.[62]
It may be these apparent prodigies,[63]
The unaccustom'd terror of this night,
200 And the persuasion of his augurers[64]
May hold him from the Capitol today.

DECIUS.   Never fear that. If he be so resolv'd,
I can o'ersway him;[65] for he loves to hear
That unicorns may be betray'd with trees,[66]
205 And bears with glasses,[67] elephants with holes,[68]
Lions with toils,[69] and men with flatterers;
But when I tell him he hates flatterers
He says he does, being then most flattered.
Let me work;
210 For I can give his humor the true bent,[70]
And I will bring him to the Capitol.

CASSIUS.   Nay, we will all of us be there to fetch him.

BRUTUS.   By the eighth hour; is that the uttermost?

CINNA.   Be that the uttermost, and fail not then.

215 **METELLUS.**   Caius Ligarius doth bear Caesar hard,[71]
Who rated[72] him for speaking well of Pompey;
I wonder none of you have thought of him.

BRUTUS.   Now, good Metellus, go along by[73] him.
He loves me well, and I have given him reasons;
220 Send him but hither, and I'll fashion[74] him.

CASSIUS.   The morning comes upon 's.[75] We'll leave you, Brutus,

60. **take th**
mourn

61. **Quite from the main opinion.** Very different from the strong opinion
62. **ceremonies.** Rituals held to predict the future
63. **apparent prodigies.** Noticeable omens
64. **augurers** (ô´gyər ərs). People who read omens to predict the future
65. **o'ersway him.** Convince him otherwise
66. **betray'd with trees.** Tricked into burying its horn into a tree and so captured
67. **glasses.** Looking glasses, or mirrors
68. **holes.** Pits dug into the ground
69. **toils.** Nets
70. **give...bent.** Put him in the right state of mind

71. **bear Caesar hard.** Dislike Caesar
72. **rated.** Chastised

73. **along by.** To
74. **fashion.** Mold; shape; convince
75. **The morning comes upon 's.** The sun is up.

And, friends, disperse yourselves; but all remember
What you have said, and show yourselves true Romans.

BRUTUS.   Good gentlemen, look fresh and merrily;
225 Let not our looks put on our purposes,
But bear it[76] as our Roman actors do,
With untir'd spirits and formal constancy.[77]
And so good morrow to you every one.

Exeunt. Manet BRUTUS.

Boy! Lucius! Fast asleep? It is no matter,
230 Enjoy the honey-heavy dew of slumber.
Thou hast no figures[78] nor no fantasies,
Which busy care draws in the brains of men;
Therefore thou sleep'st so sound.

Enter PORTIA.

PORTIA.   Brutus, my lord!

BRUTUS.   Portia! What mean you? Wherefore[79] rise you now?
235 It is not for[80] your health thus to commit
Your weak condition to the raw cold morning.

PORTIA.   Nor for yours neither. Y' have ungently, Brutus,
Stole from my bed; and yesternight[81] at supper
You suddenly arose and walk'd about,
240 Musing and sighing, with your arms across;
And when I ask'd you what the matter was,
You star'd upon me with ungentle looks.
I urg'd you further; then you scratch'd your head
And too impatiently stamp'd with your foot.
245 Yet I insisted, yet you answer'd not,
But with an angry wafter[82] of your hand
Gave sign for me to leave you. So I did,
Fearing to strengthen that impatience
Which seem'd too much enkindled; and withal[83]
250 Hoping it was but an effect of humor,[84]
Which sometime hath his hour with every man.
It will not let you eat, nor talk, nor sleep;
And could it work so much upon your shape
As it hath much prevail'd on your condition,
255 I should not know you Brutus. Dear my lord,
Make me acquainted with your cause of grief.

BRUTUS.   I am not well in health, and that is all.

PORTIA.   Brutus is wise, and were he not in health,
He would embrace the means to come by it.

76. **bear it.** Perform the role
77. **formal constancy.** Unfaltering dignity

78. **figures.** Wild imaginings

79. **Wherefore.** Why
80. **for.** Good for

81. **yesternight.** Last night

82. **wafter.** Waving

83. **withal.** Also
84. **humor.** Ill spirits

"You have some sick offense within your mind..." Brutus and his wife Portia (played by James Mason and Deborah Kerr).

260   **BRUTUS.**   Why, so I do. Good Portia, go to bed.

      PORTIA.   Is Brutus sick? and is it physical
To walk unbraced[85] and suck up the humors[86]
Of the dank morning? What, is Brutus sick?
And will he steal out of his wholesome bed
265   To dare the vile contagion of the night,
And tempt the rheumy and unpurgèd[87] air
To add unto his sickness? No, my Brutus,
You have some sick offense within your mind,
Which, by the right and virtue of my place,[88]
270   I ought to know of; and upon my knees
I charm you, by my once commended beauty,
By all your vows of love, and that great vow
Which did incorporate[89] and make us one,
That you unfold to me, yourself, your half,
275   Why you are heavy, and what men tonight
Have had resort to you; for here have been
Some six or seven, who did hide their faces
Even from darkness.

      BRUTUS.   Kneel not, gentle Portia.

      PORTIA.   I should not need, if you were gentle Brutus.
280   Within the bond of marriage, tell me, Brutus,

85. **is it physical… unbraced.** Is it good for the body to walk around with your shirt unbuttoned?
86. **humors.** Dampness and cold
87. **rheumy and unpurgèd.** Damp and impure

88. **my place.** Portia's position as his wife

89. **incorporate.** Join together

Is it excepted[90] I should know no secrets
That appertain[91] to you? Am I yourself
But, as it were, in sort or limitation?[92]
To keep with you at meals, comfort your bed,
285 And talk to you sometimes? Dwell I but in the suburbs[93]
Of your good pleasure? If it be no more,
Portia is Brutus' harlot, not his wife.

BRUTUS.   You are my true and honorable wife,
As dear to me as are the ruddy[94] drops
290 That visit my sad heart.

PORTIA.   If this were true, then should I[95] know this secret.
I grant I am a woman; but withal
A woman that Lord Brutus took to wife.
I grant I am a woman; but withal
295 A woman well reputed, Cato's[96] daughter.
Think you I am no stronger than my sex,
Being so father'd and so husbanded?
Tell me your counsels,[97] I will not disclose 'em.
I have made strong proof of my constancy,
300 Giving myself a voluntary wound
Here, in the thigh; can I bear that with patience,
And not my husband's secrets?

BRUTUS.   O ye gods !
Render me worthy of this noble wife!

Knock.

Hark, hark, one knocks! Portia, go in a while,
305 And by and by thy bosom shall partake
The secrets of my heart.
All my engagements I will construe to thee,
All the charactery of[98] my sad brows.
Leave me with haste.

Exit PORTIA.

Lucius, who's that knocks?

Enter LUCIUS *and* CAIUS LIGARIUS.

310 **LUCIUS.**   Here is a sick man that would speak with you.

BRUTUS.   Caius Ligarius, that Metellus spake of.
Boy, stand aside. Caius Ligarius, how?[99]

Exit LUCIUS.

LIGARIUS.   Vouchsafe[100] good morrow from a feeble tongue.

---

90. **excepted.** Specified; required
91. **appertain.** Relate
92. **in sort or limitation?** Only in part
93. **suburbs.** Outskirts of a city, where theaters, taverns, and houses of ill repute were to be found

whore

94. **ruddy.** Red

95. **should I.** I should

96. **Cato's.** Belonging to Marcus Porcius Cato, who was an ally of Pompey against Caesar and was known for his nobility and integrity
97. **counsels.** Secrets

98. **charactery of.** Writing found on (that is, the troubled look)

99. **how?** How are you?

100. **Vouchsafe.** Agree to accept

BRUTUS.   O, what a time have you chose out, brave Caius,
315 To wear a kerchief!¹⁰¹ Would you were not sick!

LIGARIUS.   I am not sick, if Brutus have in hand
Any <u>exploit</u> worthy the name of honor.

BRUTUS.   Such an exploit have I in hand, Ligarius,
Had you a healthful ear to hear of it.

320 **LIGARIUS.**   By all the gods that Romans bow before,
I here discard my sickness! Soul of Rome!
Brave son, deriv'd from honorable loins!¹⁰²
Thou, like an exorcist, hast conjur'd up
My mortified¹⁰³ spirit. Now bid me run,
325 And I will strive with things impossible,
Yea, get the better of them. What's to do?

BRUTUS.   A piece of work that will make sick men whole.

LIGARIUS.   But are not some whole that we must make sick?

BRUTUS.   That must we also. What it is, my Caius,
330 I shall unfold to thee, as we are going,
To whom it must be done.

LIGARIUS.   Set on your foot
And with a heart new-fir'd I follow you,
To do I know not what; but it <u>sufficeth</u>
That Brutus leads me on.

Thunder.

BRUTUS.   Follow me then.

Exeunt.

SCENE II: THE HOME OF JULIUS CAESAR

Thunder and lightning. Enter JULIUS CAESAR *in his nightgown.*

CAESAR.   Nor¹ heaven nor earth have been at peace tonight.
Thrice hath Calphurnia in her sleep cried out,
"Help, ho! they murther² Caesar!" Who's within?

Enter a SERVANT.

SERVANT.   My lord?

5 **CAESAR.**   Go bid the priests do present sacrifice,³
And bring me their opinions of success.⁴

SERVANT.   I will, my lord.

Exit.

101. **To wear a kerchief.** To be sick

ex • ploit (ek´ sploit´) *n.,* deed; heroic act

102. **loins.** Thighs. The reference is to Brutus's heritage. He is descended from Lucius Junius Brutus, who helped to establish the Roman Republic by overthrowing a king.
103. **mortified.** Deadened

suf • fice (sə fīs´) *v.,* to be enough

ACT II, SCENE II
1. **Nor.** Neither

2. **murther.** Murder

3. **do present sacrifice.** Immediately perform a sacrifice (and read the omens)
4. **opinions of success.** Predictions about whether I shall be successful

"Caesar...You shall not stir out of your house today." Calphurnia (played by Greer Garson) pleads with her husband (played by Louis Calhern) to stay home on the Ides of March.

Enter CALPHURNIA.

CALPHURNIA.   What mean you, Caesar? Think you to walk forth?
You shall not stir out of your house today.

10 **CAESAR.**   Caesar shall forth; the things that threaten'd me
Ne'er look'd but on my back; when they shall see
The face of Caesar, they are vanished.

CALPHURNIA.   Caesar, I never stood on ceremonies,[5]
Yet now they fright[6] me. There is one within,
15 Besides the things that we have heard and seen,
Recounts most horrid sights seen by the watch.[7]
A lioness hath whelped[8] in the streets,
And graves have yawn'd and yielded up their dead;
Fierce fiery warriors fight upon the clouds
20 In ranks and squadrons and right form[9] of war,

5. **stood on ceremonies.** Believed in omens
6. **fright.** Frighten

7. **watch.** Watchmen
8. **hath whelped.** Has given birth

9. **right form.** Proper formations

Which drizzled blood upon the Capitol;
The noise of battle hurtled in the air;
Horses did neigh, and dying men did groan,
And ghosts did shriek and squeal about the streets.
25 O Caesar, these things are beyond all use,[10]
And I do fear them.

CAESAR.   What can be avoided
Whose end is purpos'd by the mighty gods?
Yet Caesar shall go forth; for these predictions
Are to the world in general as to Caesar.[11]

30 CALPHURNIA.   When beggars die there are no comets seen;
The heavens themselves blaze forth the death of princes.

CAESAR.   Cowards die many times before their deaths,
The valiant never taste of death but once.
Of all the wonders that I yet have heard,
35 It seems to me most strange that men should fear,
Seeing that death, a necessary end,
Will come when it will come.

Enter a SERVANT.

                                What say the augurers?[12]

SERVANT.   They would not have you to stir forth today.
Plucking the entrails of an offering forth,[13]
40 They could not find a heart within the beast.

CAESAR.   The gods do this in shame of cowardice;
Caesar should be a beast without a heart
If he should stay at home today for fear.
No, Caesar shall not; Danger knows full well
45 That Caesar is more dangerous than he.
We are two lions litter'd[14] in one day,
And I the elder and more terrible;
And Caesar shall go forth.

CALPHURNIA.   Alas, my lord,
Your wisdom is consum'd in confidence.
50 Do not go forth today; call it my fear
That keeps you in the house, and not your own.
We'll send Mark Antony to the Senate house
And he shall say you are not well today.
Let me, upon my knee, prevail in this.

55 CAESAR.   Mark Antony shall say I am not well,
And for thy humor[15] I will stay at home.

Enter DECIUS.

10. **beyond all use.** Outside all normal experience

11. **Are to...Caesar.** Apply as much to the rest of the world as they do to me

12. **augurers.** Religious officials of ancient Rome who foretold the future by reading signs and omens
13. **Plucking...forth.** It was believed that signs could be read by examining the entrails, or inner organs, of animals used for sacrifices.

14. **litter'd.** Born

15. **for thy humor.** At your insistence, to please you

Here's Decius Brutus; he shall tell them so.

DECIUS.   Caesar, all hail! Good morrow, worthy Caesar,
I come to fetch you to the Senate house.

60   CAESAR.   And you are come in very happy time
To bear my greeting to the senators,
And tell them that I will not come today.
Cannot, is false; and that I dare not, falser:
I will not come today. Tell them so, Decius.

CALPHURNIA.   Say he is sick.

65   CAESAR.   Shall Caesar send a lie?
Have I in conquest stretch'd mine arm so far,
To be afeard to tell greybeards the truth?
Decius, go tell them Caesar will not come.

DECIUS.   Most mighty Caesar, let me know some cause,
70   Lest I be laugh'd at when I tell them so.

CAESAR.   The cause is in my will, I will not come:
That is enough to satisfy the Senate.
But for your private satisfaction,
Because I love you, I will let you know.
75   Calphurnia here, my wife, stays[16] me at home:
She dreamt tonight she saw my statue,
Which, like a fountain with an hundred spouts,
Did run pure blood; and many lusty Romans
Came smiling and did bathe their hands in it.
80   And these does she apply for[17] warnings and portents
And evils imminent, and on her knee
Hath begg'd that I will stay at home today.

DECIUS.   This dream is all amiss[18] interpreted,
It was a vision fair and fortunate.
85   Your statue spouting blood in many pipes,
In which so many smiling Romans bath'd,
Signifies that from you great Rome shall suck
Reviving blood, and that great men shall press
For tinctures, stains, relics, and cognizance.[19]
90   This by Calphurnia's dream is signified.

CAESAR.   And this way have you well expounded[20] it.

DECIUS.   I have, when you have heard what I can say;
And know it now: the Senate have concluded
To give this day a crown to mighty Caesar.
95   If you shall send them word you will not come,
Their minds may change. Besides, it were a mock

16. **stays.** Keeps

17. **apply for.** Explain as

por • tent (pôr´ tent) *n.*,
sign; omen
im • mi • nent
(i´ mə nənt) *adj.*, about
to occur

18. **amiss.** Wrongly; improperly

19. **tinctures…cognizance.**
Signs showing their allegiance
to Caesar

20. **expounded.** Explained

Apt to be render'd,[21] for someone to say
"Break up the Senate till another time,
When Caesar's wife shall meet with[22] better dreams."
100   If Caesar hide himself, shall they not whisper,
"Lo Caesar is afraid"?
Pardon me, Caesar, for my dear, dear love
To your proceeding[23] bids me tell you this;
And reason to my love is liable.[24]

105   CAESAR.   How foolish do your fears seem now, Calphurnia!
I am ashamed I did yield to them.
Give me my robe, for I will go.

Enter BRUTUS, LIGARIUS, METELLUS, CASCA, TREBONIUS, CINNA, *and* PUBLIUS.

And look where Publius is come to fetch me.

PUBLIUS.   Good morrow, Caesar.

CAESAR.   Welcome, Publius.
110   What, Brutus, are you stirr'd so early too?
Good morrow, Casca. Caius Ligarius,
Caesar was ne'er so much your enemy
As that same ague[25] which hath made you lean.
What is't a' clock?[26]

BRUTUS.   Caesar, 'tis strucken[27] eight.

115   CAESAR.   I thank you for your pains and courtesy.

Enter ANTONY.

See, Antony, that revels long a-nights,
Is notwithstanding up. Good morrow, Antony.

ANTONY.   So to most noble Caesar.

CAESAR.   Bid them prepare within;
I am to blame to be thus waited for.
120   Now, Cinna; now, Metellus; what, Trebonius:
I have an hour's talk in store for you;
Remember that you call on me today;
Be near me, that I may remember you.

TREBONIUS.   Caesar, I will; [*Aside.*] and so near will I be,
125   That your best friends shall wish I had been further.

CAESAR.   Good friends, go in, and taste some wine with me,
And we, like friends, will straightway go together.

BRUTUS.   [*Aside.*] That every like is not the same,[28] O Caesar,
The heart of Brutus earns[29] to think upon!

Exeunt.

---

21. **a mock...render'd.** Something likely to be said in mockery
22. **meet with.** Have

23. **proceeding.** Advancing; moving forward
24. **reason...liable.** My thinking is based on my love for you.

25. **ague.** Fever
26. **What is't a' clock?** What time is it?
27. **'tis strucken.** It has struck.

28. **every like...same.** Being like something is not being identical with it. Brutus is saying that some of those present are only like friends, not actually friends.
29. **earns.** Grieves

SCENE III: A STREET IN ROME NEAR THE CAPITOL

Enter ARTEMIDORUS *reading a paper.*

ARTEMIDORUS. "Caesar, beware of Brutus; take heed of
Cassius; come not near Casca; have an eye to Cinna; trust not
Trebonius; mark well Metellus Cimber; Decius Brutus loves
thee not; thou hast wrong'd Caius Ligarius. There is but one
5   mind in all these men, and it is bent against Caesar. If thou
beest[1] not immortal, look about you; security gives way to
conspiracy. The mighty gods defend thee!
                    Thy lover,[2]
                              Artemidorus."
10   Here will I stand till Caesar pass along,
And as a suitor[3] will I give him this.
My heart <u>laments</u> that virtue cannot live
Out of the teeth of emulation.[4]
If thou read this, O Caesar, thou mayest live;
15   If not, the Fates with traitors do contrive.[5]

Exit.

SCENE IV: IN FRONT OF BRUTUS'S HOUSE

Enter PORTIA *and* LUCIUS.

PORTIA.   I prithee,[1] boy, run to the Senate house;
Stay not to answer me, but get thee gone.
Why dost thou stay?

LUCIUS.   To know my errand, madam.

PORTIA.   I would have had thee there and here again
5   Ere I can tell thee what thou shouldst do there.—
O constancy,[2] be strong upon my side,
Set a huge mountain 'tween my heart and tongue!
I have a man's mind, but a woman's might.
How hard it is for women to keep counsel![3]—
Art thou here yet?

10   **LUCIUS.**   Madam, what should I do?
Run to the Capitol, and nothing else?
And so return to you, and nothing else?

PORTIA.   Yes, bring me word, boy, if thy lord look well,
For he went sickly forth; and take good note
15   What Caesar doth, what suitors press to him.

ACT II, SCENE III
1. **thou beest.** You are

2. **lover.** Friend

3. **as a suitor.** Like someone asking a favor

la • ment (lə ment´) *v.*, to grieve or regret deeply

4. **virtue…emulation.** Great and virtuous people (such as Caesar) cannot live outside the destructive reach (the teeth) of rivalry.
5. **contrive.** Plot

ACT II, SCENE IV
1. **prithee.** Pray thee; request

2. **constancy.** Will

3. **counsel.** Secrets

Hark, boy, what noise is that?

Lucius. I hear none, madam.

Portia. Prithee listen well;
I heard a bustling rumor,[4] like a fray,[5]
And the wind brings it from the Capitol.

20 **Lucius.** Sooth,[6] madam, I hear nothing.

Enter the Soothsayer.

Portia. Come hither, fellow; which way hast thou been?

Soothsayer. At mine own house, good lady.

Portia. What is't a' clock?

Soothsayer. About the ninth hour, lady.

Portia. Is Caesar yet gone to the Capitol?

25 **Soothsayer.** Madam, not yet; I go to take my stand,
To see him pass on to the Capitol.

Portia. Thou hast some suit to Caesar, hast thou not?

Soothsayer. That I have, lady, if it will please Caesar
To be so good to Caesar as to hear me:
30 I shall beseech[7] him to befriend himself.

Portia. Why, know'st thou any harm's intended towards him?

Soothsayer. None that I know will be, much that I fear may chance.[8]
Good morrow to you. Here the street is narrow;
The throng that follows Caesar at the heels,
35 Of senators, of praetors,[9] common suitors,
Will crowd a feeble man almost to death.
I'll get me to a place more void,[10] and there
Speak to great Caesar as he comes along.

Exit.

Portia. I must go in. Aye me! How weak a thing
40 The heart of woman is! O Brutus,
The heavens speed thee in thine enterprise!
Sure the boy heard me.—Brutus hath a suit
That Caesar will not grant.—O, I grow faint.—
Run, Lucius, and commend me[11] to my lord,
45 Say I am merry. Come to me again,
And bring me word what he doth say to thee.

Exeunt severally.

4. **rumor.** Noise
5. **fray.** Battle

6. **Sooth.** Truthfully

7. **beseech.** Beg; ask

8. **chance.** Occur; happen

9. **praetors.** Magistrates

10. **void.** Empty

11. **commend me.** Give my best wishes

Which is more important—loyalty to country or loyalty to a friend? If you were Brutus, and Cassius came to you with his plan, what would you do?

REFER TO TEXT ▶ ▶ ▶ ▶	▶ REASON WITH TEXT	
1a. State what Brutus decides to do at the beginning of Act II.	1b. Discuss the reasons Brutus gives for this decision.	**Understand** **Find meaning**
2a. Locate II.i.171–174 and identify the simile Brutus uses to compare the actual killing of Caesar to something else.	2b. Applying what you know about Brutus, why do you think he uses this comparison? Do you think he is attempting to describe the way Caesar will be stabbed, or is he commenting on the right or wrong nature of the act itself?	**Apply** **Use information**
3a. Describe Calphurnia's dream. Why does the dream cause her to insist that Caesar stay at home?	3b. Compare and contrast the ways Caesar and Brutus treat their wives in Act II. To what degree does each man listen to his wife's concerns or agree to respond to them?	**Analyze** **Take things apart**
4a. Identify what Brutus compares Caesar to at the end of his soliloquy in II.i.10–34.	4b. Paraphrase Brutus's soliloquy in II.i.10–34. Evaluate his reasoning. Do you think his thinking is sound, or is he stretching to come up with reasons for killing Caesar? Why do you think so?	**Evaluate** **Make judgments**
5a. Recall what proof Portia gives of her constancy and emotional strength.	5b. Explain what conclusions you can draw about the characters of Brutus and Caesar based on their interactions with their wives.	**Create** **Bring ideas together**

ANALYZE LITERATURE: Blank Verse and Rising Action

Refer to the descriptions of blank verse and iambic pentameter on page 528. Then copy the following passages from Act II on your own paper, marking the stressed and unstressed syllables. Which lines do not follow the pattern typical of blank verse?

1. Scene i, lines 61–65

2. Scene i, lines 172–174

3. Scene ii, lines 32–37

What events in Act II develop the central conflict of this play? What important decision does Brutus make and why? On the Plot Diagram you began with Act I, enter the rising action from Act II, or the events that complicate the plot of *The Tragedy of Julius Caesar*.

Temple of Vesta in the Roman Forum.

ACT III

SCENE I: ROME; IN FRONT OF THE CAPITOL, THE IDES OF MARCH

Flourish. Enter CAESAR, BRUTUS, CASSIUS, CASCA, DECIUS, METELLUS, TREBONIUS, CINNA, ANTONY, LEPIDUS, ARTEMIDORUS, PUBLIUS, POPILIUS, *and the* SOOTHSAYER.

CAESAR. The ides of March[1] are come.

SOOTHSAYER. Ay, Caesar, but not gone.

ARTEMIDORUS. Hail, Caesar! Read this schedule.

DECIUS. Trebonius doth desire you to o'er-read

ACT III, SCENE 1
1. **ides of March.** March 15

5   (At your best leisure) this his humble suit.[2]

Artemidorus.   O Caesar, read mine first; for mine's a suit
That touches Caesar nearer. Read it, great Caesar.

Caesar.   What touches us ourself shall be last serv'd.

Artemidorus.   Delay not, Caesar, read it instantly.

Caesar.   What, is the fellow mad?

10 **Publius.**   Sirrah, give place.[3]

Cassius.   What, urge you your petitions in the street?
Come to the Capitol.

Caesar enters the Capitol, the rest following.

Popilius.   I wish your enterprise today may thrive.

Cassius.   What enterprise, Popilius?

Popilius.   Fare you well.

                         Leaves him and joins Caesar.

15 **Brutus.**   What said Popilius Lena?

Cassius.   He wish'd today our enterprise might thrive.
I fear our purpose is discovered.

Brutus.   Look how he makes to[4] Caesar; mark him.

Cassius.   Casca, be sudden, for we fear prevention.
20 Brutus, what shall be done? If this be known,
Cassius or Caesar never shall turn back,
For I will slay myself.

Brutus.   Cassius, be constant;[5]
Popilius Lena speaks not of our purposes,
For look he smiles, and Caesar doth not change.

25 **Cassius.**   Trebonius knows his time; for look you, Brutus,
He draws Mark Antony out of the way.

                         Exeunt Antony *and* Trebonius.

Decius.   Where is Metellus Cimber? Let him go
And presently prefer[6] his suit to Caesar.

Brutus.   He is address'd;[7] press near and second him.

30 **Cinna.**   Casca, you are the first that rears your hand.

Caesar.   Are we all ready? What is now amiss
That Caesar and his Senate must redress?

---

2. **suit.** Request or petition

3. **Sirrah, give place.** Get out of the way. *Sirrah* was a disrespectful term of address.

4. **makes to.** Heads toward

5. **constant.** Steady

6. **presently prefer.** Immediately present
7. **address'd.** Ready

METELLUS.　　Most high, most mighty, and most <u>puissant</u> Caesar,
Metellus Cimber throws before thy seat
An humble heart. [*Kneeling.*]

35　**CAESAR.**　　　　　　I must prevent thee, Cimber.
These couchings and these lowly courtesies[8]
Might fire the blood of ordinary men,
And turn preordinance and first <u>decree</u>[9]
Into the law of children.[10] Be not fond
40　To[11] think that Caesar bears such rebel[12] blood
That will be thaw'd from the true quality
With that which melteth fools—I mean sweet words,
Low-crooked curtsies, and base spaniel fawning.
Thy brother by decree is banishèd;
45　If thou dost bend, and pray, and fawn for him,
I spurn thee like a cur[13] out of my way.
Know, Caesar doth not wrong, nor without cause
Will he be satisfied.[14]

　　METELLUS.　　Is there no voice more worthy than my own,
50　To sound more sweetly in great Caesar's ear
For the repealing of my banish'd brother?

　　BRUTUS.　　I kiss thy hand, but not in flattery, Caesar;
Desiring thee that Publius Cimber may
Have an immediate freedom of repeal.[15]

　　CAESAR.　　What, Brutus?

55　**CASSIUS.**　　　　　　Pardon, Caesar! Caesar, pardon!
As low as to thy foot doth Cassius fall,
To beg enfranchisement[16] for Publius Cimber.

　　CAESAR.　　I could be well mov'd, if I were as you;
If I could pray to move, prayers would move me;
60　But I am constant as the northern star,
Of whose true-fix'd and resting quality
There is no fellow in the firmament.[17]
The skies are painted with unnumb'red sparks,
They are all fire, and every one doth shine;
65　But there's but one in all doth hold his place.
So in the world: 'tis furnish'd well with men,
And men are flesh and blood, and apprehensive;[18]
Yet in the number I do know but one
That unassailable holds on his rank,[19]
70　Unshak'd of motion; and that I am he,
Let me a little show it, even in this—
That I was constant Cimber should be banish'd

---

puis • sant (pwĭ´ sənt)
adj., strong; powerful

8. **courtesies.** Bows
9. **preordinance and first decree.** Earlier-made laws

de • cree (dĭ krē´) *n.*,
order; rule; proclamation

10. **the law of children.** Children's games to be changed at whim
11. **fond / To.** So absurd as to
12. **rebel.** Rebellious

13. **spurn...cur.** Kick you like a dog

14. **satisfied.** Moved to change his mind

15. **freedom of repeal.** Permission to be recalled from exile

16. **enfranchisement.** Here, Cassius means reinstatement as a full citizen.

17. **no fellow...firmament.** No equal in the sky

18. **apprehensive.** Capable of reason

19. **holds on his rank.** Holds his position

"Speak hands for me!" Cassius (played by John Gielgud) stabs Caesar (played by Louis Calhern) in the 1953 film adaptation of *Julius Caesar.*

And constant do remain to keep him so.

CINNA. O Caesar—

CAESAR.   Hence! Wilt thou lift up Olympus?[20]

DECIUS. Great Caesar—

20. **Olympus.** In Greek mythology, the mountain that is home to the gods

75 CAESAR.   Doth not Brutus bootless[21] kneel?

CASCA.   <u>Speak hands for me!</u>

They stab CAESAR.

CAESAR.   *Et tu,*[22] *Brute?*—Then fall Caesar! [*Dies.*]

CINNA.   Liberty! Freedom! Tyranny is dead!
Run hence, proclaim, cry it about the streets.

80 CASSIUS.   Some to the common pulpits,[23] and cry out,
"Liberty, freedom, and enfranchisement!"[24]

BRUTUS.   People and senators, be not affrighted;[25]
Fly not, stand still; ambition's debt is paid.

CASCA.   Go to the pulpit, Brutus.

DECIUS.   And Cassius too.

85 BRUTUS.   Where's Publius?

CINNA.   Here, quite confounded with[26] this mutiny.

METELLUS.   Stand fast together, lest some friend of Caesar's
Should chance[27]—

BRUTUS.   Talk not of standing. Publius, good cheer,
90 There is no harm intended to your person,
Nor to no Roman else.[28] So tell them, Publius.

CASSIUS.   And leave us, Publius, lest that the people,
Rushing on us, should do your age some mischief.

BRUTUS.   Do so, and let no man abide[29] this deed,
95 But we the doers.

Exeunt all but the CONSPIRATORS.

Enter TREBONIUS.

CASSIUS.   Where is Antony?

TREBONIUS.   Fled to his house amaz'd.
Men, wives, and children stare, cry out, and run,
As[30] it were doomsday.

BRUTUS.   Fates, we will know your pleasures.
That we shall die, we know, 'tis but the time,
100 And drawing days out, that men stand upon.[31]

CASCA.   Why, he that cuts off twenty years of life
Cuts off so many[32] years of fearing death.

BRUTUS.   Grant that, and then is death a benefit;

---

21. **bootless.** In vain

22. *Et tu.* Latin for "and you"

23. **pulpits.** Platforms for public speakers
24. **enfranchisement.** Full citizenship rights
25. **affrighted.** Frightened

26. **confounded with.** Overwhelmed by

27. **chance.** Happen

28. **no Roman else.** Any other Roman

29. **abide.** Suffer the consequences of

30. **As.** As if

31. **stand upon.** Worry about

32. **so many.** As many

So are we Caesar's friends, that have abridg'd
105   His time of fearing death. Stoop, Romans, stoop,
And let us bathe our hands in Caesar's blood
Up to the elbows, and besmear our swords;
Then walk we forth, even to the marketplace,[33]
And waving our red weapons o'er our heads,
110   Let's all cry, "Peace, freedom, and liberty!"

CASSIUS.   Stoop then, and wash. How many ages hence
Shall this our lofty scene be acted over
In states unborn and accents[34] yet unknown!

BRUTUS.   How many times shall Caesar bleed in sport,[35]
115   That now on Pompey's basis[36] lies along
No worthier than the dust!

CASSIUS.   So oft as that shall be,
So often shall the knot[37] of us be call'd
The men that gave their country liberty.

DECIUS.   What, shall we forth?

CASSIUS.   Ay, every man away.
120   Brutus shall lead, and we will grace his heels
With the most boldest and best hearts of Rome.

Enter a SERVANT.

BRUTUS.   Soft, who comes here? A friend of Antony's.

SERVANT.   Thus, Brutus, did my master bid me kneel;
Thus did Mark Antony bid me fall down;
125   And being prostrate, thus he bade me say:
Brutus is noble, wise, valiant, and honest;
Caesar was mighty, bold, royal, and loving.
Say, I love Brutus, and I honor him;
Say, I fear'd Caesar, honor'd him, and lov'd him.
130   If Brutus will vouchsafe that Antony
May safely come to him, and be resolv'd
How Caesar hath deserv'd to lie in death,
Mark Antony shall not love Caesar dead
So well as Brutus living; but will follow
135   The fortunes and affairs of noble Brutus
Thorough the hazards of this untrod[38] state
With all true faith. So says my master Antony.

BRUTUS.   Thy master is a wise and valiant Roman,
I never thought him worse.
140   Tell him, so please him come unto this place,
He shall be satisfied; and, by my honor,

33. **marketplace.** The Forum

34. **accents.** Languages
35. **in sport.** In entertainments, such as plays
36. **Pompey's basis.** Pedestal of Pompey's statue

37. **knot.** Group

38. **untrod.** Not previously explored; new

Depart untouch'd.

SERVANT.   I'll fetch him presently.[39]

Exit SERVANT.

BRUTUS.   I know that we shall have him well to friend.[40]

CASSIUS.   I wish we may; but yet have I a mind
145 That fears him much; and my misgiving still
Falls shrewdly to the purpose.[41]

Enter ANTONY.

BRUTUS.   But here comes Antony. Welcome, Mark Antony!

ANTONY.   O mighty Caesar! dost thou lie so low?
Are all thy conquests, glories, triumphs,[42] spoils,
150 Shrunk to this little measure? Fare thee well!
I know not, gentlemen, what you intend,
Who else must be let blood,[43] who else is rank;[44]
If I myself, there is no hour so fit
As Caesar's death's hour, nor no instrument
155 Of half that worth as those your swords, made rich
With the most noble blood of all this world.
I do beseech ye, if you bear me hard,[45]
Now, whilst your purpled hands do reek and smoke,[46]
Fulfill your pleasure. Live a thousand years,
160 I shall not find myself so apt to die;
No place will please me so, no mean[47] of death,
As here by Caesar, and by you cut off,
The choice and master spirits of this age.

BRUTUS.   O Antony! beg not your death of us.
165 Though now we must appear bloody and cruel,
As by our hands and this our present act
You see we do, yet see you but our hands,
And this the bleeding business they have done.
Our hearts you see not, they are pitiful;[48]
170 And pity to the general wrong of Rome—
As fire drives out fire, so pity pity—
Hath done this deed on Caesar.[49] For your part,
To you our swords have leaden points, Mark Antony;
Our arms in strength of malice,[50] and our hearts
175 Of brothers' temper, do receive you in
With all kind love, good thoughts, and reverence.

CASSIUS.   Your voice shall be as strong as any man's
In the disposing of new dignities.[51]

39. **presently.** At once

40. **well to friend.** As a good friend

41. **my misgiving...purpose.** My suspicions usually prove to be correct.

42. **triumphs.** Processions

43. **let blood.** Bled, as was done in the past to cure disease
44. **rank.** Sick

45. **bear me hard.** Dislike me
46. **smoke.** Steam with warm blood

47. **mean.** Means

48. **pitiful.** Full of pity

49. **pity to...Caesar.** Our pity for Rome caused us to act as we have.
50. **arms...malice.** Our arms seemingly full of evil intent (because they are bloodstained)
51. **Your voice...dignities.** Your vote will be equal to ours in appointing people to political offices.

BRUTUS.   Only be patient till we have appeas'd
180 The multitude, beside themselves with fear,
And then we will deliver[52] you the cause
Why I, that did love Caesar when I strook him,
Have thus proceeded.

ANTONY.   I doubt not of your wisdom.
Let each man render me his bloody hand.
185 First, Marcus Brutus, will I shake with you;
Next, Caius Cassius, do I take your hand;
Now, Decius Brutus, yours; now yours, Metellus;
Yours, Cinna; and, my valiant Casca, yours;
Though last, not least in love, yours, good Trebonius.
190 Gentlemen all—alas, what shall I say?
My credit[53] now stands on such slippery ground
That one of two bad ways you must conceit[54] me,
Either a coward or a flatterer.
That I did love thee, Caesar, O, 'tis true;
195 If then thy spirit look upon us now,
Shall it not grieve thee dearer than thy death,
To see thy Antony making his peace,
Shaking the bloody fingers of thy foes,
Most noble! in the presence of thy corse?[55]
200 Had I as many eyes as thou hast wounds,
Weeping as fast as they stream forth thy blood,
It would become me better than to close
In terms of friendship with thine enemies.
Pardon me, Julius! Here wast thou bay'd,[56] brave hart,[57]
205 Here didst thou fall, and here thy hunters stand,
Sign'd in thy spoil, and crimson'd in thy lethe.[58]
O world! thou wast the forest to this hart,
And this indeed, O world, the heart of thee.
How like a deer, strooken[59] by many princes,
210 Dost thou here lie!

CASSIUS.   Mark Antony—

ANTONY.   Pardon me, Caius Cassius!
The enemies of Caesar shall say this:
Then, in a friend, it is cold modesty.

CASSIUS.   I blame you not for praising Caesar so,
215 But what compact mean you to have with us?
Will you be prick'd in number[60] of our friends,
Or shall we on, and not depend on you?

ANTONY.   Therefore I took your hands, but was indeed
Sway'd from the point, by looking down on Caesar.

52. **deliver.** Explain to

53. **credit.** Reputation
54. **conceit.** Perceive

55. **corse.** Body

56. **bay'd.** Chased down; brought to bay
57. **hart.** Deer, with a pun on *heart*
58. **lethe.** Blood. In Greek mythology, Lethe was a river from which the dead in Hades drank, causing them to forget and to give up their former lives.
59. **strooken.** Struck

60. **prick'd in number.** Counted as one

thinking this in his head

read in his head

thinking in his head

"Woe to the hand that shed this costly blood!" Antony (played by Marlon Brando) vows revenge against Caesar's killers.

220   Friends am I with you all, and love you all,
Upon this hope, that you shall give me reasons
Why, and wherein, Caesar was dangerous.

     BRUTUS.   Or else were this a savage spectacle.
Our reasons are so full of good regard
225   That were you, Antony, the son of Caesar,
You should be satisfied.

     ANTONY.   That's all I seek,
And am, moreover, suitor that I may
Produce his body to the marketplace,[61]

61. **suitor...marketplace.**
I ask that I may be in charge
of displaying Caesar's body to
the people in the marketplace.

And in the pulpit, as becomes a friend,

230 Speak in the order of[62] his funeral.

BRUTUS. You shall, Mark Antony.

CASSIUS. Brutus, a word with you.
[*Aside to Brutus.*] You know not what you do. Do not consent
That Antony speak in his funeral.
Know you how much the people may be mov'd
By that which he will utter?

235 **BRUTUS.** By your pardon—
I will myself into the pulpit first,
And show the reason of our Caesar's death.
What Antony shall speak, I will protest
He speaks by leave and by permission;
240 And that we are contented Caesar shall
Have all true rites and lawful ceremonies.
It shall advantage[63] more than do us wrong.

CASSIUS. I know not what may fall,[64] I like it not.

BRUTUS. Mark Antony, here take you Caesar's body.
245 You shall not in your funeral speech blame us,
But speak all good you can devise of Caesar,
And say you do't by our permission;
Else shall you not have any hand at all
About his funeral. And you shall speak
250 In the same pulpit whereto I am going,
After my speech is ended.

ANTONY. Be it so;
I do desire no more.

BRUTUS. Prepare the body then, and follow us.

Exeunt. Manet ANTONY.

✳ soliloquy

ANTONY. O, pardon me, thou bleeding piece of earth,[65]
255 That I am meek and gentle with these butchers!
Thou art the ruins of the noblest man
That ever lived in the tide of times.
Woe to the hand that shed this costly blood!
Over thy wounds now do I prophesy
260 (Which like dumb mouths do ope their ruby lips
To beg the voice and utterance of my tongue)[66]
A curse shall light upon the limbs of men;
Domestic fury and fierce civil strife
Shall cumber[67] all the parts of Italy;
265 Blood and destruction shall be so in use,

62. **in the order of.** In the ceremonies conducted for

63. **advantage.** Help; aid

64. **may fall.** May occur

65. **thou...earth.** Caesar

66. **ope...tongue.** Caesar's wounds open their red lips to beg Antony to speak out against the murder.

67. **cumber.** Help; aid

Wounds of Accusation

Elizabethans believed that the wounds of the dead would open, almost as if to speak in accusation, when the murderer or murderers were in the presence of the deceased. This belief is reflected in lines 260–261, in which Antony describes Caesar's wounds as opening like speechless mouths to beg him to speak for them. Similar scenes occur in other works of Shakespeare, most notably in *The Tragedy of Richard III*, in which Richard woos Anne over the body of her father-in-law.

And dreadful objects so familiar,
That mothers shall but smile when they behold
Their infants quartered with the hands of war;
All pity chok'd with custom of fell deeds;[68]
270 And Caesar's spirit, ranging[69] for revenge,
With Ate[70] by his side come hot from hell,
Shall in these confines with a monarch's voice
Cry "Havoc!"[71] and let slip the dogs of war,
That this foul deed shall smell above the earth
275 With carrion men, groaning for burial.

Enter Octavio's[72] SERVANT.

You serve Octavius Caesar, do you not?

SERVANT.   I do, Mark Antony.

ANTONY.   Caesar did write for him to come to Rome.

SERVANT.   He did receive his letters and is coming,
280 And bid me say to you by word of mouth—
O Caesar!— [*Seeing the body.*]

ANTONY.   Thy heart is big; get thee apart and weep.
Passion, I see, is catching, for mine eyes,
Seeing those beads of sorrow stand in thine,

68. **All pity...deeds.** Nobody will have pity anymore because everyone will be so accustomed to seeing such cruel deeds.
69. **ranging.** Roving
70. **Ate (ā´ tē).** Greek goddess of discord
71. **"Havoc!"** War cry given by a king, ordering general slaughter
72. **Octavio's.** Belonging to Gaius Octavius, grandnephew of and heir to Julius Caesar; later Augustus Caesar, the first Roman emperor

285 Began to water. Is thy master coming?

SERVANT.   He lies tonight within seven leagues of Rome.

ANTONY.   Post[73] back with speed, and tell him what hath chanc'd.[74]
Here is a mourning Rome, a dangerous Rome,
No Rome of safety for Octavius yet;
290 Hie hence,[75] and tell him so. Yet stay awhile,
Thou shalt not back till I have borne this corse
Into the marketplace. There shall I try,
In my <u>oration</u>, how the people take
The cruel issue of these bloody men,[76]
295 According to the which thou shalt discourse
To young Octavius of the state of things.[77]
Lend me your hand.

Exeunt with CAESAR'S *body.*

SCENE II: THE ROMAN FORUM

Enter BRUTUS *and* CASSIUS *with the* PLEBEIANS.[1]

PLEBEIANS.   We will be satisfied! Let us be satisfied!

BRUTUS.   Then follow me, and give me audience, friends.
Cassius, go you into the other street,
And part the numbers.[2]
Those that will hear me speak, let 'em stay here;
5 Those that will follow Cassius, go with him;
And public reasons shall be rendered
Of Caesar's death.

1. PLEBEIAN.   I will hear Brutus speak.

2. PLEBEIAN.   I will hear Cassius, and compare their reasons,
10 When severally[3] we hear them rendered.

Exit CASSIUS *with some of the* PLEBEIANS.
BRUTUS *goes into the pulpit.*

3. PLEBEIAN.   The noble Brutus is[4] ascended; silence!

BRUTUS.   Be patient till the last.[5]
Romans, countrymen, and lovers,[6] hear me for my cause, and be
silent, that you may hear. Believe me for mine honor, and have
15 respect to[7] mine honor, that you may believe. Censure[8] me in
your wisdom, and awake your senses, that you may the better
judge. If there be any in this assembly, any dear friend of
Caesar's, to him I say, that Brutus' love to Caesar was no less

Critical Viewing

Examine the staging of this scene. What can you infer about Brutus from his body language, costume, and placement in the scene? What can you infer about Antony?

"As Caesar lov'd me, I weep for him...but, as he was ambitious, I slew him." Brutus (played by James Mason) explains his actions to the crowd while Mark Antony (played by Marlon Brando) looks upon Caesar's body in the 1953 film *Julius Caesar*.

than his. If then that friend demand why Brutus rose against
20 Caesar, this is my answer: Not that I lov'd Caesar less, but that I
lov'd Rome more. Had you rather Caesar were living, and die all
slaves, than that Caesar were dead, to live all freemen? As Caesar
lov'd me, I weep for him; as he was fortunate, I rejoice at it; as he
was valiant, I honor him; but, as he was ambitious, I slew him.
25 There is tears for his love; joy for his fortune; honor for his
valor; and death for his ambition. Who is here so base that
would be a bondman?[9] If any, speak, for him have I offended.
Who is here so rude[10] that would not be a Roman? If any, speak,

val • or (vaʹ lər) *n.,* courage; bravery

9. **Who...bondman?**
Who is so low that he would choose to be a slave?
10. **rude.** Uncivilized; lacking in manners and culture

for him have I offended. Who is here so vile that will not love

30 his country? If any, speak, for him have I offended. I pause for a
reply.

ALL. None, Brutus, none.

BRUTUS. Then none have I offended. I have done no more to
Caesar than you shall do to Brutus. The question of his death is

35 enroll'd[11] in the Capitol: his glory not extenuated,[12] wherein he
was worthy; nor his offences enforc'd,[13] for which he suffer'd
death.

Enter MARK ANTONY *and others with* CAESAR'S *body.*

Here comes his body, mourn'd by Mark Antony, who, though he had
no hand in his death, shall receive the benefit of his

40 dying, a place in the commonwealth,[14] as which of you shall not?
With this I depart, that, as I slew my best lover[15] for the good of
Rome, I have the same dagger for myself, when it shall please my
country to need my death.

ALL. Live, Brutus, live, live!

45 **1. PLEBEIAN.** Bring him with triumph home unto his house.

2. PLEBEIAN. Give him a statue with his ancestors.

3. PLEBEIAN. Let him be Caesar.

4. PLEBEIAN.   Caesar's better parts
Shall be crown'd in Brutus.

1. PLEBEIAN.   We'll bring him to his house
With shouts and clamors.

BRUTUS.   My countrymen—

2. PLEBEIAN. Peace, silence! Brutus speaks.

50 **1. PLEBEIAN.**   Peace ho!

BRUTUS. Good countrymen, let me depart alone,
And, for my sake, stay here with Antony.
Do grace to Caesar's corpse, and grace his speech
Tending to Caesar's glories, which Mark Antony

55 (By our permission) is allow'd to make.
I do entreat you, not a man depart,
Save I alone, till Antony have spoke.[16]

Exit.

1. PLEBEIAN. Stay ho, and let us hear Mark Antony.

3. PLEBEIAN. Let him go up into the public chair,

11. **question…is enroll'd.**
Reasons for his death have
been recorded.
12. **extenuated.** Lessened
13. **enforc'd.** Forced; exaggerated

14. **commonwealth.**
Republic (nation ruled by
elected leaders)
15. **lover.** Friend

16. **have spoke.** Has spoken

60   We'll hear him. Noble Antony, go up.

ANTONY.   For Brutus' sake, I am beholding[17] to you.
    [*Goes into the pulpit.*]

17. **beholding.** Indebted

4. PLEBEIAN.   What does he say of Brutus?

3. PLEBEIAN.   He says, for
Brutus' sake
He finds himself beholding to us all.

4. PLEBEIAN.   'Twere best he speak no harm of Brutus here!

65 **1. PLEBEIAN.**   This Caesar was a tyrant.

3. PLEBEIAN.   Nay, that's certain:
We are blest that Rome is rid of him.

2. PLEBEIAN.   Peace, let us hear what Antony can say.

ANTONY.   You gentle Romans—

ALL.   Peace ho, let us hear him.

ANTONY.   Friends, Romans, countrymen, lend me your ears!
70   I come to bury Caesar, not to praise him.
    The evil that men do lives after them,
    The good is oft interred[18] with their bones;
    So let it be with Caesar. The noble Brutus
    Hath told you Caesar was ambitious;
75   If it were so, it was a grievous fault,
    And grievously hath Caesar answer'd it.
    Here, under leave of Brutus and the rest
    (For Brutus is an honorable man,
    So are they all, all honorable men),
80   Come I to speak in Caesar's funeral.
    He was my friend, faithful and just to me;
    But Brutus says he was ambitious,
    And Brutus is an honorable man.
    He hath brought many captives home to Rome,
85   Whose ransoms did the general coffers[19] fill;
    Did this in Caesar seem ambitious?
    When that the poor have cried, Caesar hath wept;
    Ambition should be made of sterner stuff:
    Yet Brutus says he was ambitious,
90   And Brutus is an honorable man.
    You all did see that on the Lupercal
    I thrice presented him a kingly crown,
    Which he did thrice refuse. Was this ambition?
    Yet Brutus says he was ambitious,

18. **interred.** Buried

griev • ous (grē´ vəs)
adj., very serious; grave

19. **general coffers.** The treasury of the republic

"Here's a parchment with the seal of Caesar...'tis his will." Antony (played by Marlon Brando) presents Caesar's will to the Romans.

95 And sure[20] he is an honorable man.
I speak not to disprove what Brutus spoke,
But here I am to speak what I do know.
You all did love him once, not without cause;
What cause withholds you then to mourn for him?

100 O judgment! thou art fled to brutish beasts,
And men have lost their reason. Bear with me,
My heart is in the coffin there with Caesar,
And I must pause till it come back to me.

1. PLEBEIAN.   Methinks there is much reason in his sayings.

105 **2. PLEBEIAN.**   If thou consider rightly of the matter,
Caesar has had great wrong.

3. PLEBEIAN.   Has he, masters?
I fear there will a worse come in his place.

4. PLEBEIAN.   Mark'd ye his words? He would not take the crown,
Therefore 'tis certain he was not ambitious.

110 **1. PLEBEIAN.**   If it be found so, some will dear abide it.[21]

2. PLEBEIAN.   Poor soul, his eyes are red as fire with weeping.

3. PLEBEIAN.   There's not a nobler man in Rome than Antony.

4. PLEBEIAN.   Now mark him, he begins again to speak.

ANTONY.   But yesterday the word of Caesar might
115 Have stood against the world; now lies he there,
And none so poor to[22] do him reverence.
O masters! if I were dispos'd to stir
Your hearts and minds to mutiny and rage,
I should do Brutus wrong, and Cassius wrong,
120 Who (you all know) are honorable men.
I will not do them wrong; I rather choose
To wrong the dead, to wrong myself and you,
Than I will wrong such honorable men.
But here's a parchment with the seal of Caesar,
125 I found it in his closet, 'tis his will.
Let but the commons hear this testament—
Which, pardon me, I do not mean to read—
And they would go and kiss dead Caesar's wounds,
And dip their napkins in his sacred blood;
130 Yea, beg a hair of him for memory,
And dying, mention it within their wills,
<u>Bequeathing</u> it as a rich legacy
Unto their issue.[23]

20. **sure.** Certainly

21. **some…it.** Some (the conspirators) will pay dearly for it.

22. **poor to.** Low ranking as to

be · queath (bē kwēth')
v., hand down; pass on

23. **issue.** Children; heirs

4. Plebeian.   We'll hear the will. Read it, Mark Antony.

135   **All.**   The will, the will! we will hear Caesar's will.

Antony.   Have patience, gentle friends, I must not read it.
It is not meet[24] you know how Caesar lov'd you:
You are not wood, you are not stones, but men;
And, being men, hearing the will of Caesar,
140   It will inflame you, it will make you mad.
'Tis good you know not that you are his heirs,
For if you should, O, what would come of it?

4. Plebeian.   Read the will, we'll hear it, Antony.
You shall read us the will, Caesar's will.

145   **Antony.**   Will you be patient? Will you stay[25] awhile?
I have o'ershot myself[26] to tell you of it.
I fear I wrong the honorable men
Whose daggers have stabb'd Caesar; I do fear it.

4. Plebeian.   They were traitors; honorable men!

150   **All.**   The will! the testament!

2. Plebeian.   They were villains, murderers. The will, read the will!

Antony.   You will compel me then to read the will?
Then make a ring about the corpse of Caesar,
And let me show you him that made the will.
155   Shall I descend? and will you give me leave?[27]

All.   Come down.

2. Plebeian.   Descend.

3. Plebeian.   You shall have leave.

Antony comes down from the pulpit.

4. Plebeian.   A ring, stand round.

160   **1. Plebeian.**   Stand from the hearse, stand from the body.

2. Plebeian.   Room for Antony, most noble Antony.

Antony.   Nay, press not so upon me, stand far off.

All.   Stand back; room, bear back!

Antony.   If you have tears, prepare to shed them now.
165   You all do know this mantle.[28] I remember
The first time ever Caesar put it on;
'Twas on a summer's evening, in his tent,

24. **meet.** Proper; suitable

25. **stay.** Wait
26. **o'ershot myself.** Gone too far

27. **give me leave.** Allow me to

28. **this mantle.** Caesar's toga

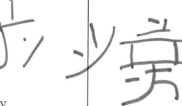

That day he overcame the Nervii.[29]
Look, in this place ran Cassius' dagger through;
170 See what a rent[30] the envious Casca made;
Through this the well-beloved Brutus stabb'd,
And as he pluck'd his cursed steel away,
Mark how the blood of Caesar followed it,
As rushing out of doors to be resolv'd
175 If Brutus so unkindly knock'd or no;[31]
For Brutus, as you know, was Caesar's angel.
Judge, O you gods, how dearly Caesar lov'd him!
This was the most unkindest cut of all;
For when the noble Caesar saw him stab,
180 Ingratitude, more strong than traitors' arms,
Quite vanquish'd[32] him. Then burst his mighty heart,
And in his mantle muffling up his face,
Even at the base of Pompey's statue
(Which all the while ran blood) great Caesar fell.
185 O, what a fall was there, my countrymen!
Then I, and you, and all of us fell down,
Whilst bloody treason flourish'd over us.
O now you weep, and I perceive you feel
The dint[33] of pity. These are gracious drops.
190 Kind souls, what weep you when you but behold
Our Caesar's vesture wounded? Look you here,

Lifting CAESAR's *mantle.*

Here is himself, marr'd as you see with traitors.[34]

1. PLEBEIAN.   O piteous spectacle!

2. PLEBEIAN.   O noble Caesar!

195 **3. PLEBEIAN.**   O woeful day!

4. PLEBEIAN.   O traitors, villains!

1. PLEBEIAN.   O most bloody sight!

2. PLEBEIAN.   We will be reveng'd!

ALL.   Revenge! About! Seek! Burn! Fire! Kill!
200 Slay! Let not a traitor live!

ANTONY.   Stay, countrymen.

1. PLEBEIAN.   Peace there, hear the noble Antony.

2. PLEBEIAN.   We'll hear him, we'll follow him, we'll die with him.

ANTONY.   Good friends, sweet friends, let me not stir you up

---

29. **Nervii** (ner´ vē ī). Belgian tribe conquered by Caesar in 57 BCE
30. **rent.** Tear

31. **Mark...no.** Caesar's blood rushed out as if hurrying to see if it was really Brutus who had made the wound.

32. **vanquish'd.** Defeated

33. **dint.** Stroke; force

34. **Kind...traitors.** If you weep when you see the holes in Caesar's clothing (vesture), then look at Caesar himself, his body stabbed by traitors.

205 To such a sudden flood of mutiny.
They that have done this deed are honorable.
What private griefs they have, alas, I know not,
That made them do it. They are wise and honorable,
And will no doubt with reasons answer you.

210 I come not, friends, to steal away your hearts.
I am no orator, as Brutus is;
But (as you know me all) a plain blunt man
That love[35] my friend, and that they know full well
That gave me public leave to speak of him.

215 For I have neither wit, nor words,[36] nor worth,
Action, nor utterance, nor the power of speech
To stir men's blood; I only speak right on.[37]
I tell you that which you yourselves do know,
Show you sweet Caesar's wounds, poor, poor, dumb mouths,

220 And bid them speak for me. But were I Brutus,
And Brutus Antony, there were an Antony
Would ruffle up your spirits, and put a tongue
In every wound of Caesar, that should move
The stones of Rome to rise and mutiny.

225 **ALL.**   We'll mutiny.

1. PLEBEIAN.   We'll burn the house of Brutus.

3. PLEBEIAN.   Away then, come, seek the conspirators.

ANTONY.   Yet hear me, countrymen, yet hear me speak.

ALL.   Peace ho, hear Antony, most noble Antony!

230 **ANTONY.**   Why, friends, you go to do you know not what.
Wherein hath Caesar thus deserv'd your loves?
Alas you know not! I must tell you then:
You have forgot the will I told you of.

ALL.   Most true. The will! Let's stay and hear the will.

235 **ANTONY.**   Here is the will, and under Caesar's seal:
To every Roman citizen he gives,
To every several man, seventy-five drachmas.[38]

2. PLEBEIAN.   Most noble Caesar! we'll revenge his death.

3. PLEBEIAN.   O royal Caesar!

240 **ANTONY.**   Hear me with patience.

ALL.   Peace ho!

ANTONY.   Moreover, he hath left you all his walks,

35. **love.** Loved

36. **words.** Fluency; ease with words

37. **right on.** Directly; from the heart; not as a trained speaker

38. **drachmas.** Silver coins

His private arbors and new-planted orchards,
On this side Tiber;³⁹ he hath left them you,
245 And to your heirs for ever—common pleasures,⁴⁰
To walk abroad and recreate⁴¹ yourselves.
Here was a Caesar! when comes such another?

1. PLEBEIAN. Never, never! Come, away, away!
We'll burn his body in the holy place,
250 And with the brands fire the traitors' houses.
Take up the body.

2. PLEBEIAN. Go fetch fire.

3. PLEBEIAN. Pluck down benches.

4. PLEBEIAN. Pluck down forms,⁴² windows,⁴³ anything.

Exeunt PLEBEIANS *with the body.*

255 **ANTONY.** Now let it work. Mischief, thou art afoot,
Take thou what course thou wilt!

Enter SERVANT.

How now, fellow?

SERVANT. Sir, Octavius is⁴⁴ already come to Rome.

ANTONY. Where is he?

SERVANT. He and Lepidus are at Caesar's house.

260 **ANTONY.** And thither will I straight to visit him;
He comes upon a wish.⁴⁵ Fortune is merry,
And in this mood will give us any thing.

SERVANT. I heard him say, Brutus and Cassius
Are rid like madmen through the gates of Rome.⁴⁶

265 **ANTONY.** Belike⁴⁷ they had some notice⁴⁸ of the people,
How I had mov'd them. Bring me to Octavius.

Exeunt.

SCENE III: A STREET IN ROME

Enter CINNA *the poet, and after him the* PLEBEIANS.

CINNA. I dreamt tonight¹ that I did feast with Caesar,
And things unluckily charge my fantasy.
I have no will to wander forth of² doors,
Yet something leads me forth.

---

39. **this side Tiber.** This side of the Tiber River
40. **pleasures.** Public places of rest and relaxation
41. **recreate.** Enjoy

42. **forms.** Benches
43. **windows.** Shutters

44. **is.** Has

45. **upon a wish.** As I wished

46. **rid...Rome.** Have run away from Rome
47. **Belike.** Most likely
48. **notice.** News

ACT III, SCENE III
1. **tonight.** Last night

2. **forth of.** Out of

5   **1. PLEBEIAN.**   What is your name?

2. PLEBEIAN.   Whither are you going?

3. PLEBEIAN.   Where do you dwell?

4. PLEBEIAN.   Are you a married man or a bachelor?

2. PLEBEIAN.   Answer every man directly.

10 **1. PLEBEIAN.**   Aye, and briefly.

4. PLEBEIAN.   Aye, and wisely.

3. PLEBEIAN.   Aye, and truly, you were best.[3]

CINNA.   What is my name? Whither am I going? Where do I dwell?
Am I a married man or a bachelor? Then to answer every
15 man directly and briefly, wisely and truly: wisely, I say, I am a
bachelor.

2. PLEBEIAN.   That's as much as to say, they are fools that marry.
You'll bear me a bang[4] for that, I fear. Proceed directly.

CINNA.   Directly, I am going to Caesar's funeral.

20 **1. PLEBEIAN.**   As a friend or an enemy?

CINNA.   As a friend.

2. PLEBEIAN.   That matter is answer'd directly.

4. PLEBEIAN.   For your dwelling—briefly.

CINNA.   Briefly, I dwell by the Capitol.

25 **3. PLEBEIAN.**   Your name, sir, truly.

CINNA.   Truly, my name is Cinna.

1. PLEBEIAN.   Tear him to pieces, he's a conspirator.

CINNA.   I am Cinna the poet, I am Cinna the poet.

4. PLEBEIAN.   Tear him for his bad verses, tear him for his bad verses.

30 **CINNA.**   I am not Cinna the conspirator.

4. PLEBEIAN.   It is no matter, his name's Cinna. Pluck but his name
out of his heart, and turn him going.[5]

3. PLEBEIAN.   Tear him, tear him! Come, brands ho, fire-brands!
To Brutus', to Cassius'; burn all! Some to Decius'
35 house, and some to Casca's; some to Ligarius'. Away, go!

Exeunt all the PLEBEIANS *dragging off* CINNA.

3. **were best.** Had better

4. **bear me a bang.** Be beaten by me

5. **turn him going.** Send him away; kill him

What do you think of the plebeians of Rome after reading Act III? Are they qualified to govern themselves in a democracy? Why or why not? What political situations that have occurred in the last hundred years might resemble that of Act III?

REFER TO TEXT ▶ ▶ ▶ ▶	▶ REASON WITH TEXT	
1a. Review Brutus's speech in III.ii.12–44. Quote what Brutus tells the crowd about Antony. What is the mood of the crowd after Brutus speaks? How does the crowd's mood change after Antony speaks?	1b. Discuss why you think that, despite Cassius's advice, Brutus allows Antony to speak at Caesar's funeral. Infer what this action reveals about Brutus. Is his action a mistake? Why or why not?	**Understand** **Find meaning**
2a. Recall Caesar's last words.	2b. Examine what Caesar's last words reveal about him. What feelings did he have for Brutus?	**Apply** **Use information**
3a. Quote a passage from both Brutus's speech and Antony's speech that you think is rhetorically effective. What is it about this passage that you think is effective in manipulating the crowd?	3b. Compare and contrast Brutus's and Antony's speeches. How are they similar or different in content, purpose, tone, and style?	**Analyze** **Take things apart**
4a. Distinguish who trusts Antony and who does not trust Antony. Which actions make him seem trustworthy? Which actions make him seem untrustworthy?	4b. Assess the impact of Antony's speech on the crowd. Do you think Antony achieves his purpose? Use evidence from the text to support your answer.	**Evaluate** **Make judgments**
5a. Describe what the crowd does following Antony's speech.	5b. Why do you think mob mentality is often considered dangerous? Propose constructive actions that the mob could have taken.	**Create** **Bring ideas together**

ANALYZE LITERATURE: Rhetorical Device, Climax, and Crisis

Read the definition of rhetorical device in the Literary Terms Handbook and give an example of a rhetorical question from Antony's speech, III. ii. 69–103. How does this device contribute to the impact of the speech?

Review the elements of plot on page 526. What is the climax of Julius Caesar? What is the crisis—the point at which the fortunes of Brutus take a turn for the worse? Note these points on your Plot Diagram.

Literature CONNECTION

Constantine Cavafy (1863–1933) is considered one of the great modern Greek poets. Born in Alexandria, a seaport in Egypt named for Alexander the Great, Cavafy had a fascination with the cultures of ancient Greece and Rome. Cavafy's poem **"The Ides of March"** alludes to an incident in the life of Julius Caesar.

CAVAFY

THE IDES OF MARCH

A Poem by **Constantine Cavafy**

Oh soul, fear things grandiose.[1]
And if you are unable to master your ambitions,
serve them with hesitation, with precaution.
And the farther you advance,
5   the more you must be questioning and careful.

And when you reach your height, Caesar finally;
when you take up the form of a man that renowned,[2]
then take great care as you go out into the street,
the striking dignitary[3] with an entourage,[4]

---

1. **grandiose** (gran´ dē ôs'). Magnificent; extremely grand
2. **when...renowned.** When you become as renowned, or famous, as Caesar
3. **dignitary.** Person in a high position
4. **entourage** (än' tů räzh´). Group of attendants or associates

10   if it happens that from the crowd

a certain Artemidoros comes near, who brings a letter,

and rushed says "Read this immediately,

it speaks of grave matters that concern you,"

don't miss the opportunity to stop; to put off

15   all talk, every task; don't miss the chance

to cast off those random praisers and scrapers[5]

(you can see them later); let even the Senate itself wait

for this, and learn at once

what gravity is in the writing of Artemidoros. ❖

---

5. **scrapers.** Those who bow so low they scrape the ground

REFER TO TEXT ▶ ▶ ▶ ▶	▶ REASON WITH TEXT	
1a. Make a list of the specific warnings Cavafy gives to those who are in a high position.	1b. Summarize the advice Cavafy gives in the poem. What does he caution people like Caesar to do?	**Understand** **Find meaning**
2a. How does Cavafy describe the information Artemidorus brings to Caesar?	2b. Contrast Cavafy's description of Artemidorus's information with that of the followers who accompany Caesar to the Senate. Do you agree with Cavafy's description of these men? Why or why not?	**Analyze** **Take things apart**
3a. Recall the title of the poem.	3b. Critique the title of the poem. Do you think it is an effective title? Why or why not? What information does the title bring to the poem? How does this associated information affect your reading of the poem?	**Evaluate** **Make judgments**

TEXT ←TO→ TEXT CONNECTION

- Recall Artemidorus's words in II. iii. 12–13 of *The Tragedy of Julius Caesar*. Does Cavafy share Artemidorus's lament? Explain.
- Do you find the tone of Cavafy's poem sorrowful or mournful, or more witty and ironic? Explain your answer.

VOCABULARY & SPELLING

UNDERSTAND THE CONCEPT

APPLY THE SKILL

Spelling Rules and Tips

Spelling errors are sometimes very easy to make. Aside from looking up every word you write in a dictionary, remembering the following rules and tips can help you avoid common spelling errors.

Remember Spelling Patterns

In the English language, spelling patterns exist for certain types of words. Three of the most common patterns are listed below.

1. **Suffixes with Y, Part I.** If you are adding a *suffix* (a letter or group of letters added to the end of a word to change its meaning) to a word that ends with *y* and that *y* follows a vowel, usually leave the *y* in place.

   EXAMPLES

   annoy → annoys → annoying → annoyed
   employ → employs → employing → employed

2. **Suffixes with Y, Part II.** If you are adding a suffix to a word that ends with *y* and that *y* follows a consonant, change the *y* to *i* before adding any ending except *–ing*.

   EXAMPLES

   easy → easiest → easier
   satisfy → satisfied → satisfying

3. **The *ie / ei* Pattern.** When a word is spelled with the letters *i* and *e* and has a long *e* sound (ē), it is usually spelled *ie* except after the letter *c*. Use *ei* when the sound is not long *e*. When the vowel combination has a long *a* sound (ā), always spell it with *ei*.

   EXAMPLES

   Long *e:* niece, receipt, yield
   (Exceptions: either, neither, weird)

   Not long *e:* counterfeit, forfeit, foreign
   (Exceptions: friend, fief, handkerchief)

   Long *a:* eight, weigh, reign

Break Words into Syllables

To remember how to correctly spell words that have several syllables, try spelling them syllable by syllable. This is especially helpful with words that have sounds that often get dropped in pronunciation.

EXAMPLES

choc-o-late
Feb-ru-a-ry
bus-i-ness
bound-a-ry

Use Mnemonic Devices

Another way to remember how to spell a word correctly is to create a **mnemonic device,** or a catchy phrase, an image, or a trick that helps you remember information. For example, you might think of the round dome in the Capitol building to remember that the seat of government is spelled *capitOL* rather than *capitAL.*

To create your own mnemonic devices, try finding a word within a word, as in the example below:

EXAMPLE

believe or *beleive?* Remember: There is a <u>lie</u> in be<u>lie</u>ve.

Another way to create a mnemonic device is to associate the word with others like it, that is, with another word that contains the same spelling pattern, word part, or root.

EXAMPLES

Reletive, relitive, or *relative?* Remember: A <u>rela</u>tive is someone <u>rela</u>ted to you.

Idiosyncrasy or *idiocincrasy?* Remember: *Idio* like <u>idio</u>t and <u>syn</u> as in <u>syn</u>onym.

Be Aware of Spell-Check Software

Spell-check software can be a useful tool in checking work you do on a computer. However, keep in mind that spell check does not always make the correct decisions. For example, words like *their, there,* and *they're* may be spelled correctly but used incorrectly.

Identify Misspelled Words

Read these sentences from Act III of *The Tragedy of Julius Caesar.* Identify the sentences with misspelled words. Rewrite the sentence with the correct spelling or spellings. If the words in a sentence are spelled correctly, write "correct."

1. "My credit now stands on such slippery ground that one of two bad ways you must conciet me, either a coward or a flaterer."
2. "Our reasons are so full of good regard that were you, Antony, the son of Caesar, you should be satisfyed."
3. "Domestic fury and fierce civil strife shall cumber all the parts of Italy."
4. "Here comes his body, mourned by Mark Antony, who, though he had no hand in his death, shall receive the benefit of his dying."
5. "If it were so, it was a grievous fault, and greiveously hath Caesar answered it."
6. "O judgement! thou art fled to brutish beasts, and men have lost thier reason."
7. "'Tis good you know not that you are his hiers, for if you should, O, what would come of it?"
8. "O now you weep, and I perceive you feel the dint of pity. These are graceous drops."
9. "O pityous spectacle! O noble Caesar! O woeful day!"
10. "Mischief, thou art afoot, take thou what course thou wilt!"

Improve Your Spelling

Rewrite the following paragraph so that all the words are spelled correctly.

In Act III, the senaters kill Caesar to stop his advancment to emperor. The people are frigtened, so Brutus speeks to them about why they killed Caesar and how the people should not think of them as cruel. When Antony speaks, however, he turns the crowd agianst the senaters by telling them they are Caesar's hiers and that he left them money and parks for there plea-sure. He does not beleive that the murder was justifyable. The crowd then trys to kill those who killed Caesar.

Create Mnemonic Devices

Create mnemonic devices for the following vocabulary words from this unit:

1. valor
2. grievous
3. corporal
4. disconsolate
5. vice

Use Correct Spelling in Your Writing

Write a review of a popular website, such as the one for the Smithsonian or the Louvre Museum in Paris. Describe its content and links. What makes it a worthwhile site to visit? What groups in particular would enjoy it? Use as many words with the spelling patterns presented in this workshop as you can to show off your understanding of letter and sound patterns. Double-check your spelling. If any words are misspelled, see if you can see a pattern that will help you remember to spell the words correctly the next time.

EXTEND THE SKILL

Now that all computer document-writing programs and many e-mail providers have a spell-checking feature, some people do not bother to check their electronic writing for incorrect words, thinking that the computer will catch the mistakes. However, spell-checking features cannot help you if the word is spelled like a word with a different meaning. Do an Internet search for commonly misspelled or confusing words. Print out the list and circle the ones that cause you trouble. When you next send an e-mail or write a paper on the computer, proofread your spellings of those words.

Temple of Athena in Paestum.

Act IV

Scene I: Antony's House in Rome, a Year and a Half Later

Enter Antony, Octavius, *and* Lepidus.[1]

ANTONY.   These many then shall die, their names are prick'd.[2]

OCTAVIUS.   Your brother too must die; consent you, Lepidus?

LEPIDUS.   I do consent—

OCTAVIUS.   Prick him down, Antony.

ACT IV, SCENE I
1. **Antony, Octavius, *and* Lepidus.** These three men now rule Rome jointly, as a triumvirate.
2. **prick'd.** Marked down on a list

LEPIDUS. Upon condition Publius shall not live,
5 Who is your sister's son, Mark Antony.

ANTONY. He shall not live; look, with a spot[3] I damn him.
But, Lepidus, go you to Caesar's house;
Fetch the will hither, and we shall determine
How to cut off some charge in legacies.[4]

10 **LEPIDUS.** What? shall I find you here?

OCTAVIUS. Or here or at the Capitol.

Exit LEPIDUS.

ANTONY. This is a slight unmeritable[5] man,
Meet[6] to be sent on errands; is it fit,
The threefold world[7] divided, he should stand
One of the three to share it?

15 **OCTAVIUS.** So you thought him,
And took his voice who should be prick'd to die
In our black sentence[8] and proscription.[9]

ANTONY. Octavius, I have seen more days than you,
And though we lay these honors on this man
20 To ease ourselves of divers sland'rous loads,[10]
He shall but bear them as the ass bears gold,
To groan and sweat under the business,
Either led or driven, as we point the way;
And having brought our treasure where we will,
25 Then take we down his load, and turn him off
(Like to the empty ass) to shake his ears
And graze in commons.[11]

OCTAVIUS. You may do your will;
But he's a tried and valiant soldier.

ANTONY. So is my horse, Octavius, and for that
30 I do appoint him store of provender.[12]
It is a creature that I teach to fight,
To wind, to stop, to run directly on,
His <u>corporal</u> motion govern'd by my spirit;
And in some taste is Lepidus but so:[13]
35 He must be taught, and train'd, and bid go forth;
A barren-spirited fellow; one that feeds
On objects, arts, and imitations,
Which, out of use and stal'd by other men,
Begin his fashion.[14] Do not talk of him
40 But as a property. And now, Octavius,
Listen great things. Brutus and Cassius

3. **spot.** Mark

4. **cut...legacies.** Reduce the amount of money left to the people in Caesar's will

5. **unmeritable.** Undeserving; lacking in worth
6. **Meet.** Appropriate
7. **threefold world.** The Roman Empire spanned Europe, Asia, and Africa.

8. **So...sentence.** You thought so, when you gave Lepidus a vote on who should get the death sentence.
9. **proscription.** Publishing of the name of a person condemned to death or exile
10. **we...loads.** We give him these honors only so that he can take the blame for various (divers) accusations (sland'rous loads).

11. **commons.** Pun referring both to a public pastureland and to the lower order of society, the common people

12. **I do appoint...provender.** I supply him with his feed.

cor • por • al
(kôr p[ə] rəl) *adj.,* having to do with the body

13. **in some...but so.** Lepidus is no different.

14. **Begin his fashion.** Antony is saying that Lepidus is a follower, one who pursues interests after others have taken them up.

Are levying powers;[15] we must straight make head;[16]
Therefore let our alliance be combin'd,[17]
Our best friends made, our means stretch'd,
45 And let us presently[18] go sit in council,
How covert matters may be best disclos'd
And open perils surest answered.[19]

OCTAVIUS.   Let us do so; for we are at the stake,
And bay'd about with many enemies,[20]
50 And some that smile have in their hearts, I fear,
Millions of mischiefs.[21]

Exeunt.

15. **levying powers.** Raising an army
16. **make head.** Raise an army
17. **combin'd.** Added to
18. **presently.** At once
19. **covert...answered.** Hidden or secret plans (made by Brutus and Cassius) may best be uncovered and dangers may best be confronted.
20. **at the stake...enemies.** Octavius compares their plight to that of a bear tied to a stake and attacked by dogs.
21. **mischiefs.** Intentions of doing harm

SCENE II: A MILITARY CAMP NEAR SARDIS IN ASIA MINOR; IN FRONT OF BRUTUS'S TENT

Drum. Enter BRUTUS, LUCILIUS, LUCIUS, *and the army.* TITINIUS *and* PINDARUS *meet them.*

BRUTUS.   Stand ho!

LUCILIUS.   Give the word ho! and stand.

BRUTUS.   What now, Lucilius, is Cassius near?

LUCILIUS.   He is at hand, and Pindarus is come
5 To do you salutation from his master.[1]

BRUTUS.   He greets me well. Your master, Pindarus,
In his own change, or by ill officers,
Hath given me some worthy cause to wish
Things done undone;[2] but if he be at hand
I shall be satisfied.[3]

10 PINDARUS.   I do not doubt
But that my noble master will appear
Such as he is, full of regard and honor.

BRUTUS.   He is not doubted. A word, Lucilius,
How he receiv'd you; let me be resolv'd.[4]

15 LUCILIUS.   With courtesy and with respect enough,
But not with such familiar instances,[5]
Nor with such free and friendly conference,[6]
As he hath us'd of old.[7]

BRUTUS.   Thou hast describ'd
A hot friend cooling. Ever note, Lucilius,

ACT IV, SCENE II
1. **To do you salutation... master.** To bring you greetings from Cassius. Pindarus is Cassius's servant.
2. **Your master...undone.** Cassius, whether by his own decision or the decisions of incompetent (ill) officers, has done some things to make me regret ever joining him in the conspiracy.
3. **if he be...satisfied.** If he is here, I will get an explanation.

4. **resolv'd.** Told in full

5. **familiar instances.** Friendly actions
6. **conference.** Discussion; talk
7. **of old.** In the past

20 When love begins to sicken and decay
It useth an enforced ceremony.[8]
There are no tricks in plain and simple faith;
But hollow[9] men, like horses hot at hand,[10]
Make gallant show and promise of their mettle;[11]

Low march within.

25 But when they should endure the bloody spur,
They fall[12] their crests, and like deceitful jades[13]
Sink in the trial.[14] Comes his army on?

LUCILIUS.   They mean this night in Sardis to be quarter'd.
The greater part, the horse in general,[15]
Are come with Cassius.

Enter CASSIUS and his powers.

30 BRUTUS.   Hark, he is arriv'd.
March gently on to meet him.

CASSIUS.   Stand ho!

BRUTUS.   Stand ho! Speak the word along.

1. SOLDIER.   Stand!

35 2. SOLDIER.   Stand!

3. SOLDIER.   Stand!

CASSIUS.   Most noble brother, you have done me wrong.

BRUTUS.   Judge me, you gods! wrong I mine enemies?
And if not so, how should I wrong a brother?

40 CASSIUS.   Brutus, this sober[16] form of yours hides wrongs,
And when you do them—

BRUTUS.   Cassius, be content,
Speak your griefs softly; I do know you well.
Before the eyes of both our armies here
(Which should perceive nothing but love from us)
45 Let us not wrangle. Bid them move away;
Then in my tent, Cassius, enlarge[17] your griefs,
And I will give you audience.

CASSIUS.   Pindarus,
Bid our commanders lead their charges[18] off
A little from this ground.

50 BRUTUS.   Lucius, do you the like, and let no man
Come to our tent till we have done our conference.

8. **enforced ceremony.**
Forced civility or formality
9. **hollow.** Phony; insincere
10. **hot at hand.** Too spirited at the beginning (as of a race)
11. **mettle.** Ability

12. **fall.** Drop
13. **deceitful jades.** Poor horses; nags
14. **Sink in the trial.** Fail to meet the challenge
15. **horse in general.** Cavalry as a whole

16. **sober.** Somber

17. **enlarge.** Expand upon

18. **charges.** Soldiers

Let Lucilius and Titinius guard our door.

Exeunt. Manent BRUTUS *and* CASSIUS, *who withdraw into* BRUTUS*'s tent, while* LUCILIUS *and* TITINIUS *mount guard without.*

SCENE III: INTERIOR OF BRUTUS'S TENT

CASSIUS.   That you have wrong'd me doth appear in this:
You have condemn'd and noted[1] Lucius Pella
For taking bribes here of the Sardians;
Wherein my letters, praying on his side,
5   Because I knew the man, was[2] slighted off.[3]

BRUTUS.   You wrong'd yourself to write in such a case.

CASSIUS.   In such a time as this it is not meet[4]
That every nice[5] offense should bear his comment.[6]

BRUTUS.   Let me tell you, Cassius, you yourself
10   Are much condemn'd to have an itching palm,
To sell and mart[7] your offices for gold
To undeservers.

CASSIUS.   I, an itching palm?
You know that you are Brutus that speaks this,
Or, by the gods, this speech were else your last.

15   BRUTUS.   The name of Cassius honors this corruption,
And <u>chastisement</u> doth therefore hide his head.[8]

CASSIUS.   Chastisement?

BRUTUS.   Remember March, the ides of March remember:
Did not great Julius bleed for justice' sake?
20   What villain touch'd his body, that did stab
And not for justice? What? shall one of us,
That struck the foremost man of all this world
But for supporting robbers, shall we now
Contaminate our fingers with base bribes?
25   And sell the mighty space of our large honors
For so much trash as may be grasped thus?
I had rather be a dog, and bay the moon,
Than such a Roman.

CASSIUS.   Brutus, bait not me,
I'll not endure it. You forget yourself
30   To hedge me in.[9] I am a soldier, I,
Older in practice, abler than yourself
To make conditions.

ACT IV, SCENE III
1. **noted.** Marked for disgrace

2. **was.** Were
3. **slighted off.** Ignored

4. **meet.** Fit; appropriate
5. **nice.** Small
6. **bear his comment.** Require criticism; *his* means "its"

7. **mart.** Market

chas • tise • ment
(chas tīz´ mənt) *n.,* scolding; condemnation

8. **The name...head.** Your name is linked to the bribery, so nobody dares chastise, or condemn, those who take the bribes.

9. **hedge me in.** Close me in; limit my freedom

BRUTUS.　　　　　　　Go to; you are not, Cassius.

CASSIUS.　I am.

BRUTUS.　I say you are not.

35 CASSIUS.　Urge me no more, I shall forget myself;
Have mind upon your health; tempt me no farther.

BRUTUS.　Away, slight man!

CASSIUS.　Is't possible?

BRUTUS.　　　　　　　Hear me, for I will speak.
Must I give way and room to your rash choler?[10]
40 Shall I be frighted when a madman stares?

CASSIUS.　O ye gods, ye gods, must I endure all this?

BRUTUS.　All this? ay, more. Fret till your proud heart break;
Go show your slaves how choleric[11] you are,
And make your bondmen[12] tremble. Must I bouge?[13]
45 Must I observe you? Must I stand and crouch
Under your testy humor?[14] By the gods,
You shall digest the venom of your spleen[15]
Though it do split you; for, from this day forth,
I'll use you for my mirth, yea, for my laughter,
When you are waspish.[16]

50 CASSIUS.　　　　　　　Is it come to this?

BRUTUS.　You say you are a better soldier:
Let it appear so; make your vaunting true,[17]
And it shall please me well. For mine own part,
I shall be glad to learn of noble men.

55 CASSIUS.　You wrong me every way; you wrong me, Brutus:
I said an elder soldier, not a better.
Did I say "better"?

BRUTUS.　　　　　If you did, I care not.

CASSIUS.　When Caesar liv'd, he durst not thus have mov'd me.[18]

BRUTUS.　Peace, peace, you durst not so have tempted him.

60 CASSIUS.　I durst not?

BRUTUS.　No.

CASSIUS.　What? durst not tempt him?

BRUTUS.　　　　　　　　For your life you durst not.

CASSIUS.　Do not presume too much upon my love,

10. **choler.** Anger

11. **choleric.** Angry
12. **bondmen.** Slaves
13. **bouge.** Budge; move
14. **testy humor.** Irritable mood
15. **spleen.** Organ considered by Elizabethans to be the seat of strong emotions

16. **I'll...waspish.** I'll laugh at you when you are ill-tempered.

17. **make...true.** Make your boasting (vaunting) true by defeating me in a fight.

18. **When...mov'd me.** Even Caesar never dared (durst) make me this angry.

"You wrong me every way; you wrong me, Brutus." Cassius (John Gielgud) and Brutus (James Mason) speak on the eve of battle.

I may do that I shall be sorry for.

65 **BRUTUS.**   You have done that you should be sorry for.
There is no terror, Cassius, in your threats;
For I am arm'd so strong in honesty
That they pass by me as the idle wind,
Which I respect[19] not. I did send to you

70 For certain sums of gold, which you denied me;
For I can raise no money by vile means.
By heaven, I had rather coin my heart
And drop my blood for drachmas[20] than to wring
From the hard hands of peasants their vile trash

19. **respect.** Fear

20. **drachmas.** Silver coins

75 By any indirection.[21] I did send
    To you for gold to pay my legions,[22]
    Which you denied me. Was that done like Cassius?
    Should I have answer'd Caius Cassius so?
    When Marcus Brutus grows so covetous
80 To lock such rascal counters[23] from his friends,
    Be ready, gods, with all your thunderbolts,
    Dash him to pieces!

    CASSIUS.   I denied you not.

    BRUTUS.   You did.

    CASSIUS.   I did not. He was but a fool that brought
85 My answer back.[24] Brutus hath riv'd[25] my heart.
    A friend should bear his friend's <u>infirmities</u>;
    But Brutus makes mine greater than they are.

    BRUTUS.   I do not, till you practice them on me.

    CASSIUS.   You love me not.

    BRUTUS.   I do not like your faults.

90 CASSIUS.   A friendly eye could never see such faults.

    BRUTUS.   A flatterer's would not, though they do appear
    As huge as high Olympus.

    CASSIUS.   Come, Antony, and young Octavius, come,
    Revenge yourselves alone on Cassius,
95 For Cassius is a-weary of the world;
    Hated by one he loves, brav'd[26] by his brother,
    Check'd like a bondman, all his faults observ'd,
    Set in a note-book, learn'd, and conn'd by rote,[27]
    To cast into my teeth. O, I could weep
100 My spirit from mine eyes! There is my dagger,
    And here my naked breast; within, a heart
    Dearer than Pluto's mine,[28] richer than gold:
    If that thou be'st a Roman, take it forth.
    I, that denied thee gold, will give my heart:
105 Strike as thou didst at Caesar; for I know,
    When thou didst hate him worst, thou lovedst him better
    Than ever thou lovedst Cassius.

    BRUTUS.   Sheathe your dagger.
    Be angry when you will, it shall have scope;[29]
    Do what you will, dishonor shall be humor.[30]
110 O Cassius, you are yoked with a lamb
    That carries anger as the flint bears fire,

21. **indirection.** Cunning or false means
22. **legions.** Military divisions with three thousand to six thousand soldiers

23. **rascal counters.** Coins of little worth

24. **He was...back.** The messenger who told you that was a fool.
25. **riv'd.** Broken

> **in • fir • mi • ty**
> (in fur´ mə tē) *n.,* sickness; weakness

26. **brav'd.** Defied

27. **conn'd by rote.** Memorized

28. **Pluto's mine.** Treasures found in the earth; Pluto, Roman god of the underworld, is here mixed up with Plutus, god of riches.

29. **scope.** Free play; range
30. **dishonor shall be humor.** I shall interpret your insults (dishonor) as due to your disposition, or temper.

Who, much enforced, shows a hasty spark,
And straight is cold again.[31]

CASSIUS.   Hath Cassius liv'd
To be but mirth and laughter to his Brutus,
115 When grief and blood ill-temper'd vexeth him?

BRUTUS.   When I spoke that, I was ill-temper'd too.

CASSIUS.   Do you confess so much? Give me your hand.

BRUTUS.   And my heart too.

CASSIUS.   O Brutus!

BRUTUS.   What's the matter?

CASSIUS.   Have not you love enough to bear with me,
120 When that rash humor which my mother gave me
Makes me forgetful?

BRUTUS.   Yes, Cassius, and from henceforth,
When you are over-earnest[32] with your Brutus,
He'll think your mother chides,[33] and leave you so.

Enter a POET, to LUCILIUS and TITINIUS, as they stand on guard.

POET.   Let me go in to see the generals.
125 There is some grudge between 'em; 'tis not meet
They be alone.

LUCILIUS.   You shall not come to them.

POET.   Nothing but death shall stay me.

                        BRUTUS *and* CASSIUS *step out of the tent.*

CASSIUS.   How now? what's the matter?

130 POET.   For shame, you generals! what do you mean?
Love, and be friends, as two such men should be,
For I have seen more years, I'm sure, than ye.

CASSIUS.   Ha, ha! how vildly[34] doth this cynic[35] rhyme!

BRUTUS.   Get you hence, sirrah; saucy[36] fellow, hence!

135 CASSIUS.   Bear with him, Brutus, 'tis his fashion.

BRUTUS.   I'll know his humor, when he knows his time.[37]
What should the wars do with these jigging[38] fools?
Companion,[39] hence!

CASSIUS.   Away, away, be gone!

                                        Exit POET.

31. **you are…cold again.**
You are allied with a mild
and gentle man; I carry anger
as the flint does fire—when
worked upon, I flare up, but
then turn cold again right
away.

32. **over-earnest.** Overly
upset
33. **He'll…chides.** He will
attribute your actions to
inherited bad temper.

34. **vildly.** Vilely; despicably
35. **cynic (si′ nik).** Worldly
philosopher
36. **saucy.** Disrespectful

37. **I'll know…his time.** I'll
accept his temperament when
he chooses an appropriate
time to display it.
38. **jigging.** Rhyming
39. **Companion.** Low person

BRUTUS. Lucilius and Titinius, bid the commanders
140 Prepare to lodge their companies tonight.

CASSIUS. And come yourselves, and bring Messala with you
Immediately to us.

Exeunt LUCILIUS *and* TITINIUS.

BRUTUS. [*To* LUCIUS *within.*] Lucius, a bowl of wine!

BRUTUS *and* CASSIUS *return into the tent.*

CASSIUS. I did not think you could have been so angry.

BRUTUS. O Cassius, I am sick of⁴⁰ many griefs.

40. **of.** From

145 **CASSIUS.** Of your philosophy you make no use,
If you give place to accidental evils.⁴¹

41. **accidental evils.** The stoic philosophers taught that one should avoid displays of emotion and cultivate indifference to the tides of fortune.

BRUTUS. No man bears sorrow better. Portia is dead.

CASSIUS. Ha? Portia?

BRUTUS. She is dead.

150 **CASSIUS.** How scap'd I killing when I cross'd you so?
O insupportable and touching loss!
Upon what sickness?

BRUTUS. Impatient of⁴² my absence,
And grief that young Octavius with Mark Antony
Have made themselves so strong—for with her death

42. **Impatient of.** Not able to endure

155 That tidings came. With this she fell distract,⁴³
And (her attendants absent) swallow'd fire.⁴⁴

43. **fell distract.** Became crazed
44. **swallow'd fire.** According to Plutarch's *Lives,* she swallowed red-hot coals.

CASSIUS. And died so?

BRUTUS. Even so.

CASSIUS. O ye immortal gods!

Enter the Boy LUCIUS *with wine and tapers.*

BRUTUS. Speak no more of her. Give me a bowl of wine.
In this I bury all unkindness, Cassius. [*Drinks.*]

160 **CASSIUS.** My heart is thirsty for that noble pledge.
Fill, Lucius, till the wine o'erswell the cup;
I cannot drink too much of Brutus' love. [*Drinks.*]

Exit LUCIUS.

Enter TITINIUS *and* MESSALA.

BRUTUS. Come in, Titinius. Welcome, good Messala.
Now sit we close about this taper here,

165 And call in question our necessities.[45]

CASSIUS.   Portia, art thou gone?

BRUTUS.   No more, I pray you.
Messala, I have here received letters
That young Octavius and Mark Antony
Come down upon us with a mighty power,
170 Bending their expedition toward Philippi.

MESSALA.   Myself have letters of the self-same tenure.[46]

BRUTUS.   With what addition?

MESSALA.   That by proscription and bills of outlawry
Octavius, Antony, and Lepidus
175 Have put to death an hundred senators.

BRUTUS.   Therein our letters do not well agree;
Mine speak of seventy senators that died
By their proscriptions, Cicero being one.

CASSIUS.   Cicero one?

MESSALA.   Cicero is dead,
180 And by that order of proscription.
Had you your letters from your wife, my lord?

BRUTUS.   No, Messala.[47]

MESSALA.   Nor nothing in your letters writ of her?

BRUTUS.   Nothing, Messala.

MESSALA.   That, methinks, is strange.

185 BRUTUS.   Why ask you? Hear you aught of her in yours?

MESSALA.   No, my lord.

BRUTUS.   Now as you are a Roman tell me true.

MESSALA.   Then like a Roman bear the truth I tell:
For certain she is dead, and by strange manner.

190 BRUTUS.   Why, farewell, Portia. We must die, Messala.
With meditating that she must die once,[48]
I have the patience to endure it now.

MESSALA.   Even so great men great losses should endure.

CASSIUS.   I have as much of this in art[49] as you,
195 But yet my nature could not bear it so.

BRUTUS.   Well, to our work alive.[50] What do you think

45. **call...necessities.**
Consider what we must do

46. **Myself...self-same tenure.** I have letters that say the same thing.

47. **No, Messala.** This statement seems contradictory, since Brutus already knows of Portia's death. Some editors believe that lines 181–195 were mistakenly added during a later revision of the play.

48. **With...once.** By thinking on the inevitability of death

49. **have...art.** Know as much of this stoic philosophy

50. **to our work alive.** Let's act like the living.

Of marching to Philippi presently?

CASSIUS.   I do not think it good.

BRUTUS.   Your reason?

CASSIUS.   This it is:
'Tis better that the enemy seek us;
200 So shall he waste his means, weary his soldiers,
Doing himself offense, whilst we, lying still,
Are full of rest, defense, and nimbleness.

BRUTUS.   Good reasons must of force give place to better:
The people 'twixt Philippi and this ground
205 Do stand but in a forc'd affection,
For they have grudg'd us contribution.
The enemy, marching along by them,
By them shall make a fuller number up,
Come on refresh'd, new-added, and encourag'd;
210 From which advantage shall we cut him off
If at Philippi we do face him there,
These people at our back.

CASSIUS.   Hear me, good brother.

BRUTUS.   Under your pardon. You must note beside
That we have tried the utmost of [51] our friends,
215 Our legions are brimful, our cause is ripe:
The enemy increaseth every day;
We, at the height, are ready to decline.
There is a tide in the affairs of men,
Which taken at the flood, leads on to fortune;
220 Omitted,[52] all the voyage of their life
Is bound in shallows[53] and in miseries.
On such a full sea are we now afloat,
And we must take the current when it serves,
Or lose our ventures.

CASSIUS.   Then with your will go on;
225 We'll along ourselves, and meet them at Philippi.

BRUTUS.   The deep of night is[54] crept upon our talk,
And nature must obey necessity,
Which we will niggard with a little rest.[55]
There is no more to say?

CASSIUS.   No more. Good night.
230 Early tomorrow will we rise, and hence.

BRUTUS.   Lucius!

---

51. **tried the utmost of.**
Gotten all the support that we
shall be able to get

52. **Omitted.** If not taken
53. **bound in shallows.**
Limited to shallow waters
(confined to a harbor)

54. **is.** Has

55. **niggard with a little
rest.** Shortchange necessity by
allowing ourselves but a little
sleep

Enter Lucius.

             My gown.

                          Exit Lucius.

                   Farewell, good Messala.
Good night, Titinius. Noble, noble Cassius,
Good night, and good repose.

CASSIUS.   O my dear brother!
This was an ill beginning of the night.

235   Never come such division 'tween our souls!
Let it not, Brutus.

Enter Lucius *with the gown.*

BRUTUS.   Everything is well.

CASSIUS.   Good night, my lord.

BRUTUS.   Good night, good brother.

TITINIUS, MESSALA.   Good night, Lord Brutus.

BRUTUS.   Farewell every one.

           Exeunt all but BRUTUS *and* LUCIUS.

Give me the gown. Where is thy instrument?[56]

LUCIUS.   Here in the tent.

240   BRUTUS.   What, thou speak'st drowsily?
Poor knave, I blame thee not, thou art o'erwatch'd.[57]
Call Claudio and some other of my men,
I'll have them sleep on cushions in my tent.

LUCIUS.   Varrus and Claudio!

Enter VARRUS *and* CLAUDIO.

245   VARRUS.   Calls my lord?

BRUTUS.   I pray you, sirs, lie in my tent and sleep;
It may be I shall raise you by and by
On business to my brother Cassius.

VARRUS.   So please you, we will stand and watch your pleasure.

250   BRUTUS.   I will not have it so. Lie down, good sirs,
It may be I shall otherwise bethink me.[58]

VARRUS *and* CLAUDIO *lie down.*

Look, Lucius, here's the book I sought for so;
I put it in the pocket of my gown.

LUCIUS.   I was sure your lordship did not give it me.

56. **instrument.** Lute, perhaps, to play a song for Brutus

57. **o'erwatch'd.** Overly tired

58. **otherwise bethink me.** Change my mind

255 BRUTUS.   Bear with me, good boy, I am much forgetful.
Canst thou hold up thy heavy eyes awhile,
And touch thy instrument a strain or two?

LUCIUS.   Ay, my lord, an't[59] please you.

BRUTUS.   It does, my boy.
I trouble thee too much, but thou art willing.

260 LUCIUS.   It is my duty, sir.

BRUTUS.   I should not urge thy duty past thy might;
I know young bloods look for a time of rest.

LUCIUS.   I have slept, my lord, already.

BRUTUS.   It was well done, and thou shalt sleep again;
265 I will not hold thee long. If I do live,
I will be good to thee.

Music, and a song.

This is a sleepy tune. O murd'rous slumber!
Layest thou thy leaden mace[60] upon my boy,
That plays thee music? Gentle knave, good night;
270 I will not do thee so much wrong to wake thee.
If thou dost nod, thou break'st thy instrument,
I'll take it from thee; and, good boy, good night.
Let me see, let me see; is not the leaf turn'd down
Where I left reading? Here it is, I think.

Enter the GHOST OF CAESAR.

275 How ill this taper burns! Ha! who comes here?
I think it is the weakness of mine eyes
That shapes this monstrous <u>apparition</u>.
It comes upon me. Art thou any thing?
Art thou some god, some angel, or some devil
280 That mak'st my blood cold, and my hair to stare?[61]
Speak to me what thou art.

GHOST.   Thy evil spirit, Brutus.

BRUTUS.   Why com'st thou?

GHOST.   To tell thee thou shalt see me at Philippi.

BRUTUS.   Well; then I shall see thee again?

285 GHOST.   Aye, at Philippi.

BRUTUS.   Why, I will see thee at Philippi then.

Exit GHOST.

59. **an't.** If it

60. **mace.** Club

ap • pa • ri • tion
(aʹ pə riʹ shən) *n.*, ghost

61. **stare.** Stand up on end

Now I have taken heart thou vanishest.
Ill spirit, I would hold more talk with thee.
Boy, Lucius! Varrus! Claudio! Sirs, awake!
290 Claudio!

Lucius. The strings, my lord, are false.[62]

Brutus. He thinks he still is at his instrument.
Lucius, awake!

Lucius. My lord?

295 **Brutus.** Didst thou dream, Lucius, that thou so criedst out?

Lucius. My lord, I do not know that I did cry.

Brutus. Yes, that thou didst. Didst thou see any thing?

Lucius. Nothing, my lord.

Brutus. Sleep again, Lucius. Sirrah Claudio!
300 [To Varrus.] Fellow thou, awake!

Varrus. My lord?

Claudio. My lord?

Brutus. Why did you so cry out, sirs, in your sleep?[63]

Varrus, Claudio. Did we, my lord?

Brutus.   Aye. Saw you any thing?

305 **Varrus.** No, my lord, I saw nothing.

Claudio. Nor I, my lord.

Brutus. Go and commend me[64] to my brother Cassius;
Bid him set on his pow'rs betimes before,[65]
And we will follow.

310 **Varrus, Claudio.** It shall be done, my lord.

Exeunt.

62. **false.** Out of tune

63. **Why did you so cry out...sleep?** The men did not cry out; Brutus is only making an excuse to ask them whether they saw anything when the ghost appeared.

64. **commend me.** Give my regards
65. **set on...before.** Advance his troops ahead of mine

MIRRORS & WINDOWS In Act IV, Brutus behaves stoically even though he is grieving the death of his wife, Portia. Have you witnessed others grieving in this way? Do you think Brutus's reaction is healthy? What do you think is a good way for people to grieve?

REFER TO TEXT ▶ ▶ ▶ ▶	▶ REASON WITH TEXT	
1a. Recall the conversation between Lepidus, Antony, and Octavius in Act IV, Scene i. What decision do they come to? What does Antony say about Caesar's will?	**1b.** Based on what you learn in this conversation, determine what kind of person Antony reveals himself to be. Do you like him? Why or why not?	**Understand** **Find meaning**
2a. Describe what Brutus and Cassius argue about in Scene iii.	**2b.** Examine the argument between Brutus and Cassius. Are they arguing over important matters? Why do you think they are arguing in this manner? Apply what you know about the two men to answer these questions.	**Apply** **Use information**
3a. Find IV.iii.218–223 and identify to what Brutus compares the choices people are given. How does this comparison reflect Brutus's attitude toward the situation he is in?	**3b.** In Scene iii, Brutus and Cassius disagree regarding how to proceed in the battle against Antony and Octavius. Outline the arguments made by Brutus and Cassius.	**Analyze** **Take things apart**
4a. What tragic news does Brutus tell Cassius? How does this news affect Brutus? How does the news affect Cassius?	**4b.** Critique the relationship between Cassius and Brutus. Is it a friendship or a working partnership? Do they have similar values? Do they respect each other? Support your answers with evidence from the text.	**Evaluate** **Make judgments**
5a. List the "low deeds" that Brutus accuses Cassius of.	**5b.** Upon hearing that Cassius seems less friendly, Brutus observes, "When love begins to sicken and decay / It useth enforced ceremony" (IV.ii.20–21). Relate this quotation to your own life. Do you agree with Brutus's statement? Have you seen people behave in a cold, civil manner as their friendship fades? Explain.	**Create** **Bring ideas together**

ANALYZE LITERATURE: Foreshadowing and Falling Action

What do you think is foreshadowed, or hinted at, by the appearance of the ghost at the end of Act IV? Is the ghost real, or does Brutus imagine it? If the ghost is not real, what does its appearance indicate about Brutus's state of mind?

What misfortunes does Brutus suffer in this act? What has happened to his relationship with Cassius? What has happened to his wife? What immediate threat does he face? Review the elements of plot on page 526 and record in your Plot Diagram key events from the falling action.

Act V

Scene I: The Battleground at Philippi, Greece

Enter Octavius, Antony, *and their army.*

Octavius.   Now, Antony, our hopes are answered.
You said the enemy would not come down,
But keep the hills and upper regions.
It proves not so: their battles[1] are at hand;
5   They mean to warn[2] us at Philippi here,
Answering before we do demand of them.

Antony.   Tut, I am in their bosoms,[3] and I know
Wherefore they do it. They could be content
To visit other places, and come down
10   With fearful bravery, thinking by this face[4]
To fasten in our thoughts that they have courage;
But 'tis not so.

Enter a Messenger.

Messenger.   Prepare you, generals.
The enemy comes on in gallant show;
Their bloody sign of battle is hung out,
15   And something to be done immediately.

Act V, Scene I
1. **battles.** Battalions; armies
2. **warn.** Challenge

3. **I am...bosoms.** I know their hearts (plans).

4. **face.** Look; appearance

ANTONY.   Octavius, lead your battle softly on
Upon the left hand of the even field.

OCTAVIUS.   Upon the right hand I, keep thou the left.

ANTONY.   Why do you cross me in this exigent?[5]

20   **OCTAVIUS.**   I do not cross you; but I will do so.

March.

Drum. Enter BRUTUS, CASSIUS, *and their army;*
LUCILIUS, TITINIUS, MESSALA, *and others.*

BRUTUS.   They stand, and would have parley.[6]

CASSIUS.   Stand fast, Titinius; we must out and talk.

OCTÁVIUS.   Mark Antony, shall we give sign of battle?

ANTONY.   No, Caesar, we will answer on their charge.[7]
25   Make forth, the generals would have some words.

OCTAVIUS.   Stir not until the signal.

BRUTUS.   Words before blows; is it so, countrymen?

OCTAVIUS.   Not that we love words better, as you do.

BRUTUS.   Good words are better than bad strokes, Octavius.

30   **ANTONY.**   In your bad strokes, Brutus, you give good words;
Witness the hole you made in Caesar's heart,
Crying, "Long live! Hail, Caesar!"

CASSIUS.   Antony,
The posture[8] of your blows are yet unknown;
But for your words, they rob the Hybla[9] bees,
And leave them honeyless.

35   **ANTONY.**   Not stingless too?

BRUTUS.   O yes, and soundless too;
For you have stol'n their buzzing, Antony,
And very wisely threat before you sting.

ANTONY.   Villains! you did not so, when your vile daggers
40   Hack'd one another[10] in the sides of Caesar.
You show'd your teeth like apes, and fawn'd like hounds,
And bow'd like bondmen, kissing Caesar's feet;
Whilst damned Casca, like a cur, behind
Strook[11] Caesar on the neck. O you flatterers!

45   **CASSIUS.**   Flatterers? Now, Brutus, thank yourself;
This tongue had not offended so today,

5. **cross...exigent.**
Contradict me in this
emergency

6. **have parley.** Speak;
confer

7. **answer on their charge.**
React when they attack

*I read:
Clitus*

8. **posture.** Strength or
nature
9. **Hybla.** Town in Sicily
known for beehives and
honey

10. **one another.** One after
the other

11. **Strook.** Struck

"Villains!" Mark Antony (Marlon Brando) leads his army into battle.

If Cassius might have rul'd.[12]

OCTAVIUS. Come, come, the cause. If arguing make us sweat,
The proof of it will turn to redder drops.
50 Look,
I draw a sword against conspirators;
When think you that the sword goes up again?[13]
Never, till Caesar's three and thirty wounds
Be well aveng'd; or till another Caesar
55 Have added slaughter to the sword of traitors.[14]

BRUTUS. Caesar, thou canst not die by traitors' hands,
Unless thou bring'st them with thee.

CASSIUS. So I hope;

12. **Cassius might have rul'd.** Cassius had urged that Antony be killed along with Caesar.

13. **goes up again.** Will be resheathed

14. **till another...sword of traitors.** Until these traitors have killed another Caesar, Octavius himself

I was not born to die on Brutus' sword.

BRUTUS.   O, if thou wert the noblest of thy strain,[15]
60 Young man, thou couldst not die more honorable.

CASSIUS.   A peevish schoolboy,[16] worthless of such honor,
Join'd with a masker[17] and a reveller!

ANTONY.   Old Cassius still!

OCTAVIUS.   Come, Antony; away!
Defiance, traitors, hurl we in your teeth.
65 If you dare fight today, come to the field;
If not, when you have stomachs.

Exeunt OCTAVIUS, ANTONY, *and army.*

CASSIUS.   Why now blow wind, swell billow, and swim bark![18]
The storm is up, and all is on the hazard.[19]

BRUTUS.   Ho, Lucilius, hark, a word with you.

LUCILIUS *and then* MESSALA *stand forth.*

LUCILIUS.   My lord.

BRUTUS *and* LUCILIUS *converse apart.*

CASSIUS.   Messala!

MESSALA.   What says my general?

70 **CASSIUS.**   Messala,
This is my birthday; as this very day
Was Cassius born. Give me thy hand, Messala.
Be thou my witness that against my will
(As Pompey was) am I compell'd to set
75 Upon[20] one battle all our liberties.
You know that I held Epicurus[21] strong,
And his opinion; now I change my mind,
And partly credit things that do <u>presage</u>.
Coming from Sardis, on our former[22] <u>ensign</u>
80 Two mighty eagles fell, and there they perch'd,
Gorging and feeding from our soldiers' hands,
Who to Philippi here consorted[23] us.
This morning are they fled away and gone,
And in their steads[24] do ravens, crows, and kites[25]
85 Fly o'er our heads, and downward look on us
As we were sickly prey. Their shadows seem
A canopy most fatal, under which
Our army lies, ready to give up the ghost.

15. **thy strain.** Your family

16. **peevish schoolboy.** Octavius was twenty-one years old at the time of the battle.
17. **masker.** One who attends masked balls

18. **swim bark.** Sail ship
19. **on the hazard.** Risked

20. **set / Upon.** Risk in
21. **Epicurus.** Greek philosopher who did not believe in omens

pre • sage (prə sāj´) *v.,* foretell; warn
en • sign (en´ sən) *n.,* flag; banner

22. **former.** Foremost
23. **consorted.** Accompanied
24. **steads.** Places
25. **kites.** Birds of prey

MESSALA.   Believe not so.

CASSIUS.   I but believe it partly,
90   For I am fresh of spirit, and resolv'd
To meet all perils very constantly.[26]

BRUTUS.   Even so, Lucilius.

CASSIUS.   Now, most noble Brutus,
The gods today stand friendly, that we may,
Lovers[27] in peace, lead on our days to age!
95   But since the affairs of men rest still incertain,[28]
Let's reason with the worst that may befall.[29]
If we do lose this battle, then is this
The very last time we shall speak together:
What are you then determined to do?

100   BRUTUS.   Even by the rule of that philosophy
By which I did blame Cato for the death
Which he did give himself[30]—I know not how,
But I do find it cowardly and vile,
For fear of what might fall, so to prevent
105   The time of life[31]—arming myself with patience
To stay the providence[32] of some high powers
That govern us below.

CASSIUS.   Then, if we lose this battle,
You are contented to be led in triumph
Thorough[33] the streets of Rome?

110   BRUTUS.   No, Cassius, no. Think not, thou noble Roman,
That ever Brutus will go bound to Rome;
He bears too great a mind.[34] But this same day
Must end that work the ides of March begun.
And whether we shall meet again I know not;
115   Therefore our everlasting farewell take:
For ever, and for ever, farewell, Cassius!
If we do meet again, why, we shall smile;
If not, why then this parting was well made.

CASSIUS.   For ever, and for ever, farewell, Brutus!
120   If we do meet again, we'll smile indeed;
If not, 'tis true this parting was well made.

BRUTUS.   Why then lead on. O, that a man might know
The end of this day's business ere it come!
But it sufficeth that the day will end,
125   And then the end is known. Come ho, away!

Exeunt.

26. **constantly.** Firmly; resolutely

27. **Lovers.** Friends
28. **incertain.** Uncertain
29. **reason…befall.** Expect the worst

30. **Even…himself.** Brutus will live by the philosophy of Stoicism, which teaches that people should endure suffering patiently. Because of his belief in Stoicism, Brutus looked down on his father-in-law, Marcus Porcius Cato, who fought with Pompey against Caesar and committed suicide rather than surrender.
31. **prevent / The time of life.** Cut short one's life by committing suicide
32. **stay the providence.** Await the pleasure
33. **Thorough.** Through
34. **Brutus…mind.** Despite his opposition to suicide, Brutus remarks that he is not dumb enough to let the enemies capture him and put him on parade in a triumph. He implies that he would kill himself if it came to that.

CULTURE CONNECTION

The Triumph When Brutus says he will never "go bound to Rome," he is referring to an element of the triumph. The triumph was a ritual procession that was the highest honor that could be given to a victorious general. The procession was led by the Senate and followed by sacrificial animals and the defeated prisoners in chains. Behind the prisoners, the victorious general rode in a chariot. The triumph was a spectacle that emphasized the glory of the victor and the humiliation of the defeated.

SCENE II: THE BATTLEGROUND AT PHILIPPI

Alarum.[1] Enter BRUTUS *and* MESSALA.

BRUTUS.   Ride, ride, Messala, ride, and give these bills[2]
Unto the legions on the other side.

Loud alarum.

Let them set on[3] at once; for I perceive
But cold demeanor[4] in Octavio's wing,
And sudden push gives them the overthrow.
Ride, ride, Messala, let them all come down.

Exeunt.

ACT V, SCENE II
1. **Alarum.** Trumpet call to battle
2. **bills.** Written orders

3. **set on.** Go forward; charge
4. **cold demeanor.** Lack of spirit; weakness

SCENE III: THE BATTLEGROUND AT PHILIPPI

Alarums. Enter CASSIUS *and* TITINIUS.

CASSIUS.   O, look, Titinius, look, the villains fly![1]
Myself have to mine own turn'd enemy.[2]
This ensign here of mine was turning back;
I slew the coward, and did take it from him.[3]

5 **TITINIUS.**   O Cassius, Brutus gave the word too early,
Who, having some advantage on Octavius,
Took it too eagerly. His soldiers fell to spoil,[4]
Whilst we by Antony are all enclos'd.[5]

Enter PINDARUS.

ACT V, SCENE III
1. **the villains fly!** Our cowardly soldiers are fleeing!
2. **Myself...enemy.** I am now forced to fight my own men.
3. **ensign...him.** The ensign (en´ sən), or flag-bearer, was running away, so Cassius killed him and took the flag himself.
4. **fell to spoil.** Brutus's soldiers won easily and started looting (rather than continuing to fight).
5. **we...enclos'd.** We are surrounded by Antony's troops.

THE TRAGEDY OF JULIUS CAESAR, ACT V, SCENE III   **625**

PINDARUS.   Fly further off, my lord, fly further off;
10   Mark Antony is in your tents, my lord;
Fly therefore, noble Cassius, fly far off.

CASSIUS.   This hill is far enough. Look, look, Titinius,
Are those my tents where I perceive the fire?

TITINIUS.   They are, my lord.

CASSIUS.   Titinius, if thou lovest me,
15   Mount thou my horse, and hide thy spurs in him
Till he have brought thee up to yonder troops
And here again, that I may rest assur'd
Whether yond troops are friend or enemy.

TITINIUS.   I will be here again, even with a thought.[6]

Exit.

20   **CASSIUS.**   Go, Pindarus, get higher on that hill;
My sight was ever thick;[7] regard Titinius,
And tell me what thou not'st about the field.

PINDARUS goes up.

This day I breathed first: time is come round,
And where I did begin, there shall I end;
25   My life is run his compass.[8] Sirrah, what news?

PINDARUS.   [*Above.*] O my lord!

CASSIUS.   What news?

PINDARUS.   Titinius is enclosed round about
With horsemen, that make to him on the spur,[9]
30   Yet he spurs on. Now they are almost on him.
Now, Titinius! Now some light. O, he lights too.
He's ta'en.[10] [*Shout.*] And hark, they shout for joy.

CASSIUS.   Come down, behold no more.
O, coward that I am, to live so long,
35   To see my best friend ta'en before my face!

PINDARUS descends.

Come hither, sirrah.
In Parthia did I take thee prisoner,
And then I swore thee, saving of thy life,
That whatsoever I did bid thee do,
40   Thou shouldst attempt it.[11] Come now, keep thine oath;
Now be a freeman, and with this good sword,
That ran through Caesar's bowels, search this bosom.

---

6. **even with a thought.** As quickly as a thought

7. **My sight...thick.** My eyesight is poor.

8. **is run his compass.** Has run its course; is finished

9. **on the spur.** At high speed

10. **some light...ta'en.** Some are dismounting, or getting off their horses. Titinius dismounts too. He is taken prisoner.

11. **in Parthia...attempt it.** When I took you prisoner in Parthia (an ancient Asian land), you swore that if I spared your life, you would do anything I asked.

Stand not to answer; here, take thou the hilts,
And when my face is cover'd, as 'tis now,
45 Guide thou the sword. [PINDARUS *stabs him.*] Caesar, thou art reveng'd,
Even with the sword that kill'd thee. [*Dies.*]

PINDARUS.   So, I am free; yet would not so have been,
Durst I have done my will. O Cassius,
Far from this country Pindarus shall run,
50 Where never Roman shall take note of him.

Exit.

Enter TITINIUS *and* MESSALA.

MESSALA.   It is but change, Titinius; for Octavius
Is overthrown by noble Brutus' power,
As Cassius' legions are by Antony.

TITINIUS.   These tidings will well comfort Cassius.

MESSALA.   Where did you leave him?

55 TITINIUS.   All disconsolate,
With Pindarus his bondman, on this hill.

MESSALA.   Is not that he that lies upon the ground?

TITINIUS.   He lies not like the living. O my heart!

MESSALA.   Is not that he?

TITINIUS.   No, this was he, Messala,
60 But Cassius is no more. O setting sun,
As in thy red rays thou dost sink tonight,
So in his red blood Cassius' day is set!
The sun of Rome is set. Our day is gone,
Clouds, dews, and dangers come; our deeds are done!
65 Mistrust of[12] my success hath done this deed.

MESSALA.   Mistrust of good success hath done this deed.
O hateful error, melancholy's child,
Why dost thou show to the apt thoughts of men
The things that are not?[13] O error, soon conceiv'd,
70 Thou never com'st unto a happy birth,
But kill'st the mother that engend'red thee![14]

TITINIUS.   What, Pindarus? Where art thou, Pindarus?

MESSALA.   Seek him, Titinius, whilst I go to meet
The noble Brutus, thrusting this report
75 Into his ears; I may say "thrusting" it;
For piercing steel, and darts envenomed,

12. **Mistrust of.** Lack of
belief in

13. **Why dost thou…not?**
Why do you, error, convince
people to believe in things
that are not true?

14. **O error…thee!** As
soon as an error is conceived
(brought into being), it kills the
person who gave birth to it.

Shall be as welcome to the ears of Brutus
As tidings of this sight.

TITINIUS.   Hie you, Messala,
And I will seek for Pindarus the while.

Exit MESSALA.

80   Why didst thou send me forth, brave Cassius?
Did I not meet thy friends? and did not they
Put on my brows this wreath of victory,[15]
And bid me give it thee? Didst thou not hear their shouts?
Alas, thou hast <u>misconstrued</u> every thing.
85   But hold thee, take this garland on thy brow;
Thy Brutus bid me give it thee, and I
Will do his bidding. Brutus, come apace,[16]
And see how I regarded Caius Cassius.
By your leave, gods!—this is a Roman's part.
90   Come, Cassius' sword, and find Titinius' heart. [*Dies.*]

Alarum. Enter BRUTUS, MESSALA, *young* CATO, STRATO, VOLUMNIUS, *and* LUCILIUS.

BRUTUS.   Where, where, Messala, doth his body lie?

MESSALA.   Lo yonder, and Titinius mourning it.

BRUTUS.   Titinius' face is upward.

CATO.   He is slain.

BRUTUS.   <u>O Julius Caesar, thou art mighty yet!</u>
95   <u>Thy spirit walks abroad, and turns our swords</u>
<u>In our own proper entrails.</u>[17]

Low alarums.

CATO.   Brave Titinius!
Look whe'er he have not crown'd dead Cassius![18]

BRUTUS.   Are yet two Romans living such as these?
The last of all the Romans, fare thee well!
100   It is impossible that ever Rome
Should breed thy fellow.[19] Friends, I owe moe[20] tears
To this dead man than you shall see me pay.
I shall find time, Cassius; I shall find time.
Come therefore, and to Thasos[21] send his body;
105   His funerals shall not be in our camp,
Lest it discomfort us. Lucilius, come,
And come, young Cato, let us to the field,
Labio and Flavio set our battles on.

15. **Put...wreath of victory.** In Rome and in Greece, victorious athletes and soldiers were often awarded a crown of laurel leaves.

mis • con • strue (mis' kən strü´) *v.,* misunderstand; misinterpret

16. **apace.** Quickly

17. **turns...entrails.** Caesar's ghost makes them put their swords into their own guts (entrails).

18. **Look...Cassius!** Notice that he has crowned the dead Cassius!

19. **fellow.** Equal
20. **moe.** More

21. **Thasos.** Nearby island

'Tis three a' clock, and, Romans, yet ere night
110 We shall try fortune in a second fight.[22]

Exeunt.

22. **ere…fight.** Before night, we'll take our chances in a second battle.

"If you dare fight today, come to the field." Octavius's and Antony's men fight against Cassius's and Brutus's army at Philippi.

Scene iv: The Battleground at Philippi

Alarum. Enter Brutus, Messala, *young* Cato, Lucilius, *and* Flavius.

Brutus.   Yet, countrymen! O yet, hold up your heads!

Exit.

Cato.   What bastard doth not? Who will go with me?
I will proclaim my name about the field.
I am the son of Marcus Cato, ho!
5   A foe to tyrants, and my country's friend.
I am the son of Marcus Cato, ho!

Enter Soldiers *and fight.*

Lucilius.   And I am Brutus, Marcus Brutus, I,
Brutus, my country's friend; know me for Brutus!

Young Cato *is slain.*

O young and noble Cato, art thou down?

10   Why, now thou diest as bravely as Titinius,
And mayst be honor'd, being Cato's son.

1. Soldier.   Yield, or thou diest.

Lucilius.   Only I yield to die;[1]
There is so much that thou wilt kill me straight:[2]
Kill Brutus, and be honor'd in his death.

15   **1. Soldier.**   We must not. A noble prisoner!

Enter Antony.

2. Soldier.   Room ho! Tell Antony, Brutus is ta'en.

1. Soldier.   I'll tell the news. Here comes the general.
Brutus is ta'en, Brutus is ta'en, my lord!

Antony.   Where is he?

20   **Lucilius.**   Safe, Antony, Brutus is safe enough.
I dare assure thee that no enemy
Shall ever take alive the noble Brutus;
The gods defend him from so great a shame!
When you do find him, or alive or dead,
25   He will be found like Brutus, like himself.

Antony.   This is not Brutus, friend, but, I assure you,
A prize no less in worth. Keep this man safe,
Give him all kindness; I had rather have
Such men my friends than enemies. Go on,
30   And see whe'er Brutus be alive or dead,
And bring us word unto Octavius' tent
How every thing is chanc'd.[3]

                                        Exeunt.

I am clitus

Scene V: The Battleground at Philippi

Enter Brutus, Dardanius, Clitus, Strato, *and* Volumnius

Brutus.   Come, poor remains of[1] friends, rest on this rock.

Clitus.   Statilius show'd the torchlight, but, my lord,
He came not back. He is or ta'en or slain.

Brutus.   Sit thee down, Clitus; slaying is the word,
5   It is a deed in fashion. Hark thee, Clitus.

Whispering.

Clitus.   What, I, my lord? No, not for all the world.

Act V, Scene IV
  1. **Only...die.** I yield only to die.
  2. **There is...straight.** You have good reason to kill me at once [since I am Brutus].

  3. **is chanc'd.** Has happened

Act V, Scene V
  1. **remains of.** Remaining

BRUTUS. Peace then, no words.

CLITUS.   I'll rather kill myself.

BRUTUS. Hark thee, Dardanius.

Whispering.

DARDANIUS.   Shall I do such a deed?

CLITUS. O Dardanius!

10 **DARDANIUS.** O Clitus!

CLITUS. What ill request did Brutus make to thee?

DARDANIUS. To kill him, Clitus. Look, he meditates.

CLITUS. Now is that noble vessel full of grief,
That it runs over even at his eyes.

15 **BRUTUS.** Come hither, good Volumnius; list[2] a word.

VOLUMNIUS. What says my lord?

BRUTUS.   Why, this, Volumnius:
The ghost of Caesar hath appear'd to me
Two several times by night; at Sardis once,
And this last night, here in Philippi fields.
I know my hour is come.

20 **VOLUMNIUS.**   Not so, my lord.

BRUTUS. Nay, I am sure it is, Volumnius.
Thou seest the world,[3] Volumnius, how it goes;
Our enemies have beat us to the pit.

Low alarums.

It is more worthy to leap in ourselves
25 Than tarry[4] till they push us. Good Volumnius,
Thou know'st that we two went to school together;
Even for that our love of old, I prithee
Hold thou my sword-hilts, whilest I run on it.

VOLUMNIUS. That's not an office[5] for a friend, my lord.

Alarum still.

30 **CLITUS.** Fly, fly, my lord, there is no tarrying here.

BRUTUS. Farewell to you, and you, and you, Volumnius.
Strato, thou hast been all this while asleep;
Farewell to thee too, Strato. Countrymen,
My heart doth joy that yet in all my life

2. **list.** Listen to

3. **Thou seest the world.** You know how things are.

4. **tarry.** Wait

5. **office.** Task

35   I found no man but he was true to me.[6]
      I shall have glory by this losing day
      More than Octavius and Mark Antony
      By this vile conquest shall attain unto.[7]
      So fare you well at once, for Brutus' tongue
40   Hath almost ended his live's history.
      Night hangs upon mine eyes, my bones would rest,
      That have but labor'd to attain this hour.

Alarum. Cry within, "Fly, fly, fly!"

CLITUS.   Fly, my lord, fly.

BRUTUS.   Hence! I will follow.

                  Exeunt CLITUS, DARDANIUS, *and* VOLUMNIUS.

      I prithee, Strato, stay thou by thy lord.
45   Thou art a fellow of a good respect;[8]
      Thy life hath had some smatch[9] of honor in it.
      Hold then my sword, and turn away thy face,
      While I do run upon it. Wilt thou, Strato?

STRATO.   Give me your hand first. Fare you well, my lord.

BRUTUS.   Farewell, good Strato. [*Runs on his sword.*]
50   Caesar, now be still,

      I kill'd not thee with half so good a will. [*Dies.*]

Alarum. Retreat. Enter ANTONY, OCTAVIUS, MESSALA, LUCILIUS, *and the army.*

OCTAVIUS.   What man is that?

MESSALA.   My master's man. Strato, where is thy master?

STRATO.   Free from the bondage you are in, Messala;
55   The conquerors can but make a fire of him;
      For Brutus only overcame himself
      And no man else hath honor by his death.

LUCILIUS.   So Brutus should be found. I thank thee, Brutus,
      That thou hast prov'd Lucilius' saying true.[10]

60 **OCTAVIUS.**   All that serv'd Brutus, I will entertain them.[11]
      Fellow, wilt thou bestow[12] thy time with me?

STRATO.   Ay, if Messala will prefer[13] me to you.

OCTAVIUS.   Do so, good Messala.

MESSALA.   How died my master, Strato?

65 **STRATO.**   I held the sword, and he did run on it.

6. **I found...to me.** I found no man who was not true to me.

7. **I shall...unto.** I shall have more glory in losing than Octavius and Antony can ever attain through their vile, or despicable, victory.

8. **respect.** Reputation
9. **smatch.** Taste

10. **prov'd...true.** See V. iv. 21–22.
11. **entertain them.** Take them into my service
12. **bestow.** Spend
13. **prefer.** Recommend

WORLD HISTORY
CONNECTION

Dante and Virgil Encounter Lucifer in Hell, 1922. Henry John Stock.

The Intrigue of Caesar Shakespeare is just one of the many writers who have been intrigued by the dramatic history of Julius Caesar. In *The Inferno,* Italian poet Dante depicts the nine circles of hell; the ninth circle, which is the last and most terrible, is reserved for traitors—those who betrayed their family and country. Special torment is given to Judas Iscariot, who betrayed Jesus, and to Brutus and Cassius, Julius Caesar's betrayers.

MESSALA.　Octavius, then take him to follow thee,
That did the latest[14] service to my master.

ANTONY.　This was the noblest Roman of them all:
All the conspirators, save only he,
70　Did that they did in envy of great Caesar;
He, only in a general honest thought
And common good to all,[15] made one of them.[16]
His life was gentle,[17] and the elements[18]
So mix'd in him that Nature might stand up
75　And say to all the world, "This was a man!"

OCTAVIUS.　According to his virtue[19] let us use[20] him,
With all respect and rites of burial.
Within my tent his bones tonight shall lie,
Most like a soldier, ordered honorably.[21]
80　So call the field[22] to rest, and let's away,
To part the glories[23] of this happy day.

Exeunt omnes.[24] ❖

14. **latest.** Last

15. **in a general...all.** With thought for the good of all
16. **made one of them.** Joined them
17. **gentle.** Noble
18. **elements.** Four substances that were believed to make up the physical universe: earth, air, fire, and water
19. **virtue.** Worth
20. **use.** Act toward
21. **ordered honorably.** Treated with honor
22. **field.** Military forces
23. **part the glories.** Divide the spoils
24. ***omnes.*** All

Antony distinguishes Brutus from the other conspirators, calling him "The noblest Roman of them all." Is Antony correct in his evaluation of Brutus? To whom might you compare Brutus today? If a person acts in the common good, does it mean he or she shouldn't pay the consequences of the action? Why or why not?

REFER TO TEXT ▶ ▶ ▶ ▶	▶ REASON WITH TEXT	
1a. Distinguish whose armies are fighting during the battle. What is the outcome of the battle? What happens to Brutus and Cassius?	**1b.** Explain what fatal error Cassius makes. How does Messala respond to Cassius's death? How does Titinius respond?	**Understand** **Find meaning**
2a. State what Brutus and Cassius say to each other at the end of Scene i.	**2b.** Based on this information, do Brutus and Cassius seem confident of victory? Why or why not? Examine how their expectations contribute to their later actions.	**Apply** **Use information**
3a. Name the three occasions when Brutus overrules Cassius on three crucial decisions in the play.	**3b.** Point out how crucial these decisions are to the outcome of the play. Which of the two men—Cassius or Brutus— do you judge to be the better military strategist? Which do you find to be the more honorable person? Why?	**Analyze** **Take things apart**
4a. Quote what Brutus says when he dies. To whom does he say it to?	**4b.** Determine whether or not you think Julius Caesar's murder was justified. Judge if the conspirators had any other options, and if so, what these could have been.	**Evaluate** **Make judgments**
5a. Review Cassius's speech at V.i.70–86 and state what event Cassius finds troubling. How does Cassius interpret this event? Review Act I, Scene iii, and list the omens that Casca relates to Cassius. How does Cassius interpret these events?	**5b.** Throughout *The Tragedy of Julius Caesar*, omens, portents, prophecies, and ghosts appear. Choose two events and explain how they are interpreted by the characters in the play. What do these interpretations reveal about the motives, ambitions, or fears of the characters? How does Shakespeare use these events to further the action of the play?	**Create** **Bring ideas together**

ANALYZE LITERATURE: Tragic Hero and Tragic Flaw

A **tragic hero** is the main character in a tragedy whose personal weakness, or **tragic flaw,** brings about the downfall of the character. Explain why Brutus can be considered the tragic hero of this play. What, in your opinion, is Brutus's tragic flaw? Give evidence to support your answer.

Literature CONNECTION

The Prince is a *treatise,* or discussion of personal beliefs, written by **Niccolò Machiavelli.** It was intended as advice for Lorenzo de' Medici, a fifteenth-century ruler of Florence, Italy, with whom Machiavelli wanted to find favor. Since that time, *The Prince* has become the most famous—and infamous—handbook on power and politics. It discusses how a ruler should conduct himself to gain and maintain power. Machiavelli concerns himself not with how a ruler should *ideally* act but with how a ruler *has* to act to be successful. Because of the cynical nature of the philosophy Machiavelli sets forth in *The Prince,* the term *Machiavellian* has come to mean "concerned with achieving power through cunning and deceit."

MACHIAVELLI

from
The Prince

A Treatise by
Niccolò Machiavelli

Chapter 15

*Of the Things
for Which Men, and Especially Princes,
Are Praised or Blamed*

It now remains to be seen what are the methods and rules for a
prince as regards his subjects and friends. And as I know that many have
written of this, I fear that my writing about it may be deemed presumptuous,
differing as I do, especially in this matter, from the opinions of others. But my
intention being to write something of use to those who understand, it
appears to me more proper to go to the real truth of the matter than
to its imagination; and many have imagined republics and
principalities which have never been seen or known to
exist in reality; for how we live is so far removed
from how we ought to live, that he who
abandons what is done for what ought
to be done, will rather learn to
bring about his own ruin
than his preservation.
A man who

wishes to make a profession of goodness in everything must necessarily come to grief among so many who are not good. Therefore it is necessary for a prince, who wishes to maintain himself, to learn how not to be good, and use this knowledge and not use it, according to the necessity of the case.

Leaving on one side, then, those things which concern only an imaginary prince, and speaking of those that are real, I state that all men, and especially princes, who are placed at a greater height, are reputed for[1] certain qualities which bring them either praise or blame. Thus one is considered liberal,[2] another *misero* or miserly (using a Tuscan term, seeing that *avaro* still means one who is rapaciously acquisitive and *misero* one who makes grudging use of his own); one a free giver, another rapacious; one cruel, another merciful; one a breaker of his word, another trustworthy; one effeminate and pusillanimous,[3] another fierce and high-spirited; one humane,[4] another haughty; one lascivious,[5] another chaste; one frank, another <u>astute</u>; one hard, another easy; one serious, another frivolous; one religious, another an unbeliever, and so on. I know that everyone will admit that it would be highly praiseworthy in a prince to possess all the above-named qualities that are reputed good, but as they cannot all be possessed or observed, human conditions not permitting of it, it is necessary that he should be <u>prudent</u> enough to avoid the scandal of those vices which would lose him the state, and guard himself if possible against those which will not lose it him, but if not able to, he can indulge them with less scruple.[6] And yet he must not mind incurring the scandal of those vices, without which it would be difficult to save the state, for if one considers well, it will be found that some things which seem virtues would, if followed, lead to one's ruin, and some others which appear vices result in one's greater security and wellbeing.

as • tute (ə stüt´)
adj., clever
pru • dent
(prü´ d'nt) *adj.*, wise

Therefore

it is necessary for a prince,

who wishes to maintain himself,

to learn how not to

be good…

---

1. **reputed for.** Known for
2. **liberal.** Generous with money and resources
3. **pusillanimous** (pyü´ sə la´ nə məs). Cowardly
4. **humane.** Merciful; considerate of human life
5. **lascivious** (lə si´ vē əs). Lustful
6. **and guard himself…scruple.** And avoid other vices if he can, but if he can't, he may indulge them without worrying

Chapter 16
Of Liberality and Niggardliness[7]

Beginning now with the first qualities above named, I say that it would be well to be considered liberal; nevertheless liberality such as the world understands it will injure you, because if used virtuously and in the proper way, it will not be known, and you will incur the disgrace of the contrary vice. But one who wishes to obtain the reputation of liberality among men, must not omit every kind of <u>sumptuous</u> display, and to such an extent that a prince of this character will consume by such means all his resources, and will be at last compelled, if he wishes to maintain his name for liberality, to impose heavy taxes on his people, become extortionate,[8] and do everything possible to obtain money. This will make his subjects begin to hate him, and he will be little esteemed being poor, so that having by this liberality injured many and benefited but few, he will feel the first little disturbance and be endangered by every peril. If he recognizes this and wishes to change his system, he incurs at once the charge of niggardliness.

A prince, therefore, not being able to exercise this virtue of liberality without risk if it be known, must not, if he be prudent, object to being called miserly. In course of time he will be thought more liberal, when it is seen that by his parsimony[9] his revenue is sufficient, that he can defend himself against those who make war on him, and undertake enterprises without burdening his people, so that he is really liberal to all those from whom he does not take, who are infinite in number, and niggardly to all to whom he does not give, who are few. In our times we have seen nothing great done except by those who have been esteemed niggardly; the others have all been ruined. Pope Julius II,[10] although he had made use of a reputation for liberality in order to attain the papacy, did not seek to retain it afterwards, so that he might be able to wage war. The present King of France[11] has carried on so many wars without imposing an extraordinary tax, because his extra expenses were covered by the parsimony he had so long practiced. The present King of Spain,[12] if he had been thought liberal, would not have engaged in and been successful in so many enterprises.

For these reasons a prince must care little for the reputation of being a miser, if he wishes to avoid robbing his subjects, if he wishes to be able to defend himself, to avoid becoming poor and contemptible, and not to be forced to become rapacious; this niggardliness is one of those <u>vices</u> which enable him to reign. If it is said that Caesar[13] attained the empire through

sump • tu • ous (sum[p][t]′ shə wəs) *adj.*, extremely comfortable or lavish; fancy

vice (vīs) *n.*, moral failing

---

7. **Liberality and Niggardliness.** Generosity and stinginess
8. **extortionate.** Extorting, or unfairly seizing, the property and goods of others
9. **parsimony** (pär′ sə mō′ nē). Thrift; quality of being careful with money
10. **Pope Julius II.** Pope who served from 1503–1513 and restored the Papal lands to the Church. He also sponsored Renaissance artists such as Michelangelo and Raphael.
11. **present King of France.** Refers to Louis XII (1462–1515)
12. **present King of Spain.** Refers to Ferdinand II (1452–1516), a king who drove the Moors from Spain and unified the country
13. **Caesar.** Julius Caesar (c.102–44 BCE)

liberality, and that many others have reached the highest positions through being liberal or being thought so, I would reply that you are either a prince already or else on the way to become one. In the first case, this liberality is harmful; in the second, it is certainly necessary to be considered liberal. Caesar was one of those who wished to attain the mastery over Rome, but if after attaining it he had lived and had not moderated his expenses, he would have destroyed that empire. And should any one reply that there have been many princes, who have done great things with their armies, who have been thought extremely liberal, I would answer by saying that the prince may either spend his own wealth and that of his subjects or the wealth of others. In the first case he must be sparing, but for the rest he must not neglect to be very liberal. The liberality is very necessary to a prince who marches with his armies, and lives by plunder, sack and ransom, and is dealing with the wealth of others, for without it he would not be followed by his soldiers. And you may be very generous indeed with what is not the property of yourself or your subjects, as were Cyrus, Caesar, and Alexander; for spending the wealth of others will not diminish your reputation, but increase it, only spending your own resources will injure you. There is nothing which destroys itself so much as liberality, for by using it you lose the power of using it, and become either poor and despicable, or, to escape poverty, rapacious and hated. And of all things that a prince must guard against, the most important are being despicable or hated, and liberality will lead you to one or the other of these conditions. It is, there-fore, wiser to have the name of a miser, which produces disgrace without hatred, than to incur of necessity the name of being rapacious, which produces both disgrace and hatred.

Chapter 18
In What Way Princes Must Keep Faith

How laudable[14] it is for a prince to keep good faith and live with integrity, and not with astuteness, everyone knows. Still the experience of our times shows those princes to have done great things who have had little regard for good faith, and have been able by astuteness to confuse men's brains, and who have ultimately overcome those who have made loyalty their foundation.

You must know, then, that there are two methods of fighting, the one by law, the other by force: the first method is that of men, the second of beasts; but as the first method is often insufficient, one must have recourse to the second. It is therefore necessary for a prince to know well how to use both the beast and the man. This was covertly taught to rulers by ancient writers, who relate how Achilles[15] and many others of those ancient princes were given to Chiron the centaur[16] to be brought up and educated under his discipline. The parable of this

---

14. **laudable.** Praiseworthy
15. **Achilles.** Mythological Greek hero of the Trojan War
16. **Chiron the centaur.** A figure of Greek mythology who had the torso and head of a man but the body of a horse

semi-animal, semi-human teacher is meant to indicate that a prince must know how to use both natures, and that the one without the other is not durable.

A prince being thus obliged to know well how to act as a beast must imitate the fox and the lion, for the lion cannot protect himself from traps, and the fox cannot defend himself from wolves. One must therefore be a fox to recognize traps, and a lion to frighten wolves. Those that wish to be only lions do not understand this. Therefore, a prudent ruler ought not to keep faith when by so doing it would be against his interest, and when the reasons which made him bind himself no longer exist. If men were all good, this precept[17] would not be a good one; but as they are bad, and would not observe their faith with you, so you are not bound to keep faith with them. Nor have legitimate grounds ever failed a prince who wished to show colorable excuse for the non-fulfillment of his promise. Of this one could furnish an infinite number of modern examples, and show how many times peace has been broken, and how many promises rendered worthless, by the faithlessness of princes, and those that have been best able to imitate the fox have succeeded best. But it is necessary to be able to disguise this character well, and to be a great feigner and dissembler;[18] and men are so simple and so ready to obey present necessities, that one who deceives will always find those who allow themselves to be deceived. I will only mention one modern instance. Alexander VI[19] did nothing else but deceive men, he thought of nothing else, and found the occasion for it; no man was ever more able to give assurances, or affirmed things with stronger oaths, and no man observed them less; however, he always succeeded in his deceptions, as he well knew this aspect of things.

It is not, therefore, necessary for a prince to have all the above-named qualities, but it is very necessary to seem to have them. I would even be bold to say that to possess them and always to observe them is dangerous, but to appear to possess them is useful. Thus it is well to seem merciful, faithful, humane, sincere, religious, and also to be so; but you must have the mind so disposed that when it is needful to be otherwise you may be able to change to the opposite qualities. And it must be understood that a prince, and especially a new prince, cannot observe all those things which are considered good in men, being often obliged, in order to maintain the state, to act against faith, against charity, against humanity, and against religion. And, therefore, he must have a mind disposed to adapt itself according to the wind, and as the variations of fortune dictate, and, as I said before, not deviate from what is good, if possible, but be able to do evil if <u>constrained</u>.

A prince must take great care that nothing goes out of his mouth which is not full of the above-named five qualities, and, to see and hear him, he should seem to be all mercy, faith, integrity, humanity, and religion. And nothing is

con • strain
(kən strān´) *v.,* force by rule or limitation

---

17. **precept.** Law or guideline
18. **feigner and dissembler.** Pretender; liar; sneak
19. **Alexander VI.** Pope who served from 1492–1503. He was ambitious, a great political strategist who used his position to help build up the power of his son and daughter. However, his religious values were lacking, and many considered him unscrupulous.

more necessary than to seem to have this last quality, for men in general judge more by the eyes than by the hands, for everyone can see, but very few have to feel. Everybody sees what you appear to be, few feel what you are, and those few will not dare to oppose themselves to the many, who have the majesty of the state to defend them; and in the actions of men, and especially of princes, from which there is no appeal, the end justifies the means. Let a prince therefore aim at conquering and maintaining the state, and the means will always be judged honorable and praised by everyone, for the vulgar[20] is always taken by appearances and the issue of the event; and the world consists only of the vulgar, and the few who are not vulgar are isolated when the many have a rallying point in the prince. A certain prince of the present time, whom it is well not to name, never does anything but preach peace and good faith, but he is really a great enemy to both, and either of them, had he observed them, would have lost him state or reputation on many occasions. ❖

---

20. **vulgar.** Common people; the general public—this word is used insultingly

REFER TO TEXT ▶ ▶ ▶ ▶ ▶	REASON WITH TEXT	
1a. List the qualities that Machiavelli argues are necessary for a successful Prince to appear to have.	1b. In your own words, explain Machiavelli's opinion of the nature of vices and virtues. Why does Machiavelli believe it is more important to appear to have these qualities than to actually have them? What specific vices does he argue are often more useful to a ruler than the corresponding virtues?	**Understand** **Find meaning**
2a. Locate Machiavelli's description of the fox and the lion. Briefly state what he says about the qualities of both animals.	2b. Relate this information to Shakespeare's Caesar and Antony. Would Machiavelli characterize each man as a lion, a fox, or a combination of both animals? Cite evidence from the play that supports lion-like or fox-like qualities in each man.	**Apply** **Use Information**
3a. Find the passage where Machiavelli states "And in the actions of men...the end justifies the means." Outline the reasons Machiavelli gives to support this claim.	3b. Relate Machiavelli's advice to your own experience. Where do you see Machiavelli's ideas in use today? Can you think of any politicians, business-people, or other leaders who subscribe to these ideas?	**Create** **Bring Ideas Together**

TEXT ←TO→ TEXT CONNECTION

- Does the portrayal of Julius Caesar in Shakespeare's play align with what Machiavelli states about him?
- Which man do you think Machiavelli would have admired more: Brutus or Antony? What advice might he have given Brutus?
- Do you agree with Machiavelli's political perspective? Why or why not?

Literature CONNECTION

In this *Newsweek* article, **Allison Samuels** interviews film actor Denzel Washington about his decision to go from making blockbuster movies to performing Shakespeare on stage. The production of *Julius Caesar* discussed in this article, directed by Daniel Sullivan, is a modern version, as far as costumes and sets, but it still retains Shakespeare's original language.

BRUTUS ON BROADWAY

Et tu, Denzel? Washington shakes up Shakespeare

Newsweek   An Article by Allison Samuels   April 18, 2005

Denzel Washington wants—no, needs—to explain why he's shown up for breakfast in a New York City cafe wearing a pink necktie. "I want you to know I didn't pick this tie out," he says as he takes his seat. "I mean, it's not that I don't like the tie. It's nice, I think—just an odd choice for me." But the two-time Academy Award winner is here to talk about what might seem an odder choice: to put his $20 million-per-film Hollywood career on hold in order to play Brutus in a Broadway production of *Julius Caesar*—memorizing line after line of Shakespeare's English and doing a grueling eight three-hour performances a week. "I recall when we began rehearsing," he says, "standing outside the theater and thinking, 'Oh, Lord, what have I done?'"

Exactly what he wanted to do, it seems. It's been three decades since Washington, 50, started acting at Fordham University, where he appeared in *Othello* and *Much Ado About Nothing*. He made his Broadway debut in the

1988 *Checkmates*; since then he's been…a bit busy. But although such stylish thrillers as *Man on Fire, Training Day* and the remake of *The Manchurian Candidate* weren't exactly five-finger exercises, in recent interviews he's been tossing around words like "jaded." "Theater is where it really all began for me," Washington says, "and I always loved Shakespeare because it was the most challenging thing you could do. I guess I saw this as a way of redeveloping muscles I haven't had to use in a while."

Meanwhile, director Daniel Sullivan had had his eye on Washington. "Over the course of years of doing Shakespeare plays, I always knew that when I did *Julius Caesar* Denzel would be perfect for Brutus," he says. "The play is really about Brutus, and I think Denzel is such an amazing actor—he's interestingly transparent, so the audience can literally see what he's thinking." The critics haven't been quite as kind: Washington received respectful, if mixed, reviews, with many noting the production could use more of his legendary charisma. "Maybe I should've tried Shakespeare in a smaller city first," he says with a laugh. "But that's the fun of it—trying something different and putting yourself out there." Washington gives Sullivan full credit for the production's modern twist—the actors are dressed in Valentino and walk through the theater aisles after Caesar's death. But he credits himself with a fresh approach to Brutus, Caesar's tortured friend turned assassin. "Through history we've read that Brutus was stoic and cerebral—basically a boring guy," says Washington. "I was, like, 'Later for that—I want this guy to have some fire.' He loved Rome and he was passionate about it. That's what drove him to do what he did. And the director was in full agreement that Brutus could use a spice."

If Washington's mood this morning is any indication, he's having the time of his life. Such previous stage work as his 1981 star turn as Malcolm X in *When the Chickens Come Home to Roost* brought in more-diverse-than-usual audiences, and Washington hopes his *Julius Caesar* will have the same effect—despite ticket prices ranging from $51.25 to $101.25. ("Premium" seats go up to $251.25.) "I'm not just doing this for the highfalutin crowd—for lack of a better word," he says. "I want all people to be able to come to see this, in particular my fans. You know, people see you in films but never any closer than that. I feel I owe something to the people who've been unwavering in their support. This is a way to say thank you." And ticket sales have been brisk, with long lines outside the theater waiting for cancellations. On a recent weeknight, the balcony of the Belasco Theatre was filled with inner-city high-school kids eager to see their first Broadway play, and even more eager to see Denzel. Sobs of joy from 15-year-old girls erupted the moment he appeared onstage, along with thunderous applause from the young men. You don't get *that* on a Hollywood set. Welcome home, Mr. Washington. ❖

REFER TO TEXT ▷ ▷ ▶ ▶	▶ REASON WITH TEXT	
1a. Review the article and quote Denzel Washington's opinion of why he wanted to perform Shakespeare and what kind of audience he hopes to attract.	1b. What can you infer about Shakespeare's accessibility from Washington's comments? Do you agree with his assessment of Shakespeare? Why or why not? Give specific examples to support your argument.	**Understand** **Find meaning**
2a. Identify the differences between performing theater and making movies that Washington and Allison Samuels give.	2b. Compare and contrast these differences. What advantages and disadvantages do you see for the actor in each setting? What advantages and disadvantages do you see for the audience?	**Analyze** **Take things apart**
3a. Samuels's article focuses on the choices Washington made in accepting the role of Brutus and performing the part. State Washington's description of how he performed Brutus.	3b. Critique Washington's choices. Do you think his method of playing Brutus would be effective? Why or why not? Do his choices in portraying Brutus support your own characterization of Brutus? Why or why not? Cite specific examples from the text to support your answers.	**Evaluate** **Make judgments**

TEXT ◀—TO—▶ TEXT CONNECTION

- Shakespeare's Brutus is a stoic, controlling or concealing his emotions; however, Denzel Washington as Brutus played the role with "some fire." In what scenes do you think Washington was best able to do that?
- Do you agree with the assertion that because Brutus is "stoic and cerebral" he's a "boring guy"? Why or why not?

EXTEND THE TEXT

Writing Options

Creative Writing Write an **obituary** for Brutus. You may want to review several obituaries in your local newspaper and note the kinds of things that are customarily included about the deceased and his or her life. What are the most important things to say about Brutus and his life?

Expository Writing *The Tragedy of Julius Caesar* is considered a classic. Many lines or phrases from the play have entered casual speech, and *"Et tu, Brute?"* is known by many people who haven't read or seen the play. Write a **critical paragraph** examining why this play has become a classic and what about it appeals to modern audiences. Use specific examples from the play to support your ideas.

Lifelong Learning

Research the History of Rome Imagine that you work for a television network that is planning a series of educational programs on the history of Rome. Your supervisor has asked you to create a time line of the most important events in Roman history. Using Internet and library resources, research questions like these: When was Rome founded? How long did the republic last, and what came after it? Under whose rule did the territory of Rome reach its largest extent? When did Rome fall? Then create your time line with a partner.

Media Literacy

Compare Film Versions View part or all of two film versions of *The Tragedy of Julius Caesar.* Joseph L. Mankiewicz's 1953 version, starring Marlon Brando and James Mason, and Stuart Burge's 1970 version, starring Charlton Heston and Jason Robards, are two that you might find. Compare the two versions. Which actors do you find more effective? Which movie has better scenery? What similarities and differences do you see between the two interpretations? Finally, imagine you are casting a new filming of *The Tragedy of Julius Caesar.* Choose Hollywood actors for the roles of Caesar, Brutus, Antony, and Cassius, and explain your choices.

 Go to **www.mirrorsandwindows.com** for more.

READING ASSESSMENT

1. What does Brutus fear could happen to Caesar if he becomes king?
    A. He might be assassinated.
    B. He might turn against Brutus.
    C. He might not want to fight on behalf of Rome.
    D. He might be corrupted by his power.
    E. He might give the senators' lands to the plebeians.

2. What is Brutus's opinion of Antony?
    A. He thinks he is honorable and wise.
    B. He likes him but thinks he wouldn't make a good leader.
    C. He does not trust him.
    D. He thinks of him "as a brother."
    E. He is dismissive of him.

3. As used in III.ii.191, the word *vesture* means
    A. body.
    B. capsule.
    C. garment.
    D. head.
    E. pride.

4. Why does Brutus ask his servant to kill him?
    A. to avenge Caesar's death
    B. to preserve his honor in the face of defeat
    C. because he has been mortally wounded
    D. to join Portia in death
    E. to prevent Antony from torturing him

5. In the excerpt from *The Prince, w*hich of the following statements best expresses the main idea of the passage?
    A. Honesty is vital to good leadership.
    B. To be successful, one must be willing to be unethical.
    C. It is better to be stingy than generous because if you are stingy, people won't expect things of you.
    D. Being generous to one's enemies is a way of avoiding war.
    E. None of the above

6. Antony's speech in III.ii.69–103 is an excellent example of persuasion. Think of how he shapes his speech, and the various reactions he elicits from his audience. Then, write a brief analysis of Antony's speech. Be sure to indicate what makes it successful as persuasion.

GRAMMAR & STYLE

Hyphens, Dashes, and Ellipses

A **hyphen** is used to form a compound word or compound expression.

EXAMPLES

compound nouns	great-grandmother, sister-in-law
compound numbers	fifty-five years old, forty-two dollars
spelled-out fractions	one-half teaspoon, three-eighths of a yard

Many compound adjectives that come before a noun require hyphens. These same words generally do not need hyphens if they come after the verb as predicate adjectives.

EXAMPLES

hit-and-run accident, Japanese-American poet

Use a hyphen with the prefixes *all–*, *ex–*, *great–*, *half–*, and *self–* and with all prefixes before a proper noun or proper adjective.

EXAMPLES

ex-girlfriend	half-baked idea
self-control	mid-August

Use a hyphen with the suffixes *–free, –elect,* and *–style.*

EXAMPLES

sugar-free gum
president-elect Michaels
Asian-style interior design

If you are in doubt as to whether a compound word is hyphenated or not, you will often be able to find the word in a dictionary.

If a word must be divided at the end of a line, here are a few rules to help you know when and how to hyphenate a word at a line break:

- Divide an already hyphenated word at the hyphen.
- Divide a word only between syllables. If you are uncertain of a word's syllables, look up the word in a dictionary.
- Do not divide a one-syllable word.
- Do not divide a word so that one letter stands alone.

A **dash** is used to show an obvious break or change in thought. Note that a dash is longer in length than a hyphen. Dashes sometimes replace other marks of punctuation, such as periods, semicolons, or commas. A dash can also be used to mean *namely, that is,* or *in other words.*

EXAMPLE

Let but the commons hear this testament—
Which, pardon me, I do not mean to read—
And they would go and kiss dead Caesar's wounds.

Ellipsis points are a series of three spaced points. Ellipsis points, or *ellipses,* are used to show that material from a quotation or a quoted passage has been left out.

EXAMPLE

original	Brutus states in Act V, "The ghost of Caesar hath appear'd to me two several times by night; at Sardis once, and this last night, here in Philippi fields. I know my hour is come."
revised	Brutus states in Act V, "The ghost of Caesar hath appear'd to me two several times by night... I know my hour is come."

To use ellipses correctly, follow these guidelines:

- If material is left out at the beginning of a sentence or passage, use ellipsis points.
- If material is left out in the middle of a sentence, use ellipsis points.
- If material is left out at the end of a sentence, use an end mark, such as a period or question mark, after the ellipsis points.

REVIEW TERMS

- **hyphen:** used to form a compound word or compound expression
- **dash:** used to show an obvious break or change in thought
- **ellipses:** series of three spaced points

Identify Placement of Hyphens and Dashes

Rewrite the following sentences, adding hyphens and dashes as needed.

1. Geraldo lived in a two room flat.
2. The forty year old wiring threatened to set the building on fire.
3. He ate frugally, but sometimes he had coffee at the Spanish speaking café on the corner.
4. He sent money usually more than he could afford to his family in Mexico.
5. People who thought he was a good for nothing didn't know him at all.
6. The announcer's sugar coated compliments could not make up for his off color remarks about the ex commissioner.
7. Last night while you were out where were you, anyway? we watched one of those reality shows on TV.
8. The recipes sent by my great aunt can and probably should be checked for accuracy and completeness.
9. To Keiko, the book was more than just a book it was torture.
10. Eighty seven people have already bought the self help kit on the home shopping network.

Use Correct Ellipses

Rewrite each of the following sentences from *The Tragedy of Julius Caesar*, correctly adding ellipsis points in place of the underlined material.

1. Caesar, I never stood on ceremonies, yet now they fright me. There is one within, <u>besides the things that we have heard and seen,</u> recounts the most horrid sights seen by the watch.

2. <u>Publius, good cheer,</u> there is no harm intended to your person, not to no Roman else.

3. And though we lay these honors on this man <u>to ease ourselves of divers sland'rous loads,</u> he shall but bear them as the ass bears gold, to groan and sweat under the business, either led or driven, as we point the way.

4. <u>Ever note, Lucilius,</u> when love begins to sicken and decay it useth an enforced ceremony.

5. There is not terror, Cassius, in your threats; for I am arm'd so strong in honesty that they pass by me as the idle wind, <u>which I respect not.</u>

Use Hyphens, Dashes, and Ellipses in Your Writing

Pretend that you are a Roman citizen who has witnessed the murder of Caesar and heard the speeches of both Brutus and Antony. Write a letter to a relative in another part of Italy about those events. In the letter, describe the scene and give your commentary on it (a good situation for using dashes). Also transcribe bits of the speeches by using ellipses to leave out the less important parts.

EXTEND THE SKILL

Imagine you are teaching a class of eighth-grade students about using hyphens, dashes, and ellipses. In a small group, create a fun activity for them that reinforces how to use these three punctuation marks correctly.

THE ANCIENT BEGINNINGS OF DRAMA

Ancient Greek drama began as part of an Athenian religious festival honoring Dionysos (dī' ə nī' səs), the god of wine and festivity. At this festival, thousands of spectators gathered in large, outdoor theaters to watch dancers, singers, and playwrights compete for prizes. Plays performed included tragedies, comedies, and satyr (sat' ər) plays, which were wild, humorous adventures dealing with ridiculous situations and characters dressed as satyrs, or creatures half human and half goat.

Greek Tragedy

Antigone (an tig' ə nē) is an example of classic Greek tragedy. Most Greek tragedies were based on well-known legends or myths. These plays typically depicted the downfall of a great character of high status. The downfall of this tragic hero was brought about by some defect in the hero's character, known as a *tragic flaw.* One of the most common tragic flaws is *hubris,* or excessive pride.

Theaters and Scenery

The audience of a Greek play sat in an amphitheater, open to the sky, with tiered, stone seats arranged in a semicircle around a central area called the *orchestra,* where the chorus performed. Behind the orchestra was a wooden building called the *skene,* from which we get our modern word *scene.* The *skene* served as part of the set, representing a temple, a shrine, a cave, or a home. Actors performed on top of the *skene* or in the area in front of it, the proscenium. Painted backgrounds on the *skene* provided scenery.

Format of Plays

Most classical Greek productions had the same format. A play opened with a *prologue* that introduced the situation and ended with the *exodus,* or exiting scene. Scenes were divided, not by the opening and closing of a curtain as they are today, but by odes spoken in unison by a *chorus,* a group of about fifteen people led by an individual called the *choragos* (kə rā' gəs). The chorus addressed the audience directly, giving information or voicing communal beliefs and values in the form of odes. A choral ode has alternating stanzas called the *strophe* (strō' fē), the *antistrophe,* and, sometimes, the *epode.* The chorus danced in one direction while singing the strophe and in the other during the antistrophe, coming to a standstill for the epode. Traditionally, the chorus opened the play by chanting an ode called the *parodos* (par' əd əs).

Delphi Amphitheater.

THE HISTORY OF OEDIPUS

Antigone is one of three tragedies written by Sophocles (säf´ ə klēz') about the family of Oedipus (ed´ ə pəs), a legendary king of Thebes. Oedipus was Antigone's father, and his story is told in the other two tragedies, *Oedipus the King* and *Oedipus at Colonus*. The following summary of the life of Oedipus will help you understand some of the references in *Antigone*.

A Tragic Setting

The story of *Oedipus the King* begins in the city of Thebes, which was founded by Cadmus. When Cadmus angered the god Apollo, Apollo placed a curse upon the city.

It was prophesied that, as part of Apollo's curse, Oedipus, the unborn son of King Laius (lī´ əs) and Queen Jocasta, would kill his father and marry his mother. When Oedipus was born, his parents, who feared the prophesy, ordered that he be abandoned and left to die. A servant, however, took pity on the child and delivered him to a shepherd, who in turn delivered the boy to King Polybus of Corinth. Oedipus was raised by Polybus, never learning of his true parentage.

A Prophecy Fulfilled

As an adult, Oedipus left Corinth to seek his fortune. On a road in central Greece, he lost his temper and killed a man and his servants. This man was King Laius, Oedipus's real father. The first part of the prophesy was unknowingly fulfilled.

Still unaware of his relationship to the man he had killed, Oedipus continued to Thebes. There he became a hero by solving the riddle of and thereby defeating the Sphinx, a monster that was terrorizing the city. As a reward, Oedipus won the hand of the widowed Queen Jocasta. By marrying Jocasta, Oedipus unknowingly fulfilled the second part of the prophecy.

A Tragic Consequence

Oedipus had ruled Thebes for almost twenty years and had four children with Jocasta when a plague struck

Oedipus and his daughter Antigone.

the city. It was a plague of infertility, indicating that someone had polluted the kingdom. In investigating the cause of the plague, Oedipus discovered that he had killed his father and married his mother. In horror, desperate not to see what he had done, he gouged out his own eyes.

Once the truth was discovered, Oedipus's daughter Antigone led him into exile, where he died. His sons, Eteocles (ē tē´ ə klēz) and Polyneices (päl' ī nē´ sēz'), killed each other while fighting for control of the kingdom. As *Antigone* opens, Oedipus's brother Creon is the new ruler of Thebes. Oedipus's remaining children, daughters Antigone and Ismene (is men´ ē), are haunted by the tragedies of their past.

Antigone

A Play by Sophocles
Translated by Dudley Fitts and Robert Fitzgerald

BUILD BACKGROUND

Literary Context The plot of *Antigone* was based on well-known Greek stories and was as familiar to Greek audiences as classic fairy tales are to us today. The play begins with Antigone facing a grim situation. Both her brothers are dead, and Polyneices, as punishment for not supporting Creon as king, has been left unburied. According to ancient Greek tradition, this was a horrifying dishonor, and Antigone feels she must bury her brother no matter what the consequences. The play centers on the conflict between Creon and Antigone. Neither is able to yield to the other, and tragic consequences result.

Reader's Context When, if ever, is it right to go against a rule or an authority?

ANALYZE LITERATURE: Chorus and Ode

In classical Greek drama, a **chorus** was a group of people who spoke directly to the audience to convey the author's viewpoint or to introduce story details. The chorus traditionally made its entrance singing a song called the *parodos,* the first of a number of **odes,** or lofty, serious lyric poems it would sing throughout the play.

SET PURPOSE

As you read, predict who might be the tragic hero, or heroine, of *Antigone* and what will lead to his or her downfall. How does the commentary provided by the Chorus aid in your prediction? Consider the purpose of the Chorus and what information it brings to the play.

MEET THE AUTHOR

Although only seven of his 125 plays have survived, **Sophocles** (c. 496–406 BCE) is considered one of the most important playwrights who ever lived. Born into a wealthy family in Athens, Greece, Sophocles was well educated, a personal friend of prominent statesmen, and popular for his grace and charm. He lived to be ninety years old—witnessing almost the entire fifth century BCE, a glorious time in the history of Athens— and remained an active leader of the great city throughout his life. He wrote all of his surviving plays after age fifty and *Oedipus at Colonus* when he was ninety. One of his last known acts was to lead a chorus in public mourning for the death of his dramatic rival, Euripides. Sophocles died that same year.

USE READING SKILLS

Sequence of Events
Sequence is the order in which things happen in a story. Identifying the sequence of events can help you understand which events lead to other events. As you read *Antigone*, keep track of the major developments, including things that may have happened before the start of the story, by making a Sequence Map like the one below.

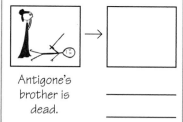

Antigone's
brother is
dead.

PREVIEW VOCABULARY

Use the context clues in the sentences below to figure out the meanings of the underlined words from the selection.

1. The judge issued a new underline{decree}, and we had no choice but to abide by it.
2. Don't try to set Patrick up on a blind date—he resents people who <u>meddle</u> in his personal life.
3. The reporter thought he had a <u>comprehensive</u> list, but several local schools were not on it.
4. Ever since Vonda went to a protest at city hall, her brother has called her an <u>anarchist</u>.
5. The cat's <u>lithe</u> body makes it easy for her to leap, pounce, and run around tight corners.

Antigone

A Play by
Sophocles

Translated by Dudley Fitts
and Robert Fitzgerald

Antigone, 1900s. Marie Spartali Stillman. Simon Carter Gallery, Woodbridge, UK.

"It is the dead, not the living, who make the longest demands...."

CAST OF CHARACTERS

ANTIGONE (an tig´ ə nē), daughter of Oedipus, former King of Thebes
ISMENE (is mē´ nē), another daughter of Oedipus
EURYDICE (yōō rid´ ə sē), wife of Creon
CREON (krē´ än), King of Thebes, uncle of Antigone and Ismene
HAIMON (hī´ mən), Creon's son, engaged to Antigone
TEIRESIAS (tī rē´ sē əs), a blind prophet
A SENTRY
A MESSENGER

CHORUS

CHORAGOS (kō rā´ gəs),
leader of the chorus
A BOY, who leads Teiresias
GUARDS
SERVANTS

Scene. *Before the palace of* CREON, *King of Thebes. A central double door, and two lateral doors. A platform extends the length of the facade, and from this platform three steps lead down into the "orchestra," or chorus-ground.* **Time.** *Dawn of the day after the repulse of the Argive[1] army from the assault on Thebes.*

Prologue

[ANTIGONE *and* ISMENE *enter from the central door of the Palace.*]

ANTIGONE. Ismene, dear sister,
You would think that we had already suffered enough
For the curse on Oedipus:
I cannot imagine any grief
5   That you and I have not gone through. And now—
Have they told you of the new <u>decree</u> of our King Creon?

ISMENE. I have heard nothing: I know
That two sisters lost two brothers, a double death
In a single hour; and I know that the Argive army
10   Fled in the night; but beyond this, nothing.

ANTIGONE. I thought so. And that is why I wanted you
To come out here with me. There is something we must do.

ISMENE. Why do you speak so strangely?

ANTIGONE. Listen, Ismene:
15   Creon buried our brother Eteocles
With military honors, gave him a soldier's funeral,
And it was right that he should; but Polyneices,
Who fought as bravely and died as miserably,—
They say that Creon has sworn
20   No one shall bury him, no one mourn for him,
But his body must lie in the fields, a sweet treasure
For carrion birds to find as they search for food.
That is what they say, and our good Creon is coming here
To announce it publicly; and the penalty—
25   Stoning to death in the public square!
                                There it is,
And now you can prove what you are:
A true sister, or a traitor to your family.

ISMENE. Antigone, you are mad! What could I possibly do?

de • cree (də krē´) *n.,* order set forth by one in authority

---

1. **Argive.** From Argos, a capital city in ancient Greece

ANTIGONE. You must decide whether you will help me or not.

30   **ISMENE.** I do not understand you. Help you in what?

ANTIGONE. Ismene, I am going to bury him. Will you come?

ISMENE. Bury him! You have just said the new law forbids it.

ANTIGONE. He is my brother. And he is your brother, too.

ISMENE. But think of the danger! Think what Creon will do!

35   **ANTIGONE.** Creon is not strong enough to stand in my way.

ISMENE. Ah sister!
Oedipus died, everyone hating him
For what his own search brought to light, his eyes
Ripped out by his own hand; and Jocasta[2] died,
40   His mother and wife at once; she twisted the cords
That strangled her life; and our two brothers died,
Each killed by the other's sword. And we are left:
But oh, Antigone,
Think how much more terrible than these
45   Our own death would be if we should go against Creon
And do what he has forbidden! We are only women;
We cannot fight with men, Antigone!
The law is strong, we must give in to the law
In this thing, and in worse. I beg the Dead
50   To forgive me, but I am helpless: I must yield
To those in authority. And I think it is dangerous business
To be always <u>meddling</u>.

ANTIGONE.   If that is what you think,
I should not want you, even if you asked to come.
You have made your choice and you can be what you want to be.
55   But I will bury him; and if I must die,
I say that this crime is holy: I shall lie down
With him in death, and I shall be as dear
To him as he to me.
                It is the dead,
Not the living, who make the longest demands:
60   We die for ever....
               You may do as you like,
Since apparently the laws of the gods mean nothing to you.

ISMENE. They mean a great deal to me; but I have no strength
To break laws that were made for the public good.

> **med • dle** (me´ d'l) *v.,* to interfere in something that is not one's business

---

2. **Jocasta** (yō kä´ stä). Jocasta, the mother of Antigone and Ismene, hanged herself when she learned that her husband, Oedipus, was actually her son.

ANTIGONE. That must be your excuse, I suppose. But as for me,
65 I will bury the brother I love.

ISMENE.   Antigone,
I am so afraid for you!

ANTIGONE.   You need not be:
You have yourself to consider, after all.

ISMENE. But no one must hear of this, you must tell no one!
I will keep it a secret, I promise!

ANTIGONE. Oh tell it! Tell everyone!
70 Think how they'll hate you when it all comes out
If they learn that you knew about it all the time!

ISMENE. So fiery! You should be cold with fear.

ANTIGONE. Perhaps. But I am doing only what I must.

ISMENE. But can you do it? I say that you cannot.

75 **ANTIGONE.** Very well: when my strength gives out, I shall do no more.

ISMENE. Impossible things should not be tried at all.

ANTIGONE. Go away, Ismene:
I shall be hating you soon, and the dead will too,
For your words are hateful. Leave me my foolish plan:
80 I am not afraid of the danger; if it means death,
It will not be the worst of deaths—death without honor.

ISMENE. Go then, if you feel that you must.
You are unwise,

But a loyal friend indeed to those who love you.

[*Exit into the Palace.* ANTIGONE *goes off, left. Enter the* CHORUS.]

Parodos

CHORUS.   [STROPHE 1]
Now the long blade of the sun, lying
Level east to west, touches with glory
Thebes of the Seven Gates.[3] Open, unlidded
Eye of golden day! O marching light
5 Across the eddy and rush of Dirce's stream.[4]
Striking the white shields of the enemy
Thrown headlong backward from the blaze of morning!

---

3. **Seven Gates.** Seven entrances through the wall that surrounded and protected Thebes
4. **Dirce's stream.** Small river into which Dirce, an early queen of Thebes, was thrown after she was murdered

"Our temples shall be sweet with hymns of praise, / And the long night shall echo with our chorus." Dinah Stabb, and behind her Rowan Wylie, rehearse a dance sequence from The Freehold's production of Sophocles' *Antigone* at the Round House, Chalk Farm, November 18, 1969.

CHORAGOS. Polyneices their commander
Roused them with windy phrases,
10 He the wild eagle screaming
Insults above our land,
His wings their shields of snow,
His crest their marshalled helms.

CHORUS.   [ANTISTROPHE 1]
Against our seven gates in a yawning ring
15 The famished spears came onward in the night;
But before his jaws were sated with our blood,
Or pinefire took the garland of our towers,
He was thrown back; and as he turned, great Thebes—

ANTIGONE, PROLOGUE   **653**

No tender victim for his noisy power—
20   Rose like a dragon behind him, shouting war.

CHORAGOS. For God hates utterly
The bray of bragging tongues;
And when he beheld their smiling,
Their swagger of golden helms,
25   The frown of his thunder blasted
Their first man from our walls.

CHORUS.   [STROPHE 2]
We heard his shout of triumph high in the air
Turn to a scream; far out in a flaming arc
He fell with his windy torch, and the earth struck him.
30   And others storming in fury no less than his
Found shock of death in the dusty joy of battle.

CHORAGOS. Seven captains at seven gates
Yielded their clanging arms to the god
That bends the battle-line and breaks it.
35   These two only, brothers in blood,
Face to face in matchless rage,
Mirroring each the other's death,
Clashed in long combat.

CHORUS.   [ANTISTROPHE 2]
But now in the beautiful morning of victory
40   Let Thebes of the many chariots sing for joy!
With hearts for dancing we'll take leave of war:
Our temples shall be sweet with hymns of praise,
And the long night shall echo with our chorus.

Scene 1

CHORAGOS. But now at last our new King is coming:
Creon of Thebes, Menoikeus'[5] son.
In this auspicious dawn of his reign
What are the new complexities
5   That shifting Fate has woven for him?
What is his counsel? Why has he summoned
The old men to hear him?

---

5. **Menoikeus** (me noi´ kē əs). Father of Creon and Jocasta

[Enter CREON *from the Palace, center. He addresses the* CHORUS *from the top step.]*

CREON. Gentlemen: I have the honor to inform you that our Ship of
State, which recent storms have threatened to destroy, has come safely
10   to harbor at last, guided by the merciful wisdom of Heaven. I have
summoned you here this morning because I know that I can depend
upon you: your devotion to King Laïos[6] was absolute; you never
hesitated in your duty to our late ruler Oedipus; and when Oedipus
died, your loyalty was transferred to his children. Unfortunately, as you
15   know, his two sons, the princes Eteocles and Polyneices, have killed each
other in battle; and I, as the next in blood, have succeeded to the full
power of the throne.

I am aware, of course, that no Ruler can expect complete loyalty from his
subjects until he has been tested in office. Nevertheless, I say to you at the
20   very outset that I have nothing but contempt for the kind of Governor
who is afraid, for whatever reason, to follow the course that he knows is
best for the State; and as for the man who sets private friendship above
the public welfare—I have no use for him, either. I call God to witness
that if I saw my country headed for ruin, I should not be afraid to speak
25   out plainly; and I need hardly remind you that I would never have any
dealings with an enemy of the people. No one values friendship more
highly than I; but we must remember that friends made at the risk of
wrecking our Ship are not real friends at all.

These are my principles, at any rate, and that is why I have made the
30   following decision concerning the sons of Oedipus: Eteocles, who died
as a man should die, fighting for his country, is to be buried with full
military honors, with all the ceremony that is usual when the greatest
heroes die; but his brother Polyneices, who broke his exile to come
back with fire and sword against his native city and the shrines of his
35   fathers' gods, whose one idea was to spill the blood of his blood and sell
his own people into slavery—Polyneices, I say, is to have no burial: no
man is to touch him or say the least prayer for him; he shall lie on the
plain, unburied; and the birds and the scavenging dogs can do with him
whatever they like.

40   This is my command, and you can see the wisdom behind it. As long as I am
King, no traitor is going to be honored with the loyal man. But whoever
shows by word and deed that he is on the side of the State—he shall have
my respect while he is living, and my <u>reverence</u> when he is dead.

CHORAGOS. If that is your will, Creon son of Menoikeus,
45   You have the right to enforce it: we are yours.

CREON. That is my will. Take care that you do your part.

CHORAGOS. We are old men: let the younger ones carry it out.

***

6. **King Laïos** (lā´ əs). Father of Oedipus

---

rev • er • ence (rev´
rən[t]s) *n.,* profound
respect, love, and awe

CREON. I do not mean that: the sentries have been appointed.

CHORAGOS. Then what is it that you would have us do?

50 **CREON.** You will give no support to whoever breaks this law.

CHORAGOS. Only a crazy man is in love with death!

CREON. And death it is; yet money talks, and the wisest
Have sometimes been known to count a few coins too many.

[*Enter* SENTRY *from left.*]

SENTRY. I'll not say that I'm out of breath from running, King, because
55 every time I stopped to think about what I have to tell you, I felt like
going back. And all the time a voice kept saying, "You fool, don't you
know you're walking straight into trouble?"; and then another voice:
"Yes, but if you let somebody else get the news to Creon first, it will be
even worse than that for you!" But good sense won out, at least I hope
60 it was good sense, and here I am with a story that makes no sense at
all; but I'll tell it anyhow, because, as they say, what's going to happen's
going to happen, and—

CREON. Come to the point. What have you to say?

Sentry. I did not do it. I did not see who did it. You must not punish me
for what someone else has done.

Creon. A <u>comprehensive</u> defense! More effective, perhaps,
65 If I knew its purpose. Come: what is it?

Sentry. A dreadful thing...I don't know how to put it—

Creon. Out with it!

Sentry.   Well, then;
The dead man—
                     Polyneices—

[*Pause. The* Sentry *is overcome, fumbles for words.* Creon *waits impassively.*]

                                 out there—
                                       someone,—

New dust on the slimy flesh!

[*Pause. No sign from* Creon.]

Someone has given it burial that way, and
70 Gone...

[*Long pause.* Creon *finally speaks with deadly control.*]

Creon. And the man who dared do this?

Sentry.   I swear I
Do not know! You must believe me!
                              Listen:
The ground was dry, not a sign of digging, no,
Not a wheeltrack in the dust, no trace of anyone.
75 It was when they relieved us this morning and one of them,
The corporal, pointed to it.
                          There it was,
The strangest—
              Look:
The body, just mounded over with light dust: you see?
Not buried really, but as if they'd covered it
80 Just enough for the ghost's peace. And no sign
Of dogs or any wild animal that had been there.
And then what a scene there was! Every man of us
Accusing the other: we all proved the other man did it,
We all had proof that we could not have done it.
85 We were ready to take hot iron in our hands,
Walk through fire, swear by all the gods,
It was not I!
I do not know who it was, but it was not I!

---

com • pre • hen •
sive (käm pri hen[t]′
siv) *adj.,* covering a
matter completely;
inclusive

[CREON'S *rage has been mounting steadily, but the* SENTRY *is too intent upon his story to notice it.*]

And then, when this came to nothing, someone said
90   A thing that silenced us and made us stare
Down at the ground: you had to be told the news,
And one of us had to do it! We threw the dice,
And the bad luck fell to me. So here I am,
No happier to be here than you are to have me:
95   Nobody likes the man who brings bad news.

CHORAGOS. I have been wondering, King: can it be that the gods
have done this?

CREON. [*Furiously*] Stop!
Must you doddering wrecks
Go out of your heads entirely! "The gods!"
100   Intolerable!
The gods favor this corpse? Why? How had he served them?
Tried to loot their temples, burn their images,
Yes, and the whole State, and its laws with it!
Is it your senile opinion that the gods love to honor bad men?
105   A pious thought!—
                No, from the very beginning
There have been those who have whispered together,
Stiff-necked <u>anarchists</u>, putting their heads together,
Scheming against me in alleys. These are the men,
And they have bribed my own guard to do this thing.
110   Money!   [*Sententiously*]
There's nothing in the world so demoralizing as money.
Down go your cities,
Homes gone, men gone, honest hearts corrupted,
Crookedness of all kinds, and all for money!
[*To* SENTRY]
115   But you—!

I swear by God and by the throne of God,
The man who has done this thing shall pay for it!
Find that man, bring him here to me, or your death
Will be the least of your problems: I'll string you up
120   Alive, and there will be certain ways to make you
Discover your employer before you die;
And the process may teach you a lesson you seem to have missed:
The dearest profit is sometimes all too dear:
That depends on the source. Do you understand me?
125   A fortune won is often misfortune.

SENTRY. King, may I speak?

---

an • ar • chist
(a´ nər kist) *n.,* one who rebels against or attempts to overthrow the government

sen • ten • tious • ly
(sen ten[t]s´ shəs lē) *adv.,* in an overly moralizing way

CREON.   Your very voice distresses me.

SENTRY. Are you sure that it is my voice, and not your <u>conscience</u>?

CREON. By God, he wants to analyze me now!

SENTRY. It is not what I say, but what has been done, that hurts you.

130   CREON. You talk too much.

SENTRY.   Maybe; but I've done nothing.

CREON. Sold your soul for some silver: that's all you've done.

SENTRY. How dreadful it is when the right judge judges wrong!

CREON. Your figures of speech
May entertain you now; but unless you bring me the man,
135   You will get little profit from them in the end.

[*Exit* CREON *into the Palace.*]

SENTRY. "Bring me the man"—!
I'd like nothing better than bring him the man!
But bring him or not, you have seen the last of me here.
At any rate, I am safe!

[*Exit* SENTRY.]

Ode I

CHORUS.   [STROPHE 1]
Numberless are the world's wonders, but none
More wonderful than man; the stormgray sea
Yields to his prows, the huge crests bear him high;
Earth, holy and inexhaustible, is graven
5   With shining furrows where his plows have gone
Year after year, the timeless labor of stallions.

                                       [ANTISTROPHE 1]

The lightboned birds and beasts that cling to cover,
The <u>lithe</u> fish lighting their reaches of dim water,
All are taken, tamed in the net of his mind;

10   The lion on the hill, the wild horse windy-maned,
Resign to him; and his blunt yoke has broken
The sultry shoulders of the mountain bull.

                                       [STROPHE 2]

Words also, and thought as rapid as air,
He fashions to his good use; <u>statecraft</u> is his,

15   And his the skill that deflects the arrows of snow,
The spears of winter rain: from every wind

He has made himself secure—from all but one:
In the late wind of death he cannot stand.

[ANTISTROPHE 2]

O clear intelligence, force beyond all measure!
20 O fate of man, working both good and evil!
When the laws are kept, how proudly his city stands!
When the laws are broken, what of his city then?
Never may the anarchic man find rest at my hearth,
Never be it said that my thoughts are his thoughts.

MIRRORS & WINDOWS

What is your opinion of Creon as a king? Would you like to live as one of his subjects? To whom in history would you compare him? Why?

REFER TO TEXT ▶ ▶ ▶ ▶	▶ REASON WITH TEXT	
1a. List the arguments given by Antigone and Ismene regarding the burial of their brother. According to Antigone, whose law is Creon defying in refusing Polyneices a proper burial?	**1b.** Identify the main reason why Antigone wants to bury her brother. Based on this information, what can you infer about her character?	**Understand** **Find meaning**
2a. Quote what Antigone says about the possibility of her own death.	**2b.** Apply what you know about Antigone's character to explain why she is willing to risk her life to bury Polyneices.	**Apply** **Use information**
3a. At the end of Scene 1, recall what the Chorus says happens when laws are kept. According to the Chorus, what happens when these laws are broken?	**3b.** Contrast the ideas Antigone, Creon, and the Choragos have about law. What are their attitudes toward the laws of the gods? What are their attitudes toward the laws of kings?	**Analyze** **Take things apart**
4a. State how Creon threatens the Sentry. How does the Sentry respond?	**4b.** Judge Antigone's decision to defy Creon's law and evaluate whether you think she is right to do so.	**Evaluate** **Make judgments**
5a. Quote what Antigone says to Ismene regarding her decision to not help Antigone.	**5b.** Are there occasions when it is acceptable to break a law if you believe it is unfair? If so, create a list of occasions where it would be acceptable. If not, create a list of reasons why such an act is unacceptable.	**Create** **Bring ideas together**

ANALYZE LITERATURE: Chorus and Ode

What important information does the Chorus reveal in the Parodos? How is the role of the Choragos different from the role of the Chorus? How do the Chorus and the Choragos describe Polyneices and his army?

Antigone and Ismene.

Scene 2

[*Re-enter* SENTRY *leading* ANTIGONE.]

CHORAGOS. What does this mean? Surely this captive woman
Is the Princess, Antigone. Why should she be taken?

SENTRY. Here is the one who did it! We caught her
In the very act of burying him.—Where is Creon?

5 CHORAGOS. Just coming from the house.

[*Enter* CREON, *center.*]

CREON.   What has happened?
Why have you come back so soon?

SENTRY. [*Expansively*]   O King,
A man should never be too sure of anything:
I would have sworn
That you'd not see me here again: your anger
10 Frightened me so, and the things you threatened me with;
But how could I tell then
That I'd be able to solve the case so soon?

No dice-throwing this time: I was only too glad to come!
Here is this woman. She is the guilty one:

15 We found her trying to bury him.
Take her, then; question her; judge her as you will.
I am through with the whole thing now, and glad of it.

CREON. But this is Antigone! Why have you brought her here?

SENTRY. She was burying him, I tell you!

CREON. [*Severely*]   Is this the truth?

20 **SENTRY.** I saw her with my own eyes. Can I say more?

CREON. The details: come, tell me quickly!

SENTRY.   It was like this:
After those terrible threats of yours, King,
We went back and brushed the dust away from the body.
The flesh was soft by now, and stinking,

25 So we sat on a hill to windward and kept guard.
No napping this time! We kept each other awake.
But nothing happened until the white round sun
Whirled in the center of the round sky over us:
Then, suddenly,

30 A storm of dust roared up from the earth, and the sky
Went out, the plain vanished with all its trees
In the stinging dark. We closed our eyes and endured it.
The whirlwind lasted a long time, but it passed;
And then we looked, and there was Antigone!

35 I have seen

"I deny nothing." Antigone (played by Vivien Leigh) and Creon (played by George Ralph) discuss Antigone's actions in the 1949 production at the New Theatre in London, England.

A mother bird come back to a stripped nest, heard
Her crying bitterly a broken note or two
For the young ones stolen. Just so, when this girl
Found the bare corpse, and all her love's work wasted,
40 She wept, and cried on heaven to damn the hands
That had done this thing.
                           And then she brought more dust
And sprinkled wine three times for her brother's ghost.
We ran and took her at once. She was not afraid.
Not even when we charged her with what she had done.
45 She denied nothing.
                        And this was a comfort to me,
And some uneasiness: for it is a good thing
To escape from death, but it is no great pleasure
To bring death to a friend.
                            Yet I always say
There is nothing so comfortable as your own safe skin!

50 CREON. [*Slowly, dangerously*] And you, Antigone,
You with your head hanging,—do you confess this thing?

ANTIGONE. I do. I deny nothing.

CREON. [*To* SENTRY]   You may go.

[*Exit* SENTRY.]

[*To* ANTIGONE] Tell me, tell me briefly:
Had you heard my proclamation touching this matter?

55 ANTIGONE. It was public. Could I help hearing it?

CREON. And yet you dared defy the law.

ANTIGONE.   I dared.
It was not God's proclamation. That final Justice
That rules the world below makes no such laws.
Your edict, King, was strong,
60 But all your strength is weakness itself against
The immortal unrecorded laws of God.
They are not merely now: they were, and shall be,
Operative forever, beyond man utterly.

I knew I must die, even without your decree:
65 I am only mortal. And if I must die
Now, before it is my time to die,
Surely this is no hardship: can anyone
Living, as I live, with evil all about me,
Think Death less than a friend? This death of mine
70 Is of no importance; but if I had left my brother

Lying in death unburied, I should have suffered.
Now I do not.

You smile at me. Ah Creon,
Think me a fool, if you like; but it may well be
That a fool convicts me of folly.

75   **CHORAGOS.** Like father, like daughter: both headstrong, deaf to reason!
She has never learned to yield.

CREON.   She has much to learn.
The inflexible heart breaks first, the toughest iron
Cracks first, and the wildest horses bend their necks
At the pull of the smallest curb.

                             Pride? In a slave?

80   This girl is guilty of a double <u>insolence</u>,
Breaking the given laws and boasting of it.
Who is the man here,
She or I, if this crime goes unpunished?
Sister's child, or more than sister's child,
85   Or closer yet in blood—she and her sister
Win bitter death for this!

[*To* SERVANTS]   Go, some of you,
Arrest Ismene. I accuse her equally.
Bring her: you will find her sniffling in the house there.
Her mind's a traitor: crimes kept in the dark
90   Cry for light, and the guardian brain shudders;
But how much worse than this
Is brazen boasting of barefaced anarchy!

ANTIGONE. Creon, what more do you want than my death?

CREON.   Nothing.
That gives me everything.

ANTIGONE.   Then I beg you: kill me.
95   This talking is a great weariness: your words
Are distasteful to me, and I am sure that mine
Seem so to you. And yet they should not seem so:
I should have praise and honor for what I have done.
All these men here would praise me
100   With their lips not frozen shut with fear of you.

[*Bitterly*]

Ah the good fortune of kings,
Licensed to say and do whatever they please!

CREON. You are alone here in that opinion.

ANTIGONE. No, they are with me. But they keep their tongues in leash.

---

in • so • lence
(in´ sə lənts) *n.,*
disrespect; haughtiness;
impudence

Greek Theaters Greek theaters seated as many as fifteen thousand people, so extreme measures were taken to make sure that everyone in the audience could see and hear the action. The actors wore elaborate costumes and large masks fitted with small brass megaphones for projecting their voices. They also wore padding, headpieces, and platform shoes to increase their size. Because of the masks, actors did not depend on facial expressions but used gestures, body movements, and tone of voice to portray the characters' feelings.

105   **CREON.** Maybe. But you are guilty, and they are not.

     ANTIGONE. There is no guilt in reverence for the dead.

     CREON. But Eteocles—was he not your brother too?

     ANTIGONE. My brother too.

     CREON.   And you insult his memory?

     ANTIGONE. [*Softly*] The dead man would not say that I insult it.

110   **CREON.** He would: for you honor a traitor as much as him.

     ANTIGONE. His own brother, traitor or not, and equal in blood.

     CREON. He made war on his country. Eteocles defended it.

     ANTIGONE. Nevertheless, there are honors due all the dead.

     CREON. But not the same for the wicked as for the just.

115   **ANTIGONE.** Ah Creon, Creon,
     Which of us can say what the gods hold wicked?

     CREON. An enemy is an enemy, even dead.

     ANTIGONE. It is my nature to join in love, not hate.

     CREON. [*Finally losing patience*] Go join them, then; if you must
       have your love,
120   Find it in hell!

     CHORAGOS. But see, Ismene comes:

[*Enter* Ismene, *guarded.*]

Those tears are sisterly, the cloud
That shadows her eyes rains down gentle sorrow.

Creon. You too, Ismene,
125   Snake in my ordered house, sucking my blood
Stealthily—and all the time I never knew
That these two sisters were aiming at my throne!

                                           Ismene,
Do you confess your share in this crime, or deny it?
Answer me.

130   **Ismene.** Yes, if she will let me say so. I am guilty.

Antigone. [*Coldly*] No, Ismene. You have no right to say so.
You would not help me, and I will not have you help me.

Ismene. But now I know what you meant; and I am here
To join you, to take my share of punishment.

135   **Antigone.** The dead man and the gods who rule the dead
      Know whose act this was. Words are not friends.

      Ismene. Do you refuse me, Antigone? I want to die with you:
        I too have a duty that I must discharge to the dead.

        Antigone. You shall not lessen my death by sharing it.

          Ismene. What do I care for life when you are dead?

        Antigone. Ask Creon. You're always hanging on his opinions.

         Ismene. You are laughing at me. Why, Antigone?

       Antigone. It's a joyless laughter, Ismene.

    Ismene.   But can I do nothing?

Antigone. Yes. Save yourself. I shall not envy you.
145   There are those who will praise you; I shall have honor, too.

Ismene. But we are equally guilty!

Antigone.   No more, Ismene.
You are alive, but I belong to Death.

Creon. [*To the* Chorus] Gentlemen, I beg you to observe these girls:
One has just now lost her mind: the other,
150   It seems, has never had a mind at all.

Ismene. Grief teaches the steadiest minds to <u>waver</u>, King.

Creon. Yours certainly did, when you assumed guilt with the guilty!

wa • ver
(wā´ vər) *v.*, to hesi-
tate; to be undecided

ISMENE. But how could I go on living without her?

CREON.   You are.
She is already dead.

ISMENE.   But your own son's bride!

155 CREON. There are places enough for him to push his plow.
I want no wicked women for my sons!

ISMENE. O dearest Haimon, how your father wrongs you!

CREON. I've had enough of your childish talk of marriage!

CHORAGOS. Do you really intend to steal this girl from your son?

160 CREON. No; Death will do that for me.

CHORAGOS.   Then she must die?

CREON. [*Ironically*] You dazzle me.
                                   —But enough of this talk!
[To Guards] You, there, take them away and guard them well:
For they are but women, and even brave men run
When they see Death coming.

[*Exit* ISMENE, ANTIGONE, *and* GUARDS.]

Ode II
CHORUS.   [STROPHE 1]
Fortunate is the man who has never tasted God's <u>vengeance</u>!
Where once the anger of heaven has struck, that house is shaken
Forever: damnation rises behind each child
Like a wave cresting out of the black northeast,
5 When the long darkness undersea roars up
And bursts drumming death upon the windwhipped sand.

                                                      [ANTISTROPHE 1]

I have seen this gathering sorrow from time long past
Loom upon Oedipus' children: generation from generation
Takes the <u>compulsive</u> rage of the enemy god.
10 So lately this last flower of Oedipus' line
Drank the sunlight! but now a passionate word
And a handful of dust have closed up all its beauty.

                                                      [STROPHE 2]

      What mortal arrogance
      Transcends the wrath of Zeus?[1]
15 Sleep cannot lull him, nor the effortless long months
Of the timeless gods: but he is young forever,

> **ven • geance**
> (ven´ jen[t]s) *n.*, act
> of taking revenge

> **com • pul • sive**
> (kəm pul´ siv) *adj.*, as
> if driven by a force

---
1. **Zeus.** Son of Cronus, chief of the Greek gods, ruler of gods and mortals

And his house is the shining day of high Olympos.[2]
　　All that is and shall be,
　　And all the past, is his.
20　No pride on earth is free of the curse of heaven.

[ANTISTROPHE 2]

　　The straying dreams of men
　　May bring them ghosts of joy:
　　But as they drowse, the waking embers burn them;
　　Or they walk with fixed eyes, as blind men walk.
25　But the ancient wisdom speaks for our own time:
　　Fate works most for woe
　　With Folly's fairest show.
　　Man's little pleasure is the spring of sorrow.

---

2. **Olympos.** Mountain in Greece; the home of the gods

MIRRORS & WINDOWS

Is Antigone getting what she deserves, or is she being treated unfairly? Explain. If you were one of Antigone's friends, what advice would you give her?

REFER TO TEXT ▶ ▶ ▶ ▶	▶ REASON WITH TEXT	
1a. Identify how Antigone responds when charged with her crime. According to Antigone, what would make her suffer more than dying?	1b. Explain what kind of person Antigone is. Give evidence from the text to support your assessment.	**Understand** **Find meaning**
2a. Review the Chorus's Ode. State the information presented by the Chorus. According to the Chorus, what happens to the family where "once the anger of heaven has struck"?	2b. Relate what you know about the "wrath of Zeus" and the story of Oedipus to predict what will happen next.	**Apply** **Use information**
3a. Recall how Ismene responds to Creon's accusations.	3b. Compare and contrast Antigone's and Ismene's ideas about and reactions to their situation.	**Analyze** **Take things apart**
4a. State the reason why Antigone believes the men around Creon do not praise her for her deeds.	4b. Assess Creon as a leader as well as a judge. What words and actions reveal his values, priorities, and moral character?	**Evaluate** **Make judgments**
5a. Identify how the Sentry feels about Antigone's arrest. Why does he bring her to Creon?	5b. What authority figures have you known or heard about that behave like Creon? Compose a list of ways to respond to such authority figures.	**Create** **Bring ideas together**

ANALYZE LITERATURE: Foil

A **foil** is a character whose attributes, or characteristics, contrast with and therefore shed light on the attributes of another character. How does Antigone react to Creon's accusation? Reread lines 121–123, in which the Choragos describes Ismene's entrance. How is Ismene a foil for Antigone?

Brave Antigone, 1882. Frederic Leighton.

Scene 3

CHORAGOS. But here is Haimon, King, the last of all your sons.
Is it grief for Antigone that brings him here,
And bitterness at being robbed of his bride?

[*Enter* HAIMON.]

CREON. We shall soon see, and no need of diviners.[1]

              —Son,

---

1. **diviners.** Those who can tell the future

def · er · ence
(deˊ fə rən[t]s) *n.,*
attitude of yielding to
another

sub · or · di · nate
(sə bôrˊ də nātˊ) *v.,*
to place in a lower class
or rank

ma · li · cious
(mə liˊ shəs) *n.,*
those who act with evil
intention

5   You have heard my final judgment on that girl:
Have you come here hating me, or have you come
With <u>deference</u> and with love, whatever I do?

HAIMON. I am your son, father. You are my guide.
You make things clear for me, and I obey you.
10   No marriage means more to me than your continuing wisdom.

CREON. Good. That is the way to behave: <u>subordinate</u>
Everything else, my son, to your father's will.
This is what a man prays for, that he may get
Sons attentive and dutiful in his house,
15   Each one hating his father's enemies,
Honoring his father's friends. But if his sons
Fail him, if they turn out unprofitably,
What has he fathered but trouble for himself
And amusement for the <u>malicious</u>?
                                  So you are right
20   Not to lose your head over this woman.
Your pleasure with her would soon grow cold, Haimon,
And then you'd have a hellcat in bed and elsewhere.
Let her find her husband in Hell!
Of all the people in this city, only she
25   Has had contempt for my law and broken it.
Do you want me to show myself weak before the people?
Or to break my sworn word? No, and I will not.
The woman dies.
I suppose she'll plead "family ties." Well, let her.
30   If I permit my own family to rebel,
How shall I earn the world's obedience?
Show me the man who keeps his house in hand,
He's fit for public authority.
                       I'll have no dealings
With lawbreakers, critics of the government:
35   Whoever is chosen to govern should be obeyed—
Must be obeyed, in all things, great and small,
Just and unjust! Oh Haimon,
The man who knows how to obey, and that man only,
Knows how to give commands when the time comes.
40   You can depend on him, no matter how fast
The spears come: he's a good soldier, he'll stick it out.
Anarchy, anarchy! Show me a greater evil!
This is why cities tumble and the great houses rain down,
This is what scatters armies!
45   No, no: good lives are made so by discipline.

We keep the laws then, and the lawmakers,

And no woman shall seduce us. If we must lose,
Let's lose to a man, at least! Is a woman stronger than we?

Choragos. Unless time has rusted my wits,
50 What you say, King, is said with point and dignity.

Haimon. [*Boyishly earnest*] Father:
Reason is God's crowning gift to man, and you are right
To warn me against losing mine. I cannot say—
I hope that I shall never want to say!—that you
55 Have reasoned badly. Yet there are other men
Who can reason, too; and their opinions might be helpful.
You are not in a position to know everything
That people say or do, or what they feel:
Your temper terrifies them—everyone
60 Will tell you only what you like to hear.
But I, at any rate, can listen; and I have heard them
Muttering and whispering in the dark about this girl.
They say no woman has ever, so unreasonably,
Died so shameful a death for a generous act:
65 "She covered her brother's body. Is this indecent?
She kept him from dogs and vultures. Is this a crime?
Death?—She should have all the honor that we can give her!"

This is the way they talk out there in the city.

You must believe me:
70 Nothing is closer to me than your happiness.
What could be closer? Must not any son
Value his father's fortune as his father does his?
I beg you, do not be unchangeable:
Do not believe that you alone can be right.
75 The man who thinks that,
The man who maintains that only he has the power
To reason correctly, the gift to speak, the soul—
A man like that, when you know him, turns out empty.

It is not reason never to yield to reason!

80 In flood time you can see how some trees bend,
And because they bend, even their twigs are safe,
While stubborn trees are torn up, roots and all.
And the same thing happens in sailing:
Make your sheet fast, never slacken—and over you go,
85 Head over heels and under: and there's your voyage.
Forget you are angry! Let yourself be moved!
I know I am young; but please let me say this:
The ideal condition
Would be, I admit, that men should be right by <u>instinct</u>;

in • stinct
(in´ stiŋ[k]t) *n.*,
impulse; natural
tendency

Describe the costumes of Haimon, Choragos, and Creon in this scene from the 1949 performance of *Antigone*. What do the costumes suggest about each character? What aspect of Greek society is the director highlighting by his choice of costumes?

"It is not reason never to yield to reason!" British actor George Ralph (1888–1960) plays King Creon of Thebes in a production of *Antigone* at the New Theatre in London, February 1949.

90 But since we are all too likely to go <u>astray</u>,
   The reasonable thing is to learn from those who can teach.

CHORAGOS. You will do well to listen to him, King,
   If what he says is sensible. And you, Haimon,
   Must listen to your father.—Both speak well.

95 CREON. You consider it right for a man of my years and experience
   To go to school to a boy?

HAIMON.   It is not right
   If I am wrong. But if I am young, and right,
   What does my age matter?

CREON. You think it right to stand up for an anarchist?

100 HAIMON. Not at all. I pay no respect to criminals.

CREON. Then she is not a criminal?

HAIMON. The City would deny it, to a man.

CREON. And the City proposes to teach me how to rule?

HAIMON. Ah. Who is it that's talking like a boy now?

105 CREON. My voice is the one voice giving orders in this City!

HAIMON. It is no City if it takes orders from one voice.

CREON. The State is the King!

HAIMON.   Yes, if the State is a desert.

[Pause]

CREON. This boy, it seems, has sold out to a woman.

HAIMON. If you are a woman: my concern is only for you.

110 CREON. So? Your "concern"! In a public brawl with your father!

HAIMON. How about you, in a public brawl with justice?

CREON. With justice, when all that I do is within my rights?

HAIMON. You have no right to trample on God's right.

CREON. [Completely out of control] Fool, adolescent fool! Taken in
   by a woman!

115 HAIMON. You'll never see me taken in by anything <u>vile</u>.

CREON. Every word you say is for her!

HAIMON. [Quietly, darkly]   And for you.
   And for me. And for the gods under the earth.

---

a • stray (ə strā´)
adv., out of the right
way; off the path

vile (vīl) *adj.,*
foul; mean; cheap;
contemptible

Democracy in Greece In this argument between Haimon and Creon, Haimon seems to be arguing for a democratic form of government, while his father advocates a dictatorship. The Athenian audience of the play would have applauded Haimon. They despised tyrants like Creon, having been ruled by tyrants up until 508 BCE, when the leader Cleisthenes (sixth century BCE) introduced democracy into Athens. A council of five hundred people was elected each year to make laws and to run the state. All male citizens had the right to vote on laws put forth by the council. Direct rule by the people or by their elected representatives flowered in Athens. The Greeks are credited with introducing democracy to the Western world. In fact, the word *democracy* comes from the Greek words *demos,* meaning "people," and *kratein,* meaning "to rule or govern."

CREON. You'll never marry her while she lives.

HAIMON. Then she must die.—But her death will cause another.

120　**CREON.** Another?
　　　Have you lost your senses? Is this an open threat?

HAIMON. There is no threat in speaking to emptiness.

CREON. I swear you'll regret this superior tone of yours!
You are the empty one!

HAIMON.　　　　　　　　If you were not my father,
125　I'd say you were perverse.

CREON. You girlstruck fool, don't play at words with me!

HAIMON. I am sorry. You prefer silence.

CREON.　　　　　　　　　　　Now, by God—!
I swear, by all the gods in heaven above us,
You'll watch it, I swear you shall!

[*To the* SERVANTS]　　　　　Bring her out!
130　Bring the woman out! Let her die before his eyes!

Here, this instant, with her bridegroom beside her!

HAIMON. Not here, no; she will not die here, King.
And you will never see my face again.
Go on raving as long as you've a friend to endure you.

[*Exit* HAIMON.]

135 **CHORAGOS.** Gone, gone.
Creon, a young man in a rage is dangerous!

CREON. Let him do, or dream to do, more than a man can.
He shall not save these girls from death.

CHORAGOS.   These girls?
You have sentenced them both?

CREON.   No, you are right.
140 I will not kill the one whose hands are clean.

CHORAGOS. But Antigone?

CREON. [*Somberly*] I will carry her far away
Out there in the wilderness, and lock her
Living in a vault of stone. She shall have food,
145 As the custom is, to absolve the State of her death.
And there let her pray to the gods of hell:
They are her only gods:
Perhaps they will show her an escape from death,
Or she may learn,
                though late,
150 That <u>piety</u> shown the dead is piety in vain.

[*Exit* CREON.]

Ode III

CHORUS.   [STROPHE]
Love, unconquerable
Waster of rich men, keeper
Of warm lights and all-night vigil
In the soft face of a girl:
5 Sea-wanderer, forest-visitor!
Even the pure Immortals cannot escape you,
And mortal man, in his one day's dusk,
Trembles before your glory.

                                              [ANTISTROPHE]

Surely you swerve upon ruin
10 The just man's <u>consenting</u> heart,
As here you have made bright anger
Strike between father and son—

pi • e • ty
(pī´ ə tē) *n.,* devoted
loyalty or duty to family
or religion

con • sent • ing
(kən sent´ iŋ) *adj.,*
agreeing; approving

And none has conquered but Love!
A girl's glance working the will of heaven:
15   Pleasure to her alone who mocks us,
Merciless Aphrodite.[2]

---

2. **Aphrodite.** Goddess of beauty and love

MIRRORS & WINDOWS

"It is not right / If I am wrong. But if I am young, and right, / What does my age matter?" Has your opinion ever been discounted because of your age? How do you think American society perceives teenagers? How can you make yourself be heard?

REFER TO TEXT ▶ ▶ ▶ ▶	▶ REASON WITH TEXT	
1a. Describe what Creon decides to do with Antigone. Why does he see Antigone as a threat? Quote specific lines he gives to justify his decision.	1b. Summarize what Creon hopes to accomplish by revising his plan for Antigone and Ismene. Why does Haimon disagree with his father's plan?	**Understand** **Find meaning**
2a. List the words Creon uses to refer to Antigone. List the words Creon uses to refer to his son, Haimon.	2b. Examine these two lists. What do these word choices reveal about Creon's attitude toward Antigone and Haimon?	**Apply** **Use information**
3a. State in your own words the main messages in the Chorus's Ode III.	3b. Compare and contrast these messages to the opinions of Haimon and Creon. What does the Chorus suggest is more powerful than Creon's law?	**Analyze** **Take things apart**
4a. Review Creon's long speech on page 670 and quote the lines where he describes the role a son should play. Does Haimon agree with him? Cite evidence from the text to support your answer.	4b. How would you describe Creon's and Haimon's relationship? Describe how Haimon's attitude toward his father changes during their conversation.	**Evaluate** **Make judgments**
5a. Recall what Haimon says to his father about reason.	5b. If you were Haimon, how would you feel about your father at the end of Scene 3? Devise a way you could change the situation to make your father see things from your point of view.	**Create** **Bring ideas together**

ANALYZE LITERATURE: Analogy

An **analogy** is a comparison of two things that are alike in some respects. Often, it is used to explain something less familiar by comparing it to something more familiar. Identify two analogies that Haimon uses in his long speech. What is the purpose of these analogies? Of what is he trying to convince Creon?

"Look upon me, friends, and pity me." Antigone (played by Vivien Leigh) is brought before Creon and the Chorus to hear her sentence in the 1949 production at the New Theatre in London, England.

Scene 4

CHORAGOS. [*As* ANTIGONE *enters guarded*] But I can no longer
　　stand in awe of this,
Nor, seeing what I see, keep back my tears,
Here is Antigone, passing to that chamber,
Where all find sleep at last.

ANTIGONE.　　　　　　　　　　　　　　　　　　　[STROPHE 1]
5　Look upon me, friends, and pity me
　Turning back at the night's edge to say
　Good-by to the sun that shines for me no longer;
　Now sleepy Death
　Summons me down to Acheron,[1] that cold shore:
10　There is no bridesong there, nor any music.

CHORUS. Yet not unpraised, not without a kind of honor,
　You walk at last into the underworld;
　Untouched by sickness, broken by no sword.
　What woman has ever found your way to death?

ANTIGONE.　　　　　　　　　　　　　　　　　　[ANTISTROPHE 1]
15　How often I have heard the story of Niobe,[2]
　Tantalos' wretched daughter, how the stone

---

1. **Acheron** (ak´ ə ron). River in the underworld over which the dead are ferried
2. **Niobe** (nī ō´ bē). Mother whose children were slain by Latona and Apollo because of her arrogance. Zeus turned her to stone, but she continued to mourn for her children, and a stream formed from her tears.

Clung fast about her, ivy-close: and they say
The rain falls endlessly
And sifting soft snow; her tears are never done.
20 I feel the loneliness of her death in mine.

CHORUS. But she was born of heaven, and you
Are woman, woman-born. If her death is yours,
A mortal woman's, is this not for you
Glory in our world and in the world beyond?

ANTIGONE.   [STROPHE 2]
25 You laugh at me. Ah, friends, friends,
Can you not wait until I am dead? O Thebes,
O men many-charioted, in love with Fortune,
Dear springs of Dirce, sacred Theban grove,
Be witnesses for me, denied all pity,
30 Unjustly judged! and think a word of love
For her whose path turns
Under dark earth, where there are no more tears.

CHORUS. You have passed beyond human daring and come at last
Into a place of stone where Justice sits.
35 I cannot tell
What shape of your father's guilt appears in this.

ANTIGONE.   [ANTISTROPHE 2]
You have touched it at last: that bridal bed
Unspeakable, horror of son and mother mingling:
Their crime, infection of all our family!
40 O Oedipus,[3] father and brother!
Your marriage strikes from the grave to murder mine.
I have been a stranger here in my own land:
All my life
The <u>blasphemy</u> of my birth has followed me.

45 CHORUS. Reverence is a virtue, but strength
Lives in established law: that must prevail.
You have made your choice,
Your death is the doing of your conscious hand.

ANTIGONE.   [EPODE]
Then let me go, since all your words are bitter,
50 And the very light of the sun is cold to me.
Lead me to my vigil, where I must have
Neither love nor <u>lamentation</u>; no song, but silence.

[CREON *interrupts impatiently.*]

---

3. **Oedipus.** Antigone's father Oedipus, who had been king of Thebes, accidentally killed his own father and married his mother, an unintentional (and prophesied) crime for which he was exiled from the city.

blas • phe • my
(blas´ fə mē) *n.,*
irreverence toward God

lam • en • ta • tion
(la' mən tā´ shən)
n., vocal expression of
sorrow

CREON. If <u>dirges</u> and planned lamentations could put off death,
Men would be singing forever.

[*To the* SERVANTS]   Take her, go!
55   You know your orders: take her to the vault
And leave her alone there. And if she lives or dies,
That's her affair, not ours: our hands are clean.

ANTIGONE. O tomb, vaulted bride-bed in eternal rock,
Soon I shall be with my own again
60   Where Persephone[4] welcomes the thin ghosts underground:
And I shall see my father again, and you, mother,
And dearest Polyneices—
                      dearest indeed
To me, since it was my hand
That washed him clean and poured the ritual wine:
65   And my reward is death before my time!

And yet, as men's hearts know, I have done no wrong,
I have not sinned before God. Or if I have,
I shall know the truth in death. But if the guilt
Lies upon Creon who judged me, then, I pray,
May his punishment equal my own.

70   CHORAGOS.   O passionate heart,
Unyielding, tormented still by the same winds!

CREON. Her guards shall have good cause to regret their delaying.

ANTIGONE. Ah! That voice is like the voice of death!

CREON. I can give you no reason to think you are mistaken.

75   ANTIGONE. Thebes, and you my fathers' gods,
And rulers of Thebes, you see me now, the last
Unhappy daughter of a line of kings,
Your kings, led away to death. You will remember
What things I suffer, and at what men's hands,
80   Because I would not <u>transgress</u> the laws of heaven.

[*To the* GUARDS, *simply*]

Come: let us wait no longer.

[*Exit* ANTIGONE, *left, guarded.*]

Ode IV

CHORUS.   [STROPHE 1]

---

4. **Persephone** (pər sef´ ə nē). Queen of the underworld and wife of Pluto, king of the underworld

dirge (dʉrj) *n.*, song or piece of writing expressing deep grief

trans • gress (tranz gres´) *v.*, go beyond set limits

All Danaë's beauty[5] was locked away
In a brazen cell where the sunlight could not come;
A small room, still as any grave, enclosed her.
Yet she was a princess too.
5   And Zeus in a rain of gold poured love upon her.
O child, child,
No power in wealth or war
Or tough sea-blackened ships
Can <u>prevail</u> against untiring Destiny!

[ANTISTROPHE 1]

pre · vail (pri vāl´)
v., grow strong; gain victory

10   And Dryas' son[6] also, that furious king,
Bore the god's prisoning anger for his pride:
Sealed up by Dionysos in deaf stone,
His madness died among echoes.
So at the last he learned what dreadful power
15   His tongue had mocked:
For he had <u>profane</u>d the revels,
And fired the wrath of the nine
<u>Implacable</u> Sisters[7] that love the sound of the flute.

[STROPHE 2]

pro · fane
(prō fān´) *v.,* violate; abuse; make impure

im · pla · ca · ble
(im pla´ kə bəl) *adj.,* unable to be appeased; relentless

And old men tell a half-remembered tale
20   Of horror done where a dark ledge splits the sea
And a double surf beats on the gray shores:
How a king's new woman, sick
With hatred for the queen he had imprisoned,
Ripped out his two sons' eyes with her bloody hands

---

5. **Danaë's beauty** (dan ā´ ē). Danaë was locked in a tower to escape a prophecy that her son would kill her father. Zeus, drawn by her beauty, visited her in the form of a shower of gold and fathered her son Perseus. Years later, Perseus killed the man he did not know was his grandfather. The story echoes that of Oedipus.

6. **Dryas' son.** Dryas' son Lycurgus was locked up and driven mad by the gods for objecting to the worship of Dionysos, the god of wine.

7. **nine Implacable Sisters.** Also called the Muses, these nine goddesses were daughters of Zeus and Mnemosyne (Memory). They inspired invention and art and were unforgiving to those who offended them.

25 While grinning Ares[8] watched the shuttle plunge
    Four times: four blind wounds crying for revenge,

    [ANTISTROPHE 2]

    Crying, tears and blood mingled. —Piteously born,
    Those sons whose mother was of heavenly birth!
    Her father was the god of the North Wind
30 And she was cradled by gales,
    She raced with young colts on the glittering hills
    And walked untrammeled in the open light:
    But in her marriage deathless Fate found means
    To build a tomb like yours for all her joy.

8. **king's…Ares.** According to the myth, King Phineas imprisoned his wife, the Queen, and allowed his jealous new wife to blind the sons of the Queen while Ares, the god of war, looked on with glee.

Why is it sometimes difficult for people to take responsibility for their actions? What kind of society would exist if no one were held accountable for his or her behavior?

REFER TO TEXT ▷ ▷ ▷ ▷ ▷	REASON WITH TEXT	
1a. Identify the event from the past that the Chorus blames for Antigone's fate. Identify Antigone's action in the present that the Chorus also blames for her fate.	**1b.** Explain why it is harder for Antigone to hear the blame the Chorus places on the present than the blame it places on the past.	**Understand** **Find meaning**
2a. Describe what happens to Antigone at the end of Scene 4.	**2b.** Examine the events to determine the purpose of the scene. What issues does it raise?	**Apply** **Use information**
3a. Quote what Antigone prays for if Creon is found to be the guilty one.	**3b.** Point out the instances in Scene 4 where blame or responsibility is discussed.	**Analyze** **Take things apart**
4a. Review the Ode at the end of Scene 4. Summarize each stanza in one sentence.	**4b.** The Chorus states, "No power in wealth or war / Or tough sea-blackened ships / Can prevail against untiring Destiny." Determine whether or not you think this statement applies to Antigone's situation.	**Evaluate** **Make judgments**
5a. Name the person to whom Antigone compares her death. How does the Chorus respond to this comparison?	**5b.** If you were Antigone, what might you have done differently in order to prevent the problems her actions caused? What would you have done differently if you had been Creon?	**Create** **Bring ideas together**

ANALYZE LITERATURE: Allusion

An **allusion** is a reference to a person, an event, an object, or a work from history or literature. Note the allusions made in Scene 4. Why might Sophocles have included these allusions in the play? Do they help the audience understand something better? If so, how? If not, what other purpose might they serve?

Scene 5

[Enter blind TEIRESIAS, *led by a boy. The opening speeches of* TEIRESIAS *should be in singsong contrast to the realistic lines of* CREON.*]*

TEIRESIAS. This is the way the blind man comes, Princes, Princes,
Lock-step, two heads lit by the eyes of one.

CREON. What new thing have you to tell us, old Teiresias?

TEIRESIAS. I have much to tell you: listen to the prophet, Creon.

5   **CREON.** I am not aware that I have ever failed to listen.

TEIRESIAS. Then you have done wisely, King, and ruled well.

CREON. I admit my debt to you. But what have you to say?

TEIRESIAS. This, Creon: you stand once more on the edge of fate.

CREON. What do you mean? Your words are a kind of dread.

10   **TEIRESIAS.** Listen, Creon:
I was sitting in my chair of augury,[1] at the place
Where the birds gather about me. They were all a-chatter,
As is their habit, when suddenly I heard
A strange note in their jangling, a scream, a
15   Whirring fury; I knew that they were fighting,
Tearing each other, dying
In a whirlwind of wings clashing. And I was afraid.
I began the rites of burnt-offering at the altar,

---

1. **chair of augury.** Seat where he practices augury, the art of telling fortunes from omens

But Hephaistos[2] failed me: instead of bright flame,
20 There was only the sputtering slime of the fat thigh-flesh
Melting: the entrails dissolved in gray smoke,
The bare bone burst from the welter. And no blaze!
This was a sign from heaven. My boy described it,
Seeing for me as I see for others.
25 I tell you, Creon, you yourself have brought
This new calamity upon us. Our hearths and altars
Are stained with the corruption of dogs and carrion birds
That glut themselves on the corpse of Oedipus' son.
The gods are deaf when we pray to them, their fire
30 Recoils from our offering, their birds of omen
Have no cry of comfort, for they are gorged
With the thick blood of the dead.

                                O my son,
These are no <u>trifles</u>! Think: all men make mistakes,
But a good man yields when he knows his course is wrong.
35 And repairs the evil. The only crime is pride.

Give in to the dead man, then: do not fight with a corpse—
What glory is it to kill a man who is dead?
Think, I beg you:
It is for your own good that I speak as I do.
40 You should be able to yield for your own good.

CREON. It seems that prophets have made me their especial province.
All my life long
I have been a kind of butt for the dull arrows
Of doddering fortunetellers!

                            No, Teiresias:
45 If your birds—if the great eagles of God himself
Should carry him stinking bit by bit to heaven,
I would not yield. I am not afraid of pollution:
No man can defile the gods.

                            Do what you will,
Go into business, make money, speculate
50 In India gold or that synthetic gold from Sardis,[3]
Get rich otherwise than by my consent to bury him.
Teiresias, it is a sorry thing when a wise man
Sells his wisdom, lets out his words for hire!

TEIRESIAS. Ah Creon! Is there no man left in the world—

55 CREON. To do what?—Come, let's have the <u>aphorism</u>!

TEIRESIAS. No man who knows that wisdom outweighs any wealth?

---

tri • fle (trī′ fəl) n., something of little value; inconsequential thing

aph • o • rism (a′ fə ri′ zəm) n., short, insightful saying

2. **Hephaistos** (hi fes′ təs). God of fire
3. **Sardis.** Where the first coins made from an alloy of gold and silver were produced

The Furies In Greek religion, the Furies or Erinyes (i rin´ ē ēz) were goddesses of vengeance, born from the blood of Uranus. Their names were Megaera (meaning envious), Tisiphone (blood avenger), and Alecto (unceasing in anger). They were most often represented as three ugly old women with the heads of dogs, bat's wings, and snakes for hair. The three Furies punished wrongs people committed against relatives, regardless of the motive. When called upon to act, they tormented their victim to death. Although cruel in their punishments, the Furies were considered to be fair in choosing their victims. Only those who committed terrible acts were pursued by the Furies. The Furies were often addressed by the euphemistic name "Eumenides," which means "Kind Ones."

CREON. As surely as bribes are baser than any baseness.

TEIRESIAS. You are sick, Creon! You are deathly sick!

CREON. As you say: it is not my place to challenge a prophet.

60 TEIRESIAS. Yet you have said my prophecy is for sale.

CREON. The generation of prophets has always loved gold.

TEIRESIAS. The generation of kings has always loved brass.

CREON. You forget yourself! You are speaking to your King.

TEIRESIAS. I know it. You are a king because of me.

65 CREON. You have a certain skill; but you have sold out.

TEIRESIAS. King, you will drive me to words that—

CREON. Say them, say them!
Only remember: I will not pay you for them.

TEIRESIAS. No, you will find them too costly.

CREON.   No doubt. Speak:
70 Whatever you say, you will not change my will.

TEIRESIAS. Then take this, and take it to heart!
The time is not far off when you shall pay back
Corpse for corpse, flesh of your own flesh.

75   You have thrust the child of this world into living night,
You have kept from the gods below the child that is theirs:
The one in a grave before her death, the other,
Dead, denied the grave. This is your crime:
And the Furies[4] and the dark gods of Hell
Are swift with terrible punishment for you.

80   Do you want to buy me now, Creon?

                            Not many days,

And your house will be full of men and women weeping,
And curses will be hurled at you from far
Cities grieving for sons unburied, left to rot
Before the walls of Thebes.

85   These are my arrows, Creon: they are all for you.
But come, child: lead me home.   [*To* BOY]
Let him waste his fine anger upon younger men.
Maybe he will learn at last
To control a wiser tongue in a better head.

[*Exit* TEIRESIAS.]

90   **CHORAGOS.** The old man has gone, King, but his words
Remain to plague us. I am old, too,
But I cannot remember that he was ever false.

CREON. That is true…. It troubles me.
Oh it is hard to give in! but it is worse
95   To risk everything for stubborn pride.

CHORAGOS. Creon: take my advice.

CREON.   What shall I do?

CHORAGOS. Go quickly: free Antigone from her vault
And build a tomb for the body of Polyneices.

CREON. You would have me do this?

CHORAGOS.   Creon, yes!
100   And it must be done at once: God moves
Swiftly to cancel the folly of stubborn men.

CREON. It is hard to deny the heart! But I
Will do it: I will not fight with destiny.

CHORAGOS. You must go yourself, you cannot leave it to others.

---

4. **Furies.** Goddesses of vengeance who punished those who sinned against their own families by
making them insane

105   **CREON.** I will go.

             —Bring axes, servants:
Come with me to the tomb. I buried her, I
Will set her free.

             Oh quickly!
My mind misgives—
The laws of the gods are mighty, and a man must serve them

110 To the last day of his life!

[*Exit* CREON.]

Paean

CHORAGOS.   [STROPHE 1]
God of many names

CHORUS.   O Iacchos

                  son
of Kadmeian Semele

        O born of the Thunder! [5]

Guardian of the West

        Regent
of Eleusis' plain[6]

        O Prince of maenad[7] Thebes
and the Dragon Field[8] by rippling Ismenos:

CHORAGOS.   [ANTISTROPHE 1]
God of many names

CHORUS.   the flame of torches
flares on our hills

            the nymphs of Iacchos
dance at the spring of Castalia:[9]
from the vine-close mountain

               come ah come in ivy:
10 *Evohe evohe!*[10] sings through the streets of Thebes

CHORAGOS.   [STROPHE 2]
God of many names

CHORUS.   Iacchos of Thebes
heavenly Child

        of Semele bride of the Thunderer!

---

   5. **Iacchos (yä´ kəs)**…**Kadmeian Semele (sem´ ə lē)**…**Thunder.** Iacchos is another name for
Dionysos. His mother was Kadmeian Semele, daughter of Kadmos, the founder of Thebes; his father was
Zeus, who controlled thunder.
   6. **Eleusis' plain.** Site of worship for Dionysos and Demeter
   7. **maenad.** Female follower of Dionysos, god of wine
   8. **Dragon Field.** Field near the River Ismenos
   9. **Castalia (kas tā´ lē ə).** Site sacred to Apollo where his followers would worship
  10. *Evohe evohe* (ē vō e)! Exclamation of triumph used during festivals of Dionysos

The shadow of plague is upon us:

come

with <u>clement</u> feet

oh come from Parnasos[11]

down the long slopes

across the lamenting water

clem • ent
(kle´ mənt) *adj.,* kind;
gentle; favorable

CHORAGOS.   [ANTISTROPHE 2]
Io[12] Fire! Chorister of the throbbing stars!
O purest among the voices of the night!
Thou son of God, blaze for us!

CHORUS. Come with choric rapture of circling Maenads
Who cry *Io Iacche!*
20   *God of many names!*

Exodos

[*Enter* MESSENGER, *left.*]

MESSENGER. Men of the line of Kadmos, you who live
Near Amphion's citadel:[13]

I cannot say
Of any condition of human life "This is fixed,
This is clearly good, or bad." Fate raises up,
5   And Fate casts down the happy and unhappy alike:
No man can foretell his Fate.

Take the case of Creon:
Creon was happy once, as I count happiness:
Victorious in battle, sole governor of the land,
Fortunate father of children nobly born.
10   And now it has all gone from him! Who can say
That a man is still alive when his life's joy fails?
He is a walking dead man. Grant him rich,
Let him live like a king in his great house:
If his pleasure is gone, I would not give
15   So much as the shadow of smoke for all he owns.

CHORAGOS. Your words hint at sorrow: what is your news for us?

MESSENGER. They are dead. The living are guilty of their death.

CHORAGOS. Who is guilty? Who is dead? Speak!

MESSENGER.   Haimon.
Haimon is dead; and the hand that killed him
Is his own hand.

---

11. **Parnasos (pär na´ səs).** Mountain in central Greece sacred to Dionysos and Apollo
12. **Io (ē´ ō).** Greek for "Behold" or "Hail"
13. **Amphion's citadel (am fī´ ənz sit´ ə del).** Fortress built magically by the King of Thebes, who used a musical instrument to move the stones into place

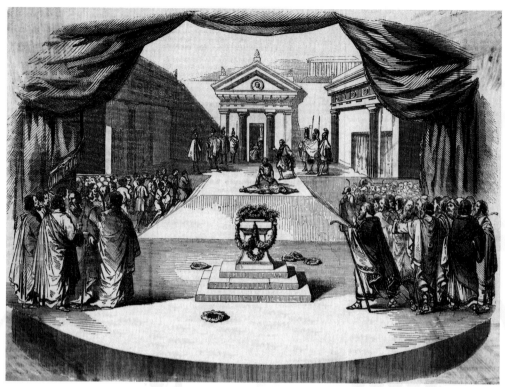

This woodcut shows the final scene of *Antigone*. Creon weeps over the body of his son, Haimon.

20   **CHORAGOS.**   His father's? or his own?

MESSENGER. His own, driven mad by the murder his father had
done.

CHORAGOS. Teiresias, Teiresias, how clearly you saw it all!

MESSENGER. This is my news: you must draw what conclusions
    you can from it.

CHORAGOS. But look: Eurydice, our Queen:
25   Has she overheard us?

[*Enter* EURYDICE *from the Palace, center.*]

EURYDICE. I have heard something, friends:
As I was unlocking the gate of Pallas'[14] shrine,
For I needed her help today, I heard a voice,
Telling of some new sorrow. And I fainted,
30   There at the temple with all my maidens about me.
But speak again: whatever it is, I can bear it:
Grief and I are no strangers.

---

14. **Pallas.** Pallas Athene, goddess of wisdom

MESSENGER.   Dearest Lady,
I will tell you plainly all that I have seen.
I shall not try to comfort you: what is the use,
35 Since comfort could lie only in what is not true?
The truth is always best.
                              I went with Creon
To the outer plain where Polyneices was lying,
No friend to pity him, his body shredded by dogs.
We made our prayers in that place to Hecate[15]
40 And Pluto,[16] that they would be merciful. And we bathed
The corpse with holy water, and we brought
Fresh-broken branches to burn what was left of it,
And upon the urn we heaped up a towering barrow
Of the earth of his own land.
                              When we were done, we ran
45 To the vault where Antigone lay on her couch of stone.
One of the servants had gone ahead,
And while he was yet far off he heard a voice
Grieving within the chamber, and he came back
And told Creon. And as the King went closer,
50 The air was full of wailing, the words lost,
And he begged us to make all haste. "Am I a prophet?"
He said, weeping, "And must I walk this road,
The saddest of all that I have gone before?
My son's voice calls me on. Oh quickly, quickly!
55 Look through the crevice there, and tell me
If it is Haimon, or some deception of the gods!"

We obeyed; and in the cavern's farthest corner
We saw her lying:
She had made a noose of her fine linen veil
60 And hanged herself. Haimon lay beside her,
His arms about her waist, lamenting her,
His love lost underground, crying out
That his father had stolen her away from him.

When Creon saw him the tears rushed to his eyes
65 And he called to him: "What have you done, child? Speak to me.
What are you thinking that makes your eyes so strange?
O my son, my son, I come to you on my knees!"
But Haimon spat in his face. He said not a word,
Staring—
                    And suddenly drew his sword
70 And lunged. Creon shrank back, the blade missed; and the boy,

---

15. **Hecate** (heˊ kə tē). A goddess of the underworld
16. **Pluto.** King of the underworld

Desperate against himself, drove it half its length
Into his own side, and fell. And as he died
He gathered Antigone close in his arms again,
Choking, his blood bright red on her white cheek.
75 And now he lies dead with the dead, and she is his
At last, his bride in the houses of the dead.

[*Exit* EURYDICE *into the Palace.*]

CHORAGOS. She has left us without a word. What can this mean?

MESSENGER. It troubles me, too; yet she knows what is best,
Her grief is too great for public lamentation,
80 And doubtless she has gone to her chamber to weep
For her dead son, leading her maidens in his dirge.

CHORAGOS. It may be so: but I fear this deep silence.

[*Pause*]

MESSENGER. I will see what she is doing. I will go in.

[*Exit* MESSENGER *into the Palace.*]

[*Enter* CREON *with attendants, bearing* HAIMON'S *body.*]

CHORAGOS. But here is the King himself: oh look at him,
85 Bearing his own damnation in his arms.

CREON. Nothing you say can touch me any more.
My own blind heart has brought me
From darkness to final darkness. Here you see
The father murdering, the murdered son—
90 And all my civic wisdom!

Haimon my son, so young, so young to die,
I was the fool, not you; and you died for me.

CHORAGOS. That is the truth; but you were late in learning it.

CREON. The truth is hard to bear. Surely a god
95 Has crushed me beneath the hugest weight of heaven,
And driven me headlong a barbaric way
To trample out the thing I held most dear.

The pains that men will take to come to pain!

[*Enter* MESSENGER *from the Palace.*]

MESSENGER. The burden you carry in your hands is heavy,
100 But it is not all: you will find more in your house.

CREON. What burden worse than this shall I find there?

MESSENGER. The Queen is dead.

CREON. O port of death, deaf world,
Is there no pity for me? And you, Angel of evil,
105 I was dead, and your words are death again.
Is it true, boy! Can it be true!
Is my wife dead? Has death bred death?

MESSENGER. You can see for yourself.

[*The doors are opened, and the body of* EURYDICE *is disclosed within.*]

CREON. Oh pity!
110 All true, all true, and more than I can bear!
O my wife, my son!

MESSENGER. She stood before the altar, and her heart
Welcomed the knife her own hand guided,
And a great cry burst from her lips for Megareus[17] dead,
115 And for Haimon dead, her sons; and her last breath
Was a curse for their father, the murderer of her sons.
And she fell, and the dark flowed in through her closing eyes.

CREON. O God, I am sick with fear.
Are there no swords here? Has no one a blow for me?

120 MESSENGER. Her curse is upon you for the deaths of both.

CREON. It is right that it should be. I alone am guilty.
I know it, and I say it. Lead me in,
Quickly, friends.
I have neither life nor substance. Lead me in.

125 CHORAGOS. You are right, if there can be right in so much wrong.
The briefest way is best in a world of sorrow.

CREON. Let it come,
Let death come quickly, and be kind to me.
I would not ever see the sun again.

130 CHORAGOS. All that will come when it will; but we, meanwhile,
Have much to do. Leave the future to itself.

CREON. All my heart was in that prayer!

CHORAGOS. Then do not pray any more: the sky is deaf.

CREON. Lead me away. I have been rash and foolish.
135 I have killed my son and my wife.
I look for comfort; my comfort lies here dead.
Whatever my hands have touched has come to nothing.

---

17. **Megareus (mə gaʹ rē əs).** Oldest son of Creon and Eurydice, killed in the civil war by Argive
forces invading Thebes

Fate has brought all my pride to a thought of dust.

[*As* CREON *is being led into the house, the* CHORAGOS *advances and speaks directly to the audience.*]

CHORAGOS. There is no happiness where there is no wisdom.
140   No wisdom but in submission to the gods.
Big words are always punished,
And proud men in old age learn to be wise. ❖

Is Creon malicious or evil, or is he just misguided? What character flaw brought about his own ruin and that of his family? What character flaws do you notice in world leaders today? Has anything about human nature changed since the time of Sophocles?

REFER TO TEXT ▶ ▶ ▶ ▶	▶ REASON WITH TEXT	
1a. State what Teiresias says happened when he began the rites of burnt-offering.	1b. Describe the events that finally persuade Creon to reverse his decision.	**Understand** Find meaning
2a. Recall what happens between Haimon and Creon in the tomb.	2b. Illustrate how the events at the end of the play affect Creon. What does he realize about himself?	**Apply** Use information
3a. Describe what happens to Antigone. What happens to Eurydice?	3b. Analyze the role of fate in *Antigone*. Which events do the characters blame on fate? List the events you think the characters brought upon themselves. Make a separate list of things the characters could not control.	**Analyze** Take things apart
4a. Name the person Teiresias blames for the calamity at the end of Scene 5.	4b. Put Creon on trial for his actions and assess his choices. What arguments would you use for the prosecution? How might you defend him?	**Evaluate** Make judgments
5a. Quote the final message of the Choragos.	5b. What message, if any, is there in this play for people today? Relate the issues presented in this play to your life, your community, or your country.	**Create** Bring ideas together

ANALYZE LITERATURE: Motif

A **motif** is any element that recurs in one or more works of literature or art. In literature, disturbances in nature commonly signify disorder in the political state. Identify lines in this scene that describe disorder in nature. What later events does this disorder foreshadow, or hint at?

Literature CONNECTION

Dahlia Ravikovitch (b. 1936) is considered one of Israel's greatest modern poets. Born in Ramat Gan, a town near Tel Aviv, Ravikovitch lived on a communal farm after her father died when she was six years old. After graduating from The Hebrew University, she worked as a journalist and a teacher. In addition to writing and publishing poetry, short stories, and children's books, Ravikovitch has translated several English works into Hebrew. Her poem **"Pride"** focuses on how fragile and vulnerable one's sense of pride can be.

Pride

A Poem by **Dahlia Ravikovitch**

Translated by Chana Bloch and Ariel Bloch

> I tell you, even rocks crack,
>
> and not because of age.
>
> For years they lie on their backs
>
> in the heat and the cold,
>
> 5   so many years,
>
> it almost seems peaceful.
>
> They don't move, so the cracks stay hidden.
>
> A kind of pride.
>
> Years pass over them, waiting.

10   Whoever is going to shatter them

hasn't come yet.

And so the moss flourishes, the seaweed

whips around,

the sea pushes through and rolls back—

15   the rocks seem motionless.

Till a little seal comes to rub against them,

comes and goes away.

And suddenly the rock has an open wound.

I told you, when rocks break, it happens by surprise.

20   And people, too. ❖

REFER TO TEXT ▷ ▷ ▷ ▶	▶ REASON WITH TEXT	
1a. List the qualities of rocks presented in the poem.	1b. Interpret how these qualities could also belong to the trait of pride. According to the poet, what qualities do rocks and pride share?	**Understand** **Find meaning**
2a. Describe the actions of the seal.	2b. Analyze the actions of the seal and identify the role the seal plays in the poem.	**Analyze** **Take things apart**
3a. Briefly summarize the description of pride in the poem.	3b. Explain whether you believe this description is more appropriate to Creon or to Antigone. Cite specific instances in the play that support your point.	**Create** **Bring ideas together**

TEXT ←TO→ TEXT CONNECTION

What message about people does the speaker convey by discussing rocks? How is the theme, or central idea, of this poem related to the theme of *Antigone?* Use quotations from both texts to support your answer.

EXTEND THE TEXT

Writing Options

Creative Writing Write a **monologue** that Creon might deliver to the people of Thebes at the end of the play. In the monologue, have Creon discuss his role in the tragedy. Try to remain true to Creon's character; in other words, make sure his way of dealing with the tragedy reflects his personality.

Expository Writing Imagine that a classmate says that he or she "just doesn't get this Greek tragedy thing." Write a one-page **literary analysis** for this classmate. In your analysis, explain what makes *Antigone* a tragic play. As part of your analysis, identify the tragic hero or heroes and the tragic flaw.

Collaborative Learning

Present a Dramatic Reading As a group, read *Antigone,* or portions of it, out loud, standing up for dramatic effect. Have a group of three or more students read the parts of the Chorus. What is the dramatic effect of hearing a group of people recite the same lines together? How is it different from hearing just one person speaking, or from reading it to yourself? Share your ideas with the group.

Media Literacy

Deliver an Expository Presentation Imagine that your class will film a performance of *Antigone*. To educate the cast and crew, research the Golden Age of Greece (477 BCE–431 BCE), a time when art, politics, drama, learning, and athleticism flourished. Select an area of focus and collect material from various sources. You might do an Internet search on Sophocles to find related information. Visit the library for picture books and videos on ancient Greece. Prepare and deliver a multimedia presentation that will help the cast and crew understand the historical context of the play.

 Go to **www.mirrorsandwindows.com** for more.

READING ASSESSMENT

1. Creon refuses to bury Polyneices because
   A. Polyneices is Antigone's brother.
   B. Polyneices insulted the gods.
   C. Polyneices killed his father and married his mother.
   D. Polyneices attacked Thebes.
   E. Polyneices refused to accept Creon's rule.

2. Who does Creon believe has committed the crime of burying Polyneices?
   A. anarchists
   B. the Sentry
   C. heretics
   D. sycophants
   E. hypocrites

3. Antigone refuses to share the blame with Ismene because
   A. Ismene knew nothing of the crime.
   B. Ismene is her sister.
   C. she doesn't want an innocent person to die.
   D. she thinks Ismene is entirely at fault.
   E. Ismene was too afraid to help her.

4. As used in line 17 of Ode IV, the word *wrath* most likely means
   A. hearth.
   B. passion.
   C. anger.
   D. jealousy.
   E. engine.

5. Of what does Creon accuse Haimon when Haimon tries to persuade him to pardon Antigone?
   A. being unreasonable
   B. profaning the gods
   C. having been bribed
   D. being a girlstruck fool
   E. None of the above

6. How is Creon's accusation of Teiresias similar to his accusation of Haimon, his own son, earlier in the play? Find the lines in the play that contain the accusations and explain how they are similar and why Creon thinks that way.

GRAMMAR & STYLE

Coordination, Subordination, and Apposition

A **clause** is a group of words that contains a subject and verb and that functions as one part of speech. An **independent clause** can stand alone as a sentence. A **coordinating conjunction** is a word used to join words, groups of words, or entire clauses of equal importance in one sentence. The most common coordinating conjunctions are *and, or, nor, for, but, yet,* and *so.*

EXAMPLES

Antigone buried her brother, <u>and</u> Creon found out.

Creon was angry with Antigone, <u>yet</u> Antigone did not back down.

A **subordinate clause** cannot stand alone; it must be attached to an independent clause. Subordinate clauses begin with subordinating conjunctions such as *after, although, because, if, unless,* and *while.* For example, "because she was proud" is a subordinate clause; it is not a complete sentence. Use subordinate clauses to combine short, choppy sentences and to add variety to your writing.

An **appositive** is a noun that is placed next to or near another noun to identify it, provide another name for it, or add information about it. An **appositive phrase** is a group of words that includes an appositive and other words that modify it, such as adjective and prepositional phrases.

EXAMPLE

Antigone, <u>Oedipus's daughter</u>, is a main character in the play. ("Oedipus's daughter" provides additional information for Antigone.)

Appositives come in two forms: *essential* (or *restrictive*) and *nonessential* (or *nonrestrictive*). If the information in an appositive impacts the meaning of the sentence by specifically identifying the noun that precedes it, then the appositive is essential and is not set off with commas. If the information in the appositive is not necessary to the meaning of the sentence, then it is called nonessential and is set off with commas.

EXAMPLES

essential: The drama <u>*Oedipus the King*</u> is famous the world over. (The appositive *Oedipus the King* specifically identifies which drama and thereby restricts the meaning of "drama" to this specific one.)

nonessential: *Oedipus the King*, <u>a drama by Sophocles</u>, is famous the world over. (The appositive "a drama by Sophocles" is not necessary to identify which particular drama, since it has already been named.)

REVIEW TERMS

- **clause:** a group of words that contains a subject and verb and that functions as one part of speech
- **independent clause:** a clause that can stand alone as a sentence
- **coordinating conjunction:** a word that links two equal phrases or sentences such as *and, or, nor, for, but, yet,* and *so*
- **subordinate clause:** a clause that cannot stand alone
- **subordinating conjunction:** a word such as *after, although, because, if, unless,* and *while*
- **appositive:** a noun that is placed next to or near another noun to identify it, provide another name for it, or add information about it
- **appositive phrase:** a group of words that includes an appositive and other words that modify it, such as adjective and prepositional phrases
- **essential/restrictive appositive:** an appositive that impacts the meaning of the sentence by specifically identifying the noun that precedes it; no commas are used
- **nonessential/nonrestrictive appositive:** an appositive that is not necessary to the meaning of the sentence; set off with commas

Identify Coordination, Subordination, and Apposition

In each of these sentences from *Antigone*, identify whether the sentence uses coordination, subordination, apposition, or a combination of the three. Note whether the appositives are essential or nonessential.

1. "Creon buried our brother Eteocles with military honors, gave him a soldier's funeral, and it was right that he should."
2. "You may do as you like, since apparently the laws of the gods mean nothing to you."
3. "Polyneices their commander roused them with windy phrases."
4. "Unfortunately, as you know, his two sons, the princes Eteocles and Polyneices, have killed each other in battle, and I, the next in blood, have succeeded to the full power of the throne."
5. "The flesh was soft by now, and stinking, so we sat on a hill to windward and kept guard."
6. "When this girl found the bare corpse, and all her love's work wasted, she wept."
7. "This death of mine is of no importance, but if I had left my brother lying in death unburied, I should have suffered."
8. "Unless time has rusted my wits, what you say, King, is said with point and dignity."
9. "If dirges and planned lamentations could put off death, men would be singing forever."
10. "You see me now, the last unhappy daughter of a line of kings, your kings, led away to death."

Fix Problems with Coordination, Subordination, and Apposition

Rewrite the following paragraph about *Antigone*, using coordination, subordination, and apposition with proper punctuation.

> Polyneices and Eteocles are brothers. They killed each other in battling over the leadership of the city. Whereas Eteocles defended Thebes. Polyneices attacked it. Creon is the new king in place of the brothers. He declares that anyone who buries Polyneices will be put to death. Antigone and her sister discuss whether or not they should violate Creon's decree. Her sister is Ismene. Despite Ismene's protests, Antigone buries Polyneices. And she is then captured and brought before Creon. Haimon is Creon's son who is engaged to marry Antigone. He tries to reason with his father. But Creon won't listen. The end result is that Antigone kills herself in her tomb. That happens before Haimon can save her. He then kills himself. And his mother kills herself. Creon's pride caused his downfall.

Use Coordination, Subordination, and Apposition in Your Writing

For a family scrapbook, write a description of a special day you spent with a family member. Use coordination, subordination, and apposition to link ideas, identify, and provide more information about your family member and the time you shared. Be sure to punctuate correctly.

EXTEND THE SKILL

Find a newspaper article about a crime or a trial. Underline where coordination, subordination, and apposition are used to describe and provide information about the topic. Compare this frequency with that of a fictional crime or law story. Make a copy of an excerpt from such a novel or short story that you have selected and review it in the same way you did the  article. What does such a comparison tell you about the appropriate writing style for each type of writing?

READING DRAMA INDEPENDENTLY
Theme: Between Friends

MRS. HALE. [Abruptly moving toward her.] *Mrs. Peters?*

MRS. PETERS. *Yes, Mrs. Hale?*

MRS. HALE. *Do you think she did it?*

MRS. PETERS. [In a frightened voice.] *Oh, I don't know.*

—from "Trifles" by Susan Glaspell

Friends are an extremely important part of people's lives. Even as people get older and change, their friendships often remain the same. Some friends come and go, but the truest friends are those who stick by not only in good times, but also in times of crisis. In the Independent Readings in this unit, friends who find themselves in challenging situations react in surprising ways. As you read, think about what you would do if you found yourself in the place of one of the characters.

USING READING SKILLS WITH DRAMA

Recognize the Sequence of Events

Sequence refers to the order in which things happen. When you read a drama, keep track of the sequence of events. You might do this by making a Time Line or Sequence Map.

- To make a Time Line, draw a line and divide it into equal parts. Label each part with a date or a time. Then add key events at the right places along the Time Line.
- To make a Sequence Map, draw a series of boxes. In each box, draw a picture that represents a key event in a selection. Then write a caption under each box that explains each event. Draw the events in the order in which they occur. Alternatively, write brief statements in the boxes about the major events. An example has been done for you based on *The Tragedy of Julius Caesar*.

Sequence Map

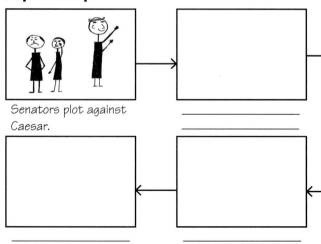

Senators plot against Caesar.

Identify Relationships

Understanding the relationships between characters and between ideas is important in getting the most out of the experience of reading drama. To keep track of the relationships between characters, it may help to make a family tree if the characters are related or a diagram with arrows making the connections if the characters are connected through other relationships. In dramas with many characters, such as Shakespearean plays, understanding these relationships can help explain the characters' actions.

To keep track of the relationships between ideas or parts of the text, you could evaluate cause and effect. When you evaluate cause and effect, you are looking for a logical relationship between an event or events and one or more results. A graphic organizer like the one below will help you to recognize relationships between causes and effects. An example has been done for you from the play *Antigone*.

Cause-and-Effect Chart

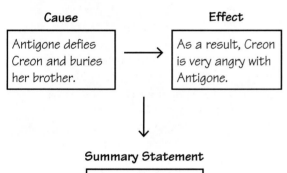

Cause	Effect
Antigone defies Creon and buries her brother.	As a result, Creon is very angry with Antigone.

Summary Statement

When Antigone chooses to disobey Creon, she puts her own life in danger.

Understand Literary Elements

Drama is different than prose because it relies on elements like dialogue and stage directions to create setting and characters. In prose, a narrator can describe a setting or a character's thoughts, but in drama, stage directions describe setting, and characters only reveal their thoughts through dialogue. While both prose and drama have plots, to figure out the plot in a drama, you need to pay attention to the lines the characters speak. As you read, look for ways the different elements work together to tell a story.

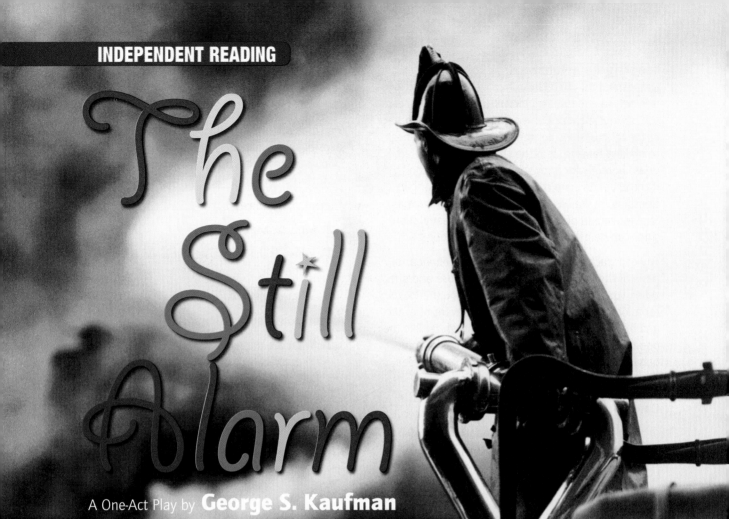

The Still Alarm

A One-Act Play by **George S. Kaufman**

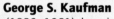

George S. Kaufman (1889–1961), born in Pittsburgh, Pennsylvania, was a celebrated playwright, director, and drama critic. **"The Still Alarm"** is a sketch from George S. Kaufman's musical revue *The Little Show*. A *revue* is a theater show of several short, humorous skits that are loosely connected. The comedy in "The Still Alarm" lies in the unusual behavior of the characters. In fact, the "Vital Note" at the beginning of the play gives the most important stage direction—the play is to be acted calmly and politely.

Calm and polite behavior is generally recommended and praised, but when is it not expected or appropriate?

[VITAL NOTE. *It is important that the entire play should be acted calmly and politely, in the manner of an English drawing-room comedy. No actor ever raises his voice; every line must be read as though it were an invitation to a cup of tea. If this direction is disregarded, the play has no point at all.*]

The scene is a hotel bedroom. Two windows in the rear wall with a bed between them. A telephone stand is at one end of the bed and a dresser is near the other. In the right wall is a door leading to the hall with a chair nearby. In the left wall is a door to another room; near it is a small table and two chairs.

ED *and* BOB *are on the stage.* ED *is getting into his overcoat as the curtain rises. Both are at the hall door.*

ED. Well, Bob, it's certainly been nice to see you again.

BOB. It was nice to see *you.*

ED. You come to town so seldom, I hardly ever get the chance to—

BOB. Well, you know how it is. A business trip is always more or less of a bore.

ED. Next time you've got to come out to the house.

BOB. I want to come out. I just had to stick around the hotel this trip.

ED. Oh, I understand. Well, give my best to Edith.

BOB. [*Remembering something.*] Oh, I say, Ed. Wait a minute.

ED. What's the matter?

BOB. I knew I wanted to show you something. [*Crosses to table. Gets roll of blueprints from drawer.*] Did you know I'm going to build?

ED. [*Follows to table.*] A house?

BOB. You bet it's a house! [*Knock on hall door.*] Come in! [*Spreads plans.*] I just got these yesterday.

ED. [*Sits.*] Well, that's fine! [*The knock is repeated—louder. Both men now give full attention to the door.*]

BOB. Come! Come in!

BELLBOY. [*Enters.*] Mr. Barclay?

BOB. Well?

BELLBOY. I've a message from the clerk, sir. For Mr. Barclay personally.

BOB. [*Crosses to boy.*] I'm Mr. Barclay. What is the message?

BELLBOY. The hotel is on fire, sir.

BOB. What's that?

BELLBOY. The hotel is on fire.

ED. This hotel?

BELLBOY. Yes, sir.

BOB. Well—is it bad?

BELLBOY. It looks pretty bad, sir.

ED. You mean it's going to burn down?

BELLBOY. We think so—yes, sir.

BOB. [*A low whistle of surprise.*] Well! We'd better leave.

BELLBOY. Yes, sir.

BOB. Going to burn down, huh?

BELLBOY. Yes, sir. If you'll step to the window you'll see.

[BOB *goes to a window.*]

BOB. Yes, that is pretty bad. H'm [*To* ED.] I say, you really ought to see this—

ED. [*Crosses to window, peers out.*] It's reached the floor right underneath.

BELLBOY. Yes, sir. The lower part of the hotel is about gone, sir.

BOB. [*Still looking out—looks up.*] Still all right up above, though. [*Turns to boy.*] Have they notified the Fire Department?

BELLBOY. I wouldn't know, sir. I'm only the bellboy.

BOB. Well, that's the thing to do, obviously [*Nods head to each one as if the previous line was a bright idea.*] notify the Fire Department. Just call them up, give them the name of the hotel—

ED. Wait a minute. I can do better than that for you. [*To the boy.*] Ring through to the Chief, and tell him that Ed Jamison told you to telephone him. [*To* BOB.] We went to school together, you know.

BOB. That's fine. [*To the boy.*] Now, get that right. Tell the Chief that Mr. Jamison said to ring him.

ED. *Ed* Jamison.

BOB. Yes, *Ed* Jamison.

BELLBOY. Yes, sir. [*Turns to go.*]

BOB. Oh! Boy! [*Pulls out handful of change; picks out a coin.*] Here you are.

BELLBOY. Thank you, sir. [*Exit* BELLBOY.]

[ED *sits at table, lights cigarette, and throws match on rug, then steps on it. There is a moment's pause.*]

BOB. Well! [*Crosses and looks out window.*] Say, we'll have to get out of here pretty soon.

ED. [*Going to window.*] How is it—no better?

BOB. Worse, if anything. It'll be up here in a few moments.

ED. What floor *is* this?

Bob. Eleventh.

Ed. Eleven. We couldn't jump, then.

Bob. Oh, no. You never could jump. [*Comes away from window to dresser.*] Well. I've got to get my things together. [*Pulls out suitcase.*]

Ed. [*Smoothing out the plans.*] Who made these for you?

Bob. A fellow here—Rawlins. [*Turns a shirt in his hand.*] I ought to call one of the other hotels for a room.

Ed. Oh, you can get in.

Bob. They're pretty crowded. [*Feels something on the sole of his foot; inspects it.*] Say, the floor's getting hot.

Ed. I know it. It's getting stuffy in the room, too. Phew! [*He looks around, then goes to the phone.*] Hello. Ice water in eleven eighteen. [*Crosses to table.*]

Bob. [*At bed.*] That's the stuff. [*Packs.*] You know, if I move to another hotel I'll never get my mail. Everybody thinks I'm stopping here.

Ed. [*Studying the plans.*] Say, this isn't bad.

Bob. [*Eagerly.*] Do you like it? [*Remembers his plight.*] Suppose I go to another hotel and there's a fire there, too!

Ed. You've got to take *some* chance.

Bob. I know, but here I'm sure. [*Phone rings.*] Oh, answer that, will you, Ed? [*To dresser and back.*]

Ed. [*Crosses to phone.*] Sure. [*At phone.*] Hello— Oh, that's good. Fine. What? Oh! Well, wait a minute. [*To* Bob.] The firemen are downstairs and some of them want to come up to this room.

Bob. Tell them, of course.

Ed. [*At phone.*] All right. Come right up. [*Hangs up, crosses and sits at table.*] Now we'll get some action.

Bob. [*Looks out of window.*] Say, there's an awful crowd of people on the street.

Ed. [*Absently, as he pores over the plans.*] Maybe there's been some kind of accident.

Bob. [*Peering out, suitcase in hand.*] No. More likely they heard about the fire. [*A knock at the door.*] Come in.

Bellboy. [*Enters.*] I beg pardon, Mr. Barclay, the firemen have arrived.

Bob. Show them in. [*Crosses to door.*]

[*The door opens. In the doorway appear two* Firemen *in full regalia. The* First Fireman *carries a hose and rubber coat; the* Second *has a violin case.*]

First Fireman. [*Very apologetically.*] Mr. Barclay.

Bob. I'm Mr. Barclay.

First Fireman. We're the firemen, Mr. Barclay. [*They remove their hats.*]

Bob. How de do?

Ed. How de do?

Bob. A great pleasure, I assure you. Really must apologize for the condition of this room, but—

First Fireman. Oh, that's all right. I know how it is at home.

Bob. May I present a friend of mine, Mr. Ed Jamison—

First Fireman. How are you?

Ed. How are you, boys? [Second Fireman *nods.*] I know your Chief.

First Fireman. Oh, is that so? He knows the Chief—dear old Chiefie. [Second Fireman *giggles.*]

Bob. [*Embarrassed.*] Well, I guess you boys want to get to work, don't you?

First Fireman. Well, if you don't mind. We would like to spray around a little bit.

Bob. May I help you?

First Fireman. Yes, if you please. [Bob *helps him into his rubber coat. At the same time the* Second Fireman, *without a word, lays the violin case on the bed, opens it, takes out the violin, and begins tuning it.*]

Bob. [*Watching him.*] I don't think I understand.

First Fireman. Well, you see, Sid doesn't get much chance to practice at home. Sometimes, at a fire, while we're waiting for a wall to fall or something, why, a fireman doesn't really have anything to do, and personally I like to see him improve himself symphonically. I hope you don't resent it. You're not antisymphonic?

Bob. Of course not— [Bob *and* Ed *nod understandingly; the* Second Fireman *is now waxing the bow.*]

It's pretty bad right now. This wall will go pretty soon now, but it'll fall out that way, so it's all right.

FIRST FIREMAN. Well, if you'll excuse me—[*To window. Turns with decision toward the window. You feel that he is about to get down to business.*]

BOB. Charming personalities.

ED. [*Follows over to the window.*] How is the fire?

FIRST FIREMAN. [*Feels the wall.*] It's pretty bad right now. This wall will go pretty soon now, but it'll fall out that way, so it's all right. [*Peers out.*] That next room is the place to fight it from. [*Crosses to door in left wall.* BOB *shows ties as* ED *crosses.*]

ED. [*Sees ties.*] Oh! Aren't those gorgeous!

FIRST FIREMAN. [*To* BOB.] Have you the key for this room?

BOB. Why, no. I've nothing to do with that room. I've just got this one. [*Folding a shirt as he talks.*]

ED. Oh, it's very comfortable.

FIRST FIREMAN. That's too bad. I had something up my sleeve, if I could have gotten in there. Oh, well, may I use your phone?

BOB. Please do. [*To* ED.] Do you think you might hold this? [*Indicates the hose.*]

ED. How?

FIRST FIREMAN. Just crawl under it. [*As he does that.*] Thanks. [*At phone.*] Hello. Let me have the clerk, please. [*To* SECOND FIREMAN.] Give us that little thing you played the night the Equitable Building burned down. [*Back to phone.*] Are you there? This is one of the firemen. Oh, *you* know. I'm in room—ah— [*Looks at* BOB.]

BOB. Eleven eighteen.

FIRST FIREMAN. Eleven eighteen, and I want to get into the next room— Oh, goody. Will you send someone up with the key? There's no one in there? Oh, supergoody! Right away. [*Hangs up.*]

BOB. That's fine. [*To* FIREMEN.] Won't you sit down?

FIRST FIREMAN. Thanks.

Ed. Have a cigar?

First Fireman. [*Takes it.*] Much obliged.

Bob. A light?

First Fireman. If you please.

Ed. [*Failing to find a match.*] Bob, have you a match?

Bob. [*Crosses to table.*] I thought there were some here. [*Hands in pockets.*]

First Fireman. Oh, never mind. [*He goes to a window, leans out, and emerges with cigar lighted.* Bob *crosses to dresser; slams drawer. The* Second Fireman *taps violin with bow.*]

First Fireman. Mr. Barclay, I think he's ready now.

Bob. Pardon me.

[*They all sit. The* Second Fireman *takes center of stage, with all the manner of a concert violinist. He goes into "Keep the Home Fires Burning."* Bob, Ed *and* First Fireman *wipe brow as lights dim to red on closing eight bars.*] ❖

Out of all the strange ways people are behaving in this play, which behavior do you think is the strangest? Have you heard of or actually witnessed people acting this way? What was the situation? What message about society do you think Kaufman is trying to get across?

Refer and Reason

1. Find a quotation that explains what Bob thinks is the proper thing to do after being informed of the fire. Analyze why Ed thinks it is important for the Fire Chief to know that Ed Jamison said to call.
2. Identify three ways in which the characters behave during the fire. Evaluate the characters' behavior. Why do you think Kaufman has them act this way?
3. Describe what Bob, Ed, and the firemen are doing at the end of the play. Explain how the effect of this play would be different if the characters acted with an emotion other than calm indifference. Choose a new emotion and suggest how that emotion would alter the play's performance.

Writing Options

1. Write your own one-act play that highlights unexpected and atypical behavior under particular circumstances. The situation can be simple, such as shopping for groceries, or it can be frightening, such as being onboard an airplane with engine trouble. Choose the tone you want to set for the play. Describe how the stage is set and how the actors are supposed to deliver their lines.
2. Imagine you are the bellboy at the hotel, and you survived the fire. Write a one-page personal narrative about your experience with Bob and Ed. You'll have to use your imagination, as not much information is given about the bellboy.

 Go to **www.mirrorsandwindows.com** for more.

Trifles

A One-Act Play by **Susan Glaspell**

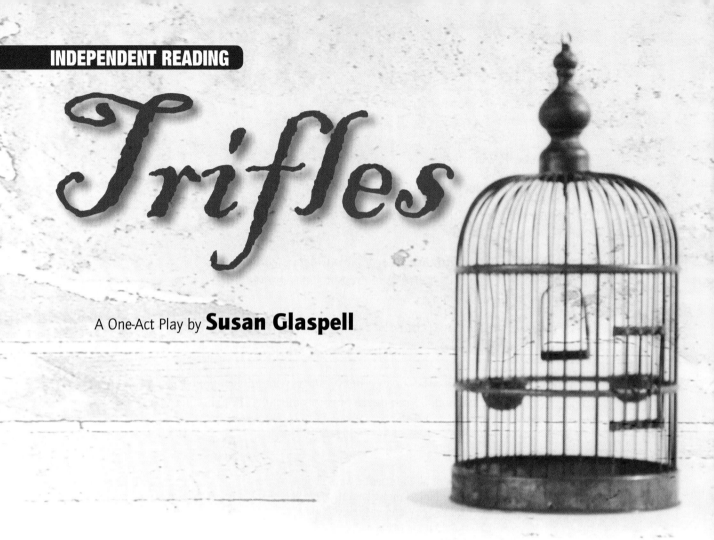

Susan Glaspell (1876–1948) was born in Davenport, Iowa. After graduating from Drake University, she worked for a time as a reporter for the *Des Moines Daily News.* Her short play **"Trifles"** was based on a murder trial she covered for the newspaper. After marrying playwright and novelist George Cram Cook, Glaspell moved to Provincetown, Massachusetts, where the couple founded the Provincetown Players, an influential theater group that helped launch the career of playwright Eugene O'Neill. In 1931, Glaspell won a Pulitzer Prize for her play *Alison's House*, after which she wrote no more plays. Glaspell's work is noted for its Midwestern regionalism and concern with women's issues, such as women's struggle against patriarchy.

SCENE. *The kitchen in the now abandoned farmhouse of John Wright, a gloomy kitchen, and left without having been put in order—unwashed pans under the sink, a loaf of bread outside the bread-box, a dish-towel on the table—other signs of incompleted work. At the rear the outer door opens and the* SHERIFF *comes in followed by the* COUNTY ATTORNEY *and* HALE. *The* SHERIFF *and* HALE *are men in middle life, the* COUNTY ATTORNEY *is a young man; all are much bundled up and go at once to the stove. They are followed by the two women—the* SHERIFF's *wife first; she is a slight wiry woman, a thin nervous face.* MRS. HALE *is larger and would ordinarily be called more comfortable looking, but she is disturbed now and looks fearfully about as she enters. The women have come in slowly, and stand close together near the door.*

COUNTY ATTORNEY. [*Rubbing his hands.*] This feels good. Come up to the fire, ladies.

MRS. PETERS. [*After taking a step forward.*] I'm not—cold.

SHERIFF. [*Unbuttoning his overcoat and stepping away from the stove as if to mark the beginning of official business.*] Now, Mr. Hale, before we move things about, you explain to Mr. Henderson just what you saw when you came here yesterday morning.

COUNTY ATTORNEY. By the way, has anything been moved? Are things just as you left them yesterday?

SHERIFF. [*Looking about.*] It's just the same. When it dropped below zero last night I thought I'd better send Frank out this morning to make a fire for us—no use getting pneumonia with a big case on, but I told him not to touch anything except the stove—and you know Frank.

COUNTY ATTORNEY. Somebody should have been left here yesterday.

SHERIFF. Oh—yesterday. When I had to send Frank to Morris Center for that man who went crazy—I want you to know I had my hands full yesterday. I knew you could get back from Omaha by today and as long as I went over everything here myself—

COUNTY ATTORNEY. Well, Mr. Hale, tell just what happened when you came here yesterday morning.

HALE. Harry and I had started to town with a load of potatoes. We came along the road from my place and as I got here I said, "I'm going to see if I can't get John Wright to go in with me on a party telephone." I spoke to Wright about it once before and he put me off, saying folks talked too much anyway, and all he asked was peace and quiet—I guess you know about how much he talked himself; but I thought maybe if I went to the house and talked about it before his wife, though I said to Harry that I didn't know as what his wife wanted made much difference to John—

COUNTY ATTORNEY. Let's talk about that later, Mr. Hale. I do want to talk about that, but tell now just what happened when you got to the house.

HALE. I didn't hear or see anything; I knocked at the door, and still it was all quiet inside. I knew they must be up, it was past eight o'clock. So I knocked again, and I thought I heard somebody say, "Come in." I wasn't sure. I'm not sure yet, but I opened the door—this door [*Indicating the door by which the two women are still standing.*] and there in that rocker—[*Pointing to it.*] sat Mrs. Wright.

[*They all look at the rocker.*]

COUNTY ATTORNEY. What—was she doing?

HALE. She was rockin' back and forth. She had her apron in her hand and was kind of—pleating it.

COUNTY ATTORNEY. And how did she—look?

HALE. Well, she looked queer.

COUNTY ATTORNEY. How do you mean—queer?

HALE. Well, as if she didn't know what she was going to do next. And kind of done up.

COUNTY ATTORNEY. How did she seem to feel about your coming?

HALE. Why, I don't think she minded—one way or other. She didn't pay much attention. I said, "How do, Mrs. Wright, it's cold, ain't it?" And she said, "Is it?"—and went on kind of pleating at her apron. Well, I was surprised: she didn't ask me to come up to the stove, or to set down, but just sat there, not even looking at me, so I said, "I want to see John." And then she—laughed. I guess you would call it a laugh. I thought of Harry and the team outside, so I said a little sharp: "Can't I see John?" "No," she says, kind o' dull like. "Ain't he home?" says I. "Yes," says she, "he's home." "Then why can't I see him?" I asked her, out of patience. "Cause he's dead," says she. "*Dead?*" says I. She just nodded her head, not getting a bit excited, but rockin' back and forth. "Why—where is he?" says I, not knowing what to say. She just pointed upstairs—like that. [*Himself pointing to the room above.*] I got up, with the idea of going up there. I walked from there to here—then I says, "Why, what did he die of?" "He died of a rope round his neck," says she, and just went on pleatin' at her apron. Well, I went out and called Harry. I thought I might—need help. We went upstairs and there he was lyin'—

COUNTY ATTORNEY. I think I'd rather have you go into that upstairs, where you can point it all out. Just go on now with the rest of the story.

HALE. Well, my first thought was to get that rope off. It looked…[*Stops, his face twitches.*]…but Harry, he went up to him, and he said, "No, he's dead all right, and we'd better not touch anything." So we went back downstairs. She was still sitting that same way. "Has anybody been notified?" I asked. "No," says she, unconcerned. "Who did this, Mrs. Wright?" said Harry. He said it business-like—and she stopped pleatin' of her apron. "I don't know," she says. "You don't *know?*" says Harry. "No," says she. "Weren't you sleepin' in the bed with him?" says Harry. "Yes," says she, "but I was on the inside." "Somebody slipped a rope round his neck and strangled him and you didn't wake up?" says Harry. "I didn't wake up," she said after him. We must 'a looked as if we didn't see how that could be, for after a minute she said, "I sleep sound." Harry was going to ask her more questions but I said maybe we ought to let her tell her story first to the coroner, or the sheriff, so Harry went fast as he could to Rivers' place, where there's a telephone.

COUNTY ATTORNEY. And what did Mrs. Wright do when she knew that you had gone for the coroner?

HALE. She moved from that chair to this one over here [*Pointing to a small chair in the corner.*] and just sat there with her hands held together and looking down. I got a feeling that I ought to make some conversation, so I said I had come in to see if John wanted to put in a telephone, and at that she started to laugh, and then she stopped and looked at me—scared. [*The* COUNTY ATTORNEY, *who has had his notebook out, makes a note.*] I dunno, maybe it wasn't scared. I wouldn't like to say it was. Soon Harry got back, and then Dr. Lloyd came, and you, Mr. Peters, and so I guess that's all I know that you don't.

COUNTY ATTORNEY. [*Looking around.*] I guess we'll go upstairs first—and then out to the barn and around there. [*To the* SHERIFF.] You're convinced that there was nothing important here—nothing that would point to any motive.

SHERIFF. Nothing here but kitchen things.

[*The* COUNTY ATTORNEY, *after again looking around the kitchen, opens the door of a cupboard closet. He gets up on a chair and looks on a shelf. Pulls his hand away, sticky.*]

COUNTY ATTORNEY. Here's a nice mess.

[*The women draw nearer.*]

MRS. PETERS. [*To the other woman.*] Oh, her fruit; it did freeze. [*To the Lawyer.*] She worried about that when it turned so cold. She said the fire'd go out and her jars would break.

SHERIFF. Well, can you beat the women! Held for murder and worryin' about her preserves.

COUNTY ATTORNEY. I guess before we're through she may have something more serious than preserves to worry about.

HALE. Well, women are used to worrying over trifles.

[*The two women move a little closer together.*]

COUNTY ATTORNEY. [*With the gallantry of a young politician.*] And yet, for all their worries, what would we do without the ladies? [*The women do not unbend. He goes to the sink, takes a dipperful of water from the pail and pouring it into a basin, washes his hands. Starts to wipe them on the roller-towel, turns it for a cleaner place.*] Dirty towels! [*Kicks his foot against the pans under the sink.*] Not much of a housekeeper, would you say, ladies?

MRS. HALE. [*Stiffly.*] There's a great deal of work to be done on a farm.

COUNTY ATTORNEY. To be sure. And yet [*With a little bow to her.*] I know there are some Dickson county farmhouses which do not have such roller towels.

[*He gives it a pull to expose its length again.*]

MRS. HALE. Those towels get dirty awful quick. Men's hands aren't always as clean as they might be.

COUNTY ATTORNEY. Ah, loyal to your sex, I see. But you and Mrs. Wright were neighbors. I suppose you were friends, too.

MRS. HALE. [*Shaking her head.*] I've not seen much of her of late years. I've not been in this house—it's more than a year.

COUNTY ATTORNEY. And why was that? You didn't like her?

MRS. HALE. I liked her all well enough. Farmers' wives have their hands full, Mr. Henderson. And then—

COUNTY ATTORNEY. Yes—?

MRS. HALE. [*Looking about.*] It never seemed a very cheerful place.

COUNTY ATTORNEY. No—it's not cheerful. I shouldn't say she had the homemaking instinct.

MRS. HALE. Well, I don't know as Wright had, either.

COUNTY ATTORNEY. You mean that they didn't get on very well?

MRS. HALE. No. I don't mean anything. But I don't think a place'd be any cheerfuller for John Wright's being in it.

COUNTY ATTORNEY. I'd like to talk more of that a little later. I want to get the lay of things upstairs now.

[*He goes to the left, where three steps lead to a stair door.*]

SHERIFF. I suppose anything Mrs. Peters does'll be all right. She was to take in some clothes for her, you know, and a few little things. We left in such a hurry yesterday.

COUNTY ATTORNEY. Yes, but I would like to see what you take, Mrs. Peters, and keep an eye out for anything that might be of use to us.

MRS. PETERS. Yes, Mr. Henderson.

[*The women listen to the men's steps on the stairs, then look about the kitchen.*]

MRS. HALE. I'd hate to have men coming into my kitchen, snooping around and criticising.

[*She arranges the pans under sink which the Lawyer had shoved out of place.*]

MRS. PETERS. Of course it's no more than their duty.

MRS. HALE. Duty's all right, but I guess that deputy sheriff that came out to make the fire might have got a little of this on. [*Gives the roller towel a pull.*] Wish I'd thought of that sooner. Seems mean to talk about her for not having things slicked up when she had to come away in such a hurry.

MRS. PETERS. [*Who has gone to a small table in the left rear corner of the room, and lifted one end of a towel that covers a pan.*] She had bread set.

[*Stands still.*]

MRS. HALE. [*Eyes fixed on a loaf of bread beside the bread-box, which is on a low shelf at the other side of the room. Moves slowly toward it.*] She was going to put this in there. [*Picks up loaf, then abruptly drops it. In a manner of returning to familiar things.*] It's a shame about her fruit. I wonder if it's all gone. [*Gets up on the chair and looks.*] I think there's some here that's all right, Mrs. Peters. Yes—here; [*Holding it toward the window.*] this is cherries, too. [*Looking again.*] I declare I believe that's the only one. [*Gets down, bottle in her hand. Goes to the sink and wipes it off on the outside.*] She'll feel awful bad after all her hard work in the hot weather. I remember the afternoon I put up my cherries last summer.

[*She puts the bottle on the big kitchen table, center of the room. With a sigh, is about to sit down in the rocking-chair. Before she is seated realizes what chair it is; with a slow look at it, steps back. The chair which she has touched rocks back and forth.*]

MRS. PETERS. Well, I must get those things from the front room closet. [*She goes to the door at the right, but after looking into the other room, steps back.*] You coming with me, Mrs. Hale? You could help me carry them.

[*They go in the other room; reappear, MRS. PETERS carrying a dress and skirt, MRS. HALE following with a pair of shoes.*]

MRS. PETERS. My, it's cold in there.

[*She puts the clothes on the big table and hurries to the stove.*]

MRS. HALE. [*Examining the skirt.*] Wright was close. I think maybe that's why she kept so much to herself. She didn't even belong to the Ladies Aid. I suppose she felt she couldn't do her part, and then you don't enjoy things when you feel shabby. She used to wear pretty clothes and be lively, when she was Minnie Foster, one of the town girls singing in the choir. But that— oh, that was thirty years ago. This all you was to take in?

MRS. PETERS. She said she wanted an apron. Funny thing to want, for there isn't much to get you dirty in jail, goodness knows. But I suppose just to make her feel more natural. She said they was in the top drawer in this cupboard. Yes, here. And then her little shawl that always hung behind the door. [*Opens stair door and looks.*] Yes, here it is.

[*Quickly shuts door leading upstairs.*]

MRS. HALE. [*Abruptly moving toward her.*] Mrs. Peters?

MRS. PETERS. Yes, Mrs. Hale?

MRS. HALE. Do you think she did it?

MRS. PETERS. [*In a frightened voice.*] Oh, I don't know.

MRS. HALE. Well, I don't think she did. Asking for an apron and her little shawl. Worrying about her fruit.

MRS. PETERS. [*Starts to speak, glances up, where footsteps are heard in the room above. In a low voice.*] Mr. Peters says it looks bad for her. Mr. Henderson is awful sarcastic in a speech and he'll make fun of her sayin' she didn't wake up.

MRS. HALE. Well, I guess John Wright didn't wake when they was slipping that rope under his neck.

MRS. PETERS. No, it's strange. It must have been done awful crafty and still. They say it was such a—funny way to kill a man, rigging it all up like that.

MRS. HALE. That's just what Mr. Hale said. There was a gun in the house. He says that's what he can't understand.

MRS. PETERS. Mr. Henderson said coming out that what was needed for the case was a motive; something to show anger, or—sudden feeling.

MRS. HALE. [*Who is standing by the table.*] Well, I don't see any signs of anger around here. [*She puts her hand on the dish-towel which lies on the table, stands looking down at table, one half of which is clean, the other half messy.*] It's wiped to here. [*Makes a move as if to finish work, then turns and looks at loaf of bread outside the bread-box. Drops towel. In that voice of coming back to familiar things.*] Wonder how they are finding things upstairs. I hope she had it a little more red-up up there. You know, it seems kind of *sneaking*. Locking her up in town and then coming out here and trying to get her own house to turn against her!

MRS. PETERS. But Mrs. Hale, the law is the law.

MRS. HALE. I s'pose 'tis. [*Unbuttoning her coat.*] Better loosen up your things, Mrs. Peters. You won't feel them when you go out.

[MRS. PETERS *takes off her fur tippet, goes to hang it on hook at back of room, stands looking at the under part of the small corner table.*]

MRS. PETERS. She was piecing a quilt.

[*She brings the large serving basket and they look at the bright pieces.*]

MRS. HALE. It's log cabin pattern. Pretty, isn't it? I wonder if she was goin' to quilt it or just knot it?

[*Footsteps have been heard coming down the stairs. The* SHERIFF *enters followed by* HALE *and the* COUNTY ATTORNEY.]

SHERIFF. They wonder if she was going to quilt it or just knot it!

[*The men laugh, the women look abashed.*]

COUNTY ATTORNEY. [*Rubbing his hands over the stove.*] Frank's fire didn't do much up there, did it? Well, let's go out to the barn and get that cleared up.

[*The men go outside.*]

MRS. HALE. [*Resentfully.*] I don't know as there's anything so strange, our takin' up our time with little things while we're waiting for them to get the evidence. [*She sits down at the big table smoothing out a block with decision.*] I don't see as it's anything to laugh about.

MRS. PETERS. [*Apologetically.*] Of course they've got awful important things on their minds.

[*Pulls up a chair and joins* MRS. HALE *at the table.*]

MRS. HALE. [*Examining another block.*] Mrs. Peters, look at this one. Here, this is the one she was working on, and look at the sewing! All the rest of it has been so nice and even. And look at this! It's all over the place! Why, it looks as if she didn't know what she was about!

[*After she had said this they look at each other, then start to glance back at the door. After an instant* Mrs. Hale *has pulled at a knot and ripped the sewing.*]

Mrs. Peters. Oh, what are you doing, Mrs. Hale?

Mrs. Hale. [*Mildly.*] Just pulling out a stitch or two that's not sewed very good. [*Threading a needle.*] Bad sewing always made me fidgety.

Mrs. Peters. [*Nervously.*] I don't think we ought to touch things.

Mrs. Hale. I'll just finish up this end. [*Suddenly stopping and leaning forward.*] Mrs. Peters?

Mrs. Peters. Yes, Mrs. Hale?

Mrs. Hale. What do you suppose she was so nervous about?

Mrs. Peters. Oh—I don't know. I don't know as she was nervous. I sometimes sew awful queer when I'm just tired. [Mrs. Hale *starts to say something, looks at* Mrs. Peters, *then goes on sewing.*] Well I must get these things wrapped up. They may be through sooner than we think. [*Putting apron and other things together.*] I wonder where I can find a piece of paper, and string.

Mrs. Hale. In that cupboard, maybe.

Mrs. Peters. [*Looking in cupboard.*] Why, here's a bird-cage. [*Holds it up.*] Did she have a bird, Mrs. Hale?

Mrs. Hale. Why, I don't know whether she did or not—I've not been here for so long. There was a man around last year selling canaries cheap, but I don't know as she took one; maybe she did. She used to sing real pretty herself.

Mrs. Peters. [*Glancing around.*] Seems funny to think of a bird here. But she must have had one, or why would she have a cage? I wonder what happened to it.

Mrs. Hale. I s'pose maybe the cat got it.

Mrs. Peters. No, she didn't have a cat. She's got that feeling some people have about cats—being afraid of them. My cat got in her room and she was real upset and asked me to take it out.

Mrs. Hale. My sister Bessie was like that. Queer, ain't it?

Mrs. Peters. [*Examining the cage.*] Why, look at this door. It's broke. One hinge is pulled apart.

Mrs. Hale. [*Looking too.*] Looks as if someone must have been rough with it.

Mrs. Peters. Why, yes.

[*She brings the cage forward and puts it on the table.*]

Winter Landscape, 1920. Stanley Royle. Private collection. The Bridgeman Art Library International.

MRS. HALE. I wish if they're going to find any evidence they'd be about it. I don't like this place.

MRS. PETERS. But I'm awful glad you came with me, Mrs. Hale. It would be lonesome for me sitting here alone.

MRS. HALE. It would, wouldn't it? [*Dropping her sewing.*] But I tell you what I do wish, Mrs. Peters. I wish I had come over sometimes when *she* was here. I—[*Looking around the room.*]—wish I had.

MRS. PETERS. But of course you were awful busy, Mrs. Hale—your house and your children.

MRS. HALE. I could've come. I stayed away because it weren't cheerful—and that's why I ought to have come. I—I've never liked this place. Maybe because it's down in a hollow and you don't see the road. I dunno what it is, but it's a lonesome place and always was. I wish I had come over to see Minnie Foster sometimes. I can see now—[*Shakes her head.*]

MRS. PETERS. Well, you mustn't reproach yourself, Mrs. Hale. Somehow we just don't see how it is with other folks until—something comes up.

"But, Mrs. Peters—look at it! Its neck! Look at its neck! It's all—to the other side."

MRS. HALE.
Not having children
makes less work—but it makes a
quiet house, and Wright out to work all day, and no
company when he did come in. Did you know John Wright, Mrs. Peters?

MRS. PETERS. Not to know him; I've seen him in town. They say he was a good man.

MRS. HALE. Yes—good; he didn't drink, and kept his word as well as most, I guess, and paid his debts. But he was a hard man, Mrs. Peters. Just to pass the time of day with him—[*Shivers.*] Like a raw wind that gets to the bone. [*Pauses, her eye falling on the cage.*] I should think she would a wanted a bird. But what do you suppose went with it?

MRS. PETERS. I don't know, unless it got sick and died.

[*She reaches over and swings the broken door, swings it again, both women watch it.*]

MRS. HALE. You weren't raised round here, were you? [Mrs. Peters *shakes her head.*] You didn't know—her?

MRS. PETERS. Not till they brought her yesterday.

MRS. HALE. She—come to think of it, she was kind of like a bird herself—real sweet and pretty, but kind of timid and—fluttery. How—she—did—change. [*Silence; then as if struck by a happy thought and relieved to get back to everyday things.*] Tell you what, Mrs. Peters, why don't you take the quilt in with you? It might take up her mind.

MRS. PETERS. Why, I think that's a real nice idea, Mrs. Hale. There couldn't possibly be any objection to it, could there? Now, just what would I take? I wonder if her patches are in here—and her things.

[*They look in the sewing basket.*]

MRS. HALE. Here's some red. I expect this has got sewing things in it. [*Brings out a fancy box.*] What a pretty box. Looks like something somebody would give you. Maybe her scissors are in here. [*Opens box. Suddenly puts her hand to her nose.*] Why— [MRS. PETERS *bends nearer, then turns her face away.*] There's something wrapped up in this piece of silk.

MRS. PETERS. Why, this isn't her scissors.

Mrs. Hale. [*Lifting the silk.*] Oh, Mrs. Peters—it's—

[Mrs. Peters *bends closer.*]

Mrs. Peters. It's the bird.

Mrs. Hale. [*Jumping up.*] But, Mrs. Peters—look at it! Its neck! Look at its neck! It's all—to the other side.

Mrs. Peters. Somebody—wrung—its—neck.

[*Their eyes meet. A look of growing comprehension, of horror. Steps are heard outside.* Mrs. Hale *slips box under quilt pieces, and sinks into her chair. Enter* Sheriff *and* County Attorney. Mrs. Peters *rises.*]

County Attorney. [*As one turning from serious things to little pleasantries.*] Well, ladies, have you decided whether she was going to quilt it or knot it?

Mrs. Peters. We think she was going to—knot it.

County Attorney. Well, that's interesting, I'm sure. [*Seeing the bird-cage.*] Has the bird flown?

Mrs. Hale. [*Putting more quilt pieces over the box.*] We think the—cat got it.

County Attorney. [*Preoccupied.*] Is there a cat?

[Mrs. Hale *glances in a quick covert way at* Mrs. Peters.]

Mrs. Peters. Well, not now. They're superstitious, you know. They leave.

County Attorney. [*To* Sheriff Peters, *continuing an interrupted conversation.*] No sign at all of anyone having come from the outside. Their own rope. Now let's go up again and go over it piece by piece. [*They start upstairs.*] It would have to have been someone who knew just the—

[Mrs. Peters *sits down. The two women sit there not looking at one another, but as if peering into something and at the same time holding back. When they talk now it is in the manner of feeling their way over strange ground, as if afraid of what they are saying, but as if they can not help saying it.*]

Mrs. Hale. She liked the bird. She was going to bury it in that pretty box.

Mrs. Peters. [*In a whisper.*] When I was a girl—my kitten—there was a boy took a hatchet, and before my eyes—and before I could get there—[*Covers her face an instant.*] If they hadn't held me back I would have—[*Catches herself, looks upstairs where steps are heard, falters weakly.*]—hurt him.

Mrs. Hale. [*With a slow look around her.*] I wonder how it would seem never to have had any children around. [*Pause.*] No, Wright wouldn't like the bird—a thing that sang. She used to sing. He killed that, too.

Mrs. Peters. [*Moving uneasily.*] We don't know who killed the bird.

Mrs. Hale. I knew John Wright.

MRS. PETERS. It was an awful thing was done in this house that night, Mrs. Hale. Killing a man while he slept, slipping a rope around his neck that choked the life out of him.

MRS. HALE. His neck. Choked the life out of him.

[Her hand goes out and rests on the bird-cage.]

MRS. PETERS. [With rising voice.] We don't know who killed him. We don't know.

MRS. HALE. [Her own feeling not interrupted.] If there'd been years and years of nothing, then a bird to sing to you, it would be awful—still, after the bird was still.

MRS. PETERS. [Something within her speaking.] I know what stillness is. When we homesteaded in Dakota, and my first baby died—after he was two years old, and me with no other then—

MRS. HALE. [Moving.] How soon do you suppose they'll be through, looking for the evidence?

MRS. PETERS. I know what stillness is. [Pulling herself back.] The law has got to punish crime, Mrs. Hale.

MRS. HALE. [Not as if answering that.] I wish you'd seen Minnie Foster when she wore a white dress with blue ribbons and stood up there in the choir and sang. [A look around the room.] Oh, I wish I'd come over here once in a while! That was a crime! That was a crime! Who's going to punish that?

MRS. PETERS. [Looking upstairs.] We mustn't—take on.

MRS. HALE. I might have known she needed help! I know how things can be—for women, I tell you, it's queer, Mrs. Peters. We live close together and we live far apart. We all go through the same things—it's all just a different kind of the same thing. [Brushes her eyes, noticing the bottle of fruit, reaches out for it.] If I was you, I wouldn't tell her her fruit was gone. Tell her it ain't. Tell her it's all right. Take this in to prove it to her. She—she may never know whether it was broke or not.

MRS. PETERS. [Takes the bottle, looks about for something to wrap it in; takes petticoat from the clothes brought from the other room, very nervously begins winding this around the bottle. In a false voice.] My, it's a good thing the men couldn't hear us. Wouldn't they just laugh! Getting all stirred up over a little thing like a—dead canary. As if that could have anything to do with—with—wouldn't they laugh!

[The men are heard coming down stairs.]

MRS. HALE. [Under her breath.] Maybe they would—maybe they wouldn't.

COUNTY ATTORNEY. No, Peters, it's all perfectly clear except a reason for doing it. But you know juries when it comes to women. If there was some definite thing. Something to show—something to make a story about—a thing that would connect up with this strange way of doing it—

[*The women's eyes meet for an instant. Enter* HALE *from outer door.*]

HALE. Well, I've got the team around. Pretty cold out there.

COUNTY ATTORNEY. I'm going to stay here a while by myself. [*To the* SHERIFF.] You can send Frank out for me, can't you? I want to go over everything. I'm not satisfied that we can't do better.

SHERIFF. Do you want to see what Mrs. Peters is going to take in?

[*The Lawyer goes to the table, picks up the apron, laughs.*]

COUNTY ATTORNEY. Oh, I guess they're not very dangerous things the ladies have picked out. [*Moves a few things about, disturbing the quilt pieces which cover the box. Steps back.*] No, Mrs. Peters doesn't need supervising. For that matter, a sheriff's wife is married to the law. Ever think of it that way, Mrs. Peters?

MRS. PETERS. Not—just that way.

SHERIFF. [*Chuckling.*] Married to the law. [*Moves toward the other room.*] I just want you to come in here a minute, George. We ought to take a look at these windows.

COUNTY ATTORNEY. [*Scoffingly.*] Oh, windows!

SHERIFF. We'll be right out, Mr. Hale.

[HALE *goes outside. The* SHERIFF *follows the* COUNTY ATTORNEY *into the other room. Then* MRS. HALE *rises, hands tight together, looking intensely at* MRS. PETERS, *whose eyes make a slow turn, finally meeting* MRS. HALE's. *A moment* MRS. HALE *holds her, then her own eyes point the way to where the box is concealed. Suddenly* MRS. PETERS *throws back quilt pieces and tries to put the box in the bag she is wearing. It is too big. She opens box, starts to take bird out, cannot touch it, goes to pieces, stands there helpless. Sound of a knob turning in the other room.* MRS. HALE *snatches the box and puts it in the pocket of her big coat. Enter* COUNTY ATTORNEY *and* SHERIFF.]

COUNTY ATTORNEY. [*Facetiously.*] Well, Henry, at least we found out that she was not going to quilt it. She was going to—what is it you call it, ladies?

MRS. HALE. [*Her hand against her pocket.*] We call it—knot it, Mr. Henderson.

CURTAIN ❖

Mrs. Peters states "The law is the law," but then helps hide the evidence. Do you believe that all crimes must be punished? Why or why not?

Literature CONNECTION

Published in *The Explicator,* a journal of literary criticism, this article by **Judith Kay Russell** explores the connection between Susan Glaspell's play "Trifles" and the Greek myth of the Fates, three women who control human destiny by spinning out the thread of life, measuring the thread for each person, and finally cutting the thread at the end of life. In Greek mythology, even the gods feared the Fates, and Zeus, the ruler of the gods, was also subject to their work.

Glaspell's "Trifles"

Literary Criticism by
Judith Kay Russell

On the surface, Susan Glaspell's one-act play "Trifles" focuses on the death of an oppressive husband at the hands of his emotionally abused wife in an isolated and remote farm in the Midwest. Beneath the surface, the collective behaviors of Mrs. Hale, Mrs. Peters, and Mrs. Wright in Glaspell's play bear strong resemblance to those of the Fates (Clotho the Spinner, Lachesis the Disposer of Lots, and Atropos the Cutter of the Thread) in Greek mythology. Although Glaspell brings new vigor to the myth, the attention given to Mrs. Hale's resewing the quilt, the change in Mrs. Peters's perspective on law and justice, and the rope placed by Mrs. Wright around her husband's neck are nonetheless grounded in the story of the Three Sisters who control the fate of men.

Mrs. Hale embodies the qualities of Clotho the Spinner, the sister who spins the thread of life. Mrs. Hale subtly suggests that Mrs. Wright is not the sole agent in the death of Mr. Wright. On the surface, Mrs. Hale's ungrammatical reference to that event, "when they was slipping the rope under his neck" (79), can be attributed to improper subject and verb agreement, which is not uncommon in certain regional dialects. However, the use of the plural pronoun and singular verb subtly suggests the involvement of more than one in a single outcome, and it foreshadows the conspiracy of the three women and their efforts to control the outcome or the fate of all characters. Furthermore, the information concerning the

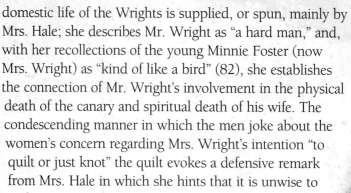

domestic life of the Wrights is supplied, or spun, mainly by Mrs. Hale; she describes Mr. Wright as "a hard man," and, with her recollections of the young Minnie Foster (now Mrs. Wright) as "kind of like a bird" (82), she establishes the connection of Mr. Wright's involvement in the physical death of the canary and spiritual death of his wife. The condescending manner in which the men joke about the women's concern regarding Mrs. Wright's intention "to quilt or just knot" the quilt evokes a defensive remark from Mrs. Hale in which she hints that it is unwise to tempt fate; she asserts, "I don't see as it's anything to laugh about" (79-80). Finally, by "just pulling out a stitch or two that's not sewed very good" and replacing it with her own stitching (80), Mrs. Hale symbolically claims her position as the person who spins the thread of life.

The second member of the Three Sisters, Lachesis the Disposer of Lots, is personified by Mrs. Peters. The viability of the thread spun by Mrs. Hale depends on the actions and reactions of Mrs. Peters. To claim her position as the member of the Fates responsible for assigning destiny, she must abandon objectivity and move toward subjectivity. Her objectivity is exemplified by her assertion that "the law is the law" and her view on physical evidence as she informs Mrs. Hale, "I don't think we ought to touch things" (79-80). The sight of the dead canary and the recognition that "somebody—wrung—its—neck" marks Mrs. Peters's initiation into subjectivity and the sisterhood (83). The discovery of the dead bird awakens Mrs. Peters's suppressed childhood memories of rage toward the "boy [who] took a hatchet" and brutally killed her kitten (83). In her mind, the kitten, Mrs. Wright, and the bird become enmeshed. Mrs. Peters realizes that the dead bird will be used to stereotype Mrs. Wright as a madwoman who overreacts to "trifles." At this point, Mrs. Peters emerges from the shadow of her role as the sheriff's wife and becomes "married to the law" (85). Her new concept of law subjectively favors justice over procedure. She claims her position as the sister who dispenses the lots in life when she moves to hide the bird and thus denies the men "something to make a story about" (85).

Mrs. Wright represents Atropos the Cutter of the Thread. Symbolically, Mrs. Wright is first linked to Atropos in Mr. Hale's description of her "rockin' back and forth" (73), a motion similar to that made by cutting with scissors. The connection to Atropos is further established when Mrs. Peters discovers the dead bird in Mrs. Wright's sewing box and exclaims, "Why, this isn't her scissors" (83). Ironically, the dead canary takes the place of the scissors: The death of the bird is directly tied to the fate of Mr. Wright. In addition, Mrs. Wright assumes mythical status through her spiritual presence and physical absence from the stage. Mr. Hale relates that in his questioning of Mrs. Wright, she admits that her husband "died of a rope round his neck," but she doesn't know how it happened because she "didn't wake up"; she is a sound sleeper (74-75). Mrs. Wright denies personal involvement in the death of her husband, yet she acknowledges that he died while she slept beside him in the bed. Mrs. Wright says, "I was on the inside" (75). Although she may be referring to her routine "inside" position of sleep behind her husband in the bed placed along the wall, Mrs. Wright's statement suggests a movement from the outside (her individual consciousness) to the inside (the collective consciousness of the Fates). Her involvement with the rope of death is the equivalent of severing the thread of life. She did not spin the thread, nor did she assign the lot; she merely contributed a part to the whole, and that collective whole becomes greater than the sum of its parts. For this reason, Mrs. Wright is correct in denying individual knowledge or responsibility in the death of her husband.

In "Trifles," Mrs. Hale weaves the story or describes the circumstances, Mrs. Peters weighs the evidence and determines the direction of justice, and Mrs. Wright carries out the verdict; although the procedure is somewhat reversed, the mythic ritual is performed nevertheless. Susan Glaspell's use of the Fates, or the Three Sisters, does not weaken her dramatization of women who are oppressed by men. Although some believe that the power of the Three Sisters rivals that of Zeus, Glaspell reminds her audience that, regardless of myth or twentieth-century law, it still takes three women to equal one man. That is the inequality on which she focuses. ❖

WORK CITED
Glaspell, Susan. "Trifles." *Plays By American Women: 1900–1930.* Ed.
    Judith E. Barlow. New York: Applause Theater Book, 1994. 70–86.

Refer and Reason

1. What theory do the women develop after seeing the bread, the irregular stitching, the broken bird cage, and the dead bird? How do they come to that conclusion?
2. Assess the amount of responsibility or blame each of these people had in what happened at the Wright household: Minnie (Mrs. Wright), John Wright, and Mrs. Hale. If you were on the jury, what verdict would you pass on Mrs. Wright?
3. "Trifles" was later turned into a short story by the title "A Jury of Her Peers." Which aspects of the story does each of these titles emphasize?

Writing Options

1. Write a newspaper article reporting this crime. Include comments from the Sheriff and Mr. and Mrs. Hale. Decide how much information Mrs. Hale would be likely to give.
2. Write the closing arguments for the prosecution and defense attorneys in Mrs. Wright's trial. The prosecution considers her guilty and deserving of a stiff sentence. The defense would be more compassionate about the circumstances leading up to the murder.

 Go to **www.mirrorsandwindows.com** for more.

TEXT ←TO→ TEXT CONNECTION

- Do you agree with the relationship Russell makes between the three women of the play and the three Fates? Why or why not?
- How has reading this literary criticism affected your understanding of the play?
- Can you think of other stories you've read or seen on television or in the movies that draw upon the idea of the Fates, perhaps using thread or scissors as symbolism?

A DOLL'S HOUSE
by Henrik Ibsen

Nora Helmer seems to be a pretty, frivolous, doll-like, young wife to the earnest, hard-working Thorvald. But unbeknownst to her husband, Nora has secretly and illegally borrowed money to pay for his convalescence in Italy. This 1879 play is considered a landmark in both theatrical realism and the women's movement.

THE TEMPEST
by William Shakespeare

"On a ship at sea: a tempestuous noise of thunder and lightening heard." So begins Shakespeare's magical and action-packed romance *The Tempest*. The tense opening scene, featuring a shipwreck on a tempest-tossed sea, leads to more suspense as the characters fall in love, plot revolts, seek revenge, and eventually reconcile—all on an island filled with magic.

HAPPY ENDINGS
by Adèle Geras

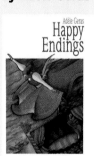

The life of sixteen-year-old Mel changes dramatically after she is cast in a summer production of Anton Chekhov's play *Three Sisters*. In this novel about a drama, you'll laugh with Mel as she uses humor and honesty to describe her first true encounter with the theater.

ST. JOAN: A CHRONICLE PLAY IN SIX SCENES AND AN EPILOGUE
by George Bernard Shaw

"Give me a horse, armor and some soldiers...These are your orders from my Lord," Joan, a nineteen-year-old village girl, tells the leaders of France. In this famous play, George Bernard Shaw presents a realistic portrait of the proud but naïve Warrior Maid, suggesting that we are often unable to tell the difference between a saint and a heretic.

THE IMPORTANCE OF BEING EARNEST
by Oscar Wilde

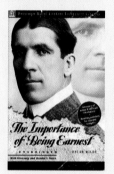

What's in a name? For Algernon and Earnest, everything. This humorous social comedy features the courtship trials of Algernon and Earnest in a crazy mix of mistaken identity, lost babies in handbags, and, of course, the importance of being named Earnest.

YOU CAN'T TAKE IT WITH YOU
by George S. Kaufman

This play, winner of the 1936 Pulitzer Prize, is about the eccentric yet lovable Sycamore family that gets along just fine until daughter Alice brings home her new boyfriend, Tony Kirby. Tony's family does not approve of the zany Sycamores. This three-act play was adapted into a film that won the Academy Award in 1938.

SPEAKING & LISTENING WORKSHOP

Deliver a Persuasive Speech

Persuasive speaking has many of the same characteristics as persuasive writing. However, your words have more immediate power when you speak them than when you write them; when you speak, you can use tone of voice and expression to emphasize your message. The goal of a persuasive speech is to change someone's mind or way of thinking about a topic. Use the following guidelines to prepare and present a persuasive speech.

1. Prepare Your Content

- Choose an issue you care about. Define your position on the issue and find evidence—statistics, facts, and quotations from reputable sources—that backs up your point of view. Identify any counterarguments to your position and explain why your point of view is best.
- Organize your ideas into a logical order. First, make an outline, then draft your speech.
- Revise your speech to include rhetorical devices such as parallelism, repetition, and rhetorical questions.

2. Practice

- To be successful in delivering your speech, you must portray yourself as the authority figure; therefore, you need to know your material well. Rehearse your speech using a tape recorder, video recorder, mirror, or practice audience. Run through the speech several times, revising as necessary. Ask a friend to critique your performance.
- Practice your speech often so you can look up and make eye contact with your audience instead of staring at your notes. Making eye contact enhances your ethos, or credibility.

3. Present Your Speech

- Speak at a normal pace, slowing down to emphasize important ideas.
- Vary your tone of voice. Your tone may go from thoughtful to angry in the same speech.
- Maintain good posture and use gestures sparingly to emphasize points. Do not fidget or rustle your papers while speaking, or you will distract your listeners.
- Use feedback from your teacher and peers to improve your speaking.

Speaking Tips

- Include in your speech details that will appeal to your audience's emotions, such as personal anecdotes or descriptions.
- Pause at certain points in your speech to allow your audience to absorb and react to key ideas.

Speaking & Listening Rubric

Your presentation will be evaluated on these elements:

Content

- ☑ clear statement of position
- ☑ thorough support of points
- ☑ effective use of rhetorical techniques

Delivery and Presentation

- ☑ appropriate use of eye contact and gestures
- ☑ effective variation of pace and tone and use of pauses

Persuasive Essay

People thrive on sharing ideas and perspectives and use persuasion as a tool to argue viewpoints, remedy injustice, weigh alternative visions, and simply present opinions, sometimes in ways that improve the human condition. In *The Tragedy of Julius Caesar,* Brutus and Antony attempt to persuade the Romans of their contrasting views on Caesar's assassination. In "A Marriage Proposal," Lomov tries to persuade Natalia and Chubukov the Oxen Meadows are his.

Persuasive language occurs everywhere – in advertising, in newspapers and magazines, on radio talk shows, and in everyday, ordinary, casual conversations. In a **persuasive essay,** the writer respectfully presents a clear position on an issue, using logic, reason, and information, to convince readers to see his or her viewpoint and, if appropriate, to take action on it.

Assignment

Write a persuasive essay, aiming to convince a larger audience to consider your viewpoint about a subject that is important to you.

❶ PREWRITE

Select Your Topic

Talk with others, read newspapers, and listen to radio commentary to consider a variety of personal, local community, or national issues. Choose a topic you feel strongly about.

Gather Information

Though your essay is based on your opinion, referring to sources will show your audience that your opinion is based on solid information and ideas. Begin to research the topic you have chosen, keeping careful track of your sources. Jot important ideas on index cards and note the sources in the top right corner of the cards. Use a separate card for each fact or quotation. Later, you can move the cards around to decide the best place for each point.

For now, use note cards to help you organize your ideas in a chart like the one on page 729. As you consider your topic, ask a friend or family member to argue against your position. This will help you identify opposing viewpoints.

Assignment
Write a persuasive essay about a subject that is important to you

Purpose
To convince your readers to understand, adopt, or support your point of view

Audience
Classmates and teachers, decision makers affected by your topic, people who may or may not agree with your position

---

Writing Rubric

A good persuasive essay:

- ☑ provides context for the issue in the **introduction** and states the writer's opinion in a **thesis statement**

- ☑ in the **body,** presents at least three points to support the thesis

- ☑ acknowledges and responds to potential opposition

- ☑ summarizes the argument, restates the thesis, and issues a call-to-action in the **conclusion**

- ☑ using appropriate, respectful diction, appeals to readers with credibility, emotion, and logic

---

Persuasive Essay Evidence Chart

Thesis: Families should not put older relatives in nursing homes.

Supporting points	Evidence
1. Health deteriorates quickly in nursing homes.	60% are in worse health after one year in a nursing home (*Eldercare*, November 2007). Not enough interaction to keep a person alert. People maintain health if they feel needed and connected with family life.
2. Nursing homes are expensive.	Costs range from $12,000 to $100,000 a year. Part-time in-home nursing care is less expensive.
3. Family needs wisdom of elderly members.	Elders are respected in many cultures. Children can learn from grandparents. Family needs to hear an older relative's stories and experiences.
Possible opposing view	**Response to opposing view**
Elders require more care than busy, stressed families can provide.	Hire part-time in-home nursing care; involve entire family, including children, in caring for older relatives

Organize Your Ideas

Now that you have support for your thesis, you can create an outline. Review your chart and organize your points in a logical order, perhaps one that presents points that build in importance. Decide when and how to appeal to your readers logically, emotionally, and ethically. Decide where best to acknowledge opposition to your argument.

Look through your index cards for additional bits of information to include. Pick strong ideas, good quotations, or surprising stories to use for your introduction and conclusion.

Write Your Thesis Statement

Using the supporting points you have identified, write a one-sentence statement that summarizes your position on the topic. This is your **thesis statement.** One student, Yan Lin, expressed her opinion in this thesis statement:

> The benefits of home care make nursing homes the last resort for elderly relatives.

What Great Writers Do

In *The Prince*, Niccolo Machiavelli humbly defers to his audience: "I fear that my writing...may be deemed presumptuous, differing as I do, especially in this matter, from the opinions of others."

Only a few lines later, however, he asserts his opinion forcefully: "He who abandons what is done for what ought to be done, will rather learn to bring about his own ruin than his preservation."

- **Introduction**
  Earn the attention and respect of your readers. Provide context for the issue, and include your thesis statement.
- **Body**
  Support your thesis with at least three points. Provide evidence for each point. Acknowledge possible opposing views and overcome these objections.
- **Conclusion**
  Rephrase your thesis, sum up your argument, and issue a call-to-action. Use vivid and powerful language to convince your readers.

❷ DRAFT

Write your essay by following this three-part framework: **introduction, body,** and **conclusion.**

Draft Your Introduction

In a persuasive essay, the introduction should provide context for the issue in a way that grabs readers' attention, perhaps with a startling image, story, or statistic. The introduction should also establish the writer's point of view in the thesis statement.

The introduction Yan wrote during the draft stage is shown in the first column of the chart on page 731. Yan presents two visual images for the reader to consider. She asks readers which image they like and is confident they will agree on the former. With this setup, she presents her thesis statement.

Draft Your Body

Establish credibility with language. Use an appropriate tone—formal, informal, or a combination of both—depending on your audience. In any case, it's best to be respectful, modest, clear, and rational. Touch your audience emotionally, with **pathos.** With **ethos,** show your audience you share their concerns. Appeal to logic, or **logos,** with examples, statistics, and facts.

Yan's first body paragraph examines one point in support of her thesis statement. See the draft of that paragraph in the left-hand column of the chart on page 731. Yan drafted three more body paragraphs, ordering her points in increasing importance. She made sure to cite the source of all information she mentioned.

What Great Writers Do

In his influential book, *On Writing Well*, William Zinsser (b. 1922) discusses style: "Getting writers to use 'I' is seldom easy. They think they must earn the right to reveal their emotions or their thoughts. Or that it's egotistical. Or that it's undignified—a fear that afflicts the academic world. Hence the professorial use of 'one'...I don't want to meet 'one'—he's a boring guy. I want [a writer] with a passion for his subject to tell me why it fascinates *him*."

At the end of his chapter on style, Zinsser writes, "Sell yourself, and your subject will exert its own appeal. Believe in your own identity and your own opinions. Writing is an act of ego, and you might as well admit it. Use its energy to keep yourself going."

Using the organizational plan you created in your Persuasive Essay Evidence Chart, write the **body** of your essay. When you state a point, support it with evidence—details, facts, anecdotes, examples, and quotations. Choose supporting arguments that will lead your audience to the main point of your conclusion.

Draft Your Conclusion

Finally, write the conclusion of your essay. A persuasive essay closes in a way that leaves readers thinking about the issue and considering the soundness of the viewpoint presented. A good conclusion summarizes the main points; restates the thesis in a strong, convincing way; and issues a call-to-action to your readers.

Does Yan do all three things in her conclusion? Look at the draft of her conclusion in the chart on page 731.

❸ REVISE

Evaluate Your Draft

Evaluate your own or a classmate's essay. Either way, think carefully about what's done well and what can be improved.

DRAFT STAGE		REVISE STAGE	
Introduction			
Picture this scene: While her daughter and son-in-law cook, an old lady helps her grandson do homework at the kitchen table. The family eats dinner together. Now picture a different scene: The same woman eats dinner alone. Lonely, walks down a stark hallway to the common room to sit with strangers. Which situation would you prefer for you're grandmother? I believe there are benefits to home care.	Draws readers' interest with a visual image Uses descriptive language Speaks directly to the reader; expresses opinion in thesis	Picture this scene: While her daughter and son-in-law cook, an ~~old lady~~ elderly woman helps her grandson do homework at the kitchen table. The family eats dinner together. Now picture a different scene: The same woman eats dinner alone from a tray. The TV in the next room blares. Lonely, she walks down a stark hallway to the common room to sit with strangers. Which situation would you prefer for your grandmother? ~~I believe there are~~ the benefits to home care make nursing homes the last resort for elderly relatives.	Replaces potentially offensive words with respectful language Adds details for a fuller image Completes a fragment by adding the subject Corrects word usage; develops and improves thesis
Body Paragraph			
A family of many generations can support each other. Teenagers and even children can help care for older people. Doing so might teach them compassion. Kids would have invaluable time with their grandparents, to listen to their stories and learn from their experiences. The grandparents would feel needed. They would gain strength from the energy of youth.	Starts with a topic sentence Supports both topic sentence and thesis	Though some may see elders as a burden, a family of many generations can support each other. Teenagers and even children can help care for older people. In fact, doing so might teach them compassion. In return, kids would have invaluable time with their grandparents, to listen to their stories and learn from their experiences. Feeling needed, grandparents would gain strength from the energy of youth.	Acknowledges opposition Adds sentence-level transitions Combines sentences
Conclusion			
Family home care is better than nursing home care. Don't steal the quality of the end of loved ones' lives by placing them in a nursing home. Visualize the life you want for them. Then start planning, with their help, to make that vision a reality.	Restates thesis Uses assertive, confident language Appeals to the reader	For health, financial, and personal reasons, family home care is ~~better than~~ preferable to nursing home care. Don't steal the quality of the end of lovedones' lives by placing them in a nursing home. Visualize the life you want for them. Then start planning, with their help, to make that vision a reality.	Summarizes essay Issues a call-to-action

REVISION CHECKLIST

Content and Organization

❑ Is the thesis clearly stated in the **introduction?**

❑ Does the essay's **body** discuss at least three supporting points? Are these points arranged in a logical order?

❑ Are opposing arguments acknowledged and successfully refuted?

❑ Does the **conclusion** restate the thesis, summarize the essay, and issue a call-to-action?

❑ Is the language respectful and appropriate for the intended audience?

Grammar and Style

❑ Is most of the essay written in active voice? (page 554)

❑ Are hyphens, dashes, and ellipses used correctly? (page 644)

❑ Are coordination, subordination, and apposition used correctly? (page 696)

Every paragraph should relate clearly back to that main idea. Use the Revision Checklist on this page to make this evaluation. Write your observations about what changes need to be made directly on the essay.

Revise for Content, Organization, and Style

Yan evaluated her draft and found a number of things to improve. Look at the chart on page 731 (this time, the right-hand column) to see how she revised the three paragraphs we looked at earlier:

• **Introduction:** Yan developed the image she tried to create for readers. She replaced potentially offensive language with respectful words. She corrected a sentence fragment and improved her thesis statement to make a better point.

• **Body:** Yan acknowledged potential opposition to her argument. She added good sentence-level transitions, deleted information that was off the topic, and combined closely related sentences.

• **Conclusion:** Yan made sure to briefly summarize her argument. Again, she strengthened her credibility by using slightly more formal language.

Review the notes you or your partner made as you evaluated your draft. Then respond to each comment and effectively revise your essay.

Proofread for Errors

The purpose of proofreading is to check specifically for remaining errors. Whether or not you found errors as you evaluated your essay, read the essay again and focus on proofreading. Use proofreader's symbols to mark any errors you find. (See Language Arts Handbook 4.1 for a list of proofreader's symbols.)

Take a look at Yan's final draft on the next page. Review how she worked through the three stages of the writing process: Prewrite, Draft, and Revise.

WRITING FOLLOW-UP

Publish and Present

• Send a copy of your essay to someone with the authority to make changes regarding the issue you have discussed.

• Develop your essay into a persuasive speech. (See the Speaking & Listening Workshop on page 727.)

Reflect

• Writing a persuasive piece requires you to think deeply and assert your position about an issue. What did you learn about your ability to take a stand?

• Pay attention to persuasive language in the world around you; find examples of effective and ineffective persuasion. What is the difference?

STUDENT MODEL

Don't Warehouse the Elderly
by Yan Lin

Picture this scene: While her daughter and son-in-law cook, an elderly woman helps her grandson do homework at the kitchen table. The family eats dinner together. Now picture a different scene: The same woman eats dinner alone from a tray. The TV in the next room blares. Lonely, she walks down a stark hallway to the common room to sit with strangers. Which situation would you prefer for your grandmother? The benefits of home care make nursing homes the last resort for elderly relatives.

Though some may see elders as a burden, a family of many generations can support each other. Teenagers and even children can help care for older people. In fact, doing so might teach them compassion. In return, kids would have invaluable time with their grandparents, to listen to their stories and learn from their experiences. The grandparents would feel needed; they would gain strength from the energy of youth.

Another benefit is that living with family is better for a person's health. According to a study published in *Eldercare*, 60 percent of nursing home residents are in worse health one year after being admitted. Nursing home residents live in tiny rooms, watching television and eating bland food. In contrast, at home, the elderly person eats meals with family, helps care for grandchildren, and joins family activities. Research shows that being needed and engaging in life make a person healthier. That is more likely to happen in a bustling family home.

Keeping older parents at home can also save money. The full-time nursing care available in nursing homes is expensive. It could cost anywhere from $12,000 to $100,000 a year, depending on the facility. If family members care for an older person at home, the family can save money by hiring a nurse part-time, if needed, for periods when relatives are not available.

Perhaps the most important reason to keep older relatives at home is that they can share with younger generations the wisdom they have accumulated. In many traditional cultures, elders are respected for their experience, but in America, too often, they are isolated with others of the same generation, unable to pass along their ideas before it is too late.

For health, financial, and personal reasons, family home care is preferable to nursing home care. Visualize the life you want for your loved ones. Then start planning, with their help, to make that vision a reality.

What is the writer's thesis?

Where does the writer acknowledge the opposing position?

What points does the writer give in support of this thesis? What evidence does she include for each supporting point?

How does the writer establish ethos?

How does the writer use logos and pathos?

What call-to-action does the writer make in the conclusion?

Reading Skills

EVALUATE AN ARGUMENT

"Make a charitable contribution to our cause." "Don't waste your money on that movie." "Buy this car instead of that one." "Vote for me." Every day, you encounter countless persuasive messages, or arguments. To make thoughtful decisions about what you will do about each of these issues, you must be able to evaluate each argument. In other words, you must be able to determine whether an argument is sound. Use these tips to help you evaluate arguments in written works:

1. Find the main idea of the selection. The main idea is the opinion, or claim, of which the author is trying to convince you.

2. Identify support for the claim. Support might come in these forms:
   • reasons, or logical statements explaining why the writer holds the opinion
   • evidence, including facts, quotations from experts, statistics, and examples
   • emotional appeals, including moving anecdotes (brief stories) and loaded language (words with strong connotations)

3. Evaluate the support. Ask yourself questions like these:
   • Are the reasons logical?
   • Does the evidence really support the claim? Is it sufficient to suggest that the claim is valid?
   • Does the argument rely on stereotypes or overgeneralizations?
   • Does the writer use highly charged emotional language or anecdotes instead of evidence?

Read the following passage from Mark Antony's funeral oration (III.ii.92–103) in *The Tragedy of Julius Caesar.*

> I thrice presented him [Caesar] a kingly crown.
> Which he did thrice refuse. Was this ambition?
> Yet Brutus says he was ambitious,
> And sure he is an honorable man.
> …Bear with me,
> My heart is in the coffin there with Caesar,
> And I must pause till it come back to me.

In this passage, Antony argues that Caesar was not ambitious, offering as evidence Caesar's refusal to become emperor when he was given the opportunity. Antony also appeals to emotion when he claims that his "heart is in the coffin there with Caesar" and pauses dramatically to regain his composure. Do you find the evidence Antony presents in defense of Caesar sound? What do you think of the way Antony appeals to emotion? Does it lead to think favorably of Caesar? Why or why not?

PRACTICE

Directions: Read the following excerpt from a speech. The questions that come after it will ask you to evaluate the speaker's argument using evidence from the text.

Nonfiction: This excerpt comes from a speech entitled "Florence Kelley Speaks Out on Child Labor and Woman's Suffrage." This speech was delivered in Philadelphia, Pennsylvania, on July 22, 1905.

We have, in this country, two million children under the age of sixteen years who are earning their bread. They vary in age from six and seven years (in the cotton mills of Georgia) and eight,
5 nine and ten years (in the coal-breakers of Pennsylvania), to fourteen, fifteen and sixteen years in more enlightened states.

No other portion of the wage earning class increased so rapidly from decade to decade as the
10 young girls from fourteen to twenty years....[N]o contingent so doubles from census period to census period (both by percent and by count of heads), as does the contingent of girls between twelve and twenty years of age. They are in
15 commerce, in offices, in manufacturing.

Tonight while we sleep, several thousand little girls will be working in textile mills, all the night through, in the deafening noise of the spindles and the looms spinning and weaving cotton and
20 wool, silks and ribbons for us to buy....

No one in this room tonight can feel free from such participation. The children make our shoes in the shoe factories; they knit our stockings, our knitted underwear in the knitting factories.
25 They spin and weave our cotton underwear in the cotton mills. Children braid straw for our hats, they spin and weave the silk and velvet wherewith we trim our hats. They stamp buckles and metal ornaments of all kinds, as well as pins and hat-
30 pins. Under the sweating system, tiny children make artificial flowers and neckwear for us to buy.

They carry bundles of garments from the factories to the tenements, little beasts of burden, robbed of school life that they may work for us.

Multiple Choice
1. The evidence in this excerpt supports the claim that
   A. children should be expected to contribute to the family income.
   B. children should not have to work long hours.
   C. child labor is a significant problem.
   D. working all night is harmful to children.

2. To which emotions does Kelley appeal?
   F. guilt and pity
   G. joy and celebration
   H. outrage and sadness
   J. grief and anger

3. Which of the following does *not* serve as factual evidence to support Kelley's claim?
   A. Two million children under the age of sixteen are working in the United States.
   B. Young girls work in the clothing factories around the country.
   C. The number of girls working in factories has increased from year to year.
   D. Some states are more enlightened than others.

4. In line 11, the word *contingent* means
   F. accidental.
   G. representative group.
   H. empirical.
   J. unnecessary.

Constructed Response
5. Evaluate the effectiveness of the evidence Kelley uses to support her claim. Refer to specific details from the speech.

Writing Skills

PERSUASIVE WRITING

Many standardized tests include sections that ask you to demonstrate your writing ability by composing an essay in response to a prompt, or topic. Sometimes, you are asked to write a persuasive, or an argumentative, piece. The purpose of this mode of writing is to persuade readers or listeners to agree with a position, change a view on an issue, or perform an action. Examples of persuasive writing include editorials, petitions, speeches, and essays. When you write a persuasive essay, keep the following tips in mind:

- Include only relevant information.
- Include an introduction (in which you identify your stance on an issue), a body (in which you support your stance to encourage others to agree with you), and a conclusion (in which you restate your stance).
- Develop concrete reasons for your positions, and support each with evidence.
- Consider and counter opposing views.
- Use vivid language that will inspire your readers to act or to agree with you.

You will be evaluated in part on your ability to use standard English, so you should also pay attention to grammar, usage, capitalization, spelling, and punctuation.

Test-Taking Tips

- Current issues in society show up every day in newspapers and television. When you hear about a new issue, practice gathering information about it and using that information to form your opinion.
- Once you've determined your opinion on an issue, practice writing letters to the editor or other persuasive pieces in which you clearly state and support your opinion.

PRACTICE

Timed Writing: 30 minutes

Think carefully about the following assignment. Allow 30 minutes to write your response to the prompt.

Assignment: Some people say high school students should devote all their time and energy to their studies and school-related activities. Other people say high school students should have part-time jobs in order to learn the basic skills that will one day be required of them in the workplace. There are both positive and negative aspects to high school students having jobs. Write a persuasive essay that argues either for or against high school students having part-time jobs.

As you write, make sure you accomplish these tasks:

- Choose a position and follow through on it.
- Give specific reasons and examples supporting your position.
- Organize the information in your essay so that it is easy to follow.
- Choose precise, descriptive words that show your insight into the subject and audience.
- Use a variety of sentence structures to make the writing interesting.
- Proofread your writing for errors in grammar, usage, spelling, punctuation, and capitalization.

Revising and Editing Skills

Some standardized tests ask you to read a draft of an essay and answer questions about how to improve it. As you read the draft, watch for errors like these:

- incorrect spellings
- disagreement between subject and verb; inconsistent verb tense; incorrect forms for irregular verbs; sentence fragments and run-ons; double negatives; and incorrect use of frequently confused words, such as *affect* and *effect*
- missing end marks, incorrect comma use, and lowercased proper nouns and proper adjectives
- unclear purpose, unclear main ideas, and lack of supporting details
- confusing order of ideas and missing transitions
- language that is inappropriate to the audience and purpose, and mood that is inappropriate for the purpose

PRACTICE

Directions: For each underlined section in the passage that follows, choose the revision that most improves the writing. If you think the original version is best, choose "MAKE NO CHANGE."

I think high school students should definitely have part-time jobs. (1) Part-time jobs are valuable <u>because they help you learn</u> responsibility and prepare for "real life." Students can also earn their own money by working after school and on weekends.

(2) I am an example of someone who has <u>benefited</u> from having a part-time job. I work at the library near my house shelving books. (3) <u>Because of my job, I know how important it is to arrive at work on time, to be polite to other people, and doing my job carefully.</u> (4) These skills will help me when I enter the <u>workforce. I've</u> also started saving the money I've earned to help pay for college.

1. A. MAKE NO CHANGE.
    B. because, they help you learn
    C. because they help students learn
    D. because they help one learn

2. F. MAKE NO CHANGE.
    G. beneffited
    H. bennefited
    J. benifited

3. A. MAKE NO CHANGE.
    B. Because of my job, I know how important it is to arrive at work on time, to be polite to other people, and to do my job carefully.
    C. Because of my job, I know how important arriving at work on time, being polite to other people, and doing my job carefully is.
    D. Because of my job, I know how important arriving at work on time is, being polite to other people is, and doing my job carefully is.

4. F. MAKE NO CHANGE.
    G. workforce and I've
    H. workforce; I've
    J. workforce, yet I've

UNIT 5
Folk Literature

TOLKIEN · LEVERTOV · GRAVES

"*I love to read their chronicles, / which such brave deeds relate;*
I love to sing their ancient rhymes, / To hear their legends told."

—Francis Brown

What stories do you remember from your childhood? As you read the stories and poems in this unit, you may find some of the situations and settings unfamiliar. Focus on the characters instead; you may have more in common than you think.

CERVANTES   WHITE   BRENTS

INTRODUCTION TO FOLK LITERATURE

That was a time when words were like
  magic.
The mind had mysterious powers,
and a word uttered by chance
might have consequences.

  —from "Magic Words" by Nalungiaq

Are there favorite bedtime stories or songs that have become a tradition in your family? Do you ever sit around a campfire and tell ghost stories? If so, then you have shared in the oral tradition that forms the basis of folk literature. The selections you'll read in this unit span cultures and generations. These selections exist because people told, and continue to tell, stories.

THE GENRE OF FOLK LITERATURE

Telling stories is not limited to a single culture or region—people around the world have been telling the same stories for generations. Long before people invented writing, they were handing down stories about their gods and heroes and experiences. **Folk literature,** or *folklore,* refers to a body of cultural knowledge and beliefs passed from one generation to the next, both orally and in writing. Much folk literature originated as part of the *oral tradition,* or the passing of a work, an idea, or a custom by word of mouth from generation to generation. Some early stories were told in the form of poems. Some were composed as songs. Still others were in the form of prose tales, the first type of fiction.

Fairy Tale Characters

One type of folk literature is fairy tales. Listed below are characters from fairy tales. Why do you think the fairy tales about these characters continue to be told to children today?

HANSEL AND GRETEL.

- Hansel and Gretel
- Rapunzel
- Aladdin
- Little Red Riding Hood
- The Elves and the Shoemaker
- Jack (as in "Jack and the Beanstalk")
- The Big Bad Wolf

TYPES OF FOLK LITERATURE

Folk literature comes in a variety of types. Sometimes, these types overlap; for example, a legend can also be an epic. The most common types of folk literature are listed below.

Myths and Legends

Myths are traditional stories, rooted in particular cultures, that deal with gods and other supernatural beings as well as with human heroes. Myths often embody religious beliefs and values and explain natural phenomena. Every early culture around the globe has produced its own myths. The Greek story "The Love of Cupid and Psyche" (page 841), the Norse story "The Death of Balder" (page 857), and the Indian story "Savitri and Satyavant" (page 852) are all examples of myths from different countries.

Legends are stories with roots in the distant past, often based on real events or characters from older times. Unlike myths, legends are popularly regarded as historical; however, they may contain elements that are fantastic or unverifiable. *Le Morte d'Arthur* (page 779) is about how the legendary character Arthur pulls the sword out of the stone to become King of England. (See Understanding Myths and Legends, page 746.)

> So when he came to the churchyard, Sir Arthur alit and tied his horse to the stile, and so he went to the tent, and found no knights there, for they were at jousting; and so he handled the sword by the handles, and lightly and fiercely pulled it out of the stone, and took his horse and rode his way until he came to his brother Sir Kay, and delivered him the sword.
>
> —from *Le Morte d'Arthur*
> by Sir Thomas Malory

Folk Tales

Folk tales are brief stories passed by word of mouth from generation to generation. In this unit, "Naked Truth and Resplendent Parable" (page 790) is a Yiddish folk tale. **Tall tales** are also folk tales. Tall tales are often lighthearted or humorous and contain highly exaggerated, unrealistic elements. The stories of Paul Bunyan and Pecos Bill are tall tales.

Fairy tales are stories that deal with mischievous spirits and other supernatural occurrences, often in medieval settings. The name is generally applied to stories of the kind collected by Charles Perrault in France and the Brothers Grimm in Germany or told by Hans Christian Andersen of Denmark. "Cinderella" and "The Little Mermaid" are famous examples. (See Understanding Folk Tales, page 788.)

Parables are very brief stories told to teach a moral lesson. The most famous parables are those told by Jesus in the Bible. **Fables** are brief stories, often with animal characters, also told to express a moral. Famous fables include those of Aesop and Jean de La Fontaine.

Folk Songs and Spirituals

Folk songs are traditional or composed songs typically made up of stanzas, a refrain, and a simple melody. A form of folk literature, folk songs are expressions of commonly shared ideas or feelings and may be narrative or lyric in style. Traditional folk songs are anonymous works that have been transmitted orally. **Spirituals** are religious songs from the African-American folk tradition. In Unit 2, "Go Down, Moses" is an example of a spiritual.

Popular Spirituals

Choose one of the spirituals below and research its history and lyrics. Try to find a recording and listen to its melody. Then write a paragraph on why you think the song is still sung today.

- "There is a Balm in Gilead"
- "Swing Low, Sweet Chariot"
- "Wade in the Water"
- "Let Us Break Bread Together"
- "Oh Freedom"

Epics

An **epic** is a long story, often told in verse, involving heroes and gods. Epics have often been passed on orally and may have anonymous authors. Grand in length and scope, an epic provides a portrait of an entire culture, of the legends, beliefs, values, laws, arts, and ways of life of a people. The Finnish epic *The Kalevala* (page 808) is an example of an epic poem. (See Understanding Epics, page 806.)

FOLK LITERATURE READING MODEL

BEFORE READING | DURING READING | AFTER READING

BUILD BACKGROUND

- **Connect** your own knowledge and experiences to what you read. Many myths and legends were created to explain the changing seasons or the origins of thunder and lightning. What do you know about those natural phenomena?
- Read the **Build Background** and **Meet the Author** sections. Based on these sections, what do you think the poem or story will involve?

ANALYZE LITERATURE

- The **Analyze Literature** feature will focus on one or more literary techniques that are used in the selection. Make note of how the author handles these elements as you read.

SET PURPOSE

- Much folk literature has a moral or lesson in it. Use background information and the title of the piece to predict what the moral or lesson will be.

USE READING SKILLS

- Before reading, apply reading skills such as determining the author's purpose, analyzing text structure, previewing new vocabulary, and using context clues.

BEFORE READING | DURING READING | AFTER READING

USE READING STRATEGIES

- **Ask questions** about things that you don't understand or that seem unusual or interesting.
- **Make predictions** about what's going to happen next. As you read, gather more clues that will either confirm or change your predictions.
- **Visualize** by forming pictures in your mind to help you see the characters, actions, or other elements.
- **Make inferences,** or educated guesses, about what is not stated directly.
- **Clarify,** or check that you understand, what you read. Go back and reread any confusing or difficult parts before continuing.

ANALYZE LITERATURE

- What literary elements stand out as you read the poem or story?

MAKE CONNECTIONS

- Notice where there are **connections** between the story and your life or the world beyond the poem or story. Have you encountered references to this story in other places? How can the lesson be applied to modern life?

BEFORE READING | DURING READING | AFTER READING

REFER TO TEXT

- Recall the **facts.** Remember **details** like characters' names, locations or settings, and any other things that you can recall.
- Determine the **sequence of events,** or the order in which things happened.

REASON WITH TEXT

- **Apply** your ideas about the poem's or story's elements to see if they help you answer any additional questions.
- **Analyze** the text by breaking down information into smaller units and figuring out how those pieces fit into the story as a whole.

- **Evaluate** the text. **Draw conclusions** by bringing together what you have read and using this material to make a decision or form an opinion.

ANALYZE LITERATURE

- Review how the author's use of literary elements enhanced your understanding or enjoyment of the poem or story.

EXTEND THE TEXT

- Take your reading beyond the poem or story by exploring ideas through writing or doing other creative projects.

MAGIC WORDS

A Poem by Nalungiaq

BEFORE READING

Translated by Edward Field

BUILD BACKGROUND

Cultural Context "Magic Words" is taken from the oral tradition of the Inuit people. This poem teaches that words have a great deal of power to bring things into existence. Although people today might scoff at the idea that words literally have magical power, the poem reminds readers that words can create objects, people, animals, and places in the imagination. The poem can be read as a celebration of the power of literature to bring worlds of the imagination into existence. It expresses an Inuit priest's or shaman's belief that at one time words had magical powers that they no longer have today.

Reader's Context How is magic similar to the imagination?

ANALYZE LITERATURE: Oral Tradition

An **oral tradition** is a work, an idea, or a custom that is passed by word of mouth from generation to generation. In traditional cultures around the globe, ideas, values, beliefs, customs, news, and history are transmitted orally. Often, the works that are part of an oral tradition contain miraculous or magical elements.

SET PURPOSE

The Inuit lived in close harmony with nature, despite living in one of the bleakest regions of the world, an isolated area of Canada above the Arctic Circle. As you read, consider how this tight relationship with nature is revealed in the poem. Also look for miraculous or magical elements in the poem that reflect the oral tradition in which it originated.

MEET THE AUTHOR

Nalungiaq, an Inuit (Eskimo) woman, reported that she learned the song "Magic Words" from an elderly uncle named Unaraluk. Unaraluk was a shaman, a kind of sorcerer or priest. The song was first written down by Danish explorer Knud Rasmussen. Rasmussen, who was part Inuit and spoke the Inuit language, lived for some time with the Netsilik people during his expedition across arctic America, known as the Fifth Thule Expedition (1921–1924). He collected many Netsilik legends and tales in the desire to learn about the unique view such an isolated people had developed of their world and the universe. Poet Edward Field translated many of these stories. "Magic Words" is also included in Jerome Rothenberg's collection of traditional Native American poetry, *Shaking the Pumpkin.*

USE READING SKILLS

Main Idea The **main idea** of a piece of writing is the central point that the author develops with supporting details. In some cases, the main idea is actually stated. If it isn't stated, you will have to infer it.

In poetry, the main idea is often a central theme that is developed with imagery and, sometimes, explanation or example. A good way of finding the main idea of a selection is to gather important details into a Main Idea Map like the one below. As you read "Magic Words," use the details to help determine the main idea.

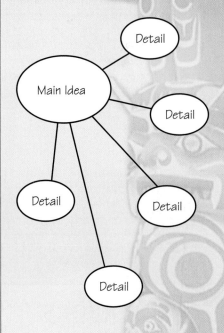

MAGIC WORDS

A Poem by **Nalungiaq**

Translated by Edward Field

In the very earliest times,
when both people and animals lived on earth,
a person could become an animal if he wanted to
and an animal could become a human being.
5   Sometimes we were people
and sometimes animals
and there was no difference.
All spoke the same, the universal tongue.
That was a time when words were like magic.
10   The mind had mysterious powers,
and a word uttered by chance
might have consequences.
It would suddenly come alive
and what people wanted to happen could happen—
15   all you had to do was say it.
Nobody could explain this.
That's just the way it was. ❖

DURING READING

USE READING STRATEGIES

Make Inferences What can you infer about the Inuit's relationship with nature by the ideas expressed in these first few lines?

DURING READING

ANALYZE LITERATURE

Oral Tradition Which lines in particular convey a sense of magic so frequently found in oral traditions?

MIRRORS & WINDOWS

"That was a time when words were like magic." In what ways have you witnessed the magic, or power, of words? How do words have power for you personally?

AFTER READING

REFER TO TEXT ▶ ▶ ▶ ▶	▶ REASON WITH TEXT	
1a. Recall the time the speaker of the poem is talking about, according to line 1. What observation does the speaker make in line 8 about language in that time?	**1b.** Does the speaker think that life today is different? How do you know?	**Understand** **Find meaning**
2a. According to lines 3 and 4, what could people and animals do in that time?	**2b.** What might this suggest about the way of life of the earliest Inuit people?	**Apply** **Use information**
3a. State the strange consequences that used to result from a word "uttered by chance."	**3b.** Identify evidence the speaker offers that people in earlier times lived in close harmony with nature and had powers they do not have today.	**Analyze** **Take things apart**
4a. Quote what people had to do to make their wishes happen.	**4b.** Determine whether you think people in ancient times felt they had the magical powers described in the poem, or whether that impression was created by the people of later generations. Explain.	**Evaluate** **Make judgments**
5a. Summarize what was magical about words in those times.	**5b.** Explain how words still perform magically every time a person reads a poem, story, or play.	**Create** **Bring ideas together**

ANALYZE LITERATURE: Oral Tradition

Stories from oral traditions are passed down through retellings often for centuries before they are written down. How might "Magic Words" have been affected by having been retold so many times, then transcribed and translated into an entirely different language?

EXTEND THE TEXT

Writing Options

Creative Writing Strange things, such as people turning into animals, often happen in dreams. Recall a dream you had once, and write a one-page **dream report** describing it. Dreams disappear quickly. If you cannot recall one, you may wish to keep a notebook beside your bed so that when you wake up, you can immediately write down what happened in your dream.

Descriptive Writing "Magic Words" focuses on the idea that words can be used to create people, places, and things that did not exist before. Writers use words to create magic all the time. Try doing some of this magic yourself. Close your eyes and create a place in your imagination. Then write a one-paragraph **description** of your place.

Collaborative Learning

Practice Storytelling Many children's stories, such

as "Cinderella," "The Frog Prince," and "Beauty and the Beast," contain elements of magic. Work with other students to brainstorm a list of such stories. You may want to consult the children's section in your school or community library. Take turns telling these stories to one another orally. Then discuss how stories change when they are told orally and not written down.

Lifelong Learning

Conduct an Interview Interview an older person—a grandparent, a neighbor, or a resident of a local nursing home—to learn what life was like long before you were born. Prepare a list of questions. Ask the person's permission to record the interview. When your interview is complete, play back the recording and transcribe, or write down, everything that was said. Then use one of the experiences of the person you interviewed to write a brief fictional story or a poem.

 Go to **www.mirrorsandwindows.com** for more.

Understanding Myths and Legends

MYTHS AND LEGENDS

Nearly every day, you encounter an example of the influence of ancient myths and age-old legends on our modern world. Did you have cereal this morning? The word "cereal" derives from Cerealia, a festival for Ceres, the Roman goddess of the harvest. Do you wear Nike shoes? "Nike" is the name of the Greek goddess of victory. For Valentine's Day, you may see cards decorated with a Cupid, a mischievous child with a bow and arrow. "Cupid" is the name of the young Roman god who is the son of Venus, the goddess of love. What do the situations listed above have in common? They each contain a reference to a myth or legend, a story told and retold over decades or centuries.

Myths

Myths are traditional stories, rooted in particular cultures, that deal with gods and other supernatural beings as well as with human heroes. Myths often embody religious beliefs and values and explain natural phenomena. Every early culture around the globe has produced its own myths.

In the Greek myth "Damon and Pythias" (page 848), the hero Pythias proves his loyalty to his friend Damon by risking his life for Damon. The Greek myth "Orpheus" (page 748) tells the story of "the most famous poet and musician who ever lived." In the Norse myth "The Death of Balder" (page 857), a god is killed by a piece of mistletoe.

Legends

Legends are stories that often have mythic qualities and sometimes serve as morality lessons or transmitters of cultural norms. Some are based on real historical figures, whereas others have a less certain origin. Even the legends about real people, however, are embellished with fantastic and sometimes superhuman aspects. As the stories are told over the years, they often change to reflect the cultures of the storytellers. For instance, the stories of King Arthur of England show him to be a good Christian king, who sends his knights on a quest for the Holy Grail, the drinking vessel used by Christ. It is widely believed, however, that the real Arthur was probably a Welsh chieftain who lived during the pre-Christian era.

Words from Mythology

Many words in the English language came from mythology. Some of them are listed below. Do you recognize any of them?

- **meander:** This word is derived from the ancient Greek river Maiandros or Maeander, which was known for its crooked and winding course, and means "a bend in a river." The verb form of *meander* means "to wander aimlessly."

- **narcissism:** This word means "to love oneself." It comes from the story of Narcissus, who fell in love with himself after seeing his own reflection in a pool.

- **nemesis:** This word means "someone who wants to bring about vengeance." It comes from the name of the goddess of vengeance.

- **stoical:** This word comes from a school of Greek philosophy that believed that people hoping to be wise should be free of joy, grief, and passions. As it is used today, *stoical* typically means "impassive" or "not showing emotion or pain."

ELEMENTS OF MYTHS AND LEGENDS

Archetypes

A young lad goes on a quest for adventure. At first, the idea seems thrilling, but soon the adventures turn more dangerous and challenging. Along the way, the lad is aided by a wise old mentor who teaches him the skills he will need. However, the forces of evil eventually kill the mentor, leaving the young man to finish the quest on his own. Through many trials, the lad succeeds and realizes he has become a mature, capable man.

Does this story sound familiar? The reason this plot sounds so familiar is that it is the basis of an archetypal story.

An **archetype** is a story, character, or theme that represents a familiar pattern repeated throughout literature and across cultures. The psychologist Carl Jung

popularized the term to refer to the idea of a "collective unconscious," which refers to the way in which certain compelling experiences have been encoded into the human consciousness and passed down through generations. Perhaps that is why today's readers can so readily grasp the universal meaning of traditional forms of literature. We respond emotionally to familiar symbols—the hero, the mentor, the quest—precisely because our minds are ready to understand their significance.

For example, the story above involves the archetypal themes of a quest and growing up. It also includes the archetypal characters of the boy hero becoming a man and the wise old mentor who must die before the boy can truly become the hero. Other archetypal themes, characters, and symbols include death and rebirth, initiation, "boy-meets-girl," the thief who aids the poor, the damsel in distress, and the trickster.

Many myths and legends are based on archetypes that we immediately recognize, even though our actual experiences do not involve noble quests, talking animals, or magical beings.

Tricksters

The mythical trickster character can be found in many cultures across the globe. The trickster, who is either an animal or a shape-shifter, is more than an annoyance to the mythical gods: He is often responsible for bringing important gifts to humanity, such as fire. In some instances, the trickster is also a creator, though he may bring disease, war, or other problems.

These are some of the most famous tricksters:

- Hare (African; becomes Br'er Rabbit in the *Uncle Remus* stories and basis for Bugs Bunny)
- Coyote (Southwestern Native American)
- Anansi (West African; usually in spider form)
- Eshu (African, particularly Yoruba)
- Eris (Greek; the goddess of discord)
- Maui (Hawaiian)

MYTHS AND LEGENDS IN MODERN SETTINGS

Myths and legends endure in the modern world because they precisely capture ideas about certain aspects of life. The stories have remained popular over the ages for their ability to entertain, as well as to create a common understanding. You will find these stories in film, theater, comic book form, among others. Listed below are just a few of the modern adaptations that exist today:

Morpheus from the movie *The Matrix.*

- The Disney movie *Mulan* is based on the legend of a person by the same name, found on page 838.
- *The Odyssey* is modernized in the film *O Brother, Where Art Thou.*
- Characters named from Greek mythology (Morpheus, Niobe, the Oracle) appear in the movie *The Matrix.*
- Cerberus, the creature who guards the entrance to the underworld, is referenced in the three-headed dog in *Harry Potter and the Sorcerer's Stone.*
- The story of Poseidon, god of the sea, is told in the film *The Poseidon Adventure.*

Orpheus

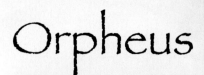

BUILD BACKGROUND

Cultural Context Dionysus (dī ō nī´ səs), the god of wine and revelry, plays an important role in **"Orpheus."** His followers were the Maenads, a wild group of women, and he demanded that sacrifice be paid to him. In the myth you will read, Dionysus becomes angry with Orpheus, whose values contradict his. Other Greek gods mentioned in the selection include Hades (hā´ dēz), the god of the underworld; and Helios (hē´ lē əs) or Apollo, the sun god.

Underlying the myth of Orpheus is one of the most common human desires: immortality. The myth has been told and retold, perhaps most famously by the Roman poet Ovid in his *Metamorphoses*, and the Orpheus story has been the subject of numerous paintings and musical compositions.

Reader's Context   Where have you read about or seen the influence of Greek mythology? List some specific examples.

ANALYZE LITERATURE: Plot and Conflict

The **plot** of a literary work is a series of events related to a central **conflict,** or struggle. A typical plot involves the introduction of a conflict, its development, and its eventual resolution. The conflict may involve a struggle between characters, a struggle between the main character and a force of nature, or a clash between a character and society. Conflict can also unfold internally, when two or more emotions come into collision within a character.

SET PURPOSE

One indicator of an interesting plot is the presence of *suspense,* or a feeling of uncertainty and tension about what will happen next. As you read, look for the central conflict in the plot, as well as for ways it creates suspense.

MEET THE AUTHOR

Robert Graves (1895–1985), like so many of his generation, was profoundly influenced by his experiences as a soldier in World War I, and this influence is apparent in much of his writing. His classic autobiography, *Goodbye to All That,* focuses on his own wartime nightmare. Although he was born in England and served that country in battle, Graves spent most of his adult life on the island of Majorca, Spain. There, he wrote lyric poetry, fiction, and nonfiction works related to history, often that of the Classical Era (the height of the cultures of ancient Greece and Rome). He was also known for his studies in mythology.

USE READING SKILLS

Importance of Details In "Orpheus," you will find details that consist mainly of references to people and places in Greek mythology. You could easily become bogged down by these details if you are unfamiliar with them. That's why it is necessary for you to be able to determine which details are important to your understanding of the myth and which are not. Use a graphic organizer like the one below to record the myth's major and minor details. If you come across a major detail you do not understand, do some research to figure out what it means.

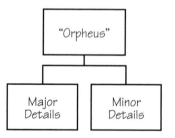

PREVIEW VOCABULARY

Use the context clues in the sentences below to figure out the meanings of the underlined words from the selection.

1. The <u>plaintive</u> song about the death of a friend brought tears to my eyes.
2. Mateo stared <u>reverently</u> at the majestic canyon stretching out before him.

Orpheus Singing His Lament for Eurydice, c. 1865–70. Jean-Baptiste-Camille Corot. Kimbell Art Museum, Fort Worth, Texas.

ORPHEUS

A Myth Retold by **Robert Graves**

Tearfully, the Muses collected his limbs and buried them at Leibethra,
at the foot of Mount Olympus, where the nightingales now sing
sweeter than anywhere else in the world.

Orpheus, son of the Thracian King Oeagrus and the Muse Calliope,[1] was the most famous poet and musician who ever lived. Apollo presented him with a lyre, and the Muses taught him its use, so that he not only enchanted wild beasts, but made the trees

USE READING SKILLS

Importance of Details
How important are the muses to the myth so far? Do you know what a muse is? How can you find out?

---

1. **Calliope** (kə li´ ə pē). Muse of eloquence and epic poetry

Descent to the Underworld In classical mythology, the descent to the underworld (called *katabasis* in Greek) is a key theme associated with the greatest of heroes. Most heroes must descend into the underworld in order to obtain necessary knowledge. The twelfth and final labor of Hercules, for example, tells of the hero's descent to Hades to capture the three-headed dog Cerberus. In Homer's *The Odyssey*, the hero Odysseus interviews the shades of the dead after digging a large pit and performing a sacrifice. Virgil's Roman epic the *Aeneid* pictures the hero Aeneas descending to the underworld, where he acquires guidance and encouragement from his dead father, enabling Aeneas to carry out his epic mission: the founding of Rome.

and rocks move from their places to follow the sound of his music. At Zone in Thrace[2] a number of ancient mountain oaks are still standing in the pattern of one of his dances, just as he left them.

After a visit to Egypt, Orpheus joined the Argonauts,[3] with whom he sailed to Colchis, his music helping them to overcome many difficulties—and, on his return, married Eurydice, whom some called Agriope, and settled among the savage Cicones of Thrace.

One day, near Tempe, in the valley of the river Peneius, Eurydice met Aristaeus, who tried to force her. She trod on a serpent as she fled, and died of its bite; but Orpheus boldly descended into Tartarus,[4] hoping to fetch her back. He used the passage which opens at Aornum in Thesprotis and, on his arrival, not only charmed the ferryman Charon, the Dog Cerberus,[5] and the three Judges of the Dead with his <u>plaintive</u> music, but temporarily suspended the tortures of the damned; and so far soothed the savage heart of Hades that he won leave to restore Eurydice to the upper world. Hades made a single condition: that Orpheus might not look behind him until she was safely back under the light of the sun. Eurydice followed Orpheus up through the dark passage, guided by the sounds of his lyre, and it was only when he reached the sunlight again that he turned to see whether she were still behind him, and so lost her for ever.

When Dionysus invaded Thrace, Orpheus neglected to honor him, but taught other sacred mysteries and preached the evil of sacrificial murder to the men of Thrace, who listened <u>reverently</u>. Every morning he would rise to greet the dawn on the summit of Mount Pangaeum, preaching that Helius, whom he

USE READING STRATEGIES

Make Inferences Why does Orpheus go into Tartarus? What inferences can you make about his character based on this action?

ANALYZE LITERATURE

Conflict Describe the conflict between Orpheus and Dionysus in this paragraph. How do you think the conflict will be resolved?

2. **Thrace.** Ancient region in the Balkan Peninsula of Greece, north of the Aegean Sea

3. **Argonauts.** Men who sail with the hero Jason to search for the Golden Fleece in Greek mythology

4. **Tartarus.** Infernal abyss below Hades, which is the home of the dead, and ruled by Hades, the god of the underworld

5. **Charon, the dog Cerberus.** Charon was the boatman who led the dead across the river Styx into Hades; Cerberus was a three-headed dog that guarded the gate of Hades.

plain • tive (plān´ tiv) *adj.,* mournful; sad
rev • er • ent • ly (rev´ rənt lē) *adv.,* in a manner suggesting deep respect, love, or awe

Orpheus, 1865. Gustave Moreau. Musée d'Orsay, Paris.

Critical Viewing

Critique the use of light in this painting. What parts does the artist choose to highlight? What does he choose to hide in shadows? What do these choices suggest about the focus and mood of the painting?

named Apollo, was the greatest of all gods. In vexation, Dionysus set the Maenads[6] upon him at Deium in Macedonia. First waiting until their husbands had entered Apollo's temple, where Orpheus served as priest, they seized the weapons stacked outside, burst in, murdered their husbands, and tore Orpheus limb from limb. His head they threw into the river Hebrus, but it floated, still singing, down to the sea, and was carried to the island of Lesbos.

Tearfully, the Muses collected his limbs and buried them at Leibethra, at the foot of Mount Olympus,[7] where the nightingales now sing sweeter than anywhere else in the world. The Maenads had attempted to cleanse themselves of Orpheus's blood in the river Helicorn; but the River-god dived under the ground and disappeared for the space of nearly four miles, emerging with a different name, the Baphyra. Thus he avoided becoming an accessory to the murder. ❖

---

6. **Maenads** (mē´ nadz). Wild group of women who worshiped Dionysus, the god of revelry
7. **Mount Olympus.** Mountain where the gods live

Based on this myth, what is your impression of Greek culture? What kinds of things about Greek culture might be similar to American culture today? What is different?

REFER TO TEXT ▶ ▶ ▶ ▶	▶ REASON WITH TEXT	
1a. Who is Orpheus, and for what is he best known?	1b. Describe how Orpheus's talents help him during his life.	**Understand** **Find meaning**
2a. Recall the condition Hades establishes when Orpheus and Eurydice are about to depart from the underworld.	2b. Apply what you know about Hades to determine why he establishes this condition.	**Apply** **Use information**
3a. What happens to Orpheus at the hands of Dionysus?	3b. Infer why Dionysus is angry with Orpheus.	**Analyze** **Take things apart**
4a. What is your opinion of Orpheus's character? What is your opinion of Dionysus?	4b. Judge whether or not Orpheus deserved his fate. Support your answer with evidence from the text.	**Evaluate** **Make judgments**
5a. Why do you think the Greeks might have told this myth?	5b. Explain what general truth or truths the myth of Orpheus conveys to you. Use the text to support your explanation.	**Create** **Bring ideas together**

ANALYZE LITERATURE: Plot and Conflict

Review the elements of plot in the Understanding Plot section of Unit 1. If you were to make a Plot Diagram of "Orpheus," what would all the parts be? What conflict or conflicts exist in "Orpheus"?

LEVERTOV

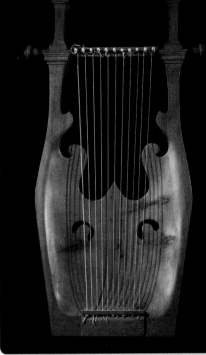

Literature CONNECTION

Denise Levertov's poem **"Tree Telling of Orpheus,"** which first appeared in *Stony Brook* (1968), makes many allusions to the myth of Orpheus. Levertov (1923–1997) was an American poet who was born in Essex, England, where she grew up and was educated at home by her mother. During World War II, Levertov worked as a civilian nurse in London. Her first book of poetry, *The Double Image,* was published in 1946. Levertov published more than a dozen books of poetry and two volumes of essays.

Tree Telling of Orpheus

A Lyric Poem by **Denise Levertov**

White dawn. Stillness.　　　　When the rippling began
　　　I took it for sea-wind, coming to our valley with rumors
　　　of salt, of treeless horizons. But the white fog
didn't stir; the leaves of my brothers remained outstretched,
5　　unmoving.
　　　　　　Yet the rippling drew nearer—and then
my own outermost branches began to tingle, almost as if
fire had been lit below them, too close, and their twig-tips
were drying and curling.
10　　　　　　　　Yet I was not afraid, only
　　　　　　　　deeply alert.

I was the first to see him,[1] for I grew
　　　　　out on the pasture slope, beyond the forest.
He was a man, it seemed: the two
15　　moving stems, the short trunk, the two
arm-branches, flexible, each with five leafless
　　　　　　　　　　twigs at their ends,

---

1. **him.** Orpheus, the poet-musician of Greek mythology

and the head that's crowned by brown or gold grass,
bearing a face not like the beaked face of a bird,
20   more like a flower's.
                                He carried a burden made of
some cut branch bent while it was green,
strands of a vine tight-stretched across it. From this,
when he touched it, and from his voice
25   which unlike the wind's voice had no need of our
leaves and branches to complete its sound,
                                            came the ripple.
But it was now no longer a ripple (he had come near and
stopped in my first shadow) it was a wave that bathed me
30   as if rain
                            rose from below and around me
                    instead of falling.
And what I felt was no longer a dry tingling:
        I seemed to be singing as he sang, I seemed to know
35   what the lark knows; all my sap
                    was mounting towards the sun that by now
                        had risen, the mist was rising, the grass
was drying, yet my roots felt music moisten them
deep under earth.

40   He came still closer, leaned on my trunk:
                        the bark thrilled like a leaf still-folded.
Music! There was no twig of me not
                                        trembling with joy and fear.
Then as he sang
45   it was no longer sounds only that made the music:
he spoke, and as no tree listens I listened, and language
                        came into my roots
                                        out of the earth,
                    into my bark
50   out of the air,
                        into the pores of my greenest shoots
                                gently as dew
and there was no word he sang but I knew its meaning.
He told of journeys,
55   of where sun and moon go while we stand in dark,
        of an earth-journey he dreamed he would take some day
deeper than roots…
He told of the dreams of man, wars, passions, griefs,
                and I, a tree, understood words—ah, it seemed
60   my thick bark would split like a sapling's that

Fire he sang,
that trees fear, and I, a tree, rejoiced
in its flames.
New buds broke forth from me
though it was full summer.

                                        grew too fast in the spring
                when a late frost wounds it.
                                        Fire he sang,
                that trees fear, and I, a tree, rejoiced in its flames.
65   New buds broke forth from me though it was full summer.
                        As though his lyre[2] (now I knew its name)
                        were both frost and fire, its chords flamed
                up to the crown of me.
                                        I was seed again.
70   I was fern in the swamp.
                                                I was coal.

                And at the heart of my wood
                (so close I was to becoming man or a god)
                        there was a kind of silence, a kind of sickness,
75   something akin to what men call boredom,
                                                                something
                (the poem descended a scale, a stream over stones)
                                that gives to a candle a coldness
                                        in the midst of its burning, he said.
80   It was then,
                        when in the blaze of his power that
                                        reached me and changed me
                        I thought I should fall my length,
                that the singer began
85   to leave me.   Slowly
                        moved from my noon shadow
                                        to open light,

---

2. **lyre.** A small stringed instrument of the harp family, used by the ancient
Greeks to accompany singers

words leaping and dancing over his shoulders
back to me
90   <u>rivery</u> sweep of lyre-tones becoming
slowly again
                ripple.
And I
           in terror
95   but not in doubt of
                          what I must do
in <u>anguish</u>, in haste,
                wrenched from the earth root after root,
the soil heaving and cracking, the moss tearing <u>asunder</u>—
100 and behind me the others: my brothers
forgotten since dawn. In the forest
they too had heard,
and were pulling their roots in pain
out of a thousand years' layers of dead leaves,
105   rolling the rocks away,
                  breaking themselves
                       out of
                   their depths.
You would have thought we would lose the sound of the lyre,
110   of the singing
so dreadful the storm-sounds were, where there was no storm,
        no wind but the rush of our
      branches moving, our trunks breasting the air.
        But the music!
115   The music reached us.
Clumsily,
      stumbling over our own roots,
            rustling our leaves
                in answer,
120 we moved, we followed.

All day we followed, up hill and down.
            We learned to dance,
for he would stop, where the ground was flat,
           and words he said
125 taught us to leap and to wind in and out
around one another   in figures   the lyre's measure designed.

---

riv • er • y (ri′ vər ē) *adj.*, riverlike
an • **guish** (aŋ′ gwish) *n.*, great suffering from worry or pain
a • **sun** • **der** (ə sun′ dər) *adv.*, into pieces or parts

Orpheus Leading Eurydice from the Underworld, 1861. Jean Baptiste Camille Corot. Museum of Fine Arts, Houston, Texas, United States.

The singer
        laughed till he wept to see us, he was so glad.
                  At sunset

130   we came to this place I stand in, this <u>knoll</u>
with its ancient grove that was bare grass then.
        In the last light of that day his song became
farewell. •
      He stilled our longing.
135   He sang our sun-dried roots back into earth,

knoll (nōl) *n.,* mound

watered them: all-night rain of music so quiet

we could almost

not hear it in the

moonless dark.

140   By dawn he was gone.

We have stood here since,

in our new life.

We have waited.

He does not return.

145   It is said he made his earth-journey, and lost
what he sought.

It is said they <u>felled</u> him

and cut up his limbs for firewood.

And it is said

150   his head still sang and was swept out to sea singing.
Perhaps he will not return.

But what we have lived

comes back to us.

We see more.

155

We feel, as our rings increase,

something that lifts our branches, that stretches our furthest

leaf-tips

further.

The wind, the birds,

160

do not sound poorer but clearer,

recalling our agony, and the way we danced.
The music! ❖

---

fell (fel) *v.,* knock or cut down

REFER TO TEXT ▶ ▶ ▶ ▶	▶ REASON WITH TEXT	
1a. State what the trees are doing in lines 93–108.	1b. Explain why the trees are following the musician.	**Understand** **Find meaning**
2a. What parts of the myth of Orpheus are retold in lines 145–150?	2b. Decide how accurately the poem portrays the myth of Orpheus. Support your answer with evidence from both texts.	**Evaluate** **Make judgments**
3a. What does the musician do for the trees?	3b. Summarize the effect of the music on the trees.	**Create** **Bring ideas together**

TEXT ◄—^{TO}—► TEXT CONNECTION

- How does "Tree Telling of Orpheus" affect the way you understand the myth?
- What effect does the shift in point of view in Levertov's poem have on the emotional impact of the Orpheus myth? Explain your answer.
- How is reading a poem different from reading a myth?

EXTEND THE TEXT

Writing Options

Creative Writing Imagine that you are a friend of Orpheus and Eurydice and are outraged at what happened to Eurydice. Write a **letter of appeal** to the gods explaining why you think Hades should not have been so strict in enforcing his "single condition."

Descriptive Writing For an encyclopedia of famous mythological characters, write a brief **character sketch** of Orpheus, based on what you learned about him from the myth and the poem. A character sketch is a description of a character in a story. The character sketch should include a description of the character's physical appearance, as well as attributes of his or her personality. Be sure to use evidence from the texts to support your ideas.

Collaborative Learning

Re-create a Greek Myth In a small group, choose a myth that would be interesting to re-create in a short play. You can find the texts of most myths on the Internet, or in anthologies located in the library. After selecting a myth, designate roles for the group members such as playwright, director, actors, and stage manager. Assign someone to create and manage props and costumes, if desired. Construct a script and practice your roles. Finally, present your play to the rest of the class.

Lifelong Learning

Write a Personality Quiz Choose a character from Greek mythology, and do some research on the character's personality traits. Using your research, write a personality quiz for a teen magazine with a title like "Find Your Inner Apollo" or "Hopeless Romantic or Mournful Musician: How Much Do You Resemble Orpheus?" Write at least five multiple-choice questions that achieve the purpose of your quiz. To find ideas for your questions, try doing an Internet search for personality quizzes. Include an answer key that tells readers about their personalities based on their answers.

 Go to **www.mirrorsandwindows.com** for more.

READING ASSESSMENT

1. Eurydice died as the result of which of the following?
   - A. a fall from a great height
   - B. a drowning accident
   - C. a snakebite
   - D. an illness
   - E. an act of disobedience

2. On page 750, the word *plaintive* most nearly means
   - A. sad.
   - B. critical.
   - C. irritated.
   - D. amused.
   - E. plain.

3. Hades allows Eurydice to return to the land of the living on the condition that Orpheus
   - A. give up his art.
   - B. not look back during the journey.
   - C. pay a tax to Charon, the boatman.
   - D. worship Apollo.
   - E. None of the above

4. In "Tree Telling of Orpheus," how do the trees react to hearing Orpheus's music?
   - A. They sway with the music and fall down.
   - B. They uproot themselves and follow Orpheus.
   - C. They shake wildly and shed all of their leaves.
   - D. They drop pine cones onto Orpheus.
   - E. They spontaneously burst into flame.

5. Which phrase from "Tree Telling of Orpheus" contains an example of alliteration?
   - A. "the two moving stems, the short trunk, the two arm-branches"
   - B. "I took it for sea-wind, coming to our valley with rumors of salt, of treeless horizons"
   - C. "it seemed my thick bark would split like a sapling's that grew too fast in the spring"
   - D. "his head still sang and was swept out to sea singing"
   - E. All of the above

6. What conflicts does Orpheus face in this myth? Identify at least two external conflicts that Orpheus experiences.

from **Sundiata: An Epic of Old Mali**
An Epic Legend by D. T. Niane

from **The Once and Future King**
A Legend by T. H. White

COMPARING LITERATURE

BUILD BACKGROUND

Literary Context These two stories blend fact and fiction to tell of heroes emerging in times of darkness.

In the thirteenth century, the Mandinka of western Africa suffered under the tyrant Sumanguru. The excerpt from **Sundiata: An Epic of Old Mali** tells of the emergence of a great hero who would defeat Sumanguru and create the peaceable kingdom of what is now called Mali.

The excerpt from **The Once and Future King** describes how an unknown squire shocked the kingdom by passing a test that would make him king.

As you read the selections, consider the following questions:
• What heroic traits does each main character possess?
• What values, beliefs, traditions, and rituals are expressed in each story?
• What makes each main character an unlikely hero?

Reader's Context When have you achieved something others thought impossible? What motivated you to succeed?

USE READING SKILLS

Cause and Effect When you evaluate cause and effect, you look for a logical relationship between a cause or causes and one or more effects. Use a Cause-and-Effect Chart like the one below while you read the selections to help you keep track of events in the stories and figure out the reasons why certain things happen.

Effects

Cause

COMPARE LITERATURE: Legend and Archetype

A **legend** is a story that is passed down over generations, often based on real events or characters from the past. As you read about Sundiata and King Arthur, consider which elements in the selections might be historical and which are probably not.

An **archetype** is a type of character, image, theme, symbol, plot, or other element that has appeared in the literature of the world from

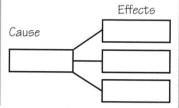

ancient times until today. An example of an archetype is the idea of characters going on a journey or quest to learn about themselves. As you read, think about which elements of the stories could be archetypes.

MEET THE AUTHORS

WHITE

Djibril Tamsir (D. T.) Niane (b. 1932) is a West African historian who comes from a long line of griots (grē´ ōs'), or African storytellers, who pass on the history and legends of their people. In *Sundiata: An Epic of Old Mali,* Niane retells the story of Sundiata in prose for a Western audience.

Terence Hanbury (T. H.) White (1906–1964) was born in India, then moved to England as a child and lived there for the rest of his life. White is best known for his four-novel series *The Once and Future King*, an adaptation of the King Arthur legend. His unique tone — at first humorous and playful and later more satirical — made White's version of the tale original.

COMPARING LITERATURE

from SUNDIATA

An Epic of Old Mali

An Epic Legend by **D. T. Niane**

Naré Maghan was very perplexed. Could it be that the stiff-jointed son of Sogolon was the one the hunter soothsayer had foretold?

Characters

Sogolon Djata (sō´ gō lōn jä´ tä), or **Sundiata** (sün jä´ tä), hero of the story, destined to become a great king and founder of the united kingdom of Mali; also called Mari (mä´ rē) Djata

Naré Maghan (nä´ rä mä gän´), Sundiata's father and a king, or chieftain, of the Mande people

Sogolon (sō´ gō lōn), one of the king's wives and Sundiata's mother; also called Sogolon Kedjou (ke´ jü)

Sassouma Bérété (sä sü´ mä be re tä´) and **Namandjé** (nä män jä´), the king's other wives

Kolonkan (kō lōn´ kän) and **Djamarou** (jä´ mä rü), Sundiata's sisters

Dankaran Touman (däŋ´ kä rän tü´ män), Sundiata's older half-brother, son of Sassouma

Boukari (bü kä´ rē), Sundiata's younger half-brother, son of Namandjé; also called Manding (män´ diŋ) Boukari

Gnankouman Doua (nyän kü´ män dü´ ä), the king's griot; also called Doua

Balla Fasséké (bä´ lä fä sä kä´), Sundiata's griot and counselor

Farakourou (fä rä kü´ rü), master blacksmith and soothsayer

Nounfaïri (nün´ fä ir' ē), Farakourou's father, also a blacksmith and soothsayer

God has his mysteries which none can fathom. You, perhaps, will be a king. You can do nothing about it. You, on the other hand, will be unlucky, but you can do nothing about that either. Each man finds his way already marked out for him and he can change nothing of it.

USE READING STRATEGIES

Visualize Sketch or describe in your own words Sogolon Djata's appearance.

Sogolon's son had a slow and difficult childhood. At the age of three he still crawled along on all-fours while children of the same age were already walking. He had nothing of the great beauty of his father Naré Maghan. He had a head so big that he seemed unable to support it; he also had large eyes which would open wide whenever anyone entered his mother's house. He was <u>taciturn</u> and used to spend the whole day just sitting in the middle of the house. Whenever his mother went out he would crawl on all fours to rummage about in the calabashes[1] in search of food, for he was very greedy.

<u>Malicious</u> tongues began to blab. What three-year-old has not yet taken his first steps? What three-year-old is not the despair of his parents through his whims and shifts of mood? What three-year-old is not the joy of his circle through his backwardness in talking? Sogolon Djata (for it was thus that they called him, prefixing his mother's name to his), Sogolon Djata, then, was very different from others of his own age. He spoke little and his severe face never relaxed into a smile. You would have thought that he was already thinking, and what amused children of his age bored him. Often Sogolon would make some of them come to him to keep him company. These children

were already walking and she hoped that Djata, seeing his companions walking, would be tempted to do likewise. But nothing came of it. Besides, Sogolon Djata would brain[2] the poor little things with his already strong arms and none of them would come near him any more.

The king's first wife was the first to rejoice at Sogolon Djata's infirmity. Her own son, Dankaran Touman, was already eleven. He was a fine and lively boy, who spent the day running about the village with those of his own age. He had even begun his initiation in the bush.[3] The king had had a bow made for him and he used to go behind the town to practice archery with his companions. Sassouma was quite happy and snapped her fingers at Sogolon, whose child was still crawling on the ground. Whenever the latter happened to pass by her house, she would say, "Come, my son, walk, jump, leap about. The jinn didn't promise you anything out of the ordinary, but I prefer a son who walks on his two legs to a lion that crawls on the ground."

She spoke thus whenever Sogolon went by her door. The <u>innuendo</u> would go straight home and then she would burst into laughter, that <u>diabolical</u> laughter which a jealous woman knows how to use so well.

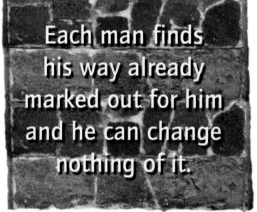

Each man finds his way already marked out for him and he can change nothing of it.

---

1. **calabashes** (ka´ lə bash' es). Utensils made from the shells of gourds
2. **brain.** Used here as a verb, it means to hit on the head.
3. **initiation in the bush.** Rite of passage into manhood, which began at age twelve and involved learning tribal lore

tac • i • turn (ta´ sə tʉrn') *adj.*, not willing to talk much
ma • li • cious (mə li´ shəs) *adj.*, mean-spirited
in • nu • en • do (in' yə wen´ dō[']) *n.*, indirect remark or hint, usually negative or suggestive
di • a • bol • i • cal (dī' ə bä´ li kəl) *adj.*, devilish; inhumanly cruel or wicked

Her son's infirmity weighed heavily upon Sogolon Kedjou; she had resorted to all her talent as a sorceress to give strength to her son's legs, but the rarest herbs had been useless. The king himself lost hope.

How impatient man is! Naré Maghan became imperceptibly estranged but Gnankouman Doua never ceased reminding him of the hunter's words. Sogolon became pregnant again. The king hoped for a son, but it was a daughter called Kolonkan. She resembled her mother and had nothing of her father's beauty. The disheartened king debarred Sogolon from[4] his house and she lived in semi-disgrace for a while. Naré Maghan married the daughter of one of his allies, the king of the Kamaras. She was called Namandjé and her beauty was legendary. A year later she brought a boy into the world. When the king consulted soothsayers[5] on the destiny of this son he received the reply that Namandjé's child would be the right hand of some mighty king. The king gave the newly-born the name of Boukari. He was to be called Manding Boukari or Manding Bory later on.

Naré Maghan was very perplexed. Could it be that the stiff-jointed son of Sogolon was the one the hunter sooth-sayer had foretold?

"The Almighty has his mysteries," Gnankouman Doua would say and, taking up the hunter's words, added, "The silk-cotton tree emerges from a tiny seed."

One day Naré Maghan came along to the house of Nounfaïri, the blacksmith seer[6] of Niani. He was an old, blind man. He received the king in the anteroom which served as his workshop. To the king's question he replied, "When the seed germinates growth is not always easy; great trees grow slowly but they plunge their roots deep into the ground."

USE READING STRATEGIES

Make Inferences
Why does the birth of Namandje's child confuse Naré Maghan? What might it mean for Sogolon Djata?

"But has the seed really germinated?" said the king.

"Of course," replied the blind seer. "Only the growth is not as quick as you would like it; how impatient man is."

This interview and Doua's confidence gave the king some assurance. To the great displeasure of Sassouma Bérété the king restored Sogolon to favor and soon another daughter was born to her. She was given the name of Djamarou.

However, all Niani talked of nothing else but the stiff-legged son of Sogolon. He was now seven and he still crawled to get about. In spite of all the king's affection, Sogolon was in despair. Naré Maghan aged and he felt his time coming to an end. Dankaran Touman, the son of Sassouma Bérété, was now a fine youth.

One day Naré Maghan made Mari Djata come to him and he spoke to the child as one speaks to an adult. "Mari Djata, I am growing old and soon I shall be no more among you, but before death takes me off I am going to give you the present each king gives his successor. In Mali every prince has his own griot.[7] Doua's father was my father's griot, Doua is mine and the son of Doua, Balla Fasséké here, will be your griot. Be inseparable friends from this day forward. From his mouth you will hear the history of your ancestors, you will learn the art of governing Mali according to the principles which our ancestors have bequeathed to us. I have served my term and done my duty too. I have done everything which a king of Mali ought to do. I am handing an enlarged kingdom over to you and I leave you sure allies. May your destiny be accomplished, but never forget that Niani is your capital and Mali the cradle of your ancestors."

---

4. **debarred...from.** Prohibited from entering
5. **soothsayers.** Individuals who predict the future
6. **seer (sē´ər).** Person with exceptional spiritual and moral insight
7. **griot (grē´ō').** In West African culture, a keeper of memories, stories, songs, and historical information, as well as an adviser to the ruler

The child, as if he had understood the whole meaning of the king's words, beckoned Balla Fasséké to approach. He made room for him on the hide he was sitting on and then said, "Balla, you will be my griot."

"Yes, son of Sogolon, if it pleases God," replied Balla Fasséké.

The king and Doua exchanged glances that radiated confidence.

A short while after this interview between Naré Maghan and his son the king died. Sogolon's son was no more than seven years old. The council of elders met in the king's palace. It was no use Doua's defending the king's will which reserved the throne for Mari Djata, for the council took no account of Naré Maghan's wish. With the help of Sassouma Bérété's <u>intrigues</u>, Dankaran Touman was proclaimed king and a regency council was formed in which the queen mother was all-powerful. A short time after, Doua died.

As men have short memories, Sogolon's son was spoken of with nothing but irony and scorn. People had seen one-eyed kings, one-armed kings, and lame kings, but a stiff-legged king had never been heard tell of. No matter how great the destiny promised for Mari Djata might be, the throne could not be given to someone who had no power in his legs; if the jinn loved him, let them begin by giving him the use of his legs. Such were the remarks that Sogolon heard every day. The queen mother, Sassouma Bérété, was the source of all this gossip.

USE READING SKILLS

Cause and Effect
What important decision is made as a result of the king's death?

Having become all-powerful, Sassouma Bérété persecuted Sogolon because the late Naré Maghan had preferred her. She banished Sogolon and her son to a back yard of the palace. Mari Djata's mother now occupied an old hut which had served as a lumber-room of Sassouma's.

in • trigue (in' trēg´) *n.*, secret or underhanded plot

The wicked queen mother allowed free passage to all those inquisitive people who wanted to see the child that still crawled at the age of seven. Nearly all the inhabitants of Niani filed into the palace and the poor Sogolon wept to see herself thus given over to public ridicule. Mari Djata took on a ferocious look in front of the crowd of sightseers. Sogolon found a little consolation only in the love of her eldest daughter, Kolonkan. She was four and she could walk. She seemed to understand all her mother's miseries and already she helped her with the housework. Sometimes, when Sogolon was attending to the chores, it was she who stayed beside her sister Djamarou, quite small as yet.

Sogolon Kedjou and her children lived on the queen mother's leftovers, but she kept a little garden in the open ground behind the village. It was there that she passed her brightest moments looking after her onions and gnougous.[8] One day she happened to be short of condiments and went to the queen mother to beg a little baobab leaf.[9]

"Look you," said the malicious Sassouma, "I have a calabash full. Help yourself, you poor woman. As for me, my son knew how to walk at seven and it was he who went and picked these baobab leaves. Take them then, since your son is unequal to mine." Then she laughed derisively with that fierce laughter which cuts through your flesh and penetrates right to the bone.

Sogolon Kedjou was dumbfounded. She had never imagined that hate could be so strong in a human being. With a lump in her throat she left Sassouma's. Outside her hut Mari Djata, sitting on his useless legs, was blandly eating out of a calabash. Unable to contain herself any longer, Sogolon burst into sobs and seizing a piece of wood, hit her son.

"Oh son of misfortune, will you never walk? Through your fault I have just suffered the greatest affront of my life! What have I done, God, for you to punish me in this way?"

Mari Djata seized the piece of wood and, looking at his mother, said, "Mother, what's the matter?"

"Shut up, nothing can ever wash me clean of this insult."

"But what then?"

"Sassouma has just humiliated me over a matter of a baobab leaf. At your age her own son could walk and used to bring his mother baobab leaves."

"Cheer up, Mother, cheer up."

"No. It's too much. I can't."

"Very well then, I am going to walk today," said Mari Djata. "Go and tell my father's smiths to make me the heaviest possible iron rod. Mother, do you want just the leaves of the baobab or would you rather I brought you the whole tree?"

USE READING STRATEGIES

Make Predictions
Predict how you think Sogolon Djata will use the iron bar.

"Ah, my son, to wipe out this insult I want the tree and its roots at my feet outside my hut."

Balla Fasséké, who was present, ran to the master smith, Farakourou, to order an iron rod.

Sogolon had sat down in front of her hut. She was weeping softly and holding her head between her two hands. Mari Djata went calmly back to his calabash of rice and began eating again as if nothing had happened. From time to time he looked up discreetly at his mother who was murmuring in a low voice, "I want the whole tree, in front of my hut, the whole tree."

All of a sudden a voice burst into laughter behind the hut. It was the wicked Sassouma telling one of her serving women about the scene of humiliation and she was laughing loudly so that Sogolon could hear. Sogolon fled into the hut and hid her face under the blankets so as not to have before her eyes this

---

8. **gnougous** (nü´ güz"). Type of root vegetable
9. **baobab** (baü´ bab') **leaf.** Leaf used to flavor food

heedless boy, who was more preoccupied with eating than with anything else. With her head buried in the bed-clothes Sogolon wept and her body shook violently. Her daughter, Sogolon Djamarou, had come and sat down beside her and she said, "Mother, Mother, don't cry. Why are you crying?"

Mari Djata had finished eating and, dragging himself along on his legs, he came and sat under the wall of the hut for the sun was scorching. What was he thinking about? He alone knew.

The royal forges[10] were situated outside the walls and over a hundred smiths worked there. The bows, spears, arrows and shields of Niani's warriors came from there. When Balla Fasséké came to order the iron rod, Farakourou said to him, "The great day has arrived then?"

"Yes. Today is a day like any other, but it will see what no other day has seen."

The master of the forges, Farakourou, was the son of the old Nounfaïri, and he was a soothsayer like his father. In his workshops there was an enormous iron bar wrought by his father Nounfaïri. Everybody wondered what this bar was destined to be used for. Farakourou called six of his apprentices and told them to carry the iron bar to Sogolon's house.

When the smiths put the gigantic iron bar down in front of the hut the noise was so frightening that Sogolon, who was lying down, jumped up with a start. Then Balla Fasséké, son of Gnankouman Doua, spoke.

"Here is the great day, Mari Djata. I am speaking to you, Maghan, son of Sogolon. The waters of the Niger can efface the stain from the body, but they cannot wipe out an insult. Arise, young lion, roar, and may the bush know that from henceforth it has a master."

The apprentice smiths were still there. Sogolon had come out and everyone was watching Mari Djata. He crept on all-fours and came to the iron bar. Supporting himself on his knees and one hand, with the other hand he picked up the iron bar without any effort and stood it up vertically. Now he was resting on nothing but his knees and held the bar with both his hands. A deathly silence had gripped all those present. Sogolon Djata closed his eyes, held tight, the muscles in his arms tensed. With a violent jerk he threw his weight on to it and his knees left the ground. Sogolon Kedjou was all eyes and watched her son's legs which were trembling as though from an electric shock. Djata was sweating and the sweat ran from his brow. In a great effort he straightened up and was on his feet at one go—but the great bar of iron was twisted and had taken the form of a bow!

Then Balla Fasséké sang out the "Hymn to the Bow," striking up with his powerful voice:
"Take your bow, Simbon,[11]
Take your bow and let us go.
Take your bow, Sogolon Djata."

When Sogolon saw her son standing she stood dumb for a moment, then suddenly she sang these words of thanks to God who had given her son the use of his legs:
"Oh day, what a beautiful day,
Oh day, day of joy;

"Yes. Today is a day like any other, but it will see what no other day has seen."

---

10. **forges.** Blacksmiths' shops
11. **Simbon.** Praise name for a great hunter

Allah[12] Almighty, you never created a finer day.

So my son is going to walk!"

Standing in the position of a soldier at ease, Sogolon Djata, supported by his enormous rod, was sweating great beads of sweat. Balla Fasséké's song had alerted the whole palace and people came running from all over to see what had happened, and each stood bewildered before Sogolon's son. The queen mother had rushed there and when she saw Mari Djata standing up she trembled from head to foot. After recovering his breath

USE READING STRATEGIES

Make Inferences Why is the queen mother trembling?

---

12. **Allah.** Name for the being who is worshiped as the creator and ruler of the universe in the Islamic religion

Sogolon's son dropped the bar and the crowd stood to one side. His first steps were those of a giant. Balla Fasséké fell into step and pointing his finger at Djata, he cried:

"Room, room, make room!
The lion has walked;
Hide antelopes,
Get out of his way."

Behind Niani there was a young baobab tree and it was there that the children of the town came to pick leaves for their mothers. With all his might the son of Sogolon tore up the tree and put it on his shoulders and went back to his mother. He threw the tree in front of the hut and said, "Mother, here are some baobab leaves for you. From henceforth it will be outside your hut that the women of Niani will come to stock up." ❖

MIRRORS & WINDOWS

"Each man finds his way already marked out for him and he can change nothing of it." Do you agree or disagree with this statement? Explain your answer. What role does fate play in a person's life? What role does personal choice play? Give examples.

REFER TO TEXT ▶ ▶ ▶ ▶	▶ REASON WITH TEXT	
1a. To what animal does Balla Fasséké compare Sogolon Djata in his song?	**1b.** Discuss the qualities associated with this animal. How do these qualities apply to Sogolon Djata?	**Understand** **Find meaning**
2a. List the signs that Sogolon Djata will be a great leader. List the factors that suggest he will not.	**2b.** According to the story, how are great leaders created? Do they decide to be leaders, or are they fated to be?	**Apply** **Use information**
3a. Describe Gnankouman Doua, the seer, and Sassouma Bérété, the king's first wife.	**3b.** Review the definition of *archetype* on page 760. How might Gnankouman Doua and Sassouma Bérété be classified as archetypal characters?	**Analyze** **Take things apart**
4a. Name several adjectives that describe Sogolon Kedjou. Do the same for the king.	**4b.** Rate the behavior of Sogolon Kedjou toward her son. Is she a good mother? Why or why not? Is the king a good father? Explain.	**Evaluate** **Make judgments**
5a. What does Sogolon Djata do with the baobab tree at the end of the story?	**5b.** Based on this story, compile a list of qualities that were admired in a leader of the Mali empire. How do these qualities compare with those admired in leaders today?	**Create** **Bring ideas together**

Stained glass detail from Sainte-Chapelle, Paris, France.

from

The Once and Future King

A Legend by **T. H. White**

King Uther is dead (handwritten)

> **"We all know the family has no chance," said Sir Ector, "that is, for the sword."**

King Pellinore arrived for the important week-end in a high state of flurry.

"I say," he exclaimed, "do you know? Have you heard? Is it a secret, what?"

"Is what a secret, what?" they asked him.

"Why, the King," cried his majesty. "You know, about the King?"

"What's the matter with the King?" inquired Sir Ector. "You don't say he's comin' down to hunt with those demned hounds of his or anythin' like that?"

"He's dead," cried King Pellinore tragically. "He's dead, poor fellah, and can't hunt any more."

Sir Grummore stood up respectfully and took off his cap of maintenance.[1]

"The King is dead," he said. "Long live the King."

Everybody else felt they ought to stand up too, and the boys' nurse burst into tears.

"There, there," she sobbed. "His loyal highness dead and gone, and him such a respectful gentleman. Many's the illuminated picture I've cut out of him, from the Illustrated Missals, aye, and stuck up over the mantel. From

---

1. **cap of maintenance.** Distinctive head covering worn at one time by people who held positions of authority

the time when he was in swaddling bands,[2] right through them world towers till he was a-visiting the dispersed areas as the world's Prince Charming, there wasn't a picture of 'im but I had it out, aye, and give 'im a last thought o' nights."

"Compose yourself, Nannie," said Sir Ector.

"It is solemn, isn't it?" said King Pellinore, "what? Uther the Conqueror, 1066 to 1216."[3]

"A solemn moment," said Sir Grummore. "The King is dead. Long live the King."

"We ought to pull down the curtains," said Kay, who was always a stickler for good form, "or half-mast the banners."

"That's right," said Sir Ector. "Somebody go and tell the sergeant-at-arms."

It was obviously the Wart's[4] duty to execute this command, for he was now the junior nobleman present, so he ran out cheerfully to find the sergeant. Soon those who were left in the solar[5] could hear a voice crying out, "Nah then, one-two, special mourning fer 'is lite majesty, lower awai on the command Two!" and then the flapping of all the standards, banners, pennons, pennoncells, banderolls, guidons, streamers and cognizances[6] which made gay the snowy turrets of the Forest Sauvage.

"How did you hear?" asked Sir Ector.

"I was pricking through the purlieus[7] of the forest after that Beast, you know, when I met with a solemn friar of orders grey, and he told me. It's the very latest news."

"Poor old Pendragon," said Sir Ector.

"The King is dead," said Sir Grummore solemnly. "Long live the King."

"It is all very well for you to keep on mentioning that, my dear Grummore," exclaimed King Pellinore petulantly, "but who is this King, what, that is to live so long, what, accordin' to you?"

"Well, his heir," said Sir Grummore, rather taken aback.

"Our blessed monarch," said the Nurse tearfully, "never had no hair. Anybody that studied the loyal family knowed that."

"Good gracious!" exclaimed Sir Ector. "But he must have had a next-of-kin?"

"That's just it," cried King Pellinore in high excitement. "That's the excitin' part of it, what? No hair and no next of skin, and who's to succeed to the throne? That's what my friar was so excited about, what, and why he was asking who could succeed to what, what? What?"

"Do you mean to tell me," exclaimed Sir Grummore indignantly, "that there ain't no King of Gramarye?"

"Not a scrap of one," cried King Pellinore, feeling important. "And there have been signs and wonders of no mean might."

"I think it's a scandal," said Sir Grummore. "God knows what the dear old country is comin' to. Due to these lollards and communists, no doubt."

"What sort of signs and wonders?" asked Sir Ector.

"Well, there has appeared a sort of sword in a stone, what, in a sort of a church. Not in the church, if you see what I mean, and not in the stone, but that sort of thing, what, like you might say."

"I don't know what the Church is coming to," said Sir Grummore.

2. **swaddling bands.** Bands of cloth used to wrap a newborn baby
3. **Uther the Conqueror, 1066 to 1216.** The legendary Uther's life spans the reigns of several actual English rulers. Uther's birth corresponds with the beginning of William the Conqueror's reign, and his death corresponds with the end of King John's reign.
4. **the Wart's.** Belonging to Arthur. The Wart is the name given to Arthur by his foster family.
5. **solar.** In this case, the sunroom
6. **standards...cognizances** (käg´ nə zən[t] səz). Banners and flags used to distinguish people of importance
7. **purlieus** (pʉrl´ yüz). Outer edges of a forest

pet • u • lant • ly (pe´ chə lənt lē) *adv.,* behaving in an impatient or irritable manner

USE READING STRATEGIES

Make Inferences What does King Pellinore mean by "no hair and no next of skin"? What do these mispronunciations tell you about him?

"It's in an <u>anvil</u>," explained the King.

"The Church?"

"No, the sword."

"But I thought you said the sword was in the stone?"

"No," said King Pellinore. "The stone is outside the church."

"Look here, Pellinore," said Sir Ector. "You have a bit of a rest, old boy, and start again. Here, drink up this horn of mead[8] and take it easy."

"The sword," said King Pellinore, "is stuck through an anvil which stands on a stone. It goes right through the anvil and into the stone. The anvil is stuck to the stone. The stone stands outside a church. Give me some more mead."

"I don't think that's much of a wonder," remarked Sir Grummore. "What I wonder at is that they should allow such things to happen. But you can't tell nowadays, what with all these Saxon agitators."[9]

"My dear fellah," cried Pellinore, getting excited again, "it's not where the stone is, what, that I'm trying to tell you, but what is written on it, what, where it is."

"What?"

"Why, on its pommel."[10]

"Come on, Pellinore," said Sir Ector. "You just sit quite still with your face to the wall for a minute, and then tell us what you are talkin' about. Take it easy, old boy. No need for hurryin'. You sit still and look at the wall, there's a good chap, and talk as slow as you can."

"There are words written on this sword in this stone outside this church," cried King Pellinore piteously, "and these words are as follows. Oh, do try to listen to me, you two, instead of interruptin' all the time about nothin', for it makes a man's head go ever so."

"What are these words?" asked Kay.

"These words say this," said King Pellinore, "so far as I can understand from that old friar of orders grey."

"Go on, do," said Kay, for the King had come to a halt.

"Go on," said Sir Ector, "what do these words on this sword in this anvil in this stone outside this church, say?"

"Some red propaganda, no doubt," remarked Sir Grummore.

King Pellinore closed his eyes tight, extended his arms in both directions, and announced in capital letters, "Whoso Pulleth Out This Sword of this Stone and Anvil, is Right-wise King Born of All England."

---

8. **mead.** Alcoholic beverage made of honey, water, yeast, and malt

9. **Saxon agitators.** Ancient Germanic people who conquered parts of England

10. **pommel.** Rounded knob that forms part of the handle of some swords

> **an • vil** (an′ vəl) *n.*, a steel or iron block

"Who said that?" asked Sir Grummore.

"But the sword said it, like I tell you."

"Talkative weapon," remarked Sir Grummore skeptically.

"It was written on it," cried the King angrily. "Written on it in letters of gold."

"Why didn't you pull it out then?" asked Sir Grummore.

"But I tell you that I wasn't there. All this that I am telling you was told to me by that friar I was telling you of, like I tell you."

"Has this sword with this inscription been pulled out?" inquired Sir Ector.

"No," whispered King Pellinore dramatically. "That's where the whole excitement comes in. They can't pull this sword out at all, although they have all been tryin' like fun, and so they have had to proclaim a tournament all over England, for New Year's Day, so that the man who comes to the tournament and pulls out the sword can be King of all England for ever, what, I say?"

"Oh, father," cried Kay. "The man who pulls that sword out of the stone will be the King of England. Can't we go to the tournament, father, and have a shot?"

"Couldn't think of it," said Sir Ector.

"Long way to London," said Sir Grummore, shaking his head.

"My father went there once," said King Pellinore.

Kay said, "Oh, surely we could go? When I am knighted I shall have to go to a tournament somewhere, and this one happens at just the right date. All the best people will be there, and we should see the famous knights and great kings. It does not matter about the sword, of course, but think of the tournament, probably the greatest there has ever been in Gramarye, and all the things we should see and do. Dear father, let me go to this tourney, if you love me, so that I may bear

USE READING SKILLS

Cause and Effect
What causes Kay to want to go to London?

away the prize of all, in my maiden fight."

"But, Kay," said Sir Ector, "I have never been to London."

"All the more reason to go. I believe that anybody who does not go for a tournament like this will be proving that he has no noble blood in his veins. Think what people will say about us, if we do not go and have a shot at that sword. They will say that Sir Ector's family was too vulgar and knew it had no chance."

"We all know the family has no chance," said Sir Ector, "that is, for the sword."

"Lot of people in London," remarked Sir Grummore, with a wild surmise. "So they say."

He took a deep breath and goggled at his host with eyes like marbles.

"And shops," added King Pellinore suddenly, also beginning to breathe heavily.

"Dang it!" cried Sir Ector, bumping his horn mug on the table so that it spilled. "Let's all go to London, then, and see the new King!"

They rose up as one man.

"Why shouldn't I be as good a man as my father?" exclaimed King Pellinore.

"Dash it all," cried Sir Grummore. "After all…it is the capital!"

"Hurray!" shouted Kay.

"Lord have mercy," said the nurse.

At this moment the Wart came in with Merlyn, and everybody was too excited to notice that, if he had not been grown up now, he would have been on the verge of tears.

"Oh, Wart," cried Kay, forgetting for the moment that he was only addressing his squire,[11] and slipping back into the familiarity of their boyhood. "What do you think? We are all going to London for a great tournament on New Year's Day!"

"Are we?"

"Yes, and you will carry my shield and spears for the jousts, and I shall win the palm[12] of everybody and be a great knight!"

---

11. **squire.** Attendant of a knight; in this case, Arthur
12. **win the palm.** Be the winner

"Well, I am glad we are going," said the Wart, "for Merlyn is leaving us too."

"Oh, we shan't need Merlyn."

"He is leaving us," repeated the Wart.

"Leavin' us?" asked Sir Ector. "I thought it was we that were leavin'?"

"He is going away from the Forest Sauvage."

Sir Ector said, "Come now, Merlyn, what's all this about? I don't understand all this a bit."

"I have come to say Good-bye, Sir Ector," said the old magician. "Tomorrow my pupil Kay will be knighted, and the next week my other pupil will go away as his squire. I have outlived my usefulness here, and it is time to go."

"Now, now, don't say that," said Sir Ector. "I think you're a jolly useful chap whatever happens. You just stay and teach me, or be the librarian or something. Don't you leave an old man alone, after the children have flown."

"We shall all meet again," said Merlyn. "There is no cause to be sad."

"Don't go," said Kay.

"I must go," replied their tutor. "We have had a good time while we were young, but it is in the nature of Time to fly. There are many things in other parts of the kingdom which I ought to be attending to just now, and it is a specially busy time for me. Come, Archimedes, say Good-bye to the company."

"Good-bye," said Archimedes tenderly to the Wart.

"Good-bye," said the Wart without looking up at all.

"But you can't go," cried Sir Ector, "not without a month's notice."

"Can't I?" replied Merlyn, taking up the position always used by philosophers who propose to dematerialize. He stood on his toes, while Archimedes held tight to his shoulder—began to spin on them slowly like a top—spun faster and faster till he was only a blur of grayish light—and in a few seconds there was no one there at all.

"Good-bye, Wart," cried two faint voices outside the solar window.

"Good-bye," said the Wart for the last time—and the poor fellow went quickly out of the room.

USE READING STRATEGIES

Make Inferences How do you think the Wart, or Arthur, feels about Merlyn? What can you tell about Arthur's character from this passage?

The knighting took place in a whirl of preparations. Kay's sumptuous bath had to be set up in the box-room, between two towel-horses and an old box of selected games which contained a worn-out straw dart-board—it was called fléchette in those days—because all the other rooms were full of packing. The nurse spent the whole time constructing new warm pants for everybody, on the principle that the climate of any place outside the Forest Sauvage must be treacherous to the extreme, and, as for the sergeant, he polished all the armor till it was quite brittle and sharpened the swords till they were almost worn away.

At last it was time to set out.

Perhaps, if you happen not to have lived in the Old England of the twelfth century, or whenever it was, and in a remote castle on the borders of the Marches at that, you will find it difficult to imagine the wonders of their journey.

The road, or track, ran most of the time along the high ridges of the hills or downs, and they could look down on either side of them upon the desolate marshes where the snowy reeds sighed, and the ice crackled, and the duck in the red sunsets quacked loud on the winter air. The whole country was like that. Perhaps there would be a moory[13] marsh on one side of the ridge, and a forest of a hundred

---

13. **moory.** Nonstandard adjective form of *moor*. A moor is a wild ground often covered with heather.

re • mote (ri mōt´) *adj.*, isolated; secluded

thousand acres on the other, with all the great branches weighted in white. They could sometimes see a wisp of smoke among the trees, or a huddle of buildings far out among the impassable reeds, and twice they came to quite respectable towns which had several inns to boast of, but on the whole it was an England without civilization. The better roads were cleared of cover for a bow-shot on either side of them, lest the traveller should be slain by hidden thieves.

They slept where they could, sometimes in the hut of some cottager who was prepared to welcome them, sometimes in the castle of a brother knight who invited them to refresh themselves, sometimes in the firelight and fleas of a dirty little hovel with a bush tied to a pole outside it—this was the sign-board used at that time by inns—and once or twice on the open ground, all huddled together for warmth between their grazing chargers. Wherever they went and wherever

Merlyn, Arthur's tutor.

USE READING STRATEGIES

Visualize Use the description in this paragraph to help you visualize the journey.

they slept, the east wind whistled in the reeds, and the geese went over high in the starlight, honking at the stars.

London was full to the brim. If Sir Ector had not been lucky enough to own a little land in Pie Street, on which there stood a respectable inn, they would have been hard put to it to find a lodging. But he did own it, and as a matter of fact drew most of his dividends from that source, so they were able to get three beds between the five of them. They thought themselves fortunate.

On the first day of the tournament, Sir Kay managed to get them on the way to the lists at least an hour before the jousts could possibly begin. He had lain awake all night, imagining how he was going to beat the best barons in England, and he had not been able to eat his breakfast. Now he rode at the front of the caval-cade,[14] with pale cheeks, and Wart wished there was something he could do to calm him down.

For country people, who only knew the dismantled tilting ground[15] of Sir Ector's castle, the scene which met their eyes was ravishing. It was a huge green pit in the earth, about as big as the arena at a football match. It lay ten feet lower than the surrounding country, with sloping banks, and the snow had been swept off it. It had been kept warm with straw, which had been cleared off that morning, and now the close-worn grass sparkled green in the white landscape. Round the arena there was a world of color so dazzling and moving and twinkling as to make one blink one's eyes. The wooden grandstands were painted in scarlet and white. The silk pavilions of famous people, pitched on every side, were azure and green and saffron and checkered. The pennons and pennoncells which floated everywhere in the sharp wind were flapping with every color of the rainbow, as they strained and slapped at their flag-poles, and the barrier down the middle of the arena itself was done in chess-board squares of black and white. Most of the combatants and their friends had not yet arrived, but one could see from those few who had come how the very people would turn the scene into a bank of flowers, and how the armor would flash, and the scalloped sleeves of the heralds jig in the wind, as they raised their brazen trumpets to their lips to shake the fleecy clouds of winter with joyances and fanfares.

"Good heavens!" cried Sir Kay. "I have left my sword at home."

"Can't joust without a sword," said Sir Grummore. "Quite irregular."

"Better go and fetch it," said Sir Ector. "You have time."

"My squire will do," said Sir Kay. "What a mistake to make! Here, squire, ride hard back to the inn and fetch my sword. You shall have a shilling[16] if you fetch it in time."

The Wart went as pale as Sir Kay was, and looked as if he were going to strike him. Then he said, "It shall be done, master," and turned his ambling palfrey[17] against the stream of newcomers. He began to push his way toward their hostelry[18] as best he might.

"To offer me money!" cried the Wart to himself. "To look down at this beastly little donkey-affair off his great charger and to call me Squire! Oh, Merlyn, give me patience with the brute, and stop me from throwing his filthy shilling in his face."

When he got to the inn it was closed. Everybody had thronged to see the famous tournament, and the entire household had followed after the mob. Those were lawless days and it was not safe to leave your house—or even to go to sleep in it—unless you were certain that it was impregnable. The wooden shutters bolted over the downstairs windows were two inches thick, and the doors were double-barred.

"Now what do I do," asked the Wart, "to earn my shilling?"

He looked ruefully at the blind little inn, and began to laugh.

---

14. **cavalcade.** Procession or formal group of riders
15. **tilting ground.** Field on which a joust (a competition in which two knights on horses fight with lances) is held
16. **shilling.** Type of British coin
17. **palfrey.** Horse that is easy to ride
18. **hostelry.** Inn

---

im • preg • na • ble (im preg´ nə bəl) *adj.*, unable to be taken by force
rue • ful • ly (rü´ fəl lē) *adv.*, regretfully

"Poor Kay," he said. "All that shilling stuff was only because he was scared and miserable, and now he has good cause to be. Well, he shall have a sword of some sort if I have to break into the Tower of London.[19]

"How does one get hold of a sword?" he continued. "Where can I steal one? Could I waylay some knight even if I am mounted on an ambling pad, and take his weapons by force? There must be some swordsmith or armorer in a great town like this, whose shop would still be open."

He turned his mount and cantered off along the street. There was a quiet churchyard at the end of it, with a kind of square in front of the church door. In the middle of the square there was a heavy stone with an anvil on it, and a fine new sword was stuck through the anvil.

"Well," said the Wart, "I suppose it is some sort of war memorial, but it will have to do. I am sure nobody would grudge Kay a war memorial, if they knew his desperate straits."

He tied his reins round a post of the lych-gate,[20] strode up the gravel path, and took hold of the sword.

"Come, sword," he said. "I must cry your mercy and take you for a better cause.

"This is extraordinary," said the Wart. "I feel strange when I have hold of this sword, and I notice everything much more clearly. Look at the beautiful gargoyles of the church, and of the monastery which it belongs to. See how splendidly all the famous banners in the aisle are waving. How nobly that yew[21] holds up the red flakes of its timbers to worship God. How clean the snow is. I can smell something like fetherfew and sweet briar—and is it music that I hear?"

It was music, whether of pan-pipes or of recorders, and the light in the courtyard was so clear, without being dazzling, that one could have picked a pin out twenty yards away.

"There is something in this place," said the Wart. "There are people. Oh, people, what do you want?"

Nobody answered him, but the music was loud and the light beautiful.

"People," cried the Wart, "I must take this sword. It is not for me, but for Kay. I will bring it back."

There was still no answer, and the Wart turned back to the anvil. He saw the golden letters, which he did not read, and the jewels on the pommel, flashing in the lovely light.

USE READING SKILLS

Cause and Effect
What causes the Wart to try to pull the sword from the stone?

---

19. **Tower of London.** Fortress founded by William the Conqueror
20. **lych-gate.** Entrance to a churchyard
21. **yew.** Kind of evergreen tree

"Come, sword," said the Wart.

He took hold of the handles with both hands, and strained against the stone. There was a melodious consort[22] on the recorders, but nothing moved.

The Wart let go of the handles, when they were beginning to bite into the palms of his hands, and stepped back, seeing stars.

"It is well fixed," he said.

He took hold of it again and pulled with all his might. The music played more strongly, and the light all about the churchyard glowed like amethysts; but the sword still stuck.

"Oh, Merlyn," cried the Wart, "help me to get this weapon."

There was a kind of rushing noise, and a long chord played along with it. All round the churchyard there were hundreds of old friends. They rose over the church wall all together, like the Punch and Judy[23] ghosts of remembered days, and there were badgers and nightingales and vulgar crows and hares and wild geese and falcons and fishes and dogs and dainty unicorns and solitary wasps and corkindrills and hedgehogs and griffins and the thousand other animals he had met. They loomed round the church wall, the lovers and helpers of the Wart, and they all spoke solemnly in turn. Some of them had come from the banners in the church, where they were painted in heraldry, some from the waters and the sky and the fields about—but all, down to the smallest shrew mouse, had come to help on account of love. The Wart felt his power grow.

"Put your back into it," said a Luce (or pike) off one of the heraldic banners, "as you once did when I was going to snap you up. Remember that power springs from the nape of the neck."

"What about those forearms," asked a Badger gravely, "that are held together by a chest? Come along, my dear embryo, and find your tool."

A Merlin[24] sitting at the top of a yew tree cried out, "Now then, Captain Wart, what is the first law of the foot? I thought I once heard something about never letting go?"

"Don't work like a stalling woodpecker," urged a Tawny Owl affectionately. "Keep up a steady effort, my duck, and you will have it yet."

A white-front said, "Now, Wart, if you were once able to fly the great North Sea, surely you can co-ordinate a few little wing-muscles here and there? Fold your powers together, with the spirit of your mind, and it will come out like butter. Come along, Homo sapiens, for all we humble friends of yours are waiting here to cheer."

The Wart walked up to the great sword for the third time. He put out his right hand softly and drew it out as gently as from a scabbard.

There was a lot of cheering, a noise like a hurdy-gurdy[25] which went on and on. In the middle of this noise, after a long time, he

ANALYZE LITERATURE

Legend Which events surrounding the Wart's attempts to pull the sword out of the stone are likely not true to the original story of Arthur? Why might White have included these events in his retelling of the story?

22. **consort** (kun´ sôrt). Song
23. **Punch and Judy.** Mr. Punch and his wife, Judy, are popular characters in British puppet shows who fight constantly and comically.
24. **Merlin.** Species of small falcon; also a play on words, as Merlin is an alternative spelling of Merlyn, the wizard who is Arthur's mentor and friend
25. **hurdy-gurdy.** Musical instrument played by turning a handle

saw Kay and gave him the sword. The people at the tournament were making a frightful row.

"But this is not my sword," said Sir Kay.

"It was the only one I could get," said the Wart. "The inn was locked."

"It is a nice-looking sword. Where did you get it?"

"I found it stuck in a stone, outside a church."

Sir Kay had been watching the tilting nervously, waiting for his turn. He had not paid much attention to his squire.

"That is a funny place to find one," he said.

"Yes, it was stuck through an anvil."

"What?" cried Sir Kay, suddenly rounding upon him. "Did you just say this sword was stuck in a stone?"

"It was," said the Wart. "It was a sort of war memorial."

Sir Kay stared at him for several seconds in amazement, opened his mouth, shut it again, licked his lips, then turned his back and plunged through the crowd. He was looking for Sir Ector, and the Wart followed after him.

"Father," cried Sir Kay, "come here a moment."

"Yes, my boy," said Sir Ector. "Splendid falls these professional chaps do manage. Why, what's the matter, Kay? You look as white as a sheet."

"Do you remember that sword which the King of England would pull out?"

"Yes."

"Well, here it is. I have it. It is in my hand. I pulled it out."

Sir Ector did not say anything silly. He looked at Kay and he looked at the Wart. Then he stared at Kay again, long and lovingly, and said, "We will go back to the church."

"Now then, Kay," he said, when they were at the church door. He looked at his first-born kindly, but straight between the eyes. "Here is the stone, and you have the sword. It will make you the King of England. You are my son that I am proud of, and always will be, whatever you

do. Will you promise me that you took it out by your own might?"

Kay looked at his father. He also looked at the Wart and at the sword.

Then he handed the sword to the Wart quite quietly.

He said, "I am a liar. Wart pulled it out."

As far as the Wart was concerned, there was a time after this in which Sir Ector kept telling him to put the sword back into the stone—which he did—and in which Sir Ector and Kay then vainly tried to take it out. The Wart took it out for them, and stuck it back again once or twice. After this, there was another time which was more painful.

He saw that his dear guardian was looking quite old and powerless, and that he was kneeling down with difficulty on a gouty knee.

"Sir," said Sir Ector, without looking up, although he was speaking to his own boy.

"Please do not do this, father," said the Wart, kneeling down also. "Let me help you up, Sir Ector, because you are making me unhappy."

"Nay, nay, my lord," said Sir Ector, with some very feeble old tears. "I was never your father nor of your blood, but I wote well ye are of an higher blood than I wend ye were."

"Plenty of people have told me you are not my father," said the Wart, "but it does not matter a bit."

"Sir," said Sir Ector humbly, "will ye be my good and gracious lord when ye are King?"

"Don't!" said the Wart.

"Sir," said Sir Ector, "I will ask no more of you but that you will make my son, your foster-brother, Sir Kay, seneschal of all your lands?"

Kay was kneeling down too, and it was more than the Wart could bear.

"Oh, do stop," he cried. "Of course he can be seneschal, if I have got to be this King, and, oh, father, don't kneel down like that, because it breaks my heart. Please get up, Sir Ector, and don't make everything so horrible. Oh, dear, oh, dear, I wish I had never seen that filthy sword at all."

And the Wart also burst into tears. ❖

When the Wart pulled the sword out of the anvil, he had no idea of the significance of his actions. What does this say about his character? Do you think the Wart is the type of person who will make a good leader? Explain your answers.

REFER TO TEXT ▶ ▶ ▶ ▶	▶ REASON WITH TEXT	
1a. Who is the Wart? What is his role with regard to Sir Kay? *he is his squire*	1b. Describe what the name "the Wart" suggests about how the other members of the court treat this character. How does this treatment of the Wart make the outcome of the trip to London surprising?	**Understand** **Find meaning**
2a. Recall what Sir Kay says initially about the sword that the Wart gives him.	2b. Examine the discussion between Sir Ector and Sir Kay about the sword. How is this discussion important to the development of the theme of the story?	**Apply** **Use information**
3a. Identify two or three specific details that White includes in his description of London. *774*	3b. Infer how the description of London adds color and excitement to the narrative.	**Analyze** **Take things apart**
4a. List the misused words and plays on words that exist in the text.	4b. Describe the effect the misused words and plays on words have on the retelling. What do they convey about the characters who use them?	**Evaluate** **Make judgments**
5a. Find a quotation from the story that shows how Arthur reacts to his newly won fame.	5b. Summarize how this depiction of Arthur compares with other depictions of him that you have encountered. How does it compare with depictions of other heroes in this unit?	**Create** **Bring ideas together**

COMPARE LITERATURE: Legend and Archetype

- Which elements of the two legends do you think could have actually occurred in history? Compare the themes of the stories. How do they overlap? What do they say about the values of the cultures in which the stories originated?
- Which archetypal characters exist in the two stories? How are these characters the same? How are they different? What is it about the characters that makes them archetypes?

Whether or not King Arthur actually lived is still up for debate, but historians have found evidence that he was likely a war general sometime in the early part of the sixth century. The tales of Arthur's feats in battle were told and retold by poets and storytellers as a way of bringing hope to the chaos of England's Dark Ages. **Sir Thomas Malory** completed the manuscript of *Le Morte d'Arthur* (*The Death of Arthur*) around 1469. This work, which is divided into twenty-one books, and each book is then divided into chapters, is the most complete and engaging retelling of the Arthurian legend. Excerpted here is the account of Arthur pulling the sword from the stone and being made king.

from Le Morte d'Arthur

A Legend by **Sir Thomas Malory**

FROM BOOK I CHAPTER 5
HOW ARTHUR WAS CHOSEN KING, AND OF WONDERS AND MARVELS OF A SWORD TAKEN OUT OF A STONE BY THE SAID ARTHUR

Then stood the realm in great jeopardy long while, for every lord that was mighty of men made him strong, and many weened[1] to have been king. Then Merlin went to the Archbishop of Canterbury, and counselled him for to send for all the lords of the realm, and all the gentlemen of arms, that they should to London come by Christmas, upon pain of cursing; and for this cause: that Jehu, that was born on that night, that He would of his great mercy show some miracle, as He was come to be king of mankind for to show some miracle who should be right-wise king of this realm. So the Archbishop, by the advice of Merlin, sent for all the lords and gentlemen of arms that they should come by Christmas even unto London. And many of them made them clean of their life, that their prayer might be the more acceptable unto God.

So in the greatest church of London (whether it were Paul's or not the French book maketh no mention) all the estates were long or day in the church for to pray. And when matins[2] and the first mass was done, there was seen in the churchyard, against the high altar, a great stone four square, like unto a marble stone, and in midst thereof was like an anvil of steel a foot on high, and therein stuck a fair sword naked by the point, and letters there were written in gold about the sword that saiden thus:—WHOSO PULLETH OUT THIS SWORD OF THIS STONE AND ANVIL, IS RIGHTWISE KING BORN OF ALL ENGLAND. Then the people marveled, and told it to the Archbishop.

"I command," said the Archbishop, "that ye keep you within your church, and pray unto God still; that no man touch the sword till the high mass be all done."

So when all masses were done all the lords went to behold the stone and the sword. And when they saw the scripture, some assayed,[3] such as would have been king. But none might stir the sword nor move it.

"He is not here," said the Archbishop, "that shall achieve the sword, but doubt not God will make him known. But this is my counsel,"

1. **weened.** Thought
2. **matins.** Morning prayers
3. **assayed.** Made an attempt

said the Archbishop, "that we let purvey[4] ten knights, men of good fame, and they to keep this sword."

So it was ordained, and then there was made a cry, that every man should assay that would, for to win the sword. And upon New Year's Day the barons let make a jousts and a tournament, that all knights that would joust or tourney there might play. And all this was ordained for to keep the lords together and the commons, for the Archbishop trusted that God would make him known that should win the sword.

So upon New Year's Day, when the service was done, the barons rode unto the field, some to joust and some to tourney, and so it happed that Sir Ector, that had great livelihood about London, rode unto the jousts, and with him rode Sir Kay his son, and young Arthur that was his nourished brother; and Sir Kay was made knight at All Hallowmass afore. So as they rode to the jousts-ward, Sir Kay had lost his sword, for he had left it at his father's lodging, and so he prayed young Arthur for to ride for his sword.

"I will well," said Arthur, and rode fast after the sword. And when he came home the lady and all were out to see the jousting.

Then was Arthur wroth, and said to himself, "I will ride to the churchyard, and take the sword with me that sticketh in the stone, for my brother Sir Kay shall not be without a sword this day." So when he came to the churchyard, Sir Arthur alit and tied his horse to the stile, and so he went to the tent, and found no knights there, for they were at jousting; and so he handled the sword by the handles, and lightly and fiercely pulled it out of the stone, and took his horse and rode his way until he came to his brother Sir Kay, and delivered him the sword.

And as soon as Sir Kay saw the sword, he wist[5] well it was the sword of the stone, and so he rode to his father Sir Ector, and said; "Sir, lo here is the sword of the stone, wherefore[6] I must be king of this land."

When Sir Ector beheld the sword, he returned again and came to the church, and there they alit all three, and went into the church. And anon he made Sir Kay to swear upon a book how he came to that sword.

"Sir," said Sir Kay, "by my brother Arthur, for he brought it to me."

"How gat ye this sword?" said Sir Ector to Arthur.

"Sir, I will tell you. When I came home for my brother's sword, I found nobody at home to deliver me his sword, and so I thought my brother Sir Kay should not be swordless, and so I came hither eagerly and pulled it out of the stone without any pain."

"Found ye any knights about this sword?" said Sir Ector.

"Nay," said Arthur.

"Now," said Sir Ector to Arthur, "I understand ye must be king of this land."

"Wherefore I," said Arthur, "and for what cause?"

"Sir," said Ector, "for God will have it so, for there should never man have drawn out this

---

4. **let purvey.** Appoint
5. **wist.** Knew
6. **wherefore.** Why

sword, but he that shall be rightwise king of this land. Now let me see whether ye can put the sword there as it was, and pull it out again."

"That is no mastery," said Arthur, and so he put it in the stone; therewithal Sir Ector assayed to pull out the sword and failed.

FROM BOOK I CHAPTER 6
HOW KING ARTHUR PULLED OUT THE SWORD DIVERS TIMES

Now assay," said Sir Ector unto Sir Kay. And anon he pulled at the sword with all his might, but it would not be.

"Now shall ye assay," said Sir Ector to Arthur.

"I will well," said Arthur, and pulled it out easily. And therewithal Sir Ector knelt down to the earth, and Sir Kay.

"Alas!" said Arthur, "my own dear father and brother, why kneel ye to me?"

"Nay, nay, my lord Arthur, it is not so, I was never your father nor of your blood, but I wot[7] well ye are of an higher blood than I weened ye were." And then Sir Ector told him all, how he was betaken[8] him for to nourish him, and by whose commandment, and by Merlin's deliverance. Then Arthur made great dole[9] when he understood that Sir Ector was not his father.

"Sir," said Ector unto Arthur, "will ye be my good and gracious lord when ye are king?"

"Else were I to blame," said Arthur, "for ye are the man in the world that I am most beholding to, and my good lady and mother your wife, that as well as her own hath fostered me and kept. And if ever it be God's will that I be king as ye say, ye shall desire of me what I may do, and I shall not fail you, God forbid I should fail you."

"Sir," said Sir Ector, "I will ask no more of you, but that ye will make my son, your foster brother, Sir Kay, seneschal[10] of all your lands."

"That shall be done," said Arthur, "and more, by the faith of my body, that never man shall have that office but he, while he and I live."

Therewithal they went unto the Archbishop, and told him how the sword was achieved, and by whom. And on Twelfthday all the barons came thither, and to assay to take the sword, who that would assay. But there afore them all, there might none take it out but Arthur; wherefore there were many lords wroth, and said it was great shame unto them all and the realm, to be over-governed with a boy of no high blood born, and so they fell out at that time, that it was put off till Candlemas,[11] and then all the barons should meet there again; but alway the ten knights were ordained to watch the sword day and night, and so they set a pavilion over the stone and the sword, and five always watched.

So at Candlemas many more great lords came thither for to have won the sword, but there might none prevail. And right as Arthur did at Christmas, he did at Candlemas, and pulled out the sword easily, whereof the barons were sore agrieved and put it off in delay till the high feast of Easter. And as Arthur sped before, so did he at Easter, yet there were some of the great lords had <u>indignation</u> that Arthur should be king, and put it off in a delay till the feast of Pentecost.[12] Then the Archbishop of Canterbury by Merlin's <u>providence</u> let purvey then of the best knights that they might get, and such knights as Uther Pendragon loved best and most trusted in his days. And such knights were put about Arthur as Sir Baudwin of Britain, Sir Kay, Sir Ulfius, Sir Brastias. All these with many other, were always about Arthur, day and night, till the feast of Pentecost.

---

7. **wot.** Know
8. **betaken.** Assigned to care for
9. **dole.** Lamentation
10. **seneschal.** Steward
11. **Candlemas.** A church feast on February 2
12. **Pentecost.** The seventh Sunday after Easter

---

in • dig • na • tion (in' dig nā´shən) *n.*, anger; scorn
prov • i • dence (prä´ və dən[t]s) *n.*, benevolent guidance

FROM BOOK I CHAPTER 7
HOW KING ARTHUR WAS CROWNED, AND HOW HE MADE OFFICERS

And at the feast of Pentecost all manner of men assayed to pull at the sword that would assay, but none might prevail but Arthur, and pulled it out afore all the lords and commons that were there, wherefore all the commons cried at once, "We will have Arthur unto our king; we will put him no more in delay, for we all see that it is God's will that he shall be our king, and who that holdeth against it, we will slay him." And therewithal they kneeled at once, both rich and poor, and cried Arthur mercy because they had delayed him so long. And Arthur forgave them, and took the sword between both his hands, and offered it upon the altar where the Archbishop was, and so was he made knight of the best man that was there.

And so anon was the coronation made. And there was he sworn unto his lords and the commons for to be a true king, to stand with true justice from thenceforth the days of this life. Also then he made all lords that held of the crown to come in, and to do service as they ought to do. And many complaints were made unto Sir Arthur of great wrongs that were done since the death of King Uther, of many lands that were bereaved lords, knights, ladies, and gentlemen. Wherefore King Arthur made the lands to be given again unto them that ought them.[13] When this was done, that the king had established all the countries about London, then he let make Sir Kay Seneschal of England; and Sir Baudwin of Britain was made constable; and Sir Ulfius was made chamberlain; and Sir Brastias was made warden to wait upon the north from Trent forwards, for it was that time the most part the king's enemies. But within few years after, Arthur won all the north, Scotland, and all that were under their <u>obeisance</u>. Also Wales, a part of it, held against Arthur, but he overcame them all, as he did the remnant, through the noble prowess of himself and his knights of the Round Table. ❖

13. **ought them.** Owned them

obei • sance (ō bē´ s'n[t]s) *n.*, authority; rule

REFER TO TEXT ▶ ▶ ▶ ▶	▶ REASON WITH TEXT	
1a. List some things Arthur does when he becomes king.	**1b.** Discuss what these actions reveal about Arthur's character.	**Understand** **Find meaning**
2a. Recall how the lords first react to the idea of Arthur becoming king.	**2b.** Argue for or against whether the reaction of the lords was justified. Support your argument.	**Evaluate** **Make judgments**
3a. How is Arthur's royal heritage discovered? How does he react when he finds out Sir Ector is not his father?	**3b.** Explain how your reaction to surprising news about your family history might compare with Arthur's. What advice would you give Arthur to help him deal with this news?	**Create** **Bring ideas together**

TEXT-TO-TEXT CONNECTION

- How do the tone and mood of Malory's version of the Arthur story compare and contrast with those of T. H. White's version? What purpose do the tone and mood serve in each selection?
- Which elements of the story of Arthur from Malory's version do you see in White's version? Which account of King Arthur do you find more compelling? Why?

EXTEND THE TEXT

Writing Options

Creative Writing Imagine that you work for a company that is creating a set of collectible cards about heroes from around the world. Write a one-paragraph **description** of either Sundiata or Arthur to use on the collectible cards.

Expository Writing How is each of these stories a Cinderella story, or a tale of an unexpected hero? Write a **literary analysis** in which you state this theme and discuss how each selection develops it. Begin by writing a thesis statement that expresses the theme shared by the two selections. In your introduction, describe the plot of each selection. Devote one body paragraph to how the theme is developed in each selection, and add a brief conclusion.

Collaborative Learning

Create a Museum Exhibit With a small group, research and curate an exhibit on Sundiata and Arthur, focusing on history, art, and literature. Collect images of representative items, such as an iron rod for Sundiata and a sword for Arthur, and create an informative caption to accompany each image. Share your exhibit with the rest of the class. Analyze the audience members' responses by asking them to fill out a short survey. Make improvements based on the survey results.

Media Literacy

Analyze Visual and Sound Techniques Watch and analyze a movie about a historic or legendary hero. Think about the following questions: What visual and sound techniques did the director use to portray the life of the hero? How were camera angles, editing techniques, and lighting used? What special effects were employed, and how do you think they were accomplished? What did music and other sound effects contribute to the movie? How did the filmmaker's decisions affect your perception of the hero? Write a brief analysis that answers these questions.

 Go to **www.mirrorsandwindows.com** for more.

READING ASSESSMENT

1. In *Sundiata*, the character named Gnankouman Doua is which of the following?
    A. a warrior
    B. a king
    C. a griot
    D. a peasant
    E. a mother

2. On page 762, the word *taciturn* most nearly means
    A. mean-spirited.
    B. silent.
    C. prophetic.
    D. angry.
    E. unhappy.

3. What kind of tree does Sogolon tear up at the end of the selection from *Sundiata?*
    A. acacia
    B. cottonwood
    C. baobab
    D. oak
    E. ginkgo

4. Why do Sir Ector, Sir Kay, and the Wart journey to London?
    A. They want to do some shopping.
    B. They want to see the Tower of London.
    C. They want to attend a tournament.
    D. They want to speak to the Archbishop.
    E. They want to pull the sword out of the anvil.

5. On page 774, the word *impregnable* most nearly means
    A. inconspicuous.
    B. unable to be taken by force.
    C. resourceful.
    D. improper.
    E. broken.

6. How does the Wart describe the place where he found the sword in the stone?
    A. as a war memorial
    B. as a forest clearing
    C. as an island in a lake
    D. as a shop selling armor
    E. as a hotel room

7. What kind of people are the Wart and Sogolon Djata? What characteristics do they share? How are they different? Which one, in your opinion, will make a better leader? Why do you think so?

GRAMMAR & STYLE

Transitions

A **transition** is a word or phrase used to connect ideas and to show relationships between them. Transitions are important in writing because they link together sentences within paragraphs and paragraphs within larger works and help them flow smoothly. Transitions also work as the glue that holds ideas together. Writing that lacks transitions is choppy and sometimes difficult to follow.

It isn't necessary to use a transition between every sentence or idea, but you should use transitions between each paragraph in a longer work. Usually a transition falls at the beginning of a paragraph.

There are many different ways you can use transitions. One way is to use transitions to emphasize the points you wish to make. To make these points, use transitions such as *again, indeed, in fact, with this in mind, to repeat, for this reason,* and *surprisingly enough.*

EXAMPLE

The Wart did not know he was going to be king; <u>in fact,</u> he was more surprised than anyone.

Use transitions to show location. Words you can use for this purpose include *below, along, behind, among, over, amid, inside, beside,* and *between.*

EXAMPLE

The sword was placed in an anvil. <u>Beside</u> the anvil was a tree.

Transitions are useful when you are comparing and contrasting items. Use transitions such as *likewise, in the same way, just as, similarly, also,* and *sometimes* to compare and transitions such as *although, on the other hand, in the meantime, nevertheless,* and *yet* to contrast.

EXAMPLE

Sundiata showed courage and strength in overcoming his weakness. <u>In the same way,</u> many modern-day heroes have overcome adversity.

Use transitions to show time. Common transitions of this type include *immediately, during, finally, meanwhile, soon, as soon as, at the same time,* and *first.*

EXAMPLE

<u>First,</u> Arthur went to look for a sword for Sir Kay. <u>At the same time,</u> Sir Kay was waiting to have his turn at jousting.

Use transitions to clarify information. Such transitions include *for example, for instance, in other words, that is,* and *to clarify.*

EXAMPLE

Sundiata was not a likely candidate for a great leader. <u>For example,</u> he had very little physical strength.

Another way transitions are useful is to add information. Use words and phrases such as *additionally, along with, also, in addition, likewise, for example,* and *moreover* to accomplish this purpose.

EXAMPLE

Sir Thomas Malory wrote about the Arthurian legend. T. H. White <u>also</u> wrote about Arthur.

Use transitions to conclude or summarize. Transitions that indicate a conclusion include *as a result, in conclusion, to conclude, finally,* and *thus.*

EXAMPLE

Sundiata stood on his own two feet. <u>As a result,</u> people finally understood how he was going to be their leader.

What Great Writers Do

Notice how T. H. White uses a transition to show sequence in the following excerpt:

> The Wart took it out for them, and stuck it back again once or twice. After this, there was another time which was more painful.

Identify Transitions

In the following paragraph, locate all the transitional words or phrases. For each transition you find, identify the purpose it serves. For example, indicate whether the transition is meant to add information, show time, and so on.

Sir Thomas Malory was an English knight. While little is known about his early life, he is believed to have lived on his family's estates at Warwickshire and Northamptonshire, England. Malory fought in the Hundred Years' War between England and France, after which he took over his father's estates, for a time representing Warwickshire in the English Parliament. Later in life, however, Malory's fortunes evidently changed. Some say he committed a series of crimes, including poaching, extortion, robbery, and murder; others say he was the victim of political entanglements. In any case, Malory was arrested on several occasions and spent much of his later life in prison. In fact, he died in prison in 1471. Scholars believe that Malory did most of his writing as a prisoner.

Improve a Paragraph

The following paragraph contains few transitions and sounds abrupt and choppy. Revise the paragraph by adding transitions where necessary.

The person who pulled the sword from the stone would be the next King of England. No one had pulled the sword from the stone. There was to be a tournament, and the winner would be king. Arthur went to the tournament, as Sir Kay's squire. At the tournament, Sir Kay realized that he had forgotten his sword.

He asked Arthur to go back to the inn and get his sword. The inn was locked. Arthur was frantic. He saw a sword sticking out of an anvil in a churchyard. He knew Kay needed a sword. He went to the anvil and pulled the sword from the stone. He returned to the tournament and presented it to Kay. Kay and Sir Ector were amazed that Arthur had pulled the sword from the stone. They returned to the churchyard, and Arthur pulled the sword from the stone again and was pronounced king.

EXTEND THE SKILL

The excerpts from *Sundiata*, *The Once and Future King*, and *Le Morte d'Arthur* are all told from the third-person point of view. Choose one of the stories, pick a character from the story, and rewrite the story from the character's first-person point of view. As you write, be sure to use transitions in your story in order to  clarify the order and timing of events, the locations of objects in the story, why events occur, what these events mean, and other information that you think is interesting and important for the reader to know. After you have finished writing your story, review your story and pay particular attention to how the transitions you used help the story flow and pull the reader along.

VOCABULARY & SPELLING

Words with Multiple Meanings

In *Vocabulary Dynamics,* Gwen Harrison writes,

> People need to tell about such basic actions as eating, running, and hunting. In the beginning, words for those activities meant only those actions and nothing more. The Latin-derived word *current,* for example, originally meant "running"—not "latest" or "up-to-date," as in current events or current fashions—but simply the physical action of running. As civilizations developed, and life became more complex, words had to become more versatile to fit new situations.

In this passage, Harrison offers a reason as to why words gain multiple meanings. She suggests that as a civilization expands, words must also grow to accommodate the communication needs of the civilization and thus take on multiple meanings. In both Niane's *Sundiata: An Epic of Old Mali* and T. H. White's *The Once and Future King,* you can find examples of words that have multiple meanings. These words develop in many ways.

- **A word may gain a broader meaning over time.** For example, in the fourteenth century *succeed* commonly meant "to follow after" and to "inherit sovereignty." Today, it is often used to suggest that something has "turned out well" or "the desired object or end" has been achieved.
- **A word may gain a more narrow or specialized meaning.** The word *engine* used to mean, in a more general sense, "evil contrivance or wile." Today, it is more commonly used to refer to "a machine for converting any of various forms of energy into mechanical force and motion."
- **A word may gain positive connotations.** For example, in the thirteenth century, the word *gentle* was an adjective meaning "belonging to a family of high social station." A century later, it was being used as a verb to mean "to raise from

being common" and "to make calm and docile." Today, the most common meaning of the word is the adjective meaning "free from harshness, sternness, or violence."

- **A word may gain negative connotations.** For example, the word *vulgar* (page 771) originally referred to the "common people." Today, it has acquired more negative connotations and can describe something that is "morally crude," "offensive in language," or "lewdly or profanely indecent."
- **A word may come to be used as a different part of speech.** Verbs may be used as nouns: "to *duel*" and "to fight in a *duel*." Adjectives may be used as nouns: "the *final* tournament" and "the *final* is tomorrow." Nouns may be used as verbs: "Sogolon Djata's *brain*" and "to *brain* another with a stick." Adjectives may be used as verbs: "a *clean* sword" and "to *clean* the sword." Nouns may be used as adjectives: "Wart's *duty* to Sir Kay" and "*duty* officer" or "*duty-free* goods."

Words that are spelled alike but have different meanings and/or pronunciations are often called **homographs.** (The word *homograph* comes from Greek roots meaning "written the same.") When you come across a word that is a homograph, you need to look at the context to decide what it means and how to pronounce it. How would you pronounce each word in the examples below?

EXAMPLES

bass (a type of fish) and *bass* (having a low pitch)

wind (moving air) and *wind* (turn a crank as on a watch)

desert (dry place) and *desert* (leave behind)

Exercise A

Below are words from the selections that have multiple meanings. Each choice is a correct definition of the word. Locate the sentence in the selection and choose the definition that best fits the context in which the word is used.

1. sharp (page 774)
   A. briskly or bitterly cold
   B. quick to understand
   C. causing intense mental or physical distress
   D. ending in a point or an edge
2. present (page 765)
   A. a gift
   B. being in view or nearby
   C. to introduce
   D. to aim or to point
3. file (page 765)
   A. a steel tool
   B. to rub away
   C. to march in a single line
   D. a collection of data

Exercise B

Below are sentences from *Sundiata* and *The Once and Future King*. Do the following activities for each underlined word:

- Use a dictionary to look up the definitions.
- Choose the definition that you think best fits the context of the word in the sentence and write this definition on your paper.
- Choose another definition of the word and write this definition on your paper.
- Compare the two definitions. By referring to the examples on the preceding page, label the word as follows:
   A. developed broader meaning
   B. developed narrower meaning
   C. gained positive connotations
   D. gained negative connotations
   E. changed part of speech

1. "A <u>solemn</u> moment," said Sir Grummore. "The King is dead. Long live the King."

2. It was obviously the Wart's duty to <u>execute</u> this command.
3. They could sometimes see a wisp of smoke among the trees, or a <u>huddle</u> of buildings far out among the impassable reeds.
4. "I am sure nobody would grudge Kay a war memorial, if they knew his desperate <u>straits</u>."
5. "It is well <u>fixed</u>," he said. He took hold of it again and pulled with all his might.
6. God has his mysteries which none can <u>fathom</u>.
7. Sogolon's son had a <u>slow</u> and difficult childhood.
8. Sogolon Djata would <u>brain</u> the poor little things with his already strong arms and none of them would come near him any more.
9. Sometimes, when Sogolon was <u>attending</u> to the chores, it was she who stayed beside her sister Djamarou.
10. The noise was so frightening that Sogolon, who was lying down, jumped up with a <u>start</u>.
11. And the Wart also <u>burst</u> into tears.
12. [B]ut one could see from those few who had come how the very people would turn the scene into a <u>bank</u> of flowers...

EXTEND THE SKILL

Create a Word Dictionary for either *Sundiata* or *The Once and Future King* by choosing five words from the selection that you think may have multiple meanings. Do not choose words that were used in the examples or in the preceding exercises. Using a separate sheet of paper for each word, copy down the sentence and the page number in which the word appears and then use the dictionary to find the definition that best fits the word. Record this definition on your paper. Together with your classmates, gather together all of your words, alphabetize them, and bind them together to create a Word Dictionary for the selection.

Understanding Folk Tales

TYPES OF FOLK TALES

Long before television and video games were invented, people found entertainment in telling stories. Some stories were told for entertainment; others were told to pass important elements of a particular culture from one generation to the next. Still other stories were told to teach a lesson.

Folk tales are brief stories passed by word of mouth from generation to generation. Many folk tales can also be considered legends.

Tall tales are folk tales that are often lighthearted or humorous and contain highly exaggerated elements. The story of John Henry, the railroad man who could lay track faster than anyone else, is a tall tale based on the life of a real person. **Fairy tales** are stories that deal with mischievous spirits and other supernatural occurrences, often in medieval settings.

Stories with morals are parables and fables. A moral is a practical lesson, usually relating to the principles of right and wrong. **Parables,** or brief stories told to teach a moral lesson, were often told by Jesus in the Bible. Parables usually use everyday occurrences to teach a lesson related to spiritual matters. **Fables** are also brief stories, often with animal characters, told to express a moral. Perhaps the most famous fables are those of Aesop.

ORIGINS OF FOLK TALES

No one knows for sure when folk tales originated. It is believed that they were passed between workers to while away the hours of tedious tasks, such as spinning thread or carding wool, and passed in turn from parents to their children.

You may be surprised when you read some of the original versions of folk tales collected by Jacob and Wilhelm Grimm, or the Brothers Grimm, as they called themselves. Their first book of folk tales, entitled *Children's and Household Tales,* was published in 1812 and, despite the title, was not especially appropriate for young children. Because the Brothers

Grimm considered themselves folklorists and cultural researchers rather than authors of children's literature, these early versions of the stories are violent and dark. These original versions, however, authentically reflect the hard lives of the common folk of earlier days, when hunger and poverty were widespread.

Another famous recorder of folklore was Denmark's Hans Christian Andersen (1805–1875). His works show the influences of the fantastic stories he had read and been told as a child.

Although Andersen became the most celebrated Danish author of his time, he still felt like an outsider in the world of the upper class — a theme that appears many times in his fairy tales. "The Little Mermaid" and "The Ugly Duckling" are often considered to reflect themes from his life, such as yearning for a different life, the alienation of the outsider, and the loss of love.

Some nineteenth-century tales originated from or were influenced by folk tales from as far away as Ireland, Russia, and Japan. In fact, it is believed that the story of Cinderella, also known as "Ash-girl," may be Chinese in origin. Today, collections of folk tales from around the world are growing in popularity. Browsing through the children's picture book section of a library, you can find many folk tales from the Middle East, Latin America, Africa, and various parts of Asia.

ELEMENTS OF FOLK TALES

Folk tales have many of the same elements as other forms of literature. There are a few, however, that appear frequently.

Symbols

A **symbol** is a thing that stands for or represents both itself and something else. Writers use the following types of symbols:

- A *conventional symbol* is one with traditional, widely spread association. Such symbols include doves for peace, the color green for jealousy, and wind for change. In "Mother Holle," the ugliness of the favorite daughter is symbolic of her mean and greedy personality.
- A *personal* or *idiosyncratic symbol* is one that assumes its secondary meaning because of the special use to which it is put by a writer or storyteller.

Symbolism is a powerful part of the folk tradition, when more could be communicated with a well-chosen symbol than with lengthy explanations or written words. Some of the recurring symbols in fairy tales are beasts such as wolves; dark, scary woods; fruit, the apple in particular; and articles of clothing such as capes and shoes.

Motifs

A **motif** is any element that occurs in one or more works of literature or art. Examples of common folk tale motifs include grateful animals or the thankful dead, three wishes, the trial or quest, the evil stepmother, and the magical transformation of one thing to another. You can learn much about a literary work by studying the motifs within it.

READING FOLK TALES

When you are reading folk tales, try recording symbols and motifs in a graphic organizer like the one that follows. This can help you dig deeper into the tale to reveal what it might have meant to the original storytellers and their audiences. In the left column of the graphic organizer, list the symbols and/or motifs. In the middle column, list where else you may have encountered a similar symbol or motif, whether in another story, comic book, or movie. In the right column, speculate, or make guesses, about what it might have meant to the early storytellers. An example from "Mother Holle" is done for you.

Symbol or Motif	Similar to...	Meaning or Importance
Motif of evil stepmother who makes her step-daughter work hard	The story of "Cinderella"	The step-daughter is eventually rewarded for her hard work.

Twisted Tales

The familiarity of many fairy tales provides authors with the chance to twist and change the stories to suit their tastes. The results can be hilarious or thought-provoking. Check out these twists on age-old tales:

- *Cinderella (As If You Didn't Already Know the Story)* by Barbara Ensor
- *Politically Correct Bedtime Stories* by James Finn Garner
- *The True Story of the Three Little Pigs* by Jon Scieszka
- *Cinder Edna* by Ellen Jackson
- The musical *Into the Woods*
- *The Three Little Wolves and the Big Bad Pig* by Eugene Trivizas

Naked Truth and Resplendent Parable

BUILD BACKGROUND

Cultural Context "Naked Truth and Resplendent Parable" comes from a collection entitled *Yiddish Folktales*. A **parable** is a brief story with a moral lesson. The most well-known parables are those told by Jesus in the Bible. The word *resplendent* means "shining or beautiful." The word *Yiddish* refers to a dialect, or version of a language spoken by the people of a particular place, time, or social group. The Yiddish dialect is made up of a combination of ancient German, Slavic, and Hebrew languages and is traditionally spoken by European Jews. The roots of Yiddish reach back to the twelfth century. In modern times, distinguished authors writing in Yiddish have included Sholem Aleichem (1859–1916) and Isaac Bashevis Singer (1904–1991). Singer won the Nobel Prize for Literature in 1978.

Literature that teaches a lesson is called *didactic* literature. As you will learn in "Naked Truth and Resplendent Parable," writers and speakers in a wide spectrum of cultures and historical periods have known that storytelling is an extremely effective didactic device.

Reader's Context What characteristics of folk tales or fairy tales do you think cause these stories to be passed down from generation to generation?

ANALYZE LITERATURE: Purpose and Personification

A writer's **purpose** is his or her aim or goal. Some common purposes for writing include to entertain, to persuade, and to inform. Some writing has more than one purpose. For example, a fable might be written both to entertain readers and to persuade them to behave in a certain way.

Personification is a figure of speech in which an idea, an animal, or a thing is described as if it were a person. As you read, note how this folk tale uses personification. What contribution does personification have on the purpose of the narrative?

SET PURPOSE

Based on the rather unusual title of this folk tale, what do you predict the message of the story will be? As you read, think about why the story might have been told in the first place and why it continues to be told.

USE READING SKILLS

Main Idea The **main idea** of a piece of writing is the central point that the author develops with supporting details. In some cases, the main idea is actually stated. If it is not stated, you will have to infer it. A good way to find the main idea of the folk tale you are about to read is to gather important details into a Main Idea Map like the one below. As you read, add details to the map. When you finish reading, use the details to determine the main idea.

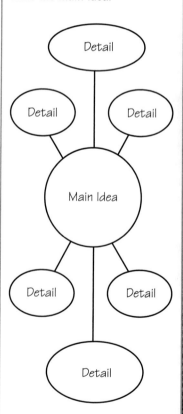

An Ashkenazi Rabbi of Jerusalem. George Sherwood Hunter.

Naked Truth and Resplendent Parable

A Yiddish Folk Tale

"Truth took Parable's advice and put on the borrowed clothes."

The great scholar known as the Vilna Gaon once asked the Preacher of Dubno,[1] "Help me to understand. What makes a parable so influential? If I recite Torah,[2] there's a small audience, but let me tell a parable and the synagogue is full. Why is that?"

The *dubner maged* replied, "I'll explain it to you by means of a parable.

"Once upon a time Truth went out about the streets as naked as the day he was born. As a result, no one would let him into their homes. Whenever people caught sight of him, they turned away or fled. One day when Truth

---

1. **Dubno.** City in western Ukraine
2. **Torah.** The first five books of the Old Testament, which comprise the most sacred text in Judaism

was sadly wandering about, he came upon Parable. Now, Parable was dressed in splendid clothes of beautiful colors. And Parable, seeing Truth, said, 'Tell me, neighbor, what makes you look so sad?' Truth replied bitterly, 'Ah, brother, things are bad. Very bad. I'm old, very old, and no one wants to acknowledge me. No one wants anything to do with me.'

"Hearing that, Parable said, 'People don't run away from you because you're old. I too am old. Very old. But the older I get, the better people like me. I'll tell you a secret: Everyone likes things to be disguised and prettied up a bit. Let me lend you some splendid clothes like mine, and you'll see that the very people who pushed you aside will invite you into their homes and be glad of your company.'

"Truth took Parable's advice and put on the borrowed clothes. And from that time on, Truth and Parable have gone hand in hand together and everyone loves them. They make a happy pair." ❖

 **MIRRORS & WINDOWS**

"Everyone likes things to be disguised and prettied up a bit." What do you think this means? Do you agree? Use specific examples from your own life or what you have you seen or heard from others to explain your answers.

AFTER READING

REFER TO TEXT ▶ ▶ ▶ ▶	▶ REASON WITH TEXT	
1a. State the question the great scholar known as the Vilna Gaon asks the Preacher of Dubno.	1b. Discuss what is humorous about the technique the Preacher of Dubno uses to answer the scholar's question.	**Understand** Find meaning
2a. List the things that happen when Truth wanders the streets naked.	2b. Examine the underlying meaning of people's reactions to Truth.	**Apply** Use information
3a. What happens when the Vilna Gaon tells a parable instead of reciting Torah?	3b. Infer why the Vilna Gaon is upset by this.	**Analyze** Take things apart
4a. Restate Parable's advice for Truth.	4b. Critique Parable's advice. Do you think Parable is telling Truth to be something he is not? Why or why not?	**Evaluate** Make judgments
5a. Identify the main idea of this folk tale.	5b. The American poet Emily Dickinson once wrote, "Tell all the truth but tell it slant, / Success in circuit lies." Summarize how this advice might relate to the main idea of this folk tale.	**Create** Bring ideas together

ANALYZE LITERATURE: Purpose and Personification

What do you think is the purpose of this folk tale? Does it accomplish its purpose? How does the use of personification advance the purpose? How would the effect of the tale be different if personification had not been used?

EXTEND THE TEXT

Writing Options

Creative Writing Imagine that you have a chance to interview the Preacher of Dubno for a TV talk show. Write a list of questions you would like to ask him about when he first heard the parable or about how the story affected the Vilna Gaon's approach to his duties in the synagogue. Then write a **transcript** of your interview, including the Preacher's responses.

Expository Writing The ancient Roman poet Horace wrote that all poetry (by which he meant literature in general) had two fundamental elements: the *dulce* (sweet or pleasing) and the *utile* (the useful or practical). In the eighteenth century, the English writer and critic Samuel Johnson echoed Horace when he said that the aim or goal of literature is "to instruct by pleasing." In two or three **paragraphs,** discuss how these value judgments in literary criticism relate to "Naked Truth and Resplendent Parable."

Media Literacy

Research a Yiddish-Language Newspaper One of the most influential twentieth-century publications in Yiddish was the newspaper called the *Jewish Daily Forward.* Together with a partner, use Internet or library resources to research the *Forward.* In your research, focus on questions such as the following: When was the newspaper founded, and where was it published? What was its circulation, and who were some of its best-known contributors and writers? Create a brief overview of the newspaper using the information you collect.

Collaborative Learning

Research Yiddish Music and Theater Use library or Internet resources to identify some audio recordings of Yiddish music or theater. Organize a presentation in which you play the music for the class as a whole and provide some background for each selection. Alternately, you might research and organize a presentation on the Broadway musical *Fiddler on the Roof* and the movie *Yentl,* both of which incorporate a number of Yiddish elements.

 Go to **www.mirrorsandwindows.com** for more.

READING ASSESSMENT

1. According to the scholar known as the Vilna Gaon, when he recites Torah in the synagogue his audience is
    A.   appreciative.
    B.   large.
    C.   small.
    D.   indifferent.
    E.   ecstatic.

2. On page 792, the word *acknowledge* most nearly means
    A.   recognize with respect.
    B.   respond with gratitude.
    C.   avoid with hostility.
    D.   regard with suspicion.
    E.   ignore with indifference.

3. In the folk tale, Parable advises Truth to do which of the following?
    A.   wear a disguise
    B.   speak more plainly
    C.   appear only on rare occasions
    D.   spend more money
    E.   tell people only what they want to hear

4. Which of the following options is an example of personification?
    A.   The *dubner maged* replied, "I'll explain it to you by means of a parable."
    B.   One day when Truth was sadly wandering about, he came upon Parable.
    C.   "I'll tell you a secret: Everyone likes things to be disguised and prettied up a bit."
    D.   All of the above
    E.   None of the above

5. Which of the following statements from the folk tale best describes its main idea?
    A.   Once upon a time, Truth went out about the streets as naked as the day he was born.
    B.   "I'll tell you a secret: Everyone likes things to be disguised and prettied up a bit."
    C.   Truth took Parable's advice and put on the borrowed clothes.
    D.   Now, Parable was dressed in splendid clothes of beautiful colors.
    E.   Parable said, "People don't run away from you because you're old. I too am old. Very old."

6. How would you state the theme, or underlying message, of this folk tale in your own words?

Mother Holle
A Fairy Tale by Jacob and Wilhelm Grimm

The Wonderful Hair
A Fairy Tale Retold by Parker Fillmore

BEFORE READING

BUILD BACKGROUND

Cultural Context In **"Mother Holle,"** two stepsisters fall into the magical realm of an old woman called Mother Holle and go through a test of character. Mother Holle is an important figure in German folklore and can appear as a maiden, a mother, or as an old woman. You may already be familiar with her Russian counterpart—Baba Yaga—an old witch who lives in a house built on chicken feet and eats naughty children.

The folk tale **"The Wonderful Hair"** is a Slavic tale about a poor man who steals a hair from a vila—or water spirit—to raise money to feed his children. Slavic folk tales come from the East European region. Because this area covers many different cultures, it is not unusual to see Russian, Serbian, Croatian, Romanian, Polish, Czech, and even Turkish influence in these tales.

Reader's Context Think of a time in your life when you were tested and discovered something new about yourself. What was the test and how did it challenge you? What did you learn about yourself after you had successfully completed the test?

USE READING SKILLS

Compare and Contrast As you read these two fairy tales, use a chart like the one below to compare and contrast the plots, characters, and settings.

	Mother Holle	The Wonder- ful Hair
Plot		
Charac- ters		
Setting		

COMPARE LITERATURE: Motif and Setting

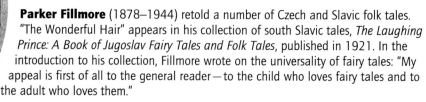

A **motif** is an element that appears in one or more works of literature or art. Examples of common motifs found in fairy tales are three wishes, helpful or mischievous elves and fairies, undertaking a trial or a quest, magical transformations, and wicked stepmothers. As you read "Mother Holle" and "The Wonderful Hair," look for motifs shared by the two fairy tales.

The **setting** of a literary work is the time and place in which it occurs. Consider the settings of the two fairy tales. Which elements of the settings are realistic? Which are imaginary?

MEET THE AUTHORS

Jacob Ludwig Carl Grimm (1785–1863) and **Wilhelm Carl Grimm** (1786–1859) were the two oldest of a family of five children born in Berlin, Germany. While studying law at the University of Marburg, the two brothers became interested in folk narratives and oral literature. The Brothers Grimm are famous for collecting folk songs and folk tales from the European oral tradition. The two hundred stories they collected convey the spirit and imagination of generations of people and have become classics of world literature. Jacob also made significant contributions to the field of linguistics in his work on the development of European languages.

BROTHERS GRIMM

Parker Fillmore (1878–1944) retold a number of Czech and Slavic folk tales. "The Wonderful Hair" appears in his collection of south Slavic tales, *The Laughing Prince: A Book of Jugoslav Fairy Tales and Folk Tales*, published in 1921. In the introduction to his collection, Fillmore wrote on the universality of fairy tales: "My appeal is first of all to the general reader—to the child who loves fairy tales and to the adult who loves them."

Mother Holle

A Fairy Tale by

Jacob and Wilhelm Grimm

Critical Viewing

Describe the woman in the painting. What can you infer about her personality based on the painting? What kind of character do you think Mother Holle will be like?

A Lonely Life, c. 1873. Hugh Cameron. National Gallery of Scotland, Edinburgh, Scotland.

"Stay with me; if you will do the work of my house properly for me, I will make you very happy."

Once upon a time there was a widow who had two daughters; one of them was beautiful and <u>industrious</u>, the other ugly and lazy. The mother, however, loved the ugly and lazy one best, because she was her own daughter, and so the other, who was only her stepdaughter, was made to do all the work

in • dus • tri • ous (in dus´ trē əs) *adj.,* constantly active or occupied; diligent

of the house, and was quite the Cinderella of the family. Her stepmother sent her out every day to sit by the well in the high road, there to spin until she made her fingers bleed. Now it chanced one day that some blood fell on to the spindle, and as the girl stopped over the well to wash it off, the spindle suddenly sprang out of her hand and fell into the well. She ran home crying to tell of her misfortune, but her stepmother spoke harshly to her, and after giving her a violent scolding, said unkindly, "As you have let the spindle fall into the well you may go yourself and fetch it out."

A girl fetches water from a well.

The girl went back to the well not knowing what to do, and at last in her distress she jumped into the water after the spindle.

She remembered nothing more until she awoke and found herself in a beautiful meadow, full of sunshine, and with countless flowers blooming in every direction.

She walked over the meadow, and presently she came upon a baker's oven full of bread, and the loaves cried out to her, "Take us out, take us out, or alas! we shall be burnt to a cinder; we were baked through long ago." So she took the bread-shovel and drew them all out.

She went on a little farther, till she came to a free full of apples. "Shake me, shake me, I pray," cried the tree; "my apples, one and all, are ripe." So she shook the tree, and the apples came falling down upon her like rain; but she continued shaking until there was not a single apple left upon it. Then she carefully gathered the apples together in a heap and walked on again.

The next thing she came to was a little house, and there she saw an old woman looking out, with such large teeth, that she was terrified, and turned to run away. But the old woman called after her, "What are you afraid of, dear child? Stay with me; if you will do the work of my house properly for me, I will make you very happy. You must be very careful, however, to make my bed in the right way, for I wish you always to shake it thoroughly, so that the feathers fly about; then they say, down there in the world, that it is snowing; for I am Mother Holle." The old woman spoke so kindly, that the girl <u>summoned</u> up courage and agreed to enter into her service.

She took care to do everything according to the old woman's bidding and every time she made the bed she shook it with all her might, so that the feathers flew about like so many snowflakes. The old woman was as good as her word: she never spoke angrily to her, and gave her roast and boiled meats every day.

So she stayed on with Mother Holle for some time, and then she began to grow unhappy. She could not at first tell why she felt sad, but she became conscious at last of great longing to go home; then she knew she was homesick, although she was a thousand times better off with Mother Holle than with her mother and sister. After waiting awhile, she went to Mother Holle and said, "I am so home-sick, that I cannot stay with you any longer, for although I am so happy here, I must return to my own people."

Then Mother Holle said, "I am pleased that you should want to go back to your own people, and as you have served me so well and faithfully, I will take you home myself."

Thereupon she led the girl by the hand up to a broad gateway. The gate was opened, and as the girl passed through, a shower of gold fell upon her, and the gold clung to her, so that she was covered with it from head to foot.

"That is a reward for your industry," said Mother Holle, and as she spoke she handed her the spindle which she had dropped into the well.

The gate was then closed, and the girl found herself back in the old world close to her mother's house. As she entered the courtyard, the cock who was perched on the well, called out:

"Cock-a-doodle-doo!

sum • mon (suˊ mən) *v.,* to call forth; to evoke

Your golden daughter's come back to you."

Then she went in to her mother and sister, and as she was so richly covered with gold, they gave her a warm welcome. She related to them all that had happened, and when the mother heard how she had come by her great riches, she thought she should like her ugly, lazy daughter to go and try her fortune. So she made the sister go and sit by the well and spin, and the girl pricked her finger and thrust her hand into a thorn-bush, so that she might drop some blood on to the spindle; then she threw it into the well, and jumped in herself.

Like her sister she awoke in the beautiful meadow, and walked over it till she came to the oven. "Take us out, take us out, or alas! we shall be burnt to a cinder; we were baked through long ago," cried the loaves as before. But the lazy girl answered, "Do you think I am going to dirty my hands for you?" and walked on.

Presently she came to the apple-tree. "Shake me, shake me, I pray; my apples, one and all, are ripe," it cried. But she only answered, "A nice thing to ask me to do, one of the apples might fall on my head," and passed on.

At last she came to Mother Holle's house, and as she had heard all about the large teeth from her sister, she was not afraid of them, and engaged herself without delay to the old woman.

The first day she was very obedient and industrious, and exerted herself to please Mother Holle, for she thought of the gold she should get in return. The next day, however, she began to dawdle over her work, and the third day she was more idle still; then she began to lie in bed in the mornings and refused to get up. Worse still, she neglected to make the old woman's bed properly, and forgot to shake it so that the feathers might fly about. So Mother Holle very soon got tired of her, and told her she might go. The lazy girl was delighted at this, and thought to herself, "The gold will soon be mine." Mother Holle led her, as she had led her sister, to the broad gateway; but as she was passing through, instead of the shower of gold, a great bucketful of pitch came pouring over her.

"That is in return for your services," said the old woman, and she shut the gate.

So the lazy girl had to go home covered with pitch, and the cock on the well called out as she saw her:

"Cock-a-doodle-doo!
 Your dirty daughter's come back to you."

But, try what she would, she could not get the pitch off and it stuck to her as long as she lived. ❖

MIRRORS & WINDOWS

In return for her hard work, Mother Holle showers the beautiful daughter in gold and says, "That is a reward for your industry." What does this suggest about the nature of hard work? Do you agree with this? Why or why not? Does hard work pay off in your life? Give an example.

REFER TO TEXT ▶ ▶ ▶ ▶	▶ **REASON WITH TEXT**	
1a. Describe the physical appearance and the personality traits of each sister.	1b. Explain how these descriptions are consistent with the actions of each sister.	**Understand** **Find meaning**
2a. What is Mother Holle's reaction to the work done by each sister?	2b. Show how Mother Holle's reaction to each sister is significant. How is her reaction related to the fate of each sister?	**Apply** **Use information**
3a. List each task the girls are asked to perform.	3b. Infer what each task symbolizes. Why do you think the girls are asked to perform each task? Is there an underlying theme connecting the tasks? If so, what is it?	**Analyze** **Take things apart**
4a. Compare and contrast the experience of each sister on the way to Mother Holle's house.	4b. Critique the actions of each sister. Do you admire the beautiful daughter? Why or why not? Do you think the ugly daughter will change her ways after her experience with Mother Holle? Why or why not?	**Evaluate** **Make judgments**
5a. Identify the ways that Mother Holle interacts with the beautiful daughter and the ugly daughter.	5b. How would you describe Mother Holle's personality? Retell the story from Mother Holle's point of view. Make sure her personality comes through in her voice.	**Create** **Bring ideas together**

THE WONDERFUL Hair

A Fairy Tale Retold by

Parker Fillmore

Ophelia, 1900. Pascal Adolphe Jean Dagnan-Bouveret.

"She will speak to you but you be careful not to answer. If you say a word to her she will be able to bewitch you."

There was once a poor man who had so many children that he was at his wit's end how to feed them all and clothe them.

"Unless something turns up soon," he thought to himself, "we shall all starve to death. Poor youngsters—I'm almost tempted to kill them with my own hands to save them from suffering the pangs of hunger!"

That night before he went to sleep he prayed God to give him help. God heard his prayer and sent an angel to him in a dream.

The angel said to him:

"Tomorrow morning when you wake, put your hand under your pillow and you will find a mirror, a red handkerchief, and an embroidered scarf. Without saying a word to any one hide these things in your shirt and go out to the woods that lie beyond the third hill from the village. There you will find a brook. Follow it until you come to a beautiful maiden who is bathing in its waters. You will know her from the great masses of golden hair that fall down over her shoulders. She will speak to you but you be careful not to answer. If you say a word to her she will be able to bewitch you. She will hold out a comb to you and ask you to comb her hair. Take the comb and do as she asks. Then part her back hair carefully and you will see one hair that is coarser than the others and as red as blood. Wrap this firmly around one of your fingers and jerk it out. Then flee as fast as you can. She will pursue you and each time as she is about to overtake you drop first the embroidered scarf, then the red handkerchief, and last the mirror. If you reach the hill nearest your own village you are safe for she can pursue you no farther. Take good care of the single hair for it has great value and you can sell it for many golden ducats."

In the morning when the poor man awoke and put his hand under his pillow he found the mirror and the handkerchief and the scarf just as the angel had said he would. So he hid them carefully in his shirt and without telling any one where he was going he went to the woods beyond the third hill from the village. Here he found the brook and followed it until he came to a pool where he saw a lovely maiden bathing.

"Good day to you!" she said politely.

The poor man remembering the angel's warning made no answer.

The maiden held out a golden comb.

"Please comb my hair for me, won't you?"

The man nodded and took the comb. Then he parted the long tresses behind and searched here and there and everywhere until he found the one hair that was blood-red in color and coarser than the others. He twisted this firmly around his finger, jerked it quickly out, and fled.

"Oh!" cried the maiden. "What are you doing? Give me back my one red hair!"

She jumped to her feet and ran swiftly after him. As she came close to him, he dropped behind him the embroidered scarf. She stooped and picked it up and examined it awhile. Then she saw the man was escaping, so she tossed the scarf aside and again ran after him. This time he dropped the red handkerchief. Its bright color caught the maiden's eye and she picked it up and lost a few more minutes admiring it while the man raced on. Then the maiden remembered him, threw away the handkerchief, and started off again in pursuit.

This time the man dropped the mirror and the maiden who of course was a Vila[1] and had never seen a mirror before picked it up and looked at it and when she saw the lovely reflection of herself she was so amazed that she kept on looking and looking. She was still looking in it and still admiring her own beauty when the man reached the third hill beyond which the maiden couldn't follow him.

So the poor man got home with the hair safely wound about his finger.

"It must be of great value," he thought to himself. "I'll take it to the city and offer it for sale there."

So the next day he went to the city and went about offering his wonderful hair to the merchants.

"What's so wonderful about it?" they asked him.

"I don't know, but I do know it's of great value," he told them.

Ioan. Stradanus inuent.   Ioan. Collaert sculp.

---

1. **Vila.** Female water spirit who bewitches passersby through song

Conspicilla, c. 1580. Jan van der Straet.

"Well," said one of them, "I'll give you one golden ducat for it."

He was a shrewd buyer and the others hearing his bid of one golden ducat decided that he must know that the hair was of much greater value. So they began to outbid him until the price offered the poor man reached one hundred golden ducats. But the poor man insisted that this was not enough.

"One hundred golden ducats not enough for one red hair!" cried the merchants.

They pretended to be disgusted that any one would refuse such a price for one red hair, but in reality they were all firmly convinced by this time that it was a magic hair and probably worth any amount of money in the world.

The whole city became excited over the wonderful hair for which all the merchants were bidding and for a time nothing else was talked about. The matter was reported to the Tsar[2] and at once he said that he himself would buy the hair for one thousand golden ducats.

One thousand golden ducats! After that there was no danger of the poor man's many children dying of starvation.

And what do you suppose the Tsar did with the hair? He had it split open very carefully and inside he found a scroll of great importance to mankind for on it were written many wonderful secrets of nature. ❖

---

2. **Tsar.** Ruler of Russia

MIRRORS & WINDOWS

One thousand golden ducats for a poor man is wealth. The Tsar, who has plenty of ducats, finds the priceless secrets of nature hidden in the Vila's hair. For the Vila, her one red hair was of greatest value to her. How do all three characters possess wealth? When have you valued something more highly than someone else? Why?

REFER TO TEXT ▶ ▶ ▶ ▶	▶ REASON WITH TEXT	
1a. What items and information does the angel give to the poor man?	1b. Explain how these items and information help the poor man gain wealth.	**Understand** **Find meaning**
2a. List the three things the poor man drops to distract the Vila.	2b. Describe the reaction the Vila has to each item. What does this suggest about the Vila's personality and what is important to her?	**Apply** **Use information**
3a. Identify examples in the story of great wealth or great poverty.	3b. Based on these examples, infer a possible theme of the story.	**Analyze** **Take things apart**
4a. How do the merchants react to the red hair?	4b. Judge the logic behind the merchants' increased bids. Why did the price of the red hair keep increasing? Do you think the price the Tsar paid for the red hair was a fair price? Why or why not?	**Evaluate** **Make judgments**
5a. What role does the angel play in helping the man gain wealth? What role does the man play in helping himself gain wealth?	5b. What relationship between the protagonist and the supernatural agent does this story suggest? How is it similar to the relationship in "Mother Holle"? How is it different?	**Create** **Bring ideas together**

COMPARE LITERATURE: Motif and Setting

Review both stories and choose a common motif. How is the motif developed in each story? In what ways is this development the same in each story? How is it different? What does the development of each motif suggest about the values of the culture? Compare the settings of both stories. What role does the setting play in each story?

EXTEND THE TEXT

Writing Options

Creative Writing Imagine you are a character from "Mother Holle" or "The Wonderful Hair." You have been invited to share your story on a national talk show. Write a **monologue** recounting your experience and how it has affected your life. Be sure to include details and colorful language to help build voice in your character and make your monologue more interesting.

Expository Writing Write a **review** of "Mother Holle" or "The Wonderful Hair" for your local newspaper. In addition to providing your opinion of the story, consider the messages that you think each story suggests and how well you think these messages come across. Also consider the characters and the development, or lack thereof, of the characters. How do the characters support the messages of the story? Be sure to include specific examples to strengthen your argument.

Media Literacy

Create a Video Game Like fairy tales, video games are often set in imaginary worlds and involve a character trying to achieve some sort of goal. Create a plan for a video game based on "Mother Holle," "The Wonderful Hair," or a different fairy tale of your choice. First, describe what the goal of the game will be. Think about what it will take to win the game and what obstacles the character will have to overcome. Next, describe or sketch the "world" or "worlds" in which your game will take place and the characters involved. Then describe the different levels of the game and what the characters will have to accomplish to move from one level to the next. Finally, present your plan to your class.

Critical Literacy

Evaluate a Modern Retelling Imagine you have been asked to write an article for a teen magazine in which you evaluate a modern retelling of a fairy tale. Look at the list of modern retellings of fairy tales in stories, cartoons, and movies on page 789 and choose one that interests you. You may also choose a retelling that is not on the list. Then write an article that discusses the ways the values, assumptions, characteristics, prejudices, and ideals of today's society are reflected in the retelling.

 Go to **www.mirrorsandwindows.com** for more.

READING ASSESSMENT

1. In "Mother Holle," how does the beautiful daughter respond to the apple tree when it asks her to shake its leaves?
   A. She tells the tree to stop talking and to shake its own leaves.
   B. She refuses to shake the tree because the apples might hurt her.
   C. Thinking that it is odd that the tree is talking to her, she walks by quickly.
   D. She does as it asks and piles the fallen apples at the base of the tree.
   E. None of the above

2. The word *industrious* on page 795 most nearly means
   A. confused.
   B. hardworking.
   C. enthusiastic.
   D. stubborn.
   E. crafty.

3. What value does the fairy tale "Mother Holle" teach?
   A. Good deeds reap good rewards.
   B. Hard work pays off.
   C. In the end, people receive their just deserts.
   D. All of the above

   E. None of the above

4. Which of the following motifs do "Mother Holle" and "The Wonderful Hair" share?
   A. a supernatural being who aids the protagonist
   B. a trial the protagonist must pass
   C. symbolic magical or non-magical objects
   D. All of the above
   E. None of the above

5. How does the Vila react after the man has pulled out her single red hair?
   A. She bursts into flames.
   B. She turns into a pile of dust.
   C. She runs after him to get her hair back.
   D. She casts a spell on him.
   E. None of the above

6. Heroic characters often embody qualities that are important to their cultures. Analyze the character of the beautiful daughter in "Mother Holle" or the father in "The Wonderful Hair." Based on information from the story, what qualities does this character possess that make him or her an ideal character in his or her society?

VOCABULARY & SPELLING

Informal and Archaic Language

A **register** is any of the varieties of language that a speaker uses in a certain social context. There are certain words and expressions that you would use in a conversation with a friend but not when talking to your friend's parents. With a child, you use a register that is nonthreatening and simple to understand. With an authority figure such as your school principal or a police officer, you use a register that is more formal—that follows the rules of standard English.

Informal English contains everyday speech and popular expressions, uses contractions, and may include sentence fragments. Two types of informal English include slang and colloquialisms.

Slang is a form of speech made up of invented words or old words that are given new meanings. Slang words fall in and out of popularity quickly.

EXAMPLES

"That movie was <u>tight, man</u>!"

"<u>Chill out</u> and tell me what the problem is."

Colloquialisms are informal expressions used in everyday speech. Many slang words or expressions start out as slang and then, once they are used by a large majority of people, become colloquialisms.

EXAMPLES

Marsha <u>let the cat out of the bag</u> when she told her sister she was engaged.

"I'm <u>in the doghouse</u> for getting home late last night."

Be sure to use formal English when you are writing essays, business letters, and other formal types of documents and to speak in formal English when you are doing something like interviewing for a job or participating in a debate. Informal English is appropriate when you are speaking with friends or writing in your journal. You can also use slang and colloquialisms as part of the dialogue in a story, as a way to create realistic characters.

Language is always changing. New words are continually introduced, and old words that are no longer used drop out. When you read words from earlier time periods, you might notice that many of the words are unfamiliar to you. Words or specific meanings of words that are rarely used in modern English may be labeled as **archaic.**

EXAMPLES

Let us go <u>presently</u>; we have no time to waste!

The man was <u>sore</u> in debt; he couldn't even afford to buy shoes.

The word *presently* is used in an archaic sense in the example above, but you can use context clues to determine that it must mean "immediately," since there is "no time to waste."

A word that is no longer used at all is **obsolete.** For example, a fever was once called an *ague,* a toilet a *donnicker,* and an unethical politician a *snollygoster.*

Encountering obsolete language is difficult because you cannot always find an obsolete word in the dictionary. If this is the case, try to use the context of the sentence to figure out what the word means. You might also be able to locate the meaning of an obsolete word on the Internet.

REVIEW TERMS

- **register:** any of the varieties of language that a speaker uses in a certain social context
- **informal English:** contains everyday speech and popular expressions, uses contractions, and may include sentence fragments
- **slang:** form of speech made up of invented words or old words that are given new meanings
- **colloquialism:** an informal expression used in everyday speech
- **archaic words:** words that are rarely used in modern English
- **obsolete words:** words that are no longer used at all in English

Exercise A

Identify each of the following items as an example of formal or informal English. Then, rewrite each example of informal English to make it more formal. Use a dictionary if necessary.

1. I gotta split. Later, girl!
2. The committee chairperson announced that the report would be released next Friday.
3. It really bugs Jean when her friends ask her for help with their homework.
4. Stash your stuff and let's get rolling for dinner.
5. Ned expects to complete his architectural training in two years.
6. We've always thought that Aunt Irma was an odd duck.
7. Bud, you've got to walk the walk if you want respect.
8. Have you seen Donnie's new wheels? So cool!
9. If you get hassled, just give me a heads-up.
10. Don't forget your umbrella. It's raining cats and dogs out!

Exercise B

In the following sentences, the underlined words are archaic. Some of these words come from the selections in this unit. Rewrite each sentence, replacing the archaic word with a more contemporary word. Use context clues and a dictionary to help.

1. He was startled to <u>behold</u> her lovely face.
2. The princess said to her wicked stepmother, "Tell me, I <u>pray</u>, why you are mistreating me."
3. The king was <u>wroth</u> to find out his orders had been disobeyed; he ordered all who had disobeyed him to be punished.
4. "Where are <u>ye</u> going?" the old man asked the traveler.
5. "We must leave <u>anon</u> or we will never escape!" cried the peasant, as the dragon chased him and his brother from the castle.
6. "As for <u>thy</u> service, <u>thou</u> will be rewarded," said the kind old woman to the servant girl.
7. "<u>Wherefore</u> did you come here?" asked the prince.

8. The knight <u>assayed</u> to climb the tower and rescue the princess, but he slipped and fell.
9. "The wicked queen will be here <u>ere</u> long. We must run!"
10. It was <u>meet</u> for them to sit politely at the table while they waited for their host to finish giving a speech.

Exercise C

Write a dialogue between two characters you have recently encountered in your reading. Choose characters from different places or regions. In your dialogue, include at least five examples of informal English. Use formal English to set up the dialogue with a narrative section. When you have finished your work, read your dialogue aloud to a small group of classmates and ask the group for feedback.

EXTEND THE SKILL

Find a document written in a formal register. You might choose a business letter or memo, a political commentary, or a textbook passage. Rewrite the document as a rap song, a journal entry, or a children's story using an informal register. Or, choose something written in an informal register, like a personal letter, and rewrite it in a formal register.

Understanding Epics

THE EPIC

Thousands of years ago, before history had been written down in books, the people of ancient Greece turned to the poets to hear the tales of the past. These poets, or bards, were masterful storytellers who would travel from village to village, singing or reciting long poetic **epics** — partly memorized, partly improvised — about the gods and heroes of days gone by. According to legend, the greatest of the ancient Greek bards was Homer. His two famous works, *The Iliad* (i´ lē əd) (page 861) and *The Odyssey* (ä´ də sē), are considered to be the most important and influential in all epic literature.

Since Homer's time, the epic has been recognized as a distinct *genre,* or type, of literature, and accordingly imitated by other authors. For example, *The Kalevala* by Elias Lönnrot (page 808) is a Finnish epic and shares many similarities with Homeric epics. All epics typically share the following characteristics:
- They are narrative poems — that is, they tell a story in verse, typically one that is taken from history or legend.
- They are grand in length and scope and provide a portrait of a culture — its beliefs, values, laws, arts, and ways of life.
- The tone and style are serious and formal.
- The subject of the tale is a battle or a great journey undertaken by a hero. Gods or other supernatural beings participate in the action.

ELEMENTS OF EPICS

Epic Hero
At the center of the epic is a larger-than-life hero, a character of great, even superhuman, strength and courage who undertakes a difficult journey or quest. Often the hero does the following:
- travels to diverse, exotic settings around the world or the universe in the course of a quest or journey
- is aided by gods or other supernatural beings
- struggles against gods, monsters, or other antagonists that test his or her strength and wit and must complete several formidable tasks before returning home

Achilles could be considered an epic hero of *The Iliad.* He is a great warrior, and his prowess in battle is widely known. Achilles must battle Hector, the greatest warrior of the Trojans, wrestle with his own pride, and still try to win the war for the Greeks. Throughout the Trojan War, the goddesses Hera and Athena favor the Greeks, and Aphrodite favors the Trojans.

The following chart lists some famous epics and the journeys their heroes take. Are any of these epics familiar to you?

Hero Story	Hero Who Goes on a Journey or Quest
The Epic of Gilgamesh	Gilgamesh, a king in ancient Babylon
The Iliad and *The Odyssey*	Achilles and Odysseus, warriors in ancient Greece
Ramayana	Rama, a warrior from ancient India
Beowulf	Beowulf, a warrior in old England
The Song of Niebelungs	Siegfried, a warrior in Germany
Orlando Furioso	Bradamante, a female Christian knight
The Lord of the Rings	Frodo, a hobbit from Middle-earth

Epic Narrator
Epics like *The Iliad* were not written but were narrated by a poet who would chant or sing the tales to the tune of a lyre, a stringed instrument. The poet-narrator often improvised, or changed details, but generally followed these conventions:
- started with an invocation — a plea to the Muse, or goddess of poetry, for inspiration
- began telling the tale *in medias res,* or "in the middle of things," filling in earlier details later, often in the form of speeches given by the main characters

- used many stock expressions, or "word formulas," such as epithets and epic similes. **Epithets** are brief descriptive phrases that emphasize an important characteristic of a person or thing. These stock expressions were easy to remember and helped the oral poets improvise on a poem as it was sung. For example, in "The Drowned Maid" from *The Kalevala,* the narrator refers to "old Väinämöinen" and "fair little hen," Aino.

Epic similes, also known as *Homeric similes,* are extended comparisons that go on for several lines. Like the epithets, these long, descriptive passages were probably memorized and repeated by the oral poets again and again each time they told the story. The excerpt below from *The Iliad* is an example.

NOAH'S ARK.

> And swift Achilles kept on coursing Hector, nonstop
> as a hound in the mountains starts a fawn from its lair,
> hunting him down the gorges, down the narrow glens
> and the fawn goes to ground, hiding deep in brush
> but the hound comes racing fast, nosing him out
> until he lands his kill.
> —from *The Iliad* by Homer

ORIGINS OF EPICS

The oldest epic poem in the world dates back to ancient Mesopotamian cultures, in what is modern-day Iraq. The *Epic of Gilgamesh* is based on a real king who ruled the city-state of Uruk around 2600 BCE. Gilgamesh visits his relative Utnapishtim who gives him a special water plant that can provide immortality. Utnapishtim is immortal himself, because he and his wife were told by the god Enki about a flood that would destroy humanity. They put a sample of every living thing on a boat and survived the flood to repopulate the earth. Does this story sound familiar? It's very similar to the account of Noah in the Bible.

Interestingly, stories of world-destroying floods and the repopulating of the earth can also be found in the myths of the Aztecs, the Norse, the Chinese, the Incas, the Greeks, and the Hindus.

The longest epic comes from India. The *Mahabharata* describes the feud between the Pandavas and the Kauravas, two families descended from King Bharata. These families supposedly lived in northern India around 1200 BCE.

Epic Films

Hollywood uses the term *epic* to refer to films that cover a long expanse of time and recreate historical events, often in an elaborate and dramatic manner. What characteristics do the following epic films have in common with epic poems you've read?

- *Gone with the Wind* (1939)
- *The Ten Commandments* (1956)
- *Cleopatra* (1963)
- *Braveheart* (1995)
- *Troy* (2004)

The Drowned Maid from *The Kalevala*

BUILD BACKGROUND

Literary Context *The Kalevala* (kä´ le vä' lä) is a Finnish epic. An *epic* is a long story, often told in verse, including heroes and gods. Väinämöinen (vī´ nə moi nən) is a powerful seer with supernatural origins who courts a young maiden, Aino (ī´ nō), in Kalevala, the "land of heroes" that is the dwelling place of the poem's chief characters.

The Kalevala is based on Finnish folklore collected by Elias Lönnrot and his colleagues. The poetic song tradition from which the epic emerged has been part of the oral tradition among speakers of Balto-Finnic languages for two thousand years. The version from which "The Drowned Maid" was drawn was first published in 1849.

Reader's Context What would be the best way to deal with the situation if someone you did not like became interested in you romantically?

ANALYZE LITERATURE: Mood and Repetition

Mood, or atmosphere, is the emotion created in the reader by all or part of a literary work. A writer can evoke in the reader an emotional response—such as fear, discomfort, longing, or anticipation—by working carefully with descriptive language and sensory details.

Repetition is the writer's intentional reuse of a sound, word, phrase, or sentence; it is an important part of oral literature because things that are repeated can be more easily remembered.

SET PURPOSE

The title of this selection, "The Drowned Maid," suggests that a young woman will drown. Make a prediction about the circumstances that will lead to her drowning. What kind of mood do you think an event such as a drowning will create? As you read, consider the mood of the piece and look for ways repetition helps create mood.

MEET THE AUTHOR

Elias Lönnrot (1802–1884) created the Finnish national epic, *The Kalevala,* from short ballads and lyric poems collected from oral tradition. He also published *Old Songs and Ballads of the Finnish People* and other collections. From 1853 to 1862, he taught Finnish language and literature at the University of Helsinki. Lönnrot promoted Finnish as a national language (Swedish had previously been predominant) and paved the way for the birth of modern Finnish literature.

USE READING SKILLS

Sequence of Events

Sequence refers to the order in which things happen. A good way to keep track of the events in a work of literature is to make a Time Line, which you can do by drawing a line and dividing it into equal parts like the one shown below. As you read "The Drowned Maid," add key events to your Time Line.

Aino gathers bath-whisks in grove.

PREVIEW VOCABULARY

An **antonym** is a word that has a meaning opposite from that of another word. In the exercise below, choose an antonym for each vocabulary word from the selection.

1. After tugging at it for several minutes, Joe was able to <u>wrench</u> the hubcap off the car.
   A. imply
   B. caress
   C. deceive
2. The poem expresses such sadness and regret that it's clear the poet <u>laments</u> the loss of his pets.
   A. rejoices
   B. decries
   C. foresees
3. The sheriff wanted to <u>detain</u> the suspect for further questioning.
   A. release
   B. distract
   C. decrease

The DROWNED *Maid*

FROM *THE KALEVALA*

An Epic by **Elias Lönnrot**

"Why are you weeping, poor girl
poor girl, young maiden?"

Aino Myth [Detail], 1891. Akseli Gallen-Kallela.
The Museum of Finnish Art, Helsinki, Finland.

1   Now, that Aino, the young maid
     young Joukahainen's sister
     went for a broom from the grove
     and for bath-whisks[1] from the scrub;
5   broke off one for her father
     another for her mother
          gathered a third too
     for her full-blooded brother.
     She was just stepping homeward
10   tripping through alders
     when old Väinämöinen came.
     He saw the maid in the grove
     the fine-hemmed in the grasses
     and uttered a word, spoke thus:
15   "Don't for anyone, young maid
          except me, young maid
     wear the beads around your neck
     set the cross upon your breast
     put your head into a braid
20   bind your hair with silk!"

     The maid put this into words:
     "Not for you nor anyone

---

1. **bath-whisks.** Tree branches used for cleaning the skin in the sauna

do I wear crosses upon
my breast, tie my hair with silk.
25   I don't care for cogware,[2] for
wheat slices I don't complain:
      I live in tight clothes
      I grow on breadcrusts
      by my good father
30   with my dear mother."

She <u>wrenched</u> the cross from her
      breast
and the rings from her finger
the beads she shook from her neck
and the red threads off her head
35   left them on the ground for the
      ground's sake
in the grove for the grove's sake
      and went weeping home
      wailing to the farm.

Her father at the window
40   sat adorning an axe haft:[3]
"Why are you weeping, poor girl
poor girl, young maiden?"

      "I have cause to weep
      woes to complain of!
45   For this I weep, my papa
for this I weep and complain:
the cross came loose from my breast
the bauble[4] shook from my belt
from my breast the silver cross
50   the copper threads off my belt."

Her brother at the gateway
is carving collar-bow wood:
"Why do you weep, poor sister
poor sister, young maid?"

55   "I have cause to weep
      woes to complain of!
For this I weep, poor brother
for this I weep and complain:
the ring slipped off my finger
60   and the beads fell from my neck
the gold ring from my finger
from my neck the silver beads."

Her sister at the floor seam
is weaving a belt of gold:
65   "Why do you weep, poor sister
      poor sister, young maid?"

      "The weeper has cause
      she who whines has woes!
For this I weep, poor sister
70   for this I weep and complain:
the gold came loose from my brows
and the silver from my hair
and the blue silks from my eyes
the red ribbons off my head."

75   Her mother on the shed step
is skimming cream off the milk:
"Why are you weeping, poor girl
      poor girl, young maiden?"

"O mamma who carried me
80   O mother who suckled me!
      There are dark causes
      very low spirits!
For this I weep, poor mother
for this, mamma, complain: I
85   went for a broom from the grove
for bath-whisk tips from the scrub
broke off one for my father
another for my mother
      gathered a third too
90   for my full-blooded brother.
I began to step homeward
was just stepping through the glade
when from the dell, from the land
burnt over, the Great One said:
95   'Don't for anyone, poor maid
      except me, poor maid
wear the beads around your neck
set the cross upon your breast
put your head into a braid
100   bind your hair with silk!'
I wrenched the cross from my breast

---

2. **cogware.** A kind of coarse cloth worn by the poorer classes
3. **haft.** Handle
4. **bauble.** Inexpensive ornamentation

wrench (rench) *v.,* twist, pull, or jerk violently

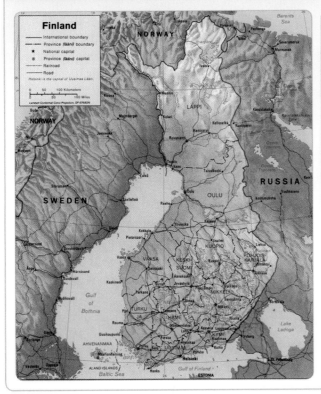

***The Kalevala's* Impact on Finland** When *The Kalevala* first appeared in print in the mid-1800s, Finland had been an autonomous state for only a quarter of a century. Before that, until 1809, Finland had been a part of the Swedish empire. The appearance of *The Kalevala* bolstered the Finns' self-confidence and faith in their language and culture and caused a stir abroad by bringing a small, relatively unknown people to the attention of other Europeans.

the beads I shook from my neck
and the blue threads from my eyes
and the red threads off my head
105   cast them on the ground for the
        ground's sake
in the grove for the grove's sake
and I put this into words:
'Not for you nor anyone
do I wear the cross upon
110   my breast, tie my head with silk.
I don't care for cogware, for
wheat slices I don't complain:
    I live in tight clothes
    I grow on breadcrusts
115   I by my good father
with my dear mother.'"

The mother put this in words
the eldest spoke to her child:
    "Don't weep, my daughter
120   fruit of my youth, don't <u>lament</u>!

One year eat melted butter:
you'll grow plumper than others;
    the next year eat pork:
you'll grow sleeker than others;
125   a third year eat cream pancakes:
you'll grow fairer than others.
Step to the shed on the hill
    open the best shed:
there is chest on top of chest
130   and box beside box.
    Open the best chest
    slam the bright lid back:
inside are six golden belts
    and seven blue skirts
135   all woven by Moon-daughter
finished off by Sun-daughter.

"Long since, when I was a maid
and lived as a lass, I went

la • ment (lə ment´) *v.,* feel or express deep sorrow

> *"Give, Moon-daughter,*
> *of your gold*
> *Sun-daughter, of your silver*
> *to this girl who has nothing*
> *to this child who begs!"*

for berries in the forest
140   raspberries under the slope.
      I heard Moon-daughter weaving
          Sun-daughter spinning
          beside blue backwoods
      at the edge of a sweet grove.
145   I went up to them
          I came close, approached;
      I began to beg of them
          I uttered and said:
      'Give, Moon-daughter, of your gold
150   Sun-daughter, of your silver
      to this girl who has nothing
          to this child who begs!'
      Moon-daughter gave of her gold
      Sun-daughter of her silver:
155   I put the gold on my brows
      on my head the good silver
          and came home a flower
      to my father's yards a joy.
      I wore them for one day, two
160   till on the third day
      I stripped the gold from my brows
      from my head the good silver
      took them to the hilltop shed

165   put them under the chest lid:
      there they have been ever since
      all this time unlooked upon.

      "Bind now the silks to your eyes
      and to your brows lift the gold
      around your neck the bright beads
170   the gold crosses on your breasts!
      Put on a shirt of linen
      one of hempen lawn[5] on top;
      pull on a skirt of broadcloth
      on top of it a silk belt
175   fine stockings of silk
          handsome leather shoes!
      Twine your hair into a braid
      tie it with ribbons of silk
      on your fingers put gold rings
180   and on your hands gold bracelets!
      Like that you will come back home
      you will step in from the shed
      to be your kinsfolk's sweetness
      the softness of all your clan:
185   you will walk the lanes a flower
      you will roam a raspberry
      more graceful than you once were
      better than you were before."

      The mother put that in words
190   that's what she said to her child
      but the daughter did not heed
      did not hear the mother's words:
      she went weeping to the yard
      pining into the farmyard.
195   She says with this word
          she spoke with this speech:
      "How do the lucky ones feel
      and how do the blessed think?
      This is how the lucky feel
200   how the blessed think—
          like water stirring
      or a ripple on a trough.
      But how do the luckless feel
      and how do the callous think?
205   This is how the luckless feel

---

5. **hempen lawn.** Cloth made of hemp, a fiber used to make rope

Young Girl on the Shore, 1912. Edvard Munch. The Munch Museum, Oslo, Norway.

how the callous think—
like hard snow under a ridge
like water in a deep well.
    Often in my gloom
210   now, often, a gloomy child
my mood is to tread dead grass
and through undergrowth to crawl
    on turf to loiter
in a bush to roll about—
215   my mood no better than tar
my heart no whiter than coal.
Better it would be for me
and better it would have been
had I not been born, not grown
220   not sprung to full size
    in these evil days
    in this joyless world.
Had I died a six-night-old

and been lost an eight-night-old
225   I would not have needed much—
    a span of linen
    a tiny field edge
a few tears from my mother
still fewer from my father
230   not even a few from my brother."

She wept one day, she wept two.
Her mother began to ask:
"Why are you weeping, poor lass
why, woebegone, complaining?"

235   "This is why I, poor lass, weep
    all my time complain:
you have given luckless me
and your own child you have pledged
made me care for an old man
240   gladden an aged man, be

refuge for a dodderer[6]
shelter for a nook-haunter.[7]
Sooner had you bidden me
go below the deep billows
245   to be sister to whitefish
and brother to the fishes!
Better to be in the sea
to dwell below the billows
to be sister to whitefish
250   and brother to the fishes
than to care for an old man
be a dodderer's refuge
one who trips on his stockings
who falls over a dry twig."

255   Then she stepped to the shed-hill
    stepped inside the shed
    opened the best chest
    slammed the bright lid back
and she found six golden belts
260   and seven blue skirts
    and she put them on
    she decks her body.
She set the gold on her brows
the silver upon her hair
265   the blue silks upon her eyes
the red threads upon her head.
    Then she stepped away
across one glade, along two;
    she roamed swamps, roamed lands
270   roamed gloomy backwoods.
    She sang as she went
    uttered as she roamed:
"In my heart there is a hurt
in my head there is an ache
275   but the hurt would not hurt more
and the ache would not more ache
if I, hapless, were to die
    were cut off, mean one
    from these great sorrows
280   from these low spirits.
Now would be the time for me
    to part from this world—
the time to go to Death, the
age to come to Tuonela:

285 father would not weep for me
mother would not take it ill
sister's face would not be wet
brother's eyes would not shed tears
though I rolled in the water
290 fell into the fishy sea
down below the deep billows
    upon the black mud."

She stepped one day, she stepped two
    till on the third day
295   she came upon sea
    faced a reedy shore:
there the night overtakes her
    the dark detains her.
There the lass wept all evening
300   whimpered all night long
on a wet rock on the shore
    at the broad bay-end.

Early in the morning she
looked out at a headland's tip:
305 three maids at the headland's tip
there were, bathing in the sea!
The maid Aino would be fourth
and the slip of a girl fifth!
She cast her shirt on willow
310 her skirt upon an aspen
her stockings on the bare ground
her shoes upon the wet rock
her beads on the sandy shore
her rings upon the shingle.
315 A rock was bright on the main
a boulder glittering gold:
she strove to swim to the rock
she would flee to the boulder.
    Then, when she got there
320   she sits herself down
    upon the bright rock
on the glittering boulder:

---

6. **dodderer.** One who trembles from weakness or old age
7. **nook-haunter.** One who haunts, or frequents, secluded or
sheltered places

de • tain (dē tān´) v., keep from going on; hold back

the rock plopped in the water
　　the boulder sank down
325　　the maid with the rock
Aino beside the boulder.

That is where the hen was lost
　　there the poor lass died.
She said while she was dying
330　spoke as she was still rolling:
"I went to bathe in the sea
arrived to swim in the main
and there I, a hen, was lost
I, a bird, untimely died:
335　　let not my father
　　ever in this world
　　draw any fishes
　　from this mighty main!
I went to wash at the shore
340　I went to bathe in the sea
and there I, a hen, was lost
I, a bird, untimely died:
　　let not my mother
　　ever in this world
345　　put water in dough
　　from the broad home-bay!
I went to wash at the shore
I went to bathe in the sea
and there I, a hen, was lost
350　I, a bird, untimely died:
　　let not my brother
　　ever in this world
　　water his war-horse
　　upon the seashore!
355　I went to wash at the shore
I went to bathe in the sea
and there I, a hen, was lost
I, a bird, untimely died:
　　let not my sister
360　　ever in this world
　　wash her eyes here, at
　　the home-bay landing!
Waters of the sea
so much blood of mine;
365　fishes of the sea
so much flesh of mine;

There the lass wept all evening
whimpered all night long
on a wet rock on the shore
at the broad bay-end.

　　brushwood on the shore
　　is a poor one's ribs;
　　grasses of the shore
370　　are her tousled hair."
Such the death of the young maid
end of the fair little hen.

Who now will carry the news
will tell it by word of mouth
375　　to the maid's famous
　　home, to the fair farm?
A bear will carry the news
will tell it by word of mouth!
But the bear does not: it was
380　lost among a herd of cows.
Who now will carry the news
will tell it by word of mouth
　　to the maid's famous
　　home, to the fair farm?
385　A wolf will carry the news
will tell it by word of mouth!
But the wolf does not: it was
lost among a flock of sheep.
Who now will carry the news

> # "Perhaps the Devil has come to stew in the pans!"

390   will tell it by word of mouth
          to the maid's famous
              home, to the fair farm?
      A fox will carry the news
      will tell it by word of mouth!
395   But the fox does not: it was
      lost among a flock of geese.
      Who now will carry the news
      will tell it by word of mouth
          to the maid's famous
400   home, to the fair farm?
      A hare will carry the news
      will tell it by word of mouth!
      The hare said for sure: "The news
      will not be lost on this man!"
405   And the hare ran off
          the long-ear lolloped
          the wry-leg rushed off
          the cross-mouth careered
          to the maid's famous
410   home, to the fair farm.

      To the sauna threshold it
      ran, on the threshold it squats.
      The sauna is full of maids;
      whisks in hand they greet: "Sly one
415   have you come here to be cooked
      pop-eye, to be roasted for
              the master's supper
              the mistress's meal
              for the daughter's snacks
420   or for the son's lunch?"

      The hare manages to say
      and the round-eye to speak out:
      "Perhaps the Devil has come
          to stew in the pans!
425   I have come carrying news
      to tell it by word of mouth:
          the fair has fallen
      the tin-breast has pined away
      sunken the silver-buckle
430   the copper-belt slipped away—
      gone into the wanton sea
          down to the vast deeps
      to be sister to whitefish
      and brother to the fishes."
435   The mother started weeping
      and a stream of tears rolling
      and then she began to say
      the woebegone to complain:
          "Don't, luckless mothers
440   ever in this world
          don't lull your daughters
          or rock your children,
      to marry against their will
      as I, a luckless mother
445   have lulled my daughters
          reared my little hens."
      The mother wept, a tear rolled:
      her plentiful waters rolled
          out of her blue eyes
450   to her luckless cheeks.
      One tear rolled, another rolled
      her plentiful waters rolled
          from her luckless cheeks
          to her ample breasts.
455   One tear rolled, another rolled
      her plentiful waters rolled
          from her ample breasts
          upon her fine hems.
      One tear rolled, another rolled
460   her plentiful waters rolled
          down from her fine hems
      upon her red-topped stockings.
      One tear rolled, another rolled
      her plentiful waters rolled

The hare brings the news of Aino's death to her mother and father.

465 down from her red-topped stockings
to her gilded[8] shoe-uppers.
One tear rolled, another rolled
her plentiful waters rolled
from her gilded shoe-uppers
470 to the ground beneath her feet;
they rolled to the ground for the
ground's sake
to the water for the water's sake.
The waters reaching the ground
began to form a river
475 and three rivers grew
from the tears she wept
that came from her head
that went from beneath her brow.
In each river grew

480 three fiery rapids;
on each rapid's foam
three crags[9] sprouted up
and on each crag's edge
a golden knoll[10] rose
485 and on each knoll's peak
there grew three birches;
in each birch's top
there were three golden cuckoos.

The cuckoos started calling:
490 the first called *love, love!*
the second *bridegroom, bridegroom!*

---

8. **gilded.** Stitched or decorated with gold
9. **crags.** Steep rugged rocks or cliffs
10. **knoll.** Small round hill

and the third *joy, joy!*
That which called *love, love!*
called out for three months
495   to the loveless girl
lying in the sea;
that which called *bridegroom,*
bridegroom!
called out for six months
to the comfortless bridegroom
500   sitting and longing;
that which called *joy, joy!*
called out for all her lifetime
to the mother without joy
weeping all her days.

505   The mother put this in words
listening to the cuckoo:
"Let a luckless mother not
listen long to the cuckoo!
When the cuckoo is calling
510   my heart is throbbing
tears come to my eyes
waters down my cheeks
flow thicker than peas
and fatter than beans:
515   by an ell my life passes
by a span my frame grows old
my whole body is blighted
when I hear the spring cuckoo." ❖

How well do you think Aino handled the situation of being betrothed to someone she did not love? Have you known anyone in a similar situation? What did he or she do? What would you do in that situation?

REFER TO TEXT ▶ ▶ ▶ ▶	▶ REASON WITH TEXT	
1a. When Väinämöinen asks Aino to wear her adornments for him, what does she do?	1b. Describe what Aino's response reveals about her feelings for Väinämöinen.	**Understand** **Find meaning**
2a. Recall where Aino goes when she leaves her home at the farm.	2b. Examine the reasons why Aino leaves home. What do Aino's reasons for leaving home tell you about her view of the situation?	**Apply** **Use information**
3a. Describe Aino's relationship with the sea.	3b. To what emotion is water linked in this selection?	**Analyze** **Take things apart**
4a. List a quotation that shows what happens to Aino when she bathes in the sea.	4b. Determine whether you think Aino's death is intentional. Explain your reasons.	**Evaluate** **Make judgments**
5a. How do you predict Aino's mother will arrange a wedding for her other daughter, now that Aino is dead?	5b. If you were Aino's mother, propose how you would view the hare after Aino's death.	**Create** **Bring ideas together**

ANALYZE LITERATURE: Mood and Repetition

Make a list of words from the epic that contribute to its mood or moods. Then classify the words according to the mood they help establish. What mood or moods are reflected most strongly? What sections of text are repeated? How does repetition help create mood?

MACKENZIE

Literature CONNECTION

Ruth MacKenzie is a singer, a writer, and an actor who has explored many creative and performing arenas. "The first time I heard the vocal sounds of Finland and Sweden, I was hooked. I wanted to house these sounds within my own body," MacKenzie said. In 1994, she studied in Finland and Sweden and worked at home in Minnesota experimenting with vocal sounds and "driving my dog nuts." MacKenzie was named Artist of the Year in 1997 by both the Minneapolis *Star Tribune* and the Minneapolis *City Pages* for her production of *Kalevala: Dream of the Salmon Maiden,* from which the song **"In the Blue Woodland"** is taken.

In the Blue Woodland

from *Kalevala: Dream of the Salmon Maiden*

Song Lyrics by **Ruth MacKenzie**

Long, long ago, in my girlhood
I went berrying, berry picking on a hillside.
Out in the cloudberries, raspberries
There I heard the Moonmaid sigh.

5   Daughter of the Moon, she sat to weaving
And her sister sun, bright, Sunsister spinning
In the far blue, the blue woodland
There I saw blue dresses of the eternities.

Anna Kuutar, kultiasi
10 Päivätär hopeitasi[1]
O how softly, how softly,
stepped into the blue, stepped into the blue woodland
Whispering these words I've kept in secret
Kept in secret but I now repeat to you.

---

1. **Anna…hopeitasi.** [Finnish] Give me good Moonmaid of your gold;
Give sweet Sunlight your silver stole.

15 Anna Kuutar, kultiasi
    Päivätär hopeitasi
    (Give me good Moonmaid of your gold
    Give sweet Sunlight your silver stole)
    Wrap me around in your bright arms
20 Give good Moon what this child desires.

    Gold on my brow and sleeves of silver
    I came to my homegates, I came home then like a flower
    Wearing the moonlight, the sunlight,
    The very sky above, gifts of light and love and power.

25   Wore them one day, then another
    Seven blue dresses, six golden girdles wait you
        As a joy to father's farmyard
    This I have kept for you, all from that distant girlhood
        But already on the third day
30 Clang the richest locker up, you behold the moon.
        Took the gold from off my forehead
    And I saved it all for you my daughter. ❖

REFER TO TEXT ▶ ▶ ▶ ▶	▶ REASON WITH TEXT	
1a. Identify whom the young girl comes across while berry picking.	1b. Discuss why the girl might have seen these figures "in the blue woodland."	**Understand** **Find meaning**
2a. List the gifts the girl in the song receives. What gifts does Aino's mother give to Aino in "The Drowned Maid"?	2b. Infer how the song answers the question in "The Drowned Maid" of why the gold and skirts were locked in a chest.	**Analyze** **Take things apart**
3a. Name the point of view used in the song. Name the point of view used in "The Drowned Maid."	3b. Critique how the difference in point of view in the two selections influences the underlying story. In your opinion, which point of view is more successful? Why? What challenges might the songwriter have faced in trying to capture a "snapshot" of *The Kalevala* in song?	**Evaluate** **Make judgments**

TEXT ← TO → TEXT CONNECTION

- Which parts of the story does each selection emphasize? Which characters are emphasized? What do you learn about Aino and her family from each version?
- Compare and contrast how each selection uses language. Which uses more modern vocabulary and sentence structures? Which is easier to understand?
- Evaluate whether Ruth MacKenzie's song is faithful to the spirit and tone of "The Drowned Maid." Explain your answer. What do both selections indicate about the values of Finnish culture? Support your answer with evidence from the text.

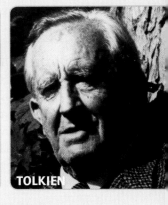

TOLKIEN

The English writer and scholar J. R. R. Tolkien (1882–1973) is best remembered for his mythological epic trilogy, *The Lord of the Rings,* first published in 1954–55. This work became immensely popular, especially among young people. Tolkien's tale combines the epic motifs of the journey, supernatural monsters, and a profound and highly suspenseful conflict of good versus evil. In the article **Lord of the Rings Inspired by an Ancient Epic,** reporter **Brian Handwerk** of *National Geographic* reveals how important an influence the Finnish national epic *The Kalevala* had on Tolkien.

LORD OF THE RINGS
Inspired by an Ancient Epic
A Magazine Article by Brian Handwerk

Generations of readers have cherished Middle-earth, the fantasy universe sprung from the mind of storyteller J. R. R. Tolkien. His magical world has been brought to life in the *Lord of the Rings* movie trilogy, the third of which, *The Return of the King,* swept every category it was nominated for at the Academy Awards ceremony last night. The movie most notably won Oscars for Best Picture and Directing, among 9 others.

While the author's imagination was vast, Tolkien's world and its cast of characters do have roots in real-world history and geography, from the world wars that dominated Tolkien's lifetime to the ancient language and legends of Finland.

Anthropologist[1] and ethnobotanist[2] Wade Davis traveled to a remote corner of Finland to uncover Tolkien influences that stretch back into the misty past of northern Europe.

Ancient Saga

Davis, a National Geographic Society explorer-in-residence, journeyed to what was once Finland's Viena Karelia region, along the Russian border, to study Finnish. By the 19th century this area was a last refuge for a unique <u>dialect</u> of the Finnish language.

Nearly all Finns at that time were speaking Finnish, Swedish, or even Russian, the region's established written languages. But a dialect still existed in this isolated region as it always had—in oral form, passed down through the

ages from one generation to the next in songs and verses, or runes.

A collection of these runes, comparable to India's *Ramayana,* or the Greek *Odyssey,* is known in Finland as the *Kalevala,* and those who sing its lyrical verses from memory are known as rune singers. These elders long

---

1. **anthropologist.** Person who studies the science of human beings
2. **ethnobotanist.** Person who studies the interaction between plants and animals and human cultures

> **di • a • lect** (dī´ ə lekt') *n.,* a variety of language spoken in a certain region and distinguishable by vocabulary, grammar, and pronunciation

carried in their minds the entire record of the Finnish language.

"In an oral tradition, the total richness of the language is no more than the vocabulary of the best storyteller," Davis explains. "In other words, at any one point in time the boundaries of the language are being stretched according to the memory of the best storyteller."

In what was the Viena Karelia region, the oral tradition of the Finnish language is still alive, but now contained in the memory of just a single storyteller. His name is Jussi Houvinen, and he is Finland's last great rune singer. This elderly man is a living link to myths and languages that have passed mouth-to-ear over the ages in an unbroken chain.

"It's an amazing thing to be in the presence of a man singing even a snippet of the poem," says Davis of his meeting with Houvinen, "because it's so powerful that even if you don't speak Finnish it's profoundly moving just to listen to it, just the <u>cadence</u> of the sounds.

"Being in his presence, and knowing how few people can today recite the poem, you felt you were in the presence of history that was about to be snuffed out." When Houvinen dies the ancient succession of rune singers will end. No one from a younger generation has been able to learn the vast breadth of the saga.

However, the *Kalevala* itself will not die with Jussi, due to the efforts of a country doctor named Elias Lönnrot.

In the early 19th century, Lönnrot became enamored of the Finnish songs and runes he found in Viena Karelia. He devoted himself to traveling the district, listening to the rune singers and committing the oral poetry to the written word. This was the genesis not only of the modern Finnish language but of the Finnish nation as an entity, creating what Davis calls "this wonderful idea of a...bardic[3] poem inspiring a modern nation."

Inspiration for Middle-earth

The *Kalevala* inspired not only Finnish nationalism but also a young English scholar and writer named J. R. R. Tolkien, in whose mind was already taking shape a magical universe that was about to be transformed by Finnish language and legend.

In a letter to W. H. Auden, on June 7, 1955, he remembered his excitement upon discovering a Finnish grammar in Exeter College Library. "It was like discovering a complete wine-cellar filled with bottles of an amazing wine of a kind and flavor never tasted before. It quite intoxicated me; and I gave up the attempt to invent an 'unrecorded' Germanic language, and my 'own language'—or series of invented languages—became heavily Finnicized [sic] in <u>phonetic</u> pattern and structure."

The Finnish language that so delighted the young student became the inspiration for the lyrical tongue of Middle-earth's elves. Tolkien taught himself the ancient and newly codified Finnish to develop his elfin language, and so that he could read the *Kalevala* in its original Finnish. This achievement opened the door to many further influences from Finnish mythology. Parallels abound between the *Kalevala* and Tolkien's own saga, in terms of both the characters themselves and the idea of the hero's journey.

The *Kalevala* features "all the themes of pre-Christian traditions, shape-shifting, mythical demons, magical plants, animals becoming human beings," says Davis, while the story itself "is fundamentally a story of a sacred object which has power, and the pursuit of the mythic heroes who seek that power, to seek a way of understanding what that power means." Davis describes the *Kalevala* as "a journey of the soul and a journey of the spirit—and that's obviously what drew Tolkien to it."

Tolkien readers have long seen Tolkien's <u>bucolic</u> vision of rural England represented in Middle-earth's Shire, and recognized English farmers in characters such as the hobbit Sam. But those who explore the *Kalevala* may discover much of the land of the elves, and their language, in the vast snowy spruce forests of Finnish legend. ❖

---

3. **bardic.** Skilled in composing and singing tribal verse

ca • dence (kā´ d'n[t]s) *n.*, a rhythmic flow of sounds in language
pho • net • ic (fə ne´ tik) *adj.*, of or relating to spoken language or speech sounds
bu • col • ic (byü kä´ lik) *adj.*, of or relating to shepherds

REFER TO TEXT ▷ ▷ ▷ ▷ ▷	REASON WITH TEXT	
1a. List the reasons anthropologist Wade Davis traveled to Finland.	**1b.** Summarize why Davis was so impressed by Jussi Houvinen. Explain Davis's opinion about his meeting with Houvinen.	**Understand** **Find meaning**
2a. Define "runes." To which famous epics does Brian Handwerk compare the Finnish runes of *The Kalevala?*	**2b.** Examine the reasons why he might have made these comparisons.	**Apply** **Use information**
3a. State what Tolkien says in his letter to poet W. H. Auden? What did his discovery of Finnish grammar inspire Tolkien to do?	**3b.** After reading this article, compile a list of things you'd like to know about Tolkien, Lonnrot, or the information presented in the article. Then make a plan for how you can locate that information.	**Create** **Bring ideas together**

TEXT ◀—TO—▶ TEXT CONNECTION

Toward the end of the article, Wade Davis refers to several "themes" of pre-Christian traditions. List these themes. What evidence of these themes do you see in "The Drowned Maid"? Use quotations from "The Drowned Maid" to support your answer.

AFTER READING

EXTEND THE TEXT

Writing Options
Creative Writing Imagine you are Väinämöinen. Write a **love note** to Aino expressing how you feel and your response to her behavior in the grove. Then write another note with Aino's response to Väinämöinen's note.

Expository Writing Explore the moods of "The Drowned Maid" and "In the Blue Woodland." How would you describe the mood of each piece? How does the mood affect your understanding of each piece? Answer these questions in a one-page **literary analysis.** In your opening paragraph, include a thesis statement that expresses your opinion about the role mood plays in the two pieces. In your body paragraphs, use support from the selections to support your thesis. Write a conclusion that summarizes your opinions.

Collaborative Learning
Conduct Reader's Theater Along with two classmates, practice reciting the passage that describes the meeting of Väinämöinen and Aino in the grove. Have the first student play the role of the narrator, the second student play the role of Väinämöinen, and the third student play the role of Aino. Use what you know about the characters to decide what gestures, tones, facial expressions, and body postures should be used. Then present the scene to the class. Compare how the groups interpret the scene.

Critical Literacy
Research Another World Epic Research another epic besides *The Kalevala,* such as Homer's *The Iliad* or *The Odyssey*, Virgil's *Aeneid*, the Indian *Ramayana*, Dante's *The Divine Comedy,* the Old English *Beowulf,* or John Milton's *Paradise Lost.* Then gather with a few classmates and take turns presenting what your epic is about and giving a plot summary. Explain what makes your epic an epic. What heroes and gods are portrayed? What does the epic reveal about the legends, beliefs, values, laws, arts, and ways of life of the people from whose culture it arose?

 Go to **www.mirrorsandwindows.com** for more.

from *The Ingenious Hidalgo Don Quixote de la Mancha*

BEFORE READING
A Novel by Miguel de Cervantes Saavedra

BUILD BACKGROUND

Literary Context *The Ingenious Hidalgo Don Quixote de la Mancha* is a parody of a medieval romance (a tale based on legend, adventure, or the supernatural), in which an eccentric man, having spent too much time reading about knights in shining armor, decides to spend his life as a knight. *Don Quixote* is also thought to poke fun at the whole idea of a larger-than-life hero that is seen in most epics. The publication of Cervantes' *Don Quixote* in the early 1600s has often been said to mark the birth of the modern novel, and it gave to the English language the word *quixotic*, meaning "impractical" or "foolishly idealistic."

Reader's Context Which books have you read, or movies have you seen, that presented worlds so appealing that you have wanted to experience them yourself?

ANALYZE LITERATURE: Parody and Allusion

A **parody** is a literary work that closely imitates the style of another work for humorous purposes. Parodies often exaggerate elements of the original works to create a comic effect.

An **allusion** refers to a well-known person, event, object, or work from history or literature. This selection contains numerous allusions to medieval romances, myths, and historical events. As you read, use the footnotes and context to better understand the allusions.

SET PURPOSE

Since this selection is a parody, it is meant to be humorous. As you read, look for elements of humor in the selection. Consider ways in which the selection makes fun of epic heroes and medieval romances. How does the author describe Don Quixote's mind-set and adventures? What is humorous about Don Quixote's experiences?

MEET THE AUTHOR

Miguel de Cervantes Saavedra (1547–1616) was born near Madrid, Spain. In 1571, he lost the use of his left hand while serving in a naval battle. Four years later, he was captured by pirates and sold into slavery in Algiers in North Africa. There, he remained until he was ransomed in 1580. In 1585, he published his first novel, *La Galatea.* As a result of a financial disagreement with the government, Cervantes was jailed in 1597. His most famous work, *Don Quixote,* was published in two parts in 1605 and 1615.

USE READING SKILLS

Meaning of Words
Cause-and-effect clues are a type of context clue that requires the reader to make a guess based on cause and effect. Some words and phrases that signal cause and effect include *if...then, when...then, thus, therefore, because, so, due to, as a result of,* and *consequently.* For example, consider the following sentence: The valley was completely <u>inundated</u> due to heavy rains. In this sentence, heavy rainfall tends to cause flooding, especially in low-lying regions such as valleys. You can assume that *inundated* means "flooded" or "covered."

PREVIEW VOCABULARY

Use the cause-and-effect clues in the sentences below to figure out the meanings of the underlined words from the selection.

1. Due to the boy's constant <u>fabrications</u>, no one believed him when he actually told the truth.
2. The student's assignment was so <u>ingenious</u> that the teacher wished there was a grade higher than A+ to award the student.
3. The toddler became <u>enamored</u> of the toy fire truck and, as a result, insisted on sleeping with it.
4. The climb was so <u>arduous</u> that even the most experienced hikers were out of breath.
5. Because Natasha disliked me, I felt <u>enmity</u> toward her.

from *The Ingenious Hidalgo Don Quixote de la Mancha*

A Novel by **Miguel de Cervantes Saavedra**

"It is perfectly clear," replied Don Quixote, "that you are but a raw novice in this matter of adventures."

Don Quixote, 1955. Pablo Picasso.

CHAPTER 1

Concerning the famous hidalgo[1] Don Quixote de la Mancha's position, character and way of life

In a village in La Mancha, the name of which I cannot quite recall, there lived not long ago one of those country

---

1. **hidalgo.** In Spain, a member of the lower nobility

gentlemen or hidalgos who keep a lance in a rack, an ancient leather shield, a scrawny hack[2] and a greyhound for coursing. A midday stew with rather more shin of beef than leg of lamb, the leftovers for supper most nights, lardy eggs on Saturdays, lentil broth on Fridays and an occasional pigeon as a Sunday treat ate up three-quarters of his income. The rest went on a cape of black broadcloth, with breeches of velvet and slippers to match for holy days, and on weekdays he walked proudly in the finest homespun. He maintained a housekeeper the wrong side of forty, a niece the right side of twenty and a jack of all trades who was as good at saddling the nag as at plying the pruning shears. Our hidalgo himself was nearly fifty; he had a robust constitution, dried-up flesh and a withered face, and he was an early riser and a keen huntsman. His surname's said to have been Quixada, or Quesada (as if he were a jawbone, or a cheesecake[3]): concerning this detail there's some discrepancy among the authors who have written on the subject, although a credible conjecture does suggest he might have been a plaintive Quexana. But this doesn't matter much, as far as our story's concerned provided that the narrator doesn't stray one inch from the truth.

Now you must understand that during his idle moments (which accounted for most of the year) this hidalgo took to reading books of chivalry[4] with such relish and enthusiasm that

Everything he read in his books took possession of his imagination: enchantments, fights, battles, challenges, wounds, sweet nothings, love affairs, storms and impossible absurdities.

he almost forgot about his hunting and even running his property, and his foolish curiosity reached such extremes that he sold acres of arable land to buy these books of chivalry, and took home as many of them as he could find.

* * *

In short, our hidalgo was soon so absorbed in these books that his nights were spent reading from dusk till dawn, and his days from dawn till dusk, until the lack of sleep and the excess of reading withered his brain, and he went mad. Everything he read in his books took possession of his imagination: enchantments, fights, battles, challenges, wounds, sweet nothings, love affairs, storms and impossible absurdities. The idea that this whole fabric of famous <u>fabrications</u> was real so established itself in his mind that no history in the world was truer for him. He would declare that El Cid, Ruy Diaz,[5] had been an excellent knight, but that he couldn't be compared to the Knight of the Burning Sword, who with just one backstroke had split two fierce and enormous giants clean down the middle. He felt happier about

---

2. **hack.** Horse that is worn out from working
3. **jawbone…cheesecake.** The Spanish *quixada* once translated into "jaw." (This translation is not used anymore.) *Quesada* in Spanish means "cheese fondue."
4. **books of chivalry.** Romances about brave and heroic knights, popular in the sixteenth century
5. **El Cid, Ruy Diaz.** Hero of Spanish history and literature

fab • ri • ca • tion (fa′ bri kā′ shən) *n.*, made-up story

Don Quixote Reading a Novel. Honore Daumier.

for the common good, to become a knight errant,[6] and to travel about the world with his armor and his arms and his horse in search of adventures, and to practice all those activities that he knew from his books were practiced by knights errant, <u>redressing</u> all kinds of <u>grievances</u>, and exposing himself to perils and dangers that he would overcome and thus gain eternal fame and renown. The poor man could already see himself being crowned Emperor of Trebizond, at the very least, through the might of his arm; and so, possessed by these delightful thoughts and carried away by the strange pleasure that he derived from them, he hastened to put into practice what he so desired.

His first step was to clean a suit of armor that had belonged to his forefathers and that, covered in rust and mold, had been standing forgotten in a corner for centuries. He scoured and mended it as best he could; yet he realized that it had one important defect, which was that the headpiece was not a complete helmet but just a simple steel cap; he was <u>ingenious</u> enough, however, to overcome this problem, constructing out of cardboard something resembling a visor and face-guard which, once inserted into the steel cap, gave it the appearance of a full helmet. It's true that, to test its strength and to find out whether it could safely be exposed to attack, he drew his sword and dealt it two blows, with the first of which he destroyed in a second what it had taken him a week to create. He couldn't help being concerned about the ease with which he'd shattered it, and to guard against this danger he reconstructed it, fixing some iron bars on the

Bernardo del Carpio, because he'd slain Roland the Enchanted at Roncesvalles, by the same method used by Hercules when he suffocated Antaeus, the son of Earth—with a bear-hug. He was full of praise for the giant Morgante because, despite belonging to a proud and insolent breed, he alone was affable and well-mannered. But his greatest favorite was Reynald of Montalban, most of all when he saw him sallying forth from his castle and plundering all those he met, and when in foreign parts he stole that image of Muhammad made of solid gold, as his history records. He'd have given his housekeeper, and even his niece into the bargain, to trample the traitor Ganelon in the dust.

And so, by now quite insane, he conceived the strangest notion that ever took shape in a madman's head, considering it desirable and necessary, both for the increase of his honor and

---

6. **knight errant.** Knight traveling in search of adventures in which to exhibit military skill and generosity

re • dress (ri dres´) *v.,* set right
griev • ance (grē´ vən[t]s) *n.,* complaint
in • gen • i • ous (in jēn´ yəs) *adj.,* extremely clever

inside, which reassured him about its strength; and, preferring not to carry out any further tests, he deemed and pronounced it a most excellent visored helmet.

Then he went to visit his nag, and although it had more corns than a barleyfield and more wrong with it than Gonella's[7] horse, which *tantum pellis et ossa fuit,*[8] it seemed to him that neither Alexander's Bucephalus nor the Cid's Babieca was its equal. He spent four days considering what name to give the nag; for (he told himself) it wasn't fitting that the horse of such a famous knight errant, and such a fine horse in its own right, too, shouldn't have some name of <u>eminence</u>; and so he tried to find one that would express both what it had been before it became a knight's horse and what it was now, for it was appropriate that, since its master had changed his rank, it too should change its name, and acquire a famous and much-trumpeted one, as suited the new order and new way of life he professed. And so, after a long succession of names that he invented, eliminated and struck out, added, deleted and remade in his mind and in his imagination, he finally decided to call it *Rocinante*, that is *Hackafore*, a name which, in his opinion, was lofty and <u>sonorous</u> and expressed what the creature had been when it was a humble hack, before it became what it was now—the first and foremost of all the hacks in the world.

Having given his horse a name, and one so much to his liking, he decided to give himself a name as well, and this problem kept him busy for another eight days, at the end of which he decided to call himself *Don Quixote*, that is, *Sir Thighpiece*,[9] from which, as has already been observed, the authors of this most true history concluded that his surname must have been Quixada, and not Quesada as others had affirmed. Yet remembering that brave Amadis[10] hadn't been content to call himself Amadis alone, but had added the name of his kingdom and homeland, to make it famous, and had styled himself Amadis of Gaul, so Don Quixote,

as a worthy knight, decided to add his own country to his name and call himself *Don Quixote de la Mancha*, by doing which, in his opinion, he declared in a most vivid manner both his lineage and his homeland, and honored the latter by taking it as his surname.

Having, then, cleaned his armor, turned his steel cap into a visored helmet, baptized his nag and confirmed himself, he realized that the only remaining task was to find a lady of whom he could be <u>enamored</u>; for a knight errant without a lady-love is a tree without leaves or fruit, a body without a soul. He said to himself:

---

7. **Gonella's.** Belonging to Gonella, a jester (entertainer) at a nobleman's court in the late 1500s; often the subject of jokes

8. ***tantum pellis et ossa fuit.*** [Latin] Was all skin and bones

9. ***Sir Thighpiece.*** Another name for Don Quixote. *Quixote* in Spanish refers to the piece of armor that covers the thighs.

10. **Amadis.** Amadis of Gaul was a character in a novel popular in Western Europe in the sixteenth and seventeenth centuries

---

em • i • nence (e′ mə nən[t]s) *n.,* high importance
so • no • rous (sə nôr′əs) *adj.,* impressive in effect or style
en • am • ored (i na′ mərd) *adj.,* consumed with love

HUMANITIES
CONNECTION

The Chivalric Romance The books that inspire the actions of Don Quixote constitute a unique literary form known as *romance*. This type of writing is based on the ideal of *chivalry*, or the standards of knightly conduct, which included loyalty, honesty, gentleness, faith, courtesy, skill, and courage. A typical romance involves a series of adventures or quests undertaken by a knight, usually to win the favor of an idealized "fair lady" who is just out of reach. Don Quixote, after reading romances, wants to be a heroic knight. Unlike the knights in romances, however, Don Quixote's attempts at chivalry and bravery never turn out quite right. What makes *Don Quixote* humorous is that it plays on the expectations of readers, who look for certain qualities in knights that Don Quixote simply does not possess.

"If, for my wicked sins or my good fortune, I encounter some giant, as knights errant usually do, and I dash him down in single combat, or cleave him asunder, or in short, defeat and <u>vanquish</u> him, will it not be proper to have someone to whom I can send him as a tribute, so that he can come before my sweet lady and fall to his knees and say in humble tones of submission: 'I, my lady, am the giant Caraculiambro, the Lord of the Isle of Malindrania, vanquished in single combat by the never sufficiently praised knight Don Quixote de la Mancha, who has commanded me to present myself before Your Highness so that Your Highness may dispose of me as you will'?"

Oh my, how our worthy knight rejoiced once he'd spoken these words—even more, once he'd found someone he could call his lady! The fact was—or so it is generally believed—that in a nearby village there lived a good-looking peasant girl, with whom he'd once been in love (although it appears that she was never aware of this love, about which he never told her). She was called Aldonza Lorenzo, and this was the woman upon whom it seemed appropriate to confer the title of the lady of his thoughts; and seeking a name with some affinity with his own, which would also suggest the name of a princess and a fine lady, he decided to call her *Dulcinea del Tobaso*, because she was a native of El Tobaso: a name that, in his opinion, was musical and magical and meaningful, like all the other names he'd bestowed upon himself and his possessions.

> **van • quish** (van´ kwish) *v.,* defeat

Don Quixote Fighting the Windmill. Gustave Doré.

CHAPTER VIII

About the brave Don Quixote's success in the dreadful and unimaginable adventure of the windmills, together with other events worthy of happy memory

As he was saying this, they caught sight of thirty or forty windmills standing on the plain, and as soon as Don Quixote saw them he said to his squire:

"Fortune is directing our affairs even better than we could have wished: for you can see over there, good friend Sancho Panza, a place where stand thirty or more monstrous giants with whom I intend to fight a battle and whose lives I intend to take; and with the booty[11] we shall begin to prosper. For this is a just war, and it is a great service to God to wipe such a wicked breed from the face of the earth."

"What giants?" said Sancho Panza.

"Those giants that you can see over there," replied his master, "with long arms: there are giants with arms almost six miles long."

"Look you here," Sancho retorted, "those over there aren't giants, they're windmills, and what look to you like arms are sails—when the wind turns them they make the millstones go round."

"It is perfectly clear," replied Don Quixote, "that you are but a raw novice in this matter of adventures. They are giants; and if you are frightened, you can take yourself away and say your prayers while I engage them in fierce and <u>arduous</u> combat."

And so saying he set spurs to his steed Rocinante, not paying any attention to his squire Sancho Panza, who was shouting that what he was charging were definitely windmills not giants. But Don Quixote was so convinced

> *"Flee not, O vile and cowardly creatures, for it is but one solitary knight who attacks you."*

that they were giants that he neither heard his squire Sancho's shouts nor saw what stood in front of him, even though he was by now upon them; instead he cried:

"Flee not, O vile and cowardly creatures, for it is but one solitary knight who attacks you."

A gust of wind arose, the great sails began to move, and Don Quixote yelled:

"Though you flourish more arms than the giant Briareus,[12] I will make you pay for it."

So saying, and commending himself with all his heart to his lady Dulcinea, begging her to succor[13] him in his plight, well protected by his little round infantryman's shield, and with his lance couched, he advanced at Rocinante's top speed and charged at the windmill nearest him. As he thrust his lance into its sail the wind turned it with such violence that it smashed the lance into pieces and dragged the horse and his rider with it, and Don Quixote went rolling over the plain in a very sore[14] predicament. Sancho Panza rushed to help his master at his donkey's fastest trot and found that he couldn't stir, such was the toss that Rocinante had given him.

"For God's sake!" said Sancho. "Didn't I tell you to be careful what you were doing, didn't I tell you they were only windmills? And only someone with windmills on the brain could have failed to see that!"

---

11. **booty.** Things of value taken from those defeated in battle
12. **Briareus.** In Greek and Roman mythology, a giant with fifty heads and a hundred hands
13. **succor** (su´ kər). Relieve
14. **sore.** Miserable

---

ar • du • ous (är´ jə wəs) *adj.,* extremely difficult, usually physically

"Not at all, friend Sancho," replied Don Quixote. "Affairs of war, even more than others, are subject to continual change. All the more so as I believe, indeed I am certain, that the same sage Frestón[15] who stole my library and my books has just turned these giants into windmills, to deprive me of the glory of my victory, such is the enmity he feels for me; but in the end his evil arts will avail him little against the might of my sword."

"God's will be done," replied Sancho Panza. ❖

15. **Frestón.** In an earlier part of the novel, Don Quixote's niece tells him that all his books were burned by a magician, possibly called Frestón, who held a secret grudge. In reality, Quixote's housekeeper burned the books to try to cure his madness.

en • mi • ty (en´ mə tē) *n.,* hatred

How would you describe the narrator's attitude toward Don Quixote? What do you think of the character? Would he be someone you would choose for a friend? Why or why not?

AFTER READING

REFER TO TEXT ▶ ▶ ▶ ▶	REASON WITH TEXT	
1a. State the effect reading romances has on Don Quixote's mind. What does he hope to accomplish by becoming a knight errant?	1b. Explain Don Quixote's attitude toward himself.	**Understand** **Find meaning**
2a. List some of the ideas Don Quixote borrows from medieval romances.	2b. Apply what you know about medieval romances to illustrate why you think Cervantes chose to parody them in *Don Quixote*.	**Apply** **Use information**
3a. What is the name of Don Quixote's horse?	3b. Point out how the author's use of allusions adds to the humor in the passage about choosing the horse's name.	**Analyze** **Take things apart**
4a. Recall how Don Quixote describes the windmills to Sancho Panza.	4b. Judge Don Quixote's choices. Is he simply foolish, or is there something noble about his desire to lead an adventurous life? Describe his mental and emotional condition.	**Evaluate** **Make judgments**
5a. How does Sancho Panza react to Don Quixote's battle with the windmill?	5b. Imagine you are Sancho Panza, and propose what you would do next to help Don Quixote.	**Create** **Bring ideas together**

ANALYZE LITERATURE: Parody and Allusion

How can you tell that *Don Quixote* is a parody rather than a serious work? Which elements of epics does Cervantes poke fun of? Give examples from the text. What allusions stood out for you as you read? How do the allusions contribute to the effect of the parody?

Writing Options

Creative Writing Imagine a new misadventure and battle for Don Quixote and his companion Sancho. Create a **comic strip** for the school newspaper that relates what happens. To compose a comic strip, begin by mapping out a plot for your story. Who will the characters be? What will happen? Then, write the text. Finally, draw several rows of boxes on a piece of paper, divide the text between the boxes, and create an illustration for each piece of text.

Expository Writing For a school literary magazine, write a **parody** of a fairy tale, fable, or other well-known story. You may imitate the original author's style and content, and your parody may be humorous, satirical, or ironic. Before you begin your parody, think about what makes the style of the original author distinctive. Consider things like word choice, sentence structure, and tone, and imitate them.

Collaborative Learning

Prepare a Skit Form a group of three to five students. Find the complete edition of *The Ingenious Hidalgo Don Quixote de la Mancha* in the library and read more of the title character's misadventures. Choose one event and prepare it to be presented as a skit to the class. You may wish to use a narrator in addition to the other characters in the scene. Rewrite the material and add dialogue where necessary, but try to stay true to the tone and style of the novel. Present your skit to the class.

Lifelong Learning

Evaluate an Adaptation *Don Quixote* has been adapted to a number of artistic forms, including ballet, film, musical theater, and opera. Research and view or listen to one of the adaptations. Write a review that analyzes how the part of the story you've just read in this selection was modified in the adaptation and how successful you think the adaptation is. Which changes were necessary to make the story work in the new format? Which changes should not have been made? What would you have done to improve the adaptation? Share your review with your classmates.

 Go to **www.mirrorsandwindows.com** for more.

READING ASSESSMENT

1. What does Don Quixote do to prepare for his quest? Put the following items in the correct order.
   - _____ A. He names his horse.
   - _____ B. He chooses a name for himself.
   - _____ C. He finds the perfect lady to be his heroine.
   - _____ D. He cleans up a suit of armor.
   - _____ E. He gives "his lady" the name *Dulcinea del Tobaso.*

2. On page 827, the word *ingenious* most nearly means
   - A. spirited.
   - B. extremely clever.
   - C. eloquent.
   - D. impressive.
   - E. obnoxious.

3. Don Quixote believes that the windmills are which of the following?
   - A. ghosts
   - B. knights
   - C. robbers
   - D. giants
   - E. None of the above

4. Which of the following actions of Don Quixote does *not* reflect the excessive influence of what he's read in books?
   - A. He mistakes windmills for marauding giants.
   - B. He hires Sancho Panza as his squire.
   - C. He names himself Don Quixote de la Mancha, a name modeled after the knight Amadis of Gaul.
   - D. He eats an occasional pigeon for supper on Sundays.
   - E. He decides to become a knight errant.

5. Don Quixote's decision to become a knight errant suggests that
   - A. he has an active imagination.
   - B. he is a practical person.
   - C. he has no regard for the welfare of others.
   - D. he is shy and introverted.
   - E. he dislikes humanity.

6. Describe the character of Don Quixote for someone who has never heard of him before. Include in your description your impression of how Don Quixote looks as well as what his personality is like.

GRAMMAR & STYLE

Adjectives and Adverbs

Adjectives and adverbs—two kinds of **modifiers**—add meaning to nouns, adjectives, verbs, and adverbs.

An **adjective** is a word that modifies a noun or a pronoun. An **adverb** is a word that modifies a verb, an adjective, or another adverb.

EXAMPLES

adjective: The <u>fading</u> sunlight has washed the deck with a <u>rosy</u> glow. (*Fading* modifies the noun *sunlight; rosy* modifies the noun *glow.*)
adverb: Tall trees shade the decks <u>quite</u> thoroughly and cast shadows <u>creatively</u> on the floor. (*Quite* modifies the adverb *thoroughly; creatively* modifies the verb *cast.*)

To determine whether a modifier is an adjective or an adverb, look at the word that is modified and ask yourself, "Is this modified word a noun or a pronoun?" If the answer is yes, the modifier is an adjective. If the answer is no, the modifier is an adverb.

Some adjectives tell *how many* or *what kind* about the nouns or pronouns they modify. Other adjectives tell *which one* or *which ones.* The most commonly occurring adjectives are the articles *a, an,* and *the.*

Two or more modifiers of the same noun or pronoun that can be joined either by the word *and* or by a comma are called **coordinate adjectives.**

EXAMPLES

a <u>long and lacy</u> scarf
a <u>delicious, nourishing</u> lunch

Not all adjective pairs are coordinate, however, as in the examples below. When an adjective pair is not coordinate, do not use a comma. One way to tell if you should use a comma or not is to put the word *and* between the two words. If it makes sense, use a comma. If it doesn't make sense, do not use a comma.

EXAMPLES

<u>five silk</u> ties
the <u>large office</u> buildings

Adverbs used to describe *where, when,* and *why* are called **relative adverbs.** A relative adverb is used to introduce an adjective clause.

EXAMPLE

This is the house <u>where</u> I was born. (*Where* relates the adjective clause to the noun *house.*)

A **conjunctive adverb** is used to express relationships between independent clauses. Common conjunctive adverbs are listed below.

accordingly	instead
also	nevertheless
besides	otherwise
consequently	similarly
finally	still
furthermore	therefore
hence	thus
however	

When you use a conjunctive adverb to establish a relationship between independent clauses, make sure that you separate the clauses with a semicolon and that you use a comma after the conjunctive adverb.

EXAMPLE

Don Quixote was convinced the windmill was dangerous; <u>therefore,</u> he set off to battle against it.

REVIEW TERMS

- **modifier:** word or phrase that adds meaning to another word or phrase
- **adjective:** a word that modifies a noun or pronoun
- **adverb:** a word that modifies a verb, an adjective, or another adverb
- **coordinate adjectives:** two or more modifiers of the same noun or pronoun that can be joined either by the word *and* or by a comma
- **relative adverbs:** adverbs used to describe *where, when,* and *why*
- **conjunctive adverbs:** adverbs used to express relationships between independent clauses

Identify Adjectives and Adverbs in Literature

Identify each of the underlined words in the following passage from *Don Quixote* as either an adjective or an adverb, and name the word or words each modifies.

Oh my, how our <u>worthy</u> knight rejoiced once he'd spoken these words—even more, once he'd found someone he could call his lady! The fact was—or so it is <u>generally</u> believed—that in a <u>nearby</u> village there lived a <u>good-looking</u> <u>peasant</u> girl, with whom he'd <u>once</u> been in love (although it appears that she was <u>never</u> aware of this love, about which he never told her). She was called Aldonza Lorenzo, and this was the woman upon whom it seemed <u>appropriate</u> to confer the title of the lady of his thoughts; and seeking a name with some affinity with his own, which would also suggest the name of a princess and a <u>fine</u> lady, he decided to call her *Dulcinea del Tobaso*, because she was a native of El Tobaso: a name that, in his opinion, was <u>musical</u> and <u>magical</u> and <u>meaningful</u>, like all the other names he'd bestowed upon himself and his possessions.

Understand Adjectives

Write a sentence using each of the following words as an adjective.

1. red
2. antique
3. his
4. Russian
5. hysterical
6. those
7. running
8. fattened
9. each
10. five

Understand Adverbs

Write a sentence using each of the following words as an adverb.

1. late
2. really
3. less
4. seldom
5. when
6. instead
7. maybe
8. sadly
9. very
10. seasonally

Use Adjectives and Adverbs in Your Writing

Imagine you're writing a letter to a grandparent or an aunt or uncle about a day you spent hanging out with your best friend. In your letter, use at least two pairs of coordinate adjectives and two conjunctive adverbs. When you are finished with your letter, ask a classmate to check it to see if you used the adjectives and adverbs correctly. Make changes as necessary.

EXTEND THE SKILL

Form a small group. As a group, write a simple sentence, like "The dog ran." Each group member should then rewrite the sentence, adding either one adjective or one adverb. For example, the first group member might write "The barking dog ran." The second group member will then add to the sentence and may write "The barking dog ran quickly." Once all the group members have added to the sentence, figure out which words added are adjectives and which are adverbs and talk about how these words change a dull sentence into an interesting one.

READING FOLK LITERATURE INDEPENDENTLY

Theme: What Makes Us Human

"But all I ask of you is to love me. I would rather have you love me as an equal than adore me as a god."

—Cupid, from "The Love of Cupid and Psyche"

The stories that are passed down through the centuries often contain subtle, or not so subtle, lessons about how to be a member of a community or culture. The characteristics that society values are often either present in the main character or completely lacking in that character to serve as a warning. Over the centuries, societies have changed, but what it means to be a human has varied only slightly, and thus, these tales continue to be passed on. As you read the selections in this section, consider which values are being promoted.

USING READING SKILLS WITH FOLK LITERATURE

Make Generalizations

When you **make generalizations,** you look at the information provided and **synthesize** it, or put it together, to develop a general idea about the selection. This synthesis may draw information from various parts of a text. To make generalizations, you need to identify the supporting details. For example, in folk literature, you may want to keep track of the details that describe a character or statements about the land or culture of the people in the tale. A Generalizations Chart like the one below for "Mu-lan" will help:

Generalizations Chart

Generalization
Mu-lan is a good warrior.

↓

Example
"Generals die in a hundred battles, / Stout soldiers return after ten years."

↓

Example
"He gives out promotions in twelve ranks [...]. The Khan asks her what she desires."

↓

Example
"Traveling together for twelve years / They didn't know Mu-lan was a girl."

Draw Conclusions

Similar to generalizing, when you **draw conclusions,** you gather pieces of information and then decide what that information means. The information you gather can be supporting details or even the generalizations that you make based on those details.

Drawing conclusions is an essential part of reading. It may be helpful to use a graphic organizer such as a chart or log to keep track of the information you find while you are reading and the conclusions you draw. You could arrange the information from your generalizations into a chart like the following:

Conclusions Log

Key Idea
Mu-lan is a good warrior.
Supporting Details
"Generals die in a hundred battles, / Stout soldiers return after ten years."
"He gives out promotions in twelve ranks […]. The Khan asks her what she desires."
"Traveling together for twelve years / They didn't know Mu-lan was a girl."
Overall Conclusion
Mu-lan didn't have to go to battle, but she did. She showed her determination and skill by performing well and keeping her secret.

What Good Readers Do

Write Things Down

As you read folk literature, writing things down is very important. Possible ways to write things down include:

❏ underlining characters' names

❏ writing messages on sticky notes

❏ highlighting the setting

❏ creating a graphic organizer to keep track of plot elements

❏ using a code in the margin that shows how you respond to the characters, setting, or events. For instance, you can mark a description you like with a "+."

Framework for Folk Literature

In the stories, poems, and songs that are a part of folk literature, storytellers want to entertain their audiences and pass along cultural ideas and beliefs. The following checklist offers strategies for reading folk literature.

As you start to read...

❏ From which culture does this tale come?

❏ Who are the characters in this tale?

❏ What do the characters do?

As you continue reading...

❏ Which supporting details describe the characters?

❏ Where does the narrator or author seem to make judgments about the characters or their actions?

❏ What generalizations can you make based on the details?

After you've finished reading...

❏ What is the final result of the tale?

❏ What conclusions can you draw about the story by synthesizing the evidence?

❏ What seems to be the main message of the tale?

MU-LAN

If you lived in ancient China and the ruler called on you to go to war, you did not say no. To do so would bring punishment to your entire family. According to legend, Mu-lan saved her elderly father from going to war by disguising herself as a man and taking his place. **"Mu-lan,"** which is a ballad, was probably composed between 420 and 589 CE, a time of instability as wandering tribes from northern China fought to rule over the native Han Chinese. Though scholars disagree on the specifics of Mu-lan's life and even whether she really existed, her story has inspired operas, paintings, musical compositions, and an animated movie.

How might a person's gender be restrictive?

An Anonymous Ballad

Translated by **Hans H. Frankel**

*TRAVELING
TOGETHER FOR
TWELVE YEARS
THEY DIDN'T KNOW
MU-LAN WAS A GIRL.*

Tsiek tsiek and again *tsiek tsiek,*
Mu-lan weaves, facing the door.
You don't hear the shuttle's[1] sound,
You only hear Daughter's sighs.

5 They ask Daughter who's in her heart,
They ask Daughter who's on her mind.
"No one is on Daughter's heart,
No one is on Daughter's mind.
Last night I saw the draft posters,

10 The Khan[2] is calling many troops,
The army list is in twelve scrolls,
On every scroll there's Father's name.
Father has no grown-up son,
Mu-lan has no elder brother.

15 I want to buy a saddle and horse,
And serve in the army in Father's place."

In the East Market she buys a spirited horse,
In the West Market she buys a saddle,
In the South Market she buys a bridle,

20 In the North Market she buys a long whip.
At dawn she takes leave of Father and Mother,
In the evening camps on the Yellow River's bank.
She doesn't hear the sound of Father and Mother calling,
She only hears the Yellow River's flowing water cry *tsien tsien.*

25 At dawn she takes leave of the Yellow River,
In the evening she arrives at Black Mountain.
She doesn't hear the sound of Father and Mother calling,
She only hears Mount Yen's nomad[3] horses cry *tsiu tsiu.*
She goes ten thousand miles on the business of war,

30 She crosses passes and mountains like flying.
Northern gusts carry the rattle of army pots,
Chilly light shines on iron armor.
Generals die in a hundred battles,
Stout soldiers return after ten years.

35 On her return she sees the Son of Heaven,[4]
The Son of Heaven sits in the Splendid Hall.
He gives out promotions in twelve ranks
And prizes of a hundred thousand and more.

---

1. **shuttle's.** In weaving, a shuttle is a device used to pass a thread between other threads stretched on a loom.
2. **Khan.** A ruler of China
3. **nomad.** Roaming from place to place for pasture; wandering
4. **Son of Heaven.** Ruler

The Khan asks her what she desires.
40   "Mu-lan has no use for a minister's post.
I wish to ride a swift mount
To take me back to my home."

When Father and Mother hear Daughter is coming
They go outside the wall to meet her, leaning on each other.
45   When Elder Sister hears Younger Sister is coming
She fixes her rouge, facing the door.
When Little Brother hears Elder Sister is coming
He whets[5] the knife, quick quick, for pig and sheep.
"I open the door to my east chamber,
50   I sit on my couch in the west room,
I take off my wartime gown
And put on my old-time clothes."
Facing the window she fixes her cloudlike hair,
Hanging up a mirror she dabs on yellow flower-powder
55   She goes out the door and sees her comrades.[6]
Her comrades are all amazed and perplexed.
Traveling together for twelve years
They didn't know Mu-lan was a girl.
"The he-hare's feet go hop and skip,
60   The she-hare's eyes are muddled and fuddled.
Two hares running side by side close to the ground,
How can they tell if I am he or she?" ❖

---

5. **whets.** Sharpens
6. **comrades.** Associates or companions

Suppose a friend tells you Mu-lan should not have taken such drastic measures to save her father—that she acted impulsively. How would you respond? What kind of reputation do risk-takers like Mu-lan commonly have in American society? How should risk-takers be regarded—as courageous or foolish? Why?

Refer and Reason

1. What does Mu-lan's family ask her when they hear her sighing in the first stanza? What assumption does the family make about the reason for her sighs? What is her real reason for sighing?
2. To what are Mu-lan and her comrades from the war compared in stanza 5? What is the significance of this comparison?
3. Evaluate Mu-lan's decisions to go to war and to come home to her family rather than take a government position. What choices would you have made had you been in Mu-lan's position?

Writing Options

1. For a local newspaper, write an editorial in which you argue for or against allowing women to participate in military combat. You may want to do some research to learn arguments for each side of the question.
2. Imagine that you are Mu-lan and have been invited to a gathering of young girls after returning home from the wars. Write a short speech discussing your reasons for making the decisions you made. Also include advice to your young audience.

 Go to **www.mirrorsandwindows.com** for more.

Cupid and Psyche. John Roddam Spencer
Stanhope. Private collection.

The Love of Cupid and Psyche

In Greek mythology, gods and goddesses are portrayed in *anthropomorphic* terms: This means they are pictured as human beings with human emotions, only they are more powerful than humans and, of course, immortal (they never die). In **"The Love of Cupid and Psyche,"** the story begins with a jealous goddess, Venus, who resents the attention paid to a mortal woman, Psyche, because of Psyche's beauty.

Have you ever been resentful of someone because he or she had something you wanted? How did you deal with the situation?

A Greek Myth Retold by **Sally Benson**

There once lived a king and queen who had three daughters. The two elder daughters were beautiful, but the youngest daughter, Psyche,[1] was the loveliest maiden in the whole world. The fame of her beauty was so great that strangers from neighboring countries came in

---

1. **Psyche** (sī´ kē). The literal meaning of her name is "soul."

THE LOVE OF CUPID AND PSYCHE **841**

crowds to admire her, paying her the homage which is only due Venus[2] herself. In fact, Venus found her altars deserted, as men turned their devotion to the exquisite young girl. People sang her praises as she walked the streets, and strewed chaplets and flowers before her.

This adulation infuriated Venus. Shaking her silken locks in indignation, she exclaimed, "Am I then to be eclipsed by a mortal girl? In vain did that royal shepherd whose judgment was approved by Jupiter himself give me the palm of beauty over my illustrious rivals, Minerva and Juno.[3] I will give this Psyche cause to repent of so unlawful a beauty."

She complained to her son, Cupid, and led him to the land where Psyche lived, so that he could see for himself the insults the girl unconsciously heaped upon his mother. "My dear son," said Venus, "punish that beauty. Give thy mother a revenge as sweet as her injuries are great. Infuse into the bosom of that haughty girl a passion for some low, mean, unworthy being, so that she may reap a shame as great as her present joy and triumph."

Now, there were two fountains in Venus's garden, one of sweet waters, the other of bitter. Cupid filled two amber vases, one from each fountain and, suspending them from the top of his quiver, hastened to Psyche's chamber, where she lay asleep. He shed a few drops from the bitter fountain over her lips, though she looked so beautiful in her sleep that he was filled with pity. Then he touched her side with the point of his arrow. At the touch, she awoke and opened her eyes on Cupid, who was so startled by their blue enchantment that he wounded himself with his own arrow. He hovered over her, invisible, and to repair the damage he had done, he poured the water from the sweet fountain over her silken ringlets.

Psyche, thus frowned upon by Venus, derived no benefit from all her charms. All eyes were still cast eagerly upon her and every mouth spoke her praise, but neither king, royal youth, or common man presented himself to demand her hand in marriage. Her two elder sisters were married to royal princes, but Psyche, in her lonely apartment, wept over her beauty, sick of the flattery it aroused, while love was denied her.

Her parents, afraid that they had unwittingly incurred the anger of the gods, consulted the oracle of Apollo,[4] and received this answer: "The girl is destined for the bride of no mortal lover. Her future husband awaits her on the top of the mountain. He is a monster whom neither the gods nor men can resist."

This dreadful decree of the oracle filled all the people with dismay, and her parents abandoned themselves to grief. But Psyche said, "Why, my dear parents, do you now lament me? You should rather have grieved when the people showered undeserved honors upon me and with one voice called me 'Venus.' I now perceive I am a victim to that name. I submit. Lead me to that rock to which my unhappy fate has destined me."

She dressed herself in gorgeous robes, and her beauty was so dazzling that people turned away as it was more than they could bear. Then, followed by wailing and lamenting crowds, she and her parents ascended the mountain. On the summit, her father and mother left her alone, and returned home in tears.

While Psyche stood on the ridge of the mountain, panting with fear and sobbing aloud, the gentle Zephyrus[5] raised her from the earth and bore her with an easy motion into a flowery dale. There she lay down on a grassy bank and fell asleep. She awoke refreshed, and saw near

---

2. **Venus.** The Roman goddess of love and beauty

3. **royal shepherd...Minerva and Juno.** In Roman mythology, Jupiter was the chief god of a group of three including Juno, the queen of the gods, and Minerva, the goddess of wisdom. Paris, a prince who lived as a shepherd, was asked by Jupiter to decide who was most beautiful of three goddesses: Juno, Minerva, or Venus. Paris chose Venus.

4. **oracle of Apollo.** God of music, healing, and archery, among other things; son of Zeus (king of the gods) and Leto. An oracle was a person who revealed the will of the gods to answer people's questions.

5. **Zephyrus** (ze´ fə rəs). Greek god of the west wind

Critical Viewing

Describe what is happening
in this painting. How does the
artist create a sense of action or
movement in this painting?

by a pleasant grove of tall
and stately trees. She entered
it, and discovered a fountain
sending forth clear and crystal
waters, and near it stood a
magnificent palace that was
too stupendous to have been
the work of mortal hands.
Drawn by admiration and
wonder, she walked through
the huge doors. Inside, golden
pillars supported the vaulted
roof, and the walls were hung
with delightful paintings. She
wandered through the empty
rooms marveling at what she
saw, when suddenly a voice
addressed her. "Sovereign
lady," it said, "all that you see
is yours. We whose voices
you hear are your servants
and shall obey all your
commands with the utmost
care and diligence. Retire,
therefore, to your chamber
and repose on your bed of
down, and when you see fit,
repair to the bath. Supper
awaits you in the adjoining
alcove when it pleases you to
take your seat there."

Psyche listened with amazement, and,
going to her room, she lay down and rested.
Then, after a refreshing bath, she went to
the alcove, where a table wheeled itself into
the room without any visible aid. It was
covered with the finest delicacies and the most
wonderful wines. There even was music from
invisible performers.

Psyche Entering Cupid's Garden, 1902. John William Waterhouse. Harris Museum
and Art Gallery, Preston, Lancashire, United Kingdom.

She had not yet seen her destined husband.
He came only in the hours of darkness and fled
before dawn, but his accents were full of love
and inspired a like passion in her. She often
begged him to stay and let her behold him,
but he would not consent. On the contrary, he
charged her to make no attempt to see him, for
it was his pleasure, for the best of reasons, to

THE LOVE OF CUPID AND PSYCHE   **843**

Detail of Cupid's Head from ***Cupid Shaping His Bow.*** Parmigianino.

numerous train of attendant voices, to refresh themselves in her baths and at her table, and to show them all her treasures. The sight of all these splendid things filled her sisters with envy, and they resented the thought that she possessed such splendor which far exceeded anything they owned.

They asked her numberless questions, and begged her to tell them what sort of person her husband was. Psyche replied that he was a beautiful youth who generally spent the daytime in hunting upon the mountains. The sisters, not satisfied with this reply, soon made her confess that she had never seen him. They then proceeded to fill her bosom with dire suspicions. "Call to mind." they said, "the Pythian oracle[6] that declared that you were destined to many a direful and tremendous monster. The inhabitants of this valley say that your husband is a terrible and monstrous serpent, who nourishes you for a while with dainties that he may by and by devour you. Take our advice. Provide yourself with a lamp and a sharp knife. Put them in concealment so that your husband may not discover them, and when he is sound asleep, slip out of bed, bring forth your lamp and see for yourself whether what they say is true or not. If it is, hesitate not to cut off the monster's head, and thereby recover your liberty."

Psyche resisted these persuasions as well as she could, but they did not fail to have

remain concealed. "Why should you wish to behold me?" he asked. "Have you any doubt of my love? If you saw me, perhaps you would fear me, perhaps adore me. But all I ask of you is to love me. I would rather have you love me as an equal than adore me as a god."

This reasoning satisfied Psyche for a time and she lived quite happily alone in the huge palace. But at length she thought of her parents who were in ignorance of her fate, and of her sisters with whom she wished to share the delights of her new home. These thoughts preyed on her mind and made her think of her splendid mansion as a prison. When her husband came one night, she told him of her distress, and at last drew from him an unwilling consent that her sisters should be brought to see her.

So, calling Zephyrus, she told him of her husband's command, and he soon brought them across the mountain down to their sister's valley. They embraced her, and Psyche's eyes filled with tears of joy. "Come," she said, "enter my house and refresh yourselves." Taking them by their hands, she led them into her golden palace and committed them to the care of her

---

6. **Pythian** (pi´ thē ən) **oracle.** Oracle of Apollo

their effect on her mind, and when her sisters were gone, their words and her own curiosity were too strong for her to resist. She prepared her lamp and a sharp knife, and hid them out of sight of her husband. When he had fallen into his first sleep, she silently arose, and uncovering her lamp beheld him. He lay there, the most beautiful and charming of the gods, with his golden ringlets wandering over his snowy neck and crimson cheek. On his shoulders were two dewy wings, whiter than snow, with shining feathers.

As she leaned over with the lamp to have a closer view of his face, a drop of burning oil fell on his shoulder, and made him wince with pain. He opened his eyes and fixed them full upon her. Then, without saying a word, he spread his white wings and flew out of the window. Psyche cried out and tried to follow him, falling from the window to the ground. Cupid, beholding her as she lay in the dust, stopped his flight for an instant and said, "O foolish Psyche! Is it thus you repay my love? After having disobeyed my mother's commands and made you my wife, will you think me a monster and cut off my head? But go. Return to your sisters whose advice you seem to think better than mine. I inflict no other punishment on you than to leave you forever. Love cannot dwell with suspicion."

He soared into the air, leaving poor Psyche prostrate on the ground.

When she recovered some degree of composure, she looked around her. The palace and gardens had vanished, and she found herself in an open field not far from the city where her sisters dwelt. She went to them and told them the whole story of her misfortune, at which, pretending to grieve, they inwardly rejoiced. "For now," they said, "he will perhaps choose one of us." With this idea, without saying a word of her intentions, each of them rose early the next morning and ascended the mountain and, having reached the top, called upon Zephyrus to receive her and bear her

to his lord. Then, leaping into space, and not being sustained by Zephyrus, they fell down the precipice and were dashed to pieces.

Psyche, meanwhile, wandered day and night, without food or rest, in search of her husband. One day, seeing a lofty mountain in the distance, she sighed and said to herself, "Perhaps my love, my lord, inhabits there."

On the mountain top was a temple and she no sooner entered it than she saw heaps of corn, some in loose ears and some in sheaves, with mingled ears of barley. Scattered about lay sickles and rakes, and all the instruments of harvest, without order, as if thrown carelessly out of the weary reapers' hands in the sultry hours of the day.

Psyche put an end to this unseemly confusion by separating and sorting everything to its proper place and kind, believing that she ought to neglect none of the gods, but endeavor by her piety to engage them all in her behalf. The holy Ceres,[7] whose temple it was, finding her so religiously employed, spoke to her, "O Psyche, truly worthy of our pity, though I cannot shield you from the frowns of Venus, yet I can teach you how to best allay her displeasure. Go then, and voluntarily surrender yourself to her, and try by modesty and submission to win her forgiveness, and perhaps her favor will restore you to the husband you have lost."

Psyche obeyed the commands of Ceres and journeyed to the temple of Venus. Venus received her in a fury of anger. "Most undutiful and faithless of servants," she said, "do you at last remember that you really have a mistress? Or have you come to see your sick husband, yet laid up with the wound given him by his loving wife? You are so ill-favored and disagreeable that the only way you can merit your lover must be by dint of industry and diligence. I will make trial of your housewifery."

She ordered Psyche to be led to the storehouse of her temple, where a great quantity of

---

7. **Ceres** (sir´ ēz[']). Roman goddess of farming

wheat, barley, millet, beans and lentils, which was used as food for her pigeons, lay scattered about the floors. Then Venus said, "Take and separate all these grains into their proper parcels, and see that you get it done before evening."

Psyche, in consternation over the enormous task, sat stupid and silent. While she sat despairing, Cupid stirred up the little ant, a native of the fields, to take compassion on her. The leader of the ant-hill, followed by whole hosts of his six-legged subjects, went to work and sorted each grain to its parcel. And when all was done, the ants vanished out of sight.

At twilight. Venus returned from the banquet of the gods, crowned with roses. Seeing the task done, she exclaimed, "This is no work of yours, wicked one, but his, whom to your own and his misfortune you have enticed." So saying, she threw her a piece of black bread for her supper and went away.

Next morning Venus ordered Psyche to be called and said to her, "Behold yonder grove which stretches along the margin of the water. There you will find sheep feeding without a shepherd, with gold-shining fleeces on their backs. Go, fetch me a sample of that precious wool from every one of their fleeces."

Psyche obediently went to the river side, prepared to do her best to execute the command. But the river god inspired the reeds with harmonious murmurs, which seemed to say, "O maiden, severely tried, tempt not the dangerous flood, nor venture among formidable rams on the other side, for as long as they are under the influence of the rising sun they burn with a cruel rage to destroy mortals with their sharp horns or rude teeth. But when the noontide sun has driven the cattle to the shade, and the serene spirit of the flood has lulled them to rest, you may then cross in safety, and you will find the woolly gold sticking to the bushes and the trunks of the trees."

She followed the compassionate river god's instructions and soon returned to Venus with her arms full of the golden fleece. Venus, in a rage, cried, "I know very well it is by none of your own doings that you have succeeded in this task. And I am not satisfied yet that you have any capacity to make yourself useful. But I have another task for you. Here, take this box, and go your way to the infernal shade and give this box to Proserpina[8] and say, 'My mistress, Venus, desires you to send her a little of your beauty, for in tending her sick son, she has lost some of her own.' Be not too long on your errand, for I must paint myself with it to appear at the circle of gods and goddesses this evening."

Psyche was now sure that her destruction was at hand, being obliged to go with her own feet down to the deathly regions of Erebus.[9] So as not to delay, she went to the highest tower prepared to hurl herself headlong from it down to the shades below. But a voice from the tower said to her, "Why, poor unlucky girl, dost thou design to put an end to thy days in so dreadful a manner? And what cowardice makes thee sink under this last danger who hast been so miraculously supported in all thy former perils?"

Then the voice told her how she might reach the realms of Pluto by way of a certain cave, and how to avoid the perils of the road, how to pass by Cerberus,[10] the three-headed dog, and prevail on Charon,[11] the ferryman, to take her across the black river and bring her back again. And the voice added, "When Proserpina has given you the box filled with her beauty, of all things this is chiefly to be observed by you, that you never once open or look into the box, nor allow your curiosity to pry into the treasure of the beauty of the goddesses."

---

8. **infernal shade...Proserpina** (prə sᴜr´ pə nə). "Infernal shade" refers to the underworld, or place inhabited by the dead. Proserpina is the wife of Pluto, the ruler of the underworld.

9. **Erebus** (er´ ə bəs). In Greek mythology, the gloomy place through which the dead pass before entering the underworld

10. **Cerberus** (sᴜr´ b[ə]rəs). The three-headed dog responsible for guarding the entrance to the underworld

11. **Charon** (ker´ ən). The ferryman who carried the dead over the mythological river Styx into the underworld

Psyche, encouraged by this advice, obeyed in all things, and traveled to the kingdom of Pluto. She was admitted to the palace of Proserpina, and without accepting the delicate seat or delicious banquet that was offered her, but content with coarse bread for her food, she delivered her message from Venus. Presently the box was returned to her, shut, and filled with the precious commodity. She returned the way she came, happy to see the light of day once more.

Having got so far successfully through her dangerous task, a desire seized her to examine the contents of the box. "What," she said to herself, "shall I, the carrier of this divine beauty, not take the least bit to put on my cheeks to appear to more advantage in the eyes of my beloved husband!" She carefully opened the box, and found nothing there of any beauty at all, but an infernal and truly Stygian[12] sleep, which, being set free from its prison, took possession of her. She fell down in the road, unconscious, without sense or motion.

Cupid had recovered from his wound and was no longer able to bear the absence of his beloved Psyche. He slipped through the smallest crack in the window of his chamber and flew to the spot where Psyche lay. He gathered up the sleep from her body and closed it again in the box. Then he waked Psyche with a light touch from one of his arrows.

"Again," he said, "hast thou almost perished by the same curiosity. But now perform exactly the task imposed on you by my mother, and I will take care of the rest."

Swift as lightning, he left the earth and penetrated the heights of heaven. Here he presented himself before Jupiter with his supplication. The god lent a favoring ear, and pleaded the cause of the lovers so earnestly with Venus that he won her consent. Then he sent Mercury to bring Psyche up to the heavenly assemblage, and when she arrived, he handed her a cup of ambrosia[13] and said, "Drink this, Psyche, and be immortal. Nor shall Cupid ever break away from the knot in which he is tied, but these nuptials shall be perpetual."

Psyche became at last united to Cupid forever. ❖

---

12. **Stygian** (stĭ´ jĭ[ē-]ən). The adjective *Stygian* comes from the river Styx and means "extremely dark, gloomy, or frightening."
13. **ambrosia.** The food or drink of immortals

MIRRORS & WINDOWS

"Love cannot dwell with suspicion." What does this mean? How does this statement tie into the main idea or theme of the myth? Do you agree with this statement? Why or why not?

Refer and Reason

1. Compare Venus's plan with the actual outcome. How is the outcome ironic, or a striking reversal of what Venus had intended?
2. List the tasks Venus commands Psyche to carry out. In the third task, how does Psyche's behavior resemble her earlier mistake with Cupid?
3. Evaluate Cupid's actions at the end of the myth. What do you think of his reactions to the mistakes Psyche makes? Will he be sorry for saving Psyche, or has she learned her lesson? Explain your answers.

Writing Options

1. Twice Psyche's curiosity gets her into trouble. Imagine she writes to a newspaper asking for advice on how to deal with her curious nature. Write an advice column in which you give Psyche helpful ways to control her curiosity.
2. How do you think Venus will react to the outcome of the myth? Write a journal entry in which you have Venus express her reactions to the story's conclusion. Be sure to make your entry consistent with the way the goddess is characterized in the myth.

 Go to **www.mirrorsandwindows.com** for more.

DAMON AND PYTHIAS

Myths from countries around the world provide insight into the values that have shaped world views in particular times and places. The Greek myth **"Damon and Pythias"** revolves around issues of loyalty and friendship. The ancient Greeks considered friendship to have even greater value than romantic love. The story of friends Damon and Pythias has been adapted into poetry, drama, and film and has come to symbolize friendship that merits even the sacrifice of one's own life.

What kinds of sacrifices have you seen people make for their friends? What kinds would you be willing to make?

A Greek Myth Retold by

William F. Russell

Damon and Pythias were two noble young men who lived on the island of Sicily in a city called Syracuse. They were such close companions and were so devoted to each other that all the people of the city admired them as the highest examples of true friendship. Each trusted the other so completely that nobody could ever have persuaded one that the other had been unfaithful or dishonest, even if that had been the case.

Now it happened that Syracuse was, at that time, ruled by a famous tyrant named Dionysius, who had gained the throne for himself through treachery, and who from then on flaunted his power by behaving cruelly to his own subjects and to all strangers and enemies who were so unfortunate as to fall into his clutches. This tyrant, Dionysius, was so unjustly cruel that once, when he awoke from a restless sleep during which he dreamt that a certain man in the town had attempted to kill him, he immediately had that man put to death.

It happened that Pythias had, quite unjustly, been accused by Dionysius of trying to overthrow him, and for this supposed crime of treason Pythias was sentenced by the king to die. Try as he might, Pythias could not prove his innocence to the king's satisfaction, and so, all hope now lost, the noble youth asked only for a few days' freedom so that he could settle his business affairs and see to it that his relatives would be cared for after he was executed. Dionysius, the hardhearted tyrant, however, would not believe Pythias's promise to return and would not allow him to leave unless he left behind him a hostage, someone who would be put to death in his place if he should fail to return within the stated time.

Pythias immediately thought of his friend Damon, and he unhesitatingly sent for him in this hour of dire necessity, never thinking for a moment that his trusty companion would refuse his request. Nor did he, for Damon hastened straightaway to the palace—much to the amazement of King Dionysius—and gladly offered to be held hostage for his friend, in spite of the dangerous condition that had been attached to this favor. Therefore, Pythias was permitted to settle his earthly affairs before departing to the Land of the Shades,[1] while Damon remained behind in the dungeon, the captive of the tyrant Dionysius.

After Pythias had been released, Dionysius asked Damon if he did not feel afraid, for Pythias might very well take advantage of the opportunity he had been given and simply not return at all, and then he, Damon, would be executed in his place. But Damon replied at once with a willing smile: "There is no need for me to feel afraid, O King, since I have perfect faith in the word of my true friend, and I know that he will certainly return before the appointed time—unless, of course, he dies or is held captive by some evil force. Even so, even should the noble Pythias be captured and held against his will, it would be an honor for me to die in his place."

Such devotion and perfect faith as this was unheard of to the friendless tyrant; still, though he could not help admiring the true nobility of his captive, he nevertheless determined that Damon should certainly be put to death should Pythias not return by the appointed time.

And, as the Fates[2] would have it, by a strange turn of events, Pythias was detained far longer in his task than he had imagined. Though he never for a single minute intended to evade the sentence of death to which he had been so unjustly committed. Pythias met with several accidents and unavoidable delays. Now his time was running out and he had yet to overcome the many impediments that had

---

1. **Land of the Shades.** In ancient Greek mythology, a place where people go after death
2. **Fates.** In Greek and Roman mythology, the three goddesses who control human destiny and life

Pythias rushes back to Syracuse on horseback.

been placed in his path. At last he succeeded in clearing away all the hindrances, and he sped back the many miles to the palace of the king, his heart almost bursting with grief and fear that he might arrive too late.

Meanwhile, when the last day of the allotted time arrived, Dionysius commanded that the place of execution should be readied at once, since he was still ruthlessly determined that if one of his victims escaped him, the other should not. And so, entering the chamber in which Damon was confined, he began to utter words of sarcastic pity for the "foolish faith," as he termed it, that the young man of Syracuse had in his friend.

In reply, however, Damon merely smiled, since, in spite of the fact that the eleventh hour had already arrived, he still believed that his lifelong companion would not fail him. Even when, a short time later, he was actually led out to the site of his execution, his serenity remained the same.

Great excitement stirred the crowd that had gathered to witness the execution, for all the people had heard of the bargain that had been struck between the two friends. There was much sobbing and cries of sympathy were heard all around as the captive was brought out, though he himself somehow retained complete composure even at this moment of darkest danger.

Presently the excitement grew more intense still as a swift runner could be seen approaching the palace courtyard at an astonishing speed, and wild shrieks of relief and joy went up as Pythias, breathless and exhausted, rushed headlong through the crowd and flung himself into the arms of his beloved friend, sobbing with relief that he had, by the grace of the gods, arrived in time to save Damon's life.

This final exhibition of devoted love and faithfulness was more than even the stony heart of Dionysius, the tyrant, could resist. As the throng of spectators melted into tears at the companions' embrace, the king approached the pair and declared that Pythias was hereby pardoned and his death sentence canceled. In addition, he begged the pair to allow him to become their friend, to try to be as much a friend to them both as they had shown each other to be.

Thus did the two friends of Syracuse, by the faithful love they bore to each other, conquer the hard heart of a tyrant king, and in the annals[3] of true friendship there are no more honored names than those of Damon and Pythias—for no person can do more than be willing to lay down his life for the sake of his friend. ❖

---

3. **annals** (a´ n'lz). Records of history

"No person can do more than be willing to lay down his life for the sake of his friend." What is your reaction to this statement? What examples of one friend sacrificing something great for another can you think of from recent history or your own experiences?

Refer and Reason

1. What favor does Pythias ask of Damon? What does Dionysius think of Damon for agreeing?
2. Analyze Dionysius's behavior throughout the myth. How does he change, and what causes this change? How does the change relate to the theme, or central idea, of the myth?
3. Could a friendship like Pythias and Damon's exist today? Why or why not?

Writing Options

1. How would you compare the myth of Cupid and Psyche with the myth of Damon and Pythias? In two or three paragraphs, write a brief comparison of the two stories, focusing on such elements as plot, characterization, theme, and tone.
2. Imagine that you are Dionysius. Write an announcement you will make to the crowd as a speech either to set Pythias and Damon free or to carry out your original punishment. Explain the reasons for your decision.

 Go to **www.mirrorsandwindows.com** for more.

Savitri and Satyavant

An Indian Myth Retold by **Walker Brents**

King Asvapati's only child was a daughter named Savitri, after the deity who guides the sun. When it came time for her to be married, many men came forward petitioning for her hand, but they were all idle, boastful, vain, arrogant, easy to see through. The eligible princes who were more discerning refused to come forward, believing Savitri was an incarnation of the goddess she was named after and not for the asking as a wife.

Her father was perplexed, both flattered and bereft. "Savitri," he said, "your reputation is both a blessing and a bane. How shall we find you a husband?"

She replied, "My father, I am only human, as you well know. Perhaps in the forest I can be recognized for who I am. I request your permission to climb aboard my chariot and enter the woods. There I will search among the sages and the hermits to find the only man to be my one and all."

"Yes, my child," her father agreed. "I grant you permission to go forth into the wilderness, and find true love among those who walk the hermit's way. Return and inform me as to your choice, and I will act accordingly."

And so Savitri boarded her golden chariot, shook the horses' reins, and was off into the vast wilds where the exiles go to seek silence and truth, there to find a true companion. Eventually she came upon the hermitage of Dyumatsena, a ruler who had gone blind and had been driven from his throne by a usurper. Now he lived in exile in the jungle with his wife and child. Their son, named Satyavant, which means "truth speaker," had grown up to be wise and upright, intelligent and loving. It wasn't long after meeting him that Savitri grew to adore him, and to know him as the one who was meant to accompany her through life. She returned to her home to inform her father of her choice.

Her father had been entertaining Narada, the cosmic sage who travels from world to

Indian mythology offers many parallels to classical Greek and Roman mythology. There are numerous divinities, for example, and each one is associated with natural phenomena or with a set of human characteristics.

"Savitri and Satyavant" presents the triumph of love over obstacles—in this case, the steepest obstacle of all, death itself.

Walker Brents (b. 1959) is a poet and storyteller who has loved folklore and myths since he discovered at the age of five the myths of Hercules and the Greek gods. He has published poetry in several literary magazines.

When have you tried to change someone's mind? Were you successful? Why or why not?

Young Princess Playing a Tambura, 1770. Alfredo Dagli Orti.

world, cosmos to cosmos, seeing all time, present, past, and future, as one transparent sphere. He was there when Savitri returned, approaching her father with sparkling eyes.

Asvapati said, "My daughter, I can see by your happy countenance that your mission is accomplished. And whom among the ones you saw have you chosen?"

Monkeys in the Virgin Forest, c. 1910. Henri Rousseau.

"There is a forest-dweller named Satyavant. Born in the city of his father, who went blind and lost his kingdom, he was raised in the wilderness. It was there I came upon his hermitage. Happily I bring you news of our betrothal."

Narada's eyebrows rose up. "Satyavant? Oh yes, I have heard of him, and I know his fate. He is fine indeed, but he is doomed. A year from now he is fated to drop dead in his tracks."

"Savitri, I cannot have you wed one who is so soon to die," her father said. "Pass him over; there will be others from whom to choose." Asvapati meant well, but Savitri's eyes were steady and her mind was composed. "Father, Narada," she replied, "I assure you both I receive your words with all due respect, but I have seen the one I love, and it is Satyavant and no other. My love is of one substance with being itself, and it cannot be retracted or with-

drawn according to the mere vicissitudes of fate. My course is chosen. Satyavant is my life's love. Our life together, long or short, will be our life together."

Narada was impressed. "Such a love has a strange and challenging force, and may well prevail over omens and threats. Allow her her choice, Asvapati."

And so it was. Savitri donned a hermit's garb, and lived in the wilds with Satyavant and his aged parents. But the sands in the hourglass were flowing, day by day, and as their happy times continued, Savitri grew more and more aware of the crisis to come. Finally, the day came—one year had passed. When the sun was two hands high over the trees, Satyavant hoisted his ax and strode toward the tangled thickets. "Allow me to accompany you, Satyavant," Savitri said. It was a request she had never made before.

"Savitri, the paths are faint, and the animals are fierce. The way is arduous, and you are frail. Allow one such as myself, accustomed to wilderness life, to go forth to gather berries and fruits, and wood for fuel."

"It is true, Satyavant, that I have never asked to go with you, but today more than any other day I have a great desire to see the forest," Savitri persisted. Satyavant relented when his mother and father took her side, assuring him they would be fine by themselves, and reminding him that Savitri had hitherto made very few demands.

And so they entered the measureless wilds, to the calling of birds and the intermittent chattering of monkeys. Midday found them in a tiny clearing. Savitri sat in the shade of a blossoming tree as Satyavant chopped wood a few paces away. Suddenly, his ax fell to the ground with a thud. "Oh, Savitri," he murmured in a daze, "my head feels pierced by pinpricks of fire. I do not know up from down." Then his knees gave out; he collapsed to the dust. Savitri rushed to him and placed his head in her lap. His breathing slowly faded, and the color left his cheeks.

All was still, the birds silent, the monkeys hidden. Savitri felt a shadow draw near. She looked up and saw a dark green man with red eyes, gravely scowling as he strode toward them. In his hand he held a small noose of braided silver thread. Then she knew: "You are Death himself. You are called Yama, and have come to take my husband's soul."

He looked at her, a little surprised. Terrifyingly, but not without kindness, he spoke: "I am rarely addressed by those who breathe. I am who you say I am." He stooped over Satyavant's prone form. When he arose he held a thumb-sized fragment enclosed in the silver noose. It was Satyavant's soul. "I am bringing his inner being to the home that cannot be taken away. Your duty is now with the clay that is left behind. What did you say your name was?"

"I am Savitri."

"Very well." Yama walked a few steps, then paused at the clearing's edge. He turned toward her. "Most fear me, but you seem different." He turned to go. He heard her footsteps. He turned again. "Go, Savitri. No one living follows me." He went on, bearing Satyavant's tiny soul-image in his silver-threaded noose.

He was well on his way when he turned again. There she was, intrepidly following, steady-eyed, persistent. "You are strange," he said. "I like that. Ask me a boon, a gift, and I will grant it, except, of course, your husband's life."

"Give my father-in-law back the sight of his eyes."

"Done. Now go." And he walked on. Still she followed. They were headed south, toward Yama's realm. The vines and creepers parted before them, and closed behind them.

> "You are Death himself.
> You are called Yama,
> and have come to take
> my husband's soul."

Savitri said, "It is reported that you were the first man to die, and went to make a place where the soul is more than a mere wanderer."

Yama turned again. He had never been spoken to that way before. "You know my history. I am flattered. Ask me another boon, and I will grant it, on the condition I have already mentioned."

"Give my father-in-law back the kingdom he lost years ago."

"Granted. Now please be gone. No one has come this far before."

"I will stand here, and raise my voice, so that you hear me as you go. I have often wondered about the nature of life. Here with you, oh great Yama, I feel its depth and its beauty. As we who live speak words and phrases, you are the parentheses that enclose them. Is this not true?"

"It is true, Savitri. You are a poet. Your words reach me. Ask another boon."

"Grant me the gift of one hundred descendants."

"Very well. You will bear one hundred children." Yama strode on a few paces, then paused. When he turned to face her, his somber green countenance bore a wry smile. "I cannot grant you this boon without allowing for the earthly means of its fulfillment. Let it be said that I bestow as well as take away. Return, Savitri, to the forest clearing. There you will find your husband's life, given back."

Savitri placed her husband's head in her lap as before. The color returned to his cheeks. His chest began to rise and fall in a familiar rhythmic cycle. The birds sang and the monkeys chattered. Satyavant's lips began to move. "I dreamed a strange dream, Savitri. I dreamed a green man came, and took me away. I dreamed you followed, and won me back."

Savitri smiled. "You speak the truth, Satyavant. You are well named. But let us hurry home, and I will tell you the rest. The sun is setting, and darkness comes. The paths are overgrown, and we must return."

Back at the hermitage, her father-in-law, Dyumatsena, bounded from his hut to greet them. "Satyavant! Savitri! A miracle—my sight has returned! I see you both glowing with beauty both inside and out."

When morning came, as they prepared breakfast, a messenger arrived, bearing news of the death of the usurper, and an invitation to Dyumatsena to return to his kingdom.

Dyumatsena ruled it well until he could rule no more, and then Savitri and Satyavant governed the kingdom, and their children numbered one hundred. ❖

What was your reaction to the outcome of this myth? Is it what you expected? Does Yama give in too easily? Is Savitri really that clever? Support your answers with evidence from the text.

Refer and Reason

1. Why does Savitri go to the forest? Whom does she meet there?
2. What does the sage Narada predict to Savitri's father? Describe the way Savitri's father reacts to the prediction. What do you think about Savitri's desire to marry Satyavant, despite the prediction?
3. Summarize the three requests Savitri asks of Yama. Why does Yama grant Savitri her three requests? How does the outcome of the story compare with the outcomes of other myths you've read in this unit?

Writing Options

1. What does Satyavant's name mean? What may be the significance of his name for the theme, or underlying message, of the myth as a whole? Discuss your ideas in a short critical essay.
2. Yama calls Savitri a poet. Write a short poem of your own in which you use sensory imagery and figurative language to express a theme similar to the theme of this myth. Your poem may or may not use rhyme, but try to make the language and the rhythm as fluent and vivid as you can.

 Go to **www.mirrorsandwindows.com** for more.

The Death of Balder

A Norse Myth Retold by **Walker Brents**

Norse god Odin rides his eight-legged horse Sleipnir into the Underworld.

"The Death of Balder" is a Norse myth. Nordic countries include Scandinavia (Denmark, Sweden, and Norway), Finland, Iceland, and Greenland. Just as in ancient Greek mythology, Norse myths feature a divine king and queen. In "The Death of Balder," these roles are filled by Odin and his wife Frigga. Balder is the handsomest of all the gods in Norse mythology, and Loki, the god of mischief and malice, is Balder's antagonist. Loki falls into the category of a trickster god, or a god who breaks all the rules of nature.

In "The Death of Balder," Balder, who thinks himself invincible, finds out he is mistaken. Have you ever thought yourself invincible? What caused you to think this way, and what was the outcome?

Characters

Balder: Son of Odin and Frigga. God of light and beauty.

Hodur: Son of Odin and Frigga. Blind god of darkness and winter.

Odin: Father of gods. God of war and wisdom.

Frigga: Goddess of marriage and fertility. Mother of Balder and Hodur.

Hermod: Son of Odin. Messenger of the gods.

Loki: God of mischief. Associated with fire, earthquakes, and magic.

Hel: Daughter of Loki and ruler of the dead.

Sleipnir: Eight-legged steed of Odin who can run through air, water, land.

Of all the gods, Balder was most beloved, not only by the Aesir[1] and the Wanes,[2] but by all the creatures and trees, all the rocks, and even the grasses. All loved Balder for his beauty, his graceful ways, and his purity of being. His home in Asgard was in a grove called Peace Stead. It was a place where no crime had ever been committed, no blood had ever been spilled, and no lie had ever been told. There the birds sang more sweetly, it seemed, than anywhere else. There grew the white-blossoming chamomile flowers, also known as "Balder's Brow." There Balder walked along winding forest paths, leading on his arm his blind brother Hodur, Hodur who silently and hesitantly clambered behind, standing still frequently, speaking quietly, always taciturn. Hodur confided only in Balder, his most trusted companion.

Loki, the Norse god of Mischief.

Balder lived with his wife Nanna in a dwelling named Breidablik, where nothing unclean could enter. The gods would visit there to contemplate his wise judgments, and to spend time in his pure company.

Then, Balder began to dream disturbing dreams. In visions of the night he was visited by the specter of Hel, a frightening crone whose domain was Niflheim, the land of the dead. In visions of the night, in the cold and mists, she came to him, and in sepulchral[3] tones spoke of a place made for him in the realms of the dead.

Balder, frightened by these portents, spoke to his father Odin, chief of the gods.

Odin responded by climbing his high and lonely watchtower and consulting with the two ravens, Hugin and Munin, thought and memory, who graced his shoulders when they were not roving over the breadth of all the wide worlds. Mounting his eight-legged horse, Sleipnir, Odin journeyed into the land of the dead. He questioned the ghostly prophetess Volva, who spoke to him in such a way that his fears about Balder his son were confirmed: Balder would soon find himself in Hel's habitation.

When Odin returned to Asgard, his wife Frigga countered his gloom with encouraging news: she had roved over the Earth, and by her divine powers had obtained, from all things that grew upon the Earth, moved over the Earth, or impinged upon the Earth, the deep and solemn promise that each would not harm her son, Balder, in any way. "Hel has no arms to reach out and pull him toward her," she declared. What could Odin say? Perhaps fate could be defied. Perhaps Balder was protected.

The happy news was announced and Peace Stead quickly became the site of a raucous and joyful celebration. All the Aesir and Wanes, and the giants and dwarves gathered and engaged in reckless revelry. In giddy acknowledgment of Balder's declared immunity, they clustered around him, and each in turn threw toward

---

1. **Aesir.** Collective race for the main race of Norse gods
2. **Wanes.** Norse gods
3. **sepulchral.** Deep and hollow

him some frightening and deadly object, only to see it fall harmlessly to the ground. Balder stood smiling before them, ensconced in an invisible and protective shield, impervious and untouched. Thor threw his weighty hammer; it bounced harmlessly onto the loam.[4] Gods and giants threw axes and spears, dwarves flung rocks and brickbats; every missile fell down as if less than wind-blown dust. Peace Stead rang with their shouts of rowdy laughter as they celebrated Balder's invulnerability.

To this spontaneous carnival came Loki, the god of mischief and malice, whose mind harbored thoughts of cunning and hatred. When he saw all the laughter and fun, his festering grudges seethed and boiled. Loki began to plan. He shape-shifted into the outer semblance of an old woman, and hobbled eagerly to the threshold of Frigga's mansion.

"What can be the meaning of such jovial tumult over at Peace Stead?" he queried through his deceitful mask.

"Why," Frigga replied, "the revelers are celebrating the oath taken by all worldly elements, that none are to harm Balder: no rock, no weapon, no blade, no poison."

"All things have joined in this pledge?" wheedled Loki.

"All things that grow upon, move across, or touch the fringes of the Earth have joined together in one promise: to do no harm to Balder, whom they all love," Frigga said. "I have roamed in all places, and have solicited this oath from all entities—all, come to think of it, except for the mistletoe, a harmless and dependant sprig which is supported by the branches of the oak that grows near the threshold of Valhalla."

This was all Loki needed to hear, and he minced away gingerly, soon changing to his original form, and sprinted toward the oak tree that grew hard upon the fringes of Valhalla. There he reached upward and plucked down the mistletoe. Then he breathed upon it and uttered spells, so that it grew cold and jagged as sharpened iron.

He appeared once more at Peace Stead, alongside blind Hodur, who stood forlornly apart.

"Why," Loki asked him, "are you not participating in all this glee?"

"I have no object to throw, much less sight to aim," was Hodur's listless reply.

"Well, I can remedy that," Loki said. "Here, take this dart. Yes, that's it. Permit me now to draw back your arm and position it in the proper direction. And then, just so, we let fly…Now!"

At Loki's instigation, Hodur flung the mistletoe. It flew through space, penetrating the invisible force field of protection, striking Balder's chest and lodging there like a whetted spike.

With a heavy sigh, Balder crumpled to the ground. At first the gods just stood there, their arms at their sides. Then their smiles disappeared as shock sank in. Then grief took hold and bit deeply. They began to lament in one keening and anguished cry, "Balder is dead! Balder is dead!"

Frigga rushed over to her son's fallen form. She bent low and put her ear to his breast. Listening for the thumping of his heart, she heard only silence.

Frigga stood, addressing the crowd: "Fate can yet be defied. Whoever among you who would stand most in my favor, I would have you seek for Balder in Niflheim, Hel's cold realm, and bring Balder back among us into warmth and light!"

The messenger of the Aesir, Hermod, volunteered. "Take Sleipnir, my eight-legged steed," offered Odin. "He knows the way."

---

4. **loam.** Soil or earth

For nine days and nine nights Hermod rode, until he arrived at the crystalline bridge over the River Gjoll, which borders Niflheim. There he had words with Modgud, the grim skeletal maiden guardian. She challenged him but let him pass when she learned of his mission. Through the haunted trees and sharpened leaves of Ironwood he passed, and when he came to the gates of Hel's forbidding mansion, he dismounted, tightened the saddle-girths, remounted and dug in his spurs, so that Sleipnir leaped so high over the walls that Garm, the bloody and ferocious hellhound, could only bark and snarl uselessly many hundreds of feet below. Hermod rode up on Sleipnir to the very doorway in which Hel loomed before him, her hooded face half alive and half dead. She stood defiantly and said that if all things in creation wept for Balder, then she would relinquish her claim upon him; but if there were one thing that did not weep, then Balder would be hers.

Hermod turned back and galloped through the rugged glens. When he arrived in Asgard, all heard his news and wept relentlessly: all the gods and creatures and trees, all the rocks and even the grasses, for they all loved Balder with a deep and abiding passion. There was one being, however, who did not weep. In Jotunheim, the land of the giants, Hermod followed a raspy crow, who who entered a cave and re-emerged as an old giant woman. "I am Thokk," she croaked, "and I weep dry tears for Balder. Let Hel keep what she holds."

There was nothing to be done. Balder would stay in Niflheim until the aftermath of Ragnarok, the final battle between the gods and the giants, after which the world would be renewed. At Balder's funeral, attended by gods, giants, and dwarves, just before his body was borne out to sea aboard a flaming ship, Odin, leaned over and whispered in his dead son's ear the one secret word all creation hungers to hear: "Rebirth." ❖

MIRRORS & WINDOWS

The myth ends with one word: "Rebirth." What does this word mean to you? When have you witnessed a form of rebirth? What does this word imply about the way Odin sees the future?

Refer and Reason

1. Identify three details in the opening description of Balder that suggest that this god and his home are representative of paradise or of a mythical Golden Age of existence.
2. How is Loki characterized? How does he bring about Balder's destruction?
3. Explain the role of Thokk in the myth. What do you think Thokk may symbolize, or represent?

Writing Options

1. Suppose a friend tells you Balder deserved his fate. Write a two-paragraph response explaining whether you agree or disagree with your friend's opinion and using support from the text. As you are writing, consider the universal truths about human nature and existence that are present in the myth.
2. At Balder's funeral, his father, the god Odin whispers the word "rebirth" in Balder's ear. Assume that Balder is reborn one day. What kind of world will he re-enter? Will he take revenge on Loki or Thokk? How will he interact with the other gods or with human beings? Write another myth as a brief sequel to the myth.

 Go to **www.mirrorsandwindows.com** for more.

Achilles Defeating Hector, 1630–32. Peter Paul Rubens. Musée des Beaux-Arts, Pau, France.

from THE ILIAD

An Epic by **Homer**

Translated by **Robert Fagles**

And swift Achilles kept on coursing Hector,[1] nonstop
as a hound in the mountains starts a fawn from its lair,
hunting him down the gorges, down the narrow glens

---

1. **Hector.** A Trojan prince, son of Priam and Hecuba

The Iliad, probably composed around 800 BCE, is an epic that tells the story of the Trojan War, fought about 400 years before. *The Iliad* is marked by many stylistic features that signal its development in an oral culture: for example, frequent repetitions, as well as the use of epithets, or adjectives or phrases used to describe people and things (for example, "swift Achilles"). In its concluding books, from which this excerpt is drawn, Homer's epic focuses on the deadly conflict between Achilles, the supreme warrior of the Greeks, and Hector, a prince of Troy who is the city's most valiant defender. The duel between these champions forms the climax of the epic.

Describe a time you were particularly courageous. After the fact, how did you react to your burst of courage? How did the people around you react?

and the fawn goes to ground, hiding deep in brush
5   but the hound comes racing fast, nosing him out
until he lands his kill. So Hector could never throw
Achilles off his trail, the swift racer Achilles[2]—
time and again he'd make a dash for the Dardan Gates,
trying to rush beneath the rock-built ramparts, hoping
10   men on the heights might save him, somehow, raining spears
but time and again Achilles would intercept him quickly,
heading him off, forcing him out across the plain
and always sprinting along the city side himself—
endless as in a dream…
15   when a man can't catch another fleeing on ahead
and he can never escape nor his rival overtake him—
so the one could never run the other down in his speed
nor the other spring away. And how could Hector have fled
the fates of death so long? How unless one last time,
20   one final time Apollo[3] had swept in close beside him,
driving strength in his legs and knees to race the wind?
And brilliant Achilles shook his head at the armies,
never letting them hurl their sharp spears at Hector—
someone might snatch the glory, Achilles come in second.
25   But once they reached the springs for the fourth time,
then Father Zeus held out his sacred golden scales:
in them he placed two fates of death that lays men low—
one for Achilles, one for Hector breaker of horses—
and gripping the beam mid-haft the Father raised it high
30   and down went Hector's day of doom, dragging him down
to the strong House of Death—and god Apollo left him.
Athena[4] rushed to Achilles, her bright eyes gleaming,
standing shoulder-to-shoulder, winging orders now:
"At last our hopes run high, my brilliant Achilles—
35   Father Zeus must love you—
we'll sweep great glory back to Achaea's fleet,[5]
we'll kill this Hector, mad as he is for battle!
No way for him to escape us now, no longer—
not even if Phoebus[6] the distant deadly Archer
40   goes through torments, pleading for Hector's life,
groveling over and over before our storming Father Zeus.

---

2. **Achilles.** Hero of the Trojan war; son of Peleus
3. **Apollo.** God of music, healing, and archery, among other things; son of Zeus (king of the gods) and Leto
4. **Athena.** Goddess of wisdom and war
5. **Achaea's fleet.** Greek troops
6. **Phoebus.** Another name for Apollo

But you, you hold your ground and catch your breath
while I run Hector down and persuade the man
to fight you face-to-face."

                        So Athena commanded

45   and he obeyed, rejoicing at heart—Achilles stopped,
leaning against his ashen spearshaft barbed in bronze.
And Athena left him there, caught up with Hector at once,
and taking the build and vibrant voice of Deiphobus[7]
stood shoulder-to-shoulder with him, winging orders:

50   "Dear brother, how brutally swift Achilles hunts you—
coursing you round the city of Priam in all his lethal speed!
Come, let us stand our ground together—beat him back."

"Deiphobus!"—Hector, his helmet flashing, called out to her—
"dearest of all my brothers, all these warring years,

55   of all the sons that Priam and Hecuba produced!
Now I'm determined to praise you all the more,
you who dared—seeing me in these straits—
to venture out from the walls, all for *my* sake,
while the others stay inside and cling to safety."

60   The goddess answered quickly, her eyes blazing,
"True, dear brother—how your father and mother both
implored me, time and again, clutching my knees,
and the comrades round me begging me to stay!
Such was the fear that broke them, man for man,

65   but the heart within me broke with grief for you.
Now headlong on and fight! No letup, no lance spared!
So now, now we'll *see* if Achilles kills us both
and hauls our bloody armor back to the beaked ships
or he goes down in pain beneath your spear."

70   Athena luring him on with all her immortal cunning—
and now, at last, as the two came closing for the kill
it was tall Hector, helmet flashing, who led off:
"No more running from you in fear, Achilles!
Not as before. Three times I fled around

75   the great city of Priam—I lacked courage then
to stand your onslaught. Now my spirit stirs me
to meet you face-to-face. Now kill or be killed!
Come, we'll swear to the gods, the highest witnesses—

---

7. **Deiphobus.** Hector's brother

Athena, Greek, c. 5th century BCE. Louvre, Paris, France.

the gods will oversee our binding pacts. I swear
80   I will never mutilate you—merciless as you are—
if Zeus allows me to last it out and tear your life away.
But once I've stripped your glorious armor, Achilles,
I will give your body back to your loyal comrades.
Swear you'll do the same."

                                                    A swift dark glance
85   and the headstrong runner answered, "Hector, stop!
         You unforgivable, you…don't talk to me of pacts.
         There are no binding oaths between men and lions—
         wolves and lambs can enjoy no meeting of the minds—
         they are all bent on hating each other to the death.
90   So with you and me. No love between us. No truce
         till one or the other falls and gluts with blood
         Ares[8] who hacks at men behind his rawhide shield.
         Come, call up whatever courage you can muster.
         Life or death—now prove yourself a spearman,
95   a daring man of war! No more escape for you—
         Athena will kill you with my spear in just a moment.
         Now you'll pay at a stroke for all my comrades' grief,
         all you killed in the fury of your spear!"

                                                    With that,
         shaft poised, he hurled and his spear's long shadow flew
100   but seeing it coming glorious Hector ducked away,
         crouching down, watching the bronze tip fly past
         and stab the earth—but Athena snatched it up
         and passed it back to Achilles
         and Hector the gallant captain never saw her.
105   He sounded out a challenge to Peleus' princely son:
         "You missed, look—the great godlike Achilles!
         So you knew nothing at all from Zeus about my death—
         and yet how sure you were! All bluff, cunning with words,
         that's all you are—trying to make me fear you,
110   lose my nerve, forget my fighting strength.
         Well, you'll never plant your lance in my back
         as I flee *you* in fear—plunge it through my chest
         as I come charging in, if a god gives you the chance!
         But now it's for you to dodge *my* brazen spear—
115   I wish you'd bury it in your body to the hilt.
         How much lighter the war would be for Trojans then
         if you, their greatest scourge, were dead and gone!"

         Shaft poised, he hurled and his spear's long shadow flew
         and it struck Achilles' shield———a dead-center hit—

---

8. **Ares.** God of savage war; son of Zeus and Hera; half-brother to Apollo and
Athena

120   but off and away it glanced and Hector seethed,
his hurtling spear, his whole arm's power poured
in a wasted shot. He stood there, cast down…
he had no spear in reserve. So Hector shouted out
to Deiphobus bearing his white shield—with a ringing shout
125   he called for a heavy lance—

                              but the man was nowhere near him,
vanished—
                yes and Hector knew the truth in his heart
and the fighter cried aloud, "My time has come!
At last the gods have called me down to death.
I thought he was at my side, the hero Deiphobus—
130   he's safe inside the walls, Athena's tricked me blind.
And now death, grim death is looming up beside me,
no longer far away. No way to escape it now. This,
this was their pleasure after all, sealed long ago—
Zeus and the son of Zeus, the distant deadly Archer—
135   though often before now they rushed to my defense.
So now I meet my doom. Well let me die—
but not without struggle, not without glory, no,
in some great clash of arms that even men to come
will hear of down the years!"

                             And on that resolve
140   he drew the whetted sword that hung at his side,
tempered, massive, and gathering all his force
he swooped like a soaring eagle
launching down from the dark clouds to earth
to snatch some helpless lamb or trembling hare.
145   So Hector swooped now, swinging his whetted sword
and Achilles charged too, bursting with rage, barbaric,
guarding his chest with the well-wrought blazoned shield,
head tossing his gleaming helmet, four horns strong
and the golden plumes shook that the god of fire
150   drove in bristling thick along its ridge.
Bright as that star amid the stars in the night sky,
star of the evening, brightest star that rides the heavens,
so fire flared from the sharp point of the spear Achilles
brandished high in his right hand, bent on Hector's death,
155   scanning his splendid body—where to pierce it best?
The rest of his flesh seemed all encased in armor,
burnished, brazen—*Achilles'* armor that Hector stripped

from strong Patroclus[9] when he killed him—true,
but one spot lay exposed,
160 where collarbones lift the neckbone off the shoulders,
the open throat, where the end of life comes quickest—*there*
as Hector charged in fury brilliant Achilles drove his spear
and the point went stabbing clean through the tender neck
but the heavy bronze weapon failed to slash the windpipe—
165 Hector could still gasp out some words, some last reply…
he crashed in the dust—

           godlike Achilles gloried over him:
"Hector—surely you thought when you stripped Patroclus'
 armor
that you, you would be safe! Never a fear of me—
 far from the fighting as I was—you fool!
170 Left behind there, down by the beaked ships
his great avenger waited, a greater man by far—
that man was I, and I smashed your strength! And you—
the dogs and birds will maul you, shame your corpse
while Achaeans bury my dear friend in glory!"

175 Struggling for breath, Hector, his helmet flashing,
said, "I beg you, beg you by your life, your parents—
don't let the dogs devour me by the Argive[10] ships!
Wait, take the princely ransom of bronze and gold,
the gifts my father and noble mother will give you—
180 but give my body to friends to carry home again,
so Trojan men and Trojan women can do me honor
with fitting rites of fire once I am dead."

Staring grimly, the proud runner Achilles answered,
"Beg no more, you fawning dog—begging me by my parents!
185 Would to god my rage, my fury would drive me now
to hack your flesh away and eat you raw—
such agonies you have caused me! Ransom?
No man alive could keep the dog-packs off you,
not if they haul in ten, twenty times that ransom
190 and pile it here before me and promise fortunes more—
no, not even if Dardan Priam should offer to weigh out
your bulk in gold! Not even then will your noble mother
lay you on your deathbed, mourn the son she bore…
The dogs and birds will rend you—blood and bone!"

---

9. **Patroclus.** Achilles' best friend
10. **Argive.** Resident of the city of Argos in Greece

Portrait of Achilles, famous Greek warrior. / *Achille en Habit Militaire,* c. 1802.
Philip de Bay.

195   At the point of death, Hector, his helmet flashing,
        said, "I know you well—I see my fate before me.
        Never a chance that I could win you over…
        Iron inside your chest, that heart of yours.
        But now beware, or my curse will draw god's wrath
200   upon your head, that day when Paris[11] and lord Apollo—
        for all your fighting heart—destroy you at the Scaean Gates!"

---

11. **Paris.** Hector's brother; his elopement with Helen, queen of Sparta, triggers
the Trojan War. He kills Achilles by hitting him in the heel with an arrow.

Death cut him short. The end closed in around him.
Flying free of his limbs
his soul went winging down to the House of Death,
205 wailing his fate, leaving his manhood far behind,
his young and supple strength. But brilliant Achilles
taunted Hector's body, dead as he was, "Die, die!
For my own death, I'll meet it freely—whenever Zeus
and the other deathless gods would like to bring it on!"

210 But now their commander, swift Achilles was led away
by Achaea's kings, barely able to bring him round—
still raging for his friend—to feast with Agamemnon.[12]
As soon as the party reached the warlord's tents
they ordered the clear-voiced heralds straightaway
215 to set a large three-legged cauldron over the fire,
still in hopes of inducing Peleus' royal son
to wash the clotted bloodstains from his body.
He spurned their offer, firmly, even swore an oath:
"No, no, by Zeus—by the highest, greatest god!
220 It's sacrilege for a single drop to touch my head
till I place Patroclus on his pyre and heap his mound
and cut my hair for him—for a second grief this harsh
will never touch my heart while I am still among the living…
But now let us consent to the feasting that I loathe.
225 And at daybreak, marshal Agamemnon, rouse your troops
to fell and haul in timber, and furnish all that's fitting,
all the dead man needs for his journey down the western dark.
Then, by heaven, the tireless fire can strike his corpse—
the sooner to burn Patroclus from our sight—
230 and the men turn back to battles they must wage."

So he insisted. They hung on his words, complied,
rushed to prepare the meal, and each man feasted well
and no man's hunger lacked a share of the banquet.
When they had put aside desire for food and drink
235 each went his way and slept in his own shelter.
But along the shore as battle lines of breakers
crashed and dragged, Achilles lay down now,
groaning deep from the heart,

---

12. **Agamemnon.** Commander of the Greeks during the Trojan War

near his Myrmidon[13] force but alone on open ground
240 where over and over rollers washed along the shore.
No sooner had sleep caught him, dissolving all his grief
as mists of refreshing slumber poured around him there—
his powerful frame was bone-weary from charging Hector
straight and hard to the walls of windswept Troy—
245 than the ghost of stricken Patroclus drifted up…
He was like the man to the life, every feature,
the same tall build and the fine eyes and voice
and the very robes that used to clothe his body.
Hovering at his head the phantom rose and spoke:
250 "Sleeping, Achilles? You've forgotten me, my friend.
You never neglected me in life, only now in death.
Bury me, quickly—let me pass the Gates of Hades.
They hold me off at a distance, all the souls,
the shades of the burnt-out, breathless dead,
255 never to let me cross the river, mingle with them…
They leave me to wander up and down, abandoned, lost
at the House of Death with the all-embracing gates.
Oh give me your hand—I beg you with my tears!
Never, never again shall I return from Hades
260 once you have given me the soothing rites of fire.
Never again will you and I, alive and breathing,
huddle side-by-side, apart from loyal comrades,
making plans together—never…Grim death,
that death assigned from the day that I was born
265 has spread its hateful jaws to take me down.

                                        And you too,
your fate awaits you too, godlike as you are, Achilles—
to die in battle beneath the proud rich Trojans' walls!
But one thing more. A last request—grant it, please.
Never bury my bones apart from yours, Achilles,
270 let them lie together…
just as we grew up together in your house,
after Menoetius brought me there from Opois,
and only a boy, but banished for bloody murder
the day I killed Amphidamas' son. I was a fool—
275 I never meant to kill him—quarreling over a dice game.
Then the famous horseman Peleus took me into his halls,
he reared me with kindness, appointed me your aide.

---

13. **Myrmidon.** Ancient nation in Greek mythology

So now let a single urn, the gold two-handled urn
your noble mother gave you, hold our bones—together!"

280   And the swift runner Achilles reassured him warmly:
"Why have you returned to me here, dear brother, friend?
Why tell me of all that I must do? I'll do it all.
I will obey you, your demands. Oh come closer!
Throw our arms around each other, just for a moment—
285   take our fill of the tears that numb the heart!"

In the same breath he stretched his loving arms
but could not seize him, no, the ghost slipped underground
like a wisp of smoke…with a high thin cry.
And Achilles sprang up with a start and staring wide,
290   drove his fists together and cried in desolation, "Ah god!
So even in Death's strong house there is something left, a
ghost, a phantom—true, but no real breath of life.
All night long the ghost of stricken Patroclus
hovered over me, grieving, sharing warm tears,
295   telling me, point by point, what I must do.
Marvelous—like the man to the life!"

                       So he cried
and his outcry stirred in them all a deep desire to grieve,
and Dawn with her rose-red fingers shone upon them weeping
round the wretched corpse. ❖

When you read this selection, with which hero did you sympathize more—Achilles or Hector—and why? How do the actions of these two warriors compare with the ideas people have today about heroic acts and bravery? Would either of these two characters be considered heroes today? Why or why not?

Refer and Reason

1. What role does the goddess Athena play in this excerpt? What did you think of her actions?
2. As he is near death, what does Hector beg of Achilles? How does Achilles respond? Why does Achilles react this way? Judge whether his reaction is justified. Why or why not?
3. How is Achilles heroic in this excerpt? How is Hector heroic? Support your answers with specific references to the text.

Writing Options

1. What is your impression of Achilles' character in this selection from *The Iliad*? In two or three paragraphs, write a character sketch of the epic hero.
2. Why do heroes matter to a culture or society? In a personal essay of two or three paragraphs, discuss your ideas about heroes and heroism, with an emphasis on the role that they play in contemporary society.

 Go to **www.mirrorsandwindows.com** for more.

THE CRYSTAL CAVE
by Mary Stewart

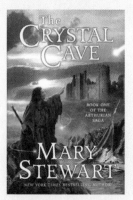

Myridden Emrys, who is nick-named Merlin, is the grandson of a king, and he is also a loner. Strange powers and mysterious visions plague him. The first volume of Stewart's Arthurian trilogy, this novel takes readers into the Dark Ages and gives them a close-up view of the powerful legendary wizard Merlin.

CUCHULAIN OF MUIRTHEMNE: THE STORY OF THE MEN OF THE RED BRANCH OF ULSTER
by Lady Augusta Gregory

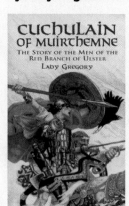

Cuchulain, called the Hound of Ulster, was the greatest of ancient Ireland's elite band of fighters, the Knights of the Red Branch. Based on stories Gregory heard in childhood in the Gaelic language, this translation has helped create new interest in the myths of old Ireland.

THE GIRL WHO MARRIED A LION AND OTHER TALES FROM AFRICA
by Alexander McCall Smith

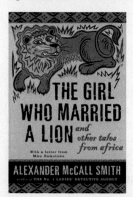

Rich in culture and voice, this collection includes forty retellings of traditional African folk tales. Readers of this book will find similarities between African folk tales and the tales of other cultures, as well as many unique differences.

SPINDLE'S END
by Robin McKinley

In this unique retelling of the fairy tale of "Sleeping Beauty," little Rosie does not know she is a prin-cess — or that she is under the spell of an evil fairy. Filled with compelling char-acters, intriguing places, and surprising twists, this novel is a must-read.

THE SWORD IN THE STONE
by T. H. White

Moving back in time, White re-creates King Arthur's child-hood, telling the story leading up to his removing the magic sword from the stone. Learning skills of jousting, hunting, and swordplay from tutor and magician, Merlin, Arthur also experiences life from different points of view when Merlin transforms him into countless animals.

FIREBIRDS: AN ANTHOLOGY OF ORIGINAL FANTASY AND SCIENCE FICTION
edited by Sharyn November

This collection of sixteen stories by popular authors offers a taste of many types of science fiction and fantasy writing. Included are humorous as well as magical stories — a young professional woman looks for her soul, the Wicked Witch of the West meets Sleeping Beauty, and two children lost on an island find a mysterious winged lady.

Prepare a Multimedia Presentation

You've heard the expression "A picture is worth a thousand words." This tends to be especially true when it comes to presenting information. In the past, there was little a person could do to enhance a presentation visually, aside from using posters, charts, graphs, and overhead projectors. Technology has made it possible to present information in colorful and compelling ways. In this workshop, you will prepare and deliver an informative presentation using a combination of text, sound, pictures, animation, and video. A multimedia presentation uses a variety of **media,** a plural form of *medium* referring to a system of communication, information, or entertainment.

1. Develop your topic

Select a topic you know well. Make an outline with at least three main subtopics. Then brainstorm details about each subtopic. You may also need to do some research.

A formal outline framework shows the most important and least important relationships among the topics and subtopics. Use an outline like the one below, which is about the game of soccer, to organize the ideas for your presentation.

> **Soccer**
> I. History of the game
>   A. Origins
>   B. Development
>   C. Modern soccer
>
> II. How it is played
>   A. Basic game
>   B. Rules
>   C. Positions

2. Create multimedia elements

Decide on a theme or design for your presentation, and use that theme or design throughout. For example, if you are doing a presentation on the destruction of the rainforest, you might want to use backgrounds and fonts that resemble the jungle. Give your pictures, photos, video, charts, and written materials a similar look and feel. Use media to emphasize key points. Avoid including too much text on a slide or an image.

3. Rehearse

Practice giving your presentation as you operate your equipment. Make sure all components are clearly audible and visible and that the room will accommodate both your needs and those of your audience.

4. Make the presentation

Do not rush through your presentation. Remember to speak clearly and loudly and to look at your audience. Allow time at the end for audience questions.

Presentation Tip

As you are choosing details for your outline, think about the types of multimedia that would work well with those details.

 Speaking and Listening Rubric

Your presentation will be evaluated on these elements:

Content and Development

☑ clear topic and goal for presenting the topic

☑ effective use of multimedia elements

☑ logical organization of ideas

☑ appropriate amount of information

Delivery

☑ appropriate volume, enunciation, and pace

☑ effective use of eye contact and audience interaction

☑ competent use of multimedia technology

Research Paper

The legend of King Arthur and the popular trilogy *Lord of the Rings* center on the drama of struggle and conquest. These fictional tales parallel conflict we see in every culture in the world, from contradictory ideas to armed warfare, from a debate of opposing values to the violence of civil unrest. No country is so unified that it is without clashing disagreement. Faced with so much conflict, people need a way to make sense of it.

When writing about a conflict, whether for a news story, persuasive essay, or research paper, a writer's mission is to clarify the roots of the conflict, present its development, and examine both sides. A good writer tries to remain objective and is ethically responsible for the truthfulness of the information. A thorough writer organizes information carefully and keeps track of all sources.

❶ PREWRITE

Select Your Topic

You may write about any conflict that has taken place in any culture at any time in history. Types of conflict include ethnic and racial tension, civil wars, clashes between new ideas and tradition, and differences in values. Brainstorm a list of conflicts about which you'd like to learn more. Then choose one that interests you.

Narrow Your Topic

Do some preliminary research on your broad topic as a way of finding a narrow area on which to focus. For example, a research paper on racial conflict in the United States could be a thousand pages long and still not cover everything, but a paper on the 1965 race riots in the Watts neighborhood of Los Angeles, California, would be manageable.

Find Sources

After you have selected your topic, find several references at the library. A good place to find credible information is in books, professional journals, and reference works such as encyclopedias, almanacs, guides, and handbooks. Start by looking at the most recent sources first, in order to have the most current information for your paper. You may also be able to find information on the Internet, but be very careful to use only articles found on reliable sites. To determine whether a site is reliable, find out who created it. If it is the website of an educational institution or professional organization, it is probably reliable.

Try to find both primary sources and secondary sources. A *primary source* is an original source such as a diary, letter, survey, interview, memoir, autobiography, or speech written by a person who actually experienced what he or she is writing about. A *secondary source* is information about an experience or a situation gathered by someone who did not experience it firsthand.

Assignment

Research a conflict and write an informative paper reporting your findings. Use sources, document them carefully, and prepare a final bibliography to accompany your paper.

Purpose

To research and analyze a conflict and inform your audience about the issues involved

Audience

Members of a community organization interested in learning more about the conflict

Writing Rubric

A successful research paper

☑ **introduces** the topic

☑ includes a **thesis statement** that expresses the main point

☑ in the **body,** supports the thesis with three to five points, using information and brief quotations from reliable sources

☑ **concludes** by restating the thesis, summarizing the body, and allowing the reader to consider both the conflict and the ideas in the paper

☑ **documents** sources correctly, both in the text and at the end of the paper

Take Notes

Once you have found sources, skim them to see if they will be useful for your research paper. When you skim, you read quickly, slowing down when you come to relevant information. For each useful source you find, create a bibliography card like the one below. (See the Language Arts Handbook, 5.6, for instruction on creating bibliographic entries.) Include on each card the location of the source in case you need to find it again; if it is a library book, include the catalog number of the item. Then, take notes from your sources on note cards. Most of your notes should be paraphrased — in your own words, not in the author's words. (Paraphrasing will help you avoid plagiarizing.) Record the author's exact words only if you think you want to quote the author, and then put the exact words in quotation marks.

Bibliography Card

Fletcher, Bill, Jr. "An Elusive Peace in the Sudan." *New York Amsterdam News.* Vol. 96, 2005: 13.

location of source: journal at library

Organize Your Ideas

As you are doing research, use a K-W-L Chart like the one on page 876 to organize your ideas and to see what information you still need to find. Continue adding to your chart until you have enough information to write your paper.

As you complete the contents of your chart, ask yourself: Have I done enough research? Does my research support my main point? Do I need more information to answer my questions? Do I need to address other questions that came up as I conducted research?

Next, create an organizational plan: Number the points of your chart in the order you will present them in your paper. Separate your note cards into groups that refer to the points of your chart. Think of each group as the material for one paragraph.

What Great Writers Do

"Write in a way that draws the reader's attention to the sense and substance of the writing, rather than to the mood and temper of the author," advised William Strunk, Jr. (1869–1946) and E. B. White (1899–1985) in their classic book, *The Elements of Style*.

Introduction

Introduce the conflict in an interesting way. State your thesis.

Body

State at least three points to prove your thesis. Develop the points with evidence, research, information, and brief quotations from your sources.

Conclusion

Restate your thesis and summarize your research. Provide a knowledgeable closing statement about the conflict.

K-W-L Chart

What I Know	What I Want to Know	What I Have Learned
• Sudan is a large country in Africa. • Darfur is a region in Sudan. • The people on both sides of the conflict have the same religion.	• Who are the people involved? • How did the conflict start? • What has happened to the people because of the conflict? • How does the future look for Darfur?	

Write Your Thesis Statement

Review your chart and state, in one sentence, the main point your research supports. This is your **thesis statement.** One student, Salvador Layton, wrote this thesis statement about his research on the Sudan conflict:

The reasons for Sudan's ethnic conflict in Darfur are complex, and the results have been devastating.

❷ DRAFT

Write your paper by following the three-part framework: **introduction, body,** and **conclusion.**

Draft Your Introduction

The **introduction** of a research paper should familiarize the reader with the topic in a highly interesting way, perhaps with a startling statistic, an anecdote, or a descriptive summary of the conflict. Provide the context in a way that leads to your thesis statement, usually the last sentence in the first paragraph, and makes an impact.

The draft of Salvador's introduction is shown in the first column of the chart on page 879. His first sentence provides concise background; his second sentence gives a significant recent development in the conflict; and his last sentence states his thesis. He doesn't fully impress on readers the magnitude of the conflict, however. What could he do to make a stronger impact?

Draft Your Body

In the **body,** state each point you want to make, and support it with evidence—facts, ideas, and quotations from your note cards. Credit the source of information and quotations in parentheses to verify your research and avoid plagiarism. Document your sources using the method explained on page 877.

What Great Writers Do

Some students question the value of studying a topic that so many others have already covered. Understand that research is invaluable for strengthening your powers of thinking. Albert Szent-Györgyi (1893–1986), a Hungarian biochemist, won the Nobel Prize for his research in medicine in 1937. He explained it this way: "Research is to see what everybody else has seen, and to think what nobody else has thought."

Salvador began the body of his paper by discussing the source of the conflict in Darfur. Look at the draft of his first body paragraph in the left-hand column of the chart on page 879. Salvador provides two more points in separate paragraphs to support his thesis statement, using facts, information, and quotations from his research.

Review the organizational plan you created from your chart and note cards. As you write the body of your paper, create topic sentences from your main points. Support the topic sentences with information from your note cards. Craft your writing style so the voice of your essay is natural and authoritative.

Draft Your Conclusion

Finally, write the **conclusion** of your research paper. A good conclusion does two things: (1) it summarizes the main point made in the body of the essay, restating the thesis, and (2) it brings the discussion to a close, leaving readers with a sense of finality.

Does Salvador do both these things in his conclusion? Look at the draft of his conclusion in the chart on page 879.

Use Proper Documentation

You need to credit authors and sources for the information that you use in your research. Documenting your sources properly allows readers to verify your research and protects you against plagiarism. Plagiarism is a serious offense that involves taking someone else's words or thoughts and pretending that they are your own.

Sources you must document include the following:

- all ideas and facts that belong to someone else, including works available electronically
- ideas or facts expressed in tables, charts, and other graphic information
- all artistic property, including works of literature, song lyrics, and ideas

There are several ways for you to incorporate sources into your writing. They are listed below.

Directly quote when passages are precise, eloquent, or unique to a source. Put the exact words in quotation marks, and reference the last name of the author of the source and the page where you found those words. When using quotations, don't let them stand alone in your paper. Blend them into your writing, and show how they contribute to your overall analysis.

EXAMPLE

The peace may not last long, however, unless it is recognized that "the Sudan is truly a multi-ethnic, multi-religious state where a politics of tolerance is the only measure through which peace and stability can be fully achieved" (Fletcher 13).

When not quoting directly, you may want to **paraphrase,** or tell in your own words, an author's ideas. In paraphrasing, you must still credit the author by referencing the author's last name and the page where you found the idea. If the author's name is unavailable, use a shortened form of the title of the work.

EXAMPLE

> By some reports, the Janjaweed have poisoned wells, killed livestock, and wrecked farming equipment so that famine will spread (Reeves 23).

If you're dealing with a lot of information that you would like to express concisely and succinctly, you can **summarize,** or recap main ideas and events. When you summarize someone else's work, be sure you do not alter its meaning in any way.

❸ REVISE

Evaluate Your Draft

You can evaluate your own writing or exchange papers with a classmate and evaluate each other's work. Either way, think carefully about what is done well and what can be improved.

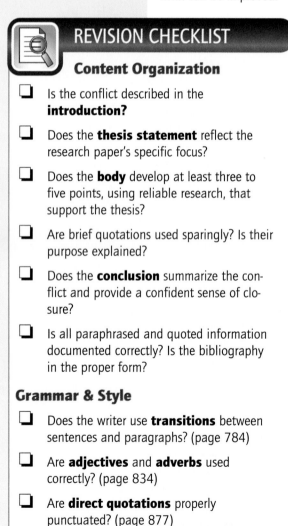

REVISION CHECKLIST

Content Organization

❑ Is the conflict described in the **introduction?**

❑ Does the **thesis statement** reflect the research paper's specific focus?

❑ Does the **body** develop at least three to five points, using reliable research, that support the thesis?

❑ Are brief quotations used sparingly? Is their purpose explained?

❑ Does the **conclusion** summarize the conflict and provide a confident sense of closure?

❑ Is all paraphrased and quoted information documented correctly? Is the bibliography in the proper form?

Grammar & Style

❑ Does the writer use **transitions** between sentences and paragraphs? (page 784)

❑ Are **adjectives** and **adverbs** used correctly? (page 834)

❑ Are **direct quotations** properly punctuated? (page 877)

Start by looking at the content and organization. In a research paper, the introduction, body, and conclusion should work together to prove the thesis. Every paragraph should relate clearly back to that main idea. Make notes directly on the research paper about what changes need to be made.

Next, check the language for errors. Go back through your draft to make sure you have correctly applied the guidelines in the Grammar & Style workshops in this unit. Use the Revision Checklist to evaluate the writing. Consider how your research writing can have authority. Because your topic has been well researched, adopt a tone of confidence.

Revise for Content, Organization, and Style

Salvador evaluated his draft and made improvements. Look at the chart on page 879 (this time, the right-hand column) to see how he revised the three paragraphs we looked at earlier:

- **Introduction:** Salvador provided context for readers who need to know where Sudan is. He added a striking fact to get readers' full attention and to create interest.
- **Body:** Salvador deleted empty phrases and wordiness. He continued to define terms. He corrected grammatical errors, making sure all verbs were in the same tense.
- **Conclusion:** Salvador worked with his sentences to improve his writing style. He punctuated in-text source citations correctly. He strengthened his assertions and created a strong closure.

DRAFT STAGE		REVISE STAGE	

Introduction

Sudan has experienced war almost continuously since 1956. In 2003, another large-scale crisis started: an ethnic conflict in Sudan's western region of Darfur. The reasons for Sudan's ethnic conflict in Darfur are complex, and I believe the results have been devastating.

Identifies the conflict
Provides background

States thesis

Sudan, the largest country in Africa, has experienced war almost continuously since 1956. In 2003, another large-scale crisis started: an ethnic conflict in Sudan's western region of Darfur. By the end of 2004, more than 350,000 people were dead, and more than a million left homeless (Reeves 22). The reasons for Sudan's ethnic conflict in Darfur are complex, and ~~I believe~~ the results have been devastating.

Adds a fact to get readers' attention; cites the source in parentheses

Deletes an empty phrase

Body Paragraph

There are many reasons but three main causes for the conflict. First, the Sudan Liberation Army and the Justice and Equality Movement were angry that the government in Khartoum neglected the poor Darfur region. The rebels attacked an airfield. The government strikes back and sends armed Arab groups in the area to "eradicate the rebellion" (Strauss 123). Most of the violence, however, was against civilians.

Provides support for the thesis

Includes research from notes

Cites source in parentheses

There are ~~many reasons but~~ three main causes for the conflict. First, the Sudan Liberation Army and the Justice and Equality Movement, two rebel groups in Darfur, were angry that the government in Khartoum, the capital of Sudan, neglected the poor Darfur region. The rebels attacked an airfield. The government ~~strikes~~ struck back and ~~sends~~ sent armed Arab groups in the area to "eradicate the rebellion" (Strauss 123). Most of the violence, however, was against civilians.

Deletes wordiness

Defines terms; provides context

Fixes grammatical error: verb tense consistency

Conclusion

The attempt to resolve the Sudan conflict has not worked. After peace talks failed, the vice president scheduled peace talks between the rebels (McLaughlin 1) The African Union increased troops in Sudan, but the number is still "woefully inadequate" (Reeves 21).

Rephrases thesis statement

Summarizes main points

Repeats key words

~~The attempt to~~ Resolving the Sudan conflict has not ~~worked~~ been easy. After peace talks failed, the vice president scheduled peace talks between the rebels (McLaughlin 1). The African Union, a peacekeeping group of African nations, increased troops in Sudan, but the number is still "woefully inadequate" (Reeves 21).

Corrects format: puts period after citation
Adds details

WRITING WORKSHOP **879**

Review the notes you or your partner made as you evaluated your draft. Then respond to each comment and effectively revise your paper.

Proofread for Errors

The purpose of proofreading is to check for remaining errors. While you can look for errors as you evaluate your research paper, you should focus on this purpose during proofreading. Use proofreaders' symbols to mark any errors you find. (See Language Arts Handbook 4.1 for a list of proofreaders' symbols.) To complete the assignment, print out a final draft and read the entire thing once more before turning it in.

Take a look at Salvador's final draft on the next page. Review how he worked through the three stages of the writing process: Prewrite, Draft, and Revise.

WRITING FOLLOW-UP

Publish and Present

- Add a cover page to your report that includes the title, your name, and the date. Display your research paper in the classroom for other students to read.
- Consider presenting the information to the members of a local community organization interested in current affairs.

Reflect

- How might you conduct research differently for your next paper? What other topics might you like to research?
- What questions do you have about documenting sources? If you have questions, where might you find answers?

STUDENT MODEL

Sudan's Darfur Region: A Culture in Conflict
by Salvador Layton

Sudan, the largest country in Africa, has experienced war almost continuously since 1956. In 2003, another large-scale crisis started: an ethnic conflict in Sudan's western region of Darfur. In less than a year, more than 350,000 people were dead and more than a million left homeless (Reeves 22). The reasons for Sudan's ethnic conflict in Darfur are complex, and the results have been devastating.

There are three main causes for the conflict. First, the Sudan Liberation Army and the Justice and Equality Movement, two rebel groups in Darfur, were angry that the government in Khartoum, the capital of Sudan, neglected the poor Darfur region. The rebels attacked an airfield. The government struck back and sent armed Arab groups in the area to "eradicate the rebellion" (Strauss 123). Most of the violence, however, was against civilians.

What is the focus of the conflict addressed in the paper?

What is the thesis statement?

Where does the writer explain causes of the conflict?

What other kinds of information does he include?

STUDENT MODEL

Second, peace talks to end the civil war between northern and southern Sudan excluded Darfur rebels. The rebels attacked again, afraid that they might be neglected again (123). Third, there were tensions between the black African Muslims who are farmers, and the Arab Muslims who are livestock herders. Drought led to fighting over land. The conflict turned violent when the Arab-led government started giving guns to the Arab tribes, which became known as the "Janjaweed" (124).

In addition, the suffering of people has been terrible beyond belief. Hundreds of thousands have died from violence, starvation, or disease. Over one million people have lost their homes and been forced to leave the area (Reeves 22). The government in Khartoum has stopped international aid organizations from entering Darfur (Booker and Colgan 8). By some reports, the Janjaweed have poisoned wells, killed livestock, and wrecked farming equipment so that famine will spread (Reeves 23).

Resolving the Sudan conflict has not been easy. After peace talks failed, the vice president scheduled peace talks between the rebels (McLaughlin 1). The African Union, a peacekeeping group of African nations, increased troops in Sudan, but the number is still "woefully inadequate" (Reeves 21). For the suffering and violence to end, the Sudan must be recognized as "a multi-ethnic, multi-religious state," and "a politics of tolerance" must be established (Fletcher 13). We can only hope that day will come soon.

Where does the writer use quotations? How are the quotations worked into the paper?

Identify three different ways the writer starts sentences. Which word choices seem especially good?

How are the sources documented? How successful is his conclusion?

Bibliography

Booker, Salih, and Ann-Louise Colgan. "Genocide in Darfur." *Nation.* Vol. 279, no. 2, 2004: 8–9.

Fletcher, Bill, Jr. "An Elusive Peace in the Sudan." *New York Amsterdam News.* Vol. 96, 2005: 13.

Hoskins, Eric. "Africa's Endless War." *Macleans's.* Vol. 117, no. 20, 2004: 26–28.

McLaughlin, Abraham. "In Darfur, Africa Left to Take Lead." *Christian Science Monitor.* Vol. 97, no. 48, 2005: 1.

Reeves, Eric. "Genocide by Attrition." *Dissent.* Winter 2005: 21–25.

Strauss, Scott. "Darfur and the Genocide Debate." *Foreign Affairs.* Vol. 84, 2005: 123–133.

Reading Skills

EVALUATE CAUSE AND EFFECT

A *cause* is something that brings about a result, or an *effect*. In other words, a cause happens first, followed by an effect. A writer, however, will sometimes explain the effect or effects first and then give information about the cause or causes. When you **evaluate cause and effect,** you look for a logical relationship between one or more causes and one or more effects. Though they are not always present in a text that explains a cause-and-effect relationship, signal words and phrases indicating cause and effect include *as a result, because, since, consequently, thus,* and *therefore.*

One way to track cause-and-effect relationships is to use a graphic organizer. The way your graphic organizer looks will depend on whether there are multiple causes or multiple effects. Read the following excerpt from "The Love of Cupid and Psyche." Then look at the Cause-and-Effect Chart below to see how to record causes and effects in a graphic organizer.

Test-Taking Tips

- As you read, pay attention to words that indicate cause and effect.
- Not all cause-and-effect relationships are obvious. Sometimes, you'll have to infer a cause or an effect using details from the text.

> Psyche, thus frowned upon by Venus, derived no benefit from all her charms. All eyes were still cast eagerly upon her and every mouth spoke her praise, but neither king, royal youth, or common man presented himself to demand her hand in marriage. Her two elder sisters were married to royal princes, but Psyche, in her lonely apartment, wept over her beauty, sick of the flattery it aroused, while love was denied her.

Here, the cause is stated first—Venus despises Psyche. The effects of this circumstance are twofold:

1. Many men admire Psyche, but no one wants to risk Venus's wrath and marry her.
2. Psyche's two sisters have married, but she is all alone and very unhappy; she resents her beauty and the empty flattery.

Cause-and-Effect Chart

Cause		Effects
Venus despises Psyche.	➡	1) Many men admire Psyche's beauty, but none of them will marry her. 2) Psyche is alone and very unhappy.

Directions: Read the following informational excerpt. The questions that come after it will ask you to evaluate cause and effect.

Nonfiction: This passage is entitled "History of Colombia" and comes from *Lonely Planet.*

Alonso de Ojeda, a companion of Christopher Columbus, landed on the Guajira Peninsula in 1499. The wealth of the local Indians promulgated the myth of El Dorado, and the shores of present-
5 day Colombia became the target of numerous expeditions. The Indians originally tolerated the arrival of the Spaniards but rebelled when the colonists tried to enslave them and confiscate their lands. Soon, a large part of what became Colombia
10 had been conquered by the Spanish, and a number of towns, including Cartagena (founded in 1533), were prospering. In 1544, the country was incorporated into the viceroyalty of Peru, where it remained until 1739 when it became a
15 part of New Granada (comprising the territories of what are today Colombia, Venezuela, Ecuador and Panama).

Along with slavery, the Spanish monopoly over commerce, taxes and duty slowly gave rise to
20 protest, particularly towards the end of the 18th century. It was during this period that the first stirrings of national autonomy occurred, but it wasn't until 1819, and the appearance of Venezuelan liberator Simón Bolívar and his army,
25 that independence was achieved. Ten years of uneasy confederation with Venezuela and Ecuador followed in the form of Gran Colombia, until regional differences between the three finally undermined the union.

30 Political currents born in the struggle for independence were formalized in 1849 when two parties (dominated by creole elites[7]) were established: the Conservatives with centralist tendencies and the Liberals with federalist leanings. The parties
35 divided the nation into partisan camps, which eventually heralded insurrection, civil chaos and war. In the course of the 19th century, the country experienced no less than 50 insurrections and eight civil wars, culminating in the bloody
40 War of the Thousand Days in 1899.

Multiple Choice

1. Colombia drew many early explorers because of the _____.
   A. wealth of the native inhabitants
   B. beauty of the landscape
   C. prosperity of the Spanish
   D. slave trade

2. Which of the following was *not* a cause for protest in Colombia near the end of the eighteenth century?
   F. Spanish control of trade
   G. poor relations with Venezuela and Ecuador
   H. disagreements over slavery
   J. financial concerns

3. Which of the following is an effect of the Spaniards conquering the land that had belonged to the Indians?
   A. Several new towns sprang up.
   B. The Indians rebelled.
   C. The country was ruled by the king or queen of Peru.
   D. All of the above

4. Which of the following is an antonym of the word *autonomy* (line 22)?
   F. independence
   G. despair
   H. slavery
   J. happiness

Constructed Response

5. Write a summary of the cause-and-effect relationship of the events described in the last paragraph of the excerpt. Use a Cause-and-Effect Chart like the one on page 882 to organize your ideas.

Writing Skills

PERSUASIVE ESSAY

Many standardized tests require you to write an essay on a prescribed topic. The writing prompt will discuss two different perspectives on a controversial issue. Then you will be asked to write an essay in which you take a position on the issue and support your position with reasons and examples. You will usually have around 30 minutes to complete your essay.

Test-Taking Tip
Choose a position on an issue. Use examples, reasons, facts, and statistics to support your position on the issue. Be sure to consider opposing views.

Scorers will take into account the fact that you had only a short amount of time to write your essay. They will evaluate your ability to:

- take a position on the issue in the prompt
- focus on the topic throughout the essay
- support your ideas logically and thoroughly
- organize ideas in a logical way
- use language clearly and effectively according to the conventions of standard written English

When you are writing a persuasive essay, first decide on what position you will take. Then, as part of your introduction, write a thesis statement that expresses your position. In body paragraphs, focus on the reasons why you believe what you do about the position you have taken, and include details like facts and personal experiences to support your reasons. As you are organizing your essay, you may want to focus on one reason in each paragraph. Don't forget to address opposing viewpoints and refute them with your own support. In your conclusion, restate your stance on the issue at hand.

PRACTICE

Timed Writing: 30 minutes

Think carefully about the issue presented below and the assignment that follows. You will have 30 minutes to write your response.

Some states are fighting for a law that prohibits people from talking on their cell phones while they are driving. Supporters of this law say talking on a cell phone while driving is distracting and can cause an accident. Opponents say talking on a cell phone is no more distracting than listening to the radio or talking to a passenger in the car. Do you think there should be a law that prohibits cell-phone use while driving?

Assignment: Take a position on whether you think there should be a law that prohibits cell-phone use while driving. You may write about either one of the two points of view given, or you may present a different point of view on this topic. Use specific reasons and examples to support your position.

Revising and Editing Skills

Some standardized tests ask you to read a draft of an essay and answer questions about how to improve it. As you read the draft, watch for errors like these:

- incorrect spellings
- disagreement between subject and verb; inconsistent verb tense; incorrect forms for irregular verbs; sentence fragments and run-ons; double negatives; and incorrect use of frequently confused words, such as *affect* and *effect*
- missing end marks, incorrect comma use, and lowercased proper nouns and proper adjectives
- unclear purpose, unclear main ideas, and lack of supporting details
- confusing order of ideas and missing transitions
- language that is inappropriate to the audience and purpose, and mood that is inappropriate for the purpose

PRACTICE

Directions: For each underlined section in the passage that follows, choose the revision that most improves the writing. If you think the original version is best, choose "MAKE NO CHANGE."

(1) My name is <u>Alex, maybe</u> you already know me. (2) I'm running for Student <u>Council</u> President. I'm going to take a few minutes to tell you why I am the best candidate. (3) <u>The first reason why you should vote for me is because I care about all of you and our school.</u> (4) Another <u>reason is I have alot</u> of experience. I hope you'll do what my campaign says: Elect Alex!

1. A. MAKE NO CHANGE.
   B. Alex; maybe
   C. Alex; and maybe
   D. Alex, however, maybe

2. F. MAKE NO CHANGE.
   G. Counsel
   H. Counsil
   J. Councel

3. A. MAKE NO CHANGE.
   B. The first reason why you should vote for me being because I care about all of you and our school.
   C. The first reason you should vote for me is, because I care about all of you and our school.
   D. The first reason you should vote for me is because I care about all of you and our school.

4. F. MAKE NO CHANGE.
   G. reason is I have a lot
   H. reason being I have alot
   J. reason was I have a lot

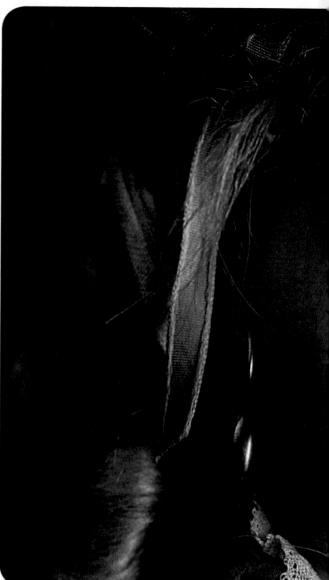

UNIT 6

Independent Reading

CISNEROS

STEINBECK

BAMBARA

> "*Books are the carriers of civilization. Without books, history is silent, literature dumb, science crippled, thought and speculation at a standstill.*"
>
> —Henry David Thoreau

What is your opinion about reading? Whether you prefer to read novels, comic books, or scientific journals, being able to read well is a skill that is essential to all walks of life. The selections in this unit are for you to read independently. As you read, remember to use the strategies and skills you've encountered in previous units.

DICKINSON

BRADBURY

GARCIÁ MÁRQUEZ

READING INDEPENDENTLY

Theme: The Examined Life

"And it occurred to him then with all the force of a revelation that, if he fell, all he was ever going to have out of life he would then, abruptly, have had."

—Tom Benecke in "Contents of the Dead Man's Pocket" by Jack Finney

One thing that separates humans from animals is self-awareness. For example, a dog eating some tasty scraps is unlikely to think, "These are good, but not as good as that stuff I ate last week," or "This is probably going straight to my hips." Those thoughts, common to humans, show self-awareness, but they are only the beginning. Examining your life requires asking deep questions about yourself—how you became who you are and where you are going in life. The selections in this section all involve some examination of life.

READING INDEPENDENTLY

As you read these selections on your own, use the following guidelines.

Before Reading
- **Preview** by reading the title of the piece; scanning any art, quotations, subheads, and sidebars in the selection; and reading the footnotes for the selection.
- **Find and make connections** to the selections by reading the introductory information. What is familiar to you?
- **Set your own purpose for reading,** and remember that you can modify that purpose as you read.

During Reading
- **Ask questions** about things that puzzle you, and make notes about things you want to remember.
- **Visualize** the setting, characters, and images while you read.
- **Make predictions** about what might happen next in the text. Adjust your predictions as you get more information.
- **Make inferences** about the information that is not specifically stated.
- **Clarify** the text by writing comments about the literary techniques or elements the author uses or any difficult vocabulary words. Also try reading the selection aloud, especially if it's poetry.

After Reading
- **Reread** the selection if you have time. Look for details you missed or forgot. If you have questions after reading the selection the first time, look for answers the second time you read.

- **Summarize** the story or poem on paper or in your head. If you can't remember a part of the story or poem, go back and **skim** or **scan** it to find the part you need to reread.
- **Review vocabulary words** that you found difficult. Try to use the words in your own sentences.
- **Ask yourself questions** about what you just read, such as what the "point" of the story or poem is. The answer to that question will likely be the theme.

What Good Readers Do

Connect to Prior Knowledge
Being aware of what you already know and thinking about it as you read can help you keep track of what's happening in the selection and will increase your knowledge. As you read, say to yourself

- ☐ I already know this about the story...
- ☐ This part of the story reminds me of...
- ☐ I think this part of the story is like...
- ☐ My experience tells me that...
- ☐ I like this description because...

APPLYING READING STRATEGIES

Note how this student used different strategies while reading the short story "Geraldine Moore the Poet" by Toni Cade Bambara (page 890).

Visualize
I can see this scene. I picture a young girl with old socks; her family might be poor.

Make Inferences
Since she's only getting paid two dollars a week for watching a dog, I'm guessing that this story is set at least twenty years ago. That's not very much for two days of dog-watching.

Clarify
The information about the hot-dog vendor makes me think that not only is Geraldine poor, but her whole neighborhood must be poor. I'm going to take note of where there are signs of poverty.

Geraldine paused at the corner to pull up her knee socks. The rubber bands she was using to hold them up made her legs itch. She dropped her books on the sidewalk while she gave a good scratch. But when she pulled the socks up again, two fingers poked right through the top of her left one.

"That stupid dog," she muttered to herself, grabbing her books and crossing against traffic. "First he chews up my gym suit and gets me into trouble, and now my socks."

Geraldine shifted her books to the other hand and kept muttering angrily to herself about Mrs. Watson's dog, which she minded two days a week for a dollar. She passed the hot-dog man on the corner and waved. He shrugged as if to say business was very bad.

Must be, she thought to herself. *Three guys before you had to pack up and forget it. Nobody's got hot-dog money around here.*

Geraldine turned down her street, wondering what her sister Anita would have for her lunch. She was glad she didn't have to eat the free lunches in high school any more. She was sick of the funny-looking tomato soup and the dried-out cheese sandwiches and those oranges that were more green than orange.

When Geraldine's mother first took sick and went away, Geraldine had been on her own except when Miss Gladys next door came in on Thursdays and cleaned the apartment and made a meat loaf so Geraldine could have dinner. But in those days Geraldine never quite managed to get breakfast for herself. So she'd sit through social studies class, scraping her feet to cover up the noise of her stomach growling.

Make Connections
I can relate to that—some school lunches are pretty bland and taste-less. I wonder why it says "she didn't have to eat the free lunches in high school any more."

Ask Questions
What happened to Geraldine's mother? What does it mean that she "went away"?

Make Predictions
I bet that with her "growling stomach" she doesn't do well in school. It would be hard to concentrate if you're so hungry.

Geraldine Moore the Poet

A Short Story by **Toni Cade Bambara**

"I can't write a poem," Geraldine said flatly,
before she even realized she was going to speak at all.
She said it very loudly, and the whole class looked up.

Toni Cade Bambara (1939–1995) found her unique voice in the creative arts, studying theater and English before working as a film writer and teaching college English. An avid civil rights activist in the 1960s and 1970s, Bambara saw her writing as a vehicle for truth in a "racist, hardheaded, heedless society" and said, "The job of the writer is to make revolution irresistible."

In **"Geraldine Moore the Poet,"** Bambara writes about an undiscovered talent while conveying another message: True poetry does not depend on the use of pretty, flowery images, or even proper grammar. Poetry is about expressing emotions or observations in one's own unique voice.

Think about the special abilities you have. How did you discover them?

Geraldine paused at the corner to pull up her knee socks. The rubber bands she was using to hold them up made her legs itch. She dropped her books on the sidewalk while she gave a good scratch. But when she pulled the socks up again, two fingers poked right through the top of her left one.

"That stupid dog," she muttered to herself, grabbing her books and crossing against traffic. "First he chews up my gym suit and gets me into trouble, and now my socks."

Geraldine shifted her books to the other hand and kept muttering angrily to herself about Mrs. Watson's dog, which she minded two days a week for a dollar. She passed the hot-dog man on the corner and waved. He shrugged as if to say business was very bad.

Must be, she thought to herself. *Three guys before you had to pack up and forget it. Nobody's got hot-dog money around here.*

Geraldine turned down her street, wondering what her sister Anita would have for her lunch. She was glad she didn't have to eat the free lunches in high school any more. She was sick of the funny-looking tomato soup and the dried-out cheese sandwiches and those oranges that were more green than orange.

When Geraldine's mother first took sick and went away, Geraldine had been on her own except when Miss Gladys next door came in on Thursdays and cleaned the apartment and made a meat loaf so Geraldine could have dinner. But in those days Geraldine never quite managed to get breakfast for herself. So she'd sit through social studies class, scraping her feet to cover up the noise of her stomach growling.

Now Anita, Geraldine's older sister, was living at home waiting for her husband to get out of the Army. She usually had some-

thing good for lunch—chicken and dumplings if she managed to get up in time, or baked ham from the night before and sweet-potato bread. But even if there was only a hot dog and some baked beans— sometimes just a TV dinner if those soap operas kept Anita glued to the TV set—anything was better than the noisy school lunchroom where monitors kept pushing you into a straight line or rushing you to the tables. Anything was better than that.

Little Sweet, 1944.
William H. Johnson.
Smithsonian American Art
Museum, Washington, DC.

Open Heart, 1995. Colin
Bootman. Private collection.

Geraldine was almost home when she stopped dead. Right outside her building was a pile of furniture and some boxes. That wasn't anything new.

She had seen people get put out in the street before, but this time the ironing board looked familiar. And she recognized the big, ugly sofa standing on its arm, its underbelly showing the hole where Mrs. Watson's dog had gotten to it.

Miss Gladys was sitting on the stoop, and she looked up and took off her glasses. "Well, Gerry," she said slowly, wiping her glasses on the hem of her dress, "looks like you'll be staying with me for a while." She looked at the men carrying out a big box with an old doll sticking up over the edge. "Anita's upstairs. Go on up and get your lunch."

Geraldine stepped past the old woman and almost bumped into the superintendent. He took off his cap to wipe away the sweat.

"Darn shame," he said to no one in particular. "Poor people sure got a hard row to hoe."

"That's the truth," said Miss Gladys, standing up with her hands on her hips to watch the men set things on the sidewalk.

Upstairs, Geraldine went into the apartment and found Anita in the kitchen.

"I dunno, Gerry," Anita said. "I just don't know what we're going to do. But everything's going to be all right soon as Ma gets well."

Anita's voice cracked as she set a bowl of soup before Geraldine.

"What's this?" Geraldine said.

"It's tomato soup, Gerry."

Geraldine was about to say something. But when she looked up at her big sister, she saw how Anita's face was getting all twisted as she began to cry.

That afternoon, Mr. Stern, the geometry teacher, started drawing cubes and cylinders on the board. Geraldine sat at her desk adding up a column of figures in her notebook—the rent, the light and gas bills, a new gym suit, some socks. Maybe they would move somewhere else, and she could have her own room. Geraldine turned the squares and triangles into little houses in the country.

"For your homework," Mr. Stern was saying with his back to the class, "set up your problems this way." He wrote GIVEN: in large letters, and then gave the formula for the first problem. Then he wrote TO FIND: and listed three items they were to include in their answers.

Geraldine started to raise her hand to ask what all these squares and angles had to do with solving real problems, like the ones she had. *Better not,* she warned herself, and sat on her hands. *Your big mouth got you in trouble last term.*

In hygiene class, Mrs. Potter kept saying that the body was a wonderful machine. Every time Geraldine looked up from her notebook, she would hear the same thing. "Right now your body is manufacturing all the proteins and tissues and energy you will need to get through tomorrow."

And Geraldine kept wondering, *How? How does my body know what it will need, when I don't even know what I'll need to get through tomorrow?*

As she headed down the hall to her next class, Geraldine remembered that she hadn't done the homework for English. Mrs. Scott had said to write a poem, and Geraldine had meant to do it at lunch-time. After all, there was nothing to it—a flower here, a raindrop there,

moon, June, rose, nose. But the men carrying off the furniture had made her forget.

"And now put away your books," Mrs. Scott was saying as Geraldine tried to scribble a poem quickly. "Today we can give King Arthur's[1] knights a rest. Let's talk about poetry."

Mrs. Scott moved up and down the aisles, talking about her favorite poems and reciting a line now and then. She got very excited whenever she passed a desk and could pick up the homework from a student who had remembered to do the assignment.

"A poem is your own special way of saying what you feel and what you see," Mrs. Scott went on, her lips moist. It was her favorite subject.

"Some poets write about the light that… that…makes the world sunny," she said, passing Geraldine's desk. "Sometimes an idea takes the form of a picture—an image."

For almost half an hour, Mrs. Scott stood at the front of the room, reading poems and talking about the lives of the great poets. Geraldine drew more houses, and designs for curtains.

"So for those who haven't done their homework, try it now," Mrs. Scott said. "Try expressing what it is like to be…to be alive in this…this glorious world."

"Oh, brother," Geraldine muttered to herself as Mrs. Scott moved up and down the aisles again, waving her hands and leaning over the students' shoulders and saying, "That's nice," or "Keep trying." Finally she came to Geraldine's desk and stopped, looking down at her.

"I can't write a poem," Geraldine said flatly, before she even realized she was going to speak at all. She said it very loudly, and the whole class looked up.

"And why not?" Mrs. Scott asked, looking hurt.

---

1. **King Arthur's.** Belonging to the legendary king of Britain and leader of the Knights of the Round Table

"I can't write a poem, Mrs. Scott, because nothing lovely's been happening in my life. I haven't seen a flower since Mother's Day, and the sun don't even shine on my side of the street. No robins come sing on my window sill."

Geraldine swallowed hard. She thought about saying that her father doesn't even come to visit any more, but changed her mind. "Just the rain comes," she went on, "and the bills come, and the men to move out our furniture. I'm sorry, but I can't write no pretty poem."

Teddy Johnson leaned over and was about to giggle and crack the whole class up, but Mrs. Scott looked so serious that he changed his mind.

"You have just said the most…the most poetic thing, Geraldine Moore," said Mrs. Scott. Her hands flew up to touch the silk scarf around her neck. "'Nothing lovely's been happening in my life.'" She repeated it so quietly that everyone had to lean forward to hear.

"Class," Mrs. Scott said very sadly, clearing her throat, "you have just heard the best poem you will ever hear." She went to the board and stood there for a long time staring at the chalk in her hand.

"I'd like you to copy it down," she said. She wrote it just as Geraldine had said it, bad grammar and all.

> Nothing lovely's been happening in my life.
> I haven't seen a flower since Mother's Day,
> And the sun don't even shine on my side of the street.
> No robins come sing on my window sill.
> Just the rain comes, and the bills come,
> And the men to move out our furniture.
> I'm sorry, but I can't write no pretty poem.

Mrs. Scott stopped writing, but she kept her back to the class for a long time—long after Geraldine had closed her notebook.

And even when the bell rang, and everyone came over to smile at Geraldine or to tap her on the shoulder or to kid her about being the school poet, Geraldine waited for Mrs. Scott to put the chalk down and turn around. Finally Geraldine stacked up her books and started to leave. Then she thought she heard a whimper—the way Mrs. Watson's dog whimpered sometimes—and she saw Mrs. Scott's shoulders shake a little. ❖

"Try expressing what it is like to be…to be alive in this…this glorious world." Is Mrs. Scott correct in her ideas about the purpose of poetry? Why or why not? What would you say to someone who thinks art and literature have nothing to do with the problems of everyday life?

Refer and Reason

1. What does Mrs. Scott assume about her students' lives when she frames her writing assignment as she does? Why can't Geraldine write a "pretty poem"?

2. Describe the effect you think Mrs. Scott's reaction to Geraldine's comments will have on Geraldine's future. How will Geraldine's comments affect Mrs. Scott's future definition of poetry?

3. Many successful individuals have attributed their success to a mentor or someone who believed in them earlier in their lives or careers. Why do you think a mentor makes a difference? Do you have a mentor? If so, how has he or she affected your life?

Writing Options

1. Pretend you are Geraldine Moore. Before you go to sleep that evening on Miss Gladys's couch, write a diary entry about the events of the day—from your sudden eviction to Mrs. Scott's emotional reaction to your words. Make sure to include your feelings about all that has happened to you.

2. Imagine you have been asked to review Geraldine Moore's poem for a collection of works by young poets. Write a one-page literary review of the poem, analyzing such aspects as its tone, theme, style, and imagery. Come up with a title for the poem that you can refer to as you write.

 Go to **www.mirrorsandwindows.com** for more.

Geraldo No Last Name

A Short Story by Sandra Cisneros

> His name was Geraldo. And his home is in another country.

Sandra Cisneros (b. 1954) writes fiction, essays, and poetry. Attending the prestigious Writers' Workshop at the University of Iowa at a time when few Hispanics were there, Cisneros sometimes felt out of place: "I knew I was a Mexican woman, but I didn't think it had anything to do with why I felt so much imbalance in my life, whereas it had everything to do with it.... That's when I decided I would write about something my classmates couldn't write about." This decision allowed Cisneros to develop her own voice, one that has led her to tremendous success.

"Geraldo No Last Name" appears in Cisneros' first novel, *The House on Mango Street* (1984), which is composed of many vignettes (literary sketches) related by a young Hispanic girl, Esperanza, who is growing up in Chicago. In "Geraldo No Last Name," Esperanza talks about an accident that affects her friend Marin.

How do you react when you hear about tragic events on the news?

She met him at a dance. Pretty too, and young. Said he worked in a restaurant, but she can't remember which one. Geraldo. That's all. Green pants and Saturday shirt. Geraldo. That's what he told her.

And how was she to know she'd be the last one to see him alive. An accident, don't you know. Hit-and-run. Marin, she goes to all those dances.

Uptown. Logan. Embassy. Palmer. Aragon. Fontana. The Manor. She likes to dance. She knows how to do cumbias and salsas and rancheras[1] even. And he was just someone she danced with. Somebody she met that night. That's right.

That's the story. That's what she said again and again. Once to the hospital people and twice to the police. No address. No name. Nothing in his pockets. Ain't it a shame.

Only Marin can't explain why it mattered, the hours and hours, for somebody she didn't even know. The hospital emergency room. Nobody but an intern working all alone. And maybe if the surgeon would've come, maybe if he hadn't lost so much blood, if the surgeon had only come, they would know who to notify and where.

But what difference does it make? He wasn't anything to her. He wasn't her boyfriend or anything like that. Just another brazer[2] who didn't speak English. Just another wetback.[3] You know the kind. The ones who always look ashamed. And what was she doing out at three a.m. anyway? Marin who was sent home with her coat and some aspirin. How does she explain?

She met him at a dance. Geraldo in his shiny shirt and green pants. Geraldo going to a dance.

What does it matter?

They never saw the kitchenettes. They never knew about the two-room flats[4] and sleeping rooms he rented, the weekly money orders sent home, the currency exchange. How could they?

His name was Geraldo. And his home is in another country. The ones he left behind are far away, will wonder, shrug, remember. Geraldo—he went north…we never heard from him again. ❖

---

1. **cumbias…rancheras.** Types of Latin music and dances
2. **brazer (brā′ zer).** From the Spanish word *bracero*, referring to a Mexican allowed into the United States temporarily to work
3. **wetback.** Offensive term for a Mexican worker who enters the United States illegally by wading or swimming the Rio Grande on the U.S.-Mexican border
4. **flats.** Apartments

MIRRORS & **W**INDOWS

"But what difference does it make [to Marin]? He wasn't anything to her." What evidence of this kind of attitude of indifference have you seen in today's society? What is your opinion about this attitude? How might this attitude be harmful? How might it be necessary?

Refer and Reason

1. Identify four things Marin knows about Geraldo. Why do you think Marin waited to see what happened to Geraldo even though she didn't know him well?
2. Describe how the hospital staff and police react to Geraldo's emergency situation and death, and what the staff does for Marin. What apparent attitudes do they have toward Geraldo and Marin? Do you think these attitudes are warranted? Explain.
3. How do you think Geraldo's family would react to his death if they knew what had happened to him? Support your answer with evidence from the text.

Writing Options

1. Retell the story in the form of a one-act play. Include dialogue between Geraldo and Marin and Marin and the people she encounters. Then, with a group of classmates, perform the play.
2. What roles do race, class, and ethnic background play in the story? Choose one of these things and examine the part it plays in the story. Consider the attitudes Marin, the hospital staff, and police have toward Geraldo's race, class, and ethnicity. Think about ways the story might have been different if Geraldo were of a different race, class, or ethnicity. Then write a three-paragraph literary analysis that explains what you've discovered.

 Go to **www.mirrorsandwindows.com** for more.

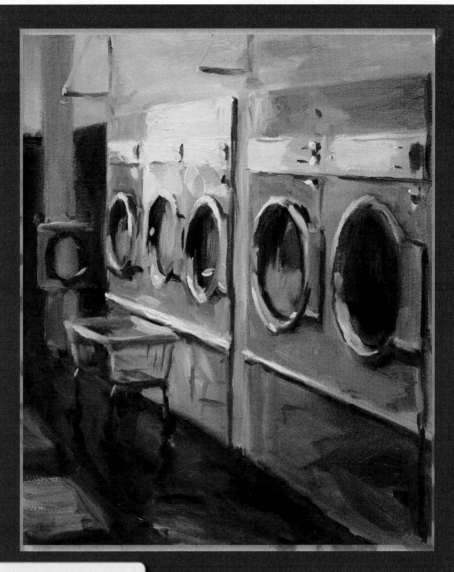

Laundromat, 2000.
Pam Ingalls.

Garrett Hongo (b. 1951) was born in Hawaii and raised in Los Angeles. He was inspired to write **"The Legend"** after seeing a TV news story about an Asian man killed in an act of street violence. The poem, he says, is about "my own needs for mercy, for a fulfillment to a broad, urban, and contemporary story that baffled me." Hongo's reference in the poem to the "weaver girl" in the final stanza recalls an Asian myth in which she is the creator of the stars.

Describe a TV news story that has had an impact on you. What makes the TV news so powerful?

The Legend

A Lyric Poem by **Garrett Hongo**

In Chicago, it is snowing softly
and a man has just done his wash for the
   week.
He steps into the twilight of early evening,
carrying a wrinkled shopping bag
5   full of neatly folded clothes,

and, for a moment, enjoys
the feel of warm laundry and crinkled
    paper,
flannellike against his gloveless hands.
There's a Rembrandt[1] glow on his face,
10 a triangle of orange in the hollow of his
    cheek,
as a last flash of sunset
blazes the storefronts and lit windows of
    the street.

He is Asian, Thai or Vietnamese,
and very skinny, dressed as one of the poor
15 in rumpled suit pants and a plaid
    mackinaw,[2]
dingy and too large.
He negotiates the slick of ice
on the sidewalk by his car,
opens the Fairlane's back door,

20 leans to place the laundry in,
and turns, for an instant,
toward the flurry of footsteps
and cries of pedestrians
as a boy—that's all he was—
25 backs from the corner package store[3]
shooting a pistol, firing it,
once, at the dumbfounded man
who falls forward,
grabbing at his chest.

30 A few sounds escape from his mouth,
a babbling no one understands
as people surround him
bewildered at his speech.
The noises he makes are nothing to them.
35 The boy has gone, lost
in the light array of foot traffic
dappling the snow with fresh prints.
Tonight, I read about Descartes'[4]
grand courage to doubt everything
40 except his own miraculous existence
and I feel so distinct
from the wounded man lying on
    the concrete
I am ashamed.

Let the night sky cover him as he dies.
45 Let the weaver girl[5] cross the bridge of
    heaven
and take up his cold hands. ❖

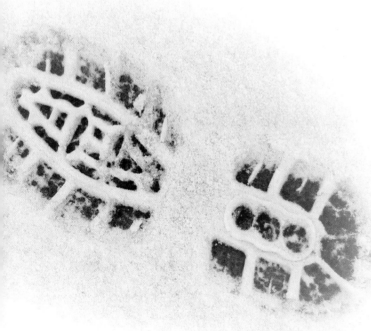

---

1. **Rembrandt.** (1606–1669) Dutch painter famous for his dramatic use of color and light
2. **mackinaw.** Short coat made of heavy fabric
3. **package store.** Liquor store
4. **Descartes.** (1596–1650) René Descartes, French philosopher who said "I think, therefore I am."
5. **weaver girl.** Creator of the stars in an Asian myth

MIRRORS & WINDOWS

What random acts of violence have you heard about on the news lately? How do you react when you hear about them? How does your reaction compare with the way the speaker of the poem reacted when he says, "I am ashamed."?

The Moon of the Milky Way.
Based on the Chinese legend of the
Herd Boy and the Weaver Maid.

PRIMARY SOURCE
CONNECTION

Garrett Hongo wrote **"Hongo Reflects on 'The Legend'"** to explain what he was trying to achieve with the poem "The Legend." He explains the allusion to the Weaver Girl. An *allusion* is a rhetorical technique in which reference is made to a person, an event, an object, or a work from history or literature. As you read, think about why Hongo chose this allusion.

Hongo Reflects on "The Legend"

A Reflection by

Garrett Hongo

What I wanted, the city could not give me. I wanted *mercy*. I wanted the universe to bend down and kiss its own creation, like a parent does to a child just after it's born, as if a tenderness were the pure expression of the world for itself. I wanted to believe that what was not given could be given, that were a man or a woman to cry out for solace, that the world, for all of its steel plants and tire factories, for all of its liquor stores and razor wire, for all of its buses that belched carcinogenic[1] poisons and people who passed you by on the freeway who cursed you with their eyes—for all of that, it would still lay its soft wings of blessing upon you if you cried out in need.

From time to time, I'd recollect a story I'd heard during childhood, probably in Hawaii, a legend about the creation of the universe. From an aunt baking *pan dulce*[2] or a cousin flinging stones with me into waves along Hau'ula Beach, into abandoned canefields or at the headboards of the Japanese graves on the promontory at the Kahuku plantation, I'd heard that, in order for the stars to turn and remain where they were, it took two creatures and their sacrifice. It took a Weaver Maid to make the stars—Being—and a Herd Boy to make sure they all stayed together or apart as they should. The Weaver Maid and the Herd Boy lived on opposite sides of the Milky Way, that band of stars that is our galaxy and which Asians see as a mighty river of stars. They call it The River of Heaven. The Herd Boy and Weaver Maid are stars on its opposite banks, the one in a cluster around Antares,[3] the other far away and down along the flow, in a spot near

---
1. **carcinogenic** (kär´ s'n ō je´ nik). Cancer-causing
2. *pan dulce* (pän´ dül´ sā). Sweet bread
3. **Antares** (an ter´ ēz´). Part of the constellation Scorpio; this bright star was named after Ares, Greek god of war.

Aldebaran.[4] They labor, dutifully fabricating the web and warp of Being, herding the star bands in an eternal solitude, celibate, without love or companionship. Yet, for one night of the year, on an evening when the star sky is said to be clearest, the universe is supposed to succumb to an overwhelming pity for the two lovers, living out lives in exile from each other, lives in deprivation of passion, without emotional compass or root in material certainties. In the form of a flock of compassionate starlings or swallows in the Japanese or Chinese versions, in the folded and gigantic wing of Crow in the Tlingit and Haida versions of the North Coast Pacific Indians, the universe, *one turning*, responds by making a footbridge across the River of Heaven out of its own interlocking bodies, out of its own need to create mercy and requital in a night of love for the effortful sacrifices of two of its children.

It is a vision of the afterlife, in a sense, a promise that the world will provide for us a reward and a reason for our struggles. It is a parable[5] about mercy and fulfillment, the response of the universe to needs of the human heart. The poem is the story of the Weaver Girl and the Herd Boy, told in inner-city, contemporary terms. It is about my own needs for mercy, for a fulfillment to a broad, urban, and contemporary story that baffled me. ❖

---

4. **Aldebaran** (al deb´ ə rən). Brightest star in the constellation Taurus

5. **parable.** Brief story that teaches a lesson

Refer and Reason

1. In the poem, how do the bystanders react after the man is shot? How does the speaker feel when he sees the wounded man? What might the reaction of the bystanders reveal about them? Why is the narrator ashamed of his own reaction?

2. Summarize in your own words the legend of the Weaver Girl. How does the universe show mercy to the Weaver Girl and the Herd Boy?

3. Identify associations that come to mind when you hear the word *legend*. Why do you think the poem is titled "The Legend"? Evaluate the speaker's attitude toward violence in contemporary society. Support your evaluation with evidence from the poem and the reflection.

Writing Options

1. The death of the man outside the Laundromat is going to be reported on the TV news. Write a transcript of the news report. You'll have to use your imagination to fill in the missing details. Remember to use the five W's—*who, what, when, where,* and *why*—in your report.

2. Imagine that you have been asked to write a column for a local newspaper after a violent act has occurred in your community. Write a reflection exploring the ways you've seen people react to violence and the possible reasons for these reactions. Also consider the ways you and your family and friends react to violence.

 Go to **www.mirrorsandwindows.com** for more.

TEXT ←TO→ TEXT CONNECTION

- In his reflection on "The Legend," Garrett Hongo says, "The poem is the story of the Weaver Girl and the Herd Boy, told in inner-city, contemporary terms." Do you agree with this assessment of the poem? Why or why not?

- What specific aspects of the poem parallel those of the Weaver Girl legend? Consider your answer in terms of theme, characters, symbolism, and other relevant elements.

New Dog

A Lyric Poem by **Mark Doty**

"New Dog" was published in 1995 in **Mark Doty's** award-winning poetry collection *Atlantis.* It tells about the wish of Wally, a dying man, for a new dog and is written with a sharp focus on the present moment. "Before Wally's diagnosis," says Doty, "lots of my work had been about memory and trying to gain some perspective on the past. Suddenly that was much less important, and I felt pushed to pay attention to now, what I could celebrate or discern in the now."

When have you been prompted to think hard about the present? What circumstances caused you to do so?

Jimi and Tony
can't keep Dino,
their cocker spaniel;
Tony's too sick,
5   the daily walks
more pressure
than pleasure,
one more obligation
that can't be met.

10   And though we already
have a dog, Wally
wants to adopt,
wants something small
and golden to sleep
15   next to him and
lick his face.
He's paralyzed now
from the waist down,

whatever's ruining him
20   moving upward, and
we don't know
how much longer
he'll be able to pet
a dog. How many men
25   want another attachment,
just as they're
leaving the world?

Wally sits up nights
and says, *I'd like*

30 *some lizards, a talking bird,*
some fish. A little rat.

So after I drive
to Jimi and Tony's
in the Village and they

35 meet me at the door and say,
We can't go through with it,
we can't give up our dog,
I drive to the shelter
—just to look—and there

40 is Beau: bounding and
practically boundless,
one brass concatenation
of tongue and tail,
unmediated energy,

45 too big, wild,

perfect. He not only
licks Wally's face
but bathes every
irreplaceable inch

50 of his head, and though
Wally can no longer
feed himself he can lift
his hand, and bring it
to rest on the rough gilt

55 flanks when they are,
for a moment, still.
I have never seen a touch
so deliberate.
It isn't about grasping;

60 the hand itself seems
almost blurred now,
softened, though
tentative only

because so much will

65 must be summoned,
such attention brought
to the work—which is all
he is now, this gesture
toward the restless splendor,

70 the unruly, the golden,
the animal, the new. ❖

MIRRORS & WINDOWS

Recall a time when you found great comfort or contentedness in something very simple. Why do you think it's important to appreciate the "simple things" in life? What are some aspects of modern society that can detract from the "simple things"? How can people find a balance?

Refer and Reason

1. About his poetic inspiration, Mark Doty says, "I wait to be haunted, as it were, by an image.... It's not enough to describe it: The image is the vehicle for something I'm trying to understand." Identify the compelling image of Wally that may have inspired this poem. What do you think Mark Doty is trying to understand?
2. Evaluate Wally's desire to form a new attachment even though he is dying. Explain your answer.
3. Compare and contrast the attitudes of Wally and the speaker toward dying. How do their attitudes compare with your own?

Writing Options

1. Imagine the speaker of "New Dog" is looking for advice on whether it's a good idea to get a new pet for Wally. Write an advice column about the benefits and drawbacks of Wally having another dog.
2. Imagine that you run a hospice organization (an organization that cares for people who are dying). Use the Internet to research the stages of dying as described by Elisabeth Kübler-Ross. Then create an outline of the presentation you will give to your employees.

Go to **www.mirrorsandwindows.com** for more.

Jack Finney (1911–1995) is best known as the author of *The Body Snatchers* (1955), the novel that became the basis for the 1956 film *Invasion of the Body Snatchers* and its 1978 remake. While working for an advertising agency in New York City, Finney began writing fiction. In **"Contents of the Dead Man's Pocket,"** New York advertising employee Tom Benecke risks his life to retrieve a sheet of paper that he believes is his key to happiness.

Think about a time when you experienced a flash of understanding about yourself or something else. What did you suddenly realize?

Contents of the Dead Man's Pocket

A Short Story by **Jack Finney**

> His teeth were exposed in a frozen grimace, the strength draining like water from his knees and calves.

At the little living-room desk Tom Benecke rolled two sheets of flimsy and a heavier top sheet, carbon paper sandwiched between them, into his portable.[1] *Inter-office Memo,* the top sheet was headed, and he typed tomorrow's date just below this; then he glanced at a creased yellow sheet, covered with his own handwriting, beside the typewriter. "Hot in here," he muttered to himself. Then, from the short hallway at his back, he heard the muffled clang of wire coat hangers in the bedroom closet, and at this reminder of what his wife was doing he thought: Hot, hell—guilty conscience.

He got up, shoving his hands into the back pockets of his gray wash slacks, stepped to the living-room window beside the desk and stood breathing on the glass, watching the expanding circlet of mist, staring down through the autumn night at Lexington Avenue, eleven stories below. He was a tall, lean, dark-haired young man in a pullover sweater, who looked as though he had played not football, probably, but basketball in college. Now he placed the heels of his hands against the top edge of the lower window frame and shoved upward. But as usual the window didn't

1. **portable.** Before the use of personal computers, small portable typewriters were popular. They can be compared to the laptops of today.

Aerial View of Times Square, c. 1990s. Franklin McMahon.

budge, and he had to lower his hands and then shoot them hard upward to jolt the window open a few inches. He dusted his hands, muttering.

But still he didn't begin his work. He crossed the room to the hallway entrance and, leaning against the doorjamb, hands shoved into his back pockets again, he called, "Clare?" When his wife answered, he said, "Sure you don't mind going alone?"

"No." Her voice was muffled, and he knew her head and shoulders were in the bedroom closet. Then the tap of her high heels sounded on the wood floor and she appeared at the end of the little hallway, wearing a slip, both hands raised to one ear, clipping on an earring. She smiled at him—a slender, very pretty girl with light brown, almost blonde, hair—her prettiness emphasized by the pleasant nature that showed in her face. "It's just that I hate you to miss this movie; you wanted to see it too."

"Yeah, I know." He ran his fingers through his hair. "Got to get this done though."

She nodded, accepting this. Then, glancing at the desk across the living room, she said, "You work too much, though, Tom—and too hard."

He smiled. "You won't mind though, will you, when the money comes rolling in and I'm known as the Boy Wizard of Wholesale Groceries?"

"I guess not." She smiled and turned back toward the bedroom.

At his desk again, Tom lighted a cigarette; then a few moments later as Clare appeared, dressed and ready to leave, he set it on the rim of the ash tray. "Just after seven," she said. "I can make the beginning of the first feature."

He walked to the front-door closet to help her on with her coat. He kissed her then and, for an instant, holding her close, smelling the perfume she had used, he was tempted to go with her; it was not actually true that he had to work tonight, though he very much wanted to. This was his own project, unannounced as yet in his office, and it could be postponed. But then they won't see it till Monday, he thought once again, and if I give it to the boss tomorrow he might read it over the weekend… "Have a good time," he said aloud. He gave his wife a little swat and opened the door for her, feeling the air from the building hallway, smelling faintly of floor wax, stream gently past his face.

He watched her walk down the hall, flicked a hand in response as she waved, and then he started to close the door, but it resisted for a moment. As the door opening narrowed, the current of warm air from the hallway, channeled through this smaller opening now, suddenly rushed past him with accelerated force. Behind him he

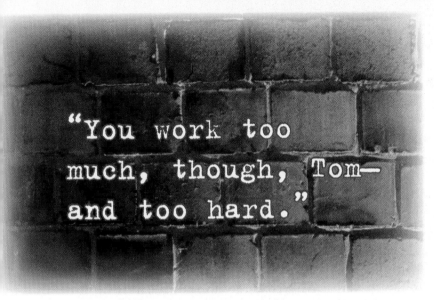

> "You work too much, though, Tom— and too hard."

heard the slap of the window curtains against the wall and the sound of paper fluttering from his desk, and he had to push to close the door.

Turning, he saw a sheet of white paper drifting to the floor in a series of arcs, and another sheet, yellow, moving toward the window, caught in the dying current flowing through the narrow opening. As he watched, the paper struck the bottom edge of the window and hung there for an instant, plastered against the glass and wood. Then as the moving air stilled completely the curtains swinging back from the wall to hang free again, he saw the yellow sheet drop to the window ledge and slide over out of sight.

He ran across the room, grasped the bottom edge of the window and tugged, staring through the glass. He saw the yellow sheet, dimly now in the darkness outside, lying on the ornamental ledge a yard below the window. Even as he watched, it was moving, scraping slowly along the ledge, pushed by the breeze that pressed steadily against the building wall. He heaved on the window with all his strength and it shot open with a bang, the window weight rattling in the casing. But the paper was past his reach and, leaning out into the night, he watched it scud steadily along the ledge to the south, half plastered against the building wall. Above the muffled sound of the street

traffic far below, he could hear the dry scrape of its movement, like a leaf on the pavement.

The living room of the next apartment to the south projected a yard or more farther out toward the street than this one; because of this the Beneckes paid seven and a half dollars less rent than their neighbors. And now the yellow sheet, sliding along the stone ledge, nearly invisible in the night, was stopped by the projecting blank wall of the next apartment. It lay motionless, then, in the corner formed by the two walls—a good five yards away, pressed firmly against the ornate corner ornament of the ledge, by the breeze that moved past Tom Benecke's face.

He knelt at the window and stared at the yellow paper for a full minute or more, waiting for it to move, to slide off the ledge and fall, hoping he could follow its course to the street, and then hurry down in the elevator and retrieve it. But it didn't move, and then he saw that the paper was caught firmly between a projection of the convoluted corner ornament and the ledge. He thought about the poker from the fireplace, then the broom, then the mop—discarding each thought as it occurred to him. There was nothing in the apartment long enough to reach that paper.

It was hard for him to understand that he actually had to abandon it—it was ridiculous— and he began to curse. Of all the papers on his desk, why did it have to be this one in particular! On four long Saturday afternoons he had stood in supermarkets counting the people who passed certain displays, and the results were scribbled on that yellow sheet. From stacks of trade publications,[2] gone over page by page in snatched half hours at work and

---

2. **trade publications.** Magazines or similar works published for and read by members of a particular trade group, such as advertisers

during evenings at home, he had copied facts, quotations and figures onto that sheet. And he had carried it with him to the Public Library on Fifth Avenue, where he'd spent a dozen lunch hours and early evenings adding more. All were needed to support and lend authority to his idea for a new grocery-store display method; without them his idea was a mere opinion. And there they all lay, in his own improvised shorthand—countless hours of work—out there on the ledge.

For many seconds he believed he was going to abandon the yellow sheet, that there was nothing else to do. The work could be duplicated. But it would take two months, and the time to present this idea, damn it, was *now*, for use in the spring displays. He struck his fist on the window ledge. Then he shrugged. Even though his plan were adopted, he told himself, it wouldn't bring him a raise in pay—not immediately, anyway, or as a direct result. It won't bring me a promotion either, he argued—not of itself.

But just the same, and he couldn't escape the thought, this and other independent projects, some already done and others planned for the future, would gradually mark him out from the score of other young men in his company. They were the way to change from a name on the payroll to a name in the minds of the company officials. They were the beginning of the long, long climb to where he was determined to be, at the very top. And he knew he was going out there in the darkness, after the yellow sheet fifteen feet beyond his reach.

By a kind of instinct, he instantly began making his intention acceptable to himself by laughing at it. The mental picture of himself sidling along the ledge outside was absurd—it was actually comical—and he smiled. He imagined himself describing it; it would make a good story at the office and, it occurred to him, would add a special interest and importance to his memorandum, which would do it no harm at all.

To simply go out and get his paper was an easy task—he could be back here with it in less than two minutes—and he knew he wasn't deceiving himself. The ledge, he saw, measuring it with his eye, was about as wide as the length of his shoe, and perfectly flat. And every fifth row of brick in the face of the building, he remembered—leaning out, he verified this—was indented half an inch, enough for the tips of his fingers, enough to maintain balance easily. It occurred to him that if this ledge and wall were only a yard aboveground—as he knelt at the window staring out, this thought was the final confirmation of his intention—he could move along the ledge indefinitely.

On a sudden impulse, he got to his feet, walked to the

front closet and took out an old tweed jacket, it would be cold outside. He put it on and buttoned it as he crossed the room rapidly toward the open window. In the back of his mind he knew he'd better hurry and get this over with before he thought too much, and at the window he didn't allow himself to hesitate.

He swung a leg over the sill, then felt for and found the ledge a yard below the window with his foot. Gripping the bottom of the window frame very tightly and carefully, he slowly ducked his head under it, feeling on his face the sudden change from the warm air of the room to the chill outside. With infinite care he brought out his other leg, his mind concentrating on what he was doing. Then he slowly stood erect. Most of the putty, dried out and brittle, had dropped off the bottom edging of the window frame, he found, and the flat wooden edging provided a good gripping surface, a half inch or more deep, for the tips of his fingers.

Now, balanced easily and firmly, he stood on the ledge outside in the slight, chill breeze, eleven stories above the street, staring into his own lighted apartment, odd and different-seeming now.

First his right hand, then his left, he carefully shifted his finger-tip grip from the puttyless window edging to an indented row of bricks directly to his right. It was hard to take the first shuffling sideways step then—to make himself move—and the fear stirred in his stomach, but he did it, again by not allowing himself time to think. And now—with his chest, stomach, and the left side of his face pressed against the rough cold brick—his lighted apartment was suddenly gone, and it was much darker out here than he had thought.

Without pause he continued—right foot, left foot, right foot, left—his shoe soles shuffling and scraping along the rough stone, never lifting from it, fingers sliding along the exposed edging of brick. He moved on the balls of his feet, heels lifted slightly; the ledge was not quite as wide as he'd expected. But leaning slightly inward toward the face of the building and pressed against it, he could feel his balance firm and secure, and moving along the ledge was quite as easy as he had thought it would be. He could hear the buttons of his jacket scraping steadily along the rough bricks and feel them catch momentarily, tugging a little, at each mortared crack. He simply did not permit himself to look down, though the compulsion to do so never left him; nor did he allow himself actually to think. Mechanically—right foot, left foot, over and again—he shuffled along crabwise, watching the projecting wall ahead loom steadily closer....

Then he reached it and, at the corner—he'd decided how he was going to pick up the paper—he lifted his right foot and placed it carefully on the ledge that ran along the projecting wall at a right angle to the ledge on which his other foot rested. And now, facing the building, he stood in the corner formed by the two walls, one foot on the ledging of each, a hand on the shoulder-high indentation of each wall. His forehead was pressed directly into the corner against the cold bricks, and now he carefully lowered first one hand, then the other, perhaps a foot farther down, to the next indentation in the row of bricks.

He simply did not permit himself to look down...

Very slowly, sliding his forehead down the trough of the brick corner and bending his knees, he lowered his body toward the paper lying between his outstretched feet. Again he lowered his fingerholds another foot and bent his knees still more, thigh muscles taut, his forehead sliding and bumping down the brick V. Half squatting now, he dropped his left hand to the next indentation and then slowly reached with his right hand toward the paper between his feet.

He couldn't quite touch it, and his knees now were pressed against the wall; he could bend them no farther. But by ducking his head another inch lower, the top of his head now pressed against the bricks, he lowered his right shoulder and his fingers had the paper by a corner, pulling it loose. At the same instant he saw, between his legs and far below, Lexington Avenue stretched out for miles ahead.

He saw, in that instant, the Loew's theater sign, blocks ahead past Fiftieth Street; the miles of traffic signals, all green now; the lights of cars and street lamps; countless neon signs; and the moving black dots of people. And a violent instantaneous explosion of absolute terror roared through him. For a motionless instant he saw himself externally—bent practically double, balanced on this narrow ledge, nearly half his body projecting out above the street far below—and he began to tremble violently, panic flaring through his mind and muscles, and he felt the blood rush from the surface of his skin.

In the fractional moment before horror paralyzed him, as he stared between his legs at that terrible length of street far beneath him, a fragment of his mind raised his body in a spasmodic jerk to an upright position again, but so violently that his head scraped hard against the wall, bouncing off it, and his body swayed outward to the knife edge of balance, and he very nearly plunged backward and fell. Then he was leaning far into the corner again, squeezing and pushing into it, not only his face but his chest and stomach, his back arching; and his fingertips clung with all the pressure of his pulling arms to the shoulder-high half-inch indentation in the bricks.

He was more than trembling now; his whole body was racked with a violent shuddering beyond control, his eyes squeezed so tightly shut it was painful, though he was past awareness of that. His teeth were exposed in a frozen grimace, the strength draining like water from his knees and calves. It was extremely likely, he knew, that he would faint, to slump down along the wall, his face scraping, and then drop backward, a limp weight, out into nothing. And to save his life he concentrated on holding onto consciousness, drawing deliberate deep breaths of cold air into his lungs, fighting to keep his senses aware.

Then he knew that he would not faint, but he could not stop shaking nor open his eyes. He stood where he was, breathing deeply, trying to hold back the terror of the glimpse he had of what lay below him; and he knew he had made a mistake in not making himself stare down at the street, getting used to it and accepting it, when he had first stepped out onto the ledge.

It was impossible to walk back. He simply could not do it. He couldn't bring himself to make the slightest movement. The strength was gone from his legs; his shivering hands— numb, cold and desperately rigid—had lost all deftness; his easy ability to move and balance

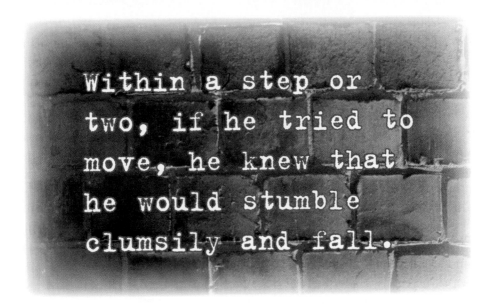

Within a step or two, if he tried to move, he knew that he would stumble clumsily and fall.

was gone. Within a step or two, if he tried to move, he knew that he would stumble clumsily and fall.

Seconds passed, with the chill faint wind pressing the side of his face, and he could hear the toned-down volume of the street traffic far beneath him. Again and again he slowed and then stopped, almost to silence; then presently, even this high, he would hear the click of the traffic signals and the subdued roar of the cars starting up again. During a lull in the street sounds, he called out. Then he was shouting *"Help!"* so loudly it rasped his throat. But he felt the steady pressure of the wind, moving between his face and the blank wall, snatch up his cries as he uttered them, and he knew they must sound directionless and distant. And he remembered how habitually, here in New York, he himself heard and ignored shouts in the night. If anyone heard him, there was no sign of it, and presently Tom Benecke knew he had to try moving; there was nothing else he could do.

Eyes squeezed shut, he watched scenes in his mind like scraps of motion-picture film—he could not stop them. He saw himself stumbling suddenly sideways as he crept along the ledge and saw his upper body arc outward, arms flailing. He saw a dangling shoestring caught between the ledge and the sole of his other shoe, saw a foot start to move, to be stopped with a jerk, and felt his balance leaving him. He saw himself falling with a terrible speed as his body revolved in the air, knees clutched tight to his chest, eyes squeezed shut, moaning softly.

Out of utter necessity, knowing that any of these thoughts might be reality in the very next seconds, he was slowly able to shut his mind against every thought but what he now began to do. With fear-soaked slowness, he slid his left foot an inch or two toward his own impossibly distant window. Then he slid the fingers of his shivering left hand a corresponding distance. For a moment he could not bring himself to lift his right foot from one ledge to the other; then he did it, and became aware of the harsh exhalation of air from his throat and realized that he was panting. As his right hand, then, began to slide along the brick edging, he was astonished to feel the yellow paper pressed to the bricks underneath his stiff fingers, and he uttered a terrible, abrupt bark that might have been a laugh or a moan. He opened his mouth and took the paper in his teeth, pulling it out from under his fingers.

By a kind of trick—by concentrating his entire mind on first his left foot, then his left hand, then the other foot, then the other hand—he was able to move, almost imperceptibly, trembling steadily, very nearly without thought. But he could feel the terrible strength of the pent-up[3] horror on just the other side of the flimsy barrier he had erected in his mind; and he knew that if it broke through he would lose this thin artificial control of his body.

During one slow step he tried keeping his eyes closed; it made him feel safer, shutting him off a little from the fearful reality of where he was. Then a sudden rush of giddiness swept over him and he had to open his eyes wide, staring sideways at the cold rough brick and angled lines of mortar, his cheek tight against the building. He kept his eyes open then, knowing that if he once let them flick outward, to stare for an instant at the lighted windows across the street, he would be past help.

He didn't know how many dozens of tiny sidling steps he had taken, his chest, belly and face pressed to the wall; but he knew the slender hold he was keeping on his mind and body was going to break. He had a sudden mental picture of his apartment on just the other side of this wall—warm, cheerful, incredibly spacious. And he saw himself striding through it, lying down on the floor on his back, arms spread wide, reveling in its unbelievable security. The impossible remoteness of this utter safety, the contrast between it and where he now stood, was more than he could bear. And the barrier broke then, and the fear of the awful height he stood on coursed through his nerves and muscles.

A fraction of his mind knew he was going to fall, and he began taking rapid blind steps with no feeling of what he was doing, sidling with a clumsy desperate swiftness, fingers scrabbling along the brick, almost hopelessly resigned to the sudden backward pull and swift

A fraction of his mind knew he was going to fall...

motion outward and down. Then his moving left hand slid onto not brick but sheer emptiness, an impossible gap in the face of the wall, and he stumbled.

His right foot smashed into his left anklebone; he staggered sideways, began falling, and the claw of his hand cracked against glass and wood, slid down it, and his finger tips were pressed hard on the puttyless edging of his window. His right hand smacked gropingly beside it as he fell to his knees; and, under the full weight and direct downward pull of his sagging body, the open window dropped shudderingly in its frame till it closed and his wrists struck the sill and were jarred off.

For a single moment he knelt, knee bones against stone on the very edge of the ledge, body swaying and touching nowhere else, fighting for balance. Then he lost it, his shoulders plunging backward, and he flung his arms forward, his hands smashing against the window casing on either side; and—his body moving backward—his fingers clutched the narrow wood stripping of the upper pane.

For an instant he hung suspended between balance and falling, his finger tips pressed onto the quarter-inch wood strips. Then, with utmost delicacy, with a focused concentration of all his senses, he increased even further the strain on his finger tips hooked to these slim edgings of wood. Elbows slowly bending, he began to draw the full weight of his upper body forward, knowing that the instant his fingers slipped off these quarter-inch strips he'd plunge backward and be falling. Elbows imperceptibly bending, body shaking with the

---

3. **pent-up.** Kept inside; not expressed

strain, the sweat starting from his forehead in great sudden drops, he pulled, his entire being and thought concentrated in his finger tips. Then suddenly, the strain slackened and ended, his chest touching the window sill, and he was kneeling on the ledge, his forehead pressed to the glass of the closed window.

Dropping his palms to the sill, he stared into his living room—at the red-brown davenport across the room, and a magazine he had left there; at the pictures on the walls and the gray rug; the entrance to the hallway; and at his papers, typewriter and desk, not two feet from his nose. A movement from his desk caught his eye and he saw that it was a thin curl of blue smoke; his cigarette, the ash long, was still burning in the ash tray where he'd left it—this was past all belief—only a few minutes before.

His head moved, and in faint reflection from the glass before him he saw the yellow paper clenched in his front teeth. Lifting a hand from the sill he took it from his mouth; the moistened corner parted from the paper, and he spat it out.

For a moment, in the light from the living room, he stared wonderingly at the yellow sheet in his hand and then crushed it into the side pocket of his jacket.

He couldn't open the window. It had been pulled not completely closed, but its lower edge was below the level of the outside sill; there was no room to get his fingers underneath it. Between the upper sash and the lower was a gap not wide enough—

reaching up, he tried—to get his fingers into; he couldn't push it open. The upper window panel, he knew from long experience, was impossible to move, frozen tight with dried paint.

Very carefully observing his balance, the finger tips of his left hand again hooked to the narrow stripping of the window casing, he drew back his right hand, palm facing the glass, and then struck the glass with the heel of his hand.

His arm rebounded from the pane, his body tottering, and he knew he didn't dare strike a harder blow.

But in the security and relief of his new position, he simply smiled; with only a sheet of glass between him and the room just before him, it was not possible that there wasn't a way past it. Eyes narrowing, he thought for a few moments about what to do. Then his eyes widened, for nothing occurred to him. But still he felt calm: the trembling, he realized, had stopped. At the back of his mind there still lay the thought that once he was again in his home, he could give release to his feelings. He actually *would* lie on the floor, rolling, clenching tufts of the rug in his hands. He would literally run across the room, free to move as he liked, jumping on the floor, testing and reveling in its absolute security, letting the relief flood through him, draining the fear from his mind and body. His yearning for this was astonishingly intense, and somehow he understood that he had better keep this feeling at bay.

He took a half dollar from his pocket and struck it against the pane, but without any hope that the glass would break and with very little disappointment when it did not. After a few moments of thought he drew his leg up onto the ledge and picked loose the knot of his shoelace. He slipped off the shoe and, holding it across the instep, drew back his arm as far as he dared and struck the leather heel against the glass. The pane rattled, but he knew he'd been a long way from breaking it. His foot was cold and he slipped the shoe back on. He shouted again, experimentally, and then once more, but there was no answer.

The realization suddenly struck him that he might have to wait here till Clare came home, and for a moment the thought was funny. He could see Clare opening the front door, withdrawing her key from the lock, closing the door behind her and then glancing up to see him crouched on the other side of the window. He could see her rush across the room, face astounded and frightened, and hear himself shouting instructions: "Never mind how I got here! Just open the wind—" She couldn't open it, he remembered, she'd never been able to; she'd always had to call him. She'd have to get the building superintendent or a neighbor, and he pictured himself smiling and answering their questions as he climbed in. "I just wanted to get a breath of fresh air, so—"

He couldn't possibly wait here till Clare came home. It was the second feature she'd wanted to see, and she'd left in time to see the first. She'd be another three hours or—He glanced at his watch; Clare had been gone eight minutes. It wasn't possible, but only eight minutes ago he had kissed his wife good-by. She wasn't even at the theater yet!

It would be four hours before she could possibly be home, and he tried to picture himself kneeling out here, finger tips hooked to these narrow strippings, while first one movie, preceded by a slow listing of credits, began, developed, reached its climax and then finally ended. There'd be a newsreel[4] next, maybe, and then an animated cartoon, and then interminable scenes from coming pictures. And then, once more, the beginning of a full-length picture—while all the time he hung out here in the night.

He might possibly get to his feet, but he was afraid to try. Already his legs were cramped, his thigh muscles tired; his knees hurt, his feet felt numb and his hands were stiff. He couldn't possibly stay out here for four hours, or anywhere near it. Long before that his legs and arms would give out; he would be forced to try changing his position often—stiffly, clumsily, his co-ordination and strength gone—and he would fall. Quite realistically, he knew that he would fall; no one could stay out here on this ledge for four hours.

A dozen windows in the apartment building across the street were lighted. Looking over his shoulder, he could see the top of a man's head behind the newspaper he was reading; in another window he saw the blue-gray flicker of a television screen. No more than twenty-odd yards from his back were scores of people, and if just one of them would walk idly to his window and glance out…. For some moments he stared over his shoulder at the lighted rectangles, waiting. But no one appeared. The man reading his paper turned a page and then continued his reading. A figure passed another of the windows and was immediately gone.

In the inside pocket of his jacket he found a little sheaf of papers, and he pulled one out

---

4. **newsreel.** Short film covering the news of the day, often shown in movie theaters before the feature film. Newsreels were popular from the 1920s to the late 1940s.

and looked at it in the light from the living room. It was an old letter, an advertisement of some sort; his name and address, in purple ink, were on a label pasted to the envelope. Gripping one end of the envelope in his teeth, he twisted it into a tight curl. From his shirt pocket he brought out a book of matches. He didn't dare let go the casing with both hands but, with the twist of paper in his teeth, he opened the matchbook with his free hand; then he bent one of the matches in two without tearing it from the folder, its red-tipped end now touching the striking surface. With his thumb, he rubbed the red tip across the striking area.

He did it again, then again, and still again, pressing harder each time, and the match suddenly flared, burning his thumb. But he kept it alight, cupping the matchbook in his hand and shielding it with his body. He held the flame to the paper in his mouth till it caught. Then he snuffed out the match flame with his thumb and forefinger, careless of the burn, and replaced the book in his pocket. Taking the paper twist in his hand, he held it flame down, watching the flame crawl up the paper, till it flared bright. Then he held it behind him over the street, moving it from side to side, watching it over his shoulder, the flame flickering and guttering in the wind.

There were three letters in his pocket and he lighted each of them, holding each till the flame touched his hand and then dropping it to the street below. At one point, watching over his shoulder while the last of the letters burned, he saw the man across the street put down his paper and stand—even seeming, to Tom, to glance toward his window. But when he moved, it was only to walk across the room and disappear from sight.

There were a dozen coins in Tom Benecke's pocket and he dropped them, three or four at a time. But if they struck anyone, or if anyone noticed their falling, no one connected them with their source, and no one glanced upward.

His arms had begun to tremble from the steady strain of clinging to this narrow perch, and he did not know what to do now and was terribly frightened. Clinging to the window stripping with one hand, he again searched his pockets. But now—he had left his wallet on his dresser when he'd changed clothes—there was nothing left but the yellow sheet. It occurred to him irrelevantly that his death on the sidewalk below would be an eternal mystery; the window closed—why, how, and from where could he have fallen? No one would be able to identify his body for a time, either—the thought was somehow unbearable and increased his fear. All they'd find in his pockets would be the yellow sheet. *Contents of the dead man's pockets,* he thought, *one sheet of paper bearing penciled notations—incomprehensible.*

He understood fully that he might actually be going to die; his arms, maintaining his balance on the ledge, were trembling steadily now. And it occurred to him then with all the force of a revelation that, if he fell, all he was ever going to have out of life he would then, abruptly, have had. Nothing, then, could ever be changed; and nothing more—no least experience or pleasure—could ever be added to his life. He wished, then, that he had not allowed his wife to go off by herself tonight—and on similar nights. He thought of all the evenings he had spent away from her, working; and he regretted them. He thought wonderingly of his fierce ambition and of the direction his life had taken; he thought of the hours he'd spent by himself, filling the yellow sheet that had brought him out here. *Contents*

All they'd find in his pockets would be the yellow sheet...

of the dead man's pockets, he thought with sudden fierce anger, *a wasted life.*

He was simply not going to cling here till he slipped and fell; he told himself that now. There was one last thing he could try; he had been aware of it for some moments, refusing to think about it, but now he faced it. Kneeling here on the ledge, the finger tips of one hand pressed to the narrow strip of wood, he could, he knew, draw his other hand back a yard perhaps, fist clenched tight, doing it very slowly till he sensed the outer limit of balance, then, as hard as he was able from the distance, he could drive his fist forward against the glass. If it broke, his fist smashing through, he was safe; he might cut himself badly, and probably would, but with his arm inside the room, he would be secure. But if the glass did not break, the rebound, flinging his arm back, would topple him off the ledge. He was certain of that.

He tested his plan. The fingers of his left hand clawlike on the little stripping, he drew back his other fist until his body began teetering backward. But he had no leverage now—he could feel that there would be no force to his swing—and he moved his fist slowly forward till he rocked forward on his knees again and could sense that his swing would carry its greatest force. Glancing down, however, measuring the distance from his fist to the glass, he saw that it was less than two feet.

It occurred to him that he could raise his arm over his head, to bring it down against the glass. But, experimenting in slow motion, he knew it would be an awkward girl-like blow without the force of a driving punch, and not nearly enough to break the glass.

Facing the window, he had to drive a blow from the shoulder, he knew now, at a distance of less than two feet; and he did not know whether it would break through the heavy glass. It might; he could picture it happening, he could feel it in the nerves of his arm. And it might not; he could feel that too—feel his fist striking this glass and being instantaneously flung back by the unbreaking pane, feel the fingers of his other hand breaking loose, nails scraping along the casing as he fell.

He waited, arm drawn back, fist balled, but in no hurry to strike; this pause, he knew, might be an extension of his life. And to live even a few seconds longer, he felt, even out here on this ledge in the night, was infinitely better than to die a moment earlier than he had to. His arm grew tired, and he brought it down and rested it.

Then he knew that it was time to make the attempt. He could not kneel here hesitating indefinitely till he lost all courage to act, waiting till he slipped off the ledge. Again he drew back his arm, knowing this time that he would not bring it down till he struck. His elbow protruding over Lexington Avenue far below, the fingers of his other hand pressed down bloodlessly tight against the narrow stripping, he waited, feeling the sick tenseness and terrible excitement building. It grew and swelled toward the moment of action, his nerves tautening. He thought of Clare—just a wordless, yearning thought—and then drew his arm back just a bit more, fist so tight his fingers pained him, and knowing he was going to do it. Then with full power, with every last scrap of strength he could bring to bear, he shot his arm forward toward the glass, and he said, *"Clare!"*

> He heard the sound, felt the blow, felt himself falling forward...

He heard the sound, felt the blow, felt himself falling forward, and his hand closed on the living-room curtains, the shards and fragments of glass showering onto the floor. And then, kneeling there on the ledge, an arm thrust into the room up to the shoulder, he began picking away the protruding slivers and great wedges of glass from the window frame, tossing them in onto the rug. And, as he grasped the edges of the empty window frame and climbed into his home, he was grinning in triumph.

He did not lie down on the floor or run through the apartment, as he had promised himself; even in the first few moments it seemed to him natural and normal that he should be where he was. He simply turned to his desk, pulled the crumpled yellow sheet from his pocket and laid it down where it had been, smoothing it out; then he absently laid a pencil across it to weight it down. He shook his head wonderingly, and turned to walk toward the closet.

There he got out his topcoat and hat and, without waiting to put them on, opened the front door and stepped out, to go find his wife. He turned to pull the door closed and warm air from the hall rushed through the narrow opening again. As he saw the yellow paper, the pencil flying, scooped off the desk and, unimpeded by the glassless window, sail out into the night and out of his life, Tom Benecke burst into laughter and then closed the door behind him. ❖

How do you determine what is important in life? Is there anything important enough to die for? Why or why not?

Informational Text
CONNECTION

As this fact sheet produced by the **American Psychological Association** explains, placing work above all else can be a recipe for disaster. While some degree of stress serves to motivate a person, too much of it may result in problems ranging from strained relationships to high blood pressure. **"Mind/Body Health: Job Stress"** offers information on managing time, setting reasonable standards, and finding other healthy ways to deal with pressures at work.

 HEALTH: JOB STRESS

A fact sheet by the American Psychological Association

Jobs and careers are an important part of our lives. Along with providing a source of income, they help us fulfill our personal aims, build social networks, and serve our professions or communities. They are also a major source of emotional stress.

STRESS AT WORK

Even "dream jobs" have stressful deadlines, performance expectations, and other responsibilities. For some, stress is the motivator that ensures things get done. However, workplace stress can easily overwhelm your life. You may continually worry about a particular project, feel unfairly treated by a supervisor or co-workers, or knowingly accept more than you can handle in hopes of earning a promotion. Putting your job ahead of everything else can also affect your personal relationships, compounding the work-related pressures.

Layoffs, restructuring, or management changes can heighten anxiety about your job security. In fact, a Norwegian study showed that the mere rumor of a factory's closure caused rapid increases in workers' pulse and blood pressure. Research in the United States has found that workplace injuries and accidents tend to increase in organizations that are being downsized.

THE BODY REACTS

Along with its emotional toll, prolonged job-related stress can drastically affect your physical health. Constant preoccupation with job responsibilities often leads to erratic eating habits and not enough exercise, resulting in weight problems, high blood pressure, and elevated cholesterol levels.

Common job stressors such as perceived low rewards, a hostile work environment, and long hours can also accelerate the onset of heart disease, including the likelihood of heart attacks. This is particularly true for blue-collar and manual workers. Studies suggest that because these employees tend to have little control over their work environments, they are more likely to develop cardiovascular disease than those in traditional "white collar" jobs.

Your age is also a factor. A University of Utah

study found that as stressed workers get older, their blood pressure increases above normal levels. Interestingly, many of the study's over-60 workers reported that they did not feel upset or unduly pressured by their jobs, even though their blood pressure levels were significantly higher.

A LOSS OF MENTAL ENERGY

Job stress also frequently causes burnout, a condition marked by emotional exhaustion and negative or cynical attitudes toward others and yourself.

Burnout can lead to depression, which, in turn, has been linked to a variety of other health concerns such as heart disease and stroke, obesity and eating disorders, diabetes, and some forms of cancer. Chronic depression also reduces your immunity to other types of illnesses, and can even contribute to premature death.

WHAT YOU CAN DO

Fortunately, there are many ways to help manage job-related stress. Some programs blend relaxation techniques with nutrition and exercise. Others focus on specific issues such as time management, assertiveness training, and improving social skills.

A qualified psychologist can help you pinpoint the causes of your stress, and develop appropriate coping strategies.

Here are some other tips for dealing with stress on the job:

- **Make the most of workday breaks.** Even 10 minutes of "personal time" will refresh your mental outlook. Take a brief walk, chat with a co-worker about a non-job topic, or simply sit quietly with your eyes closed and breathe.
- **If you feel angry, walk away.** Mentally regroup by counting to 10, then look at the situation again. Walking and other physical activities will also help you work off steam.
- **Set reasonable standards for yourself and others.** Don't expect perfection. Talk to your employer about your job description. Your responsibilities and performance criteria may not accurately reflect what you are doing. Working together to make needed changes will not only benefit your emotional and physical health, but also improve the organization's overall productivity. ❖

The American Psychological Association Practice Directorate gratefully acknowledges the assistance of Sara Weiss, Ph.D., and Nancy Molitor, Ph.D., in developing this fact sheet.

Refer and Reason

1. Recall what happens to the yellow paper as Tom steps out in the hall at the end of the story. How does Tom react? Why does he react this way?
2. Identify specific lines in the story that show Tom's initial attitude toward his work and his marriage. How does Tom's attitude change by the end of the story, and why?
3. How could one justify Tom's decision to go after the paper? Do you consider those justifications to be sound? Explain.

Writing Options

1. Imagine that Tom sends an e-mail to tell you his only copy of an important paper has blown out the window and that he is thinking of going out on the ledge to get it. Write an e-mail message giving him advice.
2. You are a reporter for a Manhattan newspaper who happened to witness Tom's experience out on the ledge. Write a newspaper article describing the events. Be sure to answer the questions *who, what, when, where, why,* and *how,* as well as to include quotations from bystanders and from Tom himself.

 Go to **www.mirrorsandwindows.com** for more.

TEXT ←TO→ TEXT CONNECTION

After reading this article, what evidence from "Contents of the Dead Man's Pocket" makes clear that Tom Benecke is suffering from job stress? How does the story's ending suggest that he has recognized his problem? What changes do you think he might make in his life as a result of this experience?

from In a Sunburned Country

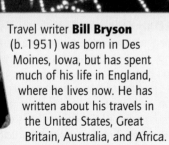

Travel writer **Bill Bryson** (b. 1951) was born in Des Moines, Iowa, but has spent much of his life in England, where he lives now. He has written about his travels in the United States, Great Britain, Australia, and Africa. Although known for the humor in his works, Bryson says he's learned that books "don't have to be funny in every line."

In a Sunburned Country covers his experience in Australia, which Bryson says is a "contrast between the wildly exotic, things you can't see anywhere else...and at the same time all the infrastructure is familiar and well-known.... It's like going to another planet without giving up the comfortable bed."

Describe a time you found yourself in an embarrassing situation.

Travel Writing by **Bill Bryson**

NATURALLY THEY PLAY DOWN THE FACT THAT EVERY TIME YOU SET YOUR FEET ON THE FLOOR SOMETHING IS LIKELY TO JUMP OUT AND SEIZE AN ANKLE.

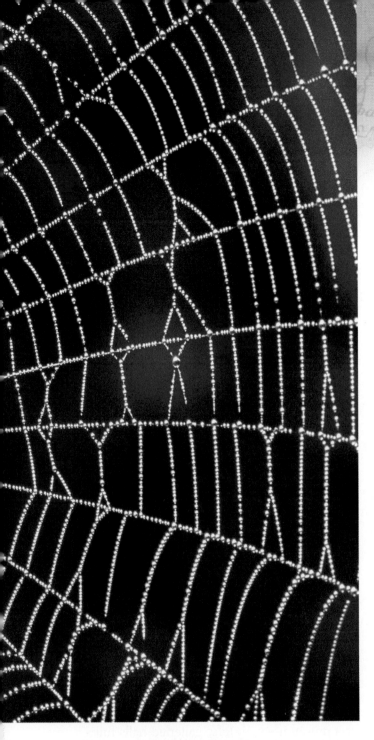

sibly took off in an airplane, and into the shaded hills above, through quiet neighborhoods of cottagey homes buried in flowering jacaranda and fragrant frangipani (and in every front garden cobwebs like trampolines, in the center of each the sort of spider that would make a brave man gasp). At every turn there was a glimpsed view of blue harbor—over a garden wall, at the bottom of a sloping road, suspended between close-set houses like a sheet hung to dry—and it was all the finer for being furtive. Sydney has whole districts filled with palatial houses that seem to consist of nothing but balconies and plate glass, with scarcely a leaf to block the beating sun or interrupt the view. But here on the north shore, wisely and nobly, they have sacrificed large-scale vistas for the cool shade of trees, and every resident will, I guarantee, go to heaven.

I walked for miles, through Kirribilli, Neutral Bay, and Cremorne Point, and on through the prosperous precincts of Mosman before at last I came to Balmoral with a sheltered beach overlooking Middle Harbour and a splendid waterfront park shaded with stout Moreton Bay figs, the loveliest tree in Australia by far. A sign by the water's edge noted that if you were eaten by sharks it wasn't because you hadn't been warned. Apparently shark attacks are much more likely inside the harbor than out. I don't know why. I had also read in Jan Morris's engaging and cheery book *Sydney* that the harbor teems with lethal goblin fish. What is notable about this is that in all my reading I never came across a single other reference to these rapacious creatures. This isn't to suggest, I hastily add, that Ms. Morris was being inventive; merely that it isn't possible in a single lifetime to read about all the dangers that lurk under every wattle bush or ripple of water in this wondrously venomous and toothy country.

These thoughts took on a certain relevance some hours later in the dry heat of afternoon,

After such a long spell in an airplane I was eager to stretch my shapely limbs, so I crossed the bridge to Kirribilli[1] and plunged into the old, cozily settled neighborhoods of the north shore. And what a wonderful area it is. I wandered past the little cove where my hero, the aviator Charles Kingsford Smith (about whom much more anon), once impos-

1. **Kirribilli.** Suburb of Sydney

Australia

- ——— International Border
- ——— State Border
- ◉ National Capital
- • State or Territory Capital
- • Secondary City
- ——— Railroad
- ——— Primary Road

| 0 | 200 | 400 mi |
| 0 | 200 | 400 | 600 km |

when I returned to the city dog-tired and pasted with sweat, and impulsively popped into the grand and brooding Australian Museum in its setting beside Hyde Park. I went not because it is fabulous, but because I was half crazed from the heat and it looked to be one of those buildings that are dim-lit and gratifyingly cool inside. It was both of those, and fabulous as well. It is a vast and old-fashioned place—I mean that as the most

admiring compliment; I know of no higher for a museum—with lofty galleried halls full of stuffed animals and long cases of carefully mounted insects, chunks of luminous minerals, or Aboriginal[2] artifacts. In a country such as Australia, every room is a wonder.

As you can imagine, I was particularly attracted to all those things that might hurt me,

---

2. **Aboriginal.** Of or related to the native peoples of Australia

which in an Australian context is practically everything. It really is the most extraordinarily lethal country. Naturally they play down the fact that every time you set your feet on the floor something is likely to jump out and seize an ankle. Thus my guidebook blandly observed that "only" fourteen species of Australian snakes are seriously lethal, among them the western brown, desert death adder, tiger snake, taipan, and yellow-bellied sea snake. The taipan is the one to watch out for. It is the most poisonous snake on earth, with a lunge so swift and a venom so potent that your last mortal utterance is likely to be: "I say, is that a sn—."

Even from across the room you could see at once which was the display case containing the stuffed taipan, for it had around it a clutch of small boys held in rapt silence by the frozen gaze of its beady, lazily hateful eyes. You can kill it and stuff it and put it in a case, but you can't take away the menace. According to the label, the taipan carries a venom fifty times more deadly than that of the cobra, its next nearest challenger. Amazingly, just one fatal attack is on record, at Mildura in 1989. But we knew the real story, my attentive little friends and I—that once you leave this building the taipans aren't stuffed and behind glass.

At least the taipan is five feet long and thick as a man's wrist, which gives you a reasonable chance of spotting it. What I found far more appalling was the existence of lethal small snakes, like the little desert death adder. Just eight inches long, it lies lightly buried in soft sand so that you have no hope of seeing it before setting your weary butt on its head. Even more worrying was the Point Darwin sea snake, which is not much larger than an earthworm but packs venom enough if not to kill you at least to make you very late for dinner.

But all of these are as nothing compared with the delicate and diaphanous box jellyfish, the most poisonous creature on earth. We will hear more of the unspeakable horrors of this little bag of lethality when we get to the tropics, but let me offer here just one small story. In 1992 a young man in Cairns, ignoring all the warning signs, went swimming in the Pacific waters at a place called Holloways Beach. He swam and dove, taunting his friends on the beach for their prudent cowardice, and then began to scream with an inhuman sound. It is said that there is no pain to compare with it. The young man staggered from the water, covered in livid whiplike stripes wherever the jellyfish's tentacles had brushed across him, and collapsed in quivering shock. Soon afterward emergency crews arrived, inflated him with morphine, and took him away for treatment. And here's the thing. Even unconscious and sedated he was still screaming.

Sydney has no box jellyfish, I was pleased to learn. The famous local danger is the funnel web spider, the most poisonous insect in the world with a venom that is "highly toxic and fast-acting." A single nip, if not promptly treated, will leave you bouncing around in the grip of seizures of an incomparable liveliness; then you turn blue; then you die. Thirteen deaths are on record, though none since 1981, when an antidote was devised. Also poisonous are white-tailed spiders, mouse spiders, wolf spiders, our old friend the redback ("hundreds of bites are reported each year…about a dozen known deaths"), and a reclusive but fractious type called the fiddleback. I couldn't say for sure whether I had seen any of these in the gardens I had passed earlier in the day, but then I couldn't say I hadn't since they all looked essentially the same. No one knows, incidentally, why Australia's spiders are so

A funnel web spider waits for prey at the center of its web.

extravagantly toxic; capturing small insects and injecting them with enough poison to drop a horse would appear to be the most literal case of overkill. Still, it does mean that everyone gives them lots of space.

I studied with particular alertness the funnel web since this was the creature that I was most likely to encounter in the next few days. It was about an inch and a half long, plump, hairy, and ugly. According to the label, you can identify a funnel web by "the mating organ on the male palp, deeply curved fovea, shiny carapace and lower labium studded with short blunt spines."[3] Alternatively, of course, you can just let it sting you. I carefully copied all this down before it occurred to me that if I were to awake to find any large, furry creature advancing crab-like across the sheets, I was unlikely to note any of its anatomical features, however singular and

telling. So I put away my notebook and went off to look at minerals, which aren't so exciting but do have the compensating virtue that almost never will they attack you.

I spent four days wandering around Sydney. I visited the principal museums with dutiful absorption and spent an afternoon in the admirably welcoming State Library of New South Wales, but mostly I just wandered wherever there was water. Without question, it is the harbor that makes Sydney. It's not so much a harbor as a fjord,[4] sixteen miles long and perfectly proportioned—big enough for gran-

---

3. **the mating...blunt spines.** The funnel web spider has a sexual organ on the segmented, protruding mouth part. The spider can also be identified by curved eye parts; a shiny, shieldlike back; and a lower mouth part with short spines.

4. **fjord.** Narrow inlet of sea between cliffs or steep banks

deur, small enough to have a neighborly air. Wherever you stand, the people on the far shore are almost never so distant as to seem remote; often you could hail them if you wished. Because it runs through the heart of the city from east to west, it divides Sydney into more or less equal halves, known as the northern and eastern suburbs. (And never mind that the eastern suburbs are actually in the south, or that many of the northern suburbs are decidedly eastern. Australians, never forget, started life as Britons.) To note that it is 16 miles long barely hints at its extent. Because it constantly wanders off into arms that finish in the serenest little coves, the most gently scalloped bays, the harbor shoreline actually extends to 152 miles. The consequence of this wandering nature is that one moment you are walking beside a tiny sheltered cove that seems miles from anywhere, and the next you round a headland to find before you an open expanse of water with the Opera House and Harbour Bridge and downtown skyscrapers gleaming in airy sunshine and holding center stage. It is endlessly and unbelievably beguiling.

On my last day I hiked out to Hunter's Hill, a treasured and secretive district about six miles from downtown on a long finger of land overlooking one of the quieter inner reaches of the harbor. I chose it because Jan Morris had made it sound so delightful in her book. I daresay she reached it by water, as any sensible person would. I decided to walk out along Victoria Road, which may not be the ugliest road in Australia but must be the least agreeable to walk along.

I strode for shadeless miles through zones of factories, warehouses, and railway lines, then miles more of marginal commercial districts of discount furnishers, industrial wholesalers, and dingy pubs offering surreally unappealing inducements[5] ("Meat Raffles 6-8 pm"). By the time I reached a small sign pointing down a side road to Hunter's Hill, my expectations were flag-

ging. Imagine then my satisfaction at discovering that Hunter's Hill was worth every steaming step—a lovely, hidden borough of plump stone mansions, pretty cottages, and picturesquely clustered shops of an often impressive venerability. There was a small but splendid town hall dating from 1860 and a chemist's shop[6] that had been in business since 1890, which must be a record in Australia. Every garden was a treasure and somewhere in almost every backdrop lurked a glimpse of harbor view. I could not have been more charmed.

Reluctant to retrace my steps, I decided to push on farther, through Linley Point, Lane Cove, Northwood, Greenwich, and Wollstonecraft, and rejoin the known world at the Harbour Bridge. It was a long way around and the day was sultry, but Sydney is a constantly rewarding place and I was feeling ambitious. I suppose I walked for about an hour before it dawned on me that this was actually *quite* ambitious—I had barely penetrated Linley Point and was still miles from downtown—but then I noticed on the map what appeared to be a worthwhile shortcut through a place called Tennyson Park.

I followed a side road down a residential street and about halfway along came to the entrance to the park. A wooden sign announced that what lay beyond was preserved bushland[7] and politely requested users not to stray from the path. Well, this seemed a splendid notion—an expanse of native bush in the heart of a great city—and I ventured in eagerly. I don't know what image "bush" conjures up in your mind, but this was not the brown and semibarren tract I would have expected, but a wooded glade with a sun-dappled path and tinkling brook. It appeared to be scarcely used—every few yards I would have to duck under or walk around big spider-

---

5. **unappealing inducements.** Things meant to be appealing that are not
6. **chemist's shop.** Australian term for a pharmacy or drugstore
7. **bushland.** Large area of uncleared, unsettled land in Australia

webs strung across the path—which lent the whole enterprise a sense of lucky discovery.

I guessed it would take about twenty minutes to cut through the park—or the reserve, as Australians call these things—and I was probably about halfway along when from an indeterminate distance off to the right there came the bark of a dog, tentative and experimental, as if to say, "Who's that?" It wasn't very close or intimidating, but it was clearly the bark of a big dog. Something in its timbre said: meat eater, black, very big, not too many generations removed from wolf. Almost in the same instant it was joined by the bark of a companion dog, also big, and this bark was decidedly less experimental. This bark said, "Red alert! Trespasser on our territory!" Within a minute they had worked themselves up into a considerable frenzy.

Nervously I quickened my pace. Dogs don't like me. It is a simple law of the universe, like gravity. I am not exaggerating when I say that I have never passed a dog that didn't act as if it thought I was about to take its Alpo. Dogs that have not moved from the sofa in years will, at the sniff of me passing outside, rise in fury and hurl themselves at shut windows. I have seen tiny dogs no bigger than a fluffy slipper, jerk little old ladies off their feet and drag them over open ground in a quest to get at my blood and sinew. Every dog on the face of the earth wants me dead.

And now here I was alone in an empty woods, which suddenly seemed very large and lonely, and two big and angry-sounding dogs had me in their sights. As I pushed on, two things became increasingly apparent: I was definitely the target and these dogs were not messing around. They were coming toward me, at some speed. Now the barking said, "We are going to have you, boy. You are dead meat.

You are small, pulpy pieces." You will note the absence of exclamation marks. Their barks were no longer tinged with lust and frenzy. They were statements of cold intent. "We know where you are," they said. "You cannot make it to the edge of the woods. We will be with you shortly. Somebody call forensic."

Casting worried glances at the foliage, I began to trot and then to run. It was now time to consider what I would do if the dogs burst onto the path. I picked up a rock for defense, then discarded it a few yards farther on for a stick that was lying across the path. The stick was ludicrously outsized—it must have been twelve feet long—and so rotted that it fell in half just from being picked up. As I ran, it lost another half, and another, until finally it was no more than a soft spongy stub—it would have been like defending myself with a loaf of bread—so I threw it down and picked up a big jagged rock in each hand, and quickened my pace yet again. The dogs now seemed to be moving parallel to me, as if they couldn't find a way through, but at a distance of no more than forty or fifty yards. They were furious. My unease expanded, and I began to run a little faster.

In my stumbling haste, I rounded a bend too fast and ran headlong into a giant spider's web. It fell over me like a collapsing parachute. Undulating in dismay, I tore at the cobweb, but with rocks in my hands only succeeded in banging myself in the forehead. In a small, lucid corner of my brain I remember thinking, "This really is very unfair." Somewhere else was the thought: "You are going to be the first person in history to die in the bush in the middle of a city, you poor, sad schlubb." All the rest was icy terror.

And so I trotted along, wretched and whimpering, until I rounded a bend and found, with another small and disbelieving

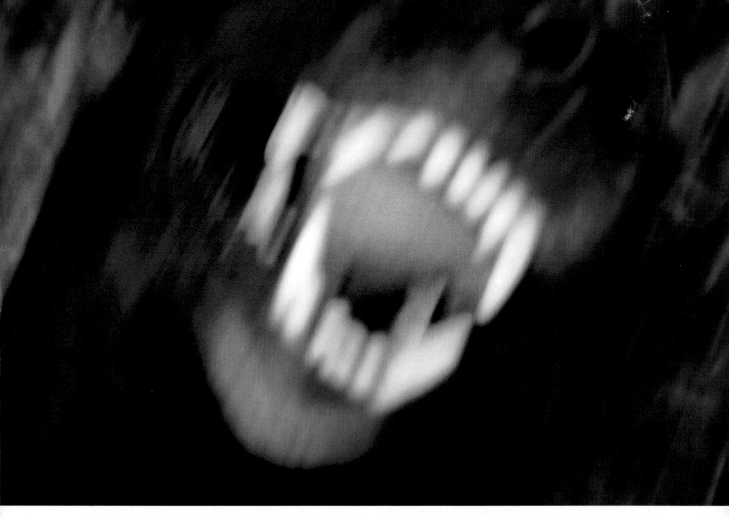

wail, that the path abruptly terminated. Before me stood nothing but impenetrable tangle—a wall of it. I looked around astounded and appalled. In my panic—doubtless while I was scraping the cobwebs from my brow with the aid of lumps of granite—I had evidently taken a wrong turn. In any case, there was no way forward and nothing behind but a narrow path leading back in the direction of two surging streaks of malice. Glancing around in desperation, I saw with unconfined joy, at the top of a twenty-foot rise, a corner of rotary clothesline. There was a home up there! I had reached the edge of the park, albeit from an unconventional direction. No matter. There was a civilized world up there. Safety! I scrambled up the hill as fast as my plump little pins[8] would carry me—the dogs were very close now—snagging myself on thorns, inhaling cobwebs, straining with every molecule of my being not to become

a headline that said, "Police find writer's torso; head still missing."

At the top of the hill stood a brick wall perhaps six feet high. Grunting extravagantly, I hauled myself onto its flat summit and dropped down on the other side. The transformation was immediate, the relief sublime. I was back in the known world, in someone's much-loved backyard. There was a set of old swings that didn't look as if they had been used in some years, flower beds, a lawn leading to a patio. The yard appeared to be fully enclosed by brick wall on three sides and a big comfortable-looking house on the fourth, which I hadn't quite anticipated. I was trespassing, of course, but there wasn't any way I was going back into those woods. Part of the view was obscured by a shed or summerhouse. With

---

8. **little pins.** Legs

luck there would be a gate beyond and I could let myself out and slip back into the world undetected. My most immediate concern was that there might be a big mean dog in here as well. Wouldn't that be richly ironic? With this in mind, I crept cautiously forward.

Now let us change the point of view just for a moment. Forgive me for getting you up, but I need to put you at the window beside the kitchen sink of this tranquil suburban home. You are a pleasant middle-aged homemaker going about your daily business—at this particular moment filling a vase with water to hold some peonies you have just cut from the bed by the drawing room[9] windows—and you see a man drop over your back wall and begin to move in a low crouch across your backyard. Frozen with fear and a peculiar detached fascination, you

are unable to move, but just stand watching as he advances stealthily across the property in a commando posture, with short, frenzied dashes between covering objects, until he is crouched beside a concrete urn at the edge of your patio only about ten feet away. It is then that he notices you staring at him.

"Oh, hello!" says the man cheerfully, straightening up and smiling in a way that he thinks looks sincere and ingratiating, but in fact merely suggests someone who has failed to take his medication. Almost at once your thoughts go to a police mug shot you saw in the evening paper earlier in the week pertaining, if you recall, to a breakout at an institution for the criminally insane at Wollongong. "Sorry to crash in on you like this," the man is saying, "but I was desperate.

---

9. **drawing room.** Reception room; formal living room

Did you hear all the racket? I thought they were going to *kill* me."

He beams foolishly and waits for you to reply, but you say nothing because you are powerless to speak. Your eyes slide over to the open back door. If you both moved for it now, you would arrive together. All kinds of thoughts start to run through your head.

"I didn't actually *see* them," the man goes on in a judicious but oddly pumped-up tone, "but I know they were after me." He looks as if he has been living rough. Smudges of dirt rim his face and one of his pant legs is torn at the knee. "They always go for me," he says, earnest now, and puzzled. "It's as if there's some kind of conspiracy to get me. I can be just walking down the street, you know, minding my own business, and suddenly from out of nowhere they just *come* for me. It's very unsettling." He shakes his head. "Is your gate unlocked?"

You haven't been listening to any of this because your hand has been moving almost imperceptibly toward the drawer containing the steak knives. As the question dawns on you, you find yourself giving a small, tight, almost involuntary nod.

"I'll just let myself out, then. Sorry to have disturbed you." At the gate he pauses. "Take it from me," he says, "you don't *ever* want to go back in those woods alone. Something terrible could happen to you back there. I love your delphiniums by the way." He smiles in a way that freezes your marrow, and says, "Well, bye, then."

And he is gone.

Six weeks later you put the house on the market. ❖

MIRRORS & WINDOWS

What kind of unrealistic expectations do people often have when they travel to a foreign country? What is your attitude toward traveling? If you were to visit a foreign country, what would you expect to do? How would you expect to be treated?

Refer and Reason

1. List the exhibits Bryson sees in the Australian Museum. Which exhibits most interest him? Why?
2. Identify positive and negative comments or details in the narrator's description of Australia. Overall, how do you think the narrator regards Australia? Given his descriptions, would you like to spend time in this place?
3. Some travel writing provides concrete advice for tourists; other travel writing, like the book from which this selection is drawn, describes one traveler's experiences. How effective is this selection as travel writing? as humor? Cite examples from the selection to support your answers.

Writing Options

1. Write a travel column about a place you have visited or even about your hometown or neighborhood. Use sensory details to evoke a sense of the place for a column that will appear in a magazine for young people. Try to convince your audience that the place is worth visiting.
2. Bryson mentions several different types of poisonous creatures native to Australia. Choose one of these creatures to research. Then create an informative fact sheet about the creature and what people should do if they encounter the creature.

 Go to **www.mirrorsandwindows.com** for more.

from Travels with Charley:

In Search of America

Narrative Nonfiction by
John Steinbeck

About fifty yards away two coyotes stood watching me, their tawny coats blending with sand and sun.

John Steinbeck (1902–1968) is best known for novels sympathetic to common people negatively affected by political, social, and environmental forces. His upbringing in Salinas, California, a farming region with a large population of migrant workers, influenced both his belief system and his love for nature.

Travels with Charley (1962), a book-length travel narrative, chronicles Steinbeck's three-month journey by truck across the United States with his poodle, Charley. In this excerpt, Steinbeck tells about his encounter with a pair of coyotes in the Mojave Desert.

What kind of experience have you had with hunting? What do you think of it?

The Mohave is a big desert and a frightening one. It's as though nature tested a man for endurance and constancy to prove whether he was good enough to get to California. The shimmering dry heat made visions of water on the flat plain. And even when you drive at high speed, the hills that mark the boundaries recede before you. Charley, always a dog for water, panted asthmatically, jarring his whole body with the effort, and a good eight inches of his tongue hung out flat as a leaf and dripping. I pulled off the road into a small gulley to give him water from my thirty-gallon tank. But before I let him drink I poured water all over him and on my hair and shoulders and shirt. The air is so dry that evaporation makes you feel suddenly cold.

I opened a can of beer from my refrigerator and sat well inside the shade of Rocinante,[1] looking out at the sunpounded plain, dotted here and there with clumps of sagebrush.

About fifty yards away two coyotes stood watching me, their tawny coats blending with sand and sun. I knew that with any quick or suspicious movement of mine they could drift into invisibility. With the most casual slowness I reached down my new rifle from its sling over my bed—the .222 with its bitter little high-speed, long-range stings. Very slowly I brought the rifle up. Perhaps in the shade of my house I was half hidden by the blinding light outside. The little rifle has a beautiful telescope sight with a wide field. The coyotes had not moved.

I got both of them in the field of my tele-scope, and the glass brought them very close. Their tongues lolled out so that they seemed to smile mockingly. They were favored animals, not starved, but well furred, the golden hair tempered with black guard hairs.[2] Their little lemon-yellow eyes were plainly visible in the glass. I moved the cross hairs to the breast of the right-hand animal, and pushed the safety. My elbows on the table steadied the gun. The cross hairs lay unmoving on the brisket.[3] And then the coyote sat down like a dog and its right rear paw came up to scratch the right shoulder.

My finger was reluctant to touch the trigger. I must be getting very old and my ancient conditioning worn thin. Coyotes are vermin. They steal chickens. They thin the ranks of quail and all other game birds. They must be killed. They are the enemy. My first shot would drop the sitting beast, and the other would whirl to fade away. I might very well pull him down with a running shot because I am a good rifleman.

---

1. **Rocinante (rō sē nän´tä).** Steinbeck's truck, named after the old horse who carried the broken-down knight Don Quixote into battle in *Don Quixote* by Miguel de Cervantes. (See the excerpt from *Don Quixote* in Unit 5.)

2. **guard hairs.** Coarse hairs that form a protective coating over the undercoat of a mammal

3. **brisket.** Lower chest of a four-legged animal

And I did not fire. My training said, "Shoot!" and my age replied, "There isn't a chicken within thirty miles, and if there are any they aren't my chickens. And this waterless place is not quail country. No, these boys are keeping their figures with kangaroo rats and jackrabbits, and that's vermin eat vermin. Why should I interfere?"

"Kill them," my training said. "Everyone kills them. It's a public service." My finger moved to the trigger. The cross was steady on the breast just below the panting tongue. I could imagine the splash and jar of angry steel, the leap and struggle until the torn heart failed, and then, not too long later, the shadow of a buzzard,[4] and another. By that time I would be long gone—out of the desert and across the Colorado River. And beside the sagebrush there would be a naked, eyeless skull, a few picked bones, a spot of black dried blood and a few rags of golden fur.

I guess I'm too old and too lazy to be a good citizen. The second coyote stood side-wise to my rifle. I moved the cross hairs to his shoulder and held steady. There was no ques-

tion of missing with that rifle at that range. I owned both animals. Their lives were mine. I put the safety on and laid the rifle on the table. Without the telescope they were not so intimately close. The hot blast of light tousled the air to shimmering.

Then I remembered something I heard long ago that I hope is true. It was unwritten law in China, so my informant told me, that when one man saved another's life he became responsible for that life to the end of its existence. For, having interfered with a course of events, the savior could not escape his responsibility. And that has always made good sense to me.

Now I had a token[5] responsibility for two live and healthy coyotes. In the delicate world of relationships, we are tied together for all time. I opened two cans of dog food and left them as a votive.[6] ❖

---

4. **buzzard.** A large bird of prey (predatory bird that eats other animals)
5. **token.** Symbolic
6. **votive.** Something offered in fulfillment of a vow or duty, often a candle lit in observance of something

 When have you made a decision that seemed right at the time, but may not have when you were younger? How do you think age and experience affect a person's morals, opinions, and choices?

Refer and Reason

1. List the reasons the narrator gives for and against killing the coyotes. Why does the narrator decide not to kill them?
2. The narrator says the Chinese belief about being forever responsible for a life one saves "has always made good sense to me." Explain whether you agree with the narrator's take on this belief.
3. Reread the narrator's depiction of the hypothetical scene that would have followed the coyotes' death. What may have been the scene following the narrator's leaving of the food? How would you describe the mood of each of these scenes?

Writing Options

1. Imagine you are responsible for turning this excerpt of Steinbeck's narrative into a cartoon for children. In this cartoon, the coyotes are talking characters. Write a dialogue between the coyotes about what they saw and what they were thinking as the narrator made his decision.
2. Think about a trip you have taken, whether across the country or across town. For a new friend you are trying to impress, write a short memoir that focuses on one memorable instance in your trip and its effect on you.

 Go to **www.mirrorsandwindows.com** for more.

Kallmunz, Stormy Atmosphere, 1904. Wassily Kandinsky.

LAND ENOUGH FOR A MAN

A Short Story by **Leo Tolstoy**

Russian writer and philosopher **Leo Tolstoy** (1829–1910), considered to be one of the world's greatest writers, penned close to one hundred volumes of novels, stories, plays, diaries, and essays.

"Land Enough for a Man" was written in 1885 and first appeared in the journal *Russian Wealth* in 1886. This story's theme reflects an attitude about greed, wealth, and worldly possessions that Tolstoy, born to a well-off family, adopted late in life.

What is your attitude toward accumulating worldly possessions? What is the appeal in doing so? What are the drawbacks?

He was afraid of dying, but unable to stop. "I've run so far," he thought. "I'd be a fool to stop now."

– 1 –

An older sister from town came to visit her younger sister in the country. The elder had married a merchant in town; the younger a peasant in the country. Drinking tea, the sisters chatted. The elder began to brag—to boast of her life in town; how spaciously and comfortably she lived, how well she dressed the children, how nicely she ate and drank, and how she went for drives, excursions, and to the theater.

The younger sister became offended and began disparaging the merchant's life and exalting her peasant life.

"I wouldn't trade my life for yours," she said. "Our life is rough, I grant you, but we haven't a worry. You may live more neatly, and, perhaps, earn a lot at your trade, but you may lose it all. Remember the proverb: loss is gain's big brother. It often goes like that: one day you're rich and the day after, you're begging in the streets. But our peasant life is more stable: a meager life, but a long one. We won't be rich, but we'll always eat."

The older sister began to speak:

"Eat—like the pigs and calves! No elegance, no manners! No matter how hard your man works, you'll live and die in manure and so will your children."

"What of it," said the younger; "that's our way. Our life may be hard, but we bow to no one, are afraid of no one. While you in town are surrounded by temptations. It's all right now, but tomorrow it may turn ugly— suddenly you'll find your man tempted by cards, or wine, or some young charmer, and everything will turn to ashes. That's what often happens, doesn't it?"

Pakhom, lying on top of the stove, listened to the women babbling.

"It's the absolute truth," he said. "We're so busy tilling mother earth from infancy, we don't get such nonsense in our heads. There's just one trouble—too little land! If I had all the land I wanted, I wouldn't fear the Devil himself!"

The women finished their tea, chatted some more about dresses, cleared the dishes, and went to bed. But the Devil sitting behind the stove had heard everything. He was delighted that the peasant wife had induced her husband to boast, and, particularly, to boast that if he had enough land even the Devil could not get him.

"All right," he thought, "we'll have a tussle, you and I; I'll give you plenty of land. And then I'll get you through your land."

Next to the peasants there lived a small landowner. She had three hundred and twenty-five acres of land. And she had always lived in peace with the peasants—never abusing them. Then she hired as overseer a retired soldier who began to harass the peasants with fines. No matter how careful Pakhom was, either his horses wandered into her oats, or his cattle got into her garden, or his calves strayed onto her meadow—and there was a fine for everything.

Pakhom would pay up and then curse and beat his family. Many were the difficulties Pakhom suffered all summer because of that overseer. Come winter, he was glad to stable the cattle—he begrudged them the fodder, but at least he was free from worry.

It was rumored that winter that the lady was selling her land, and that the innkeeper on the main road was arranging to buy it. The peasants heard this and groaned. "Well," they thought, "if the innkeeper gets the land, he'll pester us with worse fines than the lady. We can't get along without this land; we live too close."

A delegation of peasants representing the commune came to ask the lady not to sell the land to the innkeeper, but to give it to them. They promised to pay more. The lady agreed.

The peasants started making arrangements for the commune to buy the land; they held one meeting and another meeting—but the matter was still unsettled. The Evil One[1] divided them, and they were completely unable to agree. Then the peasants decided that each would buy individually as much as he could. To this, also, the lady agreed. Pakhom heard that his neighbor had bought fifty-five acres from the lady, and that she had loaned him half the money for a year. Pakhom became envious. "They're buying up all the land," he

---

1. **The Evil One.** Another name for the devil, or Satan

thought, "and I'll be left with nothing." He consulted his wife.

"People are buying," he said, "so we must buy about twenty-five acres, too. Otherwise we can't exist—the overseer is crushing us with fines."

They figured out how they could buy. They had one hundred rubles[2] put aside, and they sold the colt and half the bee swarm, hired out their son as a worker, borrowed from their brother-in-law, and raised half the money.

Pakhom gathered up the money, chose his land—forty acres including a little woods—and went to bargain with the lady. He drove a bargain for his forty acres, and sealed it with his hand and a deposit. They went to town and signed the deed with half the money paid down and the rest due in two years.

The Toast. G. K. Totybadse. Tretyakov Gallery, Moscow, Russia.

Pakhom had his own land. He borrowed seed, sowed the land he had bought: it produced well. In a year, he had settled his debts with both the lady and his brother-in-law. And so Pakhom became a landowner: he plowed and sowed his own land, mowed hay on his own land, cut timber from his own land, and pastured his herd on his own land. When Pakhom went out to plow the land which he now owned forever, or when he happened to glance over the sprouting fields and meadows, he could not rejoice enough. It seemed to him that the grass grew and the flowers flowered in a new way. When he had walked across this land before, it had been land like any land; now it had become completely exceptional.

– 3 –

So Pakhom lived and was pleased. Everything would have been fine, had the peasants not begun trespassing on his fields and meadows. He begged them politely to stop, but the trespassing continued. Either the

2. **rubles.** Russian currency

cowherds let the cattle into the meadows, or the horses got into the wheat while grazing at night. Time after time, Pakhom chased them out and forgave without pressing charges; then he became tired of it and started to complain to the district court and he knew the peasants did not do these things deliberately, but only because they were crowded, yet he thought: "One still mustn't let them or they'll ravage everything. They must be taught."

To teach them, he sued once, and then again; one was fined, then another. Pakhom's neighbors began to hold a grudge against him; they started to trespass on purpose from time to time. One went to the grove at night and cut down a dozen linden trees for bast.[3] When Pakhom walked through the woods, he looked and saw a white glimmer. He approached— there lay the discarded peelings, and there stood the little stumps. If the villain had only cut the edges of the bush, or left one standing, but he had razed them all, one after the other. Pakhom was enraged. He thought and thought: "It must be Semon," he thought. He went to search Semon's farm, found nothing, and quarreled with him. And Pakhom was even more certain Semon had done it. He filed a petition. Semon was called into court. The case dragged on and on; the peasant was acquitted for lack of evidence. Pakhom felt even more wronged and abused the elder and the judges.

"You're hand and hand with thieves," he said. "If you led honest lives, you wouldn't let thieves go free."

Pakhom quarreled with both the judges and his neighbors. The peasants started threatening to set fire to his place. Although Pakhom had more land than before, his neighbors were closing in on him.

Just then, there was a rumor that people were moving to new places. And Pakhom thought: "I have no reason to leave my land, but if some of us go, there'll be more space. I could take their land, add it to my place; life would be better. It's too crowded now."

Once when Pakhom was sitting at home, a peasant passing through dropped in. Pakhom put him up for the night, fed him, talked to him, and asked him where, pray, he came from. The peasant said he came from below, beyond the Volga, where he had been working. One thing led to another and the peasant gradually started telling how people were going there to settle. He told how his own people had gone there, joined the community, and divided off twenty-five acres a man.

"And the land is so good," he said, "that they sowed rye, and you couldn't see a horse in the stalks, it was so high; and so thick, that five handfuls make a sheaf.[4] One peasant," he said, "who hadn't a thing but his bare hands, came there and now has six horses, two cows."

Pakhom's heart took fire. He was thinking: "Why be poor and crowded here if one can live well there? We'll sell the house and land here; with this money, I'll build myself a house there and set up a whole establishment. There's only trouble in this crowded place. But I had better make the trip and look into it myself."

That summer he got ready and went. He sailed down the Volga to Samara in a steamer, then walked four hundred versts[5] on foot. When he arrived, everything was just as described. The peasants were living amply on twenty-five acres per head, and they participated willingly in the activities of the community. And whoever had money could buy, in addition to his share, as much of the very best land as he wanted at a ruble an acre; you could buy as much as you wanted!

After finding out everything, Pakhom returned home and began selling all he owned. He sold the land at profit, sold his own farm, sold his entire herd, resigned from the community, waited for spring, and set off with his family for a new place.

---

3. **bast.** Sturdy fiber used in making ropes and mats
4. **sheaf.** Cut stalks of grain bound up in a bundle
5. **versts.** Russian units of length equal to three thousand five hundred feet, or about two-thirds of a mile

Pakhom arrived at the settlement with his family, and joined the community. He stood the elders drinks and put all the papers in order. They accepted Pakhom, divided off one hundred and twenty-five acres of land in various fields as his portion for his family of five—in addition to the use of the pasture. Pakhom built himself a farm and acquired a herd. His part of the common land alone was three times as large as before. And the land was fertile. He lived ten times better than in the past. You had arable land and fodder at will. And you could keep as many cattle as you wanted.

At first, while he was busy building and settling himself, he was content; but after he became used to it, he felt crowded on this land, too. The first year, Pakhom sowed wheat on his share of the common land—it grew well. He wanted to sow wheat again, but there was not enough common land. And what there was, was not suitable. In that region, wheat is sown only on grassland or wasteland. They sow the land for a year or two, then leave it fallow until the grass grows back again. And there are many wanting that kind of land, and not enough of it for all. There were disputes over it, too; the richer peasants wanted to sow it themselves, while the poor people wanted to rent it to dealers to raise tax money. Pakhom wanted to sow more. The following year, he went to a dealer and rented land from him for a year. He sowed more—it grew well; but it was far from the village—you had to cart it about fifteen versts. He saw the peasant-dealers living in farmhouses and growing rich. "That's the thing," thought Pakhom; "if only I could buy land permanently for myself and build a farmhouse on my land. Everything would be at hand." And Pakhom began pondering over how he could buy freehold land.

So Pakhom lived for three years. He rented land and sowed wheat on it. The years were good ones, and the wheat grew well, and the surplus money accumulated. But Pakhom found it annoying to rent land from people every year and to have to move from place to place. Whenever there was a good piece of land, the peasants immediately rushed to divide up everything; if Pakhom did not hurry to buy, he had no land to sow. The third year, he and a dealer rented part of the common pasture from some peasants; he had already plowed when the peasants sued and the work was wasted. "If it had been my own land," he thought, "I'd bow to no one and there'd be no trouble."

And Pakhom began to inquire where land could be bought permanently. And he came across a peasant. The peasant had bought one thousand three hundred and fifty acres, then gone bankrupt, and was selling cheaply. Pakhom began talking terms with him. They haggled and haggled and agreed on fifteen hundred rubles, half of it payable later. They had just reached an agreement when a traveling merchant stopped at the farm for something to eat. They drank and talked. The merchant said he was returning from the far-off Bashkir country. There, he said, he bought thirteen thousand five hundred acres of land from the Bashkirs. And all for one thousand rubles. Pakhom began asking questions. The merchant recounted.

"You just have to be nice to the old men," he said. "I distributed about a hundred rubles' worth of oriental robes and carpets and a case of tea, and gave wine to whoever wanted it. And I got the land for less than ten kopecks an acre." He showed Pakhom the deed. "The land," it read, "lies along a river, and the steppe is all grass-land."

Pakhom began asking him how, where, and what.

"The land there—" said the merchant, "you couldn't walk around it in a year. The Bashkirs own it all. And the people are as silly as sheep. You can almost get it free."

"Well," Pakhom thought, "why should I buy thirteen hundred and fifty acres for my thousand rubles and saddle myself with a debt as well, when I can really get something for a thousand rubles."

– 5 –

Pakhom asked the way to the Bashkirs and as soon as he had escorted the merchant to the door, he began getting ready to go himself. He left the house in his wife's charge, made preparations, and set off with his hired hand. They went to town, bought a case of tea, gifts, wine—everything just as the merchant had said. They traveled and traveled, traversing five hundred versts. The seventh fortnight, they arrived at Bashkir camp. Everything was just as the merchant had said. They all lived in felt tents on the steppe near a stream. They them-selves neither plowed nor ate bread, but their

cattle and horses wandered over the steppes in herds. Twice a day they drove the mares to the colts tethered behind the huts; they milked the mares and made kumiss[6] out of it. The women beat the kumiss and made cheese, while all the men did was drink tea and kumiss and eat mutton and play reed pipes. They were all polite and jolly and they made merry all summer. A completely backward people, with no knowledge of Russian, but friendly.

As soon as the Bashkirs saw Pakhom, they came out of their tents and surrounded their guest. An inter-preter was found; Pakhom told him he had come for land. The Bashkirs were delighted, seized Pakhom, conducted him to one of the best tents, placed him on a carpet, put feather pillows under him, sat down in a circle around him, and began serving him tea and kumiss. They slaughtered a sheep and fed him mutton. Pakhom fetched his gifts from the wagon and began distrib-uting them among the Bashkirs. When Pakhom finished presenting his gifts to them, he divided up the tea. The Bashkirs were delighted. They jabbered and jabbered among themselves, then asked the interpreter to speak.

"They ask me to tell you that they like you," said the interpreter, "and that it is our custom to give a guest every satisfaction, and to render gifts in kind. You have presented us with gifts; now tell us what we have that you like, so we can give a gift to you."

"What I like most of all," said Pakhom, "is your land. Our land is crowded, and, further-more, all of it has been tilled, while your land is plentiful and good. I've never seen the like."

> "Well," he said. "It can be done. Choose whatever you like. Land's plentiful."

6. **kumiss.** Drink made of fermented mare's or camel's milk

The interpreter translated. The Bashkirs talked and talked among themselves. Pakhom did not understand what they were saying, but he saw that they were merry, were shouting something, and laughing. Then they became silent, turned to Pakhom, and the interpreter said, "They asked me to tell you that in return for your kindness they will be glad to give you as much land as you want. Just point it out and it will be yours."

They started to talk again and began to quarrel about something. Pakhom asked what the quarrel was about. And the interpreter said, "Some say the elder must be consulted about the land, that it can't be done without him. But others say it can be done."

– 6 –

The Bashkirs were still quarreling when, suddenly, out came a man in a fox fur cap. Everyone fell silent and stood up. And the interpreter said:

"That's the elder himself."

Pakhom immediately fetched the best robe and brought it to the elder along with five pounds of tea. The elder accepted and sat down in a seat of honor. And the Bashkirs immediately started telling him something. The elder listened and listened, requested silence with a nod, and said to Pakhom in Russian:

"Well," he said. "It can be done. Choose whatever you like. Land's plentiful."

"What does that mean: take what I want," thought Pakhom. "It has to be secured somehow. Or they'll say it's yours, then take it away."

"Thank you," he said, "for your kind words. You do have a lot of land, and I need only a little. But I'd like to know which is mine. It must be measured off somehow, and secured as mine. Our lives and deaths are in God's hands. What you, good people, are giving, your children may take back."

"You're right," said the elder; "it can be secured."

Pakhom said:

"I heard there was a merchant here. You gave him a little piece of land too, and made a deed. I should have the same thing."

The elder understood.

"It can all be done," he said. "We have a scribe, and we'll go to the town to affix the seals."

"And what is the price?" said Pakhom.

"We've only one price: a thousand rubles a day."

Pakhom did not understand.

"What kind of measure is that—a day? How many acres does it have?"

"That," he said, "we don't know. But we sell by the day; as much as you can walk around in a day is yours, and the price is a thousand rubles a day."

Pakhom was astonished.

"But look," he said, "a day's walking is a lot of land."

The elder laughed.

"It's all yours!" he said. "There's just one condition: if you're not back where you started in a day, your money is lost."

"And how," Pakhom said, "will you mark where I go?"

"Well, we'll stand on the spot you choose, and stay there while you walk off a circle; and you'll take a spade with you and, where convenient, dig holes to mark your path and pile the dirt up high; then we'll drive a plow from pit to pit. Make your circle wherever you want. What you walk around is all yours, as long as you're back where you started by sundown."

Pakhom was delighted. They decided to start off early. They chatted, drank more *kumiss,* ate mutton, drank tea again; night came on. They laid down a feather bed for Pakhom, and the Bashkirs dispersed, promising to assemble the next day at dawn to set out for the starting point before sunrise.

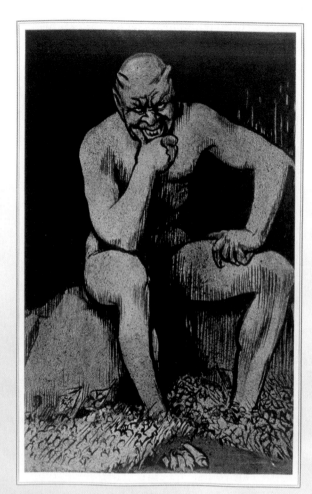

The Sleeping Partner, 1914. Louis Raemaekers. Stapleton Collection, UK.

hut with both hands holding his sides, rocking back and forth, laughing at something.

Pakhom approached him and asked: "What are you laughing at?" Then he saw that it was not the Bashkir elder, but the merchant of the other day who had come to him and told him about the land. And he had barely asked the merchant, "Have you been here long?"—when it was no longer the merchant, but the peasant who had come on foot from the south long ago. Then Pakhom saw that it was not the peasant, but the Devil himself, laughing, horns, hoofs, and all; and in front of him lay a barefoot man in shirt and trousers. And Pakhom looked closer to see what sort of man he was. He saw it was a corpse and that it was—he himself. Horrified, Pakhom woke up. "The things one dreams," he thought. He looked around; through the open door he saw the dawn; it was already turning white. "Must rouse the people," he thought; "time to go." Pakhom got up, woke his hired hand who was asleep in the wagon, ordered the horses harnessed, and went to wake the Bashkirs.

"It's time," he said, "to go to the steppe to measure off the land."

The Bashkirs got up, assembled everything, and the elder arrived. The Bashkirs began drinking *kumiss* again, and offered Pakhom tea, but he did not want to linger.

"If we're going, let's go," he said. "It's time."

– 8 –

The Bashkirs assembled, climbed on horse-back and in wagons and set off. Meanwhile, Pakhom took a spade and set off with his laborer in his own wagon. They arrived at the steppe just as day was breaking. They went up a hillock (known as a *shikhan*[7] in Bashkir). The

– 7 –

Pakhom lay on the feather bed, unable to sleep for thinking about the land. "I'll grab off a big piece of my own," he thought. "I can walk fifty versts in a day. The days are long now; there'll be quite a bit of land in fifty versts. What's poorest, I'll sell or let to the peasants, and I'll pick out the best to settle on myself. I'll get a plow and two oxen, and hire two laborers; I'll plow over a hundred acres and put cattle to graze on the rest."

All night Pakhom lay awake, drifting off to sleep only just before dawn. No sooner had he fallen asleep than he started to dream. He saw himself lying in that same hut and heard someone chuckling outside. And he wanted to see who was laughing, got up, went out of the hut, and there sat the Bashkir elder himself in front of the

---

7. *shikhan.* Small hill

Bashkirs climbed out of their wagons, slid down from their horses, and gathered in a group. The elder went to Pakhom and pointed.

"There," he said; "everything the eye encompasses is ours. Take your pick."

Pakhom's eyes glowed. It was all grassland, level as the palm of the hand, black as a poppy seed, and wherever there was a hollow, there was grass growing chest-high.

The elder took off his fox cap and put it on the ground.

"That," he said, "will be the marker. Leave from here; return here. Whatever you walk around will be yours."

Pakhom drew out his money, placed it on the cap, unfastened his belt, took off his outer coat, girded his belt tightly over his stomach again, put a bag of bread inside his jacket, tied a flask of water to his belt, drew his bootlegs tight, took the spade from his laborer, and got set to go. He pondered and pondered over which direction to take—it was good everywhere. He was thinking: "It's all the same: I'll head toward the sunrise." He turned to face the sun and paced restlessly, waiting for it to appear over the horizon. He was thinking: "I must lose no time. And walking's easier while it's still cold." As soon as the sun's rays spurted over the horizon, Pakhom flung the spade over his shoulder and started off across the steppe.

He walked neither quickly nor slowly. He covered a verst; stopped, dug out a hole, and piled the turf up so it could be seen. He walked further. He loosened up and lengthened his stride. He covered still more ground; dug still another pit.

Pakhom glanced back. The *shikhan* was clearly visible to the sun, and the people stood there, and the hoops of the cart wheels glittered. Pakhom guessed that he had covered about five versts. It was getting warmer; he took off his jacket, flung it over his shoulder; and went on. He covered another five versts. It was warm. He glanced at the sun—already breakfast time.

"One lap finished," thought Pakhom. "But there are four in a day; it's too early to turn around yet. I'll just take my boots off." He sat down, took them off, stuck them in his belt, and went on. Walking became easier. He thought, "I'll just cover about five more versts, then start veering left. This is a very nice spot, too good to leave out. The farther away it is, the better it gets." He walked straight on. When he glanced around, the *shikhan* was barely visible, the people looked like black ants, and there was something faintly glistening on it.

"Well," thought Pakhom, "I've taken enough on this side; I must turn. Besides, I've been sweating—I'm thirsty." He stopped, dug a bigger hole, stacked the turf, untied his flask, and drank. Then he veered sharply to the left. On and on he went; the grass grew taller and it became hot.

Pakhom began to feel tired; he glanced at the sun—it was already lunch time. He stopped; sat on the ground; ate bread and drank water, but did not lie down. "Lie down and you'll fall asleep," he thought. After a while, he walked on. Walking was easy at first. Eating had increased his strength. But it had gotten very hot and he was becoming sleepy. Still he pressed on, thinking—an hour of suffering for a lifetime of living.

He walked a long way in this direction too, and when he was about to turn left, he came to a damp hollow, too nice to overlook. "Flax will grow well there," he thought. Again he went straight on. He took possession of the hollow,

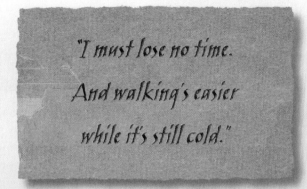

"I must lose no time. And walking's easier while it's still cold."

The Pontine Marshes, 1850s. Alexander Ivanov. State Russian Museum, St. Petersburg, Russia.

dug a hole beyond it, and turned the second corner. Pakhom glanced back at the *shikhan;* it was hazy from the heat, something seemed to be wavering in the air, and through the haze the people were barely visible on top of the *shikhan*—fifteen versts away. "Well," thought Pakhom, "I've taken long sides, I must take this one shorter." As he walked the third side, he increased his stride. He looked at the sun—it was already approaching tea-time, and he had only covered two versts on the third side. And it was still fifteen versts to the starting point. "No," he thought, "I'll have a lopsided place, but I must go straight back so I'll arrive in time, and not take anymore. There's lots of land already." Pakhom shoveled out a hole as quickly as he could and turned straight toward the *shikhan.*

– 9 –

As Pakhom walked straight toward the *shikhan,* he began having difficulties. He was perspiring, and his bare legs were cut and bruised and were beginning to fail him. He wanted to rest but could not—otherwise he would not arrive before sunset. The sun would not wait; it continued sinking, sinking. "Ah," he thought, "if only I haven't made a mistake and taken too much! What if I don't make it?" He glanced ahead at the *shikhan,* looked at the

sun: the starting point was far away, and the sun was nearing the horizon.

So Pakhom went on with difficulty; he kept increasing and increasing his stride. He walked, walked—and was still far away; he broke into a trot. He threw off his jacket, dropped his boots and flask; he threw off his cap, keeping only his spade to lean on. "Ah," he thought, "I've been too greedy, I've ruined the whole thing, I won't get there by sundown." And fear shortened his breath even more. Pakhom ran; his shirt and trousers clung to his body with sweat; his mouth was parched. His chest felt as though it had been inflated by the blacksmith's bellows; a hammer beat in his heart; and his legs no longer seemed to belong to his body— they were collapsing under him. Pakhom began to worry about dying of strain.

He was afraid of dying, but unable to stop. "I've run so far," he thought. "I'd be a fool to stop now." He ran and ran, and was very close when he heard a screeching—the Bashkirs shrieking at him—his heart became even more inflamed by their cries. Pakhom pressed forward with his remaining strength, but the sun was already reaching the horizon; and, slipping behind a cloud, it became large, red, and bloody. Now it was beginning to go down. Although the sun was close to setting, Pakhom was no longer far from the starting point either. He could already

strength, driving his body forward so that his legs could barely move fast enough to keep him from falling. Just as Pakhom ran up to the base of the *shikhan,* it suddenly became dark. He glanced around—the sun had already set. Pakhom sighed. "My work has fallen through," he thought. He was about to stop when he heard the Bashkirs still shrieking. And he remembered that though it seemed below that the sun had set, it would still be shining on top of the *shikhan.* Pakhom took a deep breath and ran up the *shikhan.* It was still light there. As Pakhom reached the top, he saw the elder sitting in front of the cap, chuckling, holding his sides with his hands. Pakhom remembered his dream and groaned; his legs gave way, and he fell forward, his hands touching the cap.

"Aiee, good man!" cried the elder. "You have acquired plenty of land!"

Pakhom's laborer ran to lift him, but the blood was flowing from his mouth and he lay dead.

The Bashkirs clicked their tongues in commiseration.

The laborer took up the spade, dug Pakhom a grave just long enough to reach from his feet to his head—six feet in all—and buried him. ❖

see the people on the *shikhan* waving their arms at him, urging him on. He saw the fox cap on the ground and the money on it; and he saw the elder sitting on the ground, holding his sides with his hands. And Pakhom remembered his dream. "There is plenty of land," he thought, "if it please God to let me live on it. Oh, I've ruined myself," he thought. "I won't make it."

Pakhom glanced at the sun, but it had touched the earth and had already begun to slip behind the horizon which cut it into an arc. Pakhom overreached his remaining

---

MIRRORS & WINDOWS

Where have you seen a lack of contentment in the world around you? Where have you seen it in your own life? Describe some consequences of always searching for more, as you have seen or experienced.

Refer and Reason

1. At the beginning of the story, all Pakhom wants is a chance to have his own land. Each time he gets more land, describe how his attitude and expectations change.
2. What is the meaning of the title? Could it have a double meaning? Explain why or why not.
3. Citing evidence from the story, compare the value Pakhom places on land and wealth with that he places on his family. What makes greed incompatible with caring for and about other people?

Writing Options

1. Imagine that at Pakhom's funeral, his widow and his sister get together to talk about how they remember Pakhom and to express their opinions about his decisions. Write the conversation these two women have.
2. The story of Pakhom teaches a lesson about greed. For a group of middle-school students, create a short parable that, like Tolstoy's tale, teaches a lesson through the experience of a single character. Your character may be based on a real person, or he or she may be entirely fictional.

 Go to **www.mirrorsandwindows.com** for more.

READING INDEPENDENTLY

Theme: Strange Happenings

"The dog ran upstairs, hysterically yelping to each door, at last realizing, as the house realized, that only silence was here."

—from "There Will Come Soft Rains"
by Ray Bradbury

It is often said that art imitates life, but how does that apply to stories of the bizarre, futuristic, or improbable? Stories that twist reality, or create an entirely different reality, can be fun for the imagination, but they can also provide instruction or warnings about modern life and society in a way that is not possible with more realistic literature. By exaggerating or distorting certain aspects of the world, those aspects may become easier to analyze and compare to life as we know it. As you read the selections in this section, think about what you can learn about real life from these tales of strange happenings.

APPLYING READING SKILLS

Use various reading skills when you read independently. Notice how reading skills are modeled for each of the following excerpts from "By the Waters of Babylon" by Stephen Vincent Benét (page 944).

> It is forbidden to cross the great river and look upon the place that was the Place of the Gods—this is most strictly forbidden. We do not even say its name though we know its name.

- **Determine Author's Approach:** The story is told from the first-person point of view, meaning that we're seeing things from the narrator's perspective. This gives us a close look inside the main character's mind to understand things as he understands them.

> We are not ignorant like the Forest People—our women spin wool on the wheel, our priests wear a white robe. We do not eat grubs from the tree; we have not forgotten the old writings, although they are hard to understand. Nevertheless, my knowledge and my lack of knowledge burned in me—I wished to know more.

- **Determine Importance of Details:** I'm not sure in what world this story is set, but the narrator mentions "the Forest People" and says they're ignorant. There might be a conflict between these people and the narrator's people. The other details, such as the priests and the wool spinning, indicate that the society is not technologically advanced and that it places importance on the priests.

> How shall I tell what I saw? I went carefully, my strung bow in my hand, my skin ready for danger. There should have been the wailings of spirits and the shrieks of demons, but there were not [...].
>
> How shall I tell what I saw? The towers are not all broken—here and there one still stands, like a great tree in a forest, and the birds nest high [...].
>
> How shall I tell what I saw? There was no smell of man left, on stone or metal.

- **Identify Parallel Structures:** By repeating "How shall I tell what I saw?" the narrator is emphasizing how astounding his discoveries in the Place of the Gods are. It might also show that he's already thinking about how to tell his people, knowing that they will find it hard to believe.

> Sometimes signs are sent by bad spirits. I waited again on the flat rock, fasting, taking no food. I was very still—I could feel the sky above me and the earth beneath. I waited till the sun was beginning to sink. Then three deer passed in the valley, going east—they did not wind me or see me. There was a white fawn with them— a very great sign.

- **Determine Author's Purpose:** The fasting and the signs in nature that the narrator waits for remind me of Native American rituals of young men going on vision quests. I think the author's purpose is to remind us of nature- and spirit-focused societies in order to contrast them with the society in this story, which in some ways seems to be more in the future than the past but lacks modern technology.

> It is known that the gods did not hunt as we do—they got their food from enchanted boxes and jars. Sometimes these are still found in the Dead Places—once, when I was a child and foolish, I opened such a jar and tasted it and found the food sweet. But my father found out and punished me for it strictly, for often that food is death.

- **Draw Conclusions:** This is proof, I think, that modern society, as we know it, experienced some huge catastrophe—maybe a nuclear war. The "enchanted boxes and jars" are just prepackaged, canned food. His father probably thinks "that food is death" because of radiation or some other sort of contamination from whatever wiped out society.

> He said, "Truth is a hard deer to hunt. If you eat too much truth at once, you may die of the truth. It was not idle that our fathers forbade the Dead Places." He was right—it is better the truth should come little by little. I have learned that, being a priest. Perhaps, in the old days, they ate knowledge too fast.

- **Find the Main Idea:** I think this is the main idea of the story—our society is making rapid technological advances, but we don't have the spiritual or moral strength to keep up with it. Perhaps the author is saying that too much knowledge when you are not ready to handle it can be a dangerous thing.

What Good Readers Do

Code the Text

Instead of writing down a short response, use a symbol or a short word to indicate your response. Use codes like the ones listed below.

+	I like this.
−	I don't like this.
√	This is important.
Yes	I agree with this.
No	I disagree with this.
?	I don't understand this.
!	This is like something I know.
*	I need to come back to this later.

By the Waters of Babylon

When gods war with gods, they use weapons we do not know.
It was fire falling out of the sky and a mist that poisoned. It
was the time of the Great Burning and the Destruction.

A Short Story by
Stephen Vincent Benét

Stephen Vincent Benét
(1898–1943) began writing at
the age of fifteen and two years
later published his first book of
poetry. In 1926, Benét began
a long narrative poem about
the Civil War, *John Brown's
Body* (1928), for which he
won a Pulitzer Prize. Benét is also known
for his stories "The Sobbin' Women" (1926), made
into the musical *Seven Brides for Seven Brothers,*
and "The Devil and Daniel Webster" (1937), made
into a play, an opera, and a movie.

"By the Waters of Babylon" is a science-fiction
story published in 1937 about a boy coming of age
in a primitive civilization set in the future, following
a "Great Burning" — a man-made disaster that
wiped out much of the population. The title of the
story refers to the ancient city of Babylon, which
crumbled into ruins amidst war and destruction.

What do you think today's world would be like after
a major nuclear war?

The north and the west and the south are
good hunting ground, but it is forbidden
to go east. It is forbidden to go to any of the
Dead Places except to search for metal, and
then he who touches the metal must be a
priest or the son of a priest. Afterwards, both
the man and the metal must be purified.
These are the rules and the laws; they are well
made. It is forbidden to cross the great river
and look upon the place that was the Place of
the Gods—this is most strictly forbidden. We
do not even say its name though we know its
name. It is there that spirits live, and demons—
it is there that there are the ashes of the Great
Burning. These things are forbidden—they
have been forbidden since the beginning of
time.

My father is a priest; I am the son of a
priest. I have been in the Dead Places near us,
with my father—at first, I was afraid. When

Interrupted Journey, c. 1971. Samuel Bak. Pucker Gallery, Boston.

my father went into the house to search for the metal, I stood by the door and my heart felt small and weak. It was a dead man's house, a spirit house. It did not have the smell of man, though there were old bones in a corner. But it is not fitting that a priest's son should show fear. I looked at the bones in the shadow and kept my voice still.

Then my father came out with the metal—a good, strong piece. He looked at me with both eyes but I had not run away. He gave me the metal to hold—I took it and did not die. So he knew that I was truly his son and would be a priest in my time. That was when I was very young—nevertheless, my brothers would not have done it, though they are good hunters. After that, they gave me the good piece of meat and the warm corner by the fire. My father watched over me—he was glad that I should be a priest. But when I boasted or wept without a reason, he punished me more strictly than my brothers. That was right.

After a time, I myself was allowed to go into the dead houses and search for metal. So I learned the ways of those houses—and if I saw bones, I was no longer afraid. The bones are light and old—sometimes they will fall into dust if you touch them. But that is a great sin.

I was taught the chants and the spells—I was taught how to stop the running of blood from a wound and many secrets. A priest must know many secrets—that was what my father said. If the hunters think we do all things by chants and spells, they may believe so—it does not hurt them. I was taught how to read in the old books and how to make the old writings—that was hard and took a long time. My knowledge made me happy—it was like a fire in my heart. Most of all, I liked to hear of the Old Days and the stories of the gods. I asked myself many questions that I could not answer, but it was good to ask them. At night, I would lie awake and listen to the wind—it seemed to me that it was the voice of the gods as they flew through the air.

We are not ignorant like the Forest People—our women spin wool on the wheel, our priests wear a white robe. We do not eat grubs from the tree; we have not forgotten the old writings, although they are hard to understand. Nevertheless, my knowledge and my lack of knowledge burned in me—I wished to know more. When I was a man at last, I came to my father and said, "It is time for me to go on my journey. Give me your leave."

He looked at me for a long time, stroking his beard; then he said at last, "Yes. It is time." That night, in the house of the priesthood, I asked for and received purification.[1] My body hurt, but my spirit was a cool stone. It was my father himself who questioned me about my dreams.

He bade[2] me look into the smoke of the fire and see—I saw and told what I saw. It was what I have always seen—a river, and, beyond it, a great Dead Place and in it the gods walking. I have always thought about that. His eyes were stern when I told him—he was no longer my father but a priest. He said, "This is a strong dream."

"It is mine," I said, while the smoke waved and my head felt light. They were singing the Star song in the outer chamber and it was like the buzzing of bees in my head.

He asked me how the gods were dressed and I told him how they were dressed. We know how they were dressed from the book, but I saw them as if they were before me. When I had finished, he threw the sticks three times and studied them as they fell.

"This is a very strong dream," he said. "It may eat you up."

"I am not afraid," I said and looked at him with both eyes. My voice sounded thin in my ears but that was because of the smoke.

He touched me on the breast and the forehead. He gave me the bow and the three arrows.

"Take them," he said. "It is forbidden to travel east. It is forbidden to cross the river. It is forbidden to go to the Place of the Gods. All these things are forbidden."

---

1. **purification.** Method of freeing from guilt or sins
2. **bade.** Asked

"All these things are forbidden," I said, but it was my voice that spoke and not my spirit. He looked at me again.

"My son," he said. "Once I had young dreams. If your dreams do not eat you up, you may be a great priest. If they eat you, you are still my son. Now go on your journey."

I went fasting,[3] as is the law. My body hurt but not my heart. When the dawn came, I was out of sight of the village. I prayed and purified myself, waiting for a sign. The sign was an eagle. It flew east.

Sometimes signs are sent by bad spirits. I waited again on the flat rock, fasting, taking no food. I was very still—I could feel the sky above me and the earth beneath. I waited till the sun was beginning to sink. Then three deer passed in the valley, going east—they did not wind me or see me. There was a white fawn with them—a very great sign.

I followed them, at a distance, waiting for what would happen. My heart was troubled about going east, yet I knew that I must go. My head hummed with my fasting—I did not even see the panther spring upon the white fawn. But, before I knew it, the bow was in my hand. I shouted and the panther lifted his head from the fawn. It is not easy to kill a panther with one arrow, but the arrow went through his eye and into his brain. He died as he tried to spring—he rolled over, tearing at the ground. Then I knew I was meant to go east—I knew that was my journey. When the night came, I made my fire and roasted meat.

It is eight suns' journey to the east and a man passes by many Dead Places. The Forest People are afraid of them, but I am not. Once

I made my fire on the edge of a Dead Place at night and, next morning, in the dead house, I found a good knife, little rusted. That was small to what came afterward but it made my heart feel big. Always when I looked for game, it was in front of my arrow, and twice I passed hunting parties of the Forest People without their knowing. So I knew my magic was strong and my journey clean, in spite of the law.

Toward the setting of the eighth sun, I came to the banks of the great river. It was half-a-day's journey after I had left the god-road—we do not use the god-roads now for they are falling apart into great blocks of stone, and the forest is safer going. A long way off, I had seen the water through trees, but the trees were thick. At last, I came out upon an open place at the top of a cliff. There was the great river below, like a giant in the sun. It is very long, very wide. It could eat all the streams we know and still be thirsty. Its name is Ou-dis-sun, the Sacred, the Long. No man of my tribe had seen it, not even my father, the priest. It was magic and I prayed.

Then I raised my eyes and looked south. It was there, the Place of the Gods.

How can I tell what it was like—you do not know. It was there, in the red light, and they were too big to be houses. It was there with the red light upon it, mighty and ruined. I knew that in another moment the gods would see me. I covered my eyes with my hands and crept back into the forest.

Surely, that was enough to do, and live. Surely it was enough to spend the night upon the cliff. The Forest People themselves do not

---

3. **fasting.** Not eating food or eating only limited amounts of food for a period of time

come near. Yet, all through the night, I knew that I should have to cross the river and walk in the places of the gods, although the gods ate me up. My magic did not help me at all, and yet there was a fire in my bowels,[4] a fire in my mind. When the sun rose, I thought, "My journey has been clean. Now I will go home from my journey." But, even as I thought so, I knew I could not. If I went to the Place of the Gods, I would surely die, but, if I did not go, I could never be at peace with my spirit again. It is better to lose one's life than one's spirit, if one is a priest and the son of a priest.

Nevertheless, as I made the raft, the tears ran out of my eyes. The Forest People could have killed me without fight, if they had come upon me then, but they did not come. When the raft was made, I said the sayings for the dead and painted myself for death. My heart was cold as a frog and my knees like water, but the burning in my mind would not let me have peace. As I pushed the raft from the shore, I began my death song—I had the right. It was a fine song.

"I am John, son of John," I sang. "My people
    are the Hill People. They are the men.
I go into the Dead Places but I am not slain.
I take the metal from the Dead Places but I am
    not blasted.
I travel upon the god-roads and am not afraid.
E-yah! I have killed the panther, I have killed
    the fawn!
E-yah! I have come to the great river. No man
    has come there before.
It is forbidden to go east, but I have gone,
    forbidden to go on the great river, but I am
    there.
Open your hearts, you spirits, and hear my
    song.
Now I go to the Place of the Gods, I shall not
    return.
My body is painted for death and my limbs
    weak, but my heart is big as I go to the
    Place of the Gods!"

All the same, when I came to the Place of the Gods, I was afraid, afraid. The current of the great river is very strong—it gripped my raft with its hands. That was magic, for the river itself is wide and calm. I could feel evil spirits about me, in the bright morning; I could feel their breath on my neck as I was swept down the stream. Never have I been so much alone—I tried to think of my knowledge, but it was a squirrel's heap of winter nuts. There was no strength in my knowledge any more and I felt small and naked as a new-hatched bird—alone upon the great river, the servant of the gods.

Yet, after a while, my eyes were opened and I saw. I saw both banks of the river—I saw that once there had been god-roads across it, though now they were broken and fallen like broken vines. Very great they were, and wonderful and broken—broken in the time of the Great Burning when the fire fell out of the sky. And always the current took me nearer to the Place of the Gods, and the huge ruins rose before my eyes.

I do not know the customs of rivers—we are the People of the Hills. I tried to guide my raft with the pole but it spun around. I thought the river meant to take me past the Place of the Gods and out into the Bitter Water of the legends. I grew angry then—my heart felt strong. I said aloud, "I am a priest and the son of a priest!" The gods heard me—they showed me how to paddle with the pole on one side of the raft. The current changed itself—I drew near to the Place of the Gods.

When I was very near, my raft struck and turned over. I can swim in our lakes—I swam to the shore. There was a great spike of rusted metal sticking out into the river—I hauled myself up upon it and sat there, panting. I had saved my bow and two arrows and the knife I found in the Dead Place but that was all. My raft went whirling downstream toward

---

4. **bowels.** Gut or intestines; inside parts

the Bitter Water. I looked after it, and thought if it had trod me under, at least I would be safely dead. Nevertheless, when I had dried my bowstring and restrung it, I walked forward to the Place of the Gods.

It felt like ground underfoot; it did not burn me. It is not true what some of the tales say, that the ground there burns forever, for I have been there. Here

and there were the marks and stains of the Great Burning, on the ruins, that is true. But they were old marks and old stains. It is not true either, what some of our priests say, that it is an island covered with fogs and enchantments. It is not. It is a great Dead Place—greater than any Dead Place we know. Everywhere in it there are god-roads, though most are cracked and broken. Everywhere there are the ruins of the high towers of the gods.

How shall I tell what I saw? I went carefully, my strung bow in my hand, my skin ready for danger. There should have been the wailings of spirits and the shrieks of demons, but there were not. It was very silent and sunny where I had landed—the wind and the rain and the birds that drop seeds had done their work—the grass grew in the cracks of the broken stone. It is a fair island—no wonder the gods built there. If I had come there, a god, I also would have built.

How shall I tell what I saw? The towers are not all broken—here and there one still stands,

like a great tree in a forest, and the birds nest high. But the towers themselves look blind, for the gods are gone. I saw a fish-hawk, catching fish in the river. I saw a little dance of white butterflies over a great heap of broken stones and columns. I went there and looked about me—there was a carved stone with cut-letters, broken in half. I can read letters but I could not understand these. They said UBTREAS.[5] There was also the shattered image of a man or a god. It had been made of white stone and he wore his hair tied back like a woman's. His name was ASHING,[6] as I read on the cracked half of a stone. I thought it wise to pray to ASHING, though I do not know that god.

How shall I tell what I saw? There was no smell of man left, on stone or metal. Nor were there many trees in that wilderness of stone. There are many pigeons, nesting and dropping in

---

5. **UBTREAS.** Probably a fragment of the word *subtreasury,* from the U.S. Subtreasury building

6. **ASHING.** Probably a fragment of the name *Washington,* from the remains of the statue of George Washington

the towers—the gods must have loved them, or, perhaps, they used them for sacrifices. There are wild cats that roam the god-roads, green-eyed, unafraid of man. At night they wail like demons, but they are not demons. The wild dogs are more dangerous, for they hunt in a pack, but them I did not meet till later. Everywhere there are the carved stones, carved with magical numbers or words.

I went North—I did not try to hide myself. When a god or demon saw me, then I would die, but meanwhile I was no longer afraid. My hunger for knowledge burned in me—there was so much that I could not understand. After awhile, I knew that my belly was hungry. I could have hunted for my meat, but I did not hunt. It is known that the gods did not hunt as we do—they got their food from enchanted boxes and jars. Sometimes these are still found in the Dead Places—once, when I was a child and foolish, I opened such a jar and tasted it and found the food sweet. But my father found out and punished me for it strictly, for often that food is death. Now, though, I had long gone past what was forbidden, and I entered the like-liest towers, looking for the food of the gods.

I found it at last in the ruins of a great temple in the mid-city. A mighty temple it must have been, for the roof was painted like the sky at night with its stars—that much I could see, though the colors were faint and dim. It went down into great caves and tunnels—perhaps they kept their slaves there. But when I started to climb down, I heard the squeaking of rats, so I did not go—rats are unclean, and there must have been many tribes of them, from the squeaking. But near there, I found food, in the heart of a ruin, behind a door that still opened. I ate only the fruits from the jars—they had a very sweet taste. There was drink, too, in bottles of glass—the drink of the gods was strong and made my head swim. After I had eaten and drunk, I slept on the top of a stone, my bow at my side.

When I woke, the sun was low. Looking down from where I lay, I saw a dog sitting on his haunches. His tongue was hanging out of his mouth; he looked as if he were laughing. He was a big dog, with a gray-brown coat, as big as a wolf. I sprang up and shouted at him but he did not move—he just sat there as if he were laughing. I did not like that. When I reached for a stone to throw, he moved swiftly out of the way of the stone. He was not afraid of me; he looked at me as if I were meat. No doubt I could have killed him with an arrow, but I did not know if there were others. Moreover, night was falling.

I looked about me—not far away there was a great, broken god-road, leading North. The towers were high enough, but not so high, and while many of the dead-houses were wrecked, there were some that stood. I went toward this god-road, keeping to the heights of the ruins, while the dog followed. When I had reached the god-road, I saw that there were others behind him. If I had slept later, they would have come upon me asleep and torn out my throat. As it was, they were sure enough of me; they did not hurry. When I went into the dead-house, they kept watch at the entrance—doubtless they thought they would have a fine hunt. But a dog cannot open a door, and I knew, from the books, that the gods did not like to live on the ground but on high.

I had just found a door I could open when the dogs decided to rush. Ha! They were surprised when I shut the door in their faces—it was a good door, of strong metal. I could hear their foolish baying beyond it, but I did not stop to answer them. I was in dark-ness—I found stairs and climbed. There were many stairs, turning around till my head was dizzy. At the top was another door—I found the knob and opened it. I was in a long, small chamber—on one side of it was a bronze door that could not be opened, for it had no handle. Perhaps there was a magic word to open it, but I did not have the word. I turned to the door in the opposite side of the wall. The lock of it was broken and I opened it and went in.

Within, there was a place of great riches. The god who lived there must have been a powerful god. The first room was a small ante-room[7]—I waited there for some time, telling the spirits of the place that I came in peace and not as a robber. When it seemed to me that they had had time to hear me, I went on. Ah, what riches! Few, even, of the windows had been broken—it was all as it had been. The great windows that looked over the city had not been broken at all though they were dusty and streaked with many years. There were coverings on the floors, the colors not greatly faded, and the chairs were soft and deep. There were pictures upon the walls, very strange, very wonderful—I remember one of a bunch of flowers in a jar—if you came close to it, you could see nothing but bits of color, but if you stood away from it, the flowers might have been picked yesterday. It made my heart feel strange to look at this picture—and to look at the figure of a bird, in some hard clay, on a table and to see it so like our birds. Everywhere there were books and writings, many in tongues that I could not read. The god who lived there must have been a wise god and full of knowledge. I felt I had a right there, as I sought knowledge also.

Nevertheless, it was strange. There was a washing-place but no water—perhaps the gods washed in air. There was a cooking-place but no wood, and though there was a machine to cook food, there was no place to put fire in

Still Life with Flowers in an Olive Jar, c. 1880. Paul Cezanne. Philadelphia Museum of Art, Philadelphia, Pennsylvania.

it. Nor were there candles or lamps—there were things that looked like lamps but they had neither oil nor wick. All these things were magic, but I touched them and lived—the magic had gone out of them. Let me tell one thing to show. In the washing-place, a thing said "Hot" but it was not hot to the touch—another thing said "Cold" but it was not cold. This must have been a strong magic but the magic was gone. I do not understand—they had ways I wish that I knew.

It was close and dry and dusty in their house of the gods. I have said the magic was gone, but that is not true—it had gone from the magic things, but it had not gone from the place. I felt the spirits about me, weighing upon me. Nor had I ever slept in a Dead Place before—and yet, tonight, I must sleep there. When I thought of it, my tongue felt dry in my throat, in spite of my wish for knowledge. Almost I would have gone down again and faced the dogs, but I did not.

I had not gone through all the rooms when the darkness fell. When it fell, I went back to the big room looking over the city and made fire. There was a place to make fire and a box with wood in it, though I do not think they cooked there. I wrapped myself in a floor-covering and slept in front of the fire—I was very tired.

---

7. **ante-room.** Reception area or waiting room

Now I tell what is very strong magic. I woke in the midst of the night. When I woke, the fire had gone out and I was cold. It seemed to me that all around me there were whisperings and voices. I closed my eyes to shut them out. Some will say that I slept again, but I do not think that I slept. I could feel the spirits drawing my spirit out of my body as a fish is drawn on a line.

Why should I lie about it? I am a priest and the son of a priest. If there are spirits, as they say, in the small Dead Places near us, what spirits must there not be in that great Place of the Gods? And would not they wish to speak? After such long years? I know that I felt myself drawn as a fish is drawn on a line. I had stepped out of my body—I could see my body asleep in front of the cold fire, but it was not I. I was drawn to look out upon the city of the gods.

It should have been dark, for it was night, but it was not dark. Everywhere there were lights—lines of light—circles and blurs of light—ten thousand torches would not have been the same. The sky itself was alight—you could barely see the stars for the glow in the sky. I thought to myself "This is strong magic," and trembled. There was a roaring in my ears like the rushing of rivers. Then my eyes grew used to the light and my ears to the sound. I knew that I was seeing the city as it had been when the gods were alive.

That was a sight indeed—yes, that was a sight: I could not have seen it in the body—my body would have died. Everywhere went the gods, on foot and in chariots—there were gods beyond number and counting and their chariots blocked the streets. They had turned night to day for their pleasure—they did not sleep with the sun. The noise of their coming and going was the noise of many waters. It was magic what they could do—it was magic what they did.

I looked out of another window—the great vines of their bridges were mended and the god-roads went East and West. Restless, restless, were the gods and always in motion! They burrowed tunnels under rivers—they flew in the air. With unbelievable tools they did giant works—no part of the earth was safe from them, for, if they wished for a thing, they summoned it from the other side of the world. And always, as they labored and rested, as they feasted and made love, there was a drum in their ears—the pulse of the giant city, beating and beating like a man's heart.

Were they happy? What is happiness to the gods? They were great, they were mighty, they were wonderful and terrible. As I looked upon them and their magic, I felt like a child—but a little more, it seemed to me, and they would pull down the moon from the sky. I saw them with wisdom beyond wisdom and knowledge beyond knowledge. And yet not all they did was well done—even I could see that—and yet their wisdom could not but grow until all was peace.

Then I saw their fate come upon them and that was terrible past speech. It came upon them as they walked the streets of their city. I have been in the fights with the Forest People—I have seen men die. But this was not like that. When gods war with gods, they use weapons we do not know. It was fire falling out of the sky and a mist that poisoned. It was the time of the Great Burning and the Destruction. They ran about like ants in the streets of their city—poor gods, poor gods! Then the towers began to fall. A few escaped—yes, a few. The legends tell it. But, even after the city became a Dead Place, for many years the poison was still in the ground. I saw it happen, I saw the last of them die. It was darkness over the broken city and I wept.

All this, I saw. I saw it as I have told it, though not in the body. When I woke in the morning, I was hungry, but I did not think first of my hunger for my heart was perplexed and confused. I knew the reason for the Dead Places but I did not see why it had happened. It seemed to me it should not have happened, with all the magic they had. I went through the house looking for an answer. There was so much in the house I could not understand—and yet I am a priest and the son of a priest. It

was like being on one side of the great river, at night, with no light to show the way.

Then I saw the dead god. He was sitting in his chair, by the window, in a room I had not entered before and, for the first moment, I thought that he was alive. Then I saw the skin on the back of his hand—it was like dry leather. The room was shut, hot and dry—no doubt that had kept him as he was. At first I was afraid to approach him—then the fear left me. He was sitting looking out over the city—he was dressed in the clothes of the gods. His age was neither young nor old—I could not tell his age. But there was wisdom in his face and great sadness. You could see that he would have not run away. He had sat at his window, watching his city die—then he himself had died. But it is better to lose one's life than one's spirit—and you could see from the face that his spirit had not been lost. I knew that, if I touched him, he would fall into dust—and yet, there was something unconquered in the face.

That is all of my story, for then I knew he was a man—I knew then that they had been men, neither gods nor demons. It is a great knowledge, hard to tell and believe. They were men—they went a dark road, but they were men. I had no fear after that—I had no fear going home, though twice I fought off the dogs, and once I was hunted for two days by the Forest People. When I saw my father again, I prayed and was purified. He touched my lips and my breast; he said, "You went away a boy. You come back a man and a priest." I said, "Father, they were men! I have been in the Place of the Gods and seen it! Now slay me, if it is the law—but still I know they were men."

He looked at me out of both eyes. He said, "The law is not always the same shape—you have done what you have done. I could not have done it my time, but you come after me. Tell!"

I told and he listened. After that, I wished to tell all the people but he showed me otherwise. He said, "Truth is a hard deer to hunt. If you eat too much truth at once, you may die

broken—but we can look at them and wonder. At least, we make a beginning. And, when I am chief priest we shall go beyond the great river. We shall go to the Place of the Gods—the place newyork—not one man but a company. We shall look for the images of the gods and find the god ASHING and the others—the gods Lincoln and Biltmore[8] and Moses.[9] But they were men who built the city, not gods or demons. They were men. I remember the dead man's face. They were men who were here before us. We must build again. ❖

of the truth. It was not idle that our fathers forbade the Dead Places." He was right—it is better the truth should come little by little. I have learned that, being a priest. Perhaps, in the old days, they ate knowledge too fast.

Nevertheless, we make a beginning. It is not for the metal alone we go to the Dead Places now—there are the books and the writings. They are hard to learn. And the magic tools are

---

8. **Biltmore.** The name of a famous hotel in New York City
9. **Moses.** Robert Moses (1888–1981) was a New York City official responsible for major public works projects in the 1930s through the 1950s. His name appears on many public buildings in the city.

"Perhaps, in the old days, they ate knowledge too fast." In what ways might people today eat knowledge too fast? How can people in the world today prevent repeating the mistakes made by the "gods" in the story?

Refer and Reason

1. John lacks the vocabulary and knowledge to interpret some of the things he sees on his journey. Identify four objects or places John describes on his journey, and explain what you think these actually are.
2. What is the Place of the Gods? Who were the gods really? What happened to them? Use the text to support your answers.
3. The story ends with the narrator saying "We must build again." Why does the narrator feel this way after his journey? In what ways was he changed by his experience in the Dead Places?

Writing Options

1. The setting of this story is very important and may seem rather strange or unusual. How do you visualize the different places the narrator goes? Imagine you will produce a movie based on this story. Using your own visualizations, write director's notes describing the film sets that will be used in the movie.
2. Imagine a publisher is going to include "By the Waters of Babylon" in an anthology, and you have been asked to write a one-paragraph critical introduction to the story. In your introduction, discuss the significance of the story's title and examine its main themes.

 Go to **www.mirrorsandwindows.com** for more.

There Will Come Soft Rains

A Short Story by **Ray Bradbury**

Ray Bradbury (b. 1920) is best known for his science fiction and fantasy stories, although he has also written children's books, poetry, and plays. His science fiction stories offer social criticism and warnings against uncontrolled technological development.

The title of the story **"There Will Come Soft Rains"** refers to a poem by Sara Teasdale about the destruction of mankind. Though it was written in 1951, this science fiction story is set in 2026. It takes place inside a house in which computers and machines do everything, and from which the owners have disappeared.

How do you imagine life in the year 2026?

> The five spots of paint—the man, the woman, the children, the ball—remained. The rest was a thin charcoaled layer.

In the living room the voice-clock sang, *Tick-tock, seven o'clock, time to get up, time to get up, seven o'clock!* as if it were afraid that nobody would. The morning house lay empty. The clock ticked on, repeating and repeating its sounds into the emptiness. *Seven-nine, breakfast time, seven-nine!*

In the kitchen the breakfast stove gave a hissing sigh and ejected from its warm interior eight pieces of perfectly browned toast, eight eggs sunnyside up, sixteen slices of bacon, two coffees, and two cool glasses of milk.

"Today is August 4, 2026," said a second voice from the kitchen ceiling, "in the City of Allendale, California." It repeated the date three times for memory's sake. "Today is Mr. Featherstone's birthday. Today is the anniversary of Tilita's marriage. Insurance is payable, as are the water, gas, and light bills."

Somewhere in the walls, relays clicked, memory tapes glided under electric eyes.

Eight-one, tick-tock, eight-one o'clock, off to school, off to work, run, run, eight-one! But no doors slammed, no carpets took the soft tread of rubber heels. It was raining outside. The weather box on the front door sang quietly: "Rain, rain, go away; rubbers, raincoats for today...." And the rain tapped on the empty house, echoing.

Outside, the garage chimed and lifted its door to reveal the waiting car. After a long wait the door swung down again.

At eight-thirty the eggs were shriveled and the toast was like stone. An aluminum wedge scraped them into the sink, where hot water whirled them down a metal throat that digested and flushed them away to the distant sea. The dirty dishes were dropped into a hot washer and emerged twinkling dry.

Nine-fifteen, sang the clock, time to clean.

Out of warrens[1] in the wall, tiny robot mice darted. The rooms were acrawl with the small cleaning animals, all rubber and metal. They thudded against chairs, whirling their mustached runners, kneading[2] the rug nap, sucking gently at hidden dust. Then, like mysterious invaders, they popped into their burrows. Their pink electric eyes faded. The house was clean.

Ten o'clock. The sun came out from behind the rain. The house stood alone in a city of rubble and ashes. This was the one house left standing. At night the ruined city gave off a radioactive[3] glow which could be seen for miles.

Ten-fifteen. The garden sprinklers whirled up in golden founts, filling the soft morning air with scatterings of brightness. The water pelted windowpanes, running down the charred west side where the house had been burned evenly free of its white paint. The entire west face of the house was black, save for five places. Here the silhouette in paint of a man mowing a lawn. Here, as in a photograph, a woman bent to pick flowers. Still farther over, their images burned on wood in one titanic instant, a small boy, hands flung into the air; higher up, the image of a thrown ball, and opposite him a girl, hands raised to catch a ball which never came down.

The five spots of paint—the man, the woman, the children, the ball—remained. The rest was a thin charcoaled layer.

The gentle sprinkler rain filled the garden with falling light.

Until this day, how well the house had kept its peace. How carefully it had inquired, "Who goes there? What's the password?" and, getting no answer from lonely foxes and whining cats, it had shut up its windows and drawn shades in a preoccupation with self-protection that bordered on a mechanical paranoia.

It quivered at each sound, the house did. If a sparrow brushed a window, the shade

---

1. **warrens.** Tunneled homes produced by small mammals
2. **kneading.** Pressing, rubbing, or squeezing
3. **radioactive.** Capable of releasing dangerous nuclear energy

snapped up. The bird, startled, flew off! No, not even a bird must touch the house!

The house was an altar with ten thousand attendants, big, small, servicing, attending, in choirs. But the gods had gone away, and the ritual of the religion continued senselessly, uselessly.

Twelve noon.

A dog whined, shivering, on the front porch.

The front door recognized the dog voice and opened. The dog, once huge and fleshy, but now gone to bone and covered with sores, moved in and through the house, tracking mud. Behind it whirred angry mice, angry at having to pick up mud, angry at inconvenience.

For not a leaf fragment blew under the door but what the wall panels flipped open and the copper scrap rats flashed swiftly out. The offending dust, hair, or paper, seized in miniature steel jaws, was raced back to the burrows. There, down tubes which fed into the cellar, it was dropped into the sighing vent of an incinerator[4] which sat like evil Baal[5] in a dark corner.

The dog ran upstairs, hysterically yelping to each door, at last realizing, as the house realized, that only silence was here.

It sniffed the air and scratched the kitchen door. Behind the door, the stove was making pancakes that filled the house with a rich baked odor and the scent of maple syrup.

The dog frothed at the mouth, lying at the door, sniffing, its eyes turned to fire. It ran wildly in circles, biting at its tail, spun in a frenzy, and died. It lay in the parlor for an hour.

Two o'clock, sang a voice.

Delicately sensing decay at last, the regiments of mice hummed out as softly as blown gray leaves in an electrical wind.

Two-fifteen.

The dog was gone.

In the cellar, the incinerator glowed suddenly and a whirl of sparks leaped up the chimney.

Two thirty-five.

Bridge[6] tables sprouted from patio walls. Playing cards fluttered onto pads in a shower of pips.[7] Drinks manifested on an oaken bench with egg-salad sandwiches. Music played.

But the tables were silent and the cards untouched.

At four o'clock the tables folded like great butterflies back through the paneled walls.

Four-thirty.

The nursery walls glowed.

Animals took shape: yellow giraffes, blue lions, pink antelopes, lilac panthers cavorting in crystal substance. The walls were glass. They looked out upon color and fantasy. Hidden films clocked through well-oiled sprockets,[8] and the walls lived. The nursery floor was woven to resemble a crisp, cereal meadow. Over this ran aluminum roaches and iron crickets, and in the hot still air butterflies of delicate red tissue wavered among the sharp aroma of animal spoors![9] There was the sound like a great matted yellow hive of bees within a dark bellows, the lazy bumble of a purring lion. And there was the patter of okapi[10] feet and the murmur of a fresh jungle rain, like other hoofs, falling upon the summer-parched grass. Now the walls dissolved into distances of parched weed, mile on mile, and warm endless sky. The animals drew away into thorn brakes and water holes.

It was the children's hour.

Five o'clock. The bath filled with clear hot water.

Six, seven, eight o'clock. The dinner dishes manipulated like magic tricks, and in the study a *click.* In the metal stand opposite the hearth where a fire now blazed up warmly, a cigar popped out, half an inch of soft gray ash on it, smoking, waiting.

---

4. **incinerator.** Furnace designed to burn waste

5. **Baal (bā´ əl).** God of the ancient Canaanites and Phoenicians

6. **Bridge.** Card game involving team strategy

7. **pips.** Figures on playing cards indicating the suit (diamonds, spades, clubs, or hearts)

8. **clocked through well-oiled sprockets.** Moved regularly through holes lined up in rows, like film in a camera

9. **spoors.** Tracks, trails, or droppings of a hunted animal

10. **okapi.** African animal with zebra-like stripes and a giraffe-like neck

Nine o'clock. The beds warmed their hidden circuits, for nights were cool here.

Nine-five. A voice spoke from the study ceiling:

"Mrs. McClellan, which poem would you like this evening?"

The house was silent.

The voice said at last, "Since you express no preference, I shall select a poem at random." Quiet music rose to back the voice. "Sara Teasdale. As I recall, your favorite…"

There will come soft rains and the smell of the
    ground,
And swallows circling with their shimmering sound;

And frogs in the pools singing at night,
And wild plum trees in tremulous[11] white;

Robins will wear their feathery fire,
Whistling their whims on a low fence-wire;

And not one will know of the war, not one
Will care at last when it is done.

Not one would mind, neither bird nor tree,
If mankind perished utterly;

And Spring herself, when she woke at dawn
Would scarcely know that we were gone.

The fire burned on the stone hearth, and the cigar fell away into a mound of quiet ash on its tray. The empty chairs faced each other between the silent walls, and the music played.

At ten o'clock the house began to die.

The wind blew. A falling tree bough crashed through the kitchen window. Cleaning solvent, bottled, shattered over the stove. The room was ablaze in an instant!

"Fire!" screamed a voice. The house lights flashed, water pumps shot water from the ceilings. But the solvent spread on the linoleum, licking, eating, under the kitchen door, while the voices took it up in chorus: "Fire, fire, fire!"

The house tried to save itself. Doors sprang tightly shut, but the windows were broken by the heat and the wind blew and sucked upon the fire.

The house gave ground as the fire in ten billion angry sparks moved with flaming ease from room to room and then up the stairs. While scurrying water rats squeaked from the walls, pistoled their water, and ran for more. And the wall sprays let down showers of mechanical rain.

But too late. Somewhere, sighing, a pump shrugged to a stop. The quenching rain ceased. The reserve water supply which had filled baths and washed dishes for many quiet days was gone.

---

11. **tremulous.** Trembling; quivering

The fire crackled up the stairs. It fed upon Picassos and Matisses[12] in the upper halls, like delicacies, baking off the oily flesh, tenderly crisping the canvases into black shavings.

Now the fire lay in beds, stood in windows, changed the colors of drapes!

And then, reinforcements.

From attic trapdoors, blind robot faces peered down with faucet mouths gushing green chemical.

The fire backed off, as even an elephant must at the sight of a dead snake. Now there were twenty snakes whipping over the floor, killing the fire with a clear cold venom of green froth.

But the fire was clever. It had sent flame outside the house, up through the attic to the pumps there. An explosion! The attic brain which directed the pumps was shattered into bronze shrapnel[13] on the beams.

The fire rushed back into every closet and felt the clothes hung there.

The house shuddered, oak bone on bone, its bared skeleton cringing from the heat, its wire, its nerves revealed as if a surgeon had torn the skin off to let the red veins and capillaries[14] quiver in the scalded air. Help, help; Fire! Run, run! Heat snapped mirrors like the first brittle winter ice. And the voices wailed Fire, fire, run, run, like a tragic nursery rhyme, a dozen voices, high, low, like children dying in a forest, alone, alone. And the voices fading as the wires popped their sheathings like hot chestnuts. One, two, three, four, five voices died.

In the nursery the jungle burned. Blue lions roared, purple giraffes bounded off. The panthers ran in circles, changing color, and ten million animals, running before the fire, vanished off toward a distant steaming river....

Ten more voices died. In the last instant under the fire avalanche, other choruses, oblivious, could be heard announcing the time, playing music, cutting the lawn by remote-control mower, or setting an umbrella frantically out and in the slamming and opening front door, a thousand things happening, like a clock shop when each clock strikes the hour insanely before or after the other, a scene of maniac confusion, yet unity; singing, screaming, a few last cleaning mice darting bravely out to carry the horrid ashes away! And one voice, with sublime disregard for the situation, read aloud in the fiery study, until all the film spools burned, until all the wires withered and the circuits cracked.

The fire burst the house and let it slam flat down, puffing out skirts of spark and smoke.

In the kitchen, an instant before the rain of fire and timber, the stove could be seen making breakfasts at a psychopathic rate, ten dozen eggs, six loaves of toast, twenty dozen bacon strips, which, eaten by fire, started the stove working again, hysterically hissing!

The crash. The attic smashing into kitchen and parlor. The parlor into cellar, cellar into subcellar. Deep freeze, armchair, film tapes, circuits, beds, and all like skeletons thrown in a cluttered mound deep under.

Smoke and silence. A great quantity of smoke.

Dawn showed faintly in the east. Among the ruins, one wall stood alone. Within the wall, a last voice said, over and over again and again, even as the sun rose to shine upon the heaped rubble and steam:

"Today is August 5, 2026, today is August 5, 2026, today is..." ❖

---

12. **Picassos and Matisses.** Works of art by Spanish artist Pablo Picasso and French artist Henri Matisse
13. **shrapnel.** Bits of shattered metal thrown from an explosion
14. **capillaries.** Small blood vessels

MIRRORS & WINDOWS

Which of the modern conveniences in the house would you like in your house? What might the disadvantages be of these modern conveniences? Do you think the kind of house described in this story will ever be a reality? Why or why not? How would it affect family life and neighborhoods if everyone had a house like the one in the story?

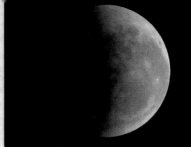

NERUDA

Literature CONNECTION

Pablo Neruda is the pen name of Neftalí Ricardo Reyes Basoalto (1904–1973), a Chilean poet who won the Nobel Prize for literature in 1971. Neruda served as a diplomat representing Chile in Argentina, Spain, and Mexico. After losing favor with the rightist government of his homeland, he went into exile in Italy, a period in his life depicted in the movie *The Postman* (1995). Neruda's poem "**House**" was published after he died in the poetry collection *Neruda at Isla Negra* (1998). The poem appears here in the English translation.

HOUSE

A Poem by **Pablo Neruda**

Perhaps this is the house I lived in
when neither I nor earth existed,
when all was moon or stone or darkness,
when still light was unborn.
5 Perhaps then this stone was
my house, my windows or my eyes.
This rose of granite[1] reminds me
of something that dwelled in me or I in it,
cave, or cosmic head of dreams,
10 cup or castle, ship or birth.
I touch the stubborn spirit of rock,
its rampart[2] pounds in the brine,[3]
and my flaws remain here,
wrinkled essence[4] that rose

15 from the depths to my soul,
and stone I was, stone I will be. Because
   of this
I touch this stone, and for me it hasn't
   died:
it's what I was, what I will be, resting
from a struggle long as time. ❖

---

1. **granite.** A tough, highly durable rock that makes up much of Earth's continents. Granite forms under intense pressure below the Earth's surface from a mixture of rock and lava.
2. **rampart.** A protective barrier
3. **brine.** Sea water
4. **essence.** The most significant quality or element of a thing or person

Refer and Reason

1. List ways in which the house seems alive. Identify passages in the story where the house is described as if it had feelings. In what ways is the house unfeeling?

2. How did you react to the house in this story? Does it seem comfortable and pleasant, or ominous and strange? What attitude does the narrator have toward the house?

3. What hints does this story give about Ray Bradbury's view of technology? How does Bradbury's view of technology compare with the view expressed in "By the Waters of Babylon"? Support your answers with evidence from the two texts.

Writing Options

1. Pretend the house is being interviewed. Write a monologue by the house recalling its day-to-day activities and its fateful end.

2. What do you think the world will be like in 2026? Will humanity destroy itself? Write the outline for a short story that addresses these questions. Include detailed descriptions of the plot, setting, conflict, and characters.

Go to **www.mirrorsandwindows.com** for more.

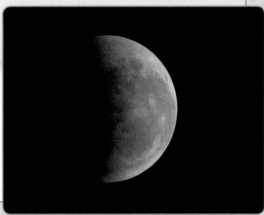

TEXT ←TO→ TEXT CONNECTION

From what point of view is "House" told? How does this choice affect your reading of the poem? From what point of view is "There Will Come Soft Rains" told? Which perspective do you find more compelling? Why? What effect does the author of each selection achieve with his choice of point of view?

Miriam

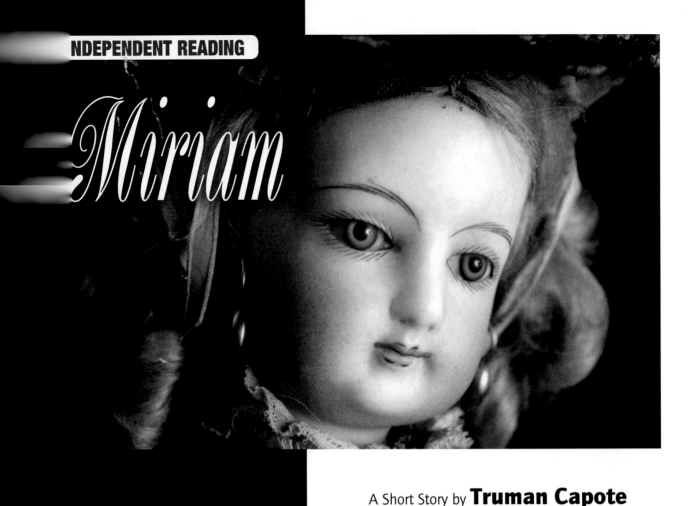

A Short Story by **Truman Capote**

Truman Capote (1924–1984) was born in New Orleans, Louisiana. His mother abandoned him, and he was raised by relatives in Alabama. Capote began to write at the age of eleven. He said, "I used to go home from school every day and I would write for about three hours. I was obsessed by it."

"Miriam" was first published in 1945. It was this story that caught the attention of publishers and landed Capote a contract with Random House. In the story, a widow is visited by a mysterious little girl who shares her first name.

Have you ever heard about or witnessed something that could not be explained? Describe your experience.

For several years, Mrs. H. T. Miller had lived alone in a pleasant apartment (two rooms with kitchenette) in a remodeled brownstone[1] near the East River.[2] She was a widow: Mr. H. T. Miller had left a reasonable amount of insurance. Her interests were narrow, she had no friends to speak of, and she rarely journeyed farther than the corner grocery. The other people in the house never seemed to notice her: her clothes were matter-of-fact, her hair iron-gray, clipped and casually waved; she did not use cosmetics, her features were plain and inconspicuous, and on her last birthday she was sixty-one. Her activities were seldom spontaneous: she kept the two rooms immaculate, smoked an

---

1. **brownstone.** A house or building made with reddish brown sandstone; a common type of apartment building in New York City
2. **East River.** The river that separates Manhattan and the Bronx from Brooklyn and Queens in New York City

Mrs. Miller's face dissolved into a mask of ugly red lines; she began to cry, and it was an unnatural, tearless sort of weeping, as though, not having wept for a long time, she had forgotten how.

occasional cigarette, prepared her own meals and tended a canary.

Then she met Miriam. It was snowing that night. Mrs. Miller had finished drying the supper dishes and was thumbing through an afternoon paper when she saw an advertisement of a picture playing at a neighborhood theatre. The title sounded good, so she struggled into her beaver coat, laced her galoshes and left the apartment, leaving one light burning in the foyer: she found nothing more disturbing than a sensation of darkness.

The snow was fine, falling gently, not yet making an impression on the pavement. The wind from the river cut only at street crossings. Mrs. Miller hurried, her head bowed, oblivious as a mole burrowing a blind path. She stopped at a drugstore and bought a package of peppermints.

A long line stretched in front of the box office; she took her place at the end. There would be (a tired voice groaned) a short wait for all seats. Mrs. Miller rummaged in her leather handbag till she collected exactly the correct change for admission. The line seemed to be taking its own time and, looking around for some distraction, she suddenly became conscious of a little girl standing under the edge of the marquee.

Her hair was the longest and strangest Mrs. Miller had ever seen: absolutely silver-white, like an albino's.[3] It flowed waist-length in smooth, loose lines. She was thin and fragilely constructed. There was a simple, special elegance in the way she stood with her thumbs in the pockets of a tailored plum-velvet coat.

Mrs. Miller felt oddly excited, and when the little girl glanced toward her, she smiled warmly. The little girl walked over and said, "Would you care to do me a favor?"

"I'd be glad to, if I can," said Mrs. Miller.

"Oh, it's quite easy. I merely want you to buy a ticket for me; they won't let me in otherwise. Here, I have the money." And gracefully she handed Mrs. Miller two dimes and a nickel.

They went over to the theatre together. An usherette directed them to a lounge; in twenty minutes the picture would be over.

"I feel just like a genuine criminal," said Mrs. Miller gaily, as she sat down. "I mean that sort of thing's against the law, isn't it? I do hope I haven't done the wrong thing. Your mother knows where you are, dear? I mean she does, doesn't she?"

The little girl said nothing. She unbuttoned her coat and folded it across her lap. Her dress underneath was prim and dark blue. A

3. **albino.** A person or an animal whose skin and hair have no pigmentation, or color

gold chain dangled about her neck, and her fingers, sensitive and musical-looking, toyed with it. Examining her more attentively, Mrs. Miller decided the truly distinctive feature was not her hair, but her eyes; they were hazel, steady, lacking any childlike quality whatsoever and, because of their size, seemed to consume her small face.

Mrs. Miller offered a peppermint. "What's your name, dear?"

"Miriam," she said, as though, in some curious way, it were information already familiar.

"Why, isn't that funny— my name's Miriam, too. And it's not a terribly common name either. Now, don't tell me your last name's Miller!"

"Just Miriam."

"But isn't that funny?"

"Moderately," said Miriam, and rolled the peppermint on her tongue.

Mrs. Miller flushed and shifted uncomfortably. "You have such a large vocabulary for such a little girl."

"Do I?"

"Well, yes," said Mrs. Miller, hastily changing the topic to: "Do you like the movies?"

"I really wouldn't know," said Miriam. "I've never been before."

Women began filling the lounge; the rumble of the newsreel bombs exploded in the distance. Mrs. Miller rose, tucking her purse under her arm. "I guess I'd better be running now if I want to get a seat," she said. "It was nice to have met you."

Miriam nodded ever so slightly.

It snowed all week. Wheels and footsteps moved soundlessly on the street, as if the business of living continued secretly behind a pale but impenetrable curtain. In the falling quiet there was no sky or earth, only snow lifting in

the wind, frosting the window glass, chilling the rooms, deadening and hushing the city. At all hours it was necessary to keep a lamp lighted, and Mrs. Miller lost track of the days: Friday was no different from Saturday and on Sunday she went to the grocery: closed, of course.

That evening she scrambled eggs and fixed a bowl of tomato soup. Then, after putting on a flannel robe and cold-creaming her face, she propped herself up in bed with a hot-water bottle under her feet. She was reading the *Times* when the doorbell rang.

At first she thought it must be a mistake and whoever it was would go away. But it rang and rang and settled to a persistent buzz. She looked at the clock: a little after eleven; it did not seem possible, she was always asleep by ten.

Climbing out of bed, she trotted barefoot across the living room. "I'm coming, please be patient." The latch was caught; she turned it this way and that way and the bell never paused an instant. "Stop it," she cried. The bolt gave way and she opened the door an inch. "What in heaven's name?"

"Hello," said Miriam.

"Oh…why, hello," said Mrs. Miller, stepping hesitantly into the hall. "You're that little girl."

"I thought you'd never answer, but I kept my finger on the button; I knew you were home. Aren't you glad to see me?"

Mrs. Miller did not know what to say. Miriam, she saw, wore the same plum-velvet coat and now she had also a beret to match; her white hair was braided in two shining plaits and looped at the ends with enormous white ribbons.

"Since I've waited so long, you could at least let me in," she said.

"It's awfully late…."

> "Why, isn't that funny—my name's Miriam, too."

Woman on a Red Couch, 1950. Jean Puy. Private collection.

Miriam regarded her blankly. "What difference does that make? Let me in. It's cold out here and I have on a silk dress." Then, with a gentle gesture, she urged Mrs. Miller aside and passed into the apartment.

She dropped her coat and beret on a chair. She was indeed wearing a silk dress. White silk. White silk in February. The skirt was beautifully pleated and the sleeves long; it made a faint rustle as she strolled about the room. "I like your place," she said. "I like the rug, blue's my favorite color." She touched a paper rose in a vase on the coffee table. "Imitation," she commented wanly. "How sad. Aren't imitations sad?" She seated herself on the sofa, daintily spreading her skirt.

"What do you want?" asked Mrs. Miller.

"Sit down," said Miriam. "It makes me nervous to see people stand."

Mrs. Miller sank to a hassock. "What do you want?" she repeated.

"You know, I don't think you're glad I came."

For a second time Mrs. Miller was without an answer; her hand motioned vaguely. Miriam giggled and pressed back on a mound of chintz pillows. Mrs. Miller observed that the girl was less pale than she remembered; her cheeks were flushed.

"How did you know where I lived?"

Miriam frowned. "That's no question at all. What's your name? What's mine?"

"But I'm not listed in the phone book."

"Oh, let's talk about something else."

Mrs. Miller said, "Your mother must be insane to let a child like you wander around at all hours of the night—and in such ridiculous clothes. She must be out of her mind."

Miriam got up and moved to a corner where a covered bird cage hung from a ceiling chain. She peeked beneath the cover. "It's a canary," she said. "Would you mind if I woke him? I'd like to hear him sing."

"Leave Tommy alone," said Mrs. Miller, anxiously. "Don't you dare wake him."

"Certainly," said Miriam. "But I don't see why I can't hear him sing." And then, "Have you anything to eat? I'm starving! Even milk and a jam sandwich would be fine."

"Look," said Mrs. Miller, arising from the hassock, "look—if I make some nice sand-wiches will you be a good child and run along home? It's past midnight, I'm sure."

"It's snowing," reproached Miriam. "And cold and dark."

"Well, you shouldn't have come here to begin with," said Mrs. Miller, struggling to control her voice. "I can't help the weather. If you want anything to eat you'll have to promise to leave."

Miriam brushed a braid against her cheek. Her eyes were thoughtful, as if weighing the proposition. She turned toward the bird cage. "Very well," she said. "I promise."

How old is she? Ten? Eleven? Mrs. Miller, in the kitchen, unsealed a jar of strawberry preserves and cut four slices of bread. She poured a glass of milk and paused to light a cigarette. *And why has she come?* Her hand shook as she held the match, fascinated, till it burned her finger. The canary was singing; singing as he did in the morning and at no other time. "Miriam," she called. "Miriam, I told you not to disturb Tommy." There was no answer. She called again; all she heard was the canary. She inhaled the cigarette and discov-ered she had lighted the cork-tip end and—oh, really, she mustn't lose her temper.

She carried the food in on a tray and set it on the coffee table. She saw first that the bird cage still wore its night cover. And Tommy was singing. It gave her a queer sensation. And no one was in the room. Mrs. Miller went through an alcove leading to her bedroom; at the door, she caught her breath.

"What are you doing?" she asked.

Miriam glanced up and in her eyes there was a look that was not ordinary. She was standing by the bureau, a jewel case opened before her. For a minute she studied Mrs. Miller, forcing their eyes to meet, and she smiled. "There's nothing good here," she said. "But I like this." Her hand held a cameo brooch. "It's charming."

"Suppose—perhaps you'd better put it back," said Mrs. Miller, feeling suddenly the need of some support. She leaned against the door frame; her head was unbear-ably heavy; a pressure weighted the rhythm of her heartbeat. The light seemed to flutter defectively. "Please, child—a gift from my husband…"

"But it's beautiful and I want it," said Miriam. *"Give it to me."*

As she stood, striving to shape a sentence which would somehow save the brooch, it came to Mrs. Miller there was no one to whom she might turn; she was alone; a fact that had not been among her thoughts for a long time. Its sheer emphasis was stunning. But here in her own room in the hushed snow-city were evidences she could not ignore or, she knew with startling clarity, resist.

Miriam ate ravenously, and when the sandwiches and milk were gone, her fingers made cobweb movements over the plate, gathering crumbs. The cameo gleamed on her blouse, the blond profile like a trick reflection of its wearer. "That was very nice," she sighed, "though now an almond cake or a cherry would be ideal. Sweets are lovely, don't you think?"

Mrs. Miller was perched precariously on the hassock, smoking a cigarette. Her hair net had slipped lopsided and loose strands straggled down her face. Her eyes were stupidly concentrated on nothing and her cheeks were mottled in red patches, as though a fierce slap had left permanent marks.

"Is there a candy—a cake?"

Mrs. Miller tapped ash on the rug. Her head swayed slightly as she tried to focus her eyes. "You promised to leave if I made the sandwiches," she said.

"Dear me, did I?"

"It was a promise and I'm tired and I don't feel well at all."

"Mustn't fret," said Miriam. "I'm only teasing."

She picked up her coat, slung it over her arm, and arranged her beret in front of a mirror. Presently she bent close to Mrs. Miller and whispered, "Kiss me good night."

"Please—I'd rather not," said Mrs. Miller.

Miriam lifted a shoulder, arched an eyebrow. "As you like," she said, and went directly to the coffee table, seized the vase containing the paper roses, carried it to where the hard surface of the floor lay bare, and hurled it downward. Glass sprayed in all directions and she stomped her foot on the bouquet.

Then slowly she walked to the door, but before closing it she looked back at Mrs. Miller with a slyly innocent curiosity.

> *Oh, it was a wonderful day—more like a holiday—and it would be so foolish to go home.*

Mrs. Miller spent the next day in bed, rising once to feed the canary and drink a cup of tea; she took her temperature and had none, yet her dreams were feverishly agitated; their unbalanced mood lingered even as she lay staring wide-eyed at the ceiling. One dream threaded through the others like an elusively mysterious theme in a complicated symphony, and the scenes it depicted were sharply outlined, as though sketched by a hand of gifted intensity: a small girl, wearing a bridal gown and a wreath of leaves, led a gray procession down a mountain path, and among them there was unusual silence till a woman at the rear asked, "Where is she taking us?" "No one knows," said an old man marching in front. "But isn't she pretty?" volunteered a third voice. "Isn't she like a frost flower…so shining and white?"

Tuesday morning she woke up feeling better; harsh slats of sunlight, slanting through Venetian blinds, shed a disrupting light on her unwholesome fancies. She opened the window to discover a thawed, mild-as-spring day; a sweep of clean new clouds crumpled against a vastly blue, out-of-season sky; and across the low line of rooftops she could see the river and smoke curving from tugboat stacks in a warm wind. A great silver truck plowed the snow-banked street, its machine sound humming on the air.

After straightening the apartment, she went to the grocer's, cashed a check and continued to Schrafft's[4] where she ate breakfast and chatted happily with the waitress. Oh, it was a wonderful day—more like a holiday—and it would be so foolish to go home.

She boarded a Lexington Avenue bus and rode up to Eighty-sixth Street; it was here that she had decided to do a little shopping.

---

4. **Schrafft's.** A restaurant chain in New York City and popular in the early twentieth century

She had no idea what she wanted or needed, but she idled along, intent only upon the passers-by, brisk and preoccupied, who gave her a disturbing sense of separateness.

It was while waiting at the corner of Third Avenue that she saw the man: an old man, bowlegged and stooped under an armload of bulging packages; he wore a shabby brown coat and a checkered cap. Suddenly she realized they were exchanging a smile: there was nothing friendly about this smile, it was merely two cold flickers of recognition. But she was certain she had never seen him before.

He was standing next to an El pillar, and as she crossed the street he turned and followed. He kept quite close; from the corner of her eye she watched his reflection wavering on the shopwindows.

Then in the middle of the block she stopped and faced him. He stopped also and cocked his head, grinning. But what could she say? Do? Here, in broad daylight, on Eighty-sixth Street? It was useless and, despising her own helplessness, she quickened her steps.

Now Second Avenue is a dismal street, made from scraps and ends; part cobblestone, part asphalt, part cement; and its atmosphere of desertion is permanent. Mrs. Miller walked five blocks without meeting anyone, and all the while the steady crunch of his footfalls in the snow stayed near. And when she came to a florist's shop, the sound was still with her. She hurried inside and watched through the glass door as the old man passed; he kept his eyes straight ahead and didn't slow his pace, but he did one strange, telling thing: he tipped his cap.

"Six white ones, did you say?" asked the florist. "Yes," she told him, "white roses." From there she went to a glassware store and selected a vase, presumably a replacement for the one Miriam had broken, though the price was intolerable and the vase itself (she thought) grotesquely vulgar. But a series of unaccountable purchases had begun as if by prearranged plan: a plan of which she had not the knowledge or control.

She bought a bag of glazed cherries, and at a place called the Knickerbocker Bakery she paid forty cents for six almond cakes.

Within the last hour the weather had turned cold again; like blurred lenses, winter clouds cast a shade over the sun, and the skeleton of an early dusk colored the sky; a damp mist mixed with the wind and the voices of a few children who romped high on mountains of gutter snow seemed lonely and cheerless. Soon the first flake fell, and when Mrs. Miller reached the brownstone house, snow was falling in a swift screen and foot tracks vanished as they were printed.

The white roses were arranged decoratively in the vase. The glazed cherries shone on a ceramic plate. The almond cakes, dusted with sugar, awaited a hand. The canary fluttered on its swing and picked at a bar of seed.

At precisely five the doorbell rang. Mrs. Miller *knew* who it was. The hem of her housecoat trailed as she crossed the floor. "Is that you?" she called.

"Naturally," said Miriam, the word resounding shrilly from the hall. "Open this door."

"Go away," said Mrs. Miller.

"Please hurry…I have a heavy package."

"Go away," said Mrs. Miller. She returned to the living room, lighted a cigarette, sat down and calmly listened to the buzzer; on and on and on. "You might as well leave. I have no intention of letting you in."

Shortly the bell stopped. For possibly ten minutes Mrs. Miller did not move. Then, hearing no sound, she concluded Miriam had gone. She tiptoed to the door and opened it a sliver; Miriam was half-reclining atop a cardboard box with a beautiful French doll cradled in her arms.

"Really, I thought you were never coming," she said peevishly. "Here, help me get this in, it's awfully heavy."

It was not spell-like compulsion that Mrs. Miller felt, but rather a curious passivity; she brought in the box, Miriam the doll. Miriam curled up on the sofa, not troubling to remove her coat or beret, and watched disinterestedly as Mrs. Miller dropped the box and stood trembling, trying to catch her breath.

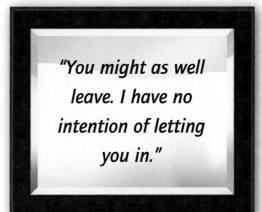

"You might as well leave. I have no intention of letting you in."

"Thank you," she said. In the daylight she looked pinched and drawn, her hair less luminous. The French doll she was loving wore an exquisite powdered wig and its idiot glass eyes sought solace in Miriam's. "I have a surprise," she continued. "Look into my box."

Kneeling, Mrs. Miller parted the flaps and lifted out another doll; then a blue dress which she recalled as the one Miriam had worn that first night at the theatre; and of the remainder she said, "It's all clothes. Why?"

"Because I've come to live with you," said Miriam, twisting a cherry stem. "Wasn't it nice of you to buy me the cherries…?"

"But you can't! For God's sake go away—go away and leave me alone!"

"…and the roses and the almond cakes? How really wonderfully generous. You know, these cherries are delicious. The last place I lived was with an old man; he was terribly poor and we never had good things to eat. But I think I'll be happy here." She paused to snuggle her doll closer. "Now, if you'll just show me where to put my things."

Mrs. Miller's face dissolved into a mask of ugly red lines; she began to cry, and it was an unnatural, tearless sort of weeping, as though, not having wept for a long time, she had forgotten how. Carefully, she edged backward till she touched the door.

She fumbled through the hall and down the stairs to a landing below. She pounded frantically on the door of the first apartment she came to: a short, redheaded man answered and she pushed past him. "Say, what the hell is this?" he said. "Anything wrong, lover?" asked a young woman who appeared from the kitchen, drying her hands. And it was to her that Mrs. Miller turned.

Girl Brushing Her Hair, 1920. Dorothy Johnstone. Private collection.

going to do something terrible. She's already stolen my cameo, but she's about to do something worse—something terrible!"

The man asked, "Is she a relative, huh?"

Mrs. Miller shook her head. "I don't know who she is. Her name's Miriam, but I don't know for certain who she is."

"You gotta calm down, honey," said the woman, stroking Mrs. Miller's arm. "Harry here'll tend to this kid. Go on, lover." And Mrs. Miller said, "The door's open—5A."

After the man left, the woman brought a towel and bathed Mrs. Miller's face. "You're very kind," Mrs. Miller said. "I'm sorry to act like such a fool, only this wicked child…"

"Sure honey," consoled the woman. "Now, you better take it easy."

Mrs. Miller rested her head in the crook of her arm: she was quiet enough to be asleep. The woman turned a radio dial; a piano and a husky voice filled the silence and the woman, tapping her foot, kept excellent time. "Maybe we oughta go up too," she said.

"I don't want to see her again. I don't want to be anywhere near her."

"Uh-huh, but what you shoulda done, you shoulda called a cop."

Presently they heard the man on the stairs. He strode into the room frowning and scratching the back of his neck. "Nobody

"Listen," she cried, "I'm ashamed behaving this way but—well, I'm Mrs. H. T. Miller and I live upstairs and…" She pressed her hands over her face. "It sounds so absurd…"

The woman guided her to a chair, while the man excitedly rattled pocket change. "Yeah?"

"I live upstairs and there's a little girl visiting me, and I suppose that I'm afraid of her. She won't leave and I can't make her and—she's there," he said, honestly embarrassed. "She musta beat it."

"Harry, you're a jerk," announced the woman. "We been sitting here the whole time and we woulda seen…" she stopped abruptly for the man's glance was sharp.

"I looked all over," he said, "and there just ain't nobody there. Nobody, understand?"

"Tell me," said Mrs. Miller, rising, "tell me, did you see a large box? Or a doll?"

"No, ma'am, I didn't."

And the woman, as if delivering a verdict, said, "Well, for cryinoutloud…."

Mrs. Miller entered her apartment softly; she walked to the center of the room and stood quite still. No, in a sense it had not changed: the roses, the cakes, and the cherries were in place. But this was an empty room, emptier than if the furnishings and familiars were not present, lifeless and petrified as a funeral parlor. The sofa loomed before her with a new strangeness: its vacancy had a meaning that would have been less penetrating and terrible had Miriam been curled on it. She gazed fixedly at the space where she remembered setting the box, and for a moment, the hassock spun desperately. And she looked through the window; surely the river was real, surely snow was falling—but then, one could not be certain witness to anything: Miriam, so vividly there— and yet, where was she? Where, where?

As though moving in a dream, she sank to a chair. The room was losing shape; it was dark and getting darker and there was nothing to be done about it; she could not lift her hand to light a lamp.

Suddenly, closing her eyes, she felt an upward surge, like a diver emerging from some deeper, greener depth. In times of terror or immense distress, there are moments when the mind waits, as though for a revelation, while a skein of calm is woven over thought; it is like a sleep, or a supernatural trance; and during this lull one is aware of a force of quiet reasoning: well, what if she had never really known a girl named Miriam? that she had been foolishly frightened on the street? In the end, like everything else, it was of no importance. For the only thing she had lost to Miriam was her identity, but now she had found again the person who lived in this room, who cooked her own meals, who owned a canary, who was someone she could trust and believe in: Mrs. H. T. Miller.

Listening in contentment, she became aware of a double sound: a bureau drawer opening and closing; she seemed to hear it long after completion—opening and closing. Then gradually, the harshness of it was replaced by the murmur of a silk dress and this, delicately faint, was moving nearer and swelling in intensity till the walls trembled with the vibration and the room was caving under a wave of whispers. Mrs. Miller stiffened and opened her eyes to a dull, direct stare.

"Hello," said Miriam. ❖

> *"I don't want to see her again. I don't want to be anywhere near her."*

MIRRORS & WINDOWS

Suppose a friend tells you Mrs. Miller had no reason to be frightened. How would you respond to your friend? If you were Mrs. Miller at the end of the story, what would you do? How have you handled frightening or unexplainable situations in the past?

DICKINSON

Literature CONNECTION

Emily Dickinson (1830–1886) was born and spent most of her life in Amherst, Massachusetts, where she lived a secluded life. At the time of her death, Dickinson had produced over one thousand poems, only seven of which had been published during her lifetime; the rest were published in 1955.

"The Only Ghost I Ever Saw" is included in Part IV, Time and Eternity, of Dickinson's second series of poems in the Project Gutenberg collection. In this poem, the speaker describes a most unusual encounter.

"The only ghost I ever saw"

A Poem by **Emily Dickinson**

The only ghost I ever saw
Was dressed in mechlin[1]—so;
He wore no sandal on his foot,
And stepped like flakes of snow.

5   His gait was soundless, like the bird,
But rapid, like the roe;[2]
His fashions quaint, mosaic,
Or, haply, mistletoe.

His conversation seldom,
10   His laughter like the breeze
That dies away in dimples
Among the pensive trees.
Our interview was transient,[3]—
Of me, himself was shy;
15   And God forbid I look behind
Since that appalling day! ❖

1. **mechlin.** A type of lace
2. **roe.** Deer
3. **transient.** Lasting only a short time

Refer and Reason

1. List the different ways Mrs. Miller reacts to Miriam's presence. What does Mrs. Miller do the first time they meet? What does she do later on? Why does her attitude toward Miriam change?
2. Summarize what happens when Mrs. Miller asks her neighbors for help. What do you think happened when the man went up to Mrs. Miller's apartment? What do the neighbors think of Mrs. Miller?
3. Who do you think Miriam is? Is she real, a ghost, or a figment of Mrs. Miller's imagination? Who is the old man? Use evidence from the text to explain your answers.

Writing Options

1. Who is Miriam? Where did she come from? Using your imagination and what you know about her from the story, write Miriam's life history in the form of several journal entries from her point of view.
2. Examine the characters of Mrs. Miller and Miriam. Consider their personality traits, mannerisms, appearances, and attitudes toward each other. Then write a compare-and-contrast essay describing the similarities and differences between these two characters. If there are aspects of the characters you don't understand, try to work out your questions in your essay.

 Go to **www.mirrorsandwindows.com** for more.

TEXT ⟶TO⟶ TEXT CONNECTION

- How does the description of the ghost in the poem compare with the way Miriam is described? Which description fits better with your idea of what a ghost should look like?
- Compare and contrast the speaker's reaction to the ghost in Emily Dickinson's poem with Mrs. Miller's reaction to Miriam. Which do you find more surprising?

A Very Old Man with Enormous Wings

A Short Story by
Gabriel García Márquez

On the following day everyone knew that a flesh-and-blood angel was held captive in Pelayo's house.

Born in Colombia in 1928, **Gabriel García Márquez** discovered his talent for writing in high school. In 1967, García Márquez published his most famous work, the novel *One Hundred Years of Solitude*.

"A Very Old Man with Enormous Wings" takes place in a rural Latin American village. The people in this fictional village are isolated from outside influences and seek understanding of their world through folklore and the supernatural. This story is an example of *magical realism*, or a kind of fiction that is for the most part realistic but that contains elements of fantasy.

When have you seen something truly unusual—something that seemed "out of this world"? How did you react to what you saw?

On the third day of rain they had killed so many crabs inside the house that Pelayo had to cross his drenched courtyard and throw them into the sea, because the newborn child had a temperature all night and they thought it was due to the stench. The world had been sad since Tuesday. Sea and sky were a single ash-gray thing and the sands of the beach, which on March nights glimmered like powdered light, had become a stew of mud and rotten shellfish. The light was so weak at noon that when Pelayo was coming back to the house after throwing away the crabs, it was hard for him to see what it was that was moving and groaning in the rear of the courtyard. He had to go very close to see that it was an old man, a very old man, lying face down in the mud, who, in spite of his

The Winged Man, 1880s. Odilon Redon. Musée des Beaux-Arts, Bordeaux, France.

tremendous efforts, couldn't get up, impeded by his enormous wings.

Frightened by that nightmare, Pelayo ran to get Elisenda, his wife, who was putting compresses on the sick child, and he took her to the rear of the courtyard. They both looked at the fallen body with mute stupor. He was dressed like a ragpicker. There were only a few faded hairs left on his bald skull and very few teeth in his mouth, and his pitiful condition of a drenched great-grandfather had taken away any sense of grandeur he might have had. His huge buzzard wings, dirty and half-plucked, were forever entangled in the mud. They looked at him so long and so closely that Pelayo and Elisenda very soon overcame their surprise and in the end found him

familiar. Then they dared speak to him, and he answered in an incomprehensible dialect with a strong sailor's voice. That was how they skipped over the inconvenience of the wings and quite intelligently concluded that he was a lonely castaway from some foreign ship wrecked by the storm. And yet, they called in a neighbor woman who knew everything about life and death to see him, and all she needed was one look to show them their mistake.

"He's an angel," she told them. "He must have been coming for the child, but the poor fellow is so old that the rain knocked him down."

On the following day everyone knew that a flesh-and-blood angel was held captive in Pelayo's house. Against the judgment of the wise neighbor woman, for whom angels in those times were the fugitive survivors of a celestial[1] conspiracy, they did not have the heart to club him to death. Pelayo watched over him all afternoon from the kitchen, armed with his bailiff's club, and before going to bed he dragged him out of the mud and locked him up with the hens in the wire chicken coop. In the middle of the night, when the rain stopped, Pelayo and Elisenda were still killing crabs. A short time afterward the child woke up without a fever and with a desire to eat. Then they felt magnanimous and decided to put the angel on a raft with fresh water and provisions for three days and leave him to his fate on the high seas. But when they went out into the courtyard with the first light of dawn, they found the whole neighborhood in front of the chicken coop having fun with the angel, without the slightest reverence, tossing him things to eat through the openings in the wire as if he weren't a supernatural creature but a circus animal.

Father Gonzaga arrived before seven o'clock, alarmed at the strange news. By that time onlookers less frivolous than those at dawn had already arrived and they were making all kinds of conjectures concerning the captive's future. The simplest among them thought that he should be named mayor of the world. Others of sterner mind felt that he should be promoted to the rank of five-star general in order to win all wars. Some visionaries hoped that he could be put to stud in order to implant on earth a race of winged wise men who could take charge of the universe. But Father Gonzaga, before becoming a priest, had been a robust woodcutter. Standing by the wire, he reviewed his catechism[2] in an instant and asked them to open the door so that he could take a close look at that pitiful man who looked more like a huge decrepit hen among the fascinated chickens. He was lying in a corner drying his open wings in the sunlight among the fruit peels and breakfast leftovers that the early risers had thrown him. Alien to the impertinences of the world, he only lifted his antiquarian eyes and murmured something in his dialect when Father Gonzaga went into the chicken coop and said good morning to him in Latin. The parish priest had his first suspicion of an imposter when he saw that he did not understand the language of God or know how to greet His ministers. Then he noticed that seen close up he was much too human: he had an unbearable smell of the outdoors, the back side of his wings was strewn with parasites and his main feathers had been mistreated by terrestrial[3] winds, and nothing about him measured up to the proud dignity of angels. Then he came out of the chicken coop and in a brief sermon warned the curious against the risks of being ingenuous. He reminded them that the devil had the bad habit of making use of carnival tricks in order to confuse the unwary. He argued that if wings were not the essential element in determining the difference between a hawk and an airplane, they were even less so in the recognition of angels. Nevertheless, he promised to write a letter to his bishop so that the latter would write to his primate so that the latter would write to the Supreme Pontiff[4] in order to get the final verdict from the highest courts.

His prudence fell on sterile hearts. The news of the captive angel spread with such rapidity that after a few hours the courtyard had the bustle of a marketplace and they had to call in troops with fixed bayonets to disperse the mob that was about to knock the house down. Elisenda, her spine all twisted from sweeping up so much marketplace trash, then got the idea of fencing in the yard and charging five cents admission to see the angel.

The curious came from far away. A traveling carnival arrived with a flying acrobat who buzzed over the crowd several times, but no

---

1. **celestial.** Of or relating to heaven
2. **catechism** (ka′ tə ki′ zəm). Summary of Christian doctrine, often in the form of questions and answers
3. **terrestrial.** Of or relating to the earth or its inhabitants
4. **Supreme Pontiff.** The Pope, head of the Catholic Church

one paid any attention to him because his wings were not those of an angel but, rather, those of a sidereal bat. The most unfortunate invalids on earth came in search of health: a poor woman who since childhood had been counting her heartbeats and had run out of numbers; a Portuguese man who couldn't sleep because the noise of the stars disturbed him; a sleepwalker who got up at night to undo the things he had done while awake; and many others with less serious ailments. In the midst of that shipwreck disorder that made the earth tremble, Pelayo and Elisenda were happy with fatigue, for in less than a week they had crammed their rooms with money and the line of pilgrims waiting their turn to enter still reached beyond the horizon.

The angel was the only one who took no part in his own act. He spent his time trying to get comfortable in his borrowed nest, befuddled by the hellish heat of the oil lamps and sacramental candles that had been placed along the wire. At first they tried to make him eat some mothballs, which, according to the wisdom of the wise neighbor woman, were the food prescribed for angels. But he turned them down, just as he turned down the papal lunches[5] that the penitents[6] brought him, and they never found out whether it was because he was an angel or because he was an old man that in the end he ate nothing but eggplant mush. His only supernatural virtue seemed to be patience. Especially during the first days, when the hens pecked at him, searching for the stellar parasites that proliferated in his wings, and the cripples pulled out feathers to touch their defective parts with, and even the most merciful threw stones at him, trying to get him to rise so they could see him standing. The only time they succeeded in arousing him was when they burned his side with an iron for branding steers, for he had been motionless for so many hours that they thought he was dead. He awoke with a start, ranting in his hermetic[7] language and with tears in his eyes, and he flapped his wings a couple of times, which brought on a whirlwind of chicken dung and lunar dust and a gale of panic that did not seem to be of this world. Although many thought that his reaction had been one not of rage but of pain, from then on they were careful not to annoy him, because the majority understood that his passivity was not that of a hero taking his ease but that of a cataclysm in repose.

Father Gonzaga held back the crowd's frivolity with formulas of maidservant inspiration while awaiting the arrival of a final

---

5. **papal lunches.** Expensive meals
6. **penitents.** People who are sorry for their sins
7. **hermetic** (hər me′ tik). Difficult or impossible for a person of ordinary understanding or knowledge to comprehend

judgment on the nature of the captive. But the mail from Rome showed no sense of urgency. They spent their time finding out if the prisoner had a navel, if his dialect had any connection with Aramaic,[8] how many times he could fit on the head of a pin, or whether he wasn't just a Norwegian with wings. Those meager letters might have come and gone until the end of time if a providential[9] event had not put an end to the priest's tribulations.

It so happened that during those days, among so many other carnival attractions, there arrived in town the traveling show of the woman who had been changed into a spider for having disobeyed her parents. The admission to see her was not only less than the admission to see the angel, but people were permitted to ask her all manner of questions about her absurd state and to examine her up and down so that no one would ever doubt the truth of her horror. She was a frightful tarantula the size of a ram and with the head of a sad maiden. What was most heartrending, however, was not her outlandish shape but the sincere affliction with which she recounted the details of her misfortune. While still practically a child she had sneaked out of her parents' house to go to a dance, and while she was coming back through the woods after having danced all night without permission, a fearful thunderclap rent the sky in two and through the crack came the lightning bolt of brimstone that changed her into a spider. Her only nourishment came from the meatballs that charitable souls chose to toss into her mouth. A spectacle like that, full of so much human truth and with such a fearful lesson,

---

8. **Aramaic.** Ancient Jewish language
9. **providential.** Occurring by or as if by an intervention of Providence, or heaven

The angel went dragging himself about here and there like a stray dying man.

was bound to defeat without even trying that of a haughty[10] angel who scarcely deigned to look at mortals. Besides, the few miracles attributed to the angel showed a certain mental disorder, like the blind man who didn't recover his sight but grew three new teeth, or the paralytic who didn't get to walk but almost won the lottery, and the leper whose sores sprouted sunflowers. Those consolation miracles, which were more like mocking fun, had already ruined the angel's reputation when the woman who had been changed into a spider finally crushed him completely. That was how Father Gonzaga was cured forever of his insomnia and Pelayo's courtyard went back to being as empty as during the time it had rained for three days and crabs walked through the bedrooms.

The owners of the house had no reason to lament. With the money they saved they built a two-story mansion with balconies and gardens and high netting so that crabs wouldn't get in during the winter, and with iron bars on the windows so that angels wouldn't get in. Pelayo also set up a rabbit warren[11] close to town and gave up his job as bailiff for good, and Elisenda bought some satin pumps with high heels and many dresses of iridescent[12] silk, the kind worn on Sunday by the most desirable women in those times. The chicken coop was the only thing that didn't receive any attention. If they washed it down with creolin[13] and burned tears of myrrh[14] inside it every so often, it was not in homage to the angel but to drive away the dungheap stench that still hung everywhere like a ghost and was turning the new house into an old one. At first, when the child learned to walk, they were careful

that he not get too close to the chicken coop. But then they began to lose their fears and got used to the smell, and before the child got his second teeth he'd gone inside the chicken coop to play, where the wires were falling apart. The angel was no less standoffish with him than with other mortals, but he tolerated the most ingenious infamies with the patience of a dog who had no illusions. They both came down with chicken pox at the same time. The doctor who took care of the child couldn't resist the temptation to listen to the angel's heart, and he found so much whistling in the heart and so many sounds in his kidneys that it seemed impossible for him to be alive. What surprised him most, however, was the logic of his wings. They seemed so natural on that completely human organism that he couldn't understand why other men didn't have them too.

When the child began school it had been some time since the sun and rain had caused the collapse of the chicken coop. The angel went dragging himself about here and there like a stray dying man. They would drive him out of the bedroom with a broom and a moment later find him in the kitchen. He seemed to be in so many places at the same time that they grew to think that he'd been duplicated, that he was reproducing himself all through the house, and the exasperated and unhinged Elisenda shouted that it was awful living in that hell full of angels. He could

---

10. **haughty.** Obviously proud
11. **rabbit warren.** Area or structure where rabbits are kept and bred
12. **iridescent.** Having a lustrous, rainbowlike play of color
13. **creolin.** Type of disinfectant
14. **myrrh.** Fragrant, bitter-tasting powder used in making incense and perfumes

scarcely eat and his antiquarian eyes had also become so foggy that he went about bumping into posts. All he had left were the bare cannulae[15] of his last feathers. Pelayo threw a blanket over him and extended him the charity of letting him sleep in the shed, and only then did they notice that he had a temperature at night, and was delirious with the tongue twisters of an old Norwegian. That was one of the few times they became alarmed, for they thought he was going to die and not even the wise neighbor woman had been able to tell them what to do with dead angels.

And yet he not only survived his worst winter, but seemed improved with the first sunny days. He remained motionless for several days in the farthest corner of the courtyard, where no one would see him, and at the beginning of December some large, stiff feathers began to grow on his wings, the feathers of a scarecrow, which looked more like another misfortune of decrepitude.[16] But he must have known the reason for those changes, for he was quite careful that no one should notice them, that no one should hear the sea chanteys[17]

that he sometimes sang under the stars. One morning Elisenda was cutting some bunches of onions for lunch when a wind that seemed to come from the high seas blew into the kitchen. Then she went to the window and caught the angel in his first attempts at flight. They were so clumsy that his fingernails opened a furrow in the vegetable patch and he was on the point of knocking the shed down with the ungainly flapping that slipped on the light and couldn't get a grip on the air. But he did manage to gain altitude. Elisenda let out a sigh of relief, for herself and for him, when she saw him pass over the last houses, holding himself up in some way with the risky flapping of a senile vulture. She kept watching him even when she was through cutting the onions and she kept on watching until it was no longer possible for her to see him, because then he was no longer an annoyance in her life but an imaginary dot on the horizon of the sea. ❖

---

15. **cannulae (kan´ yə lə).** Hollow shafts of feathers; quills
16. **decrepitude.** Quality or state of being weak and wasted
17. **sea chanteys.** Songs sung by sailors in rhythm with their work

---

 **MIRRORS & WINDOWS** When are people most often mistreated in today's society? Give examples. What causes some people to mistreat others? How does the mistreatment of others affect a whole society?

Refer and Reason

1. Describe various reactions people have to the old man. What different things do they want from him? How do they treat him?
2. This story originally had the subtitle "A Tale for Children," but many later publications of it have omitted that subtitle. Why do you think that is? Do you believe this is a story meant for children? Explain your answers.
3. Who do you think the old man is? In your opinion, is he really an angel? Why or why not? Consider the evidence from the story—including his appearance, his actions, his abilities, and what other characters think of him—in giving your answers.

Writing Options

1. Write a children's book based on this story. Before you begin, decide what you think is the theme, or central message, of García Márquez's tale, and consider how you can get this message across to young readers. Read your story to elementary schoolchildren for their reactions.
2. You and a friend disagree about whether this story is really about the old winged man or about the villagers who are affected by him. Choose your position, and write a one-page persuasive essay in which you support it.

 Go to **www.mirrorsandwindows.com** for more.

HEARTBURN

"I HAVE SOME KIND OF SMALL ANIMAL LODGED IN MY CHEST," SAID THE MAN. HE COUGHED, A SLIGHT, HOLLOW APOLOGIA TO HIS AILMENT, AND SANK BACK IN HIS CHAIR.

A Short Story by **Hortense Calisher**

Hortense Calisher (b. 1911) was born in Manhattan. She published her first story, "A Box of Ginger," in the *New Yorker* magazine. Calisher reveals her passion for writing in this exclamation: "The words! I collected them in all shapes and sizes and hung them like bangles in my mind."

"Heartburn" revolves around a conversation that takes place in a doctor's office. The patient has come down with a most unusual condition that appears to be contagious...under certain circumstances. The doctor, limited by what he thinks he knows of science, cannot take the man's ridiculous complaint seriously and soon suffers the consequences of his disbelief.

What unusual complaints or stories have you heard from people? Did you believe them?

The light, gritty wind of a spring morning blew in on the doctor's shining, cleared desk, and on the tall buttonhook[1] of a man who leaned agitatedly toward him.

"I have some kind of small animal lodged in my chest," said the man. He coughed, a slight, hollow apologia[2] to his ailment, and sank back in his chair.

---

1. **buttonhook.** Long, slender tool with a curved hook used for pulling small buttons through holes
2. **apologia.** Defense of one's actions or opinions

"Animal?" said the doctor, after a pause which had the unfortunate quality of comment. His voice, however, was practiced, deft, colored only with the careful suspension of judgment.

"Probably a form of newt or toad," answered the man, speaking with clipped distaste, as if he would disassociate himself from the idea as far as possible. His face quirked with sad foreknowledge. "Of course, you don't believe me."

The doctor looked at him noncommittally. Paraphrased, an old refrain of the poker table leapt erratically in his mind. "Nits"—no—"newts and gnats and one-eyed jacks," he thought. But already the anecdote was shaping itself, trim and perfect, for display at the clinic luncheon table. "Go on," he said.

"Why won't any of you come right out and say what you think!" the man said angrily. Then he flushed, not hectically, the doctor noted, but with the well-bred embarrassment of the normally reserved. "Sorry. I didn't mean to be rude."

"You've already had an examination?" The doctor was a neurologist, and most of his patients were referrals.

"My family doctor. I live up in Boston."

"Did you tell him—er…?" The doctor sought gingerly for a phrase.

One corner of the man's mouth lifted, as if he had watched others in the same dilemma. "I went through the routine first. Fluoroscope, metabolism, cardiograph. Even gastroscopy." He spoke, the doctor noted, with regrettable glibness of the patient who has shopped around.

"And—the findings?" said the doctor, already sure of the answer.

The man leaned forward, holding the doctor's glance with his own. A faint smile riffled through his mouth. "Positive."

"Positive!"

"Well," said the man, "machines have to be interpreted after all, don't they?" He attempted a shrug, but the quick eye of the doctor saw that the movement masked a slight contortion within his tweed suit, as if the man writhed away from himself but concealed it quickly, as one masks a hiccup with a cough. "A curious flutter in the cardiograph, a strange variation in the metabolism, an alien shadow under the fluoroscope." He coughed again and put a genteel hand over his mouth, but this time the doctor saw it clearly—the slight, cringing motion.

"You see," added the man, his eyes helpless and apologetic above the polite covering hand. "It's alive. It *travels.*"

"Yes. Yes, of course," said the doctor, soothingly now. In his mind hung the word, ovoid[3] and perfect as a drop of water about to fall. Obsession. A beautiful case. He thought again of the luncheon table.

"What did your doctor recommend?" he said.

"A place with more resources, like the Mayo Clinic. It was then that I told him I knew what it was, as I've told you. And how I acquired it." The visitor paused. "Then, of course, he was forced to pretend he believed me."

"Forced?" said the doctor.

"Well," said the visitor, "actually, I think he did believe me. People tend to believe anything these days. All the mass media information gives them the habit. It takes a strong individual to disbelieve evidence."

The doctor was confused and annoyed. Well, "What then?" he said peremptorily, ready to rise from his desk in dismissal.

"YOU SEE," ADDED THE MAN, HIS EYES HELPLESS AND APOLOGETIC ABOVE THE POLITE COVERING HAND. "IT'S ALIVE. IT TRAVELS."

---

3. **ovoid.** Egg-shaped

Again came the fleeting bodily grimace and the quick cough. "He—er…he gave me a prescription."

The doctor raised his eyebrows, in a gesture he was swift to retract as unprofessional.

"For heartburn, I think it was," added the visitor demurely.

Tipping back in his chair, the doctor tapped a pencil on the edge of the desk. "Did he suggest you seek help—on another level?"

"Many have suggested it," said the man.

"But I'm not a psychiatrist!" said the doctor irritably.

"Oh, I know that. You see, I came to you because I had the luck to hear one of your lectures at the Academy. The one on 'Overemphasis on the Non-somatic[4] Causes of Nervous Disorder.' It takes a strong man to go against the tide like that. A disbeliever. And that's what I sorely need." The visitor shuddered, this time letting the *frisson*[5] pass uncontrolled. "You see," he added, thrusting his clasped hands forward on the desk, and looking ruefully at the doctor, as if he would cushion him against his next remark, "you see—I am a psychiatrist."

The doctor sat still in his chair.

"Ah, I can't help knowing what you are thinking," said the man. "I would think the same. A streamlined version of the Napoleonic delusion."[6] He reached into his breast pocket, drew out a wallet, and fanned papers from it on the desk.

"Never mind. I believe you!" said the doctor hastily.

"Already?" said the man sadly.

Reddening, the doctor hastily looked over the collection of letters, cards of membership in professional societies, licenses, and so on—very much the same sort of thing he himself would have had to amass, he had been

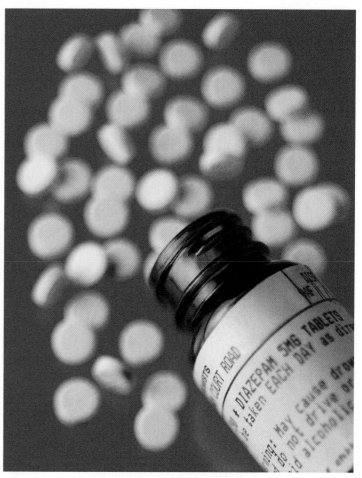

under the same necessity of proving his identity. Sanity, of course, was another matter. The documents were all issued to Dr. Curtis Retz at a Boston address. Stolen, possibly, but something in the man's manner, in fact everything in it except his unfortunate hallucination, made the doctor think otherwise. Poor guy, he thought. Occupational fatigue, perhaps. But what a form! The Boston variant, possibly. "Suppose you start from the beginning," he said benevolently.

"If you can spare the time…"

"I have no more appointments until lunch." And what a lunch that'll be, the doctor thought, already cherishing the pop-eyed scene—Travis the clinic's director (that

---

4. **Non-somatic.** Not of the body
5. *frisson* (frē sōn´). [French] Shiver or shudder
6. **Napoleonic delusion.** Unfounded belief that one has a grand position in life, as Emperor Napoleon Bonaparte of France once did

HEARTBURN **983**

plethoric Nestor[7]), and young Gruenberg (all of whose cases were unique), his hairy nostrils dilated for once in a *mise-en-scène*[8] which he did not dominate.

Holding his hands pressed formally against his chest, almost in the attitude of one of the minor placatory figures in a *Pietà*,[9] the visitor went on. "I have the usual private practice," he said, "and clinic affiliations. As a favor to an old friend of mine, headmaster of a boys' school nearby, I've acted as a guidance consultant there for some years. The school caters to boys of above average intelligence and is run along progressive lines. Nothing's ever cropped up except run-of-the-mill adolescent problems, colored a little, perhaps, by the type of parents who tend to send their children to a school like that—people who are—well—one might say, almost tediously aware of their commitments as parents."

The doctor grunted. He was that kind of parent himself.

"Shortly after the second term began, the head asked me to come down. He was worried over a sharp drop of morale which seemed to extend over the whole school—general inattention in classes, excited note-passing, nightly disturbances in the dorms—all pointing, he had thought at first, to the existence of some fancier than usual form of hazing,[10] or to one of those secret societies, sometimes laughable, sometimes with overtones of the corrupt, with which all schools are familiar. Except for one thing. One after the other, a long list of boys had been sent to the infirmary by the various teachers who presided in the dining room. Each of the boys had shown a marked debility, and what the resident doctor called 'All the stigmata of pure fright. Complete unwillingness to confide.' Each of the boys pleaded

---

7. **plethoric Nestor.** Travis is described as a merry, red-faced (*plethoric*), and wise and respectable old man (like Nestor, a king who in his old age served as a counselor to the ancient Greeks at Troy).

8. *mise-en-scène* (mē' zän' sen´). [French] Scene or setting

9. *Pietà* (pē' ā tä´). Image of Mary holding the body of Christ after he died

10. **hazing.** Harassment as a means of initiation

stubbornly for his own release, and a few broke out of their own accord. The interesting thing was that each child did recover shortly after his own release, and it was only after this that another boy was seen to fall ill. No two afflicted at the same time."

"Check the food?" said the doctor.

"All done before I got there. According to my friend, all the trouble seemed to have started with the advent of one boy, John Hallowell, a kid of about fifteen, who had come to the school late in the term with a history of having run away from four other schools. Records at these classed him as very bright, but made oblique references to 'personality difficulties' which were not defined. My friend's school, ordinarily pretty independent, had taken the boy at the insistence of old Simon Hallowell, the boy's uncle, who is a trustee. His brother, the boy's father, is well known for his marital exploits which have nourished the tabloids for years. The mother lives mostly in France and South America. One of these perennial dryads,[11] apparently, with a youthfulness maintained by money and a yearly immersion in the fountains of American plastic surgery. Only time she sees the boy…Well, you can imagine. What the feature articles call a Broken Home."

The doctor shifted in his chair.

"I won't keep you much longer," said the visitor. "I saw the boy." A violent fit of coughing interrupted him. This time his curious writhing motion went frankly unconcealed. He got up from his chair and stood at the window, gripping the sill and breathing heavily until he had regained control, and went on, one hand pulling unconsciously at his collar. "Or, at least, I think I saw him. On

my way to visit him in his room I bumped into a tall red-headed boy in a football sweater, hurrying down the hall with a windbreaker and a poncho slung over his shoulder. I asked for Hallowell's room; he jerked a thumb over his shoulder at the door just behind him, and continued past me. It never occurred to me…I was expecting some adenoidal gangler[12] with acne…or one of these sinister little angel faces, full of neurotic sensibility.

"The room was empty. Except for its finicky neatness, and a rather large amount of livestock, there was nothing unusual about it. The school, according to the current trend, is run like a farm, with the boys doing the chores, and pets are encouraged. There was a

tank with a couple of turtles near the window, beside it another, full of newts, and in one corner a large cage of well-tended, brisk white mice. Glass cases, with carefully mounted series of lepidoptera and hymenoptera, showing the metamorphic stages, hung on the walls, and on a drawing board there was a daintily executed study of Branchippus, the 'fairy shrimp.'

"While I paced the room, trying to look as if I wasn't prying, a greenish little wretch,

11. **dryads.** Magical creatures of nature in Greek mythology

12. **adenoidal gangler.** A tall, lanky person with a nasal-sounding voice

holding himself together as if he had an imaginary shawl draped around him, slunk into the half-dark room and squeaked 'Hallowell?' When he saw me he started to duck, but I detained him and found that he had had an appointment with Hallowell too. When it was clear, from his description, that Hallowell must have been the redhead I'd seen leaving, the poor urchin burst into tears.

"'I'll never get rid of it now!' he wailed. From then on it wasn't hard to get the whole maudlin story. It seems that shortly after Hallowell's arrival at school he acquired a reputation for unusual proficiency with animals and for out-of-the way lore which would impress the ingenuous. He circulated the rumor that he could swallow small animals and regurgitate them at will. No one actually saw him swallow anything, but it seems that in some mumbo-jumbo with another boy who had shown cynicism about the whole thing, it was claimed that Hallowell had, well, divested himself of something, and passed it on to the other boy, with the statement that the latter would only be able to get rid of his cargo when he in turn found a boy who would disbelieve *him*."

The visitor paused, calmer now, and leaving the window sat down again in the chair opposite the doctor, regarding him with such fixity that the doctor shifted uneasily, with the apprehension of one who is about to be asked for a loan.

"My mind turned to the elementary sort of thing we've all done at times. You know, circle of kids in the dark, piece of cooked cauliflower passed from hand to hand with the statement that the stuff is the fresh brains of some neophyte[13] who hadn't taken his initiation seriously. My young informer, Moulton his name was, swore however that this hysteria

"THE KID WAS LOOKING AT ME.
'DO YOU BELIEVE ME?'
HE SAID SUDDENLY."

(for of course, that's what I thought it) was passed on singly, from boy to boy, without any such séances.[14] He'd been home to visit his family, who are missionaries on leave, and had been infected by his roommate on his return to school, unaware that by this time the whole school had protectively turned believers, en masse.[15] His own terror came, not only from his conviction that he was possessed, but from his inability to find anybody who would take his dare. And so he'd finally come to Hallowell....

"By this time the room was getting really dark and I snapped on the light to get a better look at Moulton. Except for an occasional shudder, like a bodily tic, which I took to be the aftereffects of hard crying, he looked like a healthy enough boy who'd been scared out of his wits. I remember that a neat little monograph was already forming itself in my mind, a group study on mass psychosis, perhaps, with effective anthropological references to certain savage tribes whose dances include a rite known as 'eating evil.'

"The kid was looking at me. 'Do you believe me?' he said suddenly. 'Sir?' he added, with a naive cunning which tickled me.

"'Of course,' I said, patting his shoulder absently. 'In a way.'

"His shoulder slumped under my hand. I felt its tremor, direct misery palpitating between my fingers.

"'I thought...maybe for a man...it wouldn't be...' His voice trailed off.

"'Be the same?...I don't know,' I said slowly, for of course, I was answering, not his actual

---

13. **neophyte.** An initiate or a newcomer
14. **séances** (sā´ än[t]s´). Group sessions in which the spirits of the dead are conjured
15. **en masse** (än mas´). [French] All together or as a whole

question, but the overtone of some cockcrow of meaning that evaded me.

"He raised his head and petitioned me silently with his eyes. Was it guile, or simplicity, in his look, and was it for conviction, or the lack of it, that he arraigned me? I don't know. I've gone back over what I did then, again and again, using all my own knowledge of the mechanics of decision, and I know that it wasn't just sympathy, or a pragmatic reversal of therapy, but something intimately important for me, that made me shout with all my strength— 'Of course I don't believe you!'

"Moulton, his face contorted, fell forward on me so suddenly that I stumbled backwards, sending the tank of newts crashing to the floor. Supporting him with my arms, I hung on to him while he heaved, face downwards. At the same time I felt a tickling, sliding sensation in my own ear, and an inordinate desire to follow it with my finger, but both my hands were busy. It wasn't a minute 'til I'd gotten him onto the couch, where he drooped, a little white about the mouth, but with that chastened, purified look of the physically relieved, although he hadn't actually upchucked.

"Still watching him, I stooped to clear up the debris, but he bounded from the couch with amazing resilience.

"'I'll do it,' he said.

"'Feel better?'

"He nodded, clearly abashed, and we gathered up the remains of the tank in a sort of mutual embarrassment. I can't remember that either of us said a word, and neither of us made more than a half-hearted attempt to search for the scattered pests which had apparently sought crannies in the room. At the door we parted, muttering as formal a goodnight as possible between a grown man and a small boy. It wasn't until I reached my own room

and sat down that I realized, not only my own extraordinary behavior, but that Moulton, standing, as I suddenly recalled, for the first time quite straight, had sent after me a look of pity and speculation.

"Out of habit, I reached into my breast pocket for my pencil, in order to take notes as fresh as possible. And then I felt it…a skittering, sidling motion, almost beneath my hand. I opened my jacket and shook myself, thinking that I'd picked up something in the other room…but nothing. I sat quite still, gripping the pencil, and after an interval it came again—an inchoate[16] creeping, a twitter of movement almost *lackadaisical*, as of something inching itself lazily along—but this time on my other side. In a frenzy, I peeled off my clothes, inspected myself wildly, and enumerating to

---

16. **inchoate** (in kō´ ət). Formless

myself a reassuring abracadabra of explanation—skipped heartbeat, intercostal pressure of gas—I sat there naked, waiting. And after a moment, it came again, that wandering, aquatic motion, as if something had flipped itself over just enough to make me aware, and then settled itself, this time under the sternum, with a nudge like that of some inconceivable foetus. I jumped up and shook myself again, and as I did so I caught a glimpse of myself in the mirror in the closet door. My face, my own face, was ajar with fright, and I was standing there, hooked over, as if I were wearing an imaginary shawl."

In the silence after his visitor's voice stopped, the doctor sat there in the painful embarrassment of the listener who has played confessor, and whose expected comment is a responsibility he wishes he had evaded. The breeze from the open window fluttered the papers on the desk. Glancing out at the clean, regular façade of the hospital wing opposite, at whose evenly shaded windows the white shapes of orderlies and nurses flickered in consoling routine, the doctor wished petulantly that he had fended off the man and all his papers in the beginning. What right had the man to arraign *him?* Surprised at his own inner vehemence, he pulled himself together. "How long ago?" he said at last.

"Four months."

"And since?"

"It's never stopped." The visitor now seemed brimming with a tentative excitement, like a colleague discussing a mutually puzzling case. "Everything's been tried. Sedatives do obtain some sleep, but that's all. Purgatives. Even emetics." He laughed slightly, almost with pride. "Nothing like that works," he continued, shaking his head with the doting

fondness of a patient for some symptom which has confounded the best of them. "It's too cagey for that."

With his use of the word "it," the doctor was propelled back into that shapely sense of reality which had gone admittedly askew during the man's recital. To admit the category of "it," to dip even a slightly cooperative finger in another's fantasy, was to risk one's own equilibrium. Better not to become involved in argument with the possessed, lest one's own apertures of belief be found to have been left ajar.

"I am afraid," the doctor said blandly, "that your case is outside my field."

"As a doctor?" said his visitor. "Or as a man?"

"Let's not discuss me, if you please."

The visitor leaned intently across the desk. "Then you admit that to a certain extent, we *have* been—?"

"I admit nothing!" said the doctor, stiffening.

"Well," said the man disparagingly, "of course, that too is a kind of stand. The commonest, I've found." He sighed, pressing one hand against his collarbone. "I suppose you have a prescription too, or a recommendation. Most of them do."

The doctor did not enjoy being judged. "Why don't you hunt up young Hallowell?" he said, with malice.

"Disappeared. Don't you think I tried?" said his vis-à-vis[17] ruefully. Something furtive, hope, perhaps, spread its guileful corruption over his face. "This means you do give a certain credence—"

"Nothing of the sort!"

SPUTTERING, THE DOCTOR BEAT THE AIR AND HIS OWN PERSON WILDLY WITH HIS HANDS, AND STAGGERED UPWARD FROM HIS CHAIR.

---

17. **vis-à-vis** (vēz′ ə vē′). [French] Counterpart; person facing him

"Well then," said his interrogator, turning his palms upward.

The doctor leaned forward, measuring his words with exasperation. "Do you mean you *want* me to tell you you're crazy!"

"In my spot," answered his visitor meekly, "which would you prefer?"

Badgered to the point of commitment, the doctor stared back at his inconvenient Diogenes.[18] Swollen with irritation, he was only half conscious of an uneasy, vestigial twitching of his ear muscles, which contracted now as they sometimes did when he listened to atonal music.

"O.K., O.K….!" he shouted suddenly, slapping his hand down on the desk and thrusting his chin forward. "Have it your way then! I don't believe you!"

Rigid, the man looked back at him cataleptically, seeming, for a moment, all eye. Then, his mouth stretching in that medieval grimace, risorial and equivocal,[19] whose mask appears sometimes on one side of the stage, sometimes on the other, he fell forward on the desk, with a long, mewing sigh.

Before the doctor could reach him, he had raised himself on his arms and their foreheads touched. They recoiled, staring downward. Between them on the desk, as if one of its mahogany shadows had become animate, something seemed to move—small, seal-colored, and ambiguous. For a moment it filmed back and forth, arching in a crude, primordial inquiry; then, homing straight for the doctor, whose jaw hung down in a rictus of shock, it disappeared from view.

Sputtering, the doctor beat the air and his own person wildly with his hands, and staggered upward from his chair. The breeze blew hypnotically, and the stranger gazed back at him with such perverse calm that already he felt an assailing doubt of the lightning, untoward event. He fumbled back over his sensations of the minute before, but already piecemeal and chimerical,[20] they eluded him now, as they might forever.

"It's unbelievable," he said weakly.

His visitor put up a warding hand, shaking it fastidiously. *"Au contraire!"*[21] he relied daintily, as though by the use of another language he would remove himself still further from commitment. Reaching forward, he gathered up his papers into a sheaf, and stood up, stretching himself straight with an all-over bodily yawn of physical ease that was like an affront. He looked down at the doctor, one hand fingering his wallet. "No," he said reflectively, "guess not." He tucked the papers away. "Shall we leave it on the basis of—er—professional courtesy?" he inquired delicately.

Choking on the sludge of his rage, the doctor looked back at him, inarticulate.

Moving toward the door, the visitor paused. "After all," he said, "with your connections…try to think of it as a temporary inconvenience." Regretfully, happily, he closed the door behind him.

The doctor sat at his desk, humped forward. His hands crept to his chest and crossed. He swallowed, experimentally. He hoped it was rage. He sat there, waiting. He was thinking of the luncheon table. ❖

---

18. **Diogenes.** Ancient Greek philosopher (fourth century BCE) who believed that one needed either a great friend or a true enemy in order to get the truth

19. **risorial and equivocal.** Laughable or ridiculous (*risorial*), but at the same time deceptive or misleading in appearance (*equivocal*)

20. **chimerical** (kī mer´ i kəl). Existing only in the imagination

21. *Au contraire* (ō kän' trār´). [French] "On the contrary"

MIRRORS & WINDOWS

When has arrogance had a negative impact on your interactions with other people? Why might some people be more arrogant than others? Is arrogance always a negative thing, or can it sometimes be positive? Explain your answers.

Informational Text
CONNECTION

Information recorded by a doctor's office about a person's health is private. This information is protected by law from being shared with other parties. The following fact sheet from the **U.S. Department of Health & Human Services Office for Civil Rights** describes a person's basic right to privacy under the Health Insurance Portability and Accountability Act (HIPAA).

A **consumer document** provides information for people who use goods or services. Examples of consumer documents include fact sheets, warranties, user instructions, and product research reports. When you are reading a consumer document, pay attention to the section headings to find the information you need.

Health Information Privacy Rights

A Consumer Document from the U.S. Department of Health & Human Services Office for Civil Rights

You have privacy rights under a federal law that protects your health information. These rights are important for you to know. You can exercise these rights, ask questions about them, and file a complaint if you think your rights are being denied or your health information isn't being protected.

Who must follow this law?
- Most doctors, nurses, pharmacies, hospitals, clinics, nursing homes, and many other health care providers
- Health insurance companies, HMOs, most employer group health plans

- Certain government programs that pay for health care, such as Medicare and Medicaid

Providers and health insurers who are required to follow this law must comply with your right to...

1. **Ask to see and get a copy of your health records**
- You can ask to see and get a copy of your medical record and other health information. You may not be able to get all of your information in a few special cases. For example, if your doctor

decides something in your file might endanger you or someone else, the doctor may not have to give this information to you.

- In most cases, your copies must be given to you within 30 days, but this can be extended for another 30 days if you are given a reason.
- You may have to pay for the cost of copying and mailing if you request copies and mailing.

2. **Have corrections added to your health information**
- You can ask to change any wrong information in your file or add information to your file if it is incomplete. For example, if you and your hospital agree that your file has the wrong result for a test, the hospital must change it. Even if the hospital believes the test result is correct, you still have the right to have your disagreement noted in your file.
- In most cases the file should be changed within 60 days, but the hospital can take an extra 30 days if you are given a reason.

3. **Receive a notice that tells you how your health information is used and shared**
- You can learn how your health information is used and shared by your provider or health insurer. They must give you a notice that tells you how they may use and share your health information and how you can exercise your rights. In most cases, you should get this notice on your first visit to a provider or in the mail from your health insurer, and you can ask for a copy at any time.

4. **Decide whether to give your permission before your information can be used or shared for certain purposes**
- In general, your health information cannot be given to your employer, used or shared for things like sales calls or advertising, or used or shared for many other purposes unless you give your permission by signing an authorization form. This authorization form must tell you who will get your information and what your information will be used for.

Providers and health insurers who are required to follow this law must comply with your right to…

1. **Get a report on when and why your health information was shared**
- Under the law, your health information may be used and shared for particular reasons, like making sure doctors give good care, making sure nursing homes are clean and safe, reporting when the flu is in your area, or making required reports to the police, such as reporting gunshot wounds. In many cases, you can ask for and get a list of who your health information has been shared with for these reasons.
- You can get this report for free once a year.
- In most cases you should get the report within 60 days, but it can take an extra 30 days if you are given a reason.

2. **Ask to be reached somewhere other than home**
- You can make reasonable requests to be contacted at different places or in a different way. For example, you can have the nurse call you at your office instead of your home, or send mail to you in

an envelope instead of on a postcard. If sending information to you at home might put you in danger, your health insurer must talk, call, or write to you where you ask and in the way you ask, if the request is reasonable.

3. **Ask that your information not be shared**
   - You can ask your provider or health insurer not to share your health information with certain people, groups, or companies. For example, if you go to a clinic, you could ask the doctor not to share your medical record with other doctors or nurses in the clinic. However, they do not have to agree to do what you ask.

4. **File complaints**
   - If you believe your information was used or shared in a way that is not allowed under the privacy law, or if you were not able to exercise your rights, you can file a complaint with your provider or health insurer. The privacy notice you receive from them will tell you who to talk to and how to file a complaint. You can also file a complaint with the U.S. Government.

Refer and Reason

1. List what you learn about John Hallowell in this story. Include details about his parents, his schooling, and his actions at his new school. What role does Hallowell play in this story?
2. The "ailment" spreads very quickly through the school, but the psychiatrist could not rid himself of the problem for four months. Why might it have taken him longer?
3. Evaluate the behavior of the doctor in this story. Is he acting like a professional? Do you think he gets what he deserves? At the end of the story, what do you think he'll tell his friends at the lunch table? Explain your answers.

Writing Options

1. Write a scene for a play based on this story. Use a scene from the story, or make up a new scene, such as the arrival of Hallowell at the school or Moulton's catching the "ailment." Perform your scene for the class.
2. Write a television news report for a tabloid news show about the strange events at the boys' school. Use your imagination to fill in additional details. Remember to address the questions of *who, what, when, where, why,* and *how* in your story. Also consider your audience when you are choosing the language of your story. People who watch tabloid news shows might be interested in off-the-wall, gossipy kinds of stories.

Go to **www.mirrorsandwindows.com** for more.

TEXT ←^{TO}→ TEXT CONNECTION

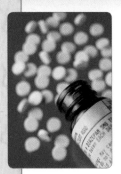

- Evaluate the usefulness of the consumer document. Could the average consumer understand it? Is the information relevant? How do the word choice, sentence structure, and organization of the document compare with these aspects of the short story? Why are there differences between the two texts?
- In "Heartburn," the doctor plans to tell the people he eats lunch with about the visit from the psychiatrist. Would this violate HIPAA rules in any way? Explain your answer. What action could the psychiatrist take against the doctor?

How could he have dreamed up this incredible happiness? He or any other human being? It was a strange, unique happiness, as though it were a private secret he had been given.

The Happy Man

A Short Story by
Naguib Mahfouz

Naguib Mahfouz (b. 1911) is an Egyptian novelist who is considered one of the most important writers in the Arab world. When Mahfouz won the Nobel Prize in 1988, his work had an audience of millions of readers, almost none of them in America. Since winning the prize, however, many of Mahfouz's books—though only a fraction of his output—have been published in English translation.

Everyone wants to be happy, but what would happen to a person who was happy all the time? In **"The Happy Man,"** Naguib Mahfouz tells the story of a man who experiences this bizarre problem. This story asks thought-provoking questions about human nature, including whether it is possible, or even desirable, to remain in a constant state of bliss.

Think of occasions on which you have felt happy. What created the feeling?

He woke up in the morning and discovered that he was happy. "What's this?" he asked himself. He could not think of any word which described his state of mind more accurately and precisely than "happy." This was distinctly peculiar when compared with the state he was usually in when he woke up. He would be half-asleep from staying so late at the newspaper office.

He would face life with a sense of strain and contemplation. Then he would get up, whetting his determination to face up to all inconveniences and withstand all difficulties.

Today he felt happy, full of happiness, as a matter of fact. There was no arguing about it. The symptoms were quite clear, and their vigor and obviousness were such as to impose themselves on his senses and mind all at once. Yes, indeed; he was happy. If this was not happiness, then what was? He felt that his limbs were well proportioned and functioning perfectly. They were working in superb harmony with each other and with the world around him. Inside him, he felt a boundless power, an imperishable energy, an ability to achieve anything with confidence, precision, and obvious success. His heart was overflowing with love for people, animals, and things, and with an all-engulfing sense of optimism and joy. It was as if he were no longer troubled or bothered by fear, anxiety, sickness, death, argument, or the question of earning a living. Even more important than that, and something he could not analyze, it was a feeling which penetrated to every cell of his body and soul; it played a tune full of delight, pleasure, serenity, and peace, and hummed in its incredible melodies the whispering sound of the world, which is denied to the unhappy.

He felt drunk with ecstasy and savored it slowly with a feeling of surprise. He asked himself where it had come from and how; the past provided no explanation, and the future could not justify it. Where did it come from, then, and how?! How long would it last? Would it stay with him till breakfast? Would it give him enough time to get to the newspaper office? Just a minute though, he thought …it won't last because it can't. If it did, man would be turned into an angel or something even higher. So he told himself that he should devote his attention to savoring it, living with it, and storing up its nectar before it became a mere memory with

no way of proving it or even being sure that it had ever existed.

He ate his breakfast with a relish, and this time nothing distracted his attention while he was eating. He gave "Uncle" Bashir, who was waiting on him, such a beaming smile that the poor man felt rather alarmed and taken aback. Usually he would only look in his direction to give orders or ask questions, although, on most occasions, he treated him fairly well.

"Tell me, 'Uncle' Bashir," he asked the servant, "am I a happy man?"

The poor man was startled. He realized why his servant was confused; for the first time ever he was talking to him as a colleague or friend. He encouraged his servant to forget about his worries and asked him with unusual insistence to answer his question.

"Through God's grace and favor, you are happy," the servant replied.

"You mean, I should be happy. Anyone with my job, living in my house, and enjoying my health, should be happy. That's what you want to say. But do you think I'm really happy?"

The servant replied, "You work too hard, Sir"; after yet more insistence, "It's more than any man can stand…."

He hesitated, but his master gestured to him to continue with what he had to say.

"You get angry a lot," he said, "and have fierce arguments with your neighbors…."

He interrupted him by laughing loudly. "What about you?" he asked. "Don't you have any worries?"

"Of course, no man can be free of worry."

"You mean that complete happiness is an impossible quest?"

"That applies to life in general…."

How could he have dreamed up this incredible happiness? He or any other human being? It was a strange, unique happiness, as though it were a private secret he had been given. In the meeting hall of the newspaper building, he spotted his main rival in this world sitting down thumbing through a magazine. The man heard his footsteps but did not look up from the magazine. He had undoubtedly noticed him in some way and was therefore pretending to ignore him so as to keep his own peace of mind. At some circulation meetings,[1] they would argue so violently with each other that sparks began to fly and they would exchange bitter words. One stage more, and they would come to blows. A week ago, his rival had won in the union elections,[2] and he had lost. He had felt pierced by a sharp, poisoned arrow, and the world had darkened

before his eyes. Now here he was approaching his rival's seat; the sight of him sitting there did not make him excited, nor did the memories of their dispute spoil his composure. He approached him with a pure and carefree heart, feeling drunk with his incredible happiness; his face showed an expression full of tolerance and forgiveness. It was as though he were approaching some other man toward whom he had never had any feelings of enmity,[3] or perhaps he might be renewing a friendship again. "Good morning!" he said without feeling any compunction.[4]

The man looked up in amazement. He was silent for a few moments until he recovered, and then returned the greeting curtly. It was as though he did not believe his eyes and ears.

He sat down alongside the man. "Marvelous weather today…." he said.

"Okay…." the other replied guardedly.

"Weather to fill your heart with happiness."

His rival looked at him closely and cautiously. "I'm glad that you're so happy…." he muttered.

"Inconceivably happy…." he replied with a laugh.

"I hope," the man continued in a rather hesitant tone of voice, "that I shan't spoil your happiness at the meeting of the administrative council…."

"Not at all. My views are well-known, but I don't mind if the members adopt your point of view. That won't spoil my happiness!"

"You've changed a great deal overnight," the man said with a smile.

"The fact is that I'm happy, inconceivably happy."

1. **circulation meetings.** Meetings about newspaper circulation or distribution
2. **union elections.** Selection of officers of unions, or groups that stand up for workers' rights
3. **enmity.** Ill will; hostility; antagonism
4. **compunction.** Uneasiness brought on by a sense of guilt

temperament which causes him a good deal of trouble and leads him to trouble other people."

"Really?"

"You don't know how to make a truce; you've no concept of intermediate solutions. You work with your nerves, with the marrow in your bones. You fight bitterly, as though any problem is a matter of life and death!"

The man examined his face carefully. "I bet your dear son has changed his mind about staying in Canada?!" he asked.

"Never, never, my friend," he replied, laughing loudly. "He is still sticking to his decision...."

"But that was the principal reason for your being so sad...."

"Quite true. I've often begged him to come back out of pity for me in my loneliness and to serve his country. But he told me that he's going to open an engineering office[5] with a Canadian partner; in fact, he's invited me to join him in it. Let him live where he'll be happy. I'm quite happy here—as you can see, inconceivably happy...."

The man still looked a little doubtful. "Quite extraordinarily brave!" he said.

"I don't know what it is, but I'm happy in the full meaning of the word."

Yes indeed, this was full happiness; full, firm, weighty, and vital. As deep as absolute power, widespread as the wind, fierce as fire, bewitching as scent, transcending nature. It could not possibly last.

The other man warmed to his display of affection. "The truth is," he said, "that I always picture you as someone with a fierce and violent

"Yes, that's true."

He accepted the criticism without any difficulty and with an open heart. His wave expanded into a boundless ocean of happiness. He struggled to control an innocent, happy laugh, which the other man interpreted in a way far removed from its pure motives.

"So then," he asked, "you think it's necessary to be able to take a balanced view of events, do you?"

"Of course. I remember, by way of example, the argument we had the day before yesterday about racism. We both had the same views on the subject; it's something worth being zealous about, even to the point of anger. But what kind of anger? An intellectual anger, abstract to a certain extent; not the type which shatters your nerves, ruins your digestion, and gives you palpitations.[6] Not so?"

"That's obvious; I quite understand...."

He struggled to control a second laugh and succeeded. His heart refused to renounce one drop of its joy. Racism, Vietnam, Palestine, ...no problem could assail that fortress of happiness which was encircling his heart. When he remem-

---

5. **engineering office.** Company that contracts to plan building projects

6. **palpitations.** Rapid heartbeat

bered a problem, his heart guffawed. He was happy. It was a tyrannical[7] happiness, despising all misery and laughing at any hardship; it wanted to laugh, dance, sing, and distribute its spirit of laughter, dancing, and singing among the various problems of the world.

He could not bear to stay in his office at the newspaper; he felt no desire to work at all. He hated the very idea of thinking about his daily business and completely failed to bring his mind down from its stronghold in the kingdom of happiness. How could he possibly write about a trolley bus falling into the Nile when he was so intoxicated by this frightening happiness? Yes, it really was frightening. How could it be anything else, when there was no reason for it at all, when it was so strong that it made him exhausted and paralyzed his will; apart from the fact that it had been with him for half a day without letting up in the slightest degree?!

He left the pages of paper blank and started walking backward and forward across the room, laughing and cracking his fingers….

He felt slightly worried; it did not penetrate deep enough to spoil his happiness but paused on the surface of his mind like an abstract idea. It occurred to him that he might recall the tragedies of his life so that he could test their effect on his happiness. Perhaps they would be able to bring back some idea of balance or security, at least until his happiness began to flag a little. For example, he remembered his wife's death in all its various aspects and details. What had happened? The event appeared to him as a series of movements without any meaning or effect, as though it had happened to some other woman, the wife of another man, in some distant historical age. In fact, it had a contagious effect which prompted a smile and then even provoked laughter. He could not stop himself laughing, and there he was guffawing, ha …ha …ha!

The same thing happened when he remembered the first letter his son had sent him saying that he wanted to emigrate to Canada.

The sound of his guffaws as he paraded the bloody tragedies of the world before him would have attracted the attention of the newspaper workers and passersby in the street, had it not been for the thickness of the walls. He could do nothing to dislodge his happiness. Memories of unhappy times hit him like waves being thrown onto a sandy beach under the golden rays of the sun.

He excused himself from attending the administrative council and left the newspaper office without writing a word. After lunch, he lay down on his bed as usual but could not sleep. In fact, sleep seemed an impossibility to him. Nothing gave him any indication that it was coming, even slowly. He was in a place alight and gleaming, resounding with sleeplessness and joy. He had to calm down and relax, to quiet his senses and limbs, but how could he do it? He gave up trying to sleep and got up. He began to hum as he was walking around his house. If this keeps up, he told himself, I won't be able to sleep, just as I can't work or feel sad. It was almost time for him to go to the club, but he did not feel like meeting any friends. What was the point of exchanging views on public affairs and private worries?! What would they think if they found him laughing at every major problem? What would they say? How would they picture things? How would they explain it? No, he did not need anyone, nor did he want to spend the evening talking. He should be by himself and go for a long walk to get rid of some of his excess vitality and think about his situation. What had happened to him? How was it that this incredible happiness had overwhelmed him? How long would he have to carry it on his shoulders? Would it keep depriving him of work, friends, sleep, and peace of mind?! Should he resign himself to it? Should he abandon himself to the flood to play with him as the whim took it? Or should he look for a way out for himself through thought, action, or advice?

---

7. **tyrannical.** Oppressive; unjust

When he was called into the examination room in the clinic of his friend, the specialist in internal medicine, he felt a little alarmed. The doctor looked at him with a smile. "You don't look like someone who's complaining about being ill," he said.

"I haven't come to see you because I'm ill," he told the doctor in a hesitant tone of voice, "but because I'm happy!"

The doctor looked piercingly at him with a questioning air.

"Yes," he repeated to underline what he had said, "because I'm happy!"

There was a period of silence. On one side, there was anxiety, and on the other, questioning and amazement.

"It's an incredible feeling which can't be defined in any other way, but it's very serious...."

The doctor laughed. "I wish your illness were contagious," he said, prodding him jokingly.

"Don't treat it as a joke. It's very serious, as I told you. I'll describe it to you...."

He told him all about his happiness from the time he had woken up in the morning till he had felt compelled to visit him.

"Haven't you been taking drugs, alcohol, or tranquilizers?"

"Absolutely nothing like that."

"Have you had some success in an important sphere of your life: work ...love ...money?"

"Nothing like that either. I've twice as much to worry about as I have to make me feel glad...."

"Perhaps if you were patient for a while...."

"I've been patient all day. I'm afraid I'll be spending the night wandering around...."

The doctor gave him a precise, careful, and comprehensive examination and then shrugged his shoulders in despair. "You're a picture of health," he said.

"And so?"

"I could advise you to take a sleeping pill, but it would be better if you consulted a nerve specialist...."

The examination was repeated in the nerve specialist's clinic with the self-same precision, care, and comprehensiveness. "Your nerves are sound," the doctor told him. "They're in enviable condition!"

"Haven't you got a plausible explanation for my condition?" he asked hopefully.

"Consult a gland specialist!" the doctor replied, shaking his head.

The examination was conducted for a third time in the gland specialist's clinic with the same precision, care, and comprehensiveness. "I congratulate you!" the doctor told him. "Your glands are in good condition."

He laughed. He apologized for laughing, laughing as he did so. Laughter was his way of expressing his alarm and despair.

He left the clinic with the feeling that he was alone, alone in the hands of his tyrannical happiness, with no helper, no guide, and no friend. Suddenly, he remembered the doctor's sign he sometimes saw from the window of his office in the newspaper building. It was true that he had no confidence in psychiatrists even though he had read about the significance of psychoanalysis.[8] Apart from that, he knew that their tentacles were very long and they kept their patients tied in a sort of long association. He laughed as he remembered the method of cure through free association and the problems which it eventually uncovers. He was laughing as his feet carried him toward the psychiatrist's clinic, and imagined the doctor listening to his incredible complaints about feeling happy, when he was used to hearing people complain about hysteria, schizophrenia,[9] anxiety, and so on.

"The truth is, Doctor, that I've come to see you because I'm happy!"

---

8. **psychoanalysis.** Psychiatric counseling technique developed by Austrian physician Sigmund Freud (1856–1939). According to the theory, rejected feelings and thoughts can be brought to the conscious mind through psychoanalytic techniques such as free association and dream analysis.

9. **schizophrenia.** Major mental disorder of unknown cause typically characterized by distortions of reality

He looked at the doctor to see what effect his statement had had on him but noticed that he was keeping his composure. He felt ridiculous. "I'm inconceivably happy…." he said in a tone of confidence.

He began to tell the doctor his story, but the latter stopped him with a gesture of his hand. "An overwhelming, incredible, debilitating[10] happiness?" he asked quietly.

He stared at him in amazement and was on the point of saying something, but the doctor spoke first. "A happiness which has made you stop working," he asked, "abandon your friends, and detest going to sleep…?"

"You're a miracle!" he shouted.

"Every time you get involved in some misfortune," the psychiatrist continued quietly, "you dissolve into laughter…?"

"Sir…are you familiar with the invisible?"

"No!" he said with a smile, "nothing like that. But I get a similar case in my clinic at least once a week!"

"Is it an epidemic?" he asked.

"I didn't say that, and I wouldn't claim that it's been possible to analyze one case into its primary elements as yet."

"But is it a disease?"

"All the cases are still under treatment."

"But are you satisfied without any doubt that they aren't natural cases…?"

"That's a necessary assumption for the job; there's only…."

"Have you noticed any of them to be deranged[11] in…?" he asked anxiously, pointing to his head.

"Absolutely not," the doctor replied convincingly. "I assure you that they're all intelligent in every sense of the word…."

The doctor thought for a moment. "We should have two sessions a week, I think?" he said.

"Very well…." he replied in resignation.

"There's no sense in getting alarmed or feeling sad…."

Alarmed, sad? He smiled, and his smile kept on getting broader. A laugh slipped out, and before long, he was dissolving into laughter. He was determined to control himself, but his resistance collapsed completely. He started guffawing loudly…. ❖

---

10. **debilitating.** Causing weakness
11. **deranged.** Disturbed

How do you think happiness is generally measured? Is it even possible to measure happiness? Why or why not? What impact does worry have on happiness? What are some ways that people might cope with worry?

Refer and Reason
1. Describe what the main character feels, unexpectedly, when he wakes up one morning. Why is this state of mind so unfamiliar to him?
2. Judge whether the author believes it is possible or even desirable to be completely happy. Are there times when sadness is appropriate or necessary? Explain your answers.
3. Do you believe the main character has control over his happiness? Identify examples from the story that support your response.

Writing Options
1. Pretend that you are a friend of the main character in "The Happy Man." You hear that he is undergoing treatment for his unusual "condition," and you want to send a handmade get-well card. Write the message for your greeting card.
2. Imagine that you are going to a conference on emotional well-being and have been asked to present a case study of a happy person. Write a character sketch about the happiest person you know. Use specific examples of the ways the person expresses his or her happiness.

 Go to **www.mirrorsandwindows.com** for more.

The Hitchhiker

"All this I know. I know that I am, at this moment, perfectly sane. That it is not I who has gone mad—but something else—something utterly beyond my control."

A Radio Drama by **Lucille Fletcher**

Lucille Fletcher (1912–2000) was born in Brooklyn, New York. She wrote and broadcast more than twenty radio dramas in the 1930s and 1940s. The two most famous are *The Hitchhiker* (1941) and *Sorry, Wrong Number* (1943).

Radio plays like **The Hitchhiker** depend entirely on sound to tell a story. The main character in this radio play is traveling across the country from New York to California. For much of his journey, he travels historic U.S. Route 66, a highway that stretched from Chicago to Los Angeles and provided the perfect setting for this strange and spooky tale.

Describe a place you've seen or heard about that would work well as the setting for a ghost story.

Characters
Orson Welles, Narrator
Ronald Adams
Mother
Voice
Mechanic
Henry
Woman
Girl
Gallup Operator
Long Distance Operator
Albuquerque Operator
New York Operator
Mrs. Whitney

WELLES. [*narrating*] Good evening, this is Orson Welles….

MUSIC. *In.*

WELLES. Personally I've never met anybody who didn't like a good ghost story, but I know a lot of people who think there are a lot of people who don't like a good ghost story. For the benefit of these, at least, I go on record at the outset of this evening's entertainment with the sober assurance that, although blood may be curdled on the program, none will be spilt. There's no shooting, knifing, throttling, axing, or poisoning here. No clanking chains, no cobwebs, no bony and/or hairy hands appearing from secret panels or, better yet, bedroom curtains. If it's any part of that dear old phosphorescent[1] foolishness that people who don't like ghost stories don't like, then again, I promise you we haven't got it. What we do have is a thriller. If it's half as good as we think it is, you can call it a shocker, and we present it proudly and without apologies. After all, a story doesn't have to appeal to the heart—it can also appeal to the spine. Sometimes you want your heart to be warmed—sometimes you want your spine to tingle. The tingling, it's to be hoped, will be quite audible as you listen tonight to *The Hitchhiker*—That's the name of our story, *The Hitchhiker*—

SOUND. *Automobile wheels humming over concrete road.*

MUSIC. *Something weird and shuddery.*

ADAMS. [*narrating*] I am in an auto camp[2] on Route Sixty-Six just west of Gallup, New Mexico. If I tell it, perhaps it will help me. It will keep me from going mad. But I must tell this quickly. I am not mad now. I feel perfectly well, except that I am running a slight temperature. My name is Ronald Adams. I am thirty-six years of age, unmarried, tall, dark, with a black mustache. I drive a 1940 Ford V-8, license number 6V-7989. I was born in Brooklyn.[3] All this I know. I know that I am, at this moment, perfectly sane. That it is not I who has gone mad—but something

else—something utterly beyond my control. But I must speak quickly…very quickly. At any moment the link with life may break. This may be the last thing I ever tell on earth…the last night I ever see the stars….

MUSIC. *In.*

ADAMS. [*narrating*] Six days ago I left Brooklyn to drive to California….

MOTHER. Goodbye, son. Good luck to you, my boy….

ADAMS. Goodbye, mother. Here—give me a kiss, and then I'll go….

MOTHER. I'll come out with you to the car.

ADAMS. No. It's raining. Stay here at the door. Hey—what is this? Tears? I thought you promised me you wouldn't cry.

MOTHER. I know dear. I'm sorry. But I—do hate to see you go.

ADAMS. I'll be back. I'll only be on the coast three months.

MOTHER. Oh—it isn't that. It's just—the trip. Ronald—I really wish you weren't driving.

ADAMS. Oh—mother. There you go again. People do it every day.

MOTHER. I know. But you'll be careful, won't you. Promise me you'll be extra careful. Don't fall asleep—or drive fast—or pick up any strangers on the road….

ADAMS. Lord, no. You'd think I was still seventeen to hear you talk—

MOTHER. And wire me as soon as you get to Hollywood, won't you, son?

ADAMS. Of course I will. Now don't you worry. There isn't anything going to happen. It's just eight days of perfectly simple driving on smooth,

---

1. **phosphorescent.** Giving off light
2. **auto camp.** Highway rest area
3. **Brooklyn.** One of the five boroughs of New York City; located south of the island of Manhattan

decent, civilized roads, with a hotdog or a hamburger stand every ten miles…. [Fade]

SOUND. *Auto hum.*

MUSIC. *In.*

ADAMS. [narrating] I was in excellent spirits. The drive ahead of me, even the loneliness, seemed like a lark. But I reckoned without *him*.

MUSIC. *Changes to something weird and empty.*

ADAMS. [narrating] Crossing Brooklyn Bridge that morning in the rain, I saw a man leaning against the cables. He seemed to be waiting for a lift. There were spots of fresh rain on his shoulders. He was carrying a cheap overnight bag in one hand. He was thin, nondescript, with a cap pulled down over his eyes. He stepped off the walk right in front of me and, if I hadn't swerved hard, I'd have hit him.

SOUND. *Terrific skidding.*

MUSIC. *In.*

ADAMS. [narrating] I would have forgotten him completely, except that just an hour later, while crossing the Pulaski Skyway over the Jersey flats,[4] I saw him again. At least, he looked like the same person. He was standing now, with one thumb pointing west. I couldn't figure out how he'd got there, but I thought probably one of those fast trucks had picked him up, beaten me to the Skyway, and let him off. I didn't stop for him. Then—late that night, I saw him again.

MUSIC. *Changing.*

ADAMS. [narrating] It was on the New Pennsylvania Turnpike between Harrisburg and Pittsburgh. It's two hundred and sixty-five miles long, with a very high speed limit. I was just slowing down for one of the tunnels—when I saw him—standing under an arc light by the side of the road. I could see him quite distinctly. The bag, the cap, even the spots of fresh rain spattered over his shoulders. He hailed me this time….

VOICE. [very spooky and faint] Hall-ooo…. [It echoes as though coming through the tunnel.] Hall-ooo…!

ADAMS. [narrating] I stepped on the gas like a shot. That's lonely country through the Alleghenies,[5] and I had no intention of stopping. Besides, the coincidence, or whatever it was, gave me the willies. I stopped at the next gas station.

SOUND. *Auto tires screeching to stop…horn honk.*

MECHANIC. Yes, sir.

ADAMS. Fill her up.

MECHANIC. Certainly, sir. Check your oil, sir?

ADAMS. No, thanks.

SOUND. *Gas being put into car.*

MECHANIC. Nice night, isn't it?

ADAMS. Yes. It—hasn't been raining here recently, has it?

MECHANIC. Not a drop of rain all week.

ADAMS. I suppose that hasn't done your business any harm.

MECHANIC. Oh—people drive through here all kinds of weather. Mostly business, you know. There aren't many pleasure cars out on the Turnpike this season of the year.

ADAMS. I suppose not. [casually] What about hitchhikers?

MECHANIC. [laughing] Hitchhikers here?

ADAMS. What's the matter? Don't you ever see any?

MECHANIC. Not much. If we did, it'd be a sight for sore eyes.

ADAMS. Why?

---

4. **Pulaski Skyway…Jersey flats.** Name of an overpass that crosses a marshy area in northeastern New Jersey

5. **Alleghenies.** Mountain range in the eastern United States

Gas, 1940. Edward Hopper. The Museum of Modern Art, New York.

MECHANIC. A guy'd be a fool who started out to hitch rides on this road. Look at it. It's two hundred and sixty-five miles long, there's practically no speed limit, and it's a straightaway. Now what car is going to stop to pick up a guy under those conditions? Would you stop?

ADAMS. No. [*He answers slowly, with puzzled emphasis.*] Then you've never seen anybody?

MECHANIC. Nope. Mebbe they get the lift before the Turnpike starts—I mean, you know—just before the toll house—but then it'd be a mighty long ride. Most cars wouldn't want to pick up a guy for that long a ride. And you know—this is pretty lonesome country here—mountains, and woods…. You ain't seen anybody like that, have you?

ADAMS. No. [*quickly*] Oh no, not at all. It was—just a—technical question.

MECHANIC. I see. Well—that'll be just a dollar forty-nine—with the tax…. [*Fade*]

SOUND. *Auto hum up.*

MUSIC. *Changing.*

ADAMS. [*narrating*] The thing gradually passed from my mind, as sheer coincidence. I had a good night's sleep in Pittsburgh. I did not think about the man all next day—until just outside of Zanesville, Ohio, I saw him again.

MUSIC. *Dark, ominous note.*

ADAMS. [*narrating*] It was a bright sun-shiny afternoon. The peaceful Ohio fields, brown with the autumn stubble, lay dreaming in the golden light. I was driving slowly, drinking it in, when the road suddenly ended in a detour. In front of the barrier, he was standing.

MUSIC. *In.*

ADAMS. [*narrating*] Let me explain about his appearance before I go on. I repeat. There was nothing sinister about him. He was as drab as a

mud fence. Nor was his attitude menacing. He merely stood there, waiting, almost drooping a little, the cheap overnight bag in his hand. He looked as though he had been waiting there for hours. Then he looked up. He hailed me. He started to walk forward.

VOICE. [*far off*] Hall-ooo…Hall-ooo….

ADAMS. [*narrating*] I had stopped the car, of course, for the detour. And for a few moments, I couldn't seem to find the new road. I knew he must be thinking that I had stopped for him.

VOICE. [*sounding closer now*] Hall-ooo…Hallll…ooo….

SOUND. *Gears jamming…sound of motor turning over hard…nervous accelerator.*

VOICE. [*closer*] Hall…oooo….

ADAMS. [*with panic in his voice*] No. Not just now. Sorry….

VOICE. [*closer*] Going to California?

SOUND. *Starter starting…gears jamming.*

ADAMS. [*as though sweating blood*] No. Not today. The other way. Going to New York. Sorry…sorry….

SOUND. *Car starts with squeal of wheels on dirt… into auto hum.*

MUSIC. *In.*

ADAMS. [*narrating*] After I got the car back onto the road again, I felt like a fool. Yet the thought of picking him up, of having him sit beside me was somehow unbearable. Yet, at the same time, I felt, more than ever, unspeakably alone.

SOUND. *Auto hum up.*

ADAMS. [*narrating*] Hour after hour went by. The fields, the towns ticked off, one by one. The lights changed. I knew now that I was going to see him again. And though I dreaded the sight, I caught myself searching the side of the road, waiting for him to appear.

SOUND. *Auto hum up...car screeches to a halt... impatient honk two or three times...door being unbolted.*

SLEEPY MAN'S VOICE. Yep? What is it? What do you want?

ADAMS. [*breathless*] You sell sandwiches and pop here, don't you?

VOICE. [*cranky*] Yep. We do. In the daytime. But we're closed up now for the night.

ADAMS. I know. But—I was wondering if you could possibly let me have a cup of coffee— black coffee.

VOICE. Not at this time of night, mister. My wife's the cook and she's in bed. Mebbe further down the road—at the Honeysuckle Rest....

SOUND. *Door squeaking on hinges as though being closed.*

ADAMS. No—no. Don't shut the door. [*shakily*] Listen—just a minute ago, there was a man standing here—right beside this stand—a suspicious looking man....

WOMAN'S VOICE. [*from distance*] Henry? Who is it, Henry?

HENRY. It's nobuddy, mother. Just a feller thinks he wants a cup of coffee. Go back into bed.

Night Shadows, 1921. Edward Hopper. Whitney Museum of American Art, New York.

ADAMS. I don't mean to disturb you. But you see, I was driving along—when I just happened to look—and there he was....

HENRY. What was he doing?

ADAMS. Nothing. He ran off—when I stopped the car.

HENRY. Then what of it? That's nothing to wake a man in the middle of his sleep about. [*sternly*] Young man, I've got a good mind to turn you over to the local sheriff.

ADAMS. But—I—

HENRY. You've been taking a nip,[6] that's what you've been doing. And you haven't got anything better to do than to wake decent folk out of their hard-earned sleep. Get going. Go on.

ADAMS. But—he looked as though he were going to rob you.

HENRY. I ain't got nothin' in this stand to lose. Now—on your way before I call out Sheriff Oakes. [*Fade*]

SOUND. *Auto hum up.*

ADAMS. [*narrating*] I got into the car again, and drove on slowly. I was beginning to hate the car. If I could have found a place to stop...to rest a little. But I was in the Ozark Mountains of Missouri now. The few resort places there

---

6. **taking a nip.** Drinking something alcoholic

were closed. Only an occasional log cabin, seemingly deserted, broke the monotony of the wild wooded landscape. I had seen him at that roadside stand; I knew I would see him again—perhaps at the next turn of the road. I knew that when I saw him next, I would run him down….

SOUND. *Auto hum up.*

ADAMS. But I did not see him again until late next afternoon….

SOUND. *Warning system at train crossing.*

ADAMS. [*narrating*] I had stopped the car at a sleepy little junction just across the border into Oklahoma—to let a train pass by—when he appeared, across the tracks, leaning against a telephone pole.

SOUND. *Distant sound of train chugging…bell ringing steadily.*

ADAMS. [*narrating, very tensely*] It was a perfectly airless, dry day. The red clay of Oklahoma was baking under the southwestern sun. Yet there were spots of fresh rain on his shoulders. I couldn't stand that. Without thinking, blindly, I started the car across the tracks.

SOUND. *Train chugging closer.*

ADAMS. [*narrating*] He didn't even look up at me. He was staring at the ground. I stepped on the gas hard, veering the wheel sharply toward him. I could hear the train in the distance now, but I didn't care. Then something went wrong with the car. It stalled right on the tracks.

SOUND. *Train chugging closer. Above this, sound of car stalling.*

ADAMS. [*narrating*] The train was coming closer. I could hear its bell ringing, and the cry of its whistle. Still he stood there. And now—I knew that he was beckoning—beckoning me to my death.

SOUND. *Train chugging close. Whistle blows wildly. Then train rushes up and by with pistons going.*

ADAMS. [*narrating*] Well—I frustrated him that time. The starter had worked at last. I managed to back up. But when the train passed, he was gone. I was all alone in the hot dry afternoon.

SOUND. *Train retreating. Crickets begin to sing in background.*

MUSIC. *In.*

ADAMS. [*narrating*] After that, I knew I had to do something. I didn't know who this man was or what he wanted of me. I only knew that from now on, I must not let myself be alone on the road for one single moment.

SOUND. *Auto hum up. Slow down. Stop. Door opening.*

ADAMS. Hello, there. Like a ride?

GIRL. Well, what do you think? How far you going?

ADAMS. Amarillo…I'll take you all the way to Amarillo.

GIRL. Amarillo, Texas?

ADAMS. I'll drive you there.

GIRL. Gee!

SOUND. *Door closes—car starts.*

MUSIC. *In.*

GIRL. Mind if I take off my shoes? My dogs[7] are killing me.

ADAMS. Go right ahead.

GIRL. Gee, what a break this is. A swell car, a decent guy, and driving all the way to Amarillo. All I been getting so far is trucks.

ADAMS. Hitchhike much?

GIRL. Sure. Only it's tough sometimes, in these great open spaces, to get the breaks.

ADAMS. I should think it would be. Though I'll bet if you get a good pick-up in a fast car,

---

7. **dogs.** Feet (slang)

you can get to places faster than—say, another person, in another car?

GIRL. I don't get you.

ADAMS. Well, take me, for instance. Suppose I'm driving across the country, say, at a nice steady clip of about forty-five miles an hour. Couldn't a girl like you, just standing beside the road, waiting for lifts, beat me to town after town—provided she got picked up every time in a car doing from sixty-five to seventy miles an hour?

GIRL. I dunno. Maybe and maybe not. What difference does it make?

ADAMS. Oh—no difference. It's just a—crazy idea I had sitting here in the car.

GIRL. [*laughing*] Imagine spending your time in a swell car thinking of things like that!

ADAMS. What would you do instead?

GIRL. [*admiringly*] What would I do? If I was a good-looking fellow like yourself? Why—I'd just enjoy myself—every minute of the time. I'd sit back, and relax, and if I saw a good-looking girl along the side of the road…[*sharply*] Hey! Look out!

ADAMS. [*breathlessly*] Did you see him too?

GIRL. See who?

ADAMS. That man. Standing beside the barbed wire fence.

GIRL. I didn't see—anybody. There wasn't nothing but a bunch of steers—and the barbed wire fence. What did you think you was doing? Trying to run into the barbed wire fence?

ADAMS. There was a man there, I tell you…a thin gray man, with an overnight bag in his hand. And I was trying to—run him down.

GIRL. Run him down? You mean—kill him?

ADAMS. He's a sort of—phantom. I'm trying to get rid of him—or else prove that he's real. But

[*desperately*] you say you didn't see him back there? You're sure?

GIRL. [*queerly*] I didn't see a soul. And as far as that's concerned, mister…

ADAMS. Watch for him the next time, then. Keep watching. Keep your eyes peeled on the road. He'll turn up again—maybe any minute now. [*excitedly*] There. Look there—

SOUND. *Auto sharply veering and skidding. Girl screams.*

SOUND. *Crash of car going into barbed wire fence. Frightened lowing of steer.*

GIRL. How does this door work? I—I'm gettin' outta here.

ADAMS. Did you see him that time?

GIRL. [*sharply*] No. I didn't see him that time. And personally, mister, I don't expect never to see him. All I want to do is to go on living—and I don't see how I will very long driving with you—

ADAMS. I'm sorry. I—I don't know what came over me. [*frightened*] Please—don't go….

GIRL. So if you'll excuse me, mister—

ADAMS. You can't go. Listen, how would you like to go to California? I'll drive you to California.

GIRL. Seeing pink elephants[8] all the way? No thanks.

ADAMS. [*desperately*] I could get you a job there. You wouldn't have to be a waitress. I have friends there—my name is Ronald Adams—You can check up.

SOUND. *Door opens.*

GIRL. Uhn-hunh. Thanks just the same.

ADAMS. Listen. Please. For just one minute. Maybe you think I am half cracked. But this man. You see, I've been seeing this man all the way across the country. He's been following

---

8. **pink elephants.** Things that don't really exist

me. And if you could only help me—stay with me—until I reach the coast—

GIRL. You know what I think you need, big boy? Not a girl friend. Just a good dose of sleep…. There, I got it now.

SOUND. *Door opens…slams.*

ADAMS. No. You can't go.

GIRL. [*screams*] Leave your hands offa me, do you hear! Leave your—

ADAMS. Come back here, please, come back.

SOUND. *Struggle…slap…footsteps running away on gravel…lowing of steer.*

ADAMS. [*narrating*] She ran from me, as though I were a monster. A few minutes later, I saw a passing truck pick her up. I knew then that I was utterly alone.

SOUND. *Lowing of steer up.*

ADAMS. [*narrating*] I was in the heart of the great Texas prairies. There wasn't a car on the road after the truck went by. I tried to figure out what to do, how to get hold of myself. If I could find a place to rest. Or even, if I could sleep right here in the car for a few hours, along the side of the road…I was getting my winter overcoat out of the back seat to use as a blanket, [Hall-ooo], when I saw him coming toward me [Hall-ooo], emerging from the herd of moving steer…

VOICE. Hall-ooo…Hall-oooo…

SOUND. *Auto starting violently…up to steady hum.*

MUSIC. *In.*

ADAMS. [*narrating*] I didn't wait for him to come any closer. Perhaps I should have spoken to him then, fought it out then and there. For now he began to be everywhere. Whenever I stopped, even for a moment—for gas, for oil, for a drink of pop, a cup of coffee, a sandwich—he was there.

MUSIC. *Faster.*

ADAMS. [*narrating*] I saw him standing outside the auto camp in Amarillo that night, when I dared to slow down. He was sitting near the drinking fountain in a little camping spot just inside the border of New Mexico.

MUSIC. *Faster.*

ADAMS. [*narrating*] He was waiting for me outside the Navajo Reservation, where I stopped to check my tires. I saw him in Albuquerque where I bought twelve gallons of gas…I was afraid now, afraid to stop. I began to drive faster and faster. I was in lunar landscape now—the great arid mesa country of New Mexico. I drove through it with the indifference of a fly crawling over the face of the moon.

MUSIC. *Faster.*

ADAMS. [*narrating*] But now he didn't even wait for me to stop. Unless I drove at eighty-five miles an hour over those endless roads—he waited for me at every other mile. I would see his figure, shadowless, flitting before me, still in its same attitude, over the cold and lifeless ground, flitting over dried-up rivers, over broken stones cast up by old glacial upheavals, flitting in the pure and cloudless air….

MUSIC. *Strikes sinister note of finality.*

ADAMS. [*narrating*] I was beside myself when I finally reached Gallup, New Mexico, this morning. There is an auto camp here—cold, almost deserted at this time of year. I went inside, and asked if there was a telephone. I had the feeling that if only I could speak to someone familiar, someone I loved, I could pull myself together.

SOUND. *Nickel put in slot.*

OPERATOR. Number, please?

ADAMS. Long distance.

SOUND. *Return of nickel: buzz.*

LONG DISTANCE. This is long distance.

ADAMS. I'd like to put in a call to my home in Brooklyn, New York. My name is Ronald Adams. The number there is Beechwood 2-0828.

LONG DISTANCE. Thank you. What is your number?

ADAMS. 312.

ALBUQUERQUE OPR. Albuquerque.

LONG DISTANCE. New York for Gallup.

[*Pause*] NEW YORK OPR. New York.

LONG DISTANCE. Gallup, New Mexico, calling Beechwood 2-0828. [*Fade*]

ADAMS. I had read somewhere that love could banish demons. It was the middle of the morning. I knew Mother would be home. I pictured her, tall, white-haired, in her crisp house dress, going about her tasks. It would be enough, I thought, merely to hear the even calmness of her voice….

LONG DISTANCE. Will you please deposit three dollars and eighty-five cents for the first three minutes? When you have deposited a dollar and a half, will you please wait until I have collected the money?

SOUND. *Clunk of six coins.*

LONG DISTANCE. All right, deposit another dollar and a half.

SOUND. *Clunk of six coins.*

LONG DISTANCE. Will you please deposit the remaining twelve cents?

SOUND. *Clunk of four coins.*

LONG DISTANCE. Ready with Brooklyn—go ahead, please.

ADAMS. Hello.

MRS. WHITNEY. Mrs. Adams's residence.

ADAMS. Hello. Hello—Mother?

MRS. WHITNEY. [*very flat and rather proper… dumb, too, in a flighty sort of way*] This is Mrs. Adams's residence. Who is it you wished to speak to, please?

ADAMS. Why—who's this?

MRS. WHITNEY. This is Mrs. Whitney.

ADAMS. Whitney? I don't know any Mrs. Whitney. Is this Beechwood 2-0828?

MRS. WHITNEY. Yes.

ADAMS. Where's my mother? Where's Mrs. Adams?

MRS. WHITNEY. Mrs. Adams is not at home. She is still in the hospital.

ADAMS. The hospital!

MRS. WHITNEY. Yes. Who is this calling please? Is it a member of the family?

ADAMS. What's she in the hospital for?

MRS. WHITNEY. She's been prostrated[9] for five days. Nervous breakdown. But who is this calling?

ADAMS. Nervous breakdown? But—my mother was never nervous…

MRS. WHITNEY. It's all taken place since the death of her oldest son, Ronald.

ADAMS. The death of her oldest son, Ronald…? Hey—what is this? What number is this?

MRS. WHITNEY. This is Beechwood 2-0828. It's all been very sudden. He was killed just six days ago in an automobile accident on the Brooklyn Bridge.

OPERATOR. [*breaking in*] Your three minutes are up, sir. [*Silence*]

OPERATOR. Your three minutes are up, sir. [*pause*] Your three minutes are up, sir. [*fade*] Sir, your three minutes are up. Your three minutes are up, sir.

ADAMS. [*narrating in a strange voice*] And so, I am sitting here in this deserted auto camp in Gallup, New Mexico. I am trying to think. I am trying to get hold of myself. Otherwise, I shall go mad… Outside it is night—the vast, soulless night of New Mexico. A million stars are in the sky. Ahead of me stretch a thousand miles of empty mesa, mountains, prairies—desert. Somewhere among them, he is waiting for me. Somewhere I shall know who he is, and who…I…am….

MUSIC. *Up.* ❖

---

9. **prostrated.** Lying flat

MIRRORS & WINDOWS

"After all, a story doesn't have to appeal to the heart—it can also appeal to the spine. Sometimes you want your heart to be warmed—sometimes you want your spine to tingle." When you read a story, what do you expect to get from it? What, in your opinion, makes a story good? What makes a story bad? Explain your answers.

An *urban legend* is a modern-day legend or folk tale, a fantastic and often scary story that is spread by word-of-mouth or, more frequently in recent years, through e-mail. In this excerpt from *The Vanishing Hitchhiker,* folklore scholar **Jan Harold Brunvand** analyzes and traces the development of one classic urban legend: the tale of the "vanishing hitchhiker." This spooky story of a ghostly passenger has been passed on for generations in various forms and may even have been in Lucille Fletcher's mind when she wrote her radio drama *The Hitchhiker.*

from
The Vanishing Hitchhiker

An Anthropological Analysis by
Jan Harold Brunvand

A prime example of the adaptability of older legends is "The Vanishing Hitchhiker"—*the* classic automobile legend. This returning-ghost tale was known by the turn of the century both in the United States and abroad. It acquired the newer automobile motif by the period of the Great Depression, and thereafter spawned a number of subtypes with greatly varied and oddly interlocking details, some of which themselves stemmed from earlier folk legends. Merely sampling some of the many "Vanishing Hitchhiker" variants that have been collected over a period of some forty years can help us trace the legend's incredible development. Surely most readers already know a local "true" account (or maybe two or three) similar to Example A, as told by a teenager in Toronto, Canada, in 1973:

Example A
Well, this happened to one of my girlfriend's best friends and her father. They were driving along a country road on their way home from the cottage when they saw a young girl hitch-

hiking. They stopped and picked her up and she got in the back seat. She told the girl and her father that she just lived in the house about five miles up the road. She didn't say anything after that but just turned to watch out the window. When the father saw the house, he drove up to it and turned around to tell the girl they had arrived—but she wasn't there! Both he and his daughter were really mystified and decided to knock on the door and tell the people what had happened. They told them that they had once had a daughter who answered the description of the girl they supposedly had picked up, but she had disappeared some years ago and had last been seen hitchhiking on this very road. Today would have been her birthday.

This version has the basic elements—not necessarily "original" ones—well known in oral tradition and occasionally reported in newspapers since the early 1930s. The stable story units have been labeled in brackets in the following text from South Carolina collected by workers of the South Carolina Writers' Project (Work Projects Administration) sometime between 1935 and 1941:

Example B
A traveling man [driver] who lived in Spartanburg [authentication[1]] was on his way home one night [setting] when he saw a woman walking along the side of the road [hitchhiker]. He stopped his car and asked the woman if he could take her where she was going. She stated that she was on her way to visit her brother who lived about three miles further on the same road [her address]. He asked her to get in the car and sit by him, but she said she would sit in the back of the car [her choice of seat]. Conversation took place for a while as they rode along, but soon the woman grew quiet. The man drove on until he reached the home of the woman's brother, whom he knew [more authentication]; then stopped his car to let the woman alight. When he looked behind him, there was no one in the car [disappearance]. He thought that rather strange [curiosity or concern], so went into the house and informed the brother that a lady had gotten into his car to ride to see him, but when he arrived at the house the lady had disappeared. The brother was not alarmed at all and stated that the lady was his sister who had died two years before [identification]. He said that this traveling man was the seventh to pick up his sister on the road to visit him, but that she had never reached his house yet.

Variations on the basic story are endless, and trying to sort them out into any kind of possible chronological development is hampered by the fact that the date when a version happened to be collected and published bears little relationship to its possible age in tradition, and by the principle that

---

1. **authentication.** According to Brunvand, most urban legends contain some "authentication," bits of information that help "prove" the story's truth, such as a specific location or date or a link to a reliable source (i.e., a news story or a "friend of a friend").

legends become highly localized and rationalized with many circumstantial details whenever they are adopted into a particular context. For instance, the plot has several different twists and turns in this 1935 version (paraphrased by the collector) from Berkeley, California:

Example C

This story was heard in a Durant Avenue boarding house, told several times as a true story. It happened to a friend of the narrator. This friend was driving up Hearst Avenue one rainy night. As he came to North Gate (Hearst and Euclid avenues) he saw a girl, a student with books under her arm, waiting for the streetcar. Since these had stopped running, he offered her a ride. She lived up on Euclid. They drove out along Euclid quite a way with some conversation. As they were crossing an intersection, another car came down the steep hill and they would have crashed if the girl had not pulled on the emergency brake [a unique detail in the story]. The fellow was flabbergasted and sat looking at the other car, which pulled around him and went on. When he remembered his companion and looked over, she was gone. Since it was near her home, he assumed she had simply gotten out to walk the rest of the way; but she had left a book on the seat. The next day he went to return the book. He found her father, an English professor, at home. He said that the girl was his daughter, that she had been killed in an auto accident at the same corner one or two years ago that

very day. But since the fellow had the book, the father took it into the library, to look on the shelves for it—he found the place where it should have been vacant.

A strictly urban setting for the story allows for more precise and thorough double-checking of factual details. In 1941 Rosalie Hankey of the University of California, who was gathering materials for a lengthy study of "The Vanishing Hitchhiker," tried to verify specific accident reports from Berkeley. In one version the automobile crash in which the girl was killed was supposed to have happened in 1935 or 1936 at the corner of College and Bancroft. But in checking the Berkeley city records from 1934 to 1937, Hankey found that only a single accident involving personal injury, non-fatal, had occurred at that corner during the five-year period....

"The Vanishing Hitchhiker" is unusual among urban legends in deriving from earlier supernatural folk legends with foreign antecedents.[2] Many ghosts, in fact, are said to be on endless quests—such as The Flying Dutchman's[3]—for peace and contentment back home. Folklorist Louis C. Jones established this link to traditional ghostlore by citing a number of New York state versions—some of them associated with European immigrant story-

---

2. **antecedents.** Ancestors or forerunners. The "ancestors" of the hitchhiker tale may have been older stories from foreign countries.

3. **The Flying Dutchman's.** Refers to a legend about a phantom ship whose ghostly captain is condemned to roam the seas forever, much like the hitchhiker condemned to seek rides from place to place without ever actually arriving anywhere

tellers—reliably dated to the late nineteenth century and involving travelers on horseback. Here is one of his examples:

Example H
(Collected by Catherine S. Martin, 1943, from her mother Grace C. Martin, who lived as a girl in and near Delmar, a small town, eight miles southwest of Albany, New York. The story was current in the 1890s.)

Mother has told of tales that she has heard of a ghost rider who used to jump on young men's horses as they went past a certain woods near Delmar on their way to parties. The rider, a woman, always disappeared when they arrived at their destination. She was believed to have been a jealous one, but did little harm except riding behind the young man.

Three other versions, from Illinois (2) and Georgia (1) dated by storytellers as having been known in 1876, 1912, and 1920 place the hitchhiker in a horse-drawn vehicle; Professor Jones has also called attention to a Chinese story collected from immigrants in California in which the ghost of a beautiful young girl *walks* with a young man along the road to her parents' home, whereupon she disappears. In an interesting counterpart to the American legend, the Chinese girl walks *behind* the man (just as the hitchhiker almost invariably sits in the car's backseat or rumble seat), so that he must turn around in order to notice her disappearance. Also, the Chinese father's reaction is a clear parallel of the scene in later accounts: "Yes, that is the precise place where she was killed. It was her spirit which led you here." ❖

Refer and Reason
1. Describe what Mrs. Adams is worried about at the beginning of the play. Were her fears justified? Why or why not? Explain what happened on the Brooklyn Bridge.
2. List details that make the hitchhiker frightening. Who is the hitchhiker? Identify specific passages from the text to support your answers.
3. Describe how the legend of the vanishing hitchhiker evolved over time. How might it continue to change in the future? For example, what might be different about the story if it is told by a person living one hundred years from now?

Writing Options
1. A parody is a literary work that imitates another work for humorous purposes. Write a parody of *The Hitchhiker*, making the story funny rather than spooky. To create a humorous mood, use exaggeration, repetition, and embellishment of the plot structure and style. Share your parody with your class.
2. Think of a popular ghost story and rewrite it in the form of a short radio play aimed at teenagers. Try to recreate the eerie mood of the story by including music and sound effects, descriptions by the narrator, and dialogue.

 Go to **www.mirrorsandwindows.com** for more.

TEXT ←TO→ TEXT CONNECTION
- Compare and contrast the story told in *The Hitchhiker* with the urban legends about a vanishing hitchhiker. What is the primary difference between the two?
- After reading about the urban legends, do you think they influenced Lucille Fletcher's radio drama at all? Explain your answer.

THE GREATEST SURVIVAL STORIES EVER TOLD
edited by Lamar Underwood

In settings ranging from the Arctic Circle to the Antarctic and from the Brazilian wilderness to the Australian Outback, the protagonists of these fiction and nonfiction stories survive shipwrecks, airplane crashes, and grizzly bear attacks. In one selection, a man battles a twenty-square-mile army of killer ants; in another, a lighthouse keeper attempts to fend off a horde of giant maritime rats.

METAMORPHOSIS
by Franz Kafka

Imagine waking up one morning and discovering you can't roll over and get out of bed. That's what happens to Gregor Samsa, when overnight he turns into a large bug! Unable to communicate, and wounded when his father pelts him with apples in a fit of rage, Gregor grows weaker and weaker. Take your turn at trying to decipher Kafka's message — or is there one?

THE ILLUSTRATED MAN
by Ray Bradbury

Although the illustrated man's exotic tattoos seem normal during the day, at night they come to life, telling stories about the future. These classic stories range from the fantastic to frightening, but they all ask probing questions about the human condition.

CITY OF THE BEASTS
by Isabel Allende

Accompanying his grandmother on an expedition to the Amazon rainforest of South America, fifteen-year-old Alexander Cold meets Nadia, a girl who is native to the region, and the adventures begin. They encounter the People of the Mist, are led by a magical shaman and his ghost wife to the City of the Beasts, face nine-foot-tall creatures, and uncover a sinister plot against the native people.

TRAVELS WITH CHARLEY: IN SEARCH OF AMERICA
by John Steinbeck

By age 58, John Steinbeck had become saddened by what he saw happening to the America he loved; so, he set out to rediscover his country. He traveled highways and country roads, crisscrossing the country over four months in a pickup, accompanied only by his French poodle friend, Charley.

ALL QUIET ON THE WESTERN FRONT
by Erich Maria Remarque

Paul Baumer and his school friends volunteer for the German army in 1919 at the urging of their teacher. But, when these "Iron Youth" reach the front lines, they find the horror of trench warfare and mustard gas, not honor and glory. All that matters is survival and loyalty to their comrades.

Analyze a Media Presentation

A multimedia presentation uses a variety of **media,** a plural form of *medium* referring to a system of communication, information, or entertainment. From documentaries to nightly news broadcasts to political commentaries, the media can play a large part in shaping your view of the world. Use the following strategies to evaluate information presented by the media and form your own opinions about it.

Identify purpose

Determine whether the presentation is intended to inform, entertain, or persuade. Be alert to a presentation that has a different purpose than you originally thought. If the nightly news, for example, tries to persuade you to take a certain position on something, you will want to take a more critical approach to watching the news.

Evaluate support

Generalizations offered in media presentations should always be supported by details, including facts, statistics, quotations, reasons, and examples. If a statement is made but it is not backed up by support, don't automatically assume the statement is true.

Analyze sources

If a statement is supported by facts or other details, consider the source of the facts or details. Is it a reputable, trustworthy source? Also consider whether support is offered for both sides of an issue.

Be aware of biased language

Although news coverage designed to inform should be objective, sometimes word choices reveal a reporter's bias. Be aware that bias exists, and look for biased language when you are watching a media presentation.

EXAMPLES

objective: Lawmakers passed the bill.
biased: Lawmakers finally passed the bill.

TRY IT YOURSELF

Watch a news broadcast, and analyze it using the strategies listed above. Prepare notes on your observations, and participate in a class discussion about evaluating media presentations. As you watch the news broadcast, pay special attention to the following:

1. major issues or stories presented

2. the types of support used as evidence for facts

3. the credibility of the sources of support

4. the objectivity or bias of the reporter's language

Listening Tip
Be especially wary of Internet sources, as anyone can publish anything on the Internet and not everything is factual.

Speaking & Listening Rubric

You will be evaluated on these elements:

☑ how much you participate in the class discussion

☑ the insightfulness of your comments

☑ your ability to listen to classmates' ideas

☑ your responses to classmates' ideas

Short Story

Assignment
Write a short story about a strange happening
Purpose
To entertain and/or enlighten your readers
Audience
Classmates, teachers, and readers of a teen literary magazine

Supernatural phenomena, science fiction, and ghost stories give readers a thrill. But authors such as Ray Bradbury and Gabriel García Márquez also create stories that allow readers to examine everyday life. The world may not be empty of humans, as in "There Will Come Soft Rains," but many people ponder the consequences of technology. Strange creatures don't often wash up on shore, as one does in "A Very Old Man with Enormous Wings," but many people live in communities that share decision-making. Strange as it might sound, "out-of-this-world" stories help readers interpret the world around them.

In a **short story,** an author can create a fictional world to explore scenarios from the bizarre to the commonplace. Stories about strange happenings often combine realistic and unrealistic elements. For example, an author might place ordinary people in fantastic settings, or unusual characters in familiar settings.

❶ PREWRITE

Select Your Conflict
Think of a **conflict** around which the plot of your story will revolve. Your main character can come into conflict with something external — another character, the environment, or society's expectations, for example — or with something internal within himself or herself. Brainstorm a list of conflicts from your life, your friends' lives, and the stories you have heard and read.

Plan Your Story
The basic building blocks of a story are characters, setting, plot, point of view, and theme. **Characters** should be believable — they should talk and act in realistic ways even if they take unusual forms (aliens or animals, for example). In a short story, you won't be able to develop all of your characters fully. Focus on creating one or two believable major characters. Freewrite for ten minutes about the appearance, personality, age, and situation of each major character. Minor characters need only be developed as much as necessary for their roles in your story.

You can choose any **setting** — time and place — for your story. Brainstorm some sensory details that will give your readers a sense of the context in which the action takes place.

The story's **theme** is its central idea. The theme, or themes, gives a story rich meaning. Themes can be implied rather than stated directly.

The **plot** of your story should introduce the conflict you have chosen, develop it to a high point of intensity (called the climax), and resolve it. A Plot Chart, like the one on the right created by student Nicholas McLean about his story, "The Mosh-tube," can help you plan how to introduce, develop, and resolve the conflict.

Writing Rubric

A successful short story

☑ **introduces** a conflict, presents believable characters, establishes a consistent point of view, and describes the setting

☑ **develops** the conflict, plot, and characters; uses sensory details; and includes effective dialogue

☑ **resolves** the conflict or shows the results of not resolving the conflict

Plot Chart

The Mosh-tube	
	Story Details
Exposition	Devloid works on a project on the moon.
Inciting Incident	He discovers a rare and dangerous "mosh-tube."
Rising Action	Branx warns Devloid that mosh-tube travel is forbidden.
Climax, or Crisis	Devloid enters mosh-tube, becomes bodiless, and encounters Rahn Meitu.
Falling Action	Rahn Meitu changes Devloid.
Resolution	Devloid has done something irreversible.
Dénouement	Devloid returns to the moon.

❷ DRAFT

Write your essay by following this three-part framework: **opening, middle,** and **end.**

Draft Your Opening

A story's opening must introduce the main characters, the setting, and the situation. At the same time, the opening needs to grab readers' interest. Follow the outline in your Plot Chart and write the opening that will let you develop your story.

The draft of the opening Nicholas wrote is shown in the first column of the chart on page 1021. His first sentence creates suspense through the main character's reaction to a discovery. He introduces a second character and, through their interaction, Nicholas reveals what that discovery was. This successfully sets up the conflict Nicholas will develop in the middle.

Draft Your Middle

Develop your conflict and the characters involved in it. Use vivid description—sensory details and imagery—to convey information. Let each character speak in a way that illustrates his or her personality. Punctuate dialogue correctly by enclosing the speaker's words and end punctuation inside quotation marks; start a new paragraph each time the speaker changes.

Read the draft of a section from the middle of Nicholas' story in the left-hand column of the chart on page 1021. By now, he has developed his plot by focusing on his characters' reactions to the conflict. His main character grapples with the conflict both internally and externally. The action is rising, and Nicholas is ready to build the story to its climax.

Review your Plot Chart. As you write the middle, take your story through the plot elements you planned in your chart. Build suspense or believable drama into each section to keep your readers' interest. Stay focused on the plot, adding only information relevant to it.

- **Opening**
  Catch the readers' attention with an exciting event or intriguing description. Establish the setting and mood. Introduce your main character and the conflict.
- **Middle**
  Develop the conflict to a high point of intensity as your main character gets deeper into the action. Use sensory details to create the feeling that the action is happening in a real time and place. Include dialogue where appropriate.
- **End**
  Resolve the conflict in a believable way, tie up loose ends, and give the story closure.

Draft Your End

A short story often ends in a dramatic way that either resolves the conflict or shows the results of not resolving the conflict. In either case, the ending should provide satisfying— surprising, startling, high-impact—closure for readers.

Does Nicholas do these things in his conclusion? Look at the draft of his conclusion in the chart on page 1021.

❸ REVISE

Evaluate Your Draft

You can evaluate your own writing or exchange papers with a classmate and evaluate each other's work. Either way, think carefully about what's done well and what can be improved.

Start by looking at the content and organization. Make sure that the opening, middle, and end work together to create a unified story. Each paragraph should focus on the conflict and further the plot. Use the Revision Checklist on page 1022 to make this evaluation. Make notes directly on the story about what changes need to be made.

Next, check the language for errors. Go back through your draft to make sure you have used grammar and punctuation correctly. Think about how to make your story riveting. One way to achieve this is to use imagery. Help readers envision the action by showing instead of telling.

Revise for Content, Organization, and Style

Nicholas evaluated his draft and found ways to improve it. Look at the chart on page 1021 (this time, the right-hand column) to see his revisions:

- **Opening:** Nicholas created a more visual sense of the setting. He added details and dialogue to develop characters. Nicholas correctly punctuated his dialogue.
- **Middle:** Nicholas deleted details that, upon rereading, seemed irrelevant to his purpose. Since he is writing from a limited third-person point of view, he rewrote lines to show the story only through Devloid's eyes.
- **End:** Nicholas expressed a line of information with imagery and description. He transitioned from one paragraph to the next to create a smoother flow. He added a last line that strengthened the ending's dramatic surprise.

Review the notes you or your partner made as you evaluated your draft. Then respond to each comment and revise your story.

What Great Writers Do

"When I read Ray Bradbury as a kid," says Stephen King, in *On Writing: A Memoir of the Craft*, "I wrote like Ray Bradbury— everything green and wondrous and seen through a lens smeared with the grease of nostalgia." After reading other authors, he says, "I wrote stories in my teenage years where all these styles merged, creating a kind of hilarious stew. This sort of stylist blending is a necessary part of developing one's own style..."

DRAFT STAGE		REVISE STAGE	
Opening Kyle trembled as he studied his display console. "What is it?" Branx clung to the railing above the cramped lunar intelligence station. "Is that…?" Branx stared at the image. "I didn't think they existed anymore". "A mosh-tube," Devloid said.	Identifies main character Establishes setting Introduces conflict	Kyle Devloid trembled as he studied his display console. "What is it, Lieutenant?" Private Branx clung to the railing above the cramped lunar intelligence station. "Is that…?" Branx stared at the image. "I didn't think they existed anymore." "A mosh-tube," Devloid said.	Further describes character Adds character details Punctuates dialogue correctly
Middle He sighed and pressed the call button. Branx appeared instantly. "Sir?" Branx asked, wiping the buttons of his jacket. "I'm going in." "It's too dangerous! We can't afford to lose you." Devloid grabbed Branx's collar. "Tell no one. Wait for my return. Record all observations," Devloid said. With wide eyes, Branx took his seat at the controls. He clamped his helmet closed, ripped open the space-station door, and launched through the atmosphere and into the mosh-tube.	Allows character interaction to further the plot Lets actions reveal characters' personalities Builds to the climax	He sighed and pressed the call button. Branx appeared instantly. "Sir?" ~~Branx asked, wiping the buttons of his jacket.~~ "I'm going in." "It's too dangerous! We can't afford to lose you." Devloid grabbed Branx's collar. "Tell no one. Wait for my return. Record all observations," Devloid said. ~~With wide eyes Branx took~~ Devloid pushed Branx into his seat at the controls. He clamped his helmet closed, ripped open the space-station door, launched through the atmosphere and into the mosh-tube.	Deletes irrelevant details Maintains a consistent point-of-view; tells the story from Devloid's perspective
End He knew his mosh-tube might save humanity or ruin it. The thought was as freeing as it was frightening. He knew the being's name. "Rahn Meitu," Devloid whispered. "It's you. You're…" "Hush. It will happen now." The white light came over him.	Brings story to its resolution Ties up loose ends; concludes by explaining one mystery but leaves a mystery for readers to ponder	He knew his mosh-tube might save humanity or ruin it. ~~The thought was as freeing as it was frightening.~~ ~~He knew~~ Then how did he know the being's name? "Rahn Meitu," Devloid whispered. "It's you. You're…" "Hush. It will happen now." The white light came over him. A moment later, Branx was shaking him.	Transitions from one section to the next Adds a line for a stronger surprise ending

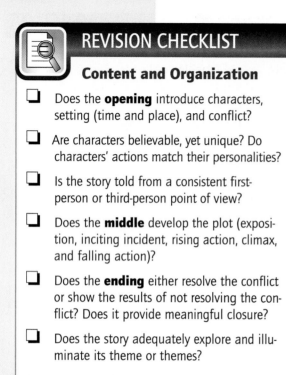

REVISION CHECKLIST

Content and Organization

- ❏ Does the **opening** introduce characters, setting (time and place), and conflict?

- ❏ Are characters believable, yet unique? Do characters' actions match their personalities?

- ❏ Is the story told from a consistent first-person or third-person point of view?

- ❏ Does the **middle** develop the plot (exposition, inciting incident, rising action, climax, and falling action)?

- ❏ Does the **ending** either resolve the conflict or show the results of not resolving the conflict? Does it provide meaningful closure?

- ❏ Does the story adequately explore and illuminate its theme or themes?

Grammar and Style

- ❏ Is the point of view consistent?

- ❏ Is dialogue capitalized properly?

- ❏ Are commas used correctly?

- ❏ Is there a variety of sentence types?

Proofread for Errors

The purpose of proofreading is to check for remaining errors. You may have corrected errors as you evaluated your story, but it's important to focus on this purpose during proofreading. Use proofreader's symbols to mark any errors you find. (See Language Arts Handbook 4.1 for a list of proofreader's symbols.) To complete the assignment, print out a final draft and read the entire thing once more before turning it in.

Take a look at Nicholas' final draft on the next page. Review how he worked through the three stages of the writing process: Prewrite, Draft, and Revise.

WRITING FOLLOW-UP

Publish and Present

- Find a literary magazine you like that accepts short story submissions for no charge. Follow the guidelines and submit your story.
- Adapt your short story by writing it as a script. Then, using actors, costumes, props, and sound effects, have your script performed.

Reflect

- How did writing a short story change the way you think? Write a journal entry about your creative process.
- Writers are avid readers. Keep a journal of the novels and short stories you read; record specific aspects you like or dislike.

STUDENT MODEL

The Mosh-tube
by Nicholas McLean

Kyle Devloid trembled as he studied his display console, no longer trained on the moon's surface but on a blue glow just above it.

"What is it, Lieutenant?" Private Branx clung to the railing above the cramped lunar intelligence station. "Is that…?" Branx stared at the image. "I didn't think they existed anymore."

"A mosh-tube," Devloid said. "You can't mention this to anyone."

"No, sir," Branx said.

What is the central conflict? How do you think the conflict will be resolved?

A historic mosh-tube—inches from the moon! He'd worked a lifetime for this discovery, but now it seemed as if the mosh-tube had found him.

"Sir, it's forbidden to enter a mosh-tube," Branx said, as if reading Devloid's mind. "Its spliced chemical could change the solar system."

"Impressive, Branx," Devloid said. "Now, get back to the bridge before I charge you with insubordination."

"Yes, sir." Branx released the bridge valve and floated out. Devloid stared into the screen. The mosh-tube called him.

No one had entered a mosh-tube since 2317—a child, by accident. He had returned a moment later but was never again normal. "Run, me too. Run, me too," he blubbered for days, wanting to go back. Devloid knew the child had seen, and been ruined by, the mystery of the mosh-tube.

The mosh-tube glowed. Entering was a stupid risk, but he longed to see it for himself. Run, me too – what did it mean? In the name of science, he needed a witness. He sighed and pressed the call button. Branx appeared instantly.

"Sir?"

"I'm going in."

"It's too dangerous! We can't afford to lose you."

Devloid grabbed Branx's collar. "Tell no one. Wait for my return. Record all observations," Devloid said.

Devloid pushed Branx into his seat at the controls. He clamped his helmet closed, ripped open the space-station door, and launched through the atmosphere and into the mosh-tube.

Inside, darkness glowed with light. He reached for his Testing Module but found he had no arm and, in fact, no body. Where was he? Was he alone? No. He instantly sensed a life form.

"My name is…" Devloid began with difficulty.

"I know," replied the being, touching Devloid somehow. Suddenly, Devloid knew everything. He knew his life was over. He'd be like the child, never the same again. He knew his mosh-tube might save humanity or ruin it.

"Rahn Metu," Devloid whispered. "It's you. You're…"

"Hush. It will happen now."

The white light came over him. A moment later, Branx was shaking him.

How does the writer convey information about the setting— where and when this story takes place?

From what point of view is the story told?

What do you know about the characters? What information does the writer provide to develop the main and minor characters?

Does the dialogue seem believable? Why or why not? How is the dialogue punctuated?

Where does the writer use sensory details?

How can you tell the story is being resolved and arriving at its closure?

Reading Skills

CLASSIFY AND SYNTHESIZE INFORMATION

Classifying and synthesizing are ways to organize the information and ideas in a text. To **classify** information is to put items that share one or more characteristics into categories, or groups. In the excerpt below from John Steinbeck's *Travels with Charley,* the information could be classified into "pros" and "cons"—the reasons why the narrator should shoot the coyotes and the reasons why he should not.

> My finger was reluctant to touch the trigger. I must be getting very old and my ancient conditioning worn thin. Coyotes are vermin. They steal chickens. They thin the ranks of quail and all other game birds. They must be killed. They are the enemy. My first shot would drop the sitting beast, and the other would whirl to fade away. I might very well pull him down with a running shot because I am a good rifleman.
>
> And I did not fire. My training said, "Shoot!" and my age replied, "There isn't a chicken within thirty miles, and if there are any they aren't my chickens. And this waterless place is not quail country. No, these boys are keeping their figures with kangaroo rats and jackrabbits, and that's vermin eat vermin. Why should I interfere?"

You can organize the information you are classifying from the excerpt above into a graphic organizer like the one below:

Pro and Con Chart

Pros of Shooting the Coyotes	Cons of Shooting the Coyotes
Coyotes are vermin.	Coyotes also eat vermin.
Coyotes steal chickens.	There are no chickens around that belong to the narrator.
Coyotes kill quail and other game birds.	There are no quail in the area.
It would be easy enough to pull the trigger.	There's no reason for the narrator to interfere with the natural order.

Synthesizing is a lot like putting together a puzzle—it involves looking at different pieces of a text and figuring out how the pieces affect the work and your understanding of it as a whole. With fiction, you can use synthesizing to find details in a story related to its characters, setting, theme, plot, and so on. Once you have gathered these details, you can see how they fit together to make a story. With nonfiction, synthesizing can help you find the main idea of a text.

PRACTICE

Directions: Read the passage below. The questions that follow will ask you to make sense of the ideas by classifying and synthesizing information.

Nonfiction: This passage is taken from the article "Sweet 16: Not for driving: Teen death rates call for drastic action," written by Patrick Welsh and published in *USA Today*.

Two weeks ago, after a 16-year-old student at Churchill High School in Montgomery County, Md., was killed while driving from a party where alcohol was being served, parents met to discuss
5 how to stop teen drinking and driving.

As well intentioned as such forums may be, they dodge the plain fact that the surest way to reduce the number of teen traffic deaths—nearly 8,000 last year—is to reduce the number of teens on the
10 road. The best place to start is with 16-year-olds.

In the U.S., 16-year-olds have a crash rate five times greater than that of 18-year-olds. Although the driving experience of 16- and 18-year-olds has to be taken into account, immaturity plays
15 an even bigger role, especially among boys. The immaturity factor is so strong that, according to the Insurance Institute for Highway Safety, driver-education courses have had little or no effect on teen accidents.

20 Yet in most states, teens are allowed to get a permit at 15 and a license at 16. If the permit age were pushed up to 16, and if kids were required to hold the permit for a year before getting a license, there would be a substantial reduction in
25 the deaths of teen drivers and their passengers. In England, the driving age is 17, and in Germany, it is 18. Both countries have lower teen fatality rates than the United States.

Multiple Choice

1. Into which of the following categories could information in this article be classified?
   A. fact and opinion
   B. cause and effect
   C. problem and solution
   D. All of the above

2. Which of the following is a synonym for the word *forum* (line 6)?
   F. argument
   G. lecture
   H. conference
   J. discussion

3. Which of the following details do *not* contribute to an understanding of the main idea of the excerpt?
   A. In the U.S., 16-year-olds have a crash rate five times greater than that of 18-year-olds.
   B. If the permit age were pushed up to 16, and if kids were required to hold the permit for a year before getting a license, there would be a substantial reduction in the deaths of teen drivers and their passengers.
   C. Two weeks ago, after a 16-year-old student at Churchill High School in Montgomery County, Md., was killed while driving from a party where alcohol was being served, parents met to discuss how to stop teen drinking and driving.
   D. In England, the driving age is 17, and in Germany, it is 18. Both countries have lower teen fatality rates than the United States.

Constructed Response

4. To synthesize ideas, it sometimes helps to create a subheading for each paragraph. What subheadings would you give the paragraphs included in the excerpt, and why? Support your answer with details from the passage.

Test-Taking Tip
Since you only have 30 minutes, you'll need to use your time wisely. You probably won't have a lot of time to revise, so take a few minutes before you begin writing to plan your essay.

Writing Skills

PERSUASIVE ESSAY

Some standardized tests, including one of the college entrance exams, require that students write an essay on a prescribed topic. The writing prompt will discuss two different perspectives on a controversial issue. Then you will be asked to write an essay in which you take a position on the issue and support your position with reasons and examples. You will have 30 minutes to complete your essay.

Scorers will take into account the fact that you had only 30 minutes to write your essay. They will evaluate your ability to:
- take a position on the issue in the prompt
- focus on the topic throughout the essay
- support your ideas logically and thoroughly
- organize ideas in a logical way
- use language clearly and effectively according to the conventions of standard written English

PRACTICE

Timed Writing: 30 minutes

Think carefully about the following assignment. Allow 30 minutes to write your response to the prompt.

Assignment: Many people like to use the Internet to download music by popular artists for free. A common argument in favor of this practice is that the artists make plenty of money from the sale of their CDs. Many popular artists believe they should be paid for all their music, whether it is purchased on CD or downloaded off the Internet, because they own the copyrights to the music. Do you think people should be able to download music for free, or should the artists be paid for all uses of their music?

In your essay, take a position on this question. You may write about either one of the two points of view given, or you may present a different point of view on this question. Use specific reasons and examples to support your position.

Revising and Editing Skills

Some standardized tests ask you to read a draft of an essay and answer questions about how to improve it. As you read the draft, watch for errors like these:
- incorrect spellings
- disagreement between subject and verb; inconsistent verb tense; incorrect forms for irregular verbs; sentence fragments and run-ons; double negatives; and incorrect use of frequently confused words, such as *affect* and *effect*
- missing end marks, incorrect comma use, and lowercased proper nouns and proper adjectives

- unclear purpose, unclear main ideas, and lack of supporting details
- confusing order of ideas and missing transitions
- language that is inappropriate to the audience and purpose, and mood that is inappropriate for the purpose

After checking for errors, read each test question and decide which answer is best.

PRACTICE

Directions: For each underlined section in the passage that follows, choose the revision that most improves the writing. If you think the original version is best, choose "MAKE NO CHANGE."

(1) The future is in the hands of the youth of today, and the youth of today is in the hands of their teachers. (2) I'm not saying that parents or other adult role models are not important. But teachers play a huge role in the development of children. (3) About how a good education is important is a thing we're always hearing. Now's the time you can do something. (4) You can back this up with bucks. Higher salaries for our teachers. (5) Here, are the most important reasons we should pay teachers at Lincoln High School more.

1. A. MAKE NO CHANGE.
   B. the youth of today is in the hands of they're teachers.
   C. youth of today, is in the hands of their teachers.
   D. the youth of today are in the hands of their teachers.

2. F. MAKE NO CHANGE.
   G. is not
   H. are
   J. is

3. A. MAKE NO CHANGE.
   B. The importance of how education should be good is what we're always hearing about.
   C. We're always hearing about the importance of a good education.
   D. The thing we're hearing about always is the importance of a good education.

4. F. MAKE NO CHANGE.
   G. bucks, higher
   H. bucks—that is, higher
   J. bucks that means higher

5. A. MAKE NO CHANGE.
   B. Here are
   C. Here; are
   D. Here, are,

Language Arts Handbook

1.1 The Reading Process

The reading process begins before you actually start to read. All readers use a reading process, even if they don't think about it. By becoming aware of this process, you can become a more effective reader. The reading process can be broken down into three stages: before reading, during reading, and after reading.

BEFORE READING

BUILD BACKGROUND

- Think about the **context** you as a reader bring to the selection based on your knowledge and experiences. What do you know about the topic? What do you want to know?

SET PURPOSE

- **Preview** the text to set a purpose for reading. Skim the first few paragraphs and glance through the selection to figure out what it's about and who the main characters are. What can you learn from the art or photos?

USE READING SKILLS

- Apply **reading skills** such as determining the author's purpose, analyzing text structure, and previewing new vocabulary.

DURING READING

USE READING STRATEGIES

- **Ask questions** about things that seem unusual or interesting, like why a character might have behaved in an unexpected way.
- **Visualize** by forming pictures in your mind to help you see the characters or actions.
- **Make predictions** about what's going to happen next. As you read, gather more clues that will either confirm or change your prediction.
- **Make inferences,** or educated guesses, about what is not stated directly. Things may be implied or hinted at, or they may be left out altogether.
- **Clarify.** Check that you understand what you read. Reread any difficult parts.

ANALYZE LITERATURE

- Determine what literary elements stand out as you read the selection. Ask whether the characters are engaging and lifelike. Determine if there is a strong central conflict or theme.

MAKE CONNECTIONS

- Notice where there are **connections** between the story and your life or the world beyond the story. Be aware of feelings or thoughts you have while reading the story.

AFTER READING

REFER TO TEXT

- Think about the facts. **Remember details** like characters' names, locations or settings, and any other things that you can recall.
- Determine the **sequence of events** or the order in which things happened.
- **Reread** the story to pick up any details you may have missed the first time around.
- Try to **summarize** the story in a sentence or two based on the events.

REASON WITH TEXT

- **Analyze** the text by breaking down information into smaller pieces and figuring out how those pieces fit into the story as a whole. Your knowledge of literary tools can help you analyze the author's technique.
- **Evaluate** the text. **Synthesize** and **draw conclusions** by bringing together what you have read and using it to make a decision or form an opinion. Decide if you agree with the author's views.

Framework for Reading

Before Reading

ASK YOURSELF

- ❏ What's my purpose for reading this?
- ❏ What is this going to be about?
- ❏ How is this information organized?
- ❏ What do I already know about the topic?
- ❏ How can I apply this information to my life?

During Reading

ASK YOURSELF

- ❏ What is the best way to accomplish my purpose for reading?
- ❏ What do I want or need to find out while I'm reading?
- ❏ What is the essential information presented here?
- ❏ What is the importance of what I am reading?
- ❏ Do I understand what I just read?
- ❏ What can I do to make the meaning more clear?

After Reading

ASK YOURSELF

- ❏ What did I learn from what I have read?
- ❏ What is still confusing?
- ❏ What do I need to remember from my reading?
- ❏ What effect did this text have on me?
- ❏ What else do I want to know about this topic?

1.2 Using Reading Strategies

Reading actively means thinking about what you are reading as you read it. A **reading strategy,** or plan, helps you read actively and get more from your reading. The following strategies can be applied at each stage of the reading process: before, during, and after reading.

Reading Strategies

- Build Background
- Set Purpose
- Ask Questions
- Visualize
- Make Predictions
- Make Inferences
- Clarify
- Make Connections

BUILD BACKGROUND

Each reader brings his or her own context to a selection based on prior knowledge and experiences. What do you know about the topic? What do you want to know? Before and during reading, think about what you already know about the topic or subject matter. By connecting to your prior knowledge, you will increase your interest in and understanding of what you read. Fill in the first two columns of a K-W-L Chart before you read. Fill in the last column after you finish reading.

K-W-L Chart

What I *Know*	What I *Want to Learn*	What I have *Learned*

SET PURPOSE

Before you begin reading, think about your reason for reading the material. You might be reading from a textbook to complete a homework assignment, skimming a magazine for information about one of your hobbies, or reading a novel for your own personal enjoyment. Know why you are reading and what information you seek. Decide on your purpose for reading as clearly as you can. Be aware that the purpose of your reading may change as you read.

Preview the text to set a purpose for reading. Skim the first few paragraphs and glance through the selection to figure out what it's about and who the main characters are. What can you learn from the art or photos? Fill in a Reader's Purpose Chart at each stage of reading to set a purpose for reading and to help you attain it.

Reader's Purpose Chart

Before Reading
Set a purpose for reading

During Reading
Take notes on what you learn

After Reading
Reflect on your purpose and what you learned

ASK QUESTIONS

Think and reflect by asking questions to further your understanding of what you are reading. Asking questions helps you to pinpoint parts of the text that are confusing. You can ask questions in your head, or you may write them down. Ask questions about things that seem unusual or interesting, like why a character might have behaved in an unexpected way. What do you wonder about as you read the text? Use a Generate Questions Bookmark like the following to record your questions as you read.

Generate Questions Bookmark

Generate Questions Bookmark	
Page #	What I Wonder About

VISUALIZE

Reading is more than simply sounding out words. It is an active process that requires you to use your imagination. When you visualize, you form a picture or an image in your mind of the action and descriptions in a text. Each reader's images will be different based on his or her prior knowledge and experience. Keep in mind that there are no "right" or "wrong" visualizations. Visualize by forming pictures in your mind to help you see the characters or actions. Use a Visualization Map to draw pictures that represent key events in a selection. Write a caption under each box that explains each event. Draw the events in the order they occur.

Visualization Map

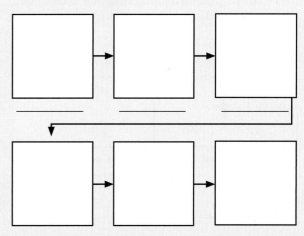

MAKE PREDICTIONS

When you **make predictions** during reading, you are making guesses about what the reading is going to be about or what might happen next. Before you read, make predictions based on clues from the page and from what you already know about the topic. Continue to make guesses as you read. The guesses do not have to be correct. When you pause during reading, gather information that helps you make more predictions and check predictions you have already made. Make predictions about what's going to happen next. As you read, gather more clues that will either confirm or change your prediction.

Prediction Chart

Guesses	Reasons	Evidence

MAKE INFERENCES

Making an inference means putting together the clues given in the text with your own prior knowledge. Make inferences, or educated guesses, about what is not stated directly. Things may be implied or hinted at, or they may be left out altogether. By paying close attention to what you read, you will be able to make inferences about what the writer is trying to communicate. Use an Inference Chart to document your conclusions.

Inference Chart

Text	What I infer
Detail from text	Conclusions I draw about the meaning

CLARIFY

Check that you understand what you read and identify text that is confusing or unclear. If you encounter problems or lose focus, it may be helpful to use **Fix-Up Ideas,** such as rereading difficult parts, reading in shorter chunks, going back and reading aloud, or changing your reading rate. (See Monitor Comprehension for more information.)

MAKE CONNECTIONS

Notice where there are **connections** between the story and your life or the world beyond the story. Be aware of feelings or thoughts you have while reading the story.

Connections Chart

Page #	Event	Reminds Me of

1.3 Using Reading Skills

Using the following skills as you read helps you to become an independent, thoughtful, and active reader who can accomplish tasks evaluated on tests, particularly standardized tests.

Reading Skills

o Identify Author's Purpose and Approach
o Skim and Scan
o Find the Main Idea
o Determine Importance of Details
o Understand Literary Elements
o Use Context Clues
o Analyze Text Organization
o Take notes
o Sequence of Events
o Compare and Contrast
o Evaluate Cause and Effect
o Classify and Reorganize Information
o Distinguish Fact from Opinion
o Identify Multiple Levels of Meaning
o Interpret Visual Aids
o Monitor Comprehension
o Summarize
o Draw Conclusions

IDENTIFY AUTHOR'S PURPOSE AND APPROACH

Author's Purpose

A writer's **purpose** is his or her aim or goal. Being able to figure out an author's purpose, or purposes, is an important reading skill. An author may write with one or more of the purposes listed in the following chart. A writer's purpose corresponds to a specific mode, or type, of writing. A writer can choose from a variety of forms while working within a mode. Once you identify what the author is trying to do, you can evaluate, or judge, how well the author achieved that purpose. For example, you may judge that the author of a persuasive essay made a good and convincing argument. Or, you may decide that the novel you are reading has a boring plot.

Purposes of Writing

Mode of Writing	Purpose	Examples
expository	to inform	news article, research report
narrative	to express thoughts or ideas, or to tell a story	personal account, memoir
descriptive	to portray a person, place, object, or event	travel brochure, personal profile
persuasive	to convince people to accept a position and respond in some way	editorial, petition

Before Reading
Identify the author's purpose, the type of writing he or she uses, and the ideas he or she wants to communicate.

During Reading
Gather ideas that the author communicates to the readers.

After Reading
Summarize the ideas the author communicates, Explain how these ideas help fulfill the author's purpose.

Author's Approach

The literary elements, the terms and techniques used in literature, make up the **author's approach** to conveying his or her main idea or theme. Understanding the author's approach in fiction involves recognizing literary elements such as *point of view, tone,* and *mood.* What perspective, or way of looking at things, does the author have? What is his or her attitude toward the subject? Is the writing serious or playful in nature? What emotions is the writer trying to evoke in the reader? (See Understand Literary Elements.)

SKIM AND SCAN

When you **skim,** you glance through material quickly to get a general idea of what it is about. Skimming is an excellent way to get a quick overview of material. It is useful for previewing a chapter in a textbook, for surveying material to see if it contains information that will be useful to you, and for reviewing material for a test or essay. When skimming, look at titles, headings, and words that appear in boldface or colored type. Also read topic sentences of paragraphs, first and last paragraphs of sections, and any summaries or conclusions. In addition, glance at illustrations, photographs, charts, maps, or other graphics.

When you **scan,** you look through written material quickly to locate particular information. Scanning is useful when, for example, you want to find an entry in an index or a definition in a textbook chapter. To scan, simply run your eye down the page, looking for a key word. When you find the key word, slow down and read carefully.

SKIM AND SCAN

To **skim** a text, preview the following:

- ❏ titles
- ❏ headings
- ❏ bold or colored type
- ❏ topic sentences
- ❏ summaries
- ❏ graphics

When you **scan** a text, you may be looking for the following:

- ❏ specific information
- ❏ key words
- ❏ main ideas
- ❏ answers to questions

FIND THE MAIN IDEA

The **main idea** is a brief statement of what you think the author wants you to know, think, or feel after reading the text. In some cases, the main idea will actually be stated. Check the first and last paragraphs for a sentence that sums up the entire passage. The author may not tell you what the main idea is, and you will have to infer it.

In general, nonfiction texts have main ideas; literary texts (poems, short stories, novels, plays, and personal essays) have themes. Sometimes, however, the term *main idea* is used to refer to the theme of a literary work, especially an essay or poem. Both deal with the central idea in a written work.

A good way to find the main or overall idea of a whole selection (or part of a selection) is to gather important details into a Main Idea Map like the one below. Use the details to determine the main or overall thought or message.

Main Idea Map

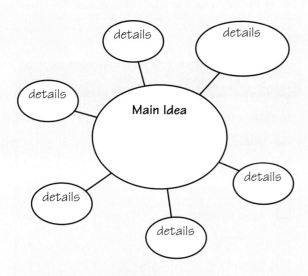

DETERMINE IMPORTANCE OF DETAILS

The main ideas are what the selection is about; the minor ideas and details provide support for the main ones. To identify supporting details, you need to do the following:

- Locate **basic facts,** such as names, dates, and events.
- **Determine the importance** of those facts to the understanding of the piece. Some facts or details will be more important than others.

- **Interpret** subtly stated details. These details can help clarify the author's stance or purpose, or they may give fuller meaning to the basic facts.
- Understand the **function** of a part of a passage. Is the author providing information, supporting a previously made point, presenting a conflicting argument, building suspense? Pay attention to how your understanding of a topic or your feelings toward it change as you read.
- Make **inferences,** or educated guesses, about how the author uses the supporting details to achieve his or her desired result. Put together clues from the text with your known prior knowledge to make inferences. A Main Idea Map or an Inference Chart can help you keep track of your ideas.

UNDERSTAND LITERARY ELEMENTS

Literary elements are the terms and techniques that are used in literature. When you read literature, you need to be familiar with the literary terms and reading skills listed below. These literary elements are explained in more detail in Understanding Fiction.

■ **Recognize Mood and Tone** The atmosphere or emotion conveyed by a literary work is called **mood.** A writer creates mood by using concrete details to describe the setting, characters, or events. **Tone** is the writer's attitude toward the subject or toward the reader of a work. Examples of different tones that a work may have include familiar, ironic, playful, sarcastic, serious, and sincere.

■ **Understand Point of View** The vantage point, or perspective, from which a story or narrative is told is referred to as **point of view.** Stories are typically written from the following points of view:

first-person point of view: narrator uses words such as *I* and *we*

second-person point of view: narrator uses *you*

third-person point of view: narrator uses words such as *he, she, it,* and *they*

■ **Analyze Character and Characterization** A **character** is a person (or sometimes an animal) who takes part in the action of a story. Characterization is the literary techniques writers use to create characters and make them come alive.

■ **Examine Plot Development** The plot is basically what happens in a story. A **plot** is a series of events related to a central conflict, or struggle. A typical plot involves the introduction of a conflict, its development, and its eventual resolution. The elements of plot include the exposition, rising action, climax, falling action, and resolution. A graphic organizer called a Plot Diagram can be used to chart the plot of a literature selection.

USE CONTEXT CLUES

You can often figure out the meaning of an unfamiliar word by using context clues. **Context clues** are words and phrases near a difficult word that provide hints about its meaning. The context in which a word is used may help you guess what it means without having to look it up in the dictionary.

Different types of context clues include the following:

- **comparison clue:** shows a comparison, or how the unfamiliar word is like something that might be familiar to you
- **contrast clue:** shows that something contrasts, or differs in meaning, from something else
- **restatement clue:** uses different words to express the same idea
- **examples clue:** gives examples of other items to illustrate the meaning of something
- **cause-and-effect clue:** tells you that something happened as a result of something else

TAKE NOTES

Writing things down helps you pay attention to the words on a page.

It is an excellent way to remember important ideas. **Taking or making notes** helps you select ideas you consider important. *Paraphrase,* or write in your own words, what you have read and put it into notes you can read later. Taking or making notes is also a quick way for you to retell what you have just read. Since you cannot write in, mark up, or highlight information in a textbook or library book, make a response bookmark like the one that follows and use it to record your thoughts and reactions. As you read, ask yourself questions, make predictions, react to ideas, identify key points, and/or write down unfamiliar words.

Response Bookmark

Page #	Questions, Predictions, Reactions, Key Points, and Unfamiliar Words

Making notes in **graphic organizers** helps you organize ideas as you read. For instance, if you are reading an essay that compares two authors, you might use a Venn Diagram or a cluster chart to collect information about each author. If you are reading about an author's life, you may construct a time line. As you read a selection, create your own method for gathering and organizing information. You might use your own version of a common graphic organizer or invent a new way to show what the selection describes.

Common Graphic Organizers

Character Chart
Sensory Details Chart
Summary Chart
Time Line
Story Strip
Plot Diagram
Pro and Con Chart
Cluster Chart
Venn Diagram
Note-Taking Chart
Cause-and-Effect Chart
Drawing Conclusions Log

ANALYZE TEXT ORGANIZATION

Text organization refers to the different ways a text may be presented or organized. If you are aware of the ways different texts are organized, you will find it easier to understand what you read. For example, familiarity with typical plot elements—the exposition, rising action, climax, falling action, and resolution—is important for understanding the events in a short story or novel. Focusing on signal words and text patterns is important for understanding nonfiction and informational text. For instance, transition words, such as *first, second, next, then,* and *finally,* might indicate that an essay is written in chronological, or time, order. Common methods of organization include the following:

Methods of Organization

Chronological Order	Events are given in the order they occur.
Order of Importance	Details are given in order of importance or familiarity.
Comparison and Contrast Order	Similarities and differences of two things are listed.
Cause and Effect Order	One or more causes are presented followed by one or more effects.

IDENTIFY SEQUENCE OF EVENTS

Sequence refers to the order in which things happen. When you read certain types of writing, such as a short story, a novel, a biography of a person's life, or a history book, keep track of the sequence of events. You might do this by making a time line or a sequence map.

Time Line

To make a time line, draw a line and divide it into equal parts like the one on the next page. Label each part with a date or a time. Then add key events at the right places along the time line.

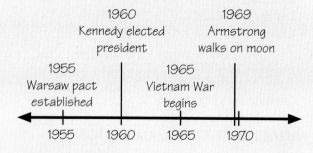

Sequence Map

In each box, draw pictures that represent key events in a selection. Then write a caption under each box that explains each event. Draw the events in the order in which they occur.

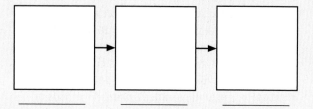

COMPARE AND CONTRAST

Comparing and contrasting are closely related processes. When you **compare** one thing to another you describe similarities between the two things; when you **contrast** two things you describe their differences. To compare and contrast, begin by listing the features of each subject. Then go down both lists and check whether each feature is shared or not. You can also show similarities and differences in a *Venn Diagram*. A Venn Diagram uses two slightly overlapping circles. The outer part of each circle shows what aspects of two things are different from each other. The inner, or shared, part of each circle shows what aspects the two things share.

Venn Diagram

Write down ideas about Topic 1 in the first circle and ideas about Topic 2 in the second circle. The area in which the circles overlap should contain ideas common to both topics.

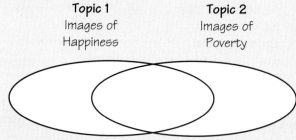

Another method is to use a Pro and Con Chart like the one below to take notes on both sides of each argument.

Pro and Con Chart

Arguments in Favor (PRO)	Arguments Against (CON)
Argument 1: Support	Argument 1: Support
Argument 2: Support	Argument 2: Support

IDENTIFY CAUSE AND EFFECT

When you evaluate **cause and effect,** you are looking for a logical relationship between a cause or causes and one or more effects. A writer may present one or more causes followed by one or more effects, or one or more effects followed by one or more causes. Transitional, or signal, words and phrases that indicate cause and effect include *one cause, another effect, as a result, consequently,* and *therefore.* As a reader, you determine whether the causes and effects in a text are reasonable. A graphic organizer like the one below will help you to recognize relationships between causes and effects. Keep track of what happens in a story and why in a chart like the one below. Use cause-and-effect signal words to help you identify causes and their effects.

Cause-and-Effect Chart

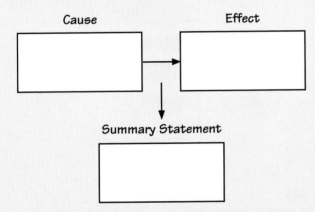

CLASSIFY AND REORGANIZE INFORMATION

To **classify** is to put into classes or categories. Items in the same category should share one or more characteristics. A writer may group things to show similarities and name the categories to clarify how one group is similar or different from another. For example, whales can be classified by their method of eating as *baleen* or *toothed.* Classifying or reorganizing the information into categories as you read increases your understanding.

The key step in classifying is choosing categories that fit your purpose. Take classification notes in a chart like the one that follows to help you organize separate types or groups and sort their characteristics.

Classification Chart

Category 1	Category 2	Category 3
Items in Category	Items in Category	Items in Category
Details and Characteristics	Details and Characteristics	Details and Characteristics

DISTINGUISH FACT FROM OPINION

A **fact** is a statement that could be proven by direct observation. Every statement of fact is either true or false. The following statement is an example of fact:

> Many Greek myths deal with human emotion. (This statement is a fact that can be proven by examining the content of Greek myths.)

An **opinion** is a statement that expresses an attitude or desire, not a fact about the world. One common type of opinion statement is a *value statement*. A value statement expresses an attitude toward something.

> Ancient Greece produced some **beautiful** and **inspiring** myths. (The adjectives used to describe myths express an attitude or opinion toward something that cannot be proven.)

Fact:	Opinion:
Proof:	Support:
Fact:	Opinion:
Proof:	Support:

IDENTIFY MULTIPLE LEVELS OF MEANING

There is often more than one purpose to a story or nonfiction work. Though there is always a main idea or theme, other levels of meaning are nonetheless important in understanding the overall meaning of the selection. As you read, take note of the multiple levels of meaning, and record them in a Levels of Meaning Chart like the one below:

Levels of Meaning Chart

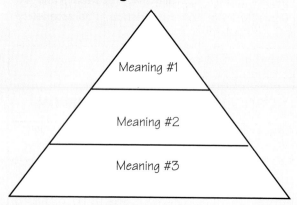

INTERPRET VISUAL AIDS

Visual aids are charts, graphs, pictures, illustrations, photos, maps, diagrams, spreadsheets, and other materials that present information. Many writers use visual aids to present data in understandable ways. Information visually presented in tables, charts, and graphs can help you find information, see trends, discover facts, and uncover patterns.

Pie Chart

A **pie chart** is a circle that stands for a whole group or set. The circle is divided into parts to show the divisions of the whole. When you look at a pie chart, you can see the relationships of the parts to one another and to the whole.

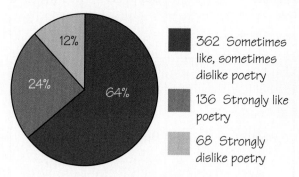

362 Sometimes like, sometimes dislike poetry

136 Strongly like poetry

68 Strongly dislike poetry

Total: 566 students

Bar Graph

A **bar graph** compares amounts of something by representing the amounts as bars of different lengths. In the bar graph below, each bar represents the value in dollars of canned goods donated by several communities to a food drive. To read the graph, simply imagine a line drawn from the edge of the bar to the bottom of the graph. Then read the number. For example, the bar graph below shows that the community of Russell Springs donated $600 worth of goods during the food drive.

DOLLAR VALUE OF DONATED GOODS TO CANNED FOOD DRIVE

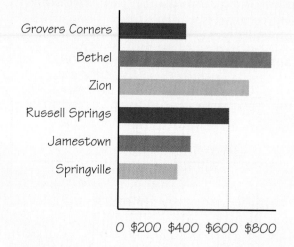

Map

A **map** is a representation, usually on a surface such as paper or a sheet of plastic, of a geographic area showing various significant features of that area.

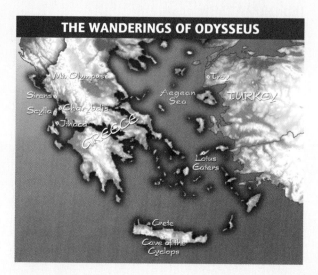

THE WANDERINGS OF ODYSSEUS

Monitor Comprehension

All readers occasionally have difficulty as they read. As you read, you should always **monitor,** or pay attention to, your progress, stopping frequently to check how well you are understanding what you are reading. If you encounter problems or lose focus, use a **fix-up idea** to get back on track. Readers who know how to apply fix-up ideas are well on the way to reading independence. They know when they are having a problem and are able to adjust and get back on track.

Fix-Up Ideas

The following **fix-up ideas** can help you "fix up" any confusion or lack of attention you experience as you read. You probably use many of these already.

☐ **Reread** If you don't understand a sentence, paragraph, or section the first time through, go back and reread it. Each time you reread a text, you understand and remember more.

☐ **Read in shorter chunks** Break a long text into shorter chunks. Read through each "chunk." Then go back and make sure you understand that section before moving on.

☐ **Read aloud** If you are having trouble keeping your focus, try reading aloud to yourself. Go somewhere private and read aloud, putting emphasis and expression in your voice. Reading aloud also allows you to untangle difficult text by talking your way through it.

☐ **Ask questions** As you read, stop and ask yourself questions about the text. These questions may help you pinpoint things that are confusing you or things that you want to come back to later. You can ask questions in your head, or jot them down in the margins or on a piece of paper.

☐ **Change your reading rate** Your reading rate is how fast or slow you read. Good readers adjust their rate to fit the situation. In some cases, when you just need to get the general idea or main points of a reading, or if the reading is simple, you will want to read through it quickly and not get bogged down. Other times, such as when a text is difficult or contains a lot of description, you will need to slow down and read carefully.

SUMMARIZE

Summarizing is giving a shortened version of something that has been said or written, stating its main points. When you summarize a selection, you are **paraphrasing,** or restating something using other words in order to make it simpler or shorter. Summarizing what you have read will help you identify, understand, and remember the main and subpoints in the text. Read and summarize short sections of a selection at a time. Then write a summary of the entire work. Use a Summary Chart like the one below.

Summary Chart

Summary of Section 1:
Summary of Section 2:
Summary of Section 3:
Summary of Section 4:
Summary of the Selection:

DRAW CONCLUSIONS

When you **draw conclusions,** you are gathering pieces of information and then deciding what that information means. Drawing conclusions is an essential part of reading. It may be helpful to use a graphic organizer such as a chart or log to keep track of the information you find while you are reading and the conclusions you draw.

Drawing Conclusions Log

Key Idea	Key Idea	Key Idea
Supporting Points	Supporting Points	Supporting Points
Overall Conclusion		

To understand what you read, you need a set of tools for dealing with words you don't know. Context clues, prior knowledge of word parts and word families, glossaries and footnotes, and dictionaries are tools that can help you unlock the meaning of unfamiliar words.

you gather from the words and sentences around the unfamiliar word, prevent you from having to look up every unknown word in the dictionary. The chart below defines the types of context clues and gives you an example of each. It also lists words that signal each type of clue.

2.1 Using Context Clues

You can often figure out the meaning of an unfamiliar word by using context clues. Context clues, or hints

Context Clues	
comparison clue	shows a comparison, or how the unfamiliar word is like something that might be familiar to you
signal words	*and, like, as, just as, as if, as though*
EXAMPLE	
Joan was as nimble as a mountain goat as she hiked along the steep, rocky trail. (A mountain goat is extremely agile and sure on its feet. *Nimble* must mean "agile.")	
contrast clue	shows that something contrasts, or differs in meaning, from something else
signal words	*but, nevertheless, on the other hand, however, although, though, in spite of*
EXAMPLE	
Hsuan is very reflective, but his friend Ku Min is known for jumping into things without thinking about them. (The word *but* signals a contrast between Hsuan's and Ku Min's ways of doing things. If Ku Min jumps in without thinking, Hsuan must think things through more thoroughly. *Reflective* must mean "thoughtful, meditative.")	
restatement clue	uses different words to express the same idea
signal words	*that is, in other words, or*
EXAMPLE	
I know Kayesha will prevail in the student council election; I have no doubt that she's going to win! (As the information after the semicolon indicates, *prevail* means "win.")	
examples clue	gives examples of other items to illustrate the meaning of something
signal words	*including, such as, for example, for instance, especially, particularly*
EXAMPLE	
Trevor has always been interested in celestial bodies such as planets, stars, and moons. (If you know enough about the examples listed, you can tell that celestial bodies are visible bodies in the sky.)	
cause-and-effect clue	tells you that something happened as a result of something else
signal words	*if/then, when/then, thus, therefore, because, so, as a result of, consequently*
EXAMPLE	
I hadn't planned on going to the party, but the host invited me in such a cordial way that I felt welcome. (If the host's cordial invitation helped the speaker feel welcome, you can guess that *cordial* means "friendly.")	

Breaking Words Into Base Words, Word Roots, Prefixes, and Suffixes

Many words are formed by adding prefixes and suffixes to main word parts called base words (if they can stand alone) or word roots (if they can't). A prefix is a letter or group of letters added to the beginning of a word to change its meaning. A suffix is a letter or group of letters added to the end of a word to change its meaning.

Word Part	Definition	Example
base word	main word part that can stand alone	form
word root	main word part that can't stand alone	struc
prefix	letter or group of letters added to the beginning of the word	pre–
suffix	letter or group of letters added to the end of the word	–tion

Common Prefixes		
Prefix	**Meaning**	**Examples**
ambi–/amphi–	both	ambidextrous, amphibian
anti–/ant–	against; opposite	antibody, antacid
bi–	two	bicycle, biped
circum–	around; about	circumnavigate, circumstance
co–/col–/com–/con–/cor–	together	cooperate, collaborate, commingle, concentrate, correlate
counter–	contrary; complementary	counteract, counterpart
de–	opposite; remove; reduce	decipher, defrost, devalue
dia–	through; apart	dialogue, diaphanous
dis–	not; opposite of	dislike, disguise
dys–	abnormal; difficult; bad	dysfunctional, dystopia
em–/en–	into or onto; cover with; cause to be; provide with	embark, empower, enslave, enfeeble
ex–	out of; from	explode, export, extend
extra–/extro–	outward; outside; beyond	extraordinary, extrovert
hyper–	too much, too many, or extreme	hyperbole, hyperactive
hypo–	under	hypodermic
il–, im–, in–, ir–	not	illogical, impossible, inoperable, irrational
	in; within; toward; on	illuminate, imperil, infiltrate, irrigate
inter–	among or between	international, intersect
intra–/intro–	into; within; inward	introvert, intramural

Common Prefixes		
Prefix	**Meaning**	**Examples**
meta–	after; changed	metamorphosis, metaphor
mis–	wrongly	mistake, misfire
non–	not	nonsense, nonsmoker
out–	in a manner that goes beyond	outrun, outmuscle
over–	excessive	overdone, overkill
per–	through, throughout	permeate, permanent
peri–	all around	perimeter, periscope
post–	after; later	postgame, postpone
pre–	before	prefix, premature
pro–	before; forward	proceed, prologue
re–	again; back	redo, recall
retro–	back	retrospect, retroactive
semi–	half; partly	semicircle, semidry
sub–/sup–	under	substandard, subfloor, support
super–	above; over; exceeding	superstar, superfluous
sym–/syn–	with; together	sympathy, synonym, synergy
trans–	across; beyond	transatlantic, transfer, transcend
ultra–	too much, too many, extreme	ultraviolet, ultrasound
un–	not	unethical, unhappy
under–	below or short of a quantity or limit	underestimate, understaffed
uni–	one	unicorn, universe

Common Suffixes		
Noun Suffixes	**Meaning**	**Examples**
–ance/–ancy/–ence/–ency	quality or state	defiance, independence, emergency
–age	action or process	marriage, voyage
–ant/–ent	one who	defendant, assistant, resident
–ar/–er/–or	one who	lawyer, survivor, liar
–dom	state or quality of	freedom, boredom
–es/–s	plural form of noun	siblings, trees
–ion/–tion	action or process	revolution, occasion
–ism	act; state; or system of belief	plagiarism, barbarism, Buddhism
–ist	one who does or believes something	ventriloquist, idealist

Common Suffixes

Noun Suffixes	Meaning	Examples
–itude, –tude	quality of, state of	multitude, magnitude
–ity/–ty	state of	longevity, infinity
–ment	action or process; state or quality; product or thing	development, government, amusement, amazement, ointment, fragment
–ness	state of	kindness, happiness

Adjective Suffixes	Meaning	Examples
–able/–ible	capable of	attainable, possible
–al	having characteristics of	personal, governmental
–er	more	higher, calmer, shorter
–est	most	lowest, craziest, tallest
–ful	full of	helpful, gleeful, woeful
–ic	having characteristics of	scientific, chronic
–ish	like	childish, reddish
–ive	performs or tends toward	creative, pensive
–less	without	hapless, careless
–ous	possessing the qualities of	generous, joyous
–y	indicates description	happy, dirty, flowery

Adverb Suffixes	Meaning	Examples
–ly	in such a way	quickly, studiously, invisibly
–ward, –ways, –wise	in such a direction	toward, sideways, crosswise

Verb Suffixes	Meaning	Examples
–ate	make or cause to be	fixate, activate
–ed	past tense of verb	walked, acted, fixed
–ify/–fy	make or cause to be	vilify, magnify, glorify
–ing	indicates action in progress (present participle); can also be a noun (gerund)	running, thinking, being
–ize	bring about; cause to be	colonize, legalize

Common Word Roots		
Word Root	**Meaning**	**Examples**
acr	highest point	acrobat
act	do	actor, reaction
ann/annu/enni	year	annual, bicentennial
aqu	water	aquarium, aquatic
aster, astr	star	asteroid, disastrous
aud	hear	audition, auditorium
bene	good	beneficial, benefactor
bibl, bibli	book	Bible
chron	time	chronic
cosm	universe; order	cosmic, cosmos
cred	believe; trust	credit, credible
cycl	circle	bicycle, cyclone
dem/demo	people	democracy
derm	skin	dermatologist
dic/dict	say	dictate, dictionary
duc/duct	lead; pull	conduct, reproduction
dyn	force, power	dynamic, dynamite
equ/equi/iqui	equal	equidistant, equitable, iniquity
fer	carry	transfer, refer
fin	end	finish, infinite
firm	firm, strong	confirm, reaffirm
flect/flex	bend	deflect, reflex, flexible
fort	strong	fortify, comfort
ge	earth	geode, geography
gress	go	progress, regress
ydr	water	hydrate
ign	fire	ignite, ignition, igneous
ject	throw	projector, eject
judic	judgment	prejudice, judicial
lect/leg	read; choose	lecture, election, collect
liber	free	liberate, liberal
loc	place	location, relocate
locut/loqu	speak	elocution, loquacious, colloquial
log/logue	word, speech, discourse	logic, dialogue

Common Word Roots		
Word Root	**Meaning**	**Examples**
luc/lumin	shine; light	translucent, illuminate
mal	bad	malevolent
man/manu	hand	manufacture, manual
metr	measure	metric
morph	form	morpheme, metamorphosis
mot	move	motor, emotion
mut	change	mutation, transmutable
nov	new	novelty, renovate
onym	name	synonym, antonym
path	feel; suffer; disease	sympathy, pathology
ped	foot, child	pedal, pediatrics
phon/phony	sound; voice; speech	symphony
phot	light	photography
physi	nature	physical, physics
pop	people	popular, populate
port	carry	transport, portable
psych	mind; soul	psychology, psychic
reg	rule	register, regulate
rupt	break	disrupt, interruption, rupture
scrib/script	write	describe, prescription
son	sound	sonic
spec/spect/spic	look	speculate, inspect, despicable
spir	breathe	spirit, inspiration
ter/terr	earth	inter, extraterrestrial, terrain
therm	heat	thermal
top	place	topography, topical
tract	draw; drag	retract, tractor, contract
typ	stamp; model	typical, type
ver	truth	veracity, verifiable
vert	turn	divert, introvert, extrovert
vid/vis	see	video, visual
viv	alive	vivacious, vivid
vol/volv	turn	evolution, revolve

2.3 Exploring Word Origins and Word Families

The English language expands constantly and gathers new words from many different sources. Understanding the source of a word can help you unlock its meaning.

One source of new words is the names of people and places associated with the thing being named. Words named for people and places are called **eponyms.**

EXAMPLES

hamburger Originally known as "Hamburg steak," the hamburger takes its name from the German city Hamburg.

spoonerism The slip of the tongue whereby the beginning sounds of words are switched is named after the Rev. William A. Spooner, who was known for such slips. For example, after a wedding, he told the groom, "It is kisstomary to cuss the bride."

Another source for new words is **acronyms.** Acronyms are words formed from the first letter or letters of the major parts of terms.

EXAMPLES

sonar, from sound navigation ranging
NATO, from North American Treaty Organization

Some words in the English language are borrowed from other languages.

EXAMPLES

deluxe (French), **Gesundheit** (German), **kayak** (Inuit)

Many words are formed by shortening longer words.

EXAMPLES

ad, from advertisement

lab, from laboratory

stereo, from stereophonic

Brand names are often taken into the English language. People begin to use these words as common nouns, even though most of them are still brand names.

EXAMPLES

Scotch tape   **Xerox**   **Rollerblade**

2.4 Using a Dictionary

When you can't figure out a word using the strategies already described, or when the word is important to the meaning of the text and you want to make sure you have it right, use a dictionary. There are many parts to a dictionary entry. Study the following sample. Then read the explanations of each part of an entry below.

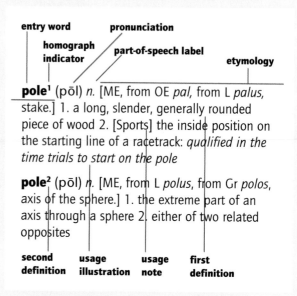

The **pronunciation** is given immediately after the entry word. The dictionary's table of contents will tell you where you can find a complete key to pronunciation symbols. In some dictionaries, a simplified pronunciation key is provided at the bottom of each page.

An abbreviation of the **part of speech** usually follows the pronunciation. This label tells how the word can be used. If a word can be used as more than one part of speech, a separate entry is provided for each part of speech.

An **etymology** is the history of the word. In the first entry, the word *pole* can be traced back through Middle English (ME) and Old English (OE) to the Latin (L) word *palus,* which means "stake." In the second entry, the word *pole* can be traced back through Middle English to the Latin word *polus,* which comes from the Greek (Gr) word *polos,* meaning "axis of the sphere."

Sometimes the entry will include a list of **synonyms,** or words that have the same or very similar meanings. The entry may also include a **usage illustration,** which is an example of how the word is used in context.

2.5 Understanding Multiple Meanings

Each definition in the entry gives a different meaning of the word. When a word has more than one meaning, the different definitions are numbered. The first definition in an entry is the most common meaning of the word, but you will have to choose the meaning that fits the context in which you have found the word. Try substituting each definition for the word until you find the one that makes the most sense. If you come across a word that doesn't seem to make sense in context, consider whether that word might have another, lesser known meaning. Can the word be used as more than one part of speech, for example, as either a noun or a verb? Does it have a broader meaning than the one that comes to your mind? For example, a line from the *Odyssey* reads "he gave me seven shining talents." The most common meaning of *talent* is "special skill or ability," but that doesn't fit here. Consulting the footnote at the bottom of the page, you would discover that the word *talent* can also refer to a type of old coin.

Keep in mind that some words not only have multiple meanings but also different pronunciations. Words that are spelled the same but are pronounced differently are called **homographs.**

2.6 Understanding Denotation and Connotation

The **denotation** of a word is its dictionary definition. Sometimes, in order to understand a passage fully, it is helpful to know the connotations of the words as well. A **connotation** of a word is an emotional association the word has in addition to its literal meaning. For example, the words *cheap* and *thrifty* both denote "tending to spend less money," but *cheap* has a negative connotation similar to "stingy," whereas *thrifty* has a positive connotation involving being responsible with money. The best way to learn the connotation of a word is to pay attention to the context in which the word appears or to ask someone more familiar with the word.

Connotation Chart

Negative	Neutral	Positive
weird	unusual	unique
freakish	different	remarkable
bizarre	uncommon	extraordinary
abnormal	rare	unequaled
strange	curious	phenomenal

3 Grammar & Style

3.1 THE SENTENCE

THE SENTENCE

From the time you entered school, you probably have been speaking and writing in sentences. In the English language, the sentence is the basic unit of meaning.

A **sentence** is a group of words that expresses a complete thought. Every sentence has two basic parts: a subject and a predicate. The **subject** tells whom or what the sentence is about. The **predicate** tells information about the subject.

EXAMPLE
> **sentence**
> The experienced detective **[subject]** |
> asked the suspect several questions **[predicate]**.

A group of words that does not have both a subject and a predicate is called a **sentence fragment.** A sentence fragment does not express a complete thought.

EXAMPLES
> **sentence fragment**
> The newspaper carrier. (The fragment does not have a predicate. The group of words does not answer the question *What did the newspaper carrier do?*)
> **sentence fragment**
> Flung the morning edition. (The fragment does not have a subject. The group of words does not answer the question *Who flung the morning edition?*)
> **sentence fragment**
> Onto the front porch. (The fragment does not have a subject or predicate. The group of words does not tell what the sentence is about or tell what the subject does.)
> **complete sentence**
> The newspaper carrier flung the morning edition onto the front porch.

FUNCTIONS OF SENTENCES

There are four different kinds of sentences: *declarative, interrogative, imperative,* and *exclamatory.* Each kind of sentence has a different purpose. You can vary the tone and mood your writing by using the four different sentence types. Read the example sentences aloud and notice how your voice changes to express each sentence's different meaning.

- A **declarative sentence** makes a statement. It ends with a period.

EXAMPLE
> Samantha is in the backyard trying to repair the lawnmower.

- An **interrogative sentence** asks a question. It ends with a question mark.

EXAMPLE
> Will she be joining you for supper later tonight?

- An **imperative sentence** gives an order or makes a request. It ends with a period or an exclamation mark. An imperative sentence has an understood subject, most often *you.*

EXAMPLES
> (You) Please take a glass of lemonade to her.
> (You) Ask Samantha how much longer she will be working.

- An **exclamatory sentence** expresses strong feeling. It ends with an exclamation point.

EXAMPLE
> Samantha is a wizard at fixing lawnmowers!

SUBJECTS AND PREDICATES

Just as the sentence is the basic building block of the English language, the subject and predicate are the basic building blocks in a sentence. The **subject** tells whom or what the sentence is about, while the **predicate** tells what the subject is, what the subject does, or what happens to the subject.

EXAMPLE
> The yellow-eyed owls **[subject]** |
> sat quietly in the oak tree **[predicate]**.

To find the subject, ask who or what performs the action of the verb.

EXAMPLE
> Who sat quietly in the oak tree? *the yellow-eyed owls* **[subject]**.
>
> What did the yellow-eyed owls do? *sat quietly in the oak tree* **[predicate]**.

SIMPLE AND COMPLETE SUBJECTS AND PREDICATES

In a sentence, the **simple subject** is the key word or words in the subject. The simple subject is usually a noun or a pronoun and does not include any modifiers. The **complete subject** includes the simple subject and all the words that modify it.

The **simple predicate** is the key verb or verb phrase that tells what the subject does, has, or is. The **complete predicate** includes the verb and all the words that modify it.

In the following sentence, a vertical line separates the complete subject and complete predicate. The simple subject is underlined once. The simple predicate is underlined twice.

EXAMPLE

Bright orange <u>tongues</u> of flame **[complete subject]** |

<u><u>danced</u></u> erratically in the center of the clearing **[complete predicate].**

Sometimes, the simple subject is also the complete subject, and the simple predicate or verb is also the complete predicate.

EXAMPLE

<u>Falcons</u> | <u><u>swooped</u></u>.

To find the simple subject and simple predicate in a sentence, first break the sentence into its two basic parts: complete subject and complete predicate. Then, identify the simple predicate by asking yourself, "What is the action of this sentence?" Finally, identify the simple subject by asking yourself, "Who or what is performing the action?" In the following sentences, the complete predicate is in parentheses. The simple predicate, or verb, appears in boldface. Remember, verbs may have as many as four words.

EXAMPLES

one-word verb
Your friend on the track team (**runs** swiftly.)
two-word verb
Your friend on the track team (**will run** swiftly in this race.)
three-word verb
All season long your friend on the track team (**has been running** swiftly.)
four-word verb
If he hadn't twisted his ankle last week, your friend on the track team (**would have been running** swiftly today.)

COMPOUND SUBJECTS AND PREDICATES

A sentence may have more than one subject or predicate. A **compound subject** has two or more simple subjects that have the same predicate. The subjects are joined by the conjunction *and, or,* or *but.*

A **compound predicate** has two or more simple predicates, or verbs, that share the same subject. The verbs are connected by the conjunction *and, or,* or *but.*

EXAMPLES

compound subject
<u>Pamela</u> and <u>Else</u> | <u><u>read</u></u> their books in the library.
compound predicate
Four maniacal <u>crows</u> | <u><u>watched</u></u> and <u><u>waited</u></u> while I washed the car.

The conjunctions *either* and *or* and *neither* and *nor* can also join compound subjects or predicates.

EXAMPLES

compound subject
Either <u>Peter</u> *or* <u>Paul</u> | <u><u>sings</u></u> the National Anthem before each game.
Neither <u>yesterday</u> *nor* today | <u><u>seemed</u></u> like a good time to start the project.
compound predicate
Her <u>dogs</u> | *either* <u><u>heard</u></u> *or* <u><u>smelled</u></u> the intruder in the basement.
The police <u>inspector</u> | *neither* <u><u>visited</u></u> *nor* <u><u>called</u></u> last night.

A sentence may also have a compound subject and a compound predicate.

EXAMPLE

compound subject and compound predicate
<u>Mandy</u> and <u>Eric</u> | <u><u>grilled</u></u> the hamburgers and <u><u>made</u></u> the coleslaw.

SENTENCE STRUCTURES

A **simple sentence** consists of one independent clause and no subordinate clauses. It may have a compound subject and a compound predicate. It may also have any number of phrases. A simple sentence is sometimes called an independent clause because it can stand by itself.

EXAMPLES

Three bears emerged from the forest.

They spotted the campers and the hikers and decided to pay a visit.

The three bears enjoyed eating the campers' fish, sandwiches, and candy bars.

A **compound sentence** consists of two sentences joined by a semicolon or by a coordinating conjunction and a comma. Each part of the compound sentence has its own subject and verb. The most common coordinating conjunctions are *and, or, nor, for, but, so,* and *yet.*

EXAMPLES

Feeding bears is dangerous and unwise, **for** it creates larger problems in the long run.

Our zoo is home to two panda bears; they were originally captured in Asia.

A **complex sentence** consists of one independent clause and one or more subordinate clauses. The subordinate clauses in the examples below are underlined.

EXAMPLES

When you finish your report, remember to print it out on paper that contains 25 percent cotton fiber.

Jim will water the lawn after he returns home from the baseball game.

If you combine a compound sentence and a complex sentence, you form a **compound-complex sentence.** This kind of sentence must have two or more independent clauses and at least one subordinate clause. In the following examples, the subordinate clauses are underlined.

EXAMPLES

Rabbits, which like to nibble on the flowers, often visit my garden early in the morning, or they wait until early evening when the dog is inside the house.

Larry enthusiastically leaps out of bed each morning after his alarm clock rings, yet he often feels sleepy in the afternoon.

3.2 THE PARTS OF SPEECH

IDENTIFYING THE PARTS OF SPEECH

Each word in a sentence performs a basic function or task. Words perform four basic tasks; they name, modify, express action or state of being, or link. By the arrangement of words in a sentence and the task that each word performs within a sentence, you can understand a sentence's meaning. To illustrate how parts of speech work together, try to decipher the following nonsense sentence.

EXAMPLE

The strutum pensundsworder sworded about the grunewaldbools of Kilargo.

What nonsense noun is the subject of the sentence? What adjective modifies the word *pensundsworder?* Which nonsense verb expresses the action in the sentence?

If you substitute real words for the nonsense words, but keep the same arrangement of words, you can identify the nouns, verb, and adjectives in the sentence.

EXAMPLE

The famous author wrote about the green hills of Africa.

There are eight different parts of speech. Each part of speech is defined in the following chart.

Part of Speech	Definition	Example
noun	A **noun** names a person, place, thing, or idea .	**Apples, oranges,** and **potato chips** were the only **items** on the **list.**
pronoun	A **pronoun** is used in place of a noun.	Fanny whispered to **her** friend as **they** waited for **their** new teacher.
verb	A **verb** expresses action or a state of being.	Playful fox cubs **tumbled** out of the den and **chased** one another across the field.
adjective	An **adjective** modifies a noun or pronoun. The most common adjectives are the articles a, an, and the.	**Tattered** curtains hung in the **dark** windows of the **gray, sagging** house.

adverb	An **adverb** modifies a verb, an adjective, or another adverb.	**Sharply** turning to the left, the bicyclist **nearly** caused an accident.
preposition	A **preposition** shows the relationship between its object—a noun or a pronoun—and another word in a sentence. Common prepositions include *after, around, at, behind, beside, off, through, until, upon,* and *with*.	**During** winter we often sit **by** the fireplace **in** the evening.
conjunction	A **conjunction** joins words or groups of words. Common conjunctions are *and, but, for, nor, or, so,* and *yet*.	**Neither** Grant **nor** Felix felt tired after two miles, **so** they ran another mile.
interjection	An **interjection** is a word used to express emotion. Common interjections are *oh, ah, well, hey,* and *wow*.	**Wow!** Did you see the dive he took from the high jump?

3.3 NOUNS

NOUNS

A **noun** is a part of speech that names a person, place, idea, or thing. In this unit, you'll learn about the different kinds of nouns and what they name.

EXAMPLES

people   Steve, editor, aunt, actor

places   homeland, Wrigley Field, St. Peter's Basilica

ideas   prejudice, subtraction, boredom, plot

things   volleyball, song, trajectory, candle

Types of Nouns	Definition	Examples
common noun	names a person, place, idea, or thing	mother, garage, plan, flower
proper noun	names a specific person, place, or thing; begins with capital letter	John Adams, Washington DC, Monroe Doctrine

concrete noun	names a thing that can be touched, seen, heard, smelled, or tasted	ruler, mirror, giggle, speech, banana
abstract noun	names an idea, a theory, a concept, or a feeling	approval, philosophy, Marxism, faith
singular noun	names one person, place, idea, or thing	governor, tree, thought, shoe
plural noun	names more than one thing	governors, trees, thoughts, shoes
possessive noun	shows ownership or possession of things or qualities	Jan's, Mrs. Wilson's, women's, intern's
compound noun	made up of two or more words	staircase, picnic table, brother-in-law
collective noun	names groups	organization, platoon, team

3.4 PRONOUNS

PRONOUNS

A **pronoun** is used in place of a noun. Sometimes a pronoun refers to a specific person or thing.

Pronouns can help your writing flow more smoothly. Without pronouns, your writing can sound awkward and repetitive. Take a look at the following examples, which show the same sentence written without and with pronouns.

EXAMPLES

without pronouns
Carrie rolled up Carrie's sleeping bag and folded Carrie's pup tent and packed the sleeping bag and the pup tent into the minivan.

with pronouns
Carrie rolled up her sleeping bag and folded her pup tent and packed them into the minivan.

The most commonly used pronouns are *personal pronouns, reflexive and intensive pronouns, demonstrative pronouns, indefinite pronouns, interrogative pronouns,* and *relative pronouns*.

Types of Pronouns	Definition	Examples
personal pronoun	used in place of the name of a person or thing	I, me, we, us, he, she, it, him, her, you, they, them
indefinite pronoun	points out a person, place, or thing, but not a specific or definite one	one, someone, anything, other, all, few, nobody
reflexive pronoun	refers back to a noun previously used; adds –self and –selves to other pronoun forms	myself, herself, yourself, themselves, ourselves
intensive pronoun	emphasizes a noun or pronoun	me myself, he himself, you yourself, they themselves, we ourselves
interrogative pronoun	asks a question	who, whose, whom, what, which
demonstrative pronoun	points out a specific person, place, idea, or thing	this, these, that, those
relative pronoun	introduces an adjective clause	that, which, who, whose, whom
singular pronoun	used in place of the name of one person or thing	I, me, you, he, she, it, him, her
plural pronoun	used in place of more than one person or thing	we, us, you, they, them
possessive pronoun	shows ownership or possession	mine, yours, his, hers, ours, theirs

PRONOUNS AND ANTECEDENTS

As you know, a *pronoun* is a word used in place of one or more nouns. The word that a pronoun stands for is called its **antecedent.** The antecedent clarifies the meaning of the pronoun. The pronoun may appear in the same sentence as its antecedent or in a following sentence.

Where is **Linda? Maria** thought **she** saw **her** in the garden. (*Linda* is the antecedent of *her. Maria* is the antecedent of *she.*)

The backyard **fence** is rather old, and **it** needs painting. (*Fence* is the antecedent of *it.*)

When you use a pronoun, be sure that it refers clearly to its antecedent. A pronoun should agree in both number (singular or plural) and gender (masculine, feminine, or neutral) with its antecedent.

EXAMPLES

number
singular   **Robert Frost** wrote many poems. "Stopping by Woods on a Snowy Evening" is perhaps **his** most well-known poem.
plural   The visiting **poets** were asked if **they** would give a reading on Saturday night.

gender
masculine   **Robert Frost** was born in California, but **he** was raised in Massachusetts and New Hampshire.
feminine   **Toni Morrison** begins **her** writing day before dawn.
neutral   The **poem** is titled "Birches," and **it** is one of my favorites.

Singular pronouns are used with some nouns that are plural in form but singular in meaning, such as *economics, electronics, gymnastics, linguistics, mathematics, measles, news,* and *physics.*

EXAMPLES

My younger brother has the **measles.** I hope I don't catch **it.** Would you like to try **gymnastics? It** is excellent exercise.

Plural pronouns are used with some nouns that are plural in form but refer to single items, such as *pliers, eyeglasses, pants, scissors,* and *shorts.*

EXAMPLES

I can't find my **eyeglasses.** Have you seen **them?** The **pants** fit you well, but **they** need hemming.

Agreement between a relative pronoun—*who, whom, whose, which,* and *that*—and its antecedent is determined by the number of the antecedent.

EXAMPLES

Marie, who has always enjoyed **her** rural life, has surprisingly decided to move to the city. (*Who* is singular because it refers to the singular noun *Marie. Her* is used to agree with *who.*)

All who wish to vote by absentee ballot should complete **their** ballots and mail **them** to the county clerk's office. (*Who* is plural because it refers to the plural pronoun *All. Their* is used to agree with *who. Them* is used to agree with *ballots.*)

PRONOUN CASES

Personal pronouns take on different forms—called *cases*—depending on how they are used in sentences. Personal pronouns can be used as subjects, direct objects, indirect objects, and objects of prepositions. In the English language, there are three case forms for personal pronouns: *nominative, objective,* and *possessive.* The following chart organizes personal pronouns by case, number, and person.

Personal Pronouns

	Nominative Case	Objective Case	Possessive Case
Singular			
first person	I	me	my, mine
second person	you	you	your, yours
third person	he, she, it	him, her, it	his, her, hers, its
Plural			
first person	we	us	our, ours
second person	you	you	your, yours
third person	they	them	their, theirs

Indefinite Pronouns

An **indefinite pronoun** points out a person, place, or thing, but not a particular or definite one. The indefinite pronouns are listed below.

Singular	Plural	Singular or Plural
another	both	all
anybody	few	any
anyone	many	more
anything	several	most
each	others	none
each other		some
either		
everybody		
everyone		
everything		
much		
neither		
nobody		
no one		
nothing		
one		
one another		
somebody		
someone		
something		

singular

Something makes a ticking noise in the night.

Everyone is welcome to join us at the picnic.

plural

Many are eager to participate in the summer festival.

Several were missing the necessary information.

3.5 VERBS

VERBS — PREDICATES

Every sentence can be divided into two parts: the **subject** and the **predicate.** The following sentence is divided between the complete subject and the complete predicate.

EXAMPLE

The tardy **student** | **raced** through the maze of hallways to class.

The subject of a sentence names whom or what the sentence is about. The predicate tells what the subject does, is, or has. A **verb** is the predicate without any complements, linkers, or modifiers. In other words, the verb is the simple predicate.

Verbs are the **expressers** of the English language. Verbs are used to express action or a state of being. They work hard to tell whether the action is completed, continuing, or will happen in the future. Verbs also express all kinds of conditions for the action. Verbs in the English language can be from one to four words long.

EXAMPLE

Lauren **volunteers** at the food pantry.

Lauren **is volunteering** at the food pantry.

Lauren **has been volunteering** at the food pantry.

Lauren **might have been volunteering** at the food pantry.

Type of Verb	Definition	Examples
action verb	names an action	howl, wobble, skitter, flutter, fly
helping verb	helps a main verb express action or a state of being	My dogs will howl when a siren sounds. A butterfly has been fluttering above the daisies.
linking verb	connects a noun with another noun, pronoun, or adjective that describes or identifies it; the most common linking verbs are formed from the verb *to be*	The butterfly is a monarch. It seems to float in the breeze.
transitive verb	has a direct object	The scientist remembered the secret code.
intransitive verb	does not have a direct object	My brother snores.
irregular verb	has a different past tense form and spelling	forget/forgot think/thought write/wrote

VERB TENSES

The Simple Tenses

Verbs have different forms, called **tenses,** which are used to tell the time in which an action takes place. In your writing and speaking, you most commonly use the simple tenses. The **simple tenses** of the verb are **present, past,** and **future.**

The **present tense** tells that an action happens now — in present time.

EXAMPLES

present tense singular
The short-order cook **flips** pancakes on the grill.

present tense plural
The short-order cooks **flip** pancakes on the grill.

present tense singular
She **listens** carefully to the instructions.

present tense plural
They **listen** carefully to the instructions.

The **past tense** tells that an action happened in the past — prior to the present time. The past tense of a regular verb is formed by adding *–d* or *–ed* to the present verb form.

EXAMPLES

past tense singular
The short-order cook **flipped** pancakes on the grill.

past tense plural
The short-order cooks **flipped** pancakes on the grill.

past tense singular
She **listened** carefully to the instructions.

past tense plural
They **listened** carefully to the instructions.

The **future tense** tells that an action will happen in the future. The future tense is formed by adding the word *will* or *shall* before the present verb form.

EXAMPLES

future tense singular
The short order cook **will (shall) flip** pancakes on the grill.

future tense plural
The short-order cooks **will (shall) flip** pancakes on the grill.

The Perfect Tenses

The **perfect tenses** of verbs also express present, past, and future time, but they show that the action continued and was completed over a period of time or that the action will be completed in the present or future. The perfect tense is formed by using *has, have,* or *had* with the past participle.

EXAMPLES

present perfect singular
Vincent **has watered** the garden. The garden **has been watered** by Vincent.

present perfect plural
Vincent and Lena **have watered** the garden. (have or has + past participle)

past perfect singular
Vincent **had watered** the garden yesterday. The garden **had been watered** yesterday by Vincent.

past perfect plural
Vincent and Lena **had watered** the garden yesterday. (had + past participle)

future perfect singular
Vincent **will have watered** the garden by now.

future perfect plural
Vincent and Lena **will have watered** the garden by now. (will have or shall have + past participle)

THE PROGRESSIVE AND EMPHATIC VERB FORMS

Each of the six tenses has another form called the progressive form. The **progressive form** of a verb is used to express continuing action or state of being. The progressive form is made of the appropriate tense of the verb *be* and the present participle of a verb.

EXAMPLES

present progressive
I **am singing.** He **is singing.** They **are singing.**

past progressive
I **was singing.** They **were singing.**

future progressive
I **will (shall) be singing.**

present perfect progressive
He **has been singing.** They **have been singing.**

past perfect progressive
I **had been singing.**

future perfect progressive
I **will (shall) have been singing.**

The **emphatic form** of a verb is used to express emphasis. Only the present and past tenses have the emphatic form.

EXAMPLES

present emphatic
I **do try** to be punctual.
It **does matter** to me.

past emphatic
I **did clean** my room.

3.6 COMPLEMENTS

COMPLEMENTS FOR ACTION VERBS

A sentence must have a subject and a verb to communicate its basic meaning. In the following sentences, the subject and verb express the total concept. There is no receiver of the verb's action.

EXAMPLES

The girls shopped.

Sandra seldom shouts.

The thunder boomed.

Many sentences that include action verbs, however, need an additional word or group of words to complete the meaning.

EXAMPLES

The musicians tuned.

The musicians tuned their instruments.

The group of words *The musicians tuned* contains a subject *(musicians)* and a verb *(tuned)*. Although the group of words may be considered a sentence, it does not express a complete thought. A word is needed to tell what the musicians tuned, such as *The musicians tuned their instruments*. The word *instruments* completes the meaning expressed by the verb *tuned*. Therefore, *instruments* is called a **complement** or a completing word. The *completers* for action verbs are **direct objects** and **indirect objects.**

Direct Objects

A **direct object** receives the action in the sentence. It usually answers the question *what?* or *whom?* To find the direct object, find the action verb in the sentence. Then ask *what?* or *whom?* about the verb.

EXAMPLES

Sam **drove Jilly** to her mother's house. (*Drove* is the action verb. Whom did Sam drive? *Jilly* is the direct object.)

The coach **blew** her **whistle**. (*Blew* is the action verb. What did the coach blow? *Whistle* is the direct object.)

Remember to use object pronouns for a direct object.

singular me, you, him, her, it
plural us, you, them

EXAMPLES

Adam invited **us** to the party.

My dog follows **me** everywhere.

Indirect Objects

Sometimes the direct object is received by someone or something. This receiver is called the **indirect object.** It comes before the direct object and tells *to whom* the action is directed or *for whom* the action is performed. Only verbs that have direct objects can have indirect objects.

EXAMPLE

Lorelei **gave** the **teacher** her project. (*Gave* is the action verb. *Project* is the direct object because it tells what Lorelei gave. *Teacher* is an indirect object. It tells to whom Lorelei gave her project.)

There are two tests that you can use to identify the indirect object: (1) Look for a noun or a pronoun that precedes the direct object. (2) Determine whether the word you think is a direct object seems to be the understood object of the preposition *to* or *for.*

COMPLEMENTS FOR LINKING VERBS

A **linking verb** connects a subject with a noun, pronoun, or adjective that describes it or identifies it. Linking verbs do not express action. Instead, they express state of being and need a noun, pronoun or adjective to complete the sentence meaning.

In each of the following sentences, the subject and verb would not be complete without the words that follow them.

EXAMPLES

Franklin D. Roosevelt **was** a popular president.

He **seemed** trustworthy and reliable.

Most linking verbs are forms of the verb *to be,* including *am, are, is, was,* and *been.* Other words that can be used as linking verbs include *appear, feel, grow, smell, taste, seem, sound, look, stay, feel, remain,* and *become.* When *to be* verbs are part of an action verb, they are helpers.

PREDICATE NOUNS AND PREDICATE PRONOUNS

A **predicate noun** is a noun that completes a sentence that uses a form of the verb *to be.* Similarly, a **predicate pronoun** is a pronoun that completes a sentence that uses a form of the verb *to be.* In fact, the relationship between the subject and the predicate noun or pronoun is so close that the sentence usually suggests an equation. Such sentences can often be reordered without changing the meaning.

EXAMPLES

predicate noun
Jacinta was the first girl to play on the boys' baseball team. (Jacinta = girl)

The first girl to play on the boys' baseball team was Jacinta. (girl = Jacinta)

predicate pronoun
The friend who took me bowling was you. (friend = you)

You were the friend who took me bowling. (You = friend)

To find a predicate noun or pronoun, ask the same question you would ask to find a direct object.

EXAMPLE

My aunt is a great **chef.** (My aunt is a what? *Chef* is the predicate noun that renames or identifies *aunt,* the subject of the sentence.)

The first contestant will probably be **you.** (The first contestant will be who? *You* is the predicate pronoun that renames or identifies contestant, the subject of the sentence.)

The ticket taker at the booth was **she.** (Think: She was the ticket taker at the booth.)

The leaders of the hike were Sara and **he.** (Think: Sara and he were the leaders of the hike.)

PREDICATE ADJECTIVES

A **predicate adjective** completes a sentence by modifying, or describing, the subject of a sentence. To find a predicate adjective, ask the same question you would ask to find a direct object.

EXAMPLE

Your directions were **precise.** (Your directions were what? *Precise* is the predicate adjective that describes *directions,* the subject of the sentence.)

3.7 SUBJECT-VERB AGREEMENT

SUBJECT AND VERB AGREEMENT

A **singular** noun describes or stands for *one* person, place, thing, or idea. A **plural noun** describes or stands for *more than one* person, place, thing, or idea.

EXAMPLES

singular nouns
beetle, mango, knife, fairy, goose
plural nouns
beetles, mangos, knives, fairies, geese

In a sentence, a verb must be singular if its subject is singular and plural if its subject is plural. In other words, a verb must agree in number with its subject.

EXAMPLES

singular subject and verb
The **beetle chews** the flowers and stems.

plural subject and verb
The **beetles chew** the flowers and stems.

singular subject and verb
A **mango adds** a delightful flavor to the salad.

plural subject and verb
The **mangos add** a delightful flavor to the salad.

singular subject and verb
A **goose protects** its goslings vigorously.

plural subject and verb
The **geese protect** their goslings vigorously.

COMPOUND SUBJECT AND VERB AGREEMENT

A **compound subject** consists of two or more subjects that share the same verb.

EXAMPLE

Tomatoes and sprouts make a sandwich taste better. (*Tomatoes and sprouts*—the compound subject—share the verb *make.*)

A compound subject must have either a singular or a plural verb, depending on how the parts of the subject are connected.

Use a singular verb:
• when the compound subject is made up of singular nouns or pronouns connected by *either/or* or *neither/nor.*

EXAMPLES

singular verb
Either sneakers or hiking boots **works** well.

Neither sandals nor flip flops **is** acceptable.

Use a plural verb:
• when the compound subject is connected by the coordinating conjunction *and.*
• when the compound subject is formed from plural nouns or pronouns.

EXAMPLES

plural verb
Flood and drought **alternate** in devastating Texas.

Either fruits or vegetables **provide** the necessary nutrients.

Neither the Red Sox nor the Blue Jays **have been** to the World Series recently.

When a compound subject consists of a singular subject and a plural subject connected by *or* or *nor,* use a verb that agrees in number with the subject that is closer to it in the sentence.

EXAMPLES

Either Ben or the Roses **distribute** the magazines. (*Roses distribute*—plural)

Neither the community nor the mayor **accepts** the budget as final. (*mayor accepts*—singular)

INDEFINITE PRONOUN AND VERB AGREEMENT

An **indefinite pronoun** does not refer to a specific person, place, or thing. Some indefinite pronouns are always singular and take singular verbs: *anybody, anyone, anything, each, either, everybody, everyone, everything, much, neither, nobody, no one, nothing, one, somebody, someone, something.*

EXAMPLES

singular

Nobody wants that jacket.

Something seems different about you.

Some indefinite pronouns are always plural and take plural verbs: *both, few, many, others, several.*

EXAMPLES

plural

Many of my friends **are** serious readers.

Several flights **leave** this airport every day.

Some indefinite pronouns can be either singular or plural, depending on their use in the sentence: *all, any, most, none, some.* They are singular when they refer to a portion or to a single person, place, or thing. They are plural when they refer to a number of individual persons, places, or things. Often the object of the preposition will signal whether the pronoun is singular or plural.

EXAMPLES

singular

None of their music **makes** sense to me.

plural

None of the lyrics **make** any sense.

3.8 MODIFIERS

ADJECTIVES AND ADVERBS

Adjectives and adverbs—two kinds of **modifiers**—add meaning to nouns, adjectives, verbs, and adverbs. An **adjective** modifies a noun or pronoun. An **adverb** modifies a verb, an adjective, or other adverb.

EXAMPLES

adjective

The **yellow** roses have rambled up the **wooden** trellis onto the roof.
(Yellow modifies the noun roses; wooden modifies the noun trellis.)

adverb

The roses are **too** thorny to be trimmed.
(Too modifies the adjective thorny.)

The roses have grown **very** slowly, but they bloom **profusely** every spring.
(Very modifies the adverb slowly; profusely modifies the verb bloom.)

To determine whether a modifier is an adjective or an adverb, you can follow these steps.

1. Look at the word that is modified.
2. Ask yourself, "Is this modified word a noun or a pronoun?" If the answer is yes, the modifier is an adjective. If the answer is no, the modifier is an adverb.

In the following example, the word *balloonist* is modified by the word *daring.* The word *balloonist* is a noun, so the word *daring* is an adjective.

EXAMPLE

The **daring balloonist** traveled around the world.

In the next example, the word *landed* is modified by the word *safely.* The word *landed* is a verb; therefore, the word *safely* is an adverb.

EXAMPLE

After surviving a storm at sea, the balloonist **landed safely** in Australia.

ADJECTIVES

Adjectives modify nouns by telling specific details about them.

EXAMPLES

noun	fence
a little more specific	picket fence
more specific yet	rickety picket fence
even more specific	old, rickety picket fence

Some adjectives tell *how many* or *what kind* about the nouns or pronouns they modify; nouns tell us *who* or *what.*

EXAMPLES

Many repairs are needed to restore the fence to its original charm.

First, we'll replace the **rotting** wood and then apply **white** paint.

Other adjectives tell *which one* or *which ones.*

EXAMPLES

Luckily, the **old** fence is in excellent condition.

These slats do not need to be replaced.

The articles *a, an,* and *the* are the most commonly occurring adjectives. *A* and *an* refer to any person, place, or thing in general. *The* refers to a specific person, place, or thing.

A **proper adjective** is formed from a proper noun. Proper adjectives are capitalized and often end in *–n, -an, -ian, -ese,* or *–ish.*

Type of Adjective	Definition	Examples
adjective	modifies nouns and pronouns; answers the questions *what kind? which one? how many?* and *how much?*	***shiny*** pennies ***hieroglyphic*** *inscription* ***dozen*** *roses* ***one*** *mistake*
article	*a* and *an* refer to an unspecified person, place, thing, or idea; *the* refers to a specific person, place, thing, or idea	***A*** *problem has developed.* *I peeled* ***an*** *orange.* ***The*** *tomatoes are ripe.*
proper adjective	is formed from proper nouns; is capitalized; often ends in *–n, –an, –ian, –ese,* or *–ish*	**Serbian** restaurant **Victorian** England **Chinese** calendar **Jewish** tradition

ADVERBS

Adverbs modify verbs, adjectives, or other adverbs. Many times adverbs will tell us *how, when, where, why* or *to what extent.*

EXAMPLES

adverbs modify verbs
Horses galloped **swiftly** across the plains. (Swiftly tells how they galloped.)

Horses **usually** stay **away** from the trainer until a bond is developed. (Usually tells when they stay away from the trainer; away tells where they stay.)

adverbs modify adjectives
This young colt is **really** frightened. (Really tells to what extent the colt is frightened.)

The trainer has **tremendous** patience in working with the colt. (Tremendous tells to what extent the trainer has patience.)

adverbs modify adverbs
Finally, the colt approaches the trainer **very** slowly. (Very tells how slowly the colt approaches the trainer.)

The colt's movements were predicted **so** accurately by the experienced trainer. (So tells how accurately the colt's movements were predicted.)

POSITION OF ADVERBS

An adverb can be placed before or after a verb it modifies. Sometimes an adverb can be separated from a verb by another word or words.

EXAMPLES

The coin collector **carefully examined** the rare silver coin.

Eager to find out when it was minted, he **looked carefully** through the magnifying glass.

He **polished** the coin **carefully** to reveal the embossed date.

Note, however, in the following examples, how changing the position of an adverb changes the meaning of the sentence.

EXAMPLES

He **only** worried about money. (He did nothing else but worry about money.)

He worried **only** about money. (He worried about nothing else but money.)

3.9 PREPOSITIONS AND CONJUNCTIONS

PREPOSITIONS AND CONJUNCTIONS

Prepositions and conjunctions are the linkers of the English language. They are used to join words and phrases to the rest of a sentence. They also show the relationships between ideas. Prepositions and conjunctions help writers vary their sentences by connecting sentence parts in different ways.

A **preposition** is used to show how its object, a noun or a pronoun, is related to other words in the sentence. Some commonly used prepositions include *above, after, against, among, around, at, behind, beneath, beside, between, down, for, from, in, on, off, toward, through, to, until, upon,* and *with.*

EXAMPLES

A bright beacon led them safely **to** the shore.

He placed the book **beside** the bed.

A **conjunction** is a word used to link related words, groups of words, or sentences. Like a preposition, a conjunction shows the relationship between the words it links. Some of the most commonly used conjunctions are *and, but, for, nor, or, yet, so, if, after, because,* *before, although, unless, while,* and *when.* Some conjunctions are used in pairs, such as *both/and, neither/nor,* and *not only/but also.*

EXAMPLES

> We went out for dinner **and** a movie on Saturday night.
>
> They played poorly **because** they did not warm up before the game.
>
> **Neither** I **nor** my brother inherited our mother's red hair.

Certain words can function as either conjunctions or prepositions. There are two important differences between a word used as a preposition and one used as a conjunction.

1. A preposition is always followed by an *object,* but a conjunction is not.

EXAMPLES

> **preposition**
> You may have a turn **after** your sister. (The noun *sister* is the object of the preposition *after.*)
>
> **conjunction**
> **After** you arrived, we had a wonderful time. (*After* is not followed by an object. It introduces a group of words, or clause, that depends on the rest of the sentence for meaning.)

2. A preposition introduces a prepositional phrase that connects parts of a sentence. A conjunction connects words or groups of words (clauses containing a subject and verb).

EXAMPLES

> **preposition**
> I never eat breakfast **before** exercising. (*Before* introduces the prepositional phrase *before exercising.*)
>
> **conjunction**
> Put on sunscreen **before** the swim meet begins. (*Before* introduces a clause, that is, a subject and verb, that modifies *put,* telling when to put on the sunscreen.)

Most Commonly Used Prepositions

aboard	between	on
about	beyond	over
above	but (meaning	past
across	"except")	since
after	by	through
against	concerning	throughout
along	down	to
amid	during	under
among	except	underneath
around	for	until
at	from	up
before	in	upon
behind	into	with
below	like	within
beside	of	without
besides	off	

Type of Conjunction	Definition	Examples
coordinating conjunction	joins words or groups of words of equal importance; coordinating conjunctions are *and, but, for, nor, or, so, yet*	Holly and Max are Labrador retrievers. They are well-behaved dogs, *for* they have taken many obedience lessons.
correlative conjunction	word pairs that join words or groups of words; correlative conjunctions include *both/and, neither/nor, either/or*	*Both* Labrador retrievers *and* golden retrievers are excellent companion dogs.
subordinating conjunction	introduces a subordinate clause and joins it to an independent clause; subordinating conjunctions include *after, although, as, as if, because, before, if, since, unless, till, when,* and *while*	*Because* Holly is growing old, she has white whiskers on her chin.

3.10 INTERJECTIONS

An **interjection** is a part of speech that expresses feeling, such as surprise, joy, relief, urgency, pain, or anger. Common interjections include *ah, aha, alas, bravo, dear me, goodness, great, ha, help, hey, hooray, hush, indeed, mercy, of course, oh, oops, ouch, phooey, really, say, see, ugh,* and *whew.*

GRAMMAR & STYLE

EXAMPLES

Hey, that's not fair!

Goodness, you don't need to get so upset.

Hush! You'll wake the baby.

Why, of course! Please do join us for dinner.

Interjections actually indicate different degrees of emotion. They may express intense or sudden emotion, as in *Wow! That was unexpected.* Notice that the strong expression of emotion stands alone in the sentence and is followed by an exclamation point. Interjections can also express mild emotion, as in *Well, that is the best we could do.* In this sentence, the interjection is part of the sentence and is set off only with a comma. Even when interjections are part of a sentence, they do not relate grammatically to the rest of the sentence.

3.11 PHRASES

A **phrase** is a group of words used as a single part of speech. A phrase lacks a subject, a verb, or both; therefore, it cannot be a sentence. There are three common kinds of phrases: prepositional phrases, verbal phrases, and appositive phrases.

PREPOSITIONAL PHRASES

A **prepositional phrase** consists of a preposition, its object, and any modifiers of that object. A prepositional phrase adds information to a sentence by relating its object to another word in the sentence. It may function as an adjective or an adverb.

EXAMPLES

adjectives

Sue planned a party **with music and dancing.** (The prepositional phrase *with music and dancing* tells what kind of party Sue planned. The phrase is used as an adjective, modifying the noun *party.*)

She found the CDs and tapes in a box **under her bed.** (The prepositional phrase *under her bed* tells in which box Sue found the CDs and tapes. The phrase is used as an adjective, modifying the object of the prepositional phrase *in a box.*)

adverbs

Albert struggled **into his jacket.** (The prepositional phrase *into his jacket* tells how Albert struggled. The phrase is used as an adverb, modifying the verb *struggled.*)

My friend is generous **with her time.** (The prepositional phrase *with her time* tells how the friend is generous. The phrase is used as an adverb, modifying the adjective *generous.*)

Use prepositional phrases to create sentence variety. When every sentence in a paragraph starts with its subject, the rhythm of the sentences becomes boring. Revise your sentences, where it is appropriate, to start some with prepositional phrases.

EXAMPLE

Chad stacked sand bags **for nearly eight hours.**

For nearly eight hours Chad stacked sand bags.

VERBAL PHRASES

Verbals are verb forms that act as namers or modifiers. There are three kinds of verbals: participles, gerunds, and infinitives.

Participial Phrases

A **participle** is a verb form ending in *–ing, –d,* or *–ed* that acts as an adjective, modifying a noun or a pronoun. A **participial phrase** is made up of a participle and all of the words related to the participle, which may include objects, modifiers, and prepositional phrases. The entire phrase acts as an adjective.

EXAMPLES

Swimming quickly toward the shore, Diego thought eagerly about a warm shower. (The participle *swimming,* the adverb *quickly,* and the prepositional phrase *toward the shore* make up the participial phrase that modifies *Diego.*)

Jeffrey picked up the clothes **scattered around his bedroom.** (The participle *scattered* and the prepositional phrase *around his bedroom* make up the participial phrase that modifies *clothes.*)

For variety, begin some of your sentences with participial phrases. However, be sure to place the participial phrase close to the word it modifies. Otherwise, you may say something you do not mean.

misplaced participial phrase

I saw the craters on the moon looking through a telescope.

revised sentence

Looking through a telescope, I saw the craters on the moon.

Gerund Phrases

A **gerund phrase** is a phrase made up of a gerund (a verb form ending in *–ing*) and all of its modifiers and complements. The entire phrase functions as a noun. This means that the phrase may be the subject, predicate nominative, direct object, indirect object, or object of the preposition in a sentence. A gerund's modifiers include adjectives, adverbs, and prepositional phrases.

EXAMPLES

Waiting for the school bus gives Henry time to read. (The gerund phrase functions as the subject of the sentence.)

One of Henry's favorite quiet times is **waiting for the school bus.** (The gerund phrase functions as the predicate nominative of the sentence.)

Jim, however, hated **waiting for the school bus** more than anything else. (The gerund phrase functions as the direct object of the sentence.)

He always stopped for snacks before **waiting for the school bus.** (The gerund phrase functions as the object of the preposition.)

Infinitive Phrases

An **infinitive phrase** is made up of an infinitive (a verb form preceded by the word *to*) and all its modifiers and complements. Infinitive phrases can function as nouns, adjectives, or adverbs.

EXAMPLES

It's pleasant **to eat strawberries with whipped cream.** (The infinitive phrase functions as an adverb.)

The general intends **to charge at the enemy's flank.** (The infinitive phrase functions as a noun.)

Sometimes the *to* of an infinitive phrase is left out; it is understood.

EXAMPLES

Eli helped **[to]** build the deck.
I'll go **[to]** turn off the porch light.

APPOSITIVE PHRASES

An **appositive phrase** is a group of words made up of an appositive and all its modifiers. The phrase renames or identifies a noun or pronoun.

EXAMPLES

Sara's house, **a cabin in a remote area,** is the site for the weekend retreat. (The appositive phrase renames the noun *house.*)

The languages **English, Spanish, and French** blasted from the loudspeakers. (The appositive phrase identifies which languages blasted from the loudspeakers.)

The first example above, *a cabin in a remote area,* is a **nonessential, or nonrestrictive, appositive phrase.** It is not necessary to the meaning of the sentence; it is not needed to identify which particular house, since we already know that it is Sara's. Therefore, it is set off with commas. The second example, *English, Spanish, and French,* is an **essential, or restrictive, appositive phrase.** It is necessary for understanding the sentence because it identifies which particular languages, since we do not already know which ones. This appositive phrase is not set off with commas.

Appositive phrases add variety to your writing because they can be placed at the beginning, in the middle, or at the end of a sentence. Using appositive phrases to combine sentences eliminates unimportant words and creates more fact-filled sentences. When you join two ideas with an appositive phrase, place the idea you wish to stress in the main clause and make the less important idea the appositive.

3.12 CLAUSES

A **clause** is a group of words that contains a subject and verb and that functions as one part of speech. There are two types of clauses—independent and subordinate.

An **independent clause,** sometimes called a *main clause,* has a subject and a verb and expresses a complete thought. Since it can stand alone as a sentence, it is called *independent.*

EXAMPLE

> Iceland has a misunderstood reputation as a land of ice, snow, and fog.

A **subordinate clause** has a subject and a verb, but it doesn't express a complete thought. It can't stand alone. It must be attached to or inserted into an independent clause. That's why subordinate clauses are also called *dependent clauses*. When you combine subordinate clauses with independent clauses, you form complete sentences.

EXAMPLES

> **Because the film was sold out,** the twins went to the mall. (The subordinate clause *because the film was sold out* is attached to an independent clause.)

> The baby **who captured everyone's attention** got the part in the commercial. (The subordinate clause *who captured everyone's attention* is inserted into the independent clause *The baby got the part in the commercial.*)

ADJECTIVE CLAUSES

There are three types of subordinate clauses: adjective clauses, adverb clauses, and noun clauses.

An **adjective clause** is a subordinate clause that functions as an adjective. It modifies a noun or pronoun. Adjective clauses are introduced most frequently with words like the following: *that, which, who, whom, whose, when, why,* and *where.* An adjective clause follows the word it modifies.

ADVERB CLAUSES

An **adverb clause** is a subordinate clause that functions as an adverb. It modifies a verb, an adjective, or another adverb.

EXAMPLES

> Virgil used the computer **every chance he could.** (*Every chance he could* modifies the verb *used*.)

> Nancy studies much harder **than her sister does.** (*Than her sister does* modifies the adverb *harder.*)

> Today, Stanley played far better **than he usually does.** (*Than he usually does* modifies the adverb *better.*)

When you use an adverb clause at the beginning of a sentence, follow it with a comma. If you use an adverb clause at the end of a sentence, you do not need to use a comma before it.

EXAMPLES

> If you're going to the grocery store, please bring home a gallon of milk.

> Please bring home a gallon of milk if you're going to the grocery store.

> Adverb clauses often, but not always, start with a subordinating conjunction such as *after, although, because, before, if, so that, unless, when, where, whether,* and *while.*

NOUN CLAUSES

A **noun clause** is a subordinate clause that functions as a noun. This means that it can function as a subject, predicate nominative, direct object, indirect object, object of a preposition, or appositive. Notice that noun clauses can have modifiers and complements. They can come at the beginning, middle, or end of a sentence. Words like these often introduce noun clauses: *that, what, whatever, where, whether, which, who, whoever, whom,* and *whose.*

EXAMPLES

> **subject**
> That the phone didn't ring was entirely surprising.

> **predicate nominative**
> This is **why she moved.**

> **direct object**
> The editor had no idea **where the** manuscript was.

> **indirect object**
> Tell **whomever you like** about the upcoming concert.

> **object of the preposition**
> Adele was greatly valued for **what she knew about human biology.**

> **appositive**
> The focus of the ad campaign, **that** frequent brushing promotes **healthy teeth,** appealed to the organization of dentists.

Too many noun clauses can make your writing sound wordy and overly formal, especially when the noun clauses are used as subjects.

INCORRECT SUBJECT-VERB AGREEMENT

A subject and its verb must agree in number. Use singular verb forms with singular subjects and plural verb forms with plural subjects.

Intervening Words

A prepositional phrase that comes between a subject and a verb does not determine whether the subject is singular or plural.

EXAMPLES

The **tree** in the backyard **sways** with the breeze. (*tree sways,* singular)

The **governor,** along with his family, **watches** the parade. (*governor watches,* singular)

The **kids** in the neighborhood **play** baseball each night. (*kids play,* plural)

The **characters** in the movie **are** not very interesting. (*characters are,* plural)

In some cases the *object* of the preposition controls the verb.

EXAMPLES

Some of the **pizza** was burned in the oven.

Some of the **pizzas** were burned in the oven.

Compound Subjects

Use a plural verb with most compound subjects connected by *and.*

EXAMPLES

Charlotte and her boss **review** the budget once a month.

Otters, beavers, and alligators **live** near bodies of water.

INCORRECT USE OF APOSTROPHES

Use an apostrophe to replace letters that have been left out in a contraction.

EXAMPLES

that's = that is
aren't = are not
we'll = we will

Use an apostrophe to show possession.

Singular Nouns

Use an apostrophe and an *s* ('*s*) to form the possessive of a singular noun, even if it ends in *s, x,* or *z.*

EXAMPLES

storm's damage
Chris's guitar
Max's spoon
jazz's history

Plural Nouns

Use an apostrophe and an *s* ('*s*) to form the possessive of a plural noun that does not end in *s.*

EXAMPLES

geese's flight
women's conference
children's laughter

Use an apostrophe alone to form the possessive of plural noun that ends in *s.*

EXAMPLES

dolphins' migration
wheels' hubcaps
jets' engines

Do not add an apostrophe or '*s* to possessive personal pronouns: *mine, yours, his, hers, its, ours,* or *theirs.* They already show ownership.

EXAMPLES

His homework is finished; **mine** is not done yet.

The red house on the corner is **theirs.**

DOUBLE NEGATIVES

Make sure that you use only one of the following negatives in each sentence: *not, nobody, none, nothing, hardly, can't, doesn't, won't, isn't, aren't.* A **double negative** is the use of two negative words together when only one is needed. Correct double negatives by removing one of the negative words or by replacing one of the negative words with a positive word.

EXAMPLES

double negative
They can't hardly afford the plane tickets.

corrected sentence
They can hardly afford the plane tickets.
They can't afford the plane tickets.

double negative
Cassidy hasn't never read *The Call of the Wild.*

corrected sentence

Cassidy hasn't ever read *The Call of the Wild.*
Cassidy has never read *The Call of the Wild.*

DANGLING AND MISPLACED MODIFIERS

Place modifying phrases and clauses as close as possible to the words they modify; otherwise, your sentences may be unclear or unintentionally humorous.

A **dangling modifier** has nothing to modify because the word it would logically modify is not present in the sentence. In the following sentence, the modifying phrase has no logical object. The sentence says that a spider was reading.

EXAMPLE

Reading in his rocking chair, a spider was spotted on the wall.

You can eliminate dangling modifiers by rewriting the sentence so that an appropriate word is provided for the modifier to modify. You can also expand a dangling phrase into a full subordinate clause.

EXAMPLES

Reading in his rocking chair, he spotted a spider on the wall.

While Frank was reading in his rocking chair, he spotted a spider on the wall.

A **misplaced modifier** is located too far from the word it should modify.

EXAMPLE

Jennifer arrived home after the two-week training session on Friday.

You can revise a misplaced modifier by moving it closer to the word it modifies.

EXAMPLES

Jennifer arrived home on Friday after the two-week training session.

On Friday Jennifer arrived home after the two-week training session.

FORMS OF *WHO* AND *WHOM*

You've already learned about the pronoun *who* earlier in this unit in the sections on interrogative and relative pronouns. *Who* and *whom* can be used to ask questions and to introduce subordinate clauses.

Knowing what form of *who* to use can sometimes be confusing. Just remember that the case of the pronoun *who* is determined by the pronoun's function in a sentence.

nominative case   who, whoever

objective case   whom, whomever

EXAMPLES

Who wrote the novel *One Hundred Years of Solitude?* (Because *who* is the subject in the sentence, the pronoun is in the nominative case.)

Did you say **who** called? (Because *who* is the subject of the subordinate clause, the pronoun is in the nominative case.)

Whoever returns my wallet will receive a reward. (Because *whoever* is the subject in the sentence, the pronoun is in the nominative case.)

Whom did you visit? (Because *whom* is the direct object in the sentence, the pronoun is in the objective case.)

SPLIT INFINITIVES

An infinitive, the base verb combined with *to,* should not be split under most circumstances. Infinitives such as *to save, to teach,* and *to hold* should not be interrupted by adverbs or other sentence components.

EXAMPLES

nonstandard
I began to seriously think about becoming a vegetarian.
standard
I began to think seriously about becoming a vegetarian.

In some cases, a modifier sounds awkward if it does not split the infinitive. In these situations, it may be best to reword the sentence to eliminate splitting the infinitive.

EXAMPLES

nonstandard
Jeff would like to nearly save the same amount of money as he did in 2001.

revised
Jeff would like to save nearly as much money as he did in 2001.

In certain cases, you may want to use a split infinitive to clarify the meaning of the sentence.

The following chart contains an alphabetic list of
words and phrases that often cause usage problems.

Word	Correct Use	Example
a, an	Use *a* before words beginning with a consonant sound. Use *an* before words beginning with a vowel sound, including a silent *h*.	While walking in the woods, Jonah saw **a** coyote. **An** orangutan has a shaggy, reddish brown coat and very long arms. It is hard to find **an** honest politician in this town.
accept, except	*Accept* is a verb meaning "to receive willingly" or "to agree." *Except* is a preposition that means "leaving out" or "but."	I wish you would **accept** this token of my appreciation. Everyone has apologized for the misunderstanding **except** the mayor.
affect, effect	*Affect* is a verb that means "to influence." The noun *effect* means "the result of an action." The verb *effect* means "to cause" or "to bring about."	You can't let the audience **affect** your concentration. We saw the **effect** of last night's storm throughout the town. Peter will **effect** the proposed reorganization when he takes office.
ain't	This word is nonstandard English. Avoid using it in speaking and writing.	**nonstandard:** I ain't going to study English this semester. **standard:** I **am not** going to study English this semester.
all ready, already	*All ready* means "entirely ready or prepared." *Already* means "previously."	Speaking with each team member, I determined that they were **all ready** to play. Sandy **already** finished her homework before soccer practice.
all right	*All right* means "satisfactory," "unhurt," "correct," or "yes, very well." The word *alright* is not acceptable in formal written English.	**All right,** let's begin the meeting. Is your ill father going to be **all right?**
a lot	*A lot* means "a great number or amount" and is always two words. Because it is imprecise, you should avoid it except in informal usage. *Alot* is not a word.	We found **a lot** of seashells on the beach. Your brother had **a lot** of help planning the surprise party.
altogether, all together	*Altogether* is an adverb meaning "thoroughly." Something done *all together* is done as a group or mass.	He was **altogether** embarrassed after tripping on the sidewalk. The family members were **all together** when they heard the good news.
anywheres, everywheres, somewheres, nowheres	Use these words and others like them without the *s*: *anywhere, everywhere, somewhere, nowhere*.	The little gray dog was **nowhere** to be found. Yolanda never goes **anywhere** without her cell phone.
at	Don't use this word after *where*.	Where are your brothers hiding?
bad, badly	*Bad* is always an adjective, and *badly* is always an adverb. Use *bad* after linking verbs.	I developed a **bad** cold after shoveling the heavy, wet snow. Tom feels **bad** about losing your favorite CD. We **badly** need to find another relief pitcher.

Word	Correct Use	Example
beside, besides	*Beside* means "next to." *Besides* means "in addition to." *Besides* can also be an adverb meaning "moreover."	The yellow plant is sitting **beside** the purple vase. I bought socks and shoes **besides** a new shirt and jacket. There is nothing worth watching on TV tonight; **besides,** I have to study for a test.
between, among	Use *between* when referring to two people or things. Use *among* when you are discussing three or more people or things.	While on vacation I divided my time **between** Paris and Brussels. The thoughtful pirate divided the loot **among** his shipmates.
bring, take	Use *bring* when you mean "to carry to." It refers to movement toward the speaker. Use *take* when you mean "to carry away." It refers to movement away from the speaker.	You need to **bring** your backpack home. Don't forget to **take** the garbage out to the curb tonight.
bust, busted	Do not use these nonstandard words as verbs to substitute for *break* or *burst.*	**nonstandard:** I busted my leg sliding into third base. The barrel busted after the extra batch was added. **standard:** I **broke** my leg sliding into third base. The barrel **burst** after the extra batch was added.
can, may	The word *can* means "able to do something." The word *may* is used to ask or give permission.	**Can** you speak a foreign language? You **may** borrow my red sweater.
choose, chose	*Choose* is the present tense and *chose* is the past tense.	I **choose** to start work at 6:00 A.M. each day. Randy **chose** to quit his job after working only three days.
could of	Use the helping verb *have* (which may sound like *could of*) with *could, might, must, should, ought,* and *would.*	**nonstandard:** We could of won the game in overtime. **standard:** We **could have** won the game in overtime.
doesn't, don't	*Doesn't* is the contraction of *does not.* It is used with singular nouns and the pronouns *he, she, it, this,* and *that. Don't* is the contraction of *do not.* Use it with plural nouns and the pronouns *I, we, they, you, these,* and *those.*	Jason **doesn't** know what to make for lunch. We **don't** answer the phone during dinner.
farther, further	Use *farther* to refer to physical distance. Use *further* to refer to greater extent in time or degree or to mean "additional."	I walked **farther** today than I did yesterday. The board members will discuss this issue **further** at the meeting. The essay requires **further** revision before it can be published.
fewer, less	Use *fewer,* which tells "how many," to refer to things that you can count individually. *Fewer* is used with plural words. Use *less* to refer to quantities that you cannot count. It is used with singular words and tells "how much."	I see **fewer** fans coming out to the ballpark each year. Jasmine has more experience and thus needs **less** training than Phil.
good, well	*Good* is always an adjective. *Well* is an adverb meaning "ably" or "capably." *Well* is also a predicate adjective meaning "satisfactory" or "in good health." Don't confuse *feel good,* which means "to feel happy or pleased," with *feel well,* which means "to feel healthy."	Charles was a **good** pilot during the war. Leslie felt **good** [pleased] after bowling three strikes in a row. Shirley paints **well** for someone with no formal training. Not feeling **well,** Samuel stayed home from school today.

Word	Correct Use	Example
had ought, hadn't ought	The verb *ought* should never be used with the helping verb *had*.	**nonstandard:** Ted had ought to find another route into town. **standard:** Ted **ought** to find another route into town. **nonstandard:** She hadn't ought climb that tree. **standard:** She **ought** not climb that tree.
hardly, scarcely	Since both of these words have negative meanings, do not use them with other negative words such as *not, no, nothing,* and *none*.	**nonstandard:** That music is so loud I can't hardly hear myself think. **standard:** That music is so loud I can **hardly** hear myself think. **nonstandard:** Shane hadn't scarcely enough gas to make it back home. **standard:** Shane had **scarcely** enough gas to make it back home.
he, she, they	Do not use these pronouns after a noun. This error is called a double subject.	**nonstandard:** Jed's brother he is a famous actor. **standard:** Jed's brother is a famous actor.
hisself, theirselves	These are incorrect forms. Use *himself* and *themselves*.	**nonstandard:** Paul talks to hisself when mowing the lawn. **standard:** Paul talks to **himself** when mowing the lawn. **nonstandard:** The panel talked among theirselves about the Holy Roman Empire. **standard:** The panel talked among **themselves** about the Holy Roman Empire.
how come	Do not use in place of *why*.	**nonstandard: How come** you didn't call me last night? **standard: Why** didn't you call me last night?
in, into	Use *in* to mean "within" or "inside." Use *into* to suggest movement toward the inside from the outside.	The children were **in** the kitchen. The children raced **into** the kitchen.
its, it's	*Its* is a possessive pronoun. *It's* is the contraction for *it is*.	The radio station held **its** annual fundraiser. **It's** too late tonight to start another game.
kind, sort, type	Use *this* or *that* to modify the singular nouns *kind, sort,* and *type*. Use *these* and *those* to modify the plural nouns *kinds, sorts,* and *types*. *Kind* should be singular when the object of the preposition following it is singular. It should be plural when the object of the preposition is plural.	This **kind** of ice cream is my favorite. These **types** of problems are difficult to solve.
kind of, sort of	Do not use these terms to mean "somewhat" or "rather."	**nonstandard:** He feels kind of sluggish today. **standard:** He feels rather sluggish today.
lay, lie	*Lay* means "to put" or "to place." *Lay* usually takes a direct object. *Lie* means "to rest" or "to be in a lying position." *Lie* never takes a direct object. (Note that the past tense of *lie* is *lay*.)	Please **lay** the blanket on the bed. I **laid** the blanket on the bed. **Lie** down on the bed and take a nap. Mary **lay** down on the bed and took a nap.
learn, teach	*Learn* means "to gain knowledge." *Teach* means "to give knowledge." Do not use them interchangeably.	Betty took lessons to **learn** how to fly a small airplane. I would like to find someone to **teach** me how to sew.

Word	Correct Use	Example
like, as	*Like* is usually a preposition followed by an object. It generally means "similar to." *As, as if,* and *as though* are conjunctions used to introduce subordinate clauses. *As* is occasionally a preposition: *He worked as a farmer.*	The alligator was motionless **like** a rock on the riverbank. The spider spun its web **as** the unsuspecting fly flew into the silky trap. Roger looks **as though** he's not feeling well.
of	This word is unnecessary after the prepositions *inside, outside,* and *off.*	The feather pillow slid **off** the bed. People gathered **outside** the stadium before the game. Please put the chattering parrot **inside** its cage.
precede, proceed	*Precede* means "to go or come before." *Proceed* means "to go forward."	The calf-roping competition will **precede** the bull-riding event. If you hear the alarm, **proceed** down the stairs and out the exit.
quiet, quite	Although these words sound alike, they have different meanings. *Quite* is an adverb meaning "positively" or "completely," whereas *quiet* is an adjective that means "making little or no noise."	The house became **quiet** after the baby finally fell asleep. Unfortunately, our bill for the car repairs was **quite** large.
real, really	*Real* is an adjective meaning "actual." *Really* is an adverb meaning "actually" or "genuinely." Do not use *real* to mean "very" or "extremely."	The table is very sturdy because it is made of **real** oak. Heather was **really** (not *real*) excited about trying out for the play.
reason . . . because	*Reason is because* is both wordy and redundant. Use *reason is that* or simply *because.*	**nonstandard:** The reason I am in a good mood is because today is Friday. **standard:** The reason for my good mood is that it is Friday. **standard:** The reason for my good mood is that today is Friday. **standard:** I am in a good mood because today is Friday.
regardless, irregardless	Use *regardless, unmindful, heedless,* or *anyway. Irregardless* is a double negative and should never be used.	**nonstandard:** Irregardless of the rain, the concert will still be held as scheduled. **standard:** Regardless of the rain, the concert will still be held as scheduled.
rise, raise	*Rise* is an intransitive verb that means "to move upward." It is an irregular verb that does not take a direct object. *Raise* is a transitive verb that means "to lift or make something go upward." It is a regular verb that takes a direct object.	The sun **rises** and sets every day. Perry **raised** his hand to ask a question.
scratch, itch	*Scratch* means "to scrape lightly to relieve itching." *Itch* means "to feel a tingling of the skin, with the desire to scratch."	The mosquito bites on my leg still **itch**. Please do not **scratch** the mosquito bites.
set, sit	*Set* is a transitive verb meaning "to place something." It always takes a direct object. *Sit* is an intransitive verb meaning "to rest in an upright position." It does not take a direct object.	Please **set** the pitcher of milk on the table. Let's **sit** outside on the back deck.
some, somewhat	*Some* is an adjective meaning "a certain unspecified quantity." *Somewhat* is an adverb meaning "slightly." Do not use *some* as an adverb.	**nonstandard:** The pressure on her schedule has eased some. **standard:** The pressure on her schedule has eased **somewhat.** **standard:** I need to find **some** index cards before starting my report.

Word	Correct Use	Example
than, then	*Than* is a conjunction used in comparisons. *Then* is an adverb that shows a sequence of events.	Hank's lawn is greener **than** Dale's lawn is. We went to the post office and **then** drove to the mall.
their, there, they're	*Their* is the possessive form of *they. There* points out a place or introduces an independent clause. *They're* is the contracted form of *they are.*	Our neighbors inspected **their** roof after the hailstorm. When you arrive at the airport, I will be **there** waiting. I don't think **they're** going to be visiting us this summer.
them	*Them* is a pronoun. It should never be used as an adjective. Use *those.*	**nonstandard:** Remember to return them books to the library. **standard:** Remember to return **those** books to the library.
this here, that there	Do not use. Simply say *this* or *that.*	**nonstandard:** This here is the best coffee shop in town. **standard: This** is the best coffee shop in town. **nonstandard:** That there is an antique rocking chair. **standard: That** is an antique rocking chair.
to, too, two	*To* is a preposition that can mean "in the direction of." *Too* is an adverb that means both "extremely, overly" and "also." *Two* is the spelling for the number 2.	Please carry the luggage **to** the car. Leah has **too** many boxes in the attic. Tony and Liz are excellent students, **too.** I bought **two** pairs of blue jeans.
try and	Use *try to* instead.	**nonstandard:** Try and find the umbrella before you leave. **standard: Try to** find the umbrella before you leave.
use to, used to	Be sure to add the *d* to *used* to form the past participle.	**nonstandard:** Rory use to enjoy singing in the choir. **standard:** Rory **used to** enjoy singing in the choir.
way, ways	Do not use *ways* for *way* when referring to distance.	**nonstandard:** We traveled a long ways from home. **standard:** We traveled a long **way** from home.
when, where	When you define a word, don't use *when* or *where.*	**nonstandard:** A *perfect game* is when a bowler throws twelve strikes resulting in a score of 300. **standard:** A *perfect game* is twelve strikes resulting in a score of 300.
where, that	Do not use *where* to mean "that."	**nonstandard:** I read where school will start a week earlier in August. **standard:** I read **that** school will start a week earlier in August.
which, that, who, whom	*Which* is used to refer only to things. Use it to introduce nonessential, or nonrestrictive, clauses that refer to things or to groups of people. Always use a comma before *which* when it introduces a nonessential clause.	Our garage, **which** was built last year, is already showing signs of wear. The panel, **which** was assembled to discuss the election, will publish its conclusions.

Word	Correct Use	Example
that	*That* is used to refer either to people or things. Use it to introduce essential, or restrictive, clauses that refer to things or groups of people. Do not use a comma before *that* when it introduces an essential clause.	The tree **that** fell in the storm was over 100 years old. An automobile **that** never needs repairs is rare.
who or whom	*Who or whom* is used to refer only to people. Use *who* or *whom* to introduce essential and nonessential clauses. Use a comma only when the pronoun introduces a nonessential clause.	Lyle is the man **who** rescued us from the fire. Abraham Lincoln, **whom** many admired, issued the Emancipation Proclamation.
who's, whose	*Who's* is a contraction for *who is* or *who has. Whose* is the possessive form of *who.*	**Who's** going to make dinner tonight? **Whose** pig is running loose in my garden?
without, unless	Do not use the preposition *without* in place of the conjunction *unless.*	**nonstandard:** I am not leaving without I have your endorsement. **standard:** I am not leaving **without** your endorsement. **standard:** I am not leaving **unless** I have your endorsement.
your, you're	*Your* is a possessive pronoun. *You're* is a contraction for the words *you are.*	Ron repaired **your** leaky kitchen faucet. **You're** very skilled at repairing things!

EDITING FOR PUNCTUATION ERRORS

When editing your work, correct all punctuation errors. Several common punctuation errors to avoid are the incorrect use of **end marks, commas, semicolons,** and colons.

Punctuation Reference Chart

Punctuation	Function	Examples
End Marks	tells the reader where a sentence ends and shows the purpose of the sentence; periods are also used for abbreviations.	Our next-door neighbor is Mrs. Ryan.
Periods	with **declarative** sentences	The weather forecast predicts rain tonight.
	with abbreviations:	
	personal names	**N.** Scott Momaday, **W. W.** Jacobs, Ursula **K.** Le Guin
	titles	**Mr.** Bruce Webber, **Mrs.** Harriet Cline, **Ms.** Steinem, **Dr.** Duvall, **Sen.** Hillary Clinton, **Gov.** George Pataki, **Capt.** Horatio Hornblower, **Prof.** Klaus
	business names	Tip Top Roofing **Co.**, Green **Bros.** Landscaping, Gigantic **Corp.**
	addresses	Oak **Dr.**, Grand **Blvd.**, Main **St.**, Kennedy **Pkwy.**, Prudential **Bldg.**
	geographical terms	Kensington, **Conn.**, San Francisco, **Calif.**, Canberra, **Aus.**
	time	**A.D.** 1500, 10 **B.C.**, 6:30 **A.M.**, 9:00 **P.M.**, 2 **hrs.** 15 **min.** **Thurs.** morning, **Jan.** 20, 21st **cent.**
	units of measurement	3 **tbsp.** olive oil 1/2 **c.** peanut butter 8 **oz.** milk 5 **ft.** 4 **in.** 20 **lbs.**
	exceptions: metric measurements, state names in postal addresses, or directional elements	**metric measurements** cc, ml, km, g, L **state postal codes** MN, WI, IA, NE, CA, NY **compass points** N, NW, S, SE
Question Marks	with **interrogative** sentences	May I have another serving of spaghetti?
Exclamation Points	with **exclamatory** sentences	Hey, be careful!
Commas	to separate words or groups of words within a sentence; to tell the reader to pause at certain spots in the sentence	Casey was confident he could hit a home run, but he struck out.

Punctuation	Function	Examples
	to separate items in a series	The magician's costume included a **silk scarf, black satin hat,** and **magic wand.**
	to combine sentences using *and, but, or, nor, yet, so,* or *for*	An infestation of beetles threatened the summer squash and zucchini crops, **yet** the sturdy plants thrived. I'll apply an organic insecticide, **or** I'll ignore the garden pest problem.
	after an introductory word, phrase, or clause	**Surprisingly,** fashions from the 1970s are making a comeback. **Frayed and tight-fitting,** denim bellbottoms remain a fashion hit.
	to set off words or phrases that interrupt sentences	Harpers Ferry, **a town in northeastern West Virginia,** was the site of John Brown's raid in 1859. The violent raid, **however,** frightened people in the North and South. **An abolitionist leader,** Brown was captured during the raid and later executed.
	between two or more adjectives that modify the same noun and that could be joined by *and*	A **warm,** [and] **spicy** aroma enticed us to enter the kitchen. Steaming bowls of chili satisfied the **tired,** [and] **hungry** travelers.
	to set off names used in direct address	**Olivia,** the zinnias and daisies need to be watered. Please remember to turn off the back porch light, **John.**
	to separate parts of a date	The United States Stock Exchange collapsed on October **28, 1929.** The stock market crash in October 1929 precipitated a severe economic crisis.
	to separate items in addresses	Gabriel García Márquez was born in **Aracataca, Colombia.** My brother will be moving to **1960 Jasmine Avenue, Liberty, Missouri 64068.**
Semicolons	to join two closely related sentences	It was a beautiful summer morning; we took advantage of it by going on a picnic.
	to join the independent clauses of a compound sentence if no coordinating conjunction is used	Marjory Stoneman Douglas was a pioneer conservationist. She formed a vigorous grassroots campaign to protect and restore the Everglades. Marjory Stoneman Douglas was a pioneer conservationist; she formed a vigorous grassroots campaign to protect and restore the Everglades.
	between independent clauses joined by a conjunction if either clause contains commas	Douglas was a writer, editor, publisher, and tireless advocate for the protection of the Everglades; and President Clinton awarded her the Medal of Freedom in 1993 for her work.
	between items in a series if the items contain commas	Members of Friends of the Everglades **wrote petitions; contacted local groups, political organizations, and governmental agencies; and gathered public support** for the restoration of the Everglades.
	between independent clauses joined by a conjunctive adverb or a transitional phrase	**conjunctive adverb** Starting in 1948, the Central and Southern Florida Project ditched and drained the Everglades; **consequently,** the four million acre wetland was reduced by half. **transitional phrase** Douglas knew that restoration of the Everglades would be a daunting task; **in other words,** she knew that it would take the combined efforts of local, state, and federal groups working in unison.

Punctuation	Function	Examples
Colons	to mean "note what follows"	Make sure you have all your paperwork in order: passport, visa, and tickets.
	to introduce a list of items	*The Tragedy of Romeo and Juliet* explores **these dominant themes:** civil strife, revenge, love, and fate. The main characters in the play are **as follows:** Romeo, Juliet, Paris, Mercutio, Tybalt, and Friar Lawrence. The role of Juliet has been played by **the following actresses:** Norma Shearer, Susan Shentall, and Olivia Hussey.
	to introduce a long or formal state-ment or a quotation	Shakespeare's prologue to *Romeo and Juliet* begins with **these memorable lines:** Two households, both alike in dignity, In fair Verona, where we lay our scene, From ancient grudge break to new mutiny, Where civil blood makes civil hands unclean. John Dryden made **the following remark about Shakespeare:** "He was the man who of all modern, and perhaps ancient poets, had the largest and most comprehen-sive soul." Nearly everyone recognizes this line by Shakespeare: "All the world's a stage."
	between two independent clauses when the second clause explains or summarizes the first clause	Shakespeare deserves the greatest of praise: his work has influenced and inspired millions of people over the centuries. For Romeo and Juliet, their love is star-crossed: If they tell their feuding parents of their love, they will be forbidden from seeing each other. On the other hand, by keeping their love secret, they follow a path that leads, tragically, to their deaths.
	between numbers that tell hours and minutes, after the greeting in a business letter, and between chapter and verse of religious works	Our English class meets Tuesdays and Thursdays from **9:00** A.M. to **10:00** A.M. Dear Juliet: Please meet me on the balcony at midnight. Ecclesiastes **3:1–8**
	not after a verb, between a prepo-sition and its object(s), or after *because* or *as*	**after a verb** **incorrect** Three of Shakespeare's most famous plays are: *Romeo and Juliet, Macbeth,* and *Hamlet.* **correct** These are three of Shakespeare's most famous plays: *Romeo and Juliet, Macbeth,* and *Hamlet.* **between a preposition and its object(s)** **incorrect** I have seen performances of Shakespeare's plays in: London, New York, and Chicago. **correct** I have seen performances of Shakespeare's plays in the following cities: London, New York, and Chicago. **after *because* or *as*** **incorrect** Shakespeare was a great playwright because: he had an extraordinary skill in depicting human nature and the universal struggles all people experience. **correct** Shakespeare was a great playwright because he had an extraordinary skill in depicting human nature and the universal struggles all people experience.
Ellipsis Points	to show that material from a quota-tion or a quoted passage has been left out	"Doing something does not require discipline...it creates its own discipline."

Punctuation	Function	Examples
	if material is left out at the beginning of a sentence or passage	. . . The very thought of hard work makes me queasy.
	if material is left out in the middle of a sentence	The very thought . . . makes me queasy.
	if material is left out at the end of a sentence	It's hard work, doing something with your life. . . . I'd rather die in peace. Here we are, all equal and alike and none of us much to write home about. . . .
Apostrophes	to form the possessive case of a singular or plural noun	the **window's** ledge, **Carlos's** father, **jazz's** beginnings, **wolves'** howls, twenty-five **cents'** worth, **countries'** treaties, **students'** textbooks
	to show joint or separate ownership	**Zack and Josh's** experiment, **Lisa and Randall's** cabin, **Sarah's** and **Jason's** schedules, **Steve's** and **John's** trumpets
	to form the possessive of an indefinite pronoun	**anyone's** guess, **each other's** notes, **everybody's** dream
	to form a contraction to show where letters, words, or numerals have been omitted	**I'm** = I am **you're** = you are **she's** = she is **o'clock** = of the clock **there're** = there are **they're** = they are
	to form the possessive of only the last word in a compound noun, such as the name of an organization or a business	brother-in-**law's** sense of humor; Teller, Teller, and **Teller's** law firm; Volunteer Nursing **Association's** office
	to form the possessive of an acronym	**NASA's** flight plan, **NATO's** alliances, **UNICEF's** contributions
	to form the plural of letters, numerals, and words referred to as words	two **A's**, **ABC's**, three **7's**, twelve **yes's**
	to show the missing numbers in a date	drought of **'02**, class of **'06**
Underlining and Italics	with titles of books, plays, long poems, periodicals, works of art, movies, radio and television series, videos, computer games, comic strips, and long musical works and recordings	**books:** *To Kill a Mockingbird; Silent Spring; Black Elk Speaks* **plays:** *The Tragedy of Romeo and Juliet; The Monsters Are Due on Maple Street* **long poems:** *Metamorphoses; Odyssey* **periodicals:** *Sports Illustrated; Wall Street Journal; The Old Farmer's Almanac* **works of art:** *The Acrobat; In the Sky; The Teacup* **movies:** *Il Postino; North by Northwest; Cast Away* **radio/television series:** *Fresh Air; West Wing; Friends; Animal Planet* **videos:** *Yoga for Strength; Cooking with Julia; Wizard of Oz* **computer games:** *Empire Earth; Age of Wonders II* **comic strips:** *Zits; Foxtrot; Overboard* **long musical works/recordings:** *Requiem; Death and the Maiden; La Traviata*
	with the names of trains, ships, aircraft, and spacecraft	**trains:** *Sunset Limited* **ships:** *Titanic* **aircraft:** *Air Force One* **spacecraft:** *Apollo 13*

Punctuation	Function	Examples
	with words, letters, symbols, and numerals referred to as such	The word *filigree* has a Latin root. People in western New York pronounce the letter *a* with a harsh, flat sound. The children learned that the symbol **+** is used in addition. Your phone number ends with four **7**'s.
	to set off foreign words or phrases that are not common in English	Did you know the word *amor* means "love"? The first Italian words I learned were *ciao* and *pronto*.
	to place emphasis on a word	Why is the soup *blue*? You're not going to borrow *my* car.
Quotation Marks	at the beginning and end of a direct quotation	"Do you want to ride together to the concert?" asked Margaret. "Don't wait for me," sighed Lillian. "I'm running late as usual."
	to enclose the titles of short works such as short stories, poems, articles, essays, parts of books and periodicals, songs, and episodes of TV series	**short stories:** "Gwilan's Harp," "Everyday Use" **poems:** "Hanging Fire," "Mirror" **articles:** "Where Stars Are Born," "Ghost of Everest" **essays:** "Thinking Like a Mountain," "It's Not Talent; It's Just Work" **parts of books:** "The Obligation to Endure," "Best Sky Sights of the Next Century" **songs:** "At the Fair," "Johnny's Garden" **episodes of TV series:** "The Black Vera Wang," "Isaac and Ishmael"
	to set off slang, technical terms, unusual expressions, invented words, and dictionary definitions	We nicknamed our dog **"Monkey"** because he moves quickly and loves to play tricks. My mother says that **"groovy"** and **"cool"** were the slang words of her generation. Did you know that the word *incident* means **"a definite, distinct occurrence"**?
Hyphens	to make a compound word or compound expression	**compound nouns:** great-grandfather Schaefer, great-uncle Tom **compound adjectives:** best-known novel, down-to-earth **used before a noun:** down-to-earth actor, real-life adventure **compound numbers:** ninety-nine years, twenty-five cents **spelled-out fractions:** one-half inch, three-eighths of a yard
	to divide an already hyphenated word at the hyphen	Finally, after much coaxing, our **great-grandfather** told his stories.
	to divide a word only between syllables	**Incorrect:** After hiking in the woods, the novice **ca-mpers** became tired and hungry. **Correct:** After hiking in the woods, the novice **camp-ers** became tired and hungry.
	with the prefixes *all-*, *ex-*, *great-*, *half-* and *self-*, and with all prefixes before a proper noun or proper adjective	**all**-purpose, **ex**-husband, **pre**-Industrial age, **great**-grandparent, **half**-baked, **self**-expression
	with the suffixes *-free*, *-elect*, and *-style*	fragrance-**free** detergent, mayor-**elect** Kingston, Southern-**style** hospitality
Dashes	to show a sudden break or change in thought	"I say it did," replied the other. "There was no thought about it; I had just— What's the matter?"

Punctuation	Function	Examples
	to mean *namely, that is,* or *in other words*	Our puppy knows only two commands — *sit* and *stay*. The hotel rates were surprisingly reasonable — less than a hundred dollars — for a double room.
Parentheses and Brackets	around material added to a sentence but not considered of major importance	Toni Cade Bambara (1939–1995) grew up in Harlem and Brooklyn, New York. The Taj Mahal (a majestic site!) is one man's tribute of love to his departed, beloved wife. More grocery stores are stocking natural food ingredients (for example, whole grains, soy products, and dried fruits).
	to punctuate a parenthetical sentence contained within another sentence.	When the quilt is dry (it shouldn't take long), please fold it and put it in the linen closet. The piping-hot funnel cakes (they were covered with powdered sugar!) just melted in our mouths. The vitamin tablets (aren't you supposed to take one every morning?) provide high doses of vitamins A and E.
	to enclose words or phrases that interrupt the sentence and are not considered essential to meaning.	They took pasta salad and fruit (how could we have forgotten dessert?) to the summer concert.
	to enclose information that explains or clarifies a detail in quoted material	A literary critic praised the author's new book, "She [Martha Grimes] never fails to delight her devoted fans with witty dialogue, elegant prose, and a cast of characters we'd like to consider our friends." Another literary critic wrote, "[Martha] Grimes is the queen of the mystery genre."

3.16 CAPITALIZATION

EDITING FOR CAPITALIZATION ERRORS

To avoid capitalization errors, check your draft for proper nouns and proper adjectives; geographical names, directions, and historical names; and titles of artworks and literary works.

Capitalization Reference Chart

Category/Rule	Examples
Proper Nouns and Proper Adjectives	
Proper Nouns	
Names of people	**S**ojourner **T**ruth, **F**ranklin **D**. **R**oosevelt, **M**artin **L**uther **K**ing **J**r.
Months, days, and holidays	**O**ctober, **W**ednesday, **M**emorial **D**ay
Names of religions, languages, races, and nationalities	**B**aptist, **C**atholicism, **C**hilean, **B**uddhism, **F**rench, **H**ispanic, **G**reek, **A**frican **A**merican
Names of clubs, organization, businesses, and institutions	**L**ittle **L**eague, **A**merican **H**eart **A**ssociation, **P**ratt-**R**ead **C**ompany, **W**ebster **B**ank
Names of awards, prizes, and medals	**E**mmy **A**ward, **N**obel **P**eace **P**rize, **P**urple **H**eart, **P**ulitzer **P**rize
Proper Adjectives	
Proper adjectives formed from proper nouns	**J**apanese gardening, **E**nglish class, **C**aribbean music, **A**laskan oil drilling
Proper nouns used as adjectives	**S**enate bill, **A**gatha **C**hristie masterpiece, **C**alifornia coast, **F**ranklin stove
I and First Words	
The pronoun *I*.	Next week **I** will leave on my trip to Yellowstone National Park.
First word of each sentence.	**T**he oldest of the U.S. national parks is noted for its beauty, wildlife, and geysers.
First word of a direct quotation.	"**T**hat mountain stands taller than any other in the state," the guide reported with pride to his group of tourists.
First lines of most poetry. (Follow the capitalization of the original poem.)	**A**nd far as the eye of God could see **D**arkness covered everything, **B**lacker than a hundred midnights **D**own in a cypress swamp.
First word in a letter salutation and the name or title of the person addressed.	**D**ear **D**ad, **M**y dear **A**unt **N**ola, **D**ear **M**adam
First word in letter closings.	**S**incerely yours, **Y**ours truly, **F**ondly, **W**arm wishes
Family Relationships and Titles of Persons	
Capitalize the titles or abbreviations that come before the names of people.	**A**dmiral Michael Chase, **M**s. Gloria Steinem, **S**enator Dodd, **M**r. and **M**rs. Douglas, **D**r. Watson, **C**hief **J**ustice Oliver Wendell Holmes
Person's title as a proper noun.	Can you meet us on Tuesday, **R**abbi? It's time to start rounds, **D**octor.
Words showing family relationships when used as titles or as substitutes for a name.	**U**ncle Fred, **G**randmother Parker, **F**ather, **C**ousin Sam
Abbreviations	
Social titles after a name.	My teacher is named **Mr.** Franks. Can't you ask **Prof.** Pardoe to help us in the soup kitchen?

Category/Rule	Examples
Abbreviate the titles of organizations.	Northeastern Manufacturing Northeastern **Mfg.** Connecticut Yard Workers **Assoc.**
Parts of government, and business, with the initials of each word in the title.	North Atlantic Treaty Organization **NATO** United States Marine Corps **USMC** International Business Machines **IBM** Southern New England Telephone **SNET**
Abbreviate address titles.	Street **St.**, Road **Rd.**, Avenue **Ave.**
Time Designations	
Time abbreviations B.C.E. (B.C.), C.E. (A.D.), A.M., and P.M.	Hatshepsut, who lived from 1503 to 1482 **B.C.E.**, was one of five women to reign as Queen of Egypt. The cruel Caligula ruled Rome until **C.E.** 41. My appointment was for 9:30 **A.M.**, and I'm not happy about waiting. We have a 7:00 **P.M.** dinner reservation at my favorite restaurant.
Geographical Names, Directions, and Historical Names	
Names of cities, states, countries, islands, and continents	**cities:** **H**onolulu, **M**oscow, **G**uatemala **C**ity **states:** **G**eorgia, **I**owa, **N**ew **M**exico **countries:** **Z**imbabwe, **B**elgium, **E**cuador **islands:** **T**ahiti, **C**ayman **I**slands, **C**yprus **continents:** **N**orth **A**merica, **E**urope, **A**frica
Names of bodies of water and geographical features	**B**lack **S**ea, **S**nake **R**iver, **S**ahara **D**esert, **M**ount **M**cKinley
Names of buildings, monuments, and bridges	**W**oolsey **H**all, **E**mpire **S**tate **B**uilding, **V**ietnam **V**eterans **M**emorial, **G**olden **G**ate **B**ridge
Names of streets and highways	**R**ailroad **A**venue, **N**ew **E**ngland **T**urnpike, **P**alm **D**rive, **R**oute 153
Sections of the country	the **S**unbelt, the **P**acific **C**oast, the **S**outheast, the **M**idwest
Names of historical events, special events, documents, and historical periods	**historical events:** **B**attle of the **B**ulge, **W**orld **W**ar I **special events:** **S**ummerfest, **B**oston **M**arathon **documents:** **M**agna **C**arta, **D**eclaration of **I**ndependence **historical periods:** **R**econstruction, **I**ndustrial **A**ge
Titles of Artworks and Literary Works	
First and last words and all important words in the titles of artworks and literary works, including books, magazines, short stories, poems, songs, movies, plays, paintings, and sculpture	*Transworld Skateboarding* (magazine), *Too Close to the Falls* (book), "The Cask of Amontillado" (short story), "Birches at Sunrise" (painting), "Polka Dots and Moonbeams" (song), *The Lion in Winter* (movie)
Titles of religious works	**H**ebrew **B**ible, **K**oran, **O**ld **T**estament

SPELLING RULES

Always check your writing for spelling errors, and try to recognize the words that give you more trouble than others. Use a dictionary when you find you have misspelled a word. Keep a list in a notebook of words that are difficult for you to spell. Write the words several times until you have memorized the correct spelling. Break down the word into syllables and carefully pronounce each individual syllable.

Some spelling problems occur when adding prefixes or suffixes to words or when making nouns plural. Other spelling problems occur when words follow certain patterns, such as those containing *ie/ei*. The following spelling rules can help you spell many words correctly.

PREFIXES AND SUFFIXES

Prefixes

A **prefix** is a letter or a group of letters added to the beginning of a word to change its meaning. When adding a prefix, do not change the spelling of the word itself.

EXAMPLES

mis– + perception = misperception
im– + possible = impossible
in– + conceivable = inconceivable
anti– + social = antisocial
al– + mighty = almighty

Suffixes

A **suffix** is a letter or a group of letters added to the end of a word to change its meaning.

The spelling of most words is not changed when the suffix *–ness* or *–ly* is added.

EXAMPLES

shy + –ness = shyness
forgive + –ness = forgiveness
eager + –ness = eagerness
strange + –ly = strangely
bad + –ly = badly
splendid + –ly = splendidly

If you are adding a suffix to a word that ends with *y* following a vowel, usually leave the *y* in place.

EXAMPLES

employ   employs   employing   employed

defray   defrays   defraying   defrayment
buoy   buoys   buoying   buoyancy

If you are adding a suffix to a word that ends with *y* following a consonant, change the *y* to *i* before adding any ending except *–ing*.

EXAMPLES

bury	buried	burying
copy	copied	copying
supply	supplied	supplying
magnify	magnified	magnifying

Double the final consonant before adding a suffix beginning with a vowel (such as *–ed, –en, –er, –ing, –ence, –ance,* or *–y*) in words ending in a single consonant preceded by a single vowel if the word is either a single syllable or ends in a stressed syllable.

EXAMPLES

regret	regrettable	regretting
quit	quitter	quitting
fan	fanned	fanning
refer	referred	referring
plot	plotted	plotting
deter	deterrence	deterring
rot	rotten	rotting

If you are adding a suffix that begins with a vowel to a word that ends with a silent *e,* usually drop the *e.*

EXAMPLES

tune	tuning
oblige	obligation
pursue	pursuable
grieve	grievous

If you are adding a suffix that begins with a consonant to a word that ends with a silent *e,* usually leave the *e* in place.

EXAMPLES

spite	spiteful
achieve	achievement
state	stately
lame	lameness

EXCEPTIONS

awe	awful
wise	wisdom
nine	ninth
due	duly

If the word ends in a soft *c* sound (spelled *ce*) or a soft *g* sound (spelled *ge*), keep the *e* when adding the suffixes *—able* or *—ous*.

EXAMPLES

acknowledge	acknowledgeable
enforce	enforceable
outrage	outrageous

PLURAL NOUNS

Plural Nouns

Most noun plurals are formed by simply adding *—s* to the end of the word.

EXAMPLES

surface + —s = surfaces
mouthful + —s = mouthfuls
platelet + —s = platelets
refrigerator + —s = refrigerators

The plural of nouns that end in *o, s, x, z, ch,* or *sh* should be formed by adding *—es.*

EXAMPLES

tomato + —es = tomatoes
loss + —es = losses
fox + —es = foxes
buzz + —es = buzzes
inch + —es = inches
flash + —es = flashes

The exception to the rule above is that musical terms and certain other words that end in *o* are usually made plural by adding *—s.* Check a dictionary if you aren't sure whether to add *—s* or *—es.*

EXAMPLES

mango + —s = mangos
piano + —s = pianos
portico + —s = porticos
solo + —s = solos
soprano + —s = sopranos
vibrato + —s = vibratos

Form the plural of nouns that end in *y* following a consonant by changing the *y* to an *i* and adding *—es.*

EXAMPLES

democracy	democracies
fairy	fairies
fallacy	fallacies
fifty	fifties
filly	fillies
signatory	signatories

Nouns that end in *f* or *fe* must be modified, changing

the *f* or *fe* to *v,* before adding *—es* to the plural form.

EXAMPLES

shelf	shelves
knife	knives
scarf	scarves
leaf	leaves
calf	calves

SPELLING PATTERNS

The ie/ei Spelling Pattern

A word spelled with the letters *i* and *e* and has a long *e* sound is usually spelled *ie* except after the letter *c.*

EXAMPLES

belief	conceive	
piece	receive	
field	deceit	

EXCEPTIONS

leisure	either	ceiling

Use *ei* when the sound is not long *e.*

EXAMPLES

forfeit	surfeit	foreign	height

EXCEPTIONS

science	mischief	sieve

If the vowel combination has a long *a* sound (as in *eight*), always spell it with *ei.*

EXAMPLES

weight	neigh	feign	vein

When two vowels are pronounced separately in a word, spell them in the order of their pronunciation.

EXAMPLES

siesta	patio	diode	conscience

The "Seed" Sound Pattern

The "seed" ending sound has three spellings: *—sede,* *—ceed,* and *—cede.*

EXAMPLES

Only one word ends in *—sede: supersede*

Three words end in *—ceed: proceed, succeed, exceed*

All other words end in *—cede: accede, concede, recede, precede, secede*

Silent Letters

Some spelling problems result from letters written but not heard when a word is spoken. Becoming familiar with the patterns in letter combinations containing silent letters will help you identify other words that fit the patterns.

- Silent *b* usually occurs with *m*.

EXAMPLES

dumb   bomb   climb   lamb

- Silent *b* also appears in *debt* and *doubt*.
- Silent *c* often appears with *s*.

EXAMPLES

scissors   scent   scenic   science

- Silent *g* often appears with *n*.

EXAMPLES

design   resign   gnome   reign
foreign

- Silent *gh* often appears at the end of a word, either alone or in combination with *t (–ght)*.

EXAMPLES

fright   freight   sought   wrought

- Silent *h* appears at the beginning of some words.

EXAMPLES

hourly   heir   honestly   honor

- Silent *h* also appears in a few other words, as in *rhythm* and *ghost*.
- Silent *k* occurs with *n*.

EXAMPLES

knack   knight   knot   kneecap
knapsack

- Silent *n* occurs with *m* at the end of some words.

EXAMPLES

condemn   solemn   column   autumn

- Silent *p* occurs with *s* at the beginning of some words.

EXAMPLES

psyche   psychosis   psaltery   psoriasis

- Silent *s* occurs with *l* in some words.

EXAMPLES

island   islet   aisle

- Silent *t* occurs with *s* in a few words.

EXAMPLES

listen   hasten   nestle

- Silent *w* occurs at the beginnings of some words.

EXAMPLES

wreak   wrong   wraith   wrapper

- Silent *w* also occurs with *s* in a few words, such as *sword* and *answer*.

Letter Combinations

Some letter combinations have a different pronunciation when combined and can cause spelling problems.

- The letters *ph* produce the *f* sound.

EXAMPLES

sphinx   photograph   alphanumeric
phosphate

- The letters *gh* produce the *f* sound usually at the end of a word. (Otherwise, they are silent.)

EXAMPLES

cough   enough   neigh   weigh

- The letter combination *tch* sounds the same as *ch*.

EXAMPLES

sketch   pitch   snitch   hatch
such   hunch   grouch   torch

If the letters *c* and *g* have soft sounds (of *s* and *j*), they will usually be followed by *e*, i, or *y*.

EXAMPLES

cyclone circle   regent giant
pediatrician   gyroscope
malicious   region
cent   outrageous

If the letters *c* and *g* have hard sounds (of *k* and *g*), they will usually be followed by *a, o,* or *u*.

EXAMPLES

candid   gasket
congeal   engorge
convey   garland
conjugate   argument
cunning   gun

Spelling Patterns of Borrowed Words

Many words borrowed from other languages follow the spelling patterns of the original language. For example, some English words borrowed from French,

Spanish, and Italian follow letter patterns of the language of origin.

- The final *t* is silent in many words borrowed from French.

EXAMPLES
croquet
parquet
ballet

- The letter combinations *eur* and *eau* appear at the end of many words with French origin.

EXAMPLES

amateur	bureau
chauffeur	plateau
grandeur	tableau

- The letter combination *oo* appears in many words borrowed from the Dutch language.

EXAMPLES
roost
cooper
toot

Many plural Italian words end in *i*.

EXAMPLES
ravioli
manicotti
linguini

Many words of Spanish origin end in *o*.

EXAMPLES
machismo
tomato
patio

Compound Nouns

A **compound noun** consists of two or more nouns used together to form a single noun. Sometimes they are written as one word *(football, uptown);* other times they are written separately *(picnic table, tennis shoes)*. Some compound nouns are connected with hyphens *(great-grandfather, fly-by-night)*. Consult a good dictionary when you are not sure of the form of compounds.

Numerals

Spell out numbers of *one hundred* or less and all numbers rounded to hundreds. Larger round numbers such as *seven thousand* or *three million* should also be spelled out.

EXAMPLES

Joe Morgan hit more than **twenty** homeruns and stole at least **thirty** bases in the same season four times in his career.

Joe DiMaggio was the first baseball player to receive an annual salary of more than **a hundred thousand** dollars.

Use a hyphen to separate compound numbers from twenty-one through ninety-nine.

EXAMPLES

forty-two birds
seventy-four candles
one hundred soldiers
sixty thousand dollars

Use a hyphen in a fraction used as a modifier, but not in a fraction used as a noun.

EXAMPLES

The glass is **two-fifths full** of water.

After an hour I had mowed **three fourths** of the backyard.

Use Arabic numerals for numbers greater than one hundred that are not rounded numbers.

EXAMPLES

Our company sent out **493,745** mailings in just **145** days this year.

My uncle boasted that he has read **1,323** books thus far in his life.

If a number appears at the beginning of a sentence, spell it out or rewrite the sentence.

EXAMPLES

incorrect
356 years ago my ancestors moved to North America.
correct
Three hundred fifty-six years ago my ancestors moved to North America.
correct
My ancestors moved to North America **356** years ago.

Use words to write the time unless you are writing the exact time (including the abbreviation A.M. or P.M.). When the word *o'clock* is used for time of day, express the number in words.

Our meeting will start at **a quarter after ten.**

At **eight-thirty** the show will begin.

I was born at **5:22 P.M.** on a Monday.

You have until **three o'clock** to finish the proposal.

Use numerals to express dates, street numbers, room numbers, apartment numbers, telephone numbers, page numbers, exact amounts of money, scores, and percentages. Spell out the word *percent*. Round dollar or cent amounts of only a few words may be expressed in words.

EXAMPLES

May 27, 1962
(402) 555-1725
5219 Perret Street
pages 49–73
seventy cents
three hundred dollars
Apartment 655
38 percent
$1.6 billion (or $1,600,000,000)
$2,634

When you write a date, do not add *–st, –nd,* or *–th.*

EXAMPLES

incorrect
August 17th, 1968   November 5th
correct
August 17, 1968   November 5 or the
                   fifth of November

COMMON SPELLING ERRORS

Pronunciation is not always a reliable guide for spelling because words are not always spelled the way they are pronounced. However, by paying attention to both letters that spell sounds and letters that are silent, you can improve some aspects of your spelling. Always check a dictionary for the correct pronunciations and spellings of words that are new to your experience.

Extra Syllables

Sometimes people misspell a word because they include an extra syllable. For example, *arthritis* is easily misspelled if it is pronounced *artheritis*, with four syllables instead of three. Pay close attention to the number of syllables in these words.

EXAMPLES

two syllables
foundry   carriage   lonely
three syllables
privilege   boundary   separate

Omitted Sounds

Sometimes people misspell a word because they do not sound one or more letters when pronouncing the word. Be sure to include the underlined letters of these words even if you don't pronounce them.

EXAMPLES

barbarous   candidate   drowned
gratitude   governor   grocery
literature   sophomore   quantity
mischievous

Homophones

Words that have the same pronunciation but different spellings and meanings are called **homophones.** An incorrect choice can be confusing to your readers. Knowing the spelling and meaning of these groups of words will improve your spelling.

EXAMPLES

allowed/aloud   compliment/complement
sole/soul   alter/altar
hear/here   some/sum
ascent/assent   lead/led
threw/through   bear/bare
night/knight   wait/weight
brake/break   pair/pear
weak/week   buy/bye/by
peace/piece   who's/whose
capital/capitol   plain/plane
coarse/course   site/sight/cite

Commonly Confused Words

Some other groups of words are not homophones, but they are similar enough in sound and spelling to create confusion. Knowing the spelling and meaning of these groups of words will also improve your spelling.

EXAMPLES

access/excess   farther/further
nauseous/nauseated   accept/except
formally/formerly   passed/past
alternate/alternative literal/literally
principle/principal   desert/dessert
loose/lose   stationary/stationery

COMMONLY MISSPELLED WORDS

Some words are often misspelled. Here is a list of 150 commonly misspelled words. If you master this list, you will avoid many errors in your spelling.

absence	enormous	parallel
abundant	enthusiastically	pastime
academically	environment	peasant
accessible	exhaust	permanent
accidentally	existence	persistent
accommodate	fascinating	phenomenon
accurate	finally	physician
acknowledgment	forfeit	pneumonia
acquaintance	fulfill	prestige
adequately	guerrilla	privilege
adolescent	guidance	procedure
advantageous	hindrance	prophesy
advisable	hypocrite	prove
ancient	independent	receipt
annihilate	influential	referred
anonymous	ingenious	rehearsal
answer	institution	relieve
apparent	interference	resistance
article	irrelevant	resources
attendance	irresistible	responsibility
bankruptcy	judgment	rhythm
beautiful	league	schedule
beggar	leisure	seize
beginning	license	separate
behavior	lightning	sergeant
biscuit	liquefy	siege
breathe	magnificent	significance
business	manageable	souvenir
calendar	maneuver	sponsor
camouflage	meadow	succeed
catastrophe	mediocre	surprise
cellar	miniature	symbol
cemetery	mischievous	synonymous
changeable	misspell	temperature
clothes	mortgage	tomorrow
colossal	mysterious	transparent
column	naïve	twelfth
committee	necessity	undoubtedly
conceivable	nickel	unmistakable
conscientious	niece	unnecessary
conscious	noticeable	vacuum
consistency	nucleus	vehicle
deceitful	nuisance	vengeance
descendant	nutritious	villain
desirable	obedience	vinegar
disastrous	occasionally	weird
discipline	occurrence	whistle
efficiency	orchestra	withhold
eighth	outrageous	yacht
embarrass	pageant	yield

SENTENCE FRAGMENTS

A sentence contains a subject and a verb and should express a complete thought. A **sentence fragment** is a phrase or clause that does not express a complete thought but that has been punctuated as though it did.

EXAMPLES

> **complete sentence**
> The hungry raccoon climbed into the garbage can.

> **sentence fragment**
> Climbed into the garbage can. (The subject is missing.)

> **sentence fragment**
> The hungry raccoon. (The verb is missing.)

> **sentence fragment**
> Into the garbage can. (The subject and verb are missing.)

RUN-ON SENTENCES

A **run-on sentence** is made up of two or more sentences that have been run together as if they were one complete thought. A run-on sentence can confuse the reader about where a thought starts or ends.

Take a look at the following examples of run-on sentences. In the first run-on, called a *fused sentence*, no punctuation mark is used between the run-on sentences. In the second run-on, called a *comma splice*, a comma is used incorrectly.

EXAMPLES

> The start of the Civil War shocked the nation many Americans thought the war would be over in a matter of days. (fused sentence)

> The United States had several forgettable presidents in the two decades prior to the Civil War, they were reluctant to deal with the slavery issue. (comma splice)

You can correct a run-on by dividing it into two separate sentences. Mark the end of each idea with a period, question mark, or exclamation point. Capitalize the first word of each new sentence.

EXAMPLE

> The start of the Civil War shocked the nation. Many Americans thought the war would be over in a matter of days.

You can also correct a run-on by using a semicolon. The second part of the sentence is not capitalized. Use a semicolon to join two sentences only if the thoughts are closely related.

EXAMPLE

> The United States had several forgettable presidents in the two decades prior to the Civil War; they were reluctant to deal with the slavery issue.

SENTENCE COMBINING AND EXPANDING

A series of short sentences in a paragraph can make your writing sound choppy and boring. The reader might also have trouble understanding how your ideas are connected. By **combining and expanding sentences** you can connect related ideas, make sentences longer and smoother, and make a paragraph more interesting to read.

One way to combine sentences is to take a key word or phrase from one sentence and insert it into another sentence.

EXAMPLES

> **short, choppy sentences**
> The squirrels scrambled up the tree trunk. They were playful.

> **combined sentence (with key word)**
> The **playful** squirrels scrambled up the tree trunk.

> **short, choppy sentences**
> We visited my grandfather in October. He lives on the West Coast.

> **combined sentence (with key phrase)**
> We visited my grandfather on the **West Coast in October.**

Another way of combining sentences is to take two related sentences and combine them by using a coordinating conjunction—*and, but, or, so, for, yet,* or *nor.* By using a coordinating conjunction, you can form a compound subject, a compound verb, or a compound sentence.

EXAMPLES

> **two related sentences**
> Jessica is from Upper Michigan. She often writes poetry about the landscape of that area.

> **combined sentence**
> Jessica is from Upper Michigan, and she often writes poetry about the landscape of that area. (compound sentence)

> **two related sentences**
> Cockroaches infested the abandoned warehouse. Rats lived there, too.

> **combined sentence**
> Cockroaches and rats infested the abandoned warehouse. (compound subject)

> **two related sentences**
> Snow fell throughout the night. It buried the mountain village.

> **combined sentence**
> Snow fell throughout the night and buried the mountain village. (compound verb)

VARYING SENTENCE STRUCTURE

Just as you probably wouldn't like to eat the same thing for breakfast every morning, your readers wouldn't enjoy reading the same sentence pattern in every paragraph. By **varying sentence structure,** you can give your sentences rhythm, create variety, and keep your readers engaged.

Sentences often begin with a subject. To vary sentence style, start some sentences with a one-word modifier, a prepositional phrase, a participial phrase, or a subordinate clause.

EXAMPLES

> **subject**
> **She** occasionally likes to fly a kite at the park.

> **one-word modifier**
> **Occasionally,** she likes to fly a kite at the park.

> **prepositional phrase**
> **During breakfast** he always reads the sports section of the paper.

> **participial phrase**
> **Recalling yesterday's game,** the coach devised a new strategy

subordinate clause
Since it may rain tomorrow, Derrick mowed the lawn tonight

WORDY SENTENCES

A **wordy sentence** includes extra words and phrases that can be difficult, confusing, or repetitive to read. When you write, use only words necessary to make your meaning clear. Revise and edit your sentences so that they are not unnecessarily wordy or complicated. Review the following examples to learn about three different ways that you can correct wordy sentences.

Replace a group of words with one word.

wordy
Sam cleaned the car **because of the fact that** he had a date that evening.

revised
Sam cleaned his car **because** he had a date that evening.

Replace a clause with a phrase.

wordy
After Josh washed his clothes in the washing machine, he looked for the ironing board.

revised
After washing his clothes, Josh looked for the ironing board.

Delete a group of unnecessary or repetitive words.

wordy
What I believe is your house will not take long to sell after it is listed.

revised
Your house will not take long to sell after it is listed.

wordy
Mr. Jones is very frugal, **and he doesn't like to spend money**.

revised
Mr. Jones is very frugal.

USING PARALLELISM

A sentence has **parallelism** when the same forms are used to express ideas of equal—or parallel—importance. Parallelism can add emphasis, balance, and rhythm to a sentence. Words, phrases, and clauses that have the same form and function in a sentence are called **parallel.**

not parallel
The soldiers **marched** into the field, **loaded** their muskets, and then **had pointed** their bayonets. (The highlighted verbs are not in the same tense.)

parallel
The soldiers **marched** into the field, **loaded** their muskets, and then **pointed** their bayonets.

not parallel
The actress is **lovely, talented**, and **sings**. (The three highlighted words include two adjectives and one verb.)

parallel
The actress is a **lovely** and **talented** singer.

MAKING PASSIVE SENTENCES ACTIVE

A verb is **active** when the subject of the verb performs the action. It is **passive** when the subject of the verb receives the action.

active
The frosty air **stung** his cheekbones.

passive
His cheekbones **were stung** by the frosty air.

USING COLORFUL LANGUAGE

When you write, use words that tell your readers exactly what you mean. **Colorful language**—such as precise and lively nouns, verbs, and modifiers—tells your readers exactly what you mean and makes your writing more interesting.

Precise nouns give your reader a clear picture of who or what is involved in the sentence.

EXAMPLES

original sentence
The **bird** sat in the **tree.**

revised sentence
The **cardinal** sat in the **elm.**

Colorful, vivid verbs describe the specific action in the sentence.

EXAMPLES

original sentence
The tiger **jumped** from behind the tree.

revised sentence
The tiger **leapt** from behind the tree.

Modifiers—adjectives and adverbs—describe the meaning of other words and make them more precise. Colorful or surprising modifiers can make your writing come alive for your readers.

EXAMPLES

original sentence
The **large** dinosaur crashed through the barrier.

revised sentence
The **massive** dinosaur crashed **forcefully** through the barrier.

4.1 The Writing Process

All writers—whether they are beginning writers, famous published writers, or somewhere in between—go through a process that leads to a complete piece of writing. The specifics of each writer's process may be unique, but for every writer, writing is a series of steps or stages.

The Writing Process

Stage	Tasks
1. Prewriting	Plan your writing: choose a topic, audience, purpose, and form; gather ideas; arrange them logically.
2. Drafting	Get your ideas down on paper.
3. Revising	Evaluate, or judge, the writing piece and suggest ways to improve it. Judging your own writing is called self-evaluation. Judging a classmate's writing is called peer evaluation.
	Work to improve the content, organization, and expression of your ideas.
	Proofread your writing for errors in spelling, grammar, capitalization, and punctuation. Correct these errors, make a final copy of your paper, and proofread it again.
Writing Follow-Up: Publish and Present	Share your work with an audience.
Reflect	Think through the writing process to determine what you learned as a writer, what you accomplished, and what you would like to strengthen the next time you write.

While writing moves through these stages, it is also a continuing cycle. You might need to go back to a previous stage before going on to the next step. Returning to a previous stage will strengthen your final work. Note also that you can take time to reflect on your writing between any of the other stages. The more you reflect on your writing, the better your writing will become.

1 PREWRITE

In the prewriting stage of the writing process you decide on a purpose, audience, topic, and form. You also begin to discover your voice and gather and organize ideas.

Prewriting Plan

Set Your Purpose	A **purpose,** or aim, is the goal that you want your writing to accomplish.
Identify Your Audience	An **audience** is the person or group of people intended to read what you write.
Find Your Voice	**Voice** is the quality of a work that tells you that one person wrote it.
Choose Your Topic	A **topic** is simply something to write about. For example, you might write about a sports hero or about a cultural event in your community.
Select a Writing Form	A **form** is a kind of writing. For example, you might write a paragraph, an essay, a short story, a poem, or a news article.

Set Your Purpose

When you choose your mode and form of writing, think about what purpose or aim you are trying to accomplish. Your purpose for writing might be to inform, to tell a story, to describe something, or to convince others to see your viewpoint. Your writing might have more than one purpose. For example, a piece of writing might inform your readers about an important event while persuading them to respond in a specific way.

Identify Your Audience

An **audience** is the person or group of people intended to read what you write. For example, you might write for yourself, a friend, a relative, or your classmates. The best writing usually is intended for a specific audience. Choosing a specific audience before writing will help you make important decisions about your work. For an audience of young children, for example, you would use simple words and ideas. For an audience of your peers in an athletic group, you would use jargon and other specialized words that your peers already know. For an adult audience, you would use more formal language.

Identify Your Audience

Use the following questions to help identify your audience.

- ☐ Who will be most interested in my topic?
- ☐ What are their interests and values?
- ☐ How much do they already know about the topic?
- ☐ What background information do they need in order to understand my ideas and point of view?
- ☐ What words, phrases, or concepts will I need to define for my audience?
- ☐ How can I capture my audience's interest from the very start?

Use Appropriate Language

Formal Versus Informal English To write effectively, you must choose your language according to your audience, purpose, and the occasion or situation. **Formal English** contains carefully constructed, complete sentences; avoids contractions; follows standard English usage and grammar; uses a serious tone; and uses sophisticated vocabulary. **Informal English** contains everyday speech and popular expressions, uses contractions, and may include sentence fragments.

Formal English is appropriate for school essays, oral or written reports, interviews, and debates. Informal English is appropriate for communication with friends, personal letters or notes, and journal entries.

EXAMPLES

formal English
I am very pleased that I received a perfect score on the math exam.

informal English
I'm so pumped that I aced that math exam!

Find Your Voice

Voice is the quality of a work that tells you that one person wrote it. Voice makes a person's writing unique. In your writing, you should strive to develop your own voice, not to imitate the voices of others. Be true to your own voice, and your experience will speak directly to the experience of others.

Select Your Topic

A **topic** is simply something to write about. For example, you might write about a sports hero or about a cultural event in your community. Here are some ideas that may help you find interesting writing topics:

Ways to Find a Writing Topic	
Check your journal	Search through your journal for ideas that you jotted down in the past. Many professional writers get their ideas from their journals.
Think about your experiences	Think about people, places, or events that affected you strongly. Recall experiences that taught you important lessons or that you felt strongly about.
Look at reference works	Reference works include printed or computerized dictionaries, atlases, almanacs, and encyclopedias.
Browse in a library	Libraries are treasure houses of information and ideas. Simply looking around in the stacks of a library can suggest good ideas for writing.
Use mass media	Newspapers, magazines, radio, television, and films can suggest good topics for writing. For example, a glance at listings for public television programs might suggest topics related to the arts, to history, or to nature.
Search the Internet	Search key words in a search engine or web browser to expand on your ideas. Make sure to keep your work original and avoid plagiarizing from websites.

Choose a Form of Writing

Another important decision that a writer needs to make is what form his or her writing will take. A form is a kind of writing. Once you've identified your topic, your purpose for writing, and your audience, a particular form of writing may become immediately obvious as the perfect one to convey your ideas. But, sometimes, an unexpected choice of form may be even more effective in presenting your topic. The following chart lists some of the many different forms of writing.

Forms of Writing

Adventure	Letter
Advertisement	Magazine article
Advice column	Memorandum
Agenda	Minutes
Apology	Movie review
Autobiography	Mystery
Biography	Myth
Book review	Narrative
Brochure	Newspaper article
Character sketch	Obituary
Children's story	Parable
Comedy	Paraphrase
Consumer report	Petition
Debate	Play
Detective story	Police/Accident report
Dialogue	Poster
Directions	Proposal
Editorial	Radio or TV spot
Epitaph	Recommendation
Essay	Research report
Eulogy	Résumé
Experiment	Science fiction
Fable	Short story
Family history	Song lyric
Fantasy	Speech
History	Sports story
Human interest story	Statement of belief
Instructions	Summary
Interview questions	Tall tale
Itinerary	Tour guide
Journal entry	Want ad

Gather Ideas

After you have identified your purpose, audience, topic, and form, the next step in the prewriting stage is to gather ideas. There are many ways to gather ideas for writing.

- **Brainstorm** When you **brainstorm,** you think of as many ideas as you can, as quickly as you can, without stopping to evaluate or criticize them. Anything goes—no idea should be rejected in the brainstorming stage.
- **Freewrite. Freewriting** is simply taking a pencil and paper and writing whatever comes into your mind. Try to write for several minutes without stopping and without worrying about spelling, grammar, usage, or mechanics.
- **Question** Ask the **reporting questions** *who, what, where, when, why,* and *how* about your topic. This questioning strategy is especially useful for gathering information about an event or for planning a story.

- **Create a Graphic Organizer** A good way to gather information is to create a **graphic organizer,** such as a Cluster Chart, Venn Diagram, Sensory Details Chart, Time Line, Story Map, or Pro-and-Con Chart. For examples, see the Language Arts Handbook, section 1, Reading Strategies and Skills.

Organize Your Ideas

Writing Paragraphs After you have gathered ideas for a piece of writing, the next step is to organize these ideas in a useful and reader-friendly way. The most basic organization of ideas occurs in forming paragraphs. A good paragraph is a carefully organized unit of writing. It develops a sequence in narrative writing or develops a particular topic in informational or persuasive writing.

Paragraphs with Topic Sentences Many paragraphs include a topic sentence that presents a main idea. The topic sentence can be placed at the beginning, middle, or end of the paragraph. Topic sentences usually appear early on in the paragraph and are commonly followed by one or more supporting sentences. Often these supporting sentences begin with transitions that relate them to the other sentences or to the topic sentence. This type of paragraph may end with a clincher sentence, which sums up what has been said in the paragraph.

EXAMPLE

Topic Sentence	*Romeo and Juliet* is probably the best known and best loved of all William Shakespeare's plays.
Supporting Details	Generations of audiences have been able to relate to the two "star-cross'd" young lovers, whose passion is doomed from the start by the bitter feuding between their families. Since Elizabethan times, the play has been interpreted in many forms, inspiring operas, ballets, musicals, and poetry. It has been translated into nearly every language and has been updated in such modern contexts as gangland New York City, the Israeli-Palestinian conflict in Jerusalem, and war-torn Sarajevo.
Clincher Sentence	The power of the story is evident in that it has been told for centuries.

Paragraphs without Topic Sentences Most paragraphs do not have topic sentences. In a narrative piece of writing, many paragraphs state a series of events, and no sentence in the paragraph sums up the events. In good narrative writing, the sequence of events appears in chronological order. Descriptive writing may contain paragraphs organized spatially—in the order in which the speaker or narrator sees, hears, feels, smells, and tastes things in a given situation.

Write Your Thesis Statement

One way to start organizing your writing, especially if you are writing an informative or persuasive essay, is to identify the main idea of what you want to say. Present this idea in the form of a sentence or two called a thesis statement. A **thesis statement** is simply a sentence that presents the main idea or the position you will take in your essay.

Example thesis for a persuasive essay

The development at Rice Creek Farm should be stopped because it will destroy one of the best natural areas near the city.

Example thesis for an informative essay

Wilma Rudolph was an athlete who succeeded in the elite sport of tennis before the world was willing to recognize her.

Methods of Organization

The ideas in your writing should be ordered and linked in a logical and easily understandable way. You can organize your writing in the following ways:

Methods of Organization	
Chronological Order	Events are given in the order they occur.
Order of Importance	Details are given in order of importance or familiarity.
Comparison and Contrast Order	Similarities and differences of two things are listed.
Cause and Effect Order	One or more causes are presented followed by one or more effects.

To link your ideas, use connective words and phrases. In informational or persuasive writing, *for example, as a result, finally, therefore,* and *in fact* are common connectives. In narrative and descriptive writing, words like *first, then, suddenly, above, beyond, in*

the distance, and *there* are common connectives. In comparison-contrast organization, common phrases include *similarly, on the other hand,* and *in contrast.* In cause-and-effect organization, linkers include *one cause, another effect, as a result, consequently, finally,* and *therefore.*

Create an Outline

An **outline** is an excellent framework for highlighting main ideas and supporting details. To create a rough outline, simply list your main ideas in some logical order. Under each main idea, list the supporting details set off by dashes.

EXAMPLE
What Is Drama?
Definition of Drama
—Tells a story
—Uses actors to play characters
—Uses a stage, properties, lights, costumes, makeup, and special effects
Types of Drama
—Tragedy
  —Definition: A play in which the main character meets a negative fate
  —Examples: *Antigone, Romeo and Juliet, Death of a Salesman*
—Comedy
  —Definition: A play in which the main character meets a positive fate
  —Examples: *A Midsummer Night's Dream, Cyrano de Bergerac, The Odd Couple*

2 DRAFT

After you have gathered your information and organized it, the next step in writing is to produce a draft. A **draft** is simply an early attempt at writing a paper. Different writers approach drafting in different ways. Some prefer to work slowly and carefully, perfecting each part as they go. Others prefer to write a discovery draft, getting all their ideas down on paper in rough form and then going back over those ideas to shape and focus them. When writing a discovery draft, you do not focus on spelling, grammar, usage, and mechanics. You can take care of those details during revision.

Draft Your Introduction

The purpose of an introduction is to capture your reader's attention and establish what you want to say. An effective introduction can start with a quotation, a question, an anecdote, an intriguing fact, or a description that hooks the reader to keep reading. An effective introduction can open with a quote, question, anecdote, fact, or description.

EXAMPLES

> "That's one small step for man, one giant leap for mankind." With these words, Neil Armstrong signaled his success as the first man to set foot on the moon...

> What would it be like if all the birds in the world suddenly stopped their singing?

> When my brother was nineteen, he volunteered in a homeless shelter making sure people had a safe place to spend the night. He told me once that he would never forget the time he met...

Draft Your Body

When writing the body of an essay, refer to your outline. Each heading in your outline will become the main idea of one of your paragraphs. To move smoothly from one idea to another, use transitional words or phrases. As you draft, include evidence from documented sources to support the ideas that you present. This evidence can be paraphrased, summarized, or quoted directly. For information on proper documentation, see the Language Arts Handbook 5.6, Documenting Sources.

Draft Your Conclusion

In the conclusion, bring together the main ideas you included in the body of your essay and create a sense of closure to the issue you raised in your thesis. There is no single right way to conclude a piece of writing. Possibilities include:

- Making a generalization
- Restating the thesis and major supporting ideas in different words
- Summarizing the points made in the rest of the essay
- Drawing a lesson or moral
- Calling on the reader to adopt a view or take an action
- Expanding on your thesis or main idea by connecting it to the reader's own interests
- Linking your thesis to a larger issue or concern

3 REVISE

Evaluate Your Draft

Self- and Peer Evaluation When you evaluate something, you examine it carefully to find its strengths and weaknesses. Evaluating your own writing is called **self-evaluation.** A **peer evaluation** is an evaluation of a piece of writing done by classmates, or peers. The following tips can help you to become a helpful peer reader, to learn to give and receive criticism, and to improve your writing.

Tips for evaluating writing

- **Check for content** Is the content, including the main idea, clear? Have any important details been left out? Do unimportant or unrelated details confuse the main point? Are the main idea and supporting details clearly connected to one another?
- **Check for organization** Are the ideas in the written work presented in a logical order?
- **Check the style and language** Is the language appropriately formal or informal? Is the tone appropriate for the audience and purpose? Have any key or unfamiliar terms been defined?

Tips for delivering helpful criticism

- **Be focused** Concentrate on content, organization, and style. At this point, do not focus on proofreading matters such as spelling and punctuation; they can be corrected during the proofreading stage.
- **Be positive** Respect the writer's feelings and genuine writing efforts. Tell the writer what you like about his or her work. Answer the writer's questions in a positive manner, tactfully presenting any changes you are suggesting.
- **Be specific** Give the writer concrete ideas for improving his or her work.

Tips for benefiting from helpful criticism

- **Tell your peer evaluator your specific concerns and questions.** If you are unsure whether you've clearly presented an idea, ask the evaluator how he or she might restate the idea.
- **Ask questions** to clarify comments that your evaluator makes. When you ask for clarification, you make sure you understand your evaluator's comments.
- **Accept your evaluator's comments graciously.** Criticism can be helpful, but you don't have to use any or all of the suggestions.

Revise for Content, Organization, and Style

After identifying weaknesses in a draft through self-evaluation and peer evaluation, the next step is to revise the draft. Here are four basic ways to improve meaning and content:

- **Adding or Expanding** Sometimes writing can be improved by adding details, examples, or transitions to connect ideas. Often a single added adjective, for example, can make a piece of writing clearer or more vivid.
- **Cutting or Condensing** Often writing can be improved by cutting unnecessary or unrelated material.
- **Replacing** Sometimes weak writing can be made stronger through more concrete, more vivid, or more precise details.
- **Moving** Often you can improve the organization of your writing by moving part of it so that related ideas appear near one another.

After you've revised the draft, ask yourself a series of questions. Think of these questions as your "revision checklist."

REVISION CHECKLIST

Content

❏ Does the writing achieve its purpose?

❏ Are the main ideas clearly stated and supported by details?

Organization

❏ Are the ideas arranged in a sensible order?

❏ Are the ideas connected to one another within paragraphs and between paragraphs?

Style

❏ Is the language appropriate to the audience and purpose?

❏ Is the mood appropriate to the purpose of the writing?

Proofread for Errors When you proofread your writing, you read it through to look for errors and to mark corrections. When you mark corrections, use the standard proofreading symbols as shown in the following chart.

Proofreader's Symbols

Symbol and Example	Meaning of Symbol
The very first time	Delete (cut) this material.
cat cradle	Insert (add) something that is missing.
George	Replace this letter or word.
All the horses king's	Move this word to where the arrow points.
french toast	Capitalize this letter.
the vice-President	Lowercase this letter.
housse	Take out this letter and close up space.
book keeper	Close up space.
gebril	Change the order of these letters.
end. "Watch out," she yelled.	Begin a new paragraph.
Love conquers all	Put a period here.
Welcome friends.	Put a comma here.
Getthe stopwatch	Put a space here.
Dear Madam	Put a colon here.
She walked he rode.	Put a semicolon here.
name-brand products	Put a hyphen here.
cats meow	Put an apostrophe here.
cat's cradle	Let it stand. (Leave as it is.)

After you have revised your draft, make a clean copy of it and proofread it for errors in spelling, grammar, and punctuation. Use the following proofreading checklist.

Proofreading Checklist

Spelling	• Are all words, including names, spelled correctly?
Grammar	• Does each verb agree with its subject? • Are verb tenses consistent and correct? • Are irregular verbs formed correctly? • Are there any sentence fragments or run-ons? • Have double negatives been avoided? • Have frequently confused words, such as affect and effect, been used correctly?
Punctuation	• Does every sentence end with an end mark? • Are commas used correctly? • Do all proper nouns and proper adjectives begin with capital letters?

Prepare Your Final Manuscript After proofreading your draft, you will prepare your final manuscript. Follow the guidelines given by your teacher or the guidelines provided here. After preparing a final manuscript according to these guidelines, proofread it one last time for errors.

Final Manuscript Preparation Checklist

❏ Keyboard your manuscript using a typewriter or word processor, or write it neatly using blue or black ink.

❏ Double-space your writing.

❏ Use one side of the paper.

❏ Leave one-inch margins on all sides of the text.

❏ Indent the first line of each paragraph.

❏ Make a cover sheet listing the title of the work, your name, the date, and the class.

❏ In the upper right-hand corner of the first page, put your name, class, and date. On every page after the first, include the page number in the heading, as follows:

EXAMPLE

Sharon Turner
English 9
March 25, 2009
p. 2

WRITING FOLLOW-UP

Publish and Present

Some writing is done just for oneself—journal writing, for example. Most writing, however, is meant to be shared with others. Here are several ways in which you can publish your writing or present it to others:

• Submit your work to a local publication, such as school literary magazine, school newspaper, or community newspaper.
• Submit your work to a regional or national publication.
• Enter your work in a contest.
• Read your work aloud to classmates, friends, or family members.
• Collaborate with other students to prepare a publication—a brochure, online literary magazine, anthology, or newspaper.
• Prepare a poster or bulletin board, perhaps in collaboration with other students, to display your writing.
• Make your own book by typing or word processing the pages and binding them together.
• Hold an oral reading of student writing as a class or school-wide project.
• Share your writing with other students in a small writers' group.

Reflect

After you've completed your writing, think through the writing process to determine what you learned as a writer, what you learned about your topic, how the writing process worked or didn't work for you, and what skills you would like to strengthen.

Reflection can be done on a self-evaluation form, in small-group discussion, or simply in silent reflection. By keeping a journal, however, you'll be able to keep track of your writing experience and pinpoint ways to make the writing process work better for you. Here are some questions to ask as you reflect on the writing process and yourself as a writer:

• Which part of the writing process did I enjoy most and least? Why? Which part of the writing process was most difficult? least difficult? Why?
• What would I change about my approach to the writing process next time?
• What have I learned in writing about this topic?
• What have I learned by using this form?

- How have I developed as a writer while writing this piece?
- What strengths have I discovered in my work?
- What aspects of my writing do I want to strengthen? How can I strengthen them?

4.2 Modes and Purposes of Writing

Types of writing generally fall within four main classifications or modes: expository, narrative, descriptive, and persuasive. Each of these modes has a specific purpose.

Mode of Writing	Purpose	Form
expository	to inform	news article, research report
narrative	to express thoughts or ideas, or to tell a story	personal account, memoir, short story
descriptive	to portray a person, place, object, or event	travel brochure, personal profile, poem
persuasive	to convince people to accept a position and respond in some way	editorial, petition, political speech

5 Research and Documentation

5.1 Critical Thinking Skills

In literature and informational texts, some things are stated as facts **(literal)** and other things are inferred or implied by the author **(inferential).** We must use **critical thinking skills** to fully understand and interpret what we read. There are six basic levels of understanding, or *cognitive domains,* which are listed below: The categories can be thought of as degrees of difficulty. That is, the first one must be mastered before the next one can take place. We apply these skills as we read a text.

Levels of Critical Thinking		
Refer to Text	**Remember**	**Recall facts:** Retrieve information presented in the text
Reason with Text	**Understand**	**Find meaning:** Interpret and explain ideas or concepts
	Apply	**Use Information:** Utilize knowledge in another situation
	Analyze	**Take things apart:** Break details down to explore interpretations and relationships
	Evaluate	**Make judgments:** Justify a decision or course of action
	Create	**Bring ideas together:** Synthesize understanding to generate new ideas, products or ways of viewing things

The paired **Refer to Text/Reason with Text** questions following the selections in this textbook are broken down into *literal* questions that refer directly to the facts in the text **(Refer to Text)** followed by *inferential* questions that ask you to apply higher levels of thinking to interpret the text **(Reason with Text).**

5.2 Research Skills

Learning is a lifelong process, one that extends far beyond school. Both in school and on your own, it is important to remember that your learning and growth are up to you. One good way to become an independent lifelong learner is to master research skills. Research is the process of gathering ideas and information. One of the best resources for research is the library.

How Library Materials Are Organized

Each book in a library is assigned a unique number, called a call number. The call number is printed on the spine (edge) of each book. The numbers serve to classify books as well as to help the library keep track of them. Libraries commonly use one of two systems for classifying books. Most school and public libraries use the Dewey Decimal System. Most college libraries use the Library of Congress Classification System (known as the LC system).

The Dewey Decimal System	
Call Numbers	**Subjects**
000–099	Reference and General Works
100–199	Philosophy, Psychology
200–299	Religion
300–399	Social Studies
400–499	Language
500–599	Science, Mathematics
600–699	Technology
700–799	Arts
800–899	Literature
900–999	History, Geography, Biography[1]

1. Biographies (920s) are arranged alphabetically by the name of the person whose life is treated in each biography.

The Library of Congress System

Call Numbers	Subjects
A	Reference and General Works
B–BJ	Philosophy, Psychology
BK–BX	Religion
C–DF	History
G	Geography, Autobiography, Recreation
H	Social Sciences
J	Political Science
K	Law
L	Education
M	Music
N	Fine Arts
P	Language, Literature
Q	Science, Mathematics
R	Medicine
S	Agriculture
T	Technology
U	Military Science
V	Naval Science
Z	Bibliography, Library Science

How to Locate Library Materials

If you know the call number of a book or the subject classification number you want, you can usually go to the bookshelves, or stacks, to obtain the book. Use the signs at the ends of the rows to locate the section you need. Then find the particular shelf that contains call numbers close to yours.

Library collections include many other types of publications besides books, such as magazines, newspapers, audio and video recordings, and government documents. Ask a librarian to tell you where to find the materials you need. To find the call numbers of books that will help you with your research, use the library's catalog. The catalog lists all the books in the library (or a group of libraries if it is part of a larger system).

Author	Wallace, David Rains, 1945–
Title	The Quetzal and the Macaw: The story of Costa Rica's National Parks
Publication info.	Sierra Club Books, 1992
No. of pages/size	xvi, 222 p. : maps : 24 cm.
ISBN	ISBN 0-87156-585-4
Subjects	National Parks and reserves—Costa Rica—History
	Costa Rica. Servicio de Parques Nacionales—History
	Nature conservation—Costa Rica—History
Dewey call number	333.78

Internet Libraries Let your fingers do the walking and visit the Internet Public library at **http://www. ipl.org/.** The Internet Public Library is the first public library of the Internet. This site provides library services to the Internet community by finding, evaluating, selecting, organizing, describing, and creating quality information resources; teaches what librarians have to contribute in a digital environment; and promotes the importance of libraries.

Computerized Catalogs Many libraries today use computerized catalogs. Systems differ from library to library, but most involve using a computer terminal to search through the library's collection. You can usually search by author, title, subject, or key word. If your library has a computerized catalog, you will need to learn how to use your library's particular system. A librarian can help you to master the system. Here is a sample book entry screen from a computerized catalog.

Computerized Catalog Searches

Search By	Example	Hints
Author	gould, stephen j	Type last name first. Type as much of the name as you know.
Title	mismeasure of man	Omit articles such as a, an, or the at the beginning of titles.
Subject	intelligence tests; ability-testing	Use the list of subjects provided by the library.
Key words	darwin; intelligence; craniology	Use related topics if you can't find anything in your subject.

Card Catalogs Like a computerized catalog, a card catalog contains basic information about each book in the library. In a card catalog the information is typed on paper cards, which are arranged alphabetically in drawers. For each book there is a title card, one author card for each author, and at least one subject card. All of these cards show the book's title, author, and call number, so you can search for a book by title, author, or subject. The following illustration shows a typical title card.

A TITLE CARD

333.78   The Quetzal and the Macaw : the story of
         Costa Rica's national parks.
         Wallace, David Rains, 1945–
         The Quetzal and the Macaw : the story of
         Costa Rica's national parks. — San
         Francisco: Sierra Club Books, 1992
         xvi, 222 p. : maps : 24 cm.
         1. National parks and reserves — Costa Rica —
         History. 2. Costa Rica. Servicio de
         Parques nacionales — History. 3. Nature
         conservation — Costa Rica — History. I. Title.
         ISBN 0-394-57456-7

When you find the entries for the books you want, write down the call number of each book and then go to the shelves. If you cannot find a particular book you need in the catalog, ask the librarian if your library can request books from another library through an interlibrary loan.

Interlibrary Loans Many libraries are part of larger library networks. In these libraries, the computerized catalog covers the collections of several libraries. If you want a book from a different library, you will need to request the book at the library's request desk or by using its computer. Ask your librarian to help you if you have questions. He or she will be able to tell you when the book will be shipped to your library.

USING REFERENCE WORKS

Most libraries have an assortment of reference works in which knowledge is collected and organized so that you can find it easily. Usually, reference works cannot be checked out of the library.

Types of Dictionaries You will find many types of dictionaries in the library reference section. The most common is a dictionary of the English language. Examples include *Merriam Webster's Collegiate Dictionary*, the *American Heritage Dictionary*, and the multi-volume *Oxford English Dictionary*. Other word dictionaries focus on slang, abbreviations and acronyms, English/foreign language translation, and spelling.

Biographical, historical, scientific, and world language dictionaries are also some of the works you will find in the reference section.

Using a Thesaurus A thesaurus is a reference book that groups synonyms, or words with similar meanings. Suppose that you are writing an essay and have a word that means almost but not quite what you want, or perhaps you find yourself using the same word over and over. A thesaurus can give you fresh and precise words to use. For example, if you look up the word *sing* in a thesaurus, you might find the following synonyms listed:

   sing (v.) carol, chant, croon, hum, vocalize,
   warble, yodel

Using Almanacs, Yearbooks, and Atlases
Almanacs and yearbooks are published each year. An almanac provides statistics and lists, often related to recent events. In an almanac you can find facts about current events, countries of the world, famous people, sports, entertainment, and many other subjects. An overview of the events of the year can be found in a yearbook. Some of the more widely used almanacs and yearbooks are *The Guinness Book of World Records;* the *Information Please, Almanac, Atlas, and Yearbook;* the *World Almanac and Book of Facts;* and the *World Book Yearbook of Events.*

An **atlas** is a collection of maps and other geographical information. Some atlases show natural features such as mountains and rivers; others show political features such as countries and cities. If you need to locate a particular feature on a map in an atlas, refer to the gazetteer, an index that lists every item shown on the map.

Using Biographical References and Encyclopedias A **biographical reference** contains information on the lives of famous people. Examples include *Who's Who*, the *Dictionary of American Biography*, and *Contemporary Authors.*

Encyclopedias provide a survey of knowledge. General encyclopedias, such as *World Book*, contain information on many different subjects. Specialized encyclopedias, such as the *LaRousse Encyclopedia of Mythology,* contain information on one particular area of knowledge. The topics in an encyclopedia are treated in articles, which are usually arranged in alphabetical order. If you look up a topic and do not find it, check the index (usually in the last volume). The index will tell you where in the encyclopedia your topic is covered.

Using Indexes, Appendices, and Glossaries

An **index** lists in alphabetical order the subjects mentioned in a book or collection of periodicals and pages where these subjects are treated. Indexes help you locate possible sources of information about your topic. An index can be at the back of a book of nonfiction, or it can be a published book itself. Indexes are available as bound books, on microfilm, and on-line on the Internet.

An **appendix** provides additional material, often in chart or table form, at the end of a book or other writing.

A **glossary** lists key words in a book and their definitions.

Primary and Secondary Sources

Primary sources are the original unedited materials created by someone directly involved in an event or speaking directly for a group. They may include first-hand documents such as diaries, interviews, works of fiction, artwork, court records, research reports, speeches, letters, surveys, and so on.

Secondary sources offer commentary or analysis of events, ideas, or primary sources. They are often written significantly later and may provide historical context or attempt to describe or explain primary sources. Examples of secondary sources include dictionaries, encyclopedias, textbooks, and books and articles that interpret or review original works.

	Primary Source	Secondary Source
Art	Painting	Article critiquing the artist's technique
History	Prisoner's diary	Book about World War II Internment Camps
Literature	Poem	Literary criticism on a particular form of poetry
Science	Research report	Analysis of results

See the Language Arts Handbook, 5.4 Media Literacy for information on using newspapers, periodicals, and other forms of media to document your research.

5.3 Internet Research

The Internet is an enormous collection of computer networks that can open a whole new world of information. With just a couple of keystrokes, you can access libraries, government agencies, high schools and universities, nonprofit and educational organizations, museums, user groups, and individuals around the world.

Keep in mind that the internet is not regulated and everything you read online may not be verified or accurate. Confirm facts from the Internet against another source. In addition, to become a good judge of Internet materials, do the following:

- **Consider the domain name of the resource.** Be sure to check out the sites you use to see if they are commercial (.com or .firm), educational (.edu), governmental (.gov), or organizational (.org or .net). Ask yourself questions like these: What bias might a commercial site have that would influence its presentation of information? Is the site sponsored by a special-interest group that slants or spins information to its advantage?

Key to Internet Domains	
.com	commercial entity
.edu	educational institution
.firm	business entity
.gov	government agency or department
.org or .net	organization

- **Consider the author's qualifications.** Regardless of the source, ask these questions: Is the author named? What expertise does he or she have? Can I locate other online information about this person? Evaluate the quality of information.
- **How accurate is the information?** Does it appear to be reliable and without errors? Is the information given without bias?
- **Check the date posted.** Is the information timely? When was the site last updated?

Keep Track of Your Search Process

Because the Internet allows you to jump from one site to the next, it's easy to lose track of how you got from place to place. A research journal, kept in a separate electronic file or in a notebook, is an excellent tool for mapping how you find information.

❏ Write a brief statement of the topic of your research.

❏ Write key words or phrases that will help you search for this information.

❏ Note the search engines that you will use.

❏ As you conduct a search, note how many "hits" or Internet sites the search engine has accessed. Determine whether you need to narrow or expand your search. Write down new key words and the results of each new search.

❏ Write down all promising sites. As you access them, evaluate the source and nature of the information and jot down your assessment.

❏ As you find the information you need, document it carefully according to the directions in "Citing Internet Resources."

❏ Keep a list of favorite websites, either in your research journal or in your browser software. This feature may be called bookmark or favorites. You can click on the name of the site in your list and return to that page without having to retype the URL (Uniform Resource Locator).

The following example shows one way to set up a research log.

Internet Research Log

Topic: _____
_____
_____
_____

Key words: _____
_____

Search engine: _____

Promising hits (titles _____
and summary of _____
sources): _____
_____

New key words or _____
phrases tried: _____

Promising hits (titles _____
and summary of _____
sources): _____
_____

Complete web _____
addresses of most _____
promising sites: _____
_____

Search Tools

A number of popular and free search engines allow you to find topics of interest. Keep in mind that each service uses slightly different methods of searching, so you may get different results using the same key words.

All the Web   http://www.alltheweb.com
AltaVista   http://www.altavista.com
Go   http://www.go.com
Yahoo   http://www.yahoo.com
Excite   http://www.excite.com
HotBot   http://www.hotbot.com
WebCrawler   http://www.webcrawler.com
Google   http://www.google.com

Search Tips

• To make searching easier, less time consuming, and more directed, narrow your subject to a key word or a group of key words. These key words are your search terms. Key search connectors, or Boolean commands, can help you limit or expand the scope of your topic.

AND (or +) narrows a search by retrieving documents that include both terms. For example: Ulysses Grant AND Vicksburg.

OR broadens a search by retrieving documents that include any of the terms. For example, Ulysses Grant OR Vicksburg OR Civil War.

NOT narrows a search by excluding documents containing certain words. For example: Ulysses Grant NOT Civil War.

- If applicable, limit your search by specifying a geographical area by using the word near. For example, golf courses near Boulder, Colorado.
- When entering a group of key words, present them in order, from the most important to the least important key word.
- If the terms of your search are not leading you to the information you need, try using synonyms. For example, if you were looking for information about how to care for your garden, you might use these terms: compost, pest control, and watering.
- Avoid opening the link to every page in your results list. Search engines typically present pages in descending order of relevancy or importance. The most useful pages will be located at the top of the list. However, skimming the text of lower order sites may give you ideas for other key words.
- If you're not getting the desired results, check your input. Common search mistakes include misspelling search terms and mistyping URLs. Remember that URLs must be typed exactly as they appear, using the exact capital or lowercase letters, spacing, and punctuation.

CITING INTERNET SOURCES

Plagiarism means to claim someone else's words or thoughts as your own. Whenever you use someone else's words or ideas, you must be careful either to put the ideas in your own words or to use quotation marks. In either case, you must give credit to the person whose ideas you are using.

5.4 Media Literacy

The term **media,** in most applications, is used as a plural of *medium,* which means a channel or system of communication, information, or entertainment. *Mass media* refers specifically to means of communication, such as newspapers, radio, or television, which are designed to reach the mass of the people. *Journalism*

is the gathering, evaluating, and disseminating, through various media, of news and facts of current interest. Originally journalism encompassed only such printed matter as newspapers and periodicals. Today, however, it includes other media used to distribute news, such as radio, television, documentary or news-reel films, the Internet, and computer news services.

Newspapers are publications usually issued on a daily or weekly basis, the main function of which is to report the news. Newspapers also provide commentary on the news, advocate various public policies, furnish special information and advice to readers, and sometimes include features such as comic strips, cartoons, and serialized books.

Periodicals are publications released at regular intervals, such as journals, magazines, or newsletters. Periodicals feature material of special interest to particular audiences. The contents of periodicals can be unrelated to current news stories — however, when dealing with the news, periodicals tend to do so in the form of commentaries or summaries.

Technical writing refers to scientific or process oriented instructional writing that is of a technical or mechanical nature. Technical writing includes instruction manuals, such as computer software manuals, how-to instructional guides, and procedural memos.

Electronic media include online magazines and journals, known as webzines or e-zines, computer news services, and many web-based newspapers that are available on the Internet. The web is by far the most widely used part of the Internet.

Multimedia is the presentation of information using the combination of text, sound, pictures, animation, and video. Common multimedia computer applications include games, learning software, presentation software, reference materials, and web pages. Most multimedia applications include links that enable users to switch between media elements and topics. The connectivity provided by these links transforms multimedia from static presentations with pictures and sound into a varied and informative interactive experience.

Visual Media In today's visually stimulating world, books and news media rely on visual arts, such as fine art, illustrations, photographs, and other visuals as well as the printed word to convey ideas. Visual arts offer insights into our world in a different way than print does. Critical viewing or careful examination of a painting or photograph can help you to comprehend its meaning and be able to compare and contrast the visual image with a literary work or other piece of writing.

5.5 Evaluating Sources

To conduct your research efficiently, you need to evaluate your sources and set priorities among them. Ideally, a source will be:

- **Unbiased.** When an author has a personal stake in what people think about a subject, he or she may withhold or distort information. Investigate the author's background to see if she or he is liable to be biased. Using loaded language and overlooking obvious counter-arguments are signs of author bias.
- **Authoritative.** An authoritative source is reliable and trustworthy. An author's reputation, especially among others who conduct research in the same field, is a sign of authority. Likewise, periodicals and publishers acquire reputations for responsible or poor editing and research.
- **Timely.** Information about many subjects changes rapidly. An astronomy text published last year may already be out of date. In other fields—for instance, algebra—older texts may be perfectly adequate. Consult with your teacher and your librarian to decide how current your sources must be.
- **Available.** Borrowing through interlibrary loan, tracing a book that is missing, or recalling a book that has been checked out to another person takes time. Make sure to allow enough time for these materials.
- **Appropriate for your level.** Find sources that present useful information that you can understand. Materials written for "young people" may be too simple to be helpful. Books written for experts may presume knowledge that you do not have. Struggling with a difficult text is often worth the effort, but if you do so, monitor your time and stay on schedule.

5.6 Documenting Sources

As you use your research in your writing, you must document your sources of information.

- Credit the sources of all ideas and facts that you use.
- Credit original ideas or facts that are expressed in text, tables, charts, and other graphic information.
- Credit all artistic property, including works of literature, song lyrics, and ideas.

Keeping a Research Journal A research journal is a notebook, electronic file, or other means to track the information you find as you conduct research. A research journal can include the following:

- A list of questions you want to research. (Such questions can be an excellent source of writing topics.)

EXAMPLES

How did the Vietnam Veterans Memorial come to be? Why is it one of the most visited memorials in America?

Where can I find more artwork by Faith Ringgold?

Why was Transcendentalism such an important literary movement in America but not in Europe?

As you conduct your research, rely on your research journal as a place to take notes on the sources you find and your evaluation of them. Keeping a research journal can be an invaluable way to track your research and to take notes.

Avoiding Plagiarizing Plagiarism is taking someone else's words or thoughts and presenting them as your own. Plagiarism is a very serious problem and has been the downfall of many students and professionals. Whenever you use someone else's writing to help you with a paper or a speech, you must be careful either to **paraphrase,** put the ideas in your own words, **summarize** the main ideas, or to use **quotation marks.** In any case, you must document your sources and give credit to the person whose ideas you are using. As you do research, make sure to include should include paraphrases, summaries, and direct quotations in your notes.

Informal and Formal Note-Taking

Informal Note-Taking Take informal notes when you want information for your own use only, and when you will not need to quote or document your sources. You would take informal notes when preparing materials to use in studying, for instance, as you watch a film or listen to a lecture.

Informal note-taking is similar to outlining. Use important ideas as headings, and write relevant details below. You will not be able to copy every word, nor is there any need to. Write phrases instead of sentences. You will also want to record information about the event or performance, including the date, time, place, speaker, and title, as applicable.

EXAMPLE

quotation

"Jerzy Kosinski came to the United States in 1957, and in 1958 he was awarded a Ford Foundation fellowship."

notes

Jerzy Kosinski

—came to US 1957

—Ford Foundation fellowship 1958

Formal Note-Taking Take formal notes when you may need to quote or document your sources. When you are keeping formal notes for a project—for instance, for a debate or a research paper—you should use 4" x 6" index cards.

Preparing Note Cards

1. Identify the source at the top right corner of the card. (Use the source numbers from your bibliography cards.)
2. Identify the subject or topic of the note on the top line of the card. (This will make it easier to organize the cards later.)
3. Use a separate card for each fact or quotation. (This will make it easier to organize the cards later.)
4. Write the pertinent source page number or numbers after the note.

Sample Note Card

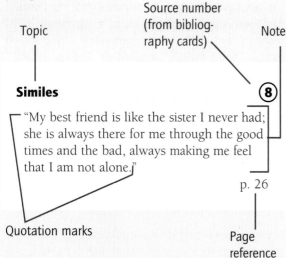

Topic

Source number (from bibliography cards)

Note

Similes ⑧

"My best friend is like the sister I never had; she is always there for me through the good times and the bad, always making me feel that I am not alone."

p. 26

Quotation marks

Page reference

Bilbliographies and Bibliography Cards

If you are writing a research paper, your teacher will ask you to include a bibliography to tell where you got your information. A bibliography is a list of sources that you used for your writing. A source is a book, a magazine, a film, or any other written or audio-visual material that you use to get information. As you work on your paper, you should be writing down on note cards the information for each source that you use.

EXAMPLE

Van Lawick-Goodall, Jane.

In the Shadow of Man

Boston: Houghton, 1971.

Peabody Institute Library

599.8

For each source used, prepare an index card with complete bibliographical information. Include all of the information in the following chart when preparing your cards.

Information to Include on a Bibliography Card	
Author(s)	Write the complete name(s) of all author(s), editor(s), and translator(s).
Title	Write the complete title. If the piece is contained in a larger work, include the title of the larger work. (For example, write the name of the encyclopedia as well as the name of the article you used.)
Publisher	Write exactly as it appears on the title page.
Place and date of publication	Copy this information from the title page or copyright page of a book. For a magazine, write the date of the issue that you used.
Location and call number	Note where you found the book. If it is in a library collection, write the call number.
Card number	Give each bibliography card that you prepare a number. Write that number in the top right-hand corner of the card and circle it. When you take notes from the source, include this number on each note card so that you will be able to identify the source of the note later on.

The following chart shows the correct form for different types of bibliography entries, following the *Modern Language Association (MLA) Style Manual.*

Forms for Bibliography Entries	
A. A book	Douglass, Frederick. *Escape from Slavery: The Boyhood of Frederick Douglass in His Own Words.* New York: Alfred A. Knopf, 1994.
B. A magazine article	Reston, James, Jr. "Orion: Where Stars Are Born." National Geographic. December 1995: 90–101.
C. An encyclopedia entry	"Lewis and Clark Expedition." Encyclopedia Americana. Jackson, Donald. 1995 ed.
D. An interview	Campbell, Silas. Personal interview. 6 February 1997.
E. Film	*The Big Heat.* Dir. Fritz Lang. With Glenn Ford and Gloria Grahame. Writ. Sidney Boehm. Based on the novel of the same title by William P. McGiven. 90 min. Columbia, 1953.

Citing Internet Sources

To document your Internet sources, use your research journal to record each site you visit (See the Language Arts Handbook, 5.3 Internet Research) or make bibliography cards as you search. An Internet source entry should include the following general pieces of information:

- Name of the author, if available, last name first, followed by a period.
- Title of the source, document, file, or page in quotation marks, followed by a period.
- Date of the material if available, followed by a period.
- Name of the database or online source, underlined, and followed by a period.
- Date the source was accessed (day, month, year), followed by a period. Although MLA style does not require the insertion of the words retrieved or accessed before the access date, you may want to include one of these words to distinguish a retrieval date from a publication date.
- Electronic address, enclosed in angle brackets (< >), followed by a period. MLA style suggests that writers avoid showing network and e-mail addresses as underlined hyperlinks. Note that when line length forces you to break a Web address, always break it after a slash mark.

The Modern Language Association Style Manual acknowledges that all source tracking information on the Internet may not be obtainable. Therefore, the manual recommends that if you cannot find some of this information, cite what is available.

Bibliography Cards for Internet Sources

EXAMPLES

Armstrong, Mark. "That's 'Sir' Mick Jagger to You." 17 June 2002. E! Online, Inc. Accessed 17 June 2003. <http://www.eonline.com/News/Items/0,1,10110,00.html>.

This site has no name of the database or online source:
Chachich, Mike. "Letters From Japan vol 1" 30 March 1994. Accessed 17 June 2003. <http://www.chachich.com/cgi-bin/catlfj?1>.

This site has no author:
"The Science Behind the Sod." 13 June 2002. MSU News Bulletin. Accessed 17 June 2003. <http://www.newsbulletin.msu.edu/june13/sod.html>.

This is the citation for an e-mail message:
Daniel Akaka (senator@akaka.senate.gov). "Oceanic Exploration Grant." E-mail to Joseph Biden (senator@biden.senate.gov). 17 June 2003.

Parenthetical Documentation Parenthetical documentation is currently the most widely used form of documentation. To use this method to document the source of a quotation or an idea, you place a brief note identifying the source in parentheses immediately after the borrowed material. This type of note is called a parenthetical citation, and the act of placing such a note is called citing a source.

The first part of a parenthetical citation refers the reader to a source in your List of Works Cited or Works Consulted. For the reader's ease in finding the source in your bibliography, you must cite the work according to how it is listed in the bibliography.

EXAMPLE PARENTHETICAL CITATIONS

A. For works listed by title, use an abbreviated title.

Sample bibliographic entry
"History." Encyclopedia Britannica: Macropædia. 1992 ed.

Sample citation
Historians go through three stages in textual criticism ("History" 615).

B. For works listed by author or editor, use the author's or editor's last name.

Sample bibliographic entry
Brown, Dee. Bury My Heart at Wounded Knee: An Indian History of the American West. New York: Holt, 1970.

Sample citation
"Big Eyes Schurz agreed to the arrest" (Brown 364).

C. When the listed name or title is stated in the text, cite only the page number.

Brown states that Big Eyes Schurz agreed to it (364).

D. For works of multiple volumes, use a colon after the volume number.

Sample bibliographic entry
Pepys, Samuel. The Diary of Samuel Pepys. Ed. Robert Latham and William Matthews. 10 vols. Berkeley: University of California Press, 1972.

Sample citation
On the last day of 1665, Pepys took the occasion of the new year to reflect, but not to celebrate (6: 341–2).

E. For works quoted in secondary sources, use the abbreviation "qtd. in."

Sample citation
According to R. Bentley, "reason and the facts outweigh a hundred manuscripts" (qtd. in "History" 615).

F. For classic works that are available in various editions, give the page number from the edition you are using, followed by a semicolon; then identify the section of the work to help people with other editions find the reference.

Footnotes and Endnotes

In addition to parenthetical documentation, footnoting and endnoting are two other accepted methods.

Footnotes Instead of putting citations in parentheses within the text, you can place them at the bottom or foot of the page; hence the term footnote. In this system, a number or symbol is placed in the text where the parenthetical citation would otherwise be, and a matching number or symbol at the bottom of the page identifies the citation. This textbook, for example, uses numbered footnotes in its literature selections to define obscure words and to provide background information.

Endnotes Many books use endnotes instead of footnotes. Endnotes are like footnotes in that a number or symbol is placed within the text, but the matching citations are compiled at the end of the book, chapter, or article rather than at the foot of the page. Footnote and endnote entries begin with the author's (or editor's) name in its usual order (first name, then last) and include publication information and a page reference.

EXAMPLE FOOTNOTE OR ENDNOTE CITATIONS

A book with one author
[1]Jean Paul-Sartre, *Being and Nothingness* (New York: The Citadel Press, 1966) 149-151.

A book with one editor and no single author
[2]Shannon Ravenel, ed., *New Stories from the South: The Year's Best,* 1992 (Chapel Hill, NC: Algonquin Books, 1992) 305.

A magazine article
[3]Andrew Gore, "Road Test: The Apple Powerbook," *MacUser,* December 1996: 72.

6 Applied English

6.1 Workplace & Consumer Documents

Applied English is English in the world of work or business, or *practical* English. Entering a new school, writing a professional letter, applying for a job, reading an instructional manual—these are but a few of the many situations you may encounter that involve **workplace and consumer documents.** You can apply English skills to many real-world situations, using your reading, writing, speaking, and listening abilities to help you be successful in any field or occupation you choose to pursue.

6.2 Writing a Step-by-Step Procedure

A **step-by-step procedure** is a how-to or process piece that uses directions to teach someone something new. Written procedures include textual information and sometimes graphics. Spoken procedures can be given as oral demonstrations. They can include textual and graphic information and other props. Examples of step-by-step procedures include an oral demonstration of how to saddle a horse; instructions on how to treat a sprained ankle; a video showing how to do the perfect lay-up in basketball; and an interactive Internet site allowing the user to design and send a bouquet of flowers.

Guidelines for Writing a Step-by-Step Procedure

- Demonstrate the steps. If you are showing how to make something, create several different samples to show each step of the procedure. For example, if you are showing how to make a wooden basket, you might want to display the raw materials, the started basket, the basket halfway finished, and then the finished product.
- Be prepared. The best way to prevent problems is to anticipate and plan for them. Rehearse an oral demonstration several times. If you are preparing the procedure in written form, go through your directions as if you knew nothing about the process. Anticipate what it would be like to learn this procedure for the first time. See if you can follow your own directions, or have a friend work through the procedure and offer suggestions for improvement.
- Acknowledge mistakes. If you are sharing a procedure "live" as an oral demonstration and you can't talk around or correct a mistake, tell your audience

what has gone wrong, and why. If you handle the situation in a calm, direct way, the audience may also learn from your mistake.
- Know your topic. The better you know it, the better you will be able to teach others.

6.3 Writing a Business Letter

A **business letter** is usually addressed to someone you do not know personally. Therefore, a formal tone is appropriate for such a letter. Following appropriate form is especially important when writing business letters. If you follow the correct form and avoid errors in spelling, grammar, usage, and mechanics, your letter will sound professional and make a good impression. Above the salutation, a business letter should contain the name and title of the person to whom you are writing and the name and address of that person's company or organization (see the model on the following page).

One common form for a business letter is the block form. In the **block form,** each part of the letter begins at the left margin. The parts are separated by line spaces.

Begin the salutation with the word *Dear,* followed by the courtesy or professional title used in the inside address, such as Ms., Mr., or Dr., and a colon. If you are not writing to a specific person, you may use a general salutation such as *Dear Sir or Madam.*

In the body of your letter, use a polite, formal tone and standard English. Make your points clearly, in as few words as possible.

End with a standard closing such as *Sincerely, Yours truly,* or *Respectfully yours.* Capitalize only the first word of the closing. Type your full name below the closing, leaving three or four blank lines for your signature. Sign your name below the closing in blue or black ink (never in red or green). Proofread your letter before you send it. Poor spelling, grammar, or punctuation can ruin an otherwise well-written business letter.

Guidelines for Writing a Business Letter

- Outline your main points before you begin.
- Word process your letter, if at all possible. Type or print it on clean 8 1/2" x 11" white or offwhite paper. Use only one side of the paper.

- Use the block form or another standard business letter form.
- Single space, leaving a blank line between each part, including paragraphs.
- Use a standard salutation and a standard closing.
- Stick to the subject. State your main idea clearly at the beginning of the letter. Keep the letter brief and informative.
- Check your spelling, grammar, usage, and punctuation carefully.

6.4 Application Letter

One of the most frequently used types of business letters is an **application letter,** which you would write to apply to a school or for a job. In an application letter, it is important to emphasize your knowledge about the business and the skills that you can bring to the position. The following is an example of a letter written to the owner of a dive shop to apply for a summer job.

EXAMPLE APPLICATION LETTER

498 Blue Key Rd.
Charleston, SC 02716

May 3, 2009

Mr. Davy Jones, Owner
Deep Sea Divers, Inc.
73 Ocean St.
Charleston, SC 02716

Dear Mr. Jones:

Please consider me for a position as a part-time clerk in your store for the coming summer. I understand that in the summer your business increases considerably and that you might need a conscientious, hardworking clerk. I can offer you considerable knowledge of snorkeling and diving equipment and experience working in a retail shop.

I will be available for work three days per week between June 1 and August 12. I am enclosing a résumé and references. Please contact me if you wish to set up an interview.

Sincerely,

Jorge Alvarez
Jorge Alvarez

6.5 Writing a Résumé

A **résumé** is a summary of a job applicant's career objectives, previous employment experience, and education. Its purpose is to help the applicant obtain the job he or she seeks. A résumé should be accompanied by a cover letter to the employer (see 6.4 Application Letter). Many helpful books and articles are available in libraries and bookstores on writing a résumé. Here are some guidelines.

Guidelines for Writing a Résumé

- Keep your information brief—to one page if possible. The goal of the resume is to give a potential employer a quick snapshot of your skills and abilities.

- Include all vital contact information—name, address, phone number, and e-mail address, if applicable—at the top of the page.
- Use headings to summarize information regarding job or career objective, education, work experience, skills, extracurricular activities, awards (if applicable), and references. Note that work experience should be listed starting with your most recent job and working backward.
- Key or type your résumé on white or cream-colored paper. Proofread it carefully for any errors; all facts must be accurate as well. Make it as neat as possible.
- You may list references, or simply state that they are available on request.

EXAMPLE RÉSUMÉ

Pat Mizos
5555 Elm Street
Anytown, NY 20111
(212) 555-5555

Objective:
To gain employment working in a summer camp program for children

Education:
Orchard High School, 2001 graduate

Major area of study: College preparatory, with concentration in science and physical education classes

Grade point average: 3.5 (B+)

Work experience:

Summer 1999	Summer youth counselor, Anytown Parks and Recreation Department
Summer 1998	Dishwasher, The Lobster Shack, Anytown, NY

Skills:
Intermediate level Spanish (3 years in high school)
Beginning level American Sign Language (1 semester at Anytown Vocational School)
Certified in CPR

Extracurricular Activities:
Swim team, tennis team, youth hotline crisis volunteer

References:
Available on request.

6.6 Writing a Memo

In businesses, schools, and other organizations, employees, students, and others often communicate by means of *memoranda,* or **memos.** For example, the director of a school drama club might write a memo to the editor of the student newspaper announcing tryouts for a new play. Some memos will be more informal than others. If you know the person to whom you are writing well or if the memo has only a social function such as announcing a party, the tone can be fairly informal. Most memos, however, have a fairly formal tone. A memo begins with a header. Often this header contains the word memorandum (the singular form of memoranda) and the following words and abbreviations:

TO:
FR: (from)
DT: (date)
RE: (regarding)
cc: (copy)

In the following example, Jack Hart, the president of the drama club at Wheaton High School, wishes to have the upcoming tryouts for his club's production of *Oklahoma!* announced in the school newspaper. He decides to write a memo to the editor of the paper, Lisa Lowry.

EXAMPLE MEMORANDUM

MEMORANDUM
TO: Lisa Lowry
FR: Jack Hart
RE: Tryouts for the spring production of Oklahoma!
DT: February 12, 2009
cc: Ms. Wise

Please include the following announcement in the upcoming issue of the Wheaton Crier: Tryouts for the Wheaton Drama Club's spring production of Oklahoma! will be held on Friday, February 26, at 6:00 p.m. in the Wheaton High School Auditorium. Students interested in performing in this musical should come to the auditorium at that time prepared to deliver a monologue less than two minutes long and to sing one song from the musical. Copies of the music and lyrics can be obtained from the sponsor of the Wheaton Drama Club, Ms. Wise. For additional information, please contact Ms. Wise or any member of the Drama Club.

Thank you.

6.7 Writing a Proposal

A **proposal** outlines a project that a person wants to complete. It presents a summary of an idea, the reasons why the idea is important, and an outline of how the project would be carried out. Because the proposal audience is people who can help carry out the proposal, a proposal is both informative and persuasive.

EXAMPLES

- You want funding for an art project that would benefit your community

- Your student council proposes a clothing drive for disaster relief

- You and a group of your friends want to help organize a summer program for teens your age

Proposal: To host a community arts day at the park behind Jordan High School that would allow high school artists to try new art forms and to exhibit their work.

Rationale: The art students at Jordan High School have shown there is a lot of talent here worth sharing. An Art Day would let everyone interested get involved, and build school and community pride. Art students could lead others through simple art projects, and people could learn new things. At the end, the art could be displayed in an art fair at the community park. Artwork and refreshments could be sold, with all proceeds going to the Jordan High School Art Scholarship.

Schedule/Preparation Outline

Present proposal to School Pride Committee	April 1
Meet with art students to organize event	April 6-15
Contact area businesses for donations	April 6-15
Advertise event and sell tickets	April 16-25
Have practice day to make sure art activities work	April 20
Hold community Arts Day	April 26

BUDGET

Expenses

Posters, mailings, tickets	$30
Art supplies	$200
Refreshments	$75

Note: Expenses will be less if we ask area businesses to help sponsor event

Total estimated expenses	$305

Income

Ticket sales (Estimated 150 tickets sold @ $3 each)	$450
Refreshment sales	$100
Earnings from art sold at exhibit	$200
Total estimated income	$750
Net proceeds	$445

Note: All proceeds will be donated to the Jordan High School Art Scholarship Fund

Guidelines for Writing a Proposal

- Keep the tone positive, courteous, and respectful.
- State your purpose and rationale briefly and clearly.
- Give your audience all necessary information. A proposal with specific details makes it clear what you want approved, and why your audience—often a committee or someone in authority—should approve it.
- Use standard, formal English.
- Format your proposal with headings, lists, and schedules to make your proposed project easy to understand and approve.

6.8 Writing a Press Release

A **press release** is an informative piece intended for publication in local news media. A press release is usually written to promote an upcoming event or to inform the community of a recent event that promotes, or strengthens, an individual or organization.

EXAMPLES

- a brief notice from the choir director telling the community of the upcoming spring concert

- an informative piece by the district public information officer announcing that your school's art instructor has been named the state Teacher of the Year

Guidelines for Writing a Press Release

- Know your purpose. What do you want your audience to know from reading your piece?
- Use the 5 *Ws* and an *H—who, what, where, why, when,* and *how—*questioning strategy to convey the important information at the beginning of your story.
- Keep the press release brief. Local media are more likely to publish or broadcast your piece if it is short and to the point.
- Include contact information such as your name, phone number, and times you can be reached. Make this information available to the media representative or, if applicable, to the reading public.
- Type your press release using conventional manuscript form. Make sure the text is double-spaced and that you leave margins of at least an inch on all sides of the page.
- At the beginning of the press release, key the day's date and the date the information is to be released. (You can type "For immediate release" or designate the date you would like the press release to be printed in the newspaper.)
- At the end of the press release, key the word "END."
- Check a previous newspaper for deadline information or call the newspaper office to make sure you get your material there on time. Address the press release to the editor.

6.9 Writing a Public Service Announcement

A **public service announcement,** or **PSA,** is a brief, informative article intended to be helpful to the community. PSAs are written by non-profit organizations and concerned citizens for print in local newspapers, for broadcast by television and radio stations, and for publication on the Internet.

EXAMPLES

- an article by the American Cancer Society outlining early warning signs of cancer

- an announcement promoting Safety Week

- an informative piece telling coastal residents what to do during a hurricane

Guidelines for Writing a Public Service Announcement

- Know your purpose. What do you want your audience to know from reading or hearing your piece?
- State your information as objectively as possible.
- As with most informative writing, use the 5 *Ws* and an *H—who, what, where, why, when,* and *how—*questioning strategy to get your important information at the beginning of your story.
- Keep your announcement brief. Local media are more likely to publish or broadcast your piece if it is short and to the point.
- Include contact information in case the media representative has any questions. You might also include contact information in the PSA itself.
- Key or type your PSA in conventional manuscript form. Make sure the text is double-spaced and that you leave margins of at least an inch on all sides of the page.
- At the end of the PSA, key "END" to designate the end of the announcement.
- Be aware of print and broadcast deadlines and make sure your material is sent on time.

7.1 Verbal and Nonverbal Communication

Human beings use both verbal and nonverbal communication to convey meaning and exchange ideas. When a person expresses meaning through words, he or she is using verbal communication. When a person expresses meaning without using words, for example by standing up straight or shaking his or her head, he or she is using nonverbal communication. When we speak to another person, we usually think that the meaning of what we say comes chiefly from the words we use. However, as much as 60% of the meaning of a message may be communicated nonverbally.

Elements of Verbal Communication

Element	Description	Guidelines for Speakers
Volume	loudness or softness	Vary your volume, but make sure that you can be heard.
Melody, Pitch	highness or lowness	Vary your pitch. Avoid speaking in a monotone (at a single pitch).
Pace	speed	Vary the speed of your delivery to suit what you are saying.
Tone	emotional quality	Suit your tone to your message, and vary it appropriately as you speak.
Enunciation	clearness with which words are spoken	When speaking before a group, pronounce your words more precisely than you would in ordinary conversation.

Elements of Nonverbal Communication

Element	Description	Guidelines for Speakers
Eye contact	Looking audience members in the eye	Make eye contact regularly with people in your audience. Try to include all audience members.
Facial expression	Using your face to show your emotions	Use expressions to emphasize your message — raised eyebrows for a question, pursed lips for concentration, eyebrows lowered for anger, and so on.
Gesture	Meaningful motions of the arms and hands	Use gestures to emphasize points. Be careful, however, not to overuse gestures. Too many can be distracting.
Posture	Position of the body	Keep your spine straight and head high, but avoid appearing stiff. Stand with your arms and legs slightly open, except when adopting other postures to express particular emotions.
Proximity	Distance from audience	Keep the right amount of distance between yourself and the audience. You should be a comfortable distance away, but not so far away that the audience cannot hear you.

7.2 Listening Skills

Learning to listen well is essential not only for success in personal life but also for success in school and, later, on the job. It is estimated that high school and college students spend over half their waking time listening to others, yet most people are rather poor listeners.

ACTIVE VERSUS PASSIVE LISTENING

Effective listening requires skill and concentration. The mind of a good listener is focused on what a speaker is trying to communicate. In other words, an effective listener is an **active listener.** Ineffective listeners view listening as a passive activity, something that simply "happens" without any effort on their part. **Passive listening** is nothing more than hearing sounds. This type of listening can cause misunderstanding and miscommunication.

ADAPTING LISTENING SKILLS

Just as different situations require different types of listening, different tasks or goals may also require different listening strategies and skills.

Listening for Comprehension

Listening for comprehension means listening for information or ideas communicated by other people. For example, you are listening for comprehension when you try to understand directions to a friend's house or your teacher's explanation of how to conduct a classroom debate.

When listening for comprehension, your goal is to reach understanding, so it is important to recognize and remember the key information or ideas presented. Concentrate on getting the **main points or major ideas** of a message rather than all the supporting details. This can prevent you from becoming overwhelmed by the amount of information presented.

You might also use a technique called **clarifying and confirming** to help you better remember and understand information. The technique involves paraphrasing or repeating back to the speaker in your own words the key information presented to make sure that you have understood correctly. If the situation prevents you from using the technique—for instance, if there is no opportunity for you to respond directly to the speaker—it can still be helpful to rephrase the information in your own words in your head to help you remember and understand it.

Listening Critically

Listening critically means listening to a message in order to comprehend and evaluate it. When listening for comprehension, you usually assume that the information presented is true. Critical listening, on the other hand, includes **comprehending and judging** the arguments and appeals in a message in order to decide whether to accept or reject them. Critical listening is most useful when you encounter a persuasive message such as a sales pitch, advertisement, campaign speech, or news editorial.

When evaluating a persuasive message, you might consider the following:

- Is the speaker trustworthy and qualified to speak about this subject?
- Does the speaker present logical arguments supported by solid facts?
- Does the speaker use unproven assumptions to make a case?
- Does the speaker use questionable motivational appeals, such as appeals to fear or to prejudice?

These questions can help you decide whether or not to be convinced by a persuasive message.

Listening to Learn Vocabulary

Listening to learn vocabulary involves a very different kind of listening because the focus is on learning new words and how to use them properly. For instance, you have a conversation with someone who has a more advanced vocabulary and use this as an opportunity to learn new words. The key to listening in order to learn vocabulary is to **pay attention to how words are used in context.** Sometimes it is possible to figure out what an unfamiliar word means based simply on how the word is used in a sentence.

Once you learn a new word, try to use it several times so it becomes more familiar and you become comfortable using it. Also be sure to look up the word in a dictionary to find out whether it has other meanings or connotations of which you are not aware.

Listening for Appreciation

Listening for appreciation means listening purely for enjoyment or entertainment. You might listen appreciatively to a singer, a comedian, a storyteller, an acting company, or a humorous speaker. Appreciation is a very individual matter and there are no rules about how to appreciate something. However, as with all forms of listening, listening for appreciation requires attention and concentration.

7.3 Collaborative Learning and Communication

Collaboration is the act of working with one or more other people to achieve a goal. Many common learning situations involve collaboration.

- Participating in a small-group discussion
- Doing a small-group project
- Tutoring another student or being tutored
- Doing peer evaluation

Guidelines for Group Discussion

- **Listen actively** during the discussion. Maintain eye contact with the speakers. Make notes on what they say. Mentally translate what they say into your own words. Think critically about whether you agree or disagree with each speaker, and why.
- **Be polite.** Wait for your turn to speak. Do not interrupt others. If your discussion has a group leader, ask to be recognized before speaking by raising your hand.

- **Participate in the discussion.** At appropriate times, make your own comments or ask questions of other speakers.
- **Stick to the discussion topic.** Do not introduce unrelated or irrelevant ideas.
- For a formal discussion, **assign roles.** Choose a group leader to guide the discussion and a secretary to record the minutes (the main ideas and proposals made by group members). Also draw up an agenda before the discussion, listing items to be discussed.

Guidelines for Projects

- **Choose a group leader** to conduct the meetings of your project group.
- **Set a goal** for the group, some specific outcome or set of outcomes that you want to bring about.
- **Make a list of tasks** that need to be performed.
- Make a schedule for completing the tasks, including dates and times for completion of each task.
- **Make an assignment sheet.** Assign certain tasks to particular group members. Be fair in distributing the work to be done.
- **Set times for future meetings.** You might want to schedule meetings to evaluate your progress toward your goal as well as meetings to actually carry out specific tasks.
- **Meet to evaluate** your overall success when the project is completed. Also look at the individual contributions of each group member.

7.4 Asking and Answering Questions

There are many situations in which you will find it useful to ask questions of a speaker, or in which you will be asked questions about a presentation. Often a formal speech or presentation will be followed by a question-and-answer period. Keep the following guidelines in mind when asking or answering questions.

Guidelines for Asking and Answering Questions

- **Wait to be recognized.** In most cases, it is appropriate to raise your hand if you have a question and to wait for the speaker or moderator to call on you.

- **Make questions clear and direct.** The longer your question, the less chance a speaker will understand it. Make your questions short and to the point.
- **Do not debate or argue.** If you disagree with a speaker, the question-and-answer period is not the time to hash out an argument. Ask to speak with the speaker privately after the presentation is over, or agree on a later time and place to meet.
- **Do not take others' time.** Be courteous to other audience members and allow them time to ask questions. If you have a follow-up question, ask the speaker if you may proceed with your follow up.
- **Do not give a speech.** Sometimes audience members are more interested in expressing their own opinion than in asking the speaker a question. Do not give in to the temptation to present a speech of your own.
- **Come prepared** for a question-and-answer period. Although you can never predict the exact questions that people will ask you, you can anticipate many questions that are likely to be asked. Rehearse aloud your answers to the most difficult questions.
- **Be patient.** It may take some time for audience members to formulate questions in response to your speech. Give the audience a moment to do so. Don't run back to your seat the minute your speech is over, or if there is an awkward pause after you invite questions.
- **Be direct and succinct.** Be sure to answer the question directly as it has been asked, and to provide a short but clear answer.

7.5 Conducting an Interview

In an interview, you meet with someone and ask him or her questions. Interviewing experts is an excellent way to gain information about a particular topic. For example, if you are interested in writing about the art of making pottery, you might interview an art teacher, a professional potter, or the owner of a ceramics shop.

When planning an interview, you should do some background research on your subject and think carefully about questions you would like to ask. Write out a list of questions, including some about the person's background as well as about your topic. Other questions might occur to you as the interview proceeds, but it is best to be prepared. For guidelines on being a good listener, see Language Arts Handbook, 7.2 Listening Skills. Here are some more tips for interviewing:

Guidelines for Conducting an Interview

- **Set up a time in advance.** Don't just try to work questions into a regular conversation. Set aside time to meet in a quiet place where both you and the person you are interviewing can focus on the interview.
- **Explain the purpose** of the interview. Be sure the person you are interviewing knows what you want to find out and why you need to know it. This will help him or her to answer your questions in a way that is more useful and helpful to you.
- **Ask mostly open-ended questions.** These are questions that allow the person you are interviewing to express a personal point of view. They cannot be answered with a simple "yes" or "no" nor a brief statement of fact. The following are all examples of open-ended questions:

  "Why did you become a professional potter?"
  "What is the most challenging thing about owning your own ceramics shop?"
  "What advice would you give to a beginning potter?"

  One of the most valuable questions to ask at the end of the interview is, "What would you like to add that I haven't asked about?" This can provide some of the most interesting or vital information of all.
- **Tape-record the interview** (if possible). Then you can review the interview at your leisure. Be sure to ask the person you are interviewing whether or not you can tape-record the session. If the person refuses, accept his or her decision.
- **Take notes** during the interview, whether or not you are also tape-recording it. Write down the main points and some key words to help you remember details. Record the person's most important statements word for word.
- Clarify spelling and get permission for quotes. Be sure to get the correct spelling of the person's name and to ask permission to quote his or her statements.
- **End the interview on time.** Do not extend the interview beyond the time limits of your appointment. The person you are interviewing has been courteous enough to give you his or her time. Return this courtesy by ending the interview on time, thanking the person for his or her help, and leaving.

- **Write up the results** of the interview as soon as possible after you conduct it. Over time, what seemed like a very clear note may become unclear or confusing. If you are unclear of something important that the person said, contact him or her and ask for clarification.

7.6 Public Speaking

The fear of speaking in public, although quite common and quite strong in some people, can be overcome by preparing a speech thoroughly and practicing positive thinking and relaxation. Learning how to give a speech is a valuable skill, one that you most likely will find much opportunity to use in the future.

The nature of a speech, whether formal or informal, is usually determined by the situation or context in which it is presented. **Formal speeches** usually call for a greater degree of preparation, might require special attire such as a suit or dress, and are often presented to larger groups who attend specifically to hear the presentation. A formal speech situation might exist when presenting an assigned speech to classmates, giving a presentation to a community group or organization, or presenting a speech at an awards ceremony. **Informal speech** situations are more casual and might include telling a story among friends, giving a pep talk to your team at halftime, or presenting a toast at the dinner table.

Types of Speeches

The following are the four main types of speeches:

- **Extemporaneous:** a speech in which the speaker refers to notes occasionally. As with writing, speeches usually have a specific purpose and message.
- **Informative:** used to share new and useful information with your audience. Informative speeches are based on fact, not opinion. Examples would include a speech on how to do something or a speech about an event.
- **Persuasive:** used to convince your audience to side with your opinion and adopt your plan. The speaker tries to persuade the audience to believe something, do something, or change their ways. Persuasive speeches use facts and research to support, analyze, and sell an opinion and plan. Martin Luther King's famous "I Have a Dream" speech and Nelson Mandela's "Glory and Hope" speech are examples of persuasive speeches.

- **Commemorative:** honors an individual for outstanding accomplishments and exemplary character. Examples would be a speech honoring someone such as a historical figure, leader, teacher, athlete, relative, or celebrity.

Guidelines for Giving a Speech

A speech should always include a beginning, a middle, and an end. The **beginning,** or introduction, of your speech should spark the audience's interest, present your central idea, and briefly preview your main points. The **middle,** or body, of your speech should expand upon each of your main points in order to support the central idea. The **end,** or conclusion, of your speech should be memorable and should give your audience a sense of completion.

- **Be sincere and enthusiastic.** Feel what you are speaking about. Apathy is infectious and will quickly spread to your audience.
- **Maintain good but relaxed posture.** Don't slouch or lean. It's fine to move around a bit; it releases normal nervous tension. Keep your hands free to gesture naturally instead of holding on to notecards, props, or the podium so much that you will "tie up" your hands.
- **Speak slowly.** Oral communication is more difficult than written language and visual images for audiences to process and understand. Practice pausing. Don't be afraid of silence. Focus on communicating with the audience. By looking for feedback from the audience, you will be able to pace yourself appropriately.
- **Maintain genuine eye contact.** Treat the audience as individuals, not as a mass of people. Look at individual faces.
- Speak in a genuine, relaxed, conversational tone. Don't act or stiffen up. Just be yourself.
- **Communicate.** Focus on conveying your message, not "getting through" the speech. Focus on communicating with the audience, not speaking at or to it.
- **Use strategic pauses.** Pause briefly before proceeding to the next major point, before direct quotations, and to allow important or more complex bits of information to sink in.
- **Remain confident and composed.** Remember that listeners are generally "for you" while you are speaking, and signs of nervousness are usually undetectable. To overcome initial nervousness, take two or three deep breaths as you are stepping up to speak.

7.7 Oral Interpretation

Oral interpretation is the process of presenting a dramatic reading of a literary work or group of works. The presentation should be sufficiently dramatic to convey to the audience a sense of the particular qualities of the work. Here are the steps you need to follow to prepare and present an oral interpretation:

Guidelines for Oral Interpretation

1. **Choose a cutting.** The cutting may be a single piece; a selection from a single piece; or several short, related pieces on a single topic or theme.
2. **Write** the introduction and any necessary transitions. The introduction should mention the name of each piece, the author, and, if appropriate, the translator. It should also present the overall topic or theme of the interpretation. Transitions should introduce and connect the parts of the interpretation.
3. **Rehearse,** using appropriate variations in volume, pitch, pace, stress, tone, gestures, facial expressions, and body language. If your cutting contains different voices (a narrator's voice and characters' voices, for example), distinguish them. Try to make your verbal and nonverbal expression mirror what the piece is saying. However, avoid movement — that's for drama. Practice in front of an audience or mirror or use a video camera or tape recorder.
4. **Present** your oral interpretation. Before actually presenting your interpretation, relax and adopt a confident attitude. If you begin to feel stage fright, try to concentrate on the work you are presenting and the audience, not on yourself.

Interpreting Poetry

Here are some additional considerations as you prepare to interpret a poem. The way you prepare your interpretation of a poem will depend on whether the poem you have chosen is a lyric poem, a narrative poem, or a dramatic poem.

- A **lyric poem** has a single speaker who reports his or her own emotions.
- A **narrative poem** tells a story. Usually a narrative poem has lines belonging to narrator, or person who is telling the story. The narrator may or may not take part in the action.

- A **dramatic poem** contains characters who speak. A dramatic poem may be a lyric, in which characters simply report emotions, or a narrative, which tells a story. A dramatic monologue presents a single speaker at a moment of crisis or self-revelation and may be either lyric or narrative.

Before attempting to dramatize any poem, read through the poem carefully several times. Make sure that you understand it well. To check your understanding, try to paraphrase the poem, or restate its ideas, line by line, in your own words.

7.8 Telling a Story

A story or narrative is a series of events linked together in some meaningful fashion. We use narratives constantly in our daily lives: to make a journal entry, to tell a joke, to report a news story, to recount an historical event, to record a laboratory experiment, and so on. When creating a narrative, consider all of the following elements:

Guidelines for Storytelling

- **Decide on your purpose.** Every story has a point or purpose. It may be simply to entertain or to share a personal experience, but it may have a moral or lesson.
- **Select a focus.** The focus for your narrative will depend largely on your purpose in telling it.
- **Choose your point of view.** The storyteller or narrator determines the point of view from which the story will be told. You can choose to speak in the *first person,* either as a direct participant in the events or as an observer (real or imagined) who witnessed the events first hand, or in the *third person* voice to achieve greater objectivity.
- **Determine sequence of events.** The sequence of events refers to the order in which they are presented. Although it might seem obvious that stories should "begin at the beginning," this is not always the best approach. Some narratives begin with the turning point of the story to create a sense of drama and capture the listener's interest. Others begin at the end of the story and present the events leading up to this point in hindsight. Wherever you choose to begin the story, your narrative should present events in a logical fashion and establish a clear sense of direction for your listeners.

- **Determine duration of events.** Duration refers to how long something lasts. Everyone has experienced an event that seemed to last for hours, when in reality it only took minutes to occur. A good storyteller can likewise manipulate the duration of events in order to affect the way listeners experience them.
- **Select details carefully.** Make them consistent with your focus and make sure they are necessary to your purpose. A well-constructed story should flow smoothly, and should not get bogged down by irrelevant or unnecessary detail. Details can also establish the tone and style of the story and affect how listeners react to the events being described.
- **Choose characters.** All stories include characters, who need to be developed so that they become real for listeners. Try to provide your listeners with vivid, concrete descriptions of the mental and physical qualities of important characters in the story. Remember that listeners need to understand and relate to the characters in order to appreciate their behavior.
- **Create dialogue.** Although it is possible to tell a story in which the characters do not speak directly, conversation and dialogue help to add life to a story. As with detail, dialogue should be used carefully. It is important that dialogue sound authentic, relate to the main action of the story, and advance the narrative.

7.9 Participating in a Debate

A debate is a contest in which two people or groups of people defend opposite sides of a proposition in an attempt to convince a judge or audience to agree with their views. Propositions are statements of fact, value, or policy that usually begin with the word "resolved." The following are examples of typical propositions for debate:

RESOLVED   That lie detector tests are inaccurate. (proposition of fact)

RESOLVED   That imagination is more important than knowledge. (proposition of value)

RESOLVED   That Congress should prohibit the sale of handguns to private citizens. (proposition of policy)

The two sides in a debate are usually called the affirmative and the negative. The affirmative takes the "pro" side of the debate and argues in favor of the proposition, while the negative takes the "con" side and argues against the proposition. Using a single proposition to focus the debate ensures that the two sides argue or clash over a common topic. This allows the participants in the debate to develop their logic and ability to argue their positions persuasively.

Suggestions for Participating in a Debate

- **Be prepared.** In a debate, it will never be possible to anticipate all the arguments your opponent might make. However, by conducting careful and through research on both sides of the issue, you should be able to prepare for the most likely arguments you will encounter. You can prepare briefs or notes on particular issues in advance of the debate to save yourself preparation time during the debate.
- **Be organized.** Because a debate involves several speeches that concern the same basic arguments or issues, it is important that you remain organized during the debate. When attacking or refuting an opponent's argument, or when advancing or defending your own argument, be sure to follow a logical organizational pattern to avoid confusing the audience or the other team.
- **Take notes** by turning a long sheet of paper sideways. Draw one column for each speaker, taking notes on each speech going down one column, and recording notes about a particular argument or issue across the page as it is discussed in each successive speech.
- **Be audience-centered.** In the argument with your opponent it is easy to forget the goal of the debate: to persuade your audience that your case is correct.
- **Prepare in advance** for the most likely arguments your opponents will raise. Use time sparingly to organize your materials and think of responses to unanticipated arguments. Save time for the end of the debate, during rebuttal speeches, when it will be more valuable.

7.10 Preparing a Multimedia Presentation

Whether you use a simple overhead projector and transparencies or a PowerPoint presentation that involves graphics, video, and sound, multimedia technology can add an important visual element to a presentation. Consider the following guidelines to create a multimedia presentation:

Guidelines for a Multimedia Presentation

- **Use effective audio-visuals** that enhance understanding. The multimedia elements should add to the verbal elements, not distract from them. Be sure the content of the presentation is understandable, and that the amount of information—both verbal and visual—will not overwhelm audience members.
- **Make sure the presentation is clearly audible and visible.** Video clips or graphics may appear blurry on a projection screen, or may not be visible to audience members in the back or on the sides of the room. Audio clips may sound muffled or may echo in a larger room or a room with different acoustics. When creating a multimedia presentation, be sure the presentation can be easily and heard from all parts of the room.
- **Become familiar with the equipment.** Well before the presentation, be sure you know how to operate the equipment you will need, that you know how to troubleshoot if the equipment malfunctions, and that the equipment you will use during the presentation is the same as that which you practiced with.
- **Check the room** to be sure it can accommodate your needs. Once you know where you will make your presentation, be sure the necessary electrical outlets and extension cords are available, that lights can be dimmed or turned off as needed, that the room can accommodate the equipment you will use, etc.
- **Rehearse with the equipment.** Make sure that you can operate the equipment while speaking at the same time. Be sure that the multimedia elements are coordinated with other parts of your presentation. If you will need to turn the lights off in the room, make sure you can operate the equipment in the dark and can still see your notecards.

8.1 Preparing for Tests

Tests are a common part of school life. You take tests in your classes to show what you have learned in each class. In addition, you might have to take one or more standardized tests each year. Standardized tests measure your skills against local, state, or national standards and may determine whether you graduate, what kind of job you can get, or which college you can attend. Learning test-taking strategies will help you succeed on the tests you are required to take.

The following guidelines will help you to prepare for and take tests on the material you have covered in class.

Preparing for a Test

- **Know what will be covered on the test.** If you have questions about what will be covered, ask your teacher.
- **Make a study plan** to allow yourself time to go over the material. Avoid last-minute cramming.
- **Review the subject matter.** Use the graphic organizers and notes you made as you read as well as notes you took in class. Review any study questions given by your teacher.
- **Make lists** of important names, dates, definitions, or events. Ask a friend or family member to quiz you on them.
- **Try to predict questions** that may be on the test. Make sure you can answer them.
- **Get plenty of sleep** the night before the test. Eat a nutritious breakfast on the morning of the test.

Taking a Test

- **Survey the test** to see how long it is and what types of questions are included.
- **Read all directions and questions carefully.** Make sure you know exactly what to do.
- **Plan your time.** Answer easy questions first. Allow extra time for complicated questions. If a question seems too difficult, skip it and go back to it later. Work quickly, but do not rush.
- **Save time for review.** Once you have finished, look back over the test. Double-check your answers, but do not change answers too readily. Your first ideas are often correct.

8.2 Answering Objective Questions

An **objective question** has a single correct answer. The following chart describes the kinds of questions you may see on objective tests. It also gives you strategies for tackling each kind of question.

Description	Guidelines
True/False. You are given a statement and asked to tell whether the statement is true or false.	<ul><li>If any part of a statement is false, then the statement is false.</li><li>Words like *all, always, never,* and *every* often appear in false statements.</li><li>Words like *some, usually, often,* and *most* often appear in true statements.</li><li>If you do not know the answer, guess. You have a 50/50 chance of being right.</li></ul>
Matching. You are asked to match items in one column with items in another column.	<ul><li>Check the directions. See if each item is used only once. Also check to see if some are not used at all.</li><li>Read all items before starting.</li><li>Match those items you know first.</li><li>Cross out items as you match them.</li></ul>
Multiple Choice. You are asked to choose the best answer from a group of answers given.	<ul><li>Read *all* choices first.</li><li>Rule out incorrect answers.</li><li>Choose the answer that is most complete or accurate.</li><li>Pay particular attention to choices such as *none of the above* or *all of the above.*</li></ul>
Short Answer. You are asked to answer the question with a word, phrase, or sentence.	<ul><li>Read the directions to find out if you are required to answer in complete sentences.</li><li>Use correct spelling, grammar, punctuation, and capitalization.</li><li>If you cannot think of the answer, move on. Something in another question might remind you of the answer.</li></ul>

8.3 Strategies for Taking Standardized Tests

Standardized tests are given to large groups of students in a school district, a state, or a country. Statewide tests measure how well students are meeting the learning standards the state has set. Other tests, such as the SAT (Scholastic Aptitude

Test) or ACT, are used to help determine admission to colleges and universities. Others must be taken to enter certain careers. These tests are designed to measure overall ability or skills acquired so far. Learning how to take standardized tests will help you to achieve your goals.

You can get better at answering standardized test questions by practicing the types of questions that will be on the test. Use the Test Practice Workshop questions in this book and other sample questions your teacher gives you to practice. Think aloud with a partner or small group about how you would answer each question. Notice how other students tackle the questions and learn from what they do.

In addition, remember these points:
- **Rule out some choices** when you are not sure of the answer. Then guess from the remaining possibilities.
- **Skip questions that seem too difficult** and go back to them later. Be aware, however, that most tests allow you to go back only within a section.
- **Follow instructions exactly.** The test monitor will read instructions to you, and instructions may also be printed in your test booklet. Make sure you know what to do.

8.4 Answering Essay Questions

An essay question asks you to write an answer that shows what you know about a particular subject. A simplified writing process like the one below will help you tackle questions like this.

1. Analyze the Question

Essay questions contain clues about what is expected of you. Sometimes you will find key words that will help you determine exactly what is being asked. See the chart below for some typical key words and their meanings.

Key Words for Essay Questions	
analyze; identify	break into parts, and describe the parts and how they are related
compare	tell how two or more subjects are similar; in some cases, also mention how they are different
contrast	tell how two or more subjects are different from each other
describe	give enough facts about or qualities of a subject to make it clear to someone who is unfamiliar with it

discuss	provide an overview and analysis; use details for support
evaluate; argue	judge an idea or concept, telling whether you think it is good or bad, or whether you agree or disagree with it
explain	make a subject clearer, providing supporting details and examples
interpret	tell the meaning and importance of an event or concept
justify	explain or give reasons for decisions; be persuasive
prove	provide factual evidence or reasons for a statement
summarize	state only the main points of an event, concept, or debate

2. Plan Your Answer

As soon as the essay prompt is clear to you, collect and organize your thoughts about it. First, gather ideas using whatever method is most comfortable for you. If you don't immediately have ideas, try freewriting for five minutes. When you **freewrite,** you write whatever comes into your head without letting your hand stop moving. You might also gather ideas in a cluster chart like the one below. Then, organize the ideas you came up with. A simple outline or chart can help.

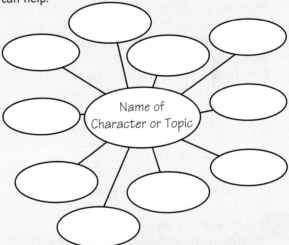

Name of Character or Topic

3. Write Your Answer

Start with a clear thesis statement in your opening paragraph. Your **thesis statement** is a single sentence that sums up your answer to the essay question. Then follow your organizational plan to provide support for your thesis. Devote one paragraph to each major point of support for your thesis. Use plenty of details as evidence for each point. Write quickly and keep moving. Don't spend too much time on any single paragraph, but try to make your answer as complete as possible. End your essay with a concluding sentence that sums up your major points.

4. Revise Your Answer

Make sure you have answered all parts of the question and included everything you were asked to include. Check to see that you have supplied enough details to support your thesis. Check for errors in grammar, spelling, punctuation, and paragraph breaks. Make corrections to your answer.

8.5 Answering Multiple-Choice Questions

On many standardized tests, questions are multiple choice and have a single correct answer. The guidelines below will help you answer these kinds of questions effectively.

- **Read each question carefully.** Pay special attention to any words that are bolded, italicized, written in all capital letters, or otherwise emphasized.
- **Read all choices** before selecting an answer.
- **Eliminate** any answers that do not make sense, that disagree with what you remember from reading a passage, or that seem too extreme. Also, if two answers have exactly the same meaning, you can eliminate both.
- **Beware of distractors.** These are incorrect answers that look attractive because they are partially correct. They might contain a common misunderstanding, or they might apply the right information in the wrong way. Distractors are based on common mistakes students make.
- **Fill in circles completely** on your answer sheet when you have selected your answer.

8.6 Answering Reading Comprehension Questions

Reading comprehension questions ask you to read a passage and answer questions about it. These questions measure how well you perform the essential reading skills. Many of the Reading Assessment questions that follow each literature selection in this book are reading comprehension questions. Use them

to help you learn how to answer these types of questions correctly. Work through each question with a partner using a "think aloud." Say out loud how you are figuring out the answer. Talk about how you can eliminate incorrect answers and determine the correct choice. You may want to make notes as you eliminate answers. By practicing this thinking process with a partner, you will be more prepared to use it silently when you have to take a standardized test.

The following steps will help you answer the reading comprehension questions on standardized tests.

- **Preview the passage and questions** and predict what the text will be about.
- **Use the reading strategies** you have learned to read the passage. Mark the text and make notes in the margins.
- **Reread the first question carefully.** Make sure you know exactly what it is asking.
- **Read the answers.** If you are sure of the answer, select it and move on. If not, go on to the next step.
- **Scan the passage** to look for key words related to the question. When you find a key word, slow down and read carefully.
- **Answer the question** and go on to the next one. Answer each question in this way.

8.7 Answering Synonym and Antonym Questions

Synonym or antonym questions give you a word and ask you to select the word that has the same meaning (for a synonym) or the opposite meaning (for an antonym). You must select the best answer even if none is exactly correct. For this type of question, you should consider all the choices to see which is best. Always notice whether you are looking for a synonym or an antonym. You will usually find both among the answers.

8.8 Answering Sentence Completion Questions

Sentence completion questions present you with a sentence that has two words missing. You must select the pair of words that best completes the sentence. The key to this kind of question is to make sure that both parts of the answer you have selected work well in the sentence.

8.9 Answering Constructed-Response Questions

In addition to multiple-choice questions, many standardized tests include **constructed-response questions** that require you to write essay answers in the test booklet. Constructed-response questions might ask you to identify key ideas or examples from the text by writing a sentence about each. In other cases, you will be asked to write a paragraph in response to a question about the selection and to use specific details from the passage to support your answer.

Other constructed-response questions ask you to apply information or ideas from a text in a new way. Another question might ask you to use information from the text in a particular imaginary situation. As you answer these questions, remember that you are being evaluated based on your understanding of the text. Although these questions may offer opportunities to be creative, you should still include ideas, details, and examples from the passage you have just read.

The following tips will help you answer constructed-response questions effectively:

- **Skim the questions first.** Predict what the passage will be about.
- **Use reading strategies** as you read. Underline information that relates to the questions and make notes. After you have finished reading, you can decide which of the details you have gathered to use in your answers.
- **List the most important points** to include in each answer. Use the margins of your test booklet or a piece of scrap paper.
- **Number the points** you have listed to show the order in which they should be included.
- **Draft your answer to fit** in the space provided. Include as much detail as possible in the space you have.
- **Revise and proofread** your answers as you have time.

Literary Terms Handbook

ACT. An **act** is a major division of a play. There are five acts in Shakespeare's *The Tragedy of Julius Caesar* (Unit 4).

ALLEGORY. An **allegory** is a work in which characters, events, or settings symbolize, or represent, something else. Spirituals such as "Go Down, Moses" (Unit 2) are often allegorical. "Go Down, Moses" is on one level about Moses demanding freedom for the Jews from the Pharaoh in Egypt, but on another level it can be read as being about slaves seeking their freedom in the United States.

ALLITERATION. **Alliteration** is the repetition of initial consonant sounds. Though alliteration usually refers to sounds at the beginnings of words, it can also be used to refer to sounds within words. The following lines from Joy Harjo's poem "Remember" (Unit 3) contain an example of alliteration:

> Remember the <u>s</u>ky you were born under,
> know each of the <u>s</u>tar's <u>s</u>tories.

ALLUSION. An **allusion** is a reference to a well-known person, event, object, or work from history or literature. For example, Langston Hughes's biography "Harriet Tubman: The Moses of Her People" (Unit 2) contains an allusion to Frederick Douglass, a former slave and influential lecturer and writer.

ANALOGY. An **analogy** is a comparison of two things that are alike in some ways but otherwise quite different. Often an analogy explains or describes something unfamiliar by comparing it to something more familiar.

ANECDOTE. An **anecdote** is usually a short account of an interesting, amusing, or biographical incident. Anecdotes are sometimes used in nonfiction writing as examples to help support an idea or opinion. In "Short Assignments" (Unit 2), Anne Lamott tells several anecdotes to underscore the idea that the writing process can be, but doesn't have to be, frustrating.

ANTAGONIST. An **antagonist** is a character or force in a literary work that is in conflict with a main character, or protagonist. The antagonist of Poe's story "The Masque of the Red Death" (Unit 1) is the Red Death, a dreaded and deadly disease. *See* Character.

APOSTROPHE. **Apostrophe,** which is common in poetry and speeches, is a method by which a speaker turns from the audience as a whole to address a single person or thing. For example, in *The Tragedy of Julius Caesar* (Unit 4), Antony turns from the audience and addresses a speech to the murdered Caesar:

> O pardon me, thou bleeding piece of earth,
> That I am meek and gentle with these butchers!
> Thou art the ruins of the noblest man
> That ever lived in the tide of times…
>   (III.i.254–257)

ARCHETYPE. An **archetype** is a story, character, or theme that represents a familiar pattern repeated throughout literature and across cultures. For example, the story in which a character sets off on a quest or journey, experiences adventure and danger, and becomes wiser may be considered archetypal. The Wart in the excerpt from T. H. White's *The Once and Future King* (Unit 5) is an archetypal character.

ARTICLE. An **article** is an informational piece of writing about a particular topic, issue, event, or series of events. Articles usually appear in newspapers, professional journals, or magazines, or on websites. An *editorial* is an article meant to give an opinion. A *review* is an article that is a critical evaluation of a work, such as a book, play, movie, or musical performance. "We Heard It Before We Saw Anything" by Julian West (Unit 2) is an example of a news article.

ASIDE. An **aside** is a statement made by a character in a play that is intended to be heard by the audience but not by other characters on the stage. In Shakespeare's *The Tragedy of Julius Caesar* (Unit 4), Caesar makes an aside to the audience:

> Nor heaven nor earth have been at peace
>   tonight.
> Thrice hath Calphurnia in her sleep cried out,
> "Help, ho! they murther Caesar!" Who's within?
>   (II.ii.1–3)

ASSONANCE. **Assonance** is the repetition of vowel sounds. An example is the repetition of the short /i/ sound in the following line from Gwendolyn Brooks's "The Bean Eaters" (Unit 3):

> Remembering, with tw<u>i</u>nkl<u>i</u>ngs and tw<u>i</u>nges

ATMOSPHERE. *See* Mood.

AUTOBIOGRAPHY. An **autobiography** is the story of a person's life, written by that person. *Desert Exile: The Uprooting of a Japanese-American Family* by Yoshiko

Uchida (Unit 2) is an example of an autobiography. *See* Biography *and* Memoir.

BALLAD. A **ballad** is a poem that tells a story and is written in four- to six-line stanzas, usually meant to be sung. Most ballads have regular rhythms and rhyme schemes and feature a refrain, or repetition of lines.

BIAS. **Bias** is a personal judgment about something, or a mental leaning in one direction or another.

BIOGRAPHY. A **biography** is the story of a person's life, told by someone other than that person. Langston Hughes's "Harriet Tubman: The Moses of Her People" (Unit 2) is a biography. *See* Autobiography.

BLANK VERSE. **Blank verse** is unrhymed poetry with a rhythmic pattern known as iambic pentameter. Shakespeare used blank verse in his plays. The following are some typical lines:

> Why, man, he doth bestride the narrow world
> Like a Colossus, and we petty men
> Walk under his huge legs, and peep about
> To find ourselves dishonorable graves.
>   (I.ii.135–138)

See Meter.

CHARACTER. A **character** is an individual that takes part in the action of a literary work. A character is usually a person but may also be a personified plant, animal, object, or imaginary creature. The main character, or protagonist, has the central role in a work and is in conflict with the antagonist.

Characters can also be classified in other ways. *Major characters* play significant roles in a work, and *minor characters* play lesser roles. A *flat character* shows only one quality, or character trait. Orpheus in the Greek myth "Orpheus" by Robert Graves (Unit 5) is a flat character. A *round character* shows the multiple character traits of a real person. A *static character* does not change during the course of the action. A *dynamic character* does change.

CHARACTERIZATION. **Characterization** is the act of creating or describing a character. Writers create characters using three major techniques: showing what characters say, do, or think; showing what other characters say or think about them; and describing what physical features, dress, and personalities the characters display. The first two methods may be considered examples of *indirect characterization,* in which the writer shows what a character is like and allows the

reader to judge the character. The third technique is considered direct characterization, in which the writer tells what the character is like. See Character.

CHORUS. In drama, a **chorus** is a group of actors who speak directly to the audience between scenes, commenting on the action of the play. In classical Greek drama, the chorus conveyed its message through a series of *odes,* or serious poems, which it sang throughout the play. See "Understanding Greek Drama and the Story of Oedipus" in Unit 4 for more information on Greek drama.

CHRONOLOGICAL ORDER. When telling a story in **chronological order,** the writer unfolds events in the order in which they occurred.

CLIMAX. The **climax** is the high point of interest and suspense in a literary work. The term also is sometimes used to describe the turning point of the action in a story or play, the point at which the rising action ends and the falling action begins. The climax in *Antigone* by Sophocles (Unit 4) occurs when Creon decides he must free Antigone, only to learn he is too late. *See* Plot.

COHERENCE. **Coherence** is the logical arrangement and progression of ideas in a piece of writing.

COMEDY. A **comedy** is any lighthearted or humorous literary work with a happy ending, especially one prepared for the stage or the screen. Comedy is often contrasted with tragedy, in which the hero meets an unhappy fate. Comedies typically show characters with human limitations, faults, and misunderstandings. The action in a comedy usually progresses from initial order to a humorous misunderstanding or confusion and back to order again. Standard elements of comedy include mistaken identities, word play, satire, and exaggerated characters and events. "A Marriage Proposal" and "The Still Alarm" (Unit 4) are both comedies. *See* Tragedy.

COMIC RELIEF. **Comic relief** is a technique used to relieve the seriousness or emotional intensity of a literary work by introducing a humorous character or situation.

CONFLICT. A **conflict** is a struggle between two forces in a literary work. A plot introduces a conflict, develops it, and eventually resolves it. There are two types of conflict: external and internal. In an *external conflict,* the main character struggles against another character, against the forces of nature, against society or social norms, or against fate. In an *internal conflict,* the main character struggles against some element within himself or herself. In Amy Tan's "Two Kinds" (Unit 1), Jing-mei is in conflict with her mother about her mother's expectations. She is also in conflict with herself about how to deal with her mother. *See* Plot.

CONNOTATION. The **connotation** of a word is the set of ideas or emotional associations it suggests, in addition to its actual meaning. For example, the word *inexpensive* has a positive connotation, whereas the word *cheap* has a negative connotation, even though both words refer to "low cost." *See* Denotation.

CONSONANCE. **Consonance** is a kind of rhyme in which the consonant sounds of two words match, but the preceding vowel sounds do not, as in the words *wind* and *sound*. The following lines from Garrett Hongo's poem "The Legend" (Unit 6) provide an example:

> at a last flash of sunset / blazes the storefronts
> and lit windows of the street

CONTEXT. The conditions under which a literary work occurs make up its **context.** Context is closely related to setting, but focuses more on the environment of the time and place. Two common types of context include historical and cultural.

COUPLET. A **couplet** is two lines of verse that rhyme. These lines from Shakespeare's *The Tragedy of Julius Caesar* (Unit 4) provide an example:

> So call the field to rest, and let's away,
> To part the glories of this happy day.
> (V.v.80-81)

A *closed couplet* is a pair of rhyming lines that present a complete statement. A pair of rhyming iambic pentameter lines is also known as a *heroic couplet.*

DEDUCTIVE REASONING. **Deductive reasoning** is a pattern of thought that starts with a general idea and, using examples and facts, moves into a precise conclusion. *See* Inductive Reasoning.

DENOTATION. The **denotation** of a word is its dictionary meaning without any emotional associations. For example, the words *dirt* and *soil* share a common denotation. However, dirt has a negative connotation of uncleanliness, whereas soil does not. *See* Connotation.

DÉNOUEMENT. *See* Plot.

DESCRIPTION. A **description** is a picture in words. *Descriptive writing* is used to portray a character, an object, or a scene. Descriptions include *sensory*

details—words and phrases that describe how things look, sound, smell, taste, or feel. In his poem "New Dog" (Unit 6), Mark Doty appeals to the sense of touch by describing the dog in the following manner:

> He not only
> licks Wally's face
> but bathes every
> irreplaceable inch
> of his head

DIALECT. A **dialect** is a version of a language spoken by the people of a particular place, time, or social group. A *regional dialect* is one spoken in a particular place. A *social dialect* is one spoken by members of a particular social group or class. The following is an example of dialect from Wilma Elizabeth McDaniel's story "Who Said We All Have to Talk Alike" (Unit 1):

> A wider worman is a free worman, especially if she don't have no children. She ought to be free to come and go like she pleases.

DIALOGUE. **Dialogue** is conversation between two or more people or characters. Plays are made up of dialogue and stage directions. Fictional works are made up of dialogue, narration, and description. When dialogue is included in fiction or nonfiction, the speaker's words are enclosed in quotation marks.

DICTION. **Diction,** when applied to writing, refers to the author's choice of words. Much of a writer's style is determined by his or her diction—the types of words that he or she chooses. *See* Style.

DRAMA. A **drama** is a story told through characters played by actors. Dramas are divided into segments called *acts.* The script of a drama is made up of dialogue spoken by the characters and stage directions. Because it is meant to be performed before an audience, drama features elements such as lighting, costumes, makeup, properties, set pieces, music, sound effects, and the movements and expressions of actors. Two major types of drama are comedy and tragedy. *See* Comedy, Dialogue, Stage Directions, *and* Tragedy.

DRAMATIC IRONY. *See* Irony.

DRAMATIC MONOLOGUE. A **dramatic monologue** is a poem written in the form of a speech by a single character to an imaginary audience.

DRAMATIC POEM. A **dramatic poem** relies heavily on literary devices such as *monologue* (speech by a single character) or *dialogue* (conversation involving two or more characters). Often dramatic poems tell stories.

Types of dramatic poetry include the dramatic monologue and the soliloquy. *See* Dramatic Monologue *and* Soliloquy.

EPIC. An **epic** is a long story, often told in verse, involving heroes and gods. Grand in length and scope, an epic provides a portrait of an entire culture—of the legends, beliefs, values, laws, arts, and ways of life of a people. *The Kalevala* and *The Illiad* (Unit 5) are examples of epics.

EPIPHANY. An **epiphany** is a moment of sudden insight in which the nature of a person, thing, or situation is revealed.

ESSAY. An **essay** is a short nonfiction work that presents a single main idea, or *thesis*, about a particular topic.

- An *expository*, or *informative*, *essay* explores a topic with the goal of informing or enlightening the reader.
- A *persuasive essay* aims to persuade the reader to accept a certain point of view. Robert MacNeil's "The Trouble with Television" (Unit 2) is an example of a persuasive essay.
- A *personal essay* explores a topic related to the life or interests of the writer. Personal essays are characterized by an intimate and informal style or tone. *How Reading Changed My Life*, excerpted in Unit 2, is a personal essay by Anna Quindlen.

ETHOS. In persuasive speaking or writing, **ethos** refers to the character of the person giving the argument. In *The Tragedy of Julius Caesar* (Unit 4), Brutus appeals to ethos when he requests, "Believe me for mine honor...." *See* Pathos *and* Logos.

EUPHEMISM. A **euphemism** is an indirect word or phrase used in place of a direct statement that might be considered too harsh or offensive. The phrase *pass away*, used instead of *die*, and the phrase *waste management*, used in place of *garbage collection*, are euphemisms. In *Desert Exile: The Uprooting of a Japanese-American Family* (Unit 2), Yoshiko Uchida considers "apartment" a euphemism since her family's living quarters in the internment camp are no more than a horse stable.

EXPOSITION. In a plot, the **exposition** provides background information, often about the characters, setting, or conflict. Exposition is also another word for *expository writing*, the type of writing that aims to inform or explain. *See* Plot.

EXTENDED METAPHOR. An **extended metaphor** is a point-by-point presentation of one thing as though it were another. The description is meant as an implied comparison, inviting the reader to associate the thing being described with something that is quite different from it.

FABLE. **Fables** are brief stories, often with animal characters, told to express morals. Famous fables include those of Aesop and Jean de La Fontaine.

FAIRY TALE. **Fairy tales** are stories that deal with mischievous spirits and other supernatural occurrences, often in medieval settings. "Mother Holle" and "The Wonderful Hair" (Unit 5) are examples of fairy tales.

FALLING ACTION. *See* Plot.

FANTASY. A **fantasy** is a literary work that contains highly unrealistic elements. Included as fantasy are stories that resemble fairy tales, involve the supernatural, or have imaginary characters and settings. Stephen Vincent Benét's "By the Waters of Babylon" (Unit 6) contains elements of fantasy. *See* Magical Realism *and* Science Fiction.

FICTION. **Fiction** is any work of prose that tells an invented or imaginary story. The primary forms of fiction are the novel and the short story. *See* Novel *and* Short Story.

FIGURATIVE LANGUAGE. **Figurative language** is writing or speech meant to be understood imaginatively instead of literally. Many writers, especially poets, use figurative language to help readers see things in new ways. Types of figurative language, or **figures of speech,** include *hyperbole, metaphor, personification, simile,* and *understatement.*

FIGURES OF SPEECH. *See* Figurative Language.

FLASHBACK. A **flashback** interrupts the chronological sequence of a literary work and presents an event that occurred earlier. Writers use flashbacks most often to provide background information about characters or situations. In the short story "Cranes" by Hwang Sun-wŏn (Unit 1), Sŏngsam remembers the time when he and his childhood friend, Tŏkchae, capture a crane. This flashback helps explain Sŏngsam's later actions concerning his treatment of Tŏkchae.

FOIL. A **foil** is a character whose traits contrast with, and therefore highlight, the traits of another character. In Shakespeare's *The Tragedy of Julius Caesar* (Unit 4), Mark Antony may be seen as a foil for Brutus in that the former is a persuasive and charismatic speaker, whereas the latter is straightforward and less showy.

FOLK LITERATURE. Folk literature, or *folklore,* refers to a body of cultural knowledge and beliefs passed from one generation to the next, both orally and in writing. Much of folk literature originated as part of the *oral tradition,* or the passing of a work, an idea, or a custom by word of mouth from generation to generation. *See* Oral Tradition, Folk Song, *and* Folk Tale.

FOLK SONG. Folk songs are traditional or composed songs typically made up of stanzas, a refrain, and a simple melody. A form of folk literature, folk songs are expressions of commonly shared ideas or feelings and may be narrative or lyric in style.

FOLK TALE. A **folk tale** is a brief story passed by word of mouth from generation to generation. Types of folk tales include fairy tales, tall tales, parables, and fables. "Naked Truth and Resplendent Parable" (Unit 5) is an example of a Yiddish folk tale. *See* Fairy Tale, Folk Tale, Tall Tale, Parable, *and* Fable.

FOOT. *See* Meter.

FORESHADOWING. Foreshadowing is the act of presenting hints to events that will occur later in a story. In the short story "The Monkey's Paw" by W. W. Jacobs (Unit 1), the sergeant-major's warning about the way the monkey's paw can alter a person's life foreshadows what the White family will experience when Mr. White uses the paw.

FREE VERSE. Free verse is poetry that does not use regular rhyme, meter, or stanza division. Free verse may contain irregular line breaks and sentence fragments and tends to mimic the rhythm of ordinary speech. Most contemporary poetry is written in free verse. "The Floral Apron" by Marilyn Chin (Unit 3) is an example of a poem written in free verse.

GENRE. A **genre** (zhän′ rə) is a type or category of literary composition. Major genres of literature include fiction, nonfiction, poetry, and drama. *See* Drama, Fiction, Poetry, *and* Prose.

HAIKU. A **haiku** is a traditional Japanese three-line poem containing five syllables in the first line, seven in the second, and five in the third. The syllable pattern is often lost when a haiku is translated into English. A haiku presents a single vivid image, often of nature or the seasons, intended to evoke in the reader a specific emotional or spiritual response.

HERO. A **hero** is a character whose actions are inspiring and courageous. In early literature, a hero was often part divine and had remarkable abilities, such as magical power, superhuman strength, or great courage. Sogolon Djata in *Sundiata: An Epic of Old Mali* (Unit 5) is one such hero. In contemporary literature, the term *hero* often refers to any main character. Former trapeze artist Anna Avalon is the hero of Louise Erdrich's story "The Leap" (Unit 1).

HYPERBOLE. Hyperbole (hī pür′ bə lē') is overstatement, or exaggeration, used for dramatic effect.

IAMB. *See* Meter.

IAMBIC PENTAMETER. *See* Meter.

IDIOM. An **idiom** is an expression that cannot be understood from the meanings of its separate words but must be learned as whole.

IMAGE. An **image** is a picture formed in the mind of a reader.

IMAGERY. Imagery is language that creates pictures by appealing to the senses of sight, sound, touch, taste, and smell. *See* Description *and* Figurative Language.

INDUCTIVE REASONING. Inductive reasoning is a pattern of thought that starts with specific details and uses them to make a general, broader conclusion. Inductive reasoning is often used in persuasive writing. *See* Deductive Reasoning.

INFORMATIONAL TEXT. An **informational text** is a form of nonfiction that aims to convey or explain information. Examples of informational texts include reference materials, articles, editorials, and how-to writing.

INTERNAL MONOLOGUE. An **internal monologue** reveals the private thoughts and emotions of the first-person narrator of a story.

IRONY. Irony is the difference between appearance and reality—in other words, what seems to be and what really is. Types of irony include the following: *dramatic irony,* in which something is known by the reader or audience but unknown to the characters; *verbal irony,* in which a character says one thing but means another; and *irony of situation,* in which an event occurs that violates the expectations of the characters, the reader, or the audience. Irony of situation occurs in R. K. Narayan's "Like the Sun" (Unit 1), when Sekhar experiences his "first test" at his morning meal.

LEGEND. A **legend** is a story that is passed down through generations and is often based on real events or characters from the past. Unlike myths, legends are usually considered to be historical; however, they may contain elements that are fantastic or unverifiable.

LOGOS. In persuasive speaking or writing, logos is based on logic or reason. A person who uses logos strives to convince the audience through a clear, logical argument that his or her position is the correct one.

LYRIC POEM. A **lyric poem** is a highly musical type of poetry that expresses the emotions of a speaker. Lyric poems are often contrasted with narrative poems, which have storytelling as their main purpose. "I Am Offering This Poem" by Jimmy Santiago Baca (Unit 3) is a lyric poem. *See* Poetry.

MAGICAL REALISM. **Magical realism** is a kind of fiction that is for the most part realistic but that contains elements of fantasy. It originated in the works of Latin American writers and reflects the fact that Latin American culture often accepts as part of everyday life incidents that Europeans would consider "fantastic occurrences." "A Very Old Man with Enormous Wings" by Gabriel García Márquez (Unit 6) is an example of magical realism.

MEMOIR. A **memoir** is a type of autobiography that focuses on one incident or period in a person's life. Memoirs are often based on a person's memories of, and reactions to, historical events. Part of Le Ly Hayslip's memoir *When Heaven and Earth Changed Places* (Unit 2) focuses on her early memories of her father in Vietnam. *See* Autobiography.

METAPHOR. A **metaphor** is a comparison in which one thing is spoken or written about as if it were another. This figure of speech invites the reader to make a comparison between the writer's actual subject—the *tenor* of the metaphor—and another thing to which the subject is likened—the *vehicle* of the metaphor. In "Poetry" (Unit 3), Nikki Giovanni uses the following metaphor to show what poetry means to her:

> a poem is pure energy
> horizontally contained
> between the mind
> of the poet and the ear of the reader

See Extended Metaphor *and* Figurative Language.

METER. **Meter** is a regular rhythmic pattern in poetry. The pattern is determined by the number of beats, or stresses, in each line. Stressed and unstressed syllables are divided into rhythmical units called *feet*. Feet commonly used in poetry are as follows:

Type of Foot	Stress Pattern	Example
iamb (iambic)	an unstressed syllable followed by a stressed syllable	**insist**
trochee (trochaic)	a stressed syllable followed by an unstressed syllable	**freedom**
anapest (anapestic)	two unstressed syllables followed by one stressed syllable	**unim-pressed**
dactyl (dactylic)	one stressed syllable followed by two unstressed syllables	**feverish**
spondee (spondaic)	two stressed syllables	**baseball**

Terms used to describe the number of feet in a line include the following:

> *monometer* for a one-foot line
> *dimeter* for a two-foot line
> *trimeter* for a three-foot line
> *tetrameter* for a four-foot line
> *pentameter* for a five-foot line
> *hexameter,* or *Alexandrine,* for a six-foot line
> *heptameter* for a seven-foot line
> *octameter* for an eight-foot line

A complete description of the meter of a line includes both the term for the type of foot used most often in the line and the term for the number of feet in the line. The most common meters are *iambic tetrameter* and *iambic pentameter.* The following are examples of each:

iambic tetrameter

Ō slow | ly, slow | ly rose | she up

iambic pentameter

The cur | few tolls | the knell | of part | ing day

MOOD. **Mood,** or atmosphere, is the emotion created in the reader by part or all of a literary work. The writer can evoke in the reader an emotional response—such as fear, discomfort, longing, or anticipation—by working carefully with descriptive language and sensory details. "The Monkey's Paw" (Unit 1) has an eerie and suspenseful mood.

MORAL. A **moral** is a lesson that relates to the principles of right and wrong and is intended to be drawn from a story or other work of literature.

MOTIF. A **motif** is any element that appears in one or more works of literature or art. Examples of common folk-tale motifs found in oral traditions throughout the world include the granting of three wishes, the trial or quest, and the magical metamorphosis, or transformation of one thing into another. "Cinderella," "The Ugly Duckling," and the Arthurian "Sword in the Stone" are examples of the transformation motif, in which persons or creatures of humble station are revealed to be exceptional. Much can be revealed about a literary work by studying the motifs within it. In *The Tragedy of Julius Caesar* (Unit 4), the motif of disorder in nature is significant because it reflects the moral disorder in Rome.

MOTIVATION. A **motivation** is a force that moves a character to think, feel, or behave in a certain way. Chee, in "Chee's Daughter" (Unit 1), is motivated by love to get his daughter back from his in-laws.

MYTH. A **myth** is a traditional story, rooted in a particular culture, that deals with gods, goddesses, and other supernatural beings, as well as human heroes. Myths often embody religious beliefs and values and explain natural phenomena. Every early culture around the globe has produced its own myths. "The Death of Balder" (Unit 5) is a Norse myth.

NARRATION. Narration is a type of writing that tells a story, or describes events.

NARRATIVE POEM. A **narrative poem** is one that tells a story. "Ex-Basketball Player" by John Updike (Unit 3) is an example of a narrative poem. *See* Poetry.

NARRATOR. A **narrator** is a character or speaker who tells a story. The writer's choice of narrator is important to the story and determines how much and what kind of information readers will be given about events and other characters. The narrator in a work of fiction may be a major or minor character or simply someone who witnessed or heard about the events

being related. A *reliable narrator* gives a trustworthy account of events. An *unreliable narrator,* such as the one in "The Moment Before the Gun Went Off" (Unit 1), cannot be trusted because he or she comments on and offers opinions about events. *See* Point of View *and* Speaker.

NONFICTION. **Nonfiction** writing explores real people's lives, places, things, events, and ideas. Essays, autobiographies, biographies, and news articles are all types of nonfiction. *See* Prose.

NOVEL. A **novel** is a long work of fiction. Often novels have involved plots, many characters, and numerous settings. An excerpt from Khaled Hosseini's novel *The Kite Runner* appears in Unit 1.

ODE. An **ode** is a poem to honor or praise someone or something.

ONOMATOPOEIA. **Onomatopoeia** is the use of words or phrases that sound like the things to which they refer. Examples of onomatopoeia include words such as *buzz, click,* and *pop.* In "Jazz Fantasia" (Unit 3), *hoo-hoo-hoo-oo* is an example of onomatopoeia.

ORAL TRADITION. The **oral tradition** is the passing of a work, an idea, or a custom by word of mouth from generation to generation. Common works found in the oral traditions of peoples around the world include folk tales, fables, fairy tales, tall tales, nursery rhymes, proverbs, legends, myths, parables, riddles, charms, spells, and ballads. *See* Folk Tale, Legend, Myth, *and* Parable.

OXYMORON. An **oxymoron** is a word or group of words that contradict themselves. Words like *bittersweet* and *pianoforte* (literally, "soft-loud") are oxymorons.

PARABLE. A **parable** is a very brief story told to teach a moral lesson. The most famous parables are those told by Jesus in the Bible.

PARADOX. A **paradox** is a seemingly contradictory statement, idea, or event that may actually be true. Some paradoxes present unresolvable contradictory ideas. An example of such a paradox is the statement, "This sentence is a lie." If the sentence is true, then it is false; if it is false, then it is true. *See* Irony *and* Oxymoron.

PARALLELISM. **Parallelism** is a rhetorical device in which a writer emphasizes the equal value or weight of two or more ideas by expressing them in the same grammatical form. *See* Rhetorical Device.

PARODY. A **parody** is a literary work that closely imitates the style of another work for humorous purposes. Parodies often exaggerate elements of the original work to create a comic effect. *The Ingenious Hidalgo Don Quixote de la Mancha* (Unit 5) is a parody of chivalric romances.

PATHOS. **Pathos** is persuasion based on arousing emotions, including passion, love, hate, joy, fear, guilt, patriotism, sympathy, pity, sorrow, envy, and anger. *See* Ethos *and* Logos.

PERSONIFICATION. **Personification** is a figure of speech in which an animal, a thing, a force of nature, or an idea is described as if it were human or is given human characteristics. For example, the tree in Denise Levertov's "Tree Telling of Orpheus" (Unit 5) can talk and move as if it were human.

PERSUASION. **Persuasion,** or *persuasive writing*, is intended to change or influence the way a reader thinks or feels about a particular issue or idea.

PLOT. A **plot** is the series of events related to a central conflict, or struggle. A plot typically introduces a conflict, develops it, and eventually resolves it. A plot often contains the following elements, although it may not include all of them and they may not appear in precisely this order:

- The **exposition,** or introduction, sets the tone or mood, introduces the characters and setting, and provides necessary background information.
- The **rising action** occurs as the conflict is developed and intensified.
- The **climax** is the high point of interest or suspense.
- The **falling action** consists of all the events that follow the climax.
- The **resolution,** or dénouement (dā' nü män´), is the point at which the central conflict is ended, or resolved.

See Climax *and* Exposition.

POETRY. **Poetry** is a major type of literature. It features imaginative and musical language carefully chosen and arranged to communicate experiences, thoughts, or emotions. It differs from prose in that it compresses meaning into fewer words and often uses meter, rhyme, and imagery. Poetry is usually arranged in lines and stanzas as opposed to sentences and paragraphs, and it can be more free in the ordering of words and the use of punctuation. Types of poetry include narra-

tive, dramatic, and lyric. *See* Dramatic Poem, Lyric Poem, Meter, Narrative Poem, *and* Rhyme.

POINT OF VIEW. **Point of view** is the vantage point, or perspective, from which a story is told — in other words, who is telling the story. In **first-person point of view,** the story is told by someone who participates in or witnesses the action; this person, called the narrator, uses words such as *I* and *we* in telling the story. **Second-person point of view** uses the word *you* and addresses the reader directly, positioning the reader in the story. In **third-person point of view,** the narrator usually stands outside the action and observes; the narrator uses words such as *he, she, it,* and *they.* There are two types of third-person point of view: limited and omniscient. In *limited point of view,* the thoughts of only the narrator or a single character are revealed. In *omniscient point of view,* the thoughts of all the characters are revealed. "Lather and Nothing Else" (Unit 1) is told from third-person limited point of view. *See* Narrator.

PRIMARY SOURCE. *See* Source.

PROPAGANDA. The intentional use of false arguments to persuade others is called **propaganda.** Propaganda most often appears in nonfiction writing. There are many types of propaganda:

- A **glittering generality** is a statement given to make something sound more appealing than it actually is.
- **Spin** is a technique of creating manipulative and misleading statements in order to slant public perception of the news.
- **Circular reasoning** is the error of trying to support an opinion by restating it in different words.
- Words that stir up strong feelings, both positive and negative, are called **loaded words.**
- **Bandwagon appeal** is a statement that plays to a person's desire to be part of the crowd — to be like everyone else and do what everyone else is doing.
- A **stereotype** is an overgeneralization about a group of people based on a lack of knowledge or experience.

PROSE. **Prose** is the broad term used to describe all writing that is not drama or poetry, including fiction and nonfiction. Types of prose writing include novels, short stories, essays, and news stories. Most biographies, autobiographies, and letters are written in prose.

PROSE POEM. A **prose poem** is a passage of prose that makes such extensive use of poetic language that the line between prose and poetry becomes blurred. "Holidays" by Jamaica Kincaid (Unit 3) is a prose poem.

PROTAGONIST. A **protagonist** has the central role in a literary work. Jonathan Iwegbu is the protagonist of Chinua Achebe's short story "Civil Peace" (Unit 1). *See* Antagonist.

PROVERBS. **Proverbs,** or *adages,* are traditional sayings, such as "You can lead a horse to water, but you can't make it drink."

PUN. A **pun** is a play on words that involves either two words that sound alike but have different meanings or a word with two or more meanings. Act I, Scene i of *The Tragedy of Julius Caesar* (Unit 4) contains several puns. One example is the line "yet if you be out, sir, I can mend you." "If you be out" means both "if your shoes are worn out" and "if you are put out, or angry."

PURPOSE. A writer's **purpose** is his or her aim, or goal. People usually write with one or more of the following purposes: to inform or explain (*expository writing*); to portray a person, place, object, or event (*descriptive writing*); to convince people to accept a position and respond in some way (*persuasive writing*); and to express thoughts or ideas, or to tell a story (*narrative writing*). *See* Description, Exposition, Narration, *and* Persuasion.

QUATRAIN. A **quatrain** is a stanza of poetry containing four lines. *See* Stanza.

REFRAIN. A **refrain** is a line or group of lines repeated in a poem or song. Many ballads contain refrains.

REPETITION. **Repetition** is a writer's intentional reuse of a sound, word, phrase, or sentence. Writers often use repetition to emphasize ideas or, especially in poetry, to create a musical effect. *See* Rhetorical Device.

RESOLUTION. *See* Plot.

RHETORICAL DEVICE. A **rhetorical device** is a technique used by a speaker or writer to achieve a particular effect, especially to persuade or influence. Common rhetorical devices include parallelism, repetition, and rhetorical questions. *See* Parallelism, Repetition, *and* Rhetorical Question.

RHETORICAL QUESTION. A **rhetorical question** is a question asked for effect but not meant to be answered. In the speech "Yonder Sky That Has Wept Tears of Compassion" (Unit 2), Chief Seattle asks rhetorical questions: "How then can we be brothers? How can

your God become our God and renew our prosperity and awaken in us dreams of returning greatness?"

RHYME. **Rhyme** is the repetition of sounds in words. Types of rhyme include the following:
- *end rhyme* (the use of rhyming words at the ends of lines)
- *internal rhyme* (the use of rhyming words within lines)
- *exact rhyme* (in which the rhyming words end with the same sound or sounds, as in *moon* and *June*)
- *slant rhyme* (in which the rhyming sounds are similar but not identical, as in *rave* and *rove*)
- *sight rhyme* (in which the words are spelled similarly but pronounced differently, as in *lost* and *ghost* or *give* and *thrive*)

RHYME SCHEME. A **rhyme scheme** is the pattern of end rhymes designated by assigning a different letter of the alphabet to each rhyme. In the following verse from "Stopping by Woods on a Snowy Evening" by Robert Frost (Unit 3), the rhyme scheme is *aaba*.

> Whose woods these are I think I know.
> His house is in the village, though;
> He will not mind me stopping here
> To watch his woods fill up with snow.

RHYTHM. **Rhythm** is the pattern of beats, or stresses, in a line of poetry. Rhythm can be regular or irregular. A regular rhythmic pattern in a poem is called a *meter.* *See* Meter.

RISING ACTION. *See* Plot.

ROMANCE. **Romance** is a term used to refer to the following four types of literature:
- medieval stories about the adventures and loves of knights
- novels and other fiction involving exotic locations and extraordinary or mysterious events and characters
- nonrealistic fiction in general
- in popular, modern usage, love stories of all kinds

SATIRE. **Satire** is humorous writing or speech intended to point out errors, falsehoods, foibles, or failings. It is written for the purpose of reforming human behavior or human institutions. The play "The Still Alarm" (Unit 4) can be considered a satire, as it ridicules the behavior of two self-absorbed men.

SCENE. A **scene** is a short section of a play that usually marks changes of time and place.

SCIENCE FICTION. Science fiction is highly imaginative fiction containing fantastic elements based on scientific principles, discoveries, or laws. Ray Bradbury's short story "There Will Come Soft Rains" (Unit 6) is an example of science fiction.

SENSORY DETAILS. *See* Description.

SESTET. *See* Stanza.

SETTING. The **setting** of a literary work is the time and place in which it occurs, together with all the details used to create a sense of a particular time and place. Writers create setting by various means. In drama, the setting is often revealed by the stage set and the costumes, though it may be revealed through what the characters say about their environs. In fiction, setting is most often revealed by means of description of such elements as landscape, scenery, buildings, furniture, clothing, the weather, and the season. It can also be revealed by how characters talk and behave. *The Once and Future King* is a novel (excerpted in Unit 5) set first in the countryside of medieval England and then in London.

SHORT STORY. A **short story** is a brief work of fiction. Short stories are typically crafted carefully to develop a plot, a conflict, characters, a setting, a mood, and a theme, all within relatively few pages. *See* Fiction *and* Genre.

SIMILE. A **simile** is a comparison of two seemingly unlike things using the word "like" or "as." Jimmy Santiago Baca uses this figure of speech in "I Am Offering This Poem" (Unit 3):

> Keep it like a warm coat
> when winter comes to cover you,
> or like a pair of thick socks
> the cold cannot bite through…

SOLILOQUY. In drama, a **soliloquy** is a speech delivered by a character alone on stage that reveals the character's thoughts and feelings. Antony's speech over the dead body of Caesar in III.i.254–275 of Shakespeare's *The Tragedy of Julius Caesar* (Unit 4) is an example of a soliloquy.

SONNET. A **sonnet** is a fourteen-line poem, usually in iambic pentameter, that follows one of a number of different rhyme schemes. The *English, Elizabethan,* or *Shakespearean* sonnet is divided into four parts: three quatrains and a final couplet. The rhyme scheme of such a sonnet is *abab cdcd efef gg.* Shakespeare's

"Shall I compare thee to a summer's day?" and Edna St. Vincent Millay's "I know I am but summer to your heart" (Unit 3) are examples. The *Italian* or *Petrarchan* sonnet is divided into two parts: an octave and a sestet. The rhyme scheme of the octave is *abbaabba.* The rhyme scheme of the sestet can be *cdecde, cdcdcd,* or *cdedce.* Longfellow's "The Broken Oar" (Unit 3) is a Petrarchan sonnet. *See* Meter, Rhyme Scheme, and Stanza.

SOURCE. A **source** is evidence of an event, an idea, or a development. A *primary source* is direct evidence, or proof that comes straight from those involved. Primary sources include official documents as well as firsthand accounts, such as diaries, letters, photographs, and paintings done by witnesses or participants.

SPEAKER. The **speaker** is the character who speaks in, or narrates, a poem—the voice assumed by the writer. The speaker and the writer of a poem are not necessarily the same person. The speaker in Denise Levertov's poem "Tree Telling of Orpheus" (Unit 5) is a tree that witnessed events in the life of the mythical character Orpheus. *See* Narrator.

SPEECH. A **speech** is a public address that was originally delivered orally. Chief Seattle's speech "Yonder Sky That Has Wept Tears of Compassion" (Unit 2) is an example of a speech.

SPIRITUALS. Spirituals are religious songs from the African-American folk tradition. "Go Down, Moses" (Unit 2) is an example. A list of spirituals still sung today is included in the Introduction to Folk Literature (Unit 5).

STAGE DIRECTIONS. Stage directions are notes included in a play, in addition to the dialogue, for the purpose of describing how something should be performed on stage. Stage directions describe setting, lighting, music, sound effects, entrances and exits, properties, and the movements of characters. They are usually printed in italics and enclosed in brackets or parentheses.

STANZA. A **stanza** is a group of lines in a poem. The following are some types of stanza:

two-line stanza	couplet
three-line stanza	triplet or tercet
four-line stanza	quatrain
five-line stanza	quintain or quintet
six-line stanza	sestet
seven-line stanza	septet
eight-line stanza	octave

STEREOTYPE. A **stereotype** is an overgeneralization about a group of people based on a lack of knowledge and experience. *See* Propaganda.

STYLE. **Style** is the manner in which something is said or written. A writer's style is characterized by such elements as word choice (or *diction*), sentence structure and length, and other recurring features that distinguish his or her work from that of another. One way to think of a writer's style is as his or her written personality.

SUSPENSE. **Suspense** is a feeling of expectation, anxiousness, or curiosity created by questions raised in the mind of a reader or viewer.

SYMBOL. A **symbol** is anything that stands for or represents both itself and something else. Writers use two types of symbols—conventional, and personal or idiosyncratic. A *conventional symbol* is one with traditional, widely recognized associations. Such symbols include doves for peace; the color green for jealousy; winter, evening, or night for old age; wind for change or inspiration. A *personal* or *idiosyncratic symbol* is one that assumes its secondary meaning because of the special use to which it is put by a writer. In Doris Lessing's "Through the Tunnel" (Unit 1), the "safe beach" symbolizes Jerry's childhood, and the "wild bay" symbolizes Jerry's desire to venture out on his own.

TALL TALE. A **tall tale** is a story, often lighthearted or humorous, that contains highly exaggerated, unrealistic elements. Stories about Paul Bunyan are tall tales.

TANKA. A **tanka** is a traditional Japanese poem consisting of five lines, with five syllables in the first and third lines and seven syllables in the other lines (5-7-5-7-7). The syllable pattern is often lost when a tanka is translated into English. Tanka uses imagery to evoke emotions in the reader, but its images are often more philosophical and less immediate than those in a haiku. *See* Haiku.

THEME. A **theme** is a central message or perception about life that is revealed through a literary work. Themes may be stated or implied. A *stated theme* is presented directly, whereas an *implied theme* must be inferred. Most works of fiction do not have a stated theme but rather several implied themes. A *universal theme* is a message about life that can be understood by people of most cultures. A theme of "Everyday Use" by Alice Walker (Unit 1) is the connection of the characters to their heritage.

THESIS. A **thesis** is a main idea that is supported in a work of nonfiction. The thesis of "The Trouble with Television" by Robert MacNeil (Unit 2) is that television has negative effects on the people who watch it too much.

TONE. **Tone** is the emotional attitude toward the reader or toward the subject implied by a literary work. Examples of the different tones that a work may have include familiar, ironic, playful, sarcastic, serious, and sincere. In the poem "Eating Alone" (Unit 3), Li-Young Lee employs a lonely, wistful tone.

TRAGEDY. A **tragedy** is a work of literature, particularly a drama, that tells the story of the fall of a person of high status. It celebrates the courage and dignity of a tragic hero in the face of inevitable doom. Sometimes that doom is made inevitable by a tragic flaw. Today, the term *tragedy* is used more loosely to mean any work that has an unhappy ending. *The Tragedy of Julius Caesar* and *Antigone* (Unit 4) are both tragedies. *See* Comedy, Tragic Hero, *and* Tragic Flaw.

TRAGIC FLAW. A **tragic flaw** is a weakness of personality that causes the tragic hero to make unfortunate choices.

TRAGIC HERO. A **tragic hero** is the main character in a tragedy. Antigone is the tragic hero in the play by the same name, written by Sophocles (Unit 4).

TRICKSTER. In folk literature, the **trickster,** who is either an animal or a shape-shifter, is a cunning or deceptive character who not only annoys the gods, but also is often responsible for bringing important gifts to humanity, such as fire.

UNDERSTATEMENT. An **understatement** is an ironic statement that de-emphasizes something important, as in "He's sort of dead, I think."

VOICE. **Voice** is the way a writer uses language to reflect his or her unique personality and attitude toward topic, form, and audience. A writer expresses voice through tone, word choice (diction), and sentence structure. *See* Diction *and* Tone.

Glossary of Vocabulary Words

A

a • bate (ə bāt´) v., decrease in force or intensity

a • stray (ə strā´) adv., out of the right way; off the path

a • troc • i • ty (ə trä´ sə tē) n., cruel, horrible act

a • vert • ed (ə vʉrt´ ed) adj., turned away

ab • solve (eb zälv´) v., forgive

af • fa • ble (a´ fə bəl) adj., being pleasant and at ease in talking with others

al • cove (al´ kōv') n., relating to a section or an area of a room that is recessed or set back

ami • a • bly (ā´ mē ə blē) adv., pleasantly

an • ar • chist (a´ nər kist) n., one who rebels against or attempts to overthrow the government

an • vil (an´ vəl) n., a steel or iron block

ap • a • thy (a´ pə thē) n., indifference; lack of emotion

aph • o • rism (a´ fə ri' zəm) n., short, insightful saying

ap • pa • ri • tion (a' pə ri´ shən) n., ghost

ap • peal (ə pēl´) v., to make an earnest request

apt • ly (apt´ lē) adv., fittingly; appropriately

ar • du • ous (är´ jə wəs) adj., extremely difficult, usually physically

ar • rest • ing (ə res´ tiŋ) adj., catching the attention; striking; impressive

as • suage (ə swāj´) v., to calm; relieve

as • tute (ə stüt´) adj., clever

at • trib • ute (a tri´ byüt') v., think of as resulting from

av • a • ri • cious (a' və ri´ shəs) adj., greedy

B

ba • ser (bā´ sər) adj., less decent

be • queath (bē kwēth´) v., hand down; pass on

be • seech • ing (bi sēch´iŋ) adj., in an earnest manner

blas • phe • mous (blas´ fə məs) adj., insulting or showing disrespect or scorn for God or anything sacred

blas • phe • my (blas´ fə mē) n., irreverence toward God

bond • age (bän´ dij) n., slavery

braised (brāzd) adj., browned by simmering

buoy • ant (boi´ ənt) adj., having power to keep something afloat

C

cal • lous • ly (ka´ ləs lē) adv., insensitively; uncaringly

ca • pac • i • ty (kə pa´ sə tē) n., ability; qualification

chas • tise • ment (chas tīz´ mənt) n., scolding; condemnation

chiv • al • ry (shi´ vəl rē) n., sense of courage and honor

cleav • er (klē´ vər) n., heavy cutting tool with a broad blade

clem • ent (kle´ mənt) adj., kind; gentle; favorable

co • er • cion (kō ʉr´ zhən) n., act of force through threats or violence

co • her • ent • ly (kō hār´ ənt lē) adv., in a way capable of being understood

co • vert (kō´ vərt[']) adj., not openly shown, engaged in, or avowed

com • mend (kə mend´) v., to praise

com • mu • nal (kə myü´ n'l) adj., of or relating to a community

com • pen • sa • tion (käm pən sā´ shən) n., payment for service

com • ply (kəm plī´) v., act in accordance with a rule or request

com • pre • hen • sive (käm pri hen[t]´ siv) adj., covering a matter completely; inclusive

com • pul • sive (kəm pul´ siv) adj., as if driven by a force

con • cede (kən sēd´) v., admit

con • science (kän[t]´ shən[t]s) n., sense of right or wrong within an individual

con • sci • en • tious (kän[t]' shē en[t]´ shəs) adj., scrupulous; governed by what one knows is right

con • sci • en • tious • ly (kän[t]' shē en[t]´ shəs lē) adv., in a manner governed by doing what one knows is right

con • sent • ing (kən sent´ iŋ) adj., agreeing; approving

con • strain (kən strān´) v., force by rule or limitation

con • stric t • ing (kən strict´ iŋ) adj., limiting; compressing

con • ten • tion (kən ten[t]´ shən) n., argument

con • tin • gent (kən tin´ jənt) n., group forming part of a larger group, such as troops

con • tri • tion (kən tri´ shən) n., remorse

con • vey (kən vā´) v., make known

con • vic • tion (kən vik´ shən) n., strong belief

cor • ol • lar • y (kôr´ ə ler' ē) *n.*, something that naturally follows; result

cor • por • al (kôr p[ə] rəl) *adj.*, having to do with the body

coun • te • nance (kaun´ t'n ən[t]s *or* kaunt´ nən[t]s) *n.*, look on a person's face; face

cull (kəl) *v.*, control the size of a herd by removal; select from a group; pick or select

cul • prit (kul´ prət) *n.*, one guilty of a crime; the cause of a problem

cur • so • ry (kʉrs´ rē *or* kʉrs´ ə rē) *adj.*, hasty; rapidly performed

D

daunt • less (dônt´ ləs) *adj.*, fearless; daring

de • cree (də krē´) *n.*, order set forth by one in authority

def • er • ence (de´ fə rən[t]s) *n.*, attitude of yielding to another

deign (dān) *v.*, condescend; consent to act below one's normal level of dignity

de • lu • sion (di lü´ zhən) *n.*, false belief or opinion

des • ti • tute (des´ tə tüt') *n.*, those living in poverty

de • tain (dē tān´) *v.*, keep from going on; hold back

de • void (də void´) *adj.*, completely without

di • a • bol • i • cal (dī' ə bä´ li kəl) *adj.*, devilish; inhumanly cruel or wicked

dirge (dʉrj) *n.*, song or piece of writing expressing deep grief

dis • card (dis kärd´) *v.*, throw away

dis • con • cert (dis' kən sʉrt´) *v.*, agitate; fluster

dis • con • so • late (dis kän[t]´ sə lət) *adj.*, unhappy; not to be comforted

dis • cord • ant (dis´ kôrd' n't) *adj.*, not harmonious

dis • fig • ure (dis fi´ gyər) *v.*, disguise

dis • man • tle (dis man´ təl) *v.*, divide into pieces

dis • put • ed (di spyüt´ əd) *adj.*, subject to disagreement or debate

di • vest • ment (dī ves[t]´ mənt) *n.*, reduction of investments for social or political reasons; selling of assets difficulty

doc • trine (däk´ trən) *n.*, teaching; belief

do • mes • tic (də mes´ tik) *adj.*, relating to the household or family

du • bi • ous • ly (dü´ bē əs lē) *adv.*, skeptically; doubtfully

du • ly (dü´ lē) *adv.*, as required; sufficiently

E

e • go • cen • trism (ē' gō sen´ tri' zəm) *n.*, self-centeredness

e • thos (ē´ thäs') *n.*, distinguishing character, sentiment, moral nature, or guiding beliefs of a person, group, or institution

ec • cen • tric (ik sen´ trik) *adj.*, odd or unusual in behavior or appearance

ed • i • fice (e´ də fəs) *n.*, massive building or structure

el • o • quent (e´ lə kwənt) *adj.*, marked by forceful and fluent expression

em • bez • zle • ment (im be´ zəl mənt) *n.*, stealing money or property entrusted to one's care

em • i • nence (e´ mə nən[t]s) *n.*, high importance

e • mit (ē mit´) *v.*, discharge; send out

en • am • ored (i na´ mərd) *adj.*, consumed with love

en • dure (in dʉr´) *v.*, live through

en • gen • der (in jen´ dər) *v.*, give birth to; produce

en • gulf (in gulf´) *v.*, swallow up; to flow over and enclose

en • mi • ty (en´ mə tē) *n.*, hatred

en • sign (en´ sən) *n.*, flag; banner

en • treat (in trēt´) *v.*, to implore; strongly urge

er • rat • ic (i ra´ tik) *adj.*, having no fixed purpose

ex • al • ta • tion (ek' sôl' tā´ shən) *n.*, feeling of great joy and pride

ex • clu • siv • i • ty (eks' klü' si´ və tē) *n.*, quality or state of being limiting or restrictive

ex • empt (ig zem[p]t´) *adj.*, excused; released

ex • ploit (ek´ sploit') *n.*, deed; heroic act

ex • tri • cate (ek´ strə kāt') *v.*, free from entanglement or difficulty

F

fab • ri • ca • tion (fa' bri kā´ shən) *n.*, made-up story

fal • ter • ing (fôl´ t[ə] riŋ) *adj.*, hesitant; uncertain; wavering

fal • ter • ing • ly (fôl´ tər iŋ lē) *adv.*, uncertainly; unsteadily

fa • nat • ic • al (fə na´ ti kəl) *adj.*, interested to the point of obsession

fawn (fôn) *v.*, flatter; show excessive friendliness

fi • as • co (fē as´ kō['])) *n.*, total failure

for • ay (fôr´ ā) *n.*, raid; attack

for • bear • ance (fôr bar´ ən[t]s) *n.*, patience

fur • tive (fʉr´ tiv) *adj.*, sneaky; stealthy

G

ghast • ly (gast´ lē) *adj.*, horrible; frightful

griev • ance (grē´ vən[t]s) *n.*, complaint

griev • ous (grē´ vəs) *adj.*, very serious; grave

H

hail (hāl) *v.*, greet joyfully

ham • per (ham´ pər) *v.*, to interfere with the operation of

hap • haz • ard • ly (hap' ha´ zərd lē) *adv.*, done in a manner marked by lack of plan, order, or direction

home • ly (hōm´ lē) *adj.*, simple; plain

hy • po • chon • dri • ac (hī' pə kän´ drē ak') *n.*, person who suffers from *hypochondria*, or depression stemming from imagined illness

I

im • mi • nent (i´ mə nənt) *adj.*, about to occur; coming soon; threatening

im • part (im pärt´) *v.*, get across; give

im • per • ti • nence (im' pʉr´ tə nən[t]s) *n.*, inappropriate, insolent action

im • pla • ca • ble (im pla´ kə bəl) *adj.*, unable to be appeased; relentless

im • preg • na • ble (im preg´ nə bəl) *adj.*, unable to be taken by force

im • pu • dence (im´ pyə dən[t]s) *n.*, quality or state of being *impudent*, or showing a lack of respect or regard for others

im • pul • sive (im pul´ siv) *adj.*, likely to act without a lot of planning or thought

in • au • di • ble (i['] nô´də bəl) *adj.*, that cannot be heard

in • cli • na • tion (in' klə nā´ shən) *n.*, tendency to do something

in • cred • u • lous (in['] kre´ jə ləs) *adj.*, showing disbelief

in • del • i • ble (in de´ lə bəl) *adj.*, permanent; incapable of being erased or removed

in • dulge (in dulj´) *v.*, take pleasure freely

in • dus • tri • ous (in dus´ trē əs) *adj.*, constantly active or occupied; diligent

in • fir • mi • ty (in fʉr´ mə tē) *n.*, sickness; weakness

in • gen • i • ous (in jēn´ yəs) *adj.*, extremely clever

in • nu • en • do (in' yə wen´ dō[']) *n.*, indirect remark or hint, usually negative or suggestive

in • qui • ry (in kwir´ ē) *n.*, investigation into a matter of public interest

in • so • lence (in´ sə lənts) *n.*, disrespect; haughtiness; impudence

in • stinct (in´ stiŋ[k]t) *n.*, impulse; natural tendency

in • ter • im (in´ tə rəm) *n.*, in-between time

in • ter • pose (in' tər pōz´) *v.*, to place or come between

in • trigue (in' trēg´) *n.*, secret or underhanded plot

in • vin • ci • ble (in['] vin[t] zə bəl) *adj.*, incapable of being conquered, overcome, or subdued

i • rate (ī rāt´) *adj.*, angry

K

la • ment (lə ment´) *v.*, feel or express deep sorrow; grieve or regret deeply

lam • en • ta • tion (la' mən tā´ shən) *n.*, vocal expression of sorrow

L

leer (lir) *v.*, cast a sidelong glance that is lustful, knowing, or mischievous

list • less • ly (list´ ləs lē) *adv.*, without energy or enthusiasm

lithe (līth) *adj.*, mild; gentle; agile

loom • ing (lüm´ iŋ) *adj.*, appearing exaggeratedly large or distorted

lu • di • crous (lü´ də krəs) *adj.*, laughably absurd or foolish

lu • mi • nous (lü´ mə nəs) *adj.*, shining; bright

M

make • shift (māk´ shift') *adj.*, crude and temporary substitute

ma • li • cious (mə li´ shəs) *adj.*, desiring to cause pain, injury, or distress to another; being mean and spiteful; *n.*, those who act with evil intention

ma • ligned (mə līngd´) *adj.*, slandered

med • dle (me´ d'l) *v.*, to interfere in something that is not one's business

me • tic • u • lous (mə ti´ kyə ləs) *adj.*, marked by extreme or excessive care in the treatment of details

mi • nute • ly (mī nüt´ lē) *adv.*, to a very small degree

mis • con • strue (mis' kən strü´) *v.*, misunderstand; misinterpret

mock (mäk) *v.*, treat with contempt or ridicule

mo • les • ta • tion (mō' les' tā´ shən) *n.*, the annoyance of or disturbance of with hostile intent

mo • men • tous (mō men´ təs) *adj.*, very important

mul • ti • tude (məl´ tə tüd') *n.*, masses; large number of people considered as a unit

myr • i • ad (mir´ ē əd) *n.*, indefinitely large number

N

nes • tle (ne´ səl) *v.*, to settle snugly or comfortably

O

ob • tuse • ness (äb tüs´ nes) *n.*, state of demonstrating slow intellect; dullness

ora • tion (ôrā´ shən) *n.*, speech

P

pal • pi • ta • tion (pal' pə tā´ shən) *n.*, throbbing or rapid beating of the heart

pen • sive (pen[t]´ siv) *adj.*, thoughtful

per • sis • tence (pər sis´ tən[t]s) *n.*, stubborn continuance; tenacity

pe • ti • tion (pə ti´ shən) *n.*, formal document containing an earnest request

pet • u • lant • ly (pe´ chə lənt lē) *adv.*, behaving in an impatient or irritable manner

pi • e • ty (pī´ ə tē) *n.*, devoted loyalty or duty to family or religion

plain • tive (plān´ tiv) *adj.*, mournful; sad

plight (plīt) *n.*, awkward or wretched situation

plum • met • ing (plu´ mət iŋ) *adj.*, dropping sharply and abruptly

pomp • ous (päm´ pəs) *adj.*, self-important

por • ous (pôr´ əs) *adj.*, having pores; allowing liquids to absorb or pass through itself

por • tent (pôr´ tent) *n.*, sign; omen

por • ten • tous (pôr ten´ təs) *adj.*, predictive; foreboding; ominous

pre • sage (prə sāj´) *v.*, foretell; warn

pre • sump • tu • ous (pri zum[p]´ chə wəs) *adj.*, arrogant; tending to assume; going too far; overstepping bounds

pre • vail (pri vāl´) *v.*, grow strong; gain victory

pri • mal (prī´ məl) *adj.*, fundamental; primitive

probe (prōb) *v.*, explore; search

pro • fane (prō fān´) *v.*, violate; abuse; make impure

pro • fuse (prə fyüs´) *adj.*, plentiful; available in great amounts

pro • sa • ic (prō zā´ ik) *adj.*, commonplace; dull

pru • dent (prü´ d'nt) *adj.*, wise

R

rau • cous (rô´ kəs) *adj.*, boisterous

re • ced • ing (ri sēd´ iŋ) *adj.*, gradually moving away

re • com • pose (rē' kəm pōz´) *v.*, restore calmness of mind

re • dress (ri dres´) *v.*, set right

re • gime (rā zhēm´ or ri jēm´) *n.*, government; administration in power

re • ju • ve • nate (ri jü´ və nāt') *v.*, make to feel young again

re • ju • ve • nat • ed (ri jü´ və nāt' əd) *adj.*, renewed; made young again

rel • ic (re´ lik) *n.*, memento from a past time

rem • nant (rem´ nənt) *n.*, small remaining part

re • mote (ri mōt´) *adj.*, isolated; secluded

rep • li • ca (re´ pli kə) *n.*, an exact copy

rep • re • hen • si • ble (re' pri hen[t]´ sə bəl) *adj.*, worthy of or deserving disapproval or censure

re • proach (ri prōch´) *v.*, accuse or blame; *n.*, disapproval

res • pite (res´ pət) *n.*, rest or temporary relief

ret • i • cent (re´ tə sənt) *adj.*, inclined to be silent or uncommunicative in speech

rev • er • ence (rev´ rən[t]s) *n.*, profound respect, love, and awe

rev • er • ent • ly (rev´ rənt lē) *adv.*, in a manner suggesting deep respect, love, or awe

rev • o • lu • tion • ar • y (re' və lü´ shə ner' ē) *n.*, one who seeks to overthrow a government

ri • fle (rī´ fəl) *v.*, shuffle; move quickly through

rue • ful • ly (rü´ fəl lē) *adv.*, regretfully

S

sa • ga • cious (sə gā´ shəs) *adj.*, wise

scald • ing (skôl´ diŋ) *adj.*, unpleasantly severe

self • pos • sessed (self' pə zest´) *adj.*, confident; composed

sen • ten • tious • ly (sen ten[t]s´ shəs lē) *adv.*, in an overly moralizing way

se • ques • tered (si kwes´ tərd) *adj.*, secluded

se • rene (sə rēn´) *adj.*, calm; peaceful

self • pos • sessed (self' pə zest´) *adj.*, confident; composed

ser • vile (sᴜr´ vīl) *adj.*, slave-like; submissive

so • no • rous (sə nôr´əs) *adj.*, impressive in effect or style

spec • tral (spek´ trəl) *adj.*, ghostlike

state • craft (stāt´ kraft´) *n.*, art of conducting state affairs

steal (stēl) *v.*, move silently or cautiously

stol • id • ly (stä´ ləd lē) *adv.*, with little emotion

sub • or • di • nate (sə bôr´ də nāt') *v.*, to place in a lower class or rank

suf • fice (sə fīs´) *v.*, to be enough

sum • mon (su´ mən) *v.*, to call forth; to evoke

sump • tu • ous (sum[p][t]´ shə wəs) *adj.*, extremely comfortable or lavish; fancy

surge (sərj) *v.*, to rise and fall

sur • ly (sʉr´ lē) *adj.*, bad-tempered; hostile

sus • te • nance (sus´ tə nən[t]s) *n.*, nourishment

T

tac • i • turn (ta´ sə tʉrn') *adj.*, not willing to talk much

taut (tôt) *adj.*, tense

tem • per • ate (tem´ pə rət) *adj.*, moderate

ten • ta • tive (ten´ tə tiv) *adj.*, hesitant; uncertain

throng (thrôŋ) *n.*, crowd; gang; group

tran • quil (traŋ´ kwəl) *adj.*, calm; serene

tran • scend (tran[t] send´) *v.*, rise above or go beyond the limits of

trans • gress (tranz gres´) *v.*, go beyond set limits

tri • fle (trī´ fəl) *n.*, something of little value; inconsequential thing

U

un • leash (un' lēsh´) *v.*, to free from; to let loose

un • per • turbed (un pər tʉrb'd´) *adj.*, not bothered

un • wiel • dy (un' wēl´ dē) *adj.*, hard to manage because of weight or shape

ush • er (u´ shər) *v.*, escort; conduct

V

val • or (va´ lər) *n.*, courage; bravery

van • quish (van´ kwish) *v.*, defeat

ven • geance (ven´ jen[t]s) *n.*, act of taking revenge

ven • ti • la • tion (ven' tə lā´ shən) *n.*, movement of air in a room

ven • ture (ven[t]´ shər) *v.*, do at some risk

ver • dant (vʉr´ d'nt) *adj.*, green with vegetation

vice (vīs) *n.*, moral failing

vig • nette (vin yet´) *n.*, a brief scene

vile (vīl) *adj.*, foul; mean; cheap; contemptible

vis • age (vi´ zij) *n.*, face; appearance

vo • li • tion (vō li´ shən) *n.*, free will

vul • gar (vul´ gər) *adj.*, lacking in cultivation, perception, or taste

W

wan • ton (wôn´ t'n) *adj.*, without appropriate restraint or shame; immoral

wa • ver (wā´ vər) *v.*, to hesitate; to be undecided

war • i • ness (war´ ē nəs) *n.*, caution

wrench (rench) *v.*, twist, pull, or jerk violently

Pronunciation Key

Vowel Sounds

a	hat	i	sit	o͞o (*or* ü)	blue, stew	ə	extra
ā	play	ī	my	oi (*or* ȯi)	boy		under
ä	star	ō	go	ou (*or* aȯ)	wow		civil
e	then	ô (*or* ȯ)	paw, born	u	up		honor
ē	me	o͝o (*or* u̇)	book, put	ʉ	burn		bogus

Consonant Sounds

b	but	j	jump	p	pop	th	the
ch	watch	k	brick	r	rod	v	valley
d	do	l	lip	s	see	w	work
f	fudge	m	money	sh	she	y	yell
g	go	n	on	t	sit	z	pleasure
h	hot	ŋ	song, sink	th	with		

Literary Acknowledgments

Americas Magazine. "Lather and Nothing Else" by Hernando Téllez. Reprinted by permission of Americas magazine.

Arte Publico Press. "Family Ties" from *My Own True Name: New and Selected Poems for Young Adults, 1984–1999* by Pat Mora. Copyright © 2000 by Pat Mora. Reprinted with permission from Arte Publico Press, University of Houston. "Immigrants" is reprinted with permission from the publisher of *Borders* by Pat Mora (Houston: Arte Publico Press—University of Houston, © 1986).

The Asia Society. "Thoughts of Hanoi" by Nguyen Thi Vinh, translated by Nguyen Ngoc Bich with Burton Raffel and W. S. Merwin. Reproduced by permission of The Asia Society.

Estate of Toni Cade Bambara. "Geraldine Moore the Poet" by Toni Cade Bambara. Copyright © 1972 by Toni Cade Bambara. Used by permission of Karma Bambara Daniel on behalf of the Estate of Toni Cade Bambara.

Bancroft Library, University of California. From *Desert Exile: The Uprooting of a Japanese-American Family,* by Yoshiko Uchida. Courtesy of The Bancroft Library, University of California, Berkeley.

Elizabeth Barnett. "I know I am but summer to your heart" by Edna St. Vincent Millay. From *Collected Poems,* HarperCollins. Copyright © 1923, 1951 by Edna St. Vincent Millay and Norma Millay Ellis. All rights reserved. Used by permission of Elizabeth Barnett, literary executor.

Susan Bergholz Literary Services. "Geraldo No Last Name" from *The House on Mango Street.* Copyright © 1984 by Sandra Cisneros. Published by Vintage Books, a division of Random House, Inc., and in hardcover by Alfred A. Knopf in 1994. Reprinted by permission of Susan Bergholz Literary Services, New York. All rights reserved.

Bibliotheca Islamica. "The Happy Man" from *God's World* by Naguib Mahfouz, translated by Akef Abadir and Roger Allen. Copyright © 1973, 1988 by Akef Abadir and Roger Allen. Reprinted by permission of Bibliotheca Islamica.

Chana Bloch. "Pride" by Dahlia Ravikovitch, translated by Chana Bloch and Ariel Bloch. From *The Window,* 1989. Reprinted by permission of Chana Bloch.

BOA Editions, Ltd. "Eating Alone" from *Rose* by Li-Young Lee. Copyright © 1986 by Li-Young Lee. Reprinted with the permission of BOA Editions, Ltd. "miss rosie" by Lucille Clifton from *Good Woman: Poems and a Memoir 1969–1980,* by Lucille Clifton, 1987. Reprinted by permission of BOA Editions, Ltd.

Brandt & Hochman Literary Agents, Inc. "By the Waters of Babylon" by Stephen Vincent Benét. Copyright © 1937 by Stephen Vincent Benét. Copyright renewed © 1965 by Thomas C. Benét, Stephanie B. Mahin, and Rachel Benét Lewis. Reprinted by permission of Brandt & Hochman Literary Agents, Inc.

Walker Brents. "The Death of Balder" retold by Walker Brents. Reprinted by permission of the author. "Savitri and Satyavant" retold by Walker Brents. Reprinted by permission of the author.

Brooks Permissions. "The Bean Eaters" from *Blacks* by Gwendolyn Brooks, copyright © 1991. Reprinted by consent of Brooks Permissions. "We Real Cool" from *Blacks* by Gwendolyn Brooks, copyright © 1991. Reprinted by Consent of Brooks Permissions.

BUG MUSIC. "Land of the Living." Written by Lucy Kaplansky and Rick Litvin. © 2002 LUCYRICKY MUSIC (ASCAP). Administered by BUG. All Rights Reserved. Used by permission.

Hortense Calisher. "Heartburn" from *The Collected Stories of Hortense Calisher* by Hortense Calisher. Reprinted by permission of the author.

Carcanet Press Limited. "Orpheus" from *The Greek Myths* by Robert Graves. Copyright © 1960 by Robert Graves. Reprinted by permission of Robert Graves and Carcanet Press.

Columbia University Press. "at dawn..." by Miyazawa Kenji, "if I were to stand..." by Okamoto Kanoko and "standing still..." by Tsukamoto Kunio from *Modern Japanese Tanka,* compiled, translated, and with an introduction by Makoto Ueda. Copyright © 1996 by Columbia University Press. Reprinted with permission of the publisher.

Don Congdon Associates, Inc. "Contents of the Dead Man's Pocket" from *The Third Level* by Jack Finney. Reprinted by permission of Don Congdon Associates, Inc. Copyright © 1956 by the Crowell Collier Publishing Company, renewed 1984 by Jack

William Morris Agency, Inc. *The Hitchhiker* by Lucille Fletcher. Copyright © 1947 by Lucille Fletcher. Reprinted by permission of William Morris Agency, Inc. on behalf of the author.

The Wylie Agency Inc. "The Leap" by Louise Erdrich, © 1990 by Louise Erdrich, reprinted with the permission of the Wylie Agency Inc.

Yale University Press. "Mu-lan" from *The Flowering Plum and the Palace Lady: Interpretations of Chinese Poetry,* translated by Han H. Frankel, 1976. Reprinted by permission of Yale University Press.

Art and Photo Credits

Unit 1

1 (left) © Doug Pearson/JAI/Corbis; (right) © Images.com/Corbis; 5 Archive Photo; 6–7 (top left to top right) © Bryan Peterson/Corbis; Fotosearch; © Tom Grill/Corbis; © Image Source/Corbis; Photo by Sanja Gjenero; © Tim Pannell/Corbis; Superstock; Photo by Nick Wang; (bottom) Superstock; 9 © Archivo Iconografico, S.A./CORBIS; 13–14 Library of Congress; 15 Image Source/Getty Images; 18 © Jagdish Agarwal/Corbis; 23 © Harris Museum and Art Gallery, Preston, Lancashire, UK /The Bridgeman Art Library International; 28 © Archivo Iconografico, S.A./CORBIS; 29 © The Art Archive/Corbis; 31 © Corbis; 32 © CORBIS; 33 © DESPOTOVIC DUSKO/ CORBIS SYGMA; 34 © image100/Corbis; 37 (left) © Craig Tuttle; (middle) Library of Congress; (right) © Guenter Rossenbach/zefa/Corbis; 43 Library of Congress; 44 Photo by Jhonattan Balcazar; 45 © 2008 Artists Rights Society (ARS), New York/ADAGP, Paris; 50 Archive Photos; (background) © Onne van der Wal/Corbis; 52 © Peter Johnson/Corbis; 55 © Contemporary African Art Collection Limited/CORBIS; 60 From *Jane Eyre* by Charlotte Bronte, Introduction by Erica Jong, copyright © 1960 by New American Library. Used by permission of Dutton Signet, a division of Penguin Group (USA) Inc.; 62 (bottom left) The University of Georgia Press; (bottom right) Photo by Robert Foothorap; 63 © Kelly-Mooney Photography/CORBIS; 64 © Kim Sayer/CORBIS; 69 © PictureArts/CORBIS; 70–75 © Bettmann/CORBIS; 76 © Strauss/Curtis/CORBIS; 81 Photo by Cristiano Galbiati; 82 Library of Congress; 86 © Bettmann/ CORBIS; 89 Photo by Chris H.; 94 Library of Congress; 95 © Fine Art Photographic Library/CORBIS; 96 © CORBIS; 98 © Gianni Dagli Orti/CORBIS; 100 © Hulton-Deutsch Collection/CORBIS; 106 Photo by Sarah Williams; 107 From *The Great Gatsby* by F. Scott Fitzgerald. Copyright © 1925 by Charles Scribner's Sons. Copyright renewed 1953 by Frances Scott Fitzgerald Lanahan. Reprinted by permission of Scribner, an imprint of Simon & Schuster Publishing; 108 © Roger Ressmeyer/CORBIS; 109 © Raymond Gehman/CORBIS; 110 © Bettmann/CORBIS; 111 © Arthur Rothstein/CORBIS; 113 Library of Congress; 114 Photo courtesy of American Quilts!; 118 © Michael Dorris; 119 © 2008 Artist Rights Society (ARS), New York/ADAGP, Paris/Archivo Iconografico, S. A./CORBIS; 121 © Terry Vine/Corbis; 122 © Rick Gayle/Corbis; 125 (left) Photo by Mo Onfire; (middle) Photo by AmandaK; (right) Archive Photos; 126 © Swim Inc 2, LLC/Corbis; 132 © Arte & Immagini srl/CORBIS; 135 © Nathan Benn/CORBIS; 136 © Tim Wright/CORBIS; 137 (top) © Richard Hamilton Smith/Corbis; (bottom) Jerry Bauer; 139 © Chester Sheard/Chester Sheard-KPA/ZUMA/Corbis; 141 © John Feingersh/Corbis; 143 © Richard Smith/Corbis; 144 © Richard Hamilton Smith/CORBIS; 146 © Paul A. Souders/CORBIS; 148 © Layne Kennedy/CORBIS; 150 (bottom) © Reuters/Corbis; (background) Photo by Image Arts; 152 © image100/Corbis; 154 © Jonathan Blair/CORBIS; 155 (middle) © Reza, Webistan/CORBIS; 157 (top) © Carl & Ann Purcell/CORBIS; (bottom) AP Photo/Bob Galbraith; 159 © Comstock Select/Corbis; 160 © Corbis; 161 © Robert Farber/Corbis; 162 Victoria & Albert Museum, London, UK, / The Bridgeman Art Library International; 163 (left) © EFE/Corbis; (middle) © Hulton-Deutsch Collection/CORBIS; (top right) © Images.com/Corbis; 167 © Ainaco/CORBIS; 169 © Douglas Kirkland/CORBIS; 171 © Carl & Ann Purcell/CORBIS; 173 © George H. H. Huey/CORBIS; 175 © Carl & Ann Purcell/CORBIS; 176 © JLP/Jose L. Pelaez/Corbis; 178 (top left) © MedioImages/ Corbis; (top right) © Darren Greenwood/Design Pics/ Corbis; 180 (bottom) Steve Miller/New York Times Co./Archive Photos; 182 © Wendy Stone/Corbis; 183 © Peter Johnson/Corbis; 185 (top) Rodney Busch; (bottom) Library of Congress; 187 © Robert McIntosh/CORBIS; 188 © James L. Amos/CORBIS; 191 © Images.com/Corbis; 192 © North Carolina Museum of Art/CORBIS; 195 (top right) National Gallery of Art, Washington, D.C.; (bottom) AP; 197 © Tim Street-Porter/Beateworks/Corbis; 198 © Gregor Schuster/zefa/Corbis; 200 (bottom) Reuters/ Stringer/Archive Photos; (background) © Daniel Sicolo/Design Pics/Corbis; 204 Jacket Cover from *Bee Season* by Myla Goldberg. Used by permission of Doubleday, a division of Random House, Inc.; From *Dracula* by Bram Stoker, introduction by Leonard Wolf, copyright © 1992 by Leonard Wolf, introduction. Used by permission of Signet, an imprint of Penguin Group (USA) Inc.; Jacket design from *Across the Grain* by Jean Ferris. Copyright © 1990 by Jean Ferris. Reprinted by permission of Farrar, Straus and Giroux, LLC.; 206 © JLP/Deimos/Corbis; 212 © Jeffrey Coolidge/Corbis

Unit 2

216–217 (left) Photo by Kashfia Rahman, KashfiaRahman06@gmail.com; (middle) © Artkey/Corbis; (right) © Richard T. Nowitz/Corbis; **218** From *Chinese Cinderella: The Secret Story of an Unwanted Daughter* by Adeline Yen Mah. Copyright © 1999 by Puffin Books. Reprinted by permission of Puffin Books, an imprint of Penguin Group (USA) Inc.; **221** Library of Congress; **222** © Bettmann/CORBIS; **224** © Bettmann/CORBIS; **227** © Bettmann/CORBIS; **229** © Flip Schulke/Corbis; **233** Thumbnail image of book cover – 60th Anniversary Edition from *Black Boy* by Richard Wright. Copyright 1937, 1942, 1944, 1945 by Richard Wright; renewed copyright © 1973 by Ellen Wright. Reprinted by permission of HarperCollins Publishers.; **234** Secker & Warburg Ltd.; **234** Jean-Loup Sieff; **235** The Random House Group; **236** (top left) © Image Source/Corbis; (bottom) © Edimédia/CORBIS; (top right) © Jack Hollingsworth/Corbis; **238** © Images.com/Corbis; **241** Jean-Loup Sieff; **242** (left) © PictureArts/CORBIS; (right) Photo by Malina; **246** Bancroft Library, UC Berkeley, Berkeley, CA; **247** © Roger Shiomura. Photo courtesy of the artist; **248** National Park Service; **249** © Corbis; **251** © Seattle Post-Intelligencer Collection; Museum and Industry/Corbis; **252** © Corbis; **255** (middle) © Bettmann/Corbis; (right) © Corbis; **260** Library of Congress; **261** Smithsonian American Art Museum, Washington, DC/Art Resource; **262** Library of Congress; **263** Harriet Tubman disguised as a man, c. 1934 or 1935. Bernarda Bryson Shahn. Art © Estate of Bernarda Bryson Shahn/Licensed by VAGA, New York, NY; **264** © Louie Psihoyos; **265** © Corbis; **266** © Bettmann/CORBIS; **269** (left) © Dave Teel/Corbis; (right) © Bettmann/Corbis; **273** © Flint/Corbis; **278** Photograph courtesy of Robert MacNeil; **279** © Images.com/Corbis; **280** (top left) Photo by H. Berends; (bottom left) Photo by Michael Bretherton; (middle) Luminis/www.stockexpert.com; (right) Andres Rodriguez/www.stockexpert.com; **281** © Images.com/Corbis; **286** UPI/CORBIS-Bettmann; **288** Superstock; **288** Photo by Sanja Gjenero; **289** © Images.com/Corbis; **291** © David Pollack/CORBIS; **292** © Blue Lantern Studio/Corbis; **295** Library of Congress; **296** © Thinkstock/Corbis; **298** (top) Photo by Yad Vashem/Photo Archives, courtesy of the U.S. Memorial Holocaust Memorial Museum Photo Archives; (bottom) AP/World Wide Photos; **300** (top) © Kevin Cruff/CORBIS; (bottom) © Carmen Redondo/CORBIS; **301** © Corbis; **307** Photo by Sue Anna Joe; **308** © Musuem of History and Industry/CORBIS; **309** © Lawrence Paul Yuxweluptun. Photo: National Gallery of Canada, Ottowa; (background) © First/zefa/Corbis; **310** © Michael T. Sedam/Corbis; **311** © image100/Corbis; **315** Photo by Craig Lewis; **318** © Rick Doyle/Corbis; **320** (top) © MAPS.com/CORBIS; (bottom) © Historical Picture Archive/CORBIS; **321** James Robert Fuller; **328** © Mallory Geitheim; **329** © Pam Ingalls/CORBIS; **333** (left) © Jose Luis Pelaez Inc/Blend Images /Corbis; (middle) © Don Hammond/Design Pics/Corbis; (right) © Thinkstock/Corbis; **334** © Ken Seet/Corbis; **340** Library of Congress; **341** © Lawrence Manning/Corbis; **343** © Christies/Handout/Reuters/Corbis; **345** © Corbis; **347** (bottom) © Piotr Redlinski/Corbis; **348** © Matt McDermott/CORBIS; **350** (top left) © James Leynse/Corbis; (bottom left) Photograph courtesy of Lucy Kaplansky; (middle) © Peter Turnley/Corbis; (right) © Najlah Feanny/Corbis; **352** Photograph courtesy of Garrison Keillor; **353** (bottom) Photograph courtesy of Le Ly Hayslip; (background) © Owen Franken/CORBIS; **355** © Steve Raymer/Corbis; **356** © Steve Raymer/Corbis; **359** (left) © Alison Wright/CORBIS; (middle) © Peter Turnley/CORBIS; (top right) © Tim Page/Corbis; (bottom right) Photo by Krzysztof Falkowski; **362** (top) Christie's Images/Superstock; (bottom) © Frank Cantor; **365–366** © David Turnley/CORBIS; **368** Book cover image for *Almost a Woman* by Esmeralda Santiago. Copyright © 1998 by Esmeralda Santiago. Reprinted by permission of Perseus Books Group.; **368** © Janet Jarman/Corbis; **370–371** Library of Congress; **372–374** © Bettmann/Corbis; **376** Reproduced by permission of the Norman Rockwell Family Agency, Inc. Book cover for Washington Square Press edition of *Warriors Don't Cry* by Melba Pattillo Beals. Used courtesy of Pocket Books, an imprint of Simon & Schuster Adult Publishing Group.; *Down and out in Paris and London* by George Orwell. Copyright © 1933. Copyright renewed 1961 by S.M. Pitt-Rivers. Reprinted by permission of Harcourt, Inc.; Jacket Cover from *A Brief History of Time* by Stephen W. Hawking. Used by permission of Bantam Books, a division of Random House, Inc.; Book cover illustration from *Silent Dancing: A Partial Remembrance of a Puerto Rican Childhood* by Judith Ortiz Cofer. Reproduced by permission of Arte Publico Press.; Cover from *Phineas Gage: A Gruesome but True Story About Brain Science* by John Fleischman. Copyright © by John Fleischman. Reprinted by permission of Houghton Mifflin Company. All rights reserved.; **379–380** UPI/CORBIS-Bettmann

Unit 3

388–389 (left) © Martyn Goddard/CORBIS; (right) © Francis G. Mayer/CORBIS; **390** Courtesy of Photofest; **391** (left) Wellesley College Library, Special Collections; (middle left) Library of Congress; (middle right) Library of Congress; (right) William Abranowitz/A+C Anthology; **393** Photo courtesy of Jimmy Santiago Baca; **394** Chalet in the Snow (oil on cardboard) by Munter, Gabrielle (1877–1962) © Private Collection/The Bridgeman Art Library; **399** Photo by Dragan Sasic; **400** Photo by James H. Evans; **401** © Martyn Goddard/CORBIS; **402** (left) © Alan Schein Photography/CORBIS; (middle) Photo by Sergei Krasii; (right) Photo by Kym Parry; **406** Photo courtesy of Joy Harjo; **407** Sunrise at Montserrat, 1935 by Masson, Andre (1896–1987) © Galerie Daniel Malingue, Paris, France/The Bridgeman Art Library; **408** (top left) © Bob Rowan; Progressive Image/Corbis; (bottom left) Photo by Danas Files; (right) Photo by AD arc; **409** Photo by Terri Heisele; **410** © Christie's Images/CORBIS; **411** Library of Congress; **412** (top) Photo by Marcela Lopez; (bottom left) William Abranowitz/A+C Anthology; (right) Photo courtesy of Marilyn Chin; **413** © Gerrit Greve/CORBIS; **414** IMAGEMORE Co., Ltd./Getty Images; **419** Photo by Philip MacKenzie; **420** (top left) Photo by Mariele Ciupa; (bottom left) Wellesly College Library, Special Collections; (bottom right) Library of Congress; **421** Victoria & Albert Museum, London/Art Resource, NY; **422** © Christie's Images/CORBIS; **423** (left) © Bettmann/CORBIS; (middle) Archive Photo; (right) AP/Irish Independent/Wide World Photos; **424** © Bettmann/CORBIS; **425** Library of Congress; **430** (top) Photo by Zeth Lorenzo; AP/Wyatt Counts/Wide World Photos; **431** Digital Vision/Photosearch; **433** © Michael Nicholson/CORBIS; **434** © Jack Hollingsworth/Corbis; **436** Archive Photos; **437** © Tim Street-Porter/Beateworks/Corbis; **439** © image100/Corbis; **441** Photo by Jonathan M.; **445** © Bloomimage/Corbis; **446** (top left) Photo by Thomas Istvan Seibel; (top right) Photo by Lynne Lancaster; (bottom left) Archive Photos; (bottom right) AP/Photo; **448** (top left) © BRECELJ BOJAN/CORBIS SYGMA; (bottom left) Photo by John Hartley; (right) © Henry Diltz/Corbis; **449** © Darren Greenwood/Design Pics/Corbis; **450** (left) Photo by Jef Geeraerts; (middle) © 1995–2007 Public Broadcasting Service (PBS); (right) AP/Photo; **454** (bottom left) Library of Congress; (bottom right) Library of Congress; **455** Van Gogh Foundation; **456** Smithsonian American Art Mueseum/Art Resource,

NY; **457** (left) SCHOMBURG CENTER/Art Resource, NY; (right) Michael Ochs Archives/Getty Images; **459** © Atlantide Phototravel/Corbis; **461** Photo by Mariajose Dominquez-Reifs; **462** (top) Photo courtesy of Brendan Curran; (bottom) Library of Congress; **463** © Images.com/Corbis; **464** © Patty Abbot/Illustration Works/Corbis; **466** Photo by Paul Martlew; **467** © Alexander Demianchuk/Reuters/Corbis; **468** © Corbis; **470** Photo by Jonathan Lindskov Naundrup-Jensen; **472** (top) William Abranowitz/A+C Anthology; (background) Library of Congress; **474** (top) © Kim M. Koza/Corbis; (bottom) © Debie Milligan; **476** Library of Congress; **478** Library of Congress; **479** Early Morning, 1964. Romare Bearden. New Britain Museum of American Art. Art © Romare Bearden Foundation/Licensed by VAGA, New York, NY; **479** © Randall Fung/Corbis; **480** (bottom) © Bettmann/CORBIS; (middle) © DLILLC/Corbis; (background) © Fabio Cardoso/Corbis; **482** (top left) Arte Público Press; (top right) © Eleonora Ghioldi/CORBIS; (bottom left) Photo by Elvis Santana, elvissantana.com; **483** (top left) © Brooks Kraft/Corbis; (right) © Tom Grill/Corbis; **484** (left) ©Anthony Cassidy/JA1/Corbis; (middle) © Bettmann/CORBIS; (right) © Michael S. Yamashita/CORBIS; **486** (top) © 2008 Artists Rights Society (ARS), New York/BONO Olso/The Cleveland Art Museum; **486** (bottom) AP/World Wide Photos; **488** *Heart to Heart: New Poems Inspired by Twentieth-Century,* edited by Jan Greenberg. Copyright © 2001 Harry N. Abrams, Inc. Reprinted by permission of Harry N. Abrams, Inc.; Book cover from *Letters to a Young Poet* by Rainer Maria Rilke. Used by permission of Vintage Books, a division of Random House, Inc.; *The Poetry of Robert Frost* edited by Edward Connery Lathem. Book cover © 1969 by Henry Holt and Company. Reprinted by permission of Henry Holt and Company, LLC.; Jacket cover from *I Shall Not be Moved* by Maya Angelou, copyright © 1993. Used by permission of Bantam Books, a division of Random House, Inc.; Book cover illustration from *What Have You Lost?* by Naomi Shihab Nye. Text copyright © 2000 by Naomi Shihab Nye. Reproduced by permission of Greenwillow Books and HarperCollins Publishers.

Unit 4

500–501 (left) © Atlantide Phototravel/CORBIS; (right) © Playboy Archive/Corbis; **502** Courtesy of Photofest; **504** © Comstock Select/Corbis; **507** ©

Gelinski; **773** © Images.com/Corbis; **775** Snark/Art Resource, NY; **779** © Bettmann/CORBIS; **780** HIP/Art Resource, NY; **788** Project Gutenberg; **789** (left) *Cinder Edna* by Ellen Jackson. Copyright © 1994 by Ellen Jackson. Used by permission of HarperCollins Publishers. HarperCollins Publishers, Inc.; (right) From *The Three Little Wolves and the Big Bad Pig* by Eugene Trivizas and Helen Oxenbury. Text copyright © 1993 by Eugene Trivizas. Illustrations © 1993 by Helen Oxenbury. Reprinted by permission of Simon & Schuster Publishing.; **790** © Hanan Isachar/Corbis; **791** © Christie's Images/CORBIS; **794** (top left) © Image Source/Corbis; (bottom left) Library of Congress; **795** A Lonely Life, c.1873 by Cameron, Hugh (1835–1918) © National Gallery of Scotland, Edinburgh, Scotland/The Bridgeman Art Library; **796** © Scheufler Collection/CORBIS; **799** © Christie's Images/CORBIS; (background) © Jupiterimages/Brand X/Corbis; **801** © Corbis; **805** Photo by Bazil Raubach; **807** (top) Library of Congress; (bottom) © Bettmann/CORBIS; **808** Library of Congress; **809** © Burstein Collection/CORBIS; **811**(right) Photo by Tero Suihkonen; **817** © DLILLC/Corbis; **819** (left) Photo by Ann Marsden; (right) Photo by Rob Waterhouse; **821** (top) © Bettmann/Corbis; (bottom) Cover from *The Fellowship of the Ring* by J.R.R Tolkien. Copyright © 1954, 1965 by J.R.R Tolkien. Copyright © renewed 1982 by Christopher R. Tolkien, Michael H.R. Tolkien, John F.R. Tolkien and Priscilla M.A.R. Tolkien. Reprinted by permission of Houghton Mifflin Company. All rights reserved. **824** (bottom) © Bettmann/Corbis; **827** © Bettmann/Corbis; **828** Photo by Michal Zacharzewski; **829** (top left) The Yorck Project/GNU Free Documentation License; (top right) The Yorck Project/GNU Free Documentation License; **830** Wellesley College Library, Special Collections; **837** © Bettmann/CORBIS; **838** © Keren Su/CORBIS; **841** Cupid and Psyche (tempera on paper laid down on canvas) by Stanhope, John Roddam Spencer (1829–1908) © Private Collection/Photo © Christie's Images/The Bridgeman Art Library; **843** Psyche entering Cupid's Garden, 1903 by Waterhouse, John William (1849–1917) © Harris Museum and Art Gallery, Preston, Lancashire, UK/The Bridgeman Art Library; **844** © Francis G. Mayer/CORBIS; **848** © Araldo de Luca/Corbis; **850** © Bettmann/Corbis; **853** © The Art Archive/Corbis; **854** © Francis G. Mayer/Corbis; **857** © Charles & Josette Lenars/CORBIS; **859** © Stockdisc/Corbis; **861** Achilles Defeating Hector, 1630–32 (oil on panel) by Rubens, Peter Paul (1577–1640) © Musee des Beaux-Arts, Pau, France/Giraudon/The Bridgeman Art Library; **861** SEF/Art Resource; **864** Athena, Greek, probably 5th century BC (marble) by © Louvre, Paris, France/Peter Willi/The Bridgeman Art Library; **868** © Historical Picture Archive/Corbis; **872** Book cover from *The Crystal Cave* by Mary Stewart. Copyright © 1970 by Mary Stewart. Reprinted by permission of HarperCollins Publishers.; "Cover" by Daniel Craig, from *Spindle's End* by Robin McKinley, copyright © 2000 by Robin McKinley. Used by permission of Ace Books, an imprint of the Berkley Publishing Group, a division of Penguin Group (USA) Inc.; From *Cuchulain of Muirthemne: The Story of the Men of the Red Branch of Ulster* by Lady Gregory. Mineola, New York: Dover Publications, Inc., 2001. Reprinted by permission of Dover Publications.; "Front Book Cover," from *The Girl Who Married a Lion: And Other Tales From Africa* by Alexander McCall Smith, copyright © 1989, 1999, 2004 by Alexander McCall Smith. Used by permission of Pantheon Books, a division of Random House, Inc. Random House, Inc.; Book Cover from *Firebirds: An Anthology of Original Fantasy and Science Fiction,* by Sharyn November. Cover art copyright © 2003 by Cliff Nielsen. Used by permission of Firebird, A Division of Penguin Young Readers Group, A Member of Penguin Group (USA) Inc., 345 Hudson Street, New York, NY 10014. All rights reserved.; **876** © MPI/Stringer/Hulton Archive/Getty Images; **879** © John Phillips/Stringer/Time & Life Pictures/Getty Images

Unit 6

886–887 (left) © Images.com/Corbis; (middle) © Todd Gipstein/CORBIS; (right) © Momatiuk-Eastcott/Corbis; **890** © William J. Weber; **891** Smithsonian American Art Museum, Washington, DC/Art Resource, NY; **892** Open Heart, 1995 (oil on board) by Bootman, Colin (Contemporary Artist) ©Private Collection/The Bridgeman Art Library; **895** (top) © David Turnley/CORBIS; (bottom) Photograph courtesy of Sandra Cisneros; **897** © Pam Ingalls/CORBIS; © Ellen Foscue Johnson; (background) Photo by Thorarinn Stefansson; **899** (top left) © Bettmann/CORBIS; (middle) © Corbis; (right) © Asian Art & Archaeology, Inc./CORBIS; **901** (top) © Alley Cat Productions/Brand X/Corbis; (bottom) © Jill Krementz; **903** (top) Don Congdon Associates, Inc.; (bottom) © Franklin McMahon/Corbis; **904** © Allen Ginsberg/CORBIS; **906** © Mark Peterson/CORBIS; **908** © Photo 24/Brand X/Corbis; **911** © Bettmann/CORBIS; **912** © Scott Speakes/Corbis; **914** © Bettmann/Corbis; **916**

Vocabulary Skills

spelling patterns, 602
spelling rules, 602–603
suffixes, 314–315, 602
synonym, 260, 274–275, 328
thesaurus use, 556–557
word origins, 306–307
word root, 314–315

Grammar & Style

adjectives, 304, 834–835
adverbs, 834–835
antecedent, 58–59
apposition, 696–697
appositive phrase, 696–697
capitalization, 304–305
clause, 104, 128, 696–697
cliché, 460–461
coherence, 336–337
colons, 258–259
commas, 128–129
comma splice, 326–327
complement, 404
complex sentence, 104
compound-complex sentence, 104
compound noun, 442
compound sentence, 104
conjunctive adverb, 834–835
coordinate adjective, 834–835
coordinating conjunction, 696–697
coordination, 696–697
dash, 644–645
demonstrative pronoun, 58
descriptive writing, 416
direct object, 404
ellipsis points, 644–645
essential/restrictive appositive,
    696–697
fused sentence, 326–327
future perfect tense, 272–273
future tense, 272–273
geographical directions, 304
geographical names, 304
gerund, 404–405
historical events, 304
hyphens, 644–645
image, 416
indefinite pronoun, 58, 442
independent clause, 104, 696–697
indirect object, 404
infinitive, 404–405

intensive pronoun, 58
interrogative pronoun, 58
irregular verbs, 284–285
linking verb, 26
literary works, 304
main idea, 336–337
modifier, 404, 834–835
nonessential/nonrestrictive apposi-
    tive, 696–697
nouns, 304
object of preposition, 404
paragraph, 336–337
parallel structure, 40–41
participial, 404–405
past participle, 284
past perfect tense, 272–273
past tense, 272–273, 284
perfect tense, 272–273
periods of time, 304
personal pronoun, 58
phrases, 104, 128, 404–405
plural, 26, 58–59
plural pronoun, 58
possessive noun, 442–443
possessive pronoun, 58
possessives, 442–443
precise language, 460–461
predicate, 26, 104
predicate nominative, 404
prepositions, 404–405
present perfect tense, 272–273
present tense, 272–273, 284
progressive form, 272–273
pronoun and antecedent agree-
    ment, 58–59
proper adjectives, 304
proper nouns, 304
reflexive pronoun, 58
relative adverb, 834–835
relative pronoun, 58
rhetorical device, 26
semicolons, 258–259
sensory details, 416–417
sentence fragments, 326–327
sentence run-ons, 326–327
sentence structure, 104–105
sentence variety, 104–105
simple sentence, 104
singular, 26, 58–59
singular pronoun, 58

special events, 304
subject, 26, 104
subject-verb agreement, 26–27
subordinate clause, 104, 696–697
subordination, 696–697
supporting details, 336–337
tense, 272–273
titles of artworks, 304
topic sentence, 336–337
transitions, 336–337, 784–785
verbs, 284–285
verb tense, 272–273
wordy sentences, 460–461

Writing

anthology, 397
applied writing
    advertisement, 477
    brochure for immigrants, 483
    business letter, 283, 409
    cartoon, 930
    contract, 166
    e-mail, 917
    greeting card, 999
    handbook on fatherhood, 479
    instructions, 335
    paraphrase, 427
    personality quiz, 759
    public service pamphlet, 487
    step-by-step instructions, 49
    thank-you letter, 479
    website, 473
    writing contest, 335
audience, 378
body, 208, 210, 378, 380, 382,
    492, 494, 730, 732, 876,
    879
cause and effect order, 277
characters, 1018
chronological order, 277, 378
cluster chart, 491
coherence, 336–337
collaborative learning, 271, 295,
    397
comparison and contrast order, 277
conclusion, 208, 210, 378, 380,
    382, 492, 494, 730, 732,
    878, 879
conflict, 1018
content, 879, 1020

persuasive writing, 219
   advertisement, 477
   closing argument, 725
   critical essay, 369, 856
   editorial, 303, 451
   movie review, 313
   persuasive article, 257
   persuasive essay, 103, 276, 728–735, 980
   reflective essay, 203
   speech, 840, 851
plot, 206, 1018
plot chart, 1019
plot element chart, 207
prewrite, 206–207, 378–379, 490–491, 728–729, 874–876, 1018–1019
proofread, 383, 494
publish and present, 210, 382, 494, 732, 880, 1022
purpose, 219, 378
reflect, 210, 383, 494, 732, 880, 1022
research paper, 874–881
revise, 208–210, 380–382, 492–494, 879–880, 1020–1022
revision checklist, 210, 382, 494, 732, 878, 1022
rubric
   lyric poem, 490
   personal narrative, 378
   persuasive essay, 728
   plot analysis, 206
   research paper, 874
   short story, 1018
sensory details, 416–417
sentence variety, 104–105
setting, 1018
student model, 211, 383, 495, 733, 880–881, 1022–1023
style, 732, 879, 1020
subject-verb agreement, 26–27
supporting details, 276, 336–337
take notes, 875
theme, 1018
thesis, 276
thesis statement, 206–207, 378, 729, 876
topic, 378, 490, 728, 874

topic sentence, 336–337
transitions, 336–337, 784–785

Research and Documentation

article, 316
bandwagon appeal, 317
bias, 317
calendar, 295
circular reasoning, 317
collaborative learning, 257, 303, 325, 415, 783, 793
create bibliography, 127
editorial, 316
fact vs. opinion, 316
glittering generality, 317
graphic aids, 316
how-to writing, 316
informational text, 316–317
loaded words, 317
media literacy
   analyze ideas of success, 79
   analyze point of view in news reporting, 49
   analyze visual and sound techniques, 783
   art exhibit, 469
   compare film versions, 643
   create a calendar, 295
   create bibliography, 458
   create flier, 103
   create video game, 803
   expository presentation, 695
   follow instructions, 335
   movie review, 313
   Native American myths, 409
   public service announcement, 25
   research Yiddish-language newspaper, 793
   television commercial, 283, 523
   website creation, 271
propaganda, 317
public awareness campaign, 325
researching
   adaptation, 833
   Antigua, 441
   Brooks and Hughes, 458
   career portfolio, 432
   Chief Seattle's speech, 313

Chinese New Year, 415
Civil Rights movement, 231
coming-of-age presentation, 39
Elie Wiesel's speeches, 303
epidemic, 91
haiku, 469
Harriet Tubman, 271
history of Rome, 643
Holocaust, 303
literacy programs, 397
mother-daughter relationships, 127
Native American myths, 409
naturalism, 103
personality quiz, 759
Poet Laureate, 451
Russian writers, 523
social conventions, 11
Sri Lanka, 325
Sundiata and Arthur, 783
time line of apartheid in South Africa, 57
time period of American history, 117
tsunami, 325
world epic, 823
World War II propaganda posters, 257
Yiddish-language newspaper, 793
Yiddish music and theater, 793
review, 316
spin, 317
stereotype, 317
television commercials, 283
website creation, 271
websites, 316

Applied English

anthology, 397
art exhibit, 469
brochure for immigrants, 483
career portfolio, 432
collaborative learning, 49, 91, 335, 403, 427, 441, 451, 458, 465, 759, 783
flier, 103
graphic novel, 49
handbook on fatherhood, 479
illustrate sonnet, 427

Speaking and Listening

Test-taking Skills

For Your Reading List

INDEX OF TITLES AND AUTHORS